INTRODUCTION TO PSYCHOLOGY

Introduction to psychology

SECOND EDITION   1961

CLIFFORD T. MORGAN   THE UNIVERSITY OF WISCONSIN

McGRAW-HILL BOOK COMPANY, INC.   •   NEW YORK   TORONTO   LONDON

The text and the displayed headings in this book are set in Times Roman, a type face designed by Stanley Morison for *The Times* of London. Gabriele Wunderlich was the picture editor; line drawings are by Joseph and Eva Cellini.

Preface

THE AIM in the second edition, essentially the same as that in the first, is to provide a textbook with broad coverage of the more important and representative areas of psychology, leaving out topics that are trivial, controversial, or of interest only to specialized groups. An attempt has been made to deal soundly with each topic selected for discussion. Many decisions about what to include and what to leave out have been difficult, and other authors would have made them differently. I hope, however, that I have succeeded in presenting a fair and well-rounded picture of psychology for the student who is getting his first serious introduction to it.

Material has been selected with the fact in mind that the overwhelming proportion of students in the introductory course will not become majors in psychology. Rather, they come to the course with heterogeneous vocational ambitions and other motives. At the same time, instructors have different tastes and habits in presenting their courses, and they must adapt to the time available for the course as well as to the needs of the students they are teaching.

In order to meet these differing needs of students and instructors, the book has been organized to be flexible in use. It provides the instructor with considerable freedom in planning both the material he will cover and the way in which he will cover it. Suggestions in "To the Instructor," immediately following this preface, include outlines of three different courses for which the book might be used: a life-oriented course, a science-oriented course, and a comprehensive course that includes all chapters in the book in a somewhat different order from that in the text. These outlines are merely examples, and they may be adapted by instructors as they choose. The chapters themselves have been written to accommodate such alternative courses and sequences, and cross references have been provided where necessary to explain each term as it appears. In addition, optional or supplementary sections of the chapters, which may be omitted or assigned as desired, are listed in "To the Instructor." Finally, the glossary at the end of the book is also an aid in using the text in different ways.

In the first edition, other psychologists, each expert in his particular field, prepared first drafts of many of the chapters. In this edition, with one exception, that plan has not been followed, partly for reasons of scheduling and partly to give the author more leeway in organizing the material. I have, however, called on some of my former collaborators for advice in revising the material. And, of course, some of their material has been carried over from the first edition with only minor changes. Hence they have made important contributions also to this edition and are still in a sense collaborators. In addition, Professor Leonard Berkowitz drafted revisions of the two chapters on social psychology. Although I edited and rewrote them and must take responsibility for them, he must be credited with most of the new ideas and content in these chapters.

Other people, many of whom must remain nameless, also contributed to the preparation of the new edition. Mrs. Jean S. Morgan typed the manuscript. Two anonymous reviewers made many helpful suggestions about organization and expression. Dozens of instructors who taught from the first edition have given me helpful criticism and comments. A tribute is due to those who prepared the charts and drawings for their inventiveness and technical skill. Also appreciated are the assistance and enthusiasm of the editorial and production staffs of the McGraw-Hill Book Company, who have spared no pains in the design and production of the book. Credit is given in the legends of illustrations to the many individuals and publishers who kindly permitted the use of their material.

Clifford T. Morgan

To the instructor

This book has been written and organized with the expectation that instructors may sometimes find it necessary to omit chapters, as well as parts of chapters, and to assign material in an order different from that in the book. Each instructor must make his selection in the light of the time available to him and the needs of his students. In the hope of simplifying this task, we offer here three possible alternative arrangements and the names of some sections that might be dropped. In the first two arrangements some chapters are omitted, while in the third all chapters are included but in a different order from that in the book. In each case the instructor may easily omit chapters that are listed in the outline. In addition, several special sections within chapters, usually at the end, are optional or supplementary. They are special in the sense that they treat rather specialized aspects of the subject of the chapter. They may be omitted, if necessary, without handicapping the study of the other parts of the chapter. These special sections are listed below by name.

LIFE-ORIENTED COURSE

The science of psychology (CHAPTER 1)

Maturation and development (CHAPTER 2)

Drives and motivation (CHAPTER 3)

Feeling and emotion (CHAPTER 4)

Frustration and conflict (CHAPTER 5)

Mental health and psychotherapy (CHAPTER 6)

Principles of learning (CHAPTER 7)

Human learning and forgetting (CHAPTER 8)

Language and thinking (CHAPTER 9)

Perception and attention (CHAPTER 10)

Intelligence and aptitudes (CHAPTER 14)

Personality (CHAPTER 15)

Social influences on behavior (CHAPTER 16)

Attitudes, beliefs, and social prejudice (CHAPTER 17)

Vocational adjustment (CHAPTER 18)

SCIENCE-ORIENTED COURSE

The science of psychology (CHAPTER 1)

Nervous system and internal environment (CHAPTER 19)

Physiological basis of behavior (CHAPTER 20)

Maturation and development (CHAPTER 2)

Drives and motivation (CHAPTER 3)

Feeling and emotion (CHAPTER 4)

Frustration and conflict (CHAPTER 5)

Principles of learning (CHAPTER 7)

Human learning and forgetting (CHAPTER 8)

Language and thinking (CHAPTER 9)

Perception and attention (CHAPTER 10)

Vision (CHAPTER 11)

Hearing and lower senses (CHAPTER 12)

Psychological measurement (CHAPTER 13)

Intelligence and aptitudes (CHAPTER 14)

Personality (CHAPTER 15)

COMPREHENSIVE COURSE

The science of psychology (CHAPTER 1)

Nervous system and internal environment (CHAPTER 19)

Physiological basis of behavior (CHAPTER 20)

Maturation and development (CHAPTER 2)

Drives and motivation (CHAPTER 3)

Feeling and emotion (CHAPTER 4)

Principles of learning (CHAPTER 7)

Human learning and forgetting (CHAPTER 8)

Language and thinking (CHAPTER 9)

Perception and attention (CHAPTER 10)

Vision (CHAPTER 11)

Hearing and lower senses (CHAPTER 12)

Psychological measurement (CHAPTER 13)

Personality (CHAPTER 15)

Frustration and conflict (CHAPTER 5)

Mental health and psychotherapy (CHAPTER 6)

Intelligence and aptitudes (CHAPTER 14)

Vocational adjustment (CHAPTER 18)

Social influences on behavior (CHAPTER 16)

Attitudes, beliefs, and social prejudice (CHAPTER 17)

SPECIAL SECTIONS

The uses of psychology (CHAPTER 1)

Factors in learning (CHAPTER 7)

Maze learning (CHAPTER 7)

Techniques of study (CHAPTER 8)

Programmed learning (CHAPTER 8)

Language and communication (CHAPTER 9)

Complex processes in animals (CHAPTER 9)

Receptor processes (CHAPTER 11)

Speech perception (CHAPTER 12)

Formulas and calculations (CHAPTER 13)

Aptitudes and interests (CHAPTER 14)

Theories of personality (CHAPTER 15)

Racial attitudes and conflicts (CHAPTER 17)

Engineering for human use (CHAPTER 18)

To the student

THE FIRST CHAPTER defines psychology and indicates what you may expect to learn in studying it. You may take it for granted, however, that psychology deals with many of the problems of everyday life and thus with many things that you have already experienced. You are therefore in a position to derive some personal benefits from the study of psychology. In a formal college course, however, it is not possible for the instructor to relate your particular case to everything that is taught. Hence, to get the most from your course, you must make many of these applications yourself. To do that, you must continually ask yourself, "How does this apply in my experience?" and "How can I put to use what I am learning?" By taking such an attitude, you will profit much more from the course than if you simply learn by rote what is assigned.

Here are some suggestions for the reading of each chapter as it is assigned. Probably the first thing you should do is read the summary. It obviously cannot cover everything that is in the chapter, but it does hit the high spots. Then, after reading the summary, it will usually prove worthwhile to skim the headings before settling down to a careful reading.

In the few minutes that it takes to do this, you can add a few details and get the over-all organization in mind.

Many students try to read textbooks the way they read novels; they sit passively, running their eyes over the words and hoping that information will sink in. This is not the way to read textbooks, however, for they are jam packed with facts and explanations. To assimilate them, you should work at the task, reading every sentence carefully and turning over in your mind what it says and what it means. To make certain that you are really working at the task and also to make reviewing easier, you would do well to make a separate outline in your own words. In writing such an outline, the main headings should be approximately the same as those in the book, but under each heading you should write brief sentences that summarize in your own words what you have read.

Many students fail to grasp the subject they are studying because they do not give sufficient attention to illustrations and tables. In this book the illustrations and tables are fully as important as the corresponding discussions in the text. When you encounter a reference to one of them, you should turn to it promptly and study it carefully. In some cases we have used illustrations to teach something not included in the text. At appropriate points in your reading, usually before going on to a new heading, you should scan the illustrations to make certain you have examined them and gleaned all you can from them.

Every technical subject uses terms whose definitions must be learned, and psychology is no exception. Ordinarily a definition is given in the text whenever a new term is introduced. Since chapters will not always be assigned in the order of their arrangement in the book, a glossary is included in the back of the book. You are especially cautioned not to neglect a definition just because the term is already familiar to you. Do not, for example, pass over words like "attitude," "personality," "intelligence," and "need" because these are words that you use in everyday speech. In psychology these and other common terms often have specialized meanings different from those commonly employed. To get the most from your study of psychology, make sure to know the *psychological definitions* of all terms.

Science is the product of scientists, and it is common practice in science to ascribe particular experiments and ideas to the scientists who have contributed them. This practice, however, can be distracting and annoying to the introductory student. In this book names are used only where they are really important or convenient in learning the subject matter. To give credit where credit is due without introducing a profusion of names, names appear in brackets when particular studies or ideas are cited. These names refer to the bibliography at the back of the book, where you can find the name and article or book on which the statement is based.

There is also a *Study Guide* that you may purchase and use as an aid in study and review. This guide contains questions and exercises that not only make the study of psychology more interesting but also permit you to assess for yourself how well you have mastered the material.

Finally, look over the "Suggestions for Further Reading" at the end of each chapter. These readings have been selected with some care to permit you to learn more about a particular topic that interests you. Each title is followed by a brief descriptive statement intended to help you decide whether it suits your purpose. Most of the suggested readings will be found in college libraries.

Contents

PART ONE

INTRODUCTION

XI

PART TWO

MOTIVATION AND ADJUSTMENT

NEUROTIC REACTIONS: Anxiety reactions Phobic reactions Obsessive-compulsive reactions Conversion reactions Dissociative reactions
PSYCHOTIC REACTIONS: Affective reactions Paranoid reactions Schizophrenic reactions Organic psychoses

PART THREE
LEARNING AND THINKING

PART SIX
GROUP PROCESSES

Introduction to psychology

THE SCIENCE
OF PSYCHOLOGY

MATURATION
& DEVELOPMENT

PART ONE
INTRODUCTION

The science of psychology

Nearly everyone feels that he would be happier and more successful if he "understood people" a little better. The businessman must manage people, the salesman must sell to people, and the physician contends not only with physical illnesses but with the behavior of the people who have them. Even the man whose work has little to do with people must get along with his wife, his children, his relatives, his fellow workmen, his friends, and his neighbors. Indeed, dealing with people effectively is vital in many aspects of vocational success and in many facets of personal happiness.

The field of psychology

This need to understand people better is both a help and a hindrance in undertaking the study of psychology. It helps because it motivates, and one must have motivation to learn. It helps too because it makes the subject more enjoyable for both the student and the teacher.

A ready-made interest in psychology can also be a hindrance in two ways. One is that it leads some students to think they know more about psychology than they really do, just because they have previously taken a keen interest in observing people. Being amateur observers, such students usually have mistaken ideas about psychological matters that need straightening out. Indeed, one of the important tasks of a course in psychology is to correct the misconceptions nearly everyone acquires in the course of living in the everyday world. Hence, as you study this book you should be prepared to find that some of your opinions may be wrong or inaccurate.

1

An interest in psychology may also lead students to expect the wrong things from a course in psychology. They may expect both too much and too little from it.

They expect too much if they look for a few patent remedies to use in solving their personal problems or in seeking success and happiness. No one learns to be a physician, lawyer, engineer, or musician in a single course. Neither can he quickly become a psychologist. In each case long years of training in the subject and in many related subjects are necessary to become professionally proficient. So, although you will learn much from this book that can be of value in understanding yourself and other people—the first course in psychology is probably as useful as any beginning college course—you must expect to acquire only the rudiments of the subject, not profound knowledge or great skill.

It is possible also to underestimate the range of topics covered in psychology. How to deal with people or to cope with personal problems, for example, is only a small part of psychology. The subject also encompasses problems of social groups, of intelligence and abilities, of work and efficiency, of learning and perception, of physiological events in the body, and of animal behavior—to name just a few. Although all these topics have something to do with understanding people, they are of interest in their own right. Many have practical significance in various phases of civilized life. You should therefore be prepared to study a subject of considerable breadth—one that touches on a wider variety of problems than most people realize.

DEFINITION OF PSYCHOLOGY. Now let us see specifically what psychology is. If you ask a psychologist to define his subject,[1] he will probably say, "*Psychology is the science of human and animal behavior,*" for that is the generally accepted definition of it. Upon hearing this definition, however, the person untrained in psychology is likely

[1] For one such definition, see Keller [1937].

to be surprised at three of the important words in it: "science," "animal," and "behavior." Is psychology really a science? he may ask. Why "behavior" rather than "mind" or "thoughts" or "feelings"? And why "animal" behavior? What has that got to do with psychology?

Let us consider separately each of these three words, beginning first with *science*. *A science is a body of systematized knowledge.* Such knowledge is gathered by carefully observing and measuring events, sometimes, but not necessarily, in experiments set up by the scientist to produce the events he is studying. The things and events observed are systematized in various ways, but principally by classifying them into categories and establishing general laws or principles that describe and predict them as accurately as possible. Science may be distinguished from art in that *art is skill or knack in doing something that is acquired by study and practice.*

Psychology, by these definitions, is both an art and a science. Since art is something an individual develops, it is difficult to learn it from books and classroom study. Moreover, artistry in psychology, as in medicine or engineering, is best developed after mastering the subject matter of the underlying science. The psychological arts, as we see them in politics, diplomacy, salesmanship, and other fields, are as yet woefully ineffective in solving our most serious problems in human relationships. On the other hand, through the valiant efforts of many research workers over the last three-quarters of a century, there is now a science of psychology—a large body of systematized knowledge—which can be taught and which is the best foundation for developing an understanding of behavior. It is for these reasons that we stress "science" in our definition of psychology and in this book.

We come now to the word *behavior.* Behavior, rather than mind, thoughts, and feelings, is the subject of psychology, because it alone can be observed, recorded, and studied. No one ever saw, heard, or touched a mind, but one can see, hear, and touch behavior. He can see and measure what a person does, or hear and record what a person says—which is vocal behavior. Anything else is something inferred. We do, indeed, infer that mental processes take place and that people think and feel, but for systematic knowledge of psychological events in people at large, we are limited to the observation of behavior.

Now, finally, the word *animal*. Science does not arbitrarily limit itself to any one realm of events or to that knowledge which has immediate practical value. In fact, nearly everyone has now learned—even our most practical politicians and businessmen—that there is ultimately great practical value in pursuing knowledge for its own sake. And animal behavior can be as fascinating a study as human behavior, if not more so. So, just as the zoologist studies the form and function of all members of the animal kingdom, the psychologist systematically observes animal as well as human behavior. Animal behavior is then a legitimate area of study in its own right (see Figure 1.1).

But there is another, equally important reason for studying animal behavior. There are many similarities between animal and human behavior. In fact, animals display, or can be taught to display in the laboratory, in more rudimentary form, of course, most of the kinds of behavior which people display. Thus a study of animal behavior is a great aid in understanding human behavior. We are able to do many important experiments with animals that we cannot do with people, because human beings do not want to be guinea pigs. Psychologists therefore frequently use animals to answer general questions about behavior. For that reason, you will find in this book many studies of animal as well as human behavior.

THE BEHAVIORAL SCIENCES. Although behavior is the subject of psychology, it is by no means the exclusive property of psychology. Several other disciplines also make the study of human and animal behavior

TEST YOURSELF. On a piece of paper write down the numbers 1 to 20. Then read each of the following statements carefully, writing down whether you think it is true or false.

1. Geniuses are usually queerer than people of average intelligence (14).

2. Only human beings, not animals, have the capacity to think (9).

3. Much of human behavior is instinctive (3).

4. Slow learners remember what they learn better than fast learners (8).

5. Intelligent people form most of their opinions by logical reasoning (9).

6. A psychologist is a person who is trained to psychoanalyze people (1, 6).

7. You can size up a person quite well in an interview (15, 18).

8. When one is working for several hours, it is better to take a few long rests than several short ones (18).

9. The study of mathematics exercises the mind so that a person can think more logically in other subjects (8).

10. Grades in college have little to do with success in business careers (8).

11. Alcohol, in small amounts, is a stimulant (5).

12. There is a clear distinction between the normal person and one who is mentally ill (5).

13. Prejudices are mainly due to lack of information (17).

14. Competition among people is characteristic of most human societies (16).

15. The feature of a job that is most important to employees is the pay they get for their work (18).

16. It is possible to classify people fairly well into introverts and extroverts (15).

17. Punishment is an effective way of eliminating undesirable behavior in children (7).

18. By watching closely a person's expression, you can tell the emotion he is experiencing (4).

19. The higher one sets his goals in life, the more he is likely to accomplish and the happier he will be (3, 5).

20. If a person is honest with you, he can usually tell you what his motives are (5).

The footnote on p. 27 answers these questions. The numbers in parentheses following each question refer to chapters in the book that discuss the respective questions.

their business. These disciplines include psychiatry, anthropology, sociology, economics, political science, and history. Taken together, they have recently come to be called the *behavioral sciences*. Each of them focuses its attention upon certain aspects of behavior. Differences among them are not always clear cut, however.

Sociology and social anthropology are concerned with the behavior of groups of people. Specialists in these fields study the cultures and social structures of various societies or groups of people living together. The sociologist typically deals with modern, literate cultures, such as our own; the anthropologist, with more primitive cultures. Each science has devised its own methods and acquired its own fund of information. At the present time, however, the lines between them are becoming fainter as they pool their knowledge and apply each other's methods.

History, of course, is a behavioral science because it attempts to reconstruct and understand the events—mostly events of human behavior—that make history. Economics and political science deal, respectively, with economic and political behavior, which are simply the aspects of behavior one sees institutionalized in trade and government. To a certain extent both subjects are historical sciences because they make use of records of events that have transpired in the past.

The natural sciences such as physics, chemistry, and biology are not primarily behavioral sciences, yet they sometimes have occasion to study behavior. Some of our most useful knowledge about human perception, for example, has come from physicists and physiologists who ventured to measure human reactions to different kinds of physical stimuli. The biologist and physiologist, who are primarly concerned with structures and functions of the body, have also contributed greatly to our knowledge of behavior by studying physiological factors related to behavior. The zoologists, finally, have been interested in the classification of

animals and have carried out many studies on the behavior of animals. In this way they have both improved zoological classification and aided the psychologist in his efforts to understand animal behavior.

It is becoming increasingly difficult to establish boundary lines to separate the behavioral sciences. Actually there are no such boundary lines; scientists of different labels work at times side by side in overlapping domains, at times separated by territory as yet unexplored. In the general area of behavioral science, psychology is a kind of meeting ground for the natural sciences, such as physics, biology, and physiology, and the social sciences, such as sociology, economics, and political science. There is a good deal of give-and-take among all these sciences, and as you study this book you will see many ways in which they complement each other.

PSYCHOLOGY AS SCIENCE. We have defined psychology as science and related it to the other behavioral sciences. What does science, and especially the science of psychology, really mean? We have said that science is a body of systematized knowledge. Now we may inquire how this knowledge is obtained and systematized.

Psychology as science is, first of all, *empirical*. That is to say, it rests on experiment and observation, rather than on argument, opinion, or belief. The psychologist does experiments which other psychologists can repeat, and he obtains data, usually making quantitative measurements, that another can, if he wishes, verify. This approach is to be distinguished from forming opinions on the basis of experience, or reporting experiences that few others have had or can have, or arguing from premises that no one can test.

Not that scientists do not have opinions or occasionally argue with one another. Indeed, scientists often disagree on the interpretation of results. Scientists must also reason by inference; for example, since $A = B$ and $B = C$, they infer that $A = C$. If the scientist had only his opinions and infer-

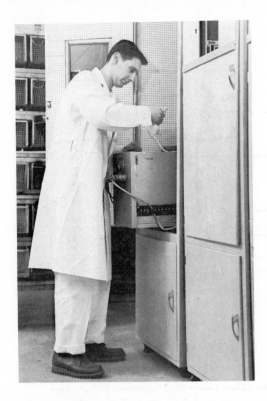

FIGURE 1.1. The experimental study of learning in the rat. An experimenter places the rat in a soundproof apparatus. Inside, the rat must push the lever every few seconds to avoid receiving a mild electric shock from the bars of the floor. At the end of an experimental session, a research assistant reads and records figures on the panel of the automatic apparatus that measure the rat's performance [Chas. Pfizer & Co., Inc.].

ences, however, he would have no science. What makes his science secure as science are the unarguable facts, the observations which he has made and which others can check, and the instances of $A = B$ and $B = C$ with which no knowledgeable person can argue. Also of crucial importance is his ability to do *research* and through it establish new observations. Without research his science would become static. He would not be able, as he now is, to erase gradually the areas of ignorance and conflicting opinion. Through research, psychology already has acquired a wealth of facts and is continuing to amass additional ones. In a later section of this chapter, we shall consider in more detail what we mean by psychological research.

Psychology is also *systematic*. Observations, though essential to science, are by themselves of little use. They can be selected to suit one's purpose or acquired without any purpose at all, piling up in a disorderly, meaningless array. What is important in science is that observations "make some sense"; they must be capable of being summarized economically by a limited number of principles. The principles may be merely a system of classification, such as we find in zoology, or they may be rather precise laws stating the order or relationship among the phenomena observed, such as we meet, for example, in physics. In any case, we attempt in science to systematize our observations in an orderly and economical way.

The effort to develop a science follows a circular path from observations to principles and back again to observations. The first part of the circle has been called induction. We make observations wherever we can, without too much rhyme or reason to them, and then attempt to formulate tentative principles that we think pretty well summarize our observations. Next we trace the part of the circle called deduction. We reason that, if our principles are correct, we should be able to predict observations not yet made. We then set out to collect new observations according to some plan that will test the adequacy of our tentative principles. Sometimes our tentative principles prove to be wholly or partly wrong; at other times, they are correct. But by systematically following the path from observations to principles to observations, we are continually formulating, modifying, and extending principles to accord with observations.

Science has many distinguishing features, but the last that we shall mention here is measurement. Almost all of us take it for granted that sciences measure things. We rank highest among the sciences the one that has developed the most precise measurements. For that reason physics is usually credited with being the most "scientific" of the sciences because its measurements are so precise. Actually, measurement is not always essential to science. In a field like zoology, for example, the important principles may consist of a systematic classification of the members of the animal kingdom.

Such a classification is not measurement in the strict sense of the word. In psychology, too, we will learn classifications of different kinds of behavior. Most of our problems, however, are questions of "more than" or "less than." We would like to know, for example, whether children of highly intelligent parents are brighter than those of less intelligent parents. To answer such a question as this, we need measurements that tell us *how intelligent* both parents and children are. Since most psychological problems are quite complex, it has not been easy to devise methods of measurement for studying them. In Chapter 13 we shall summarize the methods that have been devised. Although we usually do not delve into the details of such measurements, almost everything discussed in this book has its roots in the measurement of behavior.

Origins of scientific psychology

No science has become well established until a concerted effort to make observations and measurements—to be empirical—has gotten under way. Such effort has almost invariably met resistance from groups who feel that their beliefs might be upset or their accepted authorities challenged by new observations or by principles based on them. Historically this resistance was first shattered in settling questions about the physical world; hence physics and chemistry were first established as sciences. It took longer to overcome opposition to probing the world of living things and thus to put biology, psychology, and the social sciences on an empirical basis. Even today there is often a hue and cry when a scientist brings forth psychological data that run counter to established attitudes. Psychology has nevertheless continued to prosper as an empirical science.

NATURAL OBSERVATION. Although each science has its special methods, people have always been able to learn a great deal simply by being careful observers of what is going on around them. This method, as distinguished from the experimental method, which we shall come to in a moment, is called the method of *natural observation*. Merely by being keen observers, for example, the ancients described and classified many animals and plants, explored and charted new seas and lands, and noted many facts about human behavior.

Before the dawn of modern science, the observation and interpretation of data was the business of the *philosopher*. Beginning with the ancient Greeks, philosophers learned a great deal about the world around them, attempted to arrange their learning in an orderly way, and speculated on its meaning. Thus philosophy became the parent of our modern departments of knowledge. As philosophers increased their knowledge, they developed specialties within the field of philosophy. Natural philosophy dealt with areas now included under physics, chemistry, and the natural sciences; mental philosophy was concerned with what is now the field of psychology; and moral philosophy considered many of the social problems now encompassed by the social sciences. Thus philosophy is the parent of our modern sciences, both natural and social. This fact is still reflected in the awarding of the Ph.D. (doctor of philosophy) degree to postgraduate students in such subjects as chemistry, psychology, and economics.

EXPERIMENTAL PSYCHOLOGY. Sooner or later, the new sciences, like most children, had to leave the fold. What gave tremendous impetus to the movement, however, was the discovery of a new method, the *experimental* method. The method of natural observation limits the scientist to observing the events and things that nature has provided for him, and observing them, moreover, under nature's conditions. The experimental method, on the other hand, enables the scientist to make those events happen that he needs to observe in order to develop a science, and to do this under conditions of his own choosing.

Physicists and chemists were the first to discover and exploit the experimental method. With the aid of this method, they formulated many of the principles of physics and chemistry still taught today. In time, physicists and physiologists began to experiment on some of the problems now encompassed in psychology, such as color vision, hearing, and brain functions, which we shall study later in the book. As these problems on the fringe of psychology yielded to the experimental method, it became more and more evident that psychology, like the other sciences, could forge ahead only by developing experimental methods suited to its own unique problems.

Finally, in 1879, Prof. Wilhelm Wundt founded the first laboratory of psychology at the University of Leipzig in Germany. Perhaps the first laboratory actually came before that, because William James at Harvard was known to be doing experiments too. In any event, experimental laboratories of psychology mushroomed rapidly, once the movement got under way. In the United States, the first formal laboratory was set up at The Johns Hopkins University in 1883. Within a few more years, laboratories had been established at every major university in the country.

A science, like a child, must have time to mature. It takes thousands and thousands of experiments, performed with different methods and under different conditions, to establish a healthy body of scientific observations and principles. In the meantime, especially when the observations are scarce and new methods are developing, there is likely to be a period of "isms" characterized by different points of view which are often espoused with considerable zeal. Psychology went through such a period in which different schools of thought occupied the limelight. In the following paragraphs we shall discuss some of the most important of these schools. Four of the leaders of the schools are pictured in Figure 1.2.

FIGURE 1.2. Wilhelm Wundt (upper left) founded the first laboratory of psychology in Leipzig in 1879. William James (upper right) fostered experimentation in his laboratory at Harvard University and wrote influential books. John Dewey (lower left) was one of the leaders of functionalism and had an important influence on modern education. Sigmund Freud (lower right) developed psychoanalysis, which provided a new conception of personality and a new method of treating mental illness [Bettmann Archive].

STRUCTURALISM. The first school, or "ism," owes its origin to the time in which experimental psychology got under way. The physical scientists of the time could claim great success not only for their experimental method, but also for their atomic theory of matter. This theory, or set of principles, stated that all complex substances could be analyzed into component elements, much as elementary physics or chemistry is explained today.

It was only natural that the first experimental psychologists should follow this example, and they did. They started searching for *mental elements* into which, they hoped, all mental content could be analyzed. The element, they thought, must be a *sensation*, like red, cold, sweet, or putrid. To search for these elements and the rules for combining them, they used a special kind of experimental method called *introspection* [Boring, 1953]. A subject was trained to report as objectively as possible what he experienced in connection with a certain stimulus, disregarding the meanings he had come to associate with the particular stimulus. He might, for example, be presented with a colored light, a tone, or an odor and asked to describe it as minutely as possible. It was hoped that in this way the mental content of an experience would be reconstructed from elementary sensations.

Many valuable observations were collected in this way, and some aspects of the method are still being used. The approach, however, proved too narrow, for it was limited to reports of what a person experienced. Moreover, it gradually became apparent that one cannot think of mind as a structure made up of elementary sensations. Hence structuralism gave way to other approaches to the study of psychological events.

FUNCTIONALISM. One of these new approaches came to be known as functionalism. Two of its most influential proponents were William James [1890] and John Dewey. These men were interested in what happened in the course of psychological activities and the ends served by these activities. As the term "functionalism" implies, they sought to study the *functions* of behavior and mental processes, not merely their structure.

To study functions, the functionalists extended experimental methods to include not only the method of introspection but also the *observation of behavior*—what a person

does. Instead of limiting themselves to the description and analysis of sensory experience and of mental content, they emphasized the total activity of the individual— how he learns, how he is motivated, how he goes about solving problems, how he forgets. So functionalism had two chief characteristics: the study of the total behavior and experience of an individual, and an interest in the functions served by the things an individual does.

BEHAVIORISM. Functionalism tended to put the emphasis on the observation of behavior, but still accepted the introspection

of mental processes as a legitimate method. Another now famous psychologist, John B. Watson [1925], went a step further. He rejected completely the introspective method and insisted that psychological experiments be restricted to the study of behavior. This position characterized the school known as behaviorism.

Behaviorism also had three other important characteristics. One was an emphasis on conditioned reflexes as the elements—the building blocks—of behavior. Behaviorism, in fact, was very much like the structuralism it rejected in that it held that complex processes are built up out of more elementary ones. Its element, however, was the conditioned reflex rather than the sensation. We must leave the detailed explanation of the conditioned reflex to a later chapter, but we can describe it loosely as a relatively simple learned response to a stimulus. Watson felt that man's complex behavior was made up almost entirely of sets of conditioned reflexes.

Another closely related characteristic of behaviorism was its emphasis on learned, rather than unlearned, behavior. It blatantly denied the existence of instinct or of inborn tendencies. To Watson, almost all that a man becomes is a matter of the conditioning of reflexes. One of his most famous statements, in fact, is to the effect that he could take almost any infant and through proper training make him into a beggar, lawyer, or any other kind of person he desired.

Behaviorism, finally, was also characterized by an emphasis on animal behavior. It held that there was no important difference between man and animals, and that we could learn much about man by the study of animals, particularly since animals were easier to experiment with. This emphasis, in the hands of Watson and his students, led to an enormous amount of animal experimentation, which continues to the present day and has helped significantly in the solution of many psychological problems.

These characteristics of behaviorism have left their mark on modern psychology. Although behaviorism often went to extremes, it had an important underlying point, that the data of psychology, like those of any science, must be out in the open for all to see. In other words, the observations of psychology must be public observations which others can repeat and check. Behaviorism thus had a lot to do historically with gaining acceptance for the definition of psychology used above and throughout this book.

GESTALT PSYCHOLOGY. While behaviorism was displacing introspectionism in the United States, another school of thought was gaining ground in Germany. This was gestalt psychology [Köhler, 1947]. (*Gestalt* is a German word having no exact translation, but meaning something like *form, organization,* or *configuration.*) Gestalt psychology, like structuralism before it, was greatly influenced by concepts developing in physics. Coming along some thirty years later, however, the new concepts were now field concepts of such things as the pattern of lines making up a magnetic field. For that reason, gestalt psychologists, and particularly their modern descendants, are sometimes called *field theorists.*

Gestalt psychologists were characterized, first of all, by an opposition to "atomism." They felt that both structuralism and behaviorism had taken the wrong path in looking for elements such as sensations or conditioned reflexes. Our experiences and our behavior, they held, are not compounded from simple elements. Rather they are patterns or organizations somewhat analogous to a magnetic field, in which events in one part of the field are influenced by events in another part. A gray piece of paper, for example, is gray only in relation to its background or to something with which it is compared. On a black background it appears light; against a white background, it appears dark. A series of dots in any orderly arrangement is perceived as a pattern. When for instance, you view the dots in Figure 1.3, you do not perceive merely isolated dots. Rather

you see a square and a triangle sitting on a line. The dots are somehow organized in perception so that they are seen as a configuration. It will be possible to explain and illustrate the concept of organization better when we come to the subject of perception, but the point made by gestalt psychologists is that the patterns or forms of our experience cannot be explained by compounding elements.

Gestalt psychologists were also characterized by the use of a method called *phenomenology.* This is like the structuralists' use of introspection, but with one important difference. The structuralists believed in *trained* introspection for the purpose of dissecting the supposed elements of experience. The gestaltists, on the other hand, believed in *naïve* introspection. That is to say, they wanted to study what something looked like or meant to an observer. Put another way, they held that the raw phenomena of experience as reported without elaboration or analysis were legitimate observations. Thus phenomenology is a kind of method of natural observation applied to human perceptions.

Emphasis on the phenomenological method led early gestalt psychologists to emphasize the study of human experience and perception; they were empirical scientists who studied a wide range of problems. They

GESTALT PSYCHOLOGY EMPHASIZES THE PERCEPTION OF CONFIGURATIONS:

FIGURE 1.3. The dots are perceived not as so many isolated elements, but as a square and a triangle on a line.

have, for example, made important contributions to our understanding of learning, thought, and problem solving, which we shall take up at the appropriate time.

PSYCHOANALYSIS. Psychoanalysis is not a major school of psychology, for it originated outside the laboratory in medical practice, but it has had an impact on psychology, particularly in recent years. Moreover, it is so often confused with psychology that its nature and role need to be explained.

As almost everyone seems to know nowadays, psychoanalysis was founded by Sigmund Freud [1938]. Freud was a Viennese psychiatrist who frequently found himself confronted with patients whose problems he did not understand. At the time, psychiatry was characterized by an elaborate system of classifying mental disorders, but this system mainly put people in pigeonholes without providing very convincing explanations of the causes of the disorders or offering very effective methods of treatment.

Freud concerned himself with both problems, understanding and treatment. Being a physician, he made little use of the techniques and concepts of scientific psychology. He was also limited, so to speak, to the method of natural observation, that is, to studying whatever he could observe in the course of treating his patients. But he was a keen observer. He developed hypotheses as he went along and tried to test them in his interviewing and treatment of patients. In this sense, he was an empiricist and something of an experimentalist, even though he could not really experiment in a systematic way. Being a prolific writer, he exercised a wide influence on the thinking of psychiatrists, psychologists, modern literature, and even the general public through his books.

Out of his experience, Freud contributed two things. First of all, he developed a method of treatment, which is what the word *psychoanalysis* primarily refers to. The emphasis of this treatment is on *free association*—having the patient freely associate on his thoughts and experiences—with the objective of having the patient, with the help of the psychiatrist, analyze the causes of his difficulty. Secondly, he constructed a theory of personality, known as the Freudian, or psychoanalytic, theory. This theory is an elaborate one, stressing the role of motives, often hidden and repressed from both the individual and society.

Freud's theory of personality, rather than his method of treatment, is of the greater interest to psychology [Dollard and Miller, 1950]. The theory contains many unverified assertions, but it has nevertheless been valuable, for it has been a stimulus to further systematic research. In some cases, research has given strong support to Freud's notions, whereas in others it has not. Psychologists therefore do not subscribe fully to the theory. They merely regard it like other theories of personality—and there are others—as a deductive guide in planning research on the nature of personality.

We have now described five schools, or "isms," which have been important in the development of modern psychology. Each emphasized either a different aspect of psychology or a different method of observation. None was completely right or wrong. All had some beneficial effect on the development of the science of psychology.

Today these major schools have largely disappeared. Few psychologists, if any, identify themselves with any one school. Some lean more toward one than another, but this bias is very evident only in matters close to the frontier of psychology where one finds alternative theories about the explanation of events. But this is as it should be, for it leads people to do different kinds of experiments. Theoretical differences among psychologists do exist, and there are many unsolved problems in psychology, just as there are in physics and biology. We shall not stress the theoretical differences, or the unsolved problems, though we shall sometimes mention them. Instead our attention will focus on the basic, well-established facts and principles of modern scientific psychology.

Methods of observation

In sketching the origins of scientific psychology, we have stressed the development of the experimental method, for this was essential to put psychology on a scientific basis. The experimental method is not, however, the only sound method of making observations. Moreover, there is a legitimate place for theory and speculation in science, so long as it is bolstered by verifiable observations. In order to see scientific method in perspective, let us look in more detail at the advantages and disadvantages of different methods.

EXPERIMENTAL METHOD. Throughout this book we shall refer time and time again to experiments that illustrate or support certain principles. It is therefore well to have in mind exactly what an experiment is and why it is such an important aspect of science.

Repetition. An experiment, first of all, is something we can repeat. In elementary chemistry, for example, we can demonstrate that water is made up of oxygen and hydrogen simply by burning hydrogen (that is, combining it with oxygen) and collecting the water that results. Anyone with the proper equipment can do this experiment, and it has been done over and over again. In psychology, for example, we can demonstrate that recitation is an aid to study by having two groups of students study something, one with recitation and one without, and later measuring differences in learning. This and other experiments can be repeated.

The advantages of repetition are probably obvious. If we are able to repeat an observation over and over again, we can be sure of it beyond all reasonable doubt. So the repetition makes us more certain of our observations. Then too, the same experiment can be done by different people. A scientist in England and one in the United States can do the experiment, and though widely separated in time or place, they can agree on the same observations. Agreement between different observers is an important advantage. Indeed, it is a kind of "check-up-ability"— as one distinguished scientist, J. B. Conant, has called it—that is essential to science. Finally, the repeatability of an experiment makes it convenient. It is something we can do at will without waiting for the next opportunity to make a casual observation. This convenience lets us create such opportunities at our pleasure; it saves a lot of time that otherwise would be wasted waiting for the right observation.

Control. The experiment is also important to science because it provides control. One trouble with natural observation is that we cannot be sure of the conditions leading to a particular result. We have to take the conditions as we find them and draw the best conclusions we can. In an experiment, we can *control* the various conditions that might give us misleading results. Suppose, for example, that we try to determine whether caffeine has any effect on measured intelligence. Many factors might be considered in conducting an experiment on this question, but one important possibility is that a person might be influenced by the knowledge that he received some caffeine. We therefore wish to *control* this possibility. To do that, we select two groups of subjects of comparable intelligence and give one group pills containing caffeine and the other group pills, called *placebos,* which are identical in appearance but contain no caffeine. The group receiving the placebos is said to be the *control group* because the factor that is being tested is controlled in this group. The other group is called the *experimental group.*

We describe many experiments in this book. An important feature of each of them is control. What is controlled varies with the case. For example, let us say that we want to study the effects of heredity and environment. In order to control the factor of heredity, we try to find twins who have identical heredity; then we put them in different environments and observe how they differ psychologically. In another instance, we may be interested in an area of the brain. Then our control is to take some animals or human beings who are similar in most respects, but who differ in that some have part of the brain area removed while others do not. By comparing the behavior of the two groups, we can ascertain what that brain area has to do with behavior.

Variables. Another feature of the experiment is the use of two or more variables. A *variable, as the word implies, is something that varies.* Ideally it is a condition that varies quantitatively. In Figure 1.4, for example, one variable is altitude, which can be varied in feet, and the other variable is the light required to be just visible to an observer, which can be varied in standard light units. In many cases, however, a variable may be merely the presence or absence of a condition, or the amount of it. In the example above, caffeine was a variable because one group of subjects got it while the other group did not.

Variables may be either independent or dependent. An *independent variable* is a condition set by or selected by the experimenter—a stimulus presented, a drug administered, or so many feet of altitude. The *dependent variable* is a condition of the subject's behavior—his response to a stimulus, his score on an intelligence test, or his report of seeing or not seeing a light. The dependent variable is called dependent because its value depends, or may depend, on the value of the independent variable, the one independently set by the experimenter.

In every experiment we must have at least one independent variable and one dependent variable. Caffeine was an independent variable because we could vary its amount—which in this case was all or none—independently of other factors in the experiment. Intelligence, on the other hand, was a dependent variable, because we were interested in whether or not variations in intel-

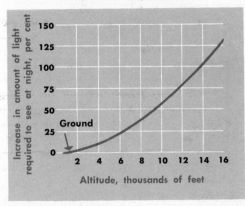

FIGURE 1.4. In plotting the results of experiments, the horizontal axis represents the independent variable, in this case altitude, and the vertical axis the dependent variable, in this case the percentage increase in the amount of light required to see at night [Millikan, 1948].

ligence could depend upon caffeine.

In some experiments, we may have more than one dependent variable. In the caffeine experiment, for example, we could have had more dependent variables by measuring other things besides intelligence, say, speed of reaction.

When the results of an experiment are presented in a graph, it is customary to let the horizontal axis (also called the abscissa or *X* axis) represent the independent variable and the vertical axis (also called the ordinate or *Y* axis) the dependent variable. Figure 1.4, for example, shows the results of an experiment on the effects of high altitude (lack of oxygen) on visual sensitivity [Millikan, 1948]. The experimenter simulated altitude by varying the amount of oxygen in a sealed chamber. Altitude, or oxygen, then, was the independent variable; it is plotted on the horizontal axis. The subjects were tested at different altitudes for the amount of light necessary to see a standard test object. This light, expressed as a percentage increase in the amount required at

THE SCIENCE OF PSYCHOLOGY 13

ground level, is the dependent variable and is plotted on the vertical axis of the graph. Thus, the convention for plotting graphs permits us to identify at a glance the independent and dependent variables.

Limitations. In many ways the experiment is the best method the scientist has, and he uses it whenever he can. The experimental method, however, has its shortcomings. It is such a good method that scientists often neglect to point out its disadvantages, but knowing them is of some value in appreciating the data it yields.

Perhaps the most obvious shortcoming is that *it cannot always be used.* Physicists, chemists, and other natural scientists do not face this difficulty often, because the lights, sounds, and chemicals that they work with never raise any objections to their experiments. People and animals are not so docile; they are not always willing to cooperate in our experiments. It is hardly possible, for example, to experiment with what makes a happy marriage—for obvious reasons. Nor is it possible to study experimentally (in people) how brain areas are important in intelligence, because a person prefers not to run the chance of being in some way handicapped by letting a scientist take away part of his brain. There are indeed many things in psychology we dare not experiment with.

A second limitation of the experiment is that *it is artificially arranged by the scientist.* In an attempt to uncover important variables, the psychologist must select the ones he wants to control. To do this, he must often be something of a detective and act on hunches or suspicions. In selecting his variables, he may be fortunate enough to pick those that are significant; but he may have bad luck and do an experiment that actually means nothing. Worse yet, he may have an experiment that seems to mean something that it really does not mean. Indeed, the scientist and psychologist must continually stand on guard against false conclusions that come from limited and somewhat artificial experiments. No matter how careful they are, they can make mistakes.

A final limitation of the experiment is that *it sometimes interferes with the very thing we are trying to study.* Physicists long ago discovered, in the field of quantum mechanics, that their experiments sometimes interfered with the behavior of small particles so that their measurements of this behavior were in error. Psychologists have even more trouble on this account.

Consider, for example, the attempt of the psychologist to find out how people fatigue when they are exposed to loud noises for a long time. He brings people into the laboratory and subjects them to loud noises (one variable). Then he measures their performance with all sorts of tests (other variables) only to find—he thinks—no fatigue. It turns out that when people know they are in an experiment they are highly motivated to perform well and will not show the fatigue they might exhibit under normal circumstances. Or, to take another example, if a psychologist brings some subjects into an experiment in which they know their personalities are being studied, they usually are not their normal selves but show quite unusual aspects of their personality. Hence the possibility that people or animals may not behave in an experiment as they normally do is something we have to consider seriously in psychological experiments.

SURVEY METHODS. What alternatives to the experimental methods do we have? One alternative has no generally accepted name, but we shall call it the survey method. Others might call it the method of systematic observation. Whatever the name, it is similar to the experimental method in that the research worker has variables he measures, but it is different in that he cannot willfully manipulate these variables. He simply makes the most systematic study he can of conditions as he finds them.

Consider the problem of studying marriage, which we have already mentioned. We cannot study marriage experimentally, but we can study it scientifically with survey techniques. The following paragraphs describe a famous study of marriage by Professor Terman of Stanford University [1938]:

Terman sought out 792 married couples. He was careful to select them from different income levels (one variable), from different age groups (another variable), from different occupations (another variable), and from different educational groups (still another variable). In fact, he had even more variables than that.

By using many subjects and collecting data from them in a systematic fashion, he was able to reach several conclusions about the causes of successful marriages. One, for example, is that the happiness of a couple depends partly on how well matched they are in strength of sex drive. By giving each couple a standardized questionnaire about their marital relations, then scoring it objectively, he was able to obtain a "happiness score." Also, by asking each spouse to rate his or her own sex drive and that of the partner, he could correlate differences in strength of sex drive with happiness. He found that happiness is greatest when the drive of the two spouses is about the same, and is less when one spouse is considerably more or less passionate than the other.

This study of marriage is an example of correlating the answers to different questions on a questionnaire given to a large representative group. In other cases, it may be possible to select groups that differ on some objective basis, and then by interviewing, to determine psychological reasons for the group differences. The following is an example drawn from an industrial situation [Katz et al., 1950]:

A large insurance company, like many companies, found that it had some groups of clerical workers within its organization that were producing a relatively large amount of work, while other groups were low producers. It wanted to know whether the leadership of the groups had anything to do with produc-

tivity. It selected twelve high-producing groups and twelve low-producing groups, matched well for number of workers in the groups, for the ages of the workers, and for the kind of work done. This matching was necessary in order to "control" such variables as size of group, age, and kind of work. The members of the groups were interviewed about their opinions of their supervisors. Did they consider the supervisor to be democratic or authoritarian? Did they consider him reasonable?

The results are summarized in Figure 1.5. Eleven out of twelve of the high-producing groups thought their supervisor was both democratic and reasonable, while none thought him to be authoritarian. Several of the low-producing groups, on the other hand, regarded their supervisor as authoritarian rather than democratic and reasonable. From such results, it could be concluded that the personality of the leader, as perceived by the subordinates, was clearly related to their production.

Survey-type methods are applicable to a large number of problems—the study of public opinion and the factors affecting it, the effects of advertising on consumer purchases, factors involved in success in college, and even such basic questions as the role of heredity and environment in the development of intelligence—to name just a few examples. Today survey methods are contributing much to the science of psychology, particularly to our knowledge of personality, social processes, and industrial problems.

CLINICAL METHODS. Some people learn a good deal about engines and automobiles not by going to school, but by fixing the machines when they break down. Similarly physicians through the years have learned much about health and disease from cases of illness that they have treated. The psychologist also learns by working with individual cases. The methods that he uses in this work are called *clinical methods*.

Such methods ordinarily are used only when people come to psychologists with

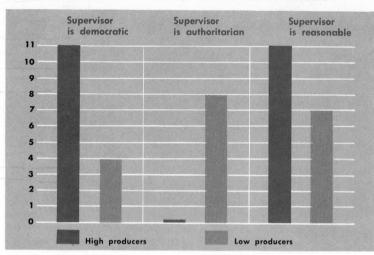

FIGURE 1.5. In this example of the survey method, most high-producing groups in the office of a large insurance company regarded their supervisors as democratic and reasonable; several of the low-producing groups considered their supervisors authoritarian [Katz et al., 1950].

problems. Little Johnny is doing badly in school and his parents bring him to the psychologist to find out why. Little Mary is throwing temper tantrums, not eating her meals, crying all night, and generally making life miserable for her parents. Jimmy, an otherwise fine young boy in high school, is caught stealing nickels from the Sunday school collection plate. Or young Mr. Doe, married for 5 years, comes in worried because he and his wife just cannot get along. Such examples could go on endlessly. All are people with problems who come to the clinical psychologist for help.

Not all clinical problems require thorough study, but when they do, the psychologist usually begins by getting a detailed account of the person's past history and of his family relations. He usually gathers this from interviews with the person and his associates. Very often he may have a specially trained social worker study the social background and environment of the person.

Then the psychologist will use tests of various kinds that have been developed through previous research. He may use intelligence tests, reading tests, interest tests, tests of emotional maturity and personality, or any of a large number he has at his command

(see Figure 1.6). From these and the biographical information, he will try to make a diagnosis of the problem—and then he will take steps to try to remedy it. The tests, the diagnosis, and the remedy will vary with the individual case. We shall study later some of the problems dealt with by psychologists.

What we are concerned with here is the clinical method as a tool in science. As a method, it combines features of natural observation, experiment, and survey. Working with individual cases, the clinician may *observe* some datum he considers to be important. By observation of cases, for example, Sigmund Freud discovered that dreams often reflect strong desires that people have but are unconscious of. In general, however, clinical observation does not provide much scientific information. It is usually too subjective, casual, uncontrolled, and lacking in precise measurement. What appear to be cause and effect in one case may not be in another. Even in a single case it is extremely difficult to separate out with certainty the significant causal factors. Probably the greatest value of clinical observation is that it suggests fruitful ideas which may be investigated more rigorously by experimental and survey methods.

THEORY IN PSYCHOLOGY. Having reviewed methods of collecting observations in psychology, we should complete the picture by indicating the role of theory in psychology.

To the layman or businessman, the word "theory" sometimes has an unsavory connotation. It may mean simply somebody's unsupported and unfounded notion of how things ought to be done. Or it may mean a set of principles obtained from books or highly artificial situations that do not work out very well in practice. Even in science, we have had some theories that turned out to be wrong or misleading.

Theory, nevertheless, is an important part of science. In fact it is one of the chief objectives of science, for science makes its greatest advances when it arrives at theories which neatly summarize many observations and predict accurately what can be expected to happen in new situations. Theory in science serves three important functions:

It serves, first, as a sort of *scientific shorthand.* A theory can summarize and generalize a lot of observations. In physics, for example, the law of gravitation is a very simple way of summarizing a host of observations about apples, stones, and feathers falling to the ground and about planets moving in their orbits. Instead of spelling out a great array of physical observations, the law of gravitation very neatly and briefly encompasses them all. In psychology, we have developed a principle—the principle of reinforcement—that the behavior of people and animals is strengthened or weakened by the use of reward or punishment, respectively. This, in a sense, is a theory that may not be entirely correct, but it is useful because it summarizes the essence of literally hundreds of experiments about learning. Hence a theory, to the extent that it states laws or principles, is a useful, shorthand way of summarizing observations.

Theory is also a *predictor.* It lets us tell in advance what will happen—given certain conditions. And the ultimate object of all science is to predict. If science were just the

FIGURE 1.6. Psychologists use tests of various kinds in measuring abilities and diagnosing personality problems [University Settlement].

collection of observations, and if one could never predict from one set of observations to another, there would be little point in science. It would do us no good to find out something, because it would never apply to any other situation. A well-developed theory is like a model house or a road map. A map, for example, depicts many of the features of a geographical area, but not all of them. Its main purpose is to tell us how we may travel in the area. Similarly, a theory lays out for us in advance many of the important features of an area of knowledge. A good map must be reasonably accurate, but it cannot tell us everything about an area. Likewise, to be useful, a theory must represent fairly well the observations it encompasses, but it need not be perfectly accurate or predict every possible detail.

There is another important use for theory, even if theory is inaccurate or wrong, and that is to *guide* us in collecting further observations in research. It was a theory about the nature of the atom that led atomic scientists to do the experiments that resulted in the atomic bomb. It was a theory, that reward and punishment are necessary for learning, that led to many experiments whose results eventually changed our methods of education. In these and many other cases, theories have been guides for research, and they have been the basis on which scientists decided how to take their next steps in making observations. When a theory is wrong or inadequate, this is soon discovered in the course of our experiments and we discard it. When it is correct or largely correct, we keep it and use it as a guide for other experiments that add further details to our knowledge.

The uses of psychology

Scientific psychology, like a baby, was of very little use when it was first born. It spent most of its early years in the laboratory making observations and devising theories to explain them. Eventually, however,

it began to be of some practical use. Its first big assignment was the development of intelligence tests in the First World War. Since then, it has taken on an increasing number of practical problems and today it spends a large part of its energies in being useful. This section will outline briefly how it does this.

First, however, we should note the phenomenal growth of psychology and of the number of psychologists in the United States. Although no one measure of growth is completely satisfactory, a rough indication can be gotten from the size of professional societies in various fields. In Table 1.1 is listed the relative size of the membership in the principal scientific societies. Membership in 1920, immediately after the First World War, is taken as the starting point and given a value of 1. Other columns in the table show at 10-year intervals the number of times membership has multiplied. Psychol-

TABLE 1.1. Relative growth of membership in various national organizations with 1920 as the base year [after Clark, 1957].

Association	1920	1930	1940	1950
Psychology	1.0	2.8	7.0	18.5
Biology	1.0	1.8	3.1	7.4*
Physics	1.0	1.9	2.9	6.9
Psychiatry	1.0	1.4	2.6	6.3
Anthropology	1.0	1.9	2.2	5.9
Mathematics	1.0	2.7	3.1	5.5
Statistics	1.0	2.3	3.2	4.4
Chemistry	1.0	1.2	1.6	4.0
Sociology	1.0	1.9	1.2	3.9
Political science	1.0	1.4	2.2	3.9
Law	1.0	2.2	2.5	3.5
Economics	1.0	1.4	1.6	3.3
Geology	1.0	1.2	1.6	2.7†

* 1949.   † 1948.

CHAPTER ONE

TABLE 1.2. Fields of specialization in psychology. The percentages of men and women in different fields, based upon more than 10,000 questionnaires returned to the National Science Foundation [based on Ogg, 1955].

Specialty	Men	Women	Total
Clinical psychology	26.3	11.8	38.1
Counseling	9.6	2.4	12.0
Educational and school psychology	6.8	3.4	10.2
Personnel and industrial psychology	9.3	0.8	10.1
Experimental psychology	8.7	1.2	9.9
Social psychology	4.3	0.6	4.9
Tests and measurements	3.0	0.6	3.6
Developmental and child psychology	1.6	1.8	3.4
Personality	2.7	0.5	3.2
Unspecialized	1.4	0.5	1.9
Human engineering	1.3	0.1	1.4
Nonpsychological	1.0	0.2	1.2
	76.0	23.9	99.9

ogy clearly outdistances all the other societies listed, having grown by a factor of 18.5 times in 30 years. By using other measures, such as the number of academic degrees granted, we would obtain slightly different results, but almost any method shows psychology to be about the fastest growing, percentagewise, of the scientific professions. This growth reflects the increasing uses of psychology in various walks of life. In 1960, there were more than 19,000 members of the American Psychological Association. If present growth trends continue, the number will double about every 10 years.

Table 1.2 shows the different fields of specialization within psychology, and thus gives an idea of the way in which psychology is being used. The different fields described there will be explained below.

CLINICAL PSYCHOLOGY. At the present time, clinical psychology is the largest field of specialization in psychology; it employs

about 38 per cent of all psychologists [Wolfle, 1948; Sanford, 1951; Clark, 1957]. When the number of individuals in clinical psychology is added to the number in counseling psychology, which is closely related, the percentage swells to about half of the entire profession.

In order to understand better what clinical psychology is, we should first distinguish among three kinds of specialists who do clinical work: psychiatrists, psychoanalysts, and clinical psychologists.

Both *psychiatrists* and *psychoanalysts* hold the M.D. degree, although there are a few nonmedical psychoanalysts. Usually, they have been trained in medicine, and then have gone into specialized training in the diagnosis and treatment of personality disorders. Such training consists largely of work in psychiatric wards and hospitals and usually does not include any substantial amount of work in psychology. The psychoanalyst is actually a psychiatrist, but he differs from other psychiatrists in that he subscribes to the general theory of personality and treatment of disorders put forth by Sigmund Freud and his followers.

The *clinical psychologist,* on the other hand, takes his basic training in normal psychology, rather than in medicine. After that, usually in the last 2 or 3 years of postgraduate work, he goes on to specialize in psychological diagnosis and psychotherapy. His training in diagnosis emphasizes the administration, scoring, and interpretation of psychological tests. His training in *psychotherapy,* like that of the psychiatrist and psychoanalyst, includes training in psychoanalytic techniques and other interview methods of helping patients solve their emotional problems. The term psychotherapy refers to *psychological methods of treating mental disorders and maladjustment,* as distinguished from shock therapy, drug therapy, and other medical methods of treatment. We shall discuss all these methods of treatment in Chapter 6.

The classification and treatment of mental illness has long been the responsibility of the psychiatrist. He began, however, to enlist the aid of psychologists in his work when he found that intelligence tests helped him estimate what he could accomplish in psychiatric care and treatment. He came to rely on psychologists even more when they developed tests for the assessment of personality. Today he regularly looks to them for aid in *personality diagnosis.* From their tests and professional opinions, as well as from his own interviews and knowledge of the case history, he arrives at a diagnosis and strategy of treatment of mental illness.

For some psychiatrists, aid in diagnosis is all that is expected or accepted from the psychologist. In other cases, the psychologist may also assist in psychotherapy. Certainly most clinical psychologists of recent vintage are trained and equipped to participate in therapeutic work. In many hospitals, especially those of the Veterans Administration and other public agencies, the need for psychotherapists has been unusually great.

In such institutions clinical psychologists frequently undertake considerable psychotherapy. This is less often the case in private practice and private hospitals; here the matter rests with the preferences of the psychiatrist in charge. It should be pointed out, however, that many psychologists, working both in hospitals and in private practice, are currently conducting psychotherapy on their own responsibility. In such cases, they first refer their patients to a physician to determine whether there are any physical complications that require medical care.

Although considerable progress has been made in the diagnosis and treatment of mental disorders, we still have a long way to go before we can feel that the problems are reasonably well in hand. There is, therefore, a pressing need for research in this area. With this everyone concerned will agree. Since the psychiatrist is trained primarily for *practice* and not for research, whereas the psychologist is typically trained in *research* and its methods, the psychologist has assumed an increasingly responsible role in the field of psychiatric research.

In recent years the idea has been gaining acceptance that psychiatric diagnosis and care should be in the hands of a psychiatric team consisting of a *psychiatrist,* a *psychologist,* and a *social worker.* In such a team, the psychiatrist has final responsibility for the care of the patient. The psychologist assumes leadership in research and assists in diagnosis and therapy. The social worker provides information about the family and background of the patient.

COUNSELING. The work of the counseling and guidance psychologist is somewhat different from that of the clinical psychologist. The counseling and guidance psychologist works with individuals having less serious problems than those requiring the services of a psychiatric team. He counsels those with emotional or personal problems who need some expert guidance. Thus he serves as a screen to separate those persons who need no more than wise counseling from those who need intensive psychiatric attention.

The counseling and guidance psychologist also helps individuals with vocational and academic problems. Working in schools, in industry, in colleges, and indeed in private practice, he administers tests of intelligence, aptitudes, interests, and personality and gives such guidance as is needed. Often this is a matter of apprising parents of the abilities and limitations of their children, or of helping a student improve his study habits, or of advising him about a vocational choice, or of helping a person work out a minor personal problem. The counseling psychologist may also engage in psychotherapy. When he does, he must always be on the alert for severe emotional problems that should be referred to a psychiatrist or clinical psychologist for a final judgment.

The employment of counseling psychologists has increased substantially in recent years. Many colleges and universities have established psychological clinics or counseling centers. Some of the larger industrial and manufacturing concerns have formal counseling programs to render aid in solving personal problems. Many schools, particularly high schools, are installing counselors whose chief duty is to help students with their vocational and personal problems. Hence this field of psychology is rapidly expanding.

EDUCATION. In carrying out their training functions, educators encounter many problems that can benefit from psychological knowledge. The study of the development of the child helps us to understand how his abilities and personality change in the course of development. Such an understanding, if put to use, enables us to know better what to teach, when to teach it, and how to teach it. Tests of intelligence and personality can, of course, be used to assess how fast the child can progress and in what direction. Psychological research on learning and the effectiveness of different methods of teaching has found application in the writing of textbooks and in classroom methods. In the colleges and universities, methods of selecting students—especially those methods that depend upon tests of aptitudes and special abilities—have required the services of persons trained in psychology. In these and other ways psychology is applied in an educational setting.

INDUSTRY. Some years ago, business and industry made relatively little use of scientific psychology. Recently, though, the situation has been changing. As Table 1.2 shows, an appreciable percentage of psychologists are now employed in personnel and industrial psychology. It is still growing, and it may well be the next one to undergo the kind of expansion experienced in clinical psychology, counseling, and educational psychology.

The first applications of psychology to industrial problems were in the use of intelligence and aptitude tests. Today many of the larger business firms have well-established programs of selection and placement that make substantial use of psychological tests. They are also finding other applications of psychology to problems of training, to supervision of personnel, to improving communications, to counseling employees, and to alleviating industrial strife. Psychologists are seldom in managerial positions enabling them to deal directly with these problems, but they are called upon as consultants. Moreover, an increasing number of businessmen are getting some training in business and industrial psychology.

There are also firms of industrial psychologists, which are growing in number and prestige. They are usually incorporated and sell their services to many different concerns. For one business, they may set up a selection program; for another, they may make recommendations concerning its training program; for another, they may examine the problems of supervision and human relations within the company; for still others, they may survey consumer attitudes toward products or the effectiveness of the company's advertising. Utilizing the services of nonstaff psychologists seems to appeal to many businesses as being more efficient than employing psychologists on a permanent basis. It has advantages for the psychologists too, allowing them to become familiar with similar problems in different enterprises and conserving their time for the solution of practical problems rather than enmeshing them in routine nonpsychological duties that are likely to be involved in regular employment. At any rate, the separate firm of psychologists is becoming an established way of putting psychology to work in industry.

GOVERNMENT.   The Federal government is the largest employer in the United States. Add to that the employees of the state and local governments, and you have a force of close to eleven million people. These employees, moreover, are highly specialized. Whether they be in the postal, diplomatic, forestry, power, law-enforcement, tax-collection, or military services, they have jobs that require special abilities and training. Being for the most part under civil service or merit systems, government employees are supposed to be selected and promoted according to fair and objective standards. It is no wonder, then, that government has taken the lead in the development and use of scientific methods of selection and placement.

We shall point out at numerous places in the book the way in which tests have been employed in the military services. By the end of the Second World War, selection tests were available for a long list of specialists such as tank men, gunners, pilots, bombardiers, riflemen, and mechanics. Research on methods of selection continues on a wide scale. Psychologists are needed for this research as well as to administer tests and to adapt them to new uses. Various agencies of the government, including the U.S. Employment Service, have also developed forms of achievement tests for evaluating and promoting personnel. Many were

devised specifically for aiding jobseekers and for aiding private employers in their task of fitting the right person to the right job.

The Second World War opened up another application of psychology to the government's problems. This is sometimes called *human engineering* or *engineering psychology*. It concerns the *design of equipment* and the tasks of individuals who operate such equipment. Thus psychologists became involved in the design of airplane cockpits, the controls of guns, or the instruments and controls of all sorts of equipment. To these problems psychologists bring their knowledge of perception, of learning, and of experimental methods of measuring human performance under various conditions. Obviously this application is of great concern to the military services, which are charged with getting the most out of very complex equipment. On the other hand, human engineers can assist in the design of civilian machines, such as automobiles, stoves, lathes, cranes, locomotives and printing presses—to name just a few. We are beginning to see more applications in this direction (see Figure 1.7).

Two other uses of psychology in government service also deserve mention. One is in the Veterans Administration, in its hospitals and centers. Here clinical and counseling psychologists take part in various services rendered veterans. The other is in several agencies of the government concerned with public attitudes and economic matters. Either directly or through major contracts with polling centers, these agencies regularly use the techniques of social psychology to gather information which guides financial and other government policies. We shall learn more about this in the next section.

SOCIAL PROBLEMS.   Last, but not least, psychology is used in the solution of social and economic problems. Many private agencies, such as the National Conference of Christians and Jews, the American Jewish Congress, and the National Association for the Advancement of Colored People, have become acquainted with the facts and principles that psychologists have uncovered concerning matters of prejudice. In some instances they employ psychologists who have conducted research on prejudice and who advise them concerning strategies for combating it. Municipal and state agencies engaged in dealing with crime and delinquency also make use of psychologists and their skills in waging their battles for healthier communities.

Aside from such social problems as prejudice, crime, and delinquency, our leaders in government are leaning more and more on information collected by polling techniques to find out what people think about important issues. During the Depression, when the government undertook to help the farmers out of their dire economic plight, psychologists made careful surveys of what farmers wanted most, what kinds of controls they were willing to accept as necessary for their own betterment, and their attitudes toward numerous policies designed to improve their lot. Often these surveys made it clear that schemes based on sound economic principles would fail solely because people held negative attitudes toward them. In other cases, campaigns were conducted to educate and inform farmers on important problems. Our Treasury Department, in its efforts to increase wartime savings and to combat inflation, often based its decision on how to sell government bonds on information about people's savings habits and attitudes collected through polling techniques. These are just a few ways in which survey methods developed by social psychologists are put to work in the interest of the general welfare and the better solution of social problems.

ANIMAL PSYCHOLOGY. A far cry from social psychology and consumer surveys, but nevertheless pertinent to a discussion of the uses of psychology, is the field of animal psychology. We have already indicated that animal behavior is of interest in its own right and helps us to understand human

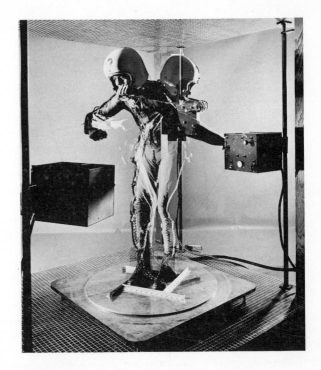

FIGURE 1.7. Simulation of man in space. Human engineers in the United States Air Force study some of man's reactions under one of the conditions to be encountered in space. The man above is on a frictionless platform, in conditions that simulate the weightlessness of space, and can move only by flailing his arms. His ability to operate controls under these conditions is also being studied [William Vandivert, © 1957]. Below, the effects of prolonged weightlessness—simulated by immersion in a tank of water—on performance of various tasks are studied [R. M. Chambers, U.S. Naval Air Development Center].

behavior. In addition, it has practical uses and appears to be having more and more as time goes on.

In many instances, animals can be used to advantage because they have better sensory acuity than man and, at the same time, often are more reliable. Watchdogs are employed to protect homes and property because of keen senses of hearing and smell. Bloodhounds can track down criminals and people who are lost because they excel in olfactory acuity. Similar abilities in other dogs have made them useful in hunting. The seeing-eye dog can be trained to take the place of a person's vision. These and many other instances are well known to everybody.

Not so well known, however, are some special uses of animals as "detectors." Canaries are very sensitive to noxious gases and have been used in coal mines and tunnels to detect such gases. In Europe, the "weather frog" is often used as a prophet of rain. When kept in an aquarium partly filled with water, it will climb up a ladder to signal rain, because it climbs only when the humidity is high. Recently, minnows have come into use to detect the pollution of streams—a problem of increasing techno-logical importance. The minnows are trained in aquariums to avoid areas in which there are traces of pollution.

Of many other uses of animal behavior, two of the more novel are illustrated in Figure 1.8. In one case, the pigeon serves as a production-line inspector. He inspects the paint job on parts passing his window. In the other case, the pigeon is used as a pilot in a homing missile, replacing complicated physical devices for steering a missile to its target. In both cases, the excellent visual acuity and the reliability of the highly trained pigeon are exploited.

We are also reading daily of the use of animals—mice, rats, dogs, monkeys—as advance "patrols" in the exploration of space. From them we learn what man can be expected to do, and not be able to do, in his space voyages.

These are just a few of the many uses, or possible uses, of animal behavior in human affairs. We shall undoubtedly see more in years to come.

CAREERS IN PSYCHOLOGY. Psychology, we have seen, is a rapidly growing field with a number of interesting possibilities for specializing and with opportunities for employ-

THE INSPECTOR IS A BIRD, AND SO IS THE DRIVER:

  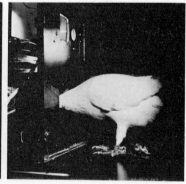

FIGURE 1.8. The pigeon as an inspector and controller. Left to right, a pigeon looks at the paint job on parts stopping in front of his window. He pecks at the window when he sees a bad job. For this he is rewarded [W. W. Cumming, Columbia Univer.; photos by Leonard Kamsler]. Far right, a pigeon is placed in the nose cone of a guided bomb.

ment in many different settings. It is one of the more popular majors in liberal arts colleges, and about 10 per cent of the students going on to graduate school for the master's degree or doctor of philosophy are in the field of psychology. It is therefore of interest to consider briefly how one becomes a psychologist and the ways in which psychologists are employed (see Table 1.3).

The person planning to become a psychologist should take a broad program of training in the natural and social sciences. Psychology is a bridge between these groups of sciences and requires some knowledge of them. Hence it is advisable to take some training in such fields as mathematics, physics, chemistry, biology, sociology, economics, and political science. Students most interested in experimental psychology and biological subjects should take additional work in the natural sciences; those most interested in the social, clinical, and industrial fields should take further work in the social and behavioral sciences. In any case, one should not concentrate too much in psychology, for that can be left to graduate training. He should take the courses required for a major, which usually include experimental psychology and statistics, but otherwise he should

By pecking at a switch whenever instruments indicate the bomb is off course he can help steer the bomb to its target [B. F. Skinner, 1960].

attempt to obtain a broad basic training in the sciences.

Unlike some fields, psychology offers little or no opportunity for employment if one has only a bachelor's degree. There are some positions here and there as assistants, which may be attractive to a girl who plans later to make a career of marriage or to a boy who needs temporary employment before going on for further training, but these positions usually have little future. There are also some industrial positions, chiefly in personnel work, open to those holding undergraduate degrees. In general, though, if one plans to make a career of psychology, one should go on to graduate school.

Standards for admission to graduate school in psychology are relatively high. To be admitted, the candidate usually must have aptitudes considerably above the average of college students—many graduate schools require that the applicant take special tests of aptitude—and his grade record ordinarily must be good too. The majority of those admitted have B to A averages, and most graduate schools do not admit C students unless there are convincing extenuating circumstances.

One does not have to be rich, or even able to afford the usual cost of college, to go to graduate school. Numerous fellowships and assistantships are available for able students. Many are offered to entering graduate students, and it is a rare student who cannot obtain substantial assistance once he is enrolled and has done satisfactory work for a year. Almost all students are self-supporting, through fellowships or assistantships, by the time they take their doctoral degrees.

Two degrees are available in graduate schools. The master's degree (usually a Master of Arts but sometimes a Master of Science), which is all some of the smaller graduate schools offer, requires 1 to 2 years of full-time work or its equivalent. The program for this degree regularly includes a core curriculum taken by all graduate students, as well as an opportunity to specialize

TABLE 1.3. Principal employer and principal function expressed as a percentage of a sample of about 13,000 psychologists [based on figures from the National Science Foundation Register, 1954–1955].

Principal employer	Principal function							
	Teaching	Testing	Administration	Research	Clinical practice	Consulting	Miscellaneous	Totals
College or university	20.0	2.1	5.8	7.4	2.9	1.0	0.4	39.6
Other educational institutions	1.0	3.5	1.7	0.4	1.5	1.0	0.1	9.2
Federal government, including Armed Forces	0.3	3.3	3.5	4.6	4.1	0.5	0.4	16.7
State and local government	0.2	5.0	2.1	0.6	3.4	0.4	0.2	11.9
Nonprofit organizations, including hospitals	0.3	2.3	1.3	1.6	2.9	0.5	0.2	9.1
Private and self-employed	1.1	1.0	1.4	2.1	1.9	1.8	0.2	9.5
Miscellaneous	0.0	0.0	0.0	0.0	0.1	0.0	3.9	4.0
Totals	22.9	17.2	15.8	16.7	16.8	5.2	5.4	100.0

somewhat in a field in which the person expects to be employed. The doctor's degree usually requires a total of 3 to 5 years of full-time work or its equivalent, including the work for the master's degree. It involves considerably more advanced and specialized work than the master's and the completion of a significant piece of research. For either lack of interest or lack of ability, roughly half of those who take master's degrees do not go on for the doctorate.

There are many employment opportunities in public and private schools, in industry, and in government for those holding the master's degree. The person must expect, however, to receive substantially less salary than if he holds the doctor's degree, and his opportunities for promotion are often limited. In some areas, however, particularly in government and industry, he has about the same opportunity to succeed as the person with a doctorate. On the other hand, for most regular teaching positions in colleges and universities and for a position of responsibility in a research organization, the doctorate is now almost mandatory. In general, a person who expects to make a lifelong career of psychology in teaching and/or research is well advised to try for the doctor's degree.

The remuneration for positions in psychology varies considerably from one situation to another. In general, it is lowest in teaching positions, somewhat higher in government, and highest in industry. On the whole, however, the financial rewards in psychology compare reasonably well with those of other professional pursuits, and the positions that are not so lucrative often have the compensation of allowing more freedom for research, writing, and independent work.

For additional information on careers in psychology, the student should consult his professor and the journal *American Psychologist*. This journal publishes annually a list of the fellowships and assistantships available to prospective graduate students. It also contains articles on the income of psychologists working in various settings.

Summary

1. Although the beginning course in psychology offers much of practical value, the student should expect to acquire from it only the rudiments, not profound knowledge or skill.

2. Psychology covers a wide range of problems, not only those of dealing with people and understanding them, but also the problems of social groups, intelligence and abilities, working efficiently, learning and perceiving, and many others. Psychology is the science of human and animal behavior.

3. Psychology is one of the behavioral sciences. These disciplines include certain aspects of history, economics, and social and political sciences, and they sometimes overlap the domains of such natural sciences as physiology and physics.

4. Like other natural and social sciences, psychology owes its parentage to philosophy. It made little headway as a science, however, until it adopted the experimental method and founded laboratories for psychological research.

5. For many years, psychological research was guided by different schools of thought: structuralism, behaviorism, gestalt psychology, functionalism, and psychoanalysis. These schools, however, have tended to disappear and merge into one as more and more factual information has accumulated.

6. The experimental method has been a cornerstone in the emergence of modern psychology, because it offers the advantages of (a) repetition, (b) control of variables, and (c) the measurement of variables. It has the limitations, however, of (a) not being feasible in every situation, (b) artificially restricting situations, and (c) sometimes interfering with the variables to be measured.

7. Experimental methods often need to be supplemented by survey methods and clinical methods. Both survey and clinical methods may be used when it is possible to measure relevant variables. When experiments are difficult or impossible, they may be the only methods that can be used.

8. Theory is essential in scientific psychology, as it is in every science. It serves (a) as a scientific shorthand, (b) as a predictor of facts, and (c) as a guide to further research.

9. Psychology, for the first few years after its establishment as a scientific subject, was mainly a pure academic science. It began to have practical applications in the First World War. Now it is one of the fastest, if not the fastest, growing of the scientific professions.

10. Clinical psychology is currently the largest single field in which psychology is being applied. It deals with research, diagnosis, and therapy in problems of abnormal behavior.

11. Other important areas in which psychology is being applied are guidance and counseling, education, industry, government, social problems, and animal psychology.

All the statements in the true-false test on page 3 are false, in some cases because of loose wording or overgeneralization. These statements, however, are typical of the assertions often heard from people who are untrained in psychology.

Boring, E. G. *A history of experimental psychology* (2d ed.). New York: Appleton-Century-Crofts, 1950.
An authoritative and well-written history of experimental psychology that is the standard work in its field.

Brown, C. W., and Ghiselli, E. E. *Scientific method in psychology.* New York: McGraw-Hill, 1955.
A unique book that describes the application of scientific method to problems in many fields of human behavior.

Clark, K. E. *America's psychologists: A survey of a growing profession.* Washington, D.C.: American Psychological Association, 1957.
A statistical survey of the characteristics of psychologists, with particular emphasis on the factors influencing the development of outstanding psychologists.

Conant, J. B. *On understanding science.* New Haven, Conn.: Yale Univer. Press, 1947.
A brief, interesting account of the development of scientific method in the physical sciences, written by a distinguished chemist and educator.

Daniel, R. S., and Louttit, C. M. *Professional problems in psychology.* Englewood Cliffs, N.J.: Prentice-Hall, 1953.
An account of the growth of psychology as a profession and a source of information for the preparation of psychological articles and books.

Gray, J. S. *Psychology applied to human affairs* (2d ed.). New York: McGraw-Hill, 1954.
A textbook covering the different fields of application of psychology.

McCormick, E. J. *Human engineering.* New York: McGraw-Hill, 1957.
The applications of experimental psychology and its methods to problems of engineering equipment for human use.

Murphy, G. *Historical introduction to modern psychology* (rev. ed.). New York: Harcourt Brace, 1949.
A highly readable overview of the history of psychology, providing a good picture of the background of many areas of modern psychology.

Rubinstein, E. A., and Lorr, M. (eds.). *Survey of clinical practice in psychology.* New York: International Univer. Press, 1954.
An account written by different authorities of the work of the clinical psychologist in various settings.

Underwood, B. J. *Psychological research.* New York: Appleton-Century-Crofts, 1957.
A textbook on methods of doing psychological research.

Watson, R. I. *Psychology as a profession.* Garden City, N.Y.: Doubleday, 1954.
A brief resume of psychology as a profession intended for the beginning student in psychology.

Wilson, J. T. et al. *Current trends in psychology and the behavioral sciences.* Pittsburgh: Univer. Pittsburgh Press, 1955.
A discussion of current research and theory in psychology and the behavioral sciences, by six experts in different fields.

Woodworth, R. S. *Contemporary schools of psychology* (rev. ed.). New York: Ronald, 1948.
A summary of the various schools of psychology, their historical origins, and their important contributions to psychological theory.

Maturation & development

A GOOD WAY TO BEGIN the study of behavior is to start with its beginnings in the life of the individual. Behavior begins long before the individual is born. The first movements of the body take place, in fact, only 8 weeks after conception, 7 months before birth. This point in time has sometimes been called the behavior zero, but even it is not the real beginning of all that matters in understanding the behavior of the individual. For that, we must go back to the origin of the individual, the moment of conception. At this point, two *germ cells,* one a *sperm cell* from the father and the other an *egg cell* (or *ovum*) from the mother, unite to form a new individual, which is called a *zygote.* This zygote receives genetic material from the father and the mother that will determine not only the physical make-up, but many of the psychological characteristics of the new individual. For that reason, the study of behavior properly begins with the study of the mechanisms of heredity.

Mechanisms of heredity

Each of the two germ cells (sperm and ovum) which unite to form the zygote consists of a dark nucleus surrounded by a light, watery substance, which is enclosed in turn in a membrane. When the two cells form a zygote, they merge their parts into a single cell of the same general structure.

29

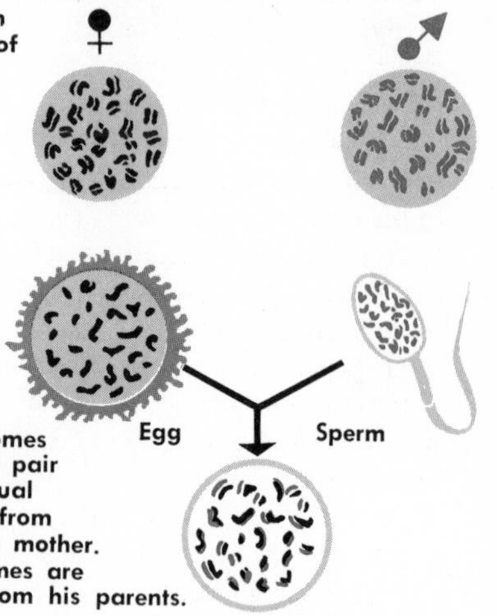

A NEW INDIVIDUAL IS FORMED BY THE UNION OF THE EGG
OF THE MOTHER AND THE SPERM OF THE FATHER:

FIGURE 2.1. The mechanism of transmission of chromosomes from the germ cells of the mother and father to the fertilized egg.

The cells of the body of men and women have 24 pairs of chromosomes.

At maturity each germ cell has only 24 single chromosomes. One member is taken randomly from each original pair.

At fertilization the chromosomes of the man and the woman pair up, so that the new individual gets 24 pairs again — half from his father and half from his mother. These two sets of chromosomes are all that a person inherits from his parents.

Egg   Sperm

The part of the zygote of principal interest to us is the nucleus, for it contains the genetic material that transmits hereditary characteristics from the parents to the new individual.

CHROMOSOMES. The genetic material consists of *chromosomes* and *genes*. The genes are the real genetic units, but they are carried on chromosomes. Hence both must be considered.

The term "chromosome" means colored body, and it is called that because it stains darkly when treated with special dyes. When thus stained it can be seen in the microscope as a twisted string of odd-sized and odd-shaped beads in the nucleus of the cell. Chromosomes are visible in most of the cells of the body, but only the chromosomes in the sperm, egg, and zygote have anything to do with inheritance, for the merger of the chromosomes of the egg cell and the sperm cell, when they form the zygote, is the only genetic link between an individual and his parents.

Each species of animal has a characteristic number of chromosomes per cell. The number, however, may vary slightly from one cell to another. In the case of man, the characteristic number is 48, although some cells with 46 chromosomes have been described. Whatever the number, the chromosomes occur in pairs. Thus human chromosomes are arranged in 24 (or 23) pairs (see Figure 2.1). The egg and sperm cells, however, pass through a stage in their production when the pairs of chromosomes split apart, leaving only one of each pair—a set of 24 single chromosomes—for each cell. The two single sets from the sperm and egg combine to make new pairs when the sperm and egg unite; therefore, in the zygote we find 24 pairs of chromosomes.

GENES. Genes are too small to be seen under the microscope, but they are contained in the chromosomes, and they are the basic units of heredity. Genes are complex chemical packets, having the unique ability to form other packets just like themselves or, in some cases, only similar to themselves. In other words, they are able to do the thing that characterizes living tissue, namely, to reproduce themselves. Genes are also able to control the chemical processes of a cell and, interacting somehow with other cells,

30   CHAPTER TWO

to determine the kind of tissues formed to make the various organs and the structure of the body. That is to say, they direct the course of development of the body. This is the basic mechanism of inheritance, for it is in this way that genes duplicate in the new individual characteristics previously found in his ancestors.

Genes always work in pairs, one member of which comes from the mother and the other from the father. A pair of genes working together directs the development of some particular characteristic of the body or of behavior. Sometimes the two genes in a pair are identical even though they come from different parents. Then there is no doubt about the characteristic they will produce. If, for example, each gene of a pair is so constituted that it will produce blue eyes, the new individual will certainly have blue eyes; or if both genes are "brown-eyed," the individual will surely have brown eyes.

Often two genes of a pair are not identical, but govern the same characteristic in a slightly different way (see Figure 2.2). One gene, for example, may produce brown eyes, the other blue eyes. The outcome then depends on which gene is dominant and which is recessive. A *dominant gene* is one whose characteristic will be dominant when paired with another gene. A *recessive gene*, conversely, is one whose characteristic will not be produced when it is paired with a dominant gene. Hence we do not see the characteristic of a recessive gene when it is paired with a dominant gene. The only way we can tell it is there is by knowing that one parent possessed the recessive characteristic or by observing that some of the offspring of the person have the recessive characteristic. This can happen only when the person's mate also has recessive genes which by chance pair with his recessive gene. Brown eyes are a good example of a dominant characteristic; blue eyes, of a recessive char-

FIGURE 2.2. The inheritance of brown and blue eyes.

Examined closely, a pair of chromosomes looks like two identical strings of beads. Each "bead" is actually a small chemical packet called a gene.

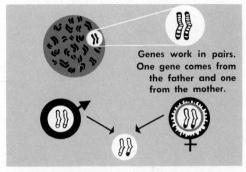

Genes work in pairs. One gene comes from the father and one from the mother.

If genes differ, one may dominate the other.

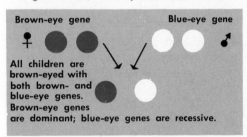

Brown-eye gene   Blue-eye gene

All children are brown-eyed with both brown- and blue-eye genes. Brown-eye genes are dominant; blue-eye genes are recessive.

If genes are alike, they work together smoothly.

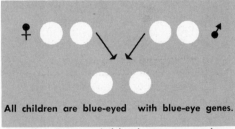

All children are blue-eyed   with blue-eye genes.

Recessive genes carried by the parent may be expressed in the offspring.

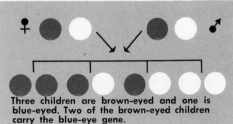

Three children are brown-eyed and one is blue-eyed. Two of the brown-eyed children carry the blue-eye gene.

TABLE 2.1. Some dominant and recessive characteristics [after Krech and Crutchfield, 1958].

Dominant characteristic	Recessive characteristic
Brown eyes	Blue eyes
Dark or brunette hair	Light, blond, or red hair
Curly hair	Straight hair
Normal hair	Baldness
Normal color vision	Color blindness
Normal sight	Night blindness
Normal hearing	Congenital deafness
Normal coloring	Albinism (lack of pigment)
Immunity to poison ivy	Susceptibility to poison ivy
Normal blood	Hemophilia (lack of blood clotting)
Extra fingers or toes	Normal number of digits
Fingers lacking one joint	Normal length of fingers
Double-jointedness	Normal joints
Dwarfing of limbs	Normally proportioned limbs

acteristic. Table 2.1 gives a list of other common characteristics that may be either dominant or recessive.

SEX DETERMINATION.   Genes also determine whether the new individual will be a male or a female. The genes concerned are found on one particular pair of chromosomes. If the two chromosomes (see Figure 2.3) are identical, that is, if both are what we call X chromosomes, the result is a female. If one of the pair is not an X chromosome but is a somewhat smaller chromosome, called a Y chromosome, the result is a male.

The sex of an individual is determined by the sperm of the father, not by the egg of the mother. Since each pair of the mother's chromosomes is an X, all eggs produced by the mother have only X chromosomes after the cells go through the process, mentioned earlier, in which the pairs of chromosomes are split apart, leaving only single ones. When the sperm of the father goes through the same process, however, half of the resulting sperms contain Y chromosomes, and the other half X chromosomes. Subsequently, the kind of sperm which fertilizes the egg determines whether the offspring will be male or female.

SEX-LINKED CHARACTERISTICS.   The chromosomes that determine sex also carry on them genes that govern other characteristics. These genes are found only on the X chromosome, not on the Y. Since the male has X as well as Y chromosomes, he consequently always possesses the characteristics produced by these genes, whether they be dominant or recessive. In the female, however, the usual rules for pairing dominant and recessive genes hold, because she has only X chromosomes. As a result, a recessive *sex-linked characteristic* always shows up in the male, but may be hidden in the female if it is paired with a dominant characteristic.

Color blindness is a good example of a sex-linked characteristic (see Figure 2.4). It happens to be recessive, but it is carried on the X chromosome. So whenever a male has the recessive gene for color blindness, he is color-blind, without exception. If he marries a normal woman carrying no genes for color blindness, all his sons will be normal because they will receive their father's Y chromosome and their mother's X chromosome. All his daughters, however will be *carriers* without displaying any color blindness, for they will receive a dominant X from their mother and a recessive X from their father. When the carrier mother marries, the possibility of

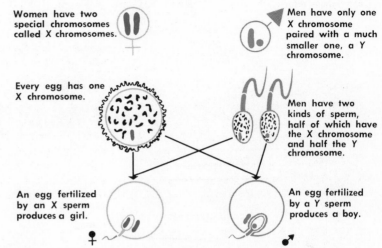

Women have two special chromosomes called X chromosomes.

Men have only one X chromosome paired with a much smaller one, a Y chromosome.

Every egg has one X chromosome.

Men have two kinds of sperm, half of which have the X chromosome and half the Y chromosome.

FIGURE 2.3. Sex determination.

An egg fertilized by an X sperm produces a girl.

An egg fertilized by a Y sperm produces a boy.

her children being color-blind depends upon whether their father is color-blind and upon which of her *X* chromosomes, the dominant or the recessive one, is passed on to the offspring. The possibilities, including the proportions expected, are given in Figure 2.4.

MULTIPLE DETERMINATION. Traits that are determined by a single pair of genes illustrate nicely the basic principles of genetics. There is a fairly long list of such traits, and some of them are named in Table 2.1. In general, they are rather simple things that depend on the presence or absence of some one thing in a tissue or organ of the body. Eye color, for example, is a matter of pigmentation of the iris. The pigmented iris is brown, the unpigmented is blue. Color blindness is probably caused by lack of a photosensitive substance in the eye, or if not that, by lack of the appropriate connections among the cells of the eye. There are even cases in which something as complex as a particular kind of feeble-mindedness can be traced to a single pair of genes, but in these cases the trouble lies in the lack of a single substance in the brain necessary for its normal functioning. Hence traits that are determined by single pairs of genes depend on the presence or absence

of some one thing in the body that affects the structure or appearance of an organ.

Many traits, obviously, depend on more than one thing. Athletic ability, intelligence, temperament, and susceptibility to mental disease are examples. Such traits have a hereditary basis, although they are not entirely determined by heredity. In so far as they are hereditary, they are multiply determined by many pairs of genes, not just one. In some cases of multiple determination, usually where the number of genes is not large, geneticists have been able to work out the rules of inheritance. In most cases of multiple determination, however, this has been impossible, just because the situation has proved too complicated. Without knowing the rules, however, it is possible to conclude from appropriate studies of inbreeding and crossbreeding that a particular trait is multiply determined. A little later we shall show some examples of psychological interest.

GENETIC CHANGE. Genes, we have seen, are the units of heredity, and a person receives his genes from his parents, who in turn received theirs from their parents, and so on back to the first man and woman. Indeed, there is an unbroken line of transmission through the germ cells of one gen-

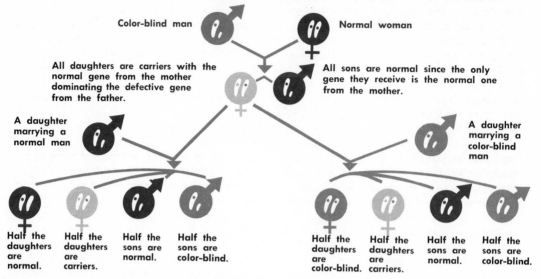

FIGURE 2.4. The inheritance of color blindness as an example of a sex-linked characteristic.

eration on through all succeeding generations. The cells of the body other than the germ plasm are outside this line (see Figure 2.7). Anything that happens to them, through injury, disease, or the acquiring of new characteristics, is irrelevant to heredity, for they never contribute their genes to the next generation.

It follows from this that acquired characteristics cannot be inherited. A person who acquires great athletic or musical skill cannot pass this on *genetically* to his child, because the skill is developed in the use of his muscle and nerve cells but has no way of modifying the genes in his germ cells. A few geneticists have contested this conclusion, notably Lamarck in the nineteenth century, when the science of genetics was still very young, and more recently Lysenko in Russia, who presumably was motivated by ideological considerations. Indeed, it would be very nice if we could improve the quality of the human (or animal) race by training individuals or by modifying them through drugs or surgery and passing on the characteristic to their offspring. Unfortunately,

the mechanisms of heredity, as we know them, make this seem completely hopeless, and there has never been any satisfactory evidence to the contrary.

It also follows from the fact of continuity of germ cells that any changes in heredity can take place only through changes in the genes. This fortunately, but also unfortunately, does sometimes happen. In the long history of the human and animal races, genes and the traits they determine have occasionally changed. By far the majority of such changes have had no lasting or beneficial effect, for they have produced traits that are incompatible with the life of the organism, either causing it to die very early in its existence or making it unsuitable for survival in its normal environment. Only a few changes, probably one in many millions, have produced traits compatible with the survival of the organism and the species.

Such changes in genes are called *mutations*. Mutations take place spontaneously in the sense that we do not always know what causes them. One cause, however, is known. This is the irradiation of germ cells

CHAPTER TWO

by charged particles. Such particles exist in abundance in the cosmic rays of the ionosphere of the earth 20 to 600 miles up. Few ever get through our atmosphere to the earth, but some do, and if they penetrate the body and hit a gene, they may knock something off it or otherwise rearrange its structure so that it is changed. Hence the trait it determines is also changed. There may be other causes of mutations, but this one has been established. In fact, it has been duplicated in the laboratory by using X rays, which are similar to the particles generated by cosmic rays, to induce genetic mutations in animals. Geneticists figure that there have been enough such spontaneous mutations in the last few hundred million years to account for the creation of new species in the animal and plant kingdoms.

FAMILY INHERITANCE. Each species of animal, man included, has its set of chromosomes and genes that determine the particular characteristics of the species. Within a species, the combination of genes an individual receives is a matter of chance. First it is chance that determines which member of a pair of genes goes into a sperm or egg when the pairs of chromosomes are divided into single sets. Consequently no two sperm or egg cells are alike, for each receives a random set of genes. Secondly, it is purely by chance that a particular sperm fuses with a particular egg to form a zygote. Since the number of genes is very large, the number of possible combinations of genes is astronomical. Hence there is an extremely small chance that any two individuals can have exactly the same genetic make-up. We may therefore expect individuals to differ widely in their heredity and thus in their traits.

Individuals of the same family, however, may be expected to have similar genes and traits. Each parent contributes half of his genes to his child, and the child in turn contributes half of his to his children. Although each half is unique, it may happen that some of the genes of a brother and sister will be identical. So too will be some of the genes of parent and child. Thus it is to be expected that brothers and sisters will resemble each other as well as their parents in some traits. There will also be resemblances between a grandparent and a grandchild, but of lesser degree, for a child on the average receives only one-quarter (one-half of one-half) of the genes of a particular grandparent.

There is only one case in which two individuals have absolutely identical heredities. This is the case of *identical twins* (or identical triplets, identical quadruplets, etc.). Identical twins are twins who develop from the same zygote. If a zygote divides into two cells, each separately goes on to form a new individual. Since each cell has the same genes as the zygote, the heredity of the two individuals will be identical. It follows from this that identical twins are always of the same sex, for each has the same sex chromosomes as the original zygote.

Not all twins, however, are identical. In fact, most twins are *fraternal twins*. These develop from two separate eggs of the mother, and hence begin as two zygotes formed independently by two different sperms. For this reason, fraternal twins are no more alike genetically than ordinary siblings born at different times. For this reason too, they may or may not be of the same sex. Hence when twins are not of the same sex, they are fraternal, not identical. The only unique thing about fraternal twins is that they are born at the same time and thus have more similar environments, both before and after birth, than brothers or sisters born at different times.

Twins are extremely useful in the study of the problems of heredity and environment, the subject we will take up next. Since identical twins have identical heredities, any differences between them must be explained on the basis of different environments. Since, on the other hand, fraternal twins are no more alike genetically than ordinary siblings, differences between fraternal twins would be attributable to genetics if their environments were identical.

Heredity and environment

With the mechanisms of heredity in mind, we are now prepared to consider a problem that has long interested almost everyone who attempts to understand human behavior. It has been called the problem of heredity *versus* environment or of nature *versus* nurture. The *"versus"* gets in these phrases because people often argue for one against the other, taking either the view that a man's hereditary nature determines pretty much what kind of person he can be or the contrary view that men are more or less equal in heredity and that the environment in which one is nurtured determines what he becomes. Such arguments, however, are quite futile, for in reality both heredity *and* environment, or nature *and* nurture, jointly fashion a person's abilities, skills, and psychological characteristics. The problem is not to choose between them but rather to define precisely how the two interacting with each other determine these characteristics.

ROLE OF HEREDITY. There is no obvious connection between genes and what a person does, so it is reasonable to ask what connection there might be between them. The link has to be the structure and function of the organs of the body, for nothing else is plausible. The genes control the development of tissues and organs of the body and hence the way in which the body functions. These functions, clearly, affect behavior, for such organs as the brain, the senses, and the muscles participate in behavior. Here, then, is the connection between genes and behavior. By keeping it in mind, we know when and when not to expect heredity to play a role in behavior.

There are several ways in which this link might work. One is through simple structure. If a person inherits short legs, stubby fingers, or a deaf ear, his abilities in some fields must be limited. This is clear, and it accounts for some of the psychological defects that are inherited as well as for hereditary limitations on the skills a person can develop. Another way for the link to work is through chemical functions. Myriad chemical substances are concerned in the body's activities—photosensitive substances take part in vision, other substances are essential to normal functioning of the brain, others for clotting of the blood, and so forth. Genes determine whether such substances are present or absent, and even how adequate they are. Some psychological characteristics like color blindness and certain kinds of feeble-mindedness are inherited because they depend on such substances.

In the case of complex psychological characteristics such as intelligence, temperament, and aptitudes, which depend partly on heredity, these two kinds of links are undoubtedly combined in many ways. The characteristics are multiply determined, we know, and this means that many genes are linked to them. They probably depend on such things as whether certain pathways are formed in the brain, the sensitivity of sense organs, the general level of activity in the brain, and the secretions of certain glands. Until we fully understand the physiological basis of inherited psychological characteristics, and also know just how genes multiply determine organ structures and functions, we will not be able to say exactly how genes are linked to behavior patterns. The possibilities, however, are clearly there. Hence we have every reason to expect heredity to play a role in behavior.

THE INSTINCT PROBLEM. In everyday speech, we often use the term "instinct." We say that a mother instinctively cares for her young, that a man has an instinct to fight, or that a father instinctively leaps into the water to save his drowning youngster. Such uses of the term, unfortunately, are loose, unscientific, and incorrect. They tend to confuse behavior that is impulsive or automatic with behavior that is inherited and unlearned. They also imply that an instinct is something that somehow explains behavior.

Because of this confusion, instinct was

long a controversial word among psychologists. Some, like John B. Watson (page 9), denounced the word because they did not believe any behavior, except simple reflexes, was inborn or unlearned. Others defended it because they were convinced that instinctive behavior did exist. Today the controversy has largely died down, partly because of the mounting evidence for the existence of instinctive patterns of behavior and partly because we define and use the term more precisely.

Instinctive behavior, it is now generally agreed, is an *inherited pattern of behavior.* We still avoid the term "instinct," however, because it implies a "something" inside the individual that makes him do things, when actually there is no such thing. Often instinctive behavior is related to a drive such as sex, but this is only one of the conditions for eliciting the behavior, not the instinct. To qualify as instinctive behavior, a pattern must meet three conditions:

1. It must be generally characteristic of a species or a breed. In other words, one must have good evidence that the behavior is genetically determined.

2. It must appear full-blown at the first appropriate opportunity without any previous training or practice. This is also a test of its being inherited, rather than learned.

3. It must continue for some time in the absence of the conditions evoking it; that is to say, it may be triggered by some stimulus but it is not controlled by the stimulus. This distinguishes it from simple reflexes, which are automatic reactions to stimuli.

To say that instinctive behavior is an inherited pattern of behavior is not to say that it is necessarily present at birth. Actually, it may appear at various times in the life cycle up to sexual maturity or even later. The body, however, takes time to develop and mature along the lines laid down by the genes. (We shall describe maturation below.) Hence patterns of behavior that depend on growth and development can be, and are, inherited even though they may not be present at birth.

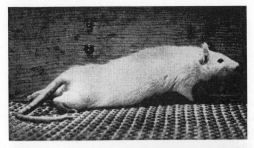

FIGURE 2.5. (Top) The stretching reaction just before delivery of the pups. (Middle) After the pups are born, the mother cleans them and eats the placenta. (Bottom) The mother has placed the pups together in a nest [Farris and Griffiths, 1949].

One example of instinctive behavior is the maternal behavior of the rat (see Figure 2.5). A pregnant rat builds a nest some time before her young are born. When they are born, she cleans them and sees to it that they are safely in the nest. When they wriggle out, she retrieves them. For many long hours a day, she keeps them warm and nurses them. Although the details of the maternal pattern vary from one species to another, the pattern is relatively consistent within a species. It also appears full-blown, in the absence of any experience or training, at the time of the first litter. Hence, it qualifies fully as instinctive behavior.

Patterns of instinctive behavior are found in many species. In general, they are more prevalent in lower animals, such as the insects, fish, and birds, than they are in mammals (animals that nurse at the breast). The most characteristic instinctive pattern in mammals is the maternal pattern just described for the rat. Because a mammal nurses her young until they are relatively capable of fending for themselves, they probably have less need for instinctive patterns, other than maternal, than many lower animals. When it comes to human beings, we cannot say with certainty that there are any instinctive behavior patterns. Man seems to have become so sophisticated in learning to adapt to his world, and in teaching his young how to adapt, that instinctive behavior is no longer a prominent human characteristic.

GENETICS AND BEHAVIOR. Instinctive behavior is only one psychological characteristic that is inherited. Tendencies to react in certain ways or abilities to learn certain things, although they are not instinctive patterns, may also be inherited. In fact, such tendencies or abilities, rather than instinctive patterns, are the principal characteristics that are inherited in higher animals and man.

There are several ways to test whether particular tendencies are inherited or learned. One is to take individuals of the same or similar heredity and raise them in different environments. The environment may be changed artificially as in the following example [quoted from Scott, 1958, p. 114]:

As we ordinarily see them, dogs respond almost continuously to human behavior. In this case it is possible to . . . separate the dogs from their human environment. At our laboratory we wished to find out how much of their behavior was native to dogs and how much was the result of the human environment. We placed groups of adult dogs in large fields where they could be watched apart from human beings and found that they reacted toward each other with the same basic behavior patterns with which they responded to people. They wagged their tails at each other, growled and barked, and fawned on any animal which was in possession of food. When all these behavior patterns were written down, they were found to be essentially the same as those exhibited by their wild ancestors, the wolves. Puppies born to these animals and kept out of contact with people showed the same behavior as the adults except that they were extremely wild and fearful toward people. The puppies literally went back to the wild in one generation. They apparently had an inherited tendency to develop fear toward strangers. As we might expect from the lasting nature of learned fears, once the puppies had developed timidity the friendly attitude of their parents had little effect in overcoming it.

Or the environment may be changed by *cross-fostering*—having the young reared by foster parents who have characteristics different from those of the natural parents. This technique has been used in both animal and human studies. It has been one of the best ways to study the inheritance of intelligence in children, which will be covered below. The following is an example of cross-fostering in animal research [quoted from Scott, 1958, p. 117]:

Hungry mice of the C strain eat peacefully side by side off the same pellet of food, whereas mice of the C57/10 strain actively compete for a single pellet. When the two strains were cross-fostered at birth, the young C mice did not take up the active habits of their foster parents and thus remained true to heredity. The mice of the other strain likewise acted in accordance with their heredity and attempted to take food away from their peaceful foster parents.

In this experiment, then, we conclude that the tendency to fight or not to fight is inherited, and it is not modified greatly by the "culture" in which the animals are reared.

Another way of studying the origin of particular tendencies is to take individuals of quite different heredities and to raise them in the same environment. Here the accent is on different heredities, and the method is most fruitful when it is possible to exaggerate differences in heredity. This is best done by selectively inbreeding individuals of similar characteristics, which is possible only in animal research. One establishes some objective test for the characteristic and then separately inbreeds individuals who score high on the test and those who score low on it. If the characteristic being measured is genetically determined, successive generations of the two separate breeds should continue to score differently on the test [quoted from Scott, 1958, p. 116].

Rats raised in cages are usually fearful and nervous when placed on a large bare table and show this by urinating and defecating. Some individuals, however, are stolid and unafraid in this situation. Selection for the two types over seven or eight generations produces distinct strains, one fearful and emotional, the other not. This and other experiments show that selection can strongly affect . . . various patterns of . . . behavior in the rat. Both the external behavior and the accompanying internal physiological and emotional reactions are changed by heredity.

SPECIES DIFFERENCES. This last method—comparing individuals of different heredities in similar environments—can be extended logically to the comparison of different species. After all, the difference between two species of animals is genetic, and by giving them the same opportunities for learning and development we can assess the role of heredity in their respective behaviors. Exactly this has been done for two species very close to home: man and ape. The paragraphs which follow describe one such study [Kellogg and Kellogg, 1933]:

A nine-month-old boy, named Donald, and a seven-month-old female chimpanzee, named Gua, were brought up together like brother and sister. The experimenters made every effort to treat the ape and their child exactly alike. They treated both with the same affection, dressed them alike, and gave them the same chance to practice different kinds of behavior like standing, walking, opening doors, eating with a spoon, and learning to use the toilet. Of course, the difference in heredity between the boy and chimpanzee is tremendous, so the experiment gives us a chance to see how much this difference can be overcome by training.

As we might expect, Gua, the chimpanzee, developed certain kinds of behavior earlier than Donald, the boy. The chimpanzee has about one-third the life span of man and matures much earlier. In the beginning of the experiment, Gua was better than Donald in such things as standing and walking (see Figure 2.6). Gua also learned to use a spoon sooner than Donald and developed the capacity to respond to verbal instructions earlier. But after 9 months, when the study was ended, Donald had caught up on almost everything except strength, and he was beginning to develop capacities such as language that Gua showed no signs of developing.

The important point in this experiment is that the ape and the child developed according to their hereditary potentials. Even though the ape's special training allowed it to develop behavior normally seen only in human beings, it very soon reached the limits of its hereditary potential and was far outstripped by the child.

Talking apes. It is often said that what sets man off from animals is his ability to use language. This is certainly true in the world as we know it, but we can ask whether it is a matter of heredity or learning. Man might by good fortune have

FIGURE 2.6. The chimpanzee and the human infant were reared together and treated alike. In many respects, the chimpanzee, Gua, developed more rapidly than Donald, but Donald caught up with and surpassed Gua, especially in the development of language [Kellogg and Kellogg, 1933].

learned language, then perpetuated it by teaching it to his offspring. Some animals may have the capacity to learn a language, but have never happened to develop it.

Several birds, like the parrot, obviously inherit the ability to talk, for they are very good at uttering clear words. But there is more to language than just talking; language, as we use it, employs words to refer to objects or situations and combines words in novel ways. Parrots, however, just "parrot"; they repeat over and over again a few simple phrases they have mimicked. Although many people with pet parrots or other talking birds have spent many hours teaching them language, no one can claim that they use language in a meaningful way. Apparently they lack the hereditary ability to do so.

Since apes are more nearly like man than other animals are, especially in body and brain structures, experimenters have tried to teach them language. So far none has succeeded very well.

One experimenter taught an orangutan to say "papa" and "cup" and to use these words with some meaning, but the process was laborious [Warden et al., 1936]. More recently, a childless couple took a newborn chimpanzee into their home and reared it as they would a child [Hayes and Hayes, 1951]. Their idea was that an ape might learn to talk if it were treated exactly like a human baby and given all the love and attention possible. After almost 3 years, however, although Viki, the chimpanzee, could occasionally use the words "mama," "papa" and "cup" meaningfully, it had not developed its linguistic skills any more than that.

So far as we know, then, apes can learn to use a few simple words only through painfully slow practice, and there is no evidence that they can ever learn to speak a variety of words or anything like sentences. So the limit of language ability in the ape is very low and can be realized only very gradually and by intensive training. Quite different, of course, is the human infant with his much greater hereditary potential for language behavior.

CHAPTER TWO

INTELLIGENCE. There are a great many studies, of both man and animals, of the inheritance of traits and abilities, such as emotionality, learning ability, mental disease, and intelligence. Some of these studies will be covered in later chapters. Here we shall round out our treatment of heredity and environment by considering just one more instance which illustrates the role of heredity in human behavior.

Intelligence is a general term covering a person's abilities in a wide range of tasks involving vocabulary, numbers, problem solving, concepts, and so on. It is measured by standardized tests, which usually involve several specific abilities, often with emphasis on verbal ability. A test score on an intelligence test can be converted into an intelligence quotient, or IQ, which indicates the testee's relative standing in the population independently of his age.

Since an intelligence quotient reflects several abilities, not just one, and each of these is itself fairly complex, we would expect that the inheritance of intelligence would be multiply determined. It would depend on many genes rather than on one or two pairs.

A natural family, consisting of parents and children all of whom are related by blood, offers us the opportunity to compare individuals who differ in inheritance by various degrees and who have relatively similar environments. To make such a comparison, we use a statistical index called a correlation coefficient (page 419), which expresses the degree to which pairs of individuals make similar scores. A correlation of 1.00 indicates perfect agreement. (Tests, however, are never perfectly reliable, so we never obtain correlations of 1.00.) A correlation of .00 indicates no relation; each pair of scores is no more alike than we would expect from chance. In between, various degrees of correlation are possible.

A natural family of three generations has the seven possible pairings listed in Table 2.2. These pairs may be grouped according to either similarity of heredity or similarity of environment. If heredity were the dominant factor in intelligence, we would expect the intelligence scores of those most similar in inheritance to be most highly correlated. If environment were the dominant factor, we would expect the highest correlation coefficient to be among those with the most similar environments.

Actually both expectations are met, as one can see by comparing different groupings in Table 2.2. The highest correlation of .88 is obtained between identical twins, who have identical heredity and almost identical environment. The correlation drops to .63 for fraternal twins of the same sex, who have about the same environments as identical twins but less similarity in heredity. This indicates that heredity is a factor. It drops again, however, from fraternal twins to siblings (brother or sister), who have about the same degree of hereditary similarity but less similarity in their environments. This indicates that environment is a factor. Sibling pairs and parent-child pairs have the same degree of hereditary similarity, and fairly similar but somewhat different environments. As one might expect, the correlation coefficients are about the same, but slightly lower for the parent-child pairs. There is another drop in correlation for grandparent-grandchild and uncle-nephew pairs, which have about the same degree of similarity of both heredity and environment but less of both than do siblings and parent-child pairs. Cousins, who have less similarity of heredity than uncles and nephews or grandparents and grandchildren, have even lower correlations.

Note that the correlations for height are about the same as those for intelligence. They tend to run a little higher for closely related individuals and a little lower for remotely related individuals. The fact, though, that the two sets of correlations closely parallel each other would make us believe that heredity plays just about as important a part in the physical characteristic of height as it does in intelligence.

From studies of this kind, we see that when heredity changes, leaving environment

TABLE 2.2. Correlations of intelligence scores (IQs) and height for individuals related by blood with different degrees of similarity of heredity and environment. Braces indicate those relationships that have about the same degree of similarity of heredity or environment.

Similarity of heredity	Relationships	Correlation of intelligence	Correlation of height	Similarity of environment
	Identical twins*	.88	.93	
	Fraternal twins (like sex)*	.63	.64	
	Siblings †,‡	.51–.53	.54–.60	
	Parents and children ‡	.49	.51	
	Grandparents and grandchildren ‡	.34	.32	
	Uncles (aunts) and nephews ‡ (nieces)	.35	.29	
	Cousins	.29	.24	

* Newman et al., 1937   † McNemar, 1942.   ‡ Burt and Howard, 1956.

relatively constant, the correlations between intelligence and IQs go down. Hence heredity is a factor in intelligence. On the other hand, when the degree of similarity of heredity remains constant and the similarity of environment changes, the correlations also go down. Hence environment is also a factor. Unfortunately, we cannot tell from such data which is the more important factor, if indeed either is; we can tell only that both are involved.

To evaluate the relative roles of heredity and environment in intelligence, we must refer to another kind of study, one that is more difficult to do. This kind of study seeks to compare the intelligence of identical twins raised apart in different environments, thereby holding heredity constant and allowing only environment to vary. This has been done in a study of 19 sets of twins [Newman et al., 1937].

Most of the 19 sets of twins were separated at less than two years of age, although one pair parted as late as six years of age. The intelligence of each set of twins was tested later, at ages varying from eleven years to fifty-nine years, but each was tested at the same age. To obtain a measure of the different environments of each twin, judges independently rated their educational advantages on a scale of 1 to 10. From such ratings the sets of twins could be divided into three general groups: those with very dissimilar environments, those with very similar environments, and those in between (see Table 2.3). Those of nearly similar environments differed hardly at all in intelligence. Those, on the other hand, who had very dissimilar environments differed by sizable amounts; on the average, it was 15 points. Those in between differed by about 5 points, which is not a particularly significant difference.

We may therefore conclude that a relatively poor environment handicaps a person's intelligence quotient. It is interesting, however, that the correlation between the IQs of identical twins reared apart was .77. This is somewhat poorer than the .88 for identical twins reared together, but it is still better than that for fraternal twins and siblings reared together. Thus both heredity and environment are important in intelligence.

It is not proper, however, to think of abilities such as intelligence as being put together with so much heredity and so much environment, like a cooking recipe. Rather the relation between heredity and environment is an *interaction*. This means that the two general variables, heredity and environment, jointly determine a trait or ability. The importance of one depends on the other. If a person of high hereditary ability, for example, is subjected to a very poor environment, his measured ability will be low. If on the other hand, his hereditary potential is low, his measured ability will be low even if he has the best of environments. In order, therefore, for him to possess high measured ability, he needs both high hereditary potential and a good environment.

Maturation and growth

Heredity, we have seen, plays its role by directing the development of the organism. This development takes time. Indeed, it is not complete until an individual is well along into adulthood. It proceeds in stages throughout life—before birth and during infancy, childhood, adolescence, and adulthood—and different processes are prominent in each of the stages. By studying these different processes and stages, we can obtain a better idea of the way in which heredity is linked to behavior. We also get a bird's-eye view of how an adult gets to be the kind of person he is. We shall begin by tracing the embryological development of an individual, since this lays the groundwork for behavior, and after that we shall consider the development of behavior.

First, we must get acquainted with the concept of *maturation,* for this concept embraces the processes going on in development. Maturation, indeed, is *the process of bringing the various parts of an organism to full development*. Actually, it is not one process, but many, for different parts de-

TABLE 2.3. Comparison of IQs of identical twins reared apart [based on Newman et al., 1937].

Number of pairs of twins	Educational advantage	Age at separation (in months)	Average difference in IQ between twins	Superiority in IQ points of group with greater advantages
6	Very unequal (5.1 on 10-point scale)	15	15.2	15.2
7	Somewhat unequal (2.4 on 10-point scale)	9	5.4	4.6
6	Relatively similar (1.6 on 10-point scale)	24	4.5	1.0

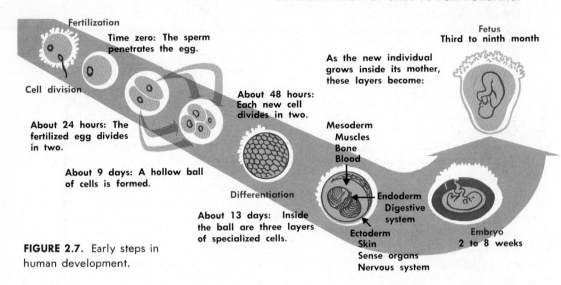

Fertilization

Time zero: The sperm penetrates the egg.

Cell division

About 24 hours: The fertilized egg divides in two.

About 48 hours: Each new cell divides in two.

About 9 days: A hollow ball of cells is formed.

Differentiation

About 13 days: Inside the ball are three layers of specialized cells.

As the new individual grows inside its mother, these layers become:

Mesoderm
Muscles
Bone
Blood

Endoderm
Digestive system

Ectoderm
Skin
Sense organs
Nervous system

Fetus
Third to ninth month

Embryo
2 to 8 weeks

FIGURE 2.7. Early steps in human development.

velop at different rates and some reach their full development before others. We may speak, for example, of the maturation of the nervous system, of the sex glands, or of walking ability, referring in each case to the processes through which the organ or the behavioral ability reaches its full development.

ORGAN DEVELOPMENT. The fertilization of an egg by a sperm takes place in a tube leading from the mother's ovary, where the egg was produced, to the womb or *uterus*. About 24 hours after fertilization, the zygote begins to divide by reproducing two cells like itself (see Figure 2.7). Each of these cells again divides in two, and the process is repeated until many cells have been produced. While this cell division is going on, the cluster of cells slowly travels down the tube to the mother's uterus (in rare cases it may remain in the tube, causing a tubular pregnancy). Usually it reaches the uterus in about 9 days, at which time it has become a hollow ball of cells. This ball, still only about 2/100 inch in diameter, attaches itself to the wall of the uterus.

The first 2 weeks of life, during which these events are taking place, is called the period of the *ovum*. During this period, all the cells being reproduced are much alike. Then a new period, the period of the *embryo* begins and lasts for about 6 weeks. At the beginning of the period, the cells of the ball differentiate into three layers, each somewhat different, called *endoderm* (inner layer), *mesoderm* (middle layer), and *ectoderm* (outer layer). Each of these layers goes on differentiating various kinds of cells to form the tissues and organs listed in Figure 2.7. At the end of the embryonic period, 2 months after conception, the cells and organs have taken the crude form of a human being, and the embryo then becomes a *fetus*. The period of the fetus lasts 7 months, from the second to the ninth month of gestation. At birth, the fetus becomes an *infant*.

TIMING OF DEVELOPMENT. When the embryo is about 6 weeks old, its heart begins to beat. About the same time, the organs necessary for behavior begin to function. At first, the *nervous system, muscles, sense organs,* and *glands* develop separately

CHAPTER TWO

and without any connection between them. At this stage of development, the muscles can be excited electrically and can be made to contract. At a little later stage, the nervous system sends down nerves to the muscles; then the nervous system can be excited electrically and contractions can be seen in the muscles. Finally, the sense organs connect with the nervous system, thus making a sensory-motor arc. At this stage, a muscular response can be produced by stimulating a sense organ. Such a response is the most rudimentary of all patterns of behavior.

The timing of these developments varies somewhat with different parts of the nervous system, different muscles, and different sense organs. Some connections between muscles and sense organs of the skin are established within 3 months after conception, and thus some reflexes are possible at this time. Connections with the eyes and ears develop more slowly, and reflexes involving these senses do not occur until about the seventh month.

MATURATION AND BEHAVIOR. One of the interesting and important things about this development is the large margin of safety that it provides. Organs mature, and connections are made, well in advance of the time they are needed. The human fetus stands practically no chance of surviving, for example, if it is born before the sixth month, yet it can make breathing movements in the fourth month. The fetus, similarly, makes walking movements with its legs in the fifth month; in the sixth month it will suck if its mouth or cheek is brushed, and it may grasp an object in its palm or even vocalize. The fetus will not need these elements of behavior until it is born, yet they are ready 2, 3, or 4 months ahead of time.

By the time the infant is born, then, most of its reflexes and elementary forms of behavior are ready for use. The breathing reactions, sucking reflexes, crying reactions to cold and discomfort, and the other behavior patterns that infants need to get along in the world are fully developed. Many other patterns that are not needed, however, are not ready; they develop slowly after birth, and may not fully mature until the child is ten or twelve years old or even later.

THE NERVOUS SYSTEM. Of all the organs of the body, the nervous system and the endocrine glands—we shall define the endocrine glands below—are among the slowest to reach complete maturity. Although the spinal cord, nerves, and lower parts of the brain are relatively mature at birth, the brain, and particularly its rind, or *cortex*, go on maturing for some time. Most infants, for example, are unable to follow moving objects with their eyes until several weeks after birth, because the pathways in the brain that are needed for this activity are not mature.

The cerebral cortex (see Chapter 19), which is important for learning and more complex behavior, is even slower to mature [Munn, 1955]. Scientists have repeatedly observed that removal of the cortex (or lack of it) at birth makes little difference in behavior at the time and for several months afterward; they have concluded, therefore, that the cortex is not functioning at that time [Sherman et al., 1936]. The ability to sit up, to crawl, and to walk all depend on the cortex, and it is not until it matures that infants are able to do these things. Most maturation of the cortex is completed by the time the child reaches the age of one to two years, but scientists can tell from electrical records of the brain's activity that some maturation goes on until a person is ten or fifteen years old [Smith, 1941].

THE ENDOCRINE GLANDS. The term *endocrine* applies to those glands of the body that empty their secretions, called *hormones*, directly into the blood rather than into cavities of the body. The glands that do the latter are called *exocrine* glands. Examples of endocrine glands are the sex glands (ovaries and testicles), the pancreas, which secretes the hormone insulin, and the thyroid glands in the neck. A familiar example of exocrine glands are the salivary glands, which secrete saliva into the mouth. Of the two kinds of glands, the endocrines are the more important in psychology, because their hormones, as we shall see (Chapters 3 and 19), affect behavior in a variety of ways.

The endocrine glands mature slowly. This may be explained in part by the fact that the supply of hormones furnished to the fetus by the mother makes it unnecessary for the fetus to secrete its own. Then, too, many of the hormones of the endocrine glands are not needed until later in life.

The sex glands are a good example. They do not mature until puberty, when boys and girls, at the age of twelve or thirteen, begin taking on the characteristics of men and women. Some of the changes that take place at that time are the growth of the beard and change of voice in boys, and the development of the breasts in girls. These changes are brought about by sex hormones. So, too, are changes in sexual motivation and the emergence of patterns of sexual behavior. This connection has been established in experiments with many different kinds of animals by injecting sex hormones into infants and noting the appearance of sexual behavior at a considerably younger age than that at which it would otherwise appear [Beach, 1949]. This is just one kind of evidence that the schedule of maturation of sexual behavior is controlled by the maturation of the sex glands.

MATURATION WITHOUT PRACTICE. The maturation of different organs of the body could conceivably be linked to behavior in two general ways: It might bring the behavior into play without the aid of any learning or practice. This surely happens in the case of reflexes and instinctive patterns, for these appear without any learning when maturation has proceeded far enough. For such patterns, we can say that the *behavior* itself matures. Maturation might, secondly, merely make a certain kind of behavior possible but leave it to learning or practice to develop the behavior. This, too, surely happens, and we

say that it is an ability or *readiness* that matures, not the behavior itself. This concept was implied in our discussion of abilities, but we shall see specific examples of it in a moment. Between these two possibilities lies an area in which the behavior, it would seem, might almost mature but would require a slight amount of practice for perfecting it. Indeed, as we shall see, the development of behavior proceeds in *all* these ways.

A number of behavior patterns mature with little or no practice required for their perfection. In few cases, if any, can we say flatly that no practice whatsoever is required, for the behavior usually becomes a little more skilled after some practice. The effect of practice can, however, be almost negligible, and when it is, maturation can be given the lion's share of the credit for the emergence of the behavior. The following paragraphs describe a classical study [Carmichael, 1927] of this question:

A psychologist took two groups of salamanders before they had begun to swim. He let one of them grow up in a tank of plain water, but he lightly anesthetized the other group by putting chloretone in their water. The chloretone kept them motionless without interfering with their growth, since salamanders are born with a yolk sac which supplies food for some time. The experimenter waited until the normal salamanders started swimming and had been swimming for 5 days. Then he transferred the anesthetized salamanders to plain water.

Within half an hour, all of them were swimming normally. To see whether this group learned rapidly in the half hour or simply required that long for the anesthetic to wear off, he also anesthetized the control animals which had already been swimming. When he returned this group to plain water, it took them a half hour to swim normally again, just as it had the group that had been under prolonged anesthesia. In this way, he demonstrated that maturation was the important, if not the sole, factor in the emergence of swim-

IN CHICKS, BOTH MATURATION AND LEARNING PLAY A PART IN PERFECTING THE SWALLOWING OF GRAIN SEIZED IN PECKING:

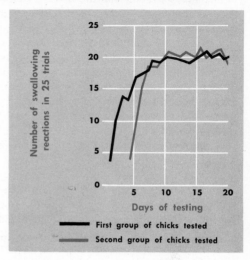

FIGURE 2.8. Improvement in swallowing reactions in chicks. Chicks were kept in the dark until they were first tested. The first group was tested 24 hours after hatching, the second group 5 days after hatching. Both groups were practically perfect in hitting the grain they pecked at, but at first they swallowed the grain on only a small proportion of the total number of trials. Note, however, that the second group caught up with the first group in two days of testing [after Cruze, 1935].

ming behavior of salamanders. The half-hour delay, during which the anesthesia wore off, involved no practice or learning.

Another study of this subject was done with baby chicks [Cruze, 1935]. Newly hatched chicks peck fairly accurately but fail to hit the grain about 25 per cent of the time. When they hit it, however, they frequently do not seize it, and even when they seize it, they often do not swallow it. The most sensitive measure of the complete eating reaction, consisting of pecking, seizing, and swallowing, is therefore the ratio of the number of swallowing reactions to the number of pecking trials. And swallowing reactions can be studied separately from accuracy of pecking.

The experimenter kept two groups of newly hatched chicks in the dark, one group for 24 hours and the other for 5 days, feeding them by hand in the meantime. At the end of the period in the dark, each group was tested for 25 pecking trials daily. On the first testing, both groups were practically perfect in hitting the grain when they pecked at it. Hence pecking, as distinguished from swallowing, de-

pended almost entirely on maturation. Each group, however, did rather poorly when scored on swallowing reactions (see Figure 2.8), making an average of less than 5 swallowing reactions in 25 trials. Each group improved as testing went on, but the second group, kept in the dark for 5 days, progressed much more rapidly than the first group, catching up to it in about 2 days. From this fact, we conclude that the development of swallowing reactions depends upon both maturation and learning.

These studies demonstrate that swimming in salamanders and pecking in chicks, both simple but essential activities, mature at the appropriate time without practice being necessary, but that swallowing in chicks is a skill which improves with practice.

Research on human beings is not so neat or unequivocal, because of the difficulty of doing controlled experiments with children, but it confirms the conclusion that basic activities are largely, if not wholly, dependent on maturation.

One study [Dennis, 1940] takes advantage of the way Hopi Indians restrict the behavior of their babies during infancy.

The Hopi Indians bind their infants tightly to a board so that the infants cannot move for most of the day. (Other groups such as the Eskimo also do this; see Figure 2.9.) Usually the infant is unbound for only an hour or two a day while he is cleaned. Hence he does not get the same opportunity to practice sitting, creeping, and walking that normal unbound infants do. Yet these bound children develop the ability to sit, creep, and walk just as rapidly as children who are never bound. It seems, then, that it takes little or no practice for a human child to develop these capacities.

The following study [Gesell and Thompson, 1929] employed the method of co-twin control:

Two girls who were identical twins, and who thus had identical heredity and the same maturational schedules, were used in an experiment. One girl, twin T, was trained in special activities such as climbing, while the other, twin C, was given no opportunity to practice these activities. After 6 weeks, twin T progressed from not being able to climb stairs at all to making five stairs in 26 seconds. At this point, control twin C was allowed to try the stairs. On her first attempt and without prior practice, she climbed all five stairs in 45 seconds. With only 2 weeks of training, twin C could make the stairs in 10 seconds. The same results were found in other types of basic activity (see Figure 2.10).

From evidence of this kind, two conclusions can be drawn: (1) Maturation, not learning, is primarily responsible for the development of such basic behavior patterns as walking, climbing, swimming (in salamanders), or pecking (in chicks). (2) To the extent that training or practice helps to perfect such patterns, it develops skill much more rapidly in the more mature individual.

READINESS FOR LEARNING. Some things, quite obviously, never are acquired merely by maturation; they have to be learned. A person does not acquire the ability to talk,

FIGURE 2.9. This picture from *Nanook of the North*, Robert Flaherty's 1922 motion picture of Eskimo life, records the practice of baby bundling, common in some Indian and Eskimo groups. Bundling restricts a baby's opportunity to practice reaching, sitting, creeping, and walking, but it does not interfere with motor development [Robert Flaherty, Revillon Frères].

to read, or to do arithmetic by maturation alone; he has to learn to do them. In such skills, nevertheless, maturation plays an essential role, for what matures is the *readiness* for learning them. Until the readiness appears in the schedule of maturation, there is no point in attempting to learn them.

The following case [Davis, 1947] dramatically illustrates this point:

A deaf-mute mother hid her young daughter from all outside social contact until she was more than six years old. The child was thus deprived of practically all opportunity to learn spoken language. When neighbors discovered the child at age six, she could not speak; she uttered only incomprehensible sounds. In 2 months of training, however, she learned many words. By that time, too, she started putting sentences together as fast as a child normally does at three years of age. Of course, she had to learn the vocabulary of English and the rules of constructing sentences, but her progress was rapid. Her case demonstrates strikingly that the capacity or readiness for learning language is something that gradually matures without practice, even though learning is required to develop skill.

There are many kinds of readiness. Generally, each appears at a characteristic age. Readiness for learning speech appears typically in a child's second year, that for learning to read at about six years. In each case, the readiness appears rather abruptly, usually over the course of a few weeks. When it appears, the child's progress in learning takes a spurt. Before he is ready, he learns slowly, and training is rather useless. When he is ready, if he has the opportunity to learn, he learns rapidly. From this fact, which will be illustrated in a moment, we infer that there is a characteristic time for the maturation of an ability or readiness to be completed.

All children, however, do not mature at the same rate. Some mature slowly, others rapidly. In general, if one ability matures slowly, others will too, though this is not always so. A child's general rate of maturation of abilities, however, is something that can be measured. It is, in fact, just what an intelligence test (for children) does measure. Most intelligence tests sample several of a child's abilities and supply an over-all score called a mental age (MA). The MA is arrived at by comparing the child's score with that of the average child at various age levels. If, for example, a child's over-all ability is the same as that of the average six-year-old, he is given an MA of 6, regardless of what his chronological age (CA) happens to be. (The IQ is simply MA/CA multiplied by 100.) Thus the MA is the measure of an individual's general level of maturation of abilities.

Now to return to the point that each readiness comes to maturity rather abruptly. This point can be demonstrated by using the MA to match children on their maturational level and then comparing them on some skill, such as reading. The following study [Morphett and Washburn, 1931] is an example:

One hundred and forty-one children were given an intelligence test when they entered the first grade. The test furnished an MA for each child. About halfway through the year, without knowing the test results, teachers rated each child on his progress in learning to read, giving him either a "satisfactory" or "unsatisfactory." In Figure 2.11 are the results. It shows that the percentage of children making satisfactory progress in reading rises sharply from zero to about 90 per cent. Most of the jump, in fact, takes place in 6 months between an MA of 5½ years and an MA of 6 years. We would not have seen this jump, however, if the CA of the children had been used, for they were all about six years old, and slight differences among them in CA were inconsequential.

The practical implication of such studies as these is that we must wait until an ability or readiness is mature before attempting to

FIGURE 2.10. Identical twins behaving almost identically [Pinney, from Monkmeyer].

teach skills that depend on the readiness. Unfortunately, our common practice in the United States of admitting children to school and programming the education of children on the basis of CA does not recognize this point. Children of six years of age vary in general readiness, that is, in MA, from 4½ or 5 up to 8 or 9. The child of low MA cannot profit from training until he is considerably older than the child of very high MA. Since the time to start training in reading is at a mental age of 6 to 6½, the common practice of admitting children to school at CA of 6 is all right for the average child, but not for the duller and brighter ones.

OPTIMUM TIME FOR PRACTICE. It does no good, we have seen, to attempt to teach a skill before the readiness for learning it has matured. So as a practical matter we should wait for the maturation of ability or readiness. Having done that, however, another important question arises. Is it possible to wait too long? If a skill is not learned or practiced when maturation makes it possible, is it more difficult to learn or perfect the skill later?

There is evidence that this is indeed true for some skills and abilities. Often there is an optimum time for learning. Behavior patterns that mature with little or no practice should be practiced; if they are not, the ability to perform deteriorates.

Deterioration without practice. Such deterioration without practice probably takes place for many of the behavior patterns that mature with little or no practice.

In one experiment [Dennis, 1941] the flying behavior of birds was studied.

The experimenter placed two baby turkey buzzards, taken from their nest, in a cage that was barely large enough to permit them to stand up, thus restricting their activity. At intervals he tested their ability to fly, but they regularly failed. Indeed, they were still unable to

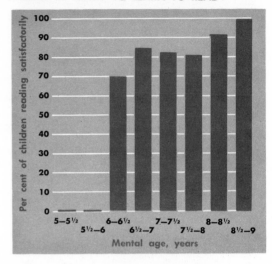

FIGURE 2.11. Reading readiness and mental age. The number of children making satisfactory progress in learning to read jumps rapidly between the mental ages of 5½ and 6 years [Morphett and Washburn, 1931].

fly long after wild buzzards judged to be the same age could be seen flying in the vicinity. Eventually, however, they did fly and joined a group of wild buzzards. The restriction, nevertheless, retarded the development of their flying skills.

In experiments of this kind, restriction of practice up to a certain point, the time when the skill normally matures, does not handicap the development of the skill. Beyond that point, however, further restriction retards or prevents the appearance of the skill.

Imprinting. The same conclusion holds for at least some kinds of learning. One example is a special kind of learning called *imprinting*, which takes place in some birds, e.g., ducks, geese, and chickens. Imprinting is very rapid learning in which an animal learns to follow or to make a response to a particular object. A gosling or chicken, for example, learns in a few experiences to follow its mother around. The stimuli for the

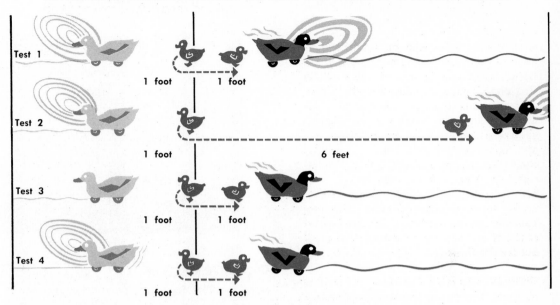

FIGURE 2.12. Four tests of the imprinting of ducklings upon the model of a male duck (dark head). In the first three tests, the duckling was first allowed 2 minutes to make a choice, and then the model chosen was moved to determine whether the duckling would follow it. In Test 1, both models were 1 foot away; in Test 2, the male was 6 feet and the female 1 foot away. In Test 3, both models were silent. In Test 4, the female model began moving at the start of the test [Ramsey and Hess, 1954].

learning are the movement of the mother and the sounds she makes. If an experimenter substitutes himself or another object for the mother at the time imprinting ordinarily takes place, the young bird will imprint on, that is, learn to follow, the substitute. Such imprinting must be learned at the right time in the bird's life; otherwise it never takes place.

The following study [Ramsay and Hess, 1954] illustrates this kind of learning:

The experimenters set up a wooden model of a duck as the object on which to imprint young ducklings. By remote control, they could make the duck move around a track and/or emit sounds of *gock, gock, gock, gock* (recorded on tape) normally made by mother ducks (see Figure 2.12). Using a standard procedure, they gave each of 92 ducklings an opportunity to become imprinted on the model duck. Later in systematic tests, by observing responses to the model, they determined whether the ducklings had in fact become imprinted on the model. Groups of ducklings were given their imprinting experiences at different times, one group within 4 hours after hatching, another group at 5 to 8 hours, and so on up to 29 to 32 hours. On later testing, the experimenters obtained the results shown in Figure 2.13. The ducklings exposed within a few hours after birth imprinted fairly well, but the optimum time for imprinting was 13 to 16 hours of age. Ducklings exposed 30 hours after hatching hardly imprinted at all.

Special training. Unfortunately, we do not have such dramatic data for human beings. So far as we know, human beings do not imprint, but the question needs further study. It is possible that something similar to it does take place. So far as other types of learning are concerned, we suspect that there is a best time for learning different skills, but the evidence for this is not yet very extensive. People who attempt to acquire athletic, musical, or linguistic skills late in life seldom achieve the proficiency of those who begin earlier when the readiness for such learning has just matured. Other evidence comes from the following study [McGraw, 1935]:

Johnny and Jimmy were twins who, it turned out later, were fraternal rather than identical. During the first year and a half of infancy, Johnny was given intensive training in a whole series of skills, first in walking, later in such things as swimming, roller skating, and tricycling. Jimmy was left to develop on his own, with even less than the normal amount of practice and training. As soon as Johnny had perfected an activity, Jimmy was tested on it. When the twins were twenty-two months old, Jimmy was trained intensively in the activities Johnny was already proficient in. After that, both were tested at regular intervals until they were six years old.

In such basic things as walking, Jimmy caught up with Johnny in very short order. Once given the chance, Jimmy showed that he could equal Johnny with little or no practice. In certain activities, however, where special techniques were helpful, Jimmy was at a disadvantage and sometimes failed to catch up with Johnny at any time. At one stage, for example, Johnny learned to climb down from a pedestal by hanging with his hands and dropping onto the mattress below. Jimmy did not learn this feat. Later, when Jimmy was trained in roller skating, he was unable to do so well as Johnny who had been taught it some months before. In general, Johnny remained superior to Jimmy in nearly every skill involving muscular coordination.

This study seems to indicate that the best time to start teaching athletic skills is during the first 2 years and that if the opportunity

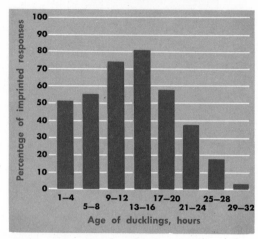

DUCKLINGS IMPRINT BEST AT 13 TO 16 HOURS OF AGE:

FIGURE 2.13. The optimum age for imprinting of ducklings [Hess, 1959].

to begin then is missed it is difficult, if not impossible, to develop these skills to the fullest later.

SENSORY DEPRIVATION AND ISOLATION. Practice at the right time in the maturational schedule, we have just seen, is needed for the fullest development of skills. It also is true that sensory experience is a requisite for normal development. An individual must be able to see, hear, and feel objects in his environment in order to acquire appropriate ways of responding to them. As yet we cannot say exactly when it is necessary to have this experience or how it depends on the maturation of any particular ability, but we do have evidence on the general point. This, like much of our evidence, comes from observing the reactions of animals, since it is so difficult to conduct the studies with infants and children. In one study [Riesen, 1950], which was really a series of studies, the subjects were chimpanzees.

The animals were kept for several months after birth in restricted visual environments. Some were kept in complete darkness. Others were allowed a little visual experience each day, such as having a light turned on periodically for a few seconds or being brought into the light for feeding and care. One chimpanzee was reared wearing translucent goggles that permitted it to see light but no forms. We must discount the results obtained with animals kept in complete darkness for several months, because these animals showed defects of the retina of the eye. This fact is itself interesting, however, for it indicates that a certain amount of light stimulation is necessary for the normal maturation of the eye.

Later, when the chimpanzees were given various visual tests, the ones that had been permitted an hour or so a day of normal visual experience did all right. Apparently this much experience was all that was required for normal development. Others with more restricted conditions, however, were retarded. They could not coordinate well in getting around in their environment. They failed to respond to objects moving toward them until they could touch them. On tasks in which they were supposed to learn to discriminate between different patterns, they were much slower, in some cases many times slower, in learning than normal animals. Eventually, but only after hundreds of hours, they were able to learn to use vision as an aid in moving about and in manipulating objects. The chimpanzee that had worn the translucent goggles was almost as poor as the other animals. Since it could see light but no form through its goggles, the important factor appeared to be lack of experience with the form and depth of objects.

Another study [Thompson and Melzack, 1956] throws additional light on the role of experience in developing emotional and social behavior:

In this study, puppies were raised singly in closed pens that admitted light from the top but denied them any experience with the outside world or with each other. As controls, litter mates of these puppies were raised as pets. These conditions were maintained for the first six to nine months of life, at which time the isolated puppies were taken out of their pens and treated like the controls. Differences between the two groups were observed and recorded.

The pups reared in isolation were markedly different. They were naïve and immature in many respects. Strange objects, such as an umbrella or a balloon, readily excited them, whereas the control pups showed little interest in the objects. The isolated pups ran around randomly and generally were more excitable than the controls. In tests of learning to solve problems, the isolated pups were greatly inferior to the controls. Even after several years, there were observable differences between the groups.

Experiments such as these are relatively recent and are still going on. We need to know more about the kinds of experiences that are important in early development. The work done so far, however, makes it clear that an environment relatively rich in stimulation is necessary for normal development. It may turn out that differences in sensory environment during the first 2 years of human life have a great deal to do with the abilities and interests the child or adult has later.

Sensory motor development

Having gained some understanding of the roles of heredity, maturation, and learning in development, we may now turn to a description of the major events that take place in development. In this section, we shall consider sensory motor development. *Motor* means moving or movement and hence is used by psychologists and physiologists to refer to human and animal movements, such as walking, swimming, steering, grasping, typing, and so on. It may be distinguished from verbal or intellectual activities that do not involve doing things.

PRENATAL DEVELOPMENT. During the prenatal period, the individual exists as an aquatic creature and as a parasite within the body of its mother. Here it is well protected from harmful stimuli and has all its needs supplied. On the whole, the uterine environment is relatively constant, and is relatively similar from one mother to another.

To the psychologist, the important feature of the fetal period is the unfolding of behavior that takes place. In a few short months—sometimes they seem long to the mother—the nervous system and other parts of the response mechanism almost completely mature. By the seventh month of prenatal life, the individual has fully developed most reflex patterns, such as turning the trunk and head, flexing and extending the limbs when touched, grasping objects that touch the palms of the hands, sucking when a nipple or similar object touches the mouth, and crying when in discomfort.

INFANCY.   Most of the features of the prenatal environment—a warm, dark, quiet, watery environment—are relatively constant and require no adjustment on the part of the fetus. Birth changes all that. The infant is suddenly thrust into a highly variable environment where food is available only at intervals, where the temperature changes from time to time, and where lights, sounds, and other stimuli impinge intermittently on him. The newborn, of course, must now breathe to get his own oxygen. He must make his own adjustments and begin to establish some independence of the environment. He must ingest and digest his own food and regulate the temperature of his own body. It usually takes a few days for the infant to make these adjustments well, and in the course of them, he may lose a little of the weight that he had accumulated before birth. The newborn is now in the stage of *infancy,* which lasts for a period of about 2 years.

SENSORY DEVELOPMENT.   At birth, the baby has rather well-developed sense organs; some are fully mature, but others are not. The senses of taste and smell appear to be mature, for newborn babies refuse to suck

and nurse when confronted with an unpleasant odor or when the milk is sour or bitter. The senses of touch and temperature also appear to be well developed at birth or soon afterward, for babies refuse milk of the wrong temperature and are sensitive to environmental temperatures. Pain, however, appears not to be so well developed as it is a few weeks later, as judged by the newborn's relative insensitivity to pinpricks and other noxious stimuli. For this reason, circumcisions may be done without anesthesia within the first few days after birth.

Hearing and vision are the two senses that lag somewhat in development. They are not fully mature at birth and they do not need to be, for the most important thing in the early weeks of life is for the infant to eat and sleep in comfort. Although it is difficult to test any sense very accurately in the baby, we do know that the newborn baby is relatively impervious to noises of various kinds. After 3 or 4 weeks, however, he begins to respond to voices and probably has reasonably normal hearing. In the case of vision, we know that a baby cannot see very well at birth, for the retina is not fully developed. He can, however, respond to light, and in the course of 10 days or so his eyes usually begin to follow any bright moving object. It may be some weeks, though, before his two eyes track a moving object smoothly, for it can take some time for the mechanisms of coordination of the eyes to mature. Complete normal vision, as we know it, probably does not mature until the child is a year or so of age.

SEQUENCE OF MOTOR DEVELOPMENT.   The most conspicuous events in the early development of the infant are motor. During the first two years, the infant gradually gains skills in controlling his body. In contrast to the newborn, for example, the child of two years is a miracle of muscular precision. He has good postural control in a wide variety of positions. In fact, he often gets into positions that seem impossible to adults. He can walk forward, backward, and sideways, and

he can go up and down a flight of steps. He
has developed a good deal of skill with his
hands—enough, in fact, to pick up a small
pellet by grasping it with his thumb and
forefinger.

If we chart carefully, as several psychologists have done, the things the infant can
do from month to month and year to year,
we can see that there is a *pattern* of development. The infant lifts his head before he sits
up, he sits before he crawls, and he crawls
before he walks. Actually, there are many
little—and, to the parent, very important—
details in this development. Yet they fit into
an orderly sequence; they make a pattern.
This pattern is almost exactly the same in
every human infant, and each infant passes
through the same steps in the course of his
development. As we might suspect, the pattern is uniform because it is largely the
result of maturation of the response mechanism.

Since there is a pattern to development in
infancy, it is possible to construct *norms* for
development. We may state, for example,
that the infant can pick up a pea-sized
object at 7 months, is able to creep at 9½
months, etc. These are ages at which the
average child displays a particular skill; we
call them norms. Many parents buy books
that give detailed norms and then watch
Junior with bated breath to see whether he
progresses on schedule. They should remember, however, that norms are only averages,
that some infants will be slower and some
faster in acquiring successive stages of skill.
They should realize, too, that speed of motor
development has very little to do with intelligence [Shirley, 1933], for the child whose
motor development is slow (but in the normal range) is as likely to have high or
normal intelligence as the one whose motor
development is rapid (see Chapter 14).

Figure 2.14 illustrates norms for the development of skills in the infant as well as
variations in the rate of development. The

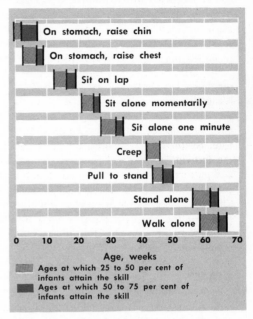

FIGURE 2.14. Norms for the development of
certain skills in the human infant [Shirley,
1933].

skills named there have been selected from
a more extensive list for which norms have
been obtained. The mark near the center of
each bar indicates the *median* age at which
the skill is attained; the median age is the
age at which one-half of a typical population
of infants attains the skill. The left-hand
end of each bar is the age at which the fastest quarter of the infants attain the skill,
while the right-hand end is the age at which
three-quarters acquire it. Note that the fastest quarter and the slowest quarter of infants
lie outside the range of the bars. Consider,
for example, the skill of sitting alone. The
median age at which children sit alone is 31
weeks or about 7 months, but one-quarter of
children can sit alone by 27 weeks, and fully
another quarter have not reached this stage
of development by 34 weeks. The full range
of ages at which this skill is attained is
considerably greater than that.

We know, then, the order in which skills appear and how each skill sets the stage for the development of succeeding patterns. It is unwise, however, to try to predict the exact age at which any specific skill will appear for any individual child.

To depict the general pattern of development for the average infant, we have drawn the series of sketches in Figure 2.15. Since these sketches tell the story well, there is no need to describe them further, but the student should study the sequence carefully.

Once the child has mastered the art of getting about, he progresses rapidly to more advanced skills, like walking up and down stairs, jumping, hopping, skipping and running. As he develops speed and accuracy he begins to coordinate all these skills into more complex activities. So the little girl who formerly used her doll carriage to steady herself as she took her first halting steps now casually wheels her "baby" to the store on a "shopping" tour. The boy who at first was content merely to balance himself on his tricycle now hitches a wagon on behind and goes tearing down the road playing fire engine.

PREHENSION. *Prehension* is a term denoting the *grasping of objects.* The simplest kind of prehension is palmar grasping: the object is grasped in the palm of the hand, as when a person hangs from the limb of a tree or takes hold of the rungs of a ladder. By using the thumb in apposition to the index finger, a finer grasp is possible, as when a person picks up a pencil or uses a pair of tweezers. This kind of prehension, which is limited to human beings and some of the apes, enables us to manipulate objects with considerable precision. It accounts for many of the feats of skill that only human beings are able to perform.

Prehensile abilities develop rather slowly in the infant. Like locomotion, they grow out of more basic patterns of behavior that must develop beforehand [Halverson, 1931].

First (see *a* in Figure 2.16) the infant makes more or less random movements in-

volving the whole arm in the general direction of the object, and frequently he misses it altogether. In time, his movements are directed at the object, and the arm is used more or less as a rake to sweep in the object with a roundabout motion. Soon (see *b*), as the infant gains more control of the various arm muscles, he can use the forearm independently of the upper arm and, eventually, the wrist separately from the arm. By this time, the reaching movement that was originally a circular pattern has become a straight-line approach.

While the infant is perfecting reaching movements, another important ability is developing. This is the ability to move the thumb in apposition to the other fingers— an ability that no other animal has except some of the apes. We see the emergence of this ability in the infant's grasping of objects. At first (see *c* in Figure 2.16), the infant squeezes an object with his fingers, without using his thumb. Later (see *d*), he curls his fingers over the object and opposes them with his thumb. Finally (see *e*), he uses only the tips of his fingers and his thumb to grasp and manipulate the object.

There is a good deal of evidence that maturation, rather than learning, is the important factor in the development of both locomotion and prehension [McGraw, 1946]. All children develop these skills in the same sequence, and there is relatively little variability in how any particular behavior pattern is expressed. After the infant gets the fundamental ability "down pat," there is considerably more variation in the way each infant uses it. Here the influence of environment comes into play, and learning increases in importance. This, of course, is seen most clearly in the different kinds of toys that boys and girls play with and the kinds of games they play.

Language development

Besides sensory motor development, there are three other aspects of development that should be considered: emotional develop-

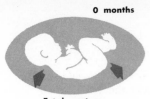

0 months

Fetal posture

THE AVERAGE CHILD DEVELOPS HIS MOTOR SKILLS ON THIS SCHEDULE:

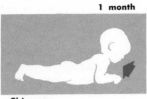

1 month

Chin up

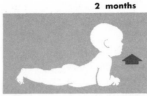

2 months

Chest up

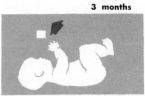

3 months

Reach and miss

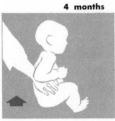

4 months

Sit with support

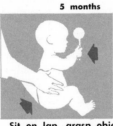

5 months

Sit on lap, grasp object

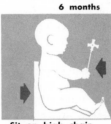

6 months

Sit on high chair, grasp dangling object

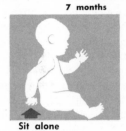

7 months

Sit alone

8 months

Stand with help

9 months

Stand holding furniture

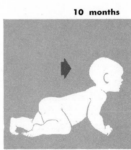

10 months

Creep

11 months

Walk when led

12 months

Pull to stand by furniture

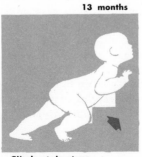

13 months

Climb stair steps

14 months

Stand alone

15 months

Walk alone

FIGURE 2.15. The sequence of motor development.

57

ment, language development, and personality development. Emotional development, however, is more conveniently treated in the chapter on feeling and emotions, and personality development fits better into the chapter on personality. Hence, at this particular point, we shall cover only the topic of language. Although language may be written or spoken, or may consist of special signaling systems such as Morse code or deaf-and-dumb signs, speech is the kind of language that ordinarily is developed and used early in life. In this account, therefore, speech development will be stressed.

EARLY VOCALIZATION. Although the infant does not use words to communicate to others until after his first year, other means of communication are in evidence as early as the first or second month. The vocalization of the newborn infant is restricted to generalized undifferentiated crying and perhaps some sort of grunting noises. Anyone who is around a young baby cannot fail to be impressed with such behavior. By his second month, the infant makes different types of cries for various states of discomfort. One cannot always tell from the cry just what is wrong, but it does communicate distress of some kind. On the other hand, gurgling and other miscellaneous sounds signify contentment and well-being. Thus, by the end of his first month, the child is using sounds to communicate his needs and feelings to those around him.

As he grows older and the relevant muscles mature, the child develops a repertory in which many other sounds appear. In Table 2.4 some of these are listed. In time he enters the so-called "babbling" stage, when he seems to enjoy making these sounds over and over again. Many of the sounds the baby makes defy written representation, even with a phonetic alphabet, but babbling is necessary and important because it pro-

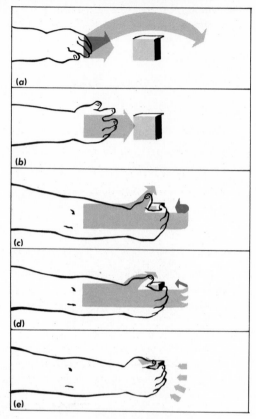

FIGURE 2.16. Five stages (a), (b), (c), (d), and (e) in the development of reaching and grasping [after Halverson, 1931].

vides practice with the vocal muscles and lets the child hear his own sounds. Indeed, feeling how sounds are made and at the same time hearing the sound helps the infant learn to associate spoken words with the objects they refer to [Lewis, 1936]. By his sixth month the baby can produce practically all the vowel and consonant sounds. These are often combined in simple ways and repeated again and again. Without understanding the significance of the sounds, the child may say "mama," or "dada," or "re-re-re." By his ninth or tenth month he can imitate sounds made by others. From

TABLE 2.4. The development of language in the infant, based on the results of eight major studies of infant development. The average age at which each kind of language behavior appears is given in months. The two numbers represent the range of average ages obtained in the different studies [modified from McCarthy, 1946].

Language behavior	Average age, months after birth
Cries, grunts, and makes other respirant sounds	0
Makes different sounds for discomfort, hunger, and pain	1
Makes vowel sounds like *ah, uh, ay*	1–2
Looks toward sound of human voice	2–4
Babbles and coos	3–4
Talks to self, using sounds like *ma, mu, do, na*	4–6
Makes sounds of pleasure and displeasure	5–6
"Sounds off" when he hears a familiar voice	6–7
Puts sounds together and repeats them over and over like *mamama-mama, booboo, dadada*	6–9
Imitates sounds made by others	9–10
Understands gestures (can wave bye-bye and often can say it)	9–12
Understands and responds to simple commands ("Hold the spoon," "Look at the doll-baby")	11–15
Imitates syllables and simple words (the first word?)	11–15
Says two different words	12
Says three to five different words	13–18
Understands and responds to the "don'ts" ("Don't touch that," "Don't spit it out")	16–20
Names one object or picture in book (cup, ball, doggy, baby, etc.)	17–24
Combines words into phrases ("Go out," "Give me milk," "Where ball")	18–24
Identifies three to five familiar objects or pictures	24
Uses phrases and simple sentences	23–24

this point on, any of these sounds can be associated with a particular object in the environment, especially if the sound and the object are presented together to the child repeatedly. Figure 2.17 indicates how this may happen.

COMPREHENSION. Many studies have shown that the child can respond to sounds long before he can make the sounds himself [McCarthy, 1946]. By his fourth month the infant reacts positively to the sound of a human voice by turning his head toward the

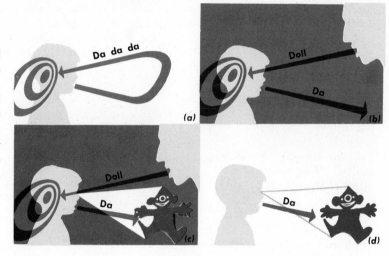

FIGURE 2.17. Associating a sound with an object. *(a)* Uttering the sound is associated with hearing it. *(b)* An adult makes a similar sound which the child imitates. *(c)* The sound is often accompanied by the object to which it refers. *(d)* Sight of the object is sufficient to produce the sound [after Allport, 1924].

direction from which he hears the sound. At six months he can distinguish between different tones of voice. He responds differently to angry and friendly voices and will stop doing something at the sound of a warning tone.

By ten months he can respond adequately to commands, especially when they are accompanied by gestures. He can wave byebye after having his hand waved for him a few times. If his mother says, "Put the spoon in the cup," and points to these objects, he quickly learns to associate the sound of the word with the object to which it refers.

GESTURES. A baby uses gestures at an early age, and these constitute an important aspect of his prespeech language behavior. By pointing or reaching, the child can convey information to others and can satisfy his wants. Turning his head or simply pushing the spoon away is a very effective method of demonstrating that he doesn't want any more. In fact, if the child can generally control his environment and get what he wants by using gestures, he may be slow to give them up and learn to use words instead.

THE USE OF WORDS. Although it may not seem so, it is relatively difficult to determine the age at which the average child utters his first word. What do we mean by the first word? Our criterion is that the sound made must refer to an object. When the child says "ball" he must mean something remotely resembling a ball; "Dada" must refer to a man. The sound must not be made randomly when his father by coincidence happens to be present. Since the development of speech is a gradual process, it is difficult, if not impossible, to pin down the age at which the first word is spoken. (Sometimes two or three words emerge at about the same time.) In combining many observations, however, we find that usually the first word is spoken between the tenth and thirteenth months.

Once the first word appears, the vocabulary increases rapidly. Nouns, generally related to things in the immediate environment, come first; then verbs; then adjectives and adverbs; with pronouns appearing last [McCarthy, 1930]. Children seem to have more difficulty in learning the correct use of pronouns than any other part of speech. Such remarks as "Pick my up" or "Me going outside" are typical.

As his vocabulary increases, the child begins to combine the words he has learned into sentences. The first type of sentence he uses consists of a single word. He may say, "Eat," to mean "Give me something to eat," or "Out," meaning "I want to go out." Sometimes people misinterpret this sort of speech, but it is reasonably efficient. Later the child begins to string two or three words together. By the age of two, he may be using the following sentences, which are incomplete but which contain all the essential words: "Where doggy go?" "No night-night!" "Me going on swing." "When baby wake up, me give bottle."

INTELLIGENCE AND SEX.   We have traced the main steps in language development in the infant. Maturation plays a part in it; so does learning. In addition, other factors enter the picture, and we ought to say a few words about them.

Intelligence is one such factor. People commonly believe that the children who talk the earliest are the most intelligent. They are partly right. One psychologist, for example, who worked with gifted children with IQs above 140[1] found that such children began talking, on the average, 4 months earlier than the average child [Terman, 1925]. Children of subnormal intelligence, on the other hand, are several months slower than the average child in beginning to talk. Indeed very feeble-minded children may never learn to talk. There are, however, many reasons why a child may be slow to talk, and if he is slow it does not necessarily mean that he is deficient in intelligence.

The sex of the child is another factor in learning to talk. Psychological studies of this factor reveal that on the whole girls are slightly ahead of boys in most measures of language skill. In such studies the influence of intelligence and socioeconomic background must be controlled, and care must

[1] Less than 2 per cent of the general population are this intelligent. For a more detailed explanation of the IQ and its meaning, see Chap. 14.

be taken not to use situations which favor one sex over the other (for example, testing with toys that only boys would be interested in). At all ages studied, girls use more words per sentence than boys, they begin to talk earlier, they articulate better, they are more easily understood, and they have larger vocabularies, especially when they are young. One study even substantiates the popular notion that girls are more talkative than boys and are so from a very early age—the difference, however, is slight [Jersild and Ritzman, 1938].

SOCIAL ENVIRONMENT.   Once the child has matured enough to control his speech mechanism, further progress depends to a great extent upon learning. And, at this early stage, how rapidly he learns depends upon the amount and kind of stimulation he gets from the environment around him.

The environment is a complex of many factors and people. The parents make up one important part of it. If the child gets what he wants from his parents by gesturing, he will be more reluctant to give up this form of communication in favor of learning to speak. If the child's parents do not bother to point out objects to him and pronounce their names, he will build his vocabulary more slowly. If they consistently use baby talk (because it is cute) or if they are sloppy in their pronunciation and sentence structure, the child will develop bad speech habits which will be extremely difficult to break. It is just as easy for a child to learn to say "thank you" and "train" as it is to learn "ta-ta" or "choo-choo," once he reaches the stage at which he can pronounce the relevant sounds. But if he is not ready (able) to pronounce a particular word correctly, no great harm will be done by waiting until he is ready.

Many studies have shown that twins are more retarded in speech development than single-birth children. One experimenter reported that five-year-old twins used sentences of about the same length as three-year-old singletons [Day, 1932]. Another study showed, however, that after twins began school they were not so far behind single children [Davis, 1932]. The likely explanation of these findings is that twins are left alone together in the home more often than single children, and consequently they do not have the advantage of stimulation from older children who are more skilled in language.

Bilingualism is another aspect of the social environment that affects speech development. If two languages are spoken in the home, or if the child is forced to learn a foreign language while he is still learning his mother tongue, he gets confused and his skill in both languages is retarded. In one study it was found that it is better for children in a home where two languages are spoken to hear each one from a different adult, each adult using one language exclusively [Smith, 1935].

One finding which has been consistently reported is the high relationship between the socioeconomic status of the family and the rate of development of language. The following study [Young, 1941] reports this finding:

The language of poor children was compared with that of well-to-do children by taking records of what they said for 6 hours. The well-to-do children, it turned out, did better than the poor children in every aspect of language that was considered. At all early ages, children of well-educated, well-to-do families had a higher level of language ability than did children from poorer, less educated families even when the factor of intelligence was excluded from the picture.

If we consider that a stimulating environment is necessary for rapid development of speech, it is easy to understand the data concerning socioeconomic background. A home with well-educated people in it is more likely to have books, pictures, music, and even a wide variety of the more prosaic articles of household furniture. If the family is well-to-do, also, the number of places to go, activities to engage in, and things available all increase proportionately. In fact, it has been found that the greater the number of toys a child has and the greater amount of travel he experiences, the faster he acquires vocabulary and learns to use sentences. Then again, well-to-do parents usually have more time to spend specifically teaching a youngster.

We can say in conclusion that the greater the variety of experiences that are made available to the child and the more time that is spent in teaching him about the world, the greater his mental development in general and his language development in particular.

Summary

1. Chromosomes and the genes carried by them are the transmitters of heredity and govern the biological characteristics of each new individual.

2. Genes always work in pairs. The characteristics they control may be either dominant or recessive. When a dominant gene is paired with a recessive gene, the characteristic of the dominant gene is expressed; a recessive characteristic is expressed only when two recessive genes are paired. Most characteristics, including height, intelligence, and emotionality, are multiply determined; they depend on a combination of genes.

3. The genes form an unbroken line of transmission from one generation through succeeding generations. What is transmitted by inheritance can be changed only by mutations in genes; acquired characteristics cannot be transmitted.

4. Since chromosomes from two parents randomly pair up in the child, each indi-

vidual is different genetically from every other, except for cases of identical twins, who begin life as a single cell. Other individuals related by blood, however, have varying degrees of common inheritance.

5. Heredity and environment jointly determine the development of behavior in the individual, though some kinds of behavior are determined more by heredity, others more by environment.

6. Instinctive behavior is an inherited pattern of behavior that appears full-blown at the first appropriate opportunity and is triggered by some stimulus situation. The principal behavioral characteristics that are inherited, however, are abilities to react in certain ways or to learn certain things.

7. Differences between species are primarily determined by inheritance. Inheritance limits ability to learn such things as language and complicated skills. For this reason, attempts to teach apes to talk have not succeeded very well.

8. Intelligence is highly correlated in identical twins, less so in brothers and sisters, and even less so in more remotely related individuals. Studies indicate that heredity and environment jointly determine a person's intelligence.

9. During the months immediately before and after birth, various organs within the individual are maturing in preparation for their normal functions. Maturation proceeds on a time schedule that is relatively similar for all normal individuals of a species. Maturation so precedes behavior that by the time a function is needed the organs for carrying it out have matured.

10. The development of reflexes and motor abilities, such as sitting, standing, and walking, as well as swimming in animals and flying in birds, is almost wholly a matter of maturation and requires little or no practice.

11. Ability or readiness for learning is also determined by maturation. Practice and learning are required for perfecting the skill, but they must await the maturation of the relevant ability.

12. In the case of some skills, there is an optimum time for practice and learning. If this time passes without the individual having an opportunity for learning the skills, he will thereafter find it difficult or impossible to acquire them.

13. Motor skills develop in a pattern that is similar for all children. This makes it possible to set up norms for the ages at which such abilities as grasping, sitting, and walking should appear. Some individuals are slower than others in their development, but they are not necessarily any less intelligent.

14. Prehension is a particularly important aspect of motor development because it is necessary for the acquisition of other skills that involve the manipulation of objects.

15. Infants begin life with no other language than their cries and grunts. As their language mechanism matures, they make more and more sounds. Even before they can use these sounds as language, they begin to comprehend the meanings of words that they hear, and they also can communicate some of their wants with gestures and cries.

16. The first word appears when the child is about one year of age; it is used as a sentence which usually means, "I want such and such." After that, vocabulary grows by leaps and bounds.

17. Language ability depends in part on maturation, but also on other factors. Those children who talk earliest will, on the average, later prove to be the most intelligent.

18. Girls tend to talk a little earlier than boys. Single children also tend to talk earlier than twins. By and large, those with a more stimulating home environment make more rapid progress in language development than those with a poorer environment.

Breckenridge, M. E., and Vincent, E. L. *Child development* (3d ed.). Philadelphia: Saunders, 1955.
A widely used text on child development.

Carmichael, L. (ed.). *Manual of child psychology* (2d ed.). New York, Wiley, 1954.
A comprehensive compilation of information on child development written by foremost authorities.

Gesell, A. T., and Ilg, F. L. *Infant and child in the culture of today*. New York: Harper, 1943.
An interesting and very readable account of the development of the child.

Hurlock, E. B. *Developmental psychology* (2d ed.). New York: McGraw-Hill, 1959.
A text covering each stage of human development from conception to old age.

Munn, N. L. *Evolution and growth of human behavior*. Boston: Houghton Mifflin, 1955.

A comprehensive text on psychological development which includes chapters on the evolutionary aspects of animal behavior.

Mussen, P. H., and Conger, J. J. *Child development and personality*. New York: Harper, 1956.
A textbook on child development that stresses the role of learning and socialization.

Scheinfeld, A. *The new heredity and you*. Philadelphia: Lippincott, 1950.
A fascinating account of the mechanisms of human heredity.

Zubek, J., and Solberg, P. A. *Human development*. New York: McGraw-Hill, 1954.
A text that treats separately each topic in psychological development and in each case gives a brief account of its background in animal behavior.

Introduction to psychology

DRIVES
& MOTIVATION

FEELING
& EMOTION

FRUSTRATION
& CONFLICT

MENTAL HEALTH
& PSYCHOTHERAPY

PART TWO
MOTIVATION & ADJUSTMENT

Drives

& motivation

ONE MAN WANTS TO BE a doctor. Another strives for power in the political world. Here is a person who is ravenously hungry and, at the moment, wants to do nothing but eat. A girl is lonely; she wants friends. A man has just committed murder, and we say that his motive was revenge. These are just a few examples of the motives and wants that play so large a part in human behavior. They run the gamut from basic wants, such as hunger and sex, to complicated, long-term motives, such as political ambition and the desire to get married. We never see these wants directly, but we know they exist from the way we feel, from what people do and say, and from what people seem to work for.

The nature of motivation

Several hundred words in our everyday vocabulary refer to people's motives. Some of the more common ones are wants, striving, desire, need, motive, goal, aspiration, drive, wish, aim, ambition, hunger, thirst, love, and revenge. Each of these words has its own connotation and is used in a certain context. Many of them can be defined with reasonable precision, and thus prove useful in the scientific study of motivation. The problem of terminology is nevertheless difficult, and the student should pay special attention to the way in which terms are defined and used in this chapter.

THE MOTIVATIONAL CYCLE. *Motivation* is a general term referring to states that motivate behavior, to the behavior motivated by these states, and to the goals or ends of such behavior. There are, in other words, three aspects of motivation: motivating states, motivated behavior, and the conditions that satisfy or alleviate the motivating conditions. Each of these aspects may be regarded as a stage in a cycle, for the first leads to the second, the second to the third, and the third to the first (see Figure 3.1). One or more terms may be used to refer to each of the three stages.

The terms used most commonly to refer to the first stage are *motive, drive,* and *need*. *Motive* is the most general term. It is derived from the same French and Latin roots that give us the word "motion." Motion means movement, and motive means to move in the sense of inciting, impelling, or supplying the power for movement. A motive, then, is whatever moves or incites to action. *Drive* is sometimes used in place of motive, for drive has a similar connotation of being an *impetus* to behavior. It will be used frequently in this chapter.

A motive or drive may arise from several causes. First, it may arise from a *need*— defined as a lack of something required for the survival, health, or well-being of the individual. *Physiological needs* are lacks in the tissues of the body of such things as food and water. There are also needs for many other things, such as companionship, prestige, and achievement. A motive or drive, secondly, may arise from a stimulus, either inside or outside the organism. Hunger pangs, environmental temperatures that are too hot or too cold, painful stimulation, or even novel stimuli that attract attention— all are instances of stimuli that may be motivating. In some physiological drives, hormones (page 597) in the blood may also be motivating. The sex and maternal drives, for example, depend in part on the presence of certain hormones. The hormones seem to activate regions of the nervous system and thus are not stimuli of the sort that activate sense organs. They nevertheless constitute motivating conditions.

The second stage of the motivational cycle is the behavior that is instigated by the motive or drive. This behavior is usually instrumental, sooner or later, in reducing the motive or drive. A hunger drive, for example, motivates an individual to explore for food. His exploratory behavior, therefore, is instrumental in satisfying or reducing the drive, but it is only a means toward the goal of satisfaction. Several kinds of instrumental behavior will be described later in the chapter.

The third stage of the motivational cycle is the reduction or satisfaction of the drive or motive. This is ordinarily achieved by reaching some *goal*. In the thirst drive, for example, lack of water in the body is a need (first stage) motivating the individual. This need arouses exploratory behavior (second stage) to find water. The goal of drinking water (third stage) when it is found satisfies the thirst and terminates the motivational cycle until the need for water builds up again.

Goals, naturally, depend on the kind of drive that is active. If a person is motivated by hunger, his goal is food; if he is motivated by the sex drive, his goal is sexual satisfaction; if he needs affection or companionship, his goal may be marriage, join-

MOTIVATION IS CYCLIC:

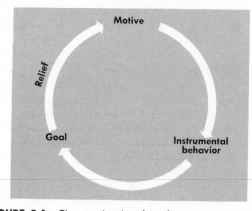

FIGURE 3.1. The motivational cycle.

ing a club, or going to the local pool room. Goals may be either positive or negative. The examples just given are of *positive goals*—goals the individual approaches or attempts to get to. *Negative goals* are those which the person tries to escape from or avoid, such as a dangerous or unpleasant situation.

In everyday speech, the term *incentive* is frequently used for the third stage of the motivational cycle. It has the additional implication, however, of being something deliberately used by someone to control motivated behavior or to exploit motives already in being. An experimental psychologist, who wishes to have a rat learn a maze, uses food as an incentive, after making the rat hungry, for motivating the rat to learn the shortest route through the maze. An employer, recognizing an employee's motive for money, may offer a bonus as an incentive to spur the employee to additional effort, that is, to increase the employee's motivation for doing good work.

In the basic physiological drives, goals are relatively fixed and unchangeable. If one is thirsty, for example, water is about the only goal that will do, although there are many forms in which the water may be consumed; if one is hungry, nothing but food will do. For more complex motives, however, any of several alternative goals may do. One may satisfy a need for recognition, for example, by becoming a pillar of the church, rising to eminence in politics, or becoming the best golf player in town. So, though goals must be appropriate to one's motives, the study of goals is itself a complex aspect of the study of motivation.

Before going on, let us illustrate these three stages in motivation by considering an incident in physiological motivation that occurred in a hospital several years ago [Wilkins and Richter, 1940].

A three-year-old boy was brought to the hospital for observation because he showed certain abnormalities of physical development. After 7 days on regular hospital diet,

the boy suddenly died. Autopsy showed that the child's adrenal glands, which are located on the top of the kidneys, were abnormal. Normally the secretions of the adrenal glands keep the salt in the body from flowing out in the urine. But in this abnormal case, the boy had lost salt faster than he could replace it on the standard hospital diet. It seemed clear that the boy died of a salt deficiency.

After the boy's death, his parents reported that he had never eaten properly. Unlike most children, he hated anything sweet, but seemed to crave salty things. He eagerly licked the salt off bacon and crackers, and although he would not eat them, he would always ask for more. One day when he was about eighteen months old, he got the salt shaker off the table and began to eat the salt voraciously. From then on, whenever he came into the kitchen, he would point to the cupboard where the salt shaker was kept and scream until someone let him have the salt. By this time his parents had discovered that he would eat fairly well if they put three or four times the normal amount of salt on his food, and in addition, let him eat about a teaspoonful of plain table salt a day.

This unfortunate case illustrates well the stages of motivation as they apply to physiological drives: (1) the boy's body had a physiological need for salt; (2) this need brought about several kinds of instrumental behavior, including the attempts to get the salt shaker from the table and the cupboard; (3) the goal was salt, and once he got it, his need was relieved and the craving temporarily disappeared. All motivation, of course, does not have an immediate physiological basis, and many needs, especially complex social needs, can go unsatisfied without resulting in death. Nevertheless, these three stages make a typical pattern of motivated behavior, both simple and complex.

CLASSIFICATION OF MOTIVES. It is convenient to divide drives into two general classes: One class, called *primary drives*, consists of unlearned drives that emerge in the course of maturation. The other class, called *secondary drives,* are those which are acquired through learning. Strictly speaking, drives themselves are probably not learned; rather the goals that satisfy the drives and the behavior that serves to attain these goals are learned. In any event, secondary drives involve a large element of learning.

Primary drives may, in turn, be divided into *physiological drives* and *general drives.* Physiological drives have their origin in some internal need or in a physiological condition within the body. General drives, although they are not rooted in any specific physiological need, also appear not to be learned. Secondary drives include *learned fears* and many of the *social motives* that characterize human motivation. These distinctions will be elaborated and illustrated in the following sections.

Physiological drives

Physiological drives, we saw above, may arise from any one of three causes: (1) stimuli, (2) tissue needs, and (3) hormonal substances in the blood. In some cases, a drive may arise from more than one of these causes; in other cases, we are not yet sure of the causes. The drives we are about to consider, however, fall roughly into these three classes in the order named.

HOMEOSTASIS. In order to understand physiological drives we should know the meaning of a concept called *homeostasis* [Cannon, 1932]. This is the *tendency of the body to maintain a balance among internal physiological conditions.* Such a balance is essential for the individual's survival. Body temperature must not get too high or too low. Blood pressure must not rise or fall beyond certain limits. The blood must not get too acidic or alkaline; it must not contain too much carbon dioxide; it must not become too concentrated; it must have a certain amount of sugar in it. If these limits

are exceeded, the individual becomes sick and he may die.

Physiologists have discovered that many *homeostatic mechanisms* are involved in keeping conditions within normal limits [Cannon, 1932]. Consider, for example, the control of body temperature. Normal body temperature in man is 98.6°F. The temperature usually stays near that point because the body can cool or heat itself. If a person's body temperature tends to get too high, he perspires and the resultant evaporation of liquid cools the body. If his temperature threatens to fall, he shivers and steps up his metabolism (page 596). Shivering burns the body's fuels faster and thus generates extra heat. In addition, many animals can insulate themselves against heat loss by fluffing their fur and creating a dead-air space around their skin. All that is left of this mechanism in human beings, however, is the goose pimples one gets when he is too cold.

Physiological mechanisms take care of many of the problems of maintaining a homeostatic balance, but the body also makes use of *regulatory behavior* [Richter, 1943]—behavior that has the effect of regulating internal physiological conditions—to maintain or restore the balance. Such regulatory behavior is behavior that is *instrumental in satisfying physiological needs.* When the body becomes depleted of water or food, for example, it cannot maintain a balance by calling on its physiological mechanisms. Rather it must obtain more water and food from the outside. It does this through motivated behavior that normally succeeds in procuring more water and food; after that, the homeostatic balance is restored. The important point, then, is that physiological drives are part of a more general physiological mechanism for maintaining homeostatic balance within the body.

Now let us consider some of the principal physiological drives.

WARMTH, COLD, AND PAIN. Warmth, cold, and pain are senses that take part in our perception of the world, and they are treated as such in Chapter 12. They may also be regarded as drives, for they can serve as powerful motives that keep a person striving to restore them to a satisfactory level. First we shall consider warmth and cold, then pain.

Warmth and *cold,* as indicated above, are regulated within limits by the physiological mechanisms of homeostasis. When the body is too hot, it perspires and does other things to reduce the production of heat; when it is too cold, it burns more fuel and keeps its loss of heat to a minimum. In addition, however, the individual may behave in such a way as to achieve a comfortable temperature. When too hot, he takes off clothes; when too cold, he puts them on. He raises or lowers the room temperature, opens or closes windows, and so on. In extreme conditions of hot or cold, he may exert most of his effort trying to obtain relief. Instances of this sort are so familiar that they need not be dwelt on. The important point is that warmth and cold are among the physiological drives.

In a part of the brain known as the *hypothalamus* (page 609) is a center for the regulation of body temperature. The hypothalamus is a relatively small region at the base of the brain immediately above the back part of the mouth. It functions in emotion, thirst, hunger, sleep, and sex—indeed in almost all physiological motivation. This center probably responds directly to the temperature of the blood circulating through it by increasing or decreasing the flow of blood throughout the body.

In addition, there are *receptors* for warmth and cold (page 301) distributed generously over the surfaces of the body. These receptors are so adapted to the temperature of the body that they are quiescent under ordinary, comfortable circumstances. When the temperature around them becomes either too hot or too cold, however, the warmth or cold receptors—there are two different kinds—are activated. Impulses from the receptors are conveyed to the brain, which instigates efforts to relieve the discomfort.

The physiological mechanism of *pain* as a drive is similar to that for warmth and cold except that there are much more specific reactions to pain. Sense organs for pain, which are probably free nerve endings (page 390), are widely distributed throughout the skin, blood vessels, and internal organs. These sense organs are usually stimulated by some injury to the tissues of the body. The individual then strives to remove the injurious stimulus. If that cannot be done or if it does not help, he looks for some way to relieve the pain.

The body is equipped with certain automatic mechanisms for avoiding pain. A sudden pain in a limb, for example, makes a person *reflexly* withdraw his limb from the source of stimulation. He does not have to think about it; he just withdraws, immediately and quickly. Sometimes when the source of pain is deep within the body, there is no way to withdraw from the source of injury. In such cases, the individual tries many techniques to reduce the pain. Modern pain-killing drugs are, of course, the most effective ways of helping such pain. But they can fail, and often they are not available. Then the individual may writhe, tear at his tissues, lie down, try to sleep, try not to move, or try to distract himself. Since none of these techniques is very effective, the individual may become preoccupied with his pain and continue endlessly his efforts to reduce it. Such pain constitutes a powerful drive that channels tremendous efforts toward one goal, the relief of pain.

Now let us turn to such drives as thirst, hunger, sleep, and sex. These drives depend mainly upon tissue needs *within* the body.

THIRST. We constantly need water because we are constantly losing it by evaporation from the skin and mouth and in the formation of urine. But what is it about the need for water that makes us thirsty and therefore motivated to drink? Thirty years ago, some physiologists declared that the throat and mouth get dry when we need water, and therefore we drink to relieve unpleasant sensations in our throats [Cannon, 1934]. Actually the problem is not so simple as that.

Certainly people will report that they drink to wet the mouth, but apparently a dry mouth and thirst are two different things. There was, for example, a man who had no salivary glands [Steggarda, 1941]. His mouth was always dry, and he would often sip water just to wet his mouth. Despite the fact that his dry mouth was never a good sign of how much he needed water, he would from time to time feel thirsty. Furthermore, he was always able to drink the right amount of water to meet his biological needs.

Dryness of the mouth can be a good sign of thirst in normal people, but it is obvious that other factors must also operate to produce thirst and permit the individual to regulate his drinking in accordance with his needs. This point has been made clear by studies done on dogs [Adolph, 1941].

By careful surgery, the esophagus—the tube from the throat to the stomach—of each dog in these experiments was brought out through the skin of the neck. Then it was opened in such a way that everything the dog drank ran out of the upper part of the opening. But still the dog could be maintained by putting food and water directly into the stomach through the lower part of the opening. When the dog was offered water, it drank just about what it needed, and then stopped, even though none of the water got into its body. Of course, after a while it drank again, and kept repeating the process until water was put into its stomach. But the important point is that the dog has some way of metering the water it

FIGURE 3.2. Sham drinking and water deficit. In experiments with fistulated dogs, which can drink water without any of it getting into the stomach, the amount of water ingested in a standard experimental period is directly proportional to the amount of water that has been lost from the body through water deprivation [after Adolph, 1941].

passes through its mouth without depending upon actual relief of its biological need.

The next step in the experiment was to put enough water directly into the dog's stomach to satisfy its biological needs and then let it drink. When the dog drank right after its stomach was filled, it drank just about the amount it needed—as judged by the amount of water that had been lost through deprivation (see Figure 3.2). But if it had to wait 15 to 30 minutes after its stomach was loaded, then it did not drink at all. So after water had been in the stomach for a short time, thirst was satisfied.

What happens that makes thirst go away when water is put into the stomach or when the animal fills itself by drinking? We do not know for certain, but the best guess is this: Lack of water makes all the cells in the body give up water. Within a center in the hypothalamus, mentioned above, are some cells that are especially sensitive to loss of water [Verney, 1947]. Through their connections with other parts of the brain, they can regulate thirst according to the relative amount of water in the body.

HUNGER.   The need for food is as obvious as the need for water. The body is always using up materials in growth, in the

THIRST IS PROPORTIONAL TO LACK OF WATER IN THE BODY:

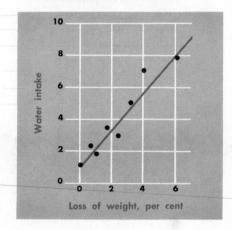

repair of tissues, and in the storage of reserve supplies. But most important is the
fact that every function of our bodies from
heartbeat to thinking requires energy, and
this energy must ultimately come from the
metabolism of food.

When people need food, they usually report that they are hungry. For some, hunger
means a feeling of strong contractions in
the stomach. But for others, there may be
no particular sensation of stomach contractions, just a general feeling of weakness
and lightheadedness. Some people have both
kinds of feeling at once. A physiologist, the
late Walter B. Cannon [1934], showed in
some very ingenious experiments that hunger and stomach contractions very often are
associated.

Cannon and his colleagues trained human
subjects to swallow a rubber balloon which
was attached to the end of a long thin rubber
tube (Figure 3.3). The experimenter blew up
the balloon until it gently filled the stomach.
Then to the end of the tube he attached a
recording pen that marked a moving tape
every time the contracting stomach com-
pressed the air in the balloon. The subject
could also make a second pen mark on the
paper by pressing a telegraph key every time
he felt a pang of hunger. So it was easy to

tell whether stomach contractions and hunger
sensations occurred at the same time or not.
They did. Not only that, the strength of the
stomach contractions and the degree of hunger both increased as time elapsed after the
last meal.

But stomach contractions are not the
whole story. First of all, some people claim
they never feel stomach contractions, but
still they report the experience of hunger.
Second, and perhaps more convincing, are
facts obtained from people who have had
their entire stomachs removed [Wangensteen
and Carlson, 1931]. They have no stomach
contractions, of course, but they still get
hungry. The same thing shows up in rats
whose stomachs are removed [Tsang, 1938].
These animals eat food eagerly, they get
restless when it is time to eat, and they
learn mazes for food rewards just like normal rats. Hunger therefore exists without
the stomach or stomach contractions, so we
must look to other factors for the explanation of hunger. Unfortunately, the exact
nature of the other factors is not known.
Many kinds of chemical changes take place
in the body when an individual is in need
of food. Some of them undoubtedly are
very important in hunger too. At the present time, we have only the barest idea of

A HUNGER PANG IS DUE TO A CONTRACTION OF STOMACH MUSCLE:

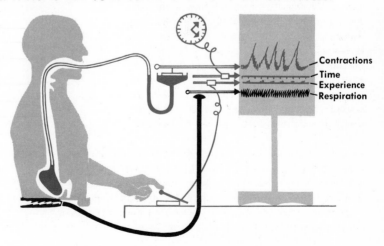

FIGURE 3.3. Hunger pangs and
contractions of the stomach.
The subject swallows a balloon connected with a marker
so that a record is made of
stomach contractions. He also
presses a key whenever he
feels a hunger pang. The record shows that spasms of the
stomach are correlated with
the subject's experience of
hunger [after Cannon, 1934].

Contractions
Time
Experience
Respiration

what these chemical changes might be and how they might do their work.

Specific hungers. Organisms not only regulate when and how much they eat; they also select what they eat. Given a chance, animals and men balance their diets and eat approximately what they need of proteins, fats, carbohydrates, vitamins, and minerals. Organisms therefore are not motivated merely by a lack of food; rather they are very specifically motivated for many particular foods. As a matter of fact, it has been questioned whether there is any such thing as general hunger apart from the sum total of specific hungers for the various food substances. But we are still far enough from answering this question to warrant treating hunger and specific hungers separately.

The best way to explain specific hungers is to describe some experiments [Davis, 1928] in which human infants were allowed to select their own diets.

The experimenter took infants from six to twelve months of age and allowed them to eat all their food from large trays containing from 12 to 20 different foods in separate containers. The babies made quite a mess of things, but they did manage to eat balanced diets. At any given meal, a baby might eat all vegetable or all butter. Sometimes, he would eat the same food for days. But over a period of time, the infants balanced out their diets by going from one food to another so that they grew as well as, or better than, infants fed according to a dietitian's formula.

The same sort of results came out of experiments with rats [Pilgrim, 1947].

The rats were given each component of the diet in a separate container (see Figure 3.4). Many of them were able to select diets that permitted them to grow as well as, or better than, rats fed on stock diets. But about one-third of the rats failed to select beneficially. In most of these cases, however, the failure was due to the fact that the rats would not eat the particular protein offered to them. If an-

other protein was substituted for that one, the animals would often eat balanced diets and grow normally.

These experiments show that animals and human beings possess mechanisms that enable them to select the kinds of food they need (see Figure 3.4).

Need and food preference. The case cited above, of the boy who suffered from salt deficiency, is an excellent example of how a specific need produces a food preference. The same sort of need can be produced experimentally in rats by surgical removal of the adrenal glands [Richter, 1936]. (These glands are described in Chapter 19.) When the adrenal glands are taken out, the rats lose salt constantly, and therefore they must eat extra amounts of it if they are to live. This they do. They will also maintain themselves by drinking large amounts of salt water in place of plain tap water. Increasing their need for salt increases their motivation for salt, and as a result, they ingest much more of it than normal, unmotivated rats (Figure 3.5).

Other specific hungers can be developed

FIGURE 3.4. Apparatus used in the study of specific hungers in rats. Each tube contains a solution of a dietary component. The amount of each component selected by the rat in any particular period can be read from the graduated markings on the tubes [C. P. Richter].

by putting the individual into a state of need [Scott and Verney, 1949]. For example, if all vitamin B is left out of the diet, the individual will develop a strong hunger for B vitamins. In pregnancy, the individual needs more fats, proteins, and certain minerals, and thus is strongly motivated to eat foods which provide them. Sometimes the motivation becomes so strong that it assumes the character of a pathological craving, and there have been extraordinary cases of pregnant women who ate plaster off the walls or ate mud, presumably to get some of the minerals they needed but could not, or did not, obtain in their ordinary diets.

In addition to specific hungers for particular foods, needs can produce *specific food aversions*. For example, the parathyroid glands situated on the thyroid glands in the neck (see Chapter 19) secrete a hormone that controls the level of calcium and phosphorus in the body. When the parathyroid glands are removed, calcium levels fall and phosphorus accumulates, so that more calcium and less phosphorus are needed. It is interesting that animals from whom the parathyroid glands have been removed eat calcium avidly but avoid phosphorus with equal fervor.

Organisms also avoid foods on which they have just been satiated [Young, 1944]. If an animal's need for protein is satisfied, it will avoid protein, although it may still be quite hungry, and highly motivated to eat a fat or carbohydrate (sugar). There are therefore *specific satiations*, as well as specific hungers.

Habit and food preference. If organisms tend to select foods that alleviate their needs, why then do people often eat inappropriate foods? We can all think of cases in which this happens. A diabetic patient, whose blood sugar may be dangerously high, may aggravate his condition by eating large amounts of sugar. Other people have been

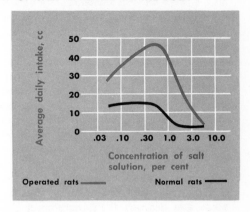

FIGURE 3.5. Salt preferences of normal rats and of rats after removal of the adrenal glands. The operated animals drank much larger quantities of salt solution until the salt concentration offered to them became quite high. Plain water was available at all times [after Bare, 1949].

known to eat sweets avidly, neglecting proteins and fats, to the detriment of their health.

There appear to be two reasons for such harmful food preferences. One is that dietary self-selection in animals and infants is not always perfect. In the experiments with rats, it will be recalled, many animals did not select foods well enough to maintain normal health and growth. The other reason is that bad habits may be learned, and these habits can distort or override natural food preferences. This fact has been demonstrated in several experiments with animals. [Scott and Verney, 1949].

In one such experiment, rats were deprived of vitamin B_1, then given their choice between food containing the vitamin and food deficient in it. As one might expect, they chose the food containing the vitamin. The experimenter, however, had mixed some licorice with this food. Licorice is not ordinarily preferred by rats, but it has a strong flavor.

DRIVES AND MOTIVATION 73

After considerable training in this situation, the rats were presented with a choice between the vitamin-deficient food with licorice and the vitamin-rich food without licorice. In other words, the licorice was switched from one food to the other. The switch fooled the rats. Now they preferred the food without the vitamin, even though they desperately needed the vitamin. The rats had learned to associate the strong flavor of licorice with the kind of food they needed, and when the licorice was in the wrong food they were misled.

In this particular experiment, the rats eventually learned that a switch had been made and changed their preferences back to the vitamin-containing food. The important point, however, is that for a time they were victims of a habit that ran counter to their natural food preferences. Situations in daily living are seldom so simple as they were in this experiment, and there are many opportunities for people to acquire habitual preferences for food.

SLEEP. Sleep is typical of physiological drives in almost every way except that it involves passive resting of the body rather than an active striving. We therefore consider the need for sleep a physiological need comparable to those for water and for food. Occasionally there is a person who does not believe sleep is a need and tries to get along without it.

One young man, for example, was convinced that sleep was only a bad habit, and resolved to prove he could stay awake indefinitely [Katz and Landis, 1935]. He sat by a time clock, punching it every 10 minutes for 7 days, when his vigil had to be terminated because he appeared on the verge of insanity. Actually, he slept quite a bit the last few days in the 10-minute intervals and often, toward the end, right through some of them. He had reached the point, however, at which he would not believe he had slept and was convinced that his clock was being tampered with in some mysterious way.

The need for sleep is real. Yet we cannot put our finger on any accumulation of waste products or special chemicals in the body that helps bring on sleep. Scientists have transfused blood from sleepy to waking dogs, but this did not make them sleepy [Kleitman, 1939]. Siamese twins with joint circulation do not always sleep at the same time. And a report of a two-headed baby that lived for a few months says that one head slept while the other was awake (Figure 3.6). Since, in these cases, sleep occurred independently of the condition of the blood, we are led to believe that sleep is regulated by centers in the brain. Such centers are discussed later in Chapter 20. For the present, all we can say is that the physiological conditions that constitute the need for sleep are poorly understood.

SEX. Sexual motivation is unique in biological motivation. It is a powerful motive, yet the survival of the individual does not depend upon it in any sense. Sexual motivation is also unique because we know more about its physiological basis than we do about the basis of other kinds of biological motivation. There is still much to be learned, particularly about sexual behavior in our own society, but as matters stand now, we have excellent information on the sexual behavior of a wide variety of different animals and in a wide variety of human societies. Sexual behavior can be understood in terms of two main factors: the sex hormones, and habits acquired through learning.

The sex hormones. The testis of the male and the ovary of the female secrete *hormones* (page 597) that are responsible for the development of the secondary sex characteristics of the body as well as for much of the sexual behavior of the two sexes. When the sex glands mature at puberty, with them develop the masculine and feminine body forms, hair distribution, vocal characteristics, and adult sex organs. At the same time, in animals as well as in human beings, interest in the opposite sex typically develops in a sharp spurt. If the

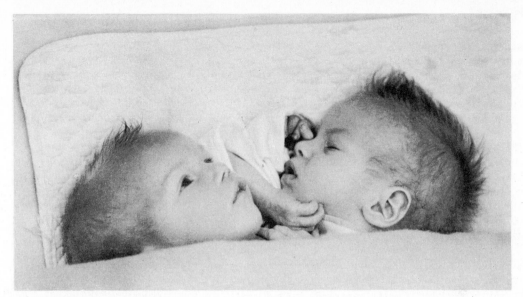

FIGURE 3.6. A two-headed baby. One head sleeps while the other is awake, indicating that sleep is controlled by the brain rather than by factors in the blood or body [Life Magazine, © Time, Inc.].

sex glands fail to develop properly or are removed in experimental animals, very few of the typical sex characteristics will show up in the individual.

One point should be clear. There is no magic about the sex hormones, especially in the case of human beings. They are not solely responsible for sexual behavior—they only help. When sexual motivation is low, extra sex hormones are not likely to help. Neither is it true that homosexuality occurs because an individual has the wrong sex hormones. Giving a homosexual an extra amount of hormone appropriate to his or her own biological sex will more likely increase the homosexuality than reverse it, if it does anything at all [Beach, 1949].

Among lower animals, such as the rat, the sex hormones are more crucial than among the higher animals, such as the chimpanzee and man [Beach, 1947a]. The spayed female rat will never mate again unless given hormones artificially. The male may continue to mate for a short while after castration, but he then becomes incapable of sexual motivation unless restored with sex hor-

mones. The comparable story for human beings is not so clear. There are cases among both sexes in which removal of the sex glands made sexual motivation disappear, but there are equal numbers of cases in which sexual motivation was unaffected by castration or ovariectomy. The picture is all the more complicated by the fact that there are men and women who are sexually impotent or frigid but who still have perfectly normal supplies of sex hormones. The information we have on monkeys and chimpanzees, however, indicates that the higher animals really do not depend crucially on sex hormones. The males in these species can be castrated without noticeable effect on sexual motivation. And it is clear that female monkeys and chimpanzees show sexual motivation at times when their hormonal supply is very low. This is not true among the lower female animals, but it is true of women.

So the sex hormones are important in the development of physical sexual characteristics and sexual motivation. However, their importance in sexual behavior is much greater among the lower animals than among the higher animals.

Habit and sexual motivation. In the sexual behavior of higher animals, such as monkeys and human beings, the sex hormones are relatively less important and *habit* and *experience* relatively more important than they are in lower animals [Beach, 1947b]. This may be illustrated by comparing the rat and the monkey. Rats reared in isolation, for example, mate normally the first time they are tested. The male rat may be inhibited by emotional situations, but the female is remarkably resistant to all but the most disturbing situations.

In monkeys and chimpanzees the story is quite different [Yerkes, 1943]. The male has to learn to mate, usually at the hands of an experienced female. The female chimpanzee, on the other hand, learns to use sexual behavior for nonsexual purposes. For example, she will often win out against a much larger male in competition for food by presenting herself sexually to the male and then making off with the food as the male focuses his attention on her.

Among human beings it is clear from many studies that sexual habits vary widely according to the level of society an individual comes from, and they are quite different in widely differing societies. Kinsey [1948] has shown, for example, that premarital intercourse is practiced more among the lower socioeconomic classes than among the higher ones. The reverse is true of masturbation. Also, studies of different cultures have shown that some societies strongly encourage homosexual practices among adolescents, whereas other cultures are even more severe than our own in the restrictions they place on homosexuality [Ford and Beach, 1951].

Habit, then, is much more important in the sexual behavior of man and higher animals than it is among the lower animals. Habits can cause sexuality to persist even when sex hormones are absent. And of course, habit frequently determines the way in which human beings express their sexual

motivation and the kinds of sexual outlets they prefer.

MATERNAL DRIVE. In Chapter 2, the maternal behavior of some animals, such as the rat, was described as instinctive behavior. In these animals, it is an unlearned pattern that is characteristic of the species. Maternal behavior is motivated behavior arising, like sex behavior, from a physiological drive. Indeed, instinctive behavior is characteristically motivated behavior associated with some identifiable drive (see Figure 3.7).

The maternal drive has its basis in a combination of hormones secreted during pregnancy and shortly thereafter. One of the important hormones in the combination is *prolactin,* a product of the pituitary gland (page 598). This gland is closely associated with the hypothalamus and concerned in the regulation of a number of physiological processes, particularly those of sex and ma-

FIGURE 3.7. Instinctive maternal behavior. Here a newborn gaur, an East Indian species of wild cattle, is being instinctively protected by its mother [Science Service].

CHAPTER THREE

ternity. The secretion of prolactin is stimulated by the presence of a fetus in the uterus. Prolactin in turn stimulates the mammary glands, which supply milk for nursing the young, but it is also important in maternal behavior. When it is injected into a virgin female rat that has been given the young of another rat, the injected rat will accept the young and care for them in much the same way that the natural mother would [Riddle et al., 1935].

General drives

If we look about us at the everyday behavior of adults, children, and animals, we can hardly escape the conclusion that relatively little of such behavior is motivated by physiological drives. True, people say they work to provide food and shelter for themselves and their families, which is a way of saying they are working to satisfy physiological drives. Yet a great deal that they do cannot be explained at all on this basis.

Think of the amount of time people spend just looking at things—at newspapers, books, television, plays, sports, canyons, mountains, and "points of interest." Think of the amount of activity that goes into playing games, skiing, boating, hiking, hunting, and touring. Most of this looking and moving about is not connected in any obvious way with the physiological drives. Neither is the play of kittens, nor the romping and whooping of children.

Despite the lack of any physiological basis for such drives, some psychologists have attempted to find a connection. In certain cases, they have succeeded, as we shall see in a moment. Moreover, they have been able to show that a number of complex social motives, to be discussed later in this chapter, are indeed derived from more basic drives, including the physiological drives. There is increasing evidence, however, for the existence of some basic, unlearned drives, which are not physiological drives in the sense used in the last section. As yet, no satisfactory term for these drives has been coined, so we are calling them general drives, just to have a name for them. They include drives for activity, for perceiving the world, for exploring and manipulating things, for contact with other people and things; they also include the fear drive. In some cases, they have a connection with physiological drives; in others, they do not. All of them, however, seem to be basic, unlearned drives that play an important part in normal behavior.

ACTIVITY.   One of the drives that is generally characteristic of all species is the drive for bodily activity. Both human beings and animals spend a good deal of time moving about for no apparent reason except that it satisfies a drive for activity. Appearances, however, may be deceiving, for activity sometimes can be explained by the presence of a physiological drive, as we shall see in a moment.

In animals, the presence of a physiological drive causes an increase in activity. Generally, whenever an animal (or human being) is hungry, thirsty, or in physiological need, it becomes more active. It runs, paces, sniffs, or explores its environment. Such changes in activity accompanying a physiological drive have been studied extensively [Reed, 1947].

One technique is to put an animal in a cage so constructed that it revolves when the animal walks. A counter mounted on the side of the cage counts the number of revolutions made in any particular period of time. In the accompanying figure (Figure 3.8) is the record of the running activity of a female rat during, between, and after periods of high sexual need (heat). At the peak of heat, the rat ran hundreds or even thousands of revolutions a day, but between periods of heat, activity greatly diminished. The sex glands were removed by spaying when the rat was about 122 days of age, and the sex cycle was thus abolished. Thereafter, activity was permanently reduced to a low level.

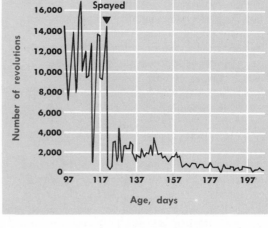

FIGURE 3.8. Activity and sexual motivation. The normal female rat shows peaks of activity when in sexual heat, which occurs about every fourth day. After the sex glands are removed by spaying, activity drops to a low level [Richter, 1927].

Similar records have been obtained in the presence of other drives such as thirst and hunger. So long as the organism remains in good health, activity increases with the presence of a physiological drive.

Activity may also have its origin in sensory stimulation [Hall, 1956]. Lights, horns, or any other strong stimulus will generally rouse an organism and make it more active. To a certain extent, the reason for this is obvious; the stimulation is annoying or disturbing. On the other hand, the stimulation does not need to be disturbing; it may merely be novel and arouse the interest or curiosity of the individual. Such curiosity is itself a drive, as will be discussed in a subsequent section.

Finally, we come to the question whether activity *qua* activity, with no physiological drive or sensory stimulation present, is a drive. The evidence shows that it is. One piece of evidence for this conclusion is that activity can be deprived; it can be pent up [Hill, 1956].

Groups of rats were confined in small cages where they had enough room to stand up or lie down, but not enough to walk around. One group was confined for 5 hours, another

for 24 hours, and a third for 46½ hours. A control group was not confined at all. After confinement, the experimental animals were placed in activity wheels, and their activity was measured for a period of an hour and a half. The amount of activity measured in this time varied with the duration of the period of confinement. Those confined for the longest time were the most active; the control group was least active.

A second kind of evidence for concluding that activity is a drive shows that activity itself can be a reward for learning a habit [Kagan and Berkun, 1954].

Two rats, an experimental subject and a control, were placed in running wheels and studied simultaneously. Each rat was provided with a lever which it could press at will throughout the period of observation. The control animal's lever, when pressed, did nothing but provide a record of lever pressing. The experimental animal's lever, on the other hand, released the brakes on both wheels so that the animals could run. By pushing the lever, the experimental animal released these brakes for a period of 30 seconds, during which the animals could run.

At the end of the 30-second period, the brakes were reapplied until the experimental animal again pushed its lever.

With this experimental design, both animals had the same opportunity for running in their respective wheels. For the experimental animal, however, the opportunity to run could be a reward for its lever pressing. Was it? The experimental animal pushed the lever significantly more—in some cases two or three times more—than the control animal. It appears then that running in the wheel was itself a reward which satisfied an activity drive.

FEAR.   Fear as a reaction to environmental situations is discussed in another chapter. Here, however, we should pause to note that fear is a drive. It must be considered a drive simply because it motivates behavior. It motivates one to try to escape a fear-producing situation or object, in other words, a *negative goal*. Fear is so powerful a drive that it may, as we shall see, interfere with the satisfaction of other drives.

We cannot always tell when fear is present, especially in sophisticated organisms that have learned to disguise it. There are, however, two general signs that may be taken as an indication of fear: One is some kind of withdrawal response—some attempt to escape or to avoid a situation. The other is some overt emotional response, such as defecation, urination, or crying. Hence these may be used as objective measures of emotional behavior.

Many fears are learned, but some appear as unlearned reactions to situations in which the individual finds himself. In general, the situations that provoke unlearned fears in animals and children involve strange noises, sights, and objects. Infants less than two years of age (page 106) tend to show fear whenever they are presented with a strange object or a loud noise. Young chimpanzees similarly show fear when they first see anything strange, even the face of a human being. Rats also are fearful, as indicated by copious urination and defecation, when

first placed in a strange enclosure, especially if it is a relatively large one. Hence we can say with reasonable assurance that strange or novel situations are the principal causes of fear in young or naïve organisms.

This point should be kept in mind as we now consider curiosity and exploratory drives.

CURIOSITY.   Several years ago it was found that a bright light has drive properties for a rat in a box. If things were so arranged that a light shining overhead could be turned off by pushing a lever in the box, the rat quickly learned to push the lever. It was thought, therefore, that light was somehow annoying to the rat; perhaps the light produced fear. Recently, however, it was shown that animals (in this case mice, but there is no reason to believe it makes a difference here) could just as easily be trained to turn a light on [Kish, 1955]. In fact, they could be taught to push a lever to produce almost any kind of novel stimulation, such as clicks of a switch, noises from a relay, or movement of a platform. Sometimes a period of habituation was required—a period in which the subjects got used to the situation, possibly to get over their fear—but after that, the novel stimulation was rewarding.

This interest in novel stimulation has been called a *curiosity drive*. It has been demonstrated in a variety of experiments with animals as well as in casual observations of children and adults. Rats will explore new mazes or areas in which they are placed, as well as strange objects in their environment. Dogs, monkeys, and children approach, handle, and explore anything new around them. For animals, the opportunity to explore is rewarding; they will readily learn to operate levers, run down alleys, or do other things merely for the sake of exploration. A curiosity drive, like other drives, can be satisfied. We see this in the fact that interest in a novel object or situation tends to diminish after some time has been spent with it.

The following experiment [Welker, 1956] demonstrates the curiosity drive:

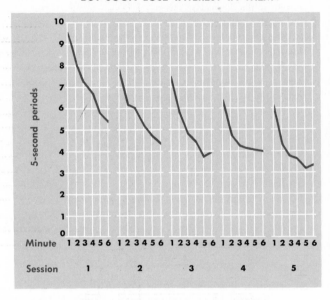

5-second periods

Minute 1 2 3 4 5 6 1 2 3 4 5 6 1 2 3 4 5 6 1 2 3 4 5 6 1 2 3 4 5 6

Session   1   2   3   4   5

FIGURE 3.9. Manipulative drive in chimpanzees. The number of 5-second periods out of 6 minutes each day during which a chimpanzee made some response to a novel set of objects. Note that interest is highest at the beginning of the period and then wanes [Welker, 1956].

Chimpanzees were presented successively with different novel objects, such as pieces of wood of different shapes, sticks that could be moved, lights that could be switched on and off, a chain, and so on. The number of times each chimp manipulated the object or made other observable responses to it was recorded for successive 5-second periods. Each set of objects was presented for 6 minutes each day, and again on successive days. When the experiment was over, the number of 5-second periods in which the chimp made some response to each set of objects was counted up. It was clear that interest was highest at the beginning of the period and waned steadily during the succeeding minutes (see Figure 3.9). When the object was presented again the next day, interest was rearoused, though not quite so much as on the preceding day, and then it gradually waned.

This sort of thing, of course, is exactly what happens when we provide children with toys. The novelty of the toy at first arouses great interest, but the novelty wears off. This is characteristic of the satisfaction of all drives. It is interesting, however, that experiments in animals permit the conclusion that such a curiosity drive, like physiological drives, is an unlearned drive that increases with deprivation and decreases with satisfaction.

MANIPULATIVE DRIVES. It is quite difficult, if not impossible, to separate what is done in exploring a novel situation from what is experienced. That is to say, we have not as yet determined whether different drives are involved, on the one hand, in just looking at or experiencing one's environment and, on the other hand, in manipulating it. So it is not possible to say whether there is a manipulative drive distinct from a curiosity or exploratory drive. We do have experiments, however, which show that a drive to manipulate objects is a relatively strong one, and like curiosity, can serve to motivate learning. The following is an example [Harlow and McClearn, 1954]:

Three monkeys were given seven problems to learn. In each problem two screw eyes were placed on a board in front of the monkey. One of the eyes could be removed from the

CHAPTER THREE

board; the other could not. Each member of the pair was of a different color. For example, in the first problem a red screw was removable and a green one was not. Other color pairs in successive problems were brown-yellow, pink-blue, black-orange, white-orchid, maple-cream, and light green–dark blue. In each case, the first-named color was removable. The monkey was scored correct if he removed the removable eye without attempting to remove the other one. But that was the only reward the monkey got. The monkeys learned to make the discrimination reasonably well, thereby demonstrating that the simple discrimination could be learned without any motivation or reward except the manipulation of the screw eyes.

These are a few of the many experiments which show the existence of a drive or drives variously called "curiosity drive," "exploratory drive," or "manipulatory drive." The experiments have been done on animals because an experimenter can know the conditions under which animals have been raised and can control precisely the conditions of experimentation; this cannot be done with children. From these experiments we can be reasonably sure that the comparable drives we have all casually observed in human beings are unlearned drives of considerable importance in accounting for the motivation of behavior.

AFFECTIONAL DRIVE. We would all agree, without much argument, that love is a powerful motive in human affairs. We love our parents, our brothers and sisters, our wives and husbands, our children, our friends, and our pets. And we love them to such a degree that almost every story, play, or magazine article intended to portray the things people do or work for has love as a major theme.

What is this thing called love? Where members of the opposite sex are concerned, it often has a large sexual component. Leaving this aside, however, love or affection for others is still a drive of considerable im-

portance. And the question is, What is this affectional drive? How does it originate? Is it innate or learned? Toward what is it directed?

Origin of affectional drive. As in the case of other drives not rooted in physiological needs or hormones, the affectional drive may develop from one or both of two sources. It may be an unlearned drive that, given the opportunity, emerges in the normal course of maturation. It may, on the other hand, be learned through experience with people, because people are instrumental in satisfying physiological drives for food, drink, etc. These two alternatives, of course, do not need to be mutually exclusive, just as maturation and learning are not mutually exclusive. It is possible that the drive is unlearned, but that the particular objects of affection are largely learned. Indeed, so far as we know now, this is correct. But to see how we arrive at this conclusion, let us consider the scientific evidence.

To study the origin of the affectional drive, it would be logical to observe the development of the drive in the human infant from birth onward. As in the study of many similar problems, however, we do not have sufficient opportunity to control the experience of the human infant. In addition, the human infant is so slow to develop its motor abilities that it is not capable at an early age of giving us measurable responses to various situations. As one investigator [Harlow, 1958] put it, "By the time the human infant's motor responses can be precisely measured, the antecedent determining conditions cannot be defined, having been lost in a jumble and jungle of confounded variables."

For these reasons, we turn again to animal subjects. The baby monkey is a very suitable subject, not only because it resembles the human infant in its form and response to other members of its species, but because its motor capabilities develop quite early. Within 2 to 10 days after birth, the baby monkey moves around on its own and manipulates objects, thus giving a meas-

FIGURE 3.10. Mother surrogates made of wire and of cloth used in experiments on affectional drive in monkeys [H. F. Harlow].

ure of what it does and does not respond to. The baby monkey can be suckled on the bottle, and thus can be brought up without any contact with other monkeys or with human beings. The following is a summary of a series of experiments [Harlow, 1958] on the development of affectional drive in baby monkeys:

The monkeys were reared singly in cages designed to provide a comfortable environment and to take adequate care of bodily needs. In one experiment, each cage was equipped with two mother surrogates. One mother surrogate (see Figure 3.10) was a cylindrical, wire-mesh tube with a block of wood at the head. This was called the "wire mother." The other "was made from a block of wood, covered with sponge rubber, and sheathed in tan cotton terry cloth." This was called the "cloth mother." It resembled a real mother much more than the wire mother did. Behind each mother was a light bulb that provided radiant heat for the infant.

Either "mother" could be outfitted with a nursing bottle placed in the center of its "breast." For one group of monkeys the bottles were placed on the cloth mothers, and for another group the bottles were placed on the wire mothers. Measurements were made of the amount of time spent with each mother. In Figure 3.11 are the results. As might be expected, those nursing on cloth mothers spent most of their time with the cloth mother and very little time with the wire mother. Those nursing on wire mothers spent *relatively* more time with the wire mother than did the first group, but from the very beginning they spent *more* time with the cloth mother than they did with the wire mother, and as the experiment progressed, they spent less and less time with the wire mother. Hence both groups showed a strong preference for the cloth mother surrogate.

BABY MONKEYS PREFER CLOTH MOTHERS:

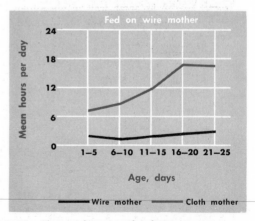

FIGURE 3.11. The preference of infant monkeys for a cloth mother [after Harlow, 1958].

This experiment brings out two interesting points. The first is that the monkeys seemed to have a drive to have contact with, or to be near, a mother. This was in addition to any physiological drive for food and water, for they spent 15 or more hours a day with a "mother" when only an hour or so was sufficient for feeding. The second point is that the choice of a mother was not associated with feeding. If the affectional drive for a mother were learned through association with feeding, one would expect those nursing on wire mothers to prefer the wire mother, yet they spent more time with the cloth mother. Apparently, there was an unlearned tendency to seek "contact comfort" with something resembling a natural mother.

Fear, curiosity, and affectional drives. Other experiments tell us how fear, curiosity, and affectional drives may conflict with one another [Harlow, 1958].

In a series of tests on the monkeys raised with mother surrogates, an infant monkey was placed in an open-field situation, a room 6 feet square, with a 6-foot ceiling, designed to evoke both fear and exploratory drives (see Figure 3.12). The room had in it a number of strange objects that usually elicit exploration and manipulation in the infant monkey. The size of the room and the strangeness of the objects could also be expected to make the animal fearful. In some tests in this situation, there was a mother surrogate; in others, there was not.

The presence or absence of a "mother" made a great difference. In her presence, indices of emotionality, based on vocalization, crouching, rocking, and sucking, were cut in half. The infant also came to use the mother as a base of operations. The infant would alternately cling to or manipulate the mother and venture out to explore the room and the objects in it, then return to the mother. The mother was a haven of safety that helped to allay fear in the strange situation, thus freeing the infant from a conflict between fear and curiosity drives.

FIGURE 3.12. Open-field situation for studying fear and exploratory drives in infant monkeys. In the absence of the mother surrogate, the monkey huddles in a corner afraid of the strange objects in the situation. [H. F. Harlow].

This experiment illustrates the interplay of affectional, fear, and exploratory drives. Fear and curiosity, we saw earlier, are conflicting drives in a novel situation. When fear is the stronger drive, it reduces curiosity and exploration. Conversely, if fear is somehow reduced, curiosity drives can take over and dominate behavior. Fear may be reduced by habituation (page 192)—becoming accustomed to the fear-provoking situation. It may be reduced, too, by the presence of an affectional object. Such an object seems to provide a feeling of security that speeds the habituation of fear and permits curiosity to prevail over fear. The object provides support for the satisfaction of curiosity drives.

This picture, derived from experiments, fits in well with casual observation. Kittens venture out from their mother to play, but they usually remain in her vicinity and return to her periodically. The human infant, after being with the mother for a while, plays happily in her vicinity, but returns frequently to tug at her apron strings. Left alone, especially in a strange situation, the infant is likely to stop playing and become afraid.

In summary, present evidence leads us to the following conclusions about affectional drive: The drive makes its appearance relatively early in the life of an infant. It is not learned; rather it appears in the normal course of maturation. It is not necessarily associated with feeding or with the satisfaction of physiological needs. It is a drive to have contact with, or to be near, some object that provides contact comfort. How much the object must resemble another individual we do not know; perhaps it need only be soft and warm. The affectional object allays fear in strange situations, providing a feeling of security, and it supports the curiosity drive.

Deprivation

At any given moment in an individual's life, some drives are quiescent or at a low ebb, while others are relatively strong. Those that are strong usually produce behavior that satisfies them; in the meantime other drives are being deprived and are increasing in strength. The strengths of various drives are thus in a state of flux, some waxing because they have been deprived, others waning because they have been satisfied.

Several factors enter into this constantly changing pattern. In the first place, after a drive such as hunger or thirst has been temporarily satisfied, it takes time for the drive again to build up enough strength to dominate behavior. This sequence is established in the physiological economy of the body and results in natural cycles or rhythms. Secondly, both man and nature impose schedules on the satisfaction of drives. Food, water, and other means of satisfying drives are only available at certain times and places, and we must therefore wait for these opportunities to satisfy our drives. In an abundant economy, these times and places are reasonably convenient, so that drives are not deprived for any lengthy period; hence they do not become excessively strong before they can be satisfied. Thirdly, there is a natural conflict between certain drives. We cannot eat and sleep at the same time; one must wait for the other. In novel situations, fear and curiosity are in conflict, and one drive must give way to the other. Finally, economic and social conditions often conspire to defeat the satisfaction of certain drives and cause them to grow more and more intense.

All these conditions of deprivation, except the last, are of little practical consequence. It may take a child some time to learn that he must wait for his meals, that he must go to the bathroom, or that he cannot immediately have whatever he wants. But he eventually learns, and in the meantime suffers no great deprivation. Indeed, most of us manage mild deprivation of drives for reasonable periods without important consequences. The problem of prolonged and severe deprivation, however, is of considerable interest. It raises such questions as, What is the effect of severe deprivation of drives? How strong can a deprived drive become? Which drives are the strongest?

COMPARATIVE STRENGTH OF DRIVES. The last question, to consider it first, is of both philosophical and practical interest. In attempting to understand human behavior, we should like to know which drives are most important in controlling behavior. Are men motivated most by fear, by hunger, by affection, or by what? If there were a simple answer to this question, it would be relatively easy to predict what a person would do in a situation, and this would be of great practical value. Unfortunately, the answer depends on several things.

One is individual differences among people. Some people never get so hungry as others; some do not have the same curiosity, fear, or affectional drive as others. So there is no one answer for everybody.

Another, and probably most important, is the degree of deprivation of a drive. Naturally, if a drive is fairly well satisfied, it is not very strong. In a society where

CHAPTER THREE

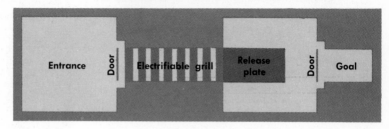

FIGURE 3.13. An obstruction box used to study the comparative strength of drives in animals. The number of times an animal will cross the electrified grid from the start box to the goal box in a specified period is the measure of drive strength. An object appropriate to a particular drive is placed in the goal box [after Warden, 1931].

such physiological drives as hunger and thirst are easily satisfied, these drives are not going to be very important, simply because they never build up any great strength. In a poverty-stricken society, however, where many people live in prolonged and severe deprivation of the hunger drive, hunger can be the most powerful motive shaping human behavior. The question, then, of which drive is the strongest can be asked only in connection with severely deprived drives. When drives are deprived, then, and become almost as strong as they can become, which are the strongest?

We know from casual observation that such drives as exploration, curiosity, or affection can sometimes be stronger than the drives of hunger or fear. Otherwise men would not risk their lives to scale unclimbed mountains or to explore new territory, or to protect those they love. This sort of casual observation, however, is anecdotal and is not very satisfactory to the scientist. Unfortunately, there is no experimental evidence on human beings, and again we must turn to animals. Several years ago the strengths of six of the drives discussed in this chapter were compared in the rat [Warden, 1931].

In order to obtain a measure of the relative strength of a drive, the experimenter trained the rats in an apparatus called an obstruction

box, shown in Figure 3.13. This apparatus consisted of a starting box, an electrified grid, and a goal box where the appropriate goal was placed. The electrified grid was the obstruction that the animals had to cross to attain their goal. The measure of the strength of a drive was the number of times they crossed the grid in a specified period. Six drives were compared: maternal, thirst, hunger, sex (female), sex (male), and exploratory. To measure the maternal drive, the experimenter placed a mother rat in the starting box, and her young pups in the goal box. In testing sex drive, the experimenter placed an animal of the opposite sex in the goal box. The female animals used were in heat, when sex drive is at its peak. In testing for exploratory drive, the experimenter placed novel objects such as sawdust and blocks of wood in the goal box. The results were exactly in the order named above (see Figure 3.14); that is, the maternal drive was the strongest, and the exploratory drive was the weakest.

Perhaps the most interesting thing about this comparison is that the maternal drive was found to be stronger than hunger or thirst, even when these latter drives were, through deprivation, extremely strong. Whether this result would hold for human beings or not, we have no way of knowing, but it shows that even in an animal as lowly as the rat, such an "unselfish" drive as the maternal drive can be stronger than the so-called "self-preservation" drives of hunger and thirst. It is also interesting that the exploratory drive, although the weakest of the six, was so strong. Rats crossed the painful electrified grill simply to explore the box and the novel objects in it. They did this about one-quarter as often as they did under maternal drive and about one-half as often as they did under sex drive. This experiment confirms the point made earlier that the exploratory (or curiosity) drive can serve as a rather powerful motive.

SEMISTARVATION IN MAN.   Although we have no similar comparison of drives in human beings, we do have a few studies of the effects of extreme deprivation of drives in man. One of these studies was conducted during the Second World War on a group of conscientious objectors who volunteered to submit to 6 months of semistarvation [Keys et al., 1950].

The subjects were placed on a diet so restricted that they lost, on the average, more than 20 per cent of their weight during the 6-month period. They were intensely hungry all the time. They were not on this regimen long before food, and the thought of food, came to dominate their lives and to submerge all other drives. They became relatively inactive, giving up almost all their former recreational activities. Their sex drives weakened; their romances broke up. They became silent and relatively unsociable, regarding outsiders with hostility and suspicion. They lost their sense of humor, no longer finding anything very funny. In short, they lost interest in everything except food. They talked mostly about eating, and they loved to read anything about food, including cookbooks. They dreamed of food and of breaking their diets. One subject went so far as to steal some food.

We may conclude then that when a drive such as hunger is exceedingly strong, it pervades all behavior, dominating the life of the person and overriding all other drives. This confirms anecdotal reports from societies where food is chronically short and from areas that have suffered famine. In Western societies, we do not see such effects of hunger because few people ever suffer

THE MATERNAL DRIVE CAN BE STRONGER THAN HUNGER OR THIRST DRIVES:

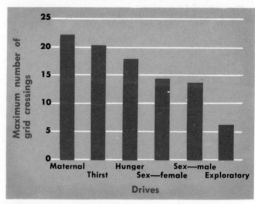

FIGURE 3.14. The relative strength of drives as measured in an obstruction box. The bars represent the number of times rats crossed an electrified grid to reach an appropriate goal object in a 20-minute period when each drive was at maximum strength [after Warden, 1931].

severe deprivation of the hunger drive. In our society, however, there are drives which are for one reason or another deprived over a long period of time in a substantial number of individuals. These drives, which include the sex drive, the curiosity drive, the drive for novel stimulation and exploration, and the affectional drive can, therefore, be expected to have some practical importance in influencing behavior.

SENSORY ISOLATION.   Occasionally we encounter a situation in which some of a man's general drives are deprived. An old and severe punishment, for example, is to place a man in solitary confinement where there is nothing to do and nothing to see. According to reports, most prisoners dread this kind of deprivation as much as, or more than, physical punishment, even though they still have enough food and have their elementary physiological needs satisfied. For this reason, solitary confinement is considered one of the worst kinds of punishment. It has been used with considerable success in warfare, e.g., by the Chinese in the Korean War, as a means of inducing or forcing a prisoner to supply intelligence information or make a false confession [Lilly, 1956]. The effects of this kind of deprivation have recently been studied in experiments with college students [Bexton et al., 1954].

The students were volunteers who undertook the experiment at an inducement of $20 a day. They lay on a comfortable bed 24 hours a day except for the time required for toilet and eating. The bed was in a small cubicle which was lighted, but quiet except for the hum of an exhaust fan. Over their eyes they wore translucent goggles, which permitted them to see light, but not objects; they wore gloves over their hands and cuffs over their forearms to reduce manual manipulation and experience. In short, everything was arranged to reduce sensory stimulation and activity to a minimum (cf. Figure 3.15).

FIGURE 3.15. The airman is in a dark, soundless room, participating in an Air Force experiment on the effects of several days of isolation from light and sound. Some of the same effects may be encountered in space flights [United States Air Force].

This might seem to be an easy way to make money, but the experiment did not last very long. Most of the subjects found that the situation became intolerable and refused to go on for more than two or three days. They began to have hallucinations, some of which were merely bizarre patterns, while others were much like dreams. They became disoriented in time and space. Their disorientation, incidentally, lasted for some time after the subjects left the cubicle. They lost their ability to think clearly; they made poor scores on problems given them to solve and were unable to concentrate on anything for very long. In brief, they began to resemble people suffering from mental disorders, and they wanted nothing more than to get out of the situation.

Experiments with the same general purpose of showing the effects of deprivation have also been conducted on subjects in tanks of water [Lilly, 1956].

The subject lies buoyant in the water, breathing through a face mask, and the environment is so arranged that sensory stimulation and activity are kept to a minimum. The subject cannot stay in the tank for more than a few hours. Before long, he finds that the lack of anything to do, anything to see, and anything to engage his attention is quite intolerable. The drives for stimulation and activity build up to a great pitch, and the experiment must be terminated.

Experiments of this kind demonstrate dramatically that the so-called "environmental drives" are extremely intense when deprived, and even though an individual might be able to survive without their satisfaction, they play as vital a role in his health and well-being as do physiological drives.

Modification of motives

There is a world of difference between the motives of a monkey and those of a man, and between those of a child and those of an adult. The drives we have been discussing, such as hunger, thirst, curiosity, and affection, are all present in the human adult, but there are others as well. Adults seem to be motivated by such things as power, status, money, achievement, and social approval—to name just a few. What is the difference, we may ask, between the drives that emerge through normal maturation and the motives that prevail in the conduct of human affairs?

A large part of the difference, surely, is learning. In the long educational process of childhood and adolescence, as well as in the adult years, people learn new goals and new fears. They also learn many ways to satisfy the physiological and general drives with which they began life. Thus, through learning, they transform rather simple drives into complex systems of motivation. But learning is a word that covers a lot of ground. To say that learning makes the difference between simple drives and complex motives is only to indicate the direction in which the answer lies. To gain a real understanding of the way in which complex motives develop requires a close look at the various factors involved. Unfortunately, we have not yet fully solved the problem of how complex motives arise; we only have some interesting clues.

ACQUIRED FEAR. When we study learning in a later chapter, we shall find that there are several kinds of learning, or at least several processes involved in it. One of these is called *conditioning*. Three elements are involved in the conditioning process: an unconditioned response, an unconditioned stimulus, and a conditioning stimulus. The unconditioned response is ordinarily an unlearned response to the unconditioned stimulus. The so-called "conditioning stimulus" is some stimulus that prior to conditioning has little or no effect on the individual. During conditioning, however, it is paired, that is, presented along with, the unconditioned stimulus. When the two stimuli are presented together—it may be once or dozens of times—the conditioning stimulus acquires the ability to elicit a response much like the unconditioned response.

The conditioning process may be illustrated by the conditioning of a fear response. An electrical shock, which is slightly painful, produces an unlearned fear response in both man and animals. The shock serves as an unconditioned stimulus for the unconditioned response, fear. By pairing the shock with some otherwise harmless stimulus—a bell, a light, or even the sight of a box— we can soon obtain a conditioned fear response to the previously innocuous stimulus, as the following experiment [Miller, 1948] illustrates:

White rats, one at a time, were placed in a white box separated from a black box by a door (see Figure 3.16). In the floor of the white compartment was a grill through which shock could be applied. First, each rat was placed in the white box for a 60-second period, during which no stimulus was applied. Then, for a period of 60 seconds, brief shocks were given every 5 seconds. At the end of this period, the door between the compartments was raised, and the shock turned on steadily. By running into the black box, the rat could escape the shock. This sequence was repeated on 10 different occasions; after that the shock was not used again.

On five subsequent occasions, rats were placed in the white box with the door raised. As one might expect, fear conditioning to the white box was strong enough to motivate them to run immediately to the black box. Following these five trials, the door was lowered, but it could be opened if the rat turned a wheel just over the door, In trying to escape, rats turned this wheel accidentally and thus discovered the means of escape. This general procedure was repeated for 16 trials. During the course of these trials, the rats learned to turn the wheel more and more promptly. After they had learned the wheel-turning response well, the wheel was adjusted so that it no longer opened the door. Instead,

CHAPTER THREE

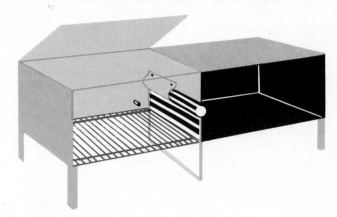

FIGURE 3.16. Apparatus for the study of acquired fears in rats [after Miller, 1948].

a lever could be depressed to open the door. The rats quickly learned this response too.

The experiment demonstrates that the fear drive can be conditioned to other stimuli, in this case, to the white box. The conditioned stimulus then becomes an incentive—a negative incentive—motivating the organism to learn habits for getting away from the incentive. The psychologist who did the experiment called the result a *learned drive,* which is a convenient shorthand for describing the phenomenon, but it is not literally correct. The drive involved, fear, was not learned; it was the unlearned response to the shock. What was new, and hence learned, was the incentive, the white box. This now evoked the fear drive, though it did not do so before conditioning. Also new, and learned under the influence of the drive, were the responses of wheel turning and lever pressing.

The process is typical. Most of the things we now fear as adults we did not fear as infants. We learned to fear them by a conditioning process. These learned fears in many cases are highly motivating and cause us to learn new habits. In the chapter on emotion, we shall see other examples of learned fears and consider in more detail the ways in which fear may be motivating.

SECONDARY GOALS. Through conditioning, we not only learn to fear new objects and situations, but we may also learn new positive goals. The process is the same, but the sign is different. Instead of learning things to avoid, we learn things to go to. We acquire new goals, called secondary goals, which we did not have before. If there is some condition that regularly precedes a primary goal, this condition may itself become a goal. Put another way, a stimulus or situation regularly connected with a primary goal becomes a secondary goal. If, for example, a mother picks up her baby each time he cries (because of hunger) in order to feed him, the baby in time acquires the goal of being picked up and may cry to be picked up even when he is not hungry. This process can be illustrated by some experiments on chimpanzees [Wolfe, 1936].

The animals were taught how to get a grape or a raisin by putting a poker chip in a small vending machine, called a Chimpomat (Figure 3.17). The experimenter simply showed a hungry chimpanzee how to insert the chip into the slot of the Chimpomat and collect his reward at the bottom. The chimpanzees learned this operation very quickly. What is more important for our purposes is the fact that after this initial learning, the chimpanzees clearly came to *value* the chips. For example, they would work as hard for the chips as they would for grapes. In one part of the study, the experimenter had the chimpanzees pull a heavily weighted box into their cages in order to get a poker chip hidden in it. As a matter of fact, the chimpanzees would pull in the weighted boxes to get chips even when they could not spend them immediately. They simply hoarded large numbers of chips and waited patiently for the chance to spend their hoard.

Later, the experimenter complicated the lives of the chimpanzees even more by teaching them to use a red chip to get food, a blue one to get water, and a white one to get out of their cages and have the freedom to run around. Then the chimpanzees would work hardest for the particular chip that would satisfy their dominant need at the moment.

The parallel between the poker chips and money is obvious, for the chimpanzees were working for poker chips in almost the same way people work for money. Money, indeed, is a secondary goal which we learn to value because it can be used to satisfy simple drives, at first for candy, a bottle of pop, or admission to the movies, and later for other things which themselves are learned as secondary goals. The principle, however, is not limited to money. Almost any thing or situation that is consistently associated with the satisfaction of primary drives will be learned as a secondary goal. The principle applies not only to money and things, but also to somewhat fuzzier goals, such as status, achievement, and values.

SOCIAL VALUES. Some of the values one acquires in this way involve other people and some do not. Those that do involve other people are called *social values*. The chimpanzees in the experiment described learned to value poker chips. A carpenter comes to value his tools, a sailor his ship and the sea, a child its toys, a soldier his gun, and a farmer his land. One can readily multiply this list of *things* people come to

FIGURE 3.17. A chimpanzee using tokens to obtain food. The chimpanzee has learned to place poker chips in the machine to obtain food—in this case, some fruit. Once the chips have acquired "value," the animal will learn to do other things to obtain chips [Yerkes Laboratories of Primate Biology, Inc. Henry W. Nissen, photographer].

value. With little trouble, however, one can also think of many social values: law observance, cleanliness, proper dress, success in school, honesty, courtesy, sexual morality, respect for one's superiors, and so on. Such social values govern the relations between people, what they strive for, what they fight for, and many of the complex details of human affairs.

A person tends to acquire social values because from the moment of his birth other people have so much to do with the satisfaction of his needs to eat, to be warm, to be dry, or to be in a comfortable position.

Thus the mother acquires social value. A little later, when the child no longer needs such physical care, he still must depend upon parents, brothers and sisters, playmates, and others for many of his needs. These people determine where and when he can play, where he can go, what clothes he shall wear, what toys he shall have, when he must sleep, whether he gets some candy, and so on. It is no wonder that he rapidly learns a host of social values and goals.

Besides this more or less inescapable learning of social values, we must also remember that every person is put through a deliberate educational process. By words and acts, parents patiently teach their children what is "right" and what is "wrong," what to aim for in the world, what to value, what to avoid, what to love, what to hate. And each parent imposes his own particular set of values on his child. Added to this are the demands that society makes. At first, society indirectly dictates to some degree what kinds of values parents instill in their children. Later, when the child lives more with people outside the home, society imposes its values through the school, the church, playmates, clubs, employment, and the various social activities in which he engages.

In considering social influences on the development of values, we should also recognize the special role that language plays. Words are stimuli; they can acquire value and pass it on to other words, people, and objects. Thus in the training of a child, the word "don't" acquires some of the negative value that punishment has, and the words "good boy" or "good girl" acquire positive value. These two kinds of words may then serve as punishments and rewards; parents can use them in shaping the attitudes, values, and future behavior of the child. Of course, it may be necessary from time to time to strengthen the values attached to these words by further training with biological rewards and punishments, and parents are always doing this too. But the important thing to remember is that when words finally do acquire value, they facilitate the whole process of acquiring new values. Unlike poker chips, for example, words are easy to carry around, so they are always available for use as rewards and punishments no matter what the situation.

SOCIAL TECHNIQUES. Motives are modified, not only by an individual's acquiring new goals, both positive and negative, but by his acquiring new habits for attaining goals. In the experiment on the conditioning of fear, cited above, the rats quickly learned the habit of pressing the bar to escape the box they had learned to fear. The chimpanzees learned similarly to operate a vending machine to satisfy their hunger drive. The learning of habits which satisfy drives goes on in many complex ways in the lives of animals and human beings. Sometimes the habits learned are so complicated and so roundabout in reaching the goal that it is difficult to tell what the goal really is. And the habits learned for attaining goals can easily be confused with the goals themselves. This is particularly true where social behavior—behavior involving other people—is concerned.

One scientist [Bechterev, 1949] who studied animal behavior for many years tells the story of a pigeon and a horse: The horse had some grain in its nose bag, and the pigeon was hungry. The pigeon was flying around the horse's head and quite by accident frightened the horse so much that it spilled some grain from the nose bag. The pigeon then swooped down and ate the spilled grain. The pigeon apparently learned very quickly, for as the scientist watched, he saw the bird repeat the trick until it had eaten liberally.

The story illustrates the use of a social technique in the satisfaction of drives. The pigeon had established a *reaction-getting habit*, using the horse as another individual, to secure what it wanted. People obviously learn such social techniques too. A child, for example, who throws a temper tantrum when he wants a piece of candy, will, if the tantrum works, quickly learn to throw a tantrum whenever he wants candy or anything else. More common is the example of the child crying for his mother to bring food. One can think of many others.

In Western society, or any highly organized society, social techniques for gaining one's ends are part and parcel of living. The school child takes the proverbial apple to the teacher in order to win her favor. The workman flatters the boss in hope of getting a raise in wages. The salesman is courteous and deferential in order to win and keep customers. The advertiser describes the virtues and low cost of his products in order to make his living. The propagandist presents the news in such a way as to win friends and turn them against his enemies. These examples illustrate the many social techniques which people learn to use to satisfy some biological or social need. Every adult in our society should be aware of the fact that he is using such techniques and that others are continually using them on him.

GENERALIZATION AND FIXATION.   In the learning that goes on in developing new goals and new techniques for attaining goals, there are two processes that are sometimes of importance.

One is *generalization*. We shall deal with it in detail in the chapter on learning. Here let us simply define it and point out its significance in the modification of motives. Generalization is a tendency to respond in the same way to all situations that are in some degree similar. This is a bit circular, because in practice we are forced to consider situations similar that are responded to in the same way. But let us take an example. Suppose that a rat has been conditioned to fear a white box, as in an earlier example. If, as a result of that conditioning, the rat now displays fear when placed in a gray box, or a larger box, or a box of a different shape, we say that generalization has taken place. The rat is giving the same fear response to situations that are somewhat similar, even though different. Or suppose that

the chimpanzee taught to operate the Chim-pomat keeps on working the apparatus just the same when it is delivering marbles as when it vends poker chips. Again we would say that the learned response has generalized to objects that are somewhat similar to, but different from, those in the original learning.

The process of generalization accounts for some of the things observed in complex motivated behavior. A person who is deathly afraid of going near the ocean may be generalizing from a childhood experience of nearly drowning in a bathtub. Or a person who is highly motivated to please people, whether they may be teachers, strangers on a bus, or anybody else, may merely be generalizing from his experience with his father, who was difficult to please and who regularly resorted to punishment whenever he was displeased. It is not difficult to think of other examples from one's own experience.

Generalization is characteristic of most learned responses. Once a response has been learned, it will be made to other objects and situations that are not exactly like the original one. Generalization is particularly characteristic of learned fears. A fear acquired in one situation usually generalizes to many others. Only through additional learning, in which an individual learns to discriminate one situation from another, is it possible to restrict generalization to things that are very similar to the one involved in original learning. The phenomenon of generalization thus accounts for many of our responses to situations and goals when there is otherwise no good reason for them.

Fixation is a second process to consider. In some respects, it is the opposite of generalization. As used here, it refers to the tendency to value certain goals, when alternative ones might do just as well. When an organism, in learning to satisfy a drive, has repeatedly found one particular object to be satisfying, it may come to prefer that object and to refuse others that might satisfy it just as well. Again let us take some examples.

Food is our general goal when we are hungry, yet there are many varieties of food that can satisfy hunger. If a rat, for example, is fed for a long time on pellets, it will not usually want to change to powdered food, even though the powder is exactly the same food in a slightly different form. Children who have been brought up on vegetable plates usually do not care for hamburger, though some of us have learned exactly the reverse preference. Examples of this kind can be found in our preferences for mates, for weather, for entertainment, for housing, and so on. Several goals may be equally valuable in satisfying a drive, but because certain ones have been attained in the past, we come to prefer them to the others. Thus we may learn to prefer certain goals and in this way our motives may be altered.

SUBSTITUTION OF DRIVES. Psychologists who have experimented with secondary goals in animals and children have noted that such goals do not continue to be goals very long unless they are backed up with the satisfaction of primary drives. If, for example, we do not pay off a chimpanzee's poker chips with food at regular intervals, the chimpanzee soon loses interest in working for poker chips. Similarly, if the rat conditioned to fear in the white box does not get a shock once in a while, it gradually loses its drive to escape from the box. This is not strange, of course, for we can cite similar cases in human affairs. We soon lose interest in money or other things if they become worthless and do not satisfy a motive.

On the other hand, organisms do continue to work for some goals after they have lost any significance in satisfying the more conspicuous drives of hunger, thirst, and the like. The poor boy who earned his first pennies to ward off hunger and discomfort often continues to work day and night at amassing a large fortune long after he has acquired enough money to meet his physical needs. A businessman who approaches retirement age with ample reserves may insist on staying on the job even though he does not need to work any more. And so on.

Indeed, in a society such as ours, where most physiological needs are met, a great deal of almost everyone's effort is devoted to goals that have little to do with the satisfaction of primary drives. Why?

We can as yet give no sure answer to the question. One proposal is that secondary goals, once acquired, become *functionally autonomous*, which is to say, they simply go on functioning on their own without being reinforced by the satisfaction of physiological drives [Allport, 1937]. This proposal, however, probably begs the question, and it was made before we learned of the great power of the so-called "general drives." What seems more plausible now is that one drive can support or substitute for another. A goal originally learned because it was associated with the satisfaction of one drive may later satisfy another, less conspicuous drive.

Some examples will make this point clear. A penniless boy who becomes a millionaire starts out with a bundle of drives, both physiological and general. To stave off hunger, he starts working, and money becomes a secondary goal. In his work, however, he finds some satisfaction for his activity drive, and since the work provides all sorts of novel situations, he also indulges his curiosity drive. The work brings him into close relationship with men who become his friends, and thus it may also satisfy his affectional drive. There may be other factors operating too, but these illustrate the point. After he has made his million, he is still motivated to work simply because the work now satisfies other drives that are strong and not so easily satisfied as the need for food and shelter. Thus the things he learned to do originally to satisfy one drive now satisfy others. Of course, he may keep on saying to himself, out of habit, that he is still motivated to make money, but he may simply be unaware of his true motives.

AGING. We have discussed a number of factors that modify motives. All those we have discussed so far are learning factors.

There are, however, some important factors that are merely a matter of aging. The activity drive is certainly a function of age, as we can attest merely by watching kittens, children, and older people. Although many adults have tried, there are few who can keep up with the activity of a growing youngster. As an individual grows older, he tends to slow down, though some persons maintain a higher level of activity for a longer time than others. Sex drive is also a function of age. It does not appear until a person enters his teens and it tends to wane after it reaches a peak. This modification of the sex drive is traceable to physiological changes taking place in the body. How other drives are affected by age is not so clear, but there is certainly a progressive change in interests throughout life, and some of these are probably due to aging rather than learning.

Complex motives

Having studied the physiological and general drives, and the ways in which motivated behavior may be modified through aging and learning, we are now in a position to consider the complex motives encountered in people every day as they go about their work and play. We can expect to see many secondary goals acquired in the course of learning how to attain primary goals. We can also expect to find drives and goals connected in diverse ways so that several secondary goals are related to a single primary drive and, conversely, several drives may be satisfied by a single goal.

This interlacing of drives and goals makes the problem of classifying complex motives difficult, if not impossible. It would be nice if we could simply list and classify all the motives found in man. Indeed psychologists have devised a number of different classifications, some of which will be described in a later chapter. Such classifications are useful for particular purposes—for making up personality tests, for counseling people with personal or vocational problems, and so on—but they are largely arbitrary. There are just too many ways in which drives and goals may be connected, and each individual has his own unique combination of them. Two individuals with the same goal, for example, may be satisfying quite different drives, or those with the same drive may satisfy it with different goals.

For this reason it is best not to attempt here to classify complex human motives. Instead, we shall consider a limited number of representative motives and see how they are derived from primary drives and learned goals. Even this limited list will not be mutually exclusive, for each of the motives has something in common with one or more of the others. It will, however, give us a general picture of some of the common human motives.

AFFILIATION. By and large, human beings are gregarious creatures. Most of their waking hours are spent with other individuals—parents, family, friends, neighbors, club members, and so on. Modern society, of course, throws people together in work, entertainment, and living, but that is not the cause of these affiliative tendencies. People in primitive societies are also gregarious. And almost all human beings seek the company of others even when there is no particular pressure to do so.

The basis of one kind of affiliation, marriage, is not hard to understand, for the sex drive plays an important part in it. Marriage is partly a means of satisfying the sex drive, but it helps satisfy many other needs as well, including both physiological and general drives. One of these is the affectional drive, which enters into many kinds of affiliation. To affiliate with clubs, churches, or certain prestigeful organizations may also satisfy other complex motives, such as the status motive, to be discussed below. In any case, affiliation with other people is a goal that satisfies, or can satisfy, many different drives. The motive to affiliate is therefore found almost universally in human cultures. (It is also characteristic of many animals.)

Closely related to affiliation, and probably a subvariety of it, is the *dependency* need. This is the need or motive to depend on others, to have someone to look up to, someone to turn to for help, someone to be accepted and loved by. Almost everyone has it in some degree. Others—a few—have it to such a degree that they can hardly do anything without depending on someone else for help or support.

The dependency motive arises in part from training in infancy and childhood. We all come into the world helpless and must depend upon our parents throughout the years of infancy, childhood, and adolescence for the satisfaction of many of our primary drives, for decisions about right and wrong, and for control of much of our behavior. Thus their presence, support, and help become secondary goals for us. When we eventually leave home and parents, we do not easily shed this dependency. We remain dependent on them, or find someone else to represent them. Adults, of course, seldom have the extreme dependency of a child, but few, if any, are able to rid themselves completely of the need to depend upon others.

SOCIAL APPROVAL. Another common motive is to seek social approval for the things we do and to avoid doing things that evoke social disapproval. In the extreme, this motive becomes one of compulsive conformity to the norms set by the group a person is in. He tries all the time to determine what is approved and what is not, and does his best to act accordingly.

This motive, too, has its roots in childhood training, when parents establish what is right and wrong for the child to do. A child learns to please his parents out of hope for the satisfaction of other drives, and perhaps also out of fear of punishment. This desire to please generalizes easily to other people. Indeed, when the child goes to school and moves into adolescence, he finds again that he can be punished and ostracized if he fails to please teachers and associates; or conversely, he finds that he can

more easily get the things he wants if he wins his associates' approval. Social approval thus is learned as a generalized secondary goal.

STATUS. Most people are motivated to have some status among their fellow men. At the minimum, this is a motive to be thought well of, to have a respectable standing among the people one knows, and not to be considered inferior. At the extreme, it can be a desire to achieve the highest possible status in one's community, one's profession, or some other standard of reference. In between, it is a desire to know just where one stands in the status system, to know who is up and who is down, and to behave accordingly. Status systems vary from one group to another. A person's particular status motives depend not only on his own make-up but also on the group he happens to be in.

Status motives may take several different forms. One is to achieve a *rank* in the hierarchy of the group. Efforts to achieve such a rank can be observed not only among members of the military profession but in most human societies. It has also been observed in groups of animals living together [Schjelderup-Ebbe, 1935]. Common barnyard hens, for example, quickly establish a "pecking order" among themselves. One hen, the most dominant, may peck most of the other hens. The least dominant hen, on the other hand, is pecked by all other hens but has no pecking rights of her own. In between, in relatively fixed rank, are hens who can peck those below them but not those above.

Such a pattern of "pecking" and ranking is almost universal in human relationships. We see it in groups of children playing together, in the size of offices and desks of businessmen, in the seating of guests at a formal luncheon, and in numerous little details of everyday life.

Other closely related examples of status motives are those for *prestige* and for *power*. The need for prestige is the need to feel better than other persons with whom one compares oneself. In daily life there are many ways in which prestige is sought and achieved. Children of five or six may consider a pair of roller skates, a new dress, or a cowboy suit a symbol of prestige. A little later, athletic prowess enters the picture as a way of achieving prestige. Among adults such symbols as dress, money, automobiles, homes, and the like are regarded as ways of feeling better than the other fellow.

The need for *power* is similar to, but not quite the same thing as, the need for prestige. There are some people who shun or ignore prestige, yet aspire to power over their fellow men. Think, for example, of the businessman who quietly and inconspicuously builds up control of an industrial empire, or consider the professional politician who holds no public office but "pulls the strings" that move the officeholder. Such individuals are displaying a desire for status, but in a different way from those who aspire to achieve prestige.

Each group, community, and society, whether primitive or modern, has its own status system. How such a system arises and what function it serves are discussed in a later chapter (page 504). So far as the individual is concerned, status is a secondary goal that stands for the satisfaction of many primary drives. Persons of a particular status can expect to make a certain amount of money, live in a certain style, and be treated in certain ways. Thus status more or less guarantees that an individual may be able to satisfy other drives. It also frees a person from the fear that he might lose some of the satisfactions that go along with his status.

SECURITY. A feeling of security, or lack of it, is also an important motive, especially in modern, complex societies. This is a feeling of being able to hold on to what one has, of being sure that he will be able to fare as well in the future as in the past. Conversely, insecurity is a haunting fear that "things may not last," that one may lose what he now has. Insecurity is thus based on fear and especially fear of not being able to satisfy one's other motives. A person may be insecure about almost anything—his status, his wife's affections, his money, or social approval for what he does, his ability to earn a living, and hence his ability to satisfy his primary drives.

In a society as highly organized as Western culture, a person depends upon many other people and upon conditions in general for his security. This means, of course, that a person's security may often be threatened or lost through no fault of his own or without any opportunity to regain it. For that reason, security takes on a special importance in people's lives—more so, in many cases, than any of the other motives we have discussed—and it is responsible for much personal unhappiness as well as social unrest. Later on (in Chapter 18), we shall see that the security motive is uppermost in the minds of employed workers and may be more important than wages, status, and other motives for working.

ACHIEVEMENT. In some cultures, particularly that of the United States, achievement is a powerful motive. This is the motive to accomplish something, to succeed at what one undertakes, and to avoid failure. We are taught that in the land of opportunity everyone can succeed at something, whether it be making money, becoming a professional—or going into politics—if only he works hard at it. And success is highly prized. Parents prod their children to make good marks in school, then to go on to college, and finally to make good at some business or profession. This is not the picture in many other cultures.

The strength of the achievement motive, like that of other complex motives, varies from individual to individual. In some people, the drive to be successful at what they undertake is tremendously strong—they have very high levels of aspiration—

while in others, it is relatively weak. On the whole, though, it is a pervasive motive in American youths and adults.

How strong the motive is depends, in part, on how successful one has been. A person usually cannot aspire to success as an athlete, scholar, or musician unless he has already had some success along the way. If he has had only modest success, he is likely to set a lower goal for himself than if he has had outstanding success.

In general, people set their goals just a little higher than they are sure of attaining, and this is healthy. In some people, however, there is a large discrepancy between the *level of aspiration* and the *level of performance,* probably because they have learned to set goals that gain the approval of their parents and associates. In others, the level of aspiration falls considerably below the capacity to achieve. This discrepancy often occurs because individuals have learned to fear failure. They do not set their goals high for fear of not attaining them.

The achievement motive has been studied intensively in recent years [McClelland et al., 1953]. We now have ways of measuring it and of distinguishing those individuals who have strong achievement motives from those who have weak ones. The origin of strong achievement motives has, as one might expect, been traced back to childhood and the kind of training the child received. The person who has a strong achievement motive is, in general, a person who was reared in a home that put strong emphasis on independence. The parents tended to be people who expected their child to solve his own problems at an early age. Thus high achievement motives spring from the child's early training in independence, or at least from his being left on his own to find out somehow for himself how to satisfy his various motives.

The motives just discussed will be treated again in more detail in later chapters, where they can be related to the study of personality and social and vocational problems. Here, we intended only to survey briefly some complex motives and to show how they are related to the primary drives described in the first part of the chapter.

UNCONSCIOUS MOTIVES. Before concluding this chapter, we should bring out one more point: *human motives are sometimes unconscious.* We mean simply that a person often does not know what his real motive is or what his goal is. He will probably be able to give some good reasons for his behavior, but often he will not be able to tell you the real motivating factor.

One explanation of this is probably obvious from the foregoing discussion. Since several drives and goals may be intertwined in any given bit of behavior, it is difficult for anyone, even a skilled observer who knows the person's life history, always to identify correctly the motive(s) behind an act.

Another explanation is that motives are, in a sense, habits. We all acquire habits of which we are largely unaware. A person, for example, may bite his nails, pull on his ears, tap on the table, or pace back and forth in front of a classroom, and not be aware of any of these habits until they are called to his attention. Complex motives may function in the same way. Moreover, motives are not so easily observed as habits, and hence, the person is less likely to be reminded of them.

A third explanation is that motives are often fashioned under unpleasant circumstances that we would like to forget. In other words, we may not want to recognize certain of our motives. Consequently, we actively forget them through a process called *repression,* which we shall take up at other points in the book. In brief, repression is a process that enables us to fool ourselves about our motives because we are not willing to admit what they really are. As a result, we disguise them by perceiving them as different from what they really are or by refusing to recognize them at all.

Summary

1. Motivation may be represented as a cycle consisting of three parts: (*a*) a drive that arouses (*b*) instrumental behavior, which leads in turn to (*c*) a goal that satisfies the drive.

2. Drives may be divided into primary drives that are unlearned and secondary drives that are acquired through learning. The primary drives, in turn, may be subdivided into physiological drives, which arise because of physiological conditions in the body, and general drives, such as activity, fear, curiosity, and affection.

3. Physiological processes within the body tend to maintain a balance called homeostasis. When this balance is disturbed, the resulting physiological need arouses regulatory behavior, like seeking food, water, or a mate, which eventually restores the balance.

4. Such drives as hunger and thirst appear to depend upon chemical conditions in the body. These conditions often produce very specific needs or hungers, for infants and animals can select particular kinds of food that are appropriate to their needs.

5. In lower animals, sexual drives depend on sex hormones, but in human beings these drives can exist in the absence of such hormones. The same is true of maternal drive.

6. General bodily activity increases when a drive, such as hunger or sex, is present. It is also a drive in its own right; it is satisfied by opportunities for exercise and serves as the basis for learning new responses.

7. The curiosity drive is aroused by novel stimulation, and the manipulative drive by the opportunity to manipulate objects. Both can serve as motivation for learning new responses. Novel situations may arouse fear as well as curiosity.

8. An affectional drive for contact comfort with a motherlike object appears to be an unlearned drive. Its satisfaction can alleviate fear and support the expression of curiosity.

9. In the comparison of primary drives in animals, the maternal drive is stronger than the thirst, hunger, and sex drives; these in turn are stronger than curiosity or exploratory drives.

10. When a drive is severely deprived, it dominates other drives, and activity is directed toward its satisfaction. Reducing sensory stimulation to a minimum causes hallucinations, restlessness, and loss of ability to concentrate. It usually cannot be tolerated very long by human subjects.

11. Under the influence of a drive, an individual learns acts that regularly lead to the appropriate goal. In learning such acts, organisms acquire new goals. Indeed, conditions that are usually present when an individual is working toward a goal themselves become learned or secondary goals.

12. Through learning, many new goals or values are acquired. Fears may also be acquired through learning. Because people, particularly parents, are so intimately a part of human learning, many of the goals acquired by human beings are "social values."

13. Activities that are learned for satisfying one drive may also serve later to satisfy other drives. Hence, in the human adult, drives and goals are interlaced in a complex way.

14. Some of the more common derived or secondary motives in man are drives for affiliation, social approval, status, security, and achievement. These motives often operate without the individual's being aware of them.

CHAPTER THREE

Suggestions for further reading

Berlyne, D. E. *Conflict arousal and curiosity*. New York: McGraw-Hill, 1960.
A systematic treatment of the role of motivation in learning, with emphasis on the curiosity and exploratory drives.

Bindra, D. *Motivation: A systematic reinterpretation*. New York: Ronald, 1958.
A textbook on motivation and theoretical analysis of the problems of motivation.

Cannon, W. B. *Bodily changes in pain, hunger, fear and rage* (2d ed.). New York: Appleton-Century-Crofts, 1929.
An account of classical experiments on some of the physiological factors in hunger and thirst.

Ford, C. S., and Beach, F. A. *Patterns of sexual behavior*. New York: Hoeber-Harper, 1951.
A good account of sexual motives and practices in animals and in different human societies.

Klineberg, O. *Social psychology* (2d ed.). New York: Holt, Rinehart and Winston, 1954.
Contains a critical analysis of the problem of instinctive behavior in man and a summary of the facts of social motivation.

McClelland, D. C. *Studies in motivation*. New York: Appleton-Century-Crofts, 1955.
A collection of articles giving a broad view of the field of motivation.

Miller, N. E. Learnable drives and rewards. In S. S. Stevens (ed.), *Handbook of experimental psychology*. New York: Wiley, 1951.
A summary of experiments on the acquisition of motives.

Morgan, C. T., and Stellar, E. *Physiological psychology* (2d ed.). New York: McGraw-Hill, 1950. Chaps. 17–20.
A textbook summary of the physiological factors in motivation.

Young, P. T. *Motivation of behavior*. New York: Wiley, 1936.
A textbook covering various aspects of motivation.

Feeling

& emotion

We HIGHLY CIVILIZED members of Western culture like to think of ourselves as rational beings who go about satisfying our motives in an intelligent way. To a certain extent we do satisfy them that way. But we are also emotional beings— more emotional than we realize. Indeed, most of the affairs of everyday life are tinged with feeling and emotion. Joys and sorrows, excitement and disappointment, love and fear, hope and dismay—all these and many more are feelings we experience in the course of a day or a week.

Without such feelings and emotions, life would be pretty dreary. Our feelings add color and spice to living; they are the sauce without which life would be dull fare. We anticipate with pleasure our Saturday night dates, we remember with a warm glow the satisfaction we got from giving a good speech, and we even recall with amusement the bitter disappointments of childhood. On the other hand, when our emotions are too intense and too easily aroused, they can get us into a good deal of trouble. They can warp our judgment, turn friends into enemies, and make us as miserable as if we were sick with fever.

Despite its practical significance, emotion is not easy to investigate scientifically. We cannot readily control or reproduce emotional situations. Nor can we always observe it objectively, for its many subtle shades are often hard to distinguish. Moreover, people are taught to hide their emotions, so we cannot know, just by seeing them, what emotion they are experiencing. For these reasons, scientific knowledge of emotion has grown slowly, and we are still far from a complete understanding of it.

This chapter is an introduction to what is now known about emotion. We shall discuss emotional development, the motivational aspects of emotion, its physiological basis, and its expression. Some of these topics are treated more fully elsewhere in the book. Emotion as motivation was mentioned in Chapter 3; it will be discussed again in Chapter 5 on frustration and conflict. It will also be encountered later when we study learning. The physiological aspects of emotion, especially the parts of the brain concerned in emotion, will be treated in more detail in Chapter 19. This chapter, then, is only a general introduction to the topic of emotion.

Just as emotion is difficult to investigate scientifically, it is also difficult to define. The word *emotion* is derived from Latin roots meaning "to move out." This conveys the idea of an outward expression of something inside, which is one aspect of emotion. "To move out" also implies a second aspect of emotion—its motivational quality. Emotion supplies the motive power for a great deal of our behavior. In addition, however, emotion is an experience; it is something we feel. Finally, it is a physiological state that can be observed with the appropriate recording equipment. We shall study all these aspects in this chapter. As for a general definition, the best we can do is follow Webster. Emotion is "a departure from the normal calm state of an organism of such nature as to include strong feeling, an impulse toward open action, and certain internal physical reactions; any one of the states designated as fear, anger, disgust, grief, joy, surprise, yearning, etc."

Emotional development

In each individual, emotions have a history much like that of other responses and of abilities. This history begins with the hereditary differences that determine emotional tendencies. It proceeds through a period of maturation during which the individual's emotional patterns of behavior gradually mature in the same sense that his basic motor abilities do. Then, interlaced with this maturation is a good deal of learning. As the individual grows up, he learns to react emotionally to new situations and to modify his emotional behavior. In this section, we shall trace the influence of these factors in emotional development.

INHERITANCE. It is fairly obvious that emotionality has some hereditary basis. As we all know, there are marked species differences in emotionality among wild and domesticated animals. Gray rats, wolves, and lions, for example, are savagely emotional, whereas their domesticated counterparts, white rats, dogs, and cats, are relatively unemotional. It is true, of course, that wild animals can be tamed to some degree, if the process is started early enough. But they seldom, if ever, become as unemotional as the commonly domesticated animals. Even when they are reared entirely in human company, many species of wild animals, such as the chimpanzee, still become dangerous by the time they reach adulthood. Conversely, if normally tame animals, such as the cat and dog, are allowed to grow up away from human beings, they become relatively wild. But they are still more tamable than otherwise wild animals.

The case for emotional inheritance does not rest on such anecdotal evidence, however. Hereditary factors in emotion have been studied experimentally. Some years ago savageness and tameness were compared in the wild gray rat and the laboratory white rat [Stone, 1932].

The white rat, gently handled in the first few months of life, easily becomes tame enough to pose no threat to the experimenter. The wild gray rat, on the other hand, improves somewhat with taming procedures, but always remains a tense, emotional animal, ready to attack and bite at the least provocation. When the two are crossbred, some of the young inherit the relatively tame disposition of the white parent, and others the savageness of the gray parent. Savageness, moreover, is linked to hair color, but to tan pigment factor rather than to gray. The hair of the wild rat appears to be gray because it consists of two colors of hair intermixed; one is a light tan, the other a brown so dark that it is practically black. These two pigment factors are separable genetically. In the crossing of white and wild gray rats, if the young inherits the tan pigment, it will be savage; if it inherits the black pigment or no pigment at all (white hair color), it will be tame. Thus it has been possible to develop a strain of black rats, which are almost as tame or tamable as the white rat and which are now frequently used in laboratories.

In another experiment [Hall, 1938], mentioned briefly in Chapter 2, rats selected from various laboratory colonies were tested in an open-field situation.

The "open field" is a large compartment that usually elicits fear, as evidenced by copious urination and defecation, when rats are first placed in it. The amount of such emotional behavior in 145 rats was objectively measured in a 2-minute test given each day for a number of days. On succeeding days, the rats habituated to the situation and showed less and less fear.

Of the original 145 rats, 7 of the most emotional females were mated with 7 of the most emotional males. Similarly, 7 of the least emotional males were mated with 7 unemotional females. This kind of inbreeding was continued for several generations. The results were striking in the first generation. The offspring of emotional animals were considerably more emotional than those of unemotional animals. In fact, the scores of one group were seven times those of the other group.

These experiments leave no doubt that savageness and fear in the rat are greatly determined by heredity. This conclusion has been confirmed in other animals, particularly in the dog [Scott, 1958]. Unfortunately, the problem has not been studied very extensively in human beings, partly because, as usual, it is difficult to do genetic experiments in man, but partly through neglect. There is one study [Jost and Sontag, 1944], however, that has some bearing on the question.

Children between six and twelve years of age were studied over a 3-year period. Various bodily states known to be associated with emotion were measured. These included skin resistance, pulse and respiration rates, and salivation. Although the measurements were not of emotionality per se, they presumably correlate with it. The study included six pairs of identical twins, as well as siblings. Correlations for the measures were computed in much the same way that we have previously described for computing correlations of intelligence. The results were:

| Identical twins | .43–.49 |
| Siblings | .26–.40 |

The range of correlations is for different physiological measures. The correlations are not high, probably because measures of bodily states vary considerably from one time to another, but those for twins and siblings are significant. The fact, too, that those for identical twins are higher than those for siblings, confirms the role of heredity in the bodily states concerned in emotion.

All indications are that emotionality is at least in part an inherited characteristic in both human beings and animals. More research on the inheritance of emotionality in human beings is sorely needed, however, in order to determine to what degree it is inherited and in what respects it is learned.

DIFFERENTIATION OF EMOTIONS. Everyone who has systematically studied the development of emotional reactions in infants agrees that this development has a fairly characteristic pattern. Different observers

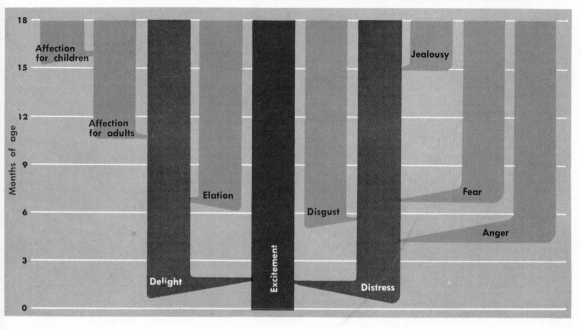

FIGURE 4.1. Development of emotional responses in the infant. The diagram summarizes studies of the order in which different identifiable expressions emerge [after Bridges, 1932].

disagree only slightly on the details. The exact age at which different emotions appear varies, of course, with the population studied. But the general pattern of development is clear. It is depicted by the diagram in Figure 4.1, which summarizes one of the early systematic studies of emotional development [Bridges, 1932]. We shall also give a brief verbal description of the process.

Infants come into the world crying, and they continue to cry periodically whenever they are hungry or uncomfortable. This is an inborn response to internal physiological needs or to discomfort. If we consider the responses to *external situations*, however, we find that almost the only emotional response that can be distinguished in the newborn infant is general *excitement*. This response consists of uncoordinated squirming, arm

waving, and kicking. It is not a specific response to any particular stimulus, but occurs whenever the environment suddenly changes.

Some time within the infant's first month or six weeks of life, this diffuse excitement begins to give way to more specific emotional reactions. The first reaction to appear has been called *distress*. This may or may not include the crying that has been going on since birth, but it is characterized by muscular tension and checked breath. Shortly afterward, something called *delight* is distinguishable. It is evidenced by smiling, gurgling, and muscular relaxation. Thus by the time the infant is six weeks to two months old, the two general emotions— distress and delight, pleasantness and unpleasantness, or call them what you wish— that will be felt and expressed through-

FEELING AND EMOTION 103

out life have made their appearance. Such development is almost wholly, if not entirely, a matter of maturation.

As the infant grows older, he develops an increasing variety of emotional responses. At three months of age, for example, he responds to unpleasant situations with general signs of distress, but responds to nursing, fondling, tickling, and rocking with smiles and general signs of delight. After that, emotions rapidly differentiate, and by the age of two years, the child has a repertory of specific reactions to different situations. This development may be regarded as a differentiation of, or refinement of, the general states of distress and delight. The order in which, and the approximate ages at which, the different patterns appear are given in Figure 4.1. Since the exact order and age vary from child to child, we have purposely made this figure inexact.

FACTORS IN EMOTIONAL DEVELOPMENT. Both maturation and learning, undoubtedly, play a part in this differentiation of emotions. From our knowledge of motor development, we may assume that maturation is relatively more important in the early stages and learning more so in the later stages. Also we can believe that the time at which an emotion appears is limited mainly by maturation and cannot be hastened much by learning or training. As yet, however, we do not have sufficient data on human beings to prove these conclusions. The later stages of emotional development in childhood and adolescence are, we can be sure, governed primarily by learning. Some of the factors involved in the modification of emotional behavior throughout this period are described below.

The child's capabilities, especially in motor activities and language, are increasing. At first, the child is frustrated by things he cannot do. He cannot reach the toy he wants, he cannot climb where he wants to, and often he cannot make his wants known. As he grows older and can do more and more things for himself, physical frustration

becomes a less frequent cause of emotional behavior.

The child also becomes increasingly familiar with the people and objects in his world. At first, his environment is limited. He sees only the face of his mother and other members of the family. Since he does not see many other people, objects, or animals, a great number of things are strange to him, and he reacts to this strangeness with fear. As he grows up and as his experience broadens, fewer and fewer things are strange to him. So this source of emotional behavior—a limited environment—also becomes less important with age.

On the other hand, the child has increasing opportunities to learn emotional reactions. He usually has the opportunity to learn unnatural fears, both by direct conditioning and by copying the fears of his parents and siblings. He also has the chance to learn emotional techniques for getting what he wants; he may, for example, learn to throw a temper tantrum whenever his wishes are frustrated. These opportunities for learning increase his repertory of emotional reactions; they alter and expand the situations that give rise to emotions.

The growing child is learning new motives and new goals. These enlarge the possibilities of his becoming frustrated and thus emotional. He learns to want all sorts of things—bicycles, clothes, money, social approval. By the time the child reaches adolescence, two general classes of goals, those connected with financial independence and those connected with social approval, have become especially important. Another thing the child learns to do is to restrain and control his emotions. Parents tend to be annoyed by a child's noisy emotional outbursts; they think he ought to learn to control his emotions. They therefore start teaching control early by punishing the child and by disapproving his expression of emotion. Teachers and other adults do the same thing. As a consequence, the child learns to avoid, or to try to avoid, displaying his emotions.

CHANGES IN EMOTIONAL EXPRESSION.
These various pressures on the child alter both the situations that give rise to emotion and the way in which emotion is expressed. Over the span from infancy to adolescence, many changes in expression take place. We shall now consider these characteristic changes.

Displays of emotion are much more frequent in children than in adolescents and adults. If you are around children very long, you will hear some kind of outburst every few minutes. First you may hear loud shouts of joy or gales of laughter; a little later, screams of anger or crying. The air is pierced periodically with some obvious expression of emotion. These outbursts, however, become less frequent as children grow up, partly perhaps because the children are maturing, but partly too because adults disapprove the outbursts, especially when they involve crying and fighting.

Emotional reactions are brief in children, but in adolescents and adults, they are more prolonged. A small child who is upset usually gets over it in a hurry. As soon as the situation causing fear or anger is done with, he is no longer afraid or mad. Later on, and especially in adolescence, this is not the case. Anger tends to be replaced by sulkiness that can go on for some time; fears are expressed as increased shyness, timidity, and jumpiness. This change occurs in part because the adolescent has been taught to restrain and contain his emotions. It occurs also because his growing intellectual ability enables him to think and brood about emotional problems. Possibly hormonal changes are also involved.

A child's emotions characteristically lack any gradation of intensity. Emotional reactions tend to be all or none. A trivial situation evokes the same screams of laughter or misery as a situation of some importance. In the growing-up process, though, emotions become graded. A small irritation is met with little signs of annoyance but no major outburst. The big scenes are saved for situations of greater import. Even then, what is important to the child may not seem important to the parent, but the older child nevertheless grades his reactions to the seeming significance of the situation.

EMOTIONAL SITUATIONS. The situations giving rise to emotional reactions change over the course of emotional development. To describe the changes that take place, we must distinguish between three general categories of emotion: pleasure, fear, and anger. Pleasure is another name for the delight seen early in infancy. Fear and anger are patterns that differentiate from distress when the infant is four to seven months of age.

Pleasure. Many different things give us pleasure, but they are all covered by one general principle: Pleasure is a reaction to the satisfaction of a drive or the achievement of a goal. This principle applies to both primary drives, including curiosity and exploration, and secondary drives, those concerned with social approval, status, etc.

Early in life, the child shows signs of pleasure when he is physically comfortable. If an infant is well fed, dry, and warm, and if there are no pins sticking in him, he is usually relaxed, smiling, and cooing. By the second or third month, he shows signs of pleasure when he sees a human face or hears a friendly voice. Still later he expresses pleasure when he exercises a new skill, such as reaching out and shaking a rattle, or when somebody plays peekaboo with him. In general, as children develop, they find pleasure in situations that are novel but not frightening and that keep them entertained and offer them some success in what they try to do.

Smiling and laughing are specific expressions of pleasure that occur, just as fear and anger do, in different situations at different ages [Washburn, 1929]. Apparently the nervous system of the infant must mature somewhat before he can smile, for smiling does not occur until the infant is about two months of age. After that, for a time, smiling is a response to being tickled or stroked. Then, smiling begins to occur when there

FIGURE 4.2. Situations evoking fear in infants and children. Groups of youngsters were exposed to four different kinds of situations: animals, noises or things that made noises, threats of illness, injury, or death, and strange things or people. The bar graphs show the percentage of each group giving a fear response in the situations [Jersild et al., 1933].

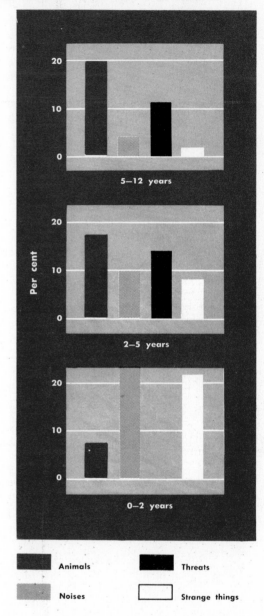

is an interesting noise or some unusual movement—as when parents wave their arms, dance, stand on their heads, or pull toys around the floor to entertain their children.

As the affectional drive matures, the child takes pleasure in having physical contact with adults—clinging to them, riding piggy back, climbing all over them, and so on. When curiosity and exploratory drives develop, the child takes pleasure in pulling things apart, playing with toys, exploring, and doing similar things. By the time adolescence arrives, and many secondary goals have been established, the boy or girl derives pleasure from social activities of various sorts and from achievement in athletics, school, or other things.

Fear. It has already been pointed out in another chapter that unlearned fears are caused primarily by things that are strange to the child. This statement, however, now needs a little qualification. Fear in infants is caused not so much by strangeness itself as by suddenness or unexpectedness. A loud noise, for example, does not necessarily elicit fear, but one that comes *suddenly* usually does. Similarly, strange objects, like stuffed animals or false faces, produce fear mainly when they appear unexpectedly. Thus the natural stimulus for fear is a strange thing that the child encounters suddenly and unexpectedly.

As children grow older, they may be afraid of imaginary creatures, of being left alone, of the dark, and of potential bodily

harm—in other words, of threats. Some of these fear-producing situations are compared at different ages in Figure 4.2. Late in childhood, children become especially fearful of social humiliation and ridicule—

CHAPTER FOUR

social threats—and are much less bothered by the noises and strange things that scared them in infancy.

Several factors are involved in this development of fear behavior. One, of course, is the conditioning of fear (page 88), but others are important too. In order to learn fear, a child need not be conditioned; he can acquire fear symbolically through the example of his parents or through their stories. This can happen whenever the child's memory and imagination are developed to the point where he is able to imagine the fearful things his parents tell him about.

Another factor is the developing perception of the world. The baby is not very discriminating, for example, about faces or animals. He can't tell one face from another or one animal from another. If he is used to one face or one animal, another is not going to appear strange. As he learns and matures, however, he comes to discriminate one face from another and becomes aware of the fact that a face is connected with a head. At that point, the face of a stranger or a disembodied face is something unexpected, and he begins to show fear of it. Hence the fear appears only when the perception of what is familiar and what is strange makes it possible. This conclusion can be illustrated by two studies; the first study [Jones and Jones, 1928] involves children and the second involves chimpanzees.

Fifty-one children and ninety adults were presented a snake and asked to handle it. Children under two years of age showed no fear of it at all and handled it as they would other things they played with. Those three or four years old were more cautious; those over four showed definite fear of it. Most of the adults were very much afraid. The investigators believed that the fears of the older children were not learned by direct contact with snakes or through stories or other training. They felt rather that the older children perceived more readily the difference between the snake and the things they were used to.

In the study of fear in chimpanzees, the experimenter observed [quoted from Hebb, 1946]:

Some of the chimpanzees of the Yerkes colony might have a paroxysm of terror at being shown a model of a human or chimpanzee head detached from the body; young infants showed no fear, increasing excitement was evident in the older (half-grown) animals, and those adults that were not frankly terrified were still considerably excited. These individual differences among adults, and the difference of response at different ages, are quite like the human differences in attitude toward snakes, the frequency and strength of fear increasing with age. . . . The increase fits in with the conception that many fears depend on some degree of intellectual development.

When the individual reaches adolescence and early adulthood, social situations take on increased importance as sources of fear [Wake, 1950]. In early adolescence (between eleven and sixteen years of age), the individual may still fear animals and potential injury or threats, but social fears are more important—fears of being left out of a group, of making a *faux pas,* of being ridiculed, or of talking to certain people. In early adulthood (eighteen to twenty-four), at least among university students, the individual attaches even more importance to social fears. Fears of animals and threats have diminished considerably, and have been replaced by fears of parental criticism or disappointment and by sexual fears pertaining to pregnancy, venereal disease, or disapproval of sexual conduct.

Perhaps the best way of summarizing the causes of fear in the later stages of growing up is to say that most fears are fears of failure or punishment—fears of failing to achieve various secondary goals that have been learned, such as success in school or social approval.

Anger. The situations that make children and adults angry have one thing in common: interference with goal-directed activity. Put another way, frustration of any want or ongoing activity is likely to provoke anger. Restraining the individual or requiring him to do things he does not want to do places him in an anger-producing situation at any age.

What varies with age is the kinds of things people do and do not want to do. We are thus led back again to the development of primary and secondary drives. In infants, simple restraint, which frustrates activity and exploratory drives, is regularly a cause for anger. In children, common provocations include: being required to sit on a toilet seat, having things taken away, having the face washed, being left alone, losing the attention of an adult, and failing to accomplish something that is being attempted. In older children and adolescents, the causes of anger shift, as we might expect, from physical constraints and frustrations to social frustrations and disappointments. Sarcasm, bossiness, shunning, or thwarting of social ambitions become frequent occasions for anger.

Social frustrations are likewise common causes of anger in adults. Most adults have learned to contain their anger, however, and hence we seldom observe outright displays of anger. More common are the mild feelings of anger that we call annoyance. One psychologist studied common annoyances and irritations by asking people to list their own annoyances for him [Cason, 1930].

From the replies of over 600 people, ranging in age from ten to ninety, he listed almost 18,000 annoyances. When account was taken of duplications, the number was reduced to about 2,600 separate annoyances. Tabulating these into various categories (see Table 4.1), he found that more than half the common annoyances are things that other people do, such as blowing their noses without handkerchiefs, coughing in one's face, smelling dirty, or treating others unkindly. Almost all these annoyances are socially disapproved behaviors or things that we just do not want done.

Only a small minority of common annoyances had to do with things rather than with people, for example, a late bus or train, but even these were mostly frustrations of some motive.

The particular way of expressing anger changes with age. Among preschool children, anger is more likely to take the form of temper tantrums, surliness, bullying, and fighting; among adolescents and adults, these expressions become more subtle, indirect, and verbal, and they include sarcasm, swearing, gossiping, and plotting. This

TABLE 4.1. Sources of annoyance. 659 individuals of both sexes ranging from ten to ninety years of age were asked to indicate the things that annoyed them [Cason, 1930].

Class of annoyance	Per cent of different annoyances
Human behavior	59.0
Things and activities not connected with people (other than clothes)	18.8
Clothes and manner of dress	12.4
Physical characteristics of people that could be altered	5.3
Physical characteristics of people that are unalterable	4.4

Most common annoyances associated with human behavior

A person blowing his nose without a handkerchief

A person coughing in one's face

A person cheating in a game

A woman spitting in public

The odor of dirty feet

A child being treated harshly

CHAPTER FOUR

change in the mode of expression of anger is obviously brought about by social pressures. Such pressures, exerted by parents, friends, associates, and the official agents of society, teach the person to suppress his natural reactions and to express his anger in ways which are socially approved.

Emotional habits and motives

Emotions can function in human life both as habits (learned reactions) and as motives. Learned emotional habits can be reactions not only to physical things and the actions of other people, but also to one's own thoughts and expectations. Emotions are also motives when they impart an impetus to behavior and give it direction toward certain goals. Let us then consider in detail how emotional habits are acquired and the role of these habits in motivation. The discussion will revolve around three basic emotional patterns: pleasure, fear, and anger.

PLEASURE. Pleasure, we have already seen, is the accompaniment of satisfying a drive. Hence the achievement of any goal, whether it be a primary goal, such as eating or drinking, or a secondary goal, such as social approval or academic achievement, is experienced as pleasant. This general principle can be extended to the relief of any tension, and indeed to relief from such emotions as fear and anger. The goal of fear is to escape a fear-producing situation or fear itself; the goal of anger is to attack, destroy, or hurt the thing provoking anger. Hence the achievement of these goals is also regarded as pleasant.

In Chapter 3 we saw that any situation regularly associated with a goal becomes a secondary goal itself. This principle applies to the pleasure we take in the achievement of goals. Anything connected with the satisfaction of drives may itself become a goal and, when achieved, gives pleasure. Thus

we like to be around people with whom we have shared satisfying experiences. We like to make money because it satisfies other needs. We like to go back to places where we formerly had a good time.

FEARS. The way in which human beings learn to fear certain things can be illustrated by describing a classic experiment [Watson and Rayner, 1920] with an infant named Albert.

Albert was an eleven-month-old boy who displayed no fear of animals. When shown a rabbit (see sketch 1 in Figure 4.3), he expressed delight and made no effort to get away. Later, however, he was shown a white rat (sketch 2), and at the same time heard a loud and sudden noise. This natural stimulus for fear had the expected effect; he shrank back. The procedure was repeated several times on different occasions. He was then presented with the white rabbit (sketch 3), which formerly had caused no fear. Now, however, he was frightened by the sight of the rabbit and attempted to get away from it. He was then tested with a number of other white furry objects, including a white beard on a man (sketch 4). All of these provoked fear.

This experiment demonstrates two points: One is the *conditioning* of fear. Any stimulus regularly present when a fear response is made can itself become a stimulus for fear. The other is the phenomenon of *generalization*. The fear that is learned is not restricted to the conditioning stimulus (page 196), but generalizes to similar objects—in this case to all white furry objects. Both conditioning and generalization are important factors in building up our repertory of learned fears.

The way in which a learned fear functions as a drive has already been illustrated in an experiment described in Chapter 3. In that experiment [Miller, 1948a], rats were conditioned to fear a white box by being shocked in it. Later, with no shock present,

A BABY LEARNS FEAR OF AN OBJECT BY ASSOCIATING IT WITH AN OBJECT HE IS AFRAID OF, THEN GENERALIZES THE FEAR TO OTHER SIMILAR OBJECTS:

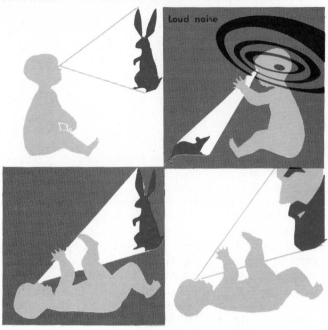

FIGURE 4.3. Conditioning and generalization of fear in the infant. (1) Before conditioning, the child approaches a white rabbit without fear. (2) A loud noise, which startles and scares the infant, is paired with the presentation of a white rat. (3) The child, after conditioning, appears to be afraid of the rabbit. (4) He is afraid of all furry white objects [Watson and Rayner, 1920].

the rats learned to turn a wheel or press a lever to escape from the box, motivated only by their acquired fear.

In just this way, people acquire many different sorts of fears. If a person has a bad fall from a height, he may go through life fearing high places. A child who is lost and terrified in a crowd of people may, even as an adult, fear being in a crowd. If at some time he is locked up in a dark closet, he may thereafter be afraid of being in a room with all the doors closed. Since people may have varied experiences of this kind, a very large number of specific fears may be found in any one person.

Parents and society deliberately use fear of punishment to enforce their will and to teach approved ways of behaving. The punishment may be something painful, such as a whipping. But most often it is the frustration of other drives—loss of money (fines, see Figure 4.4); loss of freedom (imprisonment), which frustrates a number of drives; or loss of social approval, status, and related social goals. Our government uses fear of fine or imprisonment to enforce its laws, and people use fear of loss of friends, privileges, and social prestige to control each other's behavior. Fear of loss of freedom appears to be a most potent motive for getting nations to fight. Indeed, everywhere we look, we see fear profoundly influencing what people do and what they work for.

Fears become important motives in life because we have so many opportunities to acquire them. In childhood there are physical hazards like falling down the steps and getting burned in the fire, and the child comes to fear those situations in which he has been harmed. Soon the parent starts using fear deliberately. By punishing and at the same time saying "no," a parent soon teaches an infant to fear punishment, and the signal for evoking this fear is the word "no." Later on, the teaching of fear becomes more complicated. To motivate the child, the parent may put him to bed without his supper, deny him his ice cream or popsicle, or not allow him to go out and play. Thus the child is taught to fear loss or denial of the things he wants.

ANGER. Anger, we have said, is provoked by restraints, including any interference with goal-directed activity. This means that anger is produced by frustration—by not having or getting what one wants. Frustration may not always elicit anger, but anger is usually caused by frustration or by circumstances that have previously caused frustration. Keeping this point in mind, we can note the following points about anger as a habit and as a motive.

Anger can be learned as a social technique for achieving goals. The persistence of temper tantrums in children is a good example. In many children, the temper tantrum is a natural reaction to frustration. If the baby wants something he cannot have, he gets mad and throws a tantrum. If this does not work, he will probably try other, more reasonable approaches, and the temper reaction to frustration will tend to die out. Thus he learns not to get mad, but to find other means of relieving his frustration. If, on the other hand, the temper tantrum does get him what he wants—as it often will, when parents give in because they cannot stand the annoyance of the tantrum—then the baby learns to throw tantrums whenever he is frustrated. If the tantrums continue to be successful, he will habitually get angry whenever he is frustrated, using anger as a device for getting what he wants.

There is a corollary to this: if fighting generally is successful, fighting tends to be learned. If it is not successful, it tends to drop out. This point is demonstrated in laboratory experiments with fighting mice [Scott, 1958]. When strange mice are paired up, they tend to fight. One usually wins and the other loses. The mouse that wins is more likely to fight again; the one that loses is more likely to retreat and give up without a fight. The same general principle probably applies to fighting in children. The boy who usually wins his battles is likely to become a bully who is always picking fights, but the boy who has lost a few times learns to avoid fighting if he can.

Parents and society try in various ways to suppress angry behavior. Children are usually punished for outbursts of anger. In adults, even the slightest display of anger may be frowned upon as socially disapproved behavior. So, both by failing to reward anger and by punishing its expression, society attempts to teach us not to get angry.

This raises an interesting problem. The punishment of anger is itself frustrating and hence anger-provoking. First, inability to express anger—to blow off steam— is frustrating because it prevents achievement of one's goal, namely, to attack or destroy whatever is doing the frustrating. Secondly, any sort of punishment can be frustrating, and the threat of punishment can thus be anger-provoking. Society, therefore, in its effort to suppress anger actually provokes anger. The result then is not so much to teach people not to be angry as it is to teach them not to express anger. Anger merely smolders inside instead of coming out into the open.

Anger can be conditioned and generalized in the same way as fear. We get angry at whatever keeps us from achieving our ends, and if the same thing frequently frus-

FIGURE 4.4. An example of the use of a threat of punishment to motivate behavior [Jeffrey Norton].

trates us, we acquire a conditioned hostility toward the obstacle and other things similar to it. A harsh father, for example, who frequently makes his son angry by restricting the son's activities may become such a stimulus for anger that the boy becomes generally hostile toward him even when he is doing nothing to frustrate the boy. When the boy grows up, he may be hostile to all superiors if he generalizes to them the feelings he has toward his father. Such conditioned hostility is fairly common among older children and adults.

ATTITUDES AND PREJUDICES. The tendency to react emotionally to people and things formerly associated with emotional behavior helps to account for our preferences and aversions. We prefer the kinds of things which formerly gave us pleasure, and we are averse to those which made us fearful or angry. This is also true of our attitudes and prejudices. An *attitude* is a tendency to respond positively (favorably) or negatively (unfavorably) to certain persons, objects, or situations. Hence it is a tendency to react emotionally in one direction or another. An attitude may be fearful, hostile, or pleasant. Whichever it is depends on our previous conditioning of emotional reactions to certain kinds of people or things and then the generalization of these reactions to similar people or things. This is the general way we learn our prejudices.

Attitudes and prejudices are discussed at length in a later chapter. Here we simply want to point out that they are emotionally toned tendencies learned through conditioning and generalization.

CONFLICT AND FRUSTRATION. Frustration, we have just seen, is a key to understanding anger and hostility. We have seen too that fear of punishment is frustrating and hence a source of anger. For that reason, we need to consider more carefully the common sources of frustration. This is so important a topic that the better part of the next chapter will be devoted to it. Here

we shall merely introduce a few of the main ideas. Generally speaking, sources of frustration may be classified into the three categories described below.

Environmental frustration. Environmental obstacles frustrate the satisfaction of motives by making it difficult or impossible for a person to attain his goal. These environmental obstacles may be something physical, such as a locked door or lack of money. They may be people—parents, teachers, or policemen—who prevent us from achieving our goals. In general, environmental obstacles are the most important sources of frustration for children; what usually prevents children from doing the thing they want to do is some restraint or obstacle imposed by their parents or teachers.

Personal frustration. As children grow up and move toward adulthood, *unattainable goals* loom increasingly more important as sources of frustration. These goals are largely learned goals that cannot be achieved because they are out of reach of the person's abilities. A child, for example, may learn to aspire to high academic achievement, but lack the ability to make better than a mediocre record. He may want to make the school band, the football team, to be admitted to a certain club, or to have the lead in a play, but be frustrated because he doesn't have the necessary talents. The trouble here is that one may learn goals— levels of aspiration—that are too high for one's level of performance.

Conflict frustration. The adult, as well as the child, has his share of environmental obstacles and unattainable goals, but his most important source of frustration is likely to be *motivational conflict.* This is frustration caused by a conflict of motives. The expression of anger, for example, is usually caught in such a conflict. On the one hand, a person would like to vent his anger, but on the other hand, he fears the social disapproval that would result if he did. The anger motive is thus in conflict with the motive for social approval. In Western societies, sexual motivation is often in conflict with society's standards of approved sexual behavior. There are hundreds of possible examples of motivational conflict, and more will be described later. The important point is that frustration takes place because two motives are in conflict, and it is not possible to satisfy one without frustrating the other. For this reason, many adults are forever being frustrated and hence have occasion to feel angry or hostile.

ANXIETY AND HOSTILITY. In our society, then, there is plenty of cause to feel anger, yet reason to suppress it. The consequence is a kind of smoldering anger—a hostility toward numerous things and people, depending on the particular sources of frustration in an individual's life.

There is also plenty of cause for *anxiety*. Fear, we have seen, is a reaction to a specific thing or situation. Anxiety is a general state of apprehension or uneasiness that occurs in many different situations. In other words, anxiety is a rather vague fear—an "objectless" fear, it is sometimes called. The person usually is not quite sure what he is afraid of, and it may, in fact, be rather difficult for anyone to ascertain. Anxiety is like a mosquito in the dark. You know it is near, but you do not know quite where, and you somehow cannot locate it to make the killing slap and be rid of it. Anxiety is usually less intense but more persistent than fear, although some individuals suffer brief or prolonged attacks of anxiety that are agonizingly severe.

Several sources of anxiety may be distinguished. One is linked to hostility. Since society teaches us, through threats of punishment or loss of social approval, that we should not be angry or hostile, feelings of hostility become associated with vague fears of what might happen if we expressed our feelings. Secondly, through simple conditioning of fear, we may learn to be anxious. If we have many fear-provoking experiences with parents, teachers, and associates, these can generalize to almost everyone so that we become anxious in the presence of

people generally. Human beings, thirdly, are peculiarly prone to anxiety because they have the ability to recall and imagine experiences. By thinking of fear-provoking situations that have happened or might happen, people elicit in themselves the same fear or anxiety that they would have if they were in the real situation.

For these reasons, then, people are often anxious, and some people are generally anxious a good part of the time. Thus, anxiety and hostility become prominently linked in much of everyday behavior.

Bodily states in emotion

We have described the development of emotions and the way emotions function as habits and motives. We turn now to another aspect of the subject, the bodily changes that take place in emotion. Almost anyone who has been very excited, terrified, or violently angry has experienced some of them, but he probably is not aware of all that is going on or of the reasons for his stirred-up state.

These changes, being objective ones, have been extensively studied, and we probably know more about them than any other aspect of emotion. They can be studied in two ways: by direct measurements with physiological recording devices, or by surveys of what people feel when they are stirred up. A study [Shaffer, 1947] which utilized the survey approach was done with four thousand airmen who flew in combat in the Second World War. The airmen had, at various times, been exposed to great danger, and they were asked to report on how they felt. As can be seen in Table 4.2, they were asked to say whether they "often" or "sometimes" experienced certain symptoms while flying combat missions. A wide variety of bodily changes were included in the list of symptoms: pounding of the heart, tenseness of the muscles, dryness of the mouth, "cold sweat," need to urinate, and sickness in the stomach. If one were to take the trouble to attach various measuring instruments to fliers so that their emotions could

Symptom	Percentage answering		
	"Often"	"Sometimes"	Total
Pounding heart and rapid pulse	30	56	86
Muscles very tense	30	53	83
Easily irritated, angry, or "sore"	22	58	80
Dryness of the throat or mouth	30	50	80
"Nervous perspiration" or "cold sweat"	26	53	79
"Butterflies" in the stomach	23	53	76
Sense of unreality, that this couldn't be happening.	20	49	69
Need to urinate very frequently	25	40	65
Trembling	11	53	64
Confused or rattled	3	50	53
Weak or faint	4	37	41
After mission, not being able to remember details of what happened	5	34	39
Sick to the stomach	5	33	38
Not being able to concentrate	3	32	35

TABLE 4.2. Bodily symptoms of fear in combat flying. 1,985 flying officers and 2,519 enlisted fliers of the Second World War were asked how often they experienced different symptoms in combat flying [Shaffer, 1947].

be recorded while they were in combat, one could detect an even wider variety of bodily changes and record them in detail.

AUTONOMIC CHANGES. From physiological studies of the nervous system and of bodily changes in emotion, we know that the changes that occur are initiated by a part of the nervous system called the *autonomic system* (see Figure 4.5). The changes are therefore called autonomic changes [Cannon, 1929].

The autonomic system consists of many nerves leading from the brain and spinal column (see Chapter 19) out to the various organs of the body, including particularly the blood vessels serving both the interior and exterior muscles. The autonomic system has two parts which usually work in opposition to each other. One part, the *sym-pathetic system,* increases the heart rate and blood pressure and distributes blood to the exterior muscles. It is this part that comes into play when we become emotional—or at least when we become fearful or angry. The other part of the system is called the *parasympathetic* system. It tends to be active when we are calm and relaxed. It does many things that, taken together, build up and conserve the body's stores of energy. For example, it decreases the heart rate, reduces blood pressure, and diverts blood to the digestive tract.[1]

[1] This is an oversimplified statement of the functions of the two systems. They are not always opposed to each other, and there are certain instances in which the parasympathetic system is active in emotion. Indeed, it usually increases its activity whenever the sympathetic system does.

FIGURE 4.5. Schematic diagram of the autonomic nervous system. The autonomic system consists of nerves and ganglia (see Glossary) that serve blood vessels, glands, and other internal organs of the body. It has two main divisions: the parasympathetic system, shown in color, and the sympathetic system.

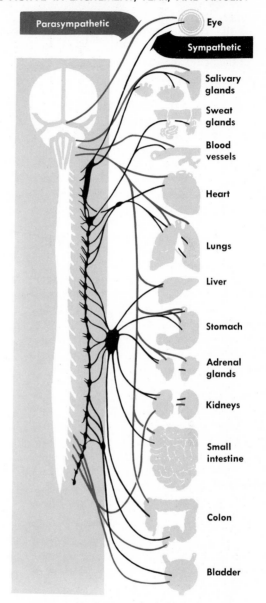

When the sympathetic part of the autonomic system steps up its discharges, as it does in emotion, it produces several symptoms that are worth noting. One set of symptoms concerns the circulation of blood. The blood vessels serving the stomach, intestines, and interior of the body tend to contract in emotion, while those serving the exterior muscles of the trunk and limbs tend to become larger. In this way, blood is diverted from digestive functions to muscular functions, and the body is thus prepared for action that may involve great muscular activity. At the same time, nervous impulses to the heart make it beat harder and faster, which means that the blood pressure goes up and the pulse rate is quickened. Thus more blood is pumped through the circulatory system to the muscles.

Besides producing changes in circulation, the sympathetic system produces several other bodily changes in emotion. Perhaps, when you have been afraid, you have felt some of them yourself. One is a change in breathing. You may hold your breath briefly, gasp, or sigh, and thus interrupt your regular breathing. Another change is in the pupil of the eye, which is ordinarily regulated by the amount of light entering the eye. In emotion, the pupil gets larger. Perhaps you have seen this if you have observed a cat or a person in great rage. Another change is a drying of the mouth. This occurs because the sympathetic system stops the secretion from the salivary glands, which ordinarily keeps the mouth moist. Still another is the change in the movements of the stomach and intestines. As can be seen in X-ray pictures or with the balloon

technique (see Figure 3.3), contractions of the stomach and intestines are stopped or reversed in strong emotion. Also the principal sphincters may involuntarily relax, causing a person to defecate or to urinate.

Another response of the sympathetic system in emotion is the discharge of the hormone *adrenalin*. This is secreted by the adrenal glands, which are located on the top of the kidneys. From this point, the hormone goes into the blood, circulates around the body, and affects many organs of the body. In the liver, it helps mobilize sugar into the blood and thus makes more energy available to the brain and muscles. Adrenalin also stimulates the heart to beat harder and thus aids the impulses of the autonomic system to the heart. (Surgeons use adrenalin to stimulate heart action when the heart has weakened or stopped.) In the skeletal muscles, adrenalin helps mobilize sugar resources so that the muscles can use them more rapidly. Thus adrenalin duplicates and reinforces many of the actions of the sympathetic system on various internal organs.

One other bodily change in emotion has recently been used extensively by psychologists in experiments on learning and personality. This change is the galvanic skin response (GSR). It is a change in the electrical resistance of the skin that can be measured by attaching a resistance meter or voltmeter to the skin. The autonomic nervous system indirectly controls the sweat glands of the skin. In strong emotional excitement, the glands increase their secretion; this is the "nervous perspiration" one feels when one is excited. Accompanying this secretion is a drop in the electrical resistance of the skin—the galvanic skin response. The GSR can be used as a fairly sensitive indicator of emotional response (page 198).

THE "LIE DETECTOR." For the past few years, the public has heard a good deal about a "lie detector" that sometimes can be used to detect a person's guilt in crime. This device makes use of several of the autonomic changes we have described above. Although there are several versions of the lie detector, it almost always affords measurements of blood pressure, respiration, and GSR. The use of such measurements to detect lying rests on the assumption that autonomic changes are not under voluntary

FIGURE 4.6. Measuring cardiac changes in "experimental anxiety." The subject periodically receives a warning tone in his earphones followed by a mild electric shock to his left hand. During the 6-second interval between the warning and the shock, cardiac changes due to anxiety are electrically recorded by an electrocardiograph through the chest electrodes. Should the experimenter wish, other indicators could be measured such as changes in muscle tension, blood pressure, breathing cycle, and electrical skin resistance [W. N. Schoenfeld, Columbia Univer.].

control—that a person can lie and hide the overt expression of emotion, but cannot control the autonomic changes that accompany fear and anxiety (see Figure 4.6).

In a lie-detection test, the subject is presented with words and questions carefully chosen to arouse emotion if he is guilty of lying but not to bother him if he is not. The subject is usually asked a series of questions, while a record is made of his physiological responses. Some of the questions are "neutral"; they are routine items like, What is your name? Where do you work? Where did you go to school? and so on. Others are "critical"; they have to do with the crime the person may have committed. Such questions are designed to evoke fear of detection or feelings of guilt about the crime. After the questions have been asked, the examiner compares the record for neutral questions with that for critical ones. If he finds that emotional responses are distinctly higher for the critical ones than for the neutral ones, he has reason to feel the person is guilty. If there is no systematic difference, he concludes otherwise.

A skilled operator who has specialized in lie detection must frame the questions, administer the test, and interpret the records if the results are to have any validity. Even so, such a test often fails to reach a conclusion. Some individuals are so emotional about being investigated for a crime that they give very strong reactions to many of the neutral questions. On the other hand, some individuals, particularly hardened criminals, may be so unafraid generally that their autonomic changes are no greater for critical questions than for neutral ones. Consequently, the lie detector does not always detect the lie. In competent hands, however, it often does, and it has never been known to "convict" an innocent person [Inbau, 1942].

DISTINGUISHING BODILY CHANGES. Although we usually can detect an emotional state through changes occurring in the body, it is quite another matter to name *what* emotional state [Lund, 1939]. Psychologists have tried for a good many years to find out whether, by measuring bodily changes, they could distinguish one emotion from another, for example, fear from anger or joy. If they had been successful, we could more easily measure emotional reactions to different situations, measure directly differences in mood and temperament among people, and correlate physiological changes with personality structure. Unfortunately, their work has been for the most part unfruitful. Although we can distinguish mild from severe emotional states, we have so far not been able to distinguish different emotions in this way with any degree of success.

PSYCHOSOMATIC REACTIONS. The bodily changes that take place in anger and fear mobilize the body's energy and strength to deal with an emergency—the fear- or anger-producing situation. Hence emotion has frequently been called an emergency reaction of the body [Cannon, 1929]. Stepped-up circulation makes energy available to the brain and muscles faster than it would otherwise be. Slowing of digestion and shunting of blood to the muscles does the same thing. In brief, each of the changes in some way makes it possible for the organism to react more quickly, exert more strength, run faster, or fight harder. Thus bodily changes help the body react more effectively in emotional emergencies.

If, on the other hand, a person is plagued with chronic anxiety or hostility that smolders on day after day and month after month, the accompanying autonomic changes also go on without any letup, and the effects are not desirable ones. In time the high heart rate and blood pressure, the increased secretion of hormones, and the alteration of digestion function can bring about actual damage to tissues and organs of the body. Or if the chronic autonomic effects do not themselves cause harm, they can make the individual more susceptible to infection or make him less able to recover from any diseases he may contract. In this way, chronic tension and anxiety bring about disorders of the body. These disorders are called psychosomatic—"psycho" meaning mind, and "somatic" meaning body—because they are induced by psychological stresses [Dunbar, 1954].

It has been demonstrated that many disorders have a psychosomatic basis in some people: peptic ulcers, high blood pressure, asthma, dermatitis, obesity, and others. Ulcers have been produced experimentally in animals merely by subjecting the animals to a regimen in which they suffer chronic anxiety. Experiments have been done with

FIGURE 4.7. Situation for studying anxiety and ulcer production. The experimental monkey on the left must press a switch every 20 seconds; otherwise he and the control monkey on the right receive an electric shock on the foot. The experimental monkey gets the ulcer [J. V. Brady].

rats, dogs, and monkeys, but perhaps those with monkeys are the most dramatic [Brady, 1958, see Figure 4.7].

Two monkeys, an experimental subject and a control, were placed side by side in specially designed chairs. Food and water were available to them, and though they were restrained, they could have lived happily in the chairs for months at a time. During alternate 6-hour periods the monkeys rested or did what they wanted. During the intervening 6-hour periods, they were subjected to the following procedure:

Both were given a gentle electric shock on the foot every 20 seconds unless the experimental monkey pressed a switch in front of him. If he did that, he could stave off the shock for 20 seconds. Hence, by pressing the switch every 20 seconds, he could completely prevent getting a shock. A switch in front of the control monkey was a dummy; so he had nothing to do. During the 6-hour experimental periods, however, both he and the experimental monkey got shocked anytime the experimental monkey went more than 20 seconds without pressing the switch.

The first time this experiment was tried,

the experimental monkey suddenly died, 23 days after the beginning of the experiment, with what appeared to be an ulcer. The experiment was subsequently repeated several times. The experimenters autopsied the monkeys that died, and sacrificed others after several weeks on the regimen. The experimental monkeys that developed ulcers have somewhat facetiously been dubbed the "executive" monkeys. They were the ones that had to "worry" about doing something, and they were punished if they failed to do the right thing regularly. Of course, the control monkeys were punished just as much; but having no control over the situation and not having learned to do anything about it, they did not have to worry about doing something. It is interesting that the experimental executive monkeys frequently got ulcers, while no control monkey ever did. Apparently the anxiety and tension the executive monkeys were under caused abnormally high secretions in the stomach, which in turn caused ulcers.

Although we have convincing proof that anxiety can induce such disorders as ulcers, we cannot conclude that all ulcers are psychosomatic. Indeed, ulcers occur in people having no obvious psychosomatic symptoms, and there are other factors besides chronic anxiety that can produce them. The same thing is true of other diseases that may be psychosomatic. For this reason, it is often difficult to determine whether a disease is wholly or partly psychosomatic. In a great many cases, there is probably a combination of causes, and the psychosomatic stress only aggravates a disorder or predisposes a person to it. Emotional stress, nonetheless, is the precipitating cause of a great many physical complaints.

GENERAL-ADAPTATION SYNDROME. Some of the bodily changes that take place in emotion also occur under other kinds of stress: overwork, prolonged exposure to cold or heat, severe burns or pain, or the ravages of disease. Therefore, we call any condition a *stress* that makes the body mobilize its resources and burn more energy than it normally does.

There appear to be three stages in the body's reaction to stress (see Figure 4.8). Taken together, they are called the *general-adaptation syndrome*. The first stage, called the *alarm reaction*, consists of the typical bodily changes in emotion that we have reviewed above. If the stress continues for some time, however, a person enters a second stage called *resistance to stress*. In this stage, the person recovers from his first burst of emotion and tries to endure the situation as best he can. Such endurance, however, puts considerable strain on his resources. Then he may eventually reach a third stage, the stage of *exhaustion*. When he arrives at this point, he has exhausted his internal resources for dealing with continued stress. We do not see this stage too frequently in emotional stresses, but in instances of exposure to severe heat or cold, the person may finally weaken and die.

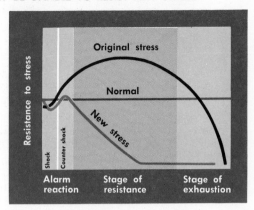

FIGURE 4.8. The general-adaptation syndrome. Responses to stress are divided into three stages: the alarm reaction, resistance, and exhaustion. The black line represents resistance to a continuous, original stress; the green line, resistance to a new kind of stress imposed in different stages of the adaptation syndrome [Selye, 1950].

This syndrome represents an attempt by the body to protect the person from stress. Unfortunately, however, an individual often pays a great price for this adaptation. It may result in such diseases as hypertension, rheumatism, arthritis, ulcers, allergies, and a host of related physical disorders. These disorders are seldom caused by psychological stress alone, yet the stress may be crucial; it may so aggravate ordinary physical causes of disorder as to produce a disorder that would not otherwise occur.

The particular diseases, whether mental or physical, that develop in reaction to stress depend upon the person's predispositions—his weak spots—and upon the kind of stress he suffers. In any case, they are apparently caused by changes in the metabolism of the body that are produced by stress. There are many such changes, but they are not yet fully understood. The most general one is a reaction of the *adrenal gland,* the organ that seems to react most promptly and most vigorously to stress.

The adrenal gland secretes two kinds of hormones, adrenalin and cortin. Adrenalin mimics the action of the sympathetic nervous system by increasing heart rate and blood pressure and by making sugar available to the brain and muscles. Cortin includes many hormones that control sodium, water, and other chemicals in the internal environment. One of the components of cortin is *cortisone,* which you may have read about in popular magazine articles. This drug, as well as the *adrenocorticotropic* hormone (ACTH), has received wide publicity as a remedy for rheumatism, arthritis, and kindred disorders. ACTH stimulates the adrenal gland to secrete cortin.

To understand how these facts relate to the general-adaptation syndrome of reaction to stress, refer again to Figure 4.8. Note that in the second stage of the adaptation syndrome, resistance to continued stress is increased. This means that *too much* adrenal secretion is being produced. In this stage, therefore, such diseases as hypertension (high blood pressure) and heart disease are prevalent. In fact, the symptoms of these diseases can be duplicated in animals by injecting an excess of adrenal hormones. On the other hand, in the later stages of adaptation to prolonged stress, the person's resources become exhausted. This is accompanied by—in part, caused by—an exhaustion of adrenal hormones. Then such diseases as rheumatism and arthritis result. It is for this reason that such drugs as ACTH (which gives added stimulation to the adrenal cortex) and cortisone (which takes the place of insufficient cortical hormone) have helped in the treatment of these diseases. These drugs compensate for the exhaustion of adrenal activity resulting from prolonged stress.

TRANQUILIZING DRUGS.   Other kinds of drugs are required for the treatment of extreme states of anxiety and emotional upset. For many years, only the sedative type of drug—a sleeping pill—was available. If an individual was greatly upset and needed calming down, he was given a sedative just as if he were tense and anxious and couldn't go to sleep. Sedatives will calm a person, but they often incapacitate him temporarily. This is because sedatives act rather generally on the nervous system to slow it down, and only incidentally calm the bodily states in emotion.

In the last few years, however, medical research has developed drugs that are relatively specific for emotional behavior. There are a number of such drugs, and each has somewhat different effects. In general, they act selectively on the parts of the nervous system concerned in emotion. They are "emotional sedatives," rather than general sedatives. They make the person tranquil without making him sleepy or greatly reducing his ability to function. Hence they are called tranquilizers or tranquilizing drugs.

By acting on the nervous system, they can save wear and tear on the body. They reduce heart rate, blood pressure, muscular tension, and other autonomic states in emotion. Thus they make the individual more comfortable, and mitigate his feelings of misery. Usually, however, they do not rid the person of his fears or the causes of anxiety. In fact, persons taking tranquilizing drugs generally report that they still worry; the tranquilizer merely keeps them from feeling so bad.

The tranquilizers developed thus far have their limitations [Wikler, 1957]. In the first place, they do not cure anything. They provide temporary relief, which often makes it possible for the physician to proceed with other forms of treatment. Secondly, some individuals seem quite resistant to the tranquilizing effects of the drugs. And finally, they may have undesirable side effects; especially when used for a long period, they may induce muscular tremor, high blood pressure, and other harmful conditions. One must therefore be cautious in using such drugs and take them only under proper medical supervision.

Emotional expression

When a person is very angry, or very much afraid, or very joyous, we usually can tell which it is by the way he behaves. What are the patterns of behavior by which we distinguish one emotion from another? And how accurate are we in telling one emotion from another?

In addressing ourselves to these questions, we shall first consider a fundamental and universal pattern of emotional response, the *startle pattern*. Then we shall consider *facial and vocal expression,* and after that *postures and gestures* as ways of expressing emotion. In the course of the discussion, we shall find that it is difficult to judge emotional expression correctly unless we also know the *emotional situations* giving rise to emotion, and this will be our last topic of the section.

THE STARTLE RESPONSE. Perhaps the most primitive of all emotional patterns is the startle response. At least, in very careful studies of many individuals, it has been found that this response is more consistent from one person to another than any other emotional pattern. You can easily observe this response by tiptoeing up to a person who is deep in thought and suddenly yelling "boo" or by shooting off a pistol when he does not expect it. The reaction you get is what psychologists call the *startle pattern* [Landis and Hunt, 1939].

The whole thing takes place very rapidly but in a consistent pattern. The first part of the reaction is a rapid closing of the eyes. The mouth widens in a suggestion of a grin. Then the head and neck are thrust forward, often with the chin tilting up, and the muscles of the neck stand out. The uniformity of this emotional reaction from one person to another makes us believe that it is an inborn reaction that is modified very little by learning and experience. The startle response is, however, the only emotional reaction about which we can say this.

FACIAL AND VOCAL EXPRESSION. Emotional patterns other than the startle pattern are not very consistent among people. They differ from one person to another and from one culture to another. Thus it is clear that each individual develops somewhat unique ways of expressing emotion. Look, for example, at Figure 4.9, which shows some children looking at a picture. Whatever the particular situation was, it was the same for all of them. Yet notice the great differences in facial expression in the different children. If you looked at each of these faces separately, you would find it difficult in many cases to say what emotion was being expressed.

If, however, emotions are classified into two general groups, those which seem pleasant and those which seem unpleasant, one can observe some consistent differences in the expression of the mouth. In general, in the unpleasant emotions, the mouth turns down; in the pleasant ones, the mouth turns up. The same thing is true of the eyes; they slant up in mirth, and droop down in sadness. Leonardo da Vinci knew this and stated it as a principle to be used in depicting emotional expression.

In order to study patterns of facial expression, psychologists have presented pictures of faces expressing various spontaneously aroused emotions and have asked people to judge what emotions were expressed. In this kind of experiment, where the judges see only the face, agreement is far from perfect. There is usually rather good agreement upon whether the emotion is pleasant or unpleasant; but it is much more difficult to agree upon whether the emotion is sorrow, fear, anger, distress, or the like. The same result obtains, in general, for *posed* expressions. When professional actors portray certain emotions and judges rate them on facial expression, agreement about the kind of emotion portrayed is not very good.

Some recent work [Engen et al., 1957, 1958] on this problem indicates that three dimensions of emotional expression can be judged with reasonable reliability (see Figure 4.10). These are *pleasantness-unpleasantness, attention-rejection,* and *sleep-tension.* The dimension of pleasantness-unpleasantness is exactly what its name implies; it is the degree to which a facial expression represents feelings of pleasantness or unpleasantness. On the attention-rejection dimension, attention is characterized by wide-open eyes, and often by flared nostrils and open mouth, as if to bring the sense organ to bear on the object. At the other extreme, rejection, the eyes, nostrils, and lips are tightly shut as if to keep out stimulation. The third dimension, sleep-tension, refers to the level of tenseness or excitement portrayed. At one extreme is the complete relaxation of sleep, and at the other end is the most emotional expression you can imagine.

People ordinarily express a good deal of emotion with their voices. Screams denote fear or surprise; groans, pain or unhappiness; sobs, sorrow; and laughter, enjoyment.

A tremor or break in the voice may denote deep sorrow; a loud, sharp, high-pitched voice usually expresses anger. In judging emotions in others, when we can hear their vocal expressions as well as see their faces, we use these cues to help us distinguish one emotion from another.

POSTURE AND GESTURES. Emotions are expressed with posture and gestures as well as with the face and voice. In fear, a person flees or is "rooted to the spot." In anger, he usually makes aggressive gestures and may even clench his fists and move to attack. In sorrow, a person tends to slump with face downward, and in joy, he holds his head high and his chest out. These signs of emotion are all taken for granted in this society.

There is some question, however, of how consistently emotion is expressed in this way. As in facial expressions, there are fairly wide individual differences among people. When judges have only the expressions of the hands and forearms to observe,

FIGURE 4.9. Differences in emotional expression. The children all see the same picture, but what emotion are they expressing? [photo by Glenn Mitchell].

CHAPTER FOUR

they agree fairly well for highly conventional expressions, such as worship, but their agreement becomes poorer for the less conventional gestures. If they are permitted to see both the facial expression and the gesture, however, their agreement improves considerably, though it is still far from perfect [Kline and Johannsen, 1935].

If one studies emotional expression in different societies, it becomes clear that such expression is largely learned. There is, indeed, a "language of emotion" that more or less characterizes each culture. The Chinese may express surprise by sticking out their tongues, disappointment by clapping their hands, and happiness by scratching their ears and cheeks. In our society, sticking out one's tongue is more likely to be a sign of anger, clapping one's hands a sign of happiness, and scratching one's ears a sign of worry. Then, too, cultures vary in the degree of emotional expression. The American Indian, for example, is relatively taciturn and expressionless, whereas the Frenchman characteristically gesticulates for even the mild emotions.

EMOTIONAL SITUATIONS.   Any single aspect of emotional expression—facial, vocal, postural, or gestural—is not a very reliable sign of the type of emotion involved. In other words, these components of expression are not uniform from one person to the next. When judges are given all of them together, however, they agree much better than when considering the components singly. Even so, they make a fair number of mistakes and may confuse such different emotions as anger and fear.

What we need to see in order to judge emotional expression most accurately is not only the pattern of expression, but the situation in which the emotion occurs. When both the situation and the expressor are known, we can do quite well at naming the emotion [Klineberg, 1954]. This is because

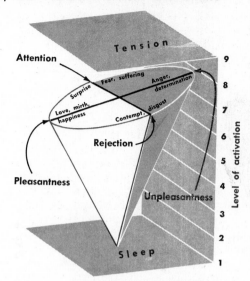

FIGURE 4.10. A solid representing three dimensions of facial expression. The top surface is sloped so that anger and fear can reach higher levels of activation than can contempt [after Schlosberg, 1954].

all of us know fairly well what our individual emotions are in different situations and thus know what the other person's should be, or is likely to be, in a similar situation. So it is by situations, more than by expression, that we are able to distinguish different emotions. In the section or emotional development, we have already described the kinds of situations that give rise to different emotions.

HUMOR AND LAUGHTER.   Smiling and laughing are distinctive expressions of emotion. In infants, we have seen, smiling is a response to tickling and stroking or to an interesting noise or unusual movement. In older children and adults, smiling and laughter occur in an increasing variety of situations. These situations appear to fall into two general categories.

One is a situation in which a person can express his superiority, hostility, sexuality, or other usually unacceptable behavior in a socially acceptable manner. Children laugh when they see a playmate in a silly or sorry predicament, or when by teasing they manage to annoy the other fellow. Thus they express superiority or hostility without the risk of being punished for it. Some adults laugh at "dirty" stories, thereby expressing sexual motivations that are otherwise socially unacceptable.

The other situation is incongruity. A person laughs when there is some contrast or incongruity between what a situation is perceived to be and what it is supposed to be. If a person falls into the water with his bathing suit on, we do not laugh, for there is nothing incongruous about that. We do laugh, however, if he falls in with his street clothes on, for this is incongruous. Such incongruity usually makes us laugh only when it occurs at someone else's expense;

it is funny only when it happens to the other fellow.

The telling of funny stories usually has elements of the first situation—superiority, hostility, or sexuality—but it relies primarily on developing an incongruity. The good storyteller manages to build up an expectation of one thing, but in his punch line he always delivers a surprise. He has something happen that we did not expect; this is the incongruity. The better the initial expectation is built up and the sharper the switch to a different outcome, the better the joke. The surprise, however, must be reasonable; it must be something that could be the outcome of the story if we hadn't been led to expect something else. Thus the incongruity must make sense. Something that is just different or completely implausible usually falls flat.

Summary

1. An emotion is any departure from the normal state of an organism; it includes feelings, impulses toward action, and certain internal physical reactions.

2. Emotional tendencies are inherited in animals and probably also in human beings. By inbreeding, it is possible to develop strains of animals that are very emotional and others that are relatively unemotional.

3. The general pattern of emotional development in infants is one of successive differentiation of emotion. At first, there is only excitement. Out of this differentiate distress and delight, and these in turn are elaborated into such emotions as anger, fear, elation, and affection for people.

4. Both maturation and learning take part in emotional development. In the later stages of this development, learning is of greater importance. The following factors are important in the later stages: increasing capabilities in motor activities and language; increasing familiarity with people and objects; increasing opportunities for learning

emotional reactions; the learning of new motives and goals; and learning to control emotions.

5. Emotional expression changes during development. Displays of emotion are more frequent, and emotional outbursts are briefer, in children than adults. As increasing control of emotions is learned, emotional reactions also become more finely graded in intensity.

6. In general, the situation giving rise to pleasure is the satisfaction of a drive or the achievement of a goal. That arousing fear is at first any strange stimulus suddenly presented, but later it is animals or threats of harm, and in adolescence it is primarily connected with social situations. Anger is aroused by any frustration or interference with goal-directed activity.

7. Emotional habits are acquired because any situation regularly associated with an emotion through conditioning comes to give rise to the emotion. Many fears are acquired in this way. Anger and hostility are also

acquired as social techniques for achieving goals. Society attempts to suppress the expression of anger, but in so doing, it actually provokes anger and hostility. Both fear and anger are easily generalized.

8. In children, the frustration of motives is primarily caused by environmental obstacles. Later, frustration may be caused by goals that are so far above a person's level of performance that he cannot attain them. In adults, much frustration comes from a conflict between motives; thus one motive cannot be satisfied without frustrating another one.

9. In rather intense emotion, numerous changes occur within the body. These changes are the result of impulses from the autonomic nervous system and, particularly, the sympathetic part of this system. In addition, the hormone adrenalin is secreted; this secretion by itself can cause many bodily changes.

10. Bodily changes in emotional situations can be measured with appropriate instruments and have practical applications in the "lie detector." It is not possible, however, to tell from such measurements what kind of emotion is involved.

11. Chronic emotional reactions can cause psychosomatic illness through continued high heart rate, blood pressure, secretions of hormones, and other reactions. Disorders sometimes caused or aggravated in this way include peptic ulcers, high blood pressure, asthma, dermatitis, and obesity.

12. Three stages in the body's reaction to severe stress may be distinguished: the alarm reaction, consisting of typical emotional reactions; a second stage of increased resistance to stress; and finally a stage of exhaustion in which internal resources for dealing with the stress are exhausted. The three stages taken together are the general-adaptation syndrome.

13. Tranquilizing drugs are emotional sedatives, for they calm anxieties and emotional reactions. They do not, by themselves, however, cure emotional illnesses, and they often have undesirable side effects.

14. Attempts to judge the kind of emotion portrayed by expressions of the face, voice, and hands alone meet with only moderate success. Best results are obtained when the observer sees not only the entire emotional pattern but also knows the situation giving rise to the emotion.

Suggestions for further reading

Cannon, W. B. *Bodily changes in pain, hunger, fear and rage* (2d ed.). New York: Appleton-Century-Crofts, 1929.
A classical description of the physiological changes in emotion.

Dollard, J., Doob, L. W., Miller, N. E., Mowrer, O. H., Sears, R. R., Ford, C. S., Hovland, C. I., and Sollenberger, R. T. *Frustration and aggression.* New Haven, Conn.: Yale Univer. Press, 1939.
An experimental and theoretical analysis of the relation between frustration and aggression.

Dunbar, F. *Mind and body: psychosomatic medicine.* New York: Random House, 1947.

A popular account, written by a physician, of the role of emotions in health and disease.

Inbau, F. E. *Lie detection and criminal investigation.* Baltimore: Williams & Wilkins, 1942.
An authoritative source on the practical use of lie-detection methods.

Lund, F. H. *Emotions.* New York: Ronald, 1939.
A text on emotions, emphasizing the physiological factors in emotion.

Rappaport, D. *Emotions and memory.* New York: International Univer. Press, 1950.
An analysis of the effects of emotion and emotional conflicts on memory.

Reymert, M. L. (ed.). *Feelings and emotion.* New York: McGraw-Hill, 1950.
A symposium of authorities summarizing modern knowledge of emotion.

Ruckmick, C. A. *The psychology of feeling and emotion.* New York: McGraw-Hill, 1936.

A good account of the history of experiments and concepts in the field of emotion.

Young, P. T. *Emotion in man and animal.* New York: Wiley, 1943.
A text and general source of information on emotion.

CHAPTER FOUR

Frustration & conflict

A MOTIVATED ORGANISM is one with a need or drive. If the need goes unsatisfied for very long, we say the organism is *deprived*. A person, for example, who goes without food all day suffers hunger deprivation. Needs, however, are usually accompanied by striving to reach a goal that would appear to satisfy the need. A person who is hunger-deprived usually tries to do something about it; he attempts to reach the nearest icebox or restaurant. In the naïve organism, striving behavior takes the form of trial-and-error behavior in random searching for the appropriate goal. In more educated organisms, the striving behavior consists of learned patterns of behavior that in the past have led to the goal.

All this, the student will recall, was spelled out in some detail in Chapter 3.

When the striving behavior of a motivated organism is blocked or thwarted by obstacles, we say the organism is *frustrated*. That is to say *mere lack of satisfaction of a need is deprivation, but the thwarting of behavior directed toward a goal is frustration*. Ordinarily, the stronger the drive, the more intense the striving behavior, and the more severe the frustration. Also, the nearer the goal or, in the case of human beings, the more clearly the goal is in mind, the greater the frustration.

Human beings have acquired many needs and learned many goals besides the physiological motives with which they are endowed. They have learned many ways of striving toward, or working toward, goals. Hence the possibilities of frustration are much greater in man than in animals. Indeed, human adjustment can be said to be a perpetual battle against frustration. For some the battle rages more savagely than for others. Some seem to be on the winning side. Others seem to lose more often than they win; these are the ones we call maladjusted, and in the extreme case, mentally ill. Thus the study of frustration and its consequences merits our serious attention.

Conflict of motives

The obstacle or barrier that frustrates the attainment of a goal is the *source of frustration*. In a complex society, there are an infinite variety of frustrations. They may, however, be classified into three main categories according to source: *environmental frustration, personal frustration,* and *conflict frustration*. These have already been described in Chapter 4 and need only be recapitulated here:

1. Environmental frustration is frustration by environmental obstacles—anything in the environment that blocks the attainment of a goal.

2. Personal frustration is frustration growing out of a person's inadequacy for

reaching his goals; the person is frustrated because he has unattainable goals. Put another way, personal frustration is due to a discrepancy between the level of aspiration and the level of performance, described in Chapter 3.

3. Conflict frustration is frustration caused by motivational conflict within the person. Because two motives somehow conflict, the satisfaction of one means the frustration of the other.

The nature of frustration may be schematized by a diagram such as that in Figure 5.1. In such a diagram, the ellipse denotes the total *environment* of the person, the dot stands for the *person,* and the vertical line represents the *thwarting* of the motive. Goals are depicted by either a + or a − sign, called a *valence*. A plus sign indicates a goal to which the person is attracted; a minus sign, a goal which repels him—punishment, threat, or something he fears or has learned to avoid. The arrow is used like a vector in physics to indicate the direction of forces acting on an individual who is under the influence of several motives. This particular method of depicting frustrating situations was devised by Lewin [1935] and helps us visualize the sources and effects of frustration. Figure 5.1 describes a situation of environmental frustration.

A PERSON ATTRACTED TO A POSITIVE GOAL MAY BE FRUSTRATED BY AN ENVIRONMENTAL BARRIER:

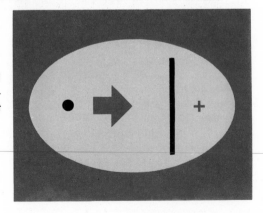

FIGURE 5.1. Frustration by environmental obstacles. A barrier (vertical line) stands between the person (dot) and the goal (+) that attracts him.

Of the three general types of frustration that we have distinguished, conflict frustration is usually the most important in determining the adjustment a person makes in life. For that reason, it deserves close study. Actually, on analysis, conflict frustration arises in three different kinds of conflicts. These have been called approach-approach conflict, avoidance-avoidance conflict, and approach-avoidance conflict.

APPROACH-APPROACH CONFLICT. As the label implies, *approach-approach conflict* is a conflict between two positive goals—goals that are equally attractive at the same time (see Figure 5.2). A physiological example is the conflict that arises when a person is hungry and sleepy at the same time. A social example is the conflict that arises when one wants to go to both a dance and a swimming party which are scheduled for the same night. The proverbial donkey is supposed to have starved to death because he stood halfway between two piles of hay and could not decide which to choose. Actually, neither donkeys nor people often "starve themselves to death" merely because they are in conflict between two positive goals. A person usually resolves such a conflict by satisfying first one goal, then the other—for example, eating and then going to bed if he is both hungry and sleepy—or by choosing one of the goals and giving up the other.

AVOIDANCE-AVOIDANCE CONFLICT. A second type of conflict, *avoidance-avoidance conflict*, is diagrammed in Figure 5.3. This involves two negative goals and is fairly common. Little Johnny must do his arithmetic or get a spanking. A student must spend the next two days studying for an examination or face the possibility of failure. A man must work at a job he intensely dislikes or take the chance of losing his income. Such conflicts are capsuled in the common saying, "caught between the devil

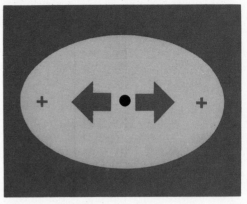

FIGURE 5.2. Approach-approach conflict. The individual is attracted at the same time by two goals that are incompatible with each other.

BEING CAUGHT BETWEEN TWO OR MORE NEGATIVE GOALS MAY CAUSE FRUSTRATION:

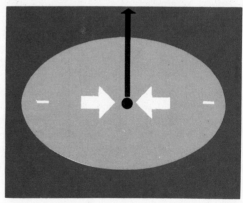

FIGURE 5.3. Avoidance-avoidance conflict. The individual is caught between two threats, fears, or situations that repel him. In addition to the negative goals shown, there are usually other barriers or negative goals to restrain the individual. Otherwise, in this type of conflict, he is inclined to "leave the field" (black arrow) in order to escape conflict.

FRUSTRATION AND CONFLICT 129

and the deep blue sea." You can probably think of many examples in your own experience of things you do not want to do but must either do or face even less desirable alternatives. Certainly such conflicts are relatively common.

Two kinds of behavior are likely to be especially conspicuous in such avoidance-avoidance conflicts. The first is *vacillation*. As we shall see below, the strength of a goal increases the closer one is to the goal. As a person approaches a negative goal, he finds it increasingly repelling. Consequently, he tends to retreat or withdraw. When he does this, he comes closer to the other negative goal and finds it, in turn, to increase in negative valence. He is like a baseball player caught in a "run down" between first and second base. He runs first one way, then the other. As he runs toward second base, he comes closer to being tagged out, but when he turns and runs back toward first base, he faces the same danger. Such vacillation is characteristic of avoidance-avoidance conflicts.

A second important feature of this kind of conflict is *an attempt to leave the conflict situation*. Theoretically, a person might escape avoidance-avoidance conflict by running away altogether from the conflict situation. People do, indeed, try to do this. In practice, however, there are additional negative goals in the periphery of the field, and these ordinarily keep a person from taking this alternative. A child, for example, who does not want either to do arithmetic or to take a spanking may think of slipping away from home. This, however, has even more serious consequences than staying in the situation and facing his problem, so he is wiser not to try it. The adult in avoidance-avoidance conflict, however, may try a quite different way of running away. This is to let his thoughts and imagination take him away from the uncomfortable situation. He may spend his time in daydreaming, instead of

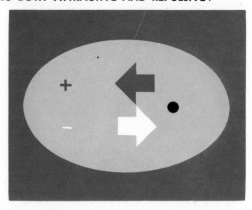

FIGURE 5.4. Approach-avoidance conflict. The individual is attracted to a positive goal, but this goal also has a fear or threat (negative goal) associated with it. Such a conflict is difficult to resolve and tends to evoke more anxiety than the approach-approach or avoidance-avoidance conflict.

facing up to his problem. A student may do this at times when he is supposed to be studying. A person may even conjure up an imaginary world, or recreate in his mind's eye the carefree world of childhood, in which there are no unpleasant tasks that have to be performed. In extreme cases, this way of leaving the conflict situation is called *fantasy* or *regression,* depending on the form it takes. We shall discuss these in later sections of this chapter.

APPROACH-AVOIDANCE CONFLICT. The third type of conflict, *approach-avoidance conflict,* is the most important of the three because it is the most difficult to resolve. In approach-avoidance conflict, a person is both repelled and attracted by the same goal object.

A young bride, for example, was brought up in an atmosphere where sexual activities were treated as ugly and sinful things. As a consequence, sexual matters have for her a negative sign (see Figure 5.4). At the same time, her normal sexual drive, as well as other social values involved in marriage, provides the marital situation with a positive sign. Now, as she enters marriage, she is caught between her sexual motives and the attitudes of her parents, which have become her own values. There is no way out of this situation except to alter her motives, which in the diagram means erasing or weakening one of the signs.

The example of the bride in conflict gives us a hint about the way in which approach-avoidance conflicts can develop. Note that the conflict arose because of the social values acquired in early training. These values serve as obstacles to the satisfaction of motives. Since they are within the person, the process of acquiring them (which we considered in Chapter 3) is regarded as one of *internalizing obstacles.* Such obstacles frustrate a person in the same way that the environmental obstacles of childhood do. The fact, however, that they are *internal,* rather than external, makes them much more difficult for the person to deal with. He may find ways of circumventing environmental obstacles, but he can hardly circumvent or get away from something that is within himself.

This analysis of frustration, depicted in Figures 5.1 to 5.4, permits us to reduce frustrating situations to their simplest elements. In everyday life, however, things are seldom this simple. More typical are conflicts in which there are many different goals, especially negative ones, surrounding a person with pressures he wishes to avoid. There are also some complex combinations of the kinds of situations we have described. One is the *double approach-avoidance conflict,* diagramed in Figure 5.5. In this, two or more goals may have both positive and negative signs. Consider, for example, the student who is in conflict between making good grades and making the college football team. Superficially, this conflict appears to be a simple case of approach-approach

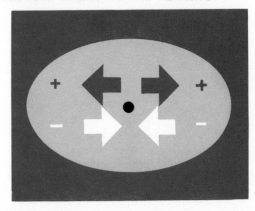

FIGURE 5.5. Double approach-avoidance conflict. Many conflicts that appear to be approach-approach or avoidance-avoidance conflicts are really double approach-avoidance conflicts.

conflict—conflict between two positive goals. The student, however, may have considerable social pressure from family and associates to achieve both goals. He may incur the disapproval of his parents if he fails to make good grades, and he may lose the esteem of his comrades if he does not make the football team. Thus failure at either one carries with it a threat. Each goal, therefore, has a negative valence as well as a positive one; hence, the student finds himself in a double approach-avoidance conflict.

The basic varieties of conflict just described have been produced and studied experimentally in rats and are illustrated in Figure 5.6.

In concluding this analysis of conflict, one additional point needs to be brought out. As we indicated above, the strength of positive and negative goals varies with psychological distance; the strength of a goal— the amount that it attracts or repels— is stronger the nearer one is to it. This fact is represented by the gradients in Figure 5.7. However, as this figure also illustrates, there is a difference between the

CONFLICTS CAN BE PRODUCED EXPERIMENTALLY IN RATS:

FIGURE 5.6. Approach-approach conflict: emerging from the center doorway, the thirsty rat can find water at either end of the runway. Avoidance-avoidance conflict: the rat attempts to avoid shock administered at both ends of the runway, but finds the center doorway closed. Approach-avoidance conflict: the thirsty rat receives both shock and water at the end of the runway. Double approach-avoidance conflict: at both ends of the runway the rat receives both shock and water [photos from McGraw-Hill Text-Film, Conflict].

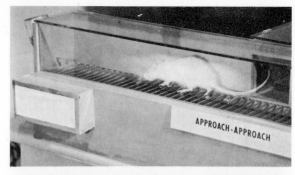

approach gradient and the *avoidance gradient:* the avoidance gradient is the steeper of the two [Brown, 1948]. This means, other things being equal, that when a person is some distance from a goal having both positive and negative valences, the positive valence seems stronger. On the other hand, when he is near such a goal, the negative valence seems stronger. Where the two gradients cross, some distance from the goal, the valences are equal. In other words, the figure indicates that a person in an approach-avoidance conflict will tend to approach the goal, but then, as the tendency to avoid becomes stronger, he will come to a stop some distance from the goal. He is thus trapped and immobile at the point where the two goal strengths are equal. He gives up near the goal without resolving the conflict.

TYPICAL CONFLICTS. If we consider the number of needs that may be distinguished in people and the many ways of satisfying them, we realize that all sorts of frustrations and conflicts are possible. Note, however, that we can expect conflict to occur whenever pleasure and pain, or reward and punishment, are associated with the same thing. That is what we mean when we refer to the conflict between positive and negative goals. If we think, then, of the goals with which individuals commonly have experienced both

CHAPTER FIVE

reward and punishment, we can identify the conflicts that are fairly common or typical. Four such conflicts which are common in American culture will be described. In foreign cultures, and even at other times in our own culture, other patterns of conflict may be more typical. The following, however, are illustrative.

Desire to achieve versus fear of failure. In Western countries, particularly in the United States, achievement is highly valued. Children are expected to make good grades in school, to excel in sports, music, or the like, and generally to "succeed" in life. Individuals are praised, bemedaled, given gifts, and most of all, paid money for superior achievement. It is not surprising, then, that the achievement motive is regarded as one of the strongest motives in individuals of our society.

The opposite of achievement is failure, which is punished in one way or another—by lack of approval, by failure to get promoted, sometimes by ridicule and ostracism. Hence the things one does for achievement take on both positive and negative valences. People get caught between the desire to achieve and the fear of failure.

Independence versus affiliation. Children, as we saw in Chapter 3, learn to depend on others; they have to in order to satisfy their needs. The people they depend on, however, have considerable authority over them, determining what they can and cannot do. When children reach adolescence, they typically develop a strong drive to be independent—to kick over the traces. This puts them in conflict, because it is difficult to be both independent and dependent. Indeed, independence means standing on their own feet, and this they may be afraid to do or not know how to do. Hence a conflict between independence and dependence is typical in adolescents. Parents themselves sometimes aggravate such a conflict by being in conflict about it themselves—criticizing the

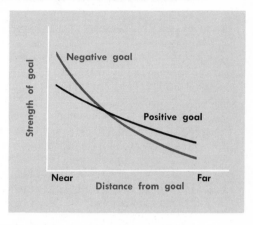

FIGURE 5.7. Gradients of goal strength for positive and negative goals. Other things being equal, goals are "stronger" the closer a person is to them. Negative goals, however, are somewhat stronger than positive ones when a person is near the goal, and positive goals are stronger than negative ones when he is far from the goal. This fact accounts for a person's being trapped in approach-avoidance conflict; he approaches the goal, then stops, and is afraid to go any closer [Brown, 1948].

adolescent one moment for being a "baby" and resenting his show of independence a moment later.

Independence is also in conflict with more general affiliative needs. One may feel strongly like standing on one's own feet, fending for oneself, and going it alone. At the same time, he may feel equally strongly a need to be approved by his parents, accepted by a group, and to have the moral support of others.

Sexual desire versus fear of sex. Among many mid-Victorians, the conflict that arose between sexual drives, on the one hand, and social or religious scruples on the other hand, was particularly strong. Today, this conflict is not so prevalent, but it is still a typical one. It may be a conflict between religious precepts and sexual interests. Or it may be a mild conflict between sexual interests and early training. Or it may concern fears of pregnancy. In any case, sex is frequently the center of an approach-avoidance conflict.

Hostility versus social approval. Another typical conflict arises between the expression of hostility and the punishing consequences of it. Many situations arise from day to day in which our impulse is to be angry or to fight back. Early in life, however, we learned, usually by being punished or scolded, not to engage in physical combat or even to lose our temper. As adults, we find ourselves in almost the same situation, except that, generally, all we provoke by displays of anger is some mild social disapproval. Still, the constraints on showing anger and hostility are strong. Consequently, we are in conflict between expressing ourselves and fearing the consequences of doing so.

These are merely examples of typical approach-avoidance conflicts. There are, of course, as many sources of conflict as there are situations and people. The kind of conflict, and its severity, varies from one individual to another and from one culture to another, because conflicts are so firmly rooted in the training and acquired motives of the individual.

Effects of frustration

What happens to a person when he is frustrated? How can we tell when he is in conflict? What are the effects on him of prolonged frustration? What does he do about them? Answering questions such as these makes a long story. There are many effects, both direct and indirect, of conflict and of the frustration induced by conflict. The rest of the chapter is devoted to describing them. We shall start with fairly general answers, and then progress to the more specific reactions to frustration.

LEARNING. One thing a frustrated person does is *learn*. He may not learn the "right" thing, the thing that would be best to alleviate his frustration, but he usually learns something connected with his frustration.

A motivated person usually varies his behavior, trying first one response, then another. Eventually he may hit upon a response that is *reinforced*—something that satisfies his motive (see page 201). If the same response is repeatedly reinforced, it is learned and becomes his regular mode of adjustment whenever he is motivated and in a similar situation. This principle of learning applies not only to simple motivated behavior, but also—and perhaps of even greater significance—to behavior learned under conditions of frustration. It accounts for the habits a person acquires as a means of reducing frustration.

Let us illustrate this principle by an example. A child at an amusement park wants a stick of candy and asks his mother for it. The mother says, "No," explaining that it is too close to suppertime. "Aw, Mom," he pleads, "can't I have one?" She continues to say "No." He pleads some more. Then, frustrated, he accuses his mother of being mean, thus attempting to browbeat her into saying "Yes." Still the answer is "No." At this point, the youngster throws what is commonly called a tantrum. He rolls on the ground screaming, beats his head against the wall, or begins to hold his breath—something that often scares mothers but shouldn't. At this point, from mental exhaustion, fear, embarrassment, or just the desire to be left alone, the mother relents and gives the child the money to buy the candy.

Thus ends one trial of a learning situation which, in less extreme form perhaps, is typical of many in life. The motive for candy made the youngster try first one approach and then another. All of them failed until he hit upon the tantrum. Since this succeeded, it was reinforced, and chances are that he used the tantrum the next time he was similarly frustrated. It takes only one or two repetitions to learn this particular mode of adjustment. Then it may become the person's habitual method of dealing with frustration. In all probability the child in this illustration will continue to use this method of adjustment until it fails. Then he may find some other mode of adjustment. Of course, as he matures, social pressures may make him vary this mode. Even then, it may be only slightly modified, and he may use some form of temper tantrum throughout life as a learned reaction to certain kinds of frustration.

There are many kinds of frustration and many opportunities to learn habitual methods of dealing with them. The opportunities, the frustrations, and the modes adopted will vary with individuals, their families, social groups, and circumstances. The important point is that through learning people tend to adopt typical, habitual responses to frustrations and that these modes of adjustment are learned according to the principles of learning that are described elsewhere (pages 199–205).

RIGIDITY. Frustrated people, then, learn habitual responses to frustration. The way they learn to respond, however, is not likely to be quite the same as that learned by people who are motivated, but not severely frustrated. The severely frustrated person, or animal, is more inclined to *fixations* of response—to rigidity of behavior. His trial-and-error behavior is not so variable and flexible. Instead of trying first one thing, then another, to solve his problem, he keeps using the same response over and over again. If the fixated response does not happen to be the correct one, or best one, for relieving a frustration, as it usually is not, he is prevented, by his rigidity, from discovering the most effective way. Hence the frustrated person reduces his chances of hitting on a response that may eliminate his frustration.

For this reason, the frustrated person often seems stupid to an observer; and the solution to his problem often seems ridiculously simple. "All he has to do is . . . ," the observer may say—and he may be right. But the frustrated person may be so blind to alternatives that he cannot see or try other methods that might prove successful.

This fixation of response as a reaction to frustration may be illustrated by the following experiment [Maier, 1949] with rats:

Rats were trained to make a discrimination between two cards in the apparatus shown in Figure 5.8. During the training process, a positive card (e.g., dark circle) was exposed in one window, a negative card (e.g., light circle) in the other. Behind the positive card was food. When an animal jumped from its position on the (white) platform to the positive

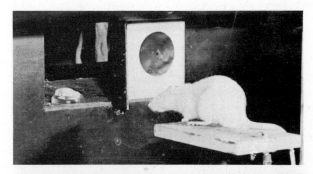

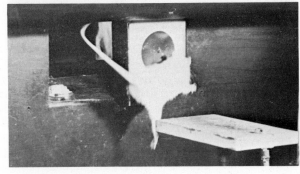

FIGURE 5.8. Fixation caused by conflict. The rat above was given an insoluble, conflict-producing problem. In this conflict, the rat developed the habit of jumping to the window on the right. Below, it jumps compulsively to that window, which is locked, while food in the left window is readily visible [Maier, 1949].

window, it knocked the card down and found the food. If it jumped to the negative card, it found the window locked, and hence fell into a net below. In time, with the positive card consistently rewarded and the negative one punished, the rats learned to discriminate the two stimuli almost perfectly.

At this point in the experiment, the procedure was changed. In order to produce frustration, the experimenter presented the rats with an insoluble problem. Instead of rewarding the formerly positive card consistently, the experimenter randomly rewarded and punished jumps to both cards. Hence, each card was now rewarded 50 per cent of the time and punished 50 per cent of the time. A rat therefore could not escape being punished 50 per cent of the time, as long as it continued jumping. This frustration procedure obviously made the animal emotional, for it squealed and defecated. Soon the animal selected a stereotyped response. It simply adopted a "position habit" of jumping to the same side all the time. Some rats jumped to the left window and some to the right, but for any particular rat, it was always the same. In many of the rats, this fixation became so rigid that, even with the other window open and with food in it in plain sight (see Figure 5.8), the rats continued to jump to the side of the fixated response.

ANXIETY. A frustrated person, we have pointed out before, is usually an anxious person, and probably also an angry one. One of the typical reactions to frustration is anger, hostility, or aggression. The other typical reaction, born of fear of not satisfying one's motives, is to be anxious and worried. One reason for this, pointed out by Horney (see page 491), is that many conflicts come about because anxiety-producing experiences have developed inherently incompatible needs within the individual. The three things—frustration, hostility, and anxiety—are so interlinked that we have not yet untangled very well which produces which. But whatever the answer proves to be, anxiety is the constant companion of frustration, particularly conflict-induced frustration. This anxiety has two important consequences:

First, anxiety causes *discomfort*. In the extreme, it causes *misery*. Anxious people, by definition, are unhappy people. At best, they are slightly uncomfortable; at worst they experience a misery comparable to the pain suffered in severe injury or physical illness. The person who is anxious may not be aware of the frustration or conflict that makes him miserable; he may not be conscious of the peculiarities in his behavior stemming from anxiety; but he is most certainly aware of his discomfort and pain. Very frequently, for example, people come to psychologists or psychiatrists solely to find relief from discomfort and misery without being aware of what causes it. From Chapter 4, you will recall that severe and prolonged anxiety can damage the internal organs of the body and be responsible for the so-called "psychosomatic" disorders.

Second, anxiety *motivates* a person to get rid of it. Anxiety is thus itself a source of avoidance behavior. Like pain, it is something the person tries to avoid or, when it wells up in him, to escape. On this point hangs much of what we have to say in the rest of the chapter. Most personality theorists, particularly Freud and Horney, regard anxiety as the key to understanding how a person copes with frustration (page 491). The frustrated person, as they view him, bends his efforts to ward off anxiety. The reduction of anxiety, indeed, becomes so important that he neglects the frustration linked with it. That, presumably, is why the anxious person is often unaware of the conflicts giving rise to the anxiety. The correctness of this view is difficult to prove, but it seems plausible and is widely accepted.

FANTASY. Sometimes it is possible to gratify a frustrated motive, at least in part, by resorting to fantasy or daydreaming. Fantasy is common among most people and is particularly prominent during adolescence. As a form of adjustment, it rarely leads to constructive action, and thus may leave a person's basic conflicts unsolved. On the other hand, if it is not overdone daydreaming about success, sexual conquests, and the like can produce a certain amount of satisfaction. A person who has been embarrassed in a social situation feels somewhat better if he indulges in a little fantasy about all the things he could have said. If a girl does not get an invitation to the junior prom, she can at least have some fun dreaming about what it would be like. It has been estimated that more than 95 per cent of college students spend some time daydreaming. Their most frequent subjects for daydreaming are academic honors, success with the opposite sex, and a future of fame and fortune.

Fantasy is rarely serious in its consequences unless it is continuously used as a way of dealing with frustrated needs. The schizophrenic form of mental illness, which we shall describe a little later in this chapter, is an example of fantasy carried too far. In this illness, the patient withdraws so deeply into fantasy that he can no longer get along in the world. In most people, a certain amount of fantasy is a harmless device for satisfying needs.

REGRESSION. Closely related to fantasy is a reaction called *regression*. This is a *retreat to early or primitive forms of behavior*. We say "early or primitive" because there is some question whether regression is one or both of these. On the one hand, regression seems to be a relapse to habits and ways of behaving that the person learned in childhood; on the other, it seems merely to represent a simpler, more primitive, and less intellectual approach to solving a problem. Whatever its interpretation, regression takes the form of a childish, rather than an adult, reaction to frustration.

Regression is frequently encountered in children of four or five years of age who are beginning to face an increasing variety of complex frustrations [Barker et al., 1941]. Perhaps the particular occasion that evokes regressive behavior is the birth of another child or the beginning of school adjustments. In any event, the child at this stage frequently reverts to baby talk and acts like a baby of two rather than a child of five.

Regression is by no means limited to children, for adults often regress too. Childish fits of anger, or pouting when one fails to get his way, may constitute regression to reactions acquired in childhood. A person who goes to bed with the slightest cold or who seems to enjoy being sick may be regressing to behavior which, in childhood, brought him affection and attention.

Extreme frustration of the sort encountered in Nazi concentration camps in the Second World War can be expected to produce regression in otherwise normal people. At least a more or less general regression to infantile behavior was reported as characteristic of the inmates of the Dachau and Buchenwald camps. The following is a quotation from a psychological study [quoted from Bettelheim, 1943, p. 443] of former prisoners in these camps:

The prisoners lived, like children, only in the immediate present; . . . they became unable to plan for the future or to give up immediate pleasure satisfactions to gain greater ones in the near future. . . . They were boastful, telling tales about what they had accomplished in their former lives, or how they succeeded in cheating foremen or guards, and how they sabotaged the work. Like children, they felt not at all set back or ashamed when it became known that they had lied about their prowess.

A more extreme form of regression is sometimes seen in schizophrenic illness (see page 154). In this disorder, the adult may talk like a child, act like a child, and live almost completely in the world of a child. Along with such behavior there is usually considerable regression in fantasy; the person lives in an imaginary world of childhood. Schizophrenia of this type will be discussed more fully in the last section of this chapter.

ALCOHOL. For many people, the drinking of alcohol is a reaction to frustration and anxiety. It is fairly obvious that alcohol has a soothing effect on anxiety. People who drink only moderately want a drink most after a frustrating day. They are likely to drink when they want to "drown their sorrows," and their behavior under the influence of alcohol is usually more relaxed and free of anxiety. True, some people become boisterous and aggressive when drunk, but this only indicates that alcohol permits them to express their aggression without the usual accompaniment of anxiety. All this is common sense and fairly common knowledge.

Experiments in recent years, however, have given us further understanding of the craving for alcohol and of its effects on anxiety. One experiment [Masserman, 1943] of this kind is presented:

Cats were taught to open a box to obtain food. After that, they were conditioned to fear the box by having blasts of air blown on them when they attempted to open it. In this way, an approach-avoidance conflict (see Figure 5.4) was set up. Next, however, the cats were forcibly fed some alcohol. Thereupon, their fear of the box disappeared; they went to it and opened it—though their drunkenness made them rather awkward about it. Even more significant was the fact that some of the "neurotic" cats, when offered plain milk together with milk containing 5 per cent alcohol, preferred alcoholic milk. Thus, as a result of approach-avoidance conflict and experience with the soothing effects of alcohol, they had developed a "craving" for alcohol. Later in the experiment, fear of the box was extinguished by appropriate training procedures (see page 196). Thereupon, the cats' craving for alcohol disappeared, and they chose to drink only pure milk.

This, and similar experiments, have given us a fairly clear picture of the role of alcohol in motivational conflicts. Alcohol reduces the painfulness of anxiety without detracting from the value of positive goals.

To put it another way, alcohol diminishes the anxiety connected with negative goals in an approach-avoidance conflict. Consequently, the conflict is temporarily resolved. It is understandable, then, that people who are afflicted with conflicts and accompanying anxieties sometimes resort to alcohol. Physiological factors may also be involved in alcoholism. Drinking is nevertheless a habit that can serve to relieve the anxiety caused by conflict.

The list of things people do or experience when they are frustrated is a long one. Still more is to come. The list may be classified, or broken down, in various ways. Our way of doing it has been, first, to present three fairly general consequences of frustration—learning, rigidity, and anxiety. These are found in some degree in almost anyone who is frustrated. Then we described three more specific reactions to frustration—fantasy, regression, and the use of alcohol—that have one thing in common: they are all *withdrawal reactions*. In employing them, an individual retreats from the field of conflict. These reactions, or at least fantasy and regression, are sometimes classified along with the defense mechanisms described in the next section.

Defense mechanisms

The concept of the *defense mechanism* comes to us from Sigmund Freud, though others have modified it in various ways. A defense mechanism is *a device—a way of behaving—that a person uses unconsciously to protect himself against ego-involving frustrations.* Actually, it is not so much the frustration he defends himself against as it is the anxiety that stems from frustration. Hence, basically, the defense mechanisms may be regarded as defenses against anxiety. At least, this is a common view.

REPRESSION. Put another way, so that we can understand what it does, a defense mechanism is a device, adopted unconsciously by the individual, *for fooling himself about his motivational conflicts*. A person can be fooled, of course, simply by not learning to recognize his own motives and goals. This undoubtedly accounts for some of the confusion people have about their conflicts. More important, however, at least in the Freudian theory of the defense mechanisms, is an active process known as *repression*. Thus to understand the defense mechanisms we must first see what repression is and does.

Repression is, in part, a kind of "forgetting" (see page 242). Through repression, a person conveniently forgets the things that might make him anxious or uncomfortable. I can easily forget to pay a bill because paying it might bring me uncomfortably close to insolvency. I can forget my dentist's appointment because I am anxious about the dentist's drills. This kind of forgetting, however, is not normal forgetting, for the memories temporarily lost can be recovered when the anxiety connected with them is reduced or eliminated—when I get my next pay check or after the date with the dentist is past. So, although repression often takes the form of forgetting, it goes deeper than that. It is a process of "pushing down" memories or thoughts that might be expressed openly, or acted upon, if they did not arouse anxiety.

The concept may be clarified by referring again to the diagrams in Figures 5.1 to 5.5. Learning, illustrated by the child's learning the tantrum, is most effective in environmental frustration (Figure 5.1), when there is merely a barrier to a positive goal. By varying his behavior, a person finds some means of penetrating or circumventing the barrier. Such learning, however, is not likely to be effective in approach-avoidance conflict involving both positive and negative goals, for the thing learned, whatever it may be, does not change the fact that the person has two mutually incompatible motives. Here the solution is to do something to alter the motives or their goals. This cannot really be done, but by fooling oneself

about some aspect of the conflict one can believe that it has been done. It is precisely this that repression takes care of.

The thing repressed may be a memory, a motive, a goal, a barrier—almost anything connected with the frustration-producing situation. If all these things are repressed at once, the person fools himself into believing that a motive and everything connected with it does not exist. This, of course, does not really resolve the conflict, but it does relieve him of the anxiety. The following incident [quoted from Cameron and Magaret, 1951, p. 367] illustrates repression as it is sometimes encountered in normal people:

A young man who had recently become engaged was walking along the street with his fiancée. Another man greeted him and began to chat in a friendly fashion. The young man realized that he must know this apparent stranger, and that both courtesy and pride required that he introduce the visitor to his fiancée. The name of the other man, however, eluded him completely; indeed, he had not even a fleeting recognition of his identity. When in his confusion he attempted at least to present his fiancée, he found that he had also forgotten her name.

Only a brief behavior analysis was necessary to make this incident comprehensible as an example of normal . . . repression. The apparent stranger was in fact a former friend of the young man; but the friendship had eventually brought frustration and disappointment in a situation identical with the one described. Some years before, our subject had become engaged to another young woman, and in his pride and happiness he had at once sought out this friend and introduced the two. Unfortunately the girl had become strongly attached to the friend and he to her; at length she broke her engagement and married the friend. The two men had not seen each other until this meeting, which repeated exactly the earlier frustrating situation. It is hardly surprising that the newly engaged man repressed all recognition of his former friend, all hints as to his identity, and even the name of the fiancée.

Such complete repression as this serves effectively as a defense mechanism against anxiety. However, repression may be less complete; it may only disguise some aspect of one of the conflicting motives: the nature of the motive, who has the motive, what the goal of the motive is, which motive is behind a particular form of behavior, or ways of circumventing the barrier to a goal. Each one of these ways of dealing with conflict is regarded as a different defense mechanism and has its own name.

REACTION FORMATION. A person may fool himself about his motivation or disguise his motivation by believing that he has *a motive that is exactly the opposite of the real motive*. This defense mechanism is called *reaction formation*. We may see it in the case of the daughter who unconsciously hates her mother but appears to be oversolicitous of her mother's health and comfort. To admit to herself that she hates her mother may be so abhorrent and may create so many anxieties that she tries to overcome the anxiety by showing excessive affection. The common quotation from Shakespeare, "The lady doth protest too much, methinks," refers to this disguise. When a person is too solicitous or too modest or too affectionate, it is very likely that he harbors aggression or other impulses that are being repressed and disguised by the opposite kind of behavior.

The following example of reaction formation is quoted from a letter received by Jules Masserman [1946, p. 35] from a "kindly, warmhearted" antivivisectionist after the publicizing of Masserman's work on alcohol addiction in cats, described above:

I read . . . your work on alcoholism. . . . I am surprised that anyone who is as well educated as you must be to hold the position that you do would stoop to such a depth as to torture helpless little cats in the pursuit

of a cure for alcoholics. . . . A drunkard does not want to be cured—a drunkard is just a weak minded idiot who belongs in the gutter and should be left there. Instead of torturing helpless little cats why not torture the drunks or better still exert your would-be noble effort toward getting a bill passed to exterminate drunks. . . . If people are such weaklings the world is better off without them. . . . If you are an example of what a noted psychiatrist should be I'm glad I am just an ordinary human being without a letter after my name. I'd rather be just myself with a clear conscience, knowing I have not hurt any living creature, and can sleep without seeing frightened, terrified dying cats—because I know they must die after you have finished with them. No punishment is too great for you and I hope I live to read about your mangled body and long suffering before you finally die—and I'll laugh long and loud.

The person who wrote this letter professed to be interested in the welfare of cats. The love of cats, however, appears to be a reaction formation serving as a disguise for some rather bitter hostility toward people.

PROJECTION. Still another common disguise that protects a person against anxiety-producing impulses is *projection*. It is a device that *disguises the source of conflict by ascribing motives to someone else*. If a student, for example, has a strong desire to cheat on an examination but is unwilling to admit it to himself because of his moral code, he may become unduly suspicious of others and accuse them of cheating when they are innocent. Or if he has a tendency to be unkind to other people yet knows that this tendency is "wrong," he may accuse other people of being unkind to him when in fact they are not.

Projection is well illustrated in a study [Sears, 1936] of the attitudes of 97 fraternity members:

The students were asked to rate certain of their fraternity brothers on four undesirable

FIGURE 5.9. The displacement of aggression. A rat that had learned to strike another rat turned to the "innocent bystander," the rubber doll, and struck it when the second rat was no longer present [N. E. Miller].

traits: stinginess, obstinacy, disorderliness, and bashfulness. After rating others, each student rated himself. Thus it was possible for the investigator to compare a student's rating of himself with other members' ratings of him. Some members seemed to be quite aware of their own traits, for their self-ratings agreed well with the ratings made by other members. From the ratings of the group, however, it appeared that certain students had one or more traits in an undesirable degree. It is interesting that these students assigned a higher degree of their own undesirable traits to other students than they did to themselves. Thus they failed to acknowledge undesirable traits in themselves and assigned them—projected them—to their fraternity brothers.

Examples of projection abound in human behavior. When a person believes incorrectly that other people are out to do him wrong, one can suspect that he is harboring strong aggressive impulses and is projecting them to other people. The unattractive spinster who will not leave her house because she is sure that men are waiting to attack her must be suspected of projecting her own thwarted sex desires. To recognize such desires in herself would make her anxious, so she defends herself by projecting the desires to someone else. In the extreme form, such projection is the mark of the mental disease called paranoia.

DISPLACEMENT. *Displacement* is still another kind of defense against anxiety-producing motives. In displacement, *the object or goal of a motive is disguised by substituting another one in place of it.* An example is the man who gets angry at his boss but is afraid to tell him off, then comes home and bawls out his wife. As another example, consider the little girl who finds her baby brother the new center of attention. Her jealousy makes her want to harm the baby. The family, however, forbids that and teaches her that hurting the baby is naughty. Unable to express her aggression against the baby, she substitutes a safer object, a doll, and may succeed in totally destroying it. Thus by displacing her aggression, she finds an acceptable outlet for it. The displacement of aggression has been demonstrated in experiments with rats [Miller, 1948]:

Two rats were placed in a box having a grill for a floor (see Figure 5.9). One rat was the "subject" in the experiment; the other rat was put there merely as an "object of aggression." Periodically the grill floor was electrified. The shock applied in this way made the rat both fearful and angry. In the course of its thrashing around, the subject struck the other rat, whereupon the shock was turned off. This procedure was repeated a number of times until the subject had learned to strike the second rat as a means of terminating the shock. Then the second rat was removed, and a rubber doll was placed in the box. In this situation, the subject turned to the "innocent bystander," the doll, and struck it. Thus aggression was displaced from the unavailable object to an available object.

RATIONALIZATION. Another defense against the anxiety aroused by conflicting motives is known as *rationalization*. In employing this mode of adjustment, an individual explains his behavior in such a way as to *conceal the motive it expresses and assign it to some other motive.* There are many examples of this mechanism. It is among the most common, socially accepted ways of reducing anxiety. A student who is motivated to have a good time may rationalize his school failures by attributing them to inadequate teaching, unfairness of the teacher, or too little time to study. A mother whose real motive is to hold onto her son as long as possible may not permit him to go out on dates, with the rationalization that his schoolwork will be hampered or that he will fall into unwholesome company. A father may beat a child because—he rationalizes—the child deserves or needs it, but his real motive may be aggression. By rationalizing his behavior, he can gratify his needs without having to take the blame.

SUBLIMATION AND COMPENSATION. Two similar forms of defense have been given special names by Freud and others who have observed them to be frequently used as modes of adjustment. One is *sublimation.* This is *the use of a substitute activity to gratify a motive.* For example, when a sexual motive cannot be directly satisfied because of external obstacles or internal conflict, the motive is sometimes said to be satisfied by finding some other outlet which seems to reduce tension. The unattractive girl with normal sexual urges may be unable to find a mate, or an attractive one may be unable to accept sexual activity. Freud believed that the frustrated urge can be partially gratified by channeling it into art, religion, music, or some aesthetic activity that is socially acceptable. Because of the passionate way in which some people embrace their aesthetic activities, Freud argued that the substitute activity is a means of satisfying sexual drives. This interpretation of sublimation is open to question, for it is doubtful whether physiological motives can be relieved by substitute activities: it is more likely that the motives involved, say, in aesthetic activities are not sexual. On the other hand, the general idea that motives may be gratified by substituting one set of activities for other, more typical activities seems to be sound and acceptable.

Compensation is also a method of adjustment which usually involves a substitute activity for a frustrated motive. However, in compensation, there is usually the *implication of failure or loss of self-esteem in one activity which is compensated for by efforts in some other realm of endeavor.* The concept of compensation does not carry with it the implication of an outlet for sexual frustration. The unattractive girl may become a bookworm and achieve high scholarship, thereby commanding the respect and prestige that she is unable to win with good looks. The man who is short may develop his skill in boxing in order to secure the recognition as a "man" that his small stature denies him. An uneducated parent may derive a great deal of substitute satisfaction by having his son well educated. Life is full of compensations through which a person achieves satisfaction that he otherwise cannot obtain. When a person's frustration stems from a feeling of social inferiority, compensation is very likely to be expressed in attempts to gain attention, as in the following example [quoted from Shaffer and Shoben, 1956, pp. 171–172]:

One high school girl, Alva B., was notably unattractive because she was overweight and had large, coarse features. Her father was a bartender, an occupation not esteemed in a conservative small town's social scheme. All these circumstances barred her from desired social relationships. In response, Alva took to an excessive use of make-up. She appeared in school well coated with cosmetics, her eyebrows plucked and penciled, and her lips drawn in a most exaggerated manner. The painting did not render her beautiful, but it made her noticed, and this was an effective substitute for social recognition. Later Alva became a cheer leader and was an excellent one, the position being perfectly suited to her need for attention.

USE OF DEFENSE MECHANISMS. The student has probably recognized a number of people, including himself, in these descriptions of people who use defense mechanisms. Almost everybody uses them some of the time. That is why it was possible to cite so many examples. Indeed, moderate use of the mechanisms is a harmless and convenient way of disposing of minor conflicts. If defense mechanisms make us feel better and make others more comfortable, as they often do, their value in reducing tension and letting us get on with important problems more than offsets the trivial self-deceptions they entail.

Not all defense mechanisms, however, are so harmless. If they are used excessively to side-step really persistent and severe sources of conflict, they can get us into a great deal of trouble. Defense mechanisms, when used to excess, have two major weaknesses.

First, they fail to solve the underlying conflict of motives. This is because they are directed at anxiety, rather than at the motivational conflicts that give rise to anxiety. They merely conceal or disguise the real problem. It is still there, ready to produce anxiety again and again. A person harboring homosexual tendencies, for example, may avoid anxiety by repressing such tendencies, yet they may be reawakened by a wide variety of stimuli. Whenever such an individual is confronted with a situation which excites the homosexual tendencies, the latent conflict is reinstated. For that reason, during the Second World War, many men with latent homosexual impulses developed severe anxieties when thrust into the intimate company of other men, although they could get along in civilian life by avoiding such contact. Hence, if a conflict is serious and persistent, defense mechanisms merely postpone its solution; the conflict is still intact and will rise again to plague the person.

A second weakness of the excessive use of defense mechanisms is that they may get the individual into new difficulties with society which in turn frustrate still other important motives of the person. While allaying anxiety from one cause, defense mechanisms can increase anxiety from other causes. The individual with excessive hostility, for example, may project this hostility to others as a mode of defense. To the people who see him, however, his projections seem queer, and when his associates show their disapproval of his behavior, another motive may be frustrated which will aggravate his anxieties even further. In the extreme form, projections become a system of delusions such as are found in the paranoid patient, who must be hospitalized because he can no longer appraise reality and has become a menace to himself and others. The neurotic patient has difficulty because his anxiety-reducing symptoms may prevent him from being gainfully employed. In these and other instances, defense mechanisms fail because they get the individual into more trouble than he had in the first place.

ABNORMAL REACTIONS.   Everyone has conflicts and frustrations; hence there is nothing abnormal about them, either in ourselves or in others. Nor, as we have said, is there anything abnormal about using defense mechanisms. On the other hand, if the mechanisms are not effective—if the person continues to suffer from a great deal of anxiety—that is abnormal. Or if he uses defense mechanisms to such an extent as to get himself into trouble with society, that too is abnormal. Actually, there is no sharp line between normal and abnormal behavior; it is just a matter of degree. Only when a person suffers from anxiety to an unusual extent or when he becomes a nuisance or a danger to other people can he be considered abnormal.

Abnormal behavior is difficult to classify, probably because each individual has his unique history and has developed his particular pattern of reacting to his environment. Hence abnormal behavior cannot be neatly pigeonholed, as can, for instance, infectious diseases, which are identified by the organism causing the disease. On the other hand, certain patterns of abnormal behavior can be described and named. These, in turn, can serve as labels for the particular combination of reactions seen in a given individual.

The two most general labels for abnormal behavior are *neurotic* and *psychotic*. The difference between these is not always clear cut, although sometimes it is. In general, the neurotic person is able to hold some form of employment and to live with his family and friends. The psychotic person, on the other hand, appears to his associates to be "peculiar," and he is more likely to be so severely handicapped or dangerous that he must be kept at home or in an institution for the mentally ill. The neurotic person suffers from a neurosis (plural neuroses), or alternatively from a psychoneurosis; the psychotic person, from a psychosis (psychoses). These will be described in the following sections.

Neurotic reactions

The *neuroses* are characterized by anxiety. Often the anxiety is obvious. The person is constantly apprehensive, worried, or complaining; he may have fits and spells when he is overcome by fear and anxiety. Sometimes the anxiety is not so obvious— the person may appear to be relatively free of anxiety—but his reactions can nevertheless be traced to anxiety and his mechanisms for avoiding it. In these cases, the person's unusual symptoms and defense mechanisms are the clue to his constant battle with anxiety. We shall make no attempt to classify or describe all the variants of neurotic behavior, for they would fill a book. The following descriptions, however, will give a general idea of what typical neurotic reactions are like.

ANXIETY REACTIONS.   Although anxiety, or the attempt to deal with it, is the mark of neurosis, in many of the neuroses it is well hidden by other symptoms. Not so in *anxiety reactions*. These are neuroses in which intense and observable anxiety is the principal symptom. The anxiety may be persistent and uncomfortably high most of the time. Or it may come as a sudden attack that lasts for a few hours or days. An abnormal state of anxiety can make a person thoroughly miserable, have him bordering on panic, and upset his health with gastric disturbances and persistent diarrhea.

Usually neither the person himself nor those around him can assign a cause to the anxiety. The anxiety may become more intense in, or be precipitated by, a stressful situation or a difficult problem. Yet it is not clear just why the person should be so anxious—at least not until his history and the situations that make him anxious have been analyzed in detail. The following case illustrates an anxiety attack and the analysis of its causes [quoted from Coleman, 1950, p. 167]:

A successful business executive developed acute anxiety attacks which occurred about once every two or three months. The patient's wife was eight years older than he, and he was no longer physically attracted to her. He had found himself increasingly interested in younger women and had begun to think how much more enjoyable it would be to have a younger, more companionable wife. During this period, he met a girl with whom he was sure he had fallen in love. It was shortly thereafter that the anxiety attacks began to occur. They were preceded by a period of several days of increased tenseness and anxiety, but the attacks came on suddenly and were very intense.

This man was . . . at a complete loss to explain his attacks. But the explanation was not difficult to find. The patient had had a poverty-stricken and insecure childhood and felt basically inferior, insecure, and threatened by a hard world. These feelings had been intensified when the patient failed college courses in his second year, even though the failure had resulted primarily from excessive outside work. He had been able to achieve some security, however, by marrying an older and very strong woman who had instilled considerable self-confidence and initiative in him. The relationship had proved very fruitful financially and the patient was living in a style which as a youth, "I hadn't dared to imagine in my wildest dreams!" His persistent thoughts about divorcing his wife, on whom he felt dependent for his security and style of life, thus represented a severe threat to the moderate adjustment he had achieved. The anxiety attacks followed.

An anxious neurotic may sometimes find a little relief from his anxiety by adopting certain physical symptoms. If he is excessively concerned with his physical welfare or constantly complaining of minor ailments, he is called *hypochondriacal*. His complaints are either groundless or grossly exaggerated, but by worrying about his health he manages to take his mind off the feelings of guilt or inadequacy that otherwise cause him to be unbearably anxious. If the person complains of general nervousness, fatigue, and insomnia, he is called a *neurasthenic*. This means, literally, "nervous weakness," and refers to the person's chronic inability to do anything. The neurasthenic, indeed, frequently claims that he is unable to work because he feels fatigued and worn out all the time. These symptoms, although they incapacitate the person, represent some gain to him, for they provide an excuse and a disguise for some underlying source of anxiety. The following case [quoted from Shaffer and Shoben, 1956, pp. 277–278] illustrates a persistent anxiety neurosis with physical symptoms:

Thomas R., an eighteen-year-old high school senior, . . . was referred to a counselor because he was failing in his studies, and had an attitude of apprehension and despair which was readily noticed by his teachers. Interviews showed that the boy's anxieties were not limited to any definite situation, but were widely generalized. He was concerned about his academic standing, especially about his father's reaction to it. Referring to his possible school failure, he said, "It will be the end for me." He felt an acute social incompetence, and said in a vague manner that he did not know much about the world, and that he had many things to learn. Thomas had little association with girls and appeared to be afraid of them, or rather of his inability to impress them as favorably as the other boys. During the preceding year he had had a few dates with a girl a little older than himself, on which he placed a high value, considering himself in love. The girl went away to college, and Thomas felt afraid of "losing" her. He was utterly unable to make decisions. The simplest problem caused him to seek advice or to feel incompetent to face the difficulty.

In addition to his anxiety, Thomas had visceral symptoms, centering around his heart. At times his heart beat very rapidly and his pulse pounded in his ears. Although several physicians examined him carefully and reported that he had no organic disorder, Thomas often rested in bed from early Saturday evening until Sunday noon because of his supposed heart disease. The intensity of Thomas's anxiety was best revealed by notes he scribbled from time to time and gave to the counselor. He wrote, "I can never be at rest and am never satisfied. I fear of not being able to control my mental and physical actions. Something is always elusive. I am more afraid of life than the basest coward. Why can't I understand people? Why can I remember only my fears, the vacant mental situations and the lonely places in my life? I seem to exist isolated. All the clean wholesome desires which make a man want to live seem to be crushed. Will I snap out of this, or will I never be a man?"

Thomas's anxiety reaction may be interpreted as a nonadjustive response to all the principal problems of late adolescence. He faces the issues of establishing his independence as a sufficient person, of financial self-support, of the choice of a vocation, and of social and sexual adjustment, quite unable to achieve a satisfactory course of action in any of them. Such an inability to adjust must have its roots in his past learning experiences. In Thomas's case, as in most, the basis was found in the attitudes and personalities of his parents.

PHOBIC REACTIONS. In the last chapter, we learned that people can acquire fears for specific situations through unique conditioning experiences. These fears are usually irrational in the sense that they are no longer justified. Most of us have acquired a few irrational fears of this kind, but we get over them or we do not allow them to overpower us. On the other hand, some acquired fears are both irrational and unusually intense; such a fear is called a *phobia*. There are many kinds of phobias, depending on what one has a fear of, and some of the more prevalent ones have names. *Claustrophobia*, for example, is an intense fear of small, enclosed places; *acrophobia*, fear of high

places; *ochlophobia*, fear of crowds. They are illustrated in Figure 5.10.

Some people who are otherwise normal and healthy have phobias. The phobias may be mild or rarely evoked, and thus cause no problem. On the other hand, a phobia may be so powerful and irrational that it alters the whole course of a person's life.

One oft-quoted example of a phobia is the case of William Ellery Leonard [1927], who was a poet and professor of literature at the University of Wisconsin.

Leonard had a phobia of going more than a few blocks away from his home and the university. For years his phobia kept him a virtual prisoner in this small geographical area. Although he knew of his fear, he did not know its underlying cause. During the course of psychoanalysis (see page 174), he was able to remember a frightening incident in his childhood. He had wandered away from his home and gone over to the railroad tracks, and a passing train had scalded him with steam. This incident was the origin of his fear. His real motive for staying near home was the fear acquired in this incident. The phobia was so powerful that it dominated his whole life. It was never completely eradicated even though he recognized its source and could be objective enough to write a book about it—*The Locomotive God.*

OBSESSIVE-COMPULSIVE REACTIONS. Another kind of neurotic reaction includes obsessions, compulsions, or both. *An obsession is an idea that constantly intrudes into a person's thoughts.* It is usually foolish and groundless, at least at the time. The person may be obsessed with the notion that he has cancer or syphilis or with the fear that he will kill himself or someone else. Or in less extreme cases, senseless phrases or ideas may run through his mind over and over again. It is thought that obsessions represent a defense against some motive or anxiety, but it is not always easy to tell just what an obsession is a defense against. Many concern sex, others aggression, but they may represent any situation or experience that makes the person very anxious.

Compulsions are similar to obsessions, except that they *are acts*, rather than ideas, *that repeatedly intrude into a person's behavior.* One compulsive person may wash his hands every few minutes; another must count all the steps he goes up; another assiduously avoids stepping on cracks in the sidewalk. Some people do not have conspicuous compulsions, but are compulsive in a more general way. They find ambiguity and uncertainty extremely uncomfortable, and they strive for orderliness of thought, of dress, or of work. Indeed any unusual

A PHOBIA IS AN INTENSE FEAR OF SOMETHING:

FIGURE 5.10. Three relatively common phobias are dramatized in these photographs: fear of small places (left); fear of high places (top) and fear of crowds (bottom) [Alfred Gescheidt].

emphasis on "doing things the right way" may be regarded as compulsive. The following case [quoted from Masserman, 1946, p. 43] illustrates a typical compulsion:

A successful executive who, for various reasons, hated the responsibility of marriage and fatherhood, was obsessed many times a day with the idea that his two children were "somehow in danger," although he knew them to be safe in a well-run private day-school to which he himself brought them every morning. As a result, he felt impelled to interrupt his office routine thrice daily by personal calls to the school principal who, incidentally, after several months began to question the sincerity of the patient's fatherly solicitude. Similarly, the patient could not return home at night without misgivings unless he brought some small present to his wife and children, although, significantly, it was almost always something they did not want.

Obsessions and compulsions are means of reducing anxieties while repressing the motives that arouse them. If someone, for example, has an obsession about cancer, it may be because he has anxieties over some past act or misconduct for which he may fear punishment. Similarly the compulsive who washes his hands every few minutes may have anxieties over a sexual transgression, and the hand washing may be an unconscious attempt to cleanse himself of guilt. In this way obsessive and compulsive individuals find some measure of relief from anxiety. But it is not complete. In fact a cycle is set up in which mounting anxiety evokes the obsession or compulsion, and this in turn temporarily relieves the anxiety until, in the course of time or circumstances, it returns again. The mechanism, however, is a defense that keeps anxiety from reaching unbearable proportions.

It is often hard to tell what the connection is between the obsession or compulsion and the original experience which the reaction represents. Occasionally the person may have some insight and know the connection.

More often he rationalizes his obsessions and compulsions to make them appear reasonable and appropriate, and thus he disguises to himself their real basis. In such circumstances, it probably will take an experienced clinician to find—after extensive probing—the source of the anxiety.

CONVERSION REACTIONS. Occasionally, when a conflict is unusually severe and repression is relatively complete, the conflict may be *converted into a physical symptom.* Hence the reaction to conflict is called a *conversion reaction.* The particular symptom that appears varies with the individual, his conflict, and his habits. It may be a paralysis of almost any part of the body, loss of feeling in a hand, a blindness or deafness, or any other sort of incapacity. The symptom is a convenient one in that it gets the individual out of work or somehow resolves the conflict he otherwise would have. It should be emphasized, however, that the symptom has no biological basis, as the physician can usually determine in a physical examination. The symptom is merely a device for coping with conflict and anxiety. Another name for a conversion reaction is *hysteria.* But the student should note that this meaning of hysteria, namely, the *conversion of a motivational conflict into a physical symptom,* is not the same as the meaning of hysteria in common parlance, which is any outbreak of uncontrolled emotional behavior. The following case illustrates a hysteria or conversion reaction:

A woman was admitted to a hospital with a paralysis of the legs. Her legs were extended rigidly and close together, like two stiff pillars. Neurological examination indicated no physical disorder, so physicians looked into other aspects of her problem. They discovered that she was the mother of several children, that she had reason to fear having any more, that her husband desired frequent intercourse, and that she had strong prohibitions against both birth control and denying her husband's sexual demands. Here were all the elements of a complex conflict situation. After interviewing the woman at length and investigating the case thoroughly, physicians concluded that her paralysis was an unconscious device for eliminating conflict.

Hysterical reactions illustrate well the process of *repression,* for in them repression is complete. In most such reactions—displacement, reaction formation, projection, and so on—some, but not all, aspects of a conflict are repressed; one goal is altered, leaving others intact. In hysteria, however the entire conflict is repressed. The individual completely rejects any thoughts and motives that may be involved and does this effectively by resorting to physical symptoms that dispose of them all. The woman with the paralyzed legs, for example, no longer had to worry about birth control, resisting her husband's sexual demands, or having more children. With her hysterical symptom, she had completely eliminated the conflict.

The particular symptom that the hysteric employs may first occur by accident or by real physical illness. A person, for example, may be in an automobile accident that causes a temporary paralysis. Although the injury is a handicap, it may also prove to be a boon in satisfying other wants. It may make the person's wife, husband, or parent become very attentive, thus giving the person the love and care he has lacked. Or the ailment may punish those who have the work and expense of taking care of him; in this way the ailment indirectly expresses aggression. In still other instances, the ailment may protect the individual from anxiety-producing situations, such as a job, school, or social relations.

An experienced doctor usually can recognize the hysterical personality, even if there are yet no full-blown physical symptoms in his patient. One of the signs is unusual naïveté. The individual is naïve because the anxiety he feels in many situations makes him avoid them and thus he either misses or represses experiences that are normal for other people. Another sign is that he is easily disturbed emotionally. When confronted with an unpleasant situation, his thoughts are blocked and confused, and he may become so disturbed that he grows ill, becomes dizzy, or faints. On a small scale, this is the kind of ailment that protects the hysteric against anxiety.

DISSOCIATIVE REACTIONS. Another set of reactions which, like conversion reactions, represent a great deal of repression are known as the *dissociative reactions.* They are called dissociative reactions because parts of the personality and memory apparatus appear to be dissociated from each other. In a mild, relatively harmless form, these may be no more than a compartmentalization of one's thinking and way of living. The businessman who is a vigorous competitor and not too scrupulous in his business affairs may be kind to his family, a fervent churchgoer, an upholder of all things righteous, and active in the philanthropic affairs of his community. In living this way, he may see no conflict whatever. He compartmentalizes his thinking and his activities so that the two personalities do not consciously get in each other's way. In more extreme form, however, the dissociative reactions are bizarre and incapacitating. They furnish the most dramatic instances of neurotic behavior.

Amnesia. One well-publicized type of dissociative reaction is seen in the *amnesia* victim. He is the subject of numerous plays, "psychological" stories, and news items. A person suffering from amnesia usually forgets his own name, where he has come from, who his relatives are, and what he has been doing for some weeks, months, or years. Amnesia can be caused by a blow on the head or injury to the brain, and in this case, recovery is not very likely, though it does occasionally occur. Amnesia as a neurotic disorder, however, represents repression in the extreme. The person, to cope with a painful conflict, unconsciously represses his memory of his own identity and things closely connected with it. As in other instances of repression, the memories are not forgotten; they are merely made unavailable to consciousness. Hence, if the source of the conflict can be discovered and something done to make it less painful for the person, he frequently can be helped to recover his memory. The following case [based on Tiegs and Katz, 1941, p, 53] is an example of amnesia:

Donald G., twenty-two, attended college at night while working to support his forty-five-year-old mother. He was in love with a girl whom he hoped to marry. Donald's mother, however, did not like the girl and tried to break them up.

The girl could see that Donald would never be able to support both her and his mother. She also knew that the three of them could never get along together under the same roof. She gave Donald a month to decide what to do about it. A week before the deadline, he suddenly disappeared. He was found two weeks later in another state, completely unable to say who he was, where he was, or what he was planning to do. He could not recall, or even recognize, the name of either his mother or his girl friend. Obviously he had developed a case of amnesia as a solution to his conflict.

This behavior was not inconsistent with his previous history. In his earlier school days, he had frequently forgotten his homework and been absent-minded. Forgetting things was already a convenient habit for him. When a major conflict developed, this mode of adjustment became a full-blown amnesia.

Some amnesias are temporary lapses accompanied by flight. The person suddenly disappears, wanders around aimlessly, or takes a long journey. During the period of flight or wandering, the person suffers from amnesia. Days or perhaps weeks later, he partly or fully recovers his memory. At this point, he may go to the police or someone else for help; or if he is fully recovered, he may contact his friends or relatives. Temporary amnesia, accompanied by flight, is

called a *fugue,* for fugue is derived from the Latin word that means "to flee."

Multiple personality. Occasionally, repression works in such a way as to dissociate two or more relatively complete personalities. The fictional story of Dr. Jekyl and Mr. Hyde is an example. In this story, one personality was evil, the other good. The transformation was accomplished by drinking a potion. In real cases of multiple personality, however, the transformation is tripped off by stress or emotional trauma, and it stems from a deep-seated conflict of motives. Though often dramatized and talked about, split or multiple personality is relatively rare. Only a few cases have been studied in detail by competent clinical authorities. A recent case is reported by Thigben and Cleckley [1957] in their fascinating book *The Three Faces of Eve.*

A woman named Eve White, age twenty-five, came to a psychiatrist complaining that she suffered painful, blinding headaches, often culminating in blackouts. In obtaining her case history, the doctor learned that she had had trouble with her husband from whom she was separated. She had a four-year-old daughter that she had been forced by financial circumstances to leave some one hundred miles from the city where she was working. The woman seemed unhappy at being separated from her daughter and was very much afraid she would lose the love of the child.

At first the case looked like one of neurosis with conversion symptoms. One day, however, the doctor received an unsigned note, which was obviously from the patient, but part of the note was in a completely different handwriting from the rest of it. The next time he saw Eve, the doctor asked about the note, but she denied sending it. All through this interview, she was agitated and uncontrolled, though previously she had been reasonably calm. Then, suddenly a strange look came over her face; she put her hands on her head briefly, and then took them away. At that moment, her whole manner changed; she cocked her head, smiled, and said, "Hi there,

Doc!" She crossed her legs coquettishly, and became an entirely new person. Indeed, she was. This was Eve Black, not Eve White. From then on, in subsequent interviews, the doctor had "two patients." For a while, he could make Eve Black appear only by using hypnotic techniques (page 172), but in time he could call out one personality or the other at will.

The two Eves, he learned, had lived side by side for years. Eve Black knew about Eve White, but not vice versa. Eve White only learned about Eve Black from sessions with the therapist. Eve White was a retiring, controlled, well-behaved, though neurotic girl. Eve Black, on the other hand, was a mischievous, "bad" girl—though not so bad as to get into any serious trouble—who frequently played pranks on Eve White. Eve Black once said to the therapist, "When I go out and get drunk, *she* wakes up with the hangover. She wonders what in the hell's made her so sick." As the therapist learned in subsequent interviews, Eve White continually struggled unconsciously against Eve Black. The bouts of headache appeared to represent her attempts to keep Eve Black from emerging and taking control.

Therapy went on for several months, and Eve White seemed to be getting better. Then the painful headaches and the blackouts became more intense. At this time, during a rather stressful interview with the therapist, a new personality, Jane, came forth. Jane's personality was the best of the three; she was more mature, lively, and competent than either of the Eves. She seemed to have healthier attitudes toward herself and others than they had.

For a time, all three personalities were in evidence from time to time; the therapist was able to call any one of them out at will. Jane developed as the dominant personality, but the therapist called on the two Eves to ferret out information from the girl's past that would help her achieve a better adjustment. Several circumstances in her childhood appeared to be connected with her multiple personality. One was the birth of twin sisters when she was about six. These she resented intensely. Four months after their birth, her grandmother died, and her mother apparently had forced her to the grandmother's coffin to kiss her grandmother "goodbye." This painful experience seemed to be the one that tripped off her dissociation of personality.

The rest of the story as told in *The Three Faces of Eve*, is that Jane managed to establish a satisfactory adjustment. As Eve White, she divorced her former husband. Then, as Jane, she fell in love with another man, who had proved understanding and helpful throughout her ordeal, and married him. The two established a home and a normal life with her little girl.

Though the psychiatric account ends there, the story does not. Jane did not turn out to be the well-integrated person it appeared she would be at the end of treatment. Under the stresses of her second marriage, she broke down and "destroyed herself," psychologically speaking. This time, though, she was able to resolve the basic conflicts that had dissociated Eve Black and Eve White and was able to establish a well-adjusted life—according to her own autobiography *The Final Face of Eve* [Lancaster, 1958].

Psychotic reactions

For a long time it was thought that neurosis and psychosis were two completely different kinds of disorders. "Once a neurotic, never a psychotic" was almost an axiom. By this, it was meant that neurosis and psychosis were such different reactions that they could not develop in the same person. Today we are not so sure about this. Certainly many patients encountered in clinical practice are difficult to classify and appear to be somewhere in between. For the present, therefore, we must consider the question unresolved.

In principle, however, we can make a distinction. Whereas the neurotic individual is characterized by anxiety or strenuous defenses against anxiety, the psychotic individual is typically one who has *lost* considerable *contact with reality*. He may simply withdraw and fail to respond to things going on around him. Or he may be so excited or depressed that his reactions are quite inappropriate to circumstances. In many instances, his thought processes may be seriously disturbed by delusions and hallucinations. In any case, he tends to live in a world of his own rather than in the real world around him. For this reason, psychosis is more severe than neurosis, and the psychotic person is more likely to require hospitalization and protective care. Most of the inmates of our mental hospitals, particularly those who stay a long time, are psychotic, not neurotic, individuals.

Psychotic reactions are classified into two categories: functional and organic. The *functional psychoses* are generally considered psychological in origin, though some of the data on the inheritance of functional psychoses (see page 482) raise doubts about this. The *organic psychoses* are those known to be caused by organic agents, such as the syphilis germ, degenerative changes in old age, alcoholism, and the like. As psychologists, we have a greater interest in the functional psychoses. These may be described under three main headings: affective reactions, paranoid reactions, and schizophrenic reactions.

AFFECTIVE REACTIONS. The major characteristic of one variety of psychosis is *extremes of mood*. Hence this is called *affective psychosis*, meaning disturbances of mood or emotion, or sometimes it is called *manic-depressive psychosis*. As the latter term implies, the mood may be either manic, depressive, or a combination of the two. The manic individual is unduly elated and active. He may sing, dance, run, talk a lot, and generally release more energy than one would think humanly possible. He may also exhibit obsessions and delusions. Frequently he is aggressive and obstreperous, breaking chairs, attacking people, using vile language, and generally putting life and property in jeopardy. Or he may try so hard to be

helpful that he is a terrible nuisance. The following case [quoted from Cameron and Magaret, 1951, p. 322] illustrates some of the typical characteristics of manic excitement.

A thirty-five-year-old biochemist was brought to the clinic by his frightened wife. To his psychiatrist, the patient explained, "I discovered that I had been drifting, broke the bonds and suddenly found myself doing things and doing them by telegraph. I was dead tired, and decided to go on a vacation; but even there it wasn't long before I was sending more telegrams. I got into high gear and started to buzz. Then a gentle hint from a friend took effect and I decided to come here and see if the changes in my personality were real." . . .

When his wife had left, the patient soon demonstrated what he meant by "high gear." He bounded down the hall, threw his medication on the floor, leaped up on a window ledge and dared anyone to get him down. When he was put in a room alone where he could be free, he promptly dismantled the bed, pounded on the walls, yelled and sang. He made a sudden sally into the hall and did a kind of hula-hula dance before he could be returned to his room. His shouting continued throughout the night. . . .

The following morning, after almost no sleep, the patient was more noisy and energetic than ever. He smashed the overhead light with his shoes and ripped off the window guard. He tore up several hospital gowns, draped himself in a loin cloth made of their fragments, said he was Tarzan, and gave wild jungle cries to prove it. "I've tasted tiger's blood!" he roared. "I'm a success and I'm the man for my boss's job. I've made a killing and this time I will keep going." He made amorous remarks to the nurses, accused them of flirting with him, and announced loudly, "At the present time I am not married; but my body is not for sale, regardless of price." From his talk it could be inferred that, far from being happily relaxed and irresponsible, the patient was in reality deeply disturbed over job competition, sexual conflicts, and his own hospitalization. A study of his personal background confirmed this inference, and indicated that, as might be expected, affectional relationships and personal status had presented recurring problems throughout his life.

In contrast to the individual who develops the manic variety of affective reaction, the depressed person feels melancholy, worthless, guilty, and hopeless. Some depressed patients cry a good deal of the time, some keep talking about terrible sins they imagine they have committed, and some are so depressed that they will take no food or water, have to be forcibly fed through a tube, and may refuse to dress or take care of their toilet needs. The extremely depressed patient is often on the verge of suicide and must be watched closely to see that he does not try suicide or otherwise harm himself.

Sometimes a manic-depressive psychosis is cyclical. The patient for a period is manic, and then swings into a depression. The cycle may be repeated either rapidly or over a period of months. It may be repeated more than once. On the other hand, manic states may never swing over into depressive ones, and vice versa. Almost any pattern of affective disturbance may be encountered.

PARANOID REACTIONS.   *Paranoia* is a psychosis marked with *delusions* and *hallucinations*. The person's hallucinations are imagined voices, music, and other sights and sounds that do not really exist. If you watch such a patient, you will frequently see him acting as though he were talking to someone you cannot see. He will claim to be seeing people and hearing things you know are not there. His delusions are thoughts of grandeur or persecution. He may tell you that he is Napoleon or George Washington and spin quite a tale to prove it. He also may have the delusion that someone is persecuting him, that someone has invented a machine that is slowly destroying him by a kind of wave, or that someone is hatching a nefarious plot to deprive him of his rights as Napoleon or as the King of England.

Two factors seem to be most important in the paranoid's peculiar mode of adjustment. One is *aggression*. In general, his attitudes, acts, and thoughts are full of aggression, and we may surmise that he has failed to adjust normally because he has been unable to give vent in normal ways to strong aggressive impulses. The other factor is *projection*. His hallucinations and delusions usually represent a projection to others of his aggressive or sexual impulses, and that is why he believes someone is plotting against him or persecuting him. The paranoid's aggression is so strong and he believes his projection of it so firmly that he is often dangerous. If not kept in custody, he may do someone harm. The following case [see Coleman, 1950, p. 271] illustrates the development of paranoid behavior:

An attractive thirty-one-year-old nurse was commissioned a second lieutenant in the Army Nurse Corps in 1942. From the beginning she failed to get along with fellow nurses or with anyone subordinate to her. Because of her social difficulties, she was frequently transferred from one post to another. In each assignment, she was overzealous in her work, interpreting ward regulations to the minutest detail, and taking the responsibilities given her far too seriously.

In her last assignment she asked for additional responsibility and was made the head nurse in one of the clinics. A few days after taking this position she started complaining to her superior officer that her fellow nurses were telling lies about her, that enlisted personnel were forming a conspiracy against her, and that her officer in charge would not cooperate with her. Feeling thus persecuted, she began to keep more and more to herself, acting tense and despondent, complaining of inability to sleep because of the noise, and crying frequently for no good reason. Several times she asked that a board of officers investigate the conspiracy against her. Finally, she was put under psychiatric care.

When she was admitted to the hospital, she seemed to be in rather good contact with reality, but fellow patients quickly discovered that they had to be unusually careful with her. Anything they said would be twisted to have some unintended meaning. She complained at length about the bad treatment she had had in the Army, and insisted there was no reason at all for her being under psychiatric observation. She was extremely critical of others, and at the same time would flare up at the slightest intimation of any criticism of herself. She managed to antagonize everyone around her. The following was typical of her conversation: "These nurses dislike me because I'm so efficient. That's why they discriminated against me. . . . And the enlisted men didn't like taking orders from me. That's why they lied about me. . . . It doesn't seem credible but they actually got together in a sort of conspiracy. . . ."

SCHIZOPHRENIC REACTIONS.　　The word *schizophrenia* means, literally, "splitting of the mind," and this is a general description of people displaying schizophrenic behavior. A little better name perhaps would be one that meant "splitting from reality," for the person cuts himself off from the outside world and lives in one of his own making a good part of the time. This psychosis used to be called *dementia praecox*, which means "youthful insanity," because it tends to develop early in life. Although people may develop it at any age, the highest rate of admissions to mental hospitals for this disease is for people in the middle twenties. The following case [Shaffer and Shoben, 1956, pp. 195–196] is quoted:

Some of the typical signs of the early stages of schizophrenia can be seen in the case of Angela B. This sixteen-year-old Italian girl had aroused the concern of her parents and of a social worker who was interested in the family by her persistent refusal to leave her home. At the time the case was referred to a psychologist, Angela had not stepped outside the house for five months. She stead-

fastly refused to do even the simplest errand and was immune to such inducements as the movies. At home she sat most of the time without apparent occupation and stubbornly refused to do her share of the housework. Once when she was given new and attractive shoes and a dress in an effort to persuade her to go out, she destroyed the gifts, cutting the shoes to pieces with a knife. The social worker asked a psychologist to interview Angela, and to give a psychological examination since there had been some suspicion of mental deficiency. The interview was held in the kitchen of Angela's home. When the psychologist entered the room, the girl retired behind the stove and refused to leave this position or to sit down. She was dressed in a very dirty cotton house dress, a dilapidated sweater, no stockings and very run-down shoes. She had better clothing, but refused to change or to wash her present garb. At first she would not talk. After she became more familiar with the psychologist's presence she spoke of commonplace matters freely, but refused to reply to any personal question. Queries were met sometimes with silence, sometimes with stereotyped answers of "I'm all right" or "It's all right," which were often quite irrelevant to the question. She resisted any attempt to administer a mental test, frequently saying, "I can't be bothered with that." During the course of the interview, however, a number of intelligence test items were given as informal questions. Angela's answers showed normal intelligence and entirely dismissed the suggestion of feeble-mindedness. Angela wore a silly smile through most of the meeting and seemed delighted to be the center of attention. Since the symptoms of seclusiveness, negativism, slovenliness, refusal to work, and superficial cheerfulness suggested an early schizophrenia, the girl was referred to a psychiatric clinic for diagnosis and help. Psychiatric interviews and placement in a girls' residential home seemed to brighten her for a time. In a few months, however, Angela returned to her withdrawing behavior, which grew so much worse that she was admitted to a mental hospital.

Several varieties of schizophrenia are simply different shades and forms of the same general kind of failure to adjust. One is *paranoid schizophrenia;* like the pure paranoid, the victim has delusions of grandeur and persecution. More often than not the delusions are of persecution. Unlike the pure paranoid, the paranoid schizophrenic has unsystematized delusions—delusions that are not too coherent and are not defended with such elaborate rationalizations. He may shift with little apparent reason from one delusion to another and show bizarre attitudes and behavior. A case of this kind [quoted from Cameron and Magaret, 1951, pp. 398–399] is presented below:

A schizophrenic young man believed that he was destined to become Emperor of the United States. "I could do a lot for the world," he said. "The United States has presidents. Will it ever have an emperor? I'll bet you think I'm nuts to ask about that. I must have the morning paper to keep track of world affairs. . . . If the people of the United States want me to rule them, I'm willing to do so; but no one has been to see me and tell me. I'll be glad to lead them." Later he spoke of hearing public announcements that he was to be crowned emperor. "It's been heard all over the country. . . . The world is in chaos. Thousands will be killed. I'm not a god or a devil, but I'm a super-natural being." All nations would come under his rule but Egypt; and Egypt would eventually fall to him through marriage. Along with these delusional convictions, the patient believed that attempts to kill him were repeatedly being made so that he lived, like Damocles, in constant greatness and in constant danger.

Another form of schizophrenic reaction is *simple schizophrenia;* this perhaps is its purest form. A person so affected has little apparent interest in the world; he is apathetic to almost all situations, is irresponsible, and withdraws from almost all social contact. He has simply withdrawn into his shell and makes no attempt to adjust to the world. He may exist for years as a vagrant, wandering from place to place, or as the family's or town's dependent, or he may get into social difficulty and be jailed or hospitalized.

Perhaps the extreme form of schizophrenia is *catatonic schizophrenia.* It is not so common as the other forms, but when it does occur, it presents a dramatic picture. The catatonic is extremely negativistic, often doing exactly the opposite of what he is asked to do. He may completely ignore people around him and refuse to say anything under any circumstances. Perhaps the most interesting thing about him, though, is his *catatonia,* which is a state of muscular rigidity. For many minutes or even hours, he may stay fixed in some absurd position— in a crouch or with arms outstretched. In fact, it is hard to see how catatonic positions can be maintained for so long, since the normal person could not hold such postures for even a short while.

Last of the schizophrenias to be mentioned is the *hebephrenic* form. In this type, the individual seems to regress to childish levels of behavior. He may giggle incessantly; in fact, everything may seem funny or foolish to him. Typically, his mood seems to bear no relation to the situation. He may talk about the death of his mother and laugh in a silly way. Or he may, for no apparent reason, begin to cry. Sometimes, while he is crying, he may report that he has no real feeling of sadness. He may talk like a child and use the sentences and words of a child. His habits of eating and perhaps of toilet may be as sloppy as those of a small child. The general pattern in hebephrenic reactions is illustrated in the following interview with a hebephrenic patient [quoted from Coleman, 1950, p. 248]:

The patient was a divorcee, 32 years of age, who had come to the hospital with bizarre delusions, hallucinations, and severe personality disintegration, and with a record of alcoholism, promiscuity, and possible incestuous relations with a brother. The following conversation shows typical hebephrenic responses to questioning:

D. How do you feel today?

P. Fine.

D. When did you come here?

P. 1416, you remember, doctor (silly giggle).

D. Do you know why you are here?

P. Well, in 1951 I changed into two men, President Truman was judge at my trial. I was convicted and hung (silly giggle). My brother and I were given back our normal bodies five years ago. I am a policewoman. I keep a dictaphone concealed on my person.

D. Can you tell me the name of this place?

P. I have not been a drinker for sixteen years. I am taking a mental rest after a "carter" assignment or "quill." You know, a "penwrap." I had contracts with Warner Brothers Studios and Eugene broke phonograph records but Mike protested. I have been with the police department for thirty-five years. I am made of flesh and blood—see, doctor (pulling up her dress).

D. Who is president now?

P. Truman. Don't you read the papers? I was raised through the facilities of the U. S. Postal Board.

D. Are you married?

P. No. I am not attracted to men (silly giggle). I have a companionship arrangement with my brother. I am a "looner" . . . a bachelor.

ORGANIC PSYCHOSES.   Any severe disturbance of thought may be regarded as a psychosis; a psychosis is usually accompanied by delusions, hallucinations, or regressive behavior. *Organic psychoses* are induced by conditions affecting the brain. For our purposes, only three need to be discussed. Two of these are so similar in their symptoms (though different in their causes) that we shall consider them together: *Senile and alcoholic psychoses.* These have different origins but symptoms that are somewhat alike. Old people may develop psychotic behavior that is characterized by delusions, defects of memory, and general disorientation. The person may imagine that he has been talking to someone who really was not there, or he may imagine that people are boring holes in his head. As his memory grows worse, he may forget what he has just said but at the same time insist that he remembers things that never happened. Very frequently in senile psychosis the person has a hard time knowing where he is, where he has been, or what is going on—he is generally disoriented. The following case [quoted from Cameron and Magaret, 1951, pp. 547–548] is an example:

A housewife, aged seventy-three years, was brought to the hospital by relatives who found it impossible to give her the care and protection she needed. According to their account, she had been "losing her memory" during the preceding three years. . . .

Up to the age of seventy years, the patient had shown nothing unusual in her behavior. She had gone about her household duties competently, maintained her social contacts reasonably well, and kept her person well groomed and clean. The first change that anyone noticed was a growing tendency to misplace articles at home, to leave packages in the stores, and to forget the purpose of an errand after she had started on it. The patient accepted these lapses good-humoredly as the forgetfulness that was natural to old age; and the family often joked about "grandma's absent-mindedness." After a few months, however, it became apparent that the forgetfulness was becoming a serious problem. The patient spent so much time searching for misplaced articles that she could not get her housework done, and she was unable to retrace her steps for the forgotten packages because she could not remember what they were or where she had been shopping. . . .

Meanwhile, the patient gave further evidence that she was undergoing general behavioral deterioration. She required a great deal of urging before she would bathe, keep her hair combed, or change her clothing. Sometimes she put on two or more of the same articles, one over the other, and sometimes she came to breakfast with her dress on backwards. She began hoarding all kinds of things under her bed—food, newspapers, kitchenware, ornaments, clothing and toilet articles. When her daughter-in-law or her husband removed these the patient at first resisted and then wept. She became progressively confused with reference to the time of day. For example, she protested at six in the evening that it was "too early for breakfast"; soon after going to bed, she would get up and insist that it was morning. . . . Not long after she had finished a meal she would ask when they were to eat, as though she had not eaten for some time.

The day before her hospitalization, the patient had disappeared from home during the afternoon; and, in spite of their frantic search of the neighborhood, her relatives could not find her. That evening she was returned cold, dirty and dishevelled, by the police, who had observed her crossing streets against traffic. . . . She arrived home cheerful and garrulous, unable to tell where she had been, to appreciate her situation, or to understand her relatives' frightened behavior. While preparing for bed, she was only with difficulty dissuaded from climbing out of the bathroom window, which she insisted was the door. These events led to a family conference, the upshot of which was that further attempts at home care were considered to be out of the question.

Chronic alcoholism can gradually destroy mental processes in somewhat the same way as advancing age. Although some features of alcoholic psychosis are unique, the general picture is similar to that of the senile psychosis. The common factor in both is probably the destruction of brain tissue. In the alcoholic, the destruction is caused by excessive alcohol. In the aged person, damage is caused by ruptured blood vessels or by loss of blood supply due to hardening of the arteries.

General paresis. This organic psychosis used to be common, especially before modern methods for the control of syphilis became available. It develops when the syphilis germ lodges in the brain and gradually destroys some of the brain tissue. The person suffering from it becomes irresponsible and unpredictable and frequently has the most extreme delusions of grandeur. He may think he is worth billions of dollars—and spend money as though he were. He may claim that he built the Empire State building with his own hands or believe that he is the son of royalty. It is fortunate that only a small percentage of people who contract syphilis develop this disease and that modern medical science is now doing an effective job of curing syphilis in its early stages.

Summary

1. Frustration is the thwarting of behavior directed toward a goal. Of three general types of frustration—environmental frustration, personal frustration, and conflict frustration—conflict frustration is usually most important in determining a person's adjustment.

2. Three types of conflict frustration may be distinguished: approach-approach conflict, avoidance-avoidance conflict, and approach-avoidance conflict. The last is the most difficult of the three to resolve, because the same goal is both positive and negative.

3. Some typical approach-avoidance conflicts are desire for achievement versus fear of failure, independence versus affiliation, sexual desire versus fear of sex, and hostility versus social approval.

4. The immediate effects of frustration include the learning of habits that relieve frustration, rigidity of behavior in frustrating situations, and anxiety. Other effects may be the use of daydreaming and fantasy

in order to achieve imaginary satisfactions, regression to earlier forms of behavior that were once satisfying, and the excessive use of alcohol to allay the painfulness of anxiety aroused by conflict.

5. A defense mechanism is a device—a way of behaving—that a person uses unconsciously to protect himself against ego-involving frustrations. Defense mechanisms are directed at the anxiety caused by conflict rather than at the conflict problem itself.

6. Repression is unconscious forgetting of aspects of a conflict that cause anxiety and discomfort. In total repression, a person so completely disguises certain motives that he is unaware of them. The motivational conflict may then reveal itself in a conversion reaction, such as paralysis or other illness.

7. Defense mechanisms in which some aspect of a motivational conflict is repressed or disguised include reaction formation, projection, displacement, rationalization, sublimation, and compensation.

8. Although everyone uses defense mechanisms to some extent, relying on them too much and too often constitutes an inadequate adjustment. Serious failures in adjustment may be classified into two categories: (a) the neuroses and (b) the psychoses.

9. The neuroses or neurotic reactions consist of (a) anxiety reactions, in which anxiety, chronic or acute, is the prominent symptom; (b) phobic reactions, involving intense irrational fears; (c) obsessive-compulsive reactions, in which ideas or acts involuntarily intrude; (d) conversion reactions, involving apparent, but not real, physical illness; and (e) dissociative reactions, in which a person represses large segments of his personality. Dissociative reactions include amnesia and multiple personality.

10. The psychoses or psychotic reactions are more severe mental illnesses than the neuroses. They may be either organic, i.e., caused by known physical diseases, or functional, i.e., without any known physiological basis.

11. The major classes of functional psychoses are (a) affective reactions, involving extreme moods of excitement or depression; (b) paranoid reactions, characterized by hallucinations and systematized delusions of persecution or grandeur; and (c) schizophrenic reactions, marked by disorientation, confused thinking, withdrawal and seclusiveness, and unsystematized delusions.

12. Of the organic psychoses, senile and alcoholic psychoses have somewhat similar symptoms: delusions, defects of memory, and general disorientation. General paresis, caused by syphilis of the nervous system, is marked by irresponsibility, unpredictability of behavior, and frequently by extreme delusions of grandeur.

Suggestions for further reading

Coleman, J. C. *Abnormal psychology and modern life* (rev. ed.). Chicago: Scott, Foresman, 1956.
A popular textbook on abnormal psychology.

Gorlow, L., and Katkovsky, W. *Readings in the psychology of adjustment.* New York: McGraw-Hill, 1959.
A selection of articles and excerpts from books on the topic of human adjustment.

Hall, C. S. *A primer of Freudian psychology.* Yonkers, N.Y.: World, 1954.
A readable introductory book on the Freudian theory of personality.

Lewin, K. *Dynamic theory of personality.* New York: McGraw-Hill, 1935. Chap. 3.
A classical description of the types of conflict.

Maier, N. R. F. *Frustration.* New York: McGraw-Hill, 1949.

An account of research on frustration and a theory of its nature and consequences.

Masserman, J. *Principle of dynamic psychiatry*. Philadelphia: Saunders, 1946.
An introduction to psychiatry.

O'Kelly, L. I., and Muckler, F. D. *Introduction to psychopathology* (2d ed.). Englewood Cliffs, N. J.: Prentice-Hall, 1955.
A standard textbook in abnormal psychology.

Shaffer, L. F., and Shoben, E. J., Jr. *The psychology of adjustment* (rev. ed.). Boston: Houghton Mifflin, 1956.
Includes a thorough, readable, and elementary treatment of the defense mechanisms.

White, R. W. *The abnormal personality* (2d ed.). New York: Ronald, 1956.
A widely used textbook on abnormal psychology.

Mental health
& psychotherapy

THE LAST CHAPTER AND this one make a pair. Chapter 5 analyzed the conflict and frustration that threaten mental health and the ways people react to them. It dealt with the *causes* and *nature* of maladjustments. This one deals with *remedies,* or at least with ways and means of treating maladjustments when they occur, and with steps that can be taken to prevent them. Unfortunately, neither the prevention nor the cure of mental illness is easy, quick, or sure. The problems involved are still largely unsolved, and we are not at all certain of the effectiveness of the methods of attack that we are now using. Nevertheless, mental health is of such importance that every intelligent person should know as much about it as he can.

The problem of mental health

Mental illness is the term generally used to describe a maladjustment which is serious enough to handicap the maladjusted person himself and to burden other people. Other almost synonymous terms are *mental disease, mental disorder,* and *behavior disorder.* In a way, although these terms are firmly intrenched in usage, they are unfortunate. Psychological maladjustments are not diseases or illnesses in the sense that physical ailments are. They are not caused by infection or a specific malfunction, nor are they exclusively "mental." That should be clear from our analysis in the last chapter.

PREVALENCE OF MENTAL ILLNESS. Mental health is a problem that concerns everyone. So many people are, have been, or will be mentally ill or seriously maladjusted that none of us can escape some personal contact with it.

Except for the number of people in hospitals, figures for the incidence of various mental disorders are at best only estimates, based on studies of certain communities. The estimates vary with the particular criterion used for deciding whether a person is badly enough maladjusted to be judged mentally ill.

Neurotics undoubtedly make up the largest single group. Those neurotic enough to be severely handicapped in social adjustment probably constitute about 5 per cent of the adult population. Extremely conservative figures give something less than 1 per cent, whereas more liberal estimates run as high as 37 per cent of adults. Another 2 or 3 per cent are alcoholics, and more than that are problem drinkers. Roughly a million individuals, or more than 1 per cent of adults, can be classified as psychotic at any one time. If we add another 2 million or so individuals who are delinquent, have criminal tendencies, or are drug addicts, the number of mentally ill and seriously maladjusted persons total about 15 million or approximately 10 per cent of the population.

These figures are only for any one given time. Over a period of years, the incidence of maladjustment is even higher. For some years past, the chances of a person spending some part of his life in a mental hospital have been about 1 in 17, or 6 per cent. And it is primarily psychotics, rather than neurotics, who are admitted to mental hospitals. Now that modern medicine has extended the life span so dramatically, many more individuals will live long enough to become victims of the senile psychoses. In view of that fact, we now estimate that about 1 individual in 10 will at some time or other be admitted to a mental hospital.

The number of patients in mental hospitals gives us another, almost shocking, idea of the seriousness of mental disease. Almost half of the hospital beds in the United States are occupied by mental patients. Otherwise said, in terms of the number of hospital beds required, mental diseases are as numerous as all other diseases combined. Beds in mental hospitals number roughly 750,000. Most mental hospital facilities are provided by the respective state and local governments. This means that a sizable share of our taxes must be used to care for the mentally ill.

Of the patients now in mental hospitals, the largest single group consists of those diagnosed as schizophrenics. Roughly 20 per cent of those admitted to mental hospitals are in this category. However, because schizophrenics have a rather poor prognosis of recovery and on the average stay in hospitals longer than most other patients, the percentage of schizophrenics in the hospital population is considerably higher than this. Next in order of numbers admitted to hospitals are the affective psychoses. Psychoneurotics usually rank third; however, these patients are more likely to recover enough to be discharged. In addition, great numbers of neurotics are treated as outpatients or as private patients of psychiatrists, and are never admitted to a hospital. As already indicated, these proportions, other things being equal, will probably change with the lengthening of the life span, so that in the future the senile psychoses will become relatively more numerous. In fact, the number of individuals over fifty years of age admitted to mental hospitals has been rising substantially in recent years, primarily because there are more older people in the population.

Environmental factors. It is frequently assumed that the stress of modern life is an important factor in mental illness. Some observers feel that, since life has become more complex, a greater number of individuals may not be able to solve their conflicts, and thus may become maladjusted or mentally ill. Whether this is true or not for all kinds of mental illness we cannot say.

It may be the case for neurotics. On the other hand, it does not seem to explain the number of admissions to mental hospitals. The figures on admissions have remained surprisingly constant for nearly a century [Goldhammer and Marshall, 1953]. Consider, for example, figures compiled from the records of the state of Massachusetts, which are given in Figure 6.1. There you see that the number of individuals (at various age levels below fifty) was about the same in the period from 1917 to 1940 as it was in 1885. Other data from different sources show almost the same thing. Perhaps this is not surprising in view of the genetic factor in some of the psychoses (page 482). In any case, the precipitating factors in psychoses apparently have not been altered appreciably in the last eighty years by changes in our culture or by our increasing understanding of mental illness.

Social class. The picture is quite different, however, if we examine the incidence of mental illness in different social classes. Over-all incidence, as well as the kind of mental illness, is definitely linked to social class. A team of research workers at Yale University has gathered the data on this question [Hollingshead and Redlich, 1958]:

The researchers classified virtually all the patients under psychiatric care at one particular time in the New Haven area. Patients "under psychiatric care" included not only those in mental hospitals, but those making regular visits to psychiatrists in clinics and private practice. The social class of each patient was determined by using certain, well-established criteria of social class: income level, occupation, educational level, housing, etc. In this way the patients were classified into one of five groups; Class I included the highest social class, Class V the lowest. There were, however, too few cases in Classes I and II to treat them separately, so these were combined. Hence comparisons were made of

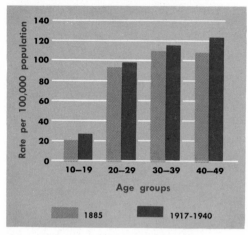

FIGURE 6.1. Admissions rates to mental hospitals in Massachusetts for 1885 and 1917–1940 per 100,000 population [after Goldhammer and Marshall, 1953].

four groups: Classes I–II, Class III, Class IV, and Class V.

Some of the results of the study were clear cut. The total incidence of cases (rate per 100,000 within a given class) was quite different for each of the four classes (see Figure 6.2). Incidence was relatively low for Classes I–II and III, rose significantly for Class IV, and then very sharply for Class V. On the other hand, the incidence of *new* cases—cases coming under psychiatric care for the first time—was more nearly the same for all four classes, although Class V was definitely higher than the others. Thus the differences among the classes was largely due to the fact that the lower classes accumulated relatively more individuals with protracted illness.

The accumulation of mental illness in the lower classes may be attributed in part to the better facilities for psychiatric treatment enjoyed by the upper classes. The major factor, however, is not that, but rather the kinds of illnesses prevalent in the different classes (see Figure 6.3). Of the patients in each class, approximately two-thirds in

Classes I–II were classified as neurotics, whereas less than 10 per cent in Class V were so classified. Class III and Class IV showed intermediate percentages. Hence the lower classes are considerably more prone to develop psychoses than neuroses; the reverse is true of the upper classes. This statement applies to individuals actually under psychiatric care. It must be remembered, however, that low-income groups are less able to afford psychiatric care and are less likely to obtain care for neurotic disorders than the high-income groups. We thus know that the true percentage of neurotic disorders in the lower classes is understated by these statistics, but we have no way of knowing what it is since we know only the number of *treated* disorders.

Among those classified as neurotic, there are also class differences. The obsessive-compulsive reactions are for the most part concentrated in the upper class (I–II), while reactions involving physical complaints are most prevalent in the lower classes. That is to say, psychosomatic anxiety reactions as well as conversion (hysterical) reactions are found in relatively greater numbers in the lower classes than in the upper classes.

The major facts emerging from this large-scale study of social class and mental disorder are certainly clear. They leave no doubt that mental illness, both as to incidence and kind, is linked to social class. What the facts mean, however, is not nearly so clear. Social-class differences include differences in genetic background, in learning experiences, in the types of stress and frustration encountered, and in the amount and kind of psychiatric care available. All these factors must somehow enter into the linkage between class and mental illness. At present, we cannot say just how they interact.

HISTORICAL BACKGROUND. Today, we recognize mental illness to be a natural phenomenon, caused by genetic and envi-

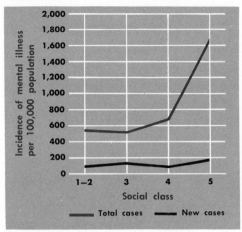

FIGURE 6.2. Relative prevalence of mental illness in different social classes. The total incidence of cases (rate per 100,000 within a given class) differs according to social class. Much of the difference is due to the accumulation of relatively more individuals with protracted illness in the lower classes [Hollingshead and Redlich, 1958].

ronmental factors. We seek to understand it just as we would any other natural phenomenon, and through objective scientific inquiry, develop methods for combating it. This has not always been so. In fact, we have been extraordinarily slow in arriving at our present conception of mental illness. Earlier chapters in the history of mental illness make fascinating, but almost unbelievable, reading [Coleman, 1956].

Ancient concepts. Among the ancients, mental disorder was attributed to demon possession. This is clear from the evidence we can put together about the cavemen of the Stone Age, living some half-million years ago, and from early writings of the Chinese, Egyptians, Hebrews, and Greeks. Early man, of course, considered all sorts of events to be the work of spirits. It was natural for him to regard the mentally ill person as one possessed by an evil spirit. Among the Hebrews, demon possession was looked upon as a punishment visited by God—a notion later revived and elaborated in the Christian tradition.

For the cavemen, the problem was to let the spirits out; to do this, they frequently *trephined* holes in the possessed person's skull. In Biblical times and later, the prescribed treatment for demon possession was *exorcism*. This involved various rituals and techniques for casting out the spirit—prayer, religious rites, weird brews and medicines, whipping, starvation, or torture.

The first rays of scientific enlightenment broke through during the Golden Age of Greece. Hippocrates (460–377 B.C.), the Greek physician regarded as the "father of medicine," repudiated the doctrine of spirit possession, asserting that mental illness was a disorder of brain function. He recognized that heredity might predispose a person to mental illness, and also that head injuries might cause certain disorders. Not all his ideas were correct—indeed some of his physiological explanations were far wide of the mark—but his belief in natural causes anticipated our modern conception of mental illness. Later Greek and Roman philosophers and physicians for the most part followed in the Hippocratic tradition.

Age of witchcraft. With the decline of Greco-Roman civilization, however, demonology was revived, modified somewhat by the theology and superstitions of the times. Exorcism also reappeared as the accepted method of treatment. In early medieval times, apparently, treatment was left to the priests, and the mentally ill were not, on the whole, treated badly. But as the idea that they were possessed of devils became more widely held, they were treated with increasing cruelty, justified on the ground that it was not only the individual, but the devils inside that were being punished.

From the fifteenth to seventeenth centuries, the period which we now think of as

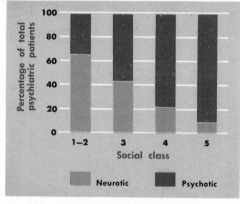

FIGURE 6.3. Kinds of mental illness prevalent in the different social classes. Neuroses predominate in the upper classes, psychoses in the lower classes [Hollingshead and Redlich, 1958].

the age of witchcraft, such misguided beliefs about mental illness saw their heyday. Victims of these beliefs, whether really ill or not, were regarded as evil. Demon possession was considered a form of God's punishment or, at worst, a sign of partnership with the devil. The possessed thereby acquired supernatural powers; they were, it was claimed, able to cause sickness, catastrophe, drought, and even to perform miracles, such as turning people into animals or vice versa. This is what was meant by "witch." Not only simple and pious people, but also prominent clergymen, both Catholic and Protestant, and other community leaders believed in witches. Martin Luther (1483–1546) wrote [Coleman, 1956]:

The greatest punishment God can inflict on the wicked . . . is to deliver them over to Satan, who with God's permission, kills them or makes them to undergo great calamities. Many devils are in woods, water, wildernesses, etc., ready to hurt and prejudice people. When these things happen, then the philosophers and physicians say, it is natural, ascribing it to the planets. . . . Men are possessed by the devil in two ways, corporally or spiritually. Those whom he possesses corporally, as mad people, he has permission from God to vex and agitate, but he has no power over their souls.

With convictions such as these, otherwise good and sensible people could harass and torture the witches and feel that they were doing God's will. This was the justification of the almost unbelievable, but true, stories of burning witches at the stake.

Not everyone believed in witchcraft or in the demonological view of mental illness. Those who did not, including many clergymen, physicians, and scientists, gradually became more vocal. Their influence was felt, and by the eighteenth century, belief in witchcraft was on its way out.

The insane asylum. In the meantime, the problem of how to care for the insane received increasing attention. Most of them were allowed loose in the community; others were kept in monasteries or prisons. Gradually the idea of a separate asylum for the insane took hold. The first asylums were established in the sixteenth century; by the eighteenth century, they were fairly common both in the United States and abroad.

At first the conditions of treatment in these asylums were little better than the patients were used to outside. The patients were crowded together in dark cells, fed poor, and often little, food, frequently placed in strait jackets, and had their heads shaved. The more violent ones were put in chains. Many were bled, doused in cold water, confined in cribs, and kept in weird contrivances. Such treatment reflected the still widespread influence of demonology and, at best, lack of understanding of the mentally ill. The following is a description of the treatment of the mentally ill in the United States during colonial times [quoted from Deutsch, 1946, p. 53]:

The mentally ill were hanged, imprisoned, tortured, and otherwise persecuted as agents of Satan. Regarded as sub-human beings, they were chained in specially devised kennels and cages like wild beasts, and thrown into prisons, bridewells and jails like criminals. They were incarcerated in workhouse dungeons or made to slave as able-bodied paupers, unclassified from the rest. They were left to wander about stark naked, driven from place to place like mad dogs, subjected to whippings as vagrants and rogues. Even the well-to-do were not spared confinement in strong rooms and cellar dungeons, while legislation usually concerned itself more with their property than their persons.

Then came the beginnings of the modern revolution in the care and treatment of the mentally ill. A physician named Pinel was placed in charge of the Paris hospital for the insane. As an experiment, he was permitted by the authorities to remove the chains of many of the hospital's inmates. He took patients out of dungeons and put them into sunny rooms, permitted them to walk around outside the hospital, and instituted a regime of kindly treatment (see Figure 6.4). The results were dramatic. Within weeks or months, many patients were pronounced cured and discharged. Others progressed more slowly, but improved enough to live relatively useful and tranquil lives in the hospital. That was in the 1790s.

Like many revolutions, Pinel's was welcomed in some quarters and distrusted or rejected in others. A few hospitals immediately followed suit. The more extreme medieval cruelties gave way to more humane treatment. Still, for another century, mental hospitals were backward custodial institutions, doing little to help their patients and often making their plight worse.

Mental health movement. This was the situation around 1900, when our modern mental health movement began. This movement got much of its initial impetus from a patient named Clifford Beers, who after several years in mental hospitals regained his mental health and wrote the book *A Mind That Found Itself*. In this book, Beers

FIGURE 6.4. Pinel removing the shackles from the inmates of La Salpetrière Asylum, Paris. This signaled a more humane and understanding approach to mental illness. [From a copy of a painting by Tony Robert-Fleury in the Central State Hospital, Indianapolis, Indiana.]

recounted his experiences, mostly of bad treatment, in mental hospitals, and told how he "found himself" in the home of a friendly attendant. He campaigned for better conditions of treatment of the mentally ill and for wider public understanding of mental health. The publication of his book and the founding of the Society for Mental Hygiene, both in 1908, were the opening guns in what has proved to be a successful campaign, although we still have a long way to go in ensuring effective treatment for all the mentally ill. Conditions in mental hospitals have improved greatly in the past fifty years. However, they are far from ideal, owing to inadequate facilities and budgets and to shortages of trained personnel.

We are more concerned, however, with the attempts to treat, and even to prevent, mental illness, which have grown out of the modern mental health movement. Such attempts were unthinkable so long as the mentally ill were regarded as witches worthy

only of punishment, or as subhuman beings to be "put away" and left in an asylum. Hence only in the last fifty years has a concerted effort been made to do something about solving the problem of mental illness.

TRENDS IN THERAPY.   *Therapy* is the general name for any method used in treating an illness. Mental illness, as we have seen, may consist of a neurosis, a functional psychosis, or an organic psychosis due to diseases of the nervous system. Different forms of therapy must be employed to treat these varieties of mental illness.

Some therapies aim at eradicating the underlying physical disease. Others involve surgery of the brain, subjecting the patient to shocks induced by electrical means or by drugs, or using drugs that restore him to a more normal state. All such therapies, naturally, are in the hands of medical specialists and are therefore classified as *medical therapy*.

Some therapeutic methods are aimed at the emotional and psychological aspects of the patient's problem. They employ interviews, discussions, play acting, and changes in the patient's environment. Since these methods of treatment involve psychological, rather than medical, techniques, and are often in the hands of psychologists, they are called *psychotherapy*.

Medical therapy is much more drastic than psychotherapy and is ordinarily restricted to severe cases of mental illness, and particularly to the psychoses. Psychotherapy, on the other hand, is used not only for psychotics and neurotics, but also for persons with less serious personality problems—delinquents and maladjusted children, people with marital, religious, scholastic, or occupational problems. Thus psychotherapy is suitable for a wide range of problems of adjustment.

At the beginning of this century, attempts to treat mental illness were mainly confined to severe psychotic disorders requiring hospitalization. The therapeutic methods were largely medical. As our understanding of mental illness grew, more reliance was put on psychotherapeutic procedures. Psychotherapy was extended first to severe neuroses, then to milder neurotic reactions encountered in people outside hospitals. The psychoanalytic movement, launched by Freud, had a great deal to do with this trend, for psychoanalysis, as one particular kind of therapy, is aimed largely at the milder neurotic disorders.

There are good reasons for this trend in psychotherapy: (1) The severely and chronically ill cost more to treat, and are less likely to benefit from treatment, than less maladjusted individuals. (2) Psychotherapists have been in short supply, and they therefore have bent their efforts where they might do the most good. (3) The treatment of less neurotic individuals offers the greatest benefit to society, for they are still active in social, economic, and political affairs. Any improvement in their adjustment is quickly reflected in their influence on associates and everyday affairs. (4) The successful treatment of mild disorders *prevents* the development of more serious ones.

Of course, if we were to achieve some dramatic breakthrough in treating severe neurotics or psychotics, this whole trend might be reversed. Otherwise, the present trend is likely to continue and to expand into widespread counseling and psychotherapy, with the aim to hold down, as much as possible, the incidence of more severe disorders.

Kinds of therapy

A physician treats many different things when he treats physical diseases. If he can diagnose the underlying cause and has the means of combating it, he may treat that. If he knows, for example, that the patient has scarlet fever, caused by a particular microorganism, he fights it with the drug most likely to kill the organism. Often he cannot do this, either because of inability to diagnose the cause or for lack of appropriate weapons. Then he may treat the symptoms by doing something to relieve fever, pain, discomfort, or other disturbing effects of the disease. The same thing is true in the treatment of mental illness, only more so. Here it is often too difficult or too expensive to discover and to treat the underlying complex causes. Hence the therapist often treats, or attempts to alleviate, the effects of the illness. He usually must choose among several possible alternatives, depending on the individual and the time available. Which he decides upon determines the kind of therapy he uses.

MEDICAL THERAPY. Since medical therapy is not the business of the psychologist, it will be described only briefly. Medical therapies for treating mental illness may be grouped into four main classes: psychosurgery, shock therapy, narcosis, and drug therapy.

Psychosurgery. Stone Age man sometimes trephined skulls to let out the "evil spirits" of the mentally ill. Though the technique was crude, the reasoning incorrect, and the results of little value, the general idea had merit. In the 1930s, a similar method was adopted for treating cases of mental illness. The method was called *psychosurgery* because it *consisted of surgery of the brain for the purpose of treating and relieving mental symptoms* [Freeman and Watts, 1950].

In psychosurgery, the particular part of the brain involved is the *frontal lobes* (see page 608). These seem to be more concerned with foresight, planning, and anticipation of the future than the other parts of the brain. They are also connected with lower emotional centers. In principle, then, if one removed tissue from the frontal lobes, or severed their connections with emotional centers, the individual might think less about the future and be less worried about it.

Psychosurgery has been used for just this purpose on several thousand individuals, mostly those suffering from depressive disorders, marked by extreme worry and agitation. At first, parts of the frontal lobes were removed, but this was much too drastic. It was dangerous, and it frequently caused such major changes in personality that the cure was worse than the disease. Later on, only the pathways between the frontal lobes and lower centers were sectioned. This operation was less drastic, but was also less effective in relieving the patient's emotional distress. Because gentler and more effective methods of treatment have been discovered, psychosurgery is not employed so often today as it was 20 years ago.

Shock therapy. Shock therapy is a name for several different kinds of therapy which put the patient for a time into an unconscious state [Jessner and Ryan, 1941]. In most cases this state is preceded by convulsions, similar to epileptic convulsions. The usefulness of the method was discovered by accident when a mental patient, who was also a diabetic, received an overdose of the antidiabetic substance insulin, and sub-

sequently showed remarkable improvement in mental symptoms. Today, no one is quite sure why or how shock treatment works. All that is known is that some patients are improved after a series of shock treatments.

The first form of shock treatment, used in the 1930s, was relatively large doses of *insulin*. Although insulin treatment often had beneficial results, it was dangerous; at the very least, it was hard on the patient. After that a convulsive drug *metrazol* was employed in place of insulin. Metrazol also is dangerous, sometimes producing convulsions violent enough to break bones. In addition, patients characteristically experience a terrifying emotional upset just prior to the convulsion. A third form of shock therapy is *electroshock*. A brief, carefully regulated jolt of electrical current is passed through the patient's brain. This, like other shock methods, causes a convulsion, then a period of unconsciousness. A patient, however, has no unpleasant experience connected with it, and indeed has little memory of the events immediately preceding the shock session. Because of its safety, its simplicity, and its acceptability to patients, electrical shock therapy is now the most widely used form of such therapy.

Shock therapy, and particularly electroshock treatment, is most effective with individuals suffering depression [Noyes, 1948]. It seems to alleviate their feelings of guilt, tendencies to suicide, and self-deprecation. Sometimes after a series of electroshock treatments, the patient seems entirely normal and can be discharged without further treatment. Often, however, shock treatment is combined with psychotherapy. The effects of the shock treatment may be only temporary, but they make him lucid and approachable enough for a therapist to make progress with psychotherapeutic techniques (see below).

Narcosis. A narcotic drug is one that in sufficient dosage puts a person to sleep. Narcotic drugs differ in several ways: how rapidly they act, how long their effects last, and how deeply they put a person to sleep.

Many years ago, before the days of shock therapy, narcosis was used extensively to keep agitated patients under control. It served this purpose, but it was not safe to use repeatedly and over long periods of time. By itself, moreover, it had little or no therapeutic value. Now that tranquilizers are available, narcosis is almost never used merely to calm or control patients.

Narcosis is currently used, however, for *narcoanalysis,* that is, in the analysis of the patient's problems. A drug often used for this purpose is *sodium amytal.* Injected in small doses, it makes the patient groggy for several minutes before he falls into a deep sleep. During the groggy or twilight state, the patient can reenact traumatic experiences [Orr, 1949] and discuss unpleasant subjects with the physician (see Figure 6.5). Thus the medical therapist can uncover deep-seated problems, and the patient can sometimes relieve his tensions. Narcoanalysis has proved particularly valuable in analyzing disorders caused by a traumatic experience, such as a pilot's terrifying experience in

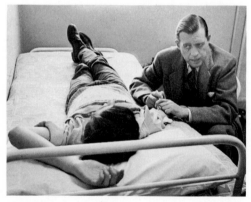

FIGURE 6.5. Narcoanalysis used as an aid in psychotherapy. This patient is receiving an injection of sodium amytal. While in a twilight state before falling asleep, the patient can reenact traumatic experiences and discuss unpleasant subjects. In this way, the therapist can uncover deep-seated problems and help the patient achieve some relief from tensions [courtesy Life Magazine, © Time, Inc.].

combat. It is also a substitute for hypnosis (see below) because it is quicker and more dependable. Sodium amytal has sometimes been called a "truth serum," for it enables a patient to remember things otherwise deeply buried by repression, but it has little or no value in eliciting confessions in criminal cases.

Chemotherapy. Chemotherapy is the name for the latest revolution in the treatment of mental illness. The best known of the chemotherapeutic drugs are the so-called "tranquilizers." Actually, there are other chemotherapeutic drugs, such as the psychomimetic drugs and "activators." The psychomimetic drugs induce some of the symptoms of psychotic behavior and may therefore help a therapist study his patient's problems. The activators are, in a sense, the opposite of tranquilizers; they can activate patients who are extremely lethargic and withdrawn. These drugs are discussed in Chapter 20.

Generally speaking, the chemotherapeutic drugs are used for two purposes: (1) to control the patient or to put him in a more relaxed state, and (2) to help the therapist analyze the patient's problems and conduct psychotherapy with him. As agents of control, these drugs merely relieve symptoms of anxiety, agitation, or depression, which in some individuals is by itself quite a feat. As aids in psychotherapy, they enable the patient to make better progress by relieving his anxiety and discomfort. In the end, however, the lasting value of chemotherapy hinges on the success of psychotherapy.

PSYCHOTHERAPY. Psychotherapy can be either a simple or a very complex process, depending on the individual's problem, how severe it is, and what can reasonably be accomplished in therapy.

The aims and over-all strategy of the psychotherapy must be decided on jointly by the patient and therapist early in the treatment; they may, however, change during the course of therapy. The therapist uses several sources of information to form his opinion of what may be accomplished in therapy. One is a *life history* of the person as given by the person himself and by his friends and relatives. Another is *physical* and *psychological* examinations of the person, including tests of intelligence, personality, and vocational abilities. A third is the picture the therapist forms of the person's problems in the course of the first few interviews.

The patient's problem, as we have already seen, may stem from (1) environmental frustrations, (2) personal frustrations, or (3) motivational conflicts. Usually all three elements are present, but the psychotherapist must decide on the particular aims of treatment. If environmental frustrations are to be the focus of treatment, then changing the situation of the patient will be a psychotherapeutic aim. If personal frustrations loom largest, then providing support temporarily will be the primary aim. If motivational conflict is the heart of the problem, as very often it is, then the principal aim will be to help the patient achieve insight and self-understanding. Let us consider briefly each of these kinds of therapy.

Changing the situation. This is the simplest goal of treatment. It is not an attempt to bring about any major change in the patient, but rather to *manipulate his situation in such a way as to relieve the stress on him.* A patient may be advised to take a vacation, change his occupation, change his educational goals, etc. Although this may be the only treatment possible in some instances, it is not likely to be satisfactory for most persons. Major changes in the environment are frequently difficult or impossible, and they sometimes make matters even worse for the patient. When the major difficulty is motivational conflict within the person, manipulating the environment is apt to bring only minor relief.

Situational changes, of course, can be important, but they are usually secondary to the treatment of the individual. For children, situational changes are frequently necessary. In simple adjustment problems

of adults, too, such changes may make the patient secure. However, for the great majority of persons who come for treatment, a good deal more is necessary. To begin by treating the situation may completely block progress toward other goals of therapy.

Providing support. If the treatment is arranged to give support to the patient but not to bring about permanent personality changes, it is called *supportive therapy*. The aim here is to help the individual through a crisis. Much of what is called *counseling* is supportive psychotherapy [Bordin, 1955]. It helps relatively normal people face specific problems of adjustment. The counselor gives information, listens to the person's problems, suggests courses of action, and reassures him about what he has done or proposes to do. In this way the counselor may support the person sufficiently to enable him to make a satisfactory adjustment.

Giving support and reassurance, however, requires an expertness that is not easily acquired. The counselor must do it subtly or he will increase rather than decrease the person's anxiety. It is usually wise to use support therapy only in certain special cases. One type is the chronic case in which illness is of such long standing, the resources for health so poor, and the environmental blocks so great that the chances of effecting a permanent change in the person are small. In such cases, supportive therapy may strengthen the person's ability to deal with some of his problems. Another type of case is that in which the person has been well adjusted most of his life, but temporarily develops a neurotic disturbance in a crisis. Here, supportive therapy may help reestablish healthy modes of adjustment.

Achieving insight. For deep-seated motivational conflicts, insight or uncovering therapy is, so far, the only appropriate one. Its aim is *to uncover the causes of a person's difficulty, to rid the patient of his neurotic defenses,* and thereby to free him for flexible adaptive behavior. Insight is not obtained through simple intellectual discovery. Rather it is a long and painstaking procedure in which the patient exposes himself to various emotional attitudes and situations [Alexander and French, 1946]. He must bring to the fore the emotional situations he has been unable to face, those which he has repressed and around which he has developed his neurotic defenses.

In actual practice, almost all psychotherapy includes some support, some insight, and eventually even some situational change. However, when the primary effort is to develop insight and to gain continuous emotional growth, the therapy is called *insight therapy*. When the effort to support the ego is greater than the effort to obtain insight, the treatment is called *supportive*.

Techniques in psychotherapy

Now let us turn to the specific techniques that psychotherapists use. There are a variety of such techniques. Some are rather specialized and are used only occasionally when the situation seems to demand them. One may be used more frequently by some therapists than by others because of differences of opinion about its relative effectiveness. Many of the techniques are difficult to distinguish clearly from one another and represent differences in emphasis rather than radical differences in method.

DIRECTIVE THERAPIES. In the early days of psychotherapy, techniques were primarily *directive*. The therapist was an authoritative prescriber. The medical practitioner prescribed medicine for physical ailments, so the psychotherapist tended to follow the same practice of prescribing for the alleviation of mental suffering. Since the patient developed his difficulties in a particular environment, the therapist was likely to prescribe a change of environment. He often considered the patient unable to plan his own life and took charge of such planning. He prescribed exercise, rest, a hobby, or certain social activities. In many cases the therapist tried to direct the patient's thinking and emotional life. Thus, in this kind of treatment, the therapist was dominant and the patient depended upon his reactions.

Reeducation. Much of the early directive therapy was called *reeducation*. Austin Riggs [1929], a leader in reeducation therapy, usually prescribed temporary environmental changes for his neurotic patients. He believed the patient should be removed from his home, social, and vocational environments because he had developed his neurotic disturbance in them. Then, in another, neutral environment, the patient went to school, so to speak, *to learn the principles of satisfactory life adjustment,* and lived on a regimented schedule of activities designed to help him develop habits of social cooperation.

Such strictly organized reeducation of the type sponsored by Riggs is seldom recommended today, but reeducation of a less directive type is frequently used. In fact, it is involved in practically all techniques and consists of developing new insights and habits of thought.

Desensitization. Closely related to reeducation is the technique of *desensitization*. This is designed to *enable the patient to be comfortable in situations in which he has previously been highly anxious.* For many patients there are situations which have been associated with pain, shame, or insecurity that cannot be approached objectively. Even patients with very good insight into their problems often are unable to change their emotional reactions to these situations. The therapy in such instances is to have the patient, under special conditions, face the anxiety-arousing situation and thus have an opportunity gradually to extinguish his emotional responses to it. If, for example, a person has a great fear of parties, therapy might consist in getting him to parties so arranged that he suffers no embarrassment and finds out that parties aren't so bad after all. Desensitization is similar in principle to the method of extinction described in Chapter 7.

Suggestion and hypnosis. Suggestion is a process in which one person gets another to accept an idea or attitude without proof or coercion. It enters into almost all situations in which one person attempts to influence another (see Chapter 16), but people are most responsive to suggestions from people of authority and prestige. Thus the therapist is in a good position to use suggestion. He may suggest that the patient has made enough progress in psychotherapy to be relieved of his nervous headaches, his nervous indigestion, or his fear of examinations, and the suggestion may be effective. In extreme conversion reactions, such as hysterical blindness or paralysis, the patient may undergo surgery, take bad-tasting medicines, or suffer other discomfort to alleviate his symptoms. In such cases the medical treatment, though of no value in itself, may have the effect of suggesting the removal of the symptom.

People are most suggestible when they are in a hypnotic state. For that reason early psychotherapists used hypnosis as a therapeutic technique. They would hypnotize the patient, and then give him *posthypnotic suggestions*—suggestions which would be effective after he awakened from the hypnotic sleep. A person suffering from hysterical paralysis of the right arm, for example, might be told under hypnosis, "When you wake up, you will be able to use your right arm. It will be completely normal again." Such suggestions as this would often work; the individual would not be paralyzed when he awoke.

One drawback of suggestion and hypnosis as aids in therapy is that many patients are difficult to hypnotize. Another shortcoming of suggestion is that it removes the symptom but not the cause. It neither produces insight nor removes the anxiety underlying the patient's symptom. Hence it does not solve his basic problem. Consequently, if symptoms are removed through suggestion, they usually appear again in somewhat different form. If neurotic headaches, for example, are alleviated through suggestion, the person

is liable to develop some other symptom, such as indigestion or backaches. For this reason, suggestive techniques are useful only in certain situations where it is important to give the patient temporary relief. If a mother has an intense fear of childbirth, for example, it may be possible through suggestion to get her through the experience without any serious disturbance.

Hypnosis has some diagnostic value in psychotherapy quite apart from the use of suggestion [Dorcus, 1956]. A person in a hypnotic state can often remember events that he has repressed and cannot recall in the normal state. The therapist may, indeed, be able to get the patient, under hypnosis, to relive terrifying experiences of the past that are now causing the patient trouble. In this way the therapist obtains necessary information to use in other phases of the treatment. Through posthypnotic suggestion, he may also be able to have the memories that have been revived under hypnosis carry over into the normal state. Thus hypnosis is a valuable technique in therapy, even though it usually does not itself effect any basic cure. The following case [based on Lecron and Bordeaux, 1947, pp. 211–212] illustrates the use of hypnosis:

A neurotic patient, Betty R., age 42, visited a psychiatrist with the complaint that she had to clear her throat every few minutes. She had had this compulsive symptom for many years. Besides being an annoyance and an embarrassment, it had kept her, she said, from becoming a successful singer. As a consequence she was forced into employment in office work, which she hated.

Under hypnosis, she was able to trace the symptom back about twenty years. She was regressed to a time at about twenty-two years of age when she had had no throat trouble, then instructed to recount any emotional experiences she could recall. She remembered attending a picnic with her fiancé, whom she was soon to marry. The two had gone canoeing on a lake, the canoe had tipped over, and she, being unable to swim, had almost drowned. She was saved when her fiancé pulled her to the canoe, which she held onto until other help arrived. He, however, was a poor swimmer and, exhausted by his efforts, himself drowned.

Reliving this experience under hypnosis, the patient began choking as though she were swallowing water. After that, she started crying and said, "I love him so, I can't stand losing him, I just can't swallow it; it sticks in my throat." Then it dawned on her, "Why, that's the reason I clear my throat!" Whereupon the therapist ended the trance.

The insight achieved through hypnosis in this case greatly aided subsequent therapy. In time the symptom disappeared, and the patient's adjustment greatly improved.

CLIENT-CENTERED THERAPY. The directive techniques just described involve explanation, direction, and control of the patient's life. They are very useful in certain situations. Psychotherapists, however, have come gradually to realize that patients cannot make fundamental changes in their adjustment merely by being told to do so or by manipulating their environments. Rather, *for psychotherapy to be of deep and lasting benefit, the patient must learn how to solve his own problems.*

Modern therapies have therefore tended to become more *nondirective*. They establish a more permissive situation in which the patient is given freedom to express his attitudes (see Figure 6.6). The most nondirective of current techniques is known as *client-centered therapy*. This is designed not to solve any particular problem of the patient but to *provide an opportunity* for him *to develop* his own *improved methods of adjustment*. The following statement expresses this attitude [quoted from Rogers, 1951, pp. 48–49]:

It has seemed clear . . . that when the counselor perceives and accepts the client as he is, when he lays aside all evaluation and enters into the perceptional frame of reference of the client, he frees the client to ex-

FIGURE 6.6. The psychotherapeutic situation. The patient talks with the psychotherapist, and together they work to understand important facts leading up to the illness and to develop ways of working out the underlying problems [National Institute of Mental Health, Public Health Service, in cooperation with St. Elizabeths Hospital, Washington, D.C.]

plore his life and experience anew, frees him to perceive in that experience new meanings and new goals. But is the therapist willing to give the client full freedom as to outcomes? Is he genuinely willing for the client to organize and direct his life? Is he willing for him to choose goals that are social or antisocial, moral or immoral? If not, it seems doubtful that therapy will be a profound experience for the client. . . . To me it appears that only as the therapist is completely willing that any outcome, any direction, may be chosen—only then does he realize the vital strength of the capacity and potentiality of the individual for constructive action.

In general, client-centered therapy may be described as a therapy in which (1) the individual, not the problem, is the focus; (2) feelings rather than intellect are attended to; (3) the present is given greater attention than the past; and (4) emotional growth takes place in the therapeutic relationship.

The method begins with some explanation of the roles of the counselor and the client and indicates that they will work out the difficulties together. The therapist takes pains to establish a relationship that is warm and permissive, that is, without pressure to follow any prescribed course and without criticism or judgment of what the patient says. The counselor's main aim is to help the person express his feelings freely. In this process, the client gains the ability to accept his feelings without fear and gradually finds it possible to express feelings that were formerly repressed. He then begins to see new relationships in his emotional attitudes and to react positively to situations to which he formerly responded negatively.

The following interchange [quoted from Cameron and Magaret, 1951, pp. 564–565] between patient (P) and therapist (T) illustrates the emphasis upon emotional attitudes which distinguishes nondirective therapy. The patient is a young man who complained of recurring periods of tension and depression at a time when his imminent induction into the Army threatened his close relationship with his mother.

P. I went home, you know. I think I have, well, a better way of getting along with Mom. I mean, take the V-12 tests, for example. She seems to understand better or something. I mean, she said I could even enlist in the Air Corps if I wanted to, and she used to just cringe when I mentioned it.

T. So it seems as if you have a new understanding with her.

P. Well, I think we've reached a pretty good understanding now. It was funny . . . once around her, I got the same old feeling back I used to have when I was younger. For the past year or so, I just haven't been feeling anything, and now I got the same old feeling of love. I didn't think I could. I thought I was just cynical and hardened or something. With a different attitude you find things easier to take. (Pause) I don't know. (Long pause).

T. Feeling pretty tense about it, aren't you?

P. Yes. Is it that obvious?

T. I am aware of it, though I guess you'd rather I weren't.

P. Well . . . of course, maybe it was just because I spent such a short time at home, and Mom thought well, I was going away pretty soon, so she was more willing to hear my side. I don't know, really. I feel I am getting back to the understanding I had as a very small person.

T. Things feel more like they used to.

P. It's just a more pleasant relationship, that's all. Take an example like this. Mom used to scream if she saw me with a cigarette— tell me I couldn't smoke, and give me all sorts of reasons and everything. And this time when I was home she offered me one! I was simply bowled over. I just couldn't understand why. (Pause) I decided maybe she just realized I was growing up or something. Oh, she let me do little things. When I was fifteen, I worked one summer at a stock exchange. She let me do that all right, she let me go, but she didn't direct me to do it. There's never been any encouragement or guidance in getting out on my own—I just went. She let me go with a tear in her eye, you know.

T. When you wanted to do things yourself, get out on your own, there was always a tear. . . .

P. Boy, that's sure the truth! I never thought about that before, but it's sure the truth. You know, a kid doesn't realize how much effect his childhood has on him, does he? You think, well, I don't have those conflicts, I didn't have a tough adolescence, you think you're apart from all that, above it, somehow. . . . (Pause) So many of the other fellows act more, well, more cold toward their folks, I think I'll always need some sort of tie, somebody to come home to that I love.

Client-centered therapy has been effective in counseling college students and in treating normal people with problems of adjustment (such as marital and vocational problems) and with mild neuroses. It has not been so successful with dependent people and those with extreme emotional difficulties.

PSYCHOANALYSIS. Psychoanalysis is a system of therapy that is somewhat nondirective, but not so much as is client-centered counseling. Its main objective is *to help the patient achieve a deep understanding of his own mechanisms of adjustment and thereby to help him solve his own basic problems.* It is designed primarily for the treatment of neuroses, but has been used with a great variety of disorders [Alexander and French, 1946]. It is usually a long, time-consuming therapy that requires 1 hour a day for 6 months to 3 years. Therefore, it is usually worthwhile only for patients with extreme, deep-seated problems who can afford the time and expense of long treatment.

The term *psychoanalyst,* you will recall, refers to and should be reserved for a psychotherapist who follows certain teachings of Sigmund Freud. Such teachings include emphasis on free association as the basic technique of therapy and the use of the phenomenon of transference to analyze the source of a patient's problems. It also makes greater use of dream analysis than other forms of therapy. (We shall define these terms below.)

Free association. Psychoanalysis begins with the therapist's explaining the general procedure, aims, and purposes of the therapy. The patient is told that he should not expect recovery in a specific period of time, that his behavior and attitudes may depend upon emotional factors of which he is unaware, and that these must be traced back to their unconscious motivations, chiefly through *free association. He is required to say whatever comes to his mind regardless of how irrelevant or objectionable it may be.* Since letting the mind go is quite different from ordinary thinking, patients frequently take some time to become able to carry on in free association. The following [quoted from Cameron and Magaret, 1951, p. 571] is an example of free association taken verbatim from an interview:

The same thing applies to the fact that they told me some time ago about loss of sleep in the beginning of the night or the last part of the night and I insisted the first was . . . I noticed for two or three nights I began waking up at 2:30 and laying awake most of the night . . . of semi-conscious . . . two—three nights . . . is that done because I'm a creature of habit on account of the suggestion of my mind . . . or am I with a nervous disease. (Pause) Thought about nearly everything . . . in general—can't recall it—nothing relating to sex . . . tried to put it out of my mind and I fight to keep it out. Got the habit of thinking about things and would dream about them . . . tried to keep things out of my mind . . . like fighting on account of the past. My mind traced right on through these lights to the fifth floor and a blond woman . . . shows my mind runs on to sex and injury . . . things like how to avoid going up in high buildings . . . afraid of how high I'd go. Didn't want to tell anybody what my trouble was. Saw it was only a four- or five-story building so I consented. It didn't bother me . . . didn't seem a real test because it wasn't high. Still no confidence in myself . . . still in the dark as to my conflicts . . . two things, one "yes" and one "no." Decided I'd adopt the good because the bad was lashing me.

During free association, the patient often shows *resistance. This is an inability to remember important events in his past or to talk about certain anxiety-charged subjects.* A great part of the analyst's task is to deal with these resistances. By continuous free association, however, the patient goes beyond his unknown resistances and overcomes them. The situation cannot be forced, but the analyst may provide some interpretations. These interpretations are considered tentative and are revised as the free associations continue. The interpretations are not offered to provide solutions but rather to clear the path of the associations and to provide for the possibility of free flow for further understanding. In this respect, psychoanalysis is sometimes quite directive.

At any time, the patient may report dreams for analysis and understanding. *Dream analysis* is considered important because dreams may provide a short road to the unconscious. They are not, however, directly interpreted but are material for more free associations. In this connection, it is not the content of the dream as reported (manifest content) that is important but rather the motivational conflicts symbolized in the dreams (latent content). Of course, only some dreams have any special significance for psychotherapy.

In one extensive study of over 10,000 dreams, the things done by the dreamer in his dream were classified into different categories [Hall, 1951]. Five categories, depicted in the drawing of Figure 6.7, were movement (34 per cent), verbal (11 per cent), sedentary (7 per cent), visual (7 per cent), and antagonistic (3 per cent). Other categories of dreams occurring reasonably often were social (6 per cent), recreational (5 per cent), manual (4 per cent), endeavor (4 per cent), and obtaining something (3 per cent). Certain of these categories, e.g. antagonistic, endeavor, and obtaining something, are more likely than others to represent motivational conflicts.

Transference. The core of psychoanalytic therapy is the *transference* that gradually develops as the analysis proceeds. Transference is *a reenactment of previous relationships with people and principally of the parent-child relationship.* It really amounts to a generalization (page 198) to the therapist of attitudes acquired toward other people. It appears when the patient and therapist have established good rapport. The therapist may, for example, become a *father figure* and be regarded emotionally by the patient much as he regarded his father. This phenomenon is called transference because it is a transfer of attitudes from one person to another. When the emotions directed toward the therapist are those of affection and dependence, the transference is called *positive;* however, a hostile attitude may be dominant, and this is referred to as *negative* transference.

Transference is significant in two ways. First, if it is positive, it can help the patient overcome his resistances. It gives him a feeling of protection so that he has the courage to seek and find repressed thoughts. Secondly, it helps the analyst understand the patient's problem. The transference substitutes a conflict between the patient and the analyst for the patient's inner conflict. Thus the analyst gets a better look at the problem. He analyzes the transference and explains its nature to the patient. The following case [quoted from Garfield, 1957, p. 258] illustrates some aspects of the transference relationship:

At one stage in therapy, the patient in this case began to make excessive demands of the therapist, requesting special examinations, medications, extra appointments, and similar types of preferment. When attempts were made to discuss this pattern of behavior, the patient immediately accused the therapist of having no interest in him, of being rejecting, and of not really trying to understand him. In this instance the patient was exhibiting patterns of behavior which he had manifested previously in other life situations. He was

FIGURE 6.7. What people dream about. In a study of over ten thousand dreams, the investigator classified the actions performed by the dreamer into categories (see text). Five categories represented in the drawing are movement, verbal, sedentary, visual, and antagonistic.

relating to the therapist as he had related previously to significant persons in his past life, and was perceiving the therapist as he had perceived other figures in the past who could not comply with his insatiable demands. Part of the therapeutic task was to help the patient understand this behavior and the motivations back of it.

The approach to the termination of the analysis is indicated in a number of ways. The patient gives evidence of having cleared up the childhood memories that have been used as resistances for important motives. The analysis cannot, however, be terminated until the transference situation has been resolved. This transference must be broken and a normal doctor-patient relationship established. This is sometimes a most difficult thing to do.

We have now described three general systems of psychotherapy: directive therapies, client-centered therapy, and psychoanalysis. There are other systems of psychotherapy, but for the most part they combine, or put a different emphasis on, various features of these systems.

Special psychotherapies

In addition to the methods we have described, psychotherapy includes a large number of special procedures. Among them are three techniques that deserve at least a brief description here: (1) psychodrama, (2) play and release therapy, and (3) group therapy.

PSYCHODRAMA. The drama in some form has been used in mental healing since ancient times. Its therapeutic values were mentioned by many philosophers, and there is evidence that, in the ancient theater, plays were sometimes presented for their therapeutic effects. *Psychodrama,* however, is a specialized technique designed *to permit patients to act out roles, situations, and fantasies related to their problems* [Moreno, 1946]. It thus affords something not normally provided by therapies in which the patient is treated alone and is able to express his feelings only in words. Psychodrama, by contrast, enables the person to express himself in realistic situations by acts, rather than mere words. It also treats the individual in social situations resembling those that in the past have been a source of his difficulties.

Usually in psychodrama, the patient may act out real situations or fantasies freely, spontaneously, and without limitation (see Figure 6.8). Trained therapeutic actors help him get started and play the roles of people significant in his problems. The patient may act out not only those situations he has experienced, but those he has feared and

FIGURE 6.8. Psychodrama, a special technique in psychotherapy. Under the guidance of members of the professional staff, patients use psychodrama to work out various problems in human relationships in front of a small audience of other patients [National Institute of Mental Health, Public Health Service, in cooperation with St. Elizabeths Hospital, Washington, D.C.].

evaded. He may portray at times himself and at other times the part of those influential in his life. As the therapy proceeds, it may become evident that he avoids certain roles and situations, and it may be necessary to direct him to live through scenes that are painful or undesirable. Psychodrama thus provides some of the same opportunities for free association and reliving of experiences as does psychoanalysis, but psychodrama uses the vehicle of the play to do it. From time to time, the therapist may analyze and interpret the situations that have been acted out.

The therapy may be carried on with or without an audience. In some situations the audience is allowed to participate in the performance and consequently acts as an aid to the therapy. In other instances the audience may be made up of patients who may themselves be the object of the therapy, since many of their own problems will be dramatized. Much of the success of this therapy depends upon a very astute chief therapist and a carefully trained staff of assistants. Even under these circumstances, however, many patients find it impossible to participate in such a dramatic procedure.

PLAY AND RELEASE THERAPY.   Recognizing that play provides unusual opportunities for relieving tension and achieving insight, therapists have devised a variety of techniques known as *play* or *release therapy* [Rogerson, 1939]. Such techniques are best employed with children. They utilize play with toys, puppet shows, drawing, modeling, and a variety of other activities (see Figure 6.9).

The greatest value of play technique is in the study of personality. The child often cannot or will not explain himself in the first person, yet he may reveal much of his inner life if allowed to play freely with toys. The child who will not tell about his own fears and conflicts may quite easily project these feelings into the dolls that he plays with. Feelings of rejection, insecurity, ambivalent attitudes toward parents, repressed hatreds, fears, and aggressions may all be freely revealed in play. Consequently, the play technique, when properly handled, may offer opportunities for understanding the child that are otherwise difficult to secure.

The play situation may also be therapeutic. In the security and permissiveness of play, the child may release feelings without fear of reprisal and thus may relieve tension. A carefully conducted play situation allows the child's feelings to come to the surface and thus helps him to learn to face them, control them, or abandon them. To the extent that the play situation is a miniature of the real one, desensitization can take place.

GROUP THERAPY. For some years now, the number of trained psychotherapists has not been sufficient for the care of all those who may profit from treatment. Partly for this reason, methods have been devised for the treatment of groups. [Klapman, 1946]. *Group therapy,* as this treatment is called, is more, however, than an economy measure; it also has values of its own. Since the patient's difficulties are frequently those of interpersonal relationships, the group serves as a therapeutic unit through which patients may be reeducated in the techniques of social adjustment.

Group therapy is sometimes a supplement to individual therapy, sometimes a substitute for it, and sometimes a sequel to it. A patient who has been under individual therapy may begin or continue group therapy when it seems to be doing him more good than individual treatment.

There are many variations of group therapy, but the usual type *consists in assembling the group under the guidance of a therapist for meetings of about an hour's duration.* The therapist attempts to remain in the background, permitting individuals in the group to talk freely. As the group conversation progresses, certain members of the group may discuss their own problems and symptoms. The perspectives of the other members are presented, and this leads gradually to each one interposing some of his own experiences, attitudes, and feelings. Certain members of the group inevitably profit more than others, but most receive some benefit. Merely learning that their own problems are not unique is of some value. The opportunity to view situations and atti-

tudes from a variety of perspectives is also helpful. It may help the individual to relieve his feelings of isolation and rejection, overcome his self-consciousness, modify a too strict conscience, give vent to aggressions, and obtain substitute gratifications.

Another value of the group method is the support it can provide. In individual therapy, some patients find dependence intolerable and are unable to accept the therapist's support. Others accept support too readily and react unfavorably when it is withdrawn. In group therapy, the members of the group support and depend upon one another, without having an obligation to any single person.

In individual therapy the situation is somewhat artificial, because the patient expresses himself to one person and is left

FIGURE 6.9. Release therapy. Emotionally disturbed adolescents release some of their feelings in finger painting [Life Magazine, © Time, Inc.].

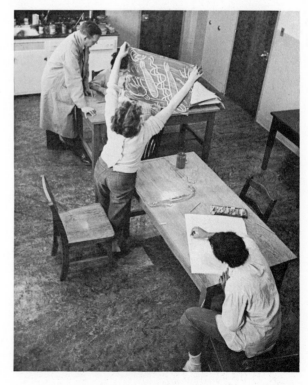

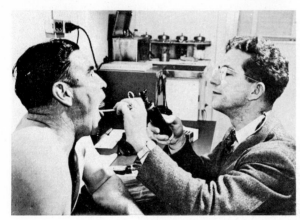

FIGURE 6.10. Patients in a mental hospital are given comprehensive examinations. Before embarking on a course of therapy, information is gathered on the patient's problem, life history, family background, and physical condition. A social worker, trained in sociology and case work, talks with members of the patient's family about his problems and life history. There is a complete medical examination. Brain waves are recorded and studied to determine whether a tumor, epilepsy, or other brain disorder is present. Psychological tests are given. The therapist interviews the patient. [(Top and bottom) National Institute of Mental Health, Public Health Service, in cooperation with St. Elizabeth's Hospital, Washington, D.C. (Middle) Standard Oil Company, New Jersey.]

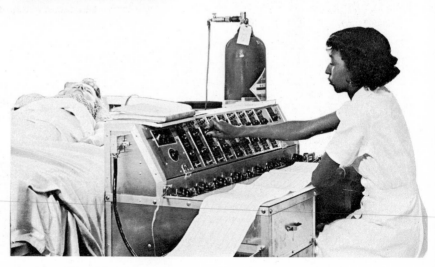

uncertain of how others will react to him. In the group, his emotional expression takes place in a situation resembling the social environment, with the members of the group representing people with special meanings for each patient. The situation thus is more real, allowing feelings to be expressed more as they are in everyday life.

Success depends partly upon the wisdom of the therapist. He must for the most part remain in the background, but he must know when to intervene, not only to provide necessary guidance, but also to prevent deleterious verbal attacks by one patient on another. He must also be skillful enough not to take over the situation and kill the spontaneity of the group.

The method has been most successful when used to supplement individual therapy or to continue treatment begun in individual therapy.

[David Linton]

Personal adjustment

Mental health, we have seen, is America's No. 1 health problem. Recognizing this, leaders in many walks of life are bending their efforts to do something about it. Research on mental health has been greatly expanded by hospitals, universities, government, and other agencies. Campaigns have been under way to educate the general public concerning the nature and magnitude of mental health problems. Many states and cities have established clinics to which children and adults can go with their adjustive problems and receive professional aid. The general purpose of the clinics is to detect emotional problems in their early stages and thereby prevent their becoming serious. Many colleges have established psychological clinics to aid students. Courses entitled mental hygiene, adjustment, etc., are being offered more widely, both in high schools and colleges and for adults in evening programs. These concerted efforts on many fronts should contribute to a general improvement in mental health.

In the end, of course, mental health is an individual problem. It is the individual who has the problem, and it is the individual who must solve the problem. Each person must learn for himself how to achieve and maintain satisfactory adjustments. Clinics,

[Mental Health Film Board]

counselors, therapists, friends, and literature can help, but they do so only by helping the person to help himself. The student who has read this chapter and the preceding one should now have a better understanding of the mental health problem and be in a position to help both others and himself. To round out this understanding, the student should be acquainted, not only with the symptoms of poor mental health, and with methods of treating it, but also with the characteristics of good mental health and of the well-adjusted personality. That is what this last section discusses. In it we cannot hope to give advice that guarantees a sound personal adjustment. We can, however, point out some of the characteristics of the well-adjusted person. Knowing them may aid the student in achieving a better personal adjustment for himself.

REALITY PRINCIPLE.   Probably the most general characteristic of the well-adjusted person is that he is "realistic" about himself. He does not fool himself greatly about his own motives, he sets goals for himself that are reasonably attainable, and he avoids unnecessary conflicts. This means that he tries to find out what he can realistically expect to achieve and adjusts his efforts and goals accordingly. He faces his personal problems objectively, much as one would go about solving a problem in arithmetic, fixing a car, or building a house. He acquaints himself with the relevant facts, makes sure that he understands what the problem is, then proceeds to make plans for solving it.

These, of course, are very general statements. Let us see more specifically how a well-adjusted person manages to deal realistically with his personal problems.

ACHIEVING SELF-UNDERSTANDING.   The maladjusted person, we have seen, is typically one who deceives himself about his real motives. He habitually practices self-deceit because he tries, with defense mechanisms, to avoid the anxiety arising from

conflict and frustration. If this is the picture of the maladjusted person, then naturally, the well-adjusted person is just the opposite.

Accepting anxiety. Healthy adjustment requires that we accept, rather than avoid, anxiety. Anxiety, being the natural outcome of experience with fear-provoking situations, can never be completely eliminated. By facing up to it, we accept it, and in the end, we have less of it.

The problem here is much like fear of dentists' chairs. Hardly anyone likes to have his teeth drilled, but some people live in mortal fear of it. Individuals, of course, differ in their sensitivity to pain, but it is doubtful whether differences of this kind have much to do with attitudes toward dentists. The important difference is one of accepting or avoiding the inevitable discomfort. Those who accept it find that it isn't so bad after all. Those who do not accept it find it ten times worse than it actually is. The same thing can be said of other situations we are anxious about. It has often been observed that the difference between the courageous soldier and the coward is that the courageous one accepts fear, while the coward lets himself be overcome by it. President Roosevelt's famous statement, "We have nothing to fear but fear itself," is another way of emphasizing this point.

Abandoning defense mechanisms. The well-adjusted person accepts a certain amount of anxiety; therefore, he also avoids using defense mechanisms to excess. These mechanisms are primarily defenses against anxiety; they are also characteristic of the maladjusted person. If one accepts and tolerates anxiety, there is little need to resort to defense mechanisms.

The adjusted person, in fact, can usually recognize, often with humor, his own tendencies to use defense mechanisms. The student who is inclined to blame his instructor for a poor grade can recognize that he is rationalizing for his failure to attend classes, keep good notes, or study. The person tempted to feel that his friends are turning against him can suspect himself of projecting his fears and dislikes to his friends. The practice of looking for such defense mechanisms can be carried too far, to the point of seeing them "under every bush." Nevertheless, recognizing them for what they really are puts one on guard against using them excessively.

Understanding motives. Since defense mechanisms are a smoke screen around one's motives, recognizing defense mechanisms puts one in a better position to understand and accept his own motives. Motives are not always easy to identify, but the well-adjusted person does a better job of it than the maladjusted one. When inclined to blame the instructor for a poor grade, he can ask himself, "What do I really want? What are my motives and goals?" An honest answer—at least a very human one—may be that he wants a good grade without doing any work. Admitting this to himself, he can see that such a combination of goals is usually unattainable. "Better get to work" or "I'll settle for a lower grade and less work" are then things he can decide without the hostility and anxiety aroused by blaming someone else.

Instructors, of course, are not infallible; they do err in assigning grades. This itself is something that needs accepting, for they almost always do their best to grade fairly. Our example serves its purpose, though, because students are far more often to blame for their poor grades than their instructors are.

ALTERING MOTIVES AND GOALS. The well-adjusted person is one who can alter his motives or goals without disguising them with defense mechanisms. Sometimes merely recognizing a motive permits one to discard it with ease. A person, for example, who continually rebels against authority, refusing to take directions from superiors and evading the rules of living, may quickly change his attitude if he realizes that his rebellion is really a reaction to an overbearing parent and that he is treating other people as though they were his father. Another per-

son, made aware of his strong prestige-seeking motives, may lose this strong interest in prestige.

Others may change their goals quite abruptly when they discover that they have taken over motives intact from other people. This may be true, for example, of vocational goals, which are often set for a young person by his parents. A boy may come to college with his heart set on being a doctor, only to be frustrated by lack of interest and ability in premedical work. After anxiety mounts to an acute stage, he may reexamine his goals and recognize that being a doctor is not his own goal at all. Then he is in a position to choose another vocational goal better suited to his own interests and abilities.

Understanding one's motives does not, on the other hand, guarantee that they will be discarded or that new, appropriate goals will be adopted. Patients in insight psychotherapy often achieve such an understanding without making much improvement. Insight, however, often makes it possible for the person to alter his motives and goals, and thus to improve his adjustment.

Not all changes in goals need to be radical ones. Some are matters of small degree. A student may settle for a B average, which he can attain, rather than be so frustrated and anxious striving for A's that he makes C's. Or he may choose a less prestigeful profession, or less remunerative job, that is less frustrating because it better suits his abilities and other motives.

REDUCING CONFLICT AND FRUSTRATION. Our society is so complex and our goals so elaborate that there is little chance, even under the best of circumstances, of being completely free of conflict and frustration. The well-adjusted person is mature enough to realize this, just as he learns to accept anxiety, and merely manages to keep conflict and frustration to a minimum. The techniques outlined in the following sections are some which serve this purpose.

Postponing satisfactions. One way to resolve a conflict, eventually, is to postpone the satisfaction of one of two competing motives. If an individual is both hungry and sleepy, he can eat first, then sleep. The student who wants excellent grades in college as well as some fun can study tonight and go out tomorrow night. The principle is simple enough. It means having a plan that postpones, but nevertheless provides for the satisfaction of, one motive until some foreseeable time. By this kind of scheduling, the conflict between motives is reduced and limited to relatively short periods of time.

Frustration tolerance. Postponing a satisfaction for a time, of course, leaves the person temporarily frustrated. Hence, he must be able to tolerate some frustration. Indeed, *frustration tolerance,* like the acceptance of anxiety, is the mark of a well-adjusted person. The healthy person accepts frustration as a normal reality of life. He learns that he cannot always have what he wants when he wants it. He stops fretting about what he cannot have and lets some of his less essential motives go unsatisfied. Once accepted for what it is, frustration is not nearly so frustrating.

Frustration tolerance, like habits and attitudes, can be acquired with practice. The individual starts with little things—the frustration of waiting for an overdue bus, of failure to find a parking place, or of being turned down for a date. When he can accept little frustrations with grace, he is ready to tackle bigger ones. The aim, of course, is not to duck problems that can be solved, but rather to tolerate the frustrations that are inevitable.

Expressing emotions. Some conflicts, we have seen, arise because emotions, particularly hostility, have been suppressed or repressed within the person. Through previous training, he has become unduly fearful of acting aggressively. The well-adjusted individual, on the other hand, is one who can express his feelings somewhat openly without fear of losing friends and alienating people. He realizes that other people expect occasional displays of impatience or anger and can take them in stride. He may even knowingly make others angry, but feel better by releasing his pent-up emotions. He manages to achieve some balance between the excessive and inconsiderate display of emotions, on the one hand, and complete restraint or repression of it, on the other.

The best way of doing this is to develop socially acceptable ways of expressing one's feelings. Without losing his temper, the skillful person can act sternly and state clearly what displeases him. By a joking retort, he can indicate displeasure and at the same time be good humored about it. By expressing emotions in a mature way, he manages not to lose the friendship and respect of others. This requires skill, and skill takes practice, but the well-adjusted person has usually learned it.

Useful work. Keeping occupied with useful work or other things is another mark of the healthy person. Most of the work one does, other than very repetitive activities, is directed toward some goal. It therefore provides the satisfaction of accomplishing something. It also takes one's mind off other things, pushing into the background motives that may cause conflict. Hence useful work is a double-barreled remedy: it satisfies certain motives while weakening others. By itself, of course, work is not a sure cure for conflict; some very maladjusted people work hard. Coupled with other measures, however, it helps a healthy person stay healthy.

Summary

1. Mental illness is the largest and most burdensome of health problems in the United States; persons suffering from mental illness occupy more than one-half of all hospital beds.

2. The relative proportion of the population in mental hospitals appears to remain relatively constant; this indicates that the genetic and environmental causes of mental illness are fairly stable. The relative incidence and the types of mental illness correlate with social class; severe, prolonged psychoses are more prevalent in the lower classes, neurotic disturbances in the upper classes.

3. The doctrine that mental illness represented possession by a devil was widely held until about one hundred and fifty years ago. During the past century and a half, however, the insane have been treated more humanely. The modern health movement, which attempts to understand and to help the mentally ill, is barely fifty years old.

4. The trend in therapy increasingly stresses psychological, rather than medical, methods of treatment, and is toward treating the mildly ill, and more readily treated, individual.

5. The treatment of an illness is called therapy. Therapy for mental illness is of two kinds: medical therapy and psychotherapy. Medical therapies consist of psychosurgery, shock therapy, narcosis, and chemotherapies. Of the first two, electroshock treatments are now the most widely used; narcosis and chemotherapy are employed more to make the patient available to psychotherapy than to produce any direct, beneficial results.

6. The aims of psychotherapy consist in some combination of (*a*) changing the situation, (*b*) providing support, (*c*) and achieving insight. The first two are effective with milder and more transient disturbances; insight therapy is usually required for major, long-lasting effects.

7. Three major varieties of therapy may be distinguished: directive therapies, client-centered therapy, and psychoanalysis. Directive therapy emphasizes changing the situation, reeducation of the individual, and desensitization to painful situations. Client-centered therapy provides a permissive situation for the patient, and attempts to help him talk out and solve his personal problem.

8. Psychoanalysis follows the teachings of Sigmund Freud. It emphasizes free association and makes use of transference of the patient's attitudes to the therapist. It may also employ dream analysis.

9. Psychodrama is a special technique that permits a patient to act out roles, situations, and fantasies in his life. Play and release therapy, used principally with children, encourages patients to exhibit their feelings in play situations. Group therapy, another special technique, permits troubled people to talk over their problems with one another under the guidance of a therapist.

10. Normal individuals may do much to improve their own personal adjustments by (*a*) attempting to achieve self-understanding, (*b*) altering their goals, and (*c*) learning various measures to reduce conflict and frustration.

11. Self-understanding is aided by (*a*) learning to accept and tolerate anxiety, (*b*) avoiding the use of defense mechanisms, and (*c*) attempting to understand one's own motives.

12. Goals may often be discarded when a person understands what they really are. Goals may also be set at more realistic and attainable levels, thereby eliminating unnecessary frustration.

13. Conflict and frustration may be minimized by (*a*) postponing satisfactions to a foreseeable time, (*b*) acquiring a frustration tolerance, (*c*) finding socially acceptable ways of venting emotions, and (*d*) keeping occupied with useful work.

Bernard, H. W. *Toward better personal adjustment*. New York: McGraw-Hill, 1951.
A text describing methods of making improved personal adjustments.

Bordin, E. S. *Psychological counseling methods*. New York: Appleton-Century, Crofts, 1955.
A textbook on counseling techniques used with individuals having minor personal problems.

Dollard, J., Auld, F., and White, A. M. *Steps in psychotherapy*. New York: Macmillan, 1953.
A case study of the progress of psychotherapy.

Dollard, J., and Miller, N. E. *Personality and psychotherapy*. New York: McGraw-Hill, 1950.
An analysis of personality and psychotherapy emphasizing the role of learning in personal adjustments.

Dorcus, R. M. (ed.). *Hypnosis and its therapeutic applications*. New York: McGraw-Hill, 1956.
A modern authoritative treatment, written by experts, of the nature and uses of hypnosis.

Freud, S. *The basic writings of Sigmund Freud* (ed. by A. A. Brill). New York: Modern Library, 1938.
A source book on the methods and theories of psychoanalysis.

Garfield, S. L. *Introductory to clinical psychology*. New York: Macmillan, 1957.
An elementary textbook describing methods of appraising personality and mental disorder, as well as psychotherapeutic methods.

Ingham, H. V., and Love, L. R. *The process of psychotherapy*. New York: McGraw-Hill, 1954.
A general summary of the practice of psychotherapy.

McKinney, F. *Psychology of personal adjustment* (rev. ed.). New York: Wiley, 1949.
A text, written for college students, on problems of improving personal adjustments.

Moreno, J. L. *The theatre of spontaneity: an introduction to psychodrama*. New York: Beacon House, 1947.
A description of psychodrama as a technique in psychotherapy.

Rogers, C. R. *Client-centered therapy*. Boston: Houghton Mifflin, 1951.
A description of the methods and results of nondirective, client-centered therapy.

Shaffer, G. W., and Lazarus, R. S. *Fundamental concepts in clinical psychology*. New York: McGraw-Hill, 1952.
A text on clinical psychology, covering diagnosis and psychotherapy.

Introduction

to psychology

PRINCIPLES
OF LEARNING

HUMAN
LEARNING
& FORGETTING

LANGUAGE
& THINKING

PART THREE
LEARNING & THINKING

Principles of learning

HOW DO ORGANISMS LEARN? Why do we learn some things easily and other things only with the greatest difficulty? How does the infant first learn? Why do some of us learn to adjust to our world and its demands, while others fail so badly at adjustment that they must be put in mental hospitals? What is the easiest way to learn the German irregular verbs?

Questions like these have probably occurred to you in the course of your studies or in reading the preceding chapters. We have already touched on the topic of learning in order to give an account of development, motivation, and emotion, but now we shall study it more systematically.

Learning is *any relatively permanent change in behavior that is a result of past experience.* This definition excludes behav-ioral changes that take place in maturation, and also changes due to disease or physical damage. Other behavioral changes resulting from experience involve learning.

It is sometimes difficult to grasp the full import of this statement because we have learned to take for granted an incalculable number of things that have been learned. Almost everything we do while we are awake has been learned. Many of our motives are learned, and so are our social values and traditions. And, of course, all that is taught in school and out, including the knowledge in this and other textbooks, was learned by somebody, sometime, somewhere.

Many psychologists therefore regard learning as *the* central process in understanding human behavior. In view of its importance, we shall devote two chapters to it. In this first chapter, we shall consider the factors involved in learning and the way it takes place in relatively naïve organisms such as animals and young children. In the next chapter, we shall consider the more sophisticated learning of older human beings—learning built upon prior learning—as well as specific problems of memorizing and forgetting. Throughout both chapters, we shall stress the learning process and leave it to the student to apply his understanding of this process to the situations that especially concern him.

Factors in learning

There are a great many phenomena of learning. All have technical names, and the conditions under which they occur are in many cases rather complicated. The student can easily become lost in a profusion of terms if he has no framework to put them in. Many of the phenomena, however, involve the same or similar factors combined in slightly different ways. By first considering the factors that are common to many learning phenomena, it will be easier to understand the phenomena when we describe them in detail. That, therefore, is the way we shall begin.

ASSOCIATION. One factor that is common to all situations in which learning takes place is *association*. The term "association," as used here, means some connection in time and place between two events. The connection usually first exists in the physical world. Fires and many other things that light up, for example, are hot. Hence the physical events of light and heat are often connected. Lightning and thunder usually occur together, and so light and sound may be connected. These connections in the physical world provide opportunities for an organism to experience two events simultaneously or in close succession. As a result, a connection is formed within the brain, and this is called an association.

We have not yet discovered what this association in the brain is [Lashley, 1950]. It very probably is not a simple connection like that formed when two wires are connected. It is more complicated than that. All we can say at present is that the process in the brain representing one event becomes associated with the process representing the other event. What this means is that, once an association has been formed, the arousal of one process gives rise to, or tends to arouse, the second process in the absence of any physical event to set off the second process. Put in symbolic form (see Figure 7.1), if S_1 and S_2 are two events in the physical world, and s_1 and s_2 are the corresponding processes in the brain, the occurrence of S_1 and S_2 together will tend to form an association of processes in the brain such that s_1 can arouse s_2 or s_2 can arouse s_1.

Sensory associations. This conception of learning was first formulated by English philosophers during the nineteenth century. The conception was called *associationism*, and they were called *associationists*. They regarded the experience s_1 aroused by the external event S_1 as a sensation, and the process s_1 aroused by S_2 in the absence of S_1 as an *idea*. An idea in this sense has also been called an *image*. The associationists then attempted to formulate laws stating the conditions under which ideas were learned by association.

Late in the nineteenth century, when experimental work on learning got under way, the language of associationism was revamped, because rigorous experimentalists could not experiment with "ideas" or "images." Although the inference that the processes aroused in sensory association are often ideas or images is probably correct (see Chapter 9), it was all too easy to lapse into loose, untestable speculation about the properties of ideas. For this reason, we stopped talking about the association of ideas and began referring simply to association, sensory association, or to *S-S* association, meaning association between two stimuli [Spence, 1951].

In the heyday of behaviorism (see page 9), those of the behaviorist persuasion went so far as to argue that there was no association between sensory experiences, and that all association was between a stimulus and a response. In recent years, however, we have had ample demonstration in our experiments that there is indeed some kind of sensory association—an association between the processes in the brain representing stimulus events the person has experienced. We shall consider some of this evidence later in the section on perceptual learning.

Stimulus-response associations. Another kind of association, an *S-R* or stimulus-response association, is more easily studied. In this case, the organism experiences two events S_1 and S_2 simultaneously or nearly so, as in sensory association, but makes some response, let us say R_2, to one of the events. R_2 is the response made to S_2 before any experience with S_1 and S_2 as connected physical events. If in time S_1 comes to call out R_2, we can be certain that an association has been formed between S_1 and R_2.

There are numerous experiments illustrating this point, some of which will be described below, but there are many everyday examples of it. One is learning the vocabulary of a foreign language. Suppose I present the following pairs of words to a person who knows English but no German:

dog	*Hund*
house	*Haus*
man	*Mann*
boy	*Knabe*

I say "dog—*Hund*," "house—*Haus*," etc. Each English word is an S_1 and the corresponding German word is an S_2. I then ask the person to say the German word of each pair right after I say it. His response is the R_2. After he has had sufficient practice, I test him by saying "dog" and having him respond with "*Hund*," and so on. If he can give this response, he has formed an associ-

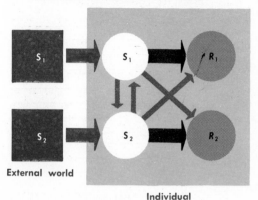

FIGURE 7.1. A schematic diagram of the associations formed in sensory-sensory (**S-S**) and stimulus-response (**S-R**) learning.

ation between S_1 and R_2—a stimulus-response association.

S-R associations lend themselves nicely to objective observation, and for this reason, they have received the greatest attention in our experiments. *S-S* associations can be studied only in roundabout ways, and therefore, they have been relatively neglected. Indeed, some psychologists have attempted to explain all association as *S-R* association, and this is one of the points on which theorists still disagree. There is an increasing body of evidence, however, that both kinds of association are formed. It may very well be that any kind of association, *S-S*, *S-R*, *R-R*, or *R-S*, can take place in the brain. Of this, however, we are not yet sure.

Contiguity. The concept of association, it is to be noted, implies *contiguity*. That is to say, for two physical events to be connected, and hence for the corresponding processes in the brain to become associated, they must occur in approximately the same time and place. They must be contiguous events. For that reason, contiguity has long been stated as a basic law governing the formation of associations.

But this raises the question of what is contiguous. Just how close in time do events have to be to become associated? How close spatially? Both questions can be, and have been, answered experimentally. Specific answers depend on a variety of experimental conditions, but in general two stimuli or a stimulus and response must be no more than a few seconds apart for them to become associated. Ideally, they should be no more than half a second apart, but some association may take place with wider gaps [Kimble, 1956]. Apparently the processes generated in the brain last only briefly, and it is necessary for the two processes to exist nearly simultaneously for association to occur.

Interference. Another aspect of forming associations deserves emphasis. This is the possibility of interference among associations. One stimulus may become associated with two different stimuli or with two different responses. If the two associations with one stimulus are incompatible, one tends to block or interfere with the other.

The learning of two languages at the same time is an example. In an earlier chapter (page 62), we noted that children who are reared in bilingual homes are slower in language development than those who learn only one language at home. A child learns language by associating a word (R_1) with some stimulus (S_1). For example, he learns to associate "hot" with the sight of the fire on the stove or a lighted match. If he at the same time must also learn to associate *heiss* (German for "hot") or *chaud* (French for "hot"), he has two different associations (R_1 and R_2) with the same visual stimulus (S_1). He cannot say them both at the same time. Hence one association interferes with the other. Consequently, neither association is built up so rapidly as it might be.

This principle, that incompatible associations interfere with each other, is a general one. It accounts, as we shall see, for several of the phenomena of learning and forgetting.

MOTIVATION. Most associations are formed when a person or animal is motivated in some way. We teach a dog tricks by making him hungry and rewarding him with food when he does what we command him to. We usually can teach a child the meaning of "hot" only after he has burned himself a time or two and has associated the sight of fire with being burned; he is already motivated to avoid the fire. In almost any learning we can think of, we can identify some motivation to learn or at least a motivation that makes learning possible. Motivation is therefore a factor in learning that has received much well-deserved study.

A common way of teaching animals and children what we want them to do is to reward or punish their behavior. If they make the response we want, we reward them with food, fondling, or a kind word. If they make an undesired response, we punish them with a spanking, a word of reproof, or deprive them of something they want. By thus rewarding and punishing their responses, we may teach them in time to associate a particular response with a command or signal.

The factor of reward and punishment is of such obvious importance in learning that it was long ago dignified by being called the *law of effect* [Thorndike, 1932]. This law states that an act that has a satisfying effect, e.g., satisfaction of a drive, escape from punishment, or relief from fear, will be learned, but that an act that has an unpleasant effect, e.g., frustration of a drive, punishment, or fear, will not be learned.

Psychologists have puzzled over whether there is anything unique about reward and punishment that causes an association to be formed. Is it the reward or punishment that forms the association or is this effect more remote? One theory, the *drive-reduction* theory, states that the satisfaction or alleviation of drives is the crucial factor in determining what responses are learned [Sheffield and Roby, 1950]. Another theory, called the *association theory* after its kinship with British associationism, holds that there is nothing unique about reward and punishment. All they do is control behavior in such a way that associations may be formed.

The issue can be illustrated by a familiar example (see Figure 7.2). We try to teach a dog to stand up in response to a hand signal. We do this when the dog is hungry and we are prepared to feed him bits of food. We hold the food out of reach but in a position where the dog can stand and look up at it; then we drop a piece of food into his mouth while he is standing. We repeat this procedure until the dog has associated standing with "hand." The drive-reduction theorist would explain the dog's learning by saying that the satisfaction of obtaining food somehow caused the response of standing to be associated with "hand." The associationist, however, would explain it by saying that all the food did was cause the animal to stand so that standing and sight of the hand were contiguous and therefore could become associated.

This is an issue that will come up later. We are introducing it now only so that we can refer to it when the occasion arises. In any case, whatever the explanation, motivation helps make it possible for associations to be formed.

VARIABILITY. Motivation is important in learning in still another way. It increases variability of behavior so that the possibilities of making a response that can be associated with a stimulus or situation are increased (see Figure 7.3).

A baby that is hungry becomes restless and cries, thereby commanding attention and getting food. At first, the crying is just an inborn response to hunger, but in time it is associated with being fed. Hence the child comes to associate the response of crying with getting attention and being fed, whether or not he is otherwise uncomfortable enough to cry. Similarly, animals that are hungry become active and forage about, exploring their environments. This increases the chances of their finding food, and if they do, the stimulus situation connected with food is associated with being hungry. Hence they learn what to do to find food when they are hungry.

These examples need not be restricted to the physiological drives. The same point also applies to the general drives of curiosity, exploration, and fear. Curiosity and exploratory drives bring the individual into wider contact with his environment, and thus enlarge the associations that may be formed. A fear drive usually is accompanied by fright reactions or at least by random, uncoordinated behavior. These reactions can be associated with getting away from the fear-provoking situation.

Motivation, then, is an aid to learning because it produces variable behavior, and certain aspects of this behavior can become associated with the situations in which the behavior takes place.

Association is a basic process in learning, and motivation is often an important condition for learning. There are circumstances, however, in which reward and punishment

FIGURE 7.2. Standing on signal. "Tricks" like this are learned by associating food with the cue of the outstretched hand. One theory says the learning occurs because food reward satisfies or reduces the hunger drive. Another theory holds that food merely gets the animal to behave so that his behavior is associated with the cue [J. V. Rae].

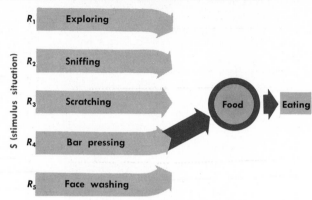

FIGURE 7.3. Variability of response in a hungry dog makes possible the selective rewarding of a particular response and hence the learning of that response [after Kimble, 1956].

do not seem to be significant and in which association between two stimuli, or a stimulus and response, is likewise not readily identified. Under these circumstances, we see at work some other factors of importance in learning.

HABITUATION. In one set of conditions, we can observe habituation.

Suppose that we have an animal in a cage—a dog, cat, rabbit, or rat—and suddenly sound a loud siren hidden in the floor of the cage. The chances are that the animal will respond with a fright reaction, such as crouching or dashing about the cage. If, however, we sound the siren at regular intervals, the animal slowly becomes accustomed to it and acts less and less frightened. This change in the animal's behavior is called *habituation* and is a simple kind of learning. It is merely learning not to respond to a situation that proves harmless. We can sometimes see this habituation in a child, as it loses its fear of strange objects (page 106), but we see the process more commonly in animals when they are being tamed.

Something like habituation can be seen in learned fears. A person who has learned to be afraid of the water or of high places may gradually lose his fear of them by being around them a great deal. In this case, the process is called *extinction*, for a learned

association becomes extinguished (see next section). Or if habituation is used deliberately to help a person get over a fear, it is sometimes called *desensitization*, which refers to the fact that the person becomes less sensitive to the fear-producing situation. Often it is difficult to distinguish between simple habituation and extinction or desensitization, especially when we do not know the person's learning history. In the pure case, however, habituation means gradually "getting used to," or learning not to respond to, situations in which there is a natural, unlearned response.

SENSITIZATION. Closely related to habituation—in fact, almost its opposite—is a process called *sensitization*.

Suppose that in the example above we have gotten our animal subject habituated to the sound of a siren. When the siren comes on, the animal no longer responds to it but goes about his business in the cage. Now suppose that through a grid in the floor of the cage we give the animal a few electric shocks. After that, if we sound the siren again, we will find that the animal again shows its original fright reaction. The shock has made the animal more "sensitive" and thus has reinstated responses that had died out.

What has happened is that the general

alertness or sensitivity of the individual has been increased by the shock without any association between the shock and siren. We often see the same sort of sensitization when a person becomes "jumpy" or unduly sensitive to annoyances because something else of importance has gone wrong.

This process has sometimes been called *pseudoconditioning* or pseudolearning because it may appear that an association has been formed between the siren and the shock when it really has not. We can prove this by presenting the shock a number of times without sounding the siren, then later sounding the siren separately, thus never giving the siren and shock a chance to become associated.

IMPRINTING. We have elsewhere described imprinting (page 50) as a rapid kind of learning that has been demonstrated in some animals, notably birds. Soon after it is hatched, a chick or gosling starts following the sound and movement of its mother, but it can be imprinted on almost any other object. The response of following an object is one that emerges through maturation; it is not learned. What is learned is the particular object to which the following response is attached. The young bird learns to follow its mother; or in experiments, it may follow a model or the experimenter (see Figure 7.4). Hence it is a discrimination among objects that is learned, not a sensory association or a response per se.

We still need to know much more about imprinting before coming to any final conclusions about it. Fear seems to play an important part in it, for animals that are not imprinted at the proper time are thereafter considerably more fearful of strange objects and movements. Also animals treated with tranquilizing drugs at the time they are given imprinting experiences do not imprint very well [Hess, 1959]. It is possible then that the following response relieves fear, and that this fear reduction becomes associated with the object which is first followed. In any case, it is an interesting instance of

FIGURE 7.4. Imprinting of goslings. The goslings have been imprinted on the experimenter, Dr. Konrad Lorenz. Though he carries a food bucket, his rhythmic sounds, not hunger, keep them with him. [Life Magazine, © 1955, Time, Inc.]

learning that occurs rapidly, at a very young age, and is closely tied to instinctive tendencies.

INHIBITION. One of the things that characterizes almost all behavior, learned or otherwise, is a tendency for responses to wane after they have been going on for some time. If we repeatedly elicit a reflex, such as an eyeblink or a knee jerk, in rapid succession, the reflex tends to become weaker on succeeding occasions. A dog that is a good retriever soon gets tired if we keep throwing the ball immediately after he has retrieved it. And a child tires of one toy after a while, and turns to another. We

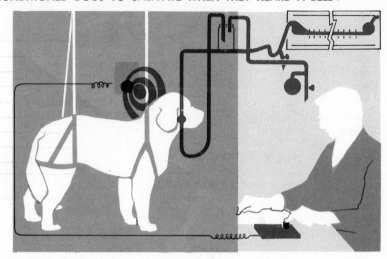

FIGURE 7.5. Pavlov's apparatus for studying the conditioned salivary response. Saliva is collected and measured by means of a tube attached to a suction cup placed in the dog's cheek near one of the salivary glands. The apparatus is in a soundproof room with a one-way vision screen between the experimenter and the dog. The experimenter can sound a bell and present food by remote control [after Pavlov, 1928].

could multiply almost endlessly examples in which an organism tends to tire of making the same response over and over again.

This tendency is so general that psychologists have postulated that the repetition of a response builds up an *inhibition* of that response. The inhibition is comparable to the fatigue we experience in doing heavy work, yet it is not physical fatigue in the usual sense, for it occurs where the effort involved is insignificant. It is more like boredom than fatigue. As we shall see, it is an important factor in learning, as well as in remembering and forgetting. It is not itself learning because it diminishes with time and rest. Yet it may be learned if conditions are so arranged that it can be associated with particular stimuli and responses.

There may be several kinds of inhibition. At least, psychologists have sometimes distinguished more than one kind. In any case, inhibition is a concept that helps us understand the phenomena of learning and forgetting.

The various factors discussed in this section provide a general introduction to the topic of learning. These factors are of varying importance in different learning situations. Now that we are familiar with them,

it will be much easier to describe and understand the phenomena of learning.

There are several different ways to classify learning, although none is completely satisfactory. For our purposes, we may distinguish three general classes of learning: classical conditioning, instrumental learning, and perceptual learning. These will constitute three of the remaining sections of the chapter. There is no sharp line between these three kinds of learning. Moreover, some instances of learning are clearly mixtures of more than one kind. Avoidance learning, for example, has elements of both classical conditioning and instrumental learning. Maze learning combines features of all three but particularly instrumental and perceptual learning. A section will be devoted to each of these hybrids.

Classical conditioning

Classical conditioning gets its name from the fact that it is the kind of learning originally studied about fifty years ago in the classical experiments of Ivan P. Pavlov (1849–1936). This famous Russian physiologist introduced the concept of conditioning and established many of its basic principles. Sometimes classical conditioning is called

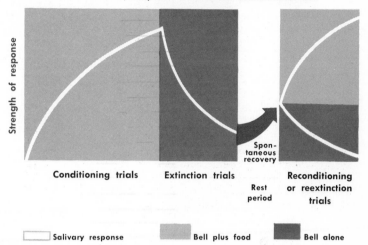

FIGURE 7.6. A schematic diagram of the course of conditioning, extinction, and spontaneous recovery [after Kimble, 1956].

Strength of response

Conditioning trials   Extinction trials   Reconditioning or reextinction trials

Spontaneous recovery

Rest period

☐ Salivary response   ▨ Bell plus food   ■ Bell alone

respondent conditioning because it involves a simple reflexlike response to a specific stimulus. We shall describe a number of Pavlov's experiments as a way of presenting a picture of the phenomena of classical conditioning.

CONDITIONING. You have probably had the experience of "watering at the mouth" when you smelled, saw, or even imagined appealing food. This phenomenon, in brief, is the one Pavlov [1927] worked with.

Pavlov devised an apparatus (see Figure 7.5) for measuring the flow of saliva. It consisted in part of tubes running from a suction cup attached to a dog's cheek arranged in such a way that it collected drops of saliva flowing from a salivary duct. The saliva displaced air in the tube and this in turn displaced a colored fluid in a calibrated instrument, which looked somewhat like a thermometer and from which very minute changes could be read. He placed the dog in a harness in a soundproof room equipped with a one-way screen through which he could see the dog, but not vice versa. By remote control, he could swing a food pan out within the dog's reach and thus reward it with food at will. He could also present the dog with

several kinds of stimuli, including the sounds of a bell, buzzer, or metronome.

In a typical experiment, he began training the dog by sounding a bell, immediately afterward presenting food, then measuring the amount of saliva secreted. After doing this a few times, he tested the effects of the training by measuring the saliva that flowed when he presented only the bell without food. He resumed the paired presentation of bell and food a few more times, and then tested with the bell alone. He found that as the training proceeded, the amount of saliva secreted in response to the bell alone gradually increased, and that this could be plotted as a learning curve.

Figure 7.6 presents such a learning curve, drawn without specifying the number of trials or the amount of saliva, for these do not concern us now. The curve (first section only) shows that pairing the bell and food gradually increased the amount of saliva secreted. It traces the course of acquiring an association between the bell and the salivary response.

Before going further, we should note certain terms that refer to the phenomena of conditioning (see Figure 7.7). Pavlov called the salivary response to food the *uncondi-*

tioned response, because it occurs without any learning. For a similar reason he called the food the *unconditioned stimulus.* The bell was two things: At the beginning of the training, it was a *conditioning stimulus,* for it was being used to condition the salivary response. After conditioning had taken place, it was called the *conditioned stimulus,* because it now had an effect it did not have before, namely, eliciting the salivary response. After conditioning, the salivary response also had a new name, the *conditioned response,* for it had now become conditioned to the sound of the bell. Pairing the unconditioned stimulus (food) with the conditioning stimulus (bell) was called a *conditioning procedure.*

EXTINCTION. Next, with a dog fully conditioned, Pavlov changed to a procedure, called an *extinction procedure,* which produces a phenomenon called *extinction.* Extinction may be illustrated as follows:

The dog was placed in the stock in the usual way. The bell was presented without the food as it was in the test trials of the conditioning procedure. In this case, however, the bell was never accompanied by food. On trial after trial, the dog heard only the bell and never saw or received food. The saliva was measured on each trial in the usual way. As the procedure was continued, the amount of saliva secreted gradually became smaller and smaller until it became relatively constant at a level little different from that at which it had been before the original conditioning. A schematic curve, showing the general course of this process, is shown in Figure 7.6.

Extinction, then, undoes the work of conditioning. It appears to weaken the association between the bell and salivary response, just as conditioning strengthened the association. We say "appears" because we shall have to qualify this statement later.

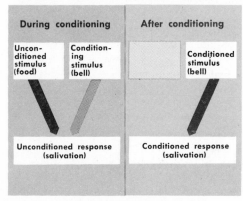

FIGURE 7.7. A schematic diagram of the conditioning process. During conditioning, a neutral stimulus (bell), called the conditioning stimulus, is paired with an unconditioned stimulus (food), which evokes an unconditioned response (salivation). As a consequence of conditioning, the bell becomes a conditioned stimulus that can evoke salivation (now the conditioned response) in the absence of the unconditioned stimulus.

REINFORCEMENT. The difference between a conditioning procedure and an extinction procedure is the presentation of the unconditioned stimulus (food) following the bell. This difference accounts for whether an association is strengthened or weakened. Pavlov therefore concluded that some reinforcement was necessary to build up and maintain a conditioned response. In this case, he called the unconditioned stimulus the *reinforcement.* From this experiment, we can derive a now well-established principle of learning, the *principle of reinforcement.* This principle is that *reinforcement is necessary for the formation of a conditioned response;* without reinforcement, the response is not formed, or if it is, it declines in strength and is extinguished. Reinforcement in this case may be defined as the presentation of the unconditioned stimulus (food), which evokes the unconditioned response (salivation) immediately following the conditioning stimulus (bell). The principle of reinforcement has been extended to instrumental learning, but we shall find that this requires a somewhat different definition of reinforcement.

Note that the reinforcement in this case is really a food reward. Hence reinforcement is a term that covers the use of reward in learning. Food is the thing that satisfies a primary physiological drive. Hence food reward can be called *primary reinforcement*. We shall see that learned goals may also serve as reinforcements in conditioning and learning, in which case we speak of *secondary reinforcement*.

SPONTANEOUS RECOVERY. Another phenomenon, called *spontaneous recovery,* may be demonstrated in experiments on conditioned responses. This term refers to the fact that a conditioned response that has been extinguished as the result of an extinction procedure may spontaneously recover some of the strength lost in extinction after an interval of rest following extinction. If, for example, a dog in whom the conditioned response has been extinguished is brought back into the experimental situation and the presentation of the bell is resumed, the amount he salivates is considerably greater than it was at the end of the previous series of extinction trials. Thus he now shows that there is some association left between the bell and salivation and that the conditioning has not been entirely erased. This is one reason why we said earlier that extinction "appears" to undo the work of conditioning.

It is possible, as indicated in Figure 7.6, to reextinguish the conditioned response by giving the dog another series of extinction trials, again bringing the response down to practically zero. After this, another rest may be followed by some spontaneous recovery, although not so much this time as before. By repeated reextinctions, the conditioned response may eventually be extinguished more or less completely and permanently.

This raises the question of what is going on in extinction. Are the associations that were formed in conditioning weakened? The answer depends on what one means by "weakened." Extinction does not subtract what has been added in conditioning. Rather, two factors, both mentioned in the preceding section, seem to be at work. One is *interference*—the learning of a new association that interferes with the original one. This is learning not to respond—at least not in a particular series of trials. Such an association, of course, is the opposite of the original one and hence competes with it. Another factor is *inhibition*—a tendency not to respond. This factor is probably also at work during original conditioning, diminishing the rate at which associations can be formed, but we usually have no way of disentangling it from the positive effects of conditioning.

Inhibition, we have seen, wears off in time. On this basis alone we would expect some spontaneous recovery. Moreover, when the animal is brought back to the experimental situation, it has no way of "knowing" whether this is a conditioning session or an extinction session. Since it has learned two associations, one of responding and the other of not responding, we might expect some tendency to respond to carry over from the conditioning session. This too would predict spontaneous recovery.

Of one thing we can be sure: extinction does not merely weaken the association formed in conditioning. This point is demonstrated by the fact of spontaneous recovery. It is also brought out if we undertake to recondition the animal, that is, to provide again the reinforcement given in original conditioning. Pavlov did this type of study, and the general results he obtained are shown in Figure 7.6. It can be seen that if a conditioning procedure follows an extinction procedure, reconditioning proceeds at a faster rate than it did in original conditioning. Indeed, an experimenter can condition, extinguish, condition, and extinguish alternately, and each time, up to a certain point, the animal will condition a little faster and extinguish a little faster than the time before. This shows that the original conditioning is not erased by extinction; instead what is taking place is a learning both to respond and not to respond. The animal is learning when to do one or the other.

This point has an important bearing on the theory of forgetting to be considered in the next chapter. It also is related to the rather striking phenomena we encounter in *partial reinforcement,* to be described later in this chapter (page 202).

STIMULUS GENERALIZATION.   Pavlov discovered very early that if he conditioned an animal to salivate to a bell, it would also salivate to the sound of a buzzer or the beat of a metronome, though to a lesser degree. Thus the animal tended to *generalize* the conditioned response to stimuli that were different from, but somewhat similar to, the one to which it was specifically conditioned. Although Pavlov described generalization of conditioned responses, the example of generalization we shall use does not come from Pavlov's laboratory but is a study [Hovland, 1937] of the conditioned galvanic skin response (GSR) in man. The student will recall from Chapter 4 that the GSR is a reflex of the sweat glands that appears in emotion. It may be evoked very easily by giving a subject an unpleasant electric shock.

In this experiment, an electric shock was the unconditioned stimulus (reinforcement) for the GSR. The experimenter began by conditioning the subject's GSR to the sound of a pure tone of a particular pitch. This was done by presenting the shock and the pure tone (the conditioning stimulus) simultaneously, or nearly so. After the GSR had been conditioned to this tone, the investigator measured the amount of conditioned GSR given to tones that were of pitches *different* from that of the original tone (now the conditioned stimulus). Figure 7.8 is a graph of the results of this experiment. The tone that was used in the original conditioning evoked the largest GSR,

and tones with pitches closer to it evoked larger GSRs than did tones with pitches more different. Thus the *greater the similarity between stimuli,* the *greater* the generalization between them.

Many responses and characteristics of people seem to be acquired through the processes of conditioning and generalization. The experiment with the GSR illustrates these processes. The GSR is a kind of index of emotional disturbance, and this is why it finds its way into lie detection (page 116). In the experiment above, the shock serving as an unconditioned stimulus elicited pain in the subject, and the conditioned stimulus elicited a fear of pain. This simple experiment serves as a model for the development of irrational fears in people. Such fears or phobias (page 147) are irrational because they are acquired through accidental conditioning to some stimulus, then generalized to situations that otherwise would not be frightening. The example of the conditioning of Albert, which we used in Chapter 4, is another case of such generalization. After conditioning to a white animal, he became fearful of all white furry objects, including a white beard.

HIGHER-ORDER CONDITIONING.   Pavlov also did something else in his experiments that helps us understand more complicated learned behavior. He discovered that he could use one conditioned response to build up another conditioned response and thus produce higher-order conditioning. One of his experiments went this way:

A dog was conditioned in the usual way to salivate to the sound of a metronome. After the dog was well conditioned, Pavlov stopped reinforcing him with food, as one would do in an extinction procedure. Before sounding the metronome, however, he thrust a card with a black square on it into the dog's view. And he did this repeatedly as in regular conditioning. After a few trials, he found that the dog started salivating when the card was presented, even though this card had never been paired with food. An association had therefore been formed between the black square and the conditioned salivary response to the metronome.

The black card in this instance was a second-order conditioned stimulus. The reinforcement for learning the conditioned response to the black card was not the primary reinforcement of food, but rather the conditioned stimulus. For this reason, the conditioned stimulus was called a *secondary reinforcement*. This is comparable to the secondary goal described in Chapter 3. There the learning situation was somewhat different, but the principle was the same. Poker chips were associated with food, and the chimps learned a new response to obtain poker chips. Here, in the conditioning of the dog, the stimulus regularly associated with food was a metronome. The animal then learned to associate a response—in this experiment the same salivary response—with that stimulus. In one case, we speak of a secondary goal because the animal worked to achieve the goal; in the other, we speak of a second-order conditioned stimulus or a secondary reinforcement. The general principle is the same, for in both cases an intervening stimulus serves as a secondary reinforcement.

Pavlov was able to carry this higher-order conditioning a step further to the conditioning of a third-order stimulus. By pairing something else with the black card, he could condition some salivation. Third-order conditioning, however, was the limit of the process, for during the higher-order conditioning trials, too much extinction to lower-order stimuli set in. While the dog was responding to the metronome and black square, it was getting no primary reinforcement with food. Thus the response to the metronome was being extinguished at the same time that the association between the

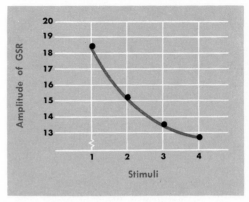

FIGURE 7.8. Generalization of a conditioned galvanic skin response. Stimulus 1 was the tone to which the GSR was originally conditioned. Stimuli 2, 3, and 4, respectively, were tones of increasingly different frequency. Note that generalization of response is less, the greater the difference in frequency [after Hovland, 1937].

square and metronome was being built up. At some point, obviously, the extinction effect has to be, and was, greater than the higher-order conditioning effect.

Instrumental learning

We seldom encounter circumstances exactly like those of the classical conditioning experiments. The value of studying such experiments is that they highlight many of the important features of any kind of learning or association, and they therefore introduce us to the more complex kinds of learning that are familiar to us. One of these has been called *instrumental learning,* or sometimes instrumental conditioning, because it involves learning a response that accomplishes something. It is instrumental in obtaining food, avoiding pain or punishment, or in achieving a goal. Classical conditioning does not accomplish anything; it is merely an association of a response with a stimulus. Sometimes the behavior involved in instru-

FIGURE 7.9. A rat in a Skinner box and a record of its learning. Each time the rat pushed the lever, the line jogged upward a notch. Note that the rat did not make its first response until about 15 minutes after being placed in the box, and did not make its second response until about 50 minutes later. The effect of food reinforcement becomes apparent, however, at about 80 minutes, when the rat began to press regularly [Chas. Pfizer & Co., Inc.].

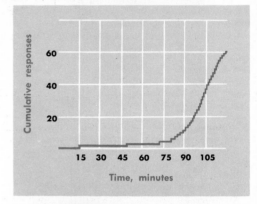

mental learning is called *operant* behavior because it "operates" on the environment [Skinner, 1938].

The response acquired in instrumental learning, generally speaking, may accomplish one or both of two ends. It may achieve the negative goal of avoiding fear or punishment, or it may lead to a positive goal of obtaining food, water, or a learned secondary goal. In some cases, it may do both at the same time. We shall begin with positive goals, then consider negative goals, and finally treat more complicated situations which involve both kinds of goals.

THE SKINNER EXPERIMENT. We have previously mentioned a learning situation in which an animal is placed in a box and can obtain food (or water) by learning to press a lever. The box was first devised and later used extensively by a psychologist named Skinner [1938], and it is therefore referred to, for convenience, as a Skinner box. A picture of a rat in such a box is presented in Figure 7.9. The lever the rat is pushing operates an electric switch, which is connected with a recording device; this device keeps a cumulative record on a time scale of the responses made by the rat. Let us begin by describing the course of learning to push a lever in such a box.

Sometime before the picture in Figure 5.9 was taken, the rat in the picture had been

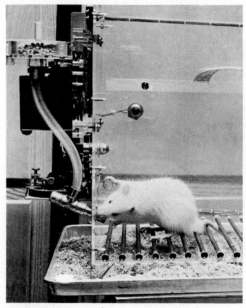

placed in the box for the first time. The rat had not eaten for 24 hours and was therefore hungry. After an initial period of habituation, the rat began to explore the box, and eventually it pressed the lever. A pellet of food was released, though the rat did not notice it at first. The rat continued exploring, stopping occasionally to wash itself, as rats do. After a while, it pressed the lever again, and the same thing happened. The third time the rat pressed the lever, it still failed to see the

CHAPTER SEVEN

pellet of food immediately, but did eventually find it. On the fourth lever response, however, the rat immediately seized the pellet of food and ate it. Thereafter the rat pressed the lever as rapidly as it could eat food and get back to push the lever again.

This whole procedure was recorded (see Figure 7.9). A device was connected to the lever in such a way that a recording pen made a jump every time the rat pressed the lever. The first jump in the black line, made about 15 minutes after the rat was put in the box, was followed by a long period during which no response occurred. Another jump in the recording line appeared at about 50 minutes, another at about 70 minutes. When the rat, after the fourth push at about 80 minutes, learned to associate the lever with food, the jumps came very close together so that the *rate of responding* appears to be a straight line with a steep slope.

This simple experiment demonstrates the basic features of instrumental learning and, indeed, of much of human learning. The organism, first of all, is *motivated by some drive*. The drive produces *general exploratory activity*. In the course of such activity, a *response happens to be made that is instrumental in achieving the appropriate goal*. This response becomes a learned response.

Just as in classical conditioning, *reinforcement* is the feature that is essential for instrumental learning to take place. However, reinforcement must be defined somewhat differently here. It is the *attainment of a goal that can satisfy a drive*. In the example of the hungry rat in the Skinner box, the reinforcement was securing food. If the animal were thirsty, the reinforcement would be obtaining water. Only because the animal received reinforcement did it learn the appropriate instrumental response. The reinforcement, however, need not be limited to physiological drives. Monkeys will similarly press a lever just for the pleasure of looking at other monkeys or, as we saw in Chapter 3, for reinforcement of curiosity and exploratory drives.

By the appropriate use of reinforcement, complicated tasks can be taught to rather simple organisms. Consider, for example, the series of pictures in Figure 7.10. If you look at them without knowing how they were obtained, you would think the pigeon is a genius. The pigeon appears to figure out that he can obtain the food at the top of the post by pulling the truck into position with the string. Actually, this trick was learned by carefully shaping the behavior of the pigeon. It was taught each stage in the solution by being rewarded each time it made an appropriate response in the direction of the correct solution. Gradually, the whole "problem-solving" sequence was learned. This and many other tricks of the sort one sees in circus acts are learned by the careful control of reinforcement.

EXTINCTION.   In both classical conditioning and instrumental learning, it is possible to *extinguish a learned response by withholding reinforcement*. If, for example, the rat no longer gets food when it presses the lever, its rate of responding gradually slows down until it stops making any responses at all. Such a procedure, we have seen previously, is called an *extinction procedure*, and its result, an *extinction curve*, is illustrated in Figure 7.11.

SECONDARY REINFORCEMENT.   The delivery of a pellet of food, like the unconditioned stimulus in a Pavlovian experiment, is a *primary reinforcement*. Secondary reinforcement is similarly common to both kinds of learning. This can be illustrated by the following example [Berch, 1951] from experiments with rats in a Skinner box.

The sound of a buzzer, in itself, is not reinforcing to a rat. If, however, the buzzer is paired with a *primary reinforcement* such as the presence of food in the mouth, it will acquire the ability to reinforce. The experimenter begins by sounding a buzzer every time a rat is given a pellet of food when it is in its home cage. Then he puts the rat in

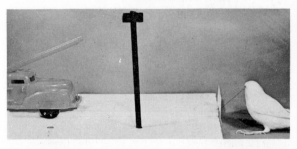

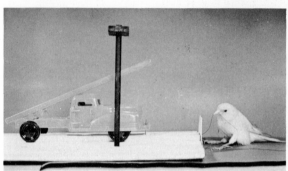

FIGURE 7.10. A complex act learned through reinforcement. The canary has been taught what appears to be reasoning or insight by a long training sequence in which correct behavior has been reinforced [David Linton].

the Skinner box and allows it to learn, for the first time, to press the lever. Instead of reinforcing the rat with food, however, the experimenter reinforces it with the buzzer that had been paired with eating food in the home cage. The buzzer now works very well as a reinforcer. The rat will learn to press the bar in a way that appears to the casual observer to be simply for the joy of hearing the buzzer. The buzzer in this case is a *secondary reinforcement*.

We now have studied **three different cases** of (positive) secondary reinforcement. The first was the learning of secondary goals (Chapter 3)—the chimps learning to acquire poker chips. The second was higher-order conditioning in the Pavlovian experiment. And now the ability of a buzzer to motivate the learning of an instrumental response. We shall be encountering others. From these various stiuations in which secondary reinforcement occurs, we can derive a general definition of the term: *Any stimulus which can motivate the learning of*

associations, because it is paired with a primary reinforcement, is a secondary reinforcement.

We can hardly overemphasize the importance of the concept of secondary reinforcement in understanding learned behavior. It helps bridge the gap between the artificial behavior of the laboratory and the behavior of real life. Secondary reinforcement explains many of the goals toward which our behavior is directed and the habits that are attached to various stimuli in the world. It thus serves both to motivate behavior and to determine what kinds of behavior are learned.

PARTIAL REINFORCEMENT.   When we described the extinction of conditioned responses, it may have occurred to you that we do not often see extinction in real life. People often forget habits—we shall deal later with forgetting—but they do not seem to stop doing something just because they receive no reinforcement for it. This raises the important question of why people often persist in their behavior without any visible reinforcement at all. One of the answers is to be found in *partial reinforcement*. Partial reinforcement, which is sometimes called "intermittent reinforcement," is reinforcement of a response some of the time, but not every time that it occurs. Hence it is a mixture of a conditioning procedure and an extinction procedure.

There are several possible arrangements of a partial reinforcement schedule. One is

a *fixed-ratio schedule* in which a reinforcement is given after every so many responses. All other responses are unreinforced. We might, for example, reinforce every third response, or every fourth, or even every hundredth. This method elicits rapid responses from an organism, for the organism gets paid as soon as it accumulates the required number of responses. The situation is comparable to piecework in human labor. Another schedule of partial reinforcement is the *fixed-interval* schedule. In this, reinforcement is given after a fixed interval of time if a response has been made within that interval. This schedule is comparable in some ways to a salary in human work. A "smart" individual on this schedule doesn't do much work; he responds frequently enough to discover what the interval is, then reduces his output to one response per interval. Most animals aren't that clever, though. They make several responses in an interval, although they slow down following a "payoff" and speed up as the end of the interval approaches.

These schedules can be made variable, rather than fixed. Subjects can be paid off after a variable number of responses—once after two responses, again after ten, and again after six, and so on. This is very much like playing a slot machine. The individual has no way of knowing when he will be paid; all he learns is that if he keeps working he will get paid at some time. The interval schedule may likewise be made variable, so that the individual will be paid first after one interval of time, then after a longer one, or shorter one, and so on.

Resistance to extinction. Partial reinforcement, especially of the ratio type, is a way of getting some responses without "paying for them." This fact has an important bearing on the extinction of responses learned under conditions of partial reinforcement, for extinction is a procedure in which responses are not paid for. An animal that has been trained on partial reinforcement extinguishes much more slowly than one that has been trained on regular reinforcement for every response.

Suppose that we put two rats, one at a time, into a Skinner box. Let us reinforce each rat 100 times and then obtain extinc-

WITHOUT REINFORCEMENT, INSTRUMENTAL RESPONSES GRADUALLY EXTINGUISH:

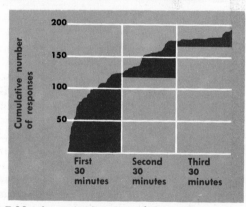

FIGURE 7.11. An extinction curve for a rat in a Skinner box. When no food is given for presses of the lever, the rate of lever pressing gradually slows down [after Skinner, 1938].

tion curves. One of the rats will be reinforced with food for every response, the other rat for every fourth response. Thus the first rat will make 100 responses to get the same amount of food for which the second rat must make 400 responses.

The extinction curves for these two rats will look something like those drawn in Figure 7.12, which were taken from two rats in exactly this way. These curves are cumulative curves—they show a running total of responses made during extinction—so they go up, rather than down, as they would if we took the number of responses per minute. When they flatten off, it means that the rats have stopped responding and that the responses are, at least for the time being, extinguished. Notice that the rat which has been reinforced for every fourth response gives many more responses during extinction than does the rat that has been reinforced every time. Indeed, reinforcing every response favors rapid extinction much more than reinforcing only occasional responses.

Practical implication. We see, then, that partial reinforcement during learning makes it much more difficult to extinguish responses. The practical implication of the effects of partial reinforcement is this: Nature seldom provides regular reinforcement for responses. An animal doesn't always find food in the same place, nor does a dog get hit by a car every time it crosses a street. And people are just as unpredictable as nature. Parents do not always punish Johnny when he gets into the cookie jar. We are not always rewarded for our good deeds, or always punished for our bad ones. Instead, we are typically rewarded or punished quite spasmodically and irregularly for the things we do. In life, then, reinforcement is usually partial or intermittent. Hence many of the things we have learned have been learned under conditions of partial reinforcement.

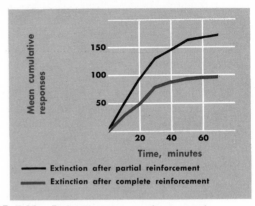

FIGURE 7.12. Extinction curves after partial and complete reinforcement. Partial reinforcement is more effective in establishing responses than 100 per cent reinforcement.

When young people first hear of the principles of reinforcement and extinction, they often say, "Ah, here is something we can apply to rearing our child. We will never pick him up when he cries; we will always catch him when he has stopped crying for a few minutes. In this way we can reinforce not-crying and extinguish crying." Unfortunately, this particular application of the basic principles of learning seldom seems to work—and for a good reason. Even the most adamant parents will give in occasionally to the persistent behavior of their children. Thus, just once in a while, a mother will pick up her baby while it is crying or allow her child to stay up late. But a child who finds that once or twice he is able to postpone his bedtime by fractious behavior is likely to be a difficult child at bedtime for several evenings afterward. The moral is that parents should be as consistent as possible, thus avoiding the undesirable effects of partial reinforcement.

There are many other applications of the principles of reinforcement and extinction to human affairs—in training animals to perform, in learning to drive a car safely, in the conduct of criminals, and even in the award of grades in school. You can probably think of many others of interest that affect your own life and the lives of others.

Avoidance learning

Up until now, we have been examining instrumental learning with positive goals. We may turn now to learning that has a negative goal—something painful, uncomfortable, or fearful that is to be escaped or avoided. Learning of this kind falls into two categories: escape learning and avoidance learning. *Escape learning* is learning to get away from or to eliminate an unpleasant situation, once the organism is in it. *Avoidance learning* is learning to avoid or to prevent the unpleasant situation before it occurs. Usually, however, the two kinds of learning are linked together. One must first learn to escape before he learns to avoid a situation. For that reason, the two kinds of learning will be treated together under avoidance learning.

STAGES IN LEARNING. Avoidance learning has been extensively studied in many kinds of experiments. An experiment [Solomon and Wynne, 1953] done with dogs will serve as an illustration:

A dog was placed in a compartment that was divided into two halves by a low fence— one the dog could easily jump over. The floor of the compartment was an electric grill through which shock could be administered to the dog. In each training trial, a buzzer was turned on, and was followed in 10 seconds by a shock on the side of the compartment the dog was in. The dog was supposed to jump over the fence to the other side of the compartment sometime within this 10-second interval. If he did, the buzzer was turned off, and all was well; if he did not, he got a shock, which was continued until he jumped

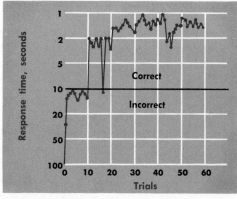

FIGURE 7.13. Acquisition of an avoidance response to a buzzer. Note the rather abrupt transition from escape learning below 10 to avoidance learning above it [Solomon and Wynne, 1953].

over the fence. Since the jumping response is instrumental in avoiding shock, it is an instrumental response, just as lever pressing is.

A learning curve for this kind of learning is shown in Figure 7.13. It is expressed as the number of correct jumps—jumps before the shock is administered—in each succeeding set of 10 trials. As can be seen in Figure 7.13, the dog in this experiment went for a number of trials without getting any correct jumps. Then relatively suddenly he began to learn, and within a few more trials, he was performing correctly almost consistently.

There is considerably more involved in such avoidance learning than can be expressed in a single graph or experiment. One point is suggested by the relatively long period during which no learning (apparently) takes place and by the relatively sudden onset of correct responses. If we were watching the dog during this period, we would get a hint of what is going on in this kind of avoidance learning. It is, we are quite sure, a two-stage process in which the dog really learns two things.

The first stage is the classical conditioning

of an emotional fear response to the buzzer. All that happens is that the buzzer, which is sounded before the shock, becomes associated with emotional reactions to shock. In the early trials of learning, one sees his association building up. When the buzzer is turned on, the dog alerts, squirms, yelps, and shows various signs of fear.

The second stage of learning, the instrumental stage, builds upon the first. This stage has two parts: *escape learning* and *avoidance learning*. While the animal is responding incorrectly, its problem is to escape. When the shock comes on, it jumps around rather aimlessly, responding in various ways, and at some time happens to jump over the barrier and escape the shock. This instrumental response to the shock is gradually learned, and takes place more and more frequently. In Figure 7.13, this learning is shown by a rise in the curve to a point just below the line representing correct avoidance responses.

Once the dog has acquired the instrumental escape response, the response can then be associated with the fear response to the buzzer. It is this association between the buzzer-aroused fear and the instrumental response that links the conditioned fear to the instrumental response. When the association becomes sufficiently strong, the animal jumps over the fence while the buzzer is sounding and before the shock begins. This is shown as an abrupt change in the learning curve; afterward, the animal rather consistently avoids the shock.

Our analysis, then, of avoidance learning is that it consists of two types of learning, classical conditioning and instrumental learning, one built on the other. First is the conditioning of fear to the buzzer, and second is learning the particular instrumental response that avoids shock (cf. the discussion of learned fear, page 109).

REINFORCEMENT AND EXTINCTION. This explanation is quite straightforward, but it raises some puzzling problems. First of all, what is the reinforcement? The quick and obvious answer might be that the electric shock is the reinforcement. But is it? Actually, what the animal seems to be learning is how not to be reinforced. In fact, when he is performing well, he is not shocked more than once every 20 or 30 trials—only when he gets a little lax and waits too long before jumping the fence. The shock then is really a partial reinforcement, for it is experienced intermittently. This, indeed, is an important characteristic of avoidance learning—that reinforcement is only partial. In considering partial reinforcement above, we saw that it is peculiarly resistant to extinction. It will come as no surprise, then, that avoidance learning is often difficult to extinguish.

But assuming that the electric shock—or more generally the painful or fearful situation—is a reinforcement, what responses are being reinforced? Two habits are involved: fear conditioning and instrumental jumping. Is the shock a reinforcement for both habits or just one? There is considerable experimental evidence on this question, but we shall give only the conclusions to be drawn from it [Solomon and Wynne, 1954]. The shock serves primarily, if not solely, as the reinforcement for the fear response to the buzzer, but the reinforcement for the jumping is relief from fear. In other words, the buzzer, by association with shock, produces a conditioned fear reaction, and then relief from fear is the satisfaction which is associated with the avoidance response.

This two-factor explanation of learning and reinforcement accounts for the fact that avoidance learning is unusually resistant to extinction. In some of the experiments with dogs, dogs have been known to jump at the sound of the buzzer for thousands of trials after the shock had been turned off completely. Some appear never to extinguish. Such a result undoubtedly varies somewhat from one species to another and with the experimental procedures used, but there can be no doubt that resistance to extinction, when an intense, traumatic stimulus is the initial reinforcement, is very great.

This resistance is very reminiscent of avoidance behavior in human beings. A person who once learned to avoid snakes or mice frequently goes on avoiding them them all his life. So it is too with the avoidance of water, high places, airplanes, and many other things. People do not easily get over habits of avoiding things.

There appear to be two reasons for this. One, already mentioned, is that avoidance learning, in the nature of the case, is learning by partial reinforcement, and habits learned in this way are resistant to extinction. The other is somewhat more subtle, but follows from the two-stage process in avoidance learning [Solomon and Wynne, 1954]. Since an avoidance response is a response to fear, it occurs as soon as fear is felt. Yet making the response relieves the fear, and this serves as a reinforcement for the response. Moreover, the avoidance response keeps the person away from the primary reinforcement, the original fear-producing situation, so that there is no chance for the fear response to be extinguished. Hence there is no extinction training of the fear response, and the avoidance response to the fear is self-perpetuating. This means that getting rid of unwanted avoidance behavior—some is very useful—can be quite a problem.

PUNISHMENT. Avoidance learning is learning motivated by punishment, that is, by the application of an unpleasant or undesirable stimulus. This punishment seems to be effective if all we want to do is teach an individual to respond to a signal to avoid punishment. The situations in which parents, policemen, and society use punishment are not always so simple. Yet punishment is widely used by society in an effort to eliminate undesirable behavior and to teach approved behavior. We punish dogs for chewing on rugs; we punish children for running into the street, lying, fighting with one another, not doing their homework, etc. Society punishes people for driving too fast or holding up banks. The use of punishment

to control behavior is indeed widespread. The question is, How well does it work? Or when, and when not, does it work?

Looking back at the experiments on avoidance learning in dogs, we may note some features of the learning situation in which punishment was effective:

1. What was punished was failure to make a response, not some already established habit. Had we punished the dog for something it had previously learned to do, the results would probably have been different.

2. Motivation to make any particular response was low. The dog was not hungry or trying to get food. It had no other motivation than to respond to shock.

3. A response for avoiding the punishment was readily available. All the dog had to do was move around a little, which was a natural response to shock and fear, and the chances were good that it would hit upon the jumping response as the avoidance response.

4. There was a definite cue, the buzzer, for impending punishment. If the dog learned to react to the cue, it successfully avoided the punishment at the appropriate time.

5. The punishment was consistently administered for failure to make the correct response. Until the animal made the desired response, the buzzer was always reinforced by shock.

6. The punishment was a strong one. The shock, though not harmful to the dog, was still strong enough to be painful and to evoke very strong fear reactions.

Each of these features of the avoidance-learning experiment is important in the use of punishment to control behavior. When any one of them, or combination of them, is altered, we get different results. In many cases, punishment can be completely ineffective in teaching new behavior. It may also cause neurotic emotional disturbances.

Punishment during extinction. Let us take a situation in which nearly all the above conditions are reversed. Let us first con-

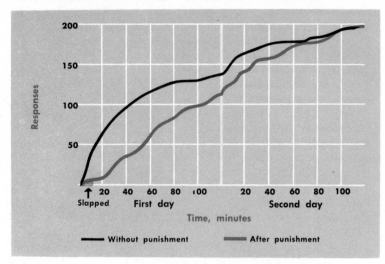

FIGURE 7.14. The effect of punishment on extinction. Punishment at first depresses the extinction curve, but in the long run the punished rat makes just as many responses as the unpunished animal [after Skinner, 1938].

sider the use of punishment to eliminate a habitual response made under conditions of high motivation [Skinner, 1938].

Two rats were trained in the usual way in a Skinner box by reinforcing them with pellets of food for pressing the lever. Then they were placed on an extinction schedule. One of the rats, however, was slapped on the paws for the first few responses made during extinction. (This was done by a device connected to the lever.) The response of the other rat, a control rat, was extinguished in the usual way.

The results of the experiment are given in Figure 7.14. The two curves in this figure are extinction curves obtained in the two rats after an equal amount of conditioning. The initial effect of the punishment (slapping) was to reduce the rate of responding. At least for a time, the punished rat responded much more slowly after the slapping than did the unpunished rat. The amazing thing, though, is that the punished rat later kept responding at about the same rate when the unpunished rat had slowed down, and that in the end, the two rats made just about the same total number of extinction responses.

This experiment has been repeated in other ways, e.g., with electric shock instead of slapping, and it nearly always gets the same results [Estes, 1944]. Punishment temporarily depresses the rate of responding, but does not lessen the total number of responses required for extinction. In the long run, therefore, nothing is gained by punishment. Extinction, rather than punishment, is required to eliminate a habit.

This result has two important, closely related implications: One is that punishment by itself does not weaken an association. It only suppresses the learned response by building up a competing fear-induced response. The other implication is that the original reinforcement of lever pressing with food built up what has been called a _reflex reserve_—a certain number of responses that will be emitted during extinction. So long as the learned response is not suppressed altogether or made impossible, this number of responses will sooner or later be made in the course of extinction. The only thing to do under such circumstances is to eliminate the behavior by letting extinction run its course.

One must be careful, however, not to overgeneralize from such experiments. The punishment was a mild one, and it was not administered regularly, so that it did not build up fear to the point of completely suppressing the habit. By giving a strong shock every time the rat pushes the lever, it is possible to suppress completely and permanently all lever-pressing behavior. If this is done, however, one has a fear-ridden, neurotic animal on his hands [Masserman, 1943]. The animal is strongly motivated to press the lever, yet is overcome with fear. Thus it experiences the kind of conflict that produces neurosis. In fact, as we saw earlier in Chapter 5, this is the kind of conflict situation that produces neurotic and maladjusted behavior.

We can conclude, however, from experiments like the one described above that *mild punishment,* administered *intermittently,* for a well-learned *habit,* when there is no obvious *alternative* to making the response, will in the long run be ineffective. These conditions are frequently encountered in human behavior. An occasional slap on the fingers, for example, will not keep a child out of the cookie jar; the only thing to do is keep the jar empty. An occasional light fine for traffic violations will not improve our driving habits, though it may bring money into the city treasury.

Punishment with alternatives. Punishment, we have just seen, will temporarily suppress a response. In doing this, it also makes behavior more variable; it increases the likelihood that some other response will be made. If things are so arranged that one of these alternatives will satisfy any existing motives and at the same time avoid punishment, then punishment can be very effective in eliminating undesirable habits and teaching desirable ones.

We regularly use punishment in this way in psychological experiments. We can, for example, provide a Skinner box with two levers. If we shock a rat on one lever, it will try the other lever, and if this never gives a shock, the rat quickly learns to use the no-shock lever. Or on a simple T maze, we can put shock on the left arm, and food on the right arm, and the animal quickly learns to go right at the T intersection. Or, as illustrated in Figure 7.15, an animal will regularly push a "correct" switch on signal to avoid shock. The important point is that when one response is punished, there is an alternative response available, and this alternative can easily be discovered when punishment has suppressed the original response and made the behavior of the individual more variable.

Cue functions of punishment. In sophisticated organisms that have acquired a large repertory of alternative responses, it is not necessary to learn a new, alternative response when punishment for one response

FIGURE 7.15. A monkey works to avoid punishment. Faced with three panels, the monkey must push the corresponding switch whenever a panel lights up. If he fails, he receives a shock; and if he pushes the wrong switch he is shocked. The apparatus in the background automatically presents lights and shocks, and records the monkey's responses. Monkeys normally perform well at this task for several hours at a time. The task is used to study the effects of drugs, fatigue, and other variables on performance [Foringer Co., Inc.].

is encountered. In this case, punishment, especially if it is mild, merely serves as a cue for selecting the correct response from among the repertory. The punishment, or some sign of punishment, merely tells the individual what is "right" and "wrong." It tells him how he is doing.

Many of the little punishments used in society serve as such cues. A low grade in an hour examination is a kind of punishment that tells a student where he stands in his mastery of the subject. Critical remarks made about a person's clothes or behavior may induce him to change his ways. In fact, all words of praise or reproof, of right and wrong, come to have cue functions, since reproof or "wrong" stands for potential punishment. So long as the person has something else he can do when he runs into a punishment cue, he can quickly learn to do the "right" thing.

Let us now summarize the conclusions we have reached about the use of punishment to eliminate undesirable habits. Punishment, first of all, does not weaken a habit that has been learned under strong motivation. If the punishment is strong enough, it may completely suppress the habit, but this leaves the individual in conflict between fear and other motives. If the punishment is mild, it temporarily suppresses the habit and makes behavior more variable so that an alternative response for achieving a goal may be learned. Without such alternative responses, mild punishment does little good. Where an individual has already learned many alternative responses, mild punishment may serve as a cue for what is "wrong" and thus indirectly encourage him to do what is "right."

Perceptual learning

In both classical conditioning and instrumental learning, the thing that is learned is, at least initially, an association of a response with a stimulus. Thus far, our attention has been focused on the response—how it is

acquired, reinforced, extinguished, and so on. Now we shall turn to the stimulus aspects of learning and consider how different responses may be associated with different stimuli and how associations between stimuli are formed. *Learning the relations between stimuli and how to discriminate between stimuli is called perceptual learning.*

CONDITIONED DISCRIMINATION. In describing Pavlov's experiments, we omitted one that is of interest here. He demonstrated that it was possible to build up a *conditioned discrimination* in which the dog responded to one stimulus but not to others. Pavlov's procedure was to reinforce one stimulus and to extinguish the response to another stimulus. To illustrate the point, we shall describe a hypothetical experiment which is similar to, but not identical with, one done by Pavlov.

A dog is first conditioned to salivate to the sound of a particular tone. The experiment is then continued by randomly presenting several different tones, one on each trial. At first, through generalization, the dog responds somewhat to all the tones, though salivating more to the conditioning tone than to others. However, the dog is reinforced only when the conditioning tone is presented, and never reinforced with any of the other tones. What this amounts to is that the response is being extinguished on all tones except the conditioning tone. As the trials go on, the amount to which the dog salivates to other tones gradually diminishes, while its salivation to the conditioned stimulus is maintained. Thus it learns to discriminate between two tones.

There is evidence, discussed below, that we do not always need to be conditioned to learn a discrimination. Both human beings and animals can notice differences in the world around them without being reinforced or extinguished on particular stimuli. The Pavlovian experiment, however, was the first to demonstrate how we (and animals) learn to *respond differentially* to different stimuli.

When, for example, a child first learns to associate words with objects, he tends at first to generalize. All animals are "bowwow," all men are "dada," and anything he can eat is a "cookee." When he finds that some animals do not bark or like his petting, that all men do not react like "dada,". or that some things don't taste at all like cookies—when he finds, in other words, that some objects are not reinforcing—his responses to them extinguish. Thus through differential reinforcement and extinction, he comes to discriminate appropriately.

DISCRIMINATIVE LEARNING. Instrumental learning, as well as conditioning, affords opportunities for acquiring such discriminations. A Skinner box, for example, may be arranged with two levers placed under two panels in which lights may be presented [Morgan, 1939]. The experimenter can so arrange things that a rat is reinforced when it pushes the lever beneath the lighted panel and is not reinforced when it pushes the lever under the dark panel. In this case, the rat learns to discriminate light from darkness by selecting the appropriate lever to push. There are many other ways in which this basic procedure may be used to teach discriminations [Munn, 1950]. Instead of levers, the experimenter may use doors, alleys, or any means of getting the animal to choose between two alternatives. Instead of lights, he may present cards of different colors or different shapes. These are incidental variations on the general principle that a discrimination may be learned by reinforcing one stimulus and not reinforcing the other one.

In learning to make discriminations, it is also possible to learn *concepts*. The term "concept" refers to a *class of objects or to some property that objects have in common.* There are many ways, for example, to make a triangle: with three lines, with three dots, with dashed lines, with the inside of the triangle completely black and its background white, and so on. There are, similarly, many ways to make a square. If an animal is repeatedly reinforced for choosing triangular objects and not reinforced for selecting square objects, it can develop a concept of "triangularity." It then consistently discriminates any kind of triangular object from any kind of square object. The learning of concepts is therefore a special case of discriminative learning. Concepts are closely related to a number of problems involved in imagination and thinking; we have therefore deferred a fuller discussion of them until Chapter 9.

INCIDENTAL LEARNING. It may have occurred to you that there is much that we may learn about stimulus situations without making any responses to them. If, for example, you are a passenger in an automobile without any responsibility for finding the way to your destination, you nevertheless learn something about the route you travel. You will notice some of the turns that are made, some of the houses you pass, and other landmarks along the way. If later you must drive the route, you will find it familiar to you. In all probability, you will find your way more easily than you could have done if you had not traveled the road before.

This kind of learning has been called *incidental learning,* because it occurs quite incidentally, without the individual's being motivated or required to make a response. It is also called *latent learning,* because it is latent until the occasion for its use arises. Some learning theorists have questioned whether such learning is truly incidental. There is always the possibility of motives and responses that are not evident to the observer. Indeed, recent research makes it seem very likely that the motivation for incidental learning may frequently be the curiosity or exploratory drive discussed in Chapter 3. But still, from the standpoint of an experimenter or an observer, the learning appears to be incidental. Incidental learning has been demonstrated in a number of experiments with animals. The following experiment [Tolman and Honzik, 1930] is a classical example of incidental learning:

Three groups of rats were run daily in a maze. One group was given food reinforcement at the end of each trial. As might be expected, they made steady progress in learning the correct path through the maze. A second group was run without any reinforcement; they simply wandered around the maze for a given period each trial. A third group was treated the same as the second group for the first 10 days. After that, however, the experimenter began rewarding them when they reached the end of the maze.

The results of this experiment are shown in Figure 7.16. All groups of rats evidently learned something, because they made fewer errors as they had more and more trials. The unreinforced groups, however, did not improve so much as the reinforced group. But when the experimenter began to reinforce the third group, their error scores suddenly dropped to about the same level as those of the first reinforced group. Apparently the unreinforced rats had learned a great deal about the maze in the early trials. They merely did not give evidence of their learning—it was latent—until they were reinforced for performing well.

This experiment has been criticized on the ground that the rats were put into the maze at its starting position and that they were taken out at the goal box. Since the maze was a strange, fear-inducing situation, the rats probably were being reinforced by being removed from the maze to their home cages. Even if this were the case, however, the fact still remains that the animals did not *perform* the maze well—did not show any appreciable learning—until food reward was introduced.

In other experiments [Buxton, 1940; Seward, 1949] attempts were made to control some of the factors for which the first experiment was criticized.

Rats were allowed to live in a maze for several days. Each rat was put in the maze and removed from it at positions different from those positions used for other rats. The rats therefore had an opportunity to explore all parts of the maze to an equal extent and were not rewarded for being taken out at the goal box. Then, on one occasion, food was put in the goal box and the rats placed directly in the goal box so that they had a chance to see that food was there. Immediately afterward, they were placed at the beginning of the maze. The result was that most of the rats made their way through the maze with very few errors.

These and similar experiments demonstrate that learning may take place when no physiological drive is rewarded or punished.

LEARNING CAN OCCUR WITHOUT REWARD, BUT REWARD IS NEEDED TO MAKE IT SHOW UP IN PERFORMANCE:

FIGURE 7.16. Latent learning of a maze. One group of rats was never rewarded and learned very little. Another group was rewarded throughout the experiment and made steady progress in learning the maze. A third group was not rewarded for the first 10 days of maze running but was rewarded regularly after that. Upon introduction of the reward, this group quickly caught up with the group that had been rewarded from the beginning [after Tolman and Honzik, 1930].

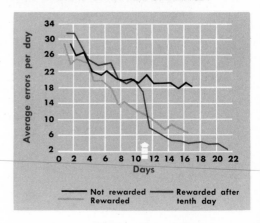

An exploratory or curiosity drive must be operating in order for the individual to "pay attention" to his environment, but he need not be motivated by physiological drives, or reinforced for any particular response, in order to learn relationships between stimuli in his visual world. <u>Reinforcement, however, is necessary for *performance*</u>. What we have previously described as instrumental learning, for example, is learning to perform a response; such learning requires reinforcement. Without reinforcement, an individual may notice many aspects of his environment and learn relations between objects in his environment, but until he is motivated and rewarded to perform, we usually do not know that learning has actually taken place. He needs reinforcement to perform.

SPONTANEOUS DISCRIMINATION. Under some circumstances, it is possible to tell that learning has taken place without using any reward to motivate performance. To do this requires some subtle measure of the effect of different stimuli on what the organism is doing. The following experiment [Thompson and Solomon, 1954] is an example:

Forty-eight rats were divided into two groups, an experimental group and a control group. Each rat was kept in a separate cage. This cage was so constructed that the experimenter could attach to it a box roughly 6 inches high, 6 inches wide, and 6 inches deep. On the wall of the box was a stimulus card. Two stimulus cards were used: one was a set of black and white stripes; the other an isosceles triangle. A box with one of these cards was attached to a cage, and the experimenter clocked the amount of time the rat looked at the card in a 100-second period. Six such periods were allowed on one day, and six more another day. For the control group, only the striped card was presented. The experimental group, however, looked at

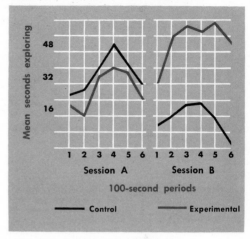

FIGURE 7.17. Spontaneous discrimination of patterns. Rats spend more time looking at a new, triangular stimulus than at black and white stripes which they are used to [Thompson and Solomon, 1954].

the striped card on the first day, and at the triangle on the second day.

The results are shown in Figure 7.17. The amount of time the rats spent looking at the cards increased during the first 500 seconds, possibly because they had to become habituated to the strange stimulus. After that it declined. When the same stimulus was presented to the control group on the second day, the rats spent very little time looking at it. Their curiosity had been "satisfied." But the experimental rats spent considerably more time looking at the new, triangular stimulus. Obviously, they knew the difference. They must have formed a discrimination between the stimuli; otherwise one group would not have been so different from the other in "looking time."

Spontaneous discriminations of this sort are probably the prerequisite for associating a particular response with a stimulus, that is, for learning what to react to in a stimulus situation. If we did not notice differences in

FIGURE 7.18. "Hypotheses" in rats. Rats were run in a maze constructed in such a way that they could choose (a) alleys that were lighted, (b) alleys having hurdles in them, or (c) the right or left alleys. Responding consistently to one cue meant a chance performance on other cues. The curves above are for one rat that early in the experiment consistently chose right alleys, i.e., the rat had a right-alley hypothesis, but later the animal learned the hurdle response, which was the correct (rewarded) one. Some rats had light-alley hypotheses; a few, hurdle hypotheses [after Krechevsky, 1932].

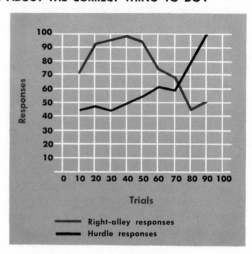

the world around us, we could not learn to respond appropriately to these differences. There is evidence, for example, that when rats are being trained for food reward to run a maze, they spontaneously discriminate a lighted alley from a dark one, or other differences in the maze, and then systematically react to these differences. They react as though they had "hypotheses" about the feature of the stimulus situation to which they should respond. In the following experiment [Krechevsky, 1932] with a maze, we see how the animals react:

There were three "hypotheses" which a rat might follow. One was simply to choose the right (or left) alley at all times. Another was to choose the alley which had a small hurdle in it, or conversely to take the one without a hurdle. The third was to turn into the alley that was lighted, or alternatively the one that was not lighted. The position of the lights and the hurdles were shifted randomly from trial to trial so that they were not consistently associated either with each other or with a particular alley. The maze consisted of four choice points between the start and the goal box, so it was possible to make up to four correct or incorrect choices on each trial.

The results for one rat are shown in Figure 7.18. It started off ignoring the hurdle, which happened to be the correct cue, and thus made a chance score of about 50 per cent on "hurdles." On the other hand, it started choosing right-hand alleys fairly consistently for the first 50 trials. Since the right-hand alley was not necessarily the correct one, the rat found it blocked about 50 per cent of the time and had to turn back and go into the one with the hurdle in it. Thus, the right-hand alley response was reinforced only about half the time, while the hurdle response was reinforced all the time. After about 70 trials, the rat gave up its preference for right-hand alley responses, then spurted ahead quickly in learning to choose the alley with the hurdle in it. Some animals in this experiment began by reacting to lighted alleys, rather than right versus left. Few, at the outset, chose hurdles.

The incidental learning of discriminations, then, plays an important part in learning to make particular responses to cues. Once the spontaneous discrimination is made, the tendency to react to one cue or another depends on a number of things: hereditary differences, chance differences among individuals, or the organism's prior experience.

It has been possible by inbreeding to develop one strain of animals that tends to choose lighted alleys in the experiment described above, for example, and another strain that tends to respond to spatial cues, that is, to choose consistently the right or left alley [Krechevsky, 1933]. Other experiments [Lawrence, 1949] indicate that previous experience with certain stimuli makes it easier to acquire a discrimination between the stimuli.

Out of such studies, a general picture of the processes involved in instrumental learning begins to emerge. Motivated by curiosity, organisms spontaneously notice differences in their environment. They learn where things are in relation to one another, and they discriminate among stimuli. When presented with a problem in which they are motivated to achieve a particular goal, they display certain preferences or "hypotheses" for one stimulus or another. By reinforcement and extinction, they abandon incorrect "hypotheses" and associate their responses with correct ones.

INSIGHTFUL LEARNING. To conclude the discussion of perceptual learning, we shall mention briefly another aspect of learning, which is to be considered at length in Chapter 9. This is *learning by insight.* All the instances of learning we have considered so far might be regarded as "stupid" learning—a more or less blind trial-and-error process or a robotlike conditioning. Even incidental learning may be regarded as a random, purposeless sort of learning.

In marked contrast to such "stupid" learning is the fact that much of human, as well as animal, learning involves reasoning and insight. Instead of being conditioned or trying to solve problems hit or miss, people frequently attempt to size up a situation and reason out the solution. They do not do things blindly; they think. Often the solution comes suddenly by *insight,* when they have correctly perceived the elements of the problem in their proper relationship. In most cases, such insightful solutions depend upon habits that the individual has previously acquired through conditioning, instrumental learning, or incidental perceptual learning. The individual thus can use his knowledge to solve similar problems without resorting to trial-and-error learning. The fullest understanding of learning by insight obviously involves the subject of thinking, and we shall discuss that subject in Chapter 9.

Maze learning

The maze has long been a favorite instrument of psychologists for studying the learning process. A maze is any apparatus consisting of a series of paths and choice points between a starting position and goal box or outlet. Mazes for animals usually consist of alleys arranged in a pattern of Ys or Ts through which the animal swims, walks, or runs. Some examples are given in Figure 7.19. Mazes have also been built for human use, but we will discuss them in the next chapter where human learning is the subject of study.

As an instrument for studying animal learning, the maze has one unique feature. It provides the opportunity to study serial learning; that is, learning a whole series of responses, not just one, leading up to a goal. This raises some interesting questions and throws light on the processes involved in problem solving. Otherwise, the maze requires instrumental learning just as a Skinner box does, but it also entails perceptual learning. Thus the maze combines serial learning with two varieties of learning we have already studied. By analyzing the processes concerned in maze learning, we gain some understanding of the mechanisms of complex trial-and-error learning such as are involved in human thinking and problem solving.

CHAINING OF RESPONSES. The simplest possible way in which the learning of a maze might take place is that each response at a choice point (a left turn or a right turn) might become associated with the response

FIGURE 7.19. Examples of mazes used in the study of maze learning [M. R. D'Amato, New York Univer.; Solomon Steiner].

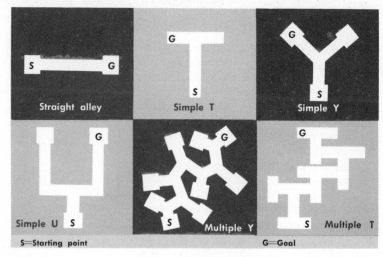

just preceding it. If, for example, a rat always had to turn left just after turning right, we might expect that the response of turning right could be a cue tripping off the succeeding response of turning left. This mechanism of forming associations would be a simple chaining of responses in a series. Watson, the behaviorist, proposed that this was the way a maze was learned. He assumed that stimuli from the contraction of muscles involved in turning left became conditioned stimuli for the response of turning right, and so on throughout the series.

Subsequent experiments have shown that Watson was only partly right. Chaining does take place, but it is only one of the factors, and probably not the most important one, in learning serial responses. Watson [Carr and Watson, 1908] himself participated in one of the experiments:

A maze was constructed so that the alleys could be lengthened or shortened without altering the pattern of turns required. Rats were trained to run the short version of the maze for food. They were trained to do this perfectly. They were then tested on the long version. If the learned behavior consisted of a chain of responses, it would be expected that the rats would run the maze very mechanically, turning at the point they were used to. Thus if the alley had been lengthened between learning and testing, one would expect the rat to turn part way down the alley whether an entrance was there or not. This, in fact, was the manner in which the rats often did behave.

This experiment, as well as others bearing on the question, indicates that chaining is one factor in serial learning. Other experiments, however, make it quite clear that this is not the only factor in serial learning. Indeed, in some circumstances, it may not be a factor at all. In one experiment [MacFarlane, 1930], rats were trained in a water maze:

The water in the maze was 8 inches deep, which is just deep enough to force a rat to swim. After the rats had learned to swim the maze fairly accurately, the experimenter put a floor between the walls of the alleys, just above the surface of the water. This did not change the appearance of the situation very much, but it did force the animals to run the maze, and thus to make quite different movements from those involved in swimming. The rats made no more errors after the switch than they had before.

CHAPTER SEVEN

This is only one of a number of experiments refuting the idea that chaining of responses is the sole, or even principal, explanation of serial maze learning.

We are left then with the conclusion that chaining of responses—a simple association of adjacent responses—may take place and can be a factor in some serial learning situations, but that other factors must also be involved.

DISCRIMINATION. An alternative explanation of serial learning is suggested by the experiments on instrumental learning described in a section above. Instead of being chained to each other, responses might be associated with stimuli in the maze. Learning a maze, then, might be little different from learning a series of discriminations. Each choice point might have something a little different about it—a crack in the floor, a difference in lighting, a familiar odor, and so on—and the animal might learn to make a turn in one direction or another on the basis of this cue. Thus an animal running the maze might be very much like a person in an automobile driving over familiar streets and roads. The driver turns correctly at each corner without reading signs or perhaps without being able to tell you why. He has learned, however, to turn "at the red house," "at the bottom of hill," "just past the gas station," or in response to other distinctive cues at the choice points.

There are several ways of proving that this kind of association does take place. One is to deprive rats of their various senses— blind them, make them deaf, or make them unable to smell [Honzik, 1936]. If serial learning depended only on response chaining and hence on internal cues from muscles, loss of peripheral sense organs should make no difference. But it does (see Figure 7.20). Actually, loss of one sense does not affect maze learning very much, for other senses can make up for the one lost, but depriving

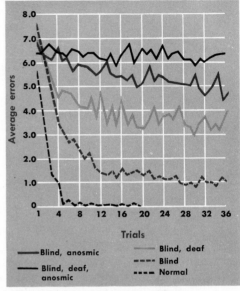

FIGURE 7.20. Maze learning with different amounts of sensory loss [after Honzik, 1936].

an animal of two or three senses seriously interferes with its maze learning. Thus it is clear that response to external stimuli is important in serial maze learning. The animal discriminates among various stimuli in the maze and learns to use these stimuli as signposts for making the appropriate correct turns.

GRADIENT OF REINFORCEMENT. Neither chaining nor discrimination, nor a combination of them, is sufficient to explain serial learning, because neither explains why a particular association is formed. The animal at the outset makes as many incorrect responses as correct ones. Why are not the incorrect ones chained together with the correct ones in the same sequence as they occur? Similarly, by making wrong turns, an animal has the opportunity to associate an incorrect response with external signposts. In either case, we cannot explain why errors are eliminated and the maze is actually learned. Something else is needed.

PRINCIPLES OF LEARNING 217

This something else is a concept known as the *gradient of reinforcement* [Hull, 1943]. The hungry animal is reinforced with food at the end of the maze. This reinforcement is closer in time to correct responses than it is to incorrect ones, because a correct turn must be made after an incorrect response, to arrive at the goal. The principle of contiguity, described earlier in the chapter, tells us that the closer two events are together, the more closely associated they will be. Hence correct turns will be more closely associated with reinforcement than incorrect turns. That is why incorrect turns are eliminated and correct ones are learned.

The effect of the nearness or remoteness of reinforcement on the learning of associations in a maze has been called the gradient of reinforcement. The word "gradient" refers to the fact that this effect is weaker at the beginning of the maze than it is near the goal. No one has directly observed a gradient of reinforcement; it is only something inferred. It is, however, logically deducible from the principles of learning developed previously.

Assuming a gradient of reinforcement, we would expect that errors close to a goal would be more quickly eliminated than those far away from the goal. In other words, in learning a maze, the elimination of errors would progress in a backward direction from the goal to the starting position. A tendency to eliminate errors in a backward direction has been observed in a number of experiments.

ANTICIPATION AND PERSEVERATION. Other things, of course, are usually not equal. One of these is ease of chaining responses. It is much easier to learn a pattern of *RLRLRL,* which is simple alternation, than one of *RRLLRRLL* or *RLRR-LLRRRLLL.* In fact, there is good reason to believe, both from theory and experiment, that a rat cannot learn a *chain* association more complicated than a simple alternation or a pattern of all *R*s and *L*s. In any case, where it is possible for a chain of

responses to be learned, we would expect this to override a gradient of reinforcement.

Another thing that is not equal is the distinctiveness of cues in the maze, and hence the ease of discrimination. Where cues are very distinctive, correct responses are learned more quickly and errors are eliminated more quickly than where they are not. This too would make a difference in the pattern of elimination of errors.

There is still another factor, however, in serial maze learning. This is stimulus generalization, a concept we have already become familiar with. It is the tendency to give the same response to stimuli that are somewhat similar. We can expect to find stimulus generalization after an association between a stimulus and a response has been formed. The more similar the stimuli, the more stimulus generalization. And a maze is a relatively homogeneous environment in which one choice point looks much like another. One would also expect stimulus generalization in the chaining of responses because the internal cues from all left responses are similar. Stimulus generalization then must be a prominent factor in serial maze learning.

How would stimulus generalization affect learning? So far as responses are concerned, it would lead to two kinds of errors: errors of perseveration and errors of anticipation. Perseverative errors are repetitions of responses made earlier in the maze; anticipative errors are repetitions of responses to be made later. In each case, the animal is simply making a response to one choice point that is correct at some other point. In popular terms, we would say that he does not know where he is, or he made the wrong turn because one intersection looked like another. Experiments with maze learning reveal that after an animal has learned some correct responses, many of the errors that still persist and are the last to be eliminated are errors of anticipation and perseveration. These are simply special cases of stimulus generalization.

To summarize briefly, the principal factors involved in the formation of associations in the serial learning of a maze are chaining of responses, discrimination of cues, a gradient of reinforcement, and stimulus generalization. Of these, the chaining of responses is generally the least important, and the gradient of reinforcement the most important.

Summary

1. Learning is any relatively permanent change in behavior that is the result of past experience.

2. The principal factor in learning is the formation of associations between events in the brain that represent external events. The associations may be between sensory processes or between sensory and motor processes. The closer two events are in time, the more easily associations are formed. If one event calls forth two different associations, the two associations may interfere with each other.

3. Most learning takes place under the influence of motivation. Motivation so controls responses that one response can be associated with stimuli connected with reward. Motivation also makes behavior more variable so that the correct response is more likely to occur.

4. Other factors involved in learning, or that closely resemble learning, are habituation, sensitization, imprinting, and inhibition.

5. Three general kinds of learning may be distinguished: classical conditioning, instrumental learning, and perceptual learning. Avoidance learning is a hybrid of classical conditioning and instrumental learning. Maze learning is a hybrid of instrumental learning and perceptual learning.

6. In classical conditioning, a neutral conditioning stimulus (e.g., a bell) is paired with an unconditioned stimulus (e.g., food) that evokes an unconditioned response (e.g., salivation). After repeated pairings of the two stimuli, the unconditioned response becomes associated with the conditioning stimulus.

7. In instrumental learning, responses that are at first made more or less randomly are learned as instrumental acts that achieve the satisfaction of some drive. In the case of avoidance learning, the instrumental act reduces fear of punishment.

8. In classical conditioning, the term "reinforcement" refers to the presentation of the unconditioned stimulus immediately following the conditioning stimulus. In instrumental learning, reinforcement refers to the reward which follows the instrumental act, or in avoidance learning to the punishment administered if the instrumental act is not performed.

9. Extinction is an experimental arrangement in which the conditioning stimulus or instrumental response is no longer reinforced. When, as a result, the unconditioned or instrumental response no longer occurs, the response is said to be extinguished. Learned responses tested after an interval of rest following extinction usually show some spontaneous recovery.

10. Stimulus generalization is the tendency to respond to stimuli that resemble the stimulus that has been reinforced. It occurs most conspicuously in conditioning, perceptual learning, and maze learning.

11. Any stimulus or situation consistently associated with primary reinforcement acquires the power to reinforce responses. Through this process, called secondary reinforcement, secondary goals are acquired. By pairing secondary reinforcers with neutral stimuli in a conditioning situation, higher-order conditioning may be obtained.

12. If conditioned or instrumental responses are reinforced only part of the time, the procedure is called partial reinforcement. Responses acquired with partial rein-

forcement are later much more difficult to extinguish than those acquired with regular reinforcement.

13. Avoidance learning can be considered two-stage learning. The first stage is the conditioning of a fear response to punishing stimulation. The second is instrumental learning that relieves the fear.

14. Punishment, in general, only temporarily eliminates learned responses; it does not reduce the total reserve of responses, as does extinction. When a response is strongly motivated and there is no alternative response, punishment is relatively ineffective in eliminating undesirable behavior.

15. Discriminations can be acquired in conditioning and instrumental learning by differentially reinforcing and extinguishing two different stimuli. Discriminations are often acquired spontaneously under the influence of the curiosity drive when there is no other reinforcement. Reinforcement, however, is usually necessary to show that any learning has taken place.

16. The solution of problems may be achieved by reasoning and insightful learning, rather than by conditioning or instrumental learning.

17. The principal factors involved in maze learning are the chaining of responses, discriminative learning, gradients of reinforcement, and stimulus generalization. Of these, the factor that may be most important in eliminating errors is the gradient of reinforcement.

Suggestions for further reading

Berlyne, D. E. *Conflict arousal and curiosity*. New York: McGraw-Hill, 1960.
A specialized but readable book that emphasizes the role of curiosity drive and of spontaneous discrimination in learning.

Deese, J. *The psychology of learning* (2d ed.). New York: McGraw-Hill, 1958.
An introductory textbook on the psychology of learning.

Guthrie, E. R. *The psychology of learning*. New York: Harper, 1952.
A textbook of learning that stresses the importance of association in learning.

Hilgard, E. R. *Theories of learning* (rev. ed.). New York: Appleton-Century-Crofts, 1956.
A scholarly, but readable, summary and evaluation of the major theories of the learning process.

Hilgard, E. R., and Marquis, D. M. *Conditioning and learning*. New York: Appleton-Century-Crofts, 1940.
A text emphasizing animal experiments in classical conditioning and instrumental learning.

Hull, C. L. *Principles of behavior*. New York: Appleton-Century-Crofts, 1943.
A rigorous and technical exposition of one of the major theories of learning, which emphasizes the principle of reinforcement.

Skinner, B. F. *Cumulative record*. New York: Appleton-Century-Crofts, 1959.
An account of an extensive research program on instrumental learning with particular emphasis on the role of reinforcement.

Woodworth, R. S., and Schlosberg, H. *Experimental psychology* (rev. ed.) New York: Holt, Rinehart and Winston, 1954.
An authoritative textbook with five chapters on learning.

Human learning & forgetting

THE LAST CHAPTER DEALT almost entirely with animal learning, for animal experiments enable us to comprehend the rudiments of learning processes. The principles we outlined in Chapter 7 are also valid for human learning, particularly the learning that takes place early in human life.

But human learning obviously goes much further than animal learning. For one thing, man is more skillful than animals in many respects. He can thread needles, drive golf balls, pound a typewriter, and perform all sorts of intricate operations for which animals simply do not have the endowment. The learning of various human skills is one of the subjects which we shall take up in this chapter. However, man excels in a number of other ways. Perhaps most im-

portant of all is his highly developed ability to use words meaningfully—a capacity that is uniquely human. This ability alone enormously enlarges the potentials of human learning, and it presents us with a whole set of phenomena not encountered in animals. This chapter will cover those phenomena and will introduce new principles that help us to understand them. Many of the principles previously introduced, however, are still of use and should be kept in mind.

Acquiring skills

Let us begin with the learning of skills—things people learn to do. If we were to study carefully the way in which a person

LEARNING CURVES CAN BE PLOTTED DIFFERENT WAYS USING SUCH MEASURES OF LEARNING AS ERRORS MADE, TIME ON TARGET, AND SPEED:

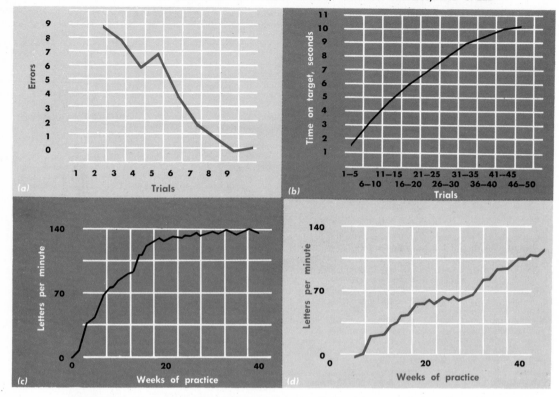

FIGURE 8.1. Four examples of learning curves. Curve (a), errors in learning a finger maze; curve (b), time on target in learning a pursuit motor skill; curve (c), learning to send by telegraph; curve (d), learning to receive by telegraph. Note the flat place, called a plateau, in curve (d) that is not present in curve (c).

learned such a skill as driving a car, probably one of the first things we would decide to measure would be how quickly the person's skill improved—the rate of his improvement. Such measures of the rate of learning with practice make up what psychologists call a *learning curve*. We saw many examples of learning curves in the last chapter, but now we shall take a closer look at them.

LEARNING CURVES. The four curves in Figure 8.1 are all learning curves. In the first one (*a*), errors or mistakes are the measure of learning, and improvement is

indicated by the *elimination of errors*. The curve happens to be one of college students learning a maze. In Figure 8.2 (left) is a student, blindfolded, tracing his way through such a maze. The student's task is to learn to find his way from one end of the maze to the other by following the "true path." Learning the correct path through a maze is charted either by the number of errors the subject makes or by the length of time it takes him to get through the maze. Curve (*a*) is a chart of the elimination of errors in learning the maze.

Another way to measure the rate of learning is to plot the *accuracy* or *correctness* of

MANY METHODS AND DEVICES ARE USED TO STUDY HUMAN LEARNING:

FIGURE 8.2. Two devices used in studying human learning. At left, a finger maze [see curve (a) in Figure 8.1]; at right, a rotary pursuit meter [see curve (b) in Figure 8.1].

performance as a function of practice. There are many ways to do this. Curve (*b*) in Figure 8.1 shows the percentage of time a learner is able to keep a small metal stylus in contact with a moving disk. A subject working at this problem is shown in Figure 8.2 (right). This apparatus is known as a rotary pursuitmeter. It is used in studies of motor learning. The curve of learning for the rotary pursuitmeter is, of course, an increasing-score curve.

Curves (*c*) and (*d*) in Figure 8.1 are curves of learning for verbal material. These curves are taken from a famous study [Bryan and Harter, 1899]—one of the earliest experimental studies of human learning—in which the ability to send and receive telegraphic code was measured as a function of practice. These two curves look much like the curve for learning the rotary pursuitmeter, that is, they are increasing-score curves. There is something special, though, about curve (*d*) that demands particular attention. Notice that about halfway through the curve there is a level place where, for a period of time, there does not seem to be much improvement. This period of little or no improvement is known as a plateau.

PLATEAUS. Plateaus do not always occur in learning curves, but when they do there are special reasons for them. One reason may be that there are several distinct stages in acquiring the skill. In Figure 8.1, for example, the plateau appears in curve (*d*) for receiving code, and not in curve (*c*) for sending code. To account for this plateau, Bryan and Harter, who did the experiment, reasoned that the learner hit the plateau because he had reached the limit of his ability to receive *letter by letter* and had not yet begun to learn to receive *word by word* or *phrase by phrase*. This means that there may be several different habits or several stages of habit involved in acquiring any particular skill; *when one stage of learning is completed before the next begins, a plateau appears in the learning curve.*

This description of the stages in acquiring habits is likely to be familiar to anyone who has tried to learn to play a musical instrument. When one begins piano lessons, for example, there is an early period during which one learns very rapidly; the fundamentals are easily acquired. But then there comes a long period during which improvement is maddeningly slow or nonexistent. Many people become discouraged at this point and quit. Others who persevere, however, find that they eventually get over the plateau and enter a new stage of learning, such as integrating the separate movements of the hands and fingers.

There are also other reasons for plateaus. Loss of motivation has been frequently suggested as a factor [Swift, 1918]. After taking piano lessons for some time, for example, a child may lose all interest in learning. Then, even if he is forced to practice regularly, his learning curve is likely to show a plateau. Plateaus do not always occur in learning, but when they do, changing the mode of practice or completely resting from practice for a period of time helps materially to overcome them.

DISTRIBUTION OF PRACTICE. One of the most important factors in learning is the rate at which a person practices a task. For an amazingly wide variety of situations, short periods of practice interspersed with periods of rest permit more efficient learning than does continuous practice [McGeoch and Irion, 1952]. This is true for simple instrumental conditioning, and it is true for such complex skills as learning to typewrite. A possible exception to this rule concerns tasks involving problem solving or inductive thinking [Cook, 1934; Ericksen, 1942], but even so, the rule of distributed practice is one of the most general in all learning.

Figure 8.3 illustrates the effect of distributed practice upon some curves of learning [Lorge, 1930]. It represents progress on a mirror-drawing task.

The subject's task was to trace a complex pattern with a pencil, viewing the pattern and his pencil in a mirror that reversed the apparent direction of movement. Thus everything the subject did appeared to be reversed. One group of subjects learned the task with massed practice; as soon as they completed one tracing of the pattern, they began an-

other. Another group was allowed 1 minute of rest between trials. A third group did only one trial a day and therefore had 24 hours' rest between trials.

Notice that there is a large and consistent difference between the learning curves of continuous, massed practice and those for distributed practice. Even an interval of 1 minute between trials was considerably superior to massed practice.

For more complicated tasks, the difference between massed and distributed practice is usually not so great as it was in this experiment. In most tasks, however, there is some optimal way in which to intersperse practice and rest to obtain the most rapid learning. There are three factors that can be varied: (1) the length of the practice period, (2) the length of the rest period, and (3) the location of the rest periods in the course of learning.

Practice periods should, in general, be short, for within certain limits, the longer they are the more they tend toward continuous practice and thus the slower the rate of learning [Kimble and Bilodeau, 1949]. On the other hand, practice periods should not be so short as to break up the task into artificial or meaningless units.

In general, the longer the rest, the more effective a given amount of practice; improvement tends to increase with the length of the rest period. Very long rest periods, however, do not make learning any more rapid [Lorge, 1930]. In other words, the optimal length of a rest period is probably quite short for most tasks, and increasing it beyond a relatively brief optimal time will not materially increase the rate of learning a task.

We can make no clear-cut recommendations about the location of rest periods, for experiments with different kinds of tasks give different results [Cook and Hilgard, 1949]. The best general summary we can make concerning distribution of practice is this: It is much more important to have short practice periods interspersed with frequent, short rest periods than to have only one or two long rest periods and one or two long practice periods.

This guiding principle for the distribution of practice has applications both to college study and to work in business or industry. Although learning a task and working at a task that we already can do well are not comparable in every respect, the same general principle applies to the distribution of periods of work and rest in vocational situations.

KNOWLEDGE OF RESULTS. Another factor of importance in learning a skill is *knowledge of results.* Ideally, a person should know on each trial exactly how well he has done. If, for example, he is shooting at targets, he should know after each shot just how close he came to the target and in what direction he was off. In learning golf, a person should be able to see exactly where his ball goes. If it is not possible to supply this kind of information, then the next best thing is knowledge of "hit or miss," that is, whether the person was correct or incorrect. This is not so helpful as information about the extent and direction of an error, but it does let him know which trials are correct, and thus provides some guidance.

A recent experiment [Baker and Young, 1960], which repeats with some modifications an old experiment [Thorndike, 1927], illustrates the value of knowledge of results in learning a simple skill. For convenience in describing the experiment, let us speak of knowledge of results as "feedback" of information.

The task of the subjects was to reproduce as accurately as possible the length of a 4-inch piece of wood. The subjects were blindfolded throughout the entire experiment and never saw the piece of wood. They could, however, feel it with their hands whenever they wanted to. To reproduce its length, they

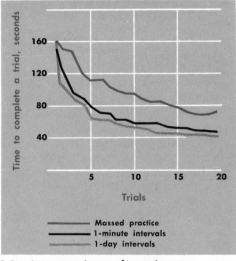

FIGURE 8.3. A comparison of continuous practice and distributed practice. The curves represent learning under three conditions: continuous practice with no rest between trials, practice with 1-minute intervals between trials, and practice with 1-day intervals between trials. Note that even a 1-minute interval favors more rapid learning than no interval at all. Intervals of 1 day are best of all [after Lorge, 1930].

inserted a pencil in a slot running from left to right and drew a line on graph paper. They were scored as correct when the line drawn was within ± .20 inch of 4 inches. Each subject drew 200 lines a day in blocks of 20 at a time; about a half-minute of rest was given between each block.

Two groups of subjects will be described. Both groups began with a pretraining day in which they drew 200 lines and received no knowledge of the results. This was to allow the experimenters to find out whether the subjects were roughly equal at the outset. On the average subjects were accurate about 12 per cent of the time. Then one group, the feedback group, had 7 days during which the subjects were told whether they were right or wrong, i.e., within ± .20 inch of the correct length, but they were not told the direction of their errors. The other group, the no-feedback group, was run for 9 days with no knowledge of results. At the end of its 7 days of knowledge of results, the feedback group was switched over to no-feedback for 7 days.

The outcome of the experiment is shown in Figure 8.4. The curves are somewhat bumpy because the number of subjects (12) was not large, but they nevertheless show clear-cut differences. The no-feedback group made no consistent progress throughout the experiment. At the end, it was performing accurately on less than 20 per cent of the trials. The feedback group, on the other hand, improved rather steadily while receiving knowledge of results, reaching about 60 per cent accuracy on the seventh day. As soon, however, as the feedback was stopped, the group's accuracy dropped abruptly to about 30 per cent. Still the feedback group performed better than the no-feedback group.

The experiment therefore shows that learning is aided by knowledge of results—indeed knowledge of results in some kinds of learning, gunnery, for example, is essential. It also shows that, even if one has to perform without feedback, he is better off if he has had feedback during the learning process.

It is also important that knowledge of results be timely. If a gunner fires a group of shots without seeing after each shot the hole that he has made in a target, he will not progress so rapidly as he will if he does see (or know) immediately the result of each shot. The reason is probably obvious; the learner needs to associate what he is doing correctly or incorrectly on each trial with the outcome of the trial. He can do this best if he learns the details of the outcome immediately. Otherwise all he knows is that he has generally been missing the mark.

Knowledge of results, then, aids learning because it permits the learner to associate the things he is doing with the outcome. The more immediately the knowledge is

given, and the more accurate and detailed it is, the faster the learning.

Knowledge of results also aids learning by being an incentive. A person who knows how he is doing is much more interested in learning than one who is not. Especially on tedious tasks, where he is likely to get bored, supplying him with some kind of record of his accomplishment helps to maintain his interest in the task. Thus knowledge of results aids learning by improving motivation for learning.

A practical application of knowledge of results is described later in the section on teaching machines.

READING VERSUS RECITATION.   There are many other variations in methods of practice that affect the rate of learning. One of particular interest to the student concerns the difference between reading and active recitation in the memorizing of verbal material. We also discuss this problem in the section of this chapter called "Techniques of Study."

There we point out that simply reading the material is vastly inferior to reading plus active recitation. In other words, if one only reads something without reciting what he has read, his learning is much less effective than if he reads and also actively recites it. As a matter of fact, if as much as 80 per cent of study time is spent in active recitation, the result is better learning than if all the time is spent reading [Gates, 1917]. This is particularly true for disconnected material, such as foreign-language vocabulary, but it is also true of highly organized, meaningful material.

We cannot make such clear statements about other modes of practice. We cannot, for example, say unequivocally that it is better to learn by reading than by listening. Many investigators have done experiments on this problem, but the results are not clear-cut. The answer probably lies in individual differences between people. Some individuals may learn better by ear than by eye, but for others the reverse may be true.

CHAPTER EIGHT

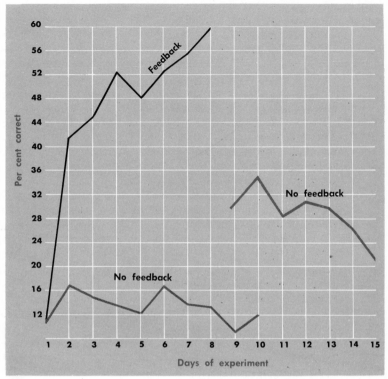

FIGURE 8.4. Effects of knowledge of results on learning. Blindfolded subjects had the task of drawing a line the same length as a piece of wood they could feel with their hands. After the first day in which no knowledge of results was given, one group, the feedback group, was told whether it was correct, i.e., within ± .20 inch of the exact length (4 inches), or not, while another group, the no-feedback group, continued with no knowledge of results. On the ninth day the feedback group was switched to no feedback. This group was at all times superior to the no-feedback group. Since the latter group was showing no improvement, it was stopped on the tenth day. [Baker and Young, 1960].

In any case, the differences are small and probably depend upon the particular situation measured.

MEANINGFULNESS OF MATERIAL. As people grow up, they acquire a large repertory of learned behavior. And as they are presented with new tasks to learn, they find that some of them are very much like tasks they have learned before. Or they find that what they have already learned helps in learning the new task. *New tasks or materials that are more easily learned because they involve old learning are meaningful tasks.* It is probably quite obvious that it is easier to learn a meaningful task than to learn a strange one.

The task of memorizing passages of words illustrates what we mean by *meaningfulness*. If you try to memorize the last paragraph, you will find it much easier than

trying to memorize the same number of words taken at random from the dictionary. Also, you would find it easier to memorize the paragraph in its correct order than to memorize it with the sentences jumbled up. But even memorizing jumbled sentences is easier than memorizing jumbled words.

In the next major section, we shall see in more detail just what is meant by meaningfulness.

WHOLE VERSUS PART LEARNING. One of the questions that faces the student and actor, or anyone who must memorize or master a large amount of material, is whether to study the material as a whole or to learn it in parts. In memorizing a poem or a part in a play, for example, should one go over the whole thing several times or take one part at a time and memorize it piecemeal? In studying a vocabulary list in a foreign language, should one keep going through the whole vocabulary list or take it in small groups? Should one master the sections of a chapter one at a time or work through the whole chapter several times?

This is the issue of *whole verus part learning*. It has been extensively studied. Some of the early experiments on memorizing poetry seemed to indicate that the whole method was superior to the part method. Later studies have not been so clear-cut. Each method has its advantages and disadvantages [McGeoch and Irion, 1952].

Part methods sometimes have these advantages: When a part is easily separable from a whole, as putting and driving are in golf, or as memorizing German vocabulary is, the part method is advantageous. When the whole is so large that one cannot go through it without running into the disadvantages of mass practice, as in rehearsing a long part in a play, the part method is preferred. The part method also has the advantage of maintaining more interest, because it gives knowledge of results and a sense of achievement more quickly. The part method, on the other hand, has the disadvantage that one must do considerably more memorizing to link the parts together after they have been learned individually. A person is also likely to get his parts mixed up or in the wrong order.

The whole method tends to be the more effective learning method under the following conditions: when the learner is intelligent enough to learn things quickly, when practice on the whole can be distributed over a number of sessions, and when the material is so meaningful that it easily hangs together. In general, the whole method of learning is more effective than one might expect, especially for a poem that is not too long. And though we cannot say that either method is always better or even usually better, the whole method probably is slightly better than the part method for most learning situations.

In the practical situation faced by the student, the best recommendation is to follow a flexible plan that combines both methods. The student should probably start with the whole method, watching out for difficult parts that need particular effort, then shift to the part method, and finally go back to the whole method again. In studying a chapter in a textbook, for example, he should read it over once, then study carefully its individual parts, and finally read it over again as a whole. The specific recommendations made in "Techniques of Study" below are based on experiments that bear out this general strategy of study.

Memory processes

This section will be more general and abstract than the last one. Our purpose will be to develop a picture of the processes of learning and remembering in the sophisticated human learner. By "sophisticated" we mean a child or adult who has learned language reasonably well and who already has a large reservoir of associations. When such a person learns new associations, he is not starting from scratch as the infant or the naïve animal is. Rather his new associations are linked with the ones he already has. As a consequence, understanding how he learns, what he remembers, and what he forgets becomes a problem of understanding how his new associations are assimilated into his old ones.

MEMORY IMAGES. As we have often emphasized, psychologists try to be as objective as possible and to base their conclusions on objective observations. They therefore have some misgivings about such concepts as "ideas," "images," and "thoughts," since these are not directly observable. From indirect evidence, however, there can be no question that images exist and that they play an important role in learning and thinking. This not only makes common sense, it is supported by considerable data.

A most dramatic example of imagery is encountered in experiments on eidetic imagery. In such experiments, a very complicated picture or design is presented to a subject for a relatively brief period of time. The subject is then asked to recall as many of the details in the stimulus as he can. People vary, of course, in their accuracy of recall, but occasionally an individual has nearly perfect recall because he is able to resurrect an image which is virtually a photographic reproduction of the original stimulus. Such an image is called *eidetic*. Eidetic imagery is rare, but it is relatively more common among children than adults.

For a test example, look at the picture in Figure 8.5 for 35 seconds. It has been placed on page 230 so that you can expose it, time yourself, and then cover it up again. Do not read further until you have inspected the picture for 35 seconds.

Now, without looking at the picture, can you spell the German word in it? In one experiment, 3 out of 30 English school children, unfamiliar with German, could spell the word forward and backward; 7 spelled it with only two mistakes. They, and other "eidetikers," often hesitate a moment before recall. During this time they seem to "project" their image on a mental screen, and inspect and read it as if it were an objective stimulus. Some subjects have recalled a page of print so accurately that they could repeat any word or line on demand, shifting to different parts of the page as the experimenter requested.

Such perfect eidetic imagery is a rare ability. Some people, though, apparently have it without knowing that they do. Edison is said to have possessed it. Its existence demonstrates that our memory for previous experiences is to some degree like a photographic process. A "print" of such an experience is somehow made in the brain and stored there. Later it can be called up by instruction or by some stimulus associated with it.

REPRODUCTION OF VISUAL FIGURES. Usually, of course, our memory of a previous experience is not so vivid. We do not carry around a perfect copy of it. Instead we remember only certain aspects of the experience. Just what it is that is remembered has been studied in a number of experiments. One such experiment [Gibson, 1929] is described below:

The subjects were directed to inspect some forms for a given period of time. Afterward they were asked to reproduce the forms. Samples of the forms used are in Figure 8.6 along with typical drawings made by subjects when later tested. In none of the cases shown is there perfect reproduction. Each shows some distortion of the original form. In each, however, various aspects of the form have been remembered, while other details have been forgotten.

In experiments of this sort, one can vary the kind of figure presented in order to determine what features of a figure are most easily remembered. The figures can vary from being very simple (triangle, circle, or square) or very familiar (outline of a face or a building) objects or designs to being a jumble of lines with no regularities at all. The latter we call nonsense figures (see Figure 8.7). As we might expect, simple and familiar figures are easily and correctly remembered, whereas nonsense figures are extremely difficult.

In trying to remember a figure, people usually make an "effort at meaning" [Bartlett, 1932]. They first try to liken it to something familiar. Indeed, if it is familiar, they simply give it a name. If not, they liken it if possible to something they already know. Children particularly do this; they tend to think of any figure as a "picture of something." If the figure does not arouse any association with a familiar object, people then are likely to "schematize" the figure, that is, to remember some order or plan to it. They tend to note geometry, symmetry, rhythm, or identical parts.

The important point here is that the learning or remembering is done in terms of already established associations. The thing remembered is, so to speak, *recoded* by identifying it with other associations. To make this clear, suppose I look at a complicated set of lines that reminds me of a face. This "association by similarity" is simple; all I have to do is remember "face." Previously I have had many associations with faces, with the eyes, nose, mouth, and other features. So far as my association is correct, I can now reproduce the original figure by drawing a face. With one simple association I have recoded the complex set of lines making up the figure. To the extent, then, that an experience can be recoded in terms of other associations, it can be quickly and easily remembered.

To the extent, on the other hand, that something is nonsense—it resembles nothing I have ever experienced before—it must be remembered either by eidetic imagery, which is rare, or by a laborious process of inspecting and memorizing every little detail. The nonsense figure in Figure 8.7, for example, is very difficult to learn. It takes almost as long to learn as a 20-digit list of numbers [Piéron, 1920].

In the chapter on development, we referred to experiments in which chimpanzees had been brought up with translucent goggles and without experience with objects in the environment. These chimpanzees had a very difficult time learning to make quite simple discriminations of geometrical figures. One possible explanation for this follows from what we have been saying. The chimps had no reservoir of associations with objects with which they could associate the forms. Hence the figures were nonsense forms to the chimps, and such figures are considerably harder to remember than forms that arouse established associations. This fits in with the general conclusion that ease of learning depends on how readily our experience can be recoded in terms of previously learned associations.

VERBAL ASSOCIATIONS.   Much of human learning, of course, is verbal. It consists of learning new associations among words. In

FIGURE 8.5. A picture test of eidetic imagery [G. W. Allport].

fact, by the time a person enters college, the great majority of his learning is done in terms of words. Having learned what words stand for in the world of objects and events, he learns new things about the world by learning to relate words in new ways. Although this learning is supplemented by diagrams, demonstrations, and laboratory work, still the brunt of the learning falls upon words.

The way in which verbal associations are formed has been the subject of considerable experimental study. As in the case of visual figures, the material used for verbal learning may vary from highly meaningful stories to nonsense syllables. The latter consist usually of three-letter words beginning and ending with a consonant and having a vowel in the middle; for example, *zeb, cor, muv, dib.* Sometimes nonsense syllables or words are longer, but then they are less likely to be nonsense, that is, to have no already established associations.

One of the common methods of studying verbal learning is known as the method of *serial anticipation.* A list of words or syllables to be learned is constructed. The words are then presented one at a time in the window of a memory drum (see Figure 8.8) for a standard interval, say, of 2 seconds. The first time the list is presented the subject has no chance of getting any of them correct because he has not seen the list before. Beginning, however, with the second run, he is asked to anticipate the syllable that follows the one he is looking at. If the list consisted of *zeb, cor, muv, dib,* etc., he would first be shown *zeb* and expected to say *cor*. A moment later *cor* would appear in the window, telling him whether he was correct or not and also giving him the cue for anticipating *muv*. And so on. This method or some variation of it has been used to study a number of the phenomena of verbal association.

Meaningfulness. The ease with which such a list of words or syllables is learned depends on their meaningfulness (see page 227). This is illustrated by the following experiment [Noble, 1952]:

A long list of two-syllable words was constructed. Some were ordinary English words; others were nonsense words. An index of "meaning" was obtained for each word by counting the average number of associations given by a group of subjects to each word in a 60-second period. Indices ranged from a low of 0.99 for the nonsense word *gojey* to 9.61 for the word *kitchen*. In this part of the study, incidentally, it turned out that some English words had lower indices of meaning than the nonsense words. The nonsense word *rompin,* for example, had a higher index than the real, but rare, English words *icon, matrix,* and *bodkin.* On the basis of these indices, two lists of words were selected. One had an average index of meaning of 1.28, the other an index of 7.85.

Subjects were then compared on their rate of learning the two lists by the method of serial anticipation described above. The list with the low index of meaning took almost three times as many trials to learn as the list with the high index.

MEMORY DISTORTS AND SIMPLIFIES THINGS:

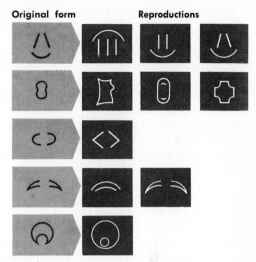

Original form   Reproductions

FIGURE 8.6. Changes in memory for forms. The forms in the left-hand column were presented to subjects; some time later, when asked to recall the forms, they reproduced those shown at the right. Note the distortions [Gibson, 1929].

DRAWINGS, AS WELL AS SYLLABLES, MAY BE NONSENSE:

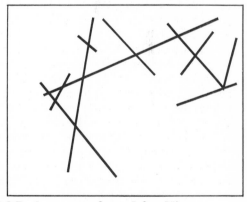

FIGURE 8.7. A nonsense figure [after Piéron, 1920].

It is to be noted that all the words in these two lists were two-syllable words, and the number of words in each list was the same. The only difference between the two sets of words was "meaningfulness." And all that was required for learning was to associate each word with the word that followed it in the sequence. Still, "meaningfulness" made one list very easy to learn; the other relatively difficult. Again we see that ease of learning depends upon making an association with an already established set of associations.

Remote associations. When a list of words is learned by the method of serial anticipation, associations are formed between each adjacent pair of items. It has been a matter of considerable interest, however, that other more remote associations are also formed, as can be seen from the following study [McGeoch, 1936]:

The experimenter had his subjects learn lists of nonsense syllables by the method of serial anticipation. He stopped the learning procedure, however, before they had fully learned the list. He then gave them a free-association test in which he presented them with the nonsense syllables in the list, but he did this in random order, not the order in which they had appeared during the training trials. He asked them, as each syllable was presented, to say the first syllable that came to mind. He then plotted the data shown in Figure 8.9. Many of the associations were, of course, correct. Some, however, belonged one step away in the list, and others two steps. Still others had varying degrees of remoteness. The curve is reasonably smooth; it shows that remote associations are formed between a syllable and other syllables farther away in the list, and that the association is weaker the farther removed the other syllables are.

This fact helps explain a phenomenon that has long been known in the learning of lists of nonsense syllables—the serial-position effect shown in Figure 8.10. This figure indicates that in the course of learning a list, the

FIGURE 8.8. A diagram of Gerbrands's memory drum, an apparatus for the study of verbal learning [Ralph Gerbrands].

early part of the list is most easily learned, the last part is next most easily learned, and the middle items in the list—actually the ones just past the middle—are the most difficult ones. A curve of this general shape is regularly obtained in learning lists by the serial-anticipation method. It holds both for nonsense syllables and for more familiar material such as a list of names [McCrary and Hunter, 1953].

To understand how remote associations are related to this serial-position effect, it must be realized that remote associations are incorrect associations. If a word has a tendency to call forth words that are one or two steps removed, rather than the next one, these are associations that interfere with the correct one. But the words near the beginning of the list have fewer words in front of them, and those near the end of the list have fewer words behind them, than the

CHAPTER EIGHT

words in the middle. We therefore expect words at the ends of a list to have fewer remote associations to interfere with the correct association than those words in the middle. Thus the serial-position effect is explained largely by interference from remote associations.

This may all seem a little academic and not too relevant to problems of learning in college. Actually this is not the case. In learning poetry, a speech, or a song, one is very apt to get ahead of himself or to say lines out of order. This is due to the remote associations formed in whatever is being learned. Remote associations also account for the fact that one usually finds it easier to learn and remember the beginning and end of something than the middle. One must therefore expect to have more trouble learning and remembering the middle part of the things he studies and to compensate for this difficulty by giving the middle part extra practice.

Statistical dependencies. The learning of lists of words or nonsense syllables may also not appear so impractical if we realize that virtually all our language consists of words arranged in lists. That is what a sentence is. In using language, we are continually associating one word with other words that precede it or follow it. The associations built up in this way give words a sequential meaning. This sequential meaning resides in the statistical structure of language. It arises from the fact that all through life we learn that certain words are more likely to follow other words.

We might expect, for example, the sequence of words, "The old brown bear . . ." to be followed by "ran," "climbed," or "growled," but not by "skyscraper," "photograph," or "pink." This simply illustrates that we learn to distinguish dependent probabilities between words. We learn that certain words are more likely to follow some

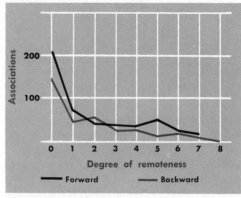

FIGURE 8.9. Remote associations in verbal learning. After partially learning a series of nonsense syllables, subjects were asked to recall the next item in the series when the syllables were presented to them in random order. When their associations were incorrect, the syllables they gave tended to be only a step or two away from the correct one in the series rather than several steps away [after McGeoch, 1936].

THE MIDDLE ITEMS IN A SERIES ARE THE HARDEST ONES TO LEARN:

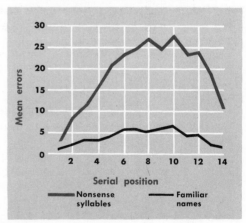

FIGURE 8.10. The serial-position effect. Difficulty in learning words or syllables varies with their position in the list. [McCrary and Hunter, 1953].

words than others. Such dependent probabilities make up the statistical structure of English and help explain why we learn meaningful English more easily than we do nonsense English. We shall consider the statistical factor in language in more detail in Chapter 9.

Transfer of training

One of the most important problems in the whole of the psychology of learning is that of the transfer of training. The fact that we are engaged in a program of academic study indicates society's implicit faith in transfer of training. The principal value that comes from formal learning in the school situation lies in the application of what we learn to problems outside the academic world. Because so much of our time is spent in formal learning of things that are intended to be useful outside the classroom, transfer of training is one of the most important applied problems in learning.

Before looking at some particular instances of the problems of transfer, we shall do well to examine the theory behind transfer of training. A general theory helps us to integrate a lot of separate facts, and this in turn helps us to apply formal knowledge to problems of daily life. So as you read about the theory of transfer of training, you might consider the ways in which it can apply to real problems.

PRINCIPLES OF TRANSFER. There are two fundamentally different consequences of transfer of training, and these need to be understood clearly. Suppose I have learned that in order to keep the attention of my class in introductory psychology I must tell a joke every 10 minutes or so. This seems to be a reasonable device, so I try it in my class in applied psychology, and it works there, too. This is an example of *positive transfer*. What I have learned to do in one situation applies equally well to another situation.

Suppose, however, that I try to carry this one step further and use the technique in a talk that I give at the faculty club. Here I discover that my jokes fall flat and the technique fails miserably. This is an example of *negative transfer*. What worked in one situation is not applicable to another situation.

Therefore, positive transfer occurs when something previously learned benefits performance or learning in a new situation. Likewise, negative transfer occurs when something previously learned hinders performance or learning in a new situation.

Similarity of stimuli. Positive transfer increases with similarity of stimuli. The more similar the stimuli in two situations, the more positive transfer there is from one to the other. This fact is the same one, expressed in different terms, that we learned in Chapter 7 under the heading of "Stimulus Generalization." In that case, you will recall, a GSR conditioned to a tone of one pitch was also evoked in lesser degree when tones of similar pitch were presented. Such stimulus generalization is a case of positive transfer.

Let us cite two more familiar examples. After a person has learned to drive one make and model of car, he usually has little difficulty in transferring to another car. Instruments on the new dashboard may be arranged somewhat differently, the windshield may be a little higher or larger, and many minor features of the two cars may be different. In general, however, the stimulus situations presented by the two cars are similar; hence transfer is good. In learning languages, if a person has studied Greek, his progress in Latin is faster; if he has studied Latin, his learning of French is made easier; and Latin is also helpful in mastering Italian or Spanish. In each case, the two languages have many similarities, and similar stimulus situations produce positive transfer of training.

Similarity of responses. The same principle also applies to cases in which there is a similarity of responses. Here, however, there is the possibility of two responses being so dissimilar that they are opposites, or near opposites. In that case, the result is negative transfer. To use again the example of driving two cars, positive transfer from one to the other usually occurs, not only because the stimulus situations are similar, but also because similar responses are required. In both cases, one uses his right foot to brake the car, his right foot to accelerate it, and his left foot to operate the clutch, if there is a clutch. To take another example, if a person has learned to play tennis, he finds it easier to learn ping-pong or badminton, because similar responses and skills are involved in all three games.

Let us consider cases in which opposite responses are required in two situations with resulting negative transfer. If one is used to steering a sled and then tries to learn to pilot a plane, one will have difficulty at first, because extending the right foot makes a sled go to the left and a plane to the right. Many people have trouble learning to steer with an outboard motor because it requires that one push the stick to the left in order to make the boat turn right, and this seems unnatural.

Negative transfer can be a matter of life and death in airplanes when a pilot has flown one type of plane for a long time and then flies a plane with rather different controls. In the new plane, he may have to do exactly the opposite of what he has been accustomed to. Airplane accidents are occasionally caused in this way [Chapanis et al., 1949]. In one incident, a pilot was undershooting the field in attempting to land. To correct his approach, he pulled back on the throttle and pushed the stick forward. This was the reverse of what he should have done, and it nosed the plane into the ground. The reason he gave afterward—he was fortunate enough to survive to tell the tale—was that he was accustomed to flying planes in which he operated the throttle with his right hand and the stick with his left hand. In this plane, the positions of the controls were different, so that he used his left hand on the throttle and his right hand on the stick. In an emergency, he had reverted

to his old habits, with almost fatal consequences.

In summary, we may say that similarity of stimuli and of responses accounts for positive transfer. A dissimilarity of responses, in which opposite or competing responses are required, accounts for negative transfer. It should be noted that virtually all learning in sophisticated human beings involves transfer, for transfer is no more than the recoding we talked about in the previous section. It is the reason, differently expressed, why meaningful words (page 231) are easier to learn by the serial-anticipation method than nonsense words are. Similarly it is the reason why we easily remember figures, like a face, that can be named or schematized. In each case, a new association is formed with already established associations. And this is all there is to transfer. In negative transfer, a similar recoding takes place; it merely happens not to serve the purpose. It constitutes an interfering association that must somehow be overcome by further learning.

TRANSFER OF TRAINING IN FORMAL EDUCATION. The whole of our formal educational program assumes that there is a certain degree of positive transfer between what is learned in school and what is needed in daily life. It is not surprising, therefore, that psychological studies of transfer of training have had a profound influence upon our contemporary notions of education.

At one time there was a fairly widespread notion that only a limited number of mental faculties needed to be trained, and that once these had been trained, they could be used in a wide variety of situations. Thus schoolboys used to study Greek, Latin, Euclid, and Aristotle, not so much because of their intrinsic value but because they were supposed to train the mind. At one time, too, there was widespread belief in the notion that one could train school children to be neat in their appearance and in the care of their belongings by teaching them to be neat in their arithmetic and spelling papers. This general notion has been called the *mental-faculty* theory of transfer or, on occasion, the *formal-discipline* theory of transfer.

This theory has been almost completely abandoned today, largely because of the results of experimental studies on transfer of training. Some years ago educational psychologists [Stroud, 1940] studied the transfer of Latin grammar to English grammar, of Euclidean geometry to the ability to solve reasoning problems, and of classical physics to the ability to understand the mechanical problems of daily life. The results were rather discouraging. In nearly every case there was some positive transfer, but it was disappointingly small. Educators have gradually relinquished the notion that one can instill an ability through sheer exercise of a faculty or general habit.

Nowadays educators are concerned not with "mental discipline," but with producing the greatest amount of positive transfer from school subjects to everyday life. Part of the technique for accomplishing this is to make school problems as realistic as possible. Hence the modern arithmetic book attempts to cast its problems in a form that makes them like the real-life experience of the child.

At the higher levels of education, positive transfer can best be increased by making it clear to the learner that what he is learning can be transferred to other situations. Even the old subjects of special delight to the adherents of formal discipline can be made useful by bringing this point home. A study of Euclidean geometry *can* aid one in improving his ability to reason if he has a good and patient teacher with a flair for pointing out what can be transferred from the formal subject to thinking in our daily experiences.

Again we point out that the practical problem of transfer is one of recoding already established associations. In teaching arithmetic we get the greatest transfer by casting problems in terms of a child's experience simply because in this way we can quickly attach the new experiences in arithmetic to the associations the child already

has with numbers, money, sticks, etc. Our frequent use of familiar examples in this textbook is a similar teaching device, used to speed the learning of new associations by attaching them to what the student already knew.

Retention

One of the most interesting problems to the student of learning is that of retention. How much of what we learn do we retain? Why do we forget? Why do we find it so difficult to remember certain common things? What produces the distortions of memory that are the common experience of everyone? These questions are all basic, and in the next few pages we shall consider some of the answers to them. Practical advice for improving retention is given later in "Techniques of Study."

Forgetting and retention are but opposite sides of the same coin. What we have forgotten is simply the difference between what we have learned and what we have retained. We can measure directly only what has been retained, of course, but sometimes our emphasis is upon "forgetting" rather than upon "retention."

MEASURING RETENTION. There are several different ways of measuring retention. We shall describe three: recall, recognition, and savings.

The *method of recall* is especially suitable for studying the retention of verbal material, such as a poem or a section of a textbook. For recall, the subject must reproduce, with a minimum of cues, something that has been learned in the past. Of the different methods we shall describe, the method of recall yields the smallest amount of measurable retention, because it is always harder to recall something "cold" than it is to relearn or to recognize something. The essay examination is an example of a recall method of measuring retention.

A second method, the *method of recognition,* is most frequently used in objective examinations consisting of true-false, multiple-choice, or similar questions. The amount of retention measured is inflated by a factor of chance, however, and for this reason the recognition method is the least useful for experimental purposes.

The method most frequently used by psychologists in experimental studies of retention is the *method of savings*. In this method the subject learns again a task that he learned some time before. The measure of retention is the difference in time or trials required for original mastery and for the second learning—the savings from the first learning. Suppose, for example, that it took me 20 repetitions to learn a certain poem. After a period of a month it took me only 10 repetitions to relearn the poem. I would then show a savings of 50 per cent. Such a method has the advantage of being very sensitive and at the same time reliable. Furthermore, it can show negative values. For example, suppose that for some reason or other I had taken 30 trials to relearn the poem; this would represent a negative savings of 50 per cent.

With this brief description of the principal methods of measuring retention, we are now ready to examine the results of research on retention.

AMOUNT OF RETENTION. How much of what we learn stays with us after a period of time? The first attempt to answer this question experimentally was made by the German psychologist Ebbinghaus. Ebbinghaus experimented on many different problems in verbal learning; he always used himself as the subject. The results of his studies were published in 1885 in a monograph, *Über das Gedächtnis*, or *Concerning Memory*.

Ebbinghaus memorized a list of nonsense syllables, such as *zeb, bep, cex, rab*. He allowed himself a period of rest, varying from a half-hour to a month, and then he learned them again. In this way he was able to measure the savings for different intervals between original learning and relearning.

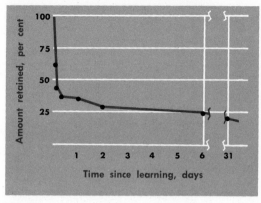

FIGURE 8.11. A classical curve of forgetting, obtained in early experiments by Ebbinghaus.

Ebbinghaus's results are shown in Figure 8.11. The savings are great for short intervals, but they decline rapidly during the first day after original learning. Thereafter the decline is much less abrupt.

This kind of curve is *negatively accelerated*, which is a way of saying that it changes more rapidly at the beginning than at the end. Such a negatively accelerated curve of retention is the rule; practically all retention curves are of this shape.

Many investigators have contrasted the retention of *meaningful material* with that of *nonsense material* [Kingsley and Garry, 1957]. Educational psychologists, for example, have studied the ability of students to remember material learned in school after periods of rest away from formal instruction. The outcome, in general, has been a negatively accelerated curve similar to that in Figure 8.11. The curve, however, usually does not fall so fast or so far as the curve for nonsense syllables, which means that meaningful material is more likely to be retained. Such studies make it quite clear that it is relatively hard to remember simple, isolated facts and relatively easy to retain meaningful material or material containing simple ideas.

This ties in with what we found earlier for ease of learning. We saw then that it was much easier to learn sense than to learn nonsense. Here we see that it is also easier to remember or retain sense than nonsense. Actually, one is the consequence of the other; the reason we don't remember nonsense or difficult material is that we never learned it very well in the first place. It was never recoded in terms of already existing associations.

Sometimes we are discouraged by the fact that we do not seem to recall very well most of the things we learn. At least we do not remember a lot that we spend a great deal of time patiently and deliberately learning. After 4 years, for example, we cannot remember the gender of German nouns, so most Americans who can speak a little German resort to a universal "der" by way of a definite article. Such forgetting, however, should not discourage us too much, for an equally remarkable fact is that we often show extraordinary degrees of savings. A rather dramatic story [Burtt, 1941] illustrates the last point:

Some years ago a psychologist undertook to read to his son passages in Greek from Sophocles's *Oedipus Tyrannus*. This is not such a remarkable thing for a professor to do, except for the fact that the son was only fifteen months old. Each day for 3 months, the professor read the same three selections of 20 lines each to the boy. When the boy was eight years old, he was required to learn by rote these selections plus some others of equal difficulty with which he had had no experience. It took the boy an average of 435 repetitions per selection to learn the new selections, and only 317 repetitions per selection to learn the old ones. Thus, even in infancy, learning of complex nonsense material (since that was surely what it was to the subject of this experiment) results in savings at a later date.

The moral of this story is, Do not be too upset about the precipitous decline in *recall* for the material that you may learn in school; there will probably be some considerable *savings* whenever you have an opportunity to use that material again or need to relearn it.

QUALITATIVE CHANGES IN RETENTION. You may have played or heard about the game of Gossip. In it, a group of individuals arrange themselves in some order. The first individual then reads a narrative to the second individual, and the second individual passes it on from memory to the third individual, and so on. Then the version at the end is compared with the original narrative. The results are usually astonishing and sometimes amusing. The "message" undergoes many changes. It is usually shortened, and becomes distorted in meaning. This game is of psychological importance because it is a useful model of certain kinds of social communication.

Gossip is also interesting because the changes that take place in the narrative as it passes from one player to another parallel the changes in memory that can happen within the same individual. If we ask a person to reproduce something after various intervals of time, we see that his memory of the thing undergoes the same losses and distortion of information. A British psychologist, Bartlett [1932], has studied these qualitative changes in great detail. In a verbal narrative, he finds that details are forgotten; the story loses much of its richness, becoming a threadbare structure. Certain phrases and words become stereotyped and appear in each repetition.

Similar changes occur in memory for perceptual objects. If subjects are shown visual forms, and later are asked to reproduce them successively, as the narrative is repeated in the game of Gossip, retention suffers from a loss of detail. There is a tendency, moreover, for the forms to become more general, more symmetrical, and more similar to familiar objects in successive reproductions. Examples of some of these changes are given in Figure 8.12.

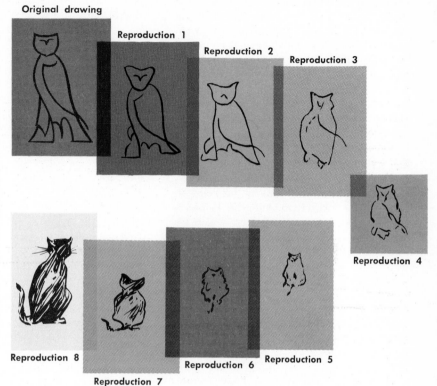

Original drawing

Reproduction 1

Reproduction 2

Reproduction 3

Reproduction 4

Reproduction 5

Reproduction 6

Reproduction 7

Reproduction 8

FIGURE 8.12. The original drawing was seen by one subject, and he was asked to reproduce it (first reproduction). Another subject looked at this reproduction and then copied it from memory (second reproduction). The same procedure was repeated throughout the series. Note how the figure changes from one reproduction to another. The distortions of memory change the figure from the conventionalized Egyptian symbol for an owl to a picture of a cat [after Bartlett, 1932].

Forgetting

If you were to ask a reasonably intelligent and well-informed person what caused forgetting, you might get the offhand reply, "Oh, just the passage of time, I guess." If pressed a little harder he might say, "Well, as time passes, the impressions of what we learn just get weaker and weaker and finally fade away."

If there is any truth at all in this notion, it cannot be the whole truth. Countless experiments have now demonstrated that it is not just the passage of time that determines how much we forget, but *it is what happens during that time.* What we do in between the time that we learn something and the time that we attempt to remember it influences how we will remember it. This

can be demonstrated in many experiments, including those to be described below.

RETENTION AFTER SLEEPING AND WAKING. Perhaps the most striking demonstration comes from a famous experiment [Jenkins and Dallenbach, 1924] in which two subjects were tested for retention of nonsense syllables after various periods of sleep and again after various periods of normal, wakeful activity. The results of this study are depicted in Figure 8.13. Sleep, as you can see, was followed by much higher retention than was wakeful activity.

This experiment has been repeated several times, and the results are always about the same [Newman, 1939]. Activity produces much more forgetting than does sleep. Furthermore, after the second hour of sleep, retention declines hardly at all.

RETROACTIVE INHIBITION. The next question is, What is there about being awake that causes more forgetting than does being asleep? We have many experiments that concern this question. They have been called experiments in *retroactive inhibition* because they show that our activity after we learn something somehow works backward to inhibit memories of what we have learned. Strictly speaking, the above experiment on sleep versus waking was one in retroactive inhibition because it showed that waking activity interfered with retention of something that was learned before the activity.

To understand this concept, it helps to realize that retroactive inhibition is just a special case of negative transfer, which we described a few pages back. Actually, retroactive inhibition is the reverse of negative transfer. *It is the harmful effect of learning or activity on the retention of learning that has gone before.* In both negative transfer and retroactive inhibition, practice or experience interferes with the learning or retention of something else.

The factors that explain negative transfer are also in large part those that explain retroactive inhibition. The important condition for negative transfer, you will recall, is that a different response to the same stimulus is required in two different situations. There are two interfering associations with the same stimulus. This same condition is important for retroactive inhibition. We may illustrate the point with an experiment on paired-associate learning.

Paired-associate learning is the name for learning in which a subject must learn to call one word when he is presented with some other word (see page 232). Suppose, for example, that we ask some subjects to associate the names of states with colors. We may regard the state names as *stimuli* and the color names as *responses,* because the subject must respond with a color ("red," for example) when he is presented with a state name ("Delaware," for example). In such an experiment, we mix up the pairs of color

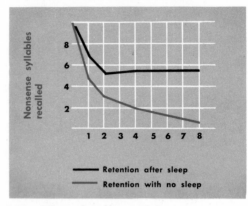

MEMORY IS BETTER PRESERVED DURING SLEEP THAN DURING WAKING:

FIGURE 8.13. Effect of waking activity compared with sleep on memory [after Jenkins and Dallenbach, 1924].

names and state names, so that the subject will not learn that one pair follows another.

After the subject has learned to perform this task with a certain degree of success, our next step in a retroactive-inhibition experiment is to give him a second task in which he must associate the *same* state names with *new* colors—"Delaware" may now, for example, be associated with "orange." The subject practices the new list of such pairs until he has learned it.

The last part of the experiment, finally, is to have the subject go back to the first list and give the color names he first learned to associate with the state-name stimuli. It should be obvious that the typical subject will find this difficult and that it will take a good deal of practice, with many errors, before he relearns the first list perfectly. In other words, he will display a great deal of retroactive inhibition on his original learning because of the second learning task. In the second task associations were formed that interfere with those learned in the first task. There are thus two interfering associations with the same stimulus.

The interfering effects of associations can carry forward as well as backward. Forward interference is called *proactive inhibition,* which is actually the same thing as negative transfer, described earlier. An experiment demonstrating proactive inhibition is merely the reverse of one on retroactive inhibition. Actually the design of the two experiments can be just the same, and all that is reversed is the effect of learning one set of associations on retention of another. In the retroactive inhibition experiment, we ask how the learning of a *second* set of color names and state names interferes with the recall of the *first* set. The interference or inhibition works both ways, both forward and backward.

THE NATURE OF FORGETTING.   In everyday life, of course, we cannot identify the stimuli and the responses involved in retroactive and proactive inhibition as we can in the experiment described above. In many experiments of this sort, however, psychologists have assured themselves that the principal factor in forgetting is interference, both retroactive and proactive, with other associations. That is to say, forgetting occurs because the stimuli involved in various learning tasks and in various aspects of waking activity are similar, and yet different responses must be made to these stimuli in different situations. *We forget because in large part associations interfere with one another.*

An example of this conclusion as well as of the proactive interference of things previously learned comes from studies [Underwood, 1957] of the recall of a series of lists:

Subjects first learned one list of 10 pairs of adjectives. Forty-eight hours later they were given a test of recall to determine how many of the pairs they remembered. A day later they were required to learn a new list of 10 pairs of adjectives. Forty-eight hours later, this list was tested for recall. A day later, a new list was learned, and so on until

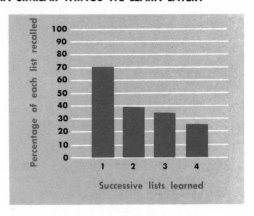

FIGURE 8.14. Proactive inhibition in the recall of lists of adjectives. Lists learned later were recalled more poorly than those learned earlier [Underwood, 1957].

four lists had been learned and tested for recall. The results are shown in Figure 8.14. The interesting thing about them is that the subjects got worse on successive lists. The more lists they learned, the less well they did on tests of recall. The conclusion drawn was that the learning of previous lists of adjectives interfered with the retention of new lists of adjectives.

This experiment happens to measure proactive inhibition—the effects of prior learning—but many experiments, conducted with different materials and under different conditions, all point to interference as the central process in forgetting. We don't just forget, we forget because new learning interferes with old learning.

It is still possible that part of our forgetting is merely a weakening of "memory traces" with the passage of time. Perhaps some of the changes in the brain that must take place in learning are somewhat temporary and simply weaken or fade with time. Certainly there is yet no clear proof that such fading cannot happen. It cannot, however, explain all the facts that psychologists have collected in their experiments.

The best and most complete explanation of forgetting now available is in terms of interference of associations.

REPRESSION AND FORGETTING. Even these, however, do not account for all forgetting. Quite frequently we see in people a type of forgetting that the psychoanalysts (see page 138) call *repression*. They discovered in their work that people with emotional conflicts tend to repress thoughts and memories that are particularly unpleasant or threatening, thereby avoiding, at least consciously, the conflicts that bother them. We described repression in Chapter 5, but we should review it briefly here.

There are many trivial examples of behavior in daily life that are easily interpreted as repression. I may forget, for example, that my wife has told me to get liver at the grocery store, because I do not like liver. We have probably all noticed that people tend to forget the names of people they do not like. As we saw in Chapter 5, however, the more important instances of repression are to be found in people who have powerful motives or strong anxieties that have not been relieved. For example, an individual may forget his early childhood experiences with sex because he has an intense anxiety about them.

As one might expect, it is difficult to produce repression in laboratory experiments because it is difficult—and undesirable—to create anxieties in people that are strong enough to cause repression. Some experimenters, however, have discovered that people tend to forget unpleasant things more rapidly than they do pleasant ones [Sharp, 1938]. It is also clear that people tend to remember better what they like and what fits in with their prejudices than they do other events [Edwards, 1942]. One investigator, moreover, was able to get people to remember material they had learned and forgotten by removing a source of anxiety connected with the memory [Zeller, 1950]. These various findings fit in with the psychoanalytic conception of repression.

Techniques of study

One of the uses of psychology that is of particular interest to college students is the improvement of methods of study. Psychologists have done considerable research on this problem, and have discovered ways in which almost every student can make some improvements, either in the time required for study or in the mastery of material studied. A summary of the practical applications of this research is given in this section for the benefit of students who may find them helpful in college study.

MOTIVATION TO STUDY. The main thing that keeps many students from developing effective study habits is lack of motivation. The students would like to do well in college, but they can't muster the fortitude to study when they should, and even when they settle down to study they can't really concentrate on the job. We know of no ready remedy for this malady, and can only offer a couple of good reasons for studying well.

First of all, the grades one makes in college are much more important than most students realize. To enter a graduate school or professional school of his choice, a student usually needs to have grades well above the average. Even business employers · pay attention to grades, and some take only students with high scholastic performance. There is evidence that those with the highest grades in college are also the ones who, on the average, succeed best in the business world [Gifford, 1928]. This may be partly a matter of ambition and ability, but it is also a result of the knowledge and good work habits acquired in college.

Secondly, being successful gives a student many satisfactions. Aside from the pleasure both a student and his parents take in a student's high grades, the good student can be a happy student because he is free of the worry that goes along with poor performance in courses. He also gets a lot of satisfaction out of knowing how to go about the job of studying and of knowing he is doing his work well.

Thirdly, once a student gets involved in a subject deeply enough to have some mastery of it, he may discover that it is fascinating in its own right. Then studying is no longer a chore; it is something the student would rather do than eat or play. He can take pleasure in knowing more and more about the subject, and in trying to unravel some of its unsolved problems. Teachers, professors, and creative people in a field usually regard their subject matter in this way. To be sure, not every subject can have a strong appeal for everyone, because individual aptitudes and interests vary, but the chances are good that some subjects will, once a person has learned how to study well enough to learn something about them.

ORGANIZING A STUDY ROUTINE. Besides motivation, what many students lack is a routine for study. They don't see to it that they have certain times and places for study, nor do they apportion their time well among their various subjects. Yet this is essential. They should make up a definite schedule for study, based on the difficulty and amount of work to be expected in each course, and then follow it reasonably well. And by all means, they should make sure that they are really studying when they are supposed to, rather than daydreaming, listening to the radio, or talking with their dormitory companions. They should take every possible step to ensure that they study when they study, play when they play, and not mix the two.

STUDY METHODS. Probably the most important things that a student can do to improve his college work are to develop strong motivation for study and have a well-organized routine. Here we shall point to some specific methods a student can use when he studies. The value of these methods will depend on the student—different techniques are suited to different students—and on the particular subject being studied.

There are, however, some good general rules that it is usually advantageous to follow.

Perhaps the best set of rules is to be found in the *Survey Q3R Method* [Robinson, 1946]. This grew out of an elaborate program at The Ohio State University that was designed to analyze and treat students' academic problems. We can rely on it as being a soundly tested system. It consists of five specific steps, labeled *Survey, Question, Read, Recite,* and *Review,* and this is why it is called the Survey Q3R Method.

Survey. When authors write textbooks, they go to some pains to organize their words under various headings so that the headings tell readers what to expect to find in each section. If you leaf through this book, for example, you will find scarcely a page without such a heading. Many students, however, ignore the headings and try to read textbooks in the same way they read novels. When they do that, they ignore much of the author's careful work and flounder in a morass of information they are not prepared to assimilate.

One important precept, then, is *use the headings.* They give the author's organization, they tell you how the material is put together, and they make it clear how topics go together and follow each other. Most important, they make it clear what the main subject of each section is going to be. When you finish reading a section, you should have located a few points that bear on the heading. Anything else in the section will be secondary or relatively unimportant. The student should also pay attention to the order of headings. Most textbooks use two or three orders of headings. This one, for example, has three.

At this point, the student who has noticed the heading of this section will realize that we have not yet come to the main idea, for that heading reads "Survey." We told you about headings in order to lead up to that point.

The first thing to do when you pick up a textbook is to run through the headings of the various chapters, for this is a way of *surveying* the book in general. In starting on a chapter, begin by surveying the various headings of sections of the chapter. In this way, you learn generally what the chapter is about and know what to expect. It is also a good idea to skim some of the sentences here and there in the chapter and to look at some of the pictures and graphs. In addition, if there is a summary, read it as part of your survey, for it will give you the most important points of the chapter before details begin to clutter up the picture.

Question. Some textbooks contain lists of review questions at the end of each chapter. (We have provided questions in a separate Study Guide designed to accompany the text). These questions are usually the most neglected parts of the book, for students do not realize their value in studying. If a book has them, read them and try to answer them. It is also valuable to *ask your own questions*. Try to turn the headings of sections into questions and read the sections with the idea of finding the answers to your questions.

Questions have several benefits. For one thing, they maintain interest in what is being read. For another, they make you actively participate in the learning process, rather than read passively. Psychological research clearly shows that active participation is a great aid in learning. Finally, questions are ways of testing yourself to see what you are learning or have learned. If you test yourself before the instructor does, you will do much better when faced with a formal examination.

Read. The next step, of course, is to read—and to read carefully. Read to answer the questions you have asked yourself. Do not read passively, as you would read a novel, but continually challenge yourself as you go along to make sure that you understand what you read. And, of course, *read to remember*. Every once in a while, remind yourself of your task—to understand and remember what you read. If you do, you will no longer voice the familiar complaint, "I forget what I read as soon as I am

through." Notice especially any words or phrases that are italicized. Authors use italics to emphasize important terms, concepts, and principles.

Also, make sure to read everything, and that means tables, graphs, and other illustrations, as well as the main text. Illustrations are used to emphasize important points in the text and to clarify them. Sometimes, in fact, a mere glance at an illustration will tell vividly what a whole page of the book is about. In other cases, illustrations convey information that cannot be expressed easily in words. In this book, for example, we occasionally tell a story with pictures that are not specifically mentioned in the text. These are just as important in the reading of the book as are the headings, paragraphs, and sentences of the text.

Recite. Recitation is one of the most important techniques of effective study, yet it is very much neglected—because it takes effort. When one just reads, he has the comfort of thinking that what is read is understood and remembered, but this is generally not true. To make certain that one understands and remembers, he should stop periodically and try to recall to himself what he has read. In other words, he should recite. At this point, for example, you might ask yourself what you have read so far in this section. Try to recall the main headings and the principal ideas under each heading. Can you give a synopsis of your reading without looking at the pages? Try to do it, then check yourself. See whether you have covered everything. If not, note your omissions and errors. Then a little later, recite again. As you read, stop at intervals to recite the substance of each major section of a chapter. When you review for examinations, again make recitation a substantial part of your procedure in preparing for them.

There are at least two good reasons for this emphasis on recitation. One is that recitation serves to keep your *attention* on the task, for you obviously cannot daydream while you are trying to recall something. Another is that it lets you *correct mistakes;* it shows you where you are weakest and where, in a second reading, you can profitably spend the most time.

Recitation is more useful for some subjects than it is for others. In general, it helps most when what you have to learn is disconnected and not too meaningful. If, for example, you have to memorize a number of rules, items, names, laws, or formulas, then recitation is of great help. On the other hand, for meaningful, storylike material, such as one finds in history or philosophy, recitation is somewhat less useful—though never useless. Hence you should vary the amount of time or the proportion of study time that you use for recitation according to the subject you are studying. Because this book contains considerable factual information, probably one-third to one-half the time spent in studying it should be spent in recitation.

Review. The fifth precept in the Survey Q3R technique is "review." If you learn something perfectly but do not review it, you will find that a few days or even hours later you will remember only a small part of it.

Here are some pointers for the best way of reviewing. *The best times for review are immediately after first studying and again just before an examination,* but it will also pay to have one or two reviews in between. The first review may be fairly brief, because there has been little time for forgetting, and it should be mainly one of recitation. The review just before the examination should also emphasize recitation, but it should be much more intensive—and usually is. Intervening reviews that are relatively brief help, and these may emphasize rereading somewhat more than recitation. Perhaps it should go without saying that reviewing should not be crammed into the last few hours before an examination. This practice makes the final task too hard, and it does not give you, at the time of examination, the mastery that you could have with a few well-spaced reviews.

TAKING LECTURE NOTES. The Survey Q3R Method applies to lectures as well as to textbooks, but not in every detail. Obviously, it is difficult or impossible to survey a lecture in advance unless the instructor does it for you—and few do that. The student must therefore provide his own organization and headings as he goes. It is important, however, to *organize.* Do this by trying to identify the lecturer's main points. *Condense his paragraphs into simple phrases or sentences, and do this in words of your own phrasing.* But sometimes this is difficult to do, and you are forced to take copious, unorganized notes to keep up with the lecture. In such circumstances, do not spend so much time trying to take neat, well-organized notes that you lose the point of the lecture; almost any kind of notes is better than none at all. Still, the more organized your notes are, the better they will be.

It is hard to say how many notes you should take. This will vary with the lecture, the lecturer, and the temperament of the student. Some students do their best by taking many notes, and others do best by taking relatively few. If you write easily, it is probably best to err on the side of taking too many.

Review is even more important for lecture notes than it is for reading. Because lecture notes are incomplete, a brief review after class usually is necessary to fill in omitted essentials and correct minor errors. Waiting too long to do that makes one forget, and he may easily wind up saying, "My lecture notes just don't make sense." It will often pay to rewrite lecture notes completely shortly after each lecture, both to provide a good review with recitation and to make it possible to understand your notes later.

Finally, let us remind you that it is important to keep lecture notes in a well-organized state. It is well to use the same kind of paper for all notes in one subject, to keep them in a notebook and not lying around in various places, and to number the pages to keep them in order. In any event, make sure to have a system that is good enough to let you find all your material quickly and to study it easily.

TAKING EXAMINATIONS.   Having read this heading, you may say, "Ah, that's what I want to know—how to take an examination." Many of us would like to know how to pass examinations without studying, but that is a bit of magic no psychologist has yet produced. In fact, the only good general rule for taking examinations is "Be prepared." And in preparation, do not bank too much on guessing what the instructor will ask. Sometimes this works, but sometimes it fails. It is a far better policy to be prepared for any reasonable question that the instructor might possibly ask.

Examinations divide themselves roughly into two classes, the *objective* and the *essay,* though there are several shades in between. You will probably want to prepare for the two types somewhat differently, and you should take them with somewhat different attitudes.

Objective examinations are usually *recognition* tests. They simply require that you recognize the right answer when you see it. It is important, however, to read and answer each question carefully. Sometimes the correct answer may hang on an all-important "not" or "always," and you may miss it if you read carelessly. It is usually best first to go straight through the examination, answering all the questions you are sure of and checking those you cannot answer immediately. When you are through, go back to the harder question. Remember that in an objective examination it is a mistake to concentrate too much on a few difficult questions, for they usually count no more than the others. If you do that, you will not have time to finish, or you will have to rush through the other questions and will make needless mistakes. If you have time at the end, carefully review your answers and correct your mistakes.

Essay examinations emphasize the ability to understand, organize, and *recall* informa-

tion. To prepare well for them, you should especially emphasize the active parts of studying—surveying and recitation. In taking the examination, remember that the instructor usually will think better of a paper if the information in it is well organized rather than rambling and discursive. So take time to organize your thoughts before you begin to write. Make sure to answer the question that the instructor asks, not a slightly different one on which you may be better prepared. Keep your answers to the point, and avoid digressions and irrelevant information—for they do not impress most instructors. Try to leave time to reread your answers at the end of the examination so that you can add important points you forgot or correct any mistakes.

Programmed learning

A student is a person who is making a business of learning. To help him to learn, a student usually has a teacher. He has a teacher presumably because he can learn faster with a teacher than without one. Similarly, he has textbooks, which have been written for the purpose of helping him to learn. The justification for both teachers and textbooks, however, is that they really do help the student to learn. How effectively do they do that?

SCIENTIFIC LEARNING PRINCIPLES.   Textbooks and teachers certainly do help students to learn; otherwise they would have been dispensed with. However, if we review what has been said in this and the preceding chapter about the science of learning, we can see that they have two serious limitations.

1. They emphasize *presentation* rather than *doing.* Teachers and textbooks tend to limit, or even to prohibit, active recitation on the part of the student. Hence they are merely stimuli. And we have seen that relatively little learning takes place when an organism is exposed to stimuli and has little it can do about them. To learn most effectively, organisms must respond. They must

somehow be motivated to do this and then have the opportunity to respond appropriately.

2. Teachers and textbooks provide no immediate *knowledge of results.* Examinations tell a student generally how well he is doing, but they provide too little information and too late. The best learning takes place when each response has a consequence—is rewarded or punished, is labeled correct or incorrect. An organism needs to know after each response how far from, or near to, being correct it is if it is to achieve mastery, and to achieve it efficiently, in a learning situation.

These two limitations might, in principle, be removed if we could provide each student with a tutor and have the tutor trained to use these principles. In practice, however, tutors are rare and they would be prohibitively expensive—at a time when an increasing number of students need to be taught and there is a shortage of teachers.

Of course movies, slides, recordings, laboratories, and demonstrations can make up for some of the things teachers and textbooks lack. They are often interesting and thus increase motivation in the student. They often incorporate skillful and efficient ways of putting things across. Audiovisual aids certainly have their place in the teaching process—in helping the student to learn—and they will be exploited more and more in the future. Even so, these aids are lacking in the two important respects we have mentioned—in providing for active recitation and knowledge of results. How then can we do something to incorporate these important elements in the learning process?

PROGRAMMED LEARNING. This problem has recently been getting a great deal of attention. All sorts of new teaching techniques have been proposed; some are being tried out, and some are going into use in educational institutions of various levels from elementary school through college. Most of the new techniques fall into one of two categories: *teaching machines* or *programmed textbooks.* Each of these approaches will be described below, but first we should note the things they have in common. There are four:

First, they involve *programmed learning.* Hence they are collectively referred to as *programmed-learning methods.* This means that they employ written scripts or programs carefully worked out to guide the student's learning [Lumsdaine and Glaser, 1960].

Next, they involve the student in tasks— they give him something to *respond* to. They do not merely present information to him. They are based on the fact that if you give someone a puzzle, or merely ask him a question, he usually will rise to the occasion. He will respond. If as soon as he has answered one question or completed one task you give him another, he will respond again. If the problems you put to the person are reasonable and interesting and are problems he knows he ought to be doing, he will tend to keep working for a long period of time— usually much longer than he manages to keep his attention on a textbook or lecture. A properly designed learning program puts questions or problems to a student that motivate him to make responses.

A third feature of programmed-learning methods is that they permit the student to *proceed at his own pace.* Lectures certainly do not do this, for they require the same amount of time from everybody. They are too slow for the fast learner and too fast for the slow learner. This is true also of recitation techniques. Learning programs, on the other hand, can be given to students individually, and each student can work away at the program as rapidly or as slowly as his abilities and work habits permit.

A fourth feature of most learning programs is that the *steps* in learning are made reasonably *small.* From what we know of animal and human learning, as well as from teaching experience, we conclude that almost every student can progress in small steps, relatively few in large ones. Small steps ensure that what a person has learned he has learned well and that he is really ready to take the next ones. With textbooks and lectures the steps taken are frequently too large, because there is not space or time to spell out every little step.

These four features of modern programmed-learning methods do much to remove the first limitation of teachers and textbooks mentioned earlier in this section—the lack of active recitation or response on the part of the learner. How well they deal with the second limitation, a lack of knowledge of results, depends on the particular programming method used. Let us look then at the two general kinds of methods: first teaching machines, then programmed textbooks.

TEACHING MACHINES. Proposals for devices that would serve as "teachers" were made more than thirty years ago. They made little headway, however, until the late 1950s. At that time, interest in them was aroused largely through the efforts of B. F. Skinner (1958) of Harvard University who designed, built, and tried out a series of machines programmed for different subjects. There are now dozens of such devices either on the market or in an experimental stage of development. They have been called teaching machines, though this is something of a misnomer since they neither teach nor take the place of the teacher. They supplement teachers and textbooks in helping students to learn. To explain what teaching machines are like, we shall refer to two prototypes designed by Skinner.

One of the principal purposes of teaching machines is to provide continuous knowledge of results, to let the individual know whether he is making the correct responses or not. Exactly how the machine does this depends on the subject being taught. It is relatively easy to provide continuous knowledge of results in a subject like arithmetic. Hence one of the first machines Skinner built was to help children learn arithmetic. His machine presents problems to the student one at a time. The student simply records his answer to each one by pressing some keys on the machine. If his answer is

correct, the machine immediately rings a bell, flashes a light, or otherwise indicates that the answer is right.

For the kind of material learned in psychology, the social sciences, and the humanities, Skinner designed a different kind of machine. For these subjects both the question and the answer are put on a tape or a disk (see Figure 8.15). The answer, however, remains covered when the question is first put to the student. The student writes his answer down at an appropriate place on the tape; then he pushes a control that uncovers the answer, and thus he can compare his answers with the correct one. By operating another control, he can move the tape or disk into position for presenting the next problem.

Teaching machines such as these clearly

FIGURE 8.15. A student studying with a teaching machine. A question or problem is presented in the left window, and he writes his answer on paper tape appearing in the right window. After that, by pushing a button, he can uncover the correct answer in the upper part of the left window. Another pushbutton controls the advance of a new problem-and-answer tape into the respective windows [B. F. Skinner].

have the advantage of telling the student exactly how he is doing. Hence they overcome the deficiency of textbooks and teachers in this respect. By providing a knowledge of results, teaching machines promote effective learning, and, furthermore, enable the student to spend time learning what he does not know rather than what he already knows. A lot of time in classroom teaching and in studying textbooks is wasted because the student is learning nothing or is going over things he already knows. (This, of course, varies considerably from student to student.) The machine can help in this situation by presenting problems that have not been answered before and by eliminating problems the student has answered correctly. In addition the tape or disk can be made to repeat a problem the student has gotten wrong, and to continue to do so until he has answered every problem correctly. Such perfect learning is seldom achieved with conventional methods.

Teaching machines, then, seem to provide two important conditions for learning that are otherwise difficult to obtain. They get the learner to respond, and they let him know where he stands in the learning process.

Machines have their limitations, however. For one, they are relatively expensive. Even the simplest machines cost several times the price of a textbook, and the more complicated ones required for college-level learning can run into hundreds of dollars. For this reason, and also because they are bulky and not really portable, one machine must serve a good many students, and the use of machines must be supervised, for example, in a library. Hence a student cannot study on his own schedule. Finally, machines require specially made programming materials such as tapes, disks, or films. All of these limitations restrict their usefulness.

PROGRAMMED TEXTBOOKS. Textbooks, of course, do not have these restrictions. They can be manufactured by well-established methods, they are sold at a cost considerably less than a machine, and they can be owned and used by the individual student. Why not use a programmed textbook instead of a teaching machine?

A learning program can indeed be printed in textbook form as well as in the form required by a teaching machine. In such a form, it can achieve the first general purpose of programmed learning methods; it can pose questions or problems for the student to solve and thus motivate him to make responses. Experiments have been done with the kinds of programs that could be used in textbook form, and with satisfactory results. They do aid learning. Hence it is probably only a matter of time until programmed textbooks become, along with teaching machines, fairly common teaching devices.

Programmed textbooks, however, are seriously limited in providing continuous knowledge of results. Keys can be supplied that enable a student to check his answers, as is done in conventional workbooks and study guides, but usually the student working with a problem must turn elsewhere in his book or to a separate sheet to make his check. He does not have a bell ring or the correct answer appear next to the answer he has just made. Nor does a textbook provide any automatic way of repeating for the student only his previously incorrect responses. Hence the programmed textbook does not supply immediate knowledge of results as effectively as a machine. Since the programmed textbook has its advantages, however, these must be balanced against its limitations. Consequently both teaching machines and programmed textbooks have a place in providing more effective teaching through programmed learning.

THE LEARNING PROGRAM. The series of statements and questions used in a teaching machine or a programmed textbook is called its *program*. How well the method teaches depends on the program. This in turn depends on whether the programmer (the teacher making up the program) knows what steps the program should take and how to set up the statements and questions. Preparing the program, like most teaching and textbook writing, is still an art rather than a science. We simply have not discovered precisely the best program for any type of teaching. Programmed learning methods, however, offer the opportunity for experimenting with different programs and finding out through research what kinds of programs are most efficient in guiding the learner to mastery of a subject—something we have seldom been able to do with conventional lectures and textbooks.

Figures 8.16 and 8.17 are examples of parts of programs that have been used in experimental work on teaching machines. Figure 8.16 reproduces a set of frames designed to teach a third- or fourth-grade pupil to spell the word "manufacture." Each of the numbered boxes is a frame appearing in a window. Note that in the first problem the child merely copies the word. That is to give him practice in making all the letters and to set the stage for spelling parts of the word. The subsequent problems, each a very small step, require him to fill in only a few letters, and each provides such a broad hint that he is very likely to get the answer right. After four such steps, he is given the problem of spelling the whole word. Even then, he has the aid of context, which incidentally exploits the factor of meaningfulness.

Another example at a somewhat higher level is part of a program for teaching high school physics (Figure 8.17). Here the sentence-completion technique is employed. Note that the first items in the program are questions that are so obvious that they can hardly be missed. Each question, however, contains within it words or hints that make it easy to answer the next question. In this way, the student tends to be responding with correct answers and at the same time learns new concepts at a fairly good rate. After he has written his answer to each item, he can uncover the correct answer to see whether he is right.

As we said above, several teaching machines and several methods of programming

1. **Manufacture** means to make or build. *Chair factories manufacture chairs.* Copy the word here:

☐ ☐ ☐ ☐ ☐ ☐ ☐ ☐ ☐ ☐

2. Part of the word is like part of the word **factory.** Both parts come from an old word meaning *make* or *build.*

m a n u ☐ ☐ ☐ ☐ u r e

FIGURE 8.16. Part of a program in experimental work on teaching machines. This set of frames is designed to teach third- or fourth-grade pupils to spell the word "manufacture" [B. F. Skinner, 1958].

3. Part of the word is like part of the word **manual.** Both parts come from an old word for *hand.* Many things used to be made by hand.

☐ ☐ ☐ ☐ f a c t u r e

4. The same letter goes in both spaces:

m ☐ n u f ☐ c t u r e

5. The same letter goes in both spaces:

m a n ☐ f a c t ☐ r e

6. **Chair factories** ☐ ☐ ☐ ☐ ☐ ☐ ☐ ☐ ☐ ☐ ☐ **chairs.**

CHAPTER EIGHT

	Word to be supplied
Sentence to be completed	

1. The important parts of a flashlight are the battery and the bulb. When we "turn on" a flashlight, we close a switch which connects the battery with the _____.   bulb

2. When we turn on a flashlight, an electric current flows through the fine wire in the _____ and causes it to grow hot.   bulb

3. When the hot wire glows brightly, we say that it gives off or sends out heat and _____.   light

4. The fine wire in the bulb is called a filament. The bulb "lights up" when the filament is heated by the passage of a(n) _____ current.   electric

5. When a weak battery produces little current, the fine wire, or _____, does not get very hot.   filament

6. A filament which is **less** hot sends out or gives off _____ light.   less

7. "Emit" means "send out." The amount of light sent out, or "emitted," by a filament depends on how _____ the filament is.   hot

8. The higher the temperature of the filament, the _____ the light emitted by it.   brighter, stronger

9. If a flashlight battery is weak, the _____ in the bulb may still glow, but with only a dull red color.   filament

10. The light from a very hot filament is colored yellow or white. The light from a filament which is not very hot is colored _____.   red

FIGURE 8.17. Part of a program for teaching high school physics with a teaching machine. The machine presents one item at a time. The student completes the item and then uncovers the corresponding word or phrase shown at the right [B. F. Skinner, 1958].

books are now in the experimental stage, and some teaching machines and programmed textbooks are gradually being introduced into our school systems. We have described only the broad outlines of a new trend in teaching techniques—one that utilizes sound scientific learning principles and that promises a kind of "break through" in education and learning.

MACHINES AND THE TEACHER. Both students and teachers, when they first hear of teaching machines and programmed textbooks, often ask whether their designers are "trying to do away with the teacher." After all, machines and books lack the personal touch of teachers, and the interaction between teacher and student supplies something a book or machine cannot. Moreover, mechanical programs are not, for the present anyway, suited to "explaining things" or to teaching complicated concepts. Programmed learning methods will probably never do away with teachers, just as machines have not done away with the workingman in industry.

If programming can be successfully developed, however, it will serve as an important adjunct to the teacher. It may motivate the student to do his "homework," which is a hard thing for teachers to do. It may get him to master the facts that require memorization or simply hard work, so that he will know these when he comes to class. It may relieve the teacher of having to present facts, rules, formulas, and the like, which the students, with proper self-instruction, can learn better for themselves. If these things can be accomplished by programming methods, then class discussions and intepretative lectures will be much more fruitful learning experiences than they now are. Programmed learning may also make the whole teaching process more economical.

Summary

1. The learning of a skill may be charted as a curve of decreasing errors or increasing accuracy. Often there are plateaus in such a curve. These usually represent a shift in the kind of learning or a change in motivation.

2. Of the many factors that affect rate of learning, four of the most important are: (*a*) whether practice is distributed over a period of time with frequent rests or massed in one period of "cramming," (*b*) whether or not immediate and accurate knowledge of results is provided, (*c*) whether time is spent in recitation *and* reading or merely in reading alone, and (*d*) whether the material to be learned is meaningful or relatively nonsensical.

3. Images are important in memory. Some young children, and more rarely adults, possess eidetic imagery; they can recall a previous experience with almost photographic accuracy. Typically, memory images are very imperfect copies of an experience.

4. Visual scenes that can easily be recoded by identifying them with previous associations, e.g., a face or house, are easily remembered, but those which resemble nothing that is familiar or those which cannot be schematized are very difficult to remember.

5. Meaningfulness is important in learning associations between words. Familiar words are easily associated; nonsense words are difficult to associate.

6. In learning lists of words by the method of anticipation—by associating each succeeding word with the word just before it—we find that remote associations between words separated in the list are formed in addition to associations between adjacent words. These remote associations interfere with the correct associations. They account in large part for the fact that the associations at the beginning and the end of the list are more easily learned than those in the middle.

7. In sentences, certain words tend to follow other words. Thus sequential associations are formed. These give language a statistical structure.

8. Transfer of training refers to the effect of learning one task on the subsequent learning of another. Transfer may be either positive or negative. When both the stimuli and the responses involved in two tasks are similar, transfer is positive. When the responses required are competing or opposite to one another, transfer is negative.

9. In formal education, there is little or no transfer between subjects that have little in common. The degree of transfer from one subject to another depends on elements the two subjects have in common.

10. There are three basic methods of measuring retention: recall, recognition, and savings. Of these, recall is the least sensitive and savings (in relearning of the same material) the most sensitive measure of retention. Even when there is little retention as measured by recall, there may be considerable retention as measured by the time required to relearn (savings).

11. Memory for a story or a picture changes qualitatively over a period of time. Details are lost, the parts remembered come

to resemble familiar objects and events, and certain features become stereotyped.

12. The most important factor in forgetting is interference of associations. Interference takes the form of retroactive inhibition, which is interference from things subsequently learned, and proactive inhibition, which is interference from associations previously learned.

13. The most important problem in studying effectively is to develop the motivation to study, but the student must somehow supply this himself. Organizing a study routine helps many students.

14. Through systematic research on techniques of study, a program of study, called Survey Q3R, has been developed. It consists of five steps: Survey, Question, Read, Recite, and Review.

15. Teachers and textbooks have two serious limitations: they emphasize presentation rather than doing, and they provide no immediate knowledge of results. To supplement them, learning programs presented through teaching machines or programmed textbooks are being developed. Such programmed learning methods give the student something to respond to, let him proceed at his own pace, and make the learning steps reasonably small.

16. Teaching machines and programmed textbooks have different advantages and limitations. The effectiveness of both depends on their programs, which must be developed through trial and error and through research. Programmed machines and textbooks are designed to supplement the teacher, not replace him.

Suggestions for further reading

Deese, J. *The psychology of learning* (2d ed.). New York: McGraw-Hill, 1958.
An introductory textbook on the psychology of learning.

Hilgard, E. R. *Theories of learning* (2d ed.). New York: Appleton-Century-Crofts, 1956.
A balanced treatment of the major theories of learning and a discussion of experiments related to these theories.

Keller, F. S., and Schoenfeld, W. N. *Principles of psychology.* New York: Appleton-Century-Crofts, 1950.
A general introduction to psychology that interprets human behavior in terms of the principles of instrumental learning.

Kingsley, H. R., and Garry, R. *Nature and conditions of learning* (2d ed.). Englewood Cliffs, N.J.: Prentice-Hall, 1957.
A textbook covering the general field of learning.

Lumsdaine, A. A., and Glaser, R. (eds.). *Teaching machines and programmed learning.* Washington, D.C.: National Education Association, 1960.
A source book of recent work on programmed learning methods.

McGeoch, J. A., and Irion, A. L. *Psychology of human learning* (rev. ed.). New York: Longmans, 1952.
A comprehensive text and reference work on human learning.

Morgan, C. T., and Deese, J. *How to study.* New York: McGraw-Hill, 1957.
A booklet describing techniques of study.

Stephens, J. M. *Educational psychology* (2d ed.). New York: Holt, Rinehart and Winston, 1956.
An application of the principles of learning to problems in education.

Woodworth, R. S., and Schlosberg, H. *Experimental psychology* (rev. ed.). New York: Holt, Rinehart and Winston, 1954.
A comprehensive text in experimental psychology containing chapters on learning, remembering, and forgetting.

Language
& thinking

Ask a man on the street, or even a college sophomore, what sets man apart from animals and he is likely to say, "People can talk and think; animals can't." That answer is just about right. Animals have some semblance of capacity to communicate and to reason, but they are separated from man by a very wide gap. Not so obvious to the man on the street is another respect in which man vastly overshadows the animals. This is the ability to form concepts. Man can react to, and think of, some general property of objects, such as redness or goodness, which he has abstracted from his previous experience.

Signs, symbols, and meaning

The three abilities just mentioned—to use language, to employ concepts, and to think—are interlinked. It is hard to discuss one without bringing in the others. But we must start somewhere, and the thing they have in common is that in all three symbols are used to convey meaning, both to others in communication and to ourselves in thinking. So we shall start with symbols and the way they acquire meaning. Then we shall be in a position to consider thinking, concept formation, and language in some detail.

SIGNS, SIGNALS, AND SYMBOLS.   The red light we encounter at traffic intersections may be perceived in two entirely different ways: simply as a red light with certain psychophysical characteristics (see Chapter 11), or as a sign not to cross the intersection. A sign is any stimulus that stands for something else. Hence any time we learn to respond to a stimulus in a certain way, the stimulus acquires the property of a sign. When Pavlov conditioned a dog to salivate in response to a bell (page 195), he was converting a stimulus into a sign—a sign of food to come. When the dog salivated to the bell, it responded *in part*—this "in part," as we shall see later, is important—as it would to food.

We should pause to note that there are subtle differences in meaning among sign, signal, and symbol [English and English, 1958]. *Sign* is the most general term; it refers to any stimulus that stands for something else. Both signal and symbol are signs, but they connote *intention* to communicate. A *signal*, strictly speaking, is a sign used to indicate that the time and place for something to happen is at hand. *Symbol* has a broader meaning; it is a sign used to stand for (represent) something else. Thus, the traffic signal and Pavlov's bell are both signals and symbols because they signal the time to do or expect something, and they represent something else. The word "stop" would similarly be both signal and symbol. But the word "house" is a symbol, not a signal, for it stands for the object house but indicates nothing about time and place. The words of a language are usually symbols because they are used by a person to communicate something for which they stand. Occasionally, however, the intent to communicate may be lacking, as when a person exclaims, "Ouch!" In this case the word is a sign, but not a symbol (or signal).

The conditioning of salivation to a bell is the simplest kind of signaling. It merely conveys one message, that food is to come. Pavlov, of course, taught his dogs more complicated signals. His next step was to use one kind of bell to signal "food," and another to signal "no food," thereby setting up a conditioned differentiation. This is comparable to the red light and green lights signaling "stop" and "go" at our traffic intersections. Sometimes animals have been taught more complex sets of signals in the laboratory or in circus training, but for sophisticated systems of signs, signals, and symbols we must look to man rather than to animals.

NATURAL SIGNS.   In general, then, learning to respond to stimuli is the learning of signs. The thing that the sign stands for is the meaning of the sign. (We shall learn more about meaning later.) Signs, however, may acquire meaning in at least two different ways. One is by the *natural relation* of events encountered in nature. We learn, for example, that the growl of a dog may be followed by a bite, that thunder is often a prelude to rain, that where there is smoke there is fire. In each case, the meaning perceived depends upon our previously having learned that certain stimuli belong together.

Animals and people learn to adapt to their environment, and to survive, by learning the meaning of these natural signs. The number of such signs, however, is limited, and there are all kinds of events for which there are no naturally occurring signs.

WORDS AS SYMBOLS.   A second class of signs includes those that have been *invented* by man and assigned to events. These signs, because they are used with intent to communicate, may be called symbols. The bell in Pavlov's experiment, of course, is such an invented symbol. It was "assigned" meaning by Pavlov's conditioning procedure. The red light at a traffic intersection is another invented symbol. In each case, the symbol has no natural relation to the event for which it stands. Since such symbols are invented, we can devise any number of them we like, and then arrange them in a system to stand for a corresponding number of events.

Many different kinds of signs have been

and can be used as symbols. In some parts of the world, including some American street corners, whistling is a well-understood symbol; in others, drumming is used extensively. Almost all societies use gestures of the hands and face as symbols. Societies which speak different languages, but are in close contact with each other—as was the case with the American Indians—may use hundreds of gestures as signals to surmount the language barrier (Figure 9.1). The most highly developed system of symbols, however, is a language in which words are spoken and written in different combinations.

A language, as we shall see later, is more than a set of words, but for the moment let us think of it as that. Each word is a stimulus that can, by conditioning or association, come to symbolize some event in our experience. The distinctive thing about language, as contrasted with naturally occurring signs, is its enormous capacity for providing discriminably different symbols. A language makes available tens or hundreds of thousands of potential symbols, whereas the symbols afforded by nature, or even by other devices of human invention, are far less numerous.

Another important thing about language is that each individual carries around with him the equipment both for generating and receiving words as stimuli. No heavy or expensive hardware is required. Our built-in equipment provides many years of trouble-free operation with a minimum cost in weight, size, and energy expenditure. It is no wonder then that words have become such a highly developed system of communicating with each other and ourselves.

More than mere equipment, however, is required. An enormously large number of

FIGURE 9.1. Some manual signs in Indian sign language. See if you can tell which sign is used to represent each of the following: fast, fight, fish, food, house, hot, hungry, snake, and snow. Correct answers are given in the footnote on p. 258 [after Tomkins, 1931].

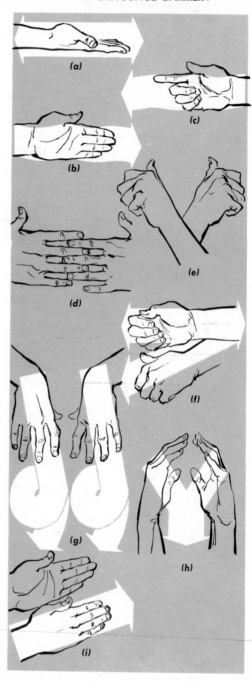

discriminations must be learned. Without these, our words would be useless. This is because an organism cannot utilize a symbol unless it can distinguish among the different things being symbolized. To have the symbols "house" and "tree" mean something, for example, an organism must be able to discriminate between the physical objects house and tree.

Though many animals are capable of learning such a simple discrimination, none seems able to learn so many fine discriminations as man can. Consider, for example, all the different objects for which we use such symbols as "house," "tree," "plant," "car," "street," and so on. Most human beings have learned to discriminate among literally thousands of such objects. And, of course, we discriminate many things besides objects, including the words in language itself. The process of learning all these discriminations requires a prodigious amount of effort and time. The process, as we shall see later, is greatly aided by language itself. In the end, though, man can use language effectively only because he learns to make so many discriminations.

THE MEANING OF MEANING. We saw previously (Chapter 7) that an association is formed whenever any two events, stimuli or responses, are repeatedly paired. Elsewhere the meaningfulness of stimuli was referred to (Chapter 8). We are now ready to see how association and meaningfulness are related.

Associative processes. First, let us again recall the Pavlovian experiment of conditioning a dog to salivate to a bell. In our paradigm of this conditioning, we represent the bell (the conditioning stimulus or CS) as forming an association with the response of salivation (the unconditioned response or UR). This seems clear enough. We should now note, however, that the dog's *unconditioned response* to food (the unconditioned stimulus or US) is more than mere salivation. The dog *eats* the food. On the other hand, to the conditioning stimulus the bell, it merely *salivates*.

The point here is that the CS only calls forth *part* of the response to the US. Apparently it takes the sight of food and perhaps other conditions as well, to get a dog to eat. This may seem sensible enough, for a dog can hardly eat food that isn't there. Yet if the conditioning process simply substituted the CS for the US in evoking the usual response to the CS, it might be expected that the dog would make some of the motions of eating food. Obviously, association is no such mechanical process.

This example from Pavlovian conditioning illustrates the general result of many different experiments. Experimenters have often compared the conditioned response with the original unconditioned response. The two are almost invariably different in some respect. Hence the association formed in learning must be only a part or *fraction* of the original response.

Salivation in bell-food conditioning is a response we can see and measure. In some circumstances, however, the associated "response" is not observable at all. This is the case in "sensory association," in which two different stimuli are paired together in the absence of any response (page 188). It was also the case in incidental learning, where the associations formed were not anything that could be discerned at the time (page 211). In both instances, by subsequently training the organism to do something that could be done only by means of association, we could demonstrate that the associations had been formed. So the association formed in learning is often not even an observable part of an original unconditioned response.

We therefore conclude (1) that an association is a process within the person that is some fraction of the original unlearned (or previously learned) process, and (2) that the process may be so small a fraction of the original one that it is not observable. The latter point is the reason we refer to the association as a process rather than a response. Further, and more important, this process *is* the meaning of the stimulus that arouses it. In other words, we say that *a stimulus is meaningful when it arouses some of the same process that may be aroused by some other stimulus.*

Mediating processes. Meanings can be meanings and nothing more. A symbol can evoke a meaning without anything else happening. I say "house" and that arouses a meaning in you, but without further instructions or without your having some problem to solve, the matter may end there.

In other cases, particularly in thinking or problem solving, a meaning is more than a mere meaning. It is a link to something else. It may be linked either (1) to a response of some kind or (2) to other meanings. If I instructed you to start out with "house" and freely associate to it, you might say, "home," "mother," "father," "children," "school," and so on. In this case the meaning of the word would be a link both to a response and to another meaning. The important point is that meanings serve as intervening links connecting psychological processes. They themselves, of course, are also psychological processes.

When we regard meaning as a link, we say it is a "mediating process." The verb "to mediate" is defined as "to be a go-between," or "to be a connecting link between." Hence to say that meanings may serve as mediating processes is to say that they may link other processes or responses together [Osgood, 1952].

To illustrate the mediation of a response, we may cite an experiment in animal learning [Tolman, 1939]. In this experiment the experimenter observed vicarious trial-and-error behavior (or VTE for short). This behavior has been described as "turning back and forth," or "crouching to jump at one door and then crouching before the other door, before finally jumping." The nice thing about VTE behavior is that it gives observable evidence of a fractional, associative process taking the place of an overt

response. It also shows how this process can mediate other responses.

Hunger-motivated rats were observed during their learning of a discrimination in a jumping apparatus. The apparatus consisted of a platform separated by a gap from two doors containing two stimulus cards. In this case the stimuli to be discriminated were a white card and a black card. When a rat jumped to the white card it was rewarded; the card fell under the weight of the rat so that the animal landed on a platform where it obtained a morsel of food. When the rat jumped to the black card, it was punished; the incorrect door was locked, so the animal bashed its nose against the door, and then fell a couple of feet into a net below.

This apparatus and procedure allowed the experimenter to observe the behavior of the rats prior to their jumping. At first, when the animals were making chance scores, indicative of no learning, they simply oriented toward a card, got set, and jumped. After several trials at this, however, they began to "VTE." This behavior, described above, was clear-cut and could be scored.

Figure 9.2 shows the results of the experiment for a single rat. One chart shows the number of correct jumps; the other shows the number of VTEs. Six trials a day were run; hence a score of three correct choices a day is chance and a score of six is perfect learning. VTE behavior appeared after 7 days (42 trials) when the animal was still performing at chance. VTE behavior increased rapidly until the animal rather suddenly showed evidence of learning. Thereafter it stayed at a high level for a few days, then diminished while the animal continued to perform the discrimination well.

VTE behavior in this experiment is evidence of a mediating process. It is interest-

Correct answers for signs in Figure 9.1 are: (*a*) hungry; (*b*) food; (*c*) fast; (*d*) fight; (*e*) house; (*f*) snake; (*g*) snow; (*h*) hot; and (*i*) fish.

ing that VTE behavior *decreases* after the discrimination has been learned. This means that the mediating process gradually becomes a smaller and less observable fraction of the original jumping response. The behavior it represents tends to "go inside" the organism. In many cases, though not in this one, the VTE response becomes either too small to see or a process entirely within the nervous system.

To recapitulate briefly, associations are formed in the course of learning to discriminate among various stimuli and responses. The associations are parts or fractions of the original responses (or sensory processes) that were paired together. Such fractional processes are what we mean by "meanings." And these meanings mediate between discriminable stimuli and the learned responses made to them. Human beings, of course, acquire so many meanings for stimuli, especially when we consider the meanings of all the words they learn to use and to respond to, that meanings, and the behavior mediated by them, are of enormous importance in understanding human "mental processes."

The thinking process

A well-known sign in certain business offices commands us to THINK. What does this mean? What does it tell us to *do*? How differently might we behave if, instead, the sign said FEAR or ACT or BELIEVE or OBEY? Do we really know how thinking differs from other experiences and reactions? An even harder question is, Can we tell when another person is thinking? What is thought? How does it start? When does it stop?

Actually, the word "think," or "thinking," as used in everyday speech, covers a very wide range of activities. At one extreme, it means little more than remember or recall. Along a road I travel frequently, for example, are signs saying, "Think—speed kills." Used in this way, "think" merely tells us to remember or to keep in mind a con-

VICARIOUS TRIAL AND ERROR TAKES THE PLACE OF ACTUAL TRIAL AND ERROR:

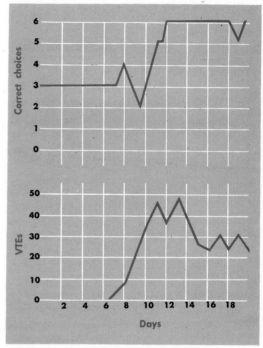

FIGURE 9.2. Correct choices and VTE behavior for a rat learning a white-black discrimination. Note that VTE behavior increases with correct choices, and then declines after the discrimination is mastered [after Tolman, 1939].

nection between fast driving and fatal accidents. Similarly, when somebody says, "Try to think of a name," he is asking us only to recall or remember something we have once learned. The processes of recall under these circumstances may actually involve some thinking, as we shall come to understand the term in this chapter, but not to any very great extent. At the other extreme, the word "think" refers to the highly rigorous and reflective activity a scientist engages in when he attempts to solve a complex problem. He may spend hours or days juggling mathematical formulas, drawing diagrams, or merely imagining various ways in which the problem might be solved.

But whether the thinking be simple or

complicated, it always seems to involve one thing: a mediating process. When we think, something links together past learning with our present responses. Mediating processes fill in the gaps between the stimulus situation and the responses we make to it. When we are solving problems, these processes substitute for things we might otherwise do overtly in a trial-and-error manner. To illustrate, let us take a common example.

Suppose that you had a jigsaw puzzle to put together. The hard way to work out the puzzle would be to try to fit the pieces together by actually trying each piece to see whether it fitted another piece. This would be solving the puzzle by plain trial-and-error. If there were many pieces in the puzzle, this would take an interminable amount of time and millions of trial-and-error fittings. You would probably do some of this, but only to choose between two or three possibilities that were very close to the correct one. Mostly you would think. The steps in your thinking would represent what you might otherwise do by trial and error. You would often think of putting the pieces together in a certain way without actually doing it. You would try putting them together in your head, and decide whether they would or would not go together before trying with your hands. Thus you would do by thinking what you might do by actually putting the pieces in place.

Your thinking *represents*, stands for, or takes the place of observable behavior and the physical rearrangement of stimuli. So the thinking process is a mediating process. To say this is to indicate how the thinking process functions—as a connector—but it does not tell us what thinking is. What goes on inside a person when he thinks? What is the thinking process? This is the question we shall deal with now.

TRACE PROCESSES.   The simplest kind of thinking process is a memory trace that lasts for some period of time and can serve in place of a stimulus cue for the solution of a simple problem. This kind of process has

THE DELAYED-REACTION TEST IS A MEANS OF STUDYING SYMBOLIC PROCESSES:

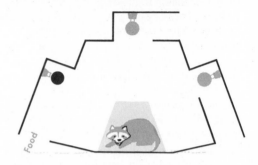

FIGURE 9.3. The delayed-reaction box [after Hunter, 1913].

been demonstrated in animals in a test called the *delayed-reaction* test. Such a test has been used with a number of different animals, but to illustrate it we shall describe an experiment [Hunter, 1913] performed with a raccoon:

The raccoon is placed in the starting box of the apparatus drawn in Figure 9.3. The box is made of wire mesh so that the animal can see out of it while being restrained. Facing the raccoon in the apparatus are three openings, each provided with a light bulb. The experiment is begun by training the animal to make the simple discrimination of going to the opening in which the bulb is lighted. The light is turned on and the screen is raised to permit the animal to walk around the box; if it goes to the correct opening, it finds food in the alley leading from the light. On successive trials, the light appears at random in one of the three possible positions, and food is presented in the lighted alley. After the raccoon has learned to go to the lighted doorway, the procedure is changed. Now the light is turned on briefly as before, but the animal is restrained in the starting cage until after it has gone off. Then, some prescribed number of seconds after the light has gone off, the raccoon is released so that it can go to the doorway that was last lighted.

CHAPTER NINE

This is a test for the existence of a mediating process because the stimulus is no longer present and the animal must use some process representing it in order to solve the problem. The length of time the animal can delay after the cessation of the stimulus serves as a measure of the rate at which the process—the "trace" of the previous stimulus—disappears.

The length of time various animals and children can delay in this kind of test and still solve the problem has been measured. In the earliest experiments with the method, rats were able to delay only 1 to 10 seconds; raccoons 10 to 15 seconds; cats 16 to 18 seconds; dogs, 1 to 3 minutes; a two-and-half-year-old child, 50 seconds; and a five-year-old child, at least 20 minutes. These figures have been revised and extended somewhat by later experiments, for much depends on how the apparatus is set up, whether there are any distractions during the period of delay, and other factors. The essential point, however, is that such a method demonstrates a simple mediating process. In order to infer from the method that such a process is taking part in the solution of the problem the test must meet the following criteria: (1) there must be some stimulus which is known to produce a characteristic, differential response; (2) the stimulus must be presented, and then withdrawn during the delay interval; and (3) there must be no other stimulus outside the body to indicate the correct response.

In some of the experiments on delayed reaction, the mediating process could readily be identified as a *posture* that oriented the head or body toward the proper box during the delay period. This was not a subtle or high-order process, but it was an effective, cue-producing process. Was it necessary? Tests by other experimenters showed that raccoons, dogs, monkeys, and children could delay successfully even when posture was radically disturbed during the delay. Later tests on rats showed that they too could delay longer, possibly up to 4 minutes, when the stimuli were made more discriminable

or the job of responding was made a little easier. So these animals, under the proper circumstances, can use mediating processes, other than postural cues. We can only guess that the process may be some kind of memory image of the correct stimulus, i.e., a "visualizing" process.

ROLE OF IMAGES. The student will recognize that the delayed-reaction experiment does not differ in principle from the experiments on eidetic imagery described in Chapter 6. In tests of eidetic imagery, a person is shown a picture or a page of print and is asked afterward to recall what he saw. Those rare individuals with eidetic ability can recall the situation with almost photographic accuracy.

Most people do not have eidetic imagery, but they usually report that they have images. Hence, even though we cannot observe another person's images objectively, we believe they exist. In some individuals, visual images apparently predominate. Auditory imagery occurs frequently, but images of muscular sensations, of pain, hunger, and other organic sensations are relatively rare. Even odors and tastes can be imagined by some individuals. Some people, on the other hand, report an almost total lack of imagery.

So far as human thinking is concerned, the question about images is not whether they exist, but what function they have in thinking. Are they the mediating processes in thinking? This issue was once hotly debated; some answered with a resounding "yes," others with a vehement "no." To answer the question scientifically, psychologists have conducted rigorous experiments on the role of images in thinking.[1]

The simplest kind of experiment is to ask a person to report on his experiences [Galton, 1907]. One can instruct him, for example, to recall his breakfast table, and ask, "What kind of images do you have?" Most people will give a fairly detailed description,

[1] For a detailed treatment of classical experiments on thinking, see Humphrey, 1951.

proving that they have images. This kind of experiment, however, only tells us what images, and how many relatively, a person may have, but it tells us little about their mediating function in thinking.

Another kind of experiment requires a person to solve some manipulative problem, such as tracing his way blindfolded through a maze with his finger or a pencil [Davis, 1932, 1933]. After he has done this, he is quizzed about his imagery. Many people in such an experiment report truly functional visual imagery; they solve the maze only by building up a "mental map" of it as they go along. Consequently they can draw the maze afterward, sometimes including the blind alleys as well as the true path. Other persons solve the maze by a purely verbal method; they count or name correct turns but do not "see" the maze as a whole in their mind's eye.

IMAGELESS THOUGHT. Experiments of the sort just described indicate that images may promote learning and that they may at times have a mediating function in thinking. There are still two other kinds of experiments on the role of images in thinking. One of these has been called the "thought experiment" and was first carried out about 1900. At that time, a group of psychologists at Würzburg, Germany, who were much interested in understanding thought and consciousness, did the experiment many times. They gave their subject a rather simple intellectual problem, such as, "Name a fruit," and then asked him to describe the images he had in arriving at the answer.

The Würzburg psychologists were surprised to discover that very few images were uncovered in this way. Moreover, images did not seem to be necessary to solve this kind of problem. If the problem were to "name a fruit," the subject could often say "apple" immediately, but yet be unable to detect any image of a fruit or apple. Apparently the thinking involved in making the appropriate response did not necessarily involve any images. Hence the possibility of *imageless*

thought was conceived, a notion that was quite controversial 50 years ago.

Two products of the imageless-thought hypothesis have proved to be of importance. One is the discovery that many of the important events in thinking may not be conscious. We cannot catch and inspect an idea or a thought as we can a bird or a butterfly. This suggests that an idea is more like a process than an object. The other product of the hypothesis is that thought often seems to be governed by a *set* that is formed before it occurs. A set is *a readiness to think or respond in a predetermined way*. If one is given a stimulus word in the experiment just mentioned, a thought seems to run off automatically, just as if one has already done his thinking before he starts! And what the thought is depends on the set. You see, for example:

$$\frac{6}{4}$$

You can give a quick answer, but whether it is 2, 10, or 24 depends on whether you are set to subtract, add, or multiply. Of course, with the appropriate instructions, we could have created any one of these sets. *Set,* as a theoretical concept, has become a most important term in the psychologists' vocabulary. We do not see set, yet in order to explain thinking we must assume that it exists.

Having gotten this far but no further, the early experimental psychologists faced a predicament. Their conception of psychology was that it was the science of *conscious experience* (see page 8), yet they established the fact that thinking could take place with no conscious content. The "higher mental processes" had eluded their search. To be sure, images did sometimes accompany thoughts, but the important thing was that images were not essential to thought. The introspective method (see page 8) had come to a blank wall, for one could not very well introspect if there were nothing to introspect about.

The conclusion then is that images may

sometimes be the mediating processes of thinking but, since thinking can go on without them, there must also be other kinds of mediating processes.

IMPLICIT RESPONSES.   When this conclusion had been reached by the early psychologists, it occurred to those of a behavioristic bent (see page 9) that some of the content of thinking might consist of small muscle movements.

Perhaps, they suggested, _implicit muscle responses_, not seen by the naked eye but sufficient in size to send back impulses to the nervous system, could be essential elements in the flow of thinking processes. This hypothesis was set forth some fifty years ago by John B. Watson as the explanation of thought.

Two steps are necessary to test the hypothesis. One is to confirm or deny the existence of implicit responses during thinking. We shall describe two experiments that concern this point. The second step is to demonstrate that such implicit responses serve as symbols or cues in the flow of thinking. This is difficult to prove, but it is a more reasonable possibility, as we shall explain below, than it might at first appear.

The idea that implicit responses take part in thinking is made plausible by the relationship between thinking and learning. Thinking begins in learning, and a good deal of learning, as we have seen earlier, is acquired by doing. One can suppose that learned responses become smaller and smaller as they are practiced and that thinking consists of these reduced movements, differentiated out of the larger movements of original learning. This is the idea of the fractional response discussed earlier.

One experiment [Jacobson, 1932] used subjects who had been taught to relax their muscles and who were lying relaxed in a darkened room:

On a signal, the subject thought of _bending his right arm_. By means of electrodes attached to the arm and connected to a galvanometer,

electrical signs of implicit muscular activity were seen to increase at this time. Control tests showed that the action currents varied consistently with the particular instructions. They died out when the subject was told to relax; they did not occur in the right arm when he was instructed to think of _bending his left arm_ or foot or to think of _extending the right arm_. Furthermore, a subject could not simultaneously relax his arm and think of bending it. Similar records were obtained while subjects thought of other activities, such as throwing a ball, turning an ice-cream freezer, and climbing a rope. In order to test the possibility that the action currents came only from the nerves and not the muscles, control experiments were run. In these experiments lightweight levers were placed directly on the muscles; when the levers moved, their action was optically magnified eightyfold. The levers told the same story as the electrodes: the muscles actually were shortening.

A similar experiment [Max, 1937], described below, employed 19 deaf-mutes who talked with their hands:

Electrodes were placed on the subjects' hands and records were taken during both sleep and waking. The records were especially watched for possible dream activity during sleep. Action currents decreased as the subjects went to sleep and stayed at a low level except for occasional bursts of activity. Were these bursts dreams? To find out, the experimenter tried awakening the subjects during bursts and asking them if they had just been dreaming. In 30 out of 33 instances, the 19 subjects answered "yes." As a control test, they were awakened 62 times during periods of electrical quiet. In 53 instances there were no dreams, but in 9 there were. Thus, in general, the bursts of activity tended to be associated with dreaming. In the waking state, deaf-mute subjects were compared with normal subjects. While solving problems in arithmetic, 84 per cent of the deaf subjects and 31 per cent of normal hearing subjects showed action currents in the hands.

Results such as these convince us that implicit movements can indeed occur during thinking. They may help answer the question, which we raised earlier, of what goes on in imageless thought.

CUE-PRODUCING RESPONSES. What purpose do such implicit responses serve? Are they just a coincidence or do they have a mediating function in thinking? Some implicit movements are undoubtedly coincidental; they simply represent an "overflow" or "leaking" of activities in the brain. Some of them, however, are probably links in the associative chains of thinking and thus are mediating processes. When they are, their function seems to be one of stimulation, that is, of providing a cue for the next element or response in the chain.

Which way, for example, do you turn your key to unlock your front door at home? The chances are that, when you think out the answer to this question, you imagine yourself putting your key in the lock and turning it. From this you get the cue to answer "right" or "left." In thinking of the event, you probably make some implicit muscle responses so that receptors in the muscles can signal the presence of muscle tension. In this case, the stimulus or cue produced by the implicit response might, because of previous conditioning, give you the answer.

Cue production from implicit responses is especially important in linguistic thinking—the thinking that is done with words. Much of human behavior is talking, reading, or writing and we solve many of our problems in terms of language. Words are among the best possible cue-producing responses because almost every word is distinctively different from other words. Except for homonyms, like "pair" and "pear," spoken words can provide many more discriminable cues than movements of arms, legs, fingers, and so on. Reduced to a *subvocal level*—to talking that is inaudible to others but sufficiently stimulating (muscularly) to oneself to permit an internal conversation—words can

serve in thinking as cue-producing responses.

We believe, then, that implicit responses can serve as mediating processes in thinking. Some of the early behaviorists, however, overstated their case when they concluded that thinking was *nothing but* a sequence of implicit responses. The evidence now available does not support such an extreme position. Rather it indicates that both images and implicit responses play a role in thinking. It also leaves room for other processes.

To explain what these other processes may be, let us point out that the brain is not a simple switchboard between incoming sensory stimulation and outgoing motor impulses. True, there are some areas that are primarily sensory and others that are principally motor in function (see Chapter 20). These areas, however, are interlinked in a variety of ways, and there are large areas, especially in the human brain, not concerned directly with sensory and motor functions. We know very little about activity in these structures, but it is plain that there is ample room for processes occurring in between sensory and motor events. These need not be manifested directly in "images," on the one hand, or "implicit responses," on the other.

These considerations, plus the facts we have covered, lead us to the conclusion that some mediating processes may be neither images nor implicit responses. Perhaps at one time, during learning, they were images or responses, but they later diminished to the point of being only connecting processes in the brain. Let us summarize, then, in a very few words: the mediating processes in thinking may be images, implicit responses, or other processes taking place in the brain.

Formation and meaning of concepts

The mediating process, whatever it is, may represent either something specific or something general. Something specific would be the particular "house I lived in as a little boy." Something general might be "redness," "government," "goodness," or the like. If it is the latter, it is a concept. *A concept is a process representing a common property of objects or events.* A common property is some feature that is the same in several otherwise different situations. It may be "redness," "triangularity," "horsiness," or any of thousands of possible characteristics of people, things, or situations.

Concepts enable us to divide things into classes. With a concept of redness, we can sort objects into the classes of "red" and "not red." With a concept of fruit, we can classify them into "fruit" and "not fruit." The common property of which we have a concept is the basis for making such classifications.

Since the number of common properties is without limit, there is no end to the number of classes or of concepts that may be formed. There are classes of classes, and classes of classes of classes. A concept can exist for any level of grouping. In the class of "dwelling unit" are subclasses of houses, apartments, and caves. In the class of "house" are subclasses of mansions and cottages. Cottages include red ones and white ones. Houses and caves can be big or little, if grouped according to the property of size.

WORDS AND CONCEPTS. In principle, one does not have to know words or a language in order to have a concept. Indeed many of our concepts are formed without the benefit of words and are poorly expressed with words. All that is necessary is that some property of objects be correctly discriminated. For example, by extensive training with all sorts of triangles, it has been possible to teach rats the concept of "triangularity." When trained, they avoid jumping to nontriangles but will jump to almost any kind of triangle, despite differences in detail among the triangles. In this case, the rats signify their concept of triangularity by their discrimination in jumping.

In practice, however, words are very im-

portant in concept formation. Language, in fact, is so closely linked to human concept formation that the definition of a concept is almost synonomous with the definition of a word [Osgood et al., 1957]. This is because most words are used as labels to refer to some common property of objects. (The exception is *proper* nouns.) To appreciate this, just select any set of words you want and ask yourself what they mean, or how they are defined. Take "red." "Red" is not the name of any one thing, but rather the name for anything having the property of "redness" regardless of its other characteristics. Hence "red" is the name for a concept, for it arouses in you the concept of redness. Take "wagon," "house," "school," "tree," or any other common noun. In each case, the concept aroused is some meaning of the property that many different objects have in common. So the meaning of words and the meaning of concepts are closely tied together, even if they are not always identical.

ABSTRACTION. In acquiring word concepts, we learn either simultaneously or successively to do two things: One is to discriminate the property that several objects have in common. This is called *abstraction.* The other is to assign a particular *word label* to the abstracted property. When the label is consistently applied to the property abstracted, the concept has been learned. Let us illustrate by taking a case of concept formation in children.

The first is the process little Johnny goes through in learning the names of things (see Figure 9.4). Suppose that whenever an apple is offered to Johnny, someone says "apple." They say nothing at all or something else whenever they offer him a ball, a cup, or a triangular block. This gives Johnny a chance to associate "apple" with the fruit of that name. In addition, he may be aided by being given an apple whenever he says "apple." The apples he associates with "apple" in this way will vary somewhat in size and shape,

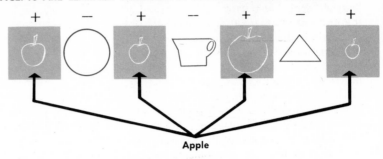

FIGURE 9.4. Concept forma- tion. A child hears the word "apple" when he sees some objects, but not others. And he is rewarded if he says "apple" when he sees some objects, but not others. In this way, he generalizes the con- cept of apple and distin- guishes it from other concepts [after Johnson, 1948].

but they will all be more or less round, they will be edible, they will have stems, etc.

Having learned this, Johnny will have the concept of apple. But it might not be the concept of apple that we know. In fact, it might turn out to be our concept of "fruit," for he might use "apple" to mean any fruit roughly of apple size that he can eat. This is because his concept of apple is any "round, juicy object he can eat." These are the com- mon properties of apples, but they are also the common properties of many fruits. He will have generalized too much, but quite justifiably. In fact, he will be exhibiting the phenomenon of stimulus generalization which we have previously encountered (page 198). Such generalization to similar objects, of course, is exactly what is required for concept formation. But to learn the right concept of "apple," he will need more training in dis- tinguishing the properties of apples from those of oranges, plums, etc. In due course he will certainly get it.

This process of concept formation will go on as rapidly as Johnny can learn to dis- criminate the differences between objects and at the same time abstract their similar- ities, thereby forming classes of objects. It will also depend on the *naming responses* available to him. Without appropriate words to label the classes, he will lack the means of responding to them. If appropriate words are available, he can attach a word meaning to each class. Thus, in concept formation,

discrimination and abstraction go hand in hand with the naming of classes.

As an illustration, consider our color con- cepts. Human beings can discriminate sev- eral thousand colors, and there are color names for dozens of them. In practice, how- ever, we use only a small number of the color concepts that are possible. A child usually is taught names for red, green, yel- low, and blue, but seldom is he taught crim- son, magenta, scarlet, or shocking pink. To him, "red" is first just a name for his red wagon-object, but he comes to use it for a class of colors of similar properties and hence to use it as a concept. The end points of the class may not be certain; he may wonder whether to call an orange-red "red," "yellow," or "orange," or he may hesitate with purple. Yet the middle points are in- stantly labeled red, and the class is named for its most frequent elements. On the other hand, lacking names for purple, magenta, etc. he may not build up these color con- cepts until the time when he has learned the words.

METHODS OF LEARNING CONCEPTS. Much of our education, both formal and informal, consists in learning concepts. Partly for this reason, concept formation has been studied extensively. One of the questions frequently asked about it is, How do people learn con- cepts? What methods do they use? Four may be distinguished.

Discriminative learning. One of the ways

CHAPTER NINE

of learning concepts is the way Johnny learned "apple" and "fruit." The person has the problem of attaching word labels to objects, and in the course of learning to do this abstracts some common property of objects. A classic experiment [Hull, 1920] illustrating this route to concept formation is as follows:

College students were presented one at a time with cards from a pack of 12. On each card was a different Chinese character. As a card was shown, the experimenter said a nonsense word, like oo, yer, or li. The first time through the pack, the subject merely repeated the nonsense word after the experimenter. Next, the cards were shuffled and again exposed serially. This time, and on succeeding runs through the pack, the subject attempted to anticipate the correct word. When wrong, he was corrected. Runs were made through the pack until the subject had learned the correct "name" for each Chinese character.

Next a second pack of 12 cards with Chinese characters was presented. The subject was instructed to use the same 12 names he had learned with the first pack, and to start guessing on the first run through the pack. He continued calling until this pack was learned. The same procedure was again followed with four more packs of 12 cards, all containing different characters.

Unbeknown to the subject, the same name was always used when a particular part, a "radical," appeared in the character. Although all characters were different, one part of the "oo" character was the same, and a character containing this common property was in each deck; the same was true of each character given a particular name. Illustrating this are two rows of characters in Figure 9.5. Those in the first row were given the same name, but each character appeared in a different deck. Similarly, each character in the second row was assigned the same name, and each character appeared in a different deck.

The learning of a concept in this experiment was measured by the number of correct guesses made on the first run of "guesses"

FIGURE 9.5. The abstraction of common elements in Chinese characters [Hull, 1920].

through the second, third, and succeeding decks. With 12 characters, chance was $1/12$, or about 8 per cent. However, the subjects' average percentage of correct responses were:

Pack number	2	3	4	5	6
Per cent correct on first trial	27	38	47	55	56

Note that the subjects were learning correctly to abstract and label some of the common parts of the characters. The task was so complex, however, that they were, on the average, far from perfect. See if you can pick out the common part or radical in the characters of each row in the figure.

The learning in this experiment is probably quite analogous to the process young children go through in learning concepts, except that it was purposely made complex enough to be difficult for college students. We shall be referring to the experiment again, so the reader should keep it in mind.

Context. A second way to learn concepts is through *context.* If we do not know the meaning of a word but see or hear it used in different contexts, we usually develop a fairly accurate idea of its meaning. The following is an example taken from an experiment on concept formation [Werner and Kaplan, 1950]. See if you can tell what a "corplum" is:

A corplum may be used for support.
Corplums may be used to close off an open place.
A corplum may be long or short, thick or thin, strong or weak.
A wet corplum does not burn.

You can make a corplum smooth with sandpaper.

The painter used a corplum to mix his paints.

These sentences were presented to subjects one at a time, after which the subjects were asked what "corplum" meant and why they thought so.

You will undoubtedly discover the concept of corplum from the statements made about it. You will find that it expresses the same concept as another word you already know. However, if you did not know the word but were familiar with the properties of corplums you would still be able to define a corplum. In fact, you would be able to write several more sentences about the properties of corplums.

Definition. A third way of learning new concepts is by *definition*. In fact, most of the concepts you learn in the later stages of your education are learned in this way. You have, for example, learned many concepts in this book by being told the definition of them. Of course, you also use a dictionary for this purpose. In any case you learn the concept by having it described in other words. Most six-year-old children, for example, have never seen a zebra, but they have a concept of zebra [Osgood et al., 1957]. They have been told that it is an animal that has stripes, that it looks and runs like a horse, is about the same size as a horse, and is usually found wild. This definition gives them a fairly accurate concept of zebra.

Classification. Another way of learning concepts is to attempt to form classes of a variety of objects. This way is frequently followed by the scientist, especially in the exploratory phases of a problem. The zoologist, for example, has developed concepts of "insect," "mammal," and so on by classifying animals according to their common characteristics. Experimenters who study concept formation often use this method, because their findings can thus be readily scored. This method is illustrated in the following experiment [Heidbreder, 1948b]:

The investigator used a pack of 144 cards. Each card contained a drawing like one of those in Figure 9.6. The drawings had been so constructed that they included three kinds of *things*, three kinds of nonsense *forms*, and three groups of numbers, namely, 3, 4, and 6. This made nine ways in which a drawing might vary, and there were 16 specimens of each class ($9 \times 16 = 144$).

The subjects (college women) were instructed to sort the cards into nine piles "according to a classification which you are to work out for yourself." Their scores were based on their consistency in classifying a card according to a particular concept. When they had finished one sorting, they were instructed to sort again using a different method of classification. In this way, their success in learning (or discovering) the different concepts of things, forms, and numbers could be scored.

FACTORS AFFECTING CONCEPT FORMATION. It is of practical, as well as academic, value to know what helps or hinders concept formation, for we would like to improve our methods of teaching concepts to people. If we went into detail, we could name a good many factors that make a difference, but for our purposes here, four will be sufficient.

Transfer. One factor, which is also important in other learning (page 234), is *transfer*. When a person already knows a concept similar to the one being learned, he can learn it rapidly. This is positive transfer. But similarity can be tricky; it can also produce negative transfer. If a new concept appears to be similar to a known concept but is also quite different in some important respect, the person may have trouble understanding the new concept. Here, to capitalize on transfer, the teacher must point out both the similarities and the differences.

Concrete versus abstract. Also affecting the ease with which we learn concepts is the relative concreteness or abstractness of the concept. Although there are exceptions,

FIGURE 9.6. Drawings used in experiment on concept formation. For further explanation, see text. (Heidbreder, 1948a.)

on the whole, *concrete concepts are easier to learn than abstract ones*. In the experiment described just above, for example, concepts of *things* were much more readily learned than concepts of forms and numbers.

In ordinary life, concrete concepts are of real objects, such as minerals, animals, trees, houses, etc. These are easier to grasp than abstract concepts, such as number, religion, and discipline. Of course, there is no absolute dividing line; differences may be only a matter of degree. And other factors listed here, such as transfer and distinctiveness, can upset the relatively greater ease of learning concrete, "thing" concepts. The teacher will do well, when he has a choice, to put his effort into teaching concrete concepts. If he realizes this and uses his imagination, he can often find a concrete approach to teaching an abstract concept. Children, for example, find abstract number concepts quite difficult to grasp. Knowing this, the teacher may use postage stamps, coins, or other familiar number objects, or have the children play an elaborate game of store in order to teach them arithmetic concepts. Using analogies between concrete and abstract concepts is an especially good way to teach an abstract subject in concrete terms—and there are many others. We have tried using some of them in this book.

Distinctiveness. A third factor in concept formation is the degree to which common elements are isolated, grouped, or otherwise made conspicuous. For want of a better term, we will call this *distinctiveness*. Anything that is done to make the common property of the concept stand out aids concept formation; whatever obscures it or embeds it in irrelevant details retards concept formation.

Two examples of this can be presented briefly. In the experiment on Chinese characters cited above, the students were very slow to learn the "concepts" because the common element was embedded in complex characters, and the characters were presented in jumbled order. If all those with the same common property had been grouped

together in twos, as they were in Figure 9.4, concept formation would have been much easier. In fact, you probably discovered the concept within a few seconds.

Another experiment demonstrates the value of isolating the property to be abstracted. In this case, the experimenter used meaningless drawings. When he outlined in red the property to be abstracted he found that concept formation proceeded much more rapidly than it did otherwise.

Worth mentioning in passing are three other factors affecting concept formation [Johnson, 1955]. One is ability to manipulate materials. If a person is allowed to rearrange, redraw, or reorganize the materials containing common properties, he is more likely to learn or discover the appropriate concepts. Another is the instruction or general purpose a person has. If he is told to try to discover a common element, that is, to search for the concept, he does better than if he is given a problem, as in the experiment with Chinese characters, of learning to use the right names. Finally, a person usually learns faster if he has all the relevant information available at the same time instead of getting it a piece at a time.

MEANING OF CONCEPTS. Concept learning is like other kinds of learning. The concept can be learned poorly or well, accurately or inaccurately. The concept one person learns may or may not be the same concept another person learns. In fact, it is quite apparent from everyday conversations with people that they often have very different concepts of the same thing. This is especially true in abstract realms like politics or religion.

Individual differences in the learning and meaning of concepts raises the question of how we can measure the meaning of a concept. How can we tell how well a concept has been learned? How can we measure differences among people in the meaning of concepts? These questions have answers, though the answers vary with our purpose and the types of concepts we are concerned with. In general, four methods of measuring the meaning of concepts may be distinguished. The first two are most useful with the kinds of concepts we attempt to teach in school, where there is some standard for deciding whether a concept is correct or not. The last two are most useful with concepts that have no such standard, but they are of interest in studying personality and social processes.

Free response. The simplest and most straightforward way of finding out what a concept means to a person is to ask him to *say* what it means. This is the free-response method. The results one gets in this way depend on the instructions given and also upon the concepts tested.

A child's concept of dog can be tested by asking him to describe a dog. His description can be scored "accurate," "too general," "abstract," "concrete," "irrelevant," etc. with a fair degree of interscorer agreement. In fact items of this kind are used on intelligence tests and scored with good reliability. When the description avoids irrelevancies and includes only the socially accepted meaning, we call it a *definition.* The description may also be pictorial, as when a child is asked to draw a triangle or a college student is asked to draw a neuron. The descriptions are influenced, of course, by the subject's skill in verbal and pictorial techniques as well as by his mastery of the concept.

Discrimination. The free-response method obviously is subjective, and it is often difficult to score reliably.[2] A more objective method makes use of a set of discriminations. A person is shown a variety of objects, or instances of people or things, and asked to indicate whether each one is or is not an instance of the concept. Alternatively, he may simply be asked to classify objects according to specified common properties. This can yield an objective score, in terms

of right and wrong answers, of the accuracy of a person's concept.

One interesting variation of the discrimination method is the *oddity method* [Cofer, 1951]. A person is given three or more items and asked to pick out the odd one—the one that does not belong. One of the virtues of this method is that one does not have to specify any particular concept. With one simple question, he can measure the meaning of several concepts as well as any confusion among concepts. The following is an example:

skyscraper   temple   cathedral   prayer

The subject is asked to pick out the odd item. Actually, in this case, there are two possible odd ones, for two concepts are involved. If the subject has a religious concept in mind, he should designate "skyscraper"; if a building concept, then "prayer." The concept the subject employs is likely to depend on the order in which the words are presented, and the first word is most important in determining the concept. With the order above, "prayer" is most likely to be considered odd. With the following order:

prayer   temple   skyscraper   cathedral

the most likely answer is "skyscraper." Of course, people who do not have very accurate concepts of some of these words may choose "temple" or "cathedral," which are never the correct odd ones in this pattern of words.

The two methods, free responses and discrimination, do not always give the same results. People frequently can give a dictionary or verbal definition of a concept, but make mistakes in choosing instances of the concept. Conversely, people may be able to identify the common (or uncommon) characteristic in a group of objects and still not be able to give a correct verbal statement of the concept. In the experiment on Chinese characters, for example, some students learned to use the correct names for characters without being able to indicate the common characteristic they named.

Disagreement in results of the two meth-

[2] Items used on intelligence tests are carefully selected; the correct answers are standardized; and the scoring is done by trained examiners.

ods is not unreasonable. If a person learns concepts by context or by definition in terms of other concepts, he is more likely to do well with the free-response method. On the other hand, a person who has learned his concepts by simple learning through experience with instances of the concept will probably do better on the discrimination method. This is one of the reasons why strictly formal education, limited to books, can turn out students who do not understand "practical" concepts and why it is a good idea to have laboratories and other more "concrete" methods of teaching concepts in addition to purely verbal instruction.

Word association. Another method of testing the meaning of concepts is particularly suited to studying personal concepts and finding out whether a person's concepts are substantially different from those of society at large. This is the word-association method. A person is given a word and asked to reply with the first association that comes to mind. Normally he will reply with a word that is in the same class of concepts as the stimulus word. If he replies with something not usually related to the stimulus word, it is an indication that his personal concepts are, in some respects, rather different from those of people in general.

Semantic differential. A fourth, more sophisticated method of measuring the meaning of concepts is called the *semantic differential* [Osgood et al., 1957]. It has only recently been developed. So far, it has been employed primarily as a research tool, but it has many possible uses. Its basic purpose

is to analyze concepts in terms of a limited number of dimensions of meaning—this will be explained below—and to compare these dimensions in various groups of people, including different national and language groups. It also may be used in attitude measurement, in mass communication, and in personality measurement.

To obtain a semantic differential two things are required: a concept and two or more scales. The concept is a word like "father," "sin," "symphony," "Russian," or "America." Each scale consists of two polar words, such as "happy-sad," "hard-soft," "slow-fast." As presented to a subject, each scale has seven spaces placed between the words at each end (see Figure 9.7). The subject is asked to place each concept at some position on each scale. Thus, the concept being judged might be "father." If the seven positions from left to right on the scale are given numbers of 1 to 7, the subject might judge "father" as a 3 on the happy-sad scale, 2 on the hard-soft scale, 5 on the slow-fast scale, etc. The subject does the same thing for "father" on the remainder of the scales, which may number anywhere from 20 to 50. He repeats this procedure with other concepts such as "sin," etc.

The result of scaling concepts in this way is a semantic differential for each concept. The differential gives the meaning of the concept by showing its position on the scales. If we desire, we can draw up a profile for each concept, showing its position on each scale. Then we can compare profiles

A SEMANTIC DIFFERENTIAL MEASURES THE MEANING OF A CONCEPT ON SEVERAL SCALES:

FIGURE 9.7. An example of a semantic differential. A person rates a concept, in this case "father," on 20 to 50 bipolar scales, three of which are illustrated [after Osgood et al., 1957].

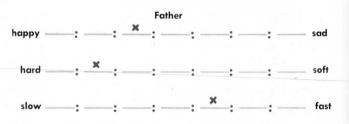

CHAPTER NINE

for different concepts. To the extent that the profiles correspond, the meaning of the two concepts is the same. To the extent that they differ, their meanings are different.

The semantic differential has been used both in this way and in other ways. It has also served as a method of analyzing the whole system of concepts used by individuals in our culture. The techniques for doing this are rather involved and they employ the statistical method of factor analysis (see page 428). From such an analysis of a large number of concepts has come the conclusion that the concepts we commonly develop are heavily weighted by three factors. These factors are best measured by scales such as fair-unfair, weak-strong, and active-passive. That is to say, these three groups of words (or words similar to them) tend to convey better than others the meanings of the concepts we hold. The three factors measured by such scales have been called *evaluation* (fair-unfair), *potency* (weak-strong), and *activity* (active-passive). These appear to be the major dimensions of meaning for a great many of our concepts.

The solution of problems

Thinking consists of mediating processes, many of them representing words and concepts. This statement summarizes what we have learned about what thinking is. It does not tell us, however, what starts it, what guides it, or what brings it to a stop. A river is more than water. It begins somewhere, it flows first in one direction and then in another, sometimes swiftly and sometimes slowly, and eventually it ends in the ocean. Thinking, too, has beginnings, courses, and ends. What explains them?

MOTIVATION.   For one thing, thinking is usually motivated. As one of the leading investigators [Wertheimer, 1959] in this area has said, thinking involves "the desire, the craving to face the true issue . . . , to go from an unclear, inadequate relation to a clear, transparent, direct confrontation." Thus he

stresses the *directedness* of thought processes. Instead of just "happening" by association, each stage in thinking is controlled by motives.

On the basis of all we now know, we ought to differentiate at least two kinds of motives in thinking: (1) a motive for the behavior immediately preceding the problem, which may be love, greed, curiosity, ambition, etc., and (2) a motive induced by the problem itself to complete or anticipate the solution of the problem. The former gets thinking started; the latter carries it through to solution.

In order to account for the thought processes of great thinkers, such as scientists, artists, writers, and inventors, we might have to postulate even a third kind of motivation: a lifelong interest in creative production or in solving challenging problems.

HABIT AND SET.   Thinking is also guided, and often impeded, by habit and set. Practice in solving problems one way tends to "set" us to solve a new problem in the same way, provided the new problem situation contains stimuli similar to those in the practiced problems. This is the secret of many trick jokes and puzzles. In one trick, you spell words and ask a person how he pronounces them. You use names beginning with Mac, like MacDonald, MacTavish. Then you slip in "machinery" and see whether he pronounces it "MacHinery." With the set for names, he may fall into your trap.

Set may be produced by immediately preceding experiences, by long-established practices, or by instructions which revive old habits (see "Transfer of Training," Chapter 8). It biases the thinker at the start of his problem and directs him away from certain families of response. It acts as an implied assumption. Like transfer of training, it can be either positive or negative in its effect. If it is helpful, we say, "How clever I am"; if a hindrance, we say, "How blind I was."

One investigator [Luchins, 1954] did a

systematic experiment on habitual set, using the problems in Table 9.1. This experiment is described in part below:

In the sixth problem, for example, the subject is required to say how he would measure 20 quarts of water when he has only three jars, holding 23, 49, and 3 quarts, respectively. Subjects do it the easy way by filling the 3-quart jar from the 23-quart jar, provided they have no interfering set. However, if they have just solved the previous problems by a longer method—that is, by filling the middle jar, from it filling the jar to the right twice and the jar to the left once, leaving the required amount in the center jar—they usually use the long method and do not notice the short one. Amazingly enough, 75 per cent of a college group were blind to the easy method after having practiced the long one only five trials!

The frequency of habitual, blind solutions is reduced by (1) warning the subject, "Don't be blind!" just before the critical sixth trial, (2) reducing the number of practice trials, and (3) separating the practice and critical trials by several days or weeks. Comparative data show that habit strength and set, as indicated by number of practice trials, can be much stronger factors than any warning against them.

Cooperative problem solving has this possible advantage: that two people may not possess the same hindering set. This is one value of "bull sessions," "group thinks," or "brain-storming."

UNCONSCIOUS FACTORS. An autobiographical account of an inventor or mathematician sometimes claims that he solved a problem while he was not even trying to think about it. After persistent labor fails, the thinker turns to other matters, only to have the solution unexpectedly appear. Poincaré [1913] and other mathematicians have reported that such unconscious solutions came to them while walking down the street or engaged in some other routine activity but seldom while intensively engaged in another mathematical problem. From what these narratives report, it appears that a concentrated thinking effort may sometimes get one into a symbolic blind alley, in which case starting over again after a rest may get one into a new path. No doubt many other factors than these we have listed do enter into human thinking. Some of these may be due to "unconscious thinking" in the sense that much of our thought is imageless.

SOLUTION BY INSIGHT. Let us summarize again. Thinking begins with some kind of problem and a motive to solve that problem. It is guided by some set or determining tendency, and it is helped—or hindered—

TABLE 9.1. Practice and test problems used by Luchins. The five practice problems require a roundabout method of solution, but the test problem can be solved easily. Most subjects, however, who acquired a set by solving practice problems first, used the long method of solving the test problem and were blind to the easy method. [Luchins, 1954].

Problem number	Given the following empty jars as measures			Obtain this amount of water
	A	B	C	
1. Practice	21	127	3	100
2. Practice	14	163	25	99
3. Practice	18	43	10	5
4. Practice	9	42	6	21
5. Practice	20	59	4	31
6. Test	23	49	3	20

by previously learned habits. It may go on even when there is no conscious awareness of it. Now we may ask how the problem gets solved.

To this there are at least three answers: by trial and error, by rote, and by insight. In attempting to solve a puzzle you sometimes stumble on the right answer. By trying first one way, then another, you finally hit on one that works. This is very much like the instrumental learning that we described in the last chapter—maze learning, for example—except that you use thought processes instead of wandering in the maze.

A second kind of solution may come by rote. If I give you a column of figures to add, you immediately start thinking according to rules you have learned, and in due time you come up with the answer. Or, if you are asked to spell a word or to give the directions for going from one place to another, you do a minimum of thinking and a lot of just plain remembering in order to give the answer. You merely reproduce what you have already learned. To understand this way of solving problems, almost all one needs to know is how the solutions were learned in the first place.

A third kind of problem solution, however, is solution by insight, which occurs neither by trial and error nor by rote. It may grow out of blind trial and error or out of rote thinking, but it represents a completely new experience to the thinker. "Aha! I have it," is a characteristic outburst when suddenly he grasps a baffling problem. He has produced a novel solution—novel for him, at least—through thinking. If the solution is truly novel, he has invented or created something that he can pass on to other members of society for them to use in their "rote-thinking" processes. As we shall see, such insight has something to do with previous learning, but it has taken a good deal of research to tell us exactly how.

The use of insight. Some problems, of course, are much more easily solved by means of insight than are others. Soldiers, for example, find it hard to get insight into

their serial numbers; nothing but simple memorizing will solve this problem. Multiplication tables, however, may be learned either by rote or by insight—learning them by rote may actually interfere with learning them by insight. Other problems, however, may be solved only by insight; or at least insight is much the easier way to solve them.

The best experiments on insight probably are those in which the subject must use tools. The following experiment is a classical example [Köhler, 1925]:

Chimpanzees were given hoes to procure bananas outside the cage beyond arm's length. Most chimpanzees explored and manipulated the hoe in trial-and-error fashion, but occasionally a chimp would suddenly run toward the hoe, put it out on the *farther* side of the banana and pull it in. This behavior was especially impressive if the chimp, just prior to the successful act, had been on the opposite side of the cage and not even looking at the hoe. Evidently he must have been *thinking* hard. The changed facial expression during solution certainly suggested that the chimp had an "Aha!" experience.

How insights develop. Many experimenters have conducted experiments on insight similar to the one cited above and have extended them to children. In general, their results show that insightful manipulation of sticks and hoes does not occur unless the subject has had previous experience in using these instruments in problem solving. In one study [Jackson, 1942] four out of six chimpanzees failed the hoe problem even though the hoe was lying in perfect position to drag the fruit in. However, chimps who were allowed to play with sticks for several days prior to the experiment did very much better, although only one achieved success on the first trial. In an experiment with children [Richardson, 1934], it was found that no child under two and one-half years solved a typical insight problem, that the percentage of successes increased as the age and specific experiences of the children increased, and that insight or understanding often occurred *after* solution instead of with it or preceding it.

The conditions which favor the appearance of sudden solutions certainly deserve much more scientific study than they have received. We need, for example, more information of the kind collected in a truly gigantic series of experiments [Harlow, 1951] on discrimination learning in monkeys and children. These researches are novel because, unlike the usual learning experiment which measures habit growth in terms of trials, the experimenter measured *transfer from problem to problem*, or from experiment to experiment (see Figure 9.8). Whereas the usual experiment stops after one problem, or at most two or three, the same subjects here continued to new ones, finally completing as many as 344 problems. Some of the later problems were similar to earlier ones, but others required the subject to *reverse* his response to the same cues.

What did the subjects learn here? Only a specific problem? Or did they learn something that transferred to the next problem and then the next? The answer is given in Figure 9.9, which is based on reversal learning. The percentage of correct responses on the *second* trial of each problem is the dependent variable. The first trial, of course, acts as an "instruction" to the subject, telling him that the problem has been changed. What he learns on the first new trial is measured by his performance on the second trial. If he learned nothing, his second trial score would be chance—in this case, 50 per cent. If he learned much, his score would approach 100 per cent. Note that the monkeys initially did little better than chance but gradually improved until in later problems they approached very near perfection on the first trial. The children started at a higher performance level, but the trend was the same.

We may conclude that (1) the amount by which a subject can profit by a single experience can, through learning, increase from nothing to everything, and (2) inter-

MONKEYS CAN SOLVE SOME FAIRLY COMPLEX PROBLEMS:

FIGURE 9.8. Problem solving in monkeys. This is the crossed-string problem; food is attached to the chain ending in left foreground, and the animal must perceive which is the correct chain to pull [H. F. Harlow].

problem improvement is a *transfer effect* from one problem to another. The name given to this process is *learning set,* which means *learning to learn.* Since performance in later problems reached near perfection, that is, there was one-trial learning or complete transfer, it is clear that sudden, insightful solutions were regularly made on problems toward the end of the series. The experimenter appropriately concluded, "These data clearly show that animals can gradually learn insight." The same statement, of course, applies to the children in the experiment. The overwhelming evidence to date, then, is that sudden solutions— with or without the "Aha!" accompaniment—grow out of and are probably due to specific conditioning and learning. In short, in learning to learn, we learn to produce insights.

ADVENTUROUS THINKING. One of the leading investigators of thinking [Bartlett, 1958] distinguishes two kinds of thinking: closed-system thinking and adventurous thinking. Closed-system thinking is guided by rules and conventions, and it is limited to certain evidence. Solving problems in arithmetic or algebra is closed-system thinking; so is the thinking involved in any problem where certain materials or facts are given and a fixed solution is required. Adventurous thinking, on the other hand, proceeds without any preestablished rules. The person himself usually formulates the problem and he is free to gather evidence and to invent tools for its solution. The creative thinking of the scientist or inventor is a special case of adventurous thinking.

The steps involved in the thinking of outstanding creative thinkers have frequently been studied through interviews, questionnaires, and introspection [Wallas, 1926]. Though each has his own way of thinking, and this depends somewhat on the kind of problems to be solved, there does seem to be a recurring pattern in such thinking. It tends to proceed in five stages: *preparation, incubation, illumination, evaluation,* and *revision.*

In the first stage, preparation, the thinker formulates his problem and collects the facts and materials he considers necessary for its solution. Very frequently he finds, like Poincaré, that he cannot solve the problem, even after hours or days of concentrated effort. Often, he deliberately or involuntarily turns away from the problem; this is stage 2, incubation. During this period, some of the ideas that were interfering with the solution of the problem tend to fade. On the other hand, things he experiences or learns in the meantime may provide the clue to the solution. During this stage, the unconscious processes may be at work. In stage 3, illumination, the thinker often has an "Aha!" insight experience. An idea for the solution may suddenly dawn on him. Next, in the evaluation stage, he determines whether the apparent solution is in fact the correct one. Frequently it turns out to be wrong, and the thinker is back where he started. In other cases, it is the right idea, but needs some

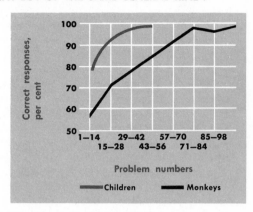

FIGURE 9.9. Discrimination learning in monkeys and children. The experiment charted here is described in the text [after Harlow, 1951].

modification or requires the solution of other, relatively minor problems. Thus, the last stage, revision, is reached.

This is far from a satisfactory description of the mental processes of the creative thinker. One day, through research, we should be able to understand the pattern better. This description does, however, provide a general picture of the steps that are frequently involved in the solution of problems by our most talented and creative people.

Logical reasoning

Our sketch of the thought processes is now nearly complete. We have seen what they are made of, that they are motivated and guided by habits and sets, and that they can arrive at solutions to problems in different ways. There is one feature of thinking, however, that we have not discussed. This is reasoning. Perhaps you are accustomed to using the words "reasoning" and "thinking" as though they were the same. We commonly do that in our everyday talk. You can remember, however, many instances of thinking that seem quite lacking in reasoning.

PUZZLES LIKE THIS ONE HELP US TO ANALYZE HOW PEOPLE SOLVE PROBLEMS:

What, then, is reasoning? A little boy was on the right track when he answered, "Putting two and two together." Reasoning certainly is not just any kind of thinking. It is solving a problem by putting two or more elements of past experience together to make something new (see Figure 9.10).

VERBAL REASONING. Most human reasoning makes use of symbols—especially verbal symbols. Since we use words so extensively to communicate our thoughts to others, we get in the habit of depending on words to think with. Yet word meanings often are vague or ambiguous, and we can be led astray by them. Also, when reasoning with verbal symbols alone, we may find it impossible to test whether our conclusion is correct, for we often lack the opportunity to compare the verbal conclusion with actuality.

To help us, society develops standards or norms for checking the results of our reasoning. People come to believe that certain statements are "reasonable" and some are not. Hence, when a person concludes with an "unreasonable" statement, people tell him so immediately and discourage him from making further foolish statements. The trouble with culturally defined standards of reasonableness is that what is reasonable to one group may be completely unreasonable to another. "It stands to reason that . . . ," a college debater argues; but as an American undergraduate, he completely forgets that the conclusion may not be obvious to, say, an Arabian or Chinese opponent.

To make the standards for reasoning as rigid as possible, philosophers and mathematicians, over the centuries, have given us rules for reasoning. These rules are called logic, and they prescribe what kinds of implications statements can have and what kinds of conclusions it is permissible to draw from them. Any reasoning that does not conform to these rules is dubbed "illogical" or "fallacious." Since so much in human affairs hangs on the question of how

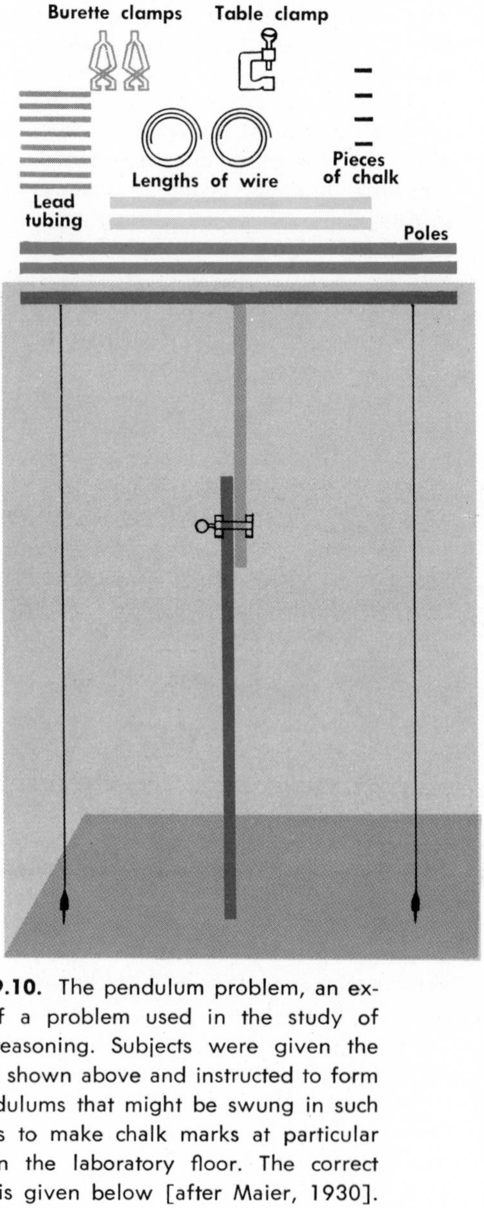

FIGURE 9.10. The pendulum problem, an example of a problem used in the study of human reasoning. Subjects were given the materials shown above and instructed to form two pendulums that might be swung in such a way as to make chalk marks at particular points on the laboratory floor. The correct solution is given below [after Maier, 1930].

logical we are in our thinking, we should study some of the psychological factors involved in the logical and illogical thinking of human beings.

LOGICAL THINKING. Suppose one conducts a test of reasoning in children and asks them this question: "If all six-year-olds are in school, and if Johnny is six, then where is Johnny?" The psychologist should not be surprised if the answer is, "I hate school," or "He's home sick with a cold," though the logician would be! To the psychologist, the child's answer is "reasonable" because it is a simple association with a stimulus, without regard to logical rules, and this is what people learn long before they learn to reason, let alone reason by the formal rules of logic.

As children grow older they learn to respond according to certain instructions and rules, to keep their associative responses within certain bounds. Suppose I test a high school student: I instruct him that whenever I say a word I want him to respond with a word that is a class name for objects of the same kind. Now I give him the word "table." He will give me back "furniture" or some comparable word, but he will not say "chair" because that would violate the rule that his response must name a class that includes "table." He has learned to follow a rule.

Now for a more complex case. In college, the student may learn the syllogism, one form of which is:

1. All *A* is *B*.
   All men are mortal.
2. All *C* is *A*.
   All farmers are men.
3. Therefore, all *C* is *B*.
   All farmers are mortal.

This, sure enough, is one of the rules of logic and the student may learn it, perhaps by rote. He will immediately encounter difficulty, however, in applying the rule to situations in daily life, because it is not easy to distinguish the syllogism from a fallacy.

The form of the syllogism above, for example, *looks* suspiciously like the following:

1. All *A* is *B*.
   All farmers are men.
2. All *B* is *C*.
   All men are mortal.
3. Therefore, all *C* is *A*.
   All mortals are farmers.

wherein the conclusion is unsound because it does not follow from (1) and (2). These are very difficult verbal discriminations even in symbol form. They become harder when put in word form. Many of the statements made in politics, business, or everyday life look like correct syllogisms when they are really fallacies. A political candidate, for example, may say:

Inflation leads to high taxes.
High taxes lead to tax scandals.
So, let's cut taxes!

and we may respond with, "I want lower taxes. Say, he makes good sense."

ILLOGICAL THINKING. One of the reasons why it is hard to think logically, then, is that it is difficult to tell verbal reasoning that follows the rules of logic from that which does not. Besides that, there are other reasons why we have trouble always being logical. Our ordinary conversation is not made from a logical mold—and how dull it would be if it were!—but rather from the interplay of personal and motivational factors. With language, we have learned to sell a magazine subscription, to persuade a reluctant parent, to hail a cab, or to stimulate a mood. Seldom do we use words in order to "think straight." Furthermore we may have received excessive training in logical confusion. A child, for example, is charged by a grownup with, "Give me one good reason why you disobeyed me!" The frightened child cannot do it, so he lies or rationalizes until the adult is satisfied with his answer.

Then, too, life itself has a way of confronting us with illogical coincidences, such as the thunderstorm on the only day we play hooky from school. Here an *animistic* reasoning, that our truancy *caused* the thunderstorm, is fostered by nature and often exploited by a moralistic parent. Society's encouragement of such fallacious reasoning is religiously systematic in some cultures and is widespread in our own, especially where cause-and-effect relationships are concerned. It not only can lead to a wrong theory of thunderstorms, it can also lead to wrong habits of reasoning which interfere with the practice of logic.

DISTORTIONS IN REASONING. Ordinarily, then, we have a strong tendency to respond to "logic" stimuli with free, associative responses, even when we may be trying our level best to be logical. And such responses tend to distort our reasoning. Some circumstances, however, are more likely than others to evoke free associations and thus distortions in reasoning. Since logical thinking is important to all of us, we ought to take a moment to look at some common distortions.

One factor is the complexity of the stimulus situation. If a logical fallacy is presented to people in a complicated way or along with a mass of complex facts and statements, they are less likely to detect it.

Another related source of distortion in reasoning is the language in which premises are expressed. An important factor in such distortion is what has been called the *atmosphere effect* [Sells, 1936]. This refers to the impression that a statement may make on a person, inclining him to give a yes or no answer quite apart from the logical implications of the statement. If, for example, the premises of a syllogism are presented in the affirmative, "All *p*'s are *q*'s, and all *q*'s are *t*'s," people tend to reject any negative conclusions containing "no" or "are not." When the premises are split, however, that is, when one is stated affirmatively and the other negatively, they tend to accept negative conclusions. Such atmosphere effects are apparently rather common; college students, at least, are amazingly subject to them.

Another important factor is what we may call the *opinion effect* on reasoning. As you might expect, numerous experiments have shown that *emotion*-producing material and words that evoke strong *prejudices, beliefs,* or *opinions* may effectively prevent discriminative, logical deductions. One of the most interesting of these is illustrated by a syllogistic test [Morgan and Morton, 1944] in two multiple-choice forms:

TABLE 9.2. Conclusions accepted by subjects in a test of syllogistic reasoning. One group of subjects was given two premises stated in neutral symbolic terms. Another group was given the same premises stated in emotionally toned sentences. They were then asked to check on a multiple-choice question the conclusions that could be drawn from these premises. See text for correct answer [modified from Morgan and Morton, 1944].

Conclusions	Per cent of subjects accepting conclusion	
	Symbolic form	Sentence form
1. Airplanes are more effective than battleships.	0	44
2. Airplanes may be more effective than battleships.	11	46
3. Airplanes are not more effective than battleships.	47	1
4. Airplanes may not be more effective than battleships.	32	0
5. None of the above conclusions seems to follow logically.	10	9

FIGURE 9.11. Development of the letter *A* from the Egyptian character *apis,* meaning sacred bull. This character seems to be the forerunner of the Phoenician character *aleph,* which meant ox. The *aleph* became the Greek *alpha* and later our *A.*

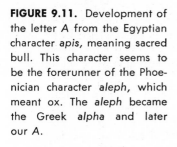

Phoenician Aleph

Roman A

Egyptian Apis

Greek Alpha

The first form was *symbolic;* it used neutral terms like *x, y,* and *z.* The second form was "emotionally toned"; it contained phrases that in 1942 evoked strong personal opinions about air power; for example, "Battleships are not as effective as certain other machines of destruction, since the British battleships *Prince of Wales* and *Repulse* were sunk by airplanes." Conclusions drawn by subjects in this experiment are given in Table 9.2. Conclusion 5 is the only correct answer, for the two premises are so stated as to imply jointly nothing whatever beyond what they say as separate sentences. Yet 90 per cent of the subjects accepted either conclusion 1 or 2, apparently because they already believed in air power: When opinions were lacking, as they were in the symbolic *x, y, z* form, the students favored conclusions 3 and 4 (probably because of atmosphere effect: negative conclusions from split negative-affirmative premises).

You would be wise to test yourself by some homemade syllogisms. See if you can distinguish the factual truth or falseness of a conclusion from the soundness or unsoundness of its logical dependence on its premises. For example:

1. All thinking is dreaming.
2. All reasoning is thinking.
3. Therefore, all reasoning is dreaming. The conclusion is false (in terms of this chapter!) but it is a logically sound deduction from the premises, one of which (1) happens to be false.

All too often, belief conquers logic when both contend in the same man. The causes are psychological. We know that they lie in the learning history of the individual. People are primarily psychological, not logical, even when they "reason."

Language and communication

Let us now take a brief look at language. We have seen that the words of our language become labels for things and concepts and that they may be incorporated into our thinking in subvocal form. Language, of course, is also employed to communicate our thinking to others. Let us see what language is made of, how it is structured, and how it is used. (For a discussion of the perception of speech, see Chapter 12).

THE STUDY OF LANGUAGE. Language, of course, may be either written or spoken. Of the two forms of language, the oral is historically the older. Later, by gradual progression from pictures to such characters as the letters of our alphabet, written language evolved (see Figure 9.11). For this reason, and because written language is usually more carefully regulated by custom and by grammarians, there are some important differences between written language and spoken language.

The basic elements of the two are, of course, different; one is based on letters and the other on sounds. Our speaking and writing vocabularies are also different—the written is usually much larger. Furthermore, our speaking and writing grammars often differ. We tend to convey different kinds of information in the two media. Finally, our written language is not so repetitive and redundant as our oral one. Despite all these differences, the two obviously have much in common, for they follow many of the same rules, and one form can easily be translated into the other by a person familiar with the language.

We should note in passing that several groups of students and scientists make it their business to study language. Some are interested in the sounds of speech, how they are made, how they are related to written symbols, and how speech may be improved; these are the *phoneticians*. Some are interested most in the meaning of words; these are the *semanticists*. Others are concerned with the rules of word form and order and with habits for speaking and writing words; these are the *grammarians*. Finally, there are specialists who compare different languages and who study the history of words and languages; these are the *philologists* and *comparative linguists*.

Psychologists can profit from the knowledge supplied by these disciplines, but their interest is somewhat different. They are not concerned with the history or grammar of language, but rather with its use as a means of communication—one of the ways in which people behave, a stimulus people perceive and respond to, and something used in learning and thinking.

LANGUAGE UNITS. Language is composed of units combined in a multitude of ways. The basic units of spoken language are called *phonemes*. These are the sounds that must be distinguished in the everyday use of language. Actually, a skilled phonetician can distinguish many more sounds than those that are called phonemes, but whenever he finds sounds that are similar and are never followed by the same sound, he groups them together into one phoneme. He does this because people do not need to distinguish sounds that are always followed by different sounds.

An example will make this point clear. Consider the sound of *k* in the two words "key" and "cool." If you say these words to yourself, you will realize that the *k* sound is different in the two words. Simply notice the position of your lips when you say them. No confusion results, however, by considering these two sounds the same, for the *k* in key is never followed by the *oo* and the *k* in cool is never followed by the *e*. Consequently, though the phonetician can distinguish these two *k*'s, we do not need to pay any attention to differences between them, for the *oo* and the *e* that follow them are our cues. For that reason, the phonetician considers the two *k*'s to be one and the same phoneme.

VERBAL CONTEXT. Phonemes, then, are the essential units of spoken language. About 40 are required to transcribe accurately any variety of English. Thus all the sentences we speak and the thousands of words we use in making these sentences can be analyzed into about 40 units. Conversely these units are combined into syllables, the syllables into words, words into sentences, and so on.

Frequency of units. If someone were given 40 units and told to construct a new oral language, one of the first decisions he would face would be how often to use each of the various units. He could, on the one hand, use each unit just as often as any other unit. In this way he could make the greatest use of the available units. He might, on the other hand, throw away all the units except one and use just that one unit. The result would not be a language—even the animals use more units than that—for it could convey one and only one message. Or he might take some middle course and use some units a good many times and other units only a few times.

It is this middle course that characterizes the languages that people use: some units are used much more frequently than others.

Of the 40 English phonemes, 9 are used to make up more than half the sounds we produce. The most frequent sound (*i* as in "bit") is used, on the average, more than 100 times as often as the least frequent sound (*z* as in "azure"). And as you probably have observed yourself, consonant sounds occur more often than vowel sounds. Indeed, only 12 consonant sounds make up about 60 per cent of all sounds produced in speech.

If we study the way in which units are combined into words, we note the same thing. Some units tend to be used more in one part of a word than in another. English words end and begin more often with consonants than with vowels. Moreover, of the consonants that begin words, more than one-half are from a group of five sounds, and of those that end words, more than one-half come from a group of eight different sounds. We use some words much more than others. It has been estimated that only 121 words make up about 60 per cent of the typical person's speech and about 45 per cent of his writing.

The fact that some units and some combinations of units (words) are used more frequently than others is not simply a statistical matter. It is related to our ability to perceive and comprehend speech. Since we hear or read some units and words much more than others, we expect and anticipate them. Thus we find it easier to perceive these than others [Howes and Solomon, 1951].

Sequence of units. Certain units not only appear more often than others, they are also more likely than others to follow certain units. That is, certain sounds tend to follow other sounds, and certain letters tend to follow other letters. Thus some *sequences* of units are more likely to occur than others. This fact helps us considerably in our perception of language. It can be illustrated by the following experiment [Miller et al., 1951]:

Subjects were shown words for very brief periods of time. The words were not those of English, but were pseudo words made up for the experiment (Table 9.3). The experimenter first constructed a list of "words" in which the letters were drawn completely at random, and presented this list to his subjects. He measured the length of visual exposure necessary for the subjects to identify the words. This list of words was called a "zero-order" list. He also used another list composed of "words" in which the letters were used as frequently as they occur in English. The letter e, for example, occurred as often in these words as it does in ordinary prose, and this was true of every other letter he used.

These words were "first-order" words. Another set of "second-order" words was formed in the same way as the "first-order" list, but in addition each letter in these words was preceded by a given letter as often as it is preceded by that letter in English. "Third-order" and "fourth-order" words were formed by the same rules except that each letter was preceded by the combination of two letters and three letters, respectively, as often as it is in English. Examples of these words are given in Table 9.3. The words begin to look more and more like English as they progress from zero-order to fourth-order. But they are all nonsense words.

TABLE 9.3. Samples of pseudo words constructed according to the statistical properties of English [selected from Miller, 1951].

Zero order	First order	Second order	Fourth order
yrulpzoc	stanugop	wallyoff	ricaning
ozhgpmtj	vtyehulo	therares	vernalit
dlegqmnw	eincaase	chevadne	mossiant
gfujxzaq	iydewakn	nermblim	bittlers
wxpaujvb	rpitcqet	onesteva	oneticul

You can probably guess what the result of the experiment was. As the pseudo words more closely approximated the sequences of letters found in English, the subjects found it easier to perceive them correctly, and the length of exposure required became shorter and shorter. You can see exactly how the results came out in Figure 9.12. Thus the fact that English uses certain sequences of units more than others and that we learn these over the years helps us in perceiving language.

At the beginning of this section, we used the phrase "verbal context" as our main heading. We are now in a position to understand this term. To perceive speech and written language, people need to perceive not merely the isolated phonemes or letters of the language, but also the frequencies and sequences in which they appear. The fact that one sound or one sequence of sounds is more likely to occur than another gives language a verbal context that makes a difference in our perception of the units of the language. Thus the stimuli or signals that make up a language are both the units of the language and the context provided by the way in which these units are combined.

VOCABULARY. Earlier in the chapter we stressed the enormous number of signs made available by a language. Actually, the English language has well over a half-million words in it. There is probably no one who knows all these words, even if we omit the thousands of technical words used only by scholars to denote their materials and concepts. In fact, most people have a surprisingly small vocabulary—considering the large number of words available—and can expand this vocabulary only under special conditions.

The number of words a person knows is usually considered to be his vocabulary; but, to be more accurate, each person has not just one, but rather several vocabularies.

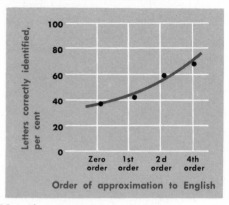

FIGURE 9.12. The recognition of pseudo words. The closer the words approximated English, the more they were correctly identified [data from Miller et al., 1951].

First of all there is the vocabulary he can *recognize*. This is almost always considerably larger than the one he can speak or write. In an earlier chapter, when we traced the development of language in the child, we pointed out that children can understand and recognize words before they can use them—at least in a way that others can understand—and this difference continues throughout life. The number of words a person can use is smaller than the number he can understand.

There is also a difference in the vocabulary that a person *can* use and that which he ordinarily uses. What this difference is varies from one person to another, but we can make some estimate of it by comparing the words we use in writing a theme or an examination paper with the words we use in everyday speech. When we try hard, which we usually do if we want to impress someone with our vocabulary, we use many more words than we do when we are speaking casually.

VERBAL DIVERSIFICATION. Language offers not only a large reservoir of words to use, but the way these words are put together can also be varied. Students of language have worked out several indices for analyzing the structure of language as it is used by people. Two of these may be mentioned briefly.

Type-token ratio. One is the type-token ratio. It is obtained by making two counts of the words a person produces in some sample of his speech or writing. One is simply the number of words; this is the number of *tokens* produced. The second is the number of different words he produces; this is the number of *types* produced. Dividing the number of types by the number of tokens gives the type-token ratio.

This ratio tends to go along with vocabulary size, for those who have limited vocabularies use a few words more often than do people who have a larger number of words at their command. It also partly describes some of the difference between written and spoken language. Written language usually has higher ratio than spoken language. When we write we generally try to choose our words with greater care and thus use different words to express shades of meaning.

Verb-adjective ratio. Another index of verbal diversification which has some interesting applications is the *verb-adjective ratio.* As its name implies, it is formed by taking the number of verbs in a sample of speech and dividing it by the number of words which qualify the action of the verb, including both adverbs and adjectives. Consequently, the higher this ratio for a sample of speech, the more "active" it is.

As one might expect, the verb-adjective ratio varies considerably with different language samples. Scientific writing makes relatively little use of verbs and has a low ratio of about 1.3. Writing which contains dialogue or has more human interest yields a higher ratio. In plays there are about nine verbs per adjective.

THE MEANING OF LANGUAGE. We have covered a few basic points concerning the way language is structured. Now we proceed to consider its meaning when it is used to communicate messages from one person to another. The primary purpose of language, of course, is to communicate meaning. How is this done?

The meaning of a message seems to be carried in two ways. One is by common experiences with words as they have been used with things and events. The child comes to know the meaning of such words as "chair," "doll," "food," "bed," and so on because these words are spoken when he is perceiving these objects directly with his senses. In this way, we build up a large number of words whose meanings we think we know and understand when we communicate with each other. This kind of meaning, which can be verified by pointing to objects or events, has been called *extensional meaning.*

A second kind of meaning is derived from the first by using dictionaries or verbal equivalents. Most of us have never seen the platypus and therefore have no extensional meaning for the word, but if we look it up in the dictionary we shall find it described in terms of words, such as *small aquatic mammal* and *bill like that of a duck,* for which we have had extensional meanings. This kind of derived meaning has been called *intentional meaning.* This kind of meaning is a general case of the meaning of concepts learned through definition referred to earlier in the chapter.

You probably take it for granted that people have somewhat different meanings in mind when they use words. That is to be expected, because many words do not have precise meanings. You might also guess that the intentional (derived) meanings of words are not so fully agreed upon as are the extensional (demonstrable) meanings. That is also true. You probably would not suspect, however, how much the meaning of a word varies from one person to another even for words which most of us think we understand. Students of language have, nevertheless, demonstrated this in a quantitative way, as we shall see.

Since language serves as communication

between people and since they manage to communicate only when the listener (or reader) has roughly the same meaning for a word as the speaker (or writer), the only practicable way to measure the meaning of a word is through agreement among people. We can devise an index of meaning, then, by determining to what extent people agree. We can let .00 stand for no agreement at all and 1.00 stand for the maximum agreement. To obtain the index of a particular word we establish how much agreement there is and divide that number by the maximum possible agreement.

One research worker [Johnson, 1944], who devised this kind of index, asked subjects to define words extensionally by accepting or rejecting the names of persons, objects, or phenomena which were offered as examples of the class of things symbolized by a word. Suppose that in a study of this kind we asked 100 subjects whether they considered Franklin D. Roosevelt an example of the class of things covered by the word "liberal." We would then count the number of "yes" responses and divide by the total possible, 100. If 100 "yes" responses were given (or 100 "no" responses), we would have complete agreement among the subjects about this particular extensional definition of liberal. If only 50 "yes" responses were given to the question, then we would have complete disagreement, since as many subjects rejected the example as accepted it. As a matter of fact, a study conducted in this manner produced an index of agreement of only .24 in the case of Roosevelt. This represents considerable disagreement. In the case of Herbert Hoover there was considerable agreement that he was not an example of the class of things covered by the word "liberal." The index for his name was .90.

Other methods of measuring the meaning of words, including those for measuring the meaning of concepts mentioned earlier, have been tried. In general, when words are considered one at a time, agreement about meaning is not very high.

MEANING IN CONTEXT. From this we might conclude that we are not very successful in communicating meaning. Actually, we are not, but things are not so bad as they seem. Part of the reason for poor agreement on the meaning of words is that the meaning of a word depends somewhat on the context in which it is used. Put another way, context supplies meaning. Since language is spoken and written according to certain rules, words occur in certain sequences more than in others. These sequences give meaning a context, and this context makes the meaning of words much more precise than it would otherwise be. How often have you heard someone exclaim, "You have quoted me out of context"? In this way, he is trying to say that you cannot tell precisely the meaning of one set of words without knowing the other words with which they are used.

Just as we were able to illustrate verbal context by building up sequences of letters and sounds, we can show the context of meaning by choosing words according to their *order* of context. This has been done in Table 9.4. In that table, the zero-order list was constructed by choosing words at random. In the first-order sentence, words occur with about the same frequency as we expect them to occur in English. This is also true of sentences of a higher order, but in the second-order sentence one word is preceded by another as often as we might expect it to be in English. In the third-order sentence, they are preceded by pairs of words as often as we might expect them in sequences in ordinary English, in the fourth-order sentence by triplets, and so on up to the seventh order. Then finally a sample of prose is given.

The method used in constructing these sentences is an interesting one, and one which you can try at home or with your friends [Miller and Selfridge, 1950]. To obtain the second-order list, a common word, such as "he," "it," or "the," is presented to a person who is asked to use the word in a sentence. The word he uses directly after the one given him is noted and then pre-

TABLE 9.4. Samples of pseudo sentences constructed according to the statistical properties of English [Miller and Selfridge, 1950].

Zero order

Betwixt trumpeter pebbly complication vigorous tipple careen obscure attractive consequence expedition pene unpunished prominence chest sweetly basin awoke photographer ungrateful.

First order

Tea realizing most so the together home and for were wanted to concert I posted he her it the walked.

Second order

Sun was nice dormitory is I like chocolate cake but I think that book is he wants to school there.

Third order

Family was large dark animal came roaring down the middle of my friends love books passionately very kiss is fine.

Fourth order

Went to the movies with a man I used to go toward Harvard Square in Cambridge is mad fun for.

Fifth order

Road in the country was insane especially in dreary rooms where they have some books to buy for studying Greek.

Seventh order

Easy if you know how to crotchet you can make a simple scarf if they knew the color that it.

Prose text

More attention has been paid to diet but mostly in relation to disease and to the growth of young children.

sented to another person who is asked to use that word in a sentence. This method is repeated, using a different person each time, until a sentence as long as is desired is obtained. The assumption which is made here is that the persons asked to form sentences will use one word following another about as frequently as the two words occur together in the English language.

In the case of the third-order sentences, persons are given two words, such as "he is," "it became," "the world," and asked to use them, as presented, in a sentence. Then the word used directly after the sequence is added to the sequence, the first word of the sequence is dropped, and the new sequence is presented to the next person to be used in a sentence. This same technique is used for fourth-order sentences, using three-word sequences; for fifth-order sentences, using four-word sequences; etc. First-order sentences are obtained by drawing words at random from all the higher-order sentences. The resulting sentences contain words occurring with about the same frequency with which they occur in common usage. The zero-order sentences can be obtained by choosing words at random from a dictionary.

When sentences constructed in this way are examined, it is easy to see that from the low to higher orders the sentences gradually begin to convey what we ordinarily accept as meaning. The higher-order sentences look meaningful in spite of the fact that they were not said by any one person intending to say something to somebody.

We should carefully notice here, however, that the meaning of our language is not all carried by verbal context as defined by the sequence in which words occur. By using the method we have described, we could construct sentences to the fifteenth order, to the twentieth order, and beyond without ever producing sentences equivalent in real meaning to sentences taken from prose text. That is, sentences which are constructed by faithfully following the statistical rules governing a language need not be good, meaningful sentences. The reason is that, although we are accustomed to using words in certain sequences, we still have a good deal of freedom in choosing a word even after lengthy sequences of previous words. This is a good thing, of course, since in order to communicate something new to another person we must be able to say something which he cannot predict with complete accuracy in advance.

DEFECTIVE LANGUAGE. The perceptions and skills involved in producing and understanding language are rather complex, and it takes an individual many years and an incalculable amount of learning to acquire them. It is therefore not surprising that such a delicate and complex function should at times result in language defects. A person may be defective in one or in several of the aspects of languages: ability to read it or to comprehend it when it is spoken, ability to produce elementary phonemes or to combine them in the sequences necessary to be intelligible, or ability to use the language with a meaning that can be understood.

Some defects in a person's language ability are the result of injury or disease of the brain. These are called *aphasias,* and we shall discuss them later in Chapter 20. Others are due to some kind of personal maladjustment. Stuttering and stammering, for example, have long been considered as stemming from emotional difficulties, although defects in functioning of the nervous system may play a part. Defects of language often appear in psychoneurotic disorders, and they are almost always prominent in the psychoses (see Chapter 5). One can, in fact, use some of the indices and relations we have described above to help in the diagnoses of the psychoses. For in some forms of mental illness, there is usually a distortion in the way words are connected with each other and in the way they are used.

Consider, for example, the case of a female schizophrenic patient presented with a block-sorting test [Cameron and Magaret, 1951, page 510]. The examiner asked her the question, "What is the difference between this group and that?" She replied:

Dividing by feeling your hand and calculating the rim. If I wrote on the blackboard by hand wouldn't give out anything at all, no chalk-mark. It's a certain light they leave careless with their work. It's light slatiness; and when I went out there to walk I found lots like that. Like those men working on the roof, keep slipping off. There's somebody copying that light all the time. How in God's name can a man keep spending money on a child and buy her clothes? And that's the way with Constance, and she going to school. They'll be going to fertilize her mind through our farm and get that light. My family took that up great. A woman in Missouri she worked on those children, boiled them and picked them and finished them. I like to do a work there.

This is an example of schizophrenic language. Such language is characteristically lacking in connectives and in precise meaning, it is filled with intrusive fragments of unrelated topics, and it is overinclusive. In brief, it does not follow very closely the rules we use to understand each other. However, as in the case of all languages, there usually are some rules that the patient is following. If one understands these rules, one can understand the speech. What this patient was trying to say has, in fact, been understood.

Complex processes in animals

It has occasionally been implied in this chapter that processes akin to human thinking are to be found in animals. Of this, as we shall see, there can be little doubt. There is also no doubt that these processes in animals are exceedingly primitive compared with those in man and that man's use of thinking processes is of a completely different order of magnitude. Nevertheless it is of interest to see just what sorts of activities related to thinking and communication are found in animals. That is our purpose here. The subject is a large one and cannot be treated comprehensively in a few pages. We can only present some selected examples.

Some of the examples come from what we generally regard as instinctive behavior. This complicates our interpretation of the behavior, but before going into that, let us look at our examples.

LIGHT-COMPASS REACTION.   One kind of behavior, called the light-compass reaction, may be observed in some insects. Those that exhibit the reaction have eyes made up of a number of elements—as bees do, for example—all pointed in different reactions. By keeping a small source of light always in such a position that it stimulates one of the elements, the animal is able to steer a straight course to some point. This kind of navigation is called the light-compass reaction because it uses the sun as a compass.

Bees use the light-compass reaction to maintain a transverse orientation toward sources of food and the beehive. When they move out from the hive in search of food, they keep the sun in a certain element of one of their faceted eyes. On the return trip, from food to home, they keep the sun in the corresponding element of the other eye. Thus they automatically return to home territory—if, they have not stayed too long. In a classical experiment with ants [Tin-

bergen, 1951], which use the same method of orientation, ants were picked up on their way home and kept in a small dark box for about 2½ hours. When subsequently released, they started off but missed their home by about the same number of degrees as the sun had moved during the intervening hours (see Figure 9.13).

Very interesting, one might say, but what does this have to do with thinking processes? Note that a very specific memory is involved. The animal must keep the sun stimulating the same (or corresponding) facet of the eye. It can do this even after an interval of hours, and even though on different trips from the home it must use different facets. It therefore holds a particular "memory trace" over a substantial period of time. In this respect it does better than many mammals on the delayed-reaction test. Some sort of mediating process therefore seems to be involved.

THE LANGUAGE OF BEES.   Bees, like ants, use the light-compass reaction for navigation. Though this is a remarkable feat, it is by no means the most wonderful of the bees' accomplishments. Bees not only can keep their orientation, they can *communicate* this orientation to other bees. Indeed, they can

THE ANT FINDS ITS WAY HOME BY USING THE SUN AS A COMPASS:

FIGURE 9.13. The light-compass reaction in the homing ant. In its trek homeward toward D, an ant was kept in the dark for 2½ hours at the spot indicated. When released, the ant started homeward again but missed its home by the number of degrees that the sun had moved in the intervening time [after Tinbergen, 1951].

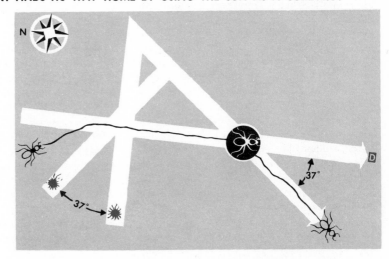

FIGURE 9.14. How bees communicate the place in which they have found food. On returning to the hive, they execute a waggle dance diagrammed in the inset. The speed of the dance (graph) communicates the distance of the food. Along the bottom of the graph is distance in thousands of meters; on the ordinate is the number of turns in a 15-second period. The direction of food (diagrams at left) is communicated by varying the angle of the dance. The sun's bearing, straight up, is used as the reference point. If, for example, food and the sun make an angle of 60 degrees with the hive, the angle of the dance is 60 degrees off the vertical [after Von Frisch, 1950].

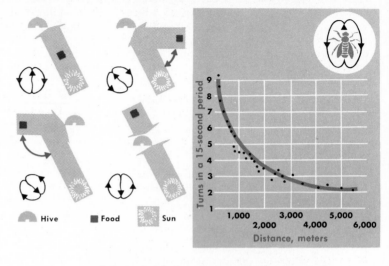

tell other bees in the hive both the direction and the distance away from the hive where they found food. This "language of bees" was discovered by the German zoologist Von Frisch [1950]. How he discovered it and learned what it is makes an interesting story:

Von Frisch once noticed that bees which had found a plentiful source of food would return to the hive and go through a particular kind of dance. This dance was repeated a greater number of times per minute if the food source were near than if it were farther away. From his observations, he was able to make a graph (see Figure 9.14) of the relationship between the distance of the food source and the number of dances per minute. Thus he showed how bees communicate the *distance* of a food source.

But this was only part of the answer. As he watched the bees, he noticed that in a part

of their dance they flew a straight course, all the time waggling their bodies. The direction of the straight course appeared to vary with the direction of the food. They seemed in this way to designate to other bees the *direction* of food. As in the light-compass reaction, they used the sun as a reference point. If the straight part of their dance led upward toward the sun, food was in the direction of the sun. If the direction of the straight "waggle" dance deviated 30 degrees to the right of the sun (see Figure 9.14), then food was to be found 30 degrees to the right. All other directions of the compass could be similarly indicated.

When Von Frisch had found this key to the language of bees, he decided to see whether he could really understand what the bees were saying. He had an assistant place a food source of sugar-water some distance from the hive, at a distance and in a direction unknown to Von Frisch. The assistant then marked the bees that located the food with a little colored shellac so that Von Frisch could know them as they returned to dance in the hive. By using a stop watch to time the number of dances per minute and a protractor to get the direction of the straight part of the dance, he was able to say, "The food has been placed so many yards from the hive and in such a direction." The assistant confirmed the fact that this was indeed the location of the food.

Thus Von Frisch was able to show that bees not only can maintain their orientation but can communicate both orientation and distance to other bees. We say "communicate" because what they do serves this purpose. Whether this is communication in the human sense of "intentionally" using signs and symbols to convey meaning, or even in the sense that my dog barks to be let into the house, we cannot say. Offhand that seems farfetched. Nevertheless bees obviously do communicate.

Communication has been studied in other animals. Experiments on the chimpanzee were described in Chapter 2. Many birds have several distinct calls, including calls representing fear, attack, and contentment. Such calls serve as signs, and thus as communication. Parrots and kindred birds, of course, can utter relatively distinct words. But serious attempts to teach them to use words meaningfully, that is, for communication, have gotten practically nowhere.

Unquestionably, however, the different sounds made by birds have meaning for birds, as the following study [Frings and Frings, 1959] illustrates:

Two experimenters in Maine watched and listened to crows for several months. They were able to distinguish four different crow calls. Moreover, with a concealed microphone, they were able to record these calls on tape, and then play them back to the crows. They discovered that one call was an assembly call, for crows gathered around the loudspeaker as soon as they heard it. Another was a dispersal call; it sent crows scattering when they heard it. The two calls thus had different meanings for these Maine crows.

The tape recordings were then sent to France to scientists studying bird calls there, where they were played to three different species of French crows. These crows, too, immediately reacted to the assembly call of the Maine crows by approaching the loudspeaker. It turned out, however, that not all crows "understand" all other crows. Recordings of French crow calls were sent to the United States, and the crows in Maine did not react to them. On the other hand, some crows in Pennsylvania did.

The explanation seems to be that crows that live and feed together, hearing each other's calls and seeing how other crows react to them, respond similarly, presumably through learning. The Pennsylvania crow winters with the southern fish crow, while the French crows associate with French crows and with other birds. They "understand" the birds with which they associate. The Maine crows have been observed not to associate with other species of birds or with other kinds of crows. They "understand" only themselves.

ALTERNATION. Earlier in this chapter the delayed-reaction test was described. It involves an immediate memory trace which serves as a mediating process for the solution of a discrimination. Two other tests designed to study thinkinglike processes in animals are tests of *delayed alternation* and of *double alternation* [Munn, 1950]. In simple alternation an animal is required to run a maze by turning first right, then left, then right, then left, etc. In double alternation, the required pattern of turns is *RRLL*, *RRLL*, *RRLL*, etc. Or it may be pushing a lever, picking up inverted cups or some other act in the same *RL* or *RRLL* sequence. The important difference between these tests and the delayed-reaction test is that the original stimulus, in addition to the symbol or substitute for it, must be inside, instead of outside, the body. That is to say, in an alternation problem, there is no flash of light to indicate the correct response after a delay. All cues for solving the problem must be furnished by the animal itself. So we can *suppose* that an internal cue for turning left is the result of just having turned right, and so on; and furthermore we can *suppose* that this cue functions the same way as does the light or other external cue in the delayed-reaction test.

If we grant these suppositions, the delayed alternation is a test of symbolic function. Rats have responded correctly in the test even though they were restrained for 15 seconds between each right and left turn; some rats have done this even though their bodies were disoriented or anesthetized during the delay interval. How long monkeys and people can delay has never been measured exactly, but of course we know that people could, with language, delay almost indefinitely.

The double-alternation test is a little different because the second R and the second L response, if successful, must be made to a symbolic cue slightly different from that of the first R or L response. How can the animal "know" to make just two rights and two lefts, instead of several, unless he can count?

This problem proves to be very difficult for rats, particularly if the test is in the temporal form and no spatial cues are supplied. The animal is required to run around the block to the right twice and then to the left twice so that all choice points are identical with respect to external stimuli. With great difficulty a few rats have learned to do one *RRLL* sequence but have not been able to extend it. Extending the sequence is possible, though, if the rats, instead of running, simply move a lever with their paws twice to the right, twice to the left, etc. In a *spatial maze*, an animal makes its sequence of turns in order without "running around the block," but the parts of the maze are interchanged and the maze reoriented in the room so that all external cues are continuously disturbed and the animal cannot make use of them to solve the problem. In studies with such a spatial maze, a few rats learned one segment of triple alternation, *RRRLLL* and of quadruple alternation, *RRRRLLLL;* at least, they could perform it part of the time, although they never really mastered it.

It is interesting that ability to solve double-alternation problems is correlated with position in the animal kingdom [Hunter and Nagge, 1931]. Raccoons can do double alternation and extend it part of a sequence (two turns), and monkeys can extend it several more turns. Using a special toy form, children above three years of age can do it, but so far no child below three has been successful. Errors are fewer with older children; five-year-olds solve it by counting—by using language—and can, of course, extend the sequences indefinitely.

ORDERLINESS. Another way to test symbolic function is to pose a problem that requires that things be done in a particular order yet provides no specific cues for the correct order. In order to learn such a problem, some memory must serve as the mediating process to "run off" responses in the correct order. In giving a motorist directions, for example, you may be able to say, "Go three blocks, turn left; then two blocks, turn right. . . ." You can do this without remembering exactly what the corners look like or having any signs to guide your thinking. Thus you are relying on memories that serve as mediating processes to give your directions.

This kind of ability to do things in correct order without specific objective cues is better in monkeys and apes than in lower animals, and far better in man than in monkeys and apes.

One of the several ways of testing this capacity in animals employs the "three-pedal box." This box has three platforms in it, arranged as you see them in Figure 9.15. The experimenter can so arrange things that the animal must push these pedals *a particular number of times in a required order* to secure a food reward. He may require the animal to push simply 1, 2, and 3, in that order, or to push them 1, 3, 1, 2, 3, 2, . . ." He can then determine the longest order that an animal can correctly master.

In Table 9.5, you see the results of experiments with different animals. Guinea pigs and rats are not very good at it, for they can, on the average master a series only one or two pushes long. The kitten is somewhat better, with three. The monkey is still better, with five to ten. And children can master much longer series than that. So you can see that the ability to remember the order in which things should be done increases markedly from lower mammals to man.

COUNTING. The ability to count develops slowly in children, usually 2 years or so after they have acquired the rudiments of language. It may be regarded as one of the more complex mental processes. Actually, there are not one but rather three ways of counting. One is *subitizing,* which is *perceiving a number of objects at a glance* without saying "one, two, three. . . ." A second is *estimating,* which is *guessing a number without counting.* And third, there is *true counting.*

You have probably heard about or seen "talking" and "counting" horses and dogs. They are often featured in vaudeville, motion pictures, or television. These animals, however, cannot count; they merely respond to cues from the trainer. Birds, however, can subitize. To see what they can do, please read the instructions near the top of page 294 (Figure 9.16). Which has the more dots, the pattern on the right or the one on the left? Birds that have been used in experiments can do just as well as you or I at this sort of counting, provided that the total number does not exceed six or seven. It is interesting, indeed, that both birds and

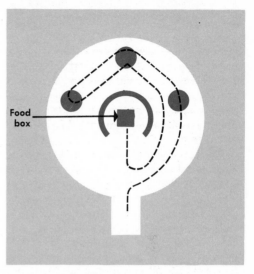

FIGURE 9.15. The three-pedal box. Problems may be arranged to require pushing of the pedals in different orders. A relatively simple problem is 1-2-3, but a more complex one is 1-2-3-2-1-2-1-3-2-1 [after Field, 1934].

people can subitize only six or seven items. Above that number, people must estimate or take time to count, whereas birds are unable to arrive at the correct answer. Birds, however, can master other difficult problems involving numbers.

For one thing, they can match from sample [Koehler, 1943]. In Figure 9.17 you see several circles, each of which has a num-

TABLE 9.5. Limits reached by various mammals tested on the three-pedal-problem apparatus. The scores represent the length of a sequence of responses that can be learned [modified from Munn, 1955].

Type of animal	Number of animals tested	Range of steps	Median	Average
Guinea pig	16	0–1	1	0.5
Rat	24	0–2	1	0.9
Kitten	62	3–7	3	3.6
Rhesus monkey	17	2–22	5	7.4
Cebus monkey	6	5–15	9½	9.8

ber of dots. On the boxes are patterns of irregularly shaped blotches. A trained bird can pick out the proper box from the total group when shown any one of the circles and open only the lid of the box that has the matching number of spots. Again, however, the total number of spots cannot exceed seven.

A bird can also learn to leave a certain number of food objects and to eat no more after he reduces the supply to that number. To train him to do this, the experimenter must shoo him away from a small pile of seeds when he has eaten all but, say, four. After sufficient training, the bird stops eating when four grains are left. Similarly, the bird can learn to leave the number of grains shown him on a cardboard. If it has three or four or five spots, the bird will leave the corresponding number of grains. This takes a little more elaborate training than the other tasks, but the bird can learn to do it. Similar techniques have been used with squirrels, and their upper limit has also been found to be seven, as with birds [Hassmann, 1952].

SOME BIRDS SUBITIZE AS WELL AS PEOPLE:

FIGURE 9.16. Take a brief glance at the two blotches, then turn to the footnote on page 296.

These, then, are some of the ways in which processes related to thinking have been studied and demonstrated in animals. It is evident that the ability to learn and utilize such processes increases as one ascends the evolutionary scale. It is also evident that it is a very long jump from animals to man.

A TRAINED BIRD CAN PICK OUT THE STIMULUS THAT HAS THE SAME NUMBER OF BLOTCHES AS A SAMPLE:

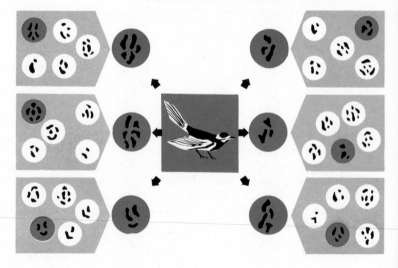

FIGURE 9.17. Matching-from-sample problems used with birds. Six different problems are shown. In green are the sample and the correct one of a group of stimuli. The bird is shown the sample and a group of irregularly shaped blotches [after Koehler, 1943].

CHAPTER NINE

Summary

1. Symbols are signs used in communication. Their meanings are learned by association. Words and language form the most highly developed system of symbols.

2. The meaning of a word or symbol is a process within the individual representing the object or thing for which the symbol stands. Such a meaning may serve as a mediating process, or connecting link, between a symbol and a response or between it and other meanings.

3. Thinking is a sequence of symbolic processes that represent past learning and experience. These processes consist in part of images and implicit muscle responses and also of central processes within the nervous system.

4. Most, if not all, people experience images, and images often help thinking. Some individuals have such vivid (eidetic) imagery that they can recall things almost perfectly. Considerable thinking, however, takes place without the benefit of images.

5. Also involved in thinking are implicit muscle movements that can be recorded with the appropriate instruments. These may be coincidental to thinking, but they may also serve as cue-producing responses that set off the next event in the thinking process.

6. A concept is a process representing a common property of objects or events. In man, language is used so extensively for labeling concepts, that the concept of a word is practically synonymous with the definition of a word.

7. Children initially learn concepts by learning at the same time to discriminate differences and common properties among objects and to use word labels for the common properties. Once some concepts are acquired in this way, concepts may also be learned (a) by gleaning meanings from the contexts in which words are used, (b) by definition in terms of other words, and (c) by classifying objects and events.

8. Several factors affect the ease with which concepts are learned, among them: (a) transfer from other concepts, (b) the extent to which a concept is abstract or concrete, and (c) the distinctiveness of the common elements.

9. The meaning of a concept may be measured in different ways: (a) by free response, which is similar to giving a word definition of it, (b) by discrimination and classification of words and objects, (c) by word associations, and (d) with a semantic differential, which is obtained by rating the position of a concept on several scales.

10. Thinking is often directed; it solves or attempts to solve problems. Such problem solving requires motivation and especially a goal toward which thinking is directed. Thinking is also directed by habits previously formed, by sets, and by unconscious factors.

11. Solutions to problems may be arrived at by (a) trial and error, (b) by rote memory (from solving similar problems in the past), or (c) by insight. Insight is a relatively sudden solution that combines past learning in a new way.

12. Adventurous, or creative, thinking is frequently characterized by five stages between perception of a problem and obtaining a solution to it: (a) preparation, (b) incubation, (c) illumination, (d) evaluation, and (e) revision.

13. Reasoning involves thinking in which elements of previous learning are combined. It has been demonstrated in animals as well as in human beings. Most reasoning in people is done with words.

14. Because words tend to have equivocal or imprecise meanings, because it is often not possible to check the results of reasoning, and because various groups and societies differ in what they consider "reasonable," reasoning is often fallacious.

15. The rules of logic have been devel-

oped to avoid such incorrect reasoning. These are seldom followed, however, in everyday reasoning, because (a) it is very difficult to discriminate logical from fallacious lines of reasoning, (b) our past experiences are often illogical, and (c) such factors as atmosphere effect and prejudice can easily distort reasoning.

16. Spoken language is composed of about 40 basic units called phonemes. Some of these units are used much more frequently than others. Moreover, certain sequences of units are more likely than others. The expected sequences of units aid us in the perception of language.

17. The way in which people use language can be quantified. Size of vocabulary is one measure, but the vocabulary a person recognizes is usually much larger than the one he uses. Verbal diversification is another measure; this indicates the ratio of the number of different words used to the total number used. Another measure is fluency.

18. Words have two kinds of meanings, extensional and intentional. Neither kind of meaning is very clear when words are used one at a time. Meanings, however, are clarified by context, that is, by the fact that some words occur more often than others and that words tend to come in expected sequences.

19. In general, the ability of animals to communicate is poor or almost lacking. A dramatic exception, however, is the ability of bees to communicate to each other the place in which they have found food. They do this by performing a dance oriented with respect to the sun.

20. The ability to use symbolic processes in the solution of problems has been demonstrated in several animals. The techniques used to do this include (a) tests of delayed alternation and double alternation, and (b) a three-pedal problem that can be complicated to require very long sequences of responses.

21. Subitizing is one way of counting; it is perceiving the correct number of objects at a glance. Certain birds and people can subitize up to six or seven items.

Suggestions for further reading

Bartlett, F. *Thinking: an experimental and social study*. London: G. Allen, 1958.
A description of some recent experiments on thinking.

Bruner, J. S., Goodnow, J., and Austin, G. A. *A study of thinking*. New York: Wiley, 1956.
A stimulating description and synthesis of experiments on concept formation.

Humphrey, G. *Thinking: an introduction to its experimental psychology*. New York: Wiley, 1951.
A text on thinking which emphasizes the classical experiments on imageless thought.

Johnson, D. M. *The psychology of thought and judgment*. New York: Harper, 1955.
A text covering thinking and problem solving.

Miller, G. A. *Language and communication*. New York: McGraw-Hill, 1951.
A psychological textbook on language.

Ogden, C. K., and Richards, I. A. *The meaning of meaning* (rev. ed.). New York: Harcourt, Brace, 1947.
The revision of a classical analysis of meaning conveyed by language.

Vinacke, W. E. *The psychology of thinking*. New York: McGraw-Hill, 1952.
A text covering experimental data on thinking and problem solving.

How many blotches were on the left side of Figure 9.16? How many on the right? When you have decided on your answer, turn back to determine whether you are correct. This is a demonstration of subitizing.

Waters, R. H., Rethlingshafer, D. A., and Caldwell, W. E. (eds.). *Principles of comparative psychology.* New York: McGraw-Hill, 1960.
A textbook describing and comparing the behavioral capacities of animals.

Wertheimer, M. *Productive thinking* (rev. ed.). New York: Harper, 1959.
Contains a theoretical analysis of thinking as well as many ideas and experiments on how to solve problems.

Woodworth, R. S., and Schlosberg, H. *Experimental psychology* (rev. ed.). New York: Holt, Rinehart and Winston, 1954.
A comprehensive text in experimental psychology containing a good summary of experiments on thinking.

Introduction

to psychology

PERCEPTION
& ATTENTION

VISION

HEARING
& LOWER
SENSES

PART FOUR
KNOWING THE WORLD

Perception

& attention

PERCEPTION IS THE process of discriminating among stimuli and of interpreting their meanings. It intervenes between sensory processes, on the one hand, and behavior, on the other. Being an intervening process, it is not directly observable. It can be investigated and understood only by observing responses made to stimuli under various conditions.

Those who are untrained in psychology often do not realize that there is much to learn about perception. They know that the sense organs are necessary for perception, but they assume that the senses merely furnish the brain with copies of the external world. Thus perception seems to be merely a photographic process of registering events in the outside world. The world seems so objective and real that they do not even suspect that there is any difference between the "real" world and the world they perceive.

There is, however, a great difference. Much that occurs in the external world never registers at all on the senses. What does register is by no means a faithful copy of the external world. It is drastically transformed by the sense organs and the transmission lines to the brain. Still further, in the brain, messages are processed and recoded so extensively that the result differs in many ways from the original stimulus. Some features of the stimulus are left out; some not in the stimulus are added.

This point will later be amply supported,

299

but it is most dramatically illustrated by the case of the visual illusion. There are many kinds of illusions, visual and otherwise, but three relatively simple examples are shown in Figure 10.1. In the upper drawing, called the Müller-Lyer illusion, one line appears to be longer than the other. But if we take a ruler and measure the lines, we will find that they are exactly the same length. The illusion is created by the direction of the arrowheads. In the second drawing, the long lines appear not to be parallel, when they actually are, as can be proved by measuring the distances between them. The third drawing illustrates the vertical-horizontal illusion. The vertical line appears to be longer than the horizontal one. Actually they are the same length.

In these illusions, our perception of the drawings is incorrect. But the illusions can be proved false only by perceiving the situation in another way, that is, by taking a ruler and measuring the lengths or spacing of the lines. Hence an *illusion is defined as a perception that does not agree with other, more trustworthy perceptions.* We trust rulers because they always give us the same results in different situations. So we rely on our perception of rulers to tell us when our visual perceptions are wrong. In other cases, it may not be so easy to discover when perceptions have played tricks on us. It took, for example, a number of centuries to gather the perceptions necessary to prove that our perception of the world as flat is false. Indeed, science may be regarded as a systematic search for better and more reliable perceptions of the world than we otherwise have. The basic point, though, is that perception is not the same as a physical copy of a stimulus situation.

Sensory discrimination

In order for an organism to perceive something, it must be able to discriminate among stimuli in its environment. In other words, a person cannot perceive something unless he can sense it. He must be able not

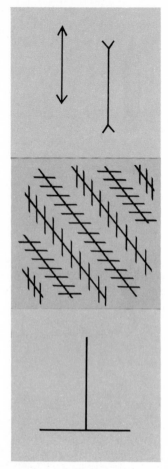

FIGURE 10.1. Some examples of illusions. The example at the top is known as the Müller-Lyer illusion; most people see the line on the left as being shorter than the one on the right. In the middle figure, the diagonal lines are really parallel, though they do not seem so. In the lower figure the vertical line looks longer than the horizontal line.

only to sense its presence, but also to discriminate some of its features—its shape, size, brightness, color, etc. Hence sensory discrimination is the first and limiting step in perception. The study of perception therefore begins with the sense organs and sensory discrimination.

SENSE ORGANS. It is often said that man has five senses: *sight, hearing, smell, taste,* and *touch.* These five, however, are only the obvious ones—the ones we know we have from everyday experience. In addition, there are several more that have been discovered by examining the organs of the body and by experimenting with their function. The fifth of the common five is a skin sense, but there are actually four skin senses: *pain, warmth, cold,* and *touch.* (The evidence for distinguishing these separate senses is given in Chapter 12.) There are also sense organs in the muscles, tendons, and joints that afford a feeling of pressure within the body. These sense organs are called *kinesthetic receptors,* and the sense they serve is *kinesthesis.* There are also, finally, other sense organs in the head associated with the hearing apparatus. These are called *vestibular receptors;* they respond to the force of gravity and to rotation of the head. They are the key sense organs in our sense of balance. The real count then is something like ten senses, rather than five. Some of these can be grouped together, and some can be further subdivided into other senses.

The sensitive elements of each sense organ are called receptors. A *receptor* is a cell that is specialized to respond to relatively small changes of a particular kind of energy. Some receptors, those for sight and smell, for example, are really nerve cells that migrated out from the brain and became specialized for their particular function. Other receptors, like those for pain, are merely the ends of nerve fibers. In other cases, such as taste, hearing, kinesthesis, and the vestibular sense, the receptor is an offshoot of skin cells that has become specialized for its particular function.

Each of these senses responds primarily to a particular kind of physical energy. Smell and taste are chemical senses, for they respond to chemical energy. Warmth and cold are thermal senses, for they respond to thermal energy. Five senses—touch, pain, kinesthesis, the vestibular sense, and hearing— are mechanical senses, for some kind of mechanical energy is required to activate them. The pain sense, however, may also be stimulated by extremes of chemical and thermal energy. The remaining sense, sight, responds to electromagnetic energy.

The range of stimuli to which each kind of receptor responds is relatively restricted. Electromagnetic energy, for example, covers a tremendous spectrum from cosmic rays, through X rays, ultraviolet rays, infrared rays, radar, radio waves, and the alternating current in house wiring (see Figure 11.1). Yet our visual receptors respond only to energy lying in the spectrum between the ultraviolet and infrared waves. Our hearing receptors, similarly, respond to vibrations between about 20 and 20,000 cycles per second, even though ultrasonic sounds go up into the millions of cycles per second. Our chemical senses also respond only to certain chemical molecules, and we are smell-blind or taste-blind to many others. In later chapters on the special senses, we shall specify more exactly the energies to which different receptors respond. The important point here is that they respond to only a very small portion of the energy changes taking place in the world around us. Much goes on that they miss. Consequently, most of the energy changes taking place in the external world are never perceived by human beings without the aid of special instruments.

THRESHOLD SENSITIVITY. Even for those energies to which a sense organ responds, no sense organ is infinitely sensitive. Each sense organ requires some minimum energy for stimulation. There are sounds that are too soft to be heard, light that is too faint to be seen, weights that are too light to be felt, and movements that are too slight to be detected. In a word, every sense has its *absolute threshold.* This is the *minimum stimulus energy* to which it can respond. It must be specified as the absolute threshold because there are other kinds of thresholds which will be described below.

Absolute thresholds may be measured in

a number of ways that have been devised for different purposes. One method, called the method of *constant stimuli,* is to present a stimulus of a given intensity to an observer and ask him to indicate whether he detects it or not. On the next trial, a somewhat different intensity is presented; again the observer merely signals "yes" or "no." The procedure is usually continued for several hundred trials until the observer piles up one hundred or so responses to each of several intensities of stimuli. A typical result is shown in Figure 10.2. This is a "frequency of seeing" curve, showing the number of times an observer saw a flash of light at each of several intensities. The threshold is taken as the intensity at which the observer was able to see the light 50 per cent of the time.

Another method, the *method of adjustment,* allows the observer to adjust the intensity of a stimulus until he just barely senses it. He is provided with a dial with which he can turn the intensity up or down. He turns it down until he cannot see or hear the stimulus, then up a little until he can, and back and forth until he is satisfied that he has the setting at which he can just detect the presence of the stimulus. This then is the threshold intensity. In order to minimize error, he is usually asked to repeat the measurement a number of times, and the average of his various readings is taken as the absolute threshold.

The absolute threshold varies with the individual, the sense involved, and with a number of conditions of observation. In vision, for example, the absolute threshold depends on the color of the light used, the size of the stimulus presented, the duration of the flash, the state of adaptation of the eye, and so on. There is, nevertheless, always an absolute threshold under any given set of conditions. Unless this is equaled or exceeded, nothing is perceived.

Even if stimuli were always above the

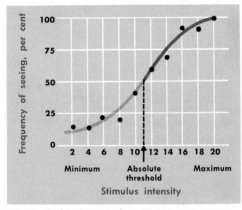

FIGURE 10.2. A frequency-of-seeing curve.

absolute threshold, we would perceive little if they were always exactly the same in intensity and quality. Stimuli must somehow be different—one stimulus must be a little more intense than another or of a different color or pitch—so that we can detect differences among them. In a word, there must be differences in stimuli that we can *discriminate.* We could not perceive a picture, for example, unless there were differences in the color and brightness of the different lines and areas in the picture.

There are limits to the discrimination of differences just as there is an absolute threshold. One stimulus—or a part of a stimulus, depending on how one arbitrarily defines stimulus—must be enough brighter, louder, different in color, etc., for us to detect the difference. The *smallest difference that can be discriminated* is known as the *differential threshold* (or sometimes the *contrast threshold* or *just-noticeable difference*). The ear, for example, can detect differences in the pitch of tones, but when the pitch difference becomes very small, there is a point, the differential threshold, beyond which it is no longer possible to discriminate differences in pitch. Similarly the eye has a differential threshold for discriminating differences in color or in brightness.

CHAPTER TEN

In general, then, our ability to perceive is limited by the differential threshold.

The differential threshold can be measured by methods similar to those used in measuring the absolute threshold. To obtain the differential threshold for pitch, for example, we can alternately present two tones of the same or different pitches and have the observer indicate whether he can or cannot tell the difference. Or we can let the observer adjust the pitch of one tone, while he listens alternately to it and a standard tone, until he finds a setting he considers to be just noticeably different.

PERCEPTUAL ATTRIBUTES.   In order to measure a differential threshold, something we have not yet mentioned is also required. This is the ability to perceive different attributes of a stimulus. An *attribute* is a *perceived quality or aspect of a stimulus*. A tone, for example, has the attributes of pitch and loudness. A patch of light has the attributes of color, brightness, and size. In making a discrimination, an observer attends to one of these attributes and ignores the others. To make a pitch discrimination, for example, he pays attention only to differences in pitch and disregards those of loudness.

An attribute, it should be emphasized, is a *perceived* aspect of a stimulus; it is "in" the observer, not the stimulus. There are, of course, certain physical characteristics of a stimulus that are related to the attribute. The pitch of a tone, for example, is related to the physical frequency of the sound vibrations reaching the ear. One, however, is not a simple replica of the other, for perceived pitch actually depends on the intensity of a tone as well as on its frequency (page 370). This fact is one of many leading to the conclusion that perception is not merely a process of copying a stimulus but rather one of interpreting it.

SENSORY SCALES.   The fact that attributes can be separately attended to and judged makes it possible to develop scales for the perceived magnitude of a particular attribute. One can ask an observer, for example, to judge how loud or how bright a stimulus is and obtain surprisingly accurate results.

There are several methods of estimating the magnitude of a stimulus. One is *fractionation*. In this method, the observer is given two stimuli, one a standard and the other a variable stimulus under his control, and asked to set the variable stimulus to a value one-half, one-third, or twice that of the other. With another somewhat similar method, *bisection,* the observer has three stimuli, two of which are fixed, and he is asked to adjust the third until it seems to him to be halfway between the other two. With another method, *absolute judgment,* the observer is asked to take numbers from, say, 1 to 20 and assign them to the magnitudes of various stimuli presented to him, using 1 for the weakest and 20 for the most intense.

Sometimes these different methods give the same results; at other times, they do not. The reasons for the discrepancies, when they occur, are fairly well understood, but need not concern us here [Stevens, 1957]. In general, it is possible to use any of these methods to construct a sensory scale. This is a scale that shows how perceived magnitude is related to physical intensity. One such scale is shown in Figure 10.3. Two points in this figure should be noted:

The first is that the scale for perceived magnitude is labeled in *brils.* This is the psychologists' term for the subjective unit of visual intensity. The perceived brightness of a light of a standard intensity of 1 milli-lambert—a unit of light intensity—is arbitrarily defined as 100 brils. Scales like this one have now been worked out for many sensory magnitudes, and each has been assigned a subjective unit. Just for the fun of it, you might try to guess what is meant by each of these units: veg, mel, sone, gust, and dol. When you have made your guesses, you can look the terms up in the Glossary at the end of the book.

The other point of importance about

Figure 10.3 is that sensory magnitude and physical magnitude are not the same. A stimulus that is ten times as intense as another is not perceived as ten times greater, but more like two times greater. The exact relationship varies somewhat with intensity. In any case, our perception of a change in intensity does not correspond in one-to-one fashion with a physical change in intensity. This again leads us to emphasize that perception is a process which is not a photographic copy of the stimulus or sensory situation.

DISCRIMINATION WITHOUT AWARENESS. We have now covered the fundamental points about sensory discrimination, but there are a couple of other problems that need to be discussed because they have received so much public attention. One is highlighted by the publicity in recent years about the possibility of using hidden television commercials. The idea here is that messages can be presented on a television screen so faintly that they will not be consciously seen by the viewer yet will in fact be "seen" and have the desired impact. In effect, this means that a stimulus can be presented below the absolute threshold, but can still be seen and serve as a "hidden persuader." Psychologists call this kind of sensing *subliminal perception.*

Offhand the idea seems self-contradictory. The word "threshold" or "liminal" means the intensity below which something cannot be sensed, yet "subliminal perception" implies that a person can see something that is below the intensity required for seeing it. Is such a thing reasonable or possible?

To answer this question, we must distinguish betwen discrimination and awareness. In principle, a person can discriminate among stimuli without being aware that he is doing so. He might be able to guess correctly when called upon without being able to say just how he managed to do it. Exactly this phenomenon has been demonstrated in a number of psychological experiments, such as the following [Miller, 1939]:

Subjects were seated so that they faced what appeared to be an ordinary mirror. Actually the mirror served as a screen on which the experimenter could project images from behind without the subjects' knowing it. Two groups of subjects were used. One group, the "naïve" subjects, were told that they were participating in an experiment on telepathy and were supposed to use the mirror like a crystal ball as something to concentrate on while trying to receive a message sent them telepathically from another room. The other group, the "sophisticated" subjects, knew that images would actually be projected on the screen. The images used for projection on the screen were five different geometrical figures, e.g., a star or wavy lines, which were then in vogue for use in experiments on extrasensory perception (see below). Each time a signal was received from the experimenter, the subject was supposed to guess which of these figures was being sent telepathically (naïve subjects) or projected on the screen (sophisticated subjects). At the beginning of the experiment, the illumination on the screen

SUBJECTIVE BRIGHTNESS IS NOT THE SAME AS PHYSICAL BRIGHTNESS:

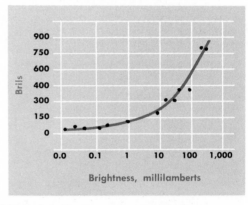

FIGURE 10.3. A subjective scale of brightness. Brils are the subjective units, and millilamberts the physical units. The same subjective scale is obtained whether the subject is asked to estimate one-third, one-half, double, or triple the brightness of a stimulus [after Hanes, 1949].

was very low; after a round of guesses, the illumination was increased a little. This procedure was continued until all the subjects could plainly see the images on the screen and were getting nearly perfect scores.

At very low levels of illumination, the subjects made very low scores. (Chance was 20 per cent.) As the illumination increased, their percentage of correct guesses increased. Both groups of subjects made better than chance scores without being able to say that they actually saw anything on the screen. The naïve subjects did this without knowing that the mirror was anything other than a "crystal." Indeed, when the illumination was finally raised to the point where they became aware of images on the screen, they were surprised. One subject's response was typical: "I was positively amazed when the setup was explained to me."

Observers watching the experiment through a one-way screen were equally astonished that the naïve subjects did not see the images at the higher illuminations, when they were plainly visible to the sophisticated subjects. Once the naïve subjects understood the setup they were again shown images at various illuminations. Now they could "see" images they had not seen before.

This general kind of experiment has been done many times in recent years. In most experiments, however, the subject is fully aware that images are being presented on the screen. One such experiment [Lazarus and McCleary, 1951] is as follows:

An electrode was attached to a subject's finger so that he could be given a light electric shock. Other electrodes were also attached to the hand so that the galvanic skin response (GSR) could be recorded. This response, it will be recalled (page 199), can readily be conditioned to a stimulus associated with electric shock. Subjects were then put through a training procedure in which a series of words were presented plainly on a screen. Some of these words (critical) were followed by a shock; others (neutral) were not. After an appropriate number of repetitions, subjects acquired a conditioned GSR to the critical words, but not to the neutral ones.

Then the testing phase of the experiment began. In this, words were flashed on the screen very briefly and at relatively weak illumination. The subject was asked to guess the word flashed. At the same time, his GSR was recorded. The experimenters found that *subjects often gave a GSR to a word when they could not guess the correct response.* In other words, they could discriminate, as indicated by the GSR response, among the critical and neutral words, without being able to report, or to be aware of, the correct response.

These and other experiments indicate that discrimination without awareness is possible. This is the basic idea of hidden persuaders. The conditions under which this is possible, however, raise some questions about the feasibility of putting it to any practical use. In the first place, in order to demonstrate the phenomenon, very accurate control of illumination is required. A relatively small increase in illumination makes the individual aware of the stimulus. In the second place, the phenomenon is most evident when the observer does not expect any stimulus to be present. Third, the subject must be attending very closely to the stimulus and be highly motivated to discriminate any cues that may be present. Fourth, the subject needs to know what the possibilities are; he knows that the stimulus is one of a number he is already familiar with. Finally, the stimulus on the screen must be the only one there; it cannot be superimposed on other objects or pictures.

It is not for us to say whether these various conditions can be attained well enough for hidden persuaders to be effective, for many technical problems are involved. But whether or not they are put to practical use, the basic problem of discrimination without awareness is an interesting one from a scientific point of view, and it has various implications for the understanding of human perception.

EXTRASENSORY PERCEPTION.   In recent years, the term *extrasensory perception* (ESP) has been widely publicized. This term refers to mental telepathy, clairvoyance, or any other means of perceiving that does not depend on the senses. Telepathy refers to one person sending a message to another by extrasensory means; clairvoyance is the name for the perception of external events without any sensory knowledge of them. Recently the term *psychokinesis* has been added to the vocabulary to cover mental influences on external events, such as making dice roll to a desired number by "concentrating" on the number. Psychologists are often asked whether there is any truth to reports that ESP has been demonstrated.

To answer this question, one must distinguish between the evidence and the possibility. Scientists must keep an open mind about all sorts of possibilities whether they seem reasonable or not or whether they are proved or not. At the present time, we see no means by which information can be perceived by an individual unless it is processed through his sense organs. It is not impossible, however, that some new form of energy or means of communication will someday be discovered. For this reason, relatively few psychologists are willing to say flatly that ESP is impossible. They have been polled on the question twice, the last time in 1952. In this poll, only 10 per cent ruled out ESP as impossible. The overwhelming majority, 73 per cent, rated it as a remote possibility or merely an unknown. Somewhat less than 3 per cent considered it an established fact.

This brings us to the evidence. If so many knowledgeable scientists are open-minded, yet unconvinced, and so few are convinced, this must mean that present evidence is suspect. And it is. There are now a large number of experiments on the question. (One journal, the *Journal of Parapsychology*, is devoted exclusively to research on ESP.) In many cases, results purporting to explain ESP have been shown to be ex-plicable in other ways. Let us consider some examples [Kennedy, 1939]:

In the original ESP experiments, a deck of 25 cards was used. In each deck were five sets of five different kinds of cards: square, circle, plus, star, and wavy lines. (These are the same symbols used in the experiment on "discrimination without awareness" reported above.) The deck was shuffled and placed face down in front of the "receiver." While studying the back of the card, the receiver guessed what it was, after which the guess was recorded and the card removed. And so on down through the deck. With the particular decks used, many receivers were able to achieve scores significantly above chance, which was 5 correct out of 25. Receivers occasionally made perfect scores. But some psychologists, suspecting an uncontrolled factor, decided to test for visual cues by repeating the experiment under reduced illumination or no illumination at all. They found that scores went down with decreasing illumination. What the observers were in fact doing was "receiving" cues from the backs of the cards; the cards had been embossed enough in the printing process to provide these cues. All the experiment really involved was discrimination without awareness.

In subsequent experiments, the procedure was changed so that the receiver could not see the cards. The cards were kept behind a screen out of view in the keeping of a "sender" and recorder. The sender turned over a card and attempted to transmit its symbol telepathically to the receiver. In this procedure, it has been demonstrated that the sender in concentrating on the card may unconsciously whisper enough to provide cues, again without awareness on the part of the receiver, and that this increases scores above chance. In other experiments, done at some considerable distance, with only a telegraph wire connecting the sender-recorder and the receiver, it has been shown that recorders who "believe" in ESP make enough unconscious errors in recording to account for what otherwise would appear to be extrasensory perception.

Thus some experiments that purport to demonstrate ESP do not support it at all. Instead the scores made by subjects are due to visual or auditory discrimination without awareness or to unintentional errors in recording. In addition, statistical mistakes have been made in some experiments. The most common mistake is to select above-average scores and to neglect average or below-average scores. In this way, results appear to be significantly above chance when they are not. In other cases, the results of an experiment simply do not hold up, for unexplainable reasons, when repeated by another investigator.

This is not to say that we can explain away every experiment that seems to support ESP. It has not been humanly possible to track down every conceivable source of error in an ESP experiment. On the other hand, because so many of the experiments have been demonstrated to be faulty, most psychologists familiar with this type of experimentation remain unconvinced that ESP has been proved.

The role of attention

One of the more obvious characteristics of perception is its selective nature. At any given moment our sense organs are bombarded by a multitude of stimuli. Yet only a few of these are perceived clearly at one time. Other stimuli or events are perceived less clearly, and the rest form a sort of hazy background of which we are partially or completely unaware. This is another way of saying that, of the various events around us, we attend to only a very few. So *attention* is a basic factor in perception.

FOCUS AND MARGIN. This factor divides our field of experience, so to speak, into a *focus* and a *margin*. In the focus of experience are the events that we perceive clearly.

Because we attend to them, they stand out from the background of our experience. Other items in the margin are dimly perceived. We are aware of their presence, but only vaguely so. Imperceptibly shading off from the margin are other items which are outside our field of attention and of which, for the moment, we are not consciously aware.

Let us illustrate the nature of attention. While watching a football game, our attention is focused on the ball carrier. We are somewhat dimly aware of the tangle of players at the scrimmage line and of the activity of the blockers, but it is the ball carrier and his movements that stand out most clearly. We are at the same time being bombarded by a number of other stimuli. Our feet may be aching with the cold, unpleasant sensations may be coming from our stomach as a result of the last hot dog we ate, and the fellow behind us may be carrying on a conversation with his girl. While the play is going on we are not aware of any of these things. Only when the play is finished or time out is called do we perceive how cold our feet are or hear the couple behind us.

SHIFTING OF ATTENTION. The fact that we do at some time hear the conversation behind us and do notice the coldness in our feet illustrates another aspect of our field of attention. Attention is constantly shifting. What is at the focus one minute is marginal the next, and still later may have passed completely from conscious awareness. Even when one activity dominates our attention, its dominance usually is not perfectly continuous. Other perceptions come fleetingly into the focus of our awareness and then are replaced again by the dominant item.

What is it that determines what we will attend to? Although attention does shift, it has a certain orderliness to it. It is not completely chaotic, for if it were we should be unable to carry out any extended activity. Actually, as a good advertising man could explain, there are certain principles that determine the direction of our attention—the principles of attention getting. These tell us what will be most clearly perceived and what may be only dimly perceived or not perceived at all. These principles concern two general classes of factors: external factors in the environment, and internal factors such as motives, set, and expectancy.

EXTERNAL FACTORS. External factors in attention may be considered under four headings: (1) intensity and size, (2) contrast, (3) repetition, and (4) movement. To this list, the factor of novelty might also be added, but this has been discussed earlier in connection with motivation (page 79).

Intensity and size. The louder a sound, the more likely a person is to attend to it. The brighter a light, the more it tends to capture his attention. By the same token, a full-page advertisement is more likely to be noticed than a half-column one. This factor of intensity or bigness is most pronounced when the person is experiencing something new or unfamiliar; then the items in the environment that are biggest, loudest, or brightest will attract his attention first. In general, if two stimuli are competing for attention, the one that is most intense will be noticed first.

Contrast. As human beings, we tend to adapt or become used to the stimulation around us. The ticking of the clock may be noticeable when we enter a room, but after a while it is not noticed at all. A room may seem hot or cold when we first enter it, but after a few minutes we are hardly aware of the temperature. On the other hand, if the clock abruptly stops ticking, we become aware of the sudden silence. As we drive along in a car, we are not aware of the hum of the engine, but if a cylinder misfires, the noise of the engine will occupy the center of our attention.

These examples illustrate the role of contrast in determining attention. Any change in the stimulation to which we have become adapted immediately captures our attention.

If we are reading in our room and someone turns on the radio in the adjoining room, we are apt to become acutely aware of it. But after a short while it drops from our awareness as we again become absorbed in our reading. Now when the radio is turned off it again receives our ATTENTION for a moment. Both the onset and the termination of a stimulus tend to acquire attention because both contrast with what has preceded them.

The word in capital letters in the above paragraph is another illustration of contrast. Most of you noticed the word as soon as you looked at this part of the page. However, if all the text were in capitals, the word would have gone unnoticed. It attracted attention because it contrasts with the words in lower-case letters.

Repetition. There are times when the repetition of a stimulus is attention-getting. A misspelled word is more likely to be noticed if it occurs twice in the same paragraph than if it occurs only once. We are more likely to hear a burst of gunfire than a single shot, or to hear our name if it is called twice. When mother calls Junior in for dinner, she shouts his name not once but several times.

The advantage of repetition is twofold. A stimulus that is repeated has a better chance of catching us during one of the periods when our attention to a task is waning. In addition, repetition increases our sensitivity or alertness to the stimulus.

Movement. Human beings, as well as most animals, are quite sensitive to objects that move in their field of vision. Our eyes are involuntarily attracted to movement in much the same way as the moth is attracted to a flame. Soldiers on a night patrol soon learn this fact and freeze in their tracks when a flare bursts. To fall flat or duck behind shelter is movement that makes their detection more likely than remaining motionless out in the open.

The field of advertising, of course, makes good use of movement as an attention getter. Some of the most effective advertising signs are those that involve movement, either blinking lights or animated figures.

INTERNAL FACTORS. The factors of intensity, contrast, repetition, and movement that attract attention are external stimulus factors. Of equal importance are internal factors, such as motives, interests, and other states within the person.

Motives. Our needs and interests govern not only what will attract our attention but also what will hold it. Even the sleepiest student in the class can be made to sit on the edge of his chair if the instructor announces that he is going to talk about "Sex Practices of American Females." Appeal to the sex drive is particularly effective in our culture because of the traditional suppression of the drive. Thus advertisements effectively use shapely girls in bathing suits to sell such unrelated items as spark plugs. In a society where food is more scarce than it is in this culture, advertisements showing food objects probably outnumber those using sex appeal.

Not only are basic motives such as sex and hunger important in directing attention, but any of the great variety of human motives and interests are effective. If a geologist and a bird fancier walk through the same fields, the geologist will notice the detailed features of the terrain, the various kinds of rocks, etc., while the bird lover will notice the number and variety of birds. If you ask the geologist about the birds, he is very apt to say that he did not notice any, much less how many or what kind. And of course the bird lover is not likely to have noted any of the geological features of the surrounding terrain.

Set or expectancy. Besides our interests and motives, set or expectancy plays a major role in selecting what we will perceive. The geologist would have been able to tell you much more about the bird life in the fields he traversed if he had known beforehand that you were going to ask him. A doctor may hear the phone ring in the night, but not hear the baby's crying. His wife, on

FIGURE 10.4. The effect of set on perception. The group of dots and lines can be perceived either as a B or as 13, depending on what a person is expecting.

the other hand, may sleep through the ringing telephone, but the slightest sound from the child probably will bring her wide awake.

When the drawing in Figure 10.4 is included in a series of two-digit numbers, subjects will report that they have seen the number 13. Another group of subjects who have been exposed to letters of the alphabet will report this drawing to be the letter B. In the one case the subjects have acquired a set or expectancy for numbers, and in the other case the set is for letters.

Of the various factors that determine attention and thus perception, expectancy is probably the most important, for our sets and expectancies largely direct and order the successions of our perceptual experiences. Without them, our perceiving would be largely at the mercy of random fluctuations in the environmental stimuli.

Perception of objects

One of the most obvious facts of our perceptual experience is that it is filled with objects. The stimulation that we are constantly receiving comes into our awareness as shapes and patterns. We do not ordinarily perceive the world about us as patches of colors, variations in brightness, and loud or high-pitched sounds. We perceive objects. We see tables, floors, walls, and buildings, and we hear automobile horns, footsteps, and words.

Some of this perception of objects is a matter of learning, as we shall see later in this chapter, but much of it is probably an unlearned property of our sense organs and nervous system. These structures tend to organize or modify our perceptions into simple patterns or objects. The measured ticking of a clock, for example, is usually not heard as such. Rather we tend involuntarily to accent the even tick-tick-tick-tick and perceive it as tick-tock, tick-tock, etc. Even when we try very hard, it is difficult to overcome such organizing tendencies in perception. They are somehow built into the way the sense organs and nervous system function. Organizing tendencies in perception take several different forms. We shall discuss them under the headings of (1) grouping, (2) figure-ground perception, (3) contour, (4) closure, and (5) apparent movement

GROUPING. One kind of organizing tendency in perception is called *grouping*. Whenever there are several different stimuli, we tend to perceive them as grouped into some pattern. In Figure 10.5, for example, are several illustrations of such grouping or patterning. They have been selected to illustrate different ways in which grouping takes place.

The role of *nearness* or *proximity* as illustrated at (*a*). Instead of seeing six vertical lines, we see three pairs of parallel lines. Items which are close together in either space or time tend to be perceived as belonging together or constituting a group.

At (*b*) and (*c*) we can see the importance of *similarity* in grouping. At (*b*) most people see one triangle formed by the dots with its apex at the top and another triangle formed by the circles with its apex at the bottom. We see these triangles because similar items, the dots and the circles respectively, tend to group together. Otherwise we would see (*b*) as a hexagon or six-pointed

WE TEND TO PERCEIVE SEVERAL DIFFERENT STIMULI AS GROUPED INTO A PATTERN:

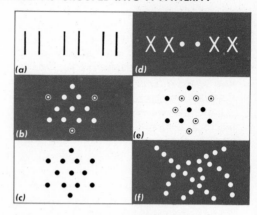

FIGURE 10.5. Examples of perceptual grouping.

star, as is the case at (*c*) where the stimuli are all the same. Another illustration of grouping according to similarity is shown at (*d*). If people are shown this figure and then asked to copy it, most of them will unconsciously draw it so that the two Xs are close together and the two circles are close together but so that the circles are farther from the Xs than in the figure. Thus they exhibit grouping due to similarity.

Grouping according to similarity, however, does not always hold. The figure at (*e*) is more easily seen as a hexagon than as one figure composed of the dots and another figure composed of the circles. In this case, similarity is competing with the principle of *symmetry* or *good figure*. Neither the circles nor the dots by themselves form a symmetrical organization. In either case certain members must be left out—a fact which most people find disturbing. In general, the tendency to group is a tendency to form a balanced or symmetrical figure that includes all the parts.

Our last principle of grouping is *continuation*. This is illustrated by the tendency of a line that starts out as a curve to be seen as continuing a smooth course. Conversely, a straight line is seen as continuing straight or, if it does change direction, as an angle rather than a curve. The figure at (*f*) illustrates continuation; we see dots in that figure as several curves and straight lines. Even though the curves and straight lines cross and have dots in common, it is only with effort that we can see a straight line suddenly becoming curved at one of these junction points.

Although all these examples have to do with vision, the same principles of grouping can be observed in the other senses. The rhythm we hear in music also depends upon grouping according to proximity in time and similarity of accents. In the sense of touch, too, there are examples of grouping.

Get a friend to help you, ask him to shut his eyes, and mark off three equally distant points on the back of his hand. Then touch a pencil to the first two points, pausing slightly before you touch the third point. Your friend will report that the first two points were closer together than were the second and third. This illusion illustrates the grouping of stimuli according to nearness or proximity in time.

The principles of grouping, taken together, explain our perception of complex patterns as units or objects. Indeed, we only see objects as objects, or units as units, because grouping processes operate in perception. Otherwise the various objects, we perceive, e.g., a face on the TV screen, a car, a tree, a book, a house, etc., etc., would not "hang together" as objects. They would be merely so many dots, lines, or blotches.

FIGURE-GROUND PERCEPTION. We have now seen that grouping is basic to our perception of objects. Closely related to the grouping tendencies is another fundamental tendency—the tendency to perceive figure and ground. The objects that fill our everyday perceptions are seen as standing out or being separate from the general background of our experience. Pictures hang *on* a wall, words are *on* a page. In this case, the pictures and words are seen as *figure,* while the wall and the page are seen as *ground.* This primitive capacity to distinguish an

FIGURE 10.6. A figure-ground, the simplest kind of perception.

object from its general sensory background is basic to all object perception.

In glancing at Figure 10.6, you automatically see the black area as being an object. Despite the fact that it may look like no object that you have ever seen, it still is seen as a unitary whole or figure that is distinct from the page. If we examine carefully our general experience of figure-ground relations, we note certain characteristics that distinguish the figure from the ground in our perception. The figure seems to have some sort of shape or object quality, while the ground tends to be formless. The ground seems to extend continuously behind the figure, or, in other words, the figure appears to be in front and the ground behind.

In Figure 10.7 is a reversible figure-ground relation. You can see it as either a vase or two profiles. When you see the vase you perceive the white area as the figure against a black ground, and conversely, to see the profiles you must perceive the black area as a figure upon a white background. It is seldom possible to see both vase and profiles simultaneously.

The figure-ground relation is also found in senses other than vision. When we listen to a symphony, the melody or theme is perceived as the figure while the chords are perceived as ground. In boogiewoogie, the pianist uses repetitive chords in the bass as ground against which to play a varied figure in the treble. In observing a person's movements, we might consider the over-all posture as the ground for, say, the finer movements of the hands and arms.

CONTOUR. We are able to separate objects or things from the general ground in our visual perception only because we can perceive contours. Contours are formed whenever there is a marked change or difference in the degree of brightness or color of the background. If we look at a piece of paper which varies in brightness from white at one border to black at the opposite border, we can perceive no contour, provided the variation in brightness is smooth and gradual. Such a paper appears very uniform to us, and if asked to say where the sheet stops being light and starts to become dark, we can only guess or be arbitrary. On the other hand, if there is a marked change, rather than a gradual change—suppose several shades are skipped—we can perceive the paper as divided into two parts, a light and a dark. The division occurs quite naturally at the place where the brightness gradient abruptly changes.

Contours give shape to the objects in our visual field because they mark off the object from other objects or from the general ground. We must be careful not to conclude, however, that contours *are* shapes. The reversible faces in Figure 10.8 show clearly the differences between contour and shape. Here both faces are formed by the same contour, but it is quite clear that both faces do not have the same shape. Contours determine shape, but by themselves are shapeless.

CLOSURE. Our perception of objects is much more complete than the sensory stimulation we receive from the object. Perception tends to fill in gaps in stimulation so that we perceive a whole object and not disjointed parts. This filling in is termed *closure*. It is a tendency to complete in perception what is physically an incomplete pattern or object.

FIGURE 10.7. A reversible figure-ground. This drawing may be perceived either as a vase or as two profiles.

In Figure 10.9, for example, the circle and square with gaps in them are seen as a "circle with gaps in it" and a "square with gaps in it," not as so many disconnected lines. If these incomplete figures were presented very rapidly, they might even be perceived as complete figures without gaps. That would also be an instance of closure. The same principle applies to the perception

DIFFERENTLY SHAPED OBJECTS MAY BE FORMED BY THE SAME CONTOUR:

FIGURE 10.8. Two different faces shaped by the same contour.

of the man on horseback in the lower part of Figure 10.9. There again we fill in the gaps and perceive an object.

APPARENT MOVEMENT. Everyone is familiar with the electric advertising signs in which arrows seem to move back and forth or patterns of lights seem to move across the sign. As you know, in most of these signs nothing really moves in the physical sense. An illusion of movement is created by lights turning off and on in sequence. Psychologists call this illusion *apparent movement.*

We can study apparent movement by having two lights arranged so that they can be turned on and off, one after the other. If the time interval between turning one light off and the other on is too long, what we see is two separate lights, one going on after the other. If we make the time interval shorter, we get apparent movement in which a single light is seen as moving back and forth. If the interval is made too short, we again see two separate lights, but this time they seem to be on simultaneously. So the interval of time between the two lights is the important thing in apparent movement. This interval, however, depends a lot upon the particular situation. A shorter time interval is needed, for example, if the lights are dim or are far apart.

Motion pictures are also examples of apparent movement. When we watch the movies we see the actors as moving about on the screen. In reality, however, there is no movement on the screen at all. What we are presented with is a rapid succession of still pictures. The projector flashes the successive frames in the film on the screen one at a time but at a very rapid rate. First there is one still picture in which the objects or people are in one position. Then the light from the projector goes off and when it comes on again there is another picture in which the objects and people are in a slightly different position. If the flashing on and off

FIGURE 10.9.
Perceptual closure.

of the projector is fast enough, we perceive apparent movement in which the objects on the screen appear to move about naturally. If the speed of the projector is too slow, we get the impression of jerkiness in the movement.

This concludes our résumé of the perception of objects. Closely related to it, however, is the perception of depth, which we shall take up in the next section.

Perception of depth

Depth perception has been a source of puzzlement to scientists and philosophers for hundreds of years. They have been bothered by the problem of how we can see a three-dimensional world with only a two-dimensional retina in each eye. Our retina is able to register images of the world only in terms of right-left or up-down, yet we perceive the world about us as having the extra dimension of depth.

We are a little more sophisticated about the problem today. We realize that the ability to perceive depth is no more amazing than any other perceptual accomplishment. As we have seen, all awareness of ourselves and of the world depends upon physical energy in various forms striking special sense organs. What our brain receives is various patterns of neural impulses, not tiny copies of various objects.

Today we view the problem of depth perception as the question, How do differences or changes in the physical stimulus relate to differences in perceptual experience? And then, How do the differences in the physical stimulus manage to stimulate our sense organs differentially so that our brain is provided with proper cues for depth? For example, when we look at a near object or at a far object, a flat object or a solid object, the retina receives different patterns of stimulation even though the profile of the objects may be the same. As we shall learn, differences in shadows, in clearness, and in the size of the image in the eye provides cues on the retina as distinctive as if the retina were able to register the third dimension directly.

Perhaps this idea can be made clearer by using an analogy. When a mathematician solves a problem involving speed and weight, he may let x stand for miles per hour and y for weight in pounds. Of course neither x nor y has any physical resemblance to what it is representing, but as long as he is consistent in his operations, his results will correspond with the physical world. His symbols will be adequate substitutes for the real objects.

In the case of perception, different cues, such as shadow and clearness, are the symbols that represent the physical world. The book lying on our desk or the automobile parked across the street form images on the retina. At the same time, senses other than vision are being stimulated too. When we reach for a book or walk to the car, all these sensory cues or symbols are somehow simultaneously perceived so that we judge correctly the distance of the book or car.

Those of you who have watched a baby reach for a rattle have noted how poor his

judgment of distance is. Even the two-year-old child, who has had an opportunity to move around in the world, sometimes appears to lack the clear depth perception of the adult. One two-year-old wanted his father to pick him up so that he could touch the moon. Depth perception probably improves as children grow older. From Chapter 2 you may recall that there is some uncertainty about the respective roles of maturation and learning in the development of perception.

Visual cues for depth perception are usually classified into monocular and binocular cues, that is, those that may be utilized by one eye alone and those that require two eyes. In addition, it is thought that kinesthetic cues (see page 301) from muscles of the eye also contribute to the perception of depth. We shall discuss all these cues in turn.

MONOCULAR CUES. *Monocular cues,* as the name suggests, are cues for depth that operate when only one eye is looking. They were first known by the ancient Greeks, and exploited by the Renaissance painters who were concerned with the problem of giving depth to their paintings. Their problem of presenting a three-dimensional world on a two-dimensional canvas is essentially the same problem that our retinas are faced with. If the artist is able to paint the scene on his canvas so that it looks essentially as the scene looks when focused on the retina, he succeeds in achieving realistic depth in his pictures. To do that he must paint objects not as they are known to be but as they look when they make an image on the retina of the eye. Let us examine some of the principles the artist uses to accomplish this.

Linear perspective. As we shall see illustrated later in the chapter, objects which are farther away project a smaller range on the retina than do near objects. In addition, the distance separating images of far objects is smaller. To understand this point, think of standing between railroad tracks and looking off into the distance. The ties become smaller and the tracks gradually become closer

FIGURE 10.10. This picture illustrates three monocular factors in depth perception. The buildings converge in the distance (linear perspective); some parts of buildings are behind others (interposition); and more distant heights are not as clear as the nearer parts (clearness) [Rockefeller Center, Inc.].

together until they appear to meet at the horizon. Figure 10.10 owes part of its depth effect to such linear perspective.

Clearness. In general, the more clearly we can see an object, the nearer the object is. The distant mountain seems farther away on a hazy day than on a clear day, because the haze in the atmosphere blurs the fine

details so that we see only the grosser features. If we can see the details, we perceive an object as relatively close, but if we can see only its general outline we perceive it is relatively far away.

Interposition. Still another monocular cue is interposition. This occurs when one thing obstructs our view of another thing. When one object is entirely in view, but another is partly covered by it, the first object is perceived as being the nearer. Interposition is illustrated in Figure 10.10.

Shadows. The pattern of shadows or of highlights in an object is very important in making the object look solid. In Figure 10.11, for example, the circle on the left looks flat, but the one on the right looks solid like a sphere. Notice that the one on the left is colored a uniform gray, while the one on the right is brightest in the center with a gradient of decreasing brightness to the edges. In the latter case, the effect is the same as shining a light on a sphere. The surface closest to the light source receives the most light, and as the surface recedes from the light less and less light falls on it. Such appearances of lighting and shading are important cues for depth perception.

In Figure 10.12 we see another example of this cue, an aerial photograph of a group of quonset huts. When the picture is turned upside down, the quonset huts look like towers. If you note carefully the differences between the quonset huts and the "towers," you will discover that the shadows are responsible for this effect. The reason, briefly, is that we are accustomed to light coming

FIGURE 10.11. Shadows as a cue in the perception of depth [Gibson, 1950].

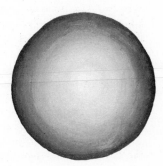

from above. Thus when the picture is turned upside down, we do not perceive the quonset huts as illuminated from below, for we are not used to light coming from this direction. Instead we see towers, because the dark areas are now of such a size and in such a position that they cannot possibly be shadows. They look more like the black-painted tops of buildings, or towers. We do not, of course, reason this out. The perception is immediate and is based on whether the dark areas appear to be shadows or not.

Movement. Whenever you move your head, you can observe that the objects in your visual field move relative to you and to one another. If you observe closely, you will find that the objects that are nearest you appear to move in the opposite direction, while distant objects appear to move in the same direction as your head. This, of course, is an obvious cue to the relative distance of objects, because whether we see real movement or move our heads, the relative amount of movement is less for far objects than for near ones. Although movement is an important cue to depth, it cannot be used by artists as can the other monocular cues.

Accommodation. Accommodation is the adjustment of the shape of the lens of the eye so that it brings an image into focus on the retina. This adjustment is accomplished by the ciliary muscles, which are so attached to the lens that they make it bulge when they contract, thus accommodating for near objects. Conversely, they let it become thinner when they relax, thus accommodating for far objects.

Many muscles of the body contain kinesthetic receptors which respond to the stretch and contraction of the muscles. It is possible that kinesthetic impulses from the ciliary muscles provide a cue to depth. It has not, however, been proved that they do. Such a cue would have to be a monocular cue, for it would be operative in each eye and would not depend on seeing with two eyes at once. This cue could work only for distances up to about 20 feet, for beyond that further accommodation is negligible.

BINOCULAR CUES. There are some cues to depth perception that depend on the fact that we have two eyes rather than just one. These are called *binocular cues.*

Retinal disparity. One such cue is *retinal disparity*—the difference in the images falling on the retinas of the two eyes. You may understand the factor of retinal disparity by considering the geometry of the situations in which the two eyes view an object (see Figure 10.13). In the center of each retina is a *fovea* that is much more sensitive than the rest of the retina. When we look at an object we fixate our eyes—point them, so to speak—so that the image of the object falls mostly on the fovea of the retina of each eye. But since the two eyes are separated from each other by several inches, they get slightly different views of any solid object, and the two images are not exactly the same. Moreover, the images are more dissimilar when the object is very close, say a few inches away, than when it is far in the distance. From these differences we get cues to depth.

These points are illustrated in Figure 10.13. The distances and sizes have been

FIGURE 10.12. Shadows and the perception of depth. If the picture is turned upside down, the quonset huts look like towers [Gibson, 1950].

CHAPTER TEN

exaggerated to make them clear. Looked at from the point of view of the observer, the left eye sees the front and left side of the cube, while the right eye sees the front and right side of the cube. Thus each eye has a different view of the cube. In addition, the two eyes see different parts of the space behind the cube, and the two eyes together see behind it. The left eye can see all the space from *A* to *F* except the distance from *B* to *C*, and the right eye can see all except the distance from *D* to *E*. This might not be true for all sizes of cubes and distances from the eye; and it certainly is not true for the space immediately behind the object. The general point, however, is that the images of the same objects falling on the two retinas are disparate—not the same.

With the pictures in Figure 10.14 and a small mirror, you can demonstrate to yourself how retinal disparity contributes to the solid appearance of objects. The figure shows the same scene photographed by a stereoscopic camera, a camera that has two lenses about as far apart as the two eyes. The picture on the left was photographed by the left lens and the one on the right by the right lens. When you look at the mirror reflection of the right-hand scene, according to the directions, the reflection appears to be physically located on top of the left-hand picture. Thus when you open both eyes, one eye sees one picture and the other eye sees the other picture and you achieve the illusion of depth. Although the right-left orientation of the objects in the right-hand scene has been reversed for the demonstration, close scrutiny of the pictures will show that they also differ in other details.

Convergence. We know that retinal disparity serves very effectively as a binocular cue to depth. We are not so sure, however, about another possible binocular cue. This is a kinesthetic cue from the muscles concerned in turning and pointing the eyes. For objects farther away than 70 feet, the lines

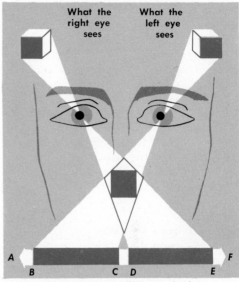

FIGURE 10.13. What we see when we look at a cube. Not only does each eye receive a different view of the cube, but together the two eyes see behind the cube. The right eye can see all the space from *A* to *F* except the distance *D* to *E*. The left eye can see all the space from *A* to *F* except the distance *B* to *C*. Hence, the two eyes together see the entire space from *A* to *F*.

of sight of the eyes are essentially parallel. For nearer objects, however, the eyes turn more and more toward each other, that is, they converge. If such convergence aids in depth perception, the cue is probably kinesthetic impulses from sense organs in the muscles that make the eyes converge.

CONFLICTING CUES. In general, the various cues to depth and distance perception work together and are mutually supporting. In cases where they conflict, one cannot see depth so clearly. When looking at a photograph, for example, most of the monocular depth cues are present, yet one does not perceive all the depth of the real scene. In this case, cues conflict. The monocular

FIGURE 10.14. Looking into the third dimension. Select a small mirror whose shortest side is at least as long as the height of the pictures. Put the mirror's edge in the space between the two pictures at right angles to the page and with its reflecting side to the right. Put your nose on or near the top edge of the mirror. Close your left eye. Look at the mirror with your right eye and adjust the mirror so that the real picture and its mirror image are aligned in the same plane. Now open the left eye. With both eyes open, focus your attention on the left-hand image. The two pictures should now appear as one three-dimensional picture [Realist, Inc.].

cues give the impression of depth, but the binocular cues make the photograph look flat. One's perception, then, is a compromise. It is possible, however, to eliminate the conflicting binocular cues, and thus to see more depth in a photograph.

To do that, roll a piece of paper into a tube. Now close one eye, and look with the other eye through the tube at the photograph in Figure 10.10. You will find that the picture seems to have much greater depth. By closing one eye, you eliminate the conflicting binocular cues, and by using the tube, you avoid seeing the edge or frame of the picture. The frame, of course, is a conflicting cue since real scenes do not have frames around them. You can increase the apparent depth even further by having some-

one else hold the picture for you. In this case, you eliminate conflicting cues coming from your arms and body.

STEREOPHONIC SOUND. Our discussion of depth perception has centered on vision. That is because man is a "visual animal" who relies more on vision than other senses for perceiving depth and distance in his environment. At times, however, he perceives depth through other senses. The most important of these is hearing. Indeed we habitually use auditory cues in judging the distance of various objects. The rumble of traffic, the sound of an automobile horn, the scream of a siren, and even the sound of a footstep are all perceived as taking place in some direction and at some dis-

CHAPTER TEN

tance from us. However, in order to discuss the specific cues we use to perceive depth in these situations we must have some knowledge of hearing and of the nature of auditory stimuli. Since these topics are discussed in Chapter 12, the consideration of auditory depth perception is also deferred to that chapter.

There is one kind of auditory depth perception, however, that fits well into our present discussion. This is so-called "stereophonic" sound, which has recently been given considerable publicity. "Stereo" means space, and "phonic" means sound; hence stereophonic refers to space-sound. The principle involved is comparable to retinal disparity in the visual domain, even though the geometry of sound and of light are somewhat different: the two ears hear a sound, so to speak, from a different point of view.

In normal listening, the sounds reaching one ear are somewhat different from those reaching the other ear. Because of reverberation in the auditorium or room, or because the source of the sound is quite complex, as it is in listening to orchestral music, the sounds reaching the two ears may be different in pitch, in loudness, in time of arrival, or in other ways that will be explained in the chapter on hearing. These differences give depth and distance to the sound.

Stereophonic recording merely attempts to reproduce the differences in the sounds reaching the two ears which a listener normally perceives when listening to live music. In making the recording, two microphones are placed some distance apart—they are the ears of the recording system—and two separate sound tracks are recorded. In playing back such a recording, the sounds picked up from these tracks are separately amplified and emitted through two speakers. To obtain the stereophonic effect, the listener must place the two speakers in different parts of the room so that each ear hears more from the speaker on its side than it does from the other. The output of the two speakers must be matched rather closely in intensity;

otherwise the output of one gets to both ears at a higher intensity than the output of the other, thus drowning out the sound of the second speaker. When the proper conditions are met, the impression of depth is remarkable. Sterephonic sound is almost as different from monophonic sound as a real view is from a flat picture.

"FACIAL VISION." Many blind people are surprisingly good at finding their way about among obstacles. They can walk along a street, make turns in halls, stop in front of people and doors, all as though they could see. Many are so extraordinary at this that they appear to have a "sixth sense" not possessed by normal people. When asked how they do it, most of them cannot say. Some report that they "feel in their faces" an obstacle that is nearby. For that reason the obstacle-avoidance ability of the blind has sometimes been called "facial vision." This term describes the blind person's feeling, but it provides no explanation of his depth perception. We now have a series of experiments [Cotzin and Dallenbach, 1950] that tell us how the blind person "sees" obstacles.

Blind persons were the subjects. To test the idea of facial vision—that air currents striking the face might be a cue—subjects had their heads covered with felt veils and hats to eliminate any possible stimulation of the face. They were then tested by being asked to walk up to an obstacle and signal when they were just in front of it. The felt covering made no difference at all in their ability to do this. In another experiment, to test the importance of auditory cues, the subjects had their ears plugged. Under these circumstances, they were no longer able to avoid running into obstacles. Thus the cue was conclusively demonstrated to be auditory. In other experiments the subjects sat listening to a loud-speaker while the experimenter approached an obstacle holding a microphone in his hands. The subjects were able to tell him when he was near the obstacle; this made it doubly certain that the cue was auditory. In still other experiments, it was established that the important auditory cues were high-pitched sounds reflected from the obstacles. High-pitched sounds reflect more sharply from objects than low-pitched sounds. They are normally made by a person as he walks along, and also by other objects emitting noise in the vicinity. When the blind person perceives these sounds as growing more intense, he knows he is near an obstacle.

We know then that blind individuals are able to avoid obstacles because they learn to perceive the reflection of high-pitched sounds. Naturally, some learn to do this better than others, and hence are better at obstacle avoidance. Some individuals, especially those of advancing age, tend to be hard of hearing for sounds of high pitch, and are therefore not so capable of avoiding obstacles.

It is interesting to note in passing that the ideas for these experiments came from experiments with bats. Bats have long been known to be very good at avoiding obstacles in the dark, but how they did it was a mystery. Two investigators [Griffin and Galambos, 1941], delving into this problem with a series of ingenious experiments, discovered that bats used "echo location" to avoid obstacles. They emit high-pitched sounds that reflect from walls, wires, and obstacles and serve as a cue to their location. By responding to the echoes, bats are able both to navigate and to locate their food in a manner that has been called "bat radar."

Perceptual constancy

The world as we perceive it is a stable world. The size of a man does not appear to change as he walks toward us, the dinner plate does not look like a circle when viewed one way and like an ellipse when viewed another, and the location of a sound does not appear to shift when we move our heads. To the layman there is nothing very sur-

THE FARTHER AWAY AN OBJECT IS, THE SMALLER ITS IMAGE ON THE RETINA:

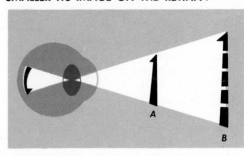

FIGURE 10.15. The size of the image on the retina depends upon the size of the object and its distance from the eye. Arrow B, which is twice as far from the eye as arrow A, must be twice as large as arrow A in order to cast the same size image on the retina.

prising about this. Why shouldn't the world of objects always look the same or remain constant?

Considered more carefully, however, this question raises some interesting problems, for often the physical stimuli from objects are not constant despite the fact that they appear to be. Indeed, as we move about in the world, the stimulation that we receive continually changes. Even the stimuli coming from the same object change markedly as we change our position with respect to it. When we stand directly in front of the window, for example, the retinal image of the window is a rectangle. But when we move to one side of the window, the image becomes a trapezoid. This is simple geometry. Despite this change in the shape of the retinal image, however, we continue to perceive the window as rectangular. Perceptually, therefore, its shape has not changed, even though its image on the retina has.

The general point is that the perceived shape of objects tends to remain the same irrespective of the positions or conditions under which we view them. This phenomenon is called *shape constancy*. Constancy in perception is not limited to shapes, however. The perceived sizes of objects, their colors, and their brightnesses also show perceptual constancy. Below we shall consider in a little more detail the problems of constancy in size and brightness. They illustrate not only the general problem of constancy but also some of the means by which perceptual constancy is achieved.

CONSTANCY OF SIZE. Since the eye works essentially like a camera, we know that the size of the image on the retina depends upon how far away the object is. The farther the object, the smaller the image. The geometry of this fact is illustrated in Figure 10.15. We can also see from this figure that an image of constant size can be produced on the retina either by a nearby small object or by a larger object at some distance.

Knowing this much about the size of retinal images, we might expect the perceived size of an object to change as we approach it. At 50 feet, it should appear much larger than it does at 100 feet. But this does not happen. The object instead appears to be about the same size irrespective of its distance. When it is far away, we do not perceive it as smaller; rather, we perceive it as being of the same size—but farther away. If depth cues are artificially reversed, familiar objects that would appear constant in size are perceived as vastly different in size (see Figure 10.16).

The constancy of object sizes in perception is closely related to our perception of distance. If the cues to depth or distance perception are present, we have good size constancy. Instead of perceiving distant objects as smaller, we perceive them as farther away. If, on the other hand, the cues to depth perception are gradually eliminated, our perception of the size of an unfamiliar object begins to correspond to the retinal image. And with all depth cues gone, constancy is completely eliminated and our perceptions and judgments of size are what one would expect them to be from the geometry of the retinal image.

For a *familiar object*, however, the elimination of depth cues does not completely destroy constancy because we know approximately the true size of the object. This knowledge gives us some degree of size constancy even in the absence of depth cues. In fact, in this case, we are able to use the size of the retinal image as a cue to the distance of the familiar object. Such a cue, it was pointed out above, is one of the monocular depth cues—linear perspective.

BRIGHTNESS CONSTANCY. Visual objects also appear constant in their degree of whiteness, grayness, or blackness. Such

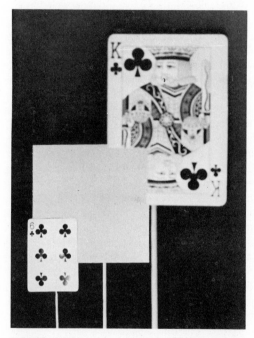

FIGURE 10.16. Size constancy destroyed by depth cues. We know that playing cards are usually the same size. They would be so perceived here if the cues to depth perception had not been reversed. The "large" card is actually much closer than the "small" card, but its corner has been cut out so that the gray card appears (by superposition) to be in front of it. If, instead, the "small" card appeared behind the gray one, the cards would look the same size [Brooks, from Monkmeyer].

brightness constancy, as we call it, tends to be independent of the illumination under which we view objects. Those objects or surfaces that appear white in a bright light still look white in dim illumination. Similarly, what looks black in dim light still looks black in more intense light. Coal looks black even in very bright sunlight, while snow continues to look white even at night. Still another example of brightness constancy is the appearance of the white paper that lies partly in a shadow. We see the paper as being uniformly white; we do not see the shadowed portion as gray, but rather as white-in-the-shadow.

We can understand why brightness is thus relatively constant if we first briefly review some of the elementary physics of light. When light falls on a surface or object, some of the light is reflected and some is absorbed. A pure white object reflects practically all the light falling on it, whereas a pure black one absorbs nearly all the incident light. Different shades of gray reflect different percentages of the incident light and absorb the rest. The greater the percentage of light reflected, the lighter the gray. The percentage of the total incident light that a surface reflects is called *albedo*.

With this background, we can now understand brightness constancy a little better. Although the absolute brightness of objects changes as the illumination changes, their albedo does not. A nearly white object that reflects 90 per cent of the incident light in sunlight still reflects 90 per cent of the available light when placed in a poorly lighted room. It is this albedo that we perceive. Since it is constant under different conditions of illumination, and since the difference in albedos of the object and its surround is constant at different illuminations, we tend to perceive these constant factors rather than the absolute change in illumination.

a compromise between what we know the object to be and the sensory image on the retina. Objects do appear to become slightly smaller as they move away from us, and white objects do not look quite as white when they are in shadow. In this sense, then, constancies are only relative. Our perceptions of objects correspond more closely to the true object, however, than to the sizes of images on the retina or to the sensory stimulus in general.

As human beings, we enjoy several advantages from perceptual constancy. It would be exceedingly difficult to move about or operate in a world where sounds changed their location when we moved our heads, and where objects changed their shapes and sizes when we viewed them from different positions and distances. Imagine what it would be like if your friends and associates had a multitude of sizes and shapes that depended upon how far away they were and from what angle you viewed them. Or imagine how difficult it would be to live in our society if the colors of things varied markedly with changes in sunlight and weather. The relative constancy of our perception of size, brightness, and color give our world a perceptual stability it otherwise would not have.

Cooperation among the senses

Most of what we have said so far has been about visual perception. That is natural because, for most of us, vision is our most important sense. Perhaps if we were four-legged animals and walked with our heads closer to the ground where the odors are more plentiful, the sense of smell might occupy more of our perceptions. As it is, however, our perceptual world is primarily a visual world. Even so, our perceived visual world owes much to our other sense organs.

PERCEPTUAL STABILITY. Perceptual constancies are not perfect. Even in the most favorable circumstances, our perceptions are

KINESTHETIC AND STATIC SENSES. We have already seen how the muscle (kinesthetic) sense may contribute to the perceived depth of the world not only as a direct cue through eye movements, but also because walking and moving about in the world provide an *understanding* of distance. The static sense in the inner ear also contributes something. It supplies the brain with information about our head movements and the relation of the head to the earth's gravity. In doing so, it is responsible for the stability of our visual world—for the fact that the world does not move or turn upside down when we move our heads or bend over. An interesting illustration of this contribution of the muscle and static senses to our visual perception is the case of the "moon illusion."

You have probably noticed how large the moon looks when it is directly on the horizon. It looks several times larger, at least, than it does when it is overhead. Of course, the moon does not really change size, nor does its distance from us change. The perceived change in size is largely an illusion. Like many of the other illusions, the moon illusion is still not completely understood, but we do know that the muscle and static senses are involved in it. We know this because the moon illusion can be made to disappear by changing the stimulation of our static- and muscle-sense organs [Boring, 1943]. You can demonstrate this for yourself. The next time you see the moon on the horizon, bend over and look at it from between your legs. You will find that the moon has shrunk and now looks about the same size as it does when overhead.

There are other ways of showing how senses other than vision modify perceptions of the visual world. If a person is seated in a dark room and is asked to adjust an illuminated rod to the vertical position, he can do this with considerable accuracy [Wapner et al., 1951]. If now an experimenter stimulates the left side of the subject's neck with an electric current—to excite artificially the kinesthetic sense organs in the neck muscles —while he is adjusting the rod to the vertical, his perception of vertical will be shifted to the left. If the right side of his neck is stimulated, the perceived vertical will shift to the right. The influence of other senses on the visually perceived vertical can be shown in a similar way. If, for example, an experimenter uses earphones to present a sound to only one ear, the subject finds that the perceived vertical shifts toward the side of the sound.

ILLUSIONS.   Usually the cues that the brain receives from the various senses mutually confirm and support each other. They fit together like the various pieces in a jigsaw puzzle. This sensory information also fits in with the knowledge and assumptions that have been acquired from past experience. All contribute in producing a clear, meaningful, and complete perception.

What happens, however, when our sensory cues do not fit together with each other, or with our knowledge and assumptions about the world—as they sometimes do not? Several things. We may experience an illusion, or we may feel confused and our perceptions may be unclear and unstable.

Look, for example, at the picture in Figure 10.17. One young man appears to be twice as tall as the other, yet both seem to be of normal build. Is the small one a midget? He does not look like one. Yet the sensory cues for size make us suspect that he is. What kind of illusion do we have here?

The key to this particular illusion is that the room is not a normal room; it is not like the rectangular rooms with which you have always had experience. Figure 10.18 shows how this room was constructed. When the door to the room is closed and you view the room with one eye through the small hole in the door, it looks like a normal room. The room has been built so as to duplicate the kind of monocular cues to depth and position you would ordinarily receive from a normal room. Consequently, it is perceived as a rectangular room. The illusion occurs despite your knowledge that the men should be about the same size.

The illusion would tend to disappear if you could step inside the room. Then your muscle and static senses would detect the slant of the floor, and you would perceive the true nature of the situation. The "larger" man would no longer look larger than the other one. Instead you would see him as standing in the slanting corner of the room.

This example illustrates a conflict of cues within the visual sense. There may, of course, be similar conflicts between two different senses. One such conflict is between the visual and static senses in the perception of the upright. The visual world may be tilted at the same time the individual is tilted, so that he has cues from his eyes and vestibular organs which may conflict. This happens to pilots in airplanes, to divers, and to persons driving cars or other vehicles.

Because this kind of conflict has practical implications, it has been studied intensively in a series of experiments extending over a period of years. The experimental technique of these experiments is shown in Figure 10.19. The individual is placed on a seat that can be tilted at will by the experimenter while surrounded by a room that may also be tilted. The subject can then ask to have the tilt of one or the other changed until he judges that he is in an upright position or until he perceives the visual world as upright.

In general, the results of experiments of this kind show that people make a compromise between visual and static cues, but visual cues tend to dominate. On the other hand, there are wide individual differences among people. Some rely primarily on visual cues, others on static cues. Each individual, under a given set of experimental conditions, is reasonably consistent in his judgments.

Experience and motivation

Psychologists have puzzled about, and at times even argued about, the roles of heredity and environment in perception. "How much," they have asked, "is the way we perceive the world due to learning and how much to the way our brain and nervous system are put together?" The general an-

swer to this question is the same as we earlier found it to be for other psychological abilities (see Chapter 2). For some aspects of perception, important limitations arise from the nervous system and the maturing of its structures. For others, learning is important. In between there is an interaction between learning processes and the perceptual abilities developed through maturation. More specifically, however, the question is, Which perceptual abilities are to be accounted for in these various ways?

MATURATION.　Almost certainly the limits of sensory discrimination—the absolute and differential thresholds—are established by neural and sensory structures. We cannot learn to see better in the dark or to improve our eyesight. All we can do is use our sensory capacities to the best advantage. The attention value of an intense stimulus, the figure-ground relation, the grouping of stimuli according to nearness and similarity, the perceiving of certain types of illusions— all these are phenomena that seem to depend upon the way our nervous system is structured. We say "seem" because we cannot prove conclusively that they do. We can only argue from the evidence that small children, primitive peoples, and even many of the lower animals give indications of having perceptions similar to ours in these respects.

Experiments on the maturation of depth perception have been done with the aid of an apparatus called a "visual cliff." This is a large box with a lid and floor of heavy glass and a patterned material covering the walls and part of the floor (see Figure 10.20). Part of the glass floor is uncovered to expose a floor several feet below which is covered with the pattern. To test depth perception, one places the subject on the covered part and observes whether he will cross the area of clear glass above the well below. The test can be given any organism as soon as it is capable of crawling or walking, and has been used with babies, rats, kittens, kids (goats), and several other animals.

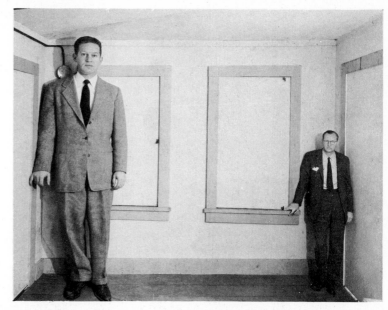

FIGURE 10.17. For an explanation of the apparent differences in size, see Figure 10.18 and text [Institute for International Social Research, Princeton, N.J.].

The results of these experiments are quite consistent. Any organism mature enough to test is able to perceive depth, as indicated by its unwillingness to cross the glass when the well beneath it is deep. On the other hand, when the well is relatively shallow, it will cross the "visual cliff." Of interest is the observation that babies and other organisms tested refuse to cross the "high cliff" even though they can touch the glass and can tell by touch that it can support them. Apparently they trust their eyes rather than their touch and kinesthetic senses.

From experiments like these we conclude that depth perception, when allowed to develop normally, matures in time to be useful at about the earliest time the organism can utilize it—as soon as it can move about. Presumably this perceptual development is largely a matter of maturation, since there is little opportunity to learn much about space before the organism can crawl or walk.

EARLY EXPERIENCE. In studies of the effects of early experience on perception (which were reviewed in Chapter 2), we have seen that some experience, and hence

learning, makes a great deal of difference in the perceptual development of an individual. Chimpanzees raised without experience with visual objects do not handle themselves well in a spatial environment, and are considerably retarded in perceptual learning. Dogs and rats raised in isolation are similarly handicapped in perceptual activities. On the other hand, it is very likely, as we shall see in a moment, that there are marked species differences in this matter. In birds and rats, space perception probably depends considerably more on maturation than it does in the chimpanzee and man.

REVERSED WORLDS. There is other evidence that our perception of space hinges considerably on our experiences. Some of it is so commonplace that we tend to overlook it. Perhaps you have had the experience of arriving late at the movies and of having to take a seat far down in front and to one side. If so, you have noticed then that the people on the screen appear distorted; their heads are elongated and flat. But if you recall, your discomfort was short-lived. After you watched the picture for a while, the distortion probably disappeared. The

FIGURE 10.18. The distorted room. This shows how the room in which the picture in Figure 10.17 was taken was constructed, and how cues from the shape of the room and the objects in it have created an illusion of size [Institute for International Social Research, Princeton, N.J.].

geometry of the situation did not change, but you came to perceive these distorted images in keeping with your past experiences. This kind of change in perception is much the same as that which occurs in size and shape constancy.

Other more direct evidence comes from experiments in which the visual world of subjects has been experimentally reversed. By using a system of lenses in front of each eye, one can invert the visual images on the retina—actually they are already inverted (see Figure 10.15) and the lenses turn them right side up—so that the world is turned upside down for the subject. The lenses also reverse right and left for the subject. Sixty years ago, the experiment was first tried of wearing such lenses for a prolonged period. It has been repeated several times since. Reports of what happens vary a little from one subject to another, but the general picture that emerges from them is as follows:

When the lenses are first put on, the effect is quite bewildering. The individual is severely disoriented, and his eye-body coordination is badly disrupted. Every time the subject moves his head, the entire world

FIGURE 10.19. Conflict between visual and static senses. When both the person and the room he is in are tilted, the resulting perception of "upright" is typically a compromise. In general, visual perception dominates, but there are wide individual differences among people [Witkin, 1959; David Linton, copyright 1950].

CHAPTER TEN

appears to swim around him. Walking and moving about are difficult. When the subject tries to avoid walking into a chair that appears to him to be on the left, he steps to the right and thus bumps directly into it. To pick up an object that appears to be on his left, he must learn to reach to his right. Sounds seem to come from the wrong direction.

After a period of two or three days, however, the world begins to stabilize itself. Walking about and locating objects in the upside-down world become easier and more automatic. The subject's head can be turned without the world seeming to move. Sounds now seem to come from the place where the object is seen to be and not from the opposite direction. One subject, an Austrian professor, rode his bicycle as usual to classes and carried on his duties quite satisfactorily.

In one experiment of this kind [Snyder and Pronko, 1952], the inverting lenses were worn for 30 days:

Before beginning the experiment, the subject was tested on a series of visual-motor tasks. One was a card-sorting task, in which the subject sorted cards into appropriate boxes. The time for completing the task was measured before, during, and after wearing the lenses, with the results shown in Figure 10.21. Performance was severely disrupted as soon as the inverting lenses were put on, but within 5 days it was back to the former level. Again when the lenses were removed, performance was slightly disrupted, but the subject quickly regained his normal proficiency.

In most of the experiments, subjects report that they gradually get accustomed to a reversed world, but that it never looks entirely normal to them. Whether this is because they only wear the lenses a few days or weeks after using normal vision for a few years, whether it is because they must always be conscious of wearing the lens and that they are seeing things differently from other people, or whether it is because there is an innate tendency to normal perception that

is only partially overcome by experience with the lenses, we do not know.

The best description of the situation comes from the words of one of the subjects when he was asked whether a particular scene looked upside down to him: "I wish you hadn't asked me. Things were all right until you popped the question at me. Now, when I recall how they *did* look *before* I put on these lenses, I must answer that they do look upside down *now*. But until the moment that you asked me I was absolutely unaware of it and hadn't given a thought to the question of whether things were right side up or upside down."

These experiments certainly demonstrate that a person can adapt to an upside-down and reversed left-right world and do this reasonably well within a comparatively short time.

Experiments in which the auditory world is reversed have also been conducted. Instead of lenses, a device called a *pseudophone* may be used. It consists of a pair of tubes that carry sounds from one side of the head to the ear on the opposite side. The results with the pseudophone are comparable to those with the inverting lenses. At first, auditory perceptions are disrupted, but within a few days, the reversal is accepted.

LEARNING. Many of our perceptions depend almost exclusively on our previous learning—on the associations we have acquired with various objects and events. Through conditioning and perceptual learning, we have come to associate people, objects, words, sound, and so on with emotions, actions, rewards, and punishments. The associations thus acquired alter our perceptions.

To a person who has lost a loved one in a hunting accident, a gun has a much different meaning from what it has to a child who is infatuated with cowboys. To the child the perception of the gun is tied up with pleasurable excitement, with fantasies of range wars and galloping horses. To the bereaved person the perception of the gun is one of sadness and fear; it makes him want to put it out of his mind. We can think of many other examples: The sound I hear, for instance, is not just a sound; it is the creaking of the stairway which signals my wife's return from the store. The apple pie in the bakery window is not just seen; one can almost smell the aroma and one's mouth begins to water in anticipation. The sight recalls memories of childhood days in grandma's kitchen and perhaps of various other experiences with apples and pies.

The effects of previous experience on perception seem to be almost irreversible. What has been learned permanently alters and influences all our subsequent perceptual behavior. Most of us have had the experience of suddenly looking at an object and failing to recognize or identify it immediately. In the fraction of a second before we recognized it, the object looked quite different from what it did after we recognized it. Yet after the moment of recognition had passed, it was impossible to visualize just what our perception had been like during that fleeting moment of uncertainty. In the same way, the trained bacteriologist can no longer perceive the slide in his microscope as he did when he was first a student. Then the slide was just so much confusion, a hodgepodge of colors and odd forms. What he now sees has been completely changed by his increased knowledge and by the fine discriminations he has learned subsequently. No longer is the perception indefinite. He notes all sorts of variations in form and color and knows their meaning.

To see how markedly knowledge of a stimulus affects perception of it, there is a simple experiment that you can perform:

Have a friend cut out a series of newspaper headlines that are unfamiliar to you. Make sure, however, that the various headlines are all the same size. Now have your friend stand at a distance from you and hold up one of the headlines for you to see. If you can read it, have him move farther away and try another headline. Keep repeating this, each time using a new headline, until

FIGURE 10.20. The "visual cliff." This is a test of depth perception that can be used with almost any organism, human or animal, as soon as it can crawl or walk. At this stage, most organisms tested have good visual depth perception [Gibson and Walk, 1960; William Vandivert, *Scientific American*].

he is just far enough away so that you can no longer read the words. Keeping this distance, have your friend read the headline to you, then look at it again. You will find that you can now read it for yourself. Your knowledge of what it says has changed your perception of it. What was perceived before as just an unintelligible blur of letters is now perceived as meaningful words.

MOTIVATION AND REWARD. Motivations, learned and unlearned, also affect the perception of situations. It is common knowledge that we seldom convince people in an argument. Where people are emotionally involved they tend to see what they want to see, hear what they want to hear, and believe what they want to believe. Love is blind, and the man in love is notoriously poor at perceiving the faults in his loved one. On the other hand, these faults are only too painfully evident to more neutral observers such as his parents. His parents "for the life of them can't understand what he sees in that bleached blonde." Such examples are simply more instances of personal motives and values influencing perception.

We must, of course, accept with caution many of the things the layman considers obvious. In this case, however, the layman's "common knowledge" is substantially correct. Our own wants and acquired values can influence our perception. Consider the following experiment [Lambert, et al., 1949]:

Nursery school children, aged three to five, were presented with a machine which had a crank on it. They received a poker chip for turning the crank 18 turns. By putting this poker chip into a slot, they could obtain candy. Before the experiment began, each child estimated the size of the poker chip by comparing it with a white disk whose size could be varied by the experimenter until the child said the two objects matched. Again, after the children had been rewarded with candy for cranking out poker chips, estimates of size were made. The poker chips now seemed significantly larger to the children. The experimenters then instituted an extinction procedure (page 201) during which the children got no candy for their efforts in

PEOPLE CAN ADJUST TO AN UPSIDE DOWN WORLD:

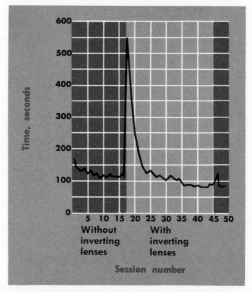

FIGURE 10.21. Effect on a psychomotor task of inverting the visual world. The graph shows the average time required for sorting packs of cards into boxes. Immediately after the subject put on the inverting lenses, the time increased enormously, but it came back to normal after the subject had had a few sessions of practice. Note the brief and slight disruption when the inverting lenses were taken off [after Snyder and Pronko, 1952].

cranking. Estimates of size were again made. The chips had shrunk back to their former size. After that, the children were again rewarded wtih candy, and the chips again increased in apparent size.

This experiment, which is only one of several that might be described, indicates that as the poker chip acquired value—represented something the child wanted—it was perceived as larger than when it had no value. The experiment supports the general conclusion that a person's motivation affects his perception of even such simple physical characteristics as size.

Generally speaking, however, it is in the

perceiving of such complex things as social and interpersonal relationships that our own internal needs and biases have their greatest effect. The concrete objects in our world do not allow us much freedom in perception. Everyone perceives them in much the same way. The table, the chair, the bookcase— everyone sees them as such. The occasional atypical individual who does not winds up in a psychiatrist's office. On the other hand, such social situations as parties, conversations, and contacts with friends or associates are often indefinite and ambiguous. Our perceptions of them are less stable and definite than are our perceptions of physical objects. How many times, for example, have we pondered over just what a friend "meant by that remark"? We all remember cases in which a remark was perceived as an insult or slight by one person but was regarded as a compliment by another. Most of us have been victims, at one time or other, of having our remarks and behavior misperceived or misinterpreted by others.

Summary

1. Perception is the process of discriminating among stimuli and of interpreting their meanings. It is not a photographic copy of a stimulus situation; rather it leaves out certain aspects of the situation and adds meanings derived from past experience.

2. Perception is limited by sensory discrimination. This takes place through some 10 different senses, each of which has receptors that are sensitive to a particular kind of energy and range of stimuli. The minimum energy of a stimulus that can be detected is the absolute threshold. The smallest difference between two stimuli that can be discriminated is the differential threshold.

3. An attribute is a perceived quality or aspect of a stimulus. It depends on physical characteristics of the stimulus but is not identical with them. Sensory scales can be constructed for each attribute to quantify the relationship between perceived magnitude and physical magnitude.

4. Under some circumstances, relatively weak stimuli may be perceived without the individual's being aware of the stimuli. The evidence for extrasensory perception, that is, perception without the use of sense organs, is not conclusive.

5. Attention is an important determinant of what is perceived. It has a focus in which events are clearly perceived and a margin in which things are less clearly perceived. It is constantly shifting from one stimulus to another.

6. External factors controlling attention are (a) intensity and size of stimuli, (b) contrast between a stimulus and its background, (c) the repetition of stimuli, and (d) movement. Internal factors controlling attention are (a) motives, needs, or interests and (b) a set or expectancy for a particular kind of stimulus.

7. Perceptual processes organize the world around a person into objects and groups of objects. Thus he tends to perceive as a group (a) those objects that are close together, (b) those that are similar to each other, (c) those that are symmetrically arranged, and (d) those that form some continuous line or pattern.

8. Objects are usually seen as figures on a ground. It is, in fact, almost impossible to "see" them any other way. Such figure-ground perception depends, in turn, on the perception of contours marking off an object from its background.

9. Perception also tends to close gaps, so that a person perceives an object even when some of its parts are missing.

10. Apparent movement is a special example of such "filling in," for it is a perception of movement when there is no movement, but merely different still objects presented in close succession.

11. Even though the retina of the eye is flat and receives a two-dimensional picture, people perceive three-dimensional depth by using several cues for depth. Most of these cues are monocular, some are binocular, and some may be kinesthetic.

12. The principal monocular cues are (a) linear perspective, (b) clearness, (c) interposition, (d) shadows, and (e) movement.

13. The chief binocular cue to depth is retinal disparity, which is a slight difference in the images projected on the two eyes when they view the same situation.

14. Kinesthetic cues from muscles involved in focusing and converging the eyes may also aid depth perception, but we are not certain of this.

15. One of the puzzling facts of perception is that it tends to be relatively constant despite a considerable change in the stimulation of the sense organs. For example, (a) shapes usually appear about the same, whether we view them from an angle or head on; (b) sizes tend to appear relatively constant, whether objects are near or far away; and (c) brightness similarly remains comparatively constant even under rather different illuminations.

16. Perceptions frequently involve the cooperation of different senses. What one hears, for example, affects what one sees, and impulses from the muscle sense can alter one's visual perception.

17. Perceptions are also modified by experience. Early experience is especially important. A person can, after a time, adjust rather well to wearing glasses that reverse left and right and turn the visual world upside down.

18. Perceptions are determined by the meaning events have acquired through previous learning, by knowledge of the stimulus situation, and by motivation. To a very considerable extent, we perceive what we want to perceive.

Suggestions for further reading

Bartley, S. H. *Principles of perception.* New York: Harper, 1958
A basic textbook on sensation and perception.

Beardslee, D. C., and Wertheimer, M. (eds.). *Readings in perception.* Princeton, N.J.: Van Nostrand, 1958.
Selected articles from the literature on perception.

Blake, R. R., and Ramsey, G. V. (eds.). *Perception: an approach to personality.* New York: Ronald, 1951.
A symposium containing discussions of various aspects of perception, especially those influenced by social and cultural factors.

Boring, E. G. *Sensation and perception in the history of experimental psychology.* New York: Appleton-Century-Crofts, 1942.
An authoritative history of concepts, problems and experiments in the field of perception.

Carr, H. A. *An introduction to space perception.* New York: Longmans, 1935.
A text summarizing the older work on depth perception.

Chapanis, A., Garner, W. R., and Morgan, C. T. *Applied experimental psychology.* New York: Wiley, 1949. Chaps. 4–9.
A text that presents applications of the principles of perception to problems of engineering design.

Gibson, J. J. *The perception of the visual world.* Boston: Houghton Mifflin, 1950.
An account with many illustrations of recent experiments in visual perception.

Köhler, W. *Gestalt psychology* (2d ed.). New York: Liveright, 1947. Chaps. 4–6.
Contains chapters on the classical work of

gestalt psychologists on organizing tendencies in perception.

Lawrence, M. *Studies in human behavior.* Princeton, N.J.: Princeton Univer. Press, 1949.
A laboratory manual that includes experiments, as well as a discussion, on perception.

Osgood, C. E. *Method and theory in experimental psychology.* New York: Oxford Univer. Press, 1953.
An advanced text covering theory and experiments in the field of perception.

Woodworth, R. S., and Schlosberg, H. *Experimental psychology* (rev. ed.). New York: Holt, Rinehart and Winston, 1954.
A text in experimental psychology containing chapters on perception and attention.

Vision

THIS CHAPTER AND the next one are about the human senses. A classification of the senses was given in Chapter 10, "Attention and Perception"; so too was a definition of different sensory thresholds. If the student has not studied Chapter 10, he should now stop and read pages 300 to 304. These pages furnish a background for the present chapter and the next one.

Why study the senses? Students frequently ask—particularly students who are interested in the arts, in business, and in the social sciences, rather than in the natural sciences—why the senses are part of the study of psychology. To them the subject seems to belong more to physics, physiology, medicine, and related disciplines. Actually, the senses are in overlapping domains. What we know about them has been contributed by research workers in several fields, and discussions of them will be found in textbooks of physics and physiology as well as psychology.

Each discipline looks at the human senses from a different point of view, depending on its central problems and interests, but they are the legitimate study of each. Psychology is interested in the senses because all that we perceive, learn, and know about the world comes to us through our senses. Hence, in order to understand fully what it is possible to perceive and to learn, we must have a knowledge of the senses and how they work. Such knowledge necessarily encompasses some of the physics of the energies that stimulate the senses and also the anatomy of the sense organs. In fact, we are forced to begin our study of the senses with at least a cursory treatment of these topics.

Otherwise we would lack the necessary background for understanding the part they play in perception. That is our principal purpose for studying them.

The eye as an instrument. We begin with the visual sense. The first thing to note here is what a marvelous instrument we have in the human eye. With this instrument a normal human being, under good conditions, can see a wire 1/16 inch in diameter at a distance of 1/4 mile. It is so sensitive that, when it is fully dark-adapted, the average person can see the flare of a match 50 miles away on a clear, dark night. In contrast, the eye can also look momentarily at the sun when it is at its zenith in the sky. If we compute the ratio of these two intensities—the flare of a match 50 miles away and the intensity of the sun—we find that the total range of intensities to which the human eye can respond is something in the order of 100,000,000,000,000:1. The average person, moreover, can see several hundred thousand different colors. Truly, then, we have in the eye an extraordinary instrument. Indeed, there are relatively few physical instruments which approach the total range of sensitivity of the human eye.

The eye also renders remarkable psychological service. It is our major source of contact with the world, and the person who is deprived of his sight has suffered a severe and irreparable loss. Not only do we learn about objects through our eyes, but we also get most of our ideas by way of them. The wealth of information which is contained in our college library, for example, is all designed for assimilation through the eyes. So our eyes are instruments of extraordinary delicacy, sensitivity, and usefulness—instruments which should excite our wonder and admiration.

The stimulus for vision

If you were asked what you see, you would probably say that you see light. This is true—you do see light. But we must distinguish between the physical stimulus that excites the eye and the psychological sensation of light that you actually experience. First we shall consider some of the physical properties of light.

ELECTROMAGNETIC RADIATION. We see objects either because they emit radiant energy or because radiant energy is reflected from them. This energy, which physicists call electromagnetic radiation, consists of electric charges moving through space at approximately 186,000 miles per second. It is difficult to explain just what these charges or electromagnetic radiations are like, but it is conventional and convenient to talk about them as though they traveled in waves. It is also possible to measure and classify radiant energy in terms of the distance from the peak of one wave to the peak of the next, that is to say, in terms of *wavelength*. Some electromagnetic radiations have wavelengths as short as 10 trillionths of an inch (the cosmic rays), some have wavelengths of many miles (radio waves), and there are all sorts of wavelengths in between (Figure 11.1). The entire range of all possible waves is called the *electromagnetic spectrum*.

VISIBLE RADIANT ENERGY. Although all radiant energy—all wavelengths of the electromagnetic spectrum—is very much the same physically, not all of it is visible. Somewhere in the middle of the spectrum, between 16 and 32 millionths of an inch in length (Figure 11.1), are the wavelengths that we can see. These are known as the *visible spectrum*. Because the word "light" implies seeing, it is only these wavelengths that are called light or light waves. Scientists use a metric scale rather than inches and feet, however, to express length. Hence the visible spectrum of wavelengths is said to extend from about 400 to 800 millimicrons (mμ). A micron is one millionth of a meter, and a millimicron is one thousandth of a micron.

As Isaac Newton discovered in 1666, it is possible to break up the visible spectrum

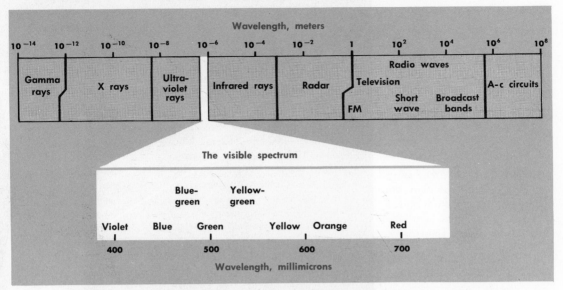

FIGURE 11.1. The electromagnetic and visible spectra. Electromagnetic waves have a spectrum from as short as 10^{-14} meters to as long as 10^8 meters. The part of the spectrum that is visible and is called light is only a tiny fraction in the neighborhood of 10^{-6} meters.

into its component wavelengths.[1] The trick for doing that is to pass a beam of sunlight through a triangular glass prism (see Figure 11.2), because such a prism bends short wavelengths (which appear violet) more than long wavelengths (which appear red). A prism, in fact, spreads all the wavelengths out in a broad band so that we can see and measure each wavelength in a bundle of light. Each wavelength of the visible spectrum has a characteristic color.

The eye and how it works

In certain respects, the eye looks and behaves like a camera (Figure 11.3). Both the eye and a camera are essentially dark chambers which admit light through an opening in front. Immediately behind the opening in each case is a lens which focuses

[1] This work was not published in full until Newton presented his *Opticks* in 1704.

images of outside objects onto the rear surface. *The surface on which the image is projected in the eye is called the retina;* in the camera, it is the photographic film.

Both the camera and the eye can be adjusted to control the amount of light falling on this surface. To control light entering a camera, the photographer adjusts the diaphragm in front of the lens. When he encounters too much light, he "stops down" the camera diaphragm, and when light is relatively dim, he increases the size of the opening in the diaphragm. The eye, however, has its own automatic (reflex) mechanism for making such an adjustment. Its diaphragm is the *iris,* which is the colored part of the eye; the iris controls the size of the opening, known as the *pupil,* which admits light to the eye. In dim light, the iris expands the pupil, thus increasing the amount of light passing through it; in bright light, the iris contracts the pupil, thus reducing the amount of light admitted. This ad-

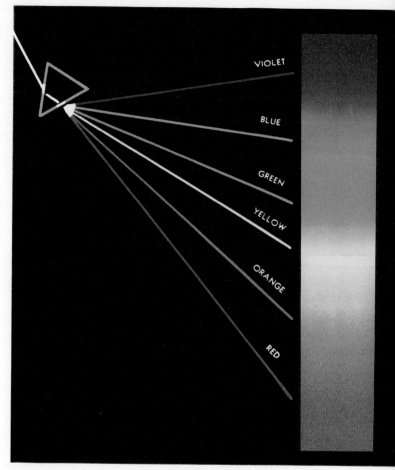

FIGURE 11.2. All the colors of the visible spectrum are produced when a prism is used to break up white light into its components [Bustanoby, 1947].

VIOLET

BLUE

GREEN

YELLOW

ORANGE

RED

justment permits a person to see in dimmer and in brighter illuminations than would otherwise be possible. You can easily observe the contraction of the pupil by having a person close his eyelids for a while and then open them. The normal pupil has a maximum range of adjustment of 2 to 8 millimeters in diameter—corresponding to a sixteenfold change in area.

From Chapter 10 you may remember that images on the retina are inverted and turned around from right to left. This happens in both the camera and the eye.

STRUCTURE OF THE EYE. Although it is helpful and instructive to compare the eye to the camera, this comparison must not be

pushed too far. A closer look at the eye reveals an organ of enormous complexity— so complex that the drawing in Figure 11.4, which is complicated enough, shows only its essential features. Unlike the camera, the eye is roughly a sphere. Its walls consist of three separate layers: the sclerotic coat, the choroid coat, and the retina.

1. The first and outer layer, the *sclerotic coat,* is a tough fibrous material that protects the eyeball and maintains its shape. In the front of the eye, this sclerotic layer becomes transparent and bulges out to form the *cornea.*

2. Underneath the sclerotic layer is the *choroid layer,* which corresponds roughly to the opaque backing on a photographic film

or to the blackening on the inside of a camera. This dark layer absorbs stray light in the eyeball and prevents light from entering the eye except through the cornea and lens.

3. The *retinal layer*, the innermost layer of the eyeball, as we have said, is like a photographic film, for it is the sensitive organ that enables us to see.

The interior of the eye is divided into two chambers: a small one in front of the lens, between it and the cornea, and a large one behind the lens, the main chamber of the eye. These chambers are filled with gelatinous fluids sometimes called humors. The chambers and the humors are shown in Figure 11.4.

RODS AND CONES. Since the retina is the sensitive organ for seeing, it deserves closer attention than the other structures of the eye. If we examine it with a microscope, we can see that it is made up of extremely tiny cells of two basic types—*rods* and *cones*. Figure 11.5 depicts these two cells; the rods are cylindrical in shape, but the cones are rather tapered. Our best estimate is that the eye contains between 110,000,000 and 125,000,000 rods, and between 6,300,-000 and 6,800,000 cones [Oesterberg, 1935]. This tremendous number of rods and cones, however, does not spread uniformly over the entire retina. Rather the cones are most numerous in a highly specialized region of the retina known as the *fovea*, and the rods occur most frequently about 20 degrees away from the fovea. As can be seen in Figure 11.4, the fovea is a slightly depressed area of the retina.

CONNECTIONS OF THE CONES AND RODS. From the rods and cones, tiny nerve fibers make connections with still other types of cells. Of these, two kinds of cells, the *bipolar* cells and the *ganglion* cells, are in a direct line with the central nervous system. Indeed, the fibers of the ganglion cells make up the optic nerve which conveys impulses from the retina to the brain. Hence the three sets of cells transmitting information about light

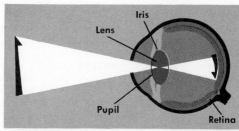
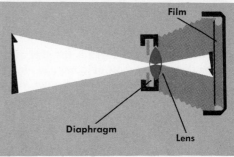

FIGURE 11.3. The eye likened to a camera. In both the eye and a camera the image is focused by a lens and is upside down and reversed on the photosensitive surface. In the eye this surface is called the retina. The part of the retina where vision is clearest is the fovea; the part where the optic nerve leaves the eye is the blind spot [see Figure 11.19].

are (1) rods and cones, (2) bipolar cells, and (3) ganglion cells.

In addition, the retina contains other types of cells, of which the *horizontal* cells are one. The interconnections among these cells and the cells in the "direct line" are so enormously complex that microanatomists have been able to trace only some of the more obvious ones, and physiologists can only surmise what function these cells serve. From the psychologist's standpoint, this network of connections allows a good many possibilities for explaining some of the curious visual phenomena that we shall discuss later. Figure 11.5 shows a diagram of some of these nervous connections in the retina.

Cornea — Pupillary opening
— Aqueous humor
Iris —
Ciliary muscle —
Lens —
— Suspensory ligament

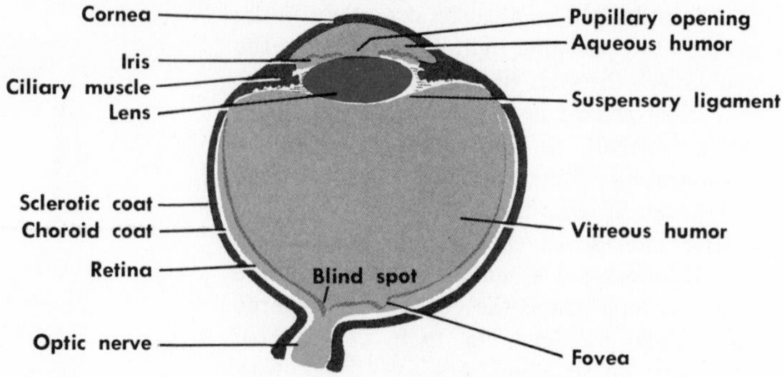

FIGURE 11.4. The anatomy of the eye. The principal parts of the eye are shown.

Sclerotic coat —
Choroid coat —
— Vitreous humor
Retina —
Blind spot
Optic nerve —
— Fovea

THE FOVEA. The fovea is the part of the retina that we use most in looking at objects, for it is the region of most distinct vision. When we want to see something very clearly, we naturally turn our head and eyes so that an image of the object falls on this part of the retina.

Some special features of this part of the eye should be noted. In the first place, the cones in the fovea are much longer and more slender than those in the periphery of the eye. In fact, foveal cones look something like rods. Since they are smaller, many more of them can be packed into the small foveal

area. A second interesting feature of the foveal cones is that they have their own individual nervous connections with the optic nerve—they have "private lines" to the brain [Polyak, 1941]. Outside the fovea, however, several cones, or several rods and cones, are usually linked together into common nerve pathways. Rods, in fact, never have private connections; there are always groups of them discharging into single nerve pathways.

A curious feature of the retina is that the *receptors point backward.* Consequently, when an image of an object is brought to a

LIGHT EXCITES THE RODS AND CONES, WHICH SEND MESSAGES VIA THE BIPOLAR AND GANGLION CELLS TO THE BRAIN:

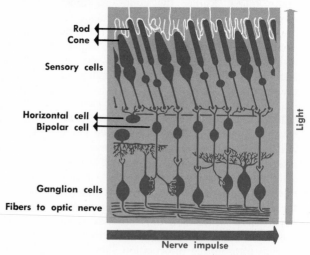

Rod
Cone
Sensory cells

FIGURE 11.5. A schematic diagram of the cells of the retina. At the top are the sensory cells, the rods and cones. These connect with bipolar cells, which connect in turn with the ganglion cells. Fibers of the ganglion cells make up the optic nerve. Note the many interconnections, especially those of the horizontal and ganglion cells.

Horizontal cell
Bipolar cell

Light

Ganglion cells
Fibers to optic nerve

Nerve impulse

CHAPTER ELEVEN

focus on the retina, the light must travel through all the nerve fibers and cell layers of the retina before it can arrive at the photosensitive cells. These intervening layers are rather transparent, but they undoubtedly blur the image a little. They do less blurring in the fovea than elsewhere in the retina because in the fovea, which is indented, they are pushed to the side.

In Figure 11.4 is a part of the retina labeled the *blind spot*. This is the point at which fibers of ganglion cells leave the retina and form the optic nerve which connects with the brain. The spot is blind because it lacks both rods and cones. Later in this chapter we shall have more to say about the blind spot.

ACCOMMODATION. In most cameras one adjusts the focus for objects at different distances by moving the lens back and forth. The lens of the eye does not work this way. *It changes its shape to focus at different distances.* Such changes are termed *accommodation.* They consist in a thickening or thinning of the lens, which is controlled by a muscle known as the *ciliary muscle.* This muscle, attached to ligaments that suspend the lens in place, so contracts and relaxes that the lens becomes thin and flat to focus the eye on far objects and becomes thick and curved to focus it on near objects (Figure 11.6).

SHAPE OF THE EYE. One of the common defects for which we wear glasses is inability to accommodate sufficiently to see objects at all distances, both near and far. Inability to see far objects clearly is called nearsightedness; the opposite is farsightedness. Accommodation normally focuses the eye for different distances, but inability to focus is usually the fault either of the shape of the eye or of the shape of the lens rather than of accommodation per se. Although eyes and their lenses are amazingly constant in shape, it does not take much distortion in shape to make them imperfect as focusing instruments. In some cases, the over-all

THE LENS CHANGES SHAPE TO FOCUS OBJECTS ON THE RETINA:

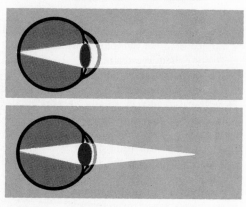

FIGURE 11.6. The accommodation of the lens. The lens flattens to focus images of objects far away, and it becomes thick to focus on nearby objects.

length of the eyeball is a little longer or shorter than it should be. In other cases, the curved surface of the cornea is a little too flat or too curved.

Farsightedness. About two-thirds of the people in America can see all right at a distance of 20 feet or more. For that reason it is possible to put blackboards at the front of classrooms in schools, signposts at considerable distances along roads, and seats far back in theaters. Some people, however, are pathologically farsighted; that is to say, they cannot see things that are very close (Figure 11.7). Usually the trouble is that the eyeball is too short. Consequently, when a farsighted person wants to look at an object that is close by, he must accommodate appreciably more than the normal person in order to bring the object to focus on his retina. If his eyeball is markedly shorter than normal, he may be quite unable to produce enough accommodation to obtain a focus. At best, in such extreme cases, a book 30 inches away always looks fuzzy. If a farsighted person reads for several hours at a time, the prolonged strain of accommodating—that is, of contracting the ciliary muscle—may bring on severe headaches and a variety of other symptoms which are collectively called eyestrain.

Nearsightedness. Exactly the reverse condition is encountered in nearsightedness. Here the difficulty is usually an abnormally long eyeball. For a person suffering nearsightedness, nearby objects come to focus on the retina with little or no accommodation in the lens, but the lens cannot flatten enough to compensate for the long eyeball and bring far objects into focus. Hence only near objects are clearly focused.

Oldsightedness. This goes by the technical name of *presbyopia,* but it is also called *oldsightedness* because it is characteristic of old people. In short, it is a farsightedness that comes on with advancing age. We often observe it in the way older people hold a newspaper far out in front of them to read. Such farsightedness is due to a hardening of the lens of the eye. This hardening process begins almost at birth and progresses throughout life. We can, in fact, guess the age of a person with rather good accuracy simply by measuring the maximum accommodation that he can accomplish with his lens.

If you would like to check this, have someone you know close one eye and hold this page at arm's length in front of the other eye. Now have him bring it slowly toward his eye and stop when the print begins to blur. Then measure the distance between his eye and the book; this distance is called the near point of vision, and from it you may estimate your subject's age by using Figure 11.8. Unfortunately there are two points that we could not get into this figure because they are so far away from the other points: the near point for fifty-year-olds averages 15 inches, and for sixty-year-olds, 39 inches. Figure 11.8, however, works only for people who have normal eyes to start with; nearsighted or farsighted people get different results.

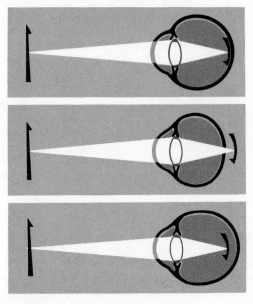

FIGURE 11.7. Farsightedness and nearsightedness. In the normal person (top) the image is focused on the retina. The farsighted person (middle) has an eyeball that is too short and focuses images on a plane behind the retina. The nearsighted person (bottom) has an eyeball that is too long and focuses images on a plane in front of the retina.

ASTIGMATISM. Another very common defect of the eye is *astigmatism.* This is usually an irregularity in the surface of the cornea, in which the cornea does not have equal curvature in all directions. As a consequence, the astigmatic person sees lines oriented in certain directions as out of focus and others oriented in other directions as in focus. This fact is utilized in test charts that are commonly used to detect astigmatism (Figure 11.9). When an astigmatic person looks at such charts at a proper distance, he reports that some lines are sharp and that others appear to run together and fuse.

Fortunately, all the optical defects that we have just described—farsightedness, near-

sightedness, oldsightedness, astigmatism—
are easily corrected with the right kinds of
glasses.

Color and brightness

Although we need all our visual abilities
to cope effectively with the visual world, our
ability to see color is probably the one that
is most impressive and the one we enjoy
most. Color is all around us in our natural
environment, and man has taken the trouble
to invent machines and dyes that add great
arrays of color to almost every feature of
daily life—neon signs, paints, fabrics, wall-
paper, etc. Without the eye's ability to discriminate many tints and shades, we could
not appreciate all this color.

In everyday speech, the word "color" is
used loosely to refer to all manner of tints
and shades. We must be more precise. To
the color scientist, color in the general sense
is some combination of three different dimensions of perception. Each of these will
be described in this section.

HUE. The first dimension to consider is
hue. Hue is the perceived dimension of color
we are referring to when we use common
color names like red, green, yellow, blue, or
combinations of them. Thus when we say
that something is red we mean that it has a
red hue; greenish-blue, a greenish-blue hue;
and so on.

Perceived hue depends primarily on wavelength of light. If there are several wavelengths mixed together, as is usually the case
with all colors except those made by a prism
(see Figure 11.2), hue depends on the wavelength that is dominant in the mixture. The
relation between wavelength and hue, however, is not completely stable. This is because the eye is not equally sensitive to all
wavelengths, and its relative sensitivity
changes with the brightness of the light (another dimension to be discussed later). But

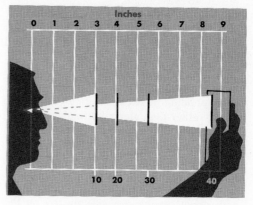

Approximate age, years

FIGURE 11.8. The near point of vision depends on age. The near point of vision is the
nearest distance one can hold, say, a printed
page and still see it clearly. This point increases with age. For a person who is fifty
years of age, it averages 15 inches; for one
who is sixty years of age, it averages 39
inches.

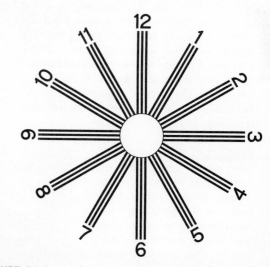

FIGURE 11.9. A chart used to test for astigmatism. The astigmatic person usually finds
that some of the sets of three lines are clear
and sharp, but that others blur and fuse into
a single blob [American Optical Company].

under arbitrarily established viewing conditions, the hue perceived can be precisely related to wavelength.

This relationship is depicted in Table 11.1 and Figure 11.10. The table lists selected wavelengths throughout the spectrum and gives the color name for the hue that the typical observer would use in viewing these wavelengths. In Figure 11.10, hues and their corresponding wavelengths are arranged in a circle, rather than along a straight scale.

Both illustrations give the wavelengths of the psychologically "pure" or *unique* colors. These are hues that observers consider not to be tinged by any other hue. Thus a unique yellow is one judged not to be tinged with green on the one side or red on the other. Unique blue is located at 477 millimicrons near the short end, wavelengthwise, of the spectrum; pure green somewhat left of center at 515 millimicrons; and pure yellow, right of center at 582 millimicrons. Pure red is an interesting case because it has no corresponding, simple wavelength. The reddest red in the visible spectrum at 700 to 780—the hue hardly changes at all between 700 and 780—is still not red enough. It requires a little blue from the other end of the spectrum to get rid of a slightly yellowish tinge and to be judged a pure red. For that reason, unique red is said to be "extraspectral," which means that it lies in the hypothetical region between the two ends of the spectrum [Dimmick and Hubbard, 1939].

COMPLEMENTARY HUES.   The extraspectral location of pure red on the color circle provides a clue to one of the basic laws of color vision, the *law of complementary colors*. Complementary colors are *hues which when mixed together are perceived as gray or white*. (Gray or white refers to the dimension of brightness, a second dimension of colors, extending from black at one extreme to white at the other.) Pure gray or white colors are colors which have no perceived hue. Complementary hues are hues that when mixed together cancel each other out and produce hueless color. The law of complementary colors states that for every hue there is a complementary hue, and that complementary hues, when mixed in the appropriate proportions, produce gray or white. As can be seen in Figure 11.10, the yellows and the blues have single complementaries in the visible spectrum, represented by white sectors. Those in the green region have no spectral complementary hues. Their complementaries are extraspectral, which is to say, they are formed out of mixtures of the red and the blue ends of the spectrum. This point is represented by the shaded sectors in Figure 11.10, the dark sector representing the extraspectral hues.

It should now be apparent why the hues are arranged in the form of a circle in Figure 11.10. This way of representing them reflects the law of complementary colors, which is operating in all our everyday perceptions of color.

TABLE 11.1. Wavelengths and color names. On the left are hues seen at the shorter wavelengths of the visible spectrum; on the right are their corresponding complementary hues seen at the longer wavelengths. The particular value of wavelength for a given hue varies with the state of adaptation of the eye. Note that the unique colors are not exactly complementary.

430 mμ	Violet	571 mμ	Green-yellow
477 mμ	Unique blue	578 mμ	Greenish yellow
482 mμ	Greenish blue	582 mμ	Unique yellow
492 mμ	Green-blue	610 mμ	Orange
495 mμ	Blue-green	660 mμ	Yellowish red
497 mμ	Bluish green		Unique red
515 mμ	Unique green		Purplish red

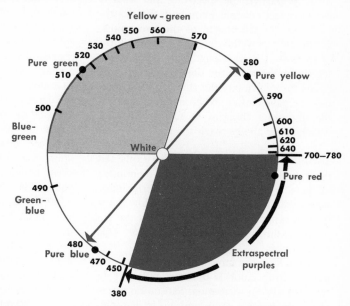

FIGURE 11.10. The color circle. This diagram shows the arrangement of various hues and their corresponding wavelengths on a circle. Points opposite each other on the unshaded sectors represent complementary hues. Those on the shaded sectors have no complementary wavelengths in the visible spectrum.

COLOR MIXTURE. What will happen if, in mixing wavelengths, we do not use wavelengths that are complementaries of each other? Ordinarily we do not have lights that are pure enough in wavelength to make complementary matches. Even when we do, they are seldom exactly the right wavelengths to match. Therefore the question is a practical one. The answer is that the resulting hue will be a hue that lies in an intermediate position on the color circle.

We can find approximately the resulting hue on the color circle by drawing a line connecting the two hues that are mixed and then making a point on the line that represents the proportions in which they are mixed. Thus if we mix a yellow and a green, we may draw a line between their respective positions on the circle. If we have mixed one part of green with two parts of yellow, we mark off one-third of the distance on that line from yellow to green. This point now designates the spoke which in turn indicates the resulting hue. If we want to know what will happen when we mix any two wavelengths, we can use this procedure to figure it out from the color circle. The same procedures may be used, though they become more complicated, for predicting the dominant hue when three, four, or even more different hues are mixed.

It will occur to some students who have had occasion to mix paints that the rules for mixing wavelengths do not seem to be the same as those for mixing paints. That is true. The perception of a mixture of yellow and blue wavelengths, for example, is gray or white, but the perception of a mixture of blue and yellow paints is green. Why?

Paints do not emit light; they reflect or absorb it. They never, however, reflect all the light that strikes them. If they are colored, they absorb some wavelengths, and it is the remaining ones that give them their color. For example, yellow paint generally absorbs violet and blue wavelengths; it reflects some green and red, somewhat more yellow-green and orange, and a lot of the yellow wavelengths. Blue paint, on the other hand, absorbs red, orange, and yellow wavelengths, and reflects the yellow-green, green, blue, and violet ones. When these two paints are mixed, the result is one of subtraction as well as addition. Each of the paints absorbs its part of the spectrum, and what is left to reflect depends upon both the absorption and the reflectance of the two paints. In the case of yellow and blue paints, most of the reflected wavelengths are green. Consequently the rules for the color mixing of paints do not violate the rules of color mixture we gave earlier. When one mixes paints the important thing is to figure out what wavelengths finally reach the eye.

SATURATION.   So far we have explained the hue dimension of color and mentioned in passing another dimension, brightness, which will be treated more fully below. Now it is time to introduce and explain the remaining dimension of perceived color. This is *saturation.*

When hues are mixed, as described above, the resulting color is different not only in hue, but also in saturation. Saturation refers to the *purity of a color,* and in fact is sometimes called purity. By purity, we do not mean uniqueness of hue or hues. We can have a very pure purple or pure yellow-green, even though these are not unique hues. By purity or saturation, we refer to the degree to which a hue is diluted or not diluted by grayness or whiteness.

The following examples should make this clear. A yellow of 580 millimicrons is the complementary hue of a blue of 480 millimicrons. Each one alone, when produced by a prism, is as pure or highly saturated as it can be. When these two hues are mixed together, however, the resulting color lies somewhere along the dashed line joining the two wavelengths in Figure 11.10. When the proportions are right, this color will lie in the center designated as white. At this point, it has no saturation or purity at all, simply because it has no detectable hue. At a point, say, one-third of the way out to the 580 point on the circle, it will have some hue—indeed, exactly the same hue as the component 580 wavelength. The saturation of the color, however, will be low because the color will have a lot of white in it. This is true because the blue has counterbalanced

some, but not all, of the yellow, thus mixing white and yellow.

Saturation, then, may be regarded on the color circle as the position of a color on the spokes of the circle. The farther out it is on a spoke, the higher its purity or saturation. The closer it is to the white neutral point in the center, the lower its saturation or purity. Translating this language into more familiar terms, the pastel or weak colors are colors that are relatively unsaturated. To make them, the mixer of paints puts a relatively small amount of dye into a base of white paint. The deep or strong colors, on the other hand, are the ones that are highly saturated. To make them, the paint mixer uses a large amount of colored dye in proportion to the base paint. In fact, the most highly saturated colors are made by using only color pigments and avoiding any white at all in the mixture.

Pure wavelengths give the highest saturation or purity that the eye is capable of seeing. On the other hand, pure wavelengths are not equally saturated. The yellows are the least saturated, the greens somewhat more, and the red and blue ends of the spectrum the most saturated of all. The reason for this is physiological. A yellow wavelength stimulates receptors for green and red as well as yellow, thereby producing the white complementary effects of green and red, as well as yellow. The effects of red and blue wavelengths, on the other hand, are more restricted to the receptors responsible for these sensations, and hence produce less white to dilute the saturation of the perceived color. (Receptor processes in color vision are covered in a later section.)

BRIGHTNESS.   The third dimension of perceived color is *brightness.* This dimension extends from black through various shades of gray. To represent it along with the dimensions of hue and saturation requires that the color circle be extended into a color solid (see Figure 11.11). To make a color solid, color circle is piled on color circle like so many layers of a cake. In this

FIGURE 11.11. The color cone or solid. When all of the colors are arranged in three dimensions, they form a color cone or color solid. At the top are colors of highest brightness, at the bottom those of lowest brightness. Around the circle are colors of different hue. The distance out from the center axis of the cone represents saturation. [More Business, copyright 1937 by the American Photoengravers Association].

solid, the up-and-down dimension represents brightness. The colors at the top are bright, those at the bottom dark. The center line of the solid runs through the centers of the various color circles and represents the points at which there is neither hue nor saturation, only varying brightnesses.

The relation of brightness to hue and saturation may be illustrated by referring again to paints. We can vary the grayness of paint by mixing black pigment with white pigment. By using all white pigment and no black, we obtain the brightest paint possible. Conversely, by using all black and no white,

we obtain a paint of low brightness. In between, varying mixtures produce different shades of gray. This is the up-and-down dimension of the solid. Grayness can in turn be mixed in varying proportions with pigments of different hues. When the proportion of colored pigment to gray pigment is low, the resulting colors are near the center of the solid and are of low saturation. When the proportion is high, the resulting color is out closer to the periphery of the circle, and its saturation is high. The remaining dimension, hue, of course, determines the position of the color around the circle.

THE MUNSELL SYSTEM. The general scheme represented by the color solid has been refined and put into useful, though complicated, form in a system known as the *Munsell system.* This system marks off distances on each of the three dimensions that are perceptually about equal—a skilled observer judges the difference between two points on one dimension to be about the same as between any other two points on each dimension—and assigns numbers to them. In this way a color of any particular hue, saturation, and brightness can be specified by a set of numbers. We need not be concerned with the number system, for it requires more explanation than is appropriate here. It is fully described, however, in the *Munsell Book of Color,* which also provides samples of various combinations of the three dimensions. In this book can be found any color known to man that can be made by mixing the pigments used in printing, though not the highly saturated colors that can be produced only with a prism. Each such color is specified by a number, which in turn can be used by paint manufacturers and others who need color standards for specifying and reproducing a particular color.

In Figure 11.12 are two pages reproduced from the *Munsell Book of Color.* Disregard the numbers and the terms used, for they refer to the intricacies of the Munsell system. They are presented, however, in order that we may summarize visually the description we have given of the color solid and its dimensions. The upper page is a slice through the solid, and hence a color circle. It shows in color what Figure 11.10 presents diagrammatically. Around the circle are colors of different hue, at the center is a neutral, hueless gray, and in between there are colors of different saturation. The lower page is a vertical slice on the red side of the solid into its center. It shows how a color of one hue, in this case red, may vary in saturation and brightness. Increasing saturation is depicted from left to right; increasing brightness from bottom to top.

Color blindness

About 1 person in 25 is color-blind, and this defect is likely to influence his everyday behavior in many ways. Some women, for example, can wear only one particular shade of lipstick, because if they use any other shade they cannot see lipstick smears on their clothes. A color-blind house painter once ruefully told us that he had to repaint half a house because the color he had used on one side of the house did not match that used on the other. Color-blind chemists have to rely on their laboratory assistants to identify colors in flame tests of metallic substances, and some electronic technicians cannot match strands of wire by their color codes.

WHAT IS COLOR BLINDNESS? It is certainly not the inability to identify a color by a particular name, for that is a question of language. Nor is it actually blindness. Most color-blind people are not really blind to color. They can usually see a great many colors, but they confuse certain critical ones. It was John Dalton, the author of the atomic theory in chemistry, who clearly recognized this fact and presented one of the earliest and best scientific accounts of the defect.

Dalton himself was so color-blind that when Oxford University conferred on him the scarlet gown of a doctor of civil laws, he wore the gown everywhere for several days, not realizing that he presented such a conspicuous appearance. This greatly astonished his friends, who knew he was a Quaker and was supposed to wear the somber garb of that sect. In 1794, at the age of twenty-eight, Dalton described to the Manchester Literary and Philosophical Society his sensations of color. Because of this classic description [Boring, 1942] of color blindness, the defect was known for more than a century afterward as *Daltonism.* He said:

All crimsons appear to me to consist chiefly of dark blue; but many of them seem to have

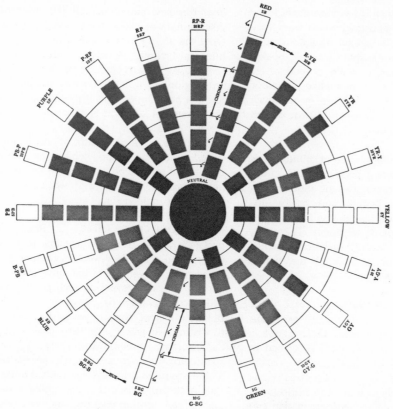

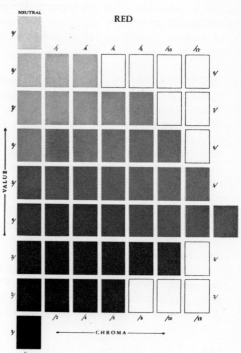

FIGURE 11.12. Two pages from the *Munsell Book of Color*, illustrating the hue, saturation, and brightness of colors. The page above shows colored samples all of the same brightness (value 5/ in Munsell terminology). They vary only in hue and saturation (chroma in Munsell terminology). The reddish sample at the top of the vertical column is designated as 10RP 5/10. The page below shows samples that all, except for the first column at the left, have the same hue (5.0 Red in the Munsell system). They differ only in brightness or in saturation (value and chroma). A very useful feature of the Munsell system is that it provides a standard nomenclature for all the colors. For example, the red sample on the right of the row 8/ (at the lower right of the page) is designated as 5.0 R 8/4.

a tinge of dark brown. I have seen specimens of crimson, claret, and mud which were very nearly alike. . . . The colour of a florid complexion appears to me that of a dull, opake, blackish blue, upon a white ground. . . . Blood appears to me . . . not unlike the colour called bottle green. . . . There is not much difference in colour between a stick of red sealing wax and green.

Reduced to essentials, color blindness is a defect that makes a person unable to tell the difference between two or more colors that most other people can easily distinguish. It is not, as is commonly supposed, a single type of deficiency. There are, on the contrary, several varieties of color blindness, and for each kind the defect exists in varying degrees.

TOTAL COLOR BLINDNESS. Total color blindness, known more technically as *achromatism,* is extremely rare. Only about a hundred cases of it have been described in the whole history of visual science. To the totally color-blind person—who, usually has other visual defects as well—the world looks like a black and white photograph. He can distinguish among white, black, and gray of various intensities, but he does not see colors as such.

TWO-COLOR VISION. By far the most common kind of color blindness is two-color vision, known as *dichromatism* [Geldard, 1953]. For people with this defect, color perception is essentially reduced to two hues: the yellows and the blues. Most of them confuse reds, greens, and yellows of certain shades with one another and are unable to distinguish clearly among bluish-greens, blues, and violets. There is also a particular shade of blue-green that dichromats confuse with gray. They never, however, confuse the yellows and blues.

Among the dichromats, visual scientists distinguish two principal varieties. One group has a defect only in color vision, not in brightness vision. This group, known as

deuteranopes, can make all the brightness discriminations called for in the color solid. Only the ability to distinguish red and green hues is lacking. A second group, called *protanopes,* cannot perceive brightness in the red region as well as normal people can. Show a protanope a red stimulus and he not only does not see it as red, he may confuse it with black.

There is a third group of dichromats, called *tritanopes,* who behave as though they could not see blue colors. So few tritanopes have been found that we know very little about their vision.

ANOMALOUS COLOR DEFECT. Besides the people who are frank dichromats, there are others who are "color-weak." Their impairment may be so slight that only the most careful tests can reveal it. Such people have little trouble with bright or vivid colors, but their defect appears when they attempt to distinguish among the very pale or light browns, tans, greens, and pinks. We call such color weakness *anomalous color defect.* There are three principal varieties of anomalous trichromats, and they are called *deuteranomalous, protanomalous,* or *tritanomalous,* depending on the kind of dichromat they most resemble.

Most kinds of color blindness are inherited, and the defect has been identified as a sex-linked recessive characteristic. The genetic mechanism of color blindness is explained and illustrated in Chapter 2. Because of the genetic relation involved, color blindness is more common among men than among women. Statistics show that about 1 man in 15 is color-blind, while less than 1 woman in 100 is so afflicted.

AWARENESS OF COLOR DEFECT. During the Second World War, it was a common experience in Air Force and Navy recruiting centers to have color-blind applicants emphatically deny their color blindness. Often they would say, "What do you mean, Doc? I can see colors. I've never had trouble with colors."

To the color-normal person it seems incomprehensible that a man can go through life unaware that he is failing to see the richness and variety of colors that others see. We must look for the explanation of this puzzling situation in several directions. In the first place, most color-blind people do see some colors. Second, a person cannot appreciate a sensation he has never sensed. A man born without taste buds will never understand the saltiness of the ocean or the sweetness of an apple. What is the tone of a 50,000-cycle sound, above the range of human hearing? Or what is the color of infrared light? We cannot give the answers to these questions because they are outside the realm of our experiences. Moreover, since we have never experienced them, we never miss the fact that we *cannot* experience them. Color-vision defects, then, often do not reveal themselves in a positive manner.

The last part of the explanation is that the color-deviant person has learned to use correct color names for many common objects. He knows that grass is green, lemons are yellow, ripe apples are red, and so on because he learned these things as a child. From experience he has learned to follow the names used by everyone else, and readily accepts correction. If you correct the mistake of a color-deviant person who says that a light green object is "pink," he will reply, "Oh, yes, it's green, I see it now." All our color names will satisfy him because this is a matter of learning anyway. The difficulty is that he has fewer color sensations than color names and he is often not sure which names to assign to his sensations.

DETECTING COLOR-VISION DEFECTS. Usually it requires special tests to find out whether a person has defective color vision. If you ask him to name the colors of common objects, the chances are that he will give you the correct names. But his defect will show up if you take him out on a dark night away from all other means of identification and ask him to pick out yellow,

green, and red lights at a distance. These principles underlie many lantern tests in use for testing color vision.

Another, and more satisfactory way, of testing color vision is with pseudoisochromatic plates (see Figure 11.13). One test, for example, consists of a card with brilliant purplish-red dots arranged in such a way as to form a number. A normal person can see the number immediately, because its color contrasts vividly with the background. But individuals with certain types of color deficiency cannot read it, because to them the dots all seem to be the same color. Now that you know how these tests work, you should be able to figure out why they are called "pseudoisochromatic."

Sensitivity of the eye

In the beginning of this chapter, we described the eye as so sensitive that a normal person can see the flare of a match at a

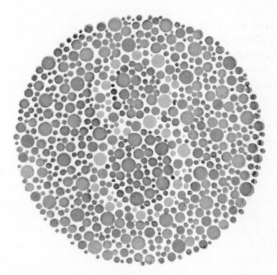

FIGURE 11.13. A plate from the Ishihara Test of color blindness. The plate is seen by a normal person as a figure 8, by the red-green blind as a figure 3, and by the totally color blind as no figure at all [C. H. Stoelting Co., Chicago, distributors of the Ishihara Test in the United States, Canada, and Mexico].

distance of 50 miles. This is true if it is a clear night, if the curvature of the earth does not get in the way, and if the eye is well dark-adapted. The sensitivity of the eye is indeed remarkable. If we measure it carefully under a variety of conditions, we can learn a few more things about vision.

DARK ADAPTATION.   Certainly everybody knows that the eye becomes more sensitive in the dark. Simply recall the times you have gone to a movie in the afternoon and found yourself unable to see your way down the aisle or into your seat until you had waited a few minutes for your eyes to get accustomed to the dark. Of course, when you come out of the dark and into a bright light again, your eyes light-adapt and lose some of their sensitivity. We can measure the course of dark adaptation by fully adapting the eye to a bright light, then putting the person in the dark and measuring his absolute threshold (see page 301) over a period of several minutes.

The resulting measurements will look something like the curve in Figure 11.14. At first the threshold is quite high—so high that a candle can be burning in a room and he will not know it unless he sees the flame itself. Sensitivity improves, however, at first very rapidly and then more slowly. After a half-hour, sensitivity is 1,000 to 100,000 times greater than it was at the beginning of dark adaptation.

Notice that the dark-adaptation curve has two segments: after an initial drop it levels out for a few minutes; then it drops more rapidly again before leveling out for good. These two segments are related to the two different receptors of the eye, the rods and cones, as we can see from measurements of spectral sensitivity.

SPECTRAL SENSITIVITY.   The term *spectral sensitivity* refers to *sensitivity at different wavelengths of the visible spectrum.* To

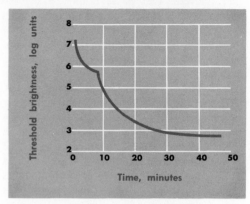

FIGURE 11.14. A typical curve of dark adaptation. After a subject has been in normal or bright illumination for some time, he is placed in the dark and asked to indicate the weakest light (threshold brightness) that he can see. Thresholds are taken repeatedly, minute after minute, and the results plotted in a curve of dark adaptation. Notice the two limbs of the curve.

measure it, lights of different wavelengths, instead of a white light, are used to obtain absolute thresholds (see page 301). Then the absolute threshold is plotted against a scale of wavelength.

The particular results one gets are a function of the state of adaptation of the eye. If the eye is kept light-adapted during the measurements by surrounding the test wavelength with a patch of light, the absolute thresholds are understandably much higher than if the eye is kept dark-adapted. In addition, the best thresholds for the light-adapted eye are in the region of 550 millimicrons, whereas those for the dark-adapted eye are around 500 millimicrons.

This difference depends upon the kind of receptors which are being stimulated, the rods or the cones [Gibson and Tyndall, 1923]. In dark adaptation, the rods are dominant; in light adaptation, the cones are. This can be demonstrated by picking two different places on the retina for making the measurements. The fovea, we know, contains only cones, so measurements made with a patch of light small enough to stimulate only the fovea provide an index of cone sensitivity. At a point about 20 angular degrees from the fovea—we learn from anatomical studies—the rods are most dense. At this position, measurements can be made of rod sensitivity by having the observer look at a special fixation light with his fovea and indicate whether or not he can at the same time see a test patch of light focused at 20 degrees from the fovea.

The results of these comparisons of the spectral sensitivity of the rods and cones are summarized in Figure 11.15. From such data we can draw the following conclusions: (1) The rods are more sensitive than the cones. (2) Each curve of sensitivity has a central region in which sensitivity is greatest, while the regions to the side are less and less sensitive. (3) The region of greatest cone sensitivity is 555 millimicrons (yellowish-green), while that of greatest rod sensitivity is approximately 505 millimicrons (bluish-green).

COLOR PERCEPTION. In measuring the thresholds plotted in Figure 11.14, we may ask a subject to report not only whether he sees the test patch of light but in addition (if he does) to indicate its color. We then discover an important difference between the two curves. In the case of the upper curve, when the subject is using his fovea, he can report correctly the color (hue) of the wavelength used in the tests. In making judgments for the lower curve, however, the subject is totally color-blind. Even though he is presented with single wavelengths, he sees them all as gray. This is the basis of the ancient saying, "When all candles bee out, all cats bee gray." And for this reason, the interval between the rod and cone curves is called the *photochromatic interval—the interval of intensities in which we can see light*

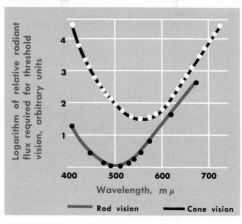

FIGURE 11.15. Thresholds for seeing at different wavelengths. The lower curve was obtained while the subject was viewing a patch of light 20 degrees from the fovea, where the rods are most numerous. The upper curve was obtained when the subject used his fovea to see with; cones are most numerous in the fovea.

but not colors. This fact is rather convincing proof that the cones are the receptors for color perception and that the rods are not.

PURKINJE EFFECT. The sensitivity curve may be plotted in another way (see Figure 11.16). Instead of recording the absolute thresholds, we may express them in relative terms by taking the best threshold—at 505 millimicrons in the rod curve and 555 millimicrons in the cone curve—and expressing all other thresholds of each curve as percentages of the maximum. This turns the curves upside down, and it also fixes the best thresholds at 100 per cent. In this form the curves are called luminosity functions. From them we can see that for cone vision (that is, for daylight levels of light adaptation) sensitivity is *relatively* better in the red and poorer in the blue than it is for rod vision (that is, for twilight levels of light adaptation) [Hecht and Williams, 1922].

Such a relative difference in the brightness of colors was discovered more than a century ago by the Bohemian physiologist Purkinje. He noticed what you may observe for yourself if you are sitting outside on a warm summer night just before the sun sets. When the sun is still shining, the reds seem relatively bright as compared with the greens and the blues. As twilight comes on, however, the reddish colors become much darker, while the blue colors hardly seem to change at all in brightness. This change in the apparent brightness of colors is called the *Purkinje shift*. The change is accounted for by the fact that the eye shifts from cone functions to rod functions in the course of dark adaptation.

Visual acuity

Objects have not only color and brightness, but also form. Sometimes it may be hard to discern form, as when we see objects in a fog or at night, but whatever we see almost invariably seems to have some form. Our perception of form usually has two aspects, size and shape. These two aspects are more or less independent, for objects of any particular shape may be large or small, and objects of any particular size may have any one of a great variety of shapes. In Chapter 10, on perception, we treated size and shape in some detail, for they illustrate well some of the general principles of perception. We shall, therefore, not consider them at this point.

Here, however we shall study the visual capacity that enables us to see size and shape. This capacity is *visual acuity—the ability of a person to perceive fine differences in the details of the visual environment*. To measure visual acuity, we always try to find a way of stating the smallest object whose shape a person can recognize when presented with it in some standard situation. There are several different ways of measuring visual acuity, but they are of two general types: one that physicians use for diagnostic purposes, and the other that laboratory scientists use in their research work in the measurement of visual activity.

EYE CHARTS. All of us, having suffered through at least a few physical examinations, are familiar with the physician's eye chart. This chart, called a Snellen chart, compares a person's visual acuity with a standard that has been established as normal.

It may be so designed that letters of different sizes on the chart represent what the normal person sees at various distances. On many charts, for example, the biggest letter can be just read at 200 feet, the next biggest letters are half as large and so can be read at 100 feet, and so on. If at 20 feet from the chart an individual can see what the normal person can see at 20 feet, he has 20/20 vision. If at 20 feet from the chart he can see only those letters that the normal person can see at 100 feet, he has 20/100 vision, which is not so good. If, on the

THE CONES ARE MOST SENSITIVE AT 555 MILLIMICRONS; THE RODS, AT 505:

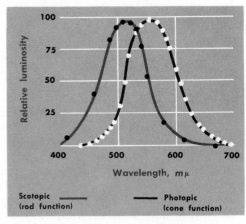

FIGURE 11.16. Relative luminosity functions. The curves represent a different way of plotting the data shown in Figure 11.15. Instead of being plotted in logarithms, each threshold is divided into the threshold at which the eye is most sensitive. This is done separately, however, for the rod and cone curves, so that the peak of each arbitrarily becomes 100 per cent.

other hand, he can see those letters that the normal person can see only at 10 feet, he has 20/10 vision, which is excellent.

Sometimes physicians prefer to use distance rather than size of letters as an index of visual acuity. For many years this kind of test was used by the United States Navy. In such examinations, the person starts walking toward the eye chart and continues until he can read the letters on it—and there is only one size of letter. The results of the test are expressed in terms of the distance at which a person sees the letters that would be seen by a normal person at 20 feet. In either case, whether distance or size of letters is used as an index, a person's acuity is compared with normal acuity at 20 feet.

It is also possible and, in fact, desirable to use test objects that are not letters. Two such objects are illustrated in Figure 11.17. One is called the *Landolt ring* and the other the *parallel bars*. Both can be used with people who cannot read; all the examinee has to do is tell where the gap is in the Landolt ring or the direction of orientation of the parallel bars. Another advantage of these test objects is that they are always the same in shape, whereas the letters of a test chart differ in size and shape and are not equally hard to recognize. For that reason, visual scientists who are interested in precise laboratory measurements prefer such test objects.

NEAR AND FAR ACUITY.   In view of what we have already said about nearsightedness and farsightedness, you will not be surprised to learn that visual acuity may vary with different distances. The acuity at 13 inches, for example, may be quite different from visual acuity at 20 feet. Beyond 20 feet, however, acuity appears to be fairly constant. To understand these facts, recall that the lens in the front of the eye has to change shape in order for the eye to focus near and far objects on the retina, and that

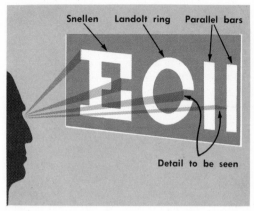

FIGURE 11.17. The Snellen letter, Landolt ring, and parallel bars. Some letters are easier to see than others, and a person may recognize a letter without seeing all of its detail. For that reason, the most careful scientific studies of visual acuity make use of the Landolt ring or parallel bars. Neither requires that a person read. He needs only to indicate the direction in which the white space points, or whether he sees two bars or one.

the ability to do this varies markedly in different individuals. Accommodation remains fairly constant, however, for objects at distances greater than 20 feet.

The fact that people may differ in their near and far acuity is sometimes of practical importance. In some industries and in many military situations, a person's visual acuity may be critical in his ability to do his job. Fliers, riflemen, and artillerymen, to mention only a few of the military specialties, must have good visual acuity. Machinists, needleworkers, many machine operators, and inspectors must also have good acuity. To select people for these positions, employers often require tests of visual acuity as part of a physical examination. If the job calls for good distance acuity, as in the case of truck drivers, it is important that the test be made at 20 feet or more, but if the job calls for good near acuity (e.g., toolmaking and watch repairing) the test should be made at distances comparable to those important in the job. Otherwise differences between near and far acuity may make the tests invalid.

RETINAL POSITION. We all use our eyes so much that we commonly overlook certain peculiarities about our seeing process and would never notice them if they were not pointed out to us. If, for example, you stare steadily at a letter on this page, it is impossible for you to read letters 2 inches away; or if you look at the road straight ahead while driving, you will not be able to read most signs along the side of the road. From such facts we know that visual acuity is not nearly so good at the side of the retina as it is at the fovea.

In Figure 11.18 you can see more precisely how visual acuity varies with the part of the retina used [Wertheim, 1894]. Acuity is best, of course, when one looks directly at an object, that is, when the image of the object falls on the fovea. At 5 degrees off the fovea, visual acuity is only half as good, and at 40, 45, or 50 degrees it is only about one-twentieth as good as it is at the fovea. You can see what it is at other positions by studying the curve in Figure 11.18. This

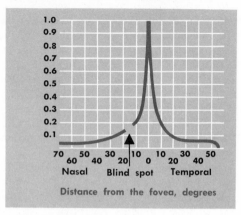

FIGURE 11.18. How visual acuity varies with the part of the retina used in viewing.

distribution is similar to that of the rods and cones, as described on page 337.

THE BLIND SPOT. Before we leave Figure 11.18, notice the part of the curve that has been left uncolored. This is the place in the retina at which blood vessels enter and the optic nerve leaves the eyeball, and it has no rods or cones. It is located about 15 degrees from the fovea, on the side of the retina toward the nose, and it is about 7 by 5 degrees in size. We cannot see anything in this area, and because of that it is called the

FIGURE 11.19. Demonstrating the blind spot. Close your left eye, and look at the cross with your right eye. Then move the book toward you or away from you until the sketch of the girl disappears, or largely disappears, from view. At this point, the image of the girl is falling on the blind spot.

blind spot. Yet if we try to find this spot in our visual field, we probably will have trouble—partly because we see with one eye what the blind spot of the other eye blanks out and also because the blind spot is so far off to the side of the fovea that we do not notice it. It is there, nonetheless, in everybody's eye, and you can prove this to yourself, if you like, by following the instructions under Figure 11.19.

AMOUNT OF LIGHT. Visual acuity improves with increasing light [Moon and Spencer, 1944]. We recognize this fact every time we turn on extra lamps to read a book or try to get as much light as we can for visual tasks. In the dark, obviously, visual acuity is zero. As some kind of light is turned on, visual acuity improves very rapidly, but then more and more light has diminishing returns, even though almost any increase in light, short of blinding intensities, improves visual acuity somewhat. This means that there is no such thing as the "best amount" of light. Rather, the important problem in everyday life is to get as much light as we need to do the kind of visual work we are going to do.

Because light is so important to visual acuity and because visual acuity is required in almost everything anybody does, the subject has been explored very intensively. There is, in fact, a special branch of engineering called *illumination engineering* that handles practical applications of the subject. Illumination engineers have provided reference handbooks to which we can go for answers to many practical questions. They have given us rules to follow in providing enough light for different visual tasks.

CONTRAST. By this time, it has probably become apparent that many factors affect visual acuity. Although we shall not be able to mention all these factors, there are two more that are interesting and have practical significance. One is *contrast.* This is the difference in brightness between an object and its immediate background. If, for example,

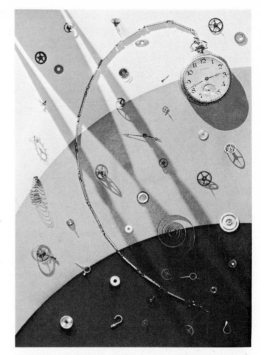

FIGURE 11.20. Visual acuity depends upon contrast. It is harder to see the watch parts against the dark background than against the lighter backgrounds. The higher the contrast between an object and its background, the more clearly one can perceive the details of the object [Luckiesh, 1944].

we are viewing dark letters on a white background, visual acuity will be better when the letters are coal black than when they are a light gray, because the black makes a greater contrast with the white than does the light gray. This means that when we are painting signs or making something we wish people to see as easily as possible or at as great a distance as possible, we should make the contrast between the dark and the light parts of the object as great as possible. In this way visual acuity is increased (see Figure 11.20).

SURROUND. A final factor to consider is the *surround* of an object we are viewing. Even though the object itself has high contrast and is illuminated by good light, visual acuity may not be what it could be if the general illumination in the room is poor. Indeed, it is relatively easy to demonstrate in the laboratory that, if the general light in a room is either much greater or much less than that on the object we are viewing, visual acuity is impaired. In Figure 11.21, you see examples of poor lighting and good lighting of the surround. The best rule is that the lighting of the surround should be about the same as the lighting of the object.

EYE MOVEMENTS IN READING. This is a convenient place to cover a point of some practical interest to the student, namely, the use of his eyes in reading. Reading, indeed, is the activity in which we employ our visual acuity for more serious purposes than the casual inspection of our environment.

As you may know, your eyes do not move continuously while you are reading. Rather they move in quick jumps, and rest intermittently for a fraction of a second at points along the line you are reading. This fact has been demonstrated in photographic records of eye movements during reading (see Figure 11.22). It is during the rest period that you perceive what you are reading. There is no way to speed up the movements, and the duration of the rests can be speeded very little. Hence your efficiency in reading depends primarily on how much and how well you perceive what you can see while your eyes are stopped.

Most people are not nearly so efficient in reading as they might be. Their most common faults are (1) not perceiving enough words at a glance and hence making too many stops along the line, and (2) retracing words and phrases they have already read. Both points are illustrated in Figure 11.22. Each vertical line shows a fixation, rest point, or glance. The numbers indicate the order of fixations on the line. The upper record is that of a good reader. Notice that the reader takes in one to two words per glance and does no retracing. The lower

SEEING IS BETTER WHEN THE BACKGROUND IS UNIFORMLY ILLUMINATED:

FIGURE 11.21. In direct lighting (above), visual acuity is poor because only part of the working area—the book the boy is reading—is illuminated. Visual acuity is much better (below) when the entire working area is illuminated [Westinghouse].

record of a poor reader shows far too many glances per line, as well as frequent reversals.

A poor reader, indeed almost any reader, can usually improve his reading speed by training and practice. To gain speed, it is necessary to expand the number of words perceived in one glance. By reading as fast

CHAPTER ELEVEN

as you can without losing the sense of what you are reading, you can gradually increase the words comprehended in a glance and thereby reduce the number of glances per line. It is best to practice fast reading on easy material—magazine articles, fiction, newspapers, etc. If you practice rapid reading, keep a record of your reading rate. Count the number of words you can read in a 1-minute period each day, and draw a chart that shows your rate of reading on successive days of practice. You must be careful to check your comprehension to make sure that you are not sacrificing understanding to increased speed. If you practice reading carefully, you can actually increase your comprehension at the same time that you are increasing your speed.

Receptor processes

This chapter has covered most of the basic phenomena of human vision: accommodation, nearsightedness and farsightedness, astigmatism, the attributes of color, complementary colors, color mixture, color blindness, thresholds of sensitivity, dark adaptation, and visual acuity. On reading about these topics it may have occurred to the student to ask "why" questions. Why, for example, are there three attributes of color? Why does the eye dark-adapt? Why do we discriminate different hues? And so on.

The answers to many questions of this sort are well understood. The answers to others are not yet available, though we are probably on the verge of obtaining them. In any case, attempts to answer them take us into the physiology of vision—the processes taking place in the retina and the rest of the visual system. Vision, in fact, is a good example of the interdisciplinary nature of most scientific fields, for research in the physiology of vision is being prosecuted just as vigorously as is work on its more psychological aspects. And it is hard to tell where one begins and the other leaves off. Hence, for those who are interested, we present here a résumé of the physiology of vision, particularly of receptor processes. This will explain the "why" of some of the phenomena we have already discussed.

A GOOD READER MAKES RELATIVELY FEW FIXATIONS AND DOES NOT RETRACE:

FIGURE 11.22. Eye movements in reading. In the picture is an ophthalmograph used for photographing the movement of the eyes in reading [Brooks, from Monkmeyer]. The film shows a record of eye movements made with such an instrument [New York Univer. Testing and Advisement Center]. The lines of print show the difference between a good reader and a poor one. Each vertical bar accompanied by a number represents a fixation.

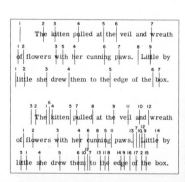

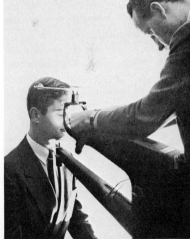

PHOTOSENSITIVE SUBSTANCES. Our first "why" question is, Why does light striking the eye give rise to a visual sensation? Why do we *see* light? The most general answer is that nerve impulses are excited in the retina and these travel to the brain, just as all sense organs initiate impulses that act as messages or signals.

In addition, however, between the moment a stimulus impinges on a receptor and the initiation of nerve impulses, there is usually an intervening event. In vision, this is a *photochemical* event [Wald, 1959]. Light strikes a substance in the receptors that is photosensitive, causing a chemical reaction to occur. This reaction in turn sets up the nerve impulse.

The fact that a photosensitive pigment is involved in vision was first discovered by Franz Boll in 1876. He noticed that the dark-adapted eye of the frog had a reddish-purple color, but that when the eye was exposed to light, the pigment bleached to a yellowish color. For this reason, the photosensitive substance was first called "visual purple," and the substance it became after exposure to light was called "visual yellow."

Today, in one species of animal or another, four different photosensitive pigments have been identified: two in the rods and two in the cones. The substances are all very similar, each being a slight variant of the other. Different substances occur in different species of animals, depending upon whether they live on land or in water, whether they are predominantly nocturnal animals with rod eyes or diurnal animals with cone eyes, or whether they have mixed eyes as human beings have. All the substances, however, behave in essentially the same way.

Rhodopsin. The best-known substance, originally called visual purple, has been renamed *rhodopsin.* This is found in the rods of most vertebrate animals. When struck by light, rhodopsin is broken down into two substances, *retinene* and *opsin* (see Figure 11.23). Retinene gives the yellowish color that was first called visual yellow. In time, retinene further decomposes to vitamin A.

Rhodopsin may then be resynthesized from either retinene and opsin or vitamin A and opsin. Various intermediate stages in these reactions are now thoroughly worked out.

This cycle of decomposition and resynthesis of photosensitive substances in the eye, sometimes called the *visual cycle,* accounts for the ability of the eye to light-adapt and dark-adapt. The light-adapted eye is one in which the substances have been depleted, at least partly, by the action of light. Photochemical materials obey a kind of probability law. The more dense the material is, the more chances there are for light to hit some of its molecules. As it thins out, fewer rays of light strike its molecules. Consequently, more light is required to decompose any given number of molecules. This is what happens in light adaptation. Conversely, when a light-adapted eye is returned to the dark, the products of decomposition of the photosensitive material have an opportunity to resynthesize. Hence, the material gradually becomes more plentiful. As it does, less light is required to "hit" its molecules. Thus the eye becomes more sensitive.

Iodopsin. You will recall from Figure 11.14 that the dark-adaptation curve for human vision has two limbs, one for rod vision and the other for cone vision. This would imply different substances in the two kinds of cells, resynthesizing at different rates. Resynthesis in the cones should be faster than it is in the rods, since the cone limb of the curve appears first. The second cone substance has been identified and named *iodopsin.* Actually, iodopsin has been obtained from the chicken retina, not from man, but we presume something very close to it is present in human cones. Very likely, it is several substances mixed together—otherwise we have difficulty explaining human color vision—but at least it is identifiably different from rhodopsin.

It is different in two ways. First of all, it resynthesizes more rapidly than rhodopsin. This has been demonstrated in extracts and appears to account for the more rapid dark

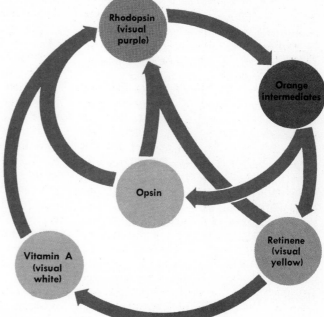

FIGURE 11.23. The visual cycle.

adaptation of the cones. Secondly, its *spectral absorption* is different. The light that decomposes rhodopsin or iodopsin is absorbed in the process, and some wavelengths are more effective than others. The proportion of light absorbed at various wavelengths, plotted as a function of wavelength, is known as the *spectral-absorption curve.* As can be seen in Figure 11.24, the two curves are different. Rhodopsin has its peak at around 500 millimicrons, iodopsin at about 560 millimicrons. On either side, absorption diminishes until it becomes negligible toward the ends of the spectrum.

If you now turn back to Figure 11.16, where the sensitivity of the eye was plotted for scotopic (rod) and photopic (cone) conditions, you will see that the similarity between the two sets of curves is remarkable. Actually, on close comparison, you will find that they are not identical, but the reasons are well known. Measurements of human sensitivity are made with light passing through the lens and optic media, whereas those of rhodopsin and iodopsin are made

in solution; therefore, corrections have to be made for the known absorption of light as it passes through the eye to the rods and cones. This correction is greatest in the blue end of the spectrum, because both the lens and the pigment of the fovea absorb some light in this region. When, however, these corrections are made, the spectral characteristics of the two photosensitive substances compare quite well with human visibility curves. This is corroborated by measurements of visibility made by electrical techniques (see below) in the eyes of various animals. These measurements, as well as corrected measurements of human spectral sensitivity, are fitted reasonably well by the lines showing the spectral absorption of rhodopsin and iodopsin.

This correlation, then, explains nicely the scotopic and photopic curves of visibility. Put another way, the absorption of photochemical substances accounts for our differences in sensitivity to lights of different wavelengths both in the dark-adapted and light-adapted eye. From this conclusion, it follows too that the Purkinje phenomenon, discussed on page 351, is similarly explained. The Purkinje shift merely represents the shift of vision from rhodopsin to iodopsin. As rhodopsin is bleached out by light, spectral sensitivity shifts over and is dependent on the absorption of the iodopsin.

Incidentally, the chemical difference between rhodopsin and iodopsin is in the opsin. When the two are decomposed by light, the resulting retinene is the same, but the opsins are slightly different chemically. For this reason the opsin going into rhodopsin is called *scotopsin,* and that in iodopsin is called *photopsin,* for they account for the differences in the scotopic and photopic visibility curves.

ELECTRICAL ACTIVITY OF THE RETINA. Decomposition of a photosensitive substance, then, is the first step in the visual process. The next one must be some sort of electrical change giving rise to nerve impulses. We as yet know relatively little about this step. We do know, however, that it occurs. Indeed, when rhodopsin extracted from the retina is bleached by light in a solution, changes in electrical potential can be recorded. Thus the act of decomposition itself is accompanied, as many chemical reactions are, by electrical changes that can in turn arouse nervous activity in the receptor cell.

Electrical activity may be recorded when the eye is stimulated by light. Indeed, such a record may be obtained in the intact human eye without injuring the eye [Granit, 1959]. This is the *electroretinogram* (ERG). An ERG is recorded when one electrode is placed on the cornea, another is placed on the side of head, and the two are connected to an appropriate amplifier and recorder while the eye is being stimulated with light. If a light is flashed on briefly, then turned off,

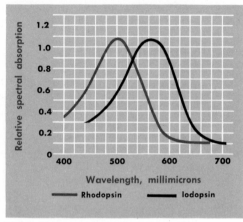

FIGURE 11.24. Spectral absorption curves for rhodopsin and iodopsin extracted from the chicken retina [after Wald, 1959]. Note the similarity to the curves in Figure 11.16.

the record looks like that in Figure 11.25. It begins with a downward deflection, the *a* wave, right after the light is turned on, then swings quickly the other way in a *b* wave, and finally, while the light is still on, goes into a long, gentle wave called the *c* wave. When the light goes off, there is a sudden deflection called the *d* wave.

The interesting part of this record is the *b* wave, for its size is proportional to the intensity of the light. One can arbitrarily select a *b* wave of a particular height and measure the intensity of light required to produce that height of *b* wave. Used in this way, the *b* wave is like an absolute threshold for a human being, when he says, "I see it."

Thus, the *b* wave may serve as a measure of the threshold of vision in a number of different situations. It has been used, for example, to obtain dark-adaptation curves, and also to determine curves of spectral sensitivity. The results obtained with this method correspond closely with those secured with psychological methods. The technique is especially valuable in the study of animal vision, for it allows one to measure thresholds of vision in animals without going to the trouble of training them to make discriminations.

THEORIES OF COLOR VISION. Before continuing with this account of the physiology of vision, we should raise a question that has puzzled visual scientists more than any other: Why do we see colors? What is the mechanism by which we can discriminate different hues from one another? Many theories designed to answer this question have been proposed, some dating back hundreds of years. We shall describe two of them. Physiological methods are bringing us much nearer to the answer to the question. It now appears that one of the theories may be rather close to the mark.

All theories of color vision have assumed that there are different kinds of cones, and that each kind of cone has its characteristic sensitivity in a certain region of the spectrum. What this means, in terms of our modern knowledge of photochemistry, is that different cones contain somewhat different photochemical substances, each with its own spectral absorption curve. For convenience, the imaginary cones have been named according to their assumed peaks of absorption. Hence a "red" cone refers to a cone assumed to be most sensitive in the red region, a "green" cone one that is supposed to be most sensitive in the green region of the spectrum, and so on.

Young-Helmholtz theory. The theory that until recently has held the limelight is named after the two men who formulated it— though they lived at different times. It is a three-cone theory [Helmholtz, 1924]. It assumes that there are three kinds of cones: "red" cones, "green" cones, and "blue" cones. It further assumes that the effects generated in these cones add up in a simple way so that an equal amount of activity in all three gives the sensation of "white."

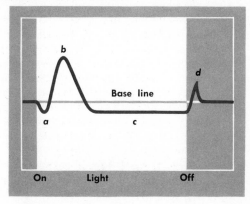

FIGURE 11.25. The electroretinogram (ERG). When a light is turned on, the electrical potential of the retina first swings in one direction (a wave), then in the other (b wave). Then follows a slower c wave. When the light is turned off, there is a sudden deflection (d wave). The b wave has been used as a measure of retinal sensitivity similar to the absolute threshold in man.

Perhaps this theory has seemed attractive and has had so much influence because of its simplicity. Indeed, this theory must be the simplest possible theory, for it is easy to show that there must be *at least* three kinds of cones to explain almost any phenomenon of color vision. The strongest support for there being a minimum of three cones comes from the data on color mixture. We can mix colors by taking three primary hues, one in the blue region of the spectrum, one in the red region, and another in the middle, green and yellow, region. It is possible to mix three hues chosen from these regions in various proportions and to reproduce any hue or saturation that human observers see. In the right mixture, they add together to produce white.

These facts of color mixture have always provided the strongest support for the Young-Helmholtz theory. Color-mixture data, however, do not prove that *only* three cones are involved in color vision. It would be perfectly possible to have four or more kinds of cones and still explain the data, merely by assuming that each color stimulates more than one cone—because their sensitivities overlap—and that the yellows cancel the blues, and the reds cancel the greens, as they do in the phenomena of complementary colors.

The Young-Helmholtz theory has always had trouble explaining many other phenomena of color vision. Why, for example, do we see yellow? The theory proposes to answer this by saying that the sensation of "yellow" is produced by the simultaneous stimulation of "red" and "green" cones, but this has never seemed very convincing. Color blindness has proved an especially difficult stumbling block for Young-Helmholtz theory. Why does color blindness run in "pairs"? The most common form of color blindness, for example, is red-green blindness, and after that yellow-blue blindness. Moreover, white-black vision is usually unimpaired in the color-blind person. How can this be when white is supposed to be the simple addition of red, green, and blue?

The theory does well with color mixture, but it is quite inadequate in accounting for many other phenomena. These too must be explained by any acceptable theory.

Hering theory. Another theory, sometimes named after its chief protagonist, Hering, is now more frequently called the *opponent-colors theory* [Hurvich and Jameson, 1957]. It assumes three *sets* of cones, all able to function in opposing ways. These are: white-black, red-green, and yellow-blue. Thus the theory assumes that the cones for brightness are separate from those for color. It further states that the processes for red oppose (cancel) those for green, while those for yellow oppose those for blue. As originally proposed, the theory held that each pair of processes took place in the same cell. It now seems more plausible to assume that there are four "color" cones and that these are linked to bipolar and ganglion cells in such a way that they function in opponent pairs.

This kind of theory has recently been gaining wider acceptance. It has always given a better explanation of color blindness than the Young-Helmholtz theory, and at the same time it does just as well with color mixture. It also handles nicely the law of complementary colors and the color circle. Now it is being supported by the work of physiologists recording electrical events in the retina.

COLOR "UNITS." By inserting extremely small electrodes, called *microelectrodes,* into the retina, physiologists have been able to record from single "units" of the retina [Granit, 1959]. They cannot see the electrode, so they cannot be certain what units or cells they record from. Chances are the units they record from in this way are not the rod or cone receptors, for it is believed that the receptors do not produce impulses. More likely, the units are bipolar cells or ganglion cells. For that reason, we speak of "units," rather than receptors.

With a microelectrode on a retinal unit, the experimenter can flash a light of a particular wavelength and record the number of impulses the flash sets off in the unit. By varying the intensity of the light, he can find some small number of impulses, say, four, that are easily counted. The intensity of light that produces this number of impulses is then regarded as the absolute threshold (see page 301). The number used is not important so long as it is kept the same throughout any one set of measurements. By varying the wavelength of the light flash and obtaining a threshold at each wavelength, the experimenter can obtain a curve of spectral sensitivity comparable to the visibility curve of the human observer. In this case, however, the curve refers to a particular neural unit in the eye, rather than to a large group of such units involved in human measurements.

Having measured the spectral sensitivity of one unit, the experimenter can move the position of his microelectrode and record from another unit. In this way he can explore the retina and measure the spectral sensitivity of a large sample of units. If the retina contains units of different spectral sensitivities, he should find that some units give one curve and other units give other curves. The eyes of many different animals have been studied in this way. The question is, What kinds of units are found?

Generally speaking, two kinds of units have been found. *Dominators* and *modulators* are the names that have been given to them. Dominators are units with broad spectral sensitivity; modulators are units with rather narrow spectral sensitivity, of the kind one would expect to serve in color vision.

Dominators. The spectral sensitivity of dominators is much like that of the rods and cones, and consequently like that of rhodopsin and iodopsin, respectively. In fact, there is hardly any doubt that the dominators are connected with the rod and cone receptors containing these different substances.

The fact that dominator units with spectral sensitivity like that of the cones exist independently of modulator units confirms the first assumption of the Hering opponent-colors theory. This is the assumption that color processes are separate from those producing white sensations, or brightness. The different assumption of the Young-Helmholtz theory that white is produced by the addition of activities in color receptors is not confirmed.

Modulators. Modulators are units whose sensitivity lies in a narrow spectral band, as shown in Figure 11.26. A modulator can be "named" according to the wavelength at which it has its peak of sensitivity. Distinguished in this way, many different modulators have been found, if one considers the dozens of animals that have been studied. Color vision, however, varies in animals. Some have none at all, some have a little and are comparable to a partially color-blind man, and some seem to have color vision comparable to normal man. In addition, some animals have photochemical substances different from man's; this accounts for different peaks of sensitivity both in the dominators and modulators. We can only guess from the structure of the retina, the extraction of photochemical pigments, and from what behavioral data may be available which animals have color vision most like that of man.

Probably several animals have, but one

THE FROG'S EYE APPEARS TO POSSESS FOUR COLOR UNITS:

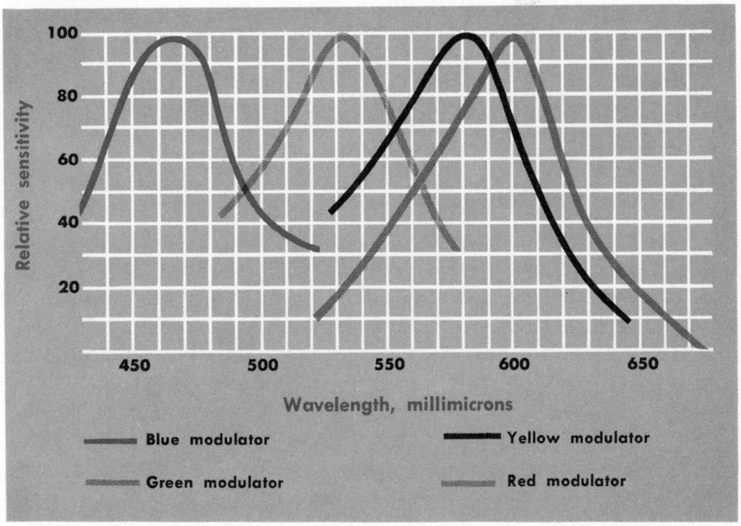

FIGURE 11.26. Modulator curves of the frog's eye. Each curve shows the sensitivity to different wavelengths of a unit touched by a microelectrode. Note that the units have their greatest sensitivities in the blue, green, yellow, and red regions of the spectrum, respectively [after Granit, 1959].

of them appears to be the frog. Like man, it has a mixed eye of both rods and cones. It also has a set of modulators that fit in with the things we know about human color vision. The modulators of the frog are shown in Figure 11.26. Reading from left to right, we first see a "blue" modulator with a peak at around 475 millimicrons. Altogether there are four, as we would expect from the opponent-colors theory.

The "green" unit is peaked at 530 millimicrons, somewhat above unique green at 515 millimicrons. Note, however, that stimulation anywhere along the spectrum, except at the extreme blue end, is likely to excite more than one receptor. According to the opponent-colors theory, we would expect unique green to lie at the point where the curves for yellow and blue cross, and hence cancel each other out. This is at 515 millimicrons where unique green is, in fact, found. At the red end of the spectrum, we can see why unique red cannot be found in the spectrum. The red and yellow units are so close together that stimulation, even beyond 650 millimicrons, mostly induces red, but still involves a yellow unit. For that reason, a little blue must be mixed with the red to cancel the tinge of yellow. Hence, unique red is extraspectral.

This, of course, is an oversimplified account of an extremely complex subject. It does show us, however, how work in physiology can explain some of the facts obtained in psychology. It also shows how we can go about testing some psychological theories.

What we learn from such physiological work may be summarized as follows: Our sensitivity to lights of different wavelength is explained by the spectral absorption of photochemical substances in the eye. Our ability to adapt to the dark and to the light is similarly explained by the decomposition and resynthesis of these substances. In addition, our ability to see colors and the laws of color mixture, including the law of complementary colors, are accounted for by a limited number of color "units" in the retina. We have not yet pinned down what these color units are, but it appears that different cones contain photochemical substances of different spectral sensitivity and that there are four types of cones, arranged in two opponent pairs, as well as "color-blind cones" that give only the experience of white or brightness.

Summary

1. Only electromagnetic energy having wavelengths between about 400 and 800 millimicrons is visible to the eye.

2. The eye has a lens that focuses an inverted image on a photosensitive surface, the retina.

3. The sensitive elements in the retina are the rods and cones. These are connected to the brain via an intricate network of cells and nerve fibers. The cones are more concentrated in the fovea of the retina, which is used in looking directly at an object. The rods are relatively more numerous in the periphery of the retina.

4. The lens of the eye changes in shape to accommodate to near or to far objects. If the lens has an irregular surface, it produces the visual defect known as astigmatism. If the eyeball is too long or too short, the person may be nearsighted or farsighted. Farsightedness increases with age.

5. Three kinds of perception are necessary to classify all colors into one scheme: (a) hue, (b) saturation, and (c) brightness. Hue is what is commonly meant by color: blue, green, yellow, red, or shades in between. Saturation is the relative amount of color, as distinguished from gray, in a stimulus. Brightness refers to the relative lightness or darkness of the stimulus.

6. Hues can be arranged in a circle, saturations as steps on the radii of the circle; and brightness as a third dimension. To portray all three, a color solid is used.

7. Certain hues are complementary, e.g., yellow and greenish-blue, and red and bluish-green. Every possible hue has a complementary hue approximately opposite it on the color circle. When hues that are not complementary are mixed, the result is an intervening hue on the color circle.

8. Total color blindness is very rare, but partial color blindness occurs in 1 out of every 25 people. Partial color blindness shows up as a confusion of certain pairs of colors. Three general kinds of color confusion have been distinguished.

9. Some individuals are color-weak rather than color-blind. Color blindness is a sex-linked hereditary characteristic that follows rules described in Chapter 2.

10. Many people are unaware that they are color-blind because they have learned the proper color names to use with objects, but their defect can be detected by any one of several tests.

11. The eye can adapt to a wide range of illuminations. In dark adaptation, there is a shift from cone function to rod function. In the course of this shift, the eye's best sensitivity to wavelengths changes from about 555 millimicrons to about 505 millimicrons.

12. Visual acuity, measured in eye examinations, is important in a number of occupations. It is better in the fovea than in the periphery of the eye; nothing at all can be seen at the blind spot.

13. Visual acuity is much better under high illumination than under dim light. It is also better when the contrast between an object and its background is high. Finally, it is better when the surrounding illumination is about the same as that on the object, and not more or less.

14. When light strikes the retina, it decomposes photosensitive substances in the rods and cones. One substance, called rhodopsin, is found in the rods; its spectral absorption corresponds to human spectral sensitivity in the dark. A second substance, iodopsin, has roughly the same spectral sensitivity as the cones.

15. Electrical records can be made in the intact human eye during stimulation by light. One of the waves, the *b* wave, recorded in this way can serve as an index of visual thresholds in various kinds of animals.

16. Two principal theories of color vision have been proposed. The Young-Helmholtz theory postulates three color receptors, respectively most sensitive in the blue, green, and red regions of the spectrum. The Hering opponent-colors theory postulates three pairs of receptors: white-black, blue-yellow, and red-green.

17. The Hering theory seems best able to explain various phenomena of color vision. It is also supported by microelectrode experiments on color "units" in the retina. These units have their respective maximum sensitivities in the blue, green, yellow, and red regions of the spectrum.

Suggestions for further reading

Bartley, S. H. *Principles of perception.* New York: Harper, 1958.
An introductory text on perception with an emphasis on vision.

Bartley, S. H. *Vision: a study of its basis.* New York: Van Nostrand, 1941.
A book emphasizing physiological processes in vision.

Boring, E. G. *Sensation and perception in the history of experimental psychology.* New York: Appleton-Century-Crofts, 1942.
An authoritative history of experimental work in vision.

Chapanis, A., Garner, W. R., and Morgan, C. T. *Applied experimental psychology.* New York: Wiley, 1949.
A text on the applications of experimental

psychology to engineering problems, including especially visual problems.

Committee on Undersea Warfare. *Human factors in undersea warfare.* Washington: National Research Council, 1949.
A study containing several chapters on vision with emphasis on applications to practical problems.

Davson, H. *The physiology of the eye.* New York: McGraw-Hill–Blakiston, 1950.
A text covering the physiological functions of the eye.

Evans, R. M. *An introduction to color.* New York: Wiley, 1948.
A readable and well-illustrated book on the fundamentals of color vision and on the everyday use of color.

Gibson, J. J. *The perception of the visual world.* Boston: Houghton Mifflin, 1950.

An analysis of the more complex phenomena of visual perception.

Hartridge, H. *Colours and how we see them.* London: G. Bell, 1949.
An interesting book covering phenomena of color vision.

Morgan, C. T., and Stellar, E. *Physiological psychology* (2d ed.). New York: McGraw-Hill, 1950.
A text that includes chapters on the physiological basis of vision.

Pirenne, M. H. *Vision and the eye.* London: Chapman and Hall, 1948.
The basic facts about vision and the eye, presented in readable fashion.

Weston, H. C. *Sight, light, and efficiency.* London: H. K. Lewis, 1949.
A book emphasizing the visual aspects of work and efficiency.

CHAPTER TWELVE

Hearing
& lower senses

VISION IS PROBABLY our most important asset in knowing and learning about our world, but hearing runs it a close second. Through hearing, we can understand speech, and speech is our chief medium for imparting and acquiring knowledge. Through hearing, too, we receive a great many signals and cues—the warning automobile horn, the chime of the clock, the fire engine's siren, the footsteps of a person approaching from behind, and many other common cues. Through hearing, many people also find a great source of enjoyment in music. Thus hearing is an important sense in appreciating our environment. In this chapter we shall consider the principles that explain how we hear.

We shall also discuss other senses, some-times called the *lower senses,* which have already been referred to in Chapter 10. They may be classified in several ways, but the classification that best suits our present purpose is the following:

Chemical senses
    Taste
    Smell
Skin senses
    Touch
    Warmth
    Cold
    Pain
Deep senses
    Muscle sense (kinesthesis)
    Vestibular sense (of equilibrium)
    Organic senses
The first part of the chapter will cover

hearing, the latter part the lower senses. The perception of speech, a specialized aspect of hearing, will be treated in the final section.

Physical basis of hearing

Before we can understand the sense of hearing, we must study the physical stimulus for hearing, because it determines in many ways what we hear. If you were asked what you hear, you probably would say, "Sound." That is true; you do hear sound. To say that, however, is not enough. You should also be able to distinguish between physical sound, which stimulates the ear, and perceived sound, which is the sound you actually experience.

SOUND WAVES. The air, as you know, is not a vacuum; it is a collection of molecules. These molecules are always moving about at random, colliding with one another and exerting pressure on one another. The more closely packed together they are, the greater the air pressure; the fewer they are, the less the pressure. When there is no sound or wind, the molecules are evenly distributed in the air around us, and thus they have a uniform pressure. When there is a sound, however, they increase and decrease in pressure, and the changes in pressure move through the air as waves do along the surface of water. It is, in fact, such changes in pressure that constitute the physical sound that we hear.

Sound waves are ordinarily generated by the vibration of a physical object in the air. When such an object vibrates, the molecules close to the object are pushed together, and thus are put under *positive pressure.* The molecules that are under positive pressure push against the molecules close to them, and these in turn transmit the pressure to neighboring molecules. A wave of positive pressure moves through the air in much the same way that ripples move on the water. Sound-pressure waves, however, travel much faster than waves of water; at sea level, they travel about 760 miles per hour, or 1,100 feet per second.

However, most objects, when they are struck, do not move in just one direction. A violin string, for example, vibrates back and forth when it is plucked. As the string moves first in one direction, a positive pressure wave begins to propagate through the air; but when the string swings back to its original position and beyond, a little vacuum (or negative pressure) is created just behind the wave of positive pressure. This vacuum moves with the speed of sound just as the positive pressure wave does. These alternations in air pressure moving along through the air are called a *sound wave,* and this sound wave is the physical stimulus for everything we hear. Different vibrations produce different sound waves. To understand the physical stimulus for hearing, then, we must understand the characteristics of sound waves.

SINE WAVES. Common observation tells us that there is an infinite variety of possible sound waves. We regard one kind of wave, however, as the simplest, because this one, called a *sine wave,* can be used in different ways to duplicate or analyze any other kind. In Figure 12.1 is a diagram of the sine wave, so called because it may be mathematically expressed by the sine function of trigonometry. It is produced when a single vibrating object moves back and forth *freely* and changes the pressure of the air. The sound that we hear when we listen to a sine wave is called a *pure tone.* Since sine waves can be produced only with special equipment, people usually hear a pure tone only in the laboratory. Some musical instruments, such as the flute, however, can produce notes that are almost pure tones.

If sound waves are changes in the pressure of air, you may wonder how we are able to take pictures of them. There are, in fact, several ways of *seeing,* as well as of hearing, sound waves. The one used most often in the laboratory is a cathode-ray oscilloscope, which has a screen very much like a television screen. If we have a microphone with which to convert sound waves into electrical signals, we can lead its wires into the oscilloscope and see the waves on the screen. The relative height of the waves represents the amount of change in air pressure, and the distance across the screen represents time. From such pictures we can make two different kinds of measurements of sine waves: (1) pitch and frequency, and (2) loudness and intensity.

PITCH AND FREQUENCY OF TONES. First, we can count how often the sine wave alternates between positive and negative pressure—how often it goes up and down—in any given period of time. This measure is called the *frequency*, and we ordinarily state it in *cycles per second*. The sound wave at the top of Figure 12.1 alternates fewer times per second than the two lower sine waves, so it has a lower frequency. To be more specific, if a sine wave goes to positive pressure, then to negative pressure, and back again 500 times in a second, its frequency is 500 cycles per second, for the sine wave has completed that many cycles in 1 second.

It is important to note the difference between frequency and pitch. The first is physical, the second psychological. As we have just pointed out, frequency is a *physical* characteristic of a tone. Pitch, on the other hand, is a *psychological* characteristic; otherwise said, pitch is a sensory *attribute* of experience. The distinction between the two is often difficult to grasp because, as we explained in Chaper 10, people tend to think of sensory experience as a carbon copy of a physical stimulus. Moreover, they do not readily understand how we can measure an attribute of experience separately from a physical stimulus. The fact, however, that pitch and frequency are different is illustrated in the following experiment [Stevens and Volkmann, 1940]:

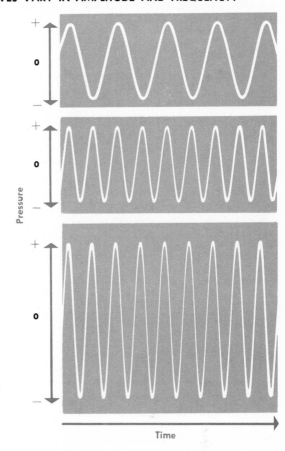

FIGURE 12.1. Three sine waves with different amplitudes and frequencies. The two upper sine waves have the same amplitude or pressure, but the middle one has a frequency twice that of the upper one. The two lower sine waves have the same frequency, but the bottom one has an amplitude twice that of the middle one.

An observer is provided with a set of earphones through which tones of different frequency can be presented to him. He is given two switches which he may depress. Pressing one turns on a standard tone of a frequency set by the experimenter. Pressing the other turns on a comparison tone whose frequency can be set by the observer merely by twisting a knob. He is instructed to set the frequency of the comparison tone so that it is perceived by him to be twice the *pitch* of the standard tone. He does this by listening first to the standard tone, then to the comparison tone, in alternation. He then adjusts the comparison tone until he is satisfied that he has set it at twice the pitch of the standard tone. The experimenter notes the frequency chosen.

The procedure is repeated with different standard tones. For example, the first standard tone might be 400 cycles per second, and the observer's choice of a tone that is twice its pitch might be roughly 1,000 cycles per second. This might serve as a standard in the next observation when the observer might choose 3,500 as being twice the pitch of 1,000 cycles per second, and so on. The numbers are only approximate, but they illustrate the point. Observations are repeated until there are many measures of "twice the pitch" throughout the audible range.

From measurements of this kind a scale can be constructed showing quantitatively the relation between frequency and pitch (see Figure 12.2). Such a scale, called a *pitch scale*, is not a straight line; rather it is curved. Pitch rises very slowly below 1,000 cycles and above 4,000 cycles. Between 1,000 and 4,000 cycles, it is more nearly proportional to frequency. Even so, a tone of 4,000 cycles has little more than twice the pitch of a 1,000-cycle tone. From 4,000 cycles to 20,000 cycles, a fivefold change in frequency, pitch increases by only 50 per cent. This fact demonstrates conclusively that pitch and frequency are not the same, because pitch does not increase or decrease in exact proportion to frequency.

This conclusion is strengthened by another fact we shall mention only briefly. The pitch of a tone depends not only on frequency, but also on intensity. The relationship between the two is complicated, but in general the pitch of a low frequency falls as it is made more intense, and that of a high frequency rises as its intensity increases. Thus the experience of pitch can be made to vary without changing frequency at all.

LOUDNESS AND THE INTENSITY OF TONES. A second kind of measure of a sound wave is its *intensity*. In Figure 12.1 intensity is shown as the height of the wave, and this height represents the pressure of the wave. The two bottom sine waves of Figure 12.1 have the same frequency but different amplitudes or intensities. Thus, while frequency gives us a measure of how often the sound wave changes from positive to negative pressure, intensity gives us a measure of how great the pressure changes are.

PITCH IS A PSYCHOLOGICAL DIMENSION OR ATTRIBUTE; FREQUENCY, A PHYSICAL DIMENSION :

FIGURE 12.2. The pitch scale. Units of pitch are called mels. The pitch of a 1,000-cycle tone is arbitrarily assigned a value of 1,000 mels. Tones that sound twice as high in pitch are assigned 2,000 mels; those that sound half as high, 500 mels. In this way, a pitch scale, relating pitch to frequency, has been constructed [after Stevens and Volkmann, 1940].

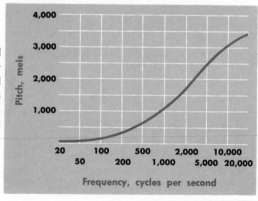

CHAPTER TWELVE

Scientists have developed a special scale for measuring the intensities of tones and sounds of all kinds. The range of sound intensities that people can hear is very great. The loudest sound that people can listen to without experiencing discomfort has a pressure about one million times as great as the weakest sound that is just audible. So if we were to measure intensities in actual sound pressures, we should have to deal with a very large scale of numbers. Consequently, we use the *decibel* (db) as our unit of measurement.

The decibel as a unit for expressing sound intensity has two main features: First, it represents a *ratio* of two intensities, not a difference between them (see Chapter 13). When two intensities are expressed in decibels, the numbers tell us that one intensity is so many times the other intensity, but they do not say what either intensity is. Secondly, a decibel is so defined that 20 decibels represents a ratio of 10 times; 40 decibels, 100 times; and so on up to 100 decibels which represents a ratio of 100,000 times. (A person familiar with logarithms can figure out for himself what any number of decibels means if he keeps in mind that the number of decibels is equal to 20 times the logarithm of the ratio of two sound pressures.)

In order for such a scale to be meaningful, it must have a starting point. Scientists have arbitrarily agreed to use a pressure of 0.0002 dyne per square centimeter—a dyne is a unit of pressure—as a starting point because this is close to the absolute threshold. When this point is used as a reference, we talk about the decibel scale as the scale of *sound-pressure level* (SPL).

For most practical purposes we can simply regard a decibel scale as a set of numbers, like a scale of temperature, and then learn that certain numbers correspond to certain loudnesses. To give you an idea what the numbers mean, Figure 12.3 shows the scale of sound-pressure level for some

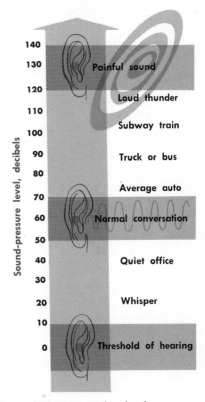

FIGURE 12.3. The sound-pressure level of familiar sounds. Each of the sounds indicated on the right has a sound-pressure level (intensity) of approximately the number of decibels shown on the left.

sounds with which you are familiar. If, when we talk about different sound-pressure levels, you are not sure what they mean, reference to this chart will at least give you a rough idea of how loud the sounds are.

As in the case of frequency, intensity is a physical characteristic; it is not the same as the psychological characteristic of loudness. The latter, like pitch, is an *attribute* of auditory experience. Although closely correlated with intensity, it does not increase or decrease in exact proportion to changes in intensity. We know this because we have been able to construct loudness scales that are comparable to the pitch scale illustrated in Figure 12.2. The shape of the scale is different, but the general point is the same. In each case, the attribute can be measured on a psychological scale that is different from the related physical scale.

Just as frequency corresponds most closely to the pitch of tones, intensity corresponds most closely to the loudness of tones. Once again, the two do not correspond perfectly. At high sound pressures, for example, a difference in intensity of 10 decibels sounds like a big difference in loudness. At low sound pressures, this much difference in intensity sounds like only a small difference in loudness. In fact, as we shall see later, decibel differences that cannot even be noticed at low intensities are easily discriminated at high intensities. `

TIMBRE AND THE COMPLEXITY OF TONES. Sine waves are extensively used in the laboratory for the study of hearing, but they are seldom encountered outside the laboratory. Rather, the sounds produced by objects in our normal environment are made up of *complex waves*. Three examples of such waves, as seen on an oscilloscope, are shown in Figure 12.4. They may be of any conceivable shape, but in general, they are either *periodic* or *aperiodic*. This means that they have a repetitive pattern occurring over and over again or they consist of waves of various heights and widths in more or less random order. In Figure 12.4, the top two tracings, one of a harmonica tone and the other of the voiced sound "oh," are examples of periodic waves; the lower tracing, of a hissing noise, illustrates an aperiodic complex wave.

In 1822 a French mathematician named Fourier showed that any periodic function can be expressed as the sum of a number of different sine waves. This fact provides a very simple technique for describing a complex periodic wave. To describe a sine wave, all we need to know is its frequency and intensity. For a complex wave, we simply

A MUSICAL TONE OR A SUSTAINED "OH" IS PERIODIC; A HISSING NOISE, APERIODIC:

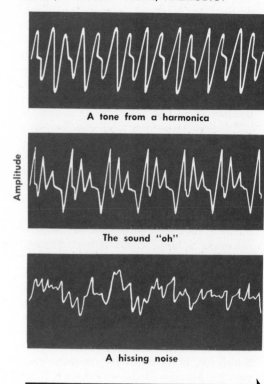

A tone from a harmonica

The sound "oh"

A hissing noise

Time

FIGURE 12.4. Oscillographic pictures of three complex sound waves. The wave at the top is a musical note played on a harmonica. The middle wave is the sustained vowel "oh." These two sound waves are periodic because the same pattern repeats itself. The sound wave at the bottom is noise; it is an aperiodic wave because it is completely irregular.

need to know the frequency and intensity of each of the sine-wave components of the complex wave. Thus we might describe the tone of a musical instrument by saying that it has a sound-pressure level of 70 decibels at 400 cycles per second, 62 decibels at 800 cycles per second, 43 decibels at 1,200 cycles per second, 29 decibels at 1,600 cycles per second, etc. This kind of description of a complex tone is known as a *Fourier analysis*.

Notice that in this example each of the frequencies involved is some multiple of the lowest frequency. All musical instruments produce complex tones of this type. The lowest frequency is called the *fundamental,* and all other frequencies are called *harmonics.* The frequency which is twice as great as the fundamental is called the *second harmonic;* that which is three times as great, the *third harmonic;* etc.

The complexity of a tone, then, is a matter of the number and the intensities of the different sine waves that make up the complete tone. The psychological counterpart of complexity is *timbre,* or *tonal quality,* and it is timbre that lets us distinguish rather easily different musical instruments and different voices from one another. A pure tone, for example, sounds very thin and lacking in tonal quality compared to the complex tone produced by an instrument such as the violin. In contrast, we would describe the violin tone as rich. The difference is that the violin tone has many strong harmonics. It is not just more timbre or less timbre, however, that distinguishes different instruments. Rather the timbres of different instruments are *different,* and we learn that each instrument has a characteristic timbre.

There are, of course, other sounds that have little or no tonal quality, and these are called *noises.* In Figure 12.4 is a picture of a noise. In that instance the noise was made by blowing air across a microphone. Notice that the picture of the noise is not periodic; it does not repeat itself in any regular pattern as do the sounds of musical instruments. That is because it is made up of many different frequencies which are not multiples or harmonics of one another; rather, the frequencies are mixed more or less randomly. When the mixture is really random, we speak of *random noise.* In other instances, such as clicks or tapping sounds, the noises are not completely random, for they contain certain dominant frequencies. They are, nevertheless, noises because they contain many frequencies that are not multiples of one another.

How the ear works

So far we have described the physical sounds that may impinge on the ears and the psychological attributes of pitch, loudness, and timbre to which they give rise. The next step is to bridge the gap between the two by describing the organs of hearing and their workings. In this way we can see how the ear translates physical sounds into nerve impulses, thereby providing the information for auditory experience.

CONDUCTION IN THE EAR. Figure 12.5 shows a cross section of the major features of the ear. The ear consists of three principal parts: the outer ear, which collects the sound; the middle ear, which transmits the sound; and the inner ear, which transforms the sound into nerve impulses.

The outer ear, or *pinna,* besides being a decoration, collects sounds, which then travel through a small air-filled duct, called the *auditory canal,* to the eardrum. The *eardrum* is a thin membrane stretched tightly across the inner end of the canal. Alternations in the pressure of the sound wave move this small membrane back and forth. The oscillation of the eardrum in turn moves three small bones, the *ossicles,* so that vibration is conducted through the middle ear to the entrance to the *cochlea* of the inner ear. The bones of the middle ear are connected like a series of levers. Hence sound is mechanically transmitted through the middle ear.

THE COCHLEA. The inner ear is by far the most complicated of the three major parts of the ear. It consists of two kinds of sense organs, one concerned in the sense of balance, and the other in hearing. The organs for balance are called the vestibular sense organs and will be discussed later in this chapter. The sense organs for hearing are contained in a bony structure. Because this structure is spiraled like a snail, it is called the *cochlea,* meaning snail shell. The cochlea has three different ducts or canals spiraling around together, separated from each other by membranes. Each duct is filled with fluid. Figure 12.6 shows a much enlarged cross section of these canals and gives their names. Sound vibrations enter them from the ossicles of the middle ear through a membrane known as the *oval window,* located at the end of the vestibular canal, but too small to show in the drawing. Thus when a sound wave moves the ossicles back and forth, this movement is transmitted to the fluid of the cochlea.

The important event that takes place in the cochlea is the stimulation of the nerve cells—called *hair cells* because they have hairs on their ends—located in the organ of Corti on the basilar membrane separating two of the canals. Pressure changes of the fluid in the canals stimulate these hair cells, causing nerve impulses to be generated and to be conducted through the auditory nerve to the brain.

The basilar membrane beneath the hair cells varies in width from one end of the cochlea to the other, and its width correlates with the frequencies of sounds to which the hair cells are most sensitive. It is narrowest at the end toward the oval window and becomes progressively wider toward the other end.

THEORIES OF HEARING.   With this last statement, we have now covered the anatomical facts of importance in understanding the function of the ear, and particularly the cochlea. Scientists have long been interested in relating these facts to our sensory experience of loudness and pitch [Wever, 1949].

Loudness is not much of a problem. We know that sense organs usually generate more and more nerve impulses as the intensity of a stimulus increases. The number of impulses generated is not always directly proportional to the intensity of a stimulus, but there is nevertheless a relationship between the two. Hence it is reasonable to assume that the loudness of a tone is deter-

SOUND TRAVELS THROUGH THE EXTERNAL AND THE MIDDLE EAR TO THE INNER EAR:

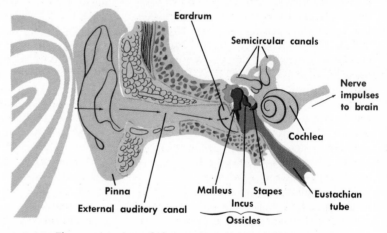

FIGURE 12.5. The human ear. The ear consists of three principal parts: the external ear, the middle ear, and the inner ear. The external ear consists of the pinna and a canal that conducts sound waves to the eardrum. The eardrum, marking the division between the external and middle ear, is set into vibration by sound waves. This vibration is transmitted by the bones of the middle ear (malleus, incus, and stapes) to the fluid of the cochlea. Sound waves in this fluid stimulate the sensory cells of the cochlea.

CHAPTER TWELVE

FIGURE 12.6. A cross-sectional diagram of the cochlea. Sound waves in the canals of the cochlea deflect the organ of Corti on the basilar membrane and in this way initiate nerve impulses in the fibers of the auditory nerve.

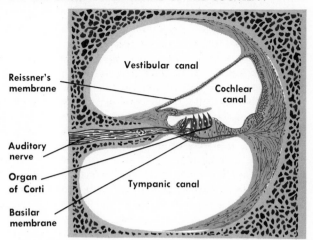

mined by the number of impulses generated and propagated down the auditory nerve to the brain. All the evidence we have both in hearing and in the other senses confirms this conclusion.

Pitch is not so easily disposed of. There are many theories of the action of the cochlea in pitch perception. At one extreme is the *Helmholtz resonance theory,* and at the other extreme the so-called *telephone theory.* The telephone theory likens the cochlea to a microphone and the auditory nerve to a telephone wire. It proposes that the pitch heard by a person is determined by the frequency of impulses traveling up the auditory nerve. The greater this frequency, the higher the pitch.

When modern methods of recording nerve impulses became available, the frequency of impulses in the auditory nerve was measured while presenting tones of different frequency to an animal (usually a cat or guinea pig). From such measurements, it became clear that the telephone theory of pitch could at best be true only for relatively low frequencies, because the auditory nerve cannot transmit distinctly different frequencies above a limit of roughly 4,000 cycles. At very low frequencies, up to 500 or possibly 1,000 cycles, a group of impulses in the

nerve corresponds to every cycle of the tone, and hence the auditory nerve behaves in somewhat the same way as a telephone wire. At higher frequencies, the nerve fibers are unable to "follow" every cycle. They therefore start "skipping" every second or third cycle of the tone. Since different fibers skip different cycles, the nerve as a whole still follows the frequency with volleys of impulses made up of different combinations of fibers. At still higher frequencies—no one knows exactly where, but probably around 4,000 cycles—this system of volleys breaks down, so that impulses in the nerve no longer correspond to individual cycles of the stimulating tone. Hence, we conclude that a telephone theory cannot be true for the perception of pitch above 4,000 cycles, if indeed it applies below that.

The Helmholtz resonance theory, as originally conceived, was that the basilar membrane consisted of fibers of different length, arranged much as the strings of a piano are arranged, and that different "strings" resonated to different frequencies of a tone. Thus the *place* stimulated in the cochlea determined the pitch experienced. For this to be true, fibers from different parts of the cochlea would have to maintain their identity and connect with different parts of the

HEARING AND LOWER SENSES 375

brain. In other words, places in the cochlea would have to be represented by a corresponding "map" in the brain.

In general, experiments support a *place theory* much better than they do the telephone theory, and most scientists concerned with the problem today take a place theory for granted. We have been able to demonstrate that different frequencies do indeed stimulate certain parts of the cochlea more than others, though the analysis in the cochlea is relatively crude. Any frequency activates a relatively large area of the cochlea, but activates one region more than another [Bekesy, 1960]. We know, too, that in the higher centers of the brain, there is a corresponding "map" representing different parts of the cochlea so that one region responds more to one frequency than to another [Ades, 1959]. These maps are not nearly so detailed at low frequencies as they are at higher ones. It is possible, then, that a telephone type of transmission of impulses plays some role in pitch perception at low frequencies. In general, however, a place theory is adequate for explaining various phenomena of pitch perception. So we are fairly confident that the position of stimulation of the basilar membrane is the principal factor in determining the perception of pitch.

The limits of hearing

We have now come to understand the stimulus for hearing and have seen how the ear converts a sound wave into a pattern of neural impulses that eventually determines what we hear. The mere fact that a physical sound exists, however, does not ensure that we shall hear anything—even when the hearing mechanism is in good working order—because there are limits to what we can hear. We cannot hear every intensity of a sound wave, nor can we hear all possible frequencies.

INTENSITY LIMITS. It is probably obvious that intensity limits a person's hearing. If a tone is too weak, we cannot hear it at all, and even though physical measurement might show that a sound wave exists, a sound wave that is too weak cannot be an adequate stimulus. As indicated in Figure 12.3, a sound-pressure level of zero decibels is approximately the lowest intensity of sound that normal human beings ever hear. However, as Figure 12.7 shows, the intensity of many frequencies must be even greater than that to reach the absolute threshold, that is, the just-audible intensity.

The curve of Figure 12.7 depicts absolute thresholds for tones of different frequencies. From it we see that hearing is best for frequencies between 1,000 and 4,000 cycles per second. At a frequency of 50 cycles per second, for example, it requires a sound pressure about 1,000 times as great for a tone to be heard as it does for a frequency of 2,000 cycles per second. Similarly at higher frequencies, greater intensities are required for hearing. Note too that there is an upper limit of sound pressure, because sound pressures that are too great arouse pain. If you will turn back to Figure 12.3, you can see that this level is approximately 130 decibels, and that it is about the same at all frequencies.

Now refer again to the curve of Figure 12.7. It suggests that tones in the middle range of frequencies are much louder than those either higher or lower. At low intensities, this is actually true. But at higher intensities, all tones tend to sound equally loud. For example, at a sound pressure level of 110 or 120 decibels, tones of all frequencies are about equally loud. Thus the differences in absolute thresholds do not carry over into differences of loudness at high sound-pressure levels.

FREQUENCY LIMITS. Just as there is a limiting range of the intensities we can hear, so is there a limiting range of frequencies. Generally speaking, we can say that the audible range of frequencies is between 20 and 20,000 cycles per second. As can be seen from Figure 12.7, however, this range is not a precisely defined one. Tones at the extremes of this range of frequencies can be heard only at very high intensities, and at lower intensities the range is considerably smaller.

So that we may have a more realistic idea of the frequency limits of hearing, the tones of a piano are also indicated in Figure 12.7. From this we can see that the range of notes is considerably narrower than the range of frequencies we can actually hear, particularly at the higher frequencies. It is, in fact, generally true that we seldom hear frequencies near the higher limits. Speech, for example, contains very few frequencies above 7,000 cycles per second. Tones at these very high frequencies hardly sound like tones at all; rather they sound weak, very thin, and almost without a real pitch. Perhaps you have noticed that even the highest notes on a piano have very little tonal character compared with the notes in the middle range of frequencies.

At very low frequencies, we can still hear sounds, but they are not tonal. Instead, we actually hear the individual pressure changes rather than a tone corresponding to the frequency of the note. A tone of 8 or 10 cycles per second, for example, is a throbbing sound. In practice, it is very difficult to produce a pure tone at these very low frequencies, and as a result, it is difficult to measure the frequency at which we no longer hear a tone. A related difficulty is that these very low frequency tones have harmonics, and the harmonics may sound tonal even though the fundamental frequency does not—at least with present techniques for producing very low tones.

INTENSITY DIFFERENCES. Our ears not only limit the range of intensities and frequencies we can hear, they also limit the amount of change or difference between two tones that we can detect. To find this limit we sound two tones, one at a time, and ask

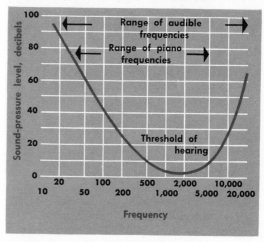

FIGURE 12.7. The absolute threshold of hearing for pure tones of different frequencies.

observers to tell us whether they are the same or different. Then we change either the intensity or the frequency, making the difference smaller or larger, until we have the difference that the observer can just detect. Psychologists have measured this limit with great care for practically all possible intensities and frequencies.

Both the frequency and the intensity of a tone affect the limit for detecting differences in intensity. Detection is poorer for weak tones than it is for loud ones. For most practical purposes, however, a number to remember is 1 decibel, for 1 decibel is a difference in intensity that we can always detect as long as sounds are reasonably loud. The other point worth noting is that detection of a difference is poorer for the very low and very high frequencies than it is for the middle ones.

FREQUENCY DIFFERENCES. Practically the same rules hold for discriminating differences in frequency, though of course the measurement is different. In this case we find the smallest difference in *frequency* (cycles per second) that a person can detect. If we express this in a percentage by dividing the difference by the frequency of one of the tones, we have a measure that is relatively constant for all kinds of tones. Actually, as in the case of intensity, the per cent that can be detected is better for high frequencies than it is for low ones, and it is better for the middle range of frequencies than it is for high tones or low tones. To demonstrate this last point, you might strike some keys on the piano, and note that it is relatively easy to tell the difference between two adjacent keys in the middle of the keyboard, but relatively hard to do it in the extreme bass or treble.

One should not confuse the ability to detect differences with the ability to identify a single note or tone—what is sometimes called absolute pitch. A very few fortunate people can identify nearly all the notes of the musical scale when they hear them played singly. Most of us have a hard time telling which octave a note is in and can identify accurately no more than 8 or 10 different ones. For most purposes, however, we do not need this ability because the important task is usually to perceive the difference between two tones rather than the identity of a single one.

MASKING. All that we have been saying about the limits of hearing assumes that people are listening in relative quiet. The limits of hearing can be quite different, however, if more than one tone is sounded at a time or if somebody is making a noise when we are trying to listen to a tone. Then it is not so easy to hear a tone or to detect a difference between two tones. Such a change in the limits of hearing is known as *masking*.

You are all familiar with the masking of sounds by other sounds in everyday life. If you are talking on the telephone and there is a noise around you or in the telephone circuit, you cannot hear so well; or if an airplane flies overhead during a lecture, you may not hear what the lecturer is saying. Research workers have measured the effects of masking on the limits of hearing as carefully as they have measured hearing in the quiet, and masking turns out to be a complex subject. The main points, however, are these: First, tones near together in frequency mask each other well—that is, each tone makes it hard for the other to be heard—but tones far apart in frequency do not mask each other very well. Secondly, low tones mask high tones better than the other way around. Consequently, if two tones are sounded together, you will be able to hear the tone of lower pitch more easily.

Dissonance and consonance

Those who are interested in music usually like to know what it is about two or more tones played together that makes them sound consonant (harmonious) or dissonant. When two or more musical notes are played together and produce a pleasing sound, we speak of the notes as being *harmonious* or *consonant;* they seem to go together. If the notes are not pleasing, we speak of *dissonance* or say that the notes are not in harmony.

What accounts for consonance and dissonance? Part of the answer is in the interaction of the harmonics of the two tones. Octave notes always sound harmonious because the harmonics of the two notes fit together. Suppose, for example, that someone plays two notes whose fundamentals are 200 and 400 cycles per second. (The 2:1 ratio means that the notes are an octave apart.) The first note has sine-wave harmonics with frequencies of 200, 400, 600, 800, 1,000, 1,200, etc., cycles per second. The second note has harmonics with frequencies of 400, 800, 1,200, 1,600, etc., cycles per second. Notice that all the harmonics of the second tone match the harmonics of the first tone. The result is that we hear a single merged tone, and the two tones together sound consonant.

As another, more complex, example of

consonant tones, let us take two notes of 200 and 300 cycles per second. This ratio of 3:2 gives a musical interval known as a perfect *fifth*. The harmonics of the lower-pitched tone are the same as above, while the harmonics of the higher-pitched tone are 300, 600, 900, 1,200, etc. The entire series of frequencies will be 200, 300, 400, 600, 800, 900, 1,000, etc. Notice that here all the frequencies are either 200 or 100 cycles apart, forming a regular pattern. This orderly relation of the harmonics also makes a consonant sound.

To illustrate a dissonant pair of notes, suppose we play a note of 100 cycles per second (which has harmonics at every even hundred cycles per second) and a note of 178 cycles per second. These two notes are a full note less than an octave apart, as a D and the C above it would be. The harmonics of the second note are 356, 534, 712, 890, 1,068, etc., cycles per second. In this case the harmonics of 712 and 890 cycles per second do not correspond with the harmonics of 700 and 900 cycles per second of the lower note. The resulting roughness makes the pair of notes sound dissonant.

We must warn you, however, that dissonance and consonance are not entirely explained merely by the presence or absence of particular harmonics. We do not know all the reasons why some combinations of tones sound harmonious and others do not. Undoubtedly, learning plays a part. So does the sequence of sounds, for a certain combination may sound harmonious in some melodies, but not in others. The relations of the harmonics are thus only one important factor in consonance.

Auditory space perception

Hearing does not provide us with very adequate information about the size or position of objects in space. Nevertheless, we can perceive the direction of sound and its distance from us fairly well. So we do have some auditory space perception.

CUES TO DIRECTION. In visual perception (see Chapter 10), the fact that we have two eyes usually helps us considerably in judging the depth of an object, but one does just as well as two for judging the direction of an object. In hearing, however, the rules are essentially reversed. To tell *direction* from auditory cues, we must have two ears, although one ear is just about as good as two for judging *depth*.

There are three types of *binaural* cues for perceiving the direction of a sound. (The term "binaural" refers to the use of two ears.) The first and most important is *time difference*. If a click is sounded off to one side of your head, the sound travels through the air at a rate of 1,100 feet per second and arrives at the nearer ear before it arrives at the farther one. This effect is shown diagrammatically in Figure 12.8. When the source of the sound is directly opposite one ear, the difference in time of arrival at the two ears is at a maximum and is about ½ millisecond (or 1/2,000 second). When the source of sound is directly ahead, then the sound wave reaches both ears at the same time. At positions in between, the difference in time of arrival at the two ears will naturally be more than zero and less than the maximum value. Thus the time difference serves as a cue to the direction of the sound. The time differences are, of course, very small, and it is remarkable that people can use them as such effective cues to the direction of a sound.

A second binaural cue is *intensity difference*. It works because intensity decreases as the square of the distance and also because the head casts a sound shadow, and the ear opposite to any sound source lies in this shadow. As you can see from Figure 12.8, the head makes a shadow because a sound coming from one side must go around the head to get to the other side, and before it gets there a great deal of it is absorbed. As a consequence, the sound reaching the farther ear is much weaker than that striking the nearer ear. Once again, as in the case of time difference, the amount of this

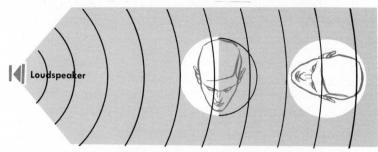

FIGURE 12.8. How we perceive the direction of a sound. Each arc represents successive crests of the sound wave as it travels from the source, which in this case is a loudspeaker. Note that when the head is facing the source, the sound wave reaches both ears at the same time, but that it reaches the nearer ear first when the head is turned away from the speaker. In addition, the ear that is farther away receives a less intense sound because of the shadow cast by the head.

shadow depends on the direction of the sound source. It is greatest when the sound source is off to the side, zero when it is directly in front, and at intermediate values when the sound source lies at other angles.

The third cue is *phase difference*. This term refers to the pressure of a sound wave at any particular place and moment. In the oscilloscopic tracing of a sound wave, for example (see Figure 12.1), any particular point along the path of alternation between positive and negative pressure is a phase. Two sounds of the same frequency composition are in the same phase when their peaks of positive pressure, and hence all other phases of the two waves, coincide exactly. They are in opposite phases when the negative peak of one corresponds to the positive peak of the other.

A difference in phase of the sine-wave tone at the two ears can come about in the same way as a difference in time of arrival. The sine wave is simply a succession of positive and negative pressures. The maximum positive pressure of the sine wave reaches one ear sooner than the other if the sound source is to one side of the head. Thus at any one time the tones at the two ears may be out of phase, but the amount by which

they will be out of phase once again depends on the exact direction of the sound source. Ordinarily, however, the phase cue is useful only at relatively low frequencies because the distance between the ears is so large relative to the wavelength of high-frequency tones that phase differences are unreliable at high frequencies.

Taken together, these three cues enable people to judge the direction of a sound rather well. When both the head and the source of sound are stationary, persons usually can tell with an accuracy of at least 20 degrees of the circle around the head where a sound comes from. When either the head or the sound source is allowed to move, they can do quite a bit better, because they then can perceive how the cues change with changes in the relative position of the head and the source. It is for this reason that people learn automatically to move their heads when they are trying to judge where a sound comes from (see Figure 12.9).

As we have just seen, the fact that we have two ears makes it possible for us to perceive the direction of a sound. With just one ear we could not perceive direction without moving our heads. For this reason, hard-of-hearing people who use a hearing

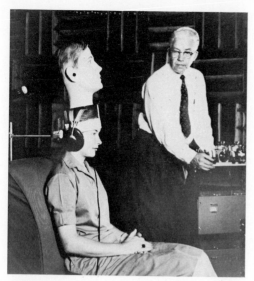

FIGURE 12.9. The study of auditory localization. Microphones in the two ears of the dummy take the place of real ears. Signals picked up by these microphones can be processed electronically—changed in intensity, phase, time of arrival—before being delivered to the subject's earphones. The dummy head is worn so that effects of the subject's moving her head can be studied [Bell Telephone Laboratories].

aid with only one earpiece always have trouble in locating the direction of a sound. Separate hearing aids, one for each ear, are coming into more general use, thereby aiding in the perception of the direction of sounds as well as increasing somewhat the loudness of what is heard.

CUES TO DISTANCE.   Only one ear is needed, however, to perceive *distance*, because the cues to distance are *intensity* and *frequency composition*, and one ear can use them as well as can two. The first of these cues depends on the fact that distance sounds are usually much weaker than near sounds. If we have not heard a sound before, we usually judge it to be farther away if it is a weak sound than if it is a loud sound. We cannot usually judge the distance

on the basis of intensity, however, unless we know what the sound is. To use this cue effectively, therefore, we must be familiar with the sound. A train whistle in the distance may be as loud as the chime of a clock nearby, and yet we know that the train is far away and the clock is close at hand. We know this, however, only because we are familiar with the two sounds and know that a train whistle would be much louder than the chime of the clock if both were at the same distance.

The other cue to distance is *frequency composition* or complexity of a sound. This, as pointed out earlier, refers to the number of frequencies that make up a sound and to the relative sound pressures of each of these frequencies. Fortunately we can use frequency composition or complexity as a cue because the air and objects in the path of a sound absorb high frequencies much more than they do low frequencies. Thus a low-frequency sound can be heard much farther away than can a high-frequency sound. Foghorns, for example, are always low-pitched because they must be heard over many miles of the sea. If a foghorn were high-pitched, it could be heard only by ships very near the horn.

Since the high frequencies in sound are absorbed more than the low frequencies, the farther away one is from the source of sound, the more the sound will appear low-pitched. When you listen to an orchestra at a distance, you cannot hear the high notes very well. Thus when you hear music being played, but can hear the low notes much better than the high notes, you judge the sound to be far away.

Deafness

We should not end this survey of hearing without saying something about deafness. Deafness is a serious problem in a civilization that depends so much on spoken communication, for the deaf or hard-of-hearing person has a difficult time communicating. Either everything must be written out for

FIGURE 12.10. Audiograms for normal hearing and two major kinds of deafness. The average threshold for normal individuals at different frequencies is taken as zero. Any particular individual does not have exactly this threshold but does not depart from it by more than a few decibels. The person with conduction deafness has a rather uniform hearing loss at all frequencies. The person with nerve deafness has a greater hearing loss at high frequencies than at low ones.

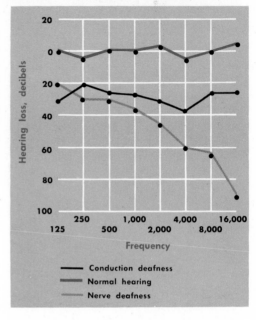

him, or he must "hear" by sign language. Some hard-of-hearing people become quite proficient at reading lips, but this procedure is at best a poor substitute for actually hearing speech.

Deafness is fairly common in our society, and until very recent years any kind of deafness was a serious handicap. It was not until the advent of the modern electronic hearing aid that partially deaf people had a sensory aid as good as that provided by eyeglasses. A totally deaf person cannot hear with a hearing aid, however, any more than a totally blind person would be able to see with glasses.

Deafness is a two-way problem; it handicaps a person as a speaker and as a listener. Because he can never hear his own voice, a deaf person eventually loses his ability to speak well. That is why many deaf people speak in a peculiar tone—they have no way of knowing whether or not their voices sound like the voices of other people. In addition, deafness can create a serious emotional problem. The deaf person tends to withdraw from people, because he cannot, without great difficulty, communicate with them and because of the irritation they show when he cannot understand them.

KINDS OF DEAFNESS. To measure deafness clinically, one uses an instrument known as the *audiometer*. This is simply a device for testing the intensity and frequency

limits of hearing that we described earlier in this chapter. It produces pure tones at several different frequencies and provides accurate control of the sound pressure at each frequency. The clinician uses it to find the minimum amount of sound (in decibels) that a person can hear at each frequency. The decibels recorded for each frequency are then plotted on a chart such as that in Figure 12.10, called an *audiogram*. This chart shows a comparison with the sound-pressure levels required for average normal hearing. The difference between the two is the measure of hearing loss.

The top curve in Figure 12.10 is a typical audiogram for a person with normal hearing. Notice that even the normal person does not hear all tones at exactly the same sound-pressure level as the *average* normal person does, for there are always individual variations from the average. The other two curves in Figure 12.10 are for two individuals who are partially deaf, that is, have sizable hearing losses. We have drawn two curves because there are two different kinds of deafness. These two kinds have different causes, and they are characterized by different patterns of hearing loss in their respective audiograms.

One kind, *conduction deafness,* has roughly the same hearing loss at all frequencies. The person suffering from conduction deafness is no more deaf at one frequency than he is at another. The term "conduction deafness" is used because such an audiogram usually indicates that something is wrong with conduction in the ear. The ear may be stopped up, the eardrum may be broken, or the ossicles of the middle ear may be damaged. The effect of conduction deafness is much the same as that of stuffing cotton in one's ears.

The lowest curve in Figure 12.10 represents the other kind of hearing loss, namely, *nerve deafness.* As its name suggests, in this type of deafness something is wrong with the auditory nervous system. Either, the nerves themselves have been damaged, or there has been damage in the cochlea, particularly to the basilar membrane. It is characteristic of nerve deafness that hearing loss is much greater at the high frequencies, which means that the nerve-deaf person can hear low-pitched sounds reasonably well but can hear high-pitched sounds very poorly or not at all. Such a person has a great deal of trouble understanding speech, because the high frequencies are very important in speech comprehension (see section on speech perception). He can hear the louder low tones, but he is not able to distinguish easily between the word sounds. Since he can hear sound but cannot comprehend speech easily, he is likely to become annoyed. Also for the same reason, this kind of deafness has sometimes been called *perception deafness.*

Nerve deafness is very common in older people. In fact, nearly all of us can expect

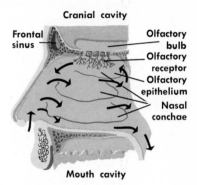

FIGURE 12.11. A cross section of the nose. Air currents inhaled through the nostrils are wafted to the upper part of the nasal cavity where they stimulate the olfactory receptors.

to have at least mild nerve deafness by the time we are sixty, just as most of us can expect to be a bit farsighted by that age. But for most people, the deafness will not be serious enough to require a hearing aid.

The chemical senses

So far, in the preceding chapter and this one, we have covered the two senses, vision and hearing, that most people would consider to be our most important ones. It remains for us to describe the others. We can divide them into three main groups: the chemical senses, the skin senses, and the deep senses. Since these senses do not figure as prominently in our lives as do vision and hearing, our descriptions will be brief. We shall begin with the chemical senses, which consist of smell and taste.

THE SMELL RECEPTORS. The receptors for smell respond to chemical substances, but only if those substances are volatile. Liquids, for example, do not stimulate the sense of smell. Smell receptors are located high up in the nasal passages leading from the nostrils to the throat (see Figure 12.11). They lie in two small patches, one on the left and one on the right, in the roofs of these passages. They are a little off the main route of air as it moves through the nose in normal breathing, and consequently our sense of smell is relatively dulled when we are breathing quietly. A sudden sniff or vigorous intake of air, however, stirs up the air in the nasal passages and brings it more directly to the receptors. This is why we see animals and people sniffing when they are trying to identify an odor.

BASIC ODORS.   Just by recalling the odors that you encounter in everyday life, you can realize that there are many shades and qualities of them. This is also true, of course, of the colors we experience. In both cases, scientists have raised the question whether the multitude of experiences might not be mixtures of a relatively few primary qualities. In color vision, it has indeed worked out that way; four psychologically unique hues mixed in various proportions can account for all perceived differences in color. Perhaps, in smell, there are similarly a few unique odors which, mixed in different proportions, might account for various discriminable odors.

Attempts have been made to discover or devise such a scheme, but they have not succeeded too well. Although research workers have devoted considerable effort to the problem, we are not yet certain what the primary odors are, or even whether there is a limited number of them. One scheme that does reasonably well is known as the Henning smell prism (see Figure 12.12). It was devised by a German research worker named Henning and is called a prism because Henning chose six basic odors and represented them in the shape of a prism. This arrangement assumes that the six basic odors may be mixed in various proportions to account for the different odors we encounter in daily experience. It is like the color circle in that all mixtures of basic odors may be regarded as falling somewhere on its surfaces between the points representing the basic odors.

Industrial chemists, who are faced with the problem of making artificial perfumes and scents, prefer a simpler fourfold classification of odors [Crocker, 1945]. According to this classification, the four basic odors and examples of them are: fragrant (musk), acid (vinegar), burnt (roast coffee), and caprylic (goaty or sweaty). Still other systems of primary odors have been proposed. Each may serve some particular purpose well, but there is little assurance that in any of them we have found the "real" primaries in the sense that the psychological primaries for color have been clearly established. Probably the biggest stumbling block to our accepting any scheme of primary odors as final is the difficulty we commonly encounter of getting individuals to agree consistently, either with themselves or with each other, in classifying different odors. This is illustrated by the following experiment [Ross and Harriman, 1949]:

HENNING CONCEIVED OF SIX BASIC ODORS, ARRANGED AS THE CORNERS OF A PRISM:

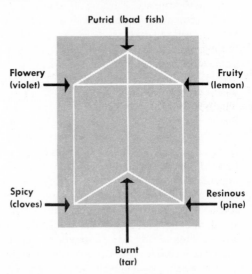

FIGURE 12.12. Henning's smell prism. Henning proposed that there are six basic odors and that they might be represented as corners on a prism. He regarded other odors as mixtures of these primary odors.

CHAPTER TWELVE

Fifteen subjects were asked to classify 32 different odors. Their instructions were to sniff the samples and to classify in groups all odors that seemed similar. They were allowed to make as many different groups as they considered necessary. In the accompanying graph (Figure 12.13) are the number of groups employed by different proportions of subjects. Only one of them could classify all odors into just 4 groups. About half of them needed 5 or 6 groups. Some subjects, however, needed as many as 12 or more groups to classify the stimuli.

SMELL SENSITIVITY.   In hearing and vision, we are able to state precisely how much energy is required for a person to detect or discriminate a stimulus. In the case of smell, our measures of sensitivity are not so precise. There are several reasons for this, but the chief one is that the smell receptors are recessed away from the main path of air through the nasal passages. The best way to get odors to the smell receptors is by sniffing, yet sniffs vary from one person to another and from one sniff to another.

Despite such limitations in measuring smell sensitivity with precision, many measurements have been made of the amounts of odorous material needed for a person to detect its presence. Thresholds of detection vary considerably for the different odors, but the impressive thing about them is that they are often so incredibly small. Anesthetic ether, which is one of the less odorous materials, requires only 6 milligrams per liter of air—a milligram is about 40 millionths of an ounce—to be detected. Artificial musk, one of the most odorous of substances, can be sensed in extraordinarily small dilutions. Only 0.00004 milligram of it in a liter of air can be smelled. This is such an enormous dilution that no physical or chemical means can be used to measure it, which means that the nose must be responding to no more than a few chemical molecules per sniff. However, impressive as this may be, the sense of smell in many animals even surpasses that in man.

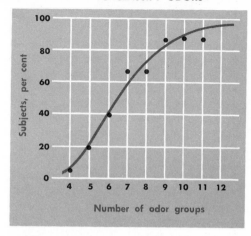

FIGURE 12.13. Number of groups required to classify olfactory stimuli. This graph summarizes an experiment in which subjects were asked to classify odors into groups according to their similarities and differences. One subject could classify all odors into four groups, but most subjects required more [after Ross and Harriman, 1949].

TASTE RECEPTORS.   The receptors for taste are specialized cells which are grouped together in little clusters known as *taste buds* (see Figure 12.14). These buds are located for the most part on the top and sides of the tongue, but a few of them are also at the back of the mouth and in the throat. If you examine the tongue closely—which you can do simply by looking at your own tongue in a mirror—you will notice a number of bumps on it, some large and some small. These bumps, called *papillae,* are richly populated with taste buds. To stimulate the taste receptors, substances must be in solutions which wash around the papillae and penetrate to the taste cells within them.

PRIMARY TASTE QUALITIES.   We have said that we are not yet certain of the primary odors. Fortunately we are clearer about the primary taste qualities. Several lines of evidence point to four qualities. These have been named *salty, sour, sweet,* and *bitter.* Part of the evidence for these qualities is the fact that the tongue is not uniformly sensitive to all stimuli. If, for example, we apply minute drops of a bitter solution, such as quinine, to different parts of the tongue, we find the bitter taste most pronounced when the drops are put at the back of the tongue. The taste of sweetness, on the other hand, is most noticeable when sugar solutions are placed on the tip of the tongue. The sides of the tongue respond mainly to sour stimuli, and the tip and part of the sides respond to salty solutions. This evidence, as well as other evidence, supports the idea of four primary taste qualities.

If we now try, however, to state what kinds of solutions give rise to the different qualities, we run into trouble. Sugars, such as common table sugar, taste sweet, but so do many other chemical compounds, such as saccharine, which have little in common, chemically, with sugar. The taste of bitter presents a similar problem. A class of compounds that the organic chemist calls *alkaloids,* which include quinine and nicotine, taste bitter, but so also do substances like some of the mineral salts that have little in common with the alkaloids. Indeed, as noted below, almost all salts other than common table salt taste either bitter or sweet. However, all this may prove only that we have not yet discovered which aspects of a chemical substance are the key ones in determining taste quality. Certainly we cannot at present state any rules for the kinds of chemical substances that produce sweet and bitter qualities of taste.

In the cases of sour and salty tastes, there is a somewhat better correlation between chemical composition and taste. All the stimuli that taste sour are acids. Moreover, the degree of sourness that we taste is fairly proportional to the total number of acid (H^+) ions present. Salty taste, similarly, is

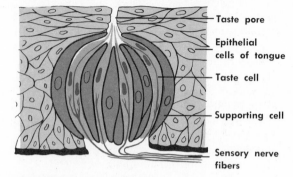

Taste pore

Epithelial cells of tongue

Taste cell

Supporting cell

Sensory nerve fibers

FIGURE 12.14. A taste bud.

usually aroused by what the chemist calls salts (meaning the chemical product of acids and alkalies). Common table salt, however, is about the only salt that has a uniquely salty taste; most other salts arouse experiences of bitter or sweet in addition to that of salt.

TASTE SENSITIVITY. Just as it is difficult to measure accurately a person's threshold for odors, so it is difficult to measure thresholds for taste. All stimuli for taste must be in solution and must reach the taste cells lying beneath the surface of the papillae. For an experimenter to control taste stimuli precisely, he must make sure that all saliva is removed from the surface to be stimulated and also that it is washed free of any solutions which have been used in preceding tests. The temperature of the tongue and the size of the area stimulated must also be carefully controlled.

When an investigator takes all these precautions, he can make measurements of taste sensitivity. From measurements that have been made, it is clear that taste sensitivity is not nearly so good, relatively, as smell sensitivity. It takes, for example, from 4 parts in 100 to 1 part in 1,000 to be easily detected. In general, our sensitivity is better for acids and bitter substances than it is for sweet and salty substances.

CHAPTER TWELVE

ADAPTATION.   All, or nearly all, our different sense organs adapt to stimuli. That is to say, they gradually become less sensitive during the course of stimulation, and the stronger the stimulation the greater is such adaptation. Some senses, such as those for hearing and for equilibrium (see below) adapt relatively little. The senses of taste and smell, however, are among those that adapt readily.

We have all noticed such adaptation. Sometimes, upon entering a room, you are almost taken aback by a strong odor. Yet, after you have been in the room for a while, you no longer notice the odor and may be unable to tell whether it is still there. Similarly, you appreciate the full flavor of your favorite food only when you first taste it. Adaptation soon sets in so that you lose some of the strength of the flavor. It is possible to measure such adaptation in the laboratory, and research workers have gathered many curves showing the rate of adaptation for various odors and tastes [Osgood, 1953].

TASTE OR SMELL?   Although we all believe that we taste with our tongues and smell with our noses, most of us do not realize that we commonly confuse taste and smell. Indeed, we often think we are identifying a flavor by taste when smell is the more important.

You can prove this by getting a friend to hold his nose while you place drops of familiar beverages on his tongue. If you place a drop of lemon juice on it, the chances are that he will say merely that it is something sour. Or if you drop a little Coca-Cola on it, he may know only that it is something bittersweet. (Potato is also indistinguishable from apple). If now you repeat the experiment without your friend holding his nose, he will immediately be able to identify the beverages as lemon juice and Coca-Cola.

Some smells, like tobacco smoke, so mask a flavor that gourmets have been known to refuse to eat in smoke-filled restaurants.

The part played by smell explains why food is so "tasteless" when a person has a stuffy head cold that greatly reduces his sensitivity to odors.

The skin senses

Vision, hearing, and the chemical senses are the sensory channels that we use most in perceiving the world. If these channels are functioning properly, we hardly need any other senses to appreciate what is going on around us. For this reason we tend to ignore what we could do, if we had to, with our skin senses. In general, we rely on our skin senses only for such simple experiences as itches and tinglings, feelings of hot and cold, and painful sensations of injury. Actually the skin senses are capable of telling us much more than that. We could, for example, identify many objects by their touch or even read braille, as the blind must do.

THE FOUR SENSES.   Let us begin our account of these senses with an experiment that has now become a common one in the psychological laboratory [Woodworth and Schlosberg, 1954]:

A subject is seated and asked to roll up the sleeve of his shirt, baring his forearm. On the undersurface of the arm a grid is stamped. The experimenter then takes a hair that can be applied with known pressure and touches the end of it first to one spot on the grid and then to another. Each time the hair is applied, the blindfolded subject reports whether or not he feels pressure. The experimenter keeps a chart corresponding to the grid stamped on the subject's arm and marks on the chart each position at which the subject reports having felt pressure (see Figure 12.15).

Having plotted all the squares on the grid where pressure is reported, the experimenter now takes a rod that has been cooled to a temperature, say of 28°C and is kept at that temperature throughout the experiment. With this rod, he goes again from square to square and charts the points at which the subject reports "cold." He then does the same thing with a rod that has been maintained at a temperature above normal, say, 35°C, and he maps all the spots for which "warm" is reported. Finally, with a fine, sharp needle applied, with a constant, light pressure, he goes over the entire grid again and plots the "pain spots."

Now let us look at the chart on which all these points are plotted (see Figure 12.15). First of all, you can see that not all areas are equally sensitive. In some places, the subject reports "pressure," in others he does not. Thus you see that the skin has a *punctate sensitivity*—it is sensitive at some points and not others. (Actually, detailed analysis shows that the skin is simply *more* sensitive or *less* sensitive from one square to another.) Secondly, you will notice that there are different maps for the different stimulators. The places of greatest sensitivity of pressure, cold, warmth, and pain are, on the whole, different. You now see that there is not one skin sense, but four different ones, and you may infer that they might represent four different kinds of receptors. This experiment is only one of several that support the conclusion that there are four skin senses.

PRESSURE OR TOUCH. The experience a subject reports when he is touched lightly with a hair is called either pressure or touch.

The amount of pressure required to elicit this experience varies greatly for different parts of the body. The tip of the tongue, the lips, the fingers, and the hands are the most sensitive areas. The arms and legs are less sensitive, while the trunk and calloused areas are the least sensitive of all. We experience pressure, it should also be noted, not only when some object touches the skin but also when hairs on the body are slightly moved.

Psychologists have studied carefully what it is about a stimulus that elicits the experience of pressure. They wanted to know in particular whether it was the weight of an object on the skin or simply a bending of the skin that aroused sensation. They have concluded that it is the latter—the deforming or bending of the skin.

If you have handy some mercury, you can demonstrate this yourself. Put some mercury in a small glass to a depth of an inch and a half or more, then dip the tip of your finger in the mercury. Mercury is rather heavy—thirteen times as heavy as water—and will exert pressure over the surface of the immersed skin. You will observe, however, that you do not feel the pressure at the tip of your finger but only at the mercury line. It is here that there is a *gradient of pressure* on your skin—a change from air pressure to the pressure exerted by the mercury. From this sort of experiment we conclude that it is a gradient of pressure, not uniformly distributed pressure, that arouses the experience of pressure.

POINTS ON THE SKIN THAT ARE USUALLY MOST SENSITIVE TO PAIN, TOUCH, HOT, OR COLD ARE DIFFERENT FOR EACH OF THESE SENSATIONS:

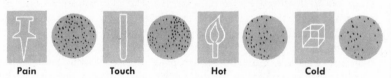

Pain   Touch   Hot   Cold

FIGURE 12.15. Mapping the sensitivity of the skin. By marking a grid on an area of the skin and then systematically stimulating different spots, one can construct a map of the sensitive spots. Maps for pain, touch, hot, and cold stimuli are usually different, indicating that there are four distinct skin senses [diagram from Gerard, 1941].

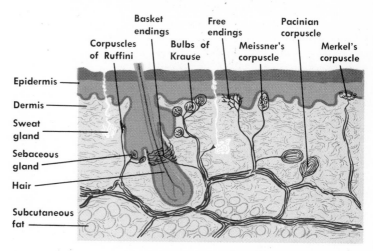

FIGURE 12.16. Structures of the human skin. Not all the structures shown in the diagram are to be found in any one area of the skin.

RECEPTORS FOR PRESSURE. For more than fifty years there have been many attempts to determine the receptors for pressure. Seldom have scientists worked so assiduously at a problem with so little success. We think that a fairly complex structure, called the *Meissner corpuscle* (see Figure 12.16), serves the pressure sense in the hairless regions of the body and that another structure, the *basket nerve ending,* does it for the roots of hairs. We also have good reason to believe that simple *free nerve endings*—endings not associated with any special structure—also convey touch impulses, because we can feel pressure in some areas of the skin where no receptors other than free nerve endings are to be found. A final answer to this problem, however, awaits further, more definitive research.

TEMPERATURE STIMULATION. In the experiment with which we began this section, the maps of "cold" spots and "warm" spots were different. This fact has been taken to mean that there are two different senses for experiencing warmth and cold. We are, in fact, rather sure of that, even though research to date has not established with certainty just what the respective receptors are. We do know, however, that the experiences

of warmth and cold are elicited by any change in the normal gradient of skin temperature. This gradient, in the case of the forearm, for example, is about 5°C and is the difference between the temperature of circulating blood (37.5°C) and that of the surface of the skin (32 or 33°C). A stimulus of 28 to 30°C, which is definitely felt as cold, increases this gradient a little, while a stimulus of 34°C, which can be felt as warm, decreases it a little. Thus it takes a change in skin temperature of only 1 or 2°C to be experienced as warmth or cold.

PAIN. A good many very diverse stimuli produce pain—a needle prick, a hard blow to the skin, scalding steam, or strong acid. For that reason, it is impossible to say in physical terms exactly what produces pain. One laboratory method of producing pain, which has proved rather precise, is to use a device that radiates heat to a given area of the skin [Wolff and Wolf, 1948]. As the radiant heat is increased in intensity, a person first reports warmth, and then at a particular intensity he reports pain. Other methods which are not quite so precise make use of pinpricks and chemical solutions.

Injury to tissues. The biological utility of pain, of course, is quite clear. This utility is illustrated by those rare individuals who have no pain sensitivity and who sometimes unknowingly incur grave injuries. One such person, a seven-year-old girl accumulated multiple scars, bruises, self-mutilations, fractures, dislocations, and other local deformities [Boyd and Nie, 1949]. On several occasions her parents smelled the odor of burning flesh and found her leaning casually on a hot stove.

Because of the close relationship between pain and bodily injury, scientists have been inclined to believe for a long time that injury to tissues is the common immediate stimulus for the sensation of pain. Recent evidence makes this view rather plausible [Hardy et al., 1951]. When an observer is asked to report pain while heat is radiated to a patch of skin on his forehead, he will usually report a sensation of pain when the temperature of his skin reaches the point at which tissues begin to break down. The amount of pain felt is not directly related to the amount of tissue damage, however. Rather, it is related to the rate of destruction, and a painful sensation results when stimulation produces a critical state in which destructive forces just begin to exceed the rate of repair.

The receptor for pain is almost certainly the unspecialized free nerve ending that is abundant in most parts of the skin, particularly where sensitivity to pain is greatest.

ADAPTATION. Like the chemical senses, those of the skin are able to adapt to stimuli within quite wide limits. Pain adapts rather incompletely—if you have ever had a bad toothache, you have discovered how slowly the sensations of pain adapt—but both touch and thermal sensitivity change appreciably during the course of stimulation. Adaptation is especially marked in the senses of warmth and cold. If, for example, one immerses his left hand in warm water and his right hand in cold water, the sensations of warm and cold, respectively, gradually die out. But then, if both hands are immersed in water at a temperature between those to which the hands are adapted, the left hand now feels cold and the right one feels warm.

The deep senses

Except when we have a stomach-ache or a headache, we are usually unaware of stimuli inside the body. Yet hidden away in the linings of internal organs, in our muscles, and in our joints is a large variety of sense organs.

SUBCUTANEOUS SENSIBILITY. Some of these sense organs are not far beneath the skin, yet are not a part of our skin senses. This fact can be demonstrated by applying an anesthetic to the skin. After the skin has become insensitive, we can still feel heavy pressure applied to the skin and some pain if the skin is pinched. There are therefore deep-pressure and pain receptors in the subcutaneous layers below the skin. It is thought that these deep-pressure receptors are the relatively large *Pacinian corpuscles* (see Figure 12.16) that are found in the regions that have deep-pressure sensitivity. As in the case of the skin senses, the receptors for deep pain are almost certainly free nerve endings.

ORGANIC SENSES. We know relatively little about receptors in the internal organs within the body cavity, mainly because these areas are so inaccessible to experimentation. But there must be cold and warm receptors in the esophagus and stomach, for we can experience cold and warmth in these parts. They also have something similar to the deep subcutaneous receptors for pressure and pain, because they yield corresponding experiences when stretched. So far as other internal organs are concerned, it is clear that we can feel pressure and pain when they are irritated or put under pressure, but we do not know to what extent these experiences arise from receptors in the organs themselves and to what extent they may arise from other tissues and the abdominal wall, which are indirectly affected by these organs.

KINESTHETIC SENSE. A bodily sense that physiologists now know a good deal about is one that most people have never heard of: kinesthesis. In some ways, it is the most important sense we have, because it provides an automatic system for coordinating our muscles in walking and in all our skilled movements. One can see how important it is only by observing a person who has been deprived of it. This sometimes happens in a form of syphilis known as *tabes dorsalis,* which attacks the sensory pathways from the kinesthetic sense organs. A patient with this disease gets no information from his muscles about their movements. He is able to walk, balance a ball, or carry out other skills only by watching carefully what his arms and legs are doing. If syphilis invades the brain stem and interrupts kinesthetic impulses from the face and mouth, uncoordinated movements of the face may also occur along with a slurring of speech, which, if severe, may make the speech unintelligible.

The kinesthetic receptors are found in three distinct places. One is in the muscles, where free nerve endings surround small muscle spindles (see Figure 12.17). These kinesthetic receptors signal the *stretch* of a muscle. A second location of kinesthetic receptors is in the tendons that connect muscles to bones. The receptors here are nerve endings that serve a specialized organ known as the *Golgi tendon organ* (see Figure 12.17). They are stimulated when a muscle contracts and puts tension on the tendon. Finally, some receptors are to be found in the linings of the joints. These are stimulated whenever a limb moves, changing the relative positions of two bones in the joint. We are still not certain about the receptors in the joints, but it is possible that they are Pacinian corpuscles—the same receptors that yield deep pressure when regions below the skin are stimulated.

THE VESTIBULAR SENSE ORGANS. Like kinesthesis, the vestibular sense is important in balance and movement, but it does not provide experiences of which we are ordi-

KINESTHETIC RECEPTORS ARE FOUND IN THE MUSCLES, TENDONS, AND JOINTS :

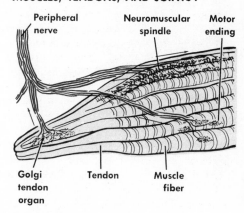

FIGURE 12.17. Kinesthetic receptors in muscle. The two kinesthetic receptors shown are the neuromuscular spindle and the Golgi tendon organ.

narily aware. The organs of the vestibular sense are well known because they are highly specialized, are reasonably large, and can be studied in detail under the microscope. They are, in fact, part of the inner ear. The inner ear is a series of cavities, only one of which, the cochlea, is concerned with hearing. The rest of the cavities constitute the vestibular organs (see Figures 12.18 and 12.19). They divide into two main groups: the *semicircular canals* and the *otolith organs.*

There are three semicircular canals, each roughly perpendicular to both the others, and they are so oriented as to represent three different planes of movements. In an enlarged part of each canal is a set of hair cells somewhat similar in general structure to those in the cochlea. These cells are encompassed by the fluid that fills the canal and are stimulated when pressure is exerted on this fluid. Such pressure occurs mainly when the head is rotated, and thus the canals are sense organs for rotation. It appears, however, that the receptors do not respond merely to continuous rotation—continuous pressure—but to changes in rate of rotation, that is, to acceleration or deceleration. So when a person is rotated, or rotates himself as some stage performers do, it is only while he is increasing speed or slowing down that the semicircular organs are stimulated.

Dancers and acrobats who do a lot of spinning have learned some tricks which help them overcome the effects of this sense during their gyrations. Watch a ballet dancer spinning, and you will see that he keeps his head as motionless as possible by fixating some object in the environment. The head whips around to pick a new fixation point while the body is still turning.

There are two other cavities making up the vestibular organ. On the walls of these cavities are thickenings which contain receptor cells. These protrude into a gelatinous mass that contains small crystals, the otoliths (*oto* means "ear," and *lith* means "stone"). These receptors appear to be positional or static receptors, for they respond merely to the tilt or position of the head and do not require rotation to be stimulated.

Vestibular reactions. The canals and the otolith organs together provide a sense of balance. Impulses from these organs help a person right himself when he has been thrown off balance. More specifically, they control a number of reflexes that automatically compensate for loss of balance. One such reflex is a movement of the head back to a normal position whenever it has been turned away from it. Another is a reflex twisting of the trunk and body to return the whole body to normal position.

Perhaps the best illustration of these effects of the vestibular sense organs is the righting reaction of the cat, an animal famed for its ability to land right side up when dropped from any height or position. A cat, when turned upside down and dropped, first twists its head around to normal position, then its trunk, and then, through some indirect reflexes, brings its four feet around to orient toward the ground. This series of reactions is controlled primarily by the vestibular receptors.

There is a special connection between the vestibular receptors and the eyes. If one turns his head quickly, his eyes ordinarily move simultaneously in the opposite direction so that they continue to fixate the same point. These are compensatory movements of the eyes that are controlled in part by the vestibular receptors. When we have been spinning around and then stop, our eyes continue to move back and forth in a movement that is called *rotation nystagmus*. The eyes drift to one side, then move quickly to the other, then drift, then jump, and so on.

THE AMPULLAE OF THE SEMICIRCULAR CANALS RESPOND TO ROTATION; THE OTOLITHS OF THE SACCULE AND UTRICLE, TO POSITION OF THE HEAD:

FIGURE 12.18. The vestibular sense organs. The three semicircular canals are so arranged that one is in each plane. Organs in the ampullae of these canals respond to rotation or movement of the head. The otolith organs located in the saccule and utricle, on the other hand, are stimulated by gravity and hence by the position of the head.

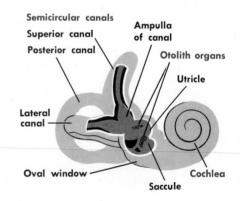

Semicircular canals
Superior canal
Posterior canal
Ampulla of canal
Otolith organs
Utricle
Lateral canal
Oval window
Saccule
Cochlea

FIGURE 12.19. The otolith organs. The sketch shows the microscopic structure of the otolith organs in the saccule and utricle. The otoliths embedded in a gelatinous substance exert pressure on the sensory hairs according to the position of the head. Stimulation of the hairs evokes impulses in sensory nerve fibers which join other fibers from the ear and end in the medulla of the brain.

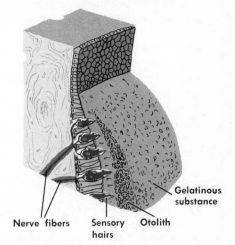

Gelatinous substance

Nerve fibers   Sensory hairs   Otolith

Such nystagmus is a reflex evoked by the stimulation that the receptors in the semicircular canals have received.

Motion sickness. Motion sickness, which causes some people so much misery, is an effect of vestibular stimulation. There are several common forms of this discomfort: train sickness, car sickness, sea sickness, and air sickness. We know that the vestibular organs are responsible for motion sickness, because the occasional individual whose vestibular system is not functioning properly does not suffer motion sickness and also because we can produce motion sickness experimentally by stimulating the vestibular impulses that evoke reflex reactions in the alimentary tract [Wendt, 1951]. Of course, other factors such as anxiety can also augment such reactions, and they therefore contribute to the direct effects of vestibular stimulation. There are now certain well-publicized drugs, e.g., Dramamine, which reduce or prevent motion sickness, but it is not yet known whether they work on the vestibular sense, alimentary tract, or some other part of the nervous system involved in the reaction.

Speech perception

Because we use speech so much for communication, speech is probably the most important class of sounds we hear. A great deal has been learned in recent years about speech perception. This knowledge has value in the design of communication devices of all sorts—telephones, public-address systems, radios—as well as in the understanding of deafness and in the teaching of speech. We shall summarize it briefly in this section.

Speech sounds are very complicated and differ from one speaker to another. Even the sounds made in speaking the same language differ considerably. A Southern accent, for example, is very different from a Brooklyn accent. But the speech of persons with widely dissimilar accents can be understood with a minimum of difficulty by the average listener. This fact poses one of the interesting questions studied by persons investigating speech as a stimulus.

Speech sounds are made by blowing air across the vocal cords, thereby setting the cords to vibrating, and then modifying the sounds produced in this way with movements of the tongue, lips, and mouth. This is not the place to discuss how speech sounds are produced. However, in order to understand how they are heard and interpreted, we must understand their physical nature.

FREQUENCY. We can analyze the various sine-wave frequencies of speech in the same way that we learned to analyze other complex sounds earlier in this chapter. Obviously, however, the frequencies of the speech sounds change from instant to instant, so that we cannot analyze a steady sound. To cope with this difficulty we can analyze many speech sounds to determine the frequencies that are contained in speech on the *average* [Licklider and Miller, 1951; Miller, 1951].

Figure 12.20 shows such an analysis of the frequencies in speech sounds of the English language. This analysis is an average for all speech sounds, and for both male and female voices. The curve shows the relative sound-pressure levels at the different frequencies. From this curve you can see that there is much greater intensity in the low frequencies than in the high ones. There are, for example, 25 decibels more sound pressure at frequencies between 200 and 500 cycles per second than at 5,000 cycles per second. From this fact you might conclude that the low frequencies are much more important in speech comprehension than the high ones, but you would be wrong.

Studies have shown that the high frequencies, although much less intense, are much more important in the comprehension of speech. In such studies, electrical circuits called filters are used to eliminate some of the frequencies while leaving the others intact (see Figure 12.21). When this is done, speech comprehension is almost as good when all the frequencies above 2,000 cycles per second are eliminated as when all frequencies below 2,000 cycles per second are eliminated. Thus we can conclude that all frequencies above 2,000 cycles per second are as important as all frequencies below that frequency. And yet Figure 12.20 clearly indicates that only a small amount of the total intensity comes from these higher frequencies. Why should this be so?

There are two reasons. One has to do with vowels, the other with consonants. Vowel sounds are composed of both low and high

MOST OF THE ENERGY OF HUMAN SPEECH IS IN THE LOW FREQUENCIES:

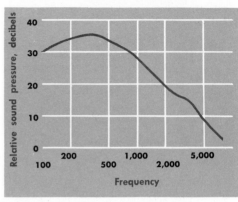

FIGURE 12.20. The average intensity of different frequencies in speech. The curve is an average of male and female voices. Note how much more intense the lower frequencies are compared with the higher frequencies.

frequencies. Although the low frequencies are more intense, the highs help us to distinguish certain of the vowels. For example, if we could hear only lows, we would not be able to discriminate between the words "fool" and "feel." The lows in the vowels are roughly the same, but the highs in "feel" are considerably higher than the highs in "fool." This difference makes it possible to discriminate the frequency patterns of different vowels.

Another reason for the importance of high frequencies is that the consonants usually contain many more high frequencies than the vowels do. Hence consonants are much more important than vowels for understanding a word or a sentence. Sounds like *sh*, *t*, and *k* are almost all high-frequency noises. Even the vocalized consonants, like *d* and *g*, have a great many high frequencies.

The consonants carry most of the information in language, because they are the sounds which allow us to distinguish different words. For example, in the following sentence we have taken all the vowels out: *Ths sctn f th chptr s bt spch.* You still have a pretty good idea of what the sentence is.

But if we take all the consonants out, and leave the vowels in, we get this unintelligible series: *i eio o e ae i aou ee.*

Since vowel sounds are vocalized and last longer than consonant sounds, they contain much more of the speech intensity. Thus we have a situation in which the loudest sounds are not the most important for comprehension or intelligibility. We might almost say that the low frequencies produce the most sound but that the high frequencies produce the most intelligibility.

AMPLITUDE. Turning this last statement around, we can say that the high-intensity sounds in speech produce the least intelligibility, while the low-intensity sounds produce the most intelligibility. This conclusion, which has some practical applications, is justified by the known effects of *amplitude distortion* on speech perception.

Amplitude distortion is any distortion of the pattern of intensities making up a series of sounds. We get relatively little amplitude distortion when sound travels through air, but it is commonly encountered in communication devices, such as public-address systems, radios, or interphones. In these devices, amplitude distortion occurs when the output of the device is not strictly proportional to the input. A loudspeaker that is overloaded, for example, causes amplitude distortion because it is limited in the sound it can put out. Hence all sounds exceeding this limit come out of the speaker at the same intensity, and the output in this region is not proportional to input.

With appropriate electrical circuits, we can arbitrarily set the limit of output of a communication device. In so doing, we are "peak clipping" the speech waves. In peak clipping, we simply cut off peaks of sound intensity exceeding a specified intensity. The process is illustrated in Figure 12.22, which shows various amounts of peak clipping from none at all up to 24 decibels. To say that speech has been clipped 24 decibels means that the only amplitudes (intensities) allowed through the system are those 24 decibels less than the peak amplitudes of speech waves.

Figure 12.23 shows the effects of peak clipping on the intelligibility of speech. The curves were obtained by having subjects write down the number of words they understood over an interphone system. Naturally, the number understood improves with an increase in intensity. That is why each curve

FIGURE 12.21. The effect on speech intelligibility of eliminating low and high frequencies in speech. The "low-pass" curve shows how word intelligibility increases as the band of transmitted frequencies increases. For that curve, all frequencies below the frequency indicated on the abscissa are passed through the system, and all higher frequencies are rejected. The "high-pass" curve indicates word intelligibility when all frequencies above a given level are transmitted and all lower frequencies are rejected. The two curves cross just below 2,000 cycles per second, indicating that frequencies above 2,000 cycles per second contribute about as much to intelligibility as those below this frequency [after French and Steinberg, 1947].

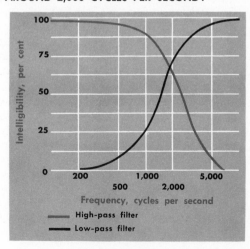

rises in S-shaped fashion from zero intelligibility to 100 per cent intelligibility. The different curves show word intelligibility for different amounts of peak clipping. After peak clipping, each speech wave has been amplified so that all curves are equated in terms of peak intensity. That is to say, the amount clipped is offset by greater amplification of the speech. Notice that the peak-clipped speech is more intelligible than the unclipped speech.

Why can we increase the intelligibility of speech by peak clipping it in this way? Essentially for the same reason that we can throw away many of the low frequencies in speech without hurting its intelligibility. The high-intensity components of speech are those of low frequency that contribute little to speech intelligibility. By clipping them off we leave room to amplify the low-intensity, high-frequency components that are more important in intelligibility.

This latter point can be demonstrated by using another kind of clipping, center clipping, illustrated in Figure 12.22. There the center containing the low-intensity components of the speech is clipped out, leaving the high-intensity components. The effect on speech intelligibility is catastrophic; center clipping of only 4 decibels makes speech completely incomprehensible. This is because the low-intensity components of higher frequency, representing consonants and the discriminable frequencies of the vowels that make speech intelligible, have been eliminated.

Naturally, one wants to avoid center clipping under any circumstances. Peak clipping, on the other hand, can be used to advantage in radios or interphones where power is limited. Under these circumstances, speech intelligibility can be substantially increased by peak clipping the high-intensity components of speech and utilizing the available power to amplify the important low-intensity components. Speech treated in

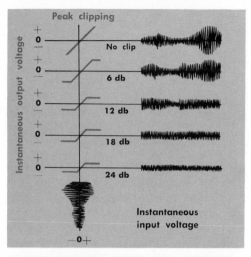

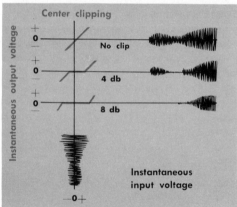

FIGURE 12.22. Two kinds of clipping. Peak clipping, shown above, rejects the high-intensity components, while allowing the low-intensity components to come through the system. Center clipping, below, rejects the low-intensity components and allows the high ones to come through. Peak clipping of 24 decibels leaves speech intelligible, but center clipping of 4 decibels makes it unrecognizable [after Licklider, 1944].

this way does not sound as good as speech presented over a high-fidelity system—it is very rough and obviously distorted—but it is quite intelligible.

FIGURE 12.23. Effects of peak clipping on the intelligibility of speech. Each curve shows word intelligibility at different intensities for different amounts of peak clipping. After peak clipping, the speech has been amplified to compensate for the clipping. Under these circumstances, peak-clipped speech is more intelligible than unclipped speech [after Licklider, 1946].

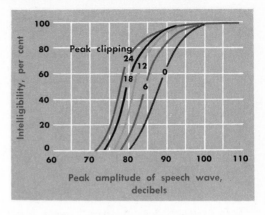

DYNAMICS OF SPEECH. We have seen that the important factor in understanding speech is its pattern of frequencies; a particular combination of frequencies makes one word sound different from another. Besides intelligibility, however, speech has some other interesting aspects. From speech sounds we recognize the voice of a friend or of a stranger. We recognize a voice on a telephone as the same voice we heard in direct conversation yesterday, even though we have never heard this particular voice on the telephone before. And we recognize that the sound of the voice over the telephone is very different from the sound of the same voice in direct conversation. We can also usually tell from the tone of voice when the speaker is angry, or happy, or disappointed. What is it in speech that allows us to recognize all these different qualities—qualities which have nothing to do with the understanding of the particular words used?

There are several factors that are important to the perception of quality. One of these is *intensity*. When people speak loudly, we recognize that they are excited or angry or perhaps having difficulty communicating. When they speak quietly, they are rarely angry. Another factor is what is called the *dynamic range*, which is the range between the loudest and weakest sounds made. The dynamic range of most voices is surprisingly small—about 30 decibels of sound-pressure level. We can, of course, hear a much wider range than that, and because the range of a voice is so small the intensity of particular

word sounds does not seem important. People differ in their dynamic ranges, however, and we can recognize this difference and use it to identify the voice of a particular person. The situation also makes a difference, and any particular person varies his dynamic range with the situation. In an oration, the dynamic range is usually reduced, sometimes to an unpleasant monotone if the speaker is inexperienced. In normal conversation the dynamic range is medium, but becomes greater when the speaker is excited.

Still a third characteristic of voice quality is *fundamental pitch*. The average female voice is higher pitched than the average male voice, but there is a wide variation in fundamental pitch from one person to another. It is the consistency of this characteristic that helps us recognize people by their voices. Pitch may change, however, under conditions of excitement or other stress. The voices of most people become higher pitched when they are excited than when they are calm.

One other characteristic of voice quality is the *rate of talking*. People vary quite a bit in their talking rate. Very slow talkers speak under 100 words per minute, whereas the fastest talkers occasionally speak over 200 words per minute. Fast talking is so well recognized as a sign of excitement that many radio and television announcers deliberately learn to talk at a very fast rate in order to give the impression of excitement. Those of you who have heard a sports announcer describing a horse race are quite familiar with this trick.

You must realize, of course, that we do not consciously analyze different voices in these various ways. What we judge about a speaker's voice is the over-all effect produced by the combination of these aspects of voice quality, and from this over-all effect we form opinions about the speaker himself or about his emotions and feelings at the time he is talking.

Summary

1. The stimulus for human hearing is alternations of air pressure called sound waves. All sound waves, no matter how complex, may be analyzed into sine waves, each of which has a certain frequency and intensity. Simple sine waves are called pure tones. Noises are sound waves that consist of many frequencies mixed more or less randomly.

2. Pitch and loudness, though correlated respectively with frequency and intensity, are psychological attributes of sounds.

3. Sound waves enter the canal of the outer ear and cause the eardrum to vibrate. This vibration is transmitted via bones to the inner ear, which contains the organ of hearing, the cochlea.

4. In the cochlea, sound waves travel through a fluid to bend the basilar membrane, thereby exciting auditory-nerve impulses. In general, the place at which the basilar membrane is bent determines pitch, and the degree of the bending determines loudness.

5. There is a lower limit of hearing below which we are unable to hear sounds. This limit is less for tones of the middle frequencies than it is for higher or lower ones. On the other hand, there is an upper limit beyond which sounds produce pain but no increase in loudness. This is about the same for all frequencies.

6. There are also limits in the ability to discriminate differences in frequency and in intensity.

7. Hearing is made more difficult if a sound is masked by another sound.

8. If the harmonics of two tones "fit" together, they are likely to sound consonant; if they do not, they may be experienced as dissonant.

9. The three principal cues to the direction of a sound—time of arrival, intensity, and phase—all depend upon differences in the sound as it arrives at the two ears. The cues to distance, however, largely depend on one ear and are (a) intensity and (b) frequency composition.

10. Deafness is fairly common. Two types can be distinguished: conductive deafness, which involves some loss in the conduction of sounds to the inner ear, and nerve deafness, which involves some defect in the basilar membrane or the auditory nerve. Nerve deafness tends to be greater for high tones than for low tones, and it is common in old age.

11. It is not certain how many qualities there are in the sense of smell, although as few as four or six will account for most odors. Taste seems to have four basic qualities: sweet, salty, sour, and bitter.

12. Smell is much more acute than taste, sometimes requiring only a few molecules per liter of air for detection. Both senses adapt fairly rapidly to continued stimulation.

13. There are four basic senses associated with the skin: warmth, cold, pressure, and pain. Several highly specialized structures in the skin have been suggested as the receptors for these senses. The best-established fact is that free nerve endings can serve as receptors for pain. Pain adapts less rapidly than the other skin senses.

14. The deep senses consist principally of the kinesthetic and vestibular senses. (*a*) Kinesthetic receptors are found in muscles, tendons, and joints. Impulses from these receptors make posture and coordination almost automatic. (*b*) The vestibular sense organs are located in the head near the cochlea and in the inner ear. They respond to the rotation of the head or to changes in its position, thus providing a sense of balance.

15. Motion sickness is an automatic disturbance resulting from stimulation of the vestibular organs.

16. On the average, speech sounds contain more of the low frequencies than of the high ones.

17. Despite this fact, the high frequencies are more important than the low ones in the comprehension of speech. This is largely because consonant sounds are high and vowel sounds are low, with the consonants being the more essential of the two in speech intelligibility.

18. For the same reason, it is possible to clip off several decibels from the peaks of speech waves without impairing speech intelligibility. If, after such peak clipping, the speech is amplified to offset the clipping, speech intelligibility is actually improved. On the other hand, as little as 4 decibels of center clipping can make speech incomprehensible.

19. The quality of a person's speech, as distinguished from its intelligibility, depends on such factors as intensity, dynamic range, fundamental pitch, and talking rate.

Suggestions for further reading

Bekesy, G. von. *Experiments in hearing.* New York: McGraw-Hill, 1960.
A well-illustrated account of significant modern experiments in hearing, particularly on the function of the cochlea.

Chapanis, A., Garner, W. R., and Morgan, C. T. *Applied experimental psychology.* New York: Wiley, 1949.
A text containing chapters on hearing, with emphasis on practical applications.

Davis, H. (ed.). *Hearing and deafness.* New York: Holt, Rinehart and Winston, 1947.
A broad survey of facts and problems of hearing and deafness, written for the intelligent layman.

Fletcher, H. *Speech and hearing in communication.* New York: Van Nostrand, 1953.
An authoritative book on speech and hearing from the standpoint of communication.

Geldard, F. A. *The human senses.* New York: Wiley, 1953.
An introductory text covering all the senses.

Hirsh, I. J. *The measurement of hearing.* New York: McGraw-Hill, 1952.
A text covering the physical and psychological aspects of the measurement of hearing.

Moncrieff, R. W. *The chemical senses.* New York: Wiley, 1946.
A summary and discussion of research on the chemical senses.

Morgan, C. T., and Stellar, E. *Physiological psychology* (2d ed.). New York: McGraw-Hill, 1950.
A text containing several chapters on the physiological aspects of hearing and the lower senses.

Osgood, C. E. *Method and theory in experimental psychology.* New York: Oxford Univer. Press, 1953.
Theories and experiments on hearing and the lower senses.

Stevens, S. S., and Davis, H. *Hearing.* New York: Wiley, 1938.
A summary of research on the psychology and physiology of hearing.

Wever, E. G. *Theory of hearing.* New York: Wiley, 1949.
An analysis of the physiological basis of hearing.

Wolff, H. G., and Wolf, S. *Pain.* Springfield,

Ill.: Charles C Thomas, 1948.
A little book covering various aspects of the topic of pain.

Woodworth, R. S., and Schlosberg, H. *Experimental psychology* (rev. ed.). New York: Holt, Rinehart and Winston, 1954.
A standard text in experimental psychology containing chapters on the different senses.

CHAPTER TWELVE

Introduction to psychology

PSYCHOLOGICAL
MEASUREMENT

INTELLIGENCE
& APTITUDES

PERSONALITY

PART FIVE
INDIVIDUAL DIFFERENCES

Psychological measurement

PROGRESS IN SCIENCE often depends upon the development of quantitative methods. Without such methods, science is limited to crude observation and classification. With them, it can greatly extend and refine the conclusions it can draw from its data. To take a simple example, people have always known that stones fall when they are dropped, but physics made little progress as a science until its early scientists began to measure how fast stones fall, how far they fall in a period of time, and whether stones fall as fast as apples or feathers.

The situation is much the same in psychology. Even the ancients recognized that some people were slow-witted and others nimble-witted, some courageous and others timid. Psychology, however, began to be a science only when it found ways of measuring such differences, attaching meaningful numbers to them, and then making useful predictions about them.

The problems of measurement are much the same in all sciences, but psychologists and behavioral scientists are probably more concerned about the logic of measurement than most physical scientists. The reason is that many of the things they want to measure are quite complex and cannot be measured on physical scales. Courage, for example, is not the same sort of thing as the length of a table; there is no simple yardstick for measuring a man's courage. Not everything psychological is so difficult to measure as courage, but much of it is. Psychologists and behavioral scientists have therefore found it necessary to invent new methods of measurement and new ways of describing the results of measurement.

The specific techniques developed for measuring things such as personality, intelligence, and attitudes are described elsewhere in the book. This chapter will cover the general rules of psychological measurement and will present statistical methods and concepts for describing and interpreting psychological data.

It is realized that many students taking introductory psychology are not well prepared to study statistical concepts. In some cases there is no need for them to learn or understand the mathematical formulas involved. For that reason, the main text of the chapter relies on words and charts for explaining the basic points. At the end of the chapter, however, is a section containing formulas and methods of calculation. This section is for the benefit of those who prefer formulas to words or who may have occasion to use the statistics described.

Kinds of measurement

The following definition of measurement is generally accepted: *Measurement is the assignment of numerals (numbers) to objects or events according to rules* [Guilford, 1954].

What this means in less formal terms is that in measuring a thing we compare it with some measuring stick—a ruler, a scale, a clock, or even the human eye—and give it a number. The number assigned depends on the rules we adopt for making the comparison. These rules vary with the purposes of our measurement or with the measuring sticks available. Many sets of rules are possible, but we need distinguish only three, and hence only three kinds of measurement (see Figure 13.1). Some writers [Stevens, 1951] distinguish four, but the fourth one, which will be mentioned below, may be regarded as a refinement of the third.

NOMINAL MEASUREMENT. A nominal measurement is nothing more than a classification of things into mutually exclusive categories so that all the things in one category are alike in some particular respect. If we took a basket of mixed fruit and sorted it into separate piles of bananas, oranges, apples, etc., we would be making the kind of classification involved in nominal measurement. All that would be necessary to complete the measurement, so to speak, would be to assign arbitrarily certain numbers to each kind of fruit. Thus bananas might be Category 1; oranges, Category 2;

MEASUREMENT INCLUDES COUNTING AND RANKING THINGS:

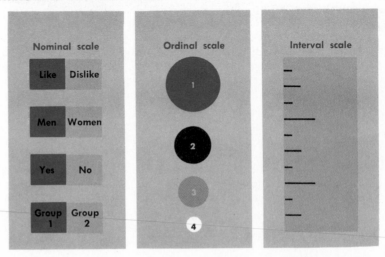

FIGURE 13.1. Three kinds of measurement.

TABLE. 13.1. Paired comparisons of vegetables. One hundred individuals were asked to express their preference between pairs of vegetables taken two at a time. All possible combinations of pairs were presented. The number in each column is the proportion of the time that the vegetable named at the top was preferred over the one named at the side. [based on Guilford, 1954].

	Carrots	Spinach	String beans	Peas	Corn
Carrots	.50	.49	.57	.71	.76
Spinach	.51	.50	.63	.68	.63
String beans	.43	.37	.50	.53	.64
Peas	.29	.32	.47	.50	.63
Corn	.24	.37	.36	.37	.50
Total preference	1.97	2.05	2.53	2.79	3.16

and apples, Category 3. This would only be using numbers instead of names, and it would have little value for scientific purposes, but it nevertheless illustrates the steps in nominal measurement.

In scientific use, nominal measurements are usually employed to designate groups that serve as independent variables (see page 13). Group 1 may be the experimental group that is given some particular treatment not given to Group 2, a control group. In making comparisons of sex differences, men would constitute one category and women another. Or in comparing achievements of the graduates of different colleges, the categories might be College 1, College 2, College 3, and so on. Nominal measurements may also be employed, on the other hand, to designate dependent variables. Simple categories like "pass-fail," "for against," or "like-dislike," which are often dependent variables in a study, are also essentially nominal measurements.

Probably the most important use of nominal measurements in psychology and the social sciences is as items on tests from which more sophisticated measurements are compounded. For example, the items on almost any objective examination or on psychological tests of intelligence and personality are nominal measurements. Each item calls for the choice of a simple category, such as *a, b, c,* or *d,* or "like" or "dislike," or "worry" or "don't worry." By making a choice, the individual places himself in one category or another on that particular item. In the typical test, of course, he makes a good many such choices. These can be counted up according to some scoring system, and his score can be compared with another person's score. In this case, the outcome is one of the following kinds of measurement.

ORDINAL MEASUREMENT. As its name implies, ordinal measurement is the rank ordering of things according to some attribute they possess or appear to possess. One method of obtaining ordinal measurements is known as the method of paired comparisons. In this, the first step is similar to the categorization described above. Things are compared two at a time, and some judgment is made of "greater" or "less," "like" or "dislike," "agree" or "disagree." Having done this for one pair, a person can make a similar comparison between one member of the pair and a third item. This process can be continued for all the items to be considered (see Table 13.1). When it has been completed, the number of times each item has been ranked above or below another item can be counted, then all the items can be ranked. This particular method has often been used by psychologists for the construction of attitude scales and other tests.

A more direct method of making ordinal measurements is simply to rank-order things. I can ask you, for example, to rank-order your preference for apples, oranges, bananas, pears, apricots, and prunes. If you assign oranges your No. 1 preference, bananas your No. 2, pears your No. 3, and so on, I have made an ordinal measurement of your preferences for this particular list of fruits. Because of its simplicity, this method of making ordinal measurements is commonly used in psychology and the social sciences. In general, however, it is not so reliable as the method of paired comparisons, primarily because a person in making each ranking cannot pay equal attention, and hence cannot do justice, to all other members of the list. The paired-comparisons method has the virtue of requiring that an objective judgment be made of only two things at a time. It also has, for reasons that will be pointed out below, the virtue of allowing the scientist to convert ordinal measurements into the third kind of measurement.

INTERVAL MEASUREMENT. An interval measurement is a measurement of the magnitude of the difference between one thing and another.

A familiar illustration of interval measurement is to be found in the reading of temperature. For this purpose, two scales are available: the Fahrenheit scale, used in households and commerce, and the centigrade scale, used in scientific measurements (see Figure 13.2). The Fahrenheit thermometer is marked off so that 32°F represents the freezing point of water and 212°F corresponds to the boiling point. The numbers between arbitrarily indicate a given expansion or contraction of the indicator liquid. A change of a particular amount in the liquid, say 1.2 millimeter, always means a change of 1° in temperature, no matter whether the difference is between 0 and 1°, between 53 and 54°, or between 154 and 155°. Equal differences along the scale represent equal differences in the behavior of

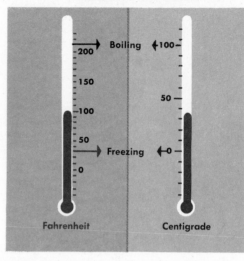

FIGURE 13.2. The Fahrenheit and centigrade temperature scales as examples of interval scales. On these scales, equal differences between numbers represent equal differences in temperature, but one cannot say that 60° is twice as hot as 30°.

the temperature-indicating liquid. The same reasoning holds for the centigrade thermometer.

What is lacking in temperature measurements, but not in many physical measurements, is the knowledge of where *zero* is. It happens that we have discovered what the zero of temperature is—about −273°C or −460°F—but the Fahrenheit or centigrade thermometers do not show this. All they do is give the true difference between any two temperatures. A ruler or a balance or a stop watch, however, are scales that have a true zero. Such scales have been called *ratio scales,* as distinguished from interval scales, for when a scale is calibrated to true zero, different ratios that are equal actually refer to equal ratios.

For example, on a scale of weight, the ratio of 100 pounds to 75 pounds is equal to a ratio of 160 pounds to 120 pounds. This is not true of interval scales, such as the thermometer. On a thermometer, 100°F is not twice as much heat as 50°F. If you are tempted to think so, note the inconsistency as soon as you convert into the centigrade scale. Since 100°F equals 38°C, and 50°F equals 10°C, you can see that 38°C is not twice 10°C. In making this conversion, you do not change the temperatures, you change only your measurement of them.

To a physicist it is of great importance whether he is making interval or ratio measurements. To a psychologist, it usually is not. The only difference is whether measurements are anchored to absolute zero, and in psychological or behavioral matters zero is seldom of any consequence. We are primarily interested in differences between people or in the correlation of differences of one kind with differences of another. Furthermore, any statistical method that is applicable to ratio measurements is usually also applicable to interval measurements. Interval measurements, then, are adequate for almost any psychological measurement.

USES OF MEASUREMENTS.   The three kinds of measurements just described clearly differ in the amount of information they convey. A nominal measurement merely tells us what qualitative category a thing is in. Ordinal measurement tells us more; it indicates that one thing has more or less of a characteristic than other things have, but not how much more or how much less. Interval measurement, on the other hand, does exactly that; it gives the magnitude of the difference between two things.

There are times when we want as much information as we can get in order to describe a person or to make a prediction precisely. In those cases, we like to use interval scales. We automatically have them, or something even better, when we measure human behavior in physical units such as weight, height, or time. On the other hand, strictly *psychological* measurements made with such instruments as intelligence tests or attitude scales do not automatically give us interval measurements.

If we want interval measurements, we must start off with nominal measurements, which is what the individual items on most psychological tests are, or with ordinal measurements, which are used in ratings scales. Then through the compounding of such measurements, and sometimes through special statistical techniques, we convert nominal or ordinal measurements into interval scales. Two of the ways in which this may be done have already been indicated (page 403). A third way requires a knowledge of the theory of probability, which will be treated in the next section.

There are two other points to be made about the use of measurements. One is that nominal or ordinal measurements may be quite sufficient for some purposes. If one wants to know, for example, whether individuals of high aptitude succeed better than those of low aptitude in a particular course of training, nominal or ordinal measurements may be as good as more precise interval measurements. In fact, in order to simplify computations, research workers sometimes reduce what was originally a set of interval measurements to ordinal ones, and get about the same result.

The other point is that the kinds of statistics we can use to summarize results or to indicate a particular person's performance depend on the kinds of measurements made. Some statistical measures, such as the arithmetic average, are simply not appropriate for ordinal measurements. This will be brought out later in the chapter when we describe ways of summarizing groups of measurements.

Distributions of measurements

For most purposes, one lone measurement is of little value. It may do for reading a thermometer, but only because we have read thermometers a good many times and know how a particular reading compares with other possible readings. We already have a frame of reference for interpreting a reading. In psychology, however, one measurement by itself does us little good. Rather we want a fair number of measurements of some kind. If we are measuring different people, we must have enough measurements to provide a frame of reference for comparing any one measurement with a group of measurements. In doing research, we especially need a relatively large number of measurements, if for no other reason than to avoid getting results that are a matter of chance or that are biased in one way or another.

When we have obtained a large number of measurements of any given type, the problem arises what to do with them. Indeed, it frequently happens that a person untrained in statistics collects a lot of measurements, and then comes to a psychologist or statistician and asks, frankly, "What do I do with them?" This is a little late to be asking the question, because the kind of measurements one makes hinges on what he expects to do with them. They can be processed in several different ways, depending on the kind of data (measurements) they are. The rest of this chapter is concerned with the processing—statistical treatment—of psychological measurements.

COUNTING OF FREQUENCIES. The first step, usually, is to find some way of organizing measurements so that one can see what they are like. To do this one counts *frequencies*. This means that he determines how many measurements of a given kind he has. For nominal measurements, this step is easy. All he needs to do is count the cases falling into each of the categories used in making the measurements. Such counting is the common way of handling and presenting many measurements of popular interest: number of automobiles purchased in March, number of people who say they will vote Republican in the next election, number of people who prefer Smell-Kleen soap, etc.

The question often arises whether one should use absolute numbers, that is, the actual counts, or express the counts in percentages. In many cases, especially those involving nominal measurements with only a few categories, one does not care about the total number of cases in each category. This was arbitrarily set to obtain a reasonable sample. What is of interest or importance is the *relative* proportion of people or things in each category. If this is the case, it is perfectly legitimate to divide the number in each category by the total number and thereby obtain the answer as a percentage rather than as a count or frequency. In doing this, though, there is one thing to remember: per cent means *per hundred,* and a percentage should ordinarily be used only when the total number of cases is close to a hundred or, of course, over a hundred. Percentages used on a small number of cases, say, 30, can be very misleading, for a change of one case may make a difference of 3 per cent, which seems much larger than it really is.

One can make counts of ordinal and interval measurements, but this involves another step that we will come to. After making a count of nominal measurements, the investigator usually finds it desirable to present them in some kind of chart so that others can immediately grasp the results. There are as many kinds of charts as there are artists to invent them, but two basic forms are commonly employed. First, there is the pie chart, which is suitable for depicting counts converted to percentages. One merely takes a circle, slices "pieces of pie" that correspond to the percentage of cases falling into a given category, and then labels the categories. From a pie chart, a reader can quickly perceive the relative proportions of cases, dollars, or whatever in each category. Another common form is the bar graph or, more technically, the histogram. It can be used either for raw counts or for percentages. It simply represents the count or percentage with relative heights of bars.

FREQUENCY DISTRIBUTIONS. The method of counting frequencies, and then of representing them with a histogram, is also the simplest way of handling interval measurements. This requires, as we indicated, an additional step: the scale on which the measurements were made must be marked off into a reasonable number of equal *intervals*. In order to illustrate this step, let us take as an example a study of the reaction time of automobile drivers. The measurements in this case were all made in terms of time, which for our purposes may be treated as an interval scale.

The study was conducted in a mock-up of an automobile, consisting of a seat, steering wheel, accelerator, and a brake pedal (see Figure 13.3). In front of the driver was a panel on which a red light could be made to appear without warning. The subject was instructed to place his foot on the brake the moment the red light appeared. An electrical circuit connected the red light and the brake, and an electric clock recorded the exact time—reaction time—between the moment the light turned red and the moment at which the brake pedal was depressed by 1 centimeter. One braking-reaction-time measurement was made on each of 200 men. The 200 measurements obtained are listed in Table 13.2.

One can look over the data in Table 13.2 and guess that the average reaction time was around 0.50 to 0.60 and estimate that the reaction times varied from about 0.45 to 0.75 seconds. Looking them over, however, is not a very satisfactory way—certainly not a precise way—of finding out what they are like. A better way is to construct a frequency distribution of the measurements.

There are two steps in forming a frequency distribution from "raw data" like those in Table 13.2. The first is to choose class intervals into which the scale of measurement may be divided. Such class intervals may be chosen quite arbitrarily so long as (1) the number of intervals is sufficiently large to permit one to see the general distribution of the measurements, and (2) all the class intervals are equal in extent from the beginning of one

FIGURE 13.3. An apparatus for measuring braking reaction time [American Automobile Association].

interval to the beginning of the next. Usually 15 to 20 intervals is a good number to take. In this case, exactly 20 class intervals covered the distance from 0.36 to 0.95, permitting each class interval to be 0.03 seconds.

The second step in constructing a frequency distribution is to tabulate or count the number of cases falling into each of the class intervals. This may be done, as illustrated in Table 13.3, by making a tally alongside each class interval for each score falling within that interval. The result is a *frequency distribution*. It is called that because it gives the frequency or count of measurements in each interval and shows how the frequencies are distributed along the scale of measurement, which in this case is a time scale. Once the counts have been made, they can be represented graphically in a histogram (see Figure 13.4).

As far as the information it shows is concerned, a frequency distribution both loses something and gains something. (1) It loses the identity of each individual measurement. We cannot identify from the distribution the score of the twenty-seventh

TABLE 13.2. Braking reaction time (in seconds) of 200 normal young men on a test of automobile driving.

0.65	0.42	0.66	0.77	0.61	0.82	0.44	0.68	0.48	0.60
0.61	0.48	0.64	0.58	0.43	0.55	0.71	0.62	0.54	0.62
0.75	0.67	0.46	0.66	0.57	0.54	0.72	0.43	0.76	0.53
0.70	0.77	0.58	0.51	0.55	0.73	0.41	0.56	0.53	0.48
0.74	0.46	0.57	0.48	0.90	0.60	0.63	0.64	0.75	0.55
0.69	0.62	0.64	0.57	0.73	0.56	0.49	0.66	0.70	0.59
0.72	0.62	0.66	0.56	0.59	0.60	0.57	0.49	0.64	0.66
0.45	0.83	0.69	0.78	0.51	0.58	0.66	0.61	0.64	0.56
0.53	0.60	0.62	0.65	0.62	0.44	0.61	0.60	0.74	0.64
0.85	0.49	0.51	0.39	0.58	0.64	0.69	0.68	0.52	0.74
0.55	0.68	0.61	0.40	0.56	0.59	0.45	0.59	0.65	0.62
0.46	0.64	0.36	0.72	0.41	0.74	0.51	0.58	0.69	0.55
0.50	0.55	0.56	0.49	0.65	0.51	0.62	0.67	0.48	0.48
0.60	0.63	0.61	0.64	0.58	0.60	0.73	0.95	0.69	0.52
0.78	0.70	0.54	0.58	0.65	0.51	0.72	0.63	0.54	0.45
0.42	0.47	0.55	0.65	0.56	0.74	0.54	0.66	0.58	0.70
0.59	0.57	0.49	0.63	0.66	0.46	0.57	0.88	0.61	0.46
0.47	0.62	0.55	0.66	0.51	0.53	0.52	0.59	0.53	0.56
0.70	0.47	0.68	0.57	0.54	0.67	0.48	0.57	0.68	0.58
0.63	0.72	0.62	0.39	0.63	0.67	0.57	0.68	0.61	0.52

man who took this test. A particular score, however, may always be recovered from our original record of measurements. (2) It also loses the precise value of any individual measurement. We cannot, for example, specify exactly the five measurements falling in the seventh class interval. Such specific knowledge is seldom of any consequence, however, for the class interval is precise enough for most practical purposes.

The frequency distribution gains for us much more than it loses. It so organizes the information in the measurements that we can immediately grasp the most important features. We can see, for example, that there were more scores in the interval from 0.60 to 0.62 seconds than in any other interval, and that with only scattered exceptions, the scores fell between 0.39 and 0.83. Then, by doing a little counting, we can see that nearly half the men (46 per cent) had scores between 0.54 and 0.65. Thus the construction of a frequency distribution has helped us to appreciate quickly the general nature of our measurements.

In passing we may note that a bar graph or histogram is not the only way to depict a frequency distribution. A simpler way, in fact, is to plot a point, instead of a bar, for the frequency of measurements in each class, and then connect each of these points with a line. The graph that results is called a *frequency polygon* (see Figure 13.4), because it still depicts frequencies, but does so with a many-sided figure. The frequency polygon, then, gives exactly the same information as the bar graph or histogram; the frequency polygon merely does it with a set of lines instead of bars.

NORMAL CURVE. All frequency polygons constructed from real measurements will show some unevenness. In general, the more measurements we take, the smoother the graph becomes, because many of the irregularities are the result of chance variations in

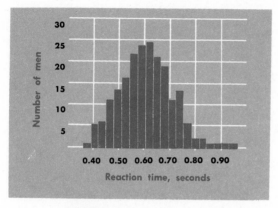
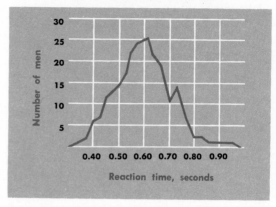

FIGURE 13.4. Histogram (left) and frequency polygon (right) of the data in Tables 13.2 and 13.3.

the population measured. It can be shown both mathematically and by experiments in probability that most ideal frequency polygons eventually approach, as the number of measurements increases and as other conditions of measurement are controlled, a shape known as the *normal curve*. The outline of this curve is shown in Figure 13.5. It is no longer a polygon, but rather a smooth bell-shaped affair. This curve depicts exactly the same thing as the frequency polygon. Any point along the curve represents the relative frequency of measurements occurring within an interval along the scale. Scale intervals are not depicted, for they are arbitrary; and the exact frequencies are not given, because they depend on the number of measurements taken. The shape of the curve is the important thing.

The normal-probability curve is considered the ideal frequency distribution because it occurs when any particular measurement is the chance outcome of a number of individual events, each having a probability of 50–50. This is the case, for example, when we toss 20 pennies at one time, and count the number of heads occurring on each toss. The count in this instance is the measurement. It can vary anywhere from zero to 20. We know from common sense, and the fact

that a penny has a 50 per cent chance of coming up heads, that *on the average* the measurement will be 10. In a very large series of measurements, however, we may expect the measurements to vary from zero to 20. They will form a frequency distribution that approximates the shape of the normal curve.

Many psychological characteristics are much like jars of pennies. Each one is made up of many individual factors combined in chance fashion so that a set of measurements very frequently gives a normal probability curve. The braking-reaction-time experiment above was one example of such a distribution. Almost any other set of measurements of human or biological characteristics, so long as they are made on an interval scale, will give a similar distribution.

The fact that measurements must be made on an interval scale to yield a normal curve provides a clue to one way of determining whether measurements are ordinal or interval. We usually have no way of knowing this in advance when we start to make up a test. In constructing an objective examination for students, for example, an instructor employs a number of items, each of which is essentially a nominal measurement. By using many items on his test and by counting the number of correct and incorrect answers, he obtains a measurement that he can regard as *ordinal*, simply because it lets him rank-order students from highest to lowest. At this point, though, he does not know whether his test is providing *interval* measurements. He does not know whether a difference between 70 and 80 is the same as the difference between 60 and 70, and hence whether it deserves a corresponding difference in the letter grades he assigns.

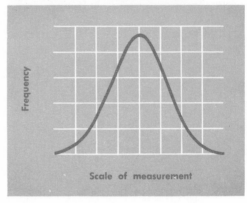

FIGURE 13.5. An idealized frequency distribution known as the normal-probability curve. The height of the curve at any point represents the relative frequency of measurements having the particular value indicated on the horizontal axis.

TABLE 13.3. Frequency distribution of the data in Table 13.2. A large number of scores may be summarized by grouping them into classes, then counting the frequency f of scores falling in each class.

Class limits, seconds	Tallies	Frequency f (number of men)
0.93–0.95	I	1
0.90–0.92	I	1
0.87–0.89	I	1
0.84–0.86	I	1
0.81–0.83	II	2
0.78–0.80	II	2
0.75–0.77	﹢﹢﹢﹢	5
0.72–0.74	﹢﹢﹢﹢ ﹢﹢﹢﹢ III	13
0.69–0.71	﹢﹢﹢﹢ ﹢﹢﹢﹢ I	11
0.66–0.68	﹢﹢﹢﹢ ﹢﹢﹢﹢ ﹢﹢﹢﹢ IIII	19
0.63–0.65	﹢﹢﹢﹢ ﹢﹢﹢﹢ ﹢﹢﹢﹢ ﹢﹢﹢﹢ I	21
0.60–0.62	etc.	25
0.57–0.59		24
0.54–0.56		22
0.51–0.53		16
0.48–0.50		13
0.45–0.47		11
0.42–0.44		6
0.39–0.41		5
0.36–0.38		1

He can find out, however, by comparing the frequency distribution of scores on the test with the shape of the normal curve. If it approximates the normal curve, reasonably well it fulfills the conditions of interval measurement, because on the normal curve equal differences are equal. Then he is justified in assigning grades on the assumption that equal differences in scores are indeed equal. Some examinations give frequency distributions like the normal curve, and some do not. We shall see the reason why in a moment.

Although the instructor seldom needs to do it, there are ways of determining how likely or probable it is that any particular frequency distribution represents a normal-probability curve. Mathematicians have worked out criteria for deciding how much a frequency distribution may depart from the normal curve and still be considered normal. One important element in their procedure for doing this is the number of measurements. A few measurements, even of the tosses of coins, will merely by chance yield a curve that looks less like a normal distribution than that produced by a large number of measurements. We need not go into the procedure, for it is complex, but we should realize that there are precise statistical ways of making such an estimate.

SKEWNESS. Two general characteristics of the normal curve distinguish it from other curves. One is its symmetry. There are an equal number of cases (frequencies) on each side of its center. A second characteristic is the concentration of frequencies in the center of the distribution. Hence, when we encounter a frequency distribution that is not reasonably symmetrical and in which the largest frequencies are not near the center, we know that we have a departure from the normal curve. Such skewness also frequently indicates a departure from an interval scale of measurements.

Frequency distributions that are not symmetrical and not "centered" are called *skewed distributions.* Two examples are shown in Figure 13.6. The one on the left is skewed to the left, and the other is skewed to the right. It has become customary to label skewness according to the side of the distribution on which measurements are spread out the most—the side that has a "tail." Curves like those in Figure 13.6 look somewhat like normal curves, but they are not normal curves because their skewness is greater than one would expect by chance.

There is usually an explanation for skewness, but it depends on the thing being measured. In the case of college examinations or psychological tests, skewness may be caused either by an unrepresentative population—one that for some reason is not normally distributed—or by unusually difficult or unusually easy items on the test. If the test is too easy, the distribution tends to skew to the left; too many individuals pile up on the high-scoring side of the distribution. If it is too difficult, it skews to the right, leaving too many individuals on the low-scoring side of the distribution. Where skewness is caused by the easiness or difficulty of the test, one usually compensates for it by "normalizing" the distribution. In other words, he does not consider equal differences in scores as deserving equal differences in grades. Rather, he divides up his "curve" unevenly so that he can assign grades more nearly like those based on a normal distribution. He should not do this, however, if he has reason to believe that the population of students, rather than the difficulty of the test, is responsible for the skewness.

Measures of frequency distributions

In the preceding section we described ways of organizing measurements into frequency distributions so that we can "get a good look at them." For some purposes, such as writing popular magazine articles or inspecting someone else's data, this may be enough. For other purposes, especially any sophisticated use of the measurements, it is not. A more precise measure of the characteristics of the distribution is then needed.

DISTRIBUTIONS OF MEASUREMENTS MAY BE SKEWED TO THE LEFT OR TO THE RIGHT :

FIGURE 13.6. Examples of skewness. A skewed curve has a longer "tail" on one side than on the other. The curve on the left is skewed to the left; the one on the right is skewed to the right.

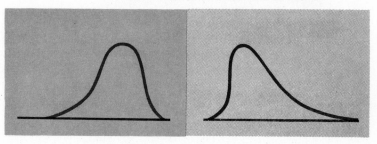

Such a measure, sometimes called a *statistic,* may be derived mathematically from the distribution and used to characterize it in an exact way. There are two general kinds of measures of frequency distributions: (1) measures of central tendency and (2) measures of variability.

MEASURES OF CENTRAL TENDENCY. Measures of *central tendency,* sometimes called measures of central value, are numbers that fix the center of the distribution. The center, of course, must be a place on the scale, and hence is a measurement, not necessarily of any one individual but at least of a hypothetical individual. To measure the center of the distribution, we must know how to define the center, and this depends on the kind of measurements we have.

Arithmetic mean. The measure of central tendency that can be used with interval measurements is the *arithmetic mean.* This is frequently called the *average,* but since average is often used loosely, it is better to call this measure the arithmetic mean. To obtain it, you simply add up all the measurements and divide by the total number. If, for example, you have a different income each month and you want to state your mean income over a 12-month period, you add up the income received for each of the 12 months, divide by 12, and thus compute your average monthly income. In the same way, you can obtain the arithmetic mean of the raw measurements of a group of interval measurements. You can do this without making any use of the frequency distribution, but there are special formulas for computing it from such a distribution.

The arithmetic mean can be used, at least meaningfully, only with interval measurements, because it gives every measurement in the distribution equal weight. Hence it implies that all magnitudes of the differences between measurements are to be trusted, which is not the case for nominal or ordinal measurements. For these kinds of measurements, one of the following measures of central tendency must be used.

Median. The *median,* very simply, *is the middle score in a group of measurements* when they have been rank-ordered from largest to smallest. If there is an even number of measurements, there is no one real middle measurement. In this case, the median is the average of the two middle measurements.

The median is the proper and ideal measure of central tendency for ordinal measurements, because the middle score is the middle rank. It may also be used, if one wishes, with interval measurements. In fact, with data that are normally distributed, it makes little difference whether one uses the median or the mean. They are identical in the ideal normal curve. The median, on the other hand, is the preferred measure for skewed distributions because it is not influenced by extreme measurements.

Mode. Mode means "most." As a measure of central tendency, it is the *category or interval that has the most cases*—the greatest frequency—*of measurements in it.* The mode is the only measure one can use with nominal measurements, for there is no proper way to calculate the other two measures. The mode can be used with other kinds of distributions, if there is any point in it; that is, if one really wants to know what class interval contains the most cases. In the ideal normal distribution, the mode will be exactly the same as the median or mean. Since, however, the mode can shift around quite a bit with chance differences in scores, especially when cases are few, the median or mean, whichever is appropriate, is almost always a better measure of central tendency.

MEASURES OF VARIABILITY. Measures of central tendency only summarize one feature of a distribution, namely, where its center is. Distributions also differ from one another in their variability. In Figure 13.7 are two hypothetical distributions, one fat and the other slender. They both have the same means (or medians) and the same number of measurements. Both are normal distributions. To measure the difference between them, we need a measure of their relative "fatness" or "leanness." Though hypothetical, they depict situations often encountered. Waitresses, for example, have about the same mean intelligence as the general population, yet the general population includes more highly intelligent persons and more feeble-minded persons than does a representative sampling of waitresses. Students in one school may, on the average, have the same aptitudes as those in another, but it may have more students with both higher aptitude and lower aptitude than has the second school. In each case, the means are the same, but the *variability* of the measurements is different. Hence we need measures of variability.

Range. Of several possible measures we might use, the simplest (but not the best) is the *range.* This is the difference between the highest and the lowest scores. For ordinal measurements, the range is of little value since differences in scores do not of themselves mean anything; only ranks are important. For interval measurements, the range is a very crude and unstable measure, for it is based on only two measures, the very extreme ones. These, in most distributions, are rather erratic, and only a small change in them changes the size of the range. So statisticians use the range only when all that is needed is a very quick and crude estimate of variability.

Standard deviation. The most useful and precise measure of variability, the one generally used by behavioral scientists, is known as the *standard deviation.* The shorthand term for referring to it is the small Greek letter σ. Briefly defined, it is the *root-mean-square of the deviations of measurements from their arithmetic mean.* A more precise algebraic definition, as well as the procedure for calculating σ, is given in the last section of this chapter. We shall stress here its properties and uses.

A standard deviation, or σ, is a number representing a distance along the scale of a frequency distribution. It is proportional to the spread of the distribution and hence

DISTRIBUTIONS MAY DIFFER IN VARIABILITY:

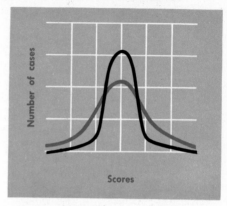

FIGURE 13.7. Distributions differing in variability. Both distributions have the same central tendency, but one is narrow and the other is robust. Consequently, they have different variabilities (standard deviations).

measures its variability. Distributions with a large σ are ones with high variability; they are relatively broad. Those with small standard deviations have low variability; the measurements are grouped closely around the mean.

The standard deviation is the measure par excellence of the variability of measurements in a distribution. The σ is such a good measure that, if the frequency distribution is reasonably normal, the distribution can be reconstructed by knowing only two numbers, the mean and the σ. This is true because mathematicians have a precise formula for the normal-probability curve, and the only two unknowns in it are the mean and the σ. Given these, one can draw the normal curve that best fits the particular frequency distribution. Thus, in so far as a distribution is normal, the mean and the σ completely describe and specify it.

This mathematical nicety has important uses. In the normal-probability curve, the σ can be used as a measuring rod to lay off distances along the scale of the distribution. The exact number of cases (the frequencies) that will be included in any given number of standard deviations is known from tables that have been constructed from the formula for the curve. The information supplied by the tables is summarized in Figure 13.8. It shows that 68.3 per cent of the cases in a normal frequency distribution lie between 1σ above and 1σ below the mean. About 95 per cent lie in the range between 2σ above and 2σ below the mean. And 99.7 per cent fall between 3σ above and 3σ below the mean. It is possible to determine from the tables the percentage of cases to be expected between any other two measurements given in terms of sigma units along the scale.

STANDARD SCORES.   One other use of the standard deviation merits special mention. It may be employed to state individual measurements in a "universal language." All that is necessary to do this is to convert any particular measurement into a sigma score (see section on formulas and calculations). The principle involved in the conversion can be seen in Figure 13.14, which appears later in the chapter (page 427), because it illustrates a number of other points as well. It is simply that, knowing the value of σ, every individual measurement has an equivalent value in σ units. This value is called the *z score*.

Closely related to the z score is the standard score, sometimes called *T score*. This is any *score derived by using the z score as a basic unit*. For example, we could arbitrarily let the mean of a distribution be 50, and then consider each standard deviation to be 10. Consequently we would have the following correspondence between z scores and standard scores:

z score	Standard score
−3	20
−2	30
−1	40
0	50
+1	60
+2	70
+3	80

Any other system for deriving standard scores is all right as long as all that is done is to add a constant (in this case 50) to z scores and/or multiply them by a constant (in this case 10).

Standard scores (T scores) and z scores constitute a kind of universal language for expressing scores because they always mean the same thing in all reasonably normal distributions, irrespective of the particular scale on which the measurements were made. From them we can quickly see where the individual stands in the distribution and can compare two or more measurements for one individual drawn from distributions having different means and different standard deviations. An example of this is the "profile" of an individual on a number of psychological tests, shown in Figure 13.9. This profile tells us how he compares with other individuals without our being concerned with the means and standard deviations on the particular tests. If for any reason we did want to know these, we could go to the tables of the normal-probability curve and find the proportion of individuals he excels or is excelled by.

CENTILE SCORES.   The last point brings us to centile scores, for it is almost a definition of a *centile score*. This is the *percentage of cases,* usually different individuals who have been measured, *falling at or below a particular person's score in the distribution.* Put another way, it is a person's rank in 100, obtained by dividing his rank by the total number of measurements in the distribution, and multiplying by 100.

A centile score (sometimes called the percentile score) has several uses. If distributions are badly skewed or there is no justification for assuming that they are distributions of interval measurements, then a centile score is a better way of indicating a person's standing in the distribution than a z score. At other times, one may have to present a score to people who do not understand the standard score or standard deviation and who do not have the time or willingness to learn. In such cases, it is better to use the centile score, since in a normal distribution one is easily converted into the other (see Figure 13.10). Notice, incidentally, that the median (z score = 0) is the 50th centile score, the −1σ point the 16th centile, the +1σ point the 84th centile, and so on.

We shall not describe the measures of variability that are appropriate for ordinal measurements, because such measures are seldom used. The easiest way to indicate the variability of ordinal measurements or of distributions that are not normal is to state the 25th, 50th (median), and 75th percentile points. The greater the skewness of the distribution, the greater the difference between the 25th and 50th centiles and the 50th and 75th centiles. In a normal distribution, these differences are equal.

Correlation

Up until now we have been concerned with the statistical treatment of frequency distributions considered one at a time. Now we come to the topic of correlation. This almost defines itself if spelled "co-relation," for it refers to the co-relation between two or more distributions of measurements. In one way or another, most of science is concerned with co-relations. In physical science, however, these are usually called "functions"; the behavior of one variable, that is, one set of measurements, is related to the behavior of another variable, that is, another set of measurements. Usually, the relationship is precise enough to permit the drawing of a line through or near all the points joining the two variables and even to summarize the relationship neatly in a mathematical formula.

Psychology sometimes has this precision too. Examples of it are to be found here and there throughout this book, particularly in the chapters on the senses. More often,

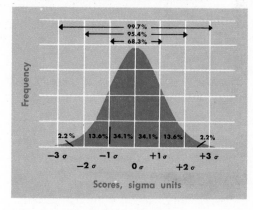

FIGURE 13.8. The distribution of scores in a normal curve. Since the normal curve has a known shape, it is possible to state the percentage of scores that lie between plus and minus 1 standard deviation, or between any other two points expressed in terms of σ units.

however, we are unable to define a function, or even to reach the point at which it is necessary to do so. Our job, typically, is to determine whether or not there is a correlation between two variables, and if so, how much of a correlation there is. Even though such correlations, when we find them, seldom have the precision of physical functions, they are nevertheless powerful tools in determining the causes of psychological phenomena and of making useful predictions from one set of measurements to another.

To make clear what it is we are trying to do in the statistics of correlation, let us take a common example of heights and weights. We know from casual observation that people differ a lot in both height and weight. If we wish, we can take any particular group of people and find their average heights and average weights. We can also measure the variability of their heights and the variability of their weights. But we know also that there must be a connection or correlation between height and weight. In general, people who are tall weigh more

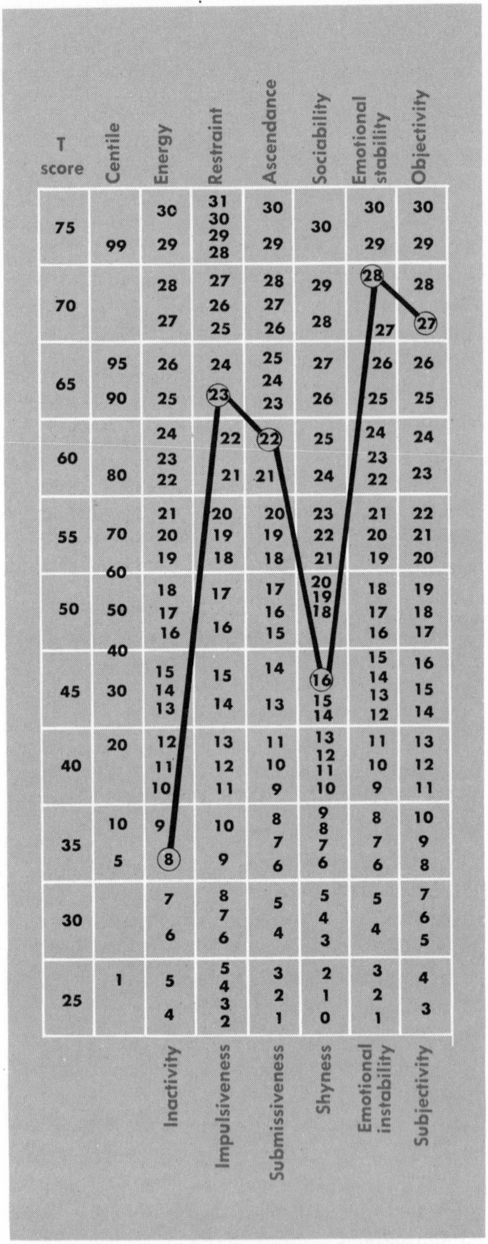

FIGURE 13.9. Profile of T scores. The scores circled and joined by lines are the scores of a single individual on different traits measured by the Guilford-Zimmerman Temperament Survey. The scores have been so arranged in each column that they show the relative position of the individual in terms of centiles or normal T scores [after Guilford, 1959].

T score	Centile	Energy	Restraint	Ascendance	Sociability	Emotional stability	Objectivity
75	99	30, 29	31, 30, 29, 28	30, 29	30	30, 29	30, 29
70		28, 27	27, 26, 25	28, 27, 26	29, 28	(28), 27	28, (27)
65	95, 90	26, 25	24, (23)	25, 24, 23	27, 26	26, 25	26, 25
60	80	24, 23, 22	22, 21	(22), 21	25, 24	24, 23, 22	24, 23
55	70, 60	21, 20, 19	20, 19, 18	20, 19, 18	23, 22, 21	21, 20, 19	22, 21, 20
50	50, 40	18, 17, 16	17, 16	17, 16, 15	20, 19, (18)	18, 17, 16	19, 18, 17
45	30	15, 14, 13	15, 14	14, 13	(16), 15, 14	15, 14, 13, 12	16, 15, 14
40	20	12, 11, 10	13, 12, 11	11, 10, 9	13, 12, 11, 10	11, 10, 9	13, 12, 11
35	10, 5	9, (8)	10, 9	8, 7, 6	9, 8, 7, 6	8, 7, 6	10, 9, 8
30		7, 6	8, 7, 6	5, 4	5, 4, 3	5, 4	7, 6, 5
25	1	5, 4	5, 4, 3, 2	3, 2, 1	2, 1, 0	3, 2, 1	4, 3
		Inactivity	Impulsiveness	Submissiveness	Shyness	Emotional instability	Subjectivity

than those who are short. Obviously, however, the correlation is not perfect, for some people only 5 feet tall weigh more than some who are 6 feet tall. So the correlation is one of degree—a statistical matter—and we therefore need a measure that expresses that degree.

For mathematical convenience, the degree of a correlation is expressed by a number between 0.00 and 1.00. Zero represents no correlation at all; 1.00 represents a perfect correlation—one comparable to the very precise functions often encountered in the physical sciences. There will be more on this later, and also on the meaning of negative correlations, such as −.50.

It is possible to obtain a measure of correlation for any two sets of measurements, whether they be nominal, ordinal, or interval. It is also possible to obtain such a measure with any combination of them, e.g., one nominal and the other interval, or one ordinal and the other interval, and so on. Each combination requires its own particular formula for calculating the answer. For simplicity, we shall discuss only the pure cases of nominal-nominal, ordinal-ordinal, and interval-interval.

CONTINGENCY. When the measurements being correlated are all in the nominal class, a measure of correlation that may be used is the *coefficient of contingency*. To illustrate this, we shall take an example from a study [Siegel, 1956] of social classes:

Of all the families in a community called Elmstown, 360 having children in high school were classified into one of five social classes. Various criteria were employed in the classification. There were too few families in each of the two upper classes (I and II) for statistical purposes, so they were lumped to-gether. Hence there were only four categories of social class. Each child in high school was enrolled in one of three designated courses: college preparatory, general, or commercial. To obtain a correlation, counts were made of each child according to his social class and his high school course. Since there were four social classes and three high school curricula, 12 combinations were possible.

Table 13.4 shows the number (frequency) of individuals in each combination—statisticians call them "cells." It is clear from the table that there is some correlation. The overwhelming proportion of those in the college-preparatory curriculum came from Classes I–II and III, and the great majority of those in Classes III, IV, and V were not in college preparatory. The greatest proportion of those in the commercial curriculum were in Classes III and IV. The computation of one particular index of correlation, the coefficient of contingency, is .39, which expresses in a number the degree of correlation.

The contingency method of measuring correlation, then, makes use of data in nominal categories. The degree to which the cases in each cell, formed by the combination of one category on one scale of measurement with a category on the second scale of measurement, departs from what might be expected by chance is the degree of correlation between the two variables.

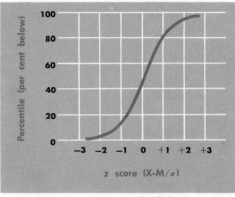

FIGURE 13.10. The use of the standard deviation to find standard scores and percentile scores. Any individual's score (X) on a test may be subtracted from the mean (M) to obtain a deviation score (x). Dividing this by the standard deviation (σ) yields a standard score (z score). Such scores may be compared with each other even when they have been derived from quite different tests. By referring to the curve above or to a table of the probability integral, one can determine the percentage of cases falling below any particular z score. This is often called the percentile score.

RANK-DIFFERENCE CORRELATION. Where ordinal measurements are the data for determining a correlation, the procedure is different. In this case, a formula has been devised that makes use of the differences in ranks on the two sets of measurements. An example is given in Table 13.5 and Figure

TABLE 13.4. The curriculum taken by high school students of different social classes in one town [from Siegel, 1956, p. 198; after Hollingshead, 1949].

Curriculum	Social class				Total
	I–II	III	IV	V	
College preparatory	23	40	16	2	81
General	11	75	107	14	207
Commercial	1	31	60	10	102
Total	35	146	183	26	390

13.11 and may be described as follows [Guilford, 1956]:

Fifteen individuals were shown at different times a series of 15 cartoons and a series of 15 limericks. When shown a cartoon, the subject was asked to rate its humor on a 5-point scale, giving 5 for "very humorous" and 1 for "not funny at all." He did the same thing for the limericks. When all the responses had been recorded, the points given by each individual on cartoons were added up to find a "cartoon score." Similarly each individual received a "limerick score." So there were two scores for every individual, a "cartoon score" and a "limerick score." The question was, How well do these scores correlate? Or what is the relationship between seeing humor in cartoons and seeing it in limericks? Since there was no reason to believe these scores met the criteria of interval measurements, the scores were transmuted to ranks. The subject scoring highest received a rank of 1, the one scoring next highest a rank of 2, and so on down

through 15. Each individual's rank on the other set of scores was determined in the same way. Then the correlation coefficient, known as *rho* was computed from the differences in ranks. It was found to be .70, which is fairly high as correlations on psychological measurements go.

One can see in Figure 13.11 that the correlation is reasonably good. Although there are some inversions, those who ranked high on one index of humor tended also to rank high on the other measurement. The conclusion, which in this case is not particularly earth-shaking, is that people show some consistency in how funny they find things in two different situations, cartoons and limericks. This experiment was of some value in research on the development of tests of humor.

The way, then, to measure the correlation between two sets of ordinal measurements is to run a rank-difference correlation, a procedure devised to make use of the ranking afforded by ordinal measurements.

TABLE 13.5. Humor scores on a cartoon test and a limerick test for 15 individuals. At the right are the rank orders of these two sets of scores [after Guilford, 1956].

Individual	Cartoon score	Limerick score	Cartoon rank	Limerick rank
A	47	75	11	8
B	71	79	4	6
C	52	85	9	5
D	48	50	10	14
E	35	49	14.5	15
F	35	59	14.5	12
G	41	75	12.5	8
H	82	91	1	3
I	72	102	3	1
J	56	87	7	4
K	59	70	6	10
L	73	92	2	2
M	60	54	5	13
N	55	75	8	8
O	41	68	12.5	11

CORRELATION COEFFICIENT. For measurements made on an interval scale, another method of computation is used. Actually, the different formulas for determining degree of correlation all arrive at about the same answer, for they have been worked out to do that. They have to be different because the kinds of data are different. In this case, the index of correlation is called the *product-moment correlation coefficient*. Its symbol is *r*, sometimes called *Pearson's r* after the English statistical psychologist who devised it. An illustration of data yielding a high correlation is given in Figure 13.12.

This example [Terman and Merrill, 1937] is drawn from the field of intelligence testing (see Chapter 14). There are two forms of the Stanford-Binet test of intelligence: Form L and Form M. A group of seven-year-old children were given the two forms of this test on two different occasions. Hence, two scores (measurements) of intelligence were available for each child. These scores were plotted on the graph in Figure 13.12 by letting each point represent a pair of scores. They are all plotted in class intervals, just as the data for reaction time were (Figure 13.4). Here, with the two scales, one for Form L and the other for Form M, at right angles to each other, the two sets of class intervals form boxes or cells. A child scoring 87 on Form L and 90 on Form M, has a single point entered in the cell made by the intersection of the class interval 85–89 on Form L and the class interval 90–94 on Form M. And so on, until all pairs of scores are plotted.

The two scales were so constructed that the same person would, ideally, make the same score on each form. If it turned out this way, the correlation between the two forms would be perfect and the correlation coefficient would be 1.00. Moreover, on the diagram one would see a perfectly straight line running from the lower left-hand corner toward the upper right-hand corner. In Figure 13.12 the scores fall around the straight line but tend to stray in one direction or another a little off the diagonal. What this

A RANK DIFFERENCE CORRELATION CAN BE DEPICTED THIS WAY:

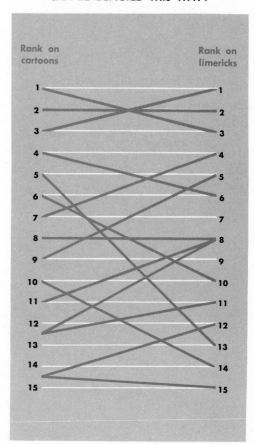

FIGURE 13.11. Each line connects the two scores made by one individual [data from Table 13.5].

means is that a person making a score on one test tends to make a somewhat different score on the other form—but not very different. Thus the correlation is not quite perfect, but is, in fact, very high—actually about .90.

Plots like that in Figure 13.12 are called *scatter diagrams*. They provide a visual picture of the degree of a correlation, because the amount of scatter, and its direction, varies with the correlation. This point is illustrated in Figure 13.13. When a correlation is zero, the points in the scatter diagram

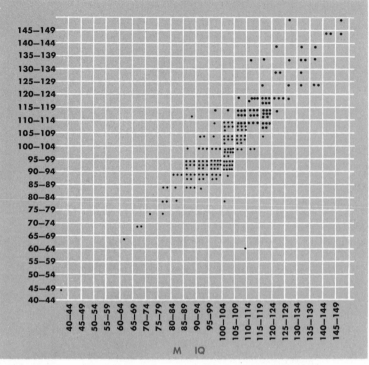

FIGURE 13.12. A scattergram of IQs obtained on Form L and Form M of the Stanford-Binet test at chronological age seven. Such a scattergram illustrates the use of correlation to express the reliability of a test, which in this case is quite high [after Terman and Merrill, 1937, p. 45].

are randomly distributed and do not line up in any particular direction. There are more points in the center of the scatter than around its fringes simply because measurements of each of the contributing frequency distributions pile up more in the center than on the "tails." If the correlation is moderate, say, .50, the scatter narrows in one direction or another, and as indicated earlier, the scatter diagram of a perfect correlation of 1.00 is a straight line.

Another way to say this is to describe the shape of the scatter diagram. It is circular when the correlation is zero. It becomes more and more elliptical as the correlation increases, and narrows down to a straight line when the correlation is perfect.

Note, too, in Figure 13.13 that the direction of the ellipse or line of the scatter diagram indicates the sign of the correlation, that is, whether it is positive or negative.

Assuming that the scales of the diagram have been arranged in the conventional way, so that high scores are at the top of the vertical scale and on the right of the horizontal scale, positive (+) correlations are indicated by a direction from the lower left-hand corner to the upper right-hand corner. Negative correlations (−) are indicated by ellipses or lines running from the upper left-hand corner to the lower right-hand corner.

There can be all degrees of negative correlation from .00 to −1.00, just as there can be degrees of positive correlation from .00 to +1.00. Minus signs and plus signs in front of a correlation of a particular size represent equally close relationships. In fact, the number, not the sign, is the index of degree of correlation. The sign merely tells us the direction of the relationship. Negative signs indicate that high scores on one set of measurements are associated with low scores on the other set, and vice versa. In positive correlations, high scores are associated with high scores, and low scores with low scores. In negative correlations, high scores are associated with low scores, and low scores with high scores.

CAUSATION AND CORRELATION. It is easy to think that a high correlation between two sets of measurements means that one of the factors measured causes the other. This, however, is usually not so. When there is a high correlation, both sets of individual differences are usually caused by some common factors. In the case of height and weight, for example, we cannot say that a person's height causes his weight, for both height and weight are caused by individual differences in genetic inheritance, nutrition, disease, etc. A correlation, in short, simply tells us that individual differences in two sets of measurements tend to vary together, not necessarily that one causes the other.

This is not to say that we never can tell anything about causation from correlation. We can. To decide, however, what causes what requires a great number of correlations, and a careful logical analysis of which variables may be the basic, underlying ones.

Sampling

The measures we have just described may be called *descriptive statistics* because they describe accurately the characteristics of a set of measurements. When we make measurements, however, we are interested not only in describing them but also in *interpreting* them. We want to make inferences from them about people in general or about the basic principles of behavior. To make such interpretations requires some additional statistics.

REPRESENTATIVE SAMPLING. The first concept that is essential to interpreting sta-

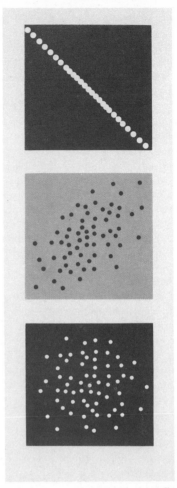

FIGURE 13.13. Scattergrams depicting different amounts of positive and negative correlation.

tistical descriptions is the concept of *sampling*. All measurement implies sampling. We usually cannot measure all cases of anything, whether it be of animal learning, of perception, of intelligence, of attitudes, of public opinion, or of anything else. There are always too many animals or people in the world and too many events to allow us to measure all cases in which we might be interested. So when we measure, whether we realize it or not, we are selecting a sample of the total possible measurements we might make.

Ordinarily we try to select a sample that is large enough and representative enough to tell us about a much larger set of measurements we were unable to make. When, for example, psychologists try to measure public opinion regarding presidential candidates, they try to get a representative sample or cross section of the population and then to take enough measurements to represent this population. From their measurements, they predict or infer the opinions of the electorate at large. In our example of intelligence-test scores, those who made the measurements were interested in getting a sample of school children representative enough to reflect the frequency distribution of intelligence among school children at large.

Biases of samples. It is not always an easy task to get representative samples. In fact, the most frequent fault with a set of measurements is that it is not representative and that we therefore cannot properly make the inferences from it that we would like. We run into this difficulty because there are always so many "biasing" factors at work. It may happen that, because of factors we are not aware of, the school children in one geographical area seem to be brighter or duller than school children in general. If we try to sample political opinion by calling people on the telephone, it may happen that people who own telephones are more often of one political opinion than another. If, as many psychologists are forced to do, we use college students for a set of measurements, it may be that they are not representative of the population in general. So various kinds of biases make it difficult to get a representative sample.

Methods of sampling. We have developed a number of different methods to try to ensure representative sampling, and some of these methods will be described in detail in later chapters (see Chapter 17). In general, they take two different forms. One we may

call *random sampling.* We use this when we know little or nothing about biasing factors in our measurement. To sample randomly, we try to see that only chance determines what is included in our sample. In making surveys of radio listening, for example, we select every two-hundredth name in the telephone directory. Or to measure intelligence, we may draw at random 2 out of every 100 names of children in each of the schools of a state. Or to study learning in rats, we select 1 out of every 10 rats in the laboratory.

The other general method of obtaining a representative sample is to do *controlled sampling.* In this case we select certain factors, such as age, sex, economic status, educational level, type of employment, etc., and deliberately balance these factors in making up our sample. In sampling public opinion, for example, we may try to see that people are selected from small towns and large towns, from poor people and rich people, from the West and East, from labor and from management—all in proportion to their numbers in the population at large. This kind of sampling, if it is done correctly, makes reasonably certain that biasing factors are controlled. Thus it is the most economical sampling method, because it is usually possible to make correct inferences from a smaller number of cases selected by controlled sampling than by random sampling.

SAMPLING ERROR.   Even when we have done our best to obtain a representative sample, we are still left with a *sampling error.* This, as its name implies, is an error due to the fact that we have only a sample of measurements from a population rather than measurements on an entire population. The error is due to chance differences in the selection of individuals from the total population. When our sample is relatively small, the error is relatively large; as the sample size increases in proportion to the population, the error decreases. As a rough general rule, the sampling error is inversely proportional to the square root of the number of measurements. In other words, the error of sampling 10 cases is about ten times as large as the error of sampling 1,000 cases.

As a result of sampling error, every measure of a frequency distribution and every measure of correlation based on distributions has some error. Consequently the mean, median, standard deviations, indices of correlation, and other measures we have described always have some error, depending on the size of the sample used. By error, we mean that the measure differs somewhat from the value we would get if we had the "true" measure of the population sampled. This fact is easy to demonstrate in practice by taking more than one sample of measurements. If, in our example of measuring braking reaction time, we had taken a second set of 200 measurements on different people, the two frequency distributions would be somewhat different. Hence their means and standard deviations would also be different.

Mathematicians have worked out formulas for estimating sampling errors. By using these formulas, we obtain numbers indicating the amount by which different samples might be expected to differ simply by chance. Whether or not we know and use such formulas, however, it must always be kept in mind that any measure we use has an error. This means that if we made the measurements over again on a new sample, each measure would have a slightly different value. That is why we should never put very much stock in small differences in means, percentages, or other measures of a distribution.

SIGNIFICANCE. This brings us to the concept of *significance*. If we are comparing two groups of measurements in an experiment, we will almost always obtain a difference between their means. Similarly, in correlating any two sets of measurements, we seldom get a correlation of zero. The question is, When is a difference or a correlation significant? By this we mean, When

is the difference from zero greater than we would expect by chance?

This question must always be answered in terms of probabilities. There are no absolute certainties in statistics. If, for example, we flip 10 pennies and get 10 heads, we may ask whether this result can be expected by chance or whether it means the coins are biased. From tables of probability, we know that 10 heads on 10 flips can be expected once in every 1,024 times, 20 heads in 20 flips once in about a million times. This may be very unlikely, but if we flip pennies several million times, we can expect this sequence to occur some time by chance. So the question of whether something is significantly different from chance must be answered in terms of chance.

In practice, we arbitrarily select two different levels of significance. One is a loose criterion of $P=.05$; another is a stricter criterion of $P=.01$, P meaning the probability expressed as a number between 0.00 and 1.00 that a result occurred by chance. These criteria mean that we will accept as really different from chance a difference that would be expected to occur 1 in 20 times or 1 in 100 times by chance. The reason for accepting the loose criterion is that it is more economical to accept it and go on to other experiments, assuming that if we are wrong, we will sooner or later find it out, than it is to continue sampling the same measurements until we are more sure of the significance of our difference. Remember that the error is proportional to the square root of the number of cases. So other things being equal, it takes several times as many measurements to establish a difference as significant at the .01 level as at the .05 level.

How do we establish significance in this way? Our formulas for estimating sampling errors can be applied to any set of data and tell us how often we might expect a given difference or a given size of correlation to occur by chance. We accept as significant then—as really different from zero—any difference greater than the amount that can be expected .05 or .01 of the time. This is why differences that might seem sizable to the unsophisticated—differences of 10 or 20 per cent in means, or correlations of .20 or more—will often be ignored by the statistician. If the number of measurements underlying these differences is not very great, it works out that they cannot be accepted as significantly different from zero.

Characteristics of "good" psychological tests

If we wish to measure the dimensions of a room or how much weight we have gained, we are accustomed to look for whatever ruler, scales, or appropriate measuring device is handy and to make our measurements without ado. We do not ask any questions about the instrument; we assume it is all right. Unfortunately, this attitude tends to carry over into things psychological. The public has heard a great deal in recent years about psychological tests and is inclined to "run to the nearest test" for the measurement of intelligence, personality, vocational aptitude, or what have you. Such an attitude has been cultivated by the unwarranted use of tests of unknown value in popular periodicals.

Tests of any kind, psychological or physical, must be used intelligently. They are invented to do a particular job. Some succeed in doing it; some do not. Even tape measures and bathroom scales often prove unreliable. In more sophisticated measurement, many tests prove to be worthless. Others are exceedingly valuable, but only when they satisfy certain requirements and are used for the purposes for which they were intended. This is especially true of psychological tests. For that reason, it is worthwhile knowing just what the characteristics of a good test are.

RELIABILITY. A good test, first of all, must be reliable. It must, in other words, be consistent in the answers it gives. If you cannot measure something twice with it and get about the same answer each time, its measurements are not worth very much. This is quite aside from the problem of sampling error discussed above. In sampling, we measure two different things (or people) from the same population. The sampling error is due to chance differences in the things (people) measured. Here we are talking about measuring the same thing (person) twice, and having the two measurements agree fairly well.

The concept of reliability can be illustrated by considering an example that, we hope, is quite unrealistic. A professor has given his class an examination, and now his somewhat odious task is to grade it. In this case he has no sampling problems because he has obtained papers from all members of the class. All he has to do is choose a measuring stick, that is, a method of scoring them. One possible method is to throw them down the stairs and, assigning a number to each step, grade each paper according to the step it falls on. If he does this, the chances are he will get a frequency distribution (which might even be a normal curve) from which he could obtain a mean and a standard deviation.

There are two obvious faults in this method of grading: it is invalid, and it is unreliable. (Validity is discussed below.) The method would be unreliable simply because it would not give the same answer twice. It would not check itself. If the professor gathered up the papers and threw them down the stairs a second time, he would not get the same score for the same paper. Assuming that the papers landed randomly on the steps, the score a person got on the second grading would bear no relation to the score on the first grading. That is why we say this method is *unreliable*.

There is a statistical method for inferring quite precisely the relative reliability or unreliability of a set of measurements. It is the correlational method we have already described. By correlating one set of scores with another set obtained by the same method, we obtain a measure of the reliability of the measurements. This, indeed, was the primary purpose of having two forms of intelligence test, Form L and Form M, in the example we used. Using two forms to test intelligence is like grading papers independently on two separate occasions. If the results correlate well, as they do in the case of intelligence, then we can assume that our measuring instrument is measuring something reliably. If they do not, our measurements are unreliable—we might as well be throwing papers down the stairs.

Reliability is a *sine qua non* of psychological measurement. If measurement is not reliable, it cannot be much of anything else. If, in other words, we cannot get the same set of scores, or almost the same set of scores, for people on two successive, independent measurements, we are not really measuring. Flipping pennies, rolling dice, or spinning roulette wheels would be just about as good. To put the matter another way, if a measuring instrument cannot be correlated rather well with itself, it is useless for making inferences about anything else.

VALIDITY. A good test or measurement must also be valid. It must correlate with something besides itself so that it is measuring something meaningful. In the simplest case, validity refers to how well a test measures what it is intended to measure. If we are trying to measure intelligence, our test should measure intelligence, not reaction time, cultural background, or something else. If it does not measure intelligence, we say that it is not a valid test of intelligence. More generally speaking, however, a test is valid to the extent, and only to the extent, that it correlates with something else. A test that correlates highly with reaction time would be a good test of reaction time, but if it does not correlate with intelligence, it is not a valid test of intelligence.

Let us return to the example of examination grading. An essay examination is generally supposed to provide a measurement of a person's knowledge of a subject and his ability to organize that knowledge. To the extent that it does this, it is a valid test. It is not supposed to measure how many words a student can write. Counting words, however, is a highly reliable measurement, and if a professor should take to counting, he could arrive at some highly reliable grades. In fact, such a method of grading would undoubtedly be about the most reliable of all methods he could use. If he used it, he might or might not have a valid test of "word production." He might even have a measurement that had some validity for measuring comprehension and organization of knowledge, since there is some correlation between the amount one writes on an essay examination and what he knows. Much more valid, however, would be some way of rating the tests for the things intended, namely, knowledge and organization, and that is what professors usually try to do.

This problem of validity of measurement is a very serious one for psychologists. It is relatively easy, although not so easy as one might suppose, to devise measuring instruments that are reliable. It is much harder to devise *valid* measures. To determine the validity of measurements, once their reliability has been established, we must use the correlational method. In this case, however, we must have some *criterion* that represents what the test in fact correlates with.

One of the major criteria of intelligence, for example, is ability to learn and to solve problems, or to put it more generally, the ability to profit by education. The criterion, then, of an intelligence test *might* be success in school. To assess the validity of an intelligence test, we might therefore correlate a person's scores on intelligence tests with his educational progress—his grades or how far he has progressed for his age. If the correlation is high, we may say that the intelligence test is valid; if it is low, the test is not so valid.

To take another example, if our purpose is to select pilots, our criterion would be whether they succeed or fail in their training for flying. When we have tests that correlate well with such success or failure, we say they are valid. If they do not correlate with the criterion, no matter how reliable they may be—no matter how well they correlate with themselves—they are invalid.

Validity, then, is a merit *index of the degree to which a test correlates with a criterion.* Usually the criterion is what we say we want to measure. Sometimes it turns out that a test is not valid for that, but is valid for some other criterion. To be valid, however, it must correlate with a criterion. Hence it can be used properly to measure or predict only that criterion.

SAMPLING OF TASKS. Good tests, thirdly, are samples of tasks. They are samples of the many things that go to make up the criterion. A lot of things, for example, go into intelligence. Hence many different measurements correlate with intelligence: speed in problem solving, ability to memorize, size of vocabulary, etc. A test of any one of these things has validity as a test of intelligence. To stick to one of them, however, is to limit the validity to a very low level. The highest validity is obtained by having in the test a fair sample of the behaviors that are involved in the criterion.

Ideally, then, to develop the most valid test, we should have to measure an infinite number of things, or at least as many as have any validity at all. This, however, would be far too expensive and impractical to do. After it was done, it would take so much time to give a test that we seldom would be able to give it properly to those who should have it, and our effort would be wasted. In practice, then, we must devise tests with a reasonable number of items, sometimes compromising the highest validity we might obtain ideally, in order to have a usable test. Nevertheless, the good test—the valid test—is one that includes as fair a sample as possible of the tasks that make up the criterion.

Having a fair sample of tasks means standardizing the way in which the test is given. We must give the test to everyone in exactly the same way and in exactly the same amount of time—if time in any way affects performance. If test procedure is not standardized, measurements may become both unreliable and invalid. Since conditions vary from time to time, we do not expect to get the same measurement twice or to have our measurements correlate as well as they might with the criterion.

STANDARDIZATION GROUP. Finally, a good test for general use as a measuring instrument should be based on a large and well-defined standardization group. For some research purposes, this may not be necessary, but it is for tests used in counseling, guidance, and making general predictions about people.

The reason for having a standardization group is that in psychological measurement we are primarily interested in comparing people. We are interested in the differences between them or in their rank order (cf. ordinal and interval measurements). A psychological trait is not like pounds and inches; it is a relative thing. It does us no good to know that John completed 83 questions on an intelligence test unless we are also told that the average number completed by other people was 60 and that fewer than 10 per cent of them completed more than 83 questions. With this information, we have a rather good picture of how John rates in comparison with other people. Without it, we simply have a meaningless fact.

For this reason, an important step in devising a test is to give it to a large number of people. The group to which it is given is called a *standardization group,* and the various scores made by people in the group are called *test norms.* The test norms tell us what the average score is and also how much variability there is among scores. There are various ways of reporting such norms, and it does not make too much difference which way is used, because the psychologist can readily convert from one form to another. This can be seen in Figure 13.14, which shows the relationship between different ways of reporting norms.

FIGURE 13.14. Statistical descriptions of a hypothetical distribution of test scores made by a standardization group. At top is the frequency distribution of raw scores that a standardization group might make on a test. The mean of this distribution, is 45; the standard deviation, 11. Raw scores may then be expressed in any of three ways: standard deviations, percentiles, or standard scores. In this case, to express them as standard scores, the mean has arbitrarily been set at 50 and the standard deviation at 10.

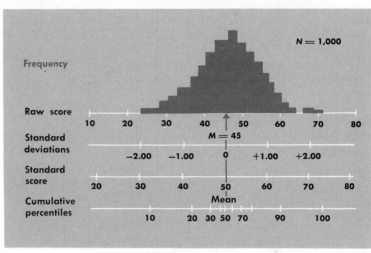

Figure 13.14 gives a distribution of scores made by a standardization group on a hypothetical test of ability. The scores range from 25 to 70. Below the scores are three scales. One shows the scores corresponding to 1σ and 2σ above and below the mean. The next scale shows standard scores. The last scale shows the percentage of persons scoring below any particular score. To a person who understands it, the standard score is particularly useful because it indicates directly the relation of the individual score to the standardization group. In this case, the mean has a standard score of 50 and each 10 points in either direction represents a standard deviation.

To illustrate these scales, let us suppose that a person made a score of 59 on our hypothetical test. By consulting the test norms, we discover that his score is about 1.3σ above the mean, that it is a score as high as, or higher than, that made by 90 per cent of the standardization group, and that it represents a standard score of 63. Test norms are expressed in any, and sometimes in all, of these ways. Age norms are usually given when the test is to be used for people of heterogeneous ages. They are omitted if the test is to be used for a relatively homogeneous group, e.g., young adults. Norms may also be given for grades in school, occupational groups, or any other classification of individuals that may be relevant.

One further point, however, is of importance. It concerns the standardization group. If our comparison of a person's score with test norms is to be a fair one, we must *know the characteristics of the standardization group*. Not any old group will do. If John is ten years old and we give him an intelligence test, it is not fair to use test norms from a standardization group of adults. The group should be children of John's own age. If we give an intelligence test to a Negro who grew up on a farm in the South, it is not proper to use norms obtained from white people living in Northern cities. So to interpret test results accurately, we must make sure that our test norms represent the kind of people with whom it is proper to compare a person's score.

One should also bear in mind that the standardization group should be reasonably large—at least several hundred and preferably a few thousand. If the group is too small, norms may be too high or too low just as a matter of chance in the selection of people for the group.

FACTOR ANALYSIS. In using tests for both practical and research purposes, we often raise the question, What does the test measure? The glib answer might be "intelligence," "personality," "scholastic aptitude," or whatever the tester *thinks* it measures. The answer might be essentially correct if validity studies have been made that show the test correlates highly with some accepted criterion for intelligence, personality, etc. Even so, there can be a deeper and more precise meaning to such a question. It could mean, What psychological factor or factors does the test measure?

Put this way, the question introduces a concept, the concept of *factor*, which is of considerable importance in psychological measurement. It may be explained as follows:

Each person possesses a number of traits. That is to say, he has abilities, aptitudes, ways of thinking and acting, etc., in which he is relatively consistent from day to day. A psychological test, if it is reliable and valid, measures some of these traits, but it does not tell us just what traits are being measured. We may guess at them by naming the particular traits a test appears to measure, but this is not a precise or scientific answer. Moreover, there are literally thousands of trait names in the dictionary, many of which are so similar that we cannot easily distinguish one trait from another. As students of human behavior, we should like to *know*, not guess at, the traits being measured by psychological tests.

A scientific approach to this problem has been devised. It is known as *factor analysis*. The details of this method are beyond the scope of this book, but the principle of it can be explained by considering a hypothetical example.

Suppose we administer six tests to a group of people. Let us call the tests A, B, C, D, E, and F. When the tests have been scored, we can calculate correlation coefficients be-

tween every possible pair of tests. There are 15 such pairs. To make the case extremely simple, let us assume that all correlations turn out to be either 1.00 or .00—something that would never happen in practice—and that they are as follows:

Tests	A	B	C	D	E
B	1.00				
C	1.00	1.00			
D	.00	.00	.00		
E	.00	.00	.00	1.00	
F	.00	.00	.00	1.00	1.00

What would such a set of correlations mean? Notice that there are two clusters of coefficients. One cluster is formed by tests A, B, and C; the other by tests D, E, and F. The tests in each cluster correlate perfectly with each other but not at all with the tests in the other cluster. Consequently we have isolated (hypothetically) two factors in the tests. Since there are only two factors, there is no need in the future to use six tests. Tests B and C measure exactly the same thing as test A, and tests E and F measure exactly the same thing as D. We can select any one test in each cluster and measure a factor. What at the outset might have seemed to be six characteristics or traits can be reduced to two.

In actual practice, we never find things so simple as we assumed them to be in the hypothetical example. Correlations making up a cluster are seldom as high as 1.00, and correlations between clusters, or tests in different clusters, are usually greater than zero. And the correlations within a cluster vary somewhat in value. Consequently, we usually cannot test a factor simply by selecting one test within a cluster. Hence more work is necessary to construct a new test that combines features of a test within a cluster. Nevertheless, our hypothetical example illustrates the principle of factor analysis. In such an analysis, a few common factors in a large number of tests may be isolated by discovering those tests that correlate highly with each other but not with other clusters of tests.

Factor analysis enables one to get "deadwood" out of tests—to eliminate tests or parts of tests that contribute nothing or add little to measuring the factors in which the tester is interested. In some cases, tests have been so constructed through factor analysis that each test measures predominantly one factor [Thurstone, 1938; Thurstone and Thurstone, 1941]. In other cases this is not desirable, for several factors are involved in a criterion, and hence need to be measured by a test designed to predict the criterion. In other instances, factor analysis has served as a powerful research tool to single out, and reduce in number, the factors being measured by particular tests. Thus it has helped greatly in the construction of good tests. Factor analysis, though a complicated technique, is a valuable tool and concept in psychology. Some of the factors it reveals have already been mentioned in Chapter 2 and will be considered again later when we study personality (page 468) and abilities (page 445).

PREDICTION FROM MEASUREMENTS. It should be pointed out, finally, that the purpose of a good test is to make successful predictions. We would not go to the trouble of constructing or administering tests if they were not supposed to predict something we did not know or could not easily measure in the first place. Sometimes the prediction is for research or scientific purposes. Very often it has important practical advantages. Several cases of such prediction will be described in later chapters, but one example here will illustrate the point.

During the Second World War, the Army was faced with the general problem of selecting men for specialized training—in this particular case, training in a tank-mechanics course. Naturally it wanted to pick men who were most likely to succeed in such training. As can be seen in Figure 13.15, there was

SPECIFIC PREDICTIONS CAN BE MADE FROM A VALIDITY COEFFICIENT:

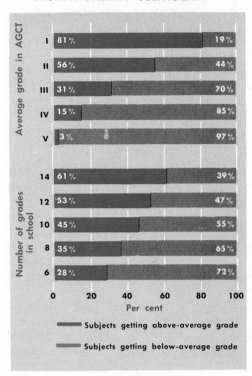

FIGURE 13.15. Predicting success in tank-mechanics school from number of grades completed in school and from scores on the Army General Classification Test. A valid test predicts what it is supposed to predict. In this case, the AGCT predicts success in tank-mechanics school better than number of grades in school completed [after Boring, 1945].

some correlation between the number of grades a man had completed in school and his success in the tank-mechanics course. Those who had completed 12 grades of school had 6 chances in 10 of doing above-average work in the course. Those, however, who had only 6 grades of school had less than 3 chances in 10 of doing this well. Consequently, the correlation between grades completed and success in the course provided some basis for prediction.

But there was a somewhat higher correlation between the Army General Classification Test and success in the tank-mechanics course. This test (which we shall discuss at more length in Chapter 14) is a test of intelligence especially designed for the purposes of the Armed Forces. The upper part of Figure 13.15 shows that men in the highest-scoring group (I) on this test had 8 chances in 10 of doing above-average work in the course. Those in the lowest-scoring group (V) had hardly any chance of doing so well. This was a considerably better prediction than that afforded by number of grades completed.

The figure illustrates the predictions one can make from reliable and valid measurements. Give a statistician a correlation coefficient between a test and a criterion, and he can make up a diagram like that in Figure 13.15 which predicts a person's chances of success from any particular score on the test. He can do this because he has the appropriate formulas that have been proved both mathematically and in practical experience to predict from one set of measurements to another. The use one makes of such predictions depends upon many practical considerations, such as the cost of training people with a low chance of success, or how much choice one has in selecting people. The important point is that valid measurements lead to useful predictions.

Formulas and calculations

For a list of the symbols used in this section and their respective definitions see the right-hand column.

MEASURES OF FREQUENCY DISTRIBUTIONS. The formula for the *arithmetic mean* is:

$$M = \frac{\Sigma X}{N} \qquad (1)$$

The formula for the standard deviation may be written in several ways. Among them are:

$$\sigma_d = \sqrt{\frac{\Sigma x^2}{N}} \qquad (2)$$

and

$$\sigma_d = \sqrt{\frac{\Sigma X^2}{N} - M^2} \qquad (3)$$

Computation of the mean by formula (1) and the standard deviation by formula (2) is illustrated in Table 13.6. The work proceeds by first obtaining the sum of the measurements (ΣX) and then calculating the mean (M). Next the column of xs can be filled in by subtracting the mean from each measurement ($X - M$), and from that the column of x^2 values can be obtained. From the sum of the deviations squared (x^2) one can then obtain the standard deviation by dividing by the number of cases (N) and taking the square root.

DEFINITION OF SYMBOLS

X The numerical value of a measurement

M Arithmetic mean

Σ Greek capital sigma used to mean "sum of"

N Number of cases in a distribution or set of measurements

σ_d Greek lower-case sigma, standard deviation of a distribution

x A measurement expressed as a deviation from the arithmetic mean

z The result of the deviation score divided by the standard deviation, x/σ

O Obtained frequency, or the number of cases counted, in the cell of a contingency table

E Expected frequency, or the number most likely to fall in the cell if the frequencies in all cells were determined by chance and hence if there were no correlation

x^2 Chi-square, a measure of the amount by which obtained frequencies (O) differ from those that would be expected by chance (E)

C Coefficient of contingency, a measure of correlation when measurements are nominal or fall into a few categories

ρ Rho, the rank-difference coefficient of correlation, a measure of correlation when measurements have been made on an ordinal scale or are expressed as ranks

r Pearson product-moment coefficient of correlation, a measure of correlation when measurements have been made on an interval scale

σ_m Standard error of a mean, a measure of the variability that may be expected among the means of different samples of the same size drawn from the same population

If a good calculator is available, the computation of the mean is the same as just described, but that of the standard deviation is faster by formula (3), which eliminates the step of converting each measurement into a deviation.

The formula for a z score is:

$$z = \frac{x}{\sigma} \qquad (4)$$

To convert a z score into any desired standard score:

$$\text{Standard score} = a + bz \qquad (5)$$

MEASURES OF CORRELATION. To calculate the coefficient of contingency, it is first necessary to obtain the quantity known as chi-square (χ^2). This calculation can be illustrated by Table 13.7 which is based on the data in Table 13.4. The first step is to determine the number that would be expected in each cell if there were no correlation between (in this instance) class and high school curriculum. This is done by multiplying the totals of the row and column intersecting on the cell and dividing by the grand total. Thus, the expected number, by chance, in the cell formed by "College preparatory" versus "Class I–II" is

$\dfrac{35 \times 81}{390} = 7.3$ For the next cell to the

right, $\dfrac{81 \times 146}{390} = 30.3$, and so on. When

TABLE 13.6. Computation of the arithmetic mean and standard deviation. The computation proceeds by getting first the sum of X and from that the mean. Then the column of Xs can be filled in and the χ^2 values computed. From the sum of χ^2 one can then obtain the standard deviation σ.

X	X − M = x	(X − M)² = χ²
40	22.5	506.25
35	17.5	306.25
33	15.5	240.25
20	2.5	6.25
19	1.5	2.25
19	1.5	2.25
19	1.5	2.25
16	−1.5	2.25
14	−3.5	12.25
11	−6.5	42.25
10	−7.5	56.25
9	−8.5	72.25
7	−10.5	110.25
7	−10.5	110.25
4	−13.5	182.25

$\Sigma X = 263$ $\chi^2 = 1,653.75$
$N = 15$

$$M = \frac{263}{15} = 17.5$$

$$\sigma = \sqrt{\frac{1653.75}{15}} = \sqrt{110.25} = 10.5$$

all the expected values—expected by chance if there were really no correlation—have been computed in this way, the following formula is used to complete the computation of chi-square:

$$\chi^2 = \Sigma \frac{(O - E)^2}{E} \qquad (6)$$

where O is the observed value—the one actually obtained in the study—and E is the expected value just computed. Chi-square

TABLE 13.7. The computation of chi-square and the contingency coefficient. Numbers in boldface are those expected by chance; other numbers are those obtained. For explanation, see text [from Siegel, 1956, p. 177].

Curriculum	Social class				Total
	I–II	III	IV	V	
College preparatory	**7.3**	**30.3**	**38.0**	**5.4**	
	23	40	16	2	81
General	**18.6**	**77.5**	**97.1**	**13.8**	
	11	75	107	14	207
Commercial	**9.1**	**38.2**	**47.9**	**6.8**	
	1	31	60	10	102
Total	35	146	183	26	390

turns out to be 69.2. To find the contingency coefficient, one then uses the formula:

$$C = \sqrt{\frac{x^2}{N + x^2}} \qquad (7)$$

The formula for the rank-difference coefficient rho is:

$$\rho = 1 - \frac{6\Sigma D^2}{N(N^2-1)} \qquad (8)$$

The D in the formula refers to a difference in ranks (see Table 13.5). Hence to compute ρ, one merely squares each rank difference, sums the squares, multiplies by 6 and divides by $N(N^2-1)$, subtracting the result from 1.

The coefficient of correlation r, sometimes called the product-moment correlation coefficient because of the way it is obtained, has a formula that may be written in any one of several ways, depending on what other measures are also being calculated and whether a calculator is available. The general formulas are:

$$r = \frac{\Sigma xy}{N\sigma_x\sigma_y} \quad \text{or} \quad \frac{\Sigma z_x z_y}{N} \quad \text{or} \quad \frac{\Sigma xy}{\sqrt{\Sigma x^2 \Sigma y^2}} \qquad (9)$$

Written this way it makes clear that the coefficient is essentially the average of the products of z scores. If a person's z score on one measurement is randomly related to his z score on another, that is, is uncorrelated, the average product moment will be zero because negative z scores will tend to cancel out positive ones. On the other hand, if the

correlation is positive, the products of negative z scores being positive, they tend to add to the products of positive scores and hence given a positive correlation.

When a good calculating machine is available, the best formula to use is one that looks forbidding, but is nevertheless easy to solve:

$$r_{xy} = \frac{N\Sigma XY - (\Sigma X)(\Sigma Y)}{\sqrt{[N\Sigma X^2 - (\Sigma X)^2][N\Sigma Y^2 - (\Sigma Y)^2]}} \qquad (10)$$

If one has previously computed the standard deviations of the two distributions by formula (3), the only additional quantity to be obtained from the measurements themselves is the sum of the products of X and Y. The rest is simple arithmetic.

It should be noted that the different coefficients C, p, and r are not exactly equivalent. In other words, a C of .50 does not have exactly the same meaning, for mathematical reasons, as an r of .50. The differences, however, are usually not very large, and methods of correction are available for determining the r that is equivalent to, say, a particular C or ρ.

SAMPLING. Sampling error of a mean may be estimated by the formula:

$$\sigma_m = \frac{\sigma_d}{\sqrt{N}} \qquad (11)$$

where the result is the standard deviation of a distribution of means that one could expect to obtain by chance if successive samples of measurements of the same number of cases were drawn from the same population. This is the basic measure involved in methods for determining whether an obtained difference in the means of two groups of measurements is significant in the sense of being greater than one would expect to obtain by chance.

Summary

1. Three kinds of measurements are commonly used in psychology: (*a*) nominal measurements, in which numbers are used to identify different categories; (*b*) ordinal measurements, in which numbers designate rank or order among the things being measured; and (*c*) interval measurements, in which numbers represent differences in magnitude.

2. The first step in organizing a set of measurements is usually to count the frequencies of measurements in each category or interval. The resulting counts may be represented graphically in a bar diagram or histogram; they constitute a frequency distribution.

3. To make a frequency distribution of interval measurements, the scale is divided into 15 or 20 intervals of equal size, and the measurements falling in each interval are tallied.

4. Frequency distributions of many psychological and biological characteristics approximate an ideal distribution known as the normal-probability curve. This is bell-shaped, being perfectly symmetrical and having more measurements near the center of the distribution than in the "tails."

5. Asymmetrical distributions are called skewed distributions. These have more of a tail on one side than on the other, and are not perfectly centered. Such distributions can result either from having some bias in the population measured or using tests that are too easy or too hard.

6. A number or statistic derived mathematically from a frequency distribution and used to characterize it in an exact way is called a measure. Two general kinds of measures are commonly employed: measures of central tendency and measures of variability.

7. Three kinds of measures of central tendency are the arithmetic mean, the median, and the mode. The arithmetic mean is the sum total of the measurements divided by the number of cases. The median is the middle score when measurements have been ranked. And the mode is the measurement that is most frequent.

8. Two kinds of measures of variability of a distribution are the range and the standard deviation. The range is the difference between the highest and lowest score; it is a very crude measure. The standard deviation is the root-mean-square deviation of measurements from the arithmetic mean; it is a precise measure of variability.

9. A measurement may be converted into a z score by dividing its deviation from the mean by the standard deviation. This is a way of stating measurements in "universal" terms independently of the particular scale of measurement or scoring used. A standard score serves a similar purpose, but it may be any score derived from a z score.

10. A score may be expressed as a centile by dividing the rank of a score in a distribution by the total number of measurements and multiplying by 100, thus reducing all scores to a rank in 100. Since this is readily understood by nearly everyone, it is a popular way of expressing scores on psychological tests.

11. A correlation coefficient states quantitatively the degree to which pairs of scores in two distributions are related. If the correlation is perfect, which it seldom is, the coefficient is 1.00. If there is no relation between the scores in the two distributions,

the coefficient is .00. The sign of the coefficient, which may be + or −, merely indicates whether the correlation is high-high and low-low or high-low and low-high, respectively.

12. Different methods of computing correlations are appropriate for different kinds of measurement: a contingency coefficient C for nominal measurements; a rank-difference correlation for ordinal measurements, and the correlation coefficient r for interval measurements.

13. In many cases of psychological measurements one wants a measure that is representative of a much larger population. To achieve this, one must be careful either to take a completely random sample or to use one of several methods that have been devised for controlling possible biases in the sample.

14. Any set of measurements is subject, by the laws of chance, to a sampling error that makes the sample depart somewhat from the true population. For this reason, one must allow for chance differences in samples in determining whether the difference between two samples is significant.

15. In order to be a worthwhile measuring instrument, a psychological test should have certain characteristics. Foremost are reliability and validity. To be reliable, a test must be able to give essentially the same results on repeated measurements of the same person or thing; to be valid, it must measure what it is intended to measure, that is, correlate well with some criterion.

16. In addition, tests used to determine the standing of a person should be administered under standardized conditions and should have norms based on a large, comparable standardization group.

17. By intercorrelating a group of tests, it is possible to isolate the basic factors being measured by the tests, and if desirable, to reconstruct tests that measure well a limited number of identifiable factors.

Suggestions for further reading

Chapanis, A., Garner, W. R., and Morgan, C. T. *Applied experimental psychology.* New York: Wiley, 1949. Chaps. 2 and 3.
A two-chapter summary of statistical methods, with special emphasis on applications to human engineering.

Dixon, W. J., and Massey, F. J., Jr. *Introduction to statistical analysis* (2d ed.). New York: McGraw-Hill, 1957.
An elementary textbook on statistics for students in all fields that requires only a knowledge of algebra.

Dornbusch, S. M., and Schmid, C. F. *A primer of social statistics.* New York: McGraw-Hill, 1955.
An elementary textbook on statistics and its uses in the social sciences.

Guilford, J. P. *Fundamental statistics in psychology and education* (3d ed.). New York: McGraw-Hill, 1956.
A widely used and comprehensive textbook on psychological statistics.

Senders, V. L. *Measurement and statistics: a basic text emphasizing behavioral science applications.* New York: Oxford Univer. Press, 1958.
A textbook that develops statistical methods around the concepts of scaling.

Stevens, S. S. Mathematics, measurement, and psychophysics. In S. S. Stevens (ed.), *Handbook of experimental psychology.* New York: Wiley, 1951.
A chapter on the theory of measurement as it relates to the science of psychology.

Underwood, B. J., Duncan, C. P., Taylor, J. A., and Cotton, J. W. *Elementary statistics.* New York: Appleton-Century-Crofts, 1954.
An elementary and readable presentation of basic statistical methods.

Yuker, H. E. *A guide to statistical calculations.* New York: Putnam, 1958.
A guide for performing calculations, requiring little knowledge of mathematics.

Intelligence & aptitudes

People differ from one another in a great many ways—in interests, abilities, motivations, personality, education, skills, and hobbies. Of all these, one of the most important is *abilities*. Most of us are accustomed to this idea and take it for granted. We know some people who are more intelligent than others; they can learn faster and solve problems more quickly. We know others who are able musicians, carpenters, golfers, mechanics, and so on. Some people have many different abilities in large amounts, some have only one in high degree, and others seem to have been skipped over entirely when the abilities were passed out.

Measures of abilities

In the everyday world, many practical decisions about people are based on some estimate of their abilities. Parents send a child to take music lessons or to college because they think (and hope) that he has the ability to profit from such education. The employer hires the man whom he considers best able to do a job. The people vote for the politician who they believe is most able to represent them. So, knowingly or not, we are forever making estimates of someone's abilities. These estimates may be crude. They may be based on all too little information about a person. Hence they often turn out to be wrong. But we make them anyway.

Psychologists decided more than fifty years ago to see whether they could provide more accurate measures of human abilities. In this effort, they were prodded first by educators and later by military leaders and businessmen who wanted more accurate measurements of abilities in order to make practical decisions about certain individuals. Today we have literally hundreds of tests of human abilities. Some of them are rather good, some are not so good, but nearly all are useful and better than subjective, everyday estimates of ability.

CHARACTERISTICS OF A GOOD TEST. In the last chapter, we discussed at length the characteristics a test should have to be considered a "good" test. A good test is one that can be used with confidence to make decisions about particular individuals in a group or about differences between groups. The characteristics of a good test apply just as well to tests of ability as to other kinds of tests. Let us review them briefly.

1. A test should be *reliable*. Different forms of the same test, or repeated measurements made with the test on the same individual, should give substantially the same results.

2. A test should be *valid*. It should correlate with the criterion which the test is used to predict. This is to say that it should measure what it is intended, or alleged, to measure. A test may be valid for one purpose and invalid for another.

3. A test should be administered according to a *standardized procedure*. If it is not, both the reliability and the validity of the test may be degraded.

4. A test should have norms based on a *standardization group*. The standardization group should be a relatively large one. It should be similar in character to the group of individuals with whom the test is subsequently used. The norms of the standardization group provide a frame of reference for interpreting the results obtained on any particular individual or group.

5. Under some circumstances, it is desirable to know the *factors* measured by the test. Such knowledge refines the interpretation to be made of any particular test result. It also enables the test constructor to improve the efficiency of his tests for different purposes.

The tests to be described in this chapter possess the first four characteristics and, in some cases, the fifth one as well.

ABILITY VERSUS ACHIEVEMENT. As the word itself implies, *ability* refers to something a person can do, not necessarily what he has done or will do. The word *achievement,* on the other hand, refers to what he has done. These two terms are therefore used to distinguish two different kinds of tests: *ability tests* and *achievement tests.* (There are other kinds of tests, too, but these are the two that concern us here.)

Note, however, that any test, by definition, measures what a person actually does, for there is no other way of testing him. Put another way, we test a person only by asking him to do something, and what he does is an achievement. Hence ability tests and achievement tests are both, in a sense, tests of achievement. The difference between them, however, depends on what we do with the results.

An ability test is used to predict future achievement or achievement in another situation. An aptitude test given to a student before he goes to college, for example, is used to predict how well he will do in college—his college achievement. It is therefore an ability test. Yet the test itself is a measure of achievement. It contains questions of knowledge or problems to solve, just as examinations in courses do. A score on such a test has little merit by itself. This test is not used to assign a grade or to "pass" a person. Its value lies in its power to predict achievement in college or a similar situation. We therefore call it an ability test. On the other hand, an examination given to a student in a course is designed to measure the knowledge gained in a course. It is therefore an achievement test, even though its results might otherwise be used to make reasonably good predictions about future achievement.

The distinction, then, between ability tests and achievement tests is a subtle one. Both measure achievement, but the ability test is designed and interpreted as a prediction of future achievement, whereas the achievement test is used to measure present knowledge or accomplishments.

KINDS OF ABILITY. Having made clear what an ability test is, we may next ask, What abilities do people have that can be measured? To this we can answer that there are a very large number of abilities—perhaps as many as there are different tasks, and hence achievements, in everyday life. Obviously, however, it is not practicable, nor would it be worthwhile, to try to measure all these specific abilities. Moreover, many tasks require certain common abilities, which is to say that high achievement on one correlates with high achievement on another. So psychologists restrict themselves in ability testing to a relatively few common abilities.

The abilities they attempt to measure fall into two general groups. One is *intellectual ability,* or aptitude for intellectual performance. Tests that measure such ability are therefore regarded as intelligence tests. Actually, intelligence tests measure several abilities, not just one, but these are the abilities that predict achievement in a wide variety of real situations, and for convenience we lump them together as "intelligence." Secondly, there are *special abilities* that are required in specific occupations or activities—mechanical, clerical, arithmetic, musical, and artistic abilities, to name just a few. We have come to call tests of such special abilities *aptitude tests,* for we frequently use them to predict achievement in some particular line of work or type of

training. Hence we have two types of tests: intelligence tests and aptitude tests, though the line between them is not at all sharp.

KINDS OF TESTS. There are now many tests of ability, and they differ in a number of ways. A few of the more significant ways in which they may differ are as follows:

1. *Group versus individual.* Some tests must be given by a trained tester to one person at a time, and these are *individual tests.* Some may be given to groups of individuals by almost anyone who can follow directions and has a stop watch; these are *group tests.* (The interpretation of both kinds of tests, however, must ordinarily be made by properly trained psychologists.)

2. *Verbal versus performance.* Most tests involve the use of written language in the instructions and in the questions answered by the testee; these are called *verbal tests,* because they use words. On the other hand, some tests have been devised for use with preschool children, illiterates, or foreign-born people who cannot read English. These tests are called *performance tests.* Instructions may be given verbally by the tester, but the test itself does not employ words or handicap a person who cannot read (see Figure 14.1).

3. *Speed versus power.* Some tests are limited in time, and the time is so set that the person who can do things quickly makes the best score. These are called *speed tests.* Other tests are designed to test the ability of a person to solve difficult problems irrespective of the time required; these are *power tests.* Sometimes power tests have time limits, but if so, they are only for administrative convenience and have been established so that the time limit makes no significant difference in a person's performance.

There are other ways in which tests may differ, and some are described in the chapter on personality, but these are the ones of importance in the study of intelligence and aptitudes. In addition, we may note that some tests give one over-all score for intelligence, whereas others provide separate scores for different abilities. Some are designed for certain age groups, and some for other age groups. Some are designed for the mentally retarded, others for the especially intelligent. Today, as we said, there are literally hundreds of tests, and the testing business is a multimillion-dollar industry.

Most of this chapter will be concerned with tests of intelligence, because these are of general interest and also because they illustrate the procedures involved in developing and using all sorts of tests of ability. In the last section, tests of aptitudes will be described.

Intelligence tests

The wide variety of tests that exist for the measurement of intelligence may be confusing to a person who is accustomed to think of intelligence as a single "real" ability, as many people do. Why, he may ask, should we not have just one test of intelligence that "really" measures intelligence?

Most tests of intelligence do, in fact, correlate reasonably well with one another, which means that they do tend to measure the same thing. Psychological research has made it clear, on the other hand, that there is more than one kind of intelligence—or that intelligence includes more than one ability. For this reason, the particular test of intelligence we use depends on what we want to find out. If we want to measure the kind of intelligence involved in doing schoolwork, we use one test; if we are interested in the kind involved in military life, we use another; and if it is intelligence useful in general business life that we want to measure, we use still other tests.

THE STANFORD-BINET TEST. The first test of intelligence to be devised was intended for use in school situations and thus stressed the abilities involved in primary education. This test was published by Alfred Binet, a French psychologist, in 1905. Binet designed the test at the request of the Paris school

FIGURE 14.1. Individual intelligence testing. The girl is doing a bead-stringing item on the Stanford-Binet test. Her task is to string the beads so that they match the example she is looking at [Brooks, from Monkmeyer]. The boy's task is to draw a line inside the "walls" of the figures as rapidly as possible and without hitting the sides [New York Univer. Testing and Advisement Center].

authorities to enable them to pick out children of low intelligence who could not profit from attending school. The test served its purpose and immediately caught the attention of American psychologists. In 1916, Terman of Stanford University brought out a revision of it intended for school children in the United States, and his revision came to be known as the Stanford-Binet test [Terman and Merrill, 1937]. It became the model for many intelligence tests that have been developed since then. For this reason, and because the now familiar IQ, or intelligence quotient, is derived from it, we can learn a good deal about intelligence tests by examining it more closely.

Mental age. The Stanford-Binet test, which is an individual test, is used with children from two to sixteen years of age. It consists of a series of subtests arranged according to age levels, that is, according to what children of each age can be expected, from test norms, to be able to pass. There are subtests for two-year-olds, others for three-year-olds, and so on. A child being tested is given the subtests in order of increasing difficulty until he reaches a point where he can pass none of the tests for a particular age level. When the results are tallied, the score he gets tells his *mental age* (MA). For example, if a child passed all the tests for age 4, half those for age 5, and none of those for age 6, his mental age would be 4½. Usually the picture is not so simple as that, but this is the principle for computing mental age.

Table 14.1 presents some of the subtests

TABLE 14.1. Some illustrative items from the Stanford-Binet test. The sample items below should be passed, on the average, at the ages indicated [from Terman and Merrill, 1937].

Age	Type of item	Example or description
2	Three-hole form board	Places form (e.g., circle) in correct hole.
	Block building	Builds tower from model after demonstration.
3	Identifying parts of the body	Points out hair, mouth, etc., on large paper doll.
4	Naming objects from memory	One of three objects (e.g., toy dog or shoe) is covered after child has seen them but is not looking; child then names object from memory.
	Picture identification	Points to correct pictures of objects on a card when asked, "Show me what we cook on," or "What do we carry when it is raining?"
7	Similarities	Answers such questions as, "In what way are coal and wood alike? Ship and automobile?"
	Copying a diamond	Copies a diamond in the record booklet.
8	Vocabulary	Defines eight words from a list.
	Memory for stories	Listens to a story, then repeats the gist of it.
9	Verbal absurdities	"I saw a well-dressed young man who was walking down the street with his hands in his pockets and twirling a brand new cane. What is foolish about that?"
	Digit reversal	Must repeat five digits backward.
Average adult	Vocabulary	Defines twenty words from a list.
	Proverbs	Explains in own words the meaning of two or more common proverbs.
	Orientation	"Which direction would you have to face so your right hand would be toward the north?"

from the Stanford-Binet test. Notice the kinds of abilities that are tested at various age levels. In the lower age levels, the tests stress information about objects, pictures, and parts of the body, as well as the perception of forms. In the higher age brackets, the tests stress more the use of words and numbers in reasoning problems. At all age levels, there are tests of vocabulary, correct use of words, and the span of memory, because these represent the more general aspects of intellectual ability.

A child's mental ability obviously increases as he grows older. When we test him at a certain age and obtain a mental-age score, we know merely the level of his ability at that age. On the average, we would expect a child's mental age to increase at the same rate as his chronological age (CA). Indeed, the test norms were established so that it could hardly be otherwise. The bright child, on the other hand, should show a more rapid increase in mental ability, so that his mental age would be greater than his chronological age. The reverse would be true of the dull child.

Intelligence quotient. This brings us to the idea that relative intelligence is a ratio between mental age and chronological age. If two children both score an MA of 5 years on the intelligence test, but one is only 4 years old and the other is 5, obviously the younger child is the brighter—in fact, much the brighter—of the two. To express this kind of difference and to do it precisely with numbers, we have the concept of the intelligence quotient (IQ). *The IQ is a ratio of mental age (MA) to chronological age (CA), multiplied by 100* to avoid the inconvenience of decimals. The formula is

$$IQ = \frac{\text{mental age}}{\text{chronological age}} \times 100 = \frac{MA}{CA} \times 100$$

Looked at in this way, the IQ shows how fast a child's abilities are growing in relation to his chronological age. Applying the IQ formula to the two children mentioned above, we find that the brighter one has an IQ of 125 and the other an IQ of 100.

The IQ is a convenient yardstick of mental ability relative to age, because it enables one to compare children of different ages even though they have different mental ages and pass subtests that are quite different in difficulty. Great care had to be taken in selecting subtests and in establishing age norms to make this possible. In fact, the test was so constructed that the distribution of IQs is about the same at all age groups. Hence it is possible to say that a child of thirteen who has an IQ of 125 and a child of five who has the same IQ are equally bright. Both, in fact, are rather bright, for only about 5 per cent of children have an IQ that high or higher.

Limitations of the test. The Stanford-Binet test is an excellent instrument for doing what it was designed to do. It has many practical uses, some of which we shall examine a little later. However, it also has some limitations. For one, it puts heavy stress upon verbal ability. The directions are given orally for the most part, and many of the subtests require the use of words. If the test were given to a person who for some reason had language difficulties, we should not get an accurate picture of his mental development. Second, the test must be administered to one individual at a time and by testers who are highly trained in its use, because, among other things, there are many props that go along with the test. This makes it inconvenient to use when large groups must be tested in a hurry or when trained testers are not available. Third, it gives a score which is indicative of over-all or general mental development, but it does not provide an adequate picture of differential development of various kinds of intellectual abilities. This is an important problem in research on basic mental abilities and is often important in establishing a diagnosis of mental illness.

Besides the limitations we have just mentioned, there is the further fact that the Stanford-Binet is not a good test to use for testing older adolescents or adults. This is because the kind of intellectual performance represented by the concept of mental age does not show any consistent increase beyond the age of sixteen. So far as the Stanford-Binet is concerned, mental age reaches a plateau at that point. You can see that this causes trouble in figuring the IQ of a person over sixteen years of age. There is an arithmetic device for getting around this trouble—in Stanford-Binet scoring you simply assume that any person older than sixteen is only sixteen—but it is much better to use a test specifically designed for adults.

WECHSLER ADULT INTELLIGENCE SCALE. The most widely used test for adults is one developed by Dr. David Wechsler [1958] of the Bellevue Psychiatric Hospital. It is called the Wechsler Adult Intelligence Scale, or WAIS for short. The WAIS, like the Stanford-Binet, is an individual test requiring many props and expert testers for its use. Also, like the Stanford-Binet, it is made up of a wide variety of subtests. In the case of WAIS, however, the subtests are grouped into two sets of categories, one *verbal* and the other *performance*. There are six verbal subtests and five performance subtests. They are:

Verbal subtests	Performance subtests
Information	Picture arrangement
General comprehension	Picture completion
Memory span	Block design
Arithmetic reasoning	Object assembly
Similarities	Digit symbol
Vocabulary	

Figure 14.2 shows examples of a block-design item and an object-assembly item.

The subtests can be separately scored so that a person's ability in the various categories can be compared. Moreover, the verbal and performance sections of the test may be independently scored to give separate IQs on each. This feature is often helpful in testing people of foreign background or of poor education who have not had a

TABLE 14.2. Distribution of intelligence quotients on the Wechsler Adult Intelligence Scale [Wechsler, 1958].

IQ	Verbal description	Per cent of adults
Above 130	Very superior	2.2
120–129	Superior	6.7
110–119	Bright normal	16.1
90–109	Average	50.0
80–89	Dull normal	16.1
70–79	Borderline	6.7
Below 70	Defective	2.2

fair opportunity to develop their verbal abilities. Such individuals frequently do better on performance tests than on verbal tests. It is also helpful in testing brain-injured persons or the mentally ill, because it sometimes makes clearer just where a person's trouble lies.

The method of computing IQs for the WAIS is different from the method we described for the Stanford-Binet. Instead of using MA and dividing that by CA, which at best is appropriate only for children, a WAIS IQ is obtained by a standard-score method (see page 414). This method, it will be recalled, requires that the mean and standard deviation of a distribution of scores be obtained and that T-score equivalents be established. In this case, the T scores are called IQs. The procedure for computing IQs is as follows:

Wechsler, by an arbitrary scoring system, secured a distribution of scores on a standardization group of 1,700 people between sixteen and sixty years of age. He computed the mean and standard deviation of this distribution. It makes no difference what these were, for they serve only as a basis for assigning equivalent IQs. He let the mean equal 100, and a standard deviation be 15. Thus a person having an IQ one standard deviation below the mean was assigned an IQ of 85; and an individual having an IQ

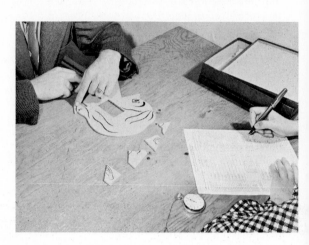

FIGURE 14.2. A veteran (left) takes a block-design item and (right) an object-assembly item on the Wechsler test for adults [New York Univer. Testing and Advisement Center].

one standard deviation above the mean was assigned 115. By defining IQs in this way, the distribution of IQs is tied directly to the normal curve. And the percentages of individuals having IQs above, below, or between any particular IQ are readily predicted from the normal curve (see Figure 13.5). The resulting distribution of IQs and the descriptive terms applied to IQs within different ranges is given in Table 14.2.

It may be of interest to the college student to have a more detailed breakdown of the distribution of above-average IQs. For IQs of 110 and up, the percentage of the population having a higher IQ is as follows:

Wechsler IQ	110	113	119	125	128	135
Per cent higher	25	20	10	5	3	1

These figures mean that about 1 per cent of people have IQs above 135, 10 per cent above 119, and so on.

In the latest revision of the Stanford-Binet, published in 1960, data have been provided for using the same type of computation of the IQ as Wechsler has in the WAIS. As compared with the MA/CA method, the Wechsler method has the advantage of providing exactly the same mean (100) and standard deviation (15) for any standardization group used. Actually, the MA/CA does not quite do this; the mean quotient, as well as the standard deviation of Stanford-Binet IQs, varies somewhat from one age group to another.

It should be noted in passing that Wechsler [1949] also developed an intelligence test for children called the Wechsler Intelligence Scale for Children, or WISC for short. The WISC has been widely used in recent years, perhaps even more than the Stanford-Binet. It is quite similar to the WAIS in its subtests and in providing separate verbal-performance IQs. Naturally the difficulty of the items is adjusted for the age and intelligence of the child being tested.

GROUP TESTS OF INTELLIGENCE. In hospitals and schools, where intelligence testing is usually only part of the handling of an individual's problem, it is convenient to use individual tests of intelligence. In these situations, too, expert personnel, specifically trained in the administration of tests, are frequently available to give the Stanford-Binet, WAIS, WISC, or some other individual test. There are many situations, however, for which a group test is either desirable or absolutely essential. One of these is the military situation, in which large groups, adding up to hundreds of thousands each year, need to be tested. Another is the mass testing of students entering colleges or other higher schools. Group tests have been devised to meet such needs.

The First World War furnished the impetus for the first large-scale effort to develop group tests. Hundreds of thousands of young men were being inducted into the service. We needed some quick method for weeding out the mentally unfit and for selecting the most able for officer training. Finally, to utilize manpower effectively, it was desirable to assign people to different battalions and technical training schools according to their abilities.

Psychologists met these needs in the First World War by devising the Army Alpha Test and the Army Beta Test. The Army Alpha Test, designed for the typical individual who can read and write, yielded scores for classifying men roughly according to intelligence. Table 14.3 shows some examples of the problems on this test. Between the two wars, the Army Alpha was frequently revised for use with both servicemen and civilians. The Army Beta was designed as a test that could be given to illiterates and foreigners not proficient in English. It emphasized nonverbal problems for which simple instructions could be given orally. Two examples of items from the Army Beta are given in Figure 14.3.

When the Second World War came along, Army psychologists took advantage of extensive research in mental testing to make a more drastic revision, which they named the Army General Classification Test (AGCT). This was given to several million servicemen upon induction into the Armed Forces. It was prepared in four different forms, which could be interchanged with one another, each form requiring about an hour to give. In addition, longer forms of the test were

TABLE 14.3. Some sample items from the Army Alpha Test.

A. If $5\frac{1}{2}$ tons of bark cost \$33, what will $3\frac{1}{2}$ cost? (   )

B. A train is harder to stop than an automobile because
     (   ) it is longer,   (   ) it is heavier,   (   ) the brakes are not so good

C. If the two words of a pair mean the same or nearly the same thing, draw a line under *same*. If they mean the opposite or nearly the opposite, draw a line under *opposite*.

comprehensive	restricted	same	opposite
allure	attract	same	opposite
latent	hidden	same	opposite
deride	ridicule	same	opposite

D. If, when you have arranged the following words to make a sentence, the sentence is true, underline *true*; if it is false, underline *false*.

people enemies arrogant many make	true	false
never who heedless those stumble are	true	false
never man the show the deeds	true	false

E. *Underline which*
     The pitcher has an important place in   tennis   football   baseball   handball

F. *Underline which*
     Dismal is to dark as cheerful is to   laugh   bright   house   gloomy

Which is the shortest path through the maze?

Complete the series.

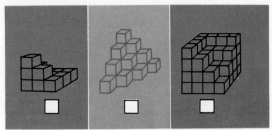

How many cubes in each pile? Write number in appropriate square.

FIGURE 14.3. Items from the Army Beta Test used during the First World War. The Beta test was used with illiterates and others for whom the Alpha was an unfair test [National Academy of Science].

devised to break down a person's performance into four different categories: (1) verbal ability, (2) spatial comprehension, (3) arithmetic computation, and (4) arithmetic reasoning.

The AGCT, like the Stanford-Binet, is so scored that the average person is assigned 100. For purposes of rough classification, the Army divided people into five groups according to score. Figure 14.4 shows the limiting scores for each group and the percentage of testees found in each group. The spread or distribution is much like that on individual tests of intelligence, but the AGCT score and the IQ are not exactly comparable. The Navy developed and used a similar NGCT, with this difference: Navy tests have an average of 50. In recent years, one test, the Armed Forces Qualification Test (AFQT), has replaced the AGCT and the NGCT.

After the First World War, several group tests were devised for use with civilians—primarily to help in selecting people for jobs in business and industry (see Chapter 18, page 564). One of the best known of these is the Otis Self-Administering Test of Mental Ability (Otis SA). This is a short four-page pencil-and-paper test that can be administered simply with a stop watch and under testing conditions that are relatively easy to

keep standard. It can be taken and scored with either a 20-minute or a 30-minute time limit. Scores on the test have been correlated with those on the Stanford-Binet so that it is possible, if one wishes, to convert them to equivalent IQs. The test is so constructed that it emphasizes verbal and reasoning factors but does not sample performance factors very well.

There are a number of other tests, used in connection with higher education, that follow the general pattern of the group tests of intelligence. There is one prepared under the sponsorship of the American Council on Education (called the ACE test) which the majority of college students take upon entering college. A similar one was used by Selective Service as a basis for the deferment of students in colleges. There are others for use at a more advanced level for students seeking entrance to medical and graduate schools. Since these latter tests are designed for the fairly specific purpose of predicting success in a particular kind of education, they have more of the earmarks of aptitude tests than of general intelligence tests, and we shall consider them later under the heading of aptitudes.

THE NATURE OF INTELLIGENCE. It seems natural to think of intelligence as one ability or attribute. We think of Mary as being "bright" and John as being "dumb." These are single labels we apply to a person. Seldom do we think of Mary as being bright in school, but very dumb in other ways—that is, that there are different kinds of intelligence. The fact that most of our tests of intelligence produce one over-all score or IQ further shapes our thinking about intelligence as a unitary thing. Is there a general intelligence as distinguished from specific abilities, or is there just a collection of abilities? What is intelligence actually?

The method of factor analysis furnishes a way of answering this question (see Chapter 13, page 428). To perform a factor analysis, research workers give a good many different tests to the same people to see how well the tests correlate with each other. For this purpose they compute correlations between subtests or individual items on tests, not just the over-all scores, in order to isolate, as best they can, the elements of intelligence. Having a lot of correlations, they then proceed, by statistical analysis, to see which items form clusters and which ones are independent of each other. It may turn out, for example, that all sorts of subtests that have to do with words may correlate with one another but not with other subtests involving numbers. In this way, they isolate *factors* in a number of tests, and in the example just cited it would be concluded that there is a verbal factor that is relatively separate from a numerical factor.

There has been a great amount of research of this kind. Each investigator obtains somewhat different results, depending on the tests he uses and the sample of people he gives them to. Various researches agree, however, in yielding *a number of different factors in intelligence*. The most extensive studies in the United States were carried out by Thurstone [Thurstone and Thurstone, 1941]. When he had finished an elaborate factor analysis of dozens of tests

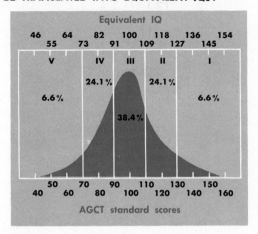

FIGURE 14.4. On the lower abscissa are scores obtained by multiplying x/σ by a constant (see Chapter 13). On the upper abscissa are equivalent IQs, obtained in this case, by taking .9 of the deviation from 100. In Roman numerals are the five groups used by the Army for rough classification of testees. The percentages indicate the relative numbers falling in each of the groups. Navy (NGCT) scores were exactly half the AGCT scores.

given to school children, he emerged with seven factors. Each factor represents a cluster of correlations between subtests and thus what is common to them. His seven factors are named and described as follows:

1. *Verbal comprehension* (V)—ability to define and understand words
2. *Word fluency* (W)—ability to think rapidly of words, as in extemporaneous speech or solving crossword puzzles
3. *Number* (N)—ability to do arithmetic problems
4. *Space* (S)—ability to draw a design from memory or to visualize relationships
5. *Memory* (M)—ability to memorize and recall
6. *Perceptual* (P)—ability to grasp visual details and to see differences and similarities among objects
7. *Reasoning* (R)—ability to find rules.

INTELLIGENCE AND APTITUDES 445

principles, or concepts for understanding or solving problems

In the course of discovering these factors, Thurstone could identify the subtests that represented each factor, for he knew which subtests were correlated and which were not. This fact enabled him to devise tests that would measure each factor as independently as possible. To do this, he rearranged his subtests, grouping together those that represented the same factor. Actually, in many instances, he tried to improve on this technique by devising new subtests that seemed to be good measures of the factors he had discovered. Now with a new set of tests, called tests of *primary mental abilities,* he could come to grips with the question of whether there is such a thing as general intelligence. Because he had obtained seven factors, he concluded that intelligence is partly made up of separate abilities. The question was whether there is a general factor, apart from the specific ones.

To settle this problem, he obtained scores on each of the tests of primary mental abilities from a large group of children, and intercorrelated these scores with one another. If there were no such thing as general intelligence, each factor measured by a test should be independent of every other, and there should be no correlations among them. The different tests *are,* in fact, *correlated*, some relatively highly and some not so much. The correlations indicate that there is some general ability that is common to all the tests of primary ability. He therefore came to the conclusion that "each of the primary factors can be regarded as a composite of an independent primary factor and a general factor which it shares with other primary factors." The answer then to our original question—What is intelligence?—is that *it is both some general ability and a number of specific abilities.*

INTERPRETATION OF TESTS. This conclusion must have considerable bearing on the interpretation of intelligence tests. Though each intelligence test may measure "general intelligence" in some degree and thus measure in part what other intelligence tests are measuring, it also reflects its own particular sample of specific abilities. None of the individual or group tests of intelligence now in common use measures these specific abilities in equal degree. Some weight several abilities more heavily than they weight others.

Actually most intelligence tests, particularly the Stanford-Binet and the Otis, are heavily weighted with verbal content. In the case of the Stanford-Binet, this came about because achievement in school, which is a rather verbal matter, was used as a criterion for selecting many of the items on the test. Group tests like the Otis are weighted by verbal and numerical ability partly because it is much easier to make up tests of these abilities than it is of other abilities. In any event, the fact is that such abilities are given greater weight. In making interpretations about individuals' abilities from an intelligence test, this fact must be kept in mind.

Another important thing to remember about intelligence tests is that *they measure present ability, not native capacity.* People have different opportunities to acquire abilities. Poor people do not have the same cultural and educational opportunities as those who are financially more fortunate. Moreover, many of the problems used in intelligence tests presuppose a cultural background. If problems concern such things as apples, organs, automobiles, baseball, and trains, then a person who grew up in a culture without these things is certainly going to be handicapped on the test, even if his native capacity is better than average. Growing up in one culture or country thus handicaps a person on intelligence tests devised for people in some other culture.

Those who devise tests try to make their items as free of such influences as possible, but no one has yet succeeded in making a completely culture-free test of intelligence. Thus tests assume a relatively common background of culture and education. Whenever a person has not had this background or is deficient in it, it is not sensible to regard his results on an intelligence test as comparable to those of other persons who have the common background. Consequently, intelligence tests are usually not suitable instruments for comparing the abilities of different races and cultural groups.

Extremes of intelligence

In Table 14.2 we presented the distribution of Wechsler IQs to be found in the general population of the United States. All the scores were arbitrarily grouped into seven categories: below 70, 70–79, 80–89, 90–109, 110–119, 120–129, and above 130. For convenience, each of these arbitrary categories was given a characteristic name such as average, superior, etc. As we shall see a little later, there are certain predictions we can make about the educational and occupational successes of each of the groups. The two extreme groups, however—namely, those below 70 and those above 130—represent special problems in our society.

FEEBLE-MINDEDNESS. Those who have IQs of less than 70 are regarded as *mentally deficient* or *defective*. On the basis of intelligence tests, we find that there are between 2 and 3 per cent of the population in this category. It has been the custom to subdivide mentally deficient individuals into three groups:
1. *Morons*, IQ 50–70
2. *Imbeciles*, IQ 20–50
3. *Idiots*, IQ below 20
If you remember that the IQ is really a ratio of mental age to chronological age and that

mental growth, as measured by the Stanford-Binet test, comes to a stop at about sixteen years of age, you can easily figure out the limits of mental age for these three groups. The moron's ultimate mental age is 8 to 12 years; that of the imbecile, 3 to 7 years; and that of the idiot, below 3 (see Table 14.4).

Knowing these limits of mental growth for the mentally deficient, you can fill in for yourself what we know to be the capacities of the deficient. The idiot will, at best, be much like a three-year-old all through life. He will never talk very well. The chances are he will be unable to master some aspects of dressing such as buttoning his clothes or tying his shoes. He can never be trusted to keep himself out of danger. He will not be able to master the simplest tasks at school or at work. The imbecile, even as an adult, will be something like the first- or second-grade child. He will be able to talk fairly well, clothe himself, and learn simple skills, but he will not profit very much from training in the higher school grades. The moron will do somewhat better and may eventually finish four to eight school grades. He will be able to learn to read and write only with difficulty. He may be able to learn a simple occupation and to look after his personal needs.

Social maturity. These descriptions of the intellectual level of the mentally deficient, however, are not a fair account of their abilities. We must remember that the IQ tests tend to weight verbal factors that are especially important in educational success but not always so important in other, more mundane daily affairs. If one studies closely

TABLE 14.4. Intelligence and social-maturity levels of the feeble-minded

	Moron	Imbecile	Idiot
Intelligence quotient	50–70	20–50	Below 20
Maximum mental age	8–12	3–7	Below 3
Age of intellectual maturity	15	10–12	6–8
Maximum social age	10–18	4–9	Below 4
Age of social maturity	20	15	10

the behavior of high-grade morons with IQs, say, of 65 to 70, one can see rather wide individual differences among them. Some can take care of themselves much better than others. In work and social situations, some seem much more intelligent than others.

For this reason one psychologist has gone to the trouble of devising another scale, the Vineland Social Maturity Scale, which weights *social* and *vocational* intelligence somewhat more than it does *verbal* intelligence [Doll, 1936]. This scale yields a *social age* (SA) which is comparable to the mental age (MA) of the Stanford-Binet test. As its name implies, this scale takes various social abilities as its standard of comparison: eating with a spoon, washing one's face unaided, being trusted with money, being able to find one's way home, etc. By checking a child on such items, the psychologist can assign a social age to each child in much the same way that a mental age is assigned.

Since the Stanford-Binet and the Vineland scales measure different things, it is not surprising that they do not correlate perfectly. In general, the ultimate social age of the mentally deficient is higher than the comparable mental age (see Table 14.4). For the moron, it is 10 to 18 years; for the imbecile, 4 to 9; and for the idiot, something below 4. Moreover, social development usually continues for a somewhat longer period than does mental growth (as tested by the Stanford-Binet).

This difference between social age and mental age has led psychologists to make a distinction between mental deficiency and feeble-mindedness. Mental deficiency is defined in terms of intelligence-test scores. Feeble-mindedness, however, is a more general term referring to the person's over-all ability to take care of himself and to make an adjustment in the world. It therefore includes both the mental and social development of the person. In many instances there is a real difference between the two. Moreover, since social development is usually greater than mental development in the feeble-minded, the person's plight is not so

bad as it might seem from the IQ score alone.

Treatment of feeble-mindedness. Feeble-mindedness is obviously a problem of some proportions in our society. Hundreds of thousands of feeble-minded children and adults are regularly lodged in special institutions throughout the country. Thousands more are living at home, constituting a burden to their family and friends. All are handicapped in the work they can do and in the kinds of lives they can lead. What can be done about feeble-mindedness?

Well-educated parents who are confronted with the fact that their child is feeble-minded are likely to think that something can be done to raise the child's IQ. Dramatic stories in the newspapers or magazines sometimes give this impression, because they seem to show that it is possible to do much with a feeble-minded child. This possibility has been carefully investigated in several psychological studies and the evidence unfortunately is against it [Goodenough, 1949]. Special training produces slight changes in IQ and in social intelligence, but seldom does anything very dramatic occur (for an exception, see the discussion of cretinism in Chapter 20). Feeble-mindedness in most cases is probably a matter of capacity, and there is little one can do to alter the mental and social capacity of the defective child. People usually deceive themselves if they think otherwise.

There is much that can be done, on the other hand, to make the most of the feeble-minded's limited capacity. Most feeble-minded persons are high-grade morons (about 60 per cent), and a minority are low-grade idiots (about 10 per cent). Whatever the grade, the training may be long and tedious, but it is worth the effort if it is relative to the capacity of the child. Gradually he can be taught some of the social skills, such as washing himself, helping with duties around the house, and doing many minor tasks that keep him from being such a burden to others. If his defect is not too severe, he can be taught some vocational skills, such as woodworking, printing, and weaving. The better institutions for the feeble-minded have facilities and teachers for training in these social and occupational skills, and each year they return to society several thousand individuals who are capable of earning a living and looking after themselves reasonably well.

Causes of feeble-mindedness. It may occur to some that we might try to find "cures" for feeble-mindedness. Research workers have indeed expended a great deal of effort in this direction, and the search continues (see Chapter 20). The possibility of finding cures, of course, depends upon the causes of feeble-mindedness. Although these are now partly understood, we have much more to learn about them.

Just as there are functional and organic psychoses (see Chapter 5), there are two general classes of feeble-mindedness. One corresponds to the functional and is called *primary* or *familial feeble-mindedness.* In this case, we can find no organic defect, no evidence of injury or disease that might have caused the feeble-mindedness. The person seems quite sound in every respect except for his intellectual deficit. In such cases, we usually find some record of feeble-mindedness occurring in other members of the family, and that is why it is often called familial. Intelligence is partly inherited (see Chapter 2 and below), and we should expect that those with low intelligence, both intellectual and social, would tend to have offspring of low intelligence.

Another kind of feeble-mindedness is caused by a biological defect; this is called *secondary feeble-mindedness.* In some cases the brain of a baby suffers a severe shortage of oxygen during pregnancy, and this may account for feeble-mindedness. In others, the child's brain is injured at birth because of some difficulty in delivery. In still others, something is wrong chemically with the reactions going on in the brain (see Chapter 20). In few of these cases of secondary feeble-mindedness have we yet found any surgery, drugs, or other agents that might be used to cure or alleviate the condition. Re-

search, however, continues to press for answers to this problem, and it is possible, though not very likely, that we shall find methods by which both primary and secondary feeble-mindedness may be helped.

THE MENTALLY GIFTED. At the top end of the distribution of IQs are the very superior (130–140) and the near genius (above 140). It is interesting to see what role persons in these categories play in society and what their problems are—and they do have unique problems. Psychologists have studied the very gifted in three ways: (1) by estimating the intelligence of gifted people who lived years ago, (2) by following the accomplishments of gifted children into adulthood, and (3) by studying the problems of very bright children in school.

Gifted leaders and writers. There is enough recorded about the lives of some of the people who have been prominent in history to make fairly reliable estimates of what their IQs would have been if they had lived in a day when they could have taken the Stanford-Binet test. If we know at what age a child began to read, when he used certain words in his vocabulary, when he mastered certain problems in arithmetic, etc., we can match these accomplishments with the standards of the Stanford-Binet test.

This sort of thing has been done for a long list of people. In Table 14.5 are their names and estimated IQs. Not all the great men of history are in this list, for we do not have enough biographical data for them. Still, it is quite plain that men who have contributed much to our literature and to our civilization are also endowed with very high intelligence.

Terman's gifted children. Even more informative is a monumental study conducted over a period of 35 years by Terman, the author of the Stanford-Binet test. Terman and his associates, having tested many thousands of children, picked out for further study a group of more than 1,500 who had IQs of 140 or more. These were the highest 1 per cent of the children. Until his death

TABLE 14.5. The IQs of some eminent men estimated from biographical data [Cox, 1926].

John Quincy Adams	165
Francis Bacon	145
Samuel Taylor Coleridge	175
René Descartes	150
Charles Dickens	145
Benjamin Franklin	145
Johann Wolfgang von Goethe	185
George Frederick Handel	145
David Hume	155
Thomas Jefferson	145
Gottfried Wilhelm von Leibnitz	185
John Stuart Mill	190
John Milton	145
Wolfgang Amadeus Mozart	150
Alfred Tennyson	155
Daniel Webster	145
William Wordsworth	150

in 1956, Terman was able to follow most of these children into their adulthood, and many of them are now in middle life. Periodically he sent them questionnaires or otherwise found out what they were doing, and thus he built up a very detailed picture of their achievements. Some of Terman's associates are continuing to follow up these gifted "children."

One interesting thing about them is the homes they came from. About a third were the children of professional people, about half came from homes of the higher business classes, and only a small proportion (7 per cent) came from the working classes.

This is quite out of proportion to the numbers of people in each of these classes, and indicates that relatively more gifted children come from the higher socioeconomic classes (see below). This fact is undoubtedly accounted for by both heredity and environment. These classes can provide a better environment for the development of intellectual abilities, and because the more successful people tend to be the more gifted, they also pass on such gifts to their children through heredity.

The later success, in fact, of Terman's gifted children is a second striking discovery of his studies. About 700 people of the original study could be contacted 25 years later. Of these, about 150 were very successful as judged by such criteria as (1) being listed in *Who's Who* or *American Men of Science,* (2) holding responsible managerial positions, or (3) receiving recognition for outstanding intellectual or professional achievement. Most of the others were less outstanding but still much more successful than people of average intelligence. On the other hand, there were some who certainly were not very successful—some who had committed crimes, some who dropped out of school early, and some who were distinctly vocational misfits and had been unsuccessful at a number of jobs. Careful comparisons of those who were very successful with those who were least successful showed that factors in personality made the differ-

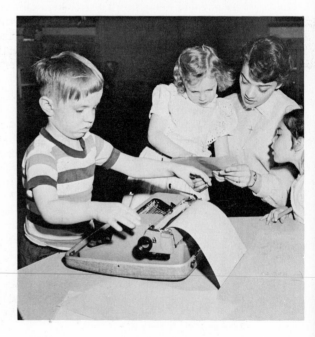

ence. The least successful were more poorly adjusted emotionally and more poorly motivated to succeed. Despite the exceptions, the most striking fact was that children of superior ability generally made an outstanding record of social and intellectual achievement.

Contrary to some common misconceptions about the genius, Terman's gifted children were above average in height, weight, and physical appearance. They also were generally better adjusted and more socially adaptable, and they had more capacity for leadership than average children. Thus Terman disproved the notion that the genius is likely to be peculiar, unadjusted, and socially backward. Some geniuses, of course, are like that—and so are some average people—but in general geniuses are less so than those of average intellectual ability.

Problems of the gifted. What we have said is true despite the many difficulties that a gifted child faces. Because he is brighter, he is more likely to be bored by children of his own age, more likely to seek the company of older children and adults and to pester them with intellectual questions. In public schools, most of which have been designed for the average child, his problem is acute because his intellectual ability and achievement usually far exceed those of other children of the same age and in the same classroom. Moreover, he usually is being taught by a teacher who is far from a genius and often is unable to match either the child's knowledge or his problem-solving ability.

Teachers faced with a child of extremely high ability are likely to consider him fresh, smart-alecky, and a show-off and hence often treat him harshly. The very bright child often finds the pace of normal education so slow and easy that he becomes bored and loses interest in the activities of the classroom. Then he may become a personality problem and a real annoyance for the schoolteacher. Some public schools, of course, are sophisticated about the problems of the gifted child, and others are becoming more so. The better ones find out early what a child's IQ is and try to include an appropriate program for gifted children (see Figure 14.5). In some instances, the gifted children are put in special classes by themselves in which they can achieve more and

FIGURE 14.5. Gifted children may be encouraged to participate in special education projects. In some school systems, children are relieved of the boredom of regular education and develop their special talents by working on special projects such as science demonstrations [Aigner, from Monkmeyer] and typewriting [Hunter College Elementary School].

be given tasks commensurate with their abilities. In other instances, special additional activities are planned for the gifted child.

Group differences in abilities

Everyday thinking is colored by notions about the abilities of different *groups* of people. Many think that Negroes and foreigners are not so intelligent as white Americans. We regard older people as much wiser than, if not as quick as, younger people. Employers think women and young people more suitable for certain positions, men and older people for other jobs. We think of people who come from "good families" of the upper socioeconomic strata as being more able than those who come from the working classes.

Psychological research, indeed, indicates that there are differences among various groups of people, but these differences are often not the same ones that the layman imagines or as great as he may think. In other chapters (Chapters 16 and 17), we shall describe differences in culture and in attitudes. Here let us see what the facts are about differences in intellectual abilities.

DIFFERENCES BETWEEN MEN AND WOMEN. In our society there is a division of labor between the sexes. Men are expected to earn a living, and women are expected to care for the home—though that pattern has been changing in the last generation. In other cultures, the economic roles of the sexes are sometimes reversed. This fact alone should make us skeptical of large inherited differences in capacities between men and women. On the other hand, there is the fact that most of the leaders in the arts and sciences and in business and industry have been men. The eminent woman is the exception rather than the rule. May we assume from this that men are more intelligent than women? Since psychologists have administered thousands of intelligence tests to both men and women,

it is easy to answer this question quantitatively.

Abilities of women. Women have a reputation for their ability to talk, and they deserve it. Girls, on the average, learn to talk at an earlier age than boys do. Later, when they can take intelligence tests, they do better on all tests involving the use of language. Thus they are superior to men in verbal abilities. Closely related to this is the fact that they generally do better on items involving social relations [Johnson and Terman, 1940].

Girls are also better on two other related kinds of abilities: perceiving details quickly and accurately and making quick, accurate manual movements. This may account, in part, for the fact that most women employed in business and industry work in clerical and secretarial jobs and also for the good record they made during the Second World War in many kinds of industrial jobs. Women also seem to have better immediate memories than men. You will recall that the Stanford-Binet has a series of tests at all age levels which measure immediate memory for a series of numbers or words. On the average, women are better in these items than are men.

Abilities of men. On the Stanford-Binet test, boys surpass girls on the items that involve spatial, numerical, and mechanical tasks. Correlated with this is the fact that they do better on tasks involving the perception of spatial relationships, the comprehension of mechanical tools and machines, and mathematical ability. Boys are better in working with numbers and in numerical-reasoning tasks.

Interpreting sex differences. We see, then, that men and women differ significantly in certain *specific abilities*. These conclusions, reached from careful analysis of tests of ability, fit in pretty well with popular conceptions of the difference in ability between men and women.

The question then arises, How did these differences come to be—through training, or by constitutional make-up? This is difficult to answer, for it is next to impossible to separate the influences of heredity and of environment on the development of specific abilities. It seems likely, however, that at least some of the differences measured on intelligence tests are due to training and environment, for as we shall see, these influences can certainly affect the abilities measured on intelligence tests.

There are two other important factors to consider in interpreting sex differences in abilities. One is that all the differences we measure are *average* differences between groups. Average differences, taken by themselves, do not tell us how a particular boy and girl are likely to compare on an ability. There is a great deal of variability in the abilities of either boys or girls, producing considerable overlap between the two distributions. In tests of language ability, for example, the average score of girls is higher than that of boys. Looking at the distribution of scores for the two groups, however, we discover that as many as 40 per cent of the boys score higher than the girls' average, that is, higher than 50 per cent of the girls. Thus average differences *between* groups are small compared to differences *within* groups. This is an important point in interpreting differences between any two groups of people.

Finally, in comparing boys and girls in intelligence, one should also remember that in over-all intelligence the two are equal. That is to say, average IQ of men and of women is the same. Intelligence tests were, in fact, constructed in such a way as to make it the same. Thus the abilities in which women exceed men are counterbalanced by those in which men surpass women. Hence differences between the sexes are restricted to specific abilities, not to the composite of specific and general abilities that we call intelligence.

AGE DIFFERENCES IN ABILITY. The United States is currently facing population changes which require an accurate evaluation of the abilities of older people. We are becoming a nation of older people. In 1830, for example, the median age of the population was 17.2 years. In 1958 the median age had increased to 29.5. Persons over forty-five years of age now comprise 29 per cent of the population; those over sixty, 13 per cent. It is therefore of interest to know what changes occur in various kinds of abilities as we grow older.

The most general statement we can make about the change in abilities with age is this: as an individual approaches maturity, all his abilities increase to a peak level and then begin to decline. Just where the peak occurs and how rapidly abilities decline depend on what is being tested. This will be evident in two examples of studies carried out on the problem:

A now classical study was performed by testing substantially all the inhabitants from ages ten to sixty in a group of New England villages. The test employed was the Army Alpha. The various subtests of the Army Alpha were analyzed to sort out different abilities. The test results on two abilities, as well as results on the total test, are shown in Figure 14.6. The solid line in that figure shows that general mental ability, as measured by the Army Alpha, rises to a peak somewhere between the ages of sixteen and twenty, and then declines rather steadily. Subtests, however, show that not all abilities behave in the same way. Tests of vocabulary, for example, which weight previous verbal learning, show no appreciably significant decline. The subtests on analogies, which weight reasoning, reach a fairly sharp peak, followed first by a rapid decline, then by a slower one.

In another, more recent study, designed to provide norms by age groups for the Wechsler Adult Intelligence Scale, we obtain roughly the same results, though the peak of intelligence is reached at a somewhat later age, in the late twenties (see Figure 14.7). Because the WAIS provides separate performance and verbal IQs, it is possible to analyze these two aspects of intelligence separately. It turns out that the peak of "performance intelligence" occurs earliest, in the mid twenties, and that for "verbal intelligence" comes in the early thirties. And after the peaks, performance intelligence declines more rapidly than verbal intelligence, which fits with the older study.

In all such studies, we have difficulty being sure that the samples are comparable at different ages, because they can be biased, say, by a tendency of younger, brighter people to migrate from a particular area. Nevertheless, the general trends seem trustworthy. As a general conclusion, we can say that the peak of intelligence is reached between the teens and the early thirties, depending upon the type of intelligence being tested, and further that older people do as well as young people in vocabulary and general information tests, but they do more poorly in tests which require the individual to work quickly or to adapt to situations which are different from those he is used to.

It is necessary to stress again the amount of variability within groups. In practically all the studies on aging there are many individuals in the oldest group who did as well as, or better than, the average performance of the best group. The implications of these

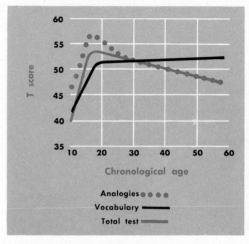

FIGURE 14.6. The relation of mental ability to age [Jones and Conrad, 1933].

findings are important. If we must make social, economic, political, or any other kind of important decisions concerning the abilities of whole groups, then we must rely on group averages. But if the problem is to select a relatively small number of *individuals*, then the decision of who shall be chosen

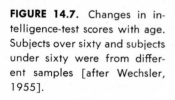

FIGURE 14.7. Changes in intelligence-test scores with age. Subjects over sixty and subjects under sixty were from different samples [after Wechsler, 1955].

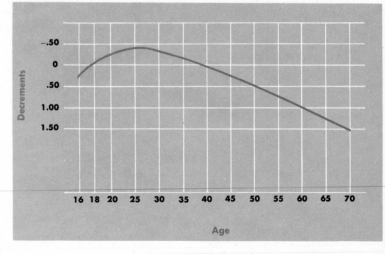

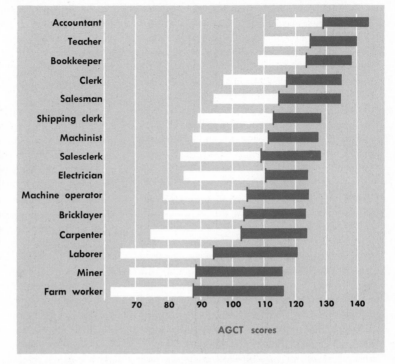

FIGURE 14.8. The ranges of AGCT scores for selected occupations. Each bar shows the range between the 10th and 90th percentiles for a sample of hundreds of men selected randomly from an occupation. Scores below the median are shown in white; those above the median in color [after Anastasi and Foley, 1958].

should not be determined by sex, race, nationality, age, or other "group" factors but should rest upon the tested abilities of the individuals.

OCCUPATIONAL LEVEL. As might be expected, people in some occupations are, on the whole, more intelligent than those in others. We have a good many studies that show this, but the one that is largest in scope comes from data obtained during the Second World War [Harrell and Harrell, 1945] (see Figure 14.8).

Accountants, lawyers, engineers, and teachers head the list with average AGCT scores above 120. At the bottom of the list are farmhands, miners, and teamsters, with scores in the neighborhood of 90. The variability, however, is large. There were some people in every occupation who scored over 130, and there were some who scored 100 or below. Again, though there is an average

difference in intelligence between groups, there is a great deal of overlap. We cannot tell too much about a person's intelligence simply by knowing his occupation.

It is not hard to understand how these occupational differences come about. In general, the higher-ranking occupations require considerably more schooling than the lower-ranking ones. The child with low intelligence tends not to finish as many years of school. When he does, he usually makes a poor grade record. This latter fact also partly explains the outcome, because the colleges and professional schools tend to admit those with higher grades and to screen out those with poorer ones. We should consider also the use of special tests of intelligence by these schools for deciding whom they will admit. This introduces a *spurious correlation;* if intelligence is used to admit a person to certain occupations, these occupations will average higher in intelligence, even if there is no necessary relation between occupation and intelligence.

A more interesting and not so easily explained difference in intelligence is among the children of parents of different occupational groupings. The children of those in the higher occupational classes tend to have higher IQs than children of parents at lower occupational levels. Illustrating this are the data in Table 14.6, taken from one study of this question. The IQs of children of professional people average about 115, while those of children of day laborers average about 95.

HOME ENVIRONMENT. The intellectual environment of children of professional parents is naturally rather different from that of children of day laborers. When we find a difference in intelligence between the two groups of children, the age-old question of heredity versus environment comes to mind. Are children of these two groups of parents different in intelligence because they have different inheritance or because they have different intellectual environments? This is an important but very difficult question, and psychologists have carried out extensive studies in an attempt to answer it. Even so, we do not have as conclusive an answer as we should like to have. Here are just a few of the most important facts bearing on the question:

In Table 14.6 are the IQs of children

tested in different age groups from 2 to 18 and arranged according to seven major occupational groups (of fathers). The differences in the youngest group (2 to 5½ years) are just about the same as those in the oldest group (15 to 18). From these data, we must conclude either that the differences are hereditary or that they are established very early in life.

In Chapter 2, when we dealt with the general question of heredity and environment, we discussed two other kinds of studies bearing on the point (see pages 41–43). One consisted of correlations of IQ between blood relatives with different degrees of similarity of heredity and environment. The other was a comparison of the IQs of identical twins reared apart and separated at different ages after birth. Both studies strongly implicated heredity as a factor in intelligence and gave it a weight equal to, or somewhat greater than, environment.

There is also the fact that when children are taken from their true parents and placed in foster homes—as many thousands of children are every year—their intelligence seems more closely related to the intelligence and educational level of the true parents than to those of the foster parents.

In one study, the correlations of the child's IQ with the intelligence and education of his true parents are of the order of .30 to .40, while correlations with the education of his foster parents are in the neighbor-

TABLE 14.6. IQs of children averaged according to the occupational grouping of their fathers [McNemar, 1942].

Father's occupation	Age of child			
	2–5½	6–9	10–14	15–18
Professional	115	115	118	116
Semiprofessional and managerial	112	107	112	117
Clerical, skilled, and business	108	105	107	110
Rural owners	98	95	92	94
Semiskilled	104	105	103	107
Slightly skilled	97	100	101	96
Day laborers	94	96	97	98

hood of zero [Hilgard, 1957]. In other studies, correlations of foster children's IQs are substantially higher with IQs of the true parents than they are with IQs of the foster parents. From this we can conclude that relative differences in intelligence are set principally by inheritance rather than by the intellectual influences of the foster home.

There are many studies, on the other hand, in which the intelligence of foster children is considerably higher than one would predict from the IQs of their true parents. In one of the more dramatic studies [Skodak and Skeels, 1949], made by Iowa University psychologists, children whose true mothers had an average IQ of 91 showed an average intelligence of more than 109 when measured at an average age of thirteen, usually 10 years or more after they had been placed in superior foster homes. Since we are not certain how high their IQs would have been had they been raised by their true parents, we cannot be sure how much of a gain this is, but it is probably fair to say that children of subnormal parents may gain as much as 10 IQ points when raised in superior homes.

This latter study, unlike the other ones presented, points to the influence of the intellectual environment. Even so, it appears that the gain is not so much as it would be were it not limited by inheritance. If, for example, one compares the IQs of foster children whose real parents were subnormal, with the IQs of true children reared in families of similar status, the foster children tend to be somewhat behind. In one study the foster children averaged 107 while the true children averaged 115.

Facts and researches on the influence of the home environment could fill a book, but these that we have cited are typical. What can we make of them? Clearly, both heredity and environment determine measured intelligence. A good environment can improve intelligence, yet poor inheritance limits how much it can be improved. So, even though no amount of favorable influence can fully overcome poor inheritance, such

influence can develop what latent intelligence there is to its fullest potentialities and can make a considerable difference in what a person may be able to do.

CULTURAL ENVIRONMENT. If the home environment of a child contributes to his intelligence, we might wonder whether other features of his culture also contribute. After all, the child lives in other environments outside the home, especially as he grows from infancy into childhood. At two or three, he starts to play with other children, and by the age of seven, he is spending a good part of his day in school. In growing up, he experiences intellectual influences from his playmates, his school, and even the community's library facilities. What effect do these influences have on intelligence?

One way of approaching this question is to compare rural and urban children, because they differ considerably in the richness of intellectual influences in their respective cultures. It is interesting, indeed, that urban children, on the average, score higher on intelligence tests than do rural children; just how much higher depends upon which particular groups are compared, but it is frequently several points. Such differences might be explained in part by the brighter families' migrating to the city, leaving the less intelligent behind. They might also be explained in part by a cultural bias of the intelligence tests; the tests may include items which are more familiar to city children than to farm children.

Undoubtedly there is something to be said for both these points, but our present data are somewhat inconclusive. On the one hand, it seems rather certain that the stimulating environment of the city, like that of a superior home, can raise substandard intelligence. We have some striking evidence for this view in a study conducted on Negro city boys of twelve years of age [Klineberg, 1935]:

Over 400 boys who had moved to the city were given intelligence tests and compared with 300-odd boys who had been born and reared in the city. The longer the boys had lived in the city, the higher the intelligence scores. Those who had been in the city only 1 to 2 years averaged only 40 (test score, not IQ), whereas those born in the city averaged 75. This is a sizable difference, and it is hard to see how it could be accounted for by selective migration. Apparently city influences affected measured intelligence.

The problem of cultural influences enters into all attempts to determine whether there are racial differences in intelligence. As you probably realize, it has long been a question whether some "races" are inferior to others in intelligence. When psychologists attempt to settle the question with research—and they have made many studies—they immediately encounter the fact that "races" other than United States–born whites have not had the same cultural environments that United States–born whites have had. There is also the fact that different groups migrating to this country come from varying socio-economic and cultural groups in their country of birth. So most studies on this question are inconclusive.

The group differences that have been most thoroughly studied are those between American Negroes and American whites. All have the same country of birth and all speak the same language—though the language habits of most Negroes differ considerably from those of most whites. Even so, Negroes on the average have inferior educational advantages and usually inferior intellectual environments. It is not surprising, then, that any large group of Negroes usually averages several points less than groups of whites on intelligence tests. This does not necessarily mean any biologically inherited inferiority in intelligence; cultural differences certainly explain part or all of the difference.

Our most comprehensive data on these racial differences come from the intelligence tests given in the First World War. In general, Negro draftees did more poorly than the whites. However, Southern draftees were poorer on the average than Northern draftees. And there were Negroes from some Northern states who averaged better than whites from some Southern states. Moreover, as we saw above, city Negroes and city whites did better than rural Negroes and rural whites. It is therefore very difficult to separate the factors of race, geography, rural-urban origin, and educational advantages. The latter three factors, however, may all be considered cultural influences, as distinguished from biological differences in the races.

Since cultural influences are of proven importance, it is safest to assume that differences between whites and Negroes are a matter of cultural environment—at least until the cultural advantages of the two groups are equal or until it is possible to get a culture-free test of any racial difference.

Aptitudes and interests

There is, as we have seen, no sharp line between intelligence tests and aptitude tests. We use intelligence tests to provide a general assessment of intellectual ability and aptitude tests to measure more specialized abilities required in specific occupations and activities. Having covered intelligence, we now turn to aptitudes and to tests used to measure them.

We shall also treat interests in this section, not because they are aptitudes, for they definitely are not, but because interests must also be taken into account in making any prediction from aptitude tests. To succeed in a given activity, a person must have both an aptitude for the activity and an interest in it. Hence in any practical use, aptitude and interest tests go hand in hand. Interests are also discussed in a different way in the chapter on personality (Chapter 15), where the focus of attention is the traits that characterize an individual.

SCHOLASTIC APTITUDES. As our definition of aptitudes implies, it has become customary to speak of aptitudes and aptitude testing when we refer to the ability or the ability test that is used for the purpose of predicting success or failure in specific training or in a line of work. If we are trying to predict success in training, we speak of *scholastic aptitude*. If it is a vocation we have in mind, we refer to the abilities required as *vocational aptitudes*.

Some aptitude tests serve two purposes— as a general intelligence test and as a scholastic-aptitude test. The data in Figure 14.8 for example, are from the Army General Classification Test, previously mentioned. This test is designed as a test of general intelligence. It also predicts fairly well whether a person is likely to succeed in officer-candidate school. Hence it can be used as a scholastic-aptitude test.

Figure 14.9 gives data on this point from the Second World War. If a person scored 140 or over on the AGCT, his chances of succeeding in officer-candidate school were better than 9 in 10. If his score was less than 110, his chances of succeeding were under 5 in 10. This illustrates the kind of prediction it is possible to make from a good scholastic-aptitude test, though such predictions depend also on the cultural background of individuals with whom it is used and on the type of training involved.

A number of scholastic-aptitude tests have been developed for various kinds of training. Probably the most widely used is the American Council on Education Psychological Examination—abbreviated ACE—which is administered to students entering the liberal arts colleges of the United States. Similar tests are available for schools of medicine, dentistry, nursing, and several other professions. More are being devised each year. Another, called the Graduate Record Examination, has been designed for students who plan to pursue graduate work for the master's or doctor's degree in such specialties as psychology, economics, engineering, and physics. There is an increasing tendency for graduate and professional

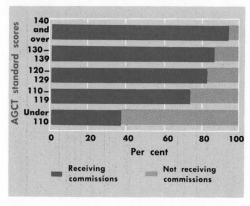

FIGURE 14.9. The prediction of success in officer-candidate school from AGCT scores. The illustration indicates the chances in 100 that an officer candidate making a certain score on the AGCT would receive a commission. Data are for 5,520 men in 14 schools. See Figure 14.4 for the distribution of AGCT scores [after Boring, 1945].

schools to require the appropriate aptitude test of all students who apply to them. If you are such a student, you should be prepared to take such a test at the time and place announced in your particular school.

VOCATIONAL APTITUDES. Scholastic-aptitude tests measure a person's aptitude for success in relatively prolonged training requiring 3, 4, or more years. The great majority of jobs in business and industry, however, do not require such training. Success in these jobs or in training for these jobs can be forecast from a knowledge of specific vocational aptitudes without too much regard for intelligence or scholastic aptitude. There are several hundred tests of vocational aptitude available today. Not all of them are good tests in the sense that they have been proved to be good predictors of vocational success. Some are. Many are slight variations of another test developed to serve some particular purpose. In fact, if time, money, and expert psychological

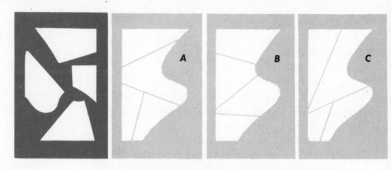

FIGURE 14.10. An example of the Minnesota paper form board, a mechanical-aptitude test. The example is like items on the test. The person being tested must indicate whether pieces on the left fit together to make A, B, or C.

talent are available, it usually is wise to modify existing tests to meet the needs of a particular business or industry. We shall describe the steps that are necessary in selecting a valid test, and then consider briefly two of the many types of tests that are available.

Validation of tests. To evaluate the ability of vocational-aptitude tests to predict success on the job, the following steps are necessary:

1. Give the test to *all* applicants for the kind of job in question until a large number of applicants, preferably several hundred, have been tested.

2. Select applicants for employment *without* considering the test results.

3. After those who are employed have been on the job long enough to be evaluated, divide them according to performance into two or more *criterion* groups. The division may be into "satisfactory" and "unsatisfactory," or it may be into several groups, such as "excellent," "good," "fair," and "poor."

4. Compare the tests results of the different groups.

This process, and particularly the last step, is designed to determine the validity of the test for the purposes intended. It is actually a way of obtaining a correlation between the test and the criterion, as described in Chapter 13. If there is such a correlation, the criterion groups will differ on their aptitude scores. And only when there is such a difference, and the difference is considerably more than one could expect by chance, is the test valid and worthy of use for selection pur-

poses. To construct a new test the steps are essentially the same as for evaluating a test, but the analysis must be made for individual items on the test rather than for the test as a whole. Items are selected that discriminate between the criterion groups; other items are discarded.

Mechanical-ability tests. Many tests that are intended for mechanics, machine operators, assembly-line workers, repairmen, and similar workers involve mechanical knowledge or ability to manipulate objects. Such

WHICH WOULD BE THE BETTER SHEARS FOR CUTTING METAL?

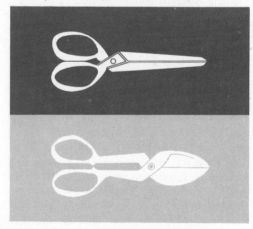

FIGURE 14.11. This is an example of an item on the Bennett-Fry Test of Mechanical Comprehension. Items on the test, however, are generally more difficult [The Psychological Corporation].

tests are called *mechanical-ability tests.* Our experience with such tests indicates that there is a relatively unique mechanical-ability factor common to the tests. People who score high on one mechanical-ability test tend to do so on another. On the other hand, different jobs require different combinations of mechanical abilities; hence there are many different tests. Some examples are given in Figures 14.10 and 14.11.

Psychomotor tests. So far there is little evidence of a general motor ability comparable to perceptual or mechanical ability. Rather, a person who has good manual dexterity is not necessarily good at the kind of coordination involved in running a tractor or an airplane. So psychomotor tests must be conceived, developed, and proved for particular jobs and occupations. These tests involve such psychomotor tasks as manual dexterity, steadiness, muscular strength, speed of response to a signal, and the coordination of many movements into a unified whole. There are many other vocational-aptitude tests for clerical and highly specialized occupations, but these examples will serve to illustrate the kinds of materials used in such tests.

Aptitudes for logical thinking. The usual aptitude tests are designed for the conventional occupations of the industrial world, particularly manufacturing and office occupations. Modern technology, however, is bringing to the fore occupations that require primarily logical thinking and problem solving. Complex automatic systems develop malfunctions which must be diagnosed by technical trouble shooters. Computers must be programmed by people who can think through intricate sequences of steps. Development engineers must design machines for all sorts of purposes.

Until recently, we have not had satisfactory tests for measuring the aptitudes involved in such jobs. We still have a long way to go. But research is being prosecuted vigorously with some promising results. One test, for example, is the LAD (Logical Analysis Device), shown in Figure 14.12. It

consists of an operator's display unit plus a central logic unit, problem-plug boards, and control and recording units. An examiner can set up various standardized problems of various degrees of complexity for an operator to solve. The operator's problem is to discover the rules for responding logically in a correct sequence.

The LAD has fairly high validity in the selection of programmers for computers. Research on its validity, and that of similar techniques, for assessing problem-solving aptitudes in engineers, technicians, and maintenance men should in time give us suitable aptitude measures for the newer occupations of our modern technology.

The use of aptitude tests. Aptitude tests are used both by the employer to select employees for his jobs and by the vocational counselor in helping a person assess his aptitudes for different types of work. The same tests are usually not suitable for both purposes. The employer, knowing exactly what jobs he has in mind, wants a test that will forecast success in his jobs as accurately as possible. He, therefore, would like a test designed specifically for his purposes, e.g.,

FIGURE 14.12. Operator's display panel for LAD. LAD is a Logical Analysis Device designed to measure aptitude for logical thinking and problem solving. This aptitude figures in such occupations as computer programming, engineering development, and trouble shooting [The Psychological Corporation].

for butter wrappers, electrical welders, or lathe operators. The counselor, on the other hand, is trying to help a person make a choice—usually a fairly general choice—among different lines of work. For this purpose, the counselor wants rather general tests that sample many different aspects of specific aptitudes. He has a large number of such general tests to choose from.

Vocational-aptitude tests, as well as the vocational-interest tests we shall describe below, are frequently available in schools and communities. A psychological clinic or student counseling service, in colleges that have one, is usually prepared to administer such tests. The U.S. Employment Service and the Veterans Administration provide testing services for those who qualify for assistance. In the larger cities, there are usually several independent agencies and individuals that offer competent testing facilities for a reasonable fee.

VOCATIONAL INTERESTS. To succeed at a job or a course of training, a person must have not only the aptitudes required for it but also a set of interests that permit him to like its various aspects. Interests, as well as aptitudes, must therefore be taken into account in choosing a vocation and the training to prepare for it. Psychologists have tried two general approaches in developing tests of interest that might serve in vocational guidance. One, developed by Strong, has been called the *empirical approach;* the other, developed by Kuder, has been called the *theoretical approach.* Each approach has its advantages and its limitations.

Strong Vocational Interest Test. The empirical approach to determining the interests required for a vocation is to measure the interests that characterize successful people already in the vocation. We find out what the interests of each vocational group are and then choose only those that *distinguish* successful people in this group from successful persons in other groups. The assumption we make is that these distinctive interests are actually necessary for success in the

TABLE 14.7. Sample items and types of items on the Strong Vocational Interest Test [Strong, 1938].

Sample occupation items			
1. Actor (not movie)	L	I	D
2. Advertiser	L	I	D
3. Architect	L	I	D
4. Army officer	L	I	D
5. Artist	L	I	D
6. Astronomer	L	I	D
7. Athletic director	L	I	D

Types of items	Number
Occupations	100
School subjects	36
Amusements	49
Activities	48
Kinds of people	47
Preference for activities	40
Comparison between items	40
Present abilities	40
Total	400

vocation. On this reasoning Professor Strong at Stanford University went about developing the Strong Vocational Interest Test. Details of his procedure are as follows:

He began by selecting several hundred items that might conceivably distinguish interests in different occupations (see Table 14.7). Items on the test concern preferences for amusements, school subjects, activities, kinds of people, etc. Most of the items are presented so that a person taking the paper-and-pencil test can indicate whether he dislikes (D), likes (L), or is indifferent to (I) the item.

Strong had several hundred people, chosen to be as representative as possible of a particular occupation or vocation, take the test so that he could find out what the interests of successful people actually were. From their responses he was able to discard many items on which there were no substantial differences among occupational groups and to retain those items that successfully discriminated among such groups. Some items, of course, discriminated between certain groups, such as doctors and lawyers, but not between others, such as physicians and chemists. They nevertheless proved useful. In the end, he was able to construct a method of scoring his test for each occupation which summarizes how well the testee's interests correspond with those of people employed in each of several occupations.

The Strong vocational test, as used in recent years, contains 400 discriminating items. It can be scored for 42 occupations in which men are employed and 24 occupations open to women. Each way of scoring gives a person's grade as A, B+, B, B—, or C. If he receives an A, his interests correspond quite well with those of successful people in the occupation, and the prognosis of success, so far as interests go, is excellent. On the other hand, a grade of C means that his interests do not correspond at all well with those of people in the occupation and that his chances of success, so far as interests go, are rather poor. Grades of B+, B, and B— are less certain and are interpreted as giving intermediate degrees of correspondence of interest. A sample of some of the occupations for which Strong scales are available is listed in Table 14.8.

Kuder Preference Record. It is both an advantage and a limitation of the Strong test that it provides scores for specific occupations. In order for a person to use its results, he must state the occupations in which he is interested and have the test separately scored for each occupation. Fortunately, machine scoring has been developed, so the results on several scales can be obtained rather quickly and cheaply. Nevertheless, the Strong test does not give a direct general picture of a person's interests. For this purpose the Kuder Preference Record is

TABLE 14.8. Some of the occupations for which the Strong Vocational Interest Test may be scored. The test is scored separately for each occupation and for men and women. Of the occupations listed below, those accompanied by an asterisk (*) are scored for women only, those accompanied by a dagger (†) are scored for both men and women, and the rest are scored for men only.

Accountant	Life-insurance sales†
Advertising man	Mathematician
Architect	Minister
Artist†	Musician
Author†	Nurse*
Aviator	Occupational
Banker	therapist*
Buyer*	Office worker†
Carpenter	Personnel manager
Chemist	Pharmacist
City school	Physician†
superintendent	Policeman
Coast guard	Printer
Dentist†	Production manager
Dietitian*	Psychologist†
Engineer	Public administrator
Farmer	Social-science teacher
Forest service	Social worker*
Housewife*	Stenographer-
Laboratory	secretary*
technician	Veterinarian
Lawyer†	YMCA-YWCA
Librarian*	secretary†

more suitable. It simply divides all interests into nine general categories: mechanical, computational, scientific, persuasive, artistic, literary, musical, social, and clerical.

A person takes the test in much the same way that he does the Strong vocational test. He indicates his likes and dislikes (see Figure 14.13) and receives a score on each of the nine interest categories. Then in order to see how his interests correspond with those of persons employed in different occupations the counselor turns to occupational norms which indicate how people in these occupations score in each of the categories.

The testee may, for example, be considering the occupation of engineering. By turning to the appropriate table, his counselor can tell him, for example, that 27 per cent of engineers score as low as he does on "scientific interests," 50 per cent as low as he on "computational interests," and so on. On the other hand, by comparing his scores with those of ministers, teachers, or members of other occupations, he may secure a profile for a different profession. The adviser, by looking at these profiles, may be able to inform the person that his interests correspond more with those of persons in sales, teaching, and social service than they do with those in engineering, science, or medicine.

The use of interest tests. Interest tests, like aptitude tests, are not infallible. People sometimes succeed in an occupation with few, if any, of the interests held by others in the occupation. All a counselor can conclude from interest tests is that the odds are strongly favorable, strongly unfavorable, or perhaps about even. Follow-up studies of people who have taken interest tests show that many more fail to succeed in a profession when their interest test indicates a poor prognosis than when the interest pattern

	Most		Least
P Visit an art gallery	●	P	●
Q Browse in a library	●	Q	○
R Visit a museum	○	R	●
S Collect autographs	○	S	●
T Collect coins	●	T	●
U Collect butterflies	●	U	○

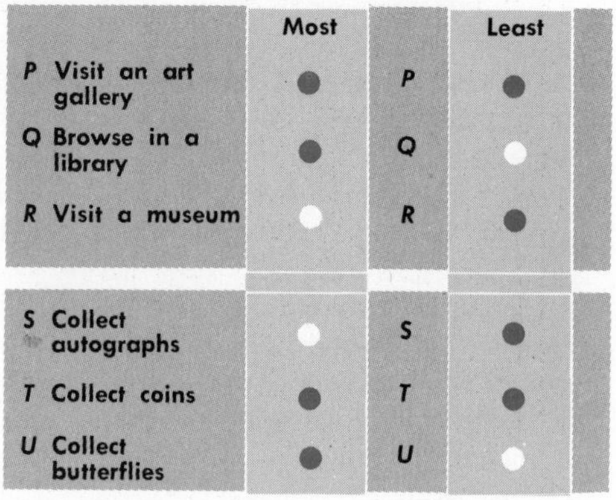

FIGURE 14.13. Two examples of items on Kuder's interest test. With a pinprick the subject indicates which of the three alternatives he likes most and which he likes least. In this case, he likes Q least and R most of P, Q, and R; and he likes S most and U least of S, T, and U [G. F. Kuder and Science Research Associates].

appears highly favorable. The student, or anyone else, who chooses an occupation after receiving strongly unfavorable advice based on interest tests is taking a considerable chance and may later regret his choice.

Summary

1. Ability tests and achievement tests are alike in that each measures present achievement or performance. Ability tests are designed, however, primarily to predict achievement in other situations.

2. Tests intended to measure intellectual ability are called intelligence tests. Those that measure special ability for a particular kind of training or for a vocation are called aptitude tests.

3. Tests of ability differ in whether they (*a*) are individual or group tests; (*b*) emphasize verbal factors or nonverbal performance factors, or (*c*) measure the speed with which a person can solve problems or the ability to solve difficult problems irrespective of time required. Tests of the latter are called power tests.

4. The Stanford-Binet Scale is an individual intelligence test devised for children of school age. It yields a score called mental age, and from this an IQ may be computed if one knows the chronological age. The Wechsler Adult Intelligence Scale is an individual test for adults.

5. There are other group tests of intelligence that may be used for testing large groups of people at the same time. The best

known of these are the Otis and the Army General Classification Test.

6. Intelligence is not a single ability. By factor analysis, it has been demonstrated that about seven abilities are involved in conventional intelligence tests. Some tests weight certain of these abilities more than other tests do.

7. Those individuals who have an IQ of less than 70 are regarded as mentally deficient. They are classified into three groups: morons, imbeciles, and idiots. Tests have been devised for measuring the social intelligence of these groups. In general, the social intelligence of mentally deficient persons is higher than their intellectual ability.

8. At the high end of the distribution of IQs are the mentally gifted. Those with IQs between 130 and 140 are considered very superior; those above 140 are regarded as near genius. Many of the outstanding leaders of history have been mentally gifted. In general, the gifted are far more successful, more physically fit, and better adjusted than those of average intelligence, though there are notable exceptions.

9. There are measurable differences in intellectual abilities among various groups in the population. Women excel men in verbal abilities, but men excel women in certain spatial and mechanical abilities. There are several other differences between men and women in specific abilities.

10. Intelligence tends to decline in old age, but some abilities decline considerably more than others.

11. People in the "higher" occupational groups are, on the average, more intelligent than those in the "lower" occupations.

12. Both the inheritance of a person and the home environment in which he is reared are related to his intelligence.

13. Scholastic-aptitude tests have been developed to estimate ability to succeed in college and other advanced training. Vocational-aptitude tests assess the likelihood of success in some particular vocation.

14. Vocational-interest tests serve as additional aids in vocational choice by measuring the degree to which a person's interests coincide with those found most frequently among persons already in a vocation.

Suggestions for further reading

Anastasi, A., and Foley, J. P., Jr. *Differential psychology* (3d ed.). New York: Macmillan, 1958.
A comprehensive text on psychological differences among groups.

Cronbach, L. J. *Essentials of psychological testing* (rev. ed.). New York: Harper, 1959.
An introduction to the field of psychological tests.

Freeman, F. S. *Theory and practice of psychological testing.* New York: Holt, Rinehart and Winston, 1950.
A text covering the principles of psychological testing.

Ghiselli, E. E., and Brown, C. W. *Personnel and industrial psychology* (2d ed.). New York: McGraw-Hill, 1955.
A standard text describing the theory and use of aptitude tests in business and industry.

Goodenough, F. *Mental testing; its history, principles and applications.* New York: Holt, Rinehart and Winston, 1949.
Another competent text discussing various aspects of psychological testing.

Klineberg, O. *Race differences.* New York: Harper, 1935.
An account of extensive psychological testing of different racial groups.

Super, D. E. *Appraising vocational fitness by means of psychological tests.* New York: Harper, 1949.
The use of tests in vocational counseling and selection.

Terman, L. M., and Oden, M. H. *The gifted group at mid-life: Thirty-five years' follow-*

up of the superior child. Stanford, Calif.: Stanford Univer. Press, 1959.
A summary of a 35-year follow-up study of a large group of gifted persons chosen as children.

Thurstone, L. L. Primary mental abilities. *Psychometr. Monogr.,* 1938, No. 1.
A description of the techniques of factor analysis as used in the development of tests of intelligence.

Tyler, L. E. *The psychology of human differences* (2d ed.). New York: Appleton-Century-Crofts, 1956.
A text covering psychological differences among various groups.

Wechsler, D. *Measurement and appraisal of adult intelligence* (4th ed.). Baltimore: Williams & Wilkins, 1958.
Information about the Wechsler Adult Intelligence Scale.

Personality

To UNDERSTAND PEOPLE better is one of the desires of almost everyone and especially of the student of psychology. A knowledge of many aspects of psychology, including development, motivation, learning, perception, intelligence, and measurement, furthers this aim. We also learn to understand people through the study of the personality of the individual. To the psychologist, this is the *study of the individual as a whole and of the interplay between him and other individuals in the normal course of living.*

Personality characteristics

When we attempt to study an individual in a real-life setting, we are immediately struck with the tremendous number of things we might observe. Every moment in the day he is doing something—sleeping, eating, writing, working, playing, talking, walking, and so on. Any attempt to describe and understand every single thing he does would involve us in a tremendously complicated, and in the end impossible, task. Once, for example, a group of psychologists attempted to record in detail the activities of a seven-year-old boy for just one day [Barker and Wright, 1951]. It took them a book of some 435 pages to do it! Think how voluminous the report would be if we attempted to do this for many individuals over a longer period of time.

We obviously must make some choices of what to study in attempting to understand personalities. To a certain extent, these choices are rather arbitrary and are made according to what we are most interested in knowing about a person. In some circumstances, we may be satisfied with only general traits of behavior. In others we may want most to characterize a person's attitudes, in others his motives, and in still others his way of dealing with personal problems.

No matter what personality characteristics are chosen for study, there are always two requirements that must be met in order to select those that are meaningful and useful. In the first place, a personality characteristic must really be *characteristic*. It does us little good, for example, to know that Mr. A was angry on a certain Tuesday morning. Anyone might have been angry in the situation he faced that particular morning, and he may not have been angry at any other time for a month. Rather, what we would like to know about Mr. A is whether he is characteristically an angry or hostile person or whether he is usually of a serene, sunny disposition and is provoked to anger only occasionally or in the most exasperating of situations. If he is usually serene, and only occasionally angry, we characterize him as a serene person.

Secondly, the aspects of personality that we choose for study should be *distinctive* ones. Almost all adult males in the United States work for a living and almost all go to barbershops to get their hair cut. It does us little good to note, therefore, that a person works for a living or gets his hair cut, for these are not characteristics that distinguish him from most other people. On the other hand, some people work harder than others or have their hair cut more often than others, so these differences do distinguish people from one another. Then we might regard "industriousness" or "well-kempt appearance" as distinguishing personality characteristics.

Confining ourselves to those aspects of personality that are characteristic and distinctive simplifies considerably the problem of studying personality. Even so, there are an enormous number of distinctive characteristics. Moreover, these characteristics are not always easily separated from each other. Is there a clear-cut distinction, for example, between honesty, on the one hand, and conscientiousness, integrity, or dependability, on the other hand? What is the difference between a person's need to depend on others and his need for affection? In these and many other instances we find that personality characteristics often overlap and are highly correlated with each other. Hence we have several possible sets of characteristics that may not be clearly different from one another. Each set, however, may serve some particular purpose in describing personality. In this section, we shall consider several sets of characteristics under the following headings: (1) traits; (2) types; (3) abilities, interests, and attitudes; (4) motives; and (5) modes of adjustment.

TRAITS. A *trait is any aspect of personality that is reasonably characteristic and distinctive.* The trait probably constitutes our most comprehensive means of characterizing a person. The problem, however, of deciding which traits are useful and which are not is a difficult one. The unabridged dictionary contains approximately eighteen thousand adjectives that are used in our language to describe how people act, think, perceive, feel, and behave [Allport and Odbert, 1936]. It also contains about four thousand words that might be accepted as traits—such words as humility, sociability, honesty, and forthrightness. Of course many of these terms are synonyms or near synonyms, and others are so rare and unusual that they are of little value. When these synonyms and rare words are carefully edited, we are left with about 170 words. This is still an unwieldy number to use for scientific purposes. It must be further reduced and refined through research. The general method that has been used to isolate limited sets of traits is the method of factor analysis described elsewhere (page 428).

In one study [Cattell, 1946], it was found that the 170-odd trait names resulting from our dictionary search could be reduced to only 12 factors. As a first step in this study, 171 traits were reduced by combining under one trait all the traits that correlated highly with another set of traits. By following this procedure, 35 broad traits or trait clusters were obtained. Then a small group of experi-enced judges rated a large group of adult men whom they knew reasonably well on each of these 35 broad traits. When all the ratings were made, they were put through a factor analysis. The result was a reduction of the 35 traits to only 12 basic traits or factors (see Table 15.1). In other words, 12

TABLE 15.1. One set of primary traits of personality obtained by the method of factor analysis. A group of experienced judges rated adult men on 35 broad traits. Factor analysis was used on the results to identify the traits that for all practical purposes were duplicates, and the long list of traits was consolidated into 12 primary traits [modified from Cattell, 1946].

	Versus	
1. **Cyclothymia** Emotionally expressive, frank, placid	**Schizothymia** Reserved, close-mouthed, anxious	
2. **General mental capacity** Intelligent, smart, assertive	**Mental defect** Unintelligent, dull, submissive	
3. **Emotionally stable** Free of neurotic symptoms, realistic about life	**Neurotic emotionality** Variety of neurotic symptoms, evasive, immature	
4. **Dominance** Self-assertive, confident, aggressive	**Submissiveness** Submissive, unsure, complaisant	
5. **Surgency** Cheerful, joyous, humorous, witty	**Desurgency** Depressed, pessimistic, dull, phlegmatic	
6. **Positive character** Persevering, attentive to people	**Dependent character** Fickle, neglectful of social chores	
7. **Adventurous cyclothymia** Likes meeting people, strong interest in opposite sex	**Withdrawn schizothymia** Shy, little interest in opposite sex	
8. **Sensitive, infantile emotionality** Dependent, immature, gregarious, attention-seeking	**Mature, tough poise** Independent-minded, self-sufficient	
9. **Socialized, cultured mind** Polished, poised, composed, introspective, sensitive	**Boorishness** Awkward, socially clumsy, crude	
10. **Trustful cyclothymia** Trustful, understanding	**Paranoia** Suspicious, jealous	
11. **Bohemian unconcernedness** Unconventional, eccentric, fitful hysterical upsets	**Conventional practicality** Conventional, unemotional	
12. **Sophistication** Logical mind, cool, aloof	**Simplicity** Sentimental mind, attentive to people	

basic or primary traits proved to be almost as good as 35 in describing personality, because a person's rating on each of the 35 traits could be predicted from his ratings on the 12 primary traits or factors (see Figure 15.1).

One should not jump to the conclusion that there are just 12 basic personality traits. The study cited is just an example, taken from many studies of the subject. The number of traits one obtains in such a study depends on several conditions, including the kinds of people observed, the settings or walks of life in which they are studied, the people doing the rating, and the number of possible traits the judges use in making their ratings.

In another study [Fiske, 1949] 128 men, who were graduate students in clinical psychology, were the subjects. Twenty-two trait descriptions were used for rating these subjects. Actually three different sets of ratings were made: one by faculty members who knew the students fairly well, another by fellow graduate students, and a third by the students themselves. Each of these sets of ratings was subjected to a factor analysis.

Out of this analysis came five basic traits, which are listed and described in Table 15.2. Though the results were slightly different for the three sets of ratings, still the same five traits appeared in all three.

Psychologists have not settled on any one set of traits, nor are they likely to, for just as there is no one "correct" picture to take of a person or a scene, so no one set of traits is to be considered final. The important thing is to have a set that is significant for a particular purpose and can be used for making comparisons among individuals.

TYPES.   Before describing other sets of personality characteristics, we should point out a fairly common error in describing personalities. This is to classify people according to types. We often hear someone say, "John is the submissive type," "Harry is the extroverted type," or "Dick is a Don Juan [type]." Such statements may serve to convey more or less correctly one of a person's rather distinctive traits, but they overstep the mark in classifying him as a type.

Such notions of *types* of personality stem

FACTOR ANALYSIS IDENTIFIES UNDERLYING TRAITS:

FIGURE 15.1. The clustering of traits. Each circle represents a possible trait on which individuals were rated. After the ratings were completed, they were correlated with each other. The number along the line joining two circles is the correlation obtained. In this case, impulsiveness, gregariousness, proneness to witticisms, and facts versus principles are highly correlated and can be considered to be essentially one trait [after Cattell, 1950].

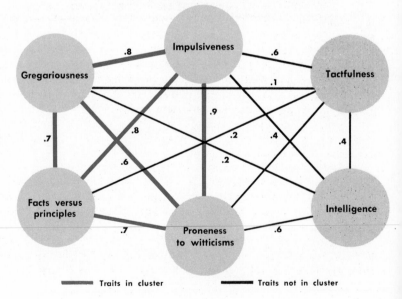

Traits in cluster   Traits not in cluster

TABLE 15.2. Five general personality traits. Twenty-two individual traits, shown on the right, were used in making ratings of 128 men. A factor analysis of the ratings yielded the five general or more basic traits listed on the left [Fiske, 1949].

General traits	Individual traits
Social adaptability	Cheerful-depressed; talkative-silent, introspective; adventurous-cautious; adaptable-rigid; placid–worrying, anxious
Emotional control	Unshakable—easily upset; self-sufficient—dependent; placid–worrying, anxious; limited overt emotional expression—marked overt emotional expression
Conformity	Readiness to cooperate—obstructiveness; serious-frivolous; trustful-suspicious; good-natured, easygoing–self-centered, selfish; conscientious—not conscientious
Inquiring intellect	Broad interests—narrow interests; independent-minded—dependent-minded; imaginative-unimaginative
Confident self-expression	Assertive-submissive; talkative–silent, introspective; marked overt interest in opposite sex—slight overt interest in opposite sex; frank, expressive–secretive, reserved

from a few dramatic instances of somebody's behavior, from contact with relatively rare personalities, or from fictional characters who have purposely been overdrawn to make them interesting and dramatic. We then unthinkingly use these rare instances as models for people in everyday life. The big bully who beats up all the kids in the community becomes a model for an "aggressive type." The relatively rare person who is the "life of the party" may be the model for the "extroverted type." And such fictional characters as Don Juan, Pollyanna, or Scrooge are presented as such distinctive personalities that they serve as models for their respective types. Actually we meet such models so rarely that they can hardly be valid ways of describing characteristic differences among people.

Another objection to typing people is that it lumps together a number of different personality traits. The "introverted type" is supposed to be withdrawn, sensitive to criticism, and inhibited in emotional expression; the "extroverted type" is supposed to be thick-skinned, spontaneous in emotional expression, and little affected by personal failures.

It more often happens, though, that one person may be as sensitive as the introvert, yet as sociable as the extrovert, and another person may be as thick-skinned as the extrovert but as ill-humored and unfriendly as the introvert. Personality, therefore, is not simple enough to be dumped into a single basket—the type. People are characterized by a number of traits. Some of these may be introvertive and some extrovertive; seldom do they all fit the pattern of any one type. Even in the rare cases where they appear to fit one pattern, it is very unlikely that all the traits will be so extreme. Most people are not extreme types or extreme in traits; rather, they fall somewhere between the extremes (see Figure 15.2). It is therefore usually not correct to characterize people by type.

ABILITIES, ATTITUDES, AND INTERESTS. Any description of personality characteristics is incomplete if it does not include such things as *abilities, attitudes,* and *interests.* It may, for example, be characteristic of a person that he is "intelligent," "conservative," and "sports-loving." Such characteristics, in fact, are usually included in the list of traits used for rating personality. In both Tables 15.1 and 15.2, you will notice that some of the trait names apply to these characteristics.

Abilities, attitudes, and interests, however, are different from other personality traits in two important respects. First, they are more often measured by objective tests, that is, by tests that can be mechanically scored and that make no use of the judgments or ratings of a judge. Secondly, they are often measured for special purposes, such as the selection of students or employees, vocational counseling, or public opinion. Since abilities, interests, and attitudes were discussed in the last chapter, however, we shall not consider them further here (see also Chapter 17).

MOTIVES. In addition to the personality characteristics we have mentioned so far, it is also possible to describe a person in terms of his motives and goals—why he does what he does. George, for example, may be quite friendly and attentive, thereby exhibiting desirable traits, but his reason for being this way may be that he wants to sell me a sizable insurance policy. Dave, on the other hand, may have the same traits simply because he likes my company. There is a world of difference. John may want very much to be my friend, but he may seem reserved and aloof because he does not have the social skills needed to show his friendship. Consequently, I may mistake his motive entirely if I judge him by his superficial traits only. We therefore need to have concepts of personality that are cast in terms of motives as well as traits. To say this is not to imply that motives and traits are mutually exclusive characteristics. On the contrary, many traits directly or indirectly describe motives. If we consider a person honest, efficient, and industrious we certainly are saying or implying something about his motives. On the other hand, it is possible to focus attention more directly on motives, leaving aside for the moment how these motives may be related to other personality characteristics.

As in the case of traits, psychologists have

AN INDIVIDUAL CANNOT BE TYPED TO FIT A NARROW CLASSIFICATION:

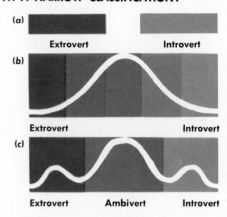

FIGURE 15.2. Conceptions of types. It is common, but incorrect, to classify people into one of two types (a) or to classify most of them into three types (c). It is more correct to think of people as distributed along a continuum, with most in the middle between two extremes (b) [after Stagner, 1948].

not yet agreed on any particular set of motives as the standard for comparing different individuals. The set employed depends on one's theoretical orientation and what one is attempting to find out about a particular individual or group. A set that has been widely used, however, particularly in interpreting the Thematic Apperception Test (see next section), is given in Table 15.3.

This set of motives was not chosen by factor analysis or any statistical method [Murray, 1938]. Rather it was arrived at in an extensive investigation of personality conducted at the Harvard Psychological Clinic. A number of young men were thoroughly tested, interviewed, and studied by a group of clinical psychologists. The investigators found that a set of motives such as that shown in the table gave them a satisfactory way of classifying and rating the motives of the young men serving as subjects.

Since the original study was conducted, psychologists skilled in the study of personality, and given appropriate information

TABLE 15.3. A classification of major personal motives [after Murray, 1938]

Motive	Goal and effects
Abasement	To submit passively to others. To seek and accept injury, blame, and criticism.
Achievement	To accomplish difficult tasks. To rival and surpass others.
Affiliation	To seek and enjoy cooperation with others. To make friends.
Aggression	To overcome opposition forcefully. To fight and revenge injury. To belittle, curse, or ridicule others.
Autonomy	To be free of restraints and obligations. To be independent and free to act according to impulse.
Counteraction	To master or make up for failure by renewed efforts. To overcome weakness and maintain pride and self-respect on a high level.
Deference	To admire and support a superior person. To yield eagerly to other people.
Defendence	To defend oneself against attack, criticism, or blame. To justify and vindicate oneself.
Dominance	To control and influence the behavior of others. To be a leader.
Exhibition	To make an impression. To be seen and heard by others. To show off.
Harmavoidance	To avoid pain, physical injury, illness, and death.
Infavoidance	To avoid humiliation. To refrain from action because of fear of failure.
Nurturance	To help and take care of sick or defenseless people. To assist others who are in trouble.
Order	To put things in order. To achieve cleanliness, arrangement, and organization.
Play	To devote one's free time to sports, games, and parties. To laugh and make a joke of everything. To be lighthearted and gay.
Rejection	To remain aloof and indifferent to an inferior person. To jilt or snub others.
Sentience	To seek and enjoy sensuous impressions and sensations. To genuinely enjoy the arts.

about a person, have been able to rate, with fairly good reliability, the strength of each of the needs in a person.

MODES OF ADJUSTMENT. Another way of characterizing people is by their typical modes of adjustment. The term *adjustment* refers to accommodating oneself to circumstances, and more particularly, to the satisfaction of needs or motives under various circumstances. There are a number of characteristic modes or ways of adjusting; these

are described at length in Chapter 5 [Murray, 1938]. Most individuals at one time or another use all the various modes. Yet they may rely on one more than on another.

A person may resort to schizoid (schizophrenic) modes of adjustment, that is, to withdrawal into a private world; another person may adopt neurotic devices, such as being extremely compulsive or orderly in his behavior or imagining that he has physical ailments that are responsible for his failures. These are examples of the poor adjustment of abnormal personalities, but the point is that different individuals, even those with rather similar needs, may adopt different characteristic modes of adjusting to their environments. Many personality tests are designed to measure these characteristic modes of adjustment.

Personality measurement

In order to make any practical use or interpretation of personality characteristics, especially for a particular individual, we must have ways of measuring them. Seldom, however, do we need exhaustive measurements of personality. Usually, we require a knowledge of certain characteristics for a particular purpose. Personnel psychologists, for example, may want to select people whose personality characteristics make them good salesmen. A military psychologist may want to measure neurotic tendencies that make people unfit for hazardous duty. Experimental psychologists may want to measure anxiety in order to control its influence in their experiments on perception or learning. There are a variety of different methods to suit these specific purposes.

PENCIL-AND-PAPER TESTS. The most convenient type of measure to use for almost any psychological purpose is a pencil-and-paper test. This may be given cheaply and quickly to large groups of people at the same time. Hence pencil-and-paper tests are rather popular, and during the last 20 years, psychologists have constructed scores of them [Guilford, 1959].

Questionnaires. Pencil-and-paper tests of personality characteristics are usually questionnaires, in which the persons being tested must answer questions or say "yes" or "no" to simple statements. Samples of statements are as follows:

I generally prefer to attend movies alone.
I occasionally cross the street to avoid meeting someone I know.
I seldom or never go out on double dates.

The person taking the test must say "yes" or "no," or "true" or "false," to each such statement, thus indicating whether he thinks it applies to him. In some questionnaires a person may also be allowed to answer "doubtful" or "uncertain."

This kind of personality test first gained widespread use during the First World War. It was used then to weed out emotionally unstable draftees. The statements in the test were chosen to reflect psychiatric symptoms that might predict future emotional breakdown. They included such items as the following:

I consider myself a very nervous person.
I frequently feel moody and depressed.

The problem of validity. A question of validity (see page 425) arises in the construction of any psychological test. In the case of personality tests, valid measurement means measurement that correlates with one or more personality characteristics. No personality test has perfect validity, but the question is whether a test has sufficient validity to be useful in drawing any conclusions from its results.

Since the First World War, personality questionnaires have grown without bounds. They are mostly designed to measure emotional maladjustment or such general traits as extroversion-introversion. When constructed by psychologists, who are conscious of the validity problem, the tests have usually been validated in some way, so that the degree of validity and the circumstances under which they are valid is known.

But many of the questionnaires in popular magazines designed to tell you whether you are a good husband, a happy person, an introvert, etc., have not been validated. Neither is there any known validity in some of the tests made up by individuals or "testing agencies" for use in selecting executives or employees in industry. Even though the items on a test may look valid, this is no guarantee that they actually are. Indeed, since validity is so hard to come by, the best assumption is that a personality test is invalid until it is proved otherwise.

An especially acute problem in developing valid personality tests is the possibility of an individual *faking* his answers on the test. A person, for example, who knows that a high score on emotional maladjustment will keep him out of the Army can deliberately get a high score. Conversely, a person who may be quite maladjusted usually can make a low score if that is necessary to get the job he is after. In the First World War, for example, a group of draftees who made abnormal scores on a personality test at the time of induction were able to make quite normal scores on it after the war was over.

Minnesota Multiphasic Personality Inventory. Despite instances of the sort described above, it is possible to construct personality tests of reasonable validity. First, the tests must be shown to correlate with a criterion when the people taking the test are being honest in their answers. Secondly, the test must be so constructed that answers are hard to fake or that faking, when it is done, can be detected. We have a number of such tests, but a good example is the Minnesota Multiphasic Personality Inventory (MMPI) [Hathaway and McKinley, 1943].

The MMPI was constructed by first giving a very large number of items to both normal people and abnormal personalities classified into seven diagnostic categories (see below). The items were fairly typical of personality questionnaires, and indeed, many of them had previously been used in other tests. As usual, the items were answered "true," "cannot say," or "false." The scores of normal individuals on each item, e.g., the number answering it "true," were then compared with those of individuals in each of the diagnostic categories. Items that did not distinguish between normals and abnormals were discarded as invalid; those that did distinguish one or more diagnostic groups from normals were retained. In other words, those that correlated with some criterion of normal-abnormal were retained as valid.

The final test contains 550 items. Some of the items are valid for one set of diagnostic categories; other items are valid for other combinations of categories. This fact is taken into account in the scoring. There are seven scales, that is, there are seven different ways of scoring the items, one for each of the categories. The names of the scales and the kinds of characteristics they measure are as follows:

1. *Hypochondriasis*—exaggerated anxiety about one's health, and pessimistic interpretation and exaggeration of minor symptoms

2. *Hysteria*—various ailments such as headaches and paralyses which have no physical basis

3. *Psychopathic deviation*—antisocial and amoral conduct

4. *Paranoia*—extreme suspiciousness of other people's motives, frequently resulting in elaborate beliefs that certain people are plotting against one

5. *Psychasthenia*—irrational thoughts that recur and/or strong compulsions to repeat seemingly meaningless acts

6. *Schizophrenia*—withdrawal into a private world of one's own, often accompanied by hallucinations and bizarre behavior

7. *Hypomania*—mild elation and excitement without any clear reason

In addition, by determining the items that distinguish between men and women, it was possible to construct a masculinity-femininity scale. Finally, scales were constructed to detect lying and placing oneself in an overly favorable light. This was done by including certain items that are traps. Take, for example, the following item: "I sometimes put off until tomorrow what I should do today." The person who is faking or trying to make the test results favorable to himself answers this "false," whereas the honest answer for most people is "true." Several checks of this sort enable the scorer to estimate the validity of the test for the particular person taking it. For an individual whose test gives valid results, the scorer can go on to construct a profile showing the relative standing of the individual on each of the various scales.

(An example of a profile, but on a different test, is given in Figure 15.3).

Allport-Vernon-Lindzey Scale. The Allport-Vernon-Lindzey Study of Values [Allport et al., 1951] is another pencil-and-paper questionnaire to test personality. It measures a person's major areas of *interest:* theoretical, economic, aesthetic, social, political, and religious.

In the first part of the test, the subject must give a yes or no answer to a series of statements, such as "The main object of scientific research should be the discovery of pure truth rather than its practical applications." If the subject agreed with this statement, his response would help make up a high score on theoretical interests; if he disagreed, his answer would count toward high economic interests. In the second part of the test, the subject must rank four alternatives in the order of his agreement with them. He would, for example, express his agreement with the following statements by indicating a rank order for them:

Do you think that a good government should aim chiefly at

(a) more aid for the poor, sick, and old?
(b) the development of manufacturing and trade?

(c) introducing more ethical principles into its policies and diplomacy?
(d) establishing a position of prestige and respect among nations?

As in the case of the MMPI, it is possible to construct a profile of the results. In this case, the profile is for the six major areas of interest. You can see an example of such a profile in Figure 15.3.

SITUATIONAL TESTS. At best pencil-and-paper questionnaires are somewhat artificial. They attempt to measure personality by asking questions about it. The ideal way to measure personality would be to sample personality itself, to observe people behaving in a fair sample of real-life situations. Situation tests have been devised which try to meet this need. In these the tester or experimenter constructs some type of real-life situation and observes personality in it.

One classical example of this kind of measure is a study [Hartshorne and May, 1928] of honesty and dishonesty in children:

Children were put in a number of situations affording an opportunity to cheat without their knowing that the experimenters could catch them. In one situation, children were given a

THE ALLPORT-VERNON-LINDZEY STUDY OF VALUES GIVES A PICTURE OF A PERSON'S MAJOR AREAS OF INTEREST:

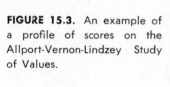

FIGURE 15.3. An example of a profile of scores on the Allport-Vernon-Lindzey Study of Values.

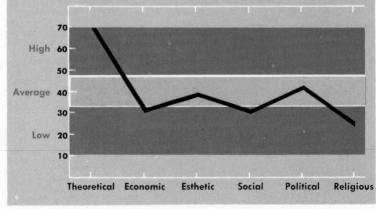

CHAPTER FIFTEEN

large number of coins to arrange in patterns. When they completed this task, they were asked to put the coins in a cupboard. An inconspicuous code on the coins, however, permitted the experimenters to tell which coins were returned and which were "stolen." Another situation presented the child with a problem so difficult—a complicated finger maze to be traced with the eyes closed—that a child had to peek or "cheat" to obtain a high score on it.

With many situations like these, the investigators exhaustively studied honesty as a personality trait in children. What they found is that honesty is not a unitary trait. Children who are honest in one situation may be dishonest in another situation, and vice versa.

Another example of the use of miniature situations to study personality is to be found in the Office of Strategic Services [Office of Strategic Services Assessment Staff, 1948]:

During the Second World War, the OSS had the task of selecting people to work as agents behind enemy lines. Psychologists developed a wide variety of situations designed to measure important personality traits for this kind of work. Candidates were given such situations as drilling a squad of men, leading a group of candidates in mock-combat conditions, and solving such problems as improvising a bridge to move heavy equipment across a stream. Then, to make the situations as stressful as possible, the psychologists deliberately made the task more difficult. In one case, for example, a candidate was to construct a tower out of heavy logs within a fairly short period of time and was assigned two helpers to do the job. The helpers, however, were stooges who deliberately failed to carry out orders. They would clumsily knock over parts of the completed structure and argue with the candidate or make insulting remarks about his intelligence, appearance, or race. Faced with such frustrations as these, many candidates broke down in tears or sputtered with rage.

Situational tests have high "face validity" because they resemble the real thing. Whether they have any real validity or not is usually open to question. In the case of the OSS studies, the exigencies of war made it impractical to validate the tests. In this case and in others, there are several obstacles to achieving high validity: (1) It may not be possible to motivate subjects as they would be motivated in real life. (2) In many cases, it is not possible to disguise the situations well enough to keep the subjects from seeing through them. Then the candidate considers the whole thing a joke. (3) The judgments of observers often do not agree with one another well enough to provide either reliable or valid measurement. For these reasons, the practical usefulness of situational tests largely remains to be demonstrated. Possibly through further research, however, tests of this kind may eventually be developed into valid measuring devices.

EXPERIMENTAL MEASUREMENTS. Scientists who are trying to discover basic principles frequently employ experimental measurements that are not practicable on a large scale. This is the case in the study of personality. Of the many kinds of experimental measurements used in research on personality, we shall give two examples.

One experiment [Postman et al., 1948] illustrates the principle that motives influence perception (also see page 329):

A group of college students first took the Allport-Vernon-Lindzey Study of Values. This test, you will remember, yields scores on six different interest areas. The experimenters chose a number of words representing each of the interest areas. To represent the economic area, they chose such words as "dollar" and "price"; to represent the religious area, they chose such words as "prayer" and "deity." Then they exposed these words very briefly on a projection screen and measured the length of exposure that was necessary for each college student correctly to identify the word. When they had collected all their measurements, they found that exposure time and interest area were correlated. That is to say, subjects with predominantly economic interests were able to recognize economic words at shorter exposures than words representing areas in which they were less interested. Thus, interest or motive was reflected in speed of recognizing words connected with these interests or motives.

Our second example [Eysenck, 1947] of the experimental measurement of personality is as follows:

A subject stands blindfolded, with a hook and thread attached to his collar. The other end of the thread is tied to a pen on a *kymograph*, which is a device that moves recording paper around a drum at some constant speed. Thus it will record any moving or swaying of the subject. Now the experimenter tells the subject that he is falling backward. If the subject is suggestible, he will start to sway. Indeed, some people are so suggestible that they would fall over if the experimenter were not prepared to catch them. In any case, the degree of suggestibility of the person is measured experimentally by the mark on the kymograph record. This measure of suggestibility can be correlated with suggestibility in other situations. In general the correlations have been small, and indicate that "suggestibility," like honesty, is not a unitary trait.

As you can see, most experimental measures of personality require an elaborate apparatus and procedure. They are therefore not useful for everyday situations. They are proving helpful, however, in establishing principles of personality and in providing suggestions for designing other, more practicable personality tests.

PERSONAL INTERVIEW.   The personality measurements discussed thus far are *objective* measurements. A measurement is objective when little or no judgment is required by the measurer; all he has to do is count or read a number. He may count, for ex-

ample, the number of times a person prefers "theoretical" over "economic" tasks, or the number of times the person cheats in an honesty test. Or he may read the number of inches a subject sways in a suggestibility test. No matter what the test situation is, so long as it can be scored by simple counting or by reading numerical measurements, the measurement is objective. An objective measurement can be made by anyone of normal intelligence who can read and count accurately.

Whenever, on the other hand, the measurement involves some judgment, rating, or interpretation made by a person, it is considered a subjective measurement. Perhaps the most familiar example to the college student is the grade given by an instructor to an essay question. The teacher does not count anything; he reads the answer and makes a subjective judgment of its quality. In general, subjective measurement is less reliable than objective measurement; it usually yields less agreement between scorers than objective measurement. Yet the difference is not always large; some scorers skilled in their task can achieve reasonably high reliability in subjective scoring. And when we lack objective means of measurement, as is sometimes the case, we are forced to do the best we can with subjective measurements.

The personal interview is one of the oldest devices for measuring personality. It is obviously subjective. Yet interviewers sometimes make reasonably good measuring instruments. Psychologists and psychiatrists, although they secure all the information they can from objective tests, usually rely on the interview to round out their picture of a personality. The interviewer tries to sample as wide a range as possible of the person's feelings and attitudes by getting him to talk about his personal experiences. In so doing, the interviewer not only notes what he hears but also observes more intangible behavior: the way a person talks about certain topics— the catch in the voice, for example, whenever mother is mentioned, or the tenseness that appears whenever certain other subjects are brought up—and in many cases what the person is careful *not* to talk about. From these varied observations, the clinician attempts to reconstruct a picture of a person's major motives, his sources of conflict, his modes of adjustment, and the over-all adequacy of his adjustment.

Although the interview is more widely used in the study of personality than any other single method, it has some serious limitations. For one thing, it depends almost entirely on the skill of the interviewer—and skill in interviewing is hard to teach. More serious than that is the difficulty of expressing the results of an interview in quantitative

TABLE 15.4. An example of a rating scale used to measure aggressive behavior toward other persons.

Instructions: Place a check mark after the category that most closely describes the subject's behavior.

A. The degree to which the subject displays hostile or aggressive behavior in his relations with others:

1. Avoids aggression even when it is called for. Never becomes angry or criticizes others.

2. Seldom becomes angry or critical of others. Will do so, however, if strongly prodded or actually attacked.

3. Shows normal amount of aggression when the circumstances seem to call for it. Is neither reluctant nor overready to show hostility.

4. Frequently engages in quarrels or arguments. Is often sarcastic. Tends to be critical of many things.

5. Almost always aggressive. Has trouble getting along with people because he is ready to argue or fight at the drop of a hat.

terms. In general the results can be communicated only in word descriptions, not in objective scores. This makes it difficult to compare people by means of the interview or even to tell whether the interviewer has, in fact, made any valid measurement. There is evidence, however, that interviewing combined with objective tests can provide more valid judgments than either one by itself.

RATING SCALES. A partial solution to the problem of expressing interview measurements in objective terms is to be found in the *rating scale*. It may be used to record impressions of personality obtained in interviews or from informal observation. There are several forms of rating scales.

One of the simpler forms lists a number of personality characteristics, such as honesty, reliability, sociability, industriousness, and emotionality, and asks the rater who knows the person being evaluated to give a rating—say, between 1 and 7—on each characteristic. Another method is to provide the rater with a number of alternative descriptions and ask him to check which alternative applies best to the person being rated. From such checks it is usually possible to convert the results into numerical scores on 5- or 7-point scales. In constructing such scales, we usually let 1 stand for one extreme of a characteristic, 7 for the other extreme, and 4 for an average amount of it. An example of such a scale is one for *aggression*, which you see in Table 15.4 (also see Figure 15.4).

Rating scales are such simple things that we can use them to record our impressions of almost any aspect of a person's personality. Their simplicity, however, should not fool us. Like any form of personality measurement, they can be unreliable and invalid. In the hands of amateurs, they usually are. Rating-scale techniques must be subjected to the same rigorous analysis of validity as other more objective forms of personality measurement.

PROJECTIVE METHODS. The last form of personality measurement to be discussed is

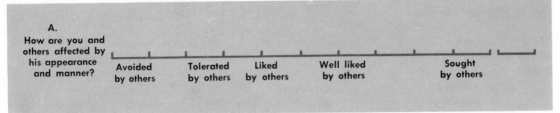

A.
How are you and others affected by his appearance and manner?

Avoided by others   Tolerated by others   Liked by others   Well liked by others   Sought by others

FIGURE 15.4. An item on a rating scale. The rater checks a point on the scale to indicate his opinion of the subject. The dash at the end means "no opportunity to observe."

the *projective method*. The method is called projective because it presents the subject with a situation, usually a visual object or picture, which gets him unknowingly to reveal some of his personality characteristics by projecting them into the situation. He is presented with the object or picture and asked to say what he sees or to tell a story about it. In his narration, he ascribes certain characteristics to the things and people he talks about and thus reveals his own characteristics. At least that is the theory of the projective test, and that is why it is called projective.

There are several different projective tests. Of these, the Thematic Apperception Test (TAT) and the Rorschach Test are two that are widely known and frequently used by clinical psychologists.

The Thematic Apperception Test consists of a series of 20 pictures [Morgan and Murray, 1935]. Each picture is ambiguous enough to permit a variety of interpretations. In Figure 15.5 is an example of the kind of picture used, though it is not one of the test pictures. When presented with a picture, the testee is asked to make up a story of what is happening in the picture. The story is supposed to begin with events leading up to the scene and end with an outcome. Most people, when they make up such stories, identify themselves with one of the characters in the picture, and their stories may be little more than thinly disguised autobiographies. In this way the testees may

reveal feelings and desires they would otherwise hesitate to discuss openly or, in some cases, would be unwilling to admit to themselves.

As generally used, the TAT has no stand-

FIGURE 15.5. An example of the Thematic Apperception Test. The subject is shown a card and instructed to tell a story about its picture. He is asked to explain the situation it represents, discuss events that led up to the situation, indicate the feelings and thoughts of the characters in the picture, and describe the outcome of the situation [Murray, 1943].

CHAPTER FIFTEEN

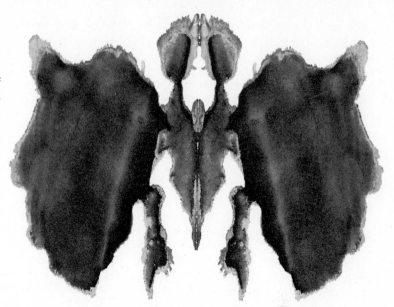

FIGURE 15.6. An example of a Rorschach ink blot. Blots similar to this one are shown to a subject with the instruction to indicate what he sees in it. After all the subject's responses are recorded, the examiner inquires more deeply into them, finding out what it was about each card that determined his responses.

ardized scoring. The tester interprets it by noting recurring themes in the stories: the characteristic needs and frustrations of the hero; the relations of the hero with members of the opposite sex, with parents, or with persons in positions of authority; and the over-all emotional tone of the stories, whether depressed or overly optimistic; and so on.

The Rorschach Test is relatively more objective and at the same time more ambiguous than the TAT.

The Rorschach [1942] consists of 10 ink blots similar to the one in Figure 15.6, although some of the blots have colored parts to them. Each card is presented to the subject with the question, "What might this be?" or "What does this remind you of?" After responding to these questions for all 10 cards, the subject goes through them again, indicating what parts of the ink blot suggested his responses.

Some of the scoring is done objectively by counting the number of times the subject responded to *part* of the blot compared with the number of times he responded to the blot as a *whole*. Counts can also be made of other things, such as the number of responses to color (in the colored blots) and

the number of responses suggesting movement. On the other hand, the clinician interprets not only number of responses in different categories, but also the pattern of the responses. This becomes somewhat subjective. Even more subjective are interpretations based on other cues, such as spontaneous remarks made during the test, signs of emotional upset, and the symbolic meaning of the responses.

Clinicians regularly use projective tests such as the Rorschach and TAT and believe they learn about an individual's personality from them. Perhaps they do. After all, the projective test is a subtle kind of interview. Unfortunately, convincing proof of the validity of the tests is lacking. We must therefore withhold judgment about their value as devices for personality measurement. Additional research on this subject is needed.

How personality develops

We have described different ways of looking at personality and different ways of measuring it. Now it is logical to raise questions about cause and effect. How do biological inheritance, on the one hand, and the social environment, on the other, contribute to personality development? In so far as learning is important, what sorts of influences mold personality? Is what a person learns early in childhood more important than what he learns later on, or vice versa? What accounts for differences in personality? Why do some people develop "good" personalities and others "poor" ones?

There are, of course, general and specific answers to these questions. To understand a particular person, we need to know what particular influences have been at work in his life, and these will be different for each person. On the other hand, we all are subject in varying degrees to many of the same sorts of influences. Thus it is possible to describe the principal influences in personality development. That is what we shall do in this section.

INHERITED PREDISPOSITIONS. Inheritance is one of the influencing factors. As in the case of most things psychological, however, personality is not directly inherited. What is inherited is a *predisposition* to develop in certain ways. This means that an individual inherits tendencies rather than a completely predetermined pattern or trait. Whether he actually becomes the kind of personality to which he is predisposed, or the degree to which he does, depends on environmental factors.

You can see some of these predispositions unfolding at an early age in infants before there has been much chance for learning to

take place. Indeed, you can often observe some striking differences among infants. One baby is extremely active, another quite sluggish. One cries and fusses most of the time, while another is so placid its mother calls the pediatrician to see whether anything is wrong. It seems obvious that such differences are to some extent innate.

The best scientific proof of inherited dispositions to develop certain kinds of personalities comes from studies of so-called "mental disease." These studies cover the inheritance of several kinds of mental disease described in Chapter 5, but one will serve as an illustration [Kallmann, 1951].

The general incidence of schizophrenia in the population of the United States is less than 1 in 100. If one parent has the disease, however, the odds increase to 10 in 100 that his child will have it. If one child in the family develops it, the odds increase further to 15 in 100 that its brother or sister will have it too. In fraternal twins, who differ as much in heredity as ordinary brothers and sisters (page 35), the odds are still 15 in 100 that one twin will become schizophrenic if the other one does. For identical twins, however, the odds jump to 85 in 100 that both twins will develop schizophrenia if one of the pair does. Similar results, with slightly different numbers, have been obtained in studying two other personality patterns (see Table 15.5).

Figures of this sort argue strongly for the inheritance of a predisposition to develop schizophrenia and certain other so-called

TABLE 15.5. The incidence of mental disease in the general population and among blood relatives of mental patients [Kallmann, 1951].

Type of mental disease	Incidence in general population, per cent	Incidence among relatives, per cent				
		Parents	Half siblings	Full siblings	Fraternal twins	Identical twins
Schizophrenia	0.9	9.3	7.1	14.2	14.5	86.2
Manic-depressive psychosis	0.4	23.4	16.7	23.0	26.3	95.7
Involutional melancholia	1.0	6.4	4.5	6.0	6.0	60.9

CHAPTER FIFTEEN

"mental diseases." To be sure, members of the same family have somewhat similar environments, but this cannot account for the different odds in fraternal and identical twins—15 as compared with 85 in 100. Moreover, identical twins *reared apart* have also been studied. They have about the same contingent odds as identical twins reared together. We must conclude, therefore, that something in the inherited biological equipment is a major factor in developing at least certain abnormal personality patterns. Of course, the fact that the odds for identical twins are 85 and not 100 leaves some room for the effects of environment.

At present we do not know how such predispositions are inherited. It is possible that the linkage is from genes to enzymes to metabolic processes in the brain (see page 599), but that is just a guess. Perhaps the endocrine glands are also involved.

ENDOCRINE GLANDS. In some cases, abnormalities of the endocrine glands show up clearly in personality. Thyroid deficiency is accompanied by sluggishness and inactivity, as well as mental deficiency if it is severe. Hyperthyroidism causes overactivity, jumpiness, and related symptoms. The role of the endocrine glands is treated in Chapter 19. So far, however, only extreme cases of deficiency or oversufficiency have been demonstrated to make a difference in personality. It stands to reason that endocrine function may subtly influence normal variations in personality, but we do not yet have much evidence on the point.

The possible relation between body structure and personality is discussed later under "Theories of Personality."

ABILITIES. Each person is endowed with certain abilities, which are gradually developed through maturation and learning. There can be little doubt that inheritance partly determines these abilities (Chapter 2). Psychologists refer to the more general abilities to learn, abstract, and solve problems as *intelligence;* they call special abilities, such as talent for music or mechanical things, *aptitudes* (Chapter 14). These abilities, as we have pointed out, are to a certain extent a part of a person's personality. They are also important influences on personality development.

A fairly common belief, which is incorrect, holds that extremely intelligent children are frail in physique and somewhat queer or neurotic in personality. There are, of course, some cases of this sort, but as a general rule this idea is wrong. Psychologists have conducted extensive studies of extremely intelligent children—geniuses—and they find that such children on the average are physically stronger, healthier, more stable emotionally, and better adjusted than normal children (Figure 15.7). This general superiority of the more intelligent, moreover, is not limited to children; it is just as true of adults.

There are probably two general reasons for this correlation. One is *biological,* the other *social.* Some individuals are better all-round biological organisms than others. The same biological factors that account for superior strength and health can be expected to produce a better-functioning nervous system and, indirectly, better intelligence. On the other hand, superior intelligence helps a person make better social adjustments. Since personality may be regarded as the composite of such adjustments, superior intelligence should be a factor in the development of a "better" personality. The brighter little Johnny is, for example, the sooner he can learn to understand that mother may be cross and grouchy because she has a headache rather than because he is a naughty, unlovable child. And the more intelligent child can learn sooner to see into the future, to delay a satisfaction now for one he may achieve a day or two hence.

Intelligence also influences personality by providing a person with means of recognition. The bright child achieves rewards from parents and teachers for his accomplishments. Another with mechanical ability may become interested in building amateur radio equipment and receive the recognition of adults and friends for his achievements. Thus intelligence and special abilities permit a child or an adult to develop areas of competence from which he acquires confidence and feelings of self-worth and self-esteem.

Abilities also seem to provide their own motivation. A person with a special talent usually has a strong motive to exercise it. The great musician Handel, for example, had a father who strongly opposed his son's interest in music. Nevertheless, even when faced with severe punishment, Handel as a child would sneak to the garret at night to practice the harpsichord. As a consequence of such strong drives to practice, children with outstanding abilities usually show them at an early age.

CULTURE. One's personality also depends, of course, upon whether he is raised in the United States or in the jungles of New Guinea, whether he lives in the city or on the farm, and whether he is reared in an upper or lower socioeconomic class. These circumstances and many others constitute the culture or subculture in which he lives. Culture largely determines the experiences a person has, the frustrations and adjustments he must deal with, and the standards of conduct required of him. Each culture has its distinctive values, morals, and ways of behaving. It dictates the rules for child training and the relationships within a family. Thus in various ways it influences personality [Linton, 1945].

Such influences are most convincingly demonstrated by the differences in cultures of primitive societies and the characteristic differences in personality associated with them.

The Balinese, for example, have been described as an introverted people who seem emotionally blunted. They do not form warm personal attachments; rather, each member seems to live within himself. The Navaho Indians are passive and forbearing in the face of physical discomfort. The Eskimos are rugged individualists. The Arapesh

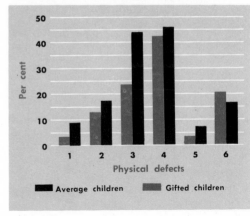

FIGURE 15.7. Physical defects of gifted and average children (control group). Green bars are for gifted children; black bars are for average children. In all cases, the height of the bar represents the percentage of children having the particular defect or characteristic. 1, frequent headaches; 2, symptoms of general weakness; 3, mouth breathing; 4, occasional or frequent colds; 5, poor or very poor hearing; 6, somewhat defective or poor vision [after Terman, 1943].

people of New Guinea seem to be without egotism or competitiveness.

In the Balinese people, the lack of emotional response has been attributed to child-rearing practices. Most of the baby tending is done by little girls, and each child may be cared for by a number of little "mothers." Such practices prevent intense family relationships from building up. In addition, the Balinese mother may make things worse by deliberately teasing her child. She will play with him up to the point of evoking love or anger, then lose interest in him or become indifferent. It is small wonder, then, that the Balinese child soon learns to inhibit emotional responses to other people.

For a more extensive discussion of the relation between personality and cultural influences, see Chapter 16.

FAMILY. The family exerts many cultural influences, for it largely determines the environment of children during their early years and decides how cultural standards are to be imposed and adhered to.

One significant influence of the family is the *affection* it gives or withholds. This is especially important, the evidence indicates, during babyhood. If a child gets fondling and affection during this period, he is more likely to be emotionally responsive later in life. Conversely, if he lacks fondling then, his emotional responsiveness may be blunted. Children, for example, who are raised from birth in orphan asylums, where they receive every physical care but little personal handling and attention, are less responsive, studies show, than are children who are placed in an orphanage after they are two years of age [Goldfarb, 1947]. Early parental influences are thus important in personality development.

The *training* and guidance given by parents also fashions personality. Parents are teachers. By rewarding some kinds of behavior and discouraging others, they help determine the personality traits, goals, and values of the child. One child may discover that his mother will let him have his own way if he throws a temper tantrum. Another child in another family may find that temper tantrums do not work, but feigning illness does. The techniques that a child develops in dealing with his parents naturally carry over into his contacts with other people. The grown man, for example, who sulks because he is angry with his wife probably learned this trait in dealing with his mother.

Probably parents' *attitudes* toward their children are as important as anything else in the way personality develops in children. Parents who are well adjusted, who love and respect their child as a person, do much to build up within the child a feeling of self-worth and self-confidence. This in turn gives the child a great advantage in facing his problems. Unfortunately, however, many parents reject their children, enmesh them in the cross fire of their own emotional problems, or take out on the children the ill-treatment that they may have experienced in their own childhood. In fact, studies have shown that many mothers and fathers unconsciously relive their own childhood problems through their children [Hilgard, 1953]. A mother may unconsciously react to her son with the same emotions and feelings that she herself felt as a child toward her older brother. If she resented and disliked her brother, her feelings toward her son may conflict. She may find herself competing with him and thus unable to give him encouragement, love, and praise. It is easy for children in such a situation to feel unwanted and unloved and thus to lack confidence and emotional security that carries over into adulthood.

Parents, finally, influence personality development by being *models.* Much of a child's learning is by imitation. By watching his father, a son learns how to act like a man, and the daughter learns how to assume the role of wife and mother by watching her mother. If the parents are poor models, the chances are that the children will find substitute models in aunts, uncles, or grandparents, or they may discover models in the comics, movies, or on television. In any case they find models with whom to identify themselves. In so doing, they may copy many of the personality traits of the parents, taking over their moral and cultural standards as well as their typical ways of adjusting to problems.

The individual and the self

In the preceding sections we have learned how personality is described, how it is measured, and how it is molded by environmental and hereditary influences. Now we come to the problem of understanding the *individual personality as a whole.* This must somehow be done by the clinical psychologist or counselor when he attempts to help an individual with his problems. Each of us tries to do it in dealing with many of the people we know intimately. There is no royal road to understanding the individual, or any set of rules for doing it. There are, however, some important points to consider, and we shall present them under the following headings: (1) individuality, (2) personality syndromes, and (3) the self.

INDIVIDUALITY. A person is not simply a profile of characteristics measured by tests or ratings, nor is he a piece of putty molded willy-nilly by environmental circumstances. Personality tests are only samples of behavior (see page 426), and environmental influences combine in different ways to affect personalities quite differently. When we have data about personality characteristics and environmental influences, these are merely windows through which we catch brief glimpses of the underlying personality. These glimpses must somehow be synthesized into a coherent picture of an individual.

Uniqueness of personality. One thing to realize is that *each person is a unique individual.* No two people—not even identical twins reared together—can be exactly alike. Each person has his unique set of abilities and habits and, except for identical twins, his unique hereditary endowment. Two individuals with similar rearing are different because endowment causes them to react differently to environmental influences. Those with similar endowments are different because they have different, or at least slightly different, environmental influences. For this reason, it is not wise in dealing with individuals to generalize glibly from one individual to another. Because Tom and Dick have similar backgrounds and even superficially similar personalities, it does not follow that the two men are to be understood in the same way. An intimate knowledge of their individual motives, traits, and modes of adjustment almost always reveals significant differences between them that make each one a unique personality.

Continuity of personality. In understanding any particular person, it should also be borne in mind that personality has a basic continuity. Habits and motives that are learned over a number of years are not easily forgotten or supplanted by new ones. Thousands and thousands of learning trials are in the history of any particular individual. Biological factors, of which the individual is partly a product, do not change greatly, at least not in the adult. In addition to learning and endowment, the roles a person is called upon to play give continuity to his personality. His family, friends, social class, and economic circumstances all are relatively constant. They continue to make demands on him for certain ways of behaving, which we call roles. These roles do not change, at least not very rapidly. (For a detailed discussion of roles, see Chapter 16.)

Three factors—endowment, learning, and social roles—lead us to expect a certain continuity, consistency, and permanency to personality. We therefore cannot expect a person to change very greatly or very quickly. What he will be tomorrow is an extension of what he is today. If he seems to be a Dr. Jekyll and Mr. Hyde—a person of changing characteristics—such an appearance is deceiving.. Beneath the exterior is a person whose motives and habits make sense in terms of the individual's past history. It is therefore best to assume that the future personality will be essentially what it has been in the past.

Personality changes. This is not to say, however, that personality never changes. Over a period of time, it usually does. In some people, it changes more than it does in others. Nearly all people gradually acquire some new habits to supplant old ones. Often they discover ways of satisfying motives that were previously frustrated. Sometimes they change their way of life, and this leads to satisfactions they did not know before or to new roles to be played. Marriage, for example, occasionally produces marked personality changes—although marriage is usually no cure for a personality problem—because it affords a new way of life and exposes a person to a different set of influences. Sometimes, too, personality changes take place as a result of intense religious experience, changing jobs, moving to a new community, achieving success in a line of work, etc. In all these cases, however, the change takes place because something has happened to change motives, satisfy motives, teach new habits, or, in a word, change a person's fundamental modes of adjustment.

Most personality changes occur gradually and with no conscious intent. Sometimes, however, there is a deliberate attempt to bring about personality changes. A person may change himself, or someone close to him may effect a change. Psychotherapy and counseling, which we discussed in Chapter 6, are organized methods for bringing about such changes. These methods are employed when a person faces a problem he feels unable to solve, or when he becomes so incapable of making social adjustments that an important personality change is urgently needed. When successful, psychotherapy and counseling techniques effect personality changes by enabling the individual to discard old habits and to learn new ones that reduce his motivational conflicts (see page 170) and provide satisfactions for his needs. Such personality changes may therefore be regarded as cases of relatively rapid learning.

PERSONALITY SYNDROMES.   Also of aid in understanding individual persons is the concept of *syndrome*. This term comes from medical terminology; it refers to a pattern of causes and symptoms of disease. In the field of personality it means a *pattern of causes and characteristics of the personality*. Although each individual's personality is unique, a person may display a syndrome which is similar in many respects to the pattern of characteristics found in other individuals.

Several personality syndromes have been described and measured. In fact, one purpose of some personality tests, such as the MMPI, is to detect such syndromes. For example, a *hypochondriacal syndrome*, which

may consist of many specific characteristics, is one of abnormal concern over bodily health. A *psychasthenic syndrome* is characterized by excessive doubt, compulsions, obsessions, and unreasonable fears. (Both these syndromes are measured on the MMPI.) Another syndrome, called the *authoritarian personality,* is marked by highly conventional behavior, desire for power, hostility, prejudice, and intolerance. This kind of personality pattern appears to have its causes in rejection or excessive domination of a child by his parents (see page 535).

Our use of the concept of syndrome does not imply, as it might seem to, the classification of people into types, which we criticized earlier in this chapter. Not everyone has a personality syndrome, and hence syndromes cannot be used to classify people. The idea of the syndrome is that some personality characteristics tend to be highly correlated and thus to form patterns. Some individuals consequently display syndromes that are similar to those of other individuals. If we are aware of a syndrome, when it exists, we have a better over-all understanding of a person than we would otherwise have.

THE SELF.   Each of us has a concept of his *self.* For most of us, the self is the real essence of the personality. Unfortunately, the self is rather elusive from the point of view of the scientist. While we are all convinced of the existence of our selves, many problems stand in the way of an objective study of them. Nevertheless, there are some conclusions that can be drawn about the self, and these are of benefit in understanding personality.

Origin of the self. For the psychologist, the self represents the individual's awareness or perception of his own personality. We learn to perceive our own body and behavior in much the same way that we learn to perceive other objects and events in the world about us (see Chapter 10, "Attention and Perception"). The beginnings of the perceived self can be traced to early infancy, when the infant first starts to learn distinctions between his own body and other objects in his environment. At birth the infant is most likely aware only of vague feelings of comfort or discomfort. Then, as his capacity for learning and memory develops and as his experience widens, the child sees that parts of his body are common to all his experiences. Muscular and organic sensations accompany all his activities, and he discovers that pinching objects such as his doll does not cause pain, whereas pinching any part of his own body does. By the time the child is two years old, his distinction between his own body and other objects is generally well established.

Self-perception. The perception of the body as a unit distinct from the changing background is probably the core around which all later self-perception takes place, but there are a number of other influences that contribute importantly to the development of self-awareness. Such awareness is fostered by giving the child a name, by holding him responsible for his behavior, and by distinguishing between possessions that are his and possessions that belong to the parents, brothers, and sisters. Since the family and society treat the child as a unit, he comes to perceive himself in this way.

The kind of experiences that the child has largely determine what his self-perception will be like. The child finds that his behavior and appearance elicit kindness or hostility, respect or rebuke, attention or indifference from parents and fellows. He hears himself described by parents and playmates in terms of various personality traits, and when these traits are consistently applied, he often accepts them as descriptions of himself. Praise and love from parents and respect and attention from playmates will contribute to the development of a picture of himself as a desirable person. On the other hand, rejection and excessive criticism at home and indifference from others can lead to a derogatory self-picture, with resulting inferiority feelings.

Of course the treatment a person receives bears some relation to his traits and abilities. The physically strong child is more apt to receive the admiration of his playmates than is the weak child. The intelligent child will have a greater opportunity for experiences of success and praise in school. Hence we would expect that the individual's perception of his own personality would tend to coincide with the way in which others perceive him. However, this is not always true. Probably in no case do we ever perceive ourselves exactly as others see us. In some cases there are marked differences between the perceived self and the real or objective personality.

Although a child may be intelligent and quite capable physically, he may, if raised by indifferent parents and subjected to constant criticism and belittlement, learn to perceive himself as an inadequate, undesirable person. Most of us have known people who constantly underrate their own performance. By the same token we have also known people with a grossly exaggerated view of their accomplishments and capabilities. Children surrounded by an admiring and doting family who excessively praise even poor performance are frequently found to have excessive self-evaluations.

The self and emotional adjustment. There are many instances in which knowing a person's self-picture helps us to understand his behavior. This is particularly true where there is a marked discrepancy between the way the person sees himself and the way others see him. Behavior is largely determined by how the person perceives a situation with reference to himself. From our vantage point we may think that John should be a popular fellow with the girls—after all, he has good looks and a ready wit—but if John does not perceive himself as having these attributes, he may be just another wallflower.

If the person's self-picture is too different from the true or objective personality, serious adjustment problems may arise. The person is constantly called upon to explain away or ignore evidence which is incompatible with his view of himself. The mediocre student who pictures himself as an intellectual giant is faced with the objective evidence of his poor grades and failures. Often, instead of changing his self-evaluation, he will use rationalizations (bright people are not interested in getting grades; they have broader interests) to explain the evidence away, or he may completely ignore it by forcing it out of his mind. When such devices are used to maintain a distorted self-perception, they are called defense mechanisms, as we saw earlier in Chapter 5. People are quite adept at fooling themselves, and there is a wide variety of defense mechanisms.

Theories of personality

Having come this far in the study of personality, the student may feel the lack of any over-all picture of personality. We have described various facets of personality and ways of measuring them. But how do the pieces fit together? What causes what? What is our general theory of personality?

The truth is that we have no general theory of personality on which psychologists are agreed. So far, personality has proved too complex, its manifestations too varied, and its determinants too numerous, for us to place the pieces together into one clear picture. Instead, we have many theories. Each is an attempt to explain the subject. None, however, manages to do it to everyone's satisfaction, for none is complete enough to encompass all that we know about personality. Each stresses certain factors, while leaving others out.

One day the problem will no doubt be solved, through research and new attempts to formulate a general theory. In the meantime, the best we can do is present several different theories. Actually, there is not room to cover all the theories that have been proposed. They are far too numerous. We can only introduce briefly seven that have had an important influence on our present conceptions of personality.

PSYCHOANALYTIC THEORY. In first mentioning psychoanalysis in Chapter 1, we pointed out that it is both a method of psychotherapy and a theory of personality. Psychoanalysis as a method is covered in Chapter 6. As a theory, it has been the most influential of all personality theories. It therefore deserves more space than some of the others. Psychoanalysis has two main themes: One is a theory of personality structure; the other is a theory of personality development [Freud, 1938].

Personality structure. Freud, the founder of psychoanalysis, considered personality to have a structure consisting of three parts: the *id,* the *ego,* and the *superego.* The id, as he conceived it, is a sort of storehouse of motives and "instinctual" reactions for satisfying motives. These motives, taken together, are called *libido.* Left to itself, the id would seek immediate satisfaction for motives as they arose, without regard to the realities of life or to morals of any kind.

The id, however, is usually bridled by the ego. This consists of elaborate ways of behaving and thinking that we have learned for dealing effectively with the world. It delays the satisfaction of motives or channels motives into socially acceptable outlets. It keeps a person working for a living, getting along with people, and generally adjusting to the realities of life. Indeed, Freud characterized the ego with the statement that it is "in the service of the reality principle."

The superego, finally, corresponds closely with what we more commonly call conscience. It consists of restraints, acquired in the course of personality development, on the activity of the ego and the id. The superego may condemn as wrong those things that the ego might do in the satisfaction of the id's motives. In addition, the superego keeps a person working toward the ideals he acquired in childhood.

Freud's conception of personality structure sums up well three major aspects of personality. In early chapters, particularly Chapter 3, we described these aspects in different terms. The first aspect, equivalent to the id, consists of unlearned physiological motives and unlearned reactions for satisfying them. The second, corresponding to the ego, is made up of learned instrumental acts for satisfying motives and also of the perceived self discussed in the section above. The third, represented by the superego, is the set of socially derived motives that affect, and sometimes conflict with, the first two factors. Thus Freud's basic ideas of personality structure, though clothed in unfamiliar terminology, are in general accord with the conclusions of experimental psychology.

It has been objected that the Freudian view of personality structure divides personality into three compartments, each seeming to be a separate personality of its own. It is indeed easy to slip into this way of viewing the id, ego, and supergo, but this was not what Freud intended. The three terms simply represent convenient concepts for summarizing major aspects of personality that have no clear lines separating them. They provide a general picture of what, in detail, becomes very complicated.

Two additional points should be kept in mind, although they are more fully treated elsewhere. First, the libido (motives, instincts) of the id is frequently blocked by the ego and superego. When it is, it may be *displaced* in other directions, and may seek outlets that are acceptable to the ego and superego. Secondly, because the id is frequently in *conflict* with the ego and superego, *anxiety* is aroused. The person then seeks ways to reduce his anxiety and learns certain ways of doing it. These methods of reducing anxiety, called *defense mechanisms,* are explained in Chapter 5.

Personality development. Freud conceived of personality as developing from infancy to adulthood through four overlapping stages. The first three stages are the pregenital stages: the oral stage, the anal stage, and the phallic stage. The fourth stage, the genital stage, is entered at puberty. It is possible, according to Freud, for the person to become fixated in any one of the pre-genital stages, if he experiences unusual frustration, insecurity, or anxiety while in that stage of development. Fixation in a pre-genital stage is characterized by certain personality syndromes in the adult.

The *oral stage* occupies much of the first year of life. During this period, the infant receives pleasure from sucking and other activities involving his mouth. If at this time he is prevented from sucking, or made anxious about it, he may acquire an *oral fixation.* In the adult, the *oral syndrome* is considered to include excessive oral behavior, greediness, dependence, and passivity.

The *anal stage* is most prominent during the second and third years of life. Largely owing to parental attempts to toilet train the child and to suppress "naughty" behavior connected with excretion, the child focuses his interest on anal activities. If training is too strict and arouses anxieties about these activities, the adult *anal syndrome* may be one of compulsiveness and excessive conformity or self-control.

After toilet training and table manners are mastered, the child focuses his interest on his sexual organs. In this pregenital *phallic stage*, the child typically develops "romantic" feelings toward the parent of the opposite sex—the boy toward his mother, and the girl toward her father. Freud called this the *Oedipus complex,* after the mythical story of King Oedipus, who, without knowing what he was doing, killed his father and married his mother. In normal development, a person gets over this complex, as he does earlier stages of development. If, however, anxieties and frustrations cause fixation in this stage, the adult may end up with a "mother complex," "father complex," or other distorted attitudes in his relations with his family and with members of the opposite sex.

During the pregenital stages, the individual tends to center interest on himself. When he enters the *genital stage* and normal heterosexual interests emerge, his interests focus more and more on others and on playing the normal roles of the adult in society.

This account, of course, is not one of fact, but rather of Freud's psychoanalytic theory. It remains to be determined just how much truth there is in the theory. Many clinicians believe they have confirmed Freud's major ideas in their experience with patients. Many do not; and some grant, at the most, that the theory accounts for certain relatively rare personality syndromes. Scientific research will ultimately provide us with an evaluation of the theory.

SUPERIORITY AND COMPENSATION.

Freud's theory emphasizes the biological drives—hunger, excretion, and sex, in particular. Most other theories place somewhat greater emphasis on social factors. One of these, put forth by Alfred Adler, an early disciple of Freud who later rejected Freudian theory, emphasizes a drive or striving for *superiority.*

It is to Adler that we owe the concept of the *inferiority complex,* a phrase now part of everyday speech. Because we strive for superiority, argued Adler, we are always seeing ways in which we fall short of our aspirations, and hence ways in which we are inferior. This itself is healthy, for feeling our weakness in first one respect and then another provides things for us "to work on." We are forever striving to overcome our inferiorities. But an inferiority complex develops when we regularly fail to overcome our weaknesses or when for any reason we come to put too much emphasis on any particular inferiority.

From Adler, too, comes the concept of *compensation* (page 142). Being aware of a weakness, we may strive especially hard to overcome it. The person who, like Theodore Roosevelt, is fragile and sickly as a child, may throw himself into physical activities and *overcompensate* for handicaps or inferiorities. In many instances, because of overcompensation, people ultimately become quite superior in things in which they were originally inferior. In addition, people may compensate for inferiority by achieving distinction in some other area. Example: the

homely girl who is a bookworm, thereby becoming superior in academic things when she fails in social affairs. This kind of compensation resembles Freud's displacement, but the difference is in the motivation. Freud's displacement is an outlet for libidinous motives; Adler's compensation is a means of satisfying the striving for superiority.

ANXIETY THEORY. Most theories give anxiety an important place in their scheme of things. Freud considered anxiety the outcome of conflict between the id and the ego. Another theorist, Karen Horney [1937], makes *basic anxiety* the central concept of her theory. Moreover, she considers this anxiety to arise from social influences in the development of the child, rather than from the conflict between biological motives and the ego or superego.

According to Horney, basic anxiety is first aroused in the child by any social situation which tends to make the child fearful. It can be instigated by threats or domination by the parent, by tension and conflict between the parents, by being required to do too much or by being mistrusted, by criticism, coldness, or indifference, and so on. Once anxiety is aroused, the child attempts to alleviate it by trial-and-error behavior, as any organism might try to solve a problem. In this way, the child learns certain ways of dealing with anxiety; these, in turn, form a pattern of "neurotic needs."

A neurotic need is thus a learned need. If the child learns to cope with anxiety by running to its mother for affection and approval, it may develop a neurotic need for affection and approval. If it managed to cope with some anxiety-producing situations by obtaining prestige or personal admiration, it may have a neurotic need for these things. According to this theory, there could be any number of neurotic needs, depending on the things the child learned to need to reduce anxiety. In any given culture, however, certain patterns of needs can be expected to arise because the sources of anxiety tend to form a repetitive pattern from one family to another and from one child to another. Hence, Horney has formulated a list of 10 needs, which include needs for such things as affection, dependency, power, prestige, achievement, and self-sufficiency.

Horney's theory, like Freud's and most others, has a place in it for *conflict*. To Horney, however, the major conflict is between needs, simply because some needs are incompatible. If a person, for example, develops both a need to have someone to depend on and a need to be self-sufficient and independent, these needs will often conflict. Most people possess neurotic needs in some degree, but when they are unable to resolve conflicts between them, some needs tend to dominate their lives. Then they are "neurotic" persons.

PSYCHOLOGICAL NEEDS. Another theorist, Henry Murray [1938], has an even longer list of needs than Horney, but he arrived at them in a different way. Although influenced considerably by Freud, he came to feel that one source of motivation, such as Freud's id, Adler's striving for superiority, or Horney's basic anxiety, oversimplified matters. He preferred to determine, as empirically as possible, the needs that could be distinguished in a representative sample of people. From extensive material, consisting of life histories, projective-test data, and interviews, gathered on 51 young men, he formulated a list of 28 needs. Some of these have already been presented in Table 15.3. He felt that a rather large number of needs were required to account for the strivings observed in people.

In Murray's theory, the psychological needs he has distinguished can be found in almost everyone, but they vary in strength. In one individual, one pattern of needs may be strong; in another individual, another pattern may predominate. To Murray, it is the strength of the needs and the pattern they form that characterize any particular individual's personality. His TAT (see above) was devised to measure these needs.

SELF-ACTUALIZATION. Another theorist, Abraham Maslow [1954], has outlined a theory that for brevity is called *self-actualization* theory. At first glance, it might seem to be a single-factor theory like Adler's striving for superiority, but it isn't. It is a multiple-factor theory which posits five levels of needs arranged in a hierarchy. Arranged from lower to higher levels, they are:

Physiological needs, such as hunger, thirst and sex

Safety needs, such as security, stability, and order

Belongingness and love needs, such as needs for affection, affiliation, and identification

Esteem needs, such as needs for prestige, success, and self-respect

Need for self-actualization

The order of listing these needs is significant in two ways: It is the order in which they tend to appear in the normal development of the person. It is also the order in which they need to be satisfied. And if needs lower in the list are not satisfied, the person never gets around to doing much about the needs higher in the list. It follows then that people in a poor society will be mostly concerned with physiological and safety needs. Those in an "affluent" society, on the other hand, will manage to satisfy the needs lower in the hierarchy and in many cases be preoccupied with the need for self-actualization. One can therefore think both of individuals and of societies as "graduating" from one level of needs to higher levels.

The need for self-actualization refers to the need to develop the full potentialities of the person. Naturally, the meaning of this need varies from person to person, for each has different potentialities. For some, it means achievement in literary or scientific fields; for others it means leadership in politics or the community; for others, it means merely living one's own life fully without being unduly restrained by social conventions. One can find "self-actualizers" among professors, businessmen, political leaders, missionaries, artists, or even among housewives. But not all individuals in any of these categories are able to achieve self-actualization; many have numerous unsatisfied needs, and their achievements are compensations that leave them frustrated and unhappy in other respects.

TRAIT THEORY.   Another theory, which may be called *trait theory* and has been espoused by Gordon Allport [1937], gives us no finite list of needs or traits. It assumes a multiplicity of needs that are never quite the same from one individual to the next. It may be distinguished from other theories in two important respects:

One is the concept of the *uniqueness of personality*. Each person, having his unique background of childhood experiences, develops a set of traits that are unique to him. For purposes of comparison, we may choose a number of traits that seem to be common to many people, and determine how the individual stands on these traits. Nevertheless, he may have traits that are unique to himself.

A second, related feature of the theory is the concept of *functional autonomy of motives*. In the course of development, each person acquires motives (see page 93) as part of satisfying other motives. These motives, according to Allport's concept of functional autonomy, continue to function autonomously without further reinforcement of the physiological conditions originally concerned in their acquisition.

Examples of what seems to be the functional autonomy of motives abound in everyday life. The poor boy who earned his first pennies to ward off hunger and discomfort continues to work day and night at amassing a large fortune long after he has acquired enough money to meet his physical needs. A businessman who approaches retirement age with ample reserves insists on staying at his job, probably because he finds that the job now satisfies needs for companionship and activities, even though his original motivation for working was to earn a living. Even the persistence of sexual interests in middle age, after hormones are no longer of much importance, has been cited as an example of functional autonomy.

CONSTITUTIONAL THEORY.   We turn, finally, to a quite different kind of theory—one which holds that personality is determined, at least in part, by the constitutional make-up of the person [Sheldon and Stevens, 1942]. It has been a common belief for centuries that body build and personality are somehow tied together. Don't you, for example, think of the big muscular fellow as being dominant and aggressive? Or the fat person as being jolly and easygoing? Or of the frail individual as being serious and tense? In Shakespeare, for example, we find Caesar saying:

Let me have men about me that are fat,
Sleek-headed men, and such as sleep o'nights.
Yond Cassius has a lean and hungry look.
He thinks too much. Such men are dangerous.

Most attempts at constitutional theories of personality have fallen into the errors of typology. They classify people into two or three types. When subjected to scrutiny, they have been discredited either on logical or factual grounds. Recently, however, constitutional theory has been reformulated by Sheldon in a more plausible, though not necessarily correct, form. Sheldon's argument proceeds in three steps: First, he proposes a system for classifying constitutional build. Second, he has a parallel system for rating temperament. (Temperament is regarded as a basic ingredient of personality, though not identical with it.) Third, he postulates a relation between constitution and temperament.

Components of body build. Sheldon distinguishes three components—not types—of body build. One component is *endomorphy,* which refers to the relative prominence in any person of the abdomen, fat, and deeper tissues. A second component is *mesomorphy,* and this refers to muscles, bones, and connective tissue. A third is *ectomorphy* and refers to relative fragility and "linearity" of body build. Actually, it is impossible in a

TABLE 15.6. Some items from a rating scale for temperament. A rater who is thoroughly familiar with a person rates him on each of the characteristics below. To the highest possible degree of a characteristic, a rater assigns a 7; to the lowest degree, a 1 [Sheldon and Stevens, 1942].

Viscerotonia	Somatotonia	Cerebrotonia
____1. Relaxation in posture and movement	____1. Assertiveness of posture and movement	____1. Restraint in posture and movement, tightness
____2. Love of physical comfort	____2. Love of physical adventure	
____3. Slow reaction	____3. The energetic characteristic	____3. Overly fast reactions
	____4. Need and enjoyment of exercise	____4. Love of privacy
		____5. Mental overintensity, hyperattentionality, apprehensiveness
	____6. Love of risk and chance	____6. Secretiveness of feeling, emotional restraint
____7. Love of polite ceremony	____7. Bold directness of manner	____7. Self-conscious motility of the eyes and face
____8. Love of society, sociophilia	____8. Physical courage for combat	____8. Fear of society, sociophobia
	____9. Competitive aggressiveness	____9. Inhibited social address
____12. Evenness of emotional flow		
____13. Tolerance	____13. The unrestrained voice	____13. Vocal restraint, and general restraint of noise
____14. Complacency		
	____16. Overmaturity of appearance	____16. Youthful intentness of manner and appearance
____17. Smooth, easy communication of feeling, extroversion of viscerotonia		

few words to give accurate definitions of the three components, but these definitions should serve as rough approximations.

It might help if one thinks of the extreme endomorphic person as appearing round, of the extreme mesomorph as being very square, and of the extreme ectomorph as being very thin. In Figure 15.8, you see some pictures of these extremes. Extremes, however, are very rare, and most people are a mixture of the three types. Each person can be described quite accurately, however, with numbers. The maximum number a person can have in each component is 7 and the minimum is 1; the average is about 4. A person who is skilled in doing the rating can take a standard photograph of a person—undressed, so that clothes will not cover up the shape of the body—and assign numbers for each component. One person, thus, might be given the designation 4-5-2, which would mean a rating of 4 on endomorphy, 5 on mesomorphy, and 2 on ectomorphy. Such a set of ratings is known as a *somatotype.*

Components of temperament. This is a modern, scientific, and rather reliable method of stating differences in body build. There remains the corresponding problem, however, of rating personality. Investigators working on this problem restricted themselves to some simple traits that, taken together, have been called *temperament.* In this case, they chose three different components of temperament, which they called respectively *viscerotonia, somatotonia,* and *cerebrotonia.* A person can get a rating on each of these temperamental variables. Such ratings are based on 20 traits in each case, some of which are listed in Table 15.6. Just as for somatotypes, a person is rated from 1 to 7 on each of these scales of temperament.

The crux of the constitutional theory is that personality or temperament is somehow determined in part by constitutional factors. If so, there should be a correlation between ratings of body build and ratings (or other measurements) of temperament.

A PERSON'S PHYSIQUE MAY BE SPECIFIED IN RELATIVE AMOUNTS OF THREE COMPONENTS:

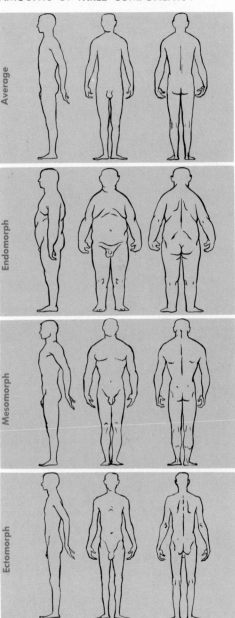

FIGURE 15.8. Sheldon's system of body components. The sketches depict extremes in endomorphy, mesomorphy, and ectomorphy, and also the average individual who has about equal proportions of all three components.

Sheldon and his coworkers have indeed reported a correlation between these ratings, and their correlations have been relatively high. It appears, however, that their results have sometimes been contaminated, because their ratings of temperament were made by individuals who knew and were influenced by constitutional theory. Other investigators, who appear to have been more careful to avoid such contamination—chiefly by using tests rather than ratings—have reported lower, but sometimes significant, correlations [Tyler, 1956]. We may conclude, then, that there is probably some correlation between body build and temperament, but that the correlation is rather small. Hence factors associated with body build are not very important determinants of temperament.

Summary

1. In studying personality, we look for characteristics that distinguish individuals from one another. One set of characteristics may serve one purpose, another set another purpose.

2. Traits are one means of characterizing personalities. Abilities, attitudes, and interests are also useful characteristics. A person's typical motives are still another; so, too, are his typical modes of adjustment.

3. Measurements of personality have been devised both for research on personality and for use in practical situations. Serving both purposes are a great variety of pencil-and-paper tests.

4. Situation tests are tests in which a person is placed in a real-life problem situation with other people and his way of dealing with the problem is observed.

5. Interviews, although often used, are not highly reliable or valid measures of personality. Somewhat more objective and valid are rating scales, which require the rating of the presence or degree of particular characteristics.

6. In recent years, projective tests such as the Rorschach and Thematic Apperception Test have come into widespread use, particularly in clinical work.

7. Personality development is affected by several factors, among them: (a) abilities, (b) culture, and (c) family and parental training.

8. The following points should be kept in mind about personality: (a) each personality is unique, (b) personality is continuous and consistent, (c) personality changes usually occur very slowly, and (d) some individuals display patterns of characteristics called syndromes.

9. The self develops through awareness of one own body and through one's being treated as a unit during childhood. A person's perception of his self has an important bearing on his relations with others and on his emotional adjustment.

10. Freud conceived of three major aspects of personality structure: (a) the id as a storehouse of motives and instinctual reactions, (b) the ego as the conscious self that attempts to cope realistically with the world, and (c) the superego as a conscience that restrains the ego and id and keeps a person working toward ideals acquired in childhood.

11. Freud and psychoanalytic theory also conceive of personality development as proceeding through the following stages: (a) oral, (b) anal, (c) phallic, and (d) genital.

12. Other theories of personality that stress motivation are: (a) Adler's theory of a drive for superiority, (b) Horney's anxiety theory, (c) Murray's need theory, and (d) Maslow's self-actualization theory.

13. Allport's theory of personality emphasizes traits.

14. Constitutional theory holds that there is a relationship between temperament and body build. Evidence to date indicates that the relationship is not very significant.

Allport, V. W. *Personality*. New York: Holt, Rinehart and Winston, 1937.
An original treatment of personality, contributing new concepts of personality.

Ferguson, L. *Personality measurement*. New York: McGraw-Hill, 1952.
A text covering different methods of measuring personality.

Guilford, J. P. *Personality*. New York: McGraw-Hill, 1959.
A text emphasizing the trait approach to personality and its measurement.

Hall, C. S., and Lindzey, G. *Theories of personality*. New York: Wiley, 1957.
A comprehensive and readable treatment of many theories of personality.

Kluckhohn, C., and Murray, H. A. *Personality: in nature, society and culture*. New York: Knopf, 1948.
A treatment of personality from the standpoint of a social anthropologist and a psychologist.

McClelland, D. C. *Personality*. New York: Sloane, 1951.
A text that offers new theoretical approaches to some of the problems of personality.

Murphy, G. *Personality*. New York: Harper, 1947.
A comprehensive, influential textbook on personality.

Nunnally, J. C. *Tests and measurements: assessment and prediction*. New York: McGraw-Hill, 1959.
A text covering both statistical methods and methods of measuring personality, interests, and abilities.

Stagner, R. *Psychology of personality* (3d ed.). New York: McGraw-Hill, 1961.
A widely used text on personality.

White, R. W. *Lives in progress: a study of the natural growth of personality*. New York: Dryden, 1952.
An intensive and interesting study of three healthy young adults, conducted in two phases, first while the subjects were in college and again 5 to 10 years later.

Introduction

to psychology

SOCIAL
INFLUENCES
ON BEHAVIOR

ATTITUDES,
BELIEFS, & SOCIAL
PREJUDICE

VOCATIONAL
ADJUSTMENT

PART SIX
GROUP PROCESSES

Social influences on behavior

DID YOU EVER STOP to think how much other people have to say about what you do? Even if you are twenty-one and relatively independent of parental control, you still cannot free yourself from the control of society. Its pressure is on the whole of your behavior, prescribing everything from the tie to wear with a particular suit to the rules of virtuous living. Ministers and elders exhort you toward moral behavior, employers and neighbors gently force you to give to the Red Cross, and in many subtle ways people dictate how you dress, what you drink, and how you enjoy yourself. Indeed, practically from the moment each of us is born, society pushes, guides, advises, and constrains us in the correct and appropriate ways of living. As Ruth Benedict [1934], the social anthropologist, has put it:

The life history of the individual is first and foremost an accommodation to the patterns and standards traditionally handed down in his community. From the moment of his birth, the customs into which he is born shape his life experience and behavior. By the time he can talk he is a little creature of his culture, and by the time he is grown and able to take part in its activities, its habits are his habits, its beliefs are his beliefs, its impossibilities are his impossibilities. Every child that is born into his group will share them with him and no child born into one on the opposite side of the globe can ever achieve the thousandth part.

So steady, so insistent, and so pervasive are cultural influences on our behavior that we rarely stop to analyze or perceive their nature. If we were dwellers in the depths of the ocean, probably the last thing we should discover would be water. Indeed, it took man a long time to discover air. Similarly it is difficult to discover and understand the culture that shapes our behavior. Yet it is necessary to do this if we are to understand human behavior at all.

Culture

The term *culture,* used in a scientific sense, refers to the *customs and traditions of a people and to the attitudes and beliefs they have about important aspects of their life.* Occasionally culture has been called "social heritage," but this gives the somewhat false impression that culture is inherited unchanged from generation to generation. A more accurate, though more imposing, definition of culture—one provided by the anthropologist Ralph Linton—is "the sum total of behavior patterns, attitudes and values, shared and transmitted by the members of a given society." This definition makes culture an important chapter in psychology.

Social anthropologists have taught us most of what we know about culture. They have focused their attention on so-called "primitive" societies or "backward" peoples—the American Indians, South Sea Islanders, Africans, and others—but they have also applied their methods to more advanced societies, including our own.[1] Thus they have been able to compare different cultures and draw conclusions about their similarities and differences.

PATTERNS OF CULTURE. The most important, perhaps, of their conclusions is that *different societies may develop altogether different solutions to the same major and recurrent problems* of life. At the same time, despite this diversity, the members of each society believe *their* way of behaving is natural and best.

As an example, consider the respective

[1] Examples of famous studies of American society are Lynd and Lynd [1929] and Hollingshead [1949].

jobs and duties a society assigns to its men and women. The eminent anthropologist Margaret Mead [1935] has observed that one primitive society, the Tchambuli of New Guinea, assigns the economic affairs of the culture to women instead of to men, as is customarily the case in our country. Tchambuli men, furthermore, are the ones concerned with the activities that we in our society expect women to perform, such as ceremonies and beautifying themselves. The beliefs in the Tchambuli culture justify this division of duties. Women are regarded as naturally easygoing, self-reliant and businesslike, while men are supposedly born to be vain and artistic. Many Americans, of course, have a completely different conception of the "fundamental nature" of men and women. But are these beliefs any more than a justification and description of our own ways of behaving?

It probably is true that most (but certainly not all) Tchambuli adults have personalities consistent with their culture's beliefs concerning the basic character of their sex. Similarly, many (but again, not all) American adults behave as we generally expect people of their sex to behave. Since most members of a culture are subjected to the same social influences throughout their

CHAPTER SIXTEEN

FIGURE 16.1. Cultural differences in eating behavior. (Left) Natives of Sumatra celebrate the painting of a house; women and children must stand and wait until the men are finished [Standard Oil Co., N.J.]. (Right) A Japanese family eats dinner [Japan Tourist Association].

lifetime, they develop characteristics that are similar and appropriate to their society.

These *widely shared ways of behaving in a society, together with the beliefs that accompany them,* have been named, for convenience, *the cultural pattern.* Such a cultural pattern, of course, is only a general characteristic of a society, and not everyone conforms to it. All Italians, for example, do not love opera, while there are some Americans who do. Yet each culture has a characteristic pattern, each has ways of behaving and believing that are common to many of its members, and thus each has a cultural pattern that differentiates it from other cultures. It is perhaps fair to say that music and opera are more important features of the Italian than of the American pattern of culture.

Novel and esoteric ways of living in different cultures are fascinating things to study (Figure 16.1). This is not the reason, however, why students of human behavior have concerned themselves with different cultural patterns. For them, cultural diversity offers a unique opportunity to study the effects of social influences upon behavior and personality development. Such influences vary more widely from society to society than they do within, say, our own society. Anthropologists have reported, for example, that societies differ greatly in the extent to which their members compete with one another for cultural goals and rewards. Some societies, such as the Kwakiutl Indians of the Pacific Northwest, compete intensely for social position and the "good things of life." In this respect, the Kwakiutl Indians are not too different from us. As often is the case in our society, their rewards are gained through individual initiative. In this way, the society fosters extreme competitiveness among its members. Among the Zuñi Indians of the American Southwest, on the other hand, excessive individual initiative and competition is frowned upon. They are therefore characteristically a mild and inoffensive people. Their culture is more preoccupied with ceremony and proper ways of doing things than with individualism or competition.

DETERMINANTS OF CULTURE. Differences in culture, we may presume, come about for some reason. The reasons might lie both in the natural conditions under which a people live—the food available to them, abundance or scarcity of resources, climate, proximity to other peoples, and so on—and in practices already established in a society that shape the personalities and habit patterns of its members. In other words, the determinants of a culture may lie both outside and inside the culture. Unfortunately, we have not succeeded too well in accounting for the various determinants of culture. We can, however, provide examples of the kinds of determinants that have been studied.

One possible determinant might be a shortage of natural resources in a society. If food and other essentials were scarce, we might expect individuals in a society to be competitive because they had learned to survive by competition for the available resources. In a study to determine the validity of this hypothesis, 13 primitive societies were studied by rank-ordering them on the abundance of food and on the competitiveness of their cultures [Newcomb, 1950]. Contrary to the hypothesis, this study suggests that there is *no* relationship between the competitiveness of a society and the scarcity of its natural resources. The shortage of "good things" for which individuals in a society compete is created, apparently, by social or internal cultural influences and is not necessarily developed by natural privations.

Let us consider a more specific case of a difference in cultural patterns. Social scientists [Whiting et al., 1958] have attempted to find out why some societies have elaborate ceremonies when a boy reaches puberty, while other societies do not have these puberty rites.

Fifty-six societies, ranging from small tribal groups to complex civilizations such as the United States, were divided into those that had harsh male initiation rites at approximately the time of puberty (such as circumcision or undergoing severe trials) and those which did not have such punishing ceremonies. The investigators found that certain sex customs were associated with these puberty rites with greater than chance frequency. Analyzing further the cultural differences, they also observed that those societies which had harsh rites also tended to prohibit

sexual relations between husband and wife for a long period after the wife gave birth. Furthermore, these societies typically prescribed that a baby son sleep with his mother for a long time after birth. These correlations led the investigators to speculate that the puberty rites are a way of asserting adult male authority over a boy. The rites are an attempt to break the boy's emotional dependence upon his mother. Perhaps they also express a rivalry for the mother characteristically existing between father and son.

CULTURAL CHANGES. Although cultures have definite patterns, these patterns are not handed down like heirlooms from one generation to the next. Rather they are constantly changing, sometimes slowly and sometimes fairly rapidly. The medieval era was for Western civilization a period of fairly slow change in culture patterns, whereas the modern period has been characterized by rapid and dramatic changes. Other cultures, similarly, have had times when changes were rapid and times when they were slow.

The reasons for cultural change are quite complex. Sometimes cultural changes are forced by *climatic conditions,* by *exhaustion of natural resources,* or, especially in modern times, *technological changes.* Today technology is stepping up the pace of cultural change, and even the most remote societies have had to yield in some measure to the force of its impact. Finally, cultural changes are brought about by an *ideology.* Some set of ideas for which there is a need in the culture takes hold and brings about major changes in cultural patterns. Christianity and communism are good examples.

On the other hand, it is not correct to assume that cultures change very rapidly or that all aspects of a culture may change, for there is always some continuity of cultural pattern. Some patterns may remain virtually unchanged while others are drastically revamped (see Figure 16.2). Witness the industrialization of Japan growing up alongside emperor worship and its cultural

FIGURE 16.2. The Hutterites, a religious sect in the North Central United States and Canada, follow their traditional patterns of dress, weaving, and goose plucking, while adopting modern methods of farming and using up-to-date commercial products [J. W. Eaton, *Scientific American*].

consequences. In cultures, as in music, the arrangement and the tempo may vary, but the underlying melody is often the same.

AWARENESS OF CULTURE. We have already pointed out that few people are aware of the cultural patterns of the society in which they live. Having their behavior molded by the culture from the moment of birth, they take for granted the stereotyped behaviors and attitudes that characterize their culture. They are therefore unaware of the extent to which culture shapes their habits and values.

It is also characteristic of cultures that no member of a society ever shares all elements of his culture. Instead, with very rare exceptions, each member knows only his particular subculture. This is because only certain aspects of a culture ordinarily influence a particular person's behavior, and he is not a part of, or greatly influenced by, other major segments of his culture.

As one illustration of this point, let us take the example of class, or cultural, mobility. In the caste and class systems of some societies, it is virtually impossible for a per-

son to move from one class to a higher one. In others, where there are few legal or economic barriers, this may still be true, simply because people in a lower stratum of society are ignorant of the cultural ways of the upper class. Even in a society such as our own, where crossing class boundaries is more freely done than in most societies, it is not so easy as it seems. To cross them, a person must discard the habits and attitudes of his childhood or early adult culture and learn the different ones of the cultural class into which he moves. This is sometimes difficult or impossible. Indeed, these hurdles of knowledge and skill within a culture are grounds for such saying as "You can't make a silk purse out of a sow's ear," and "He's from the wrong side of the tracks."

Social structure

Each culture, we have said, has its distinctive pattern. Each culture also has its own *social structure*. That is to say, it has ranks that are assigned to people, it expects certain people to do one kind of work and others to do other kinds, it expects its families to be constituted in a certain way, and it expects its members to have certain attitudes and beliefs. In some societies, this social structure is rather rigid and in others it is more flexible, but none escapes some degree of structuring.

Much of the structuring arises from differences among people in the goods and services they produce. One person makes trinkets, another makes shoes, while a third invents the steam engine. Trinkets may satisfy the rather unessential needs of a few, while the steam engine multiplies a hundredfold many different things that satisfy needs. The dependence of people upon one another is therefore not equally distributed, and some people are much more important to the society than are others.

Of all the ways in which services to a society may be unequal, those arising from sex and age are most common. These differences, therefore, structure all societies in some degree. Infants obviously contribute little and demand much, and mothers on the whole are assigned to take care of them. Children may contribute something, but still not much, and thus they are expected to treat adults with the respect befitting their different roles. Young men, in nearly all societies, are expected to be warriors in time of danger. Old men are usually the sources of wisdom and leadership. Thus individual differences in ability to meet society's needs have a lot to do with the social structure. So, too, of course, do technological differences in societies. Those societies that are more highly industrialized and have more work specialties have more elaborate social structures.

STATUS AND ROLE. As we have already implied, occupations help shape social structure. So does position in the family unit, membership in social groups, and many other factors, depending upon the particular society. What makes social structure is the fact that members of a society categorize people according to differences that are important to their needs. Thus they give to each person in the society what social scientists call a *status*—age status, sex status, occupational status, social status, and so on. Each status is a *position representing differences that are important in the exchange of goods and services and in the satisfaction of needs in the society*.

Different people may occupy a particular status at different times, and their statuses may change from time to time. Along with status, however, goes a *role*. This is a *pattern of behavior that a person is expected to exhibit in a particular status*. A father in the status of "head of a household" has a role of behavior he must play in that status. So does a person in the status of employer, or mother, or teacher, etc. Hence we must make a clear distinction between status and role; one applies to position in the social structure and the other to the behavior that goes along with that position. These concepts of status and role are key concepts in understanding social structure (see Figure 16.3).

MULTIPLE STATUS. The system by which statuses are categorized in a social structure usually permits any particular person to be categorized in many ways, e.g., as head of a household, teacher, employee, church member. A person therefore comes to have several statuses in a social structure. For some part of his life, he occupies one status; for another part, another status. In each of these statuses, moreover, he has a role to play that goes along with the particular status. He therefore finds himself in multiple statuses and multiple roles. The following illustration from Linton [1945] gives a picture of the multiple statuses a person may occupy:

Let us suppose that a man spends the day working as a clerk in a store. While he is behind the counter, his active status is that of a clerk, established by his position in our society's system of specialized occupations. The role associated with this status provides him with patterns for his relations with customers. These patterns will be well known both to him and to the customers and will enable them to transact business with a minimum of delay or misunderstanding. When he retires to the rest room for a smoke and meets other employees there, his clerk status becomes latent and he assumes another active status based upon his position in the association group composed of the store's employees as a whole. In this status his relations with other employees will be governed by a different set of culture patterns from those employed in his relations with customers. Moreover, since he probably knows most of the other employees, his exercise of these culture patterns will be modified by his personal likes and dislikes of certain individuals and by considerations of their and his own relative positions in the prestige series of the store association's members. When closing time comes, he lays aside both his clerk- and store-association statuses, and while on the way home he operates simply in terms of his status with respect to the society's age-sex system. Thus if he is a young man he will at least feel that he ought to get up and give his seat to a lady, while if he is an old one he will be quite comfortable about keeping it. As soon as he arrives at his house, a new set of statuses will be activated. These statuses derive from the kinship ties which relate him to various members of the family group. In pursuance of the roles associated with these family statuses he will try to be cordial to his mother-in-law, affectionate to his wife, and a stern disciplinarian to Junior, whose report card marks a new low. If it happens to be a lodge night, all his familial statuses will become latent at about eight o'clock. As soon as he enters the lodge room and puts on his uniform as Grand Imperial Lizard in the Ancient Order of Dinosaurs, he assumes a new status, one which has been latent since the last meeting, and performs in terms of its role until it is time for him to take off his uniform and go home.

CONFLICTS OF ROLES. Serious trouble can arise when a person is caught in a conflict of roles, and this can happen in a

A MILITARY ORGANIZATION IS AN EXTREME EXAMPLE OF A STATUS SYSTEM:

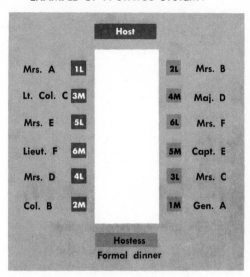

FIGURE 16.3. Status represented in a formal seating arrangement. The diagram, published in a manual for Army officers, gives the proper seating arrangements for formal dinners [Fort Benning, Ga., Infantry School].

society as complex and as mobile as ours. The blustering foreman who drives his men with an iron hand may find his methods quite unsuccessful when he climbs the ladder of executive responsibility. The student leader accustomed to the role of class president in a small-town high school may be unhappy when he becomes just another freshman in a large university. The socialite used to the manners and repartee of cocktail parties may find herself offended and uncomfortable in a gathering of farmers or laborers.

Such changes in status put a person in a conflict of roles. He finds that the role he learned in one status is no longer appropriate in a new status. He becomes uncertain of what role he should play, and when he is forced to decide on one he may have little confidence in his choice. Thus he may be thrust into motivational conflict of the sort we have previously described (see

Chapter 5). The consequences may be frustration, anxiety, hostility, and failure to adjust.

Role conflict may also occur when an individual occupies two different statuses at the same time, with these statuses imposing incompatible demands upon him. This can be seen in a situation that one investigator [Stouffer, 1949] posed for his subjects:

College students were told to imagine that they were proctoring an examination taken by fellow students. They were further instructed to imagine that they had discovered a student cheating, and to indicate what they would do, that is, what role they would play in the situation. The answers were then tabulated and analyzed. It was found that their answers depended on what they thought other students would approve of and who the imaginary cheater was. If the cheater were an ordinary student, the student proctor apparently would not be in much of a conflict. The great majority of subjects felt that both the authorities and other students would approve their reporting the violation. If, on the other hand, the cheater were a friend, the proctor would feel torn between the conflicting demands of his status as a proctor and those of his status as a friend. In this conflict, almost all subjects acknowledged that the authorities would want the cheating reported, but that other students would want the friend given "a break."

Multiple roles, however, are not always in conflict. In well-organized societies, in fact, conflicts of role are relatively rare. The structure of such societies preserves and isolates statuses so well that conflicts occur only in relatively uncommon and incongruous situations. There is the story of the Scotsman, for example, who found himself in the role of host to the murderer of his brother. Bound by the conventions of hospitality, he could resolve the conflict of the roles of host and avenger of his brother's death only by conducting the murderer outside the territory of his clan before taking

his vengeance. Such conflicts, however, are rather rare.

One reason why role conflicts are infrequent is that people usually perceive only the particular status that is most appropriate to a situation. An unscrupulous businessman who is also a regular churchgoer probably sees no incompatibility between his business behavior and the beliefs he professes on Sundays in church. During the week, functioning in the status of a businessman, he does not think in terms of his status as a churchgoer. In a sense, he usually does not become aware of other statuses he holds until he is reminded of them by situational demands or other cues [Charters and Newcomb, 1958].

SOCIAL CLASSES. So far we have described social structure in terms of statuses and roles. There is more to social structure, however, than a mere assortment of statuses. In every society, these *statuses are arranged on a scale of prestige*. That is to say, the people in the society regard some statuses more favorably than others, or they rank statuses according to their desirability (see Table 16.1). Then the awards that the community has to distribute, such as wealth, power, respect, and honors, are parceled out according to this prestige scale. Naturally, there is no one-to-one correlation, say, between wealth and prestige, for those of equal prestige may receive somewhat different shares of the wealth. But taken together, the awards of the community correspond fairly well to status on a prestige scale.

Thus the prestige scale becomes the basis for forming social classes or strata. Those high on it are largely in one class; those low on it are mainly in another class. In many societies the class system has become so formalized that it permeates all social organization and behavior. In many ancient kingdoms, for example, the classification of all members into one of three strata—nobility, freemen, and slaves—was unequivocal. Each person was one of the three. Frequently his

TABLE 16.1. The social status of occupations. When asked to rank different occupations according to social status, most groups give about the same rankings. Below are the rankings by graduate students compared with those by day laborers [from Cattell, 1942].

Occupation	Ranking by graduate students	Ranking by day laborers
Physician	1	2½
Banker, stock and loan broker	2	2½
Superintendent of state institution	3	5
Captain in Army or Navy	4	4
Manager of business	5	1
Hotelkeeper	6	7
Grade school teacher	7	10
Real-estate and insurance agents	8	14
Retail trader	9	9
Commercial traveler	10	8
Bookkeeper, cashier, and accountant	11	11
Foreman	12	6
Farm proprietor	13	16
Clerk and stenographer	14	12
Policeman	15	13
Skilled factory worker	16	15
Salesperson and clerk	17	17
Train, bus, and streetcar drivers	18	18
Waiter and domestic servant	19	20
Janitor	20	19
Laundry worker	21	24
Unskilled factory worker	22	23
Farm laborer	23	21
Casual laborer	24	25
Coal miner	25	22
Unemployed	26	26

class membership was indicated by his speech, dress, or other symbols clear to any observer. Each class was restricted to certain occupations and indeed to certain kinds of social behavior; freemen, for example, behaved in one way toward nobility, in another toward freemen, and in another toward slaves.

Our own society does not formalize classes so rigidly. It is not always easy to pick out a person's social class, nor are members of a class confined so strictly to that class and its particular occupations as are, say, members of a caste in India. In other words, we have more class mobility. There is nevertheless a definite class struc-

ture in American society. An interesting illustration of this point is to be found in a study [Warner, 1949] of the social structure in an actual American community, fictitiously called Jonesville. Mr. Walter Jones, a respected citizen of Jonesville, summarized the feelings of most people in the town in the following way:

Almost everyone in this town is rated in some way, people can rate you in just a few minutes by talking to you. It's remarkable how you can size up people in a hurry— suppose I use a rating scale of zero to 100 and rate people on it. You can be sure this is not a hypothetical thing either. Not to the people of Jonesville. People like the Caldwells and the Volmers (the Lowells and the Cabots of Jonesville) rate 100. The Shaws would be up there too. People like me, oh, a 70 maybe and people like John (a janitor) about 40, no better than that. Remember this is a social rating. If we rated them financially some of them would rank differently.

This quotation illustrates the point, but does not prove it. For proof we may go to other studies in which the attitudes of people have been scientifically sampled. One such study [Warner and Lunt, 1941] was made in a town called Yankee City, and it revealed the class structure depicted in Figure 16.4. This figure is constructed from a large number of interviews of citizens of Yankee City in which they were asked to rate their fellow townsmen on social status. For the most part, people did not think of social classes by the names used in the illustration. These were furnished by the research workers afterward. Yet it was clear enough that people distinguished three major classes and within each of them a lower and an upper part. With these they were able to classify almost everyone in the town. The percentages shown in Figure 16.4, however, would probably vary from one city or section of the country to another.

CHARACTERISTICS OF CLASS. In studies of this sort, the question arises, What criteria do the members of a community use when they rate their fellow members in social classes? The answer is never simple. *Economic criteria* are perhaps the most important, but many other factors enter into the evaluation. In Yankee City, for example, people revealed that they used all the following criteria in making their judgments: nature of occupation, kind of income (whether salary, commission, dividend, or the like), moral standing, birth and family genealogy, social relationships and organizations, and the kind of residential area in which the person lived.

But whatever the specific criteria em-

EACH SOCIETY AND COMMUNITY HAS A SOCIAL-CLASS STRUCTURE:

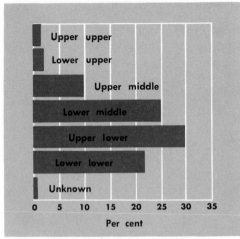

FIGURE 16.4. The class structure of Yankee City. A sample of the citizens of Yankee City, a New England community of about fifteen thousand people, were classified into six classes on the basis of interviews and other information concerning their socioeconomic status and social activities [data from Warner and Lunt, 1941].

ployed in defining social-class membership, the classes differ, as we pointed out above, in their social prestige. We are all familiar with instances of this broad principle, so it probably is of greater interest to point out the variety of ways in which status differences affect behavior.

The status hierarchy we see in any group represents a small-scale model of the social-class structure in our society as a whole. For that reason, we can study the effects of status differences by observing them in members of certain groups. This likening of a group to a society is more than a loose analogy. There are actually a great many parallels between social-class differences and status differences in smaller groups. It has frequently been shown, for example, that people from the higher social classes generally are more attractive to other people than members of the lower classes, even at grade school age [Bonney, 1944]. Essentially the same thing is true of a wide variety of groups, including military units [Masling et al., 1955] and teams of mental-health workers [Hurwitz et al., 1953]. Whatever the basis for the status differentiation, whether it be athletic ability, military rank, or occupation, in many different kinds of groups, high-status people tend to have more social prestige in their group than low-status people do. This tendency to place people on a prestige scale apparently is so strongly learned it even appears in situations that we like to believe are free of social-class effects. The following study [Strodtbeck et al., 1958] illustrates this point:

A team of investigators studied the deliberations of a mock jury, using jurors drawn by lot from regular jury pools in two large Midwestern cities. The relatively high prestige of the upper socioeconomic classes was revealed in a number of ways. For one thing, a person from the higher occupational strata was more likely than others to be chosen jury foreman. For another, practically *all* occupational groups were inclined to say that, if members of their family were involved in a jury trial, they would prefer the jury to be made up largely of people from the highest occupational ranks.

This high prestige going along with high status means that the high-status individuals often are accorded rights denied to those with lower status. One such right is the freedom to talk! High status seems to give a person the feeling that he can talk a great deal. This conclusion has come out of several studies, among them the studies of juries and mental-health workers mentioned above. In these instances, the higher the individual's status in the group, the more he participated in the group discussion.

High status under some conditions may make a person feel somewhat freer to violate group mores and to deviate from the opinions generally held by this group [Dittes and Kelley, 1956]. This "privilege" of high status

may account in part for some of the social-class differences we find in juvenile delinquency rates. Certainly middle-class youngsters are sometimes excused by the police for committing the same types of crimes or misdemeanors that send lower-class youngsters to jail.

There is one important exception to the principle that high-status persons are freer to deviate from group standards of behavior. If the high-status person occupies a position symbolizing the ideals of his group, he experiences greater pressures to conform to these ideals than the lower-status individual does. This is probably why, several years ago, Princess Margaret of England did not marry a divorced man. The marriage would have violated the teachings of the Church of England, and she had less freedom to violate these teachings than would a British commoner of her faith.

Something else that goes along with the prestige of the high-status individual is the ability to influence others in his group. He acquires some of this ability just by being allowed to talk more. In addition, people are more likely to agree with him and to believe what he says. This is another way of saying that high-status individuals are more likely to be accepted as leaders. We discuss leadership in the last section of this chapter.

SOCIAL CLASSES AND BEHAVIOR. The social classes differ not only in status and the things that go along with status, they also differ in the attitudes and personalities of their members. In regard to attitudes, political scientists, sociologists and public-opinion pollsters have long known that the social classes differ in their political beliefs and social philosophies. One of the simplest and clearest correlations is that the higher a person is, either on the occupational scale or in the social class he thinks he belongs to, the more likely he is to hold conservative political opinions.

Less well known is the fact that members of the various social classes tend to have somewhat different personalities. This is because both the physical and social environment for development of personality is largely class-determined. Indeed, the kind of home or neighborhood in which one lives, the kind of work, play, and facilities that are available, and even the minimum necessities for satisfying basic needs all go along with social class. Even more important, however, the training and education of a child differs according to social class.

Several studies of social-class differences in child-rearing practices provide some interesting information on this point [Bronfenbrenner, 1958]. In the 1930s and 1940s, research studies generally showed that middle-class parents were stricter and more frustrating in their child-rearing practices than working-class parents. Studies conducted during the 1950s, however, have come to the opposite conclusion. Middle-class parents have lately become more permissive in training their young. The reason for this change, it seems, is that the middle-class parent more often follows the advice of the "experts" in child behavior. When, in the 1930s, these experts prescribed rigid schedules for children, the mother of higher status was more likely to follow the prescription. Similarly, when the experts later advised that children be permitted greater freedom, she followed that advice too. Since most child specialists are now tending to become somewhat more conservative in this matter, advising permissiveness but within definite limits, we can expect middle-class parents to follow this pattern before their counterparts among the working class do so.

Middle- and upper-class parents, then, are more inclined to follow the advice of experts in rearing their children than working-class parents are. But there is another important difference too. The working-class parent is more likely to use physical punishment in disciplining his child than is the middle-class parent. Instead of physical punishment, the middle-class parent more frequently employs "psychological discipline" in which he tries to reason with the youngster and make

him feel guilty for doing disapproved things. This technique, the evidence indicates (see Chapter 7), is more effective in training and controlling the child. As one psychologist [Bronfenbrenner, 1958, p. 419] puts it, "These findings mean that middle class parents, though in one sense more lenient in their discipline techniques, are using methods that are actually more compelling . . . which are likely to be effective in evoking the behavior desired in the child."

The social classes also differ, of course, in their occupational goals for their children. The higher classes more often aspire to business and professional occupational status than the lower classes do. This fact is too well known to require proof. The cause is partly economic. If a working-class parent cannot afford to send his children to college and then on to medical school, but instead must have his boy's income as soon as possible, there is little sense in his boy thinking about becoming a doctor. In addition, however, there are more profound differences in motivation among the social classes.

Research with high school students has indicated, for example, that youngsters from the upper and middle social strata tend to have a higher level of achievement motivation (see page 96) than boys from the lower classes [Rosen, 1956]. Teen-agers from the higher classes more often want to do well relative to standards of excellence. The upper- and middle-class youngsters, moreover, are more likely to have some of the personal values and attributes that make for occupational success. More of them, for example, believe that it is possible for an individual to improve his status in life. More of them also think it worthwhile to postpone present pleasures in the interest of attaining future goals.

We see then that there are a number of important differences among the social classes. They differ in prestige, in attractiveness to others, in freedom to talk, in a feeling of freedom to deviate from group standards, in ability to influence others, in attitudes and beliefs, in child-rearing practices, in educational goals, and even in certain motivations.

Social groups

We have now seen that societies have cultures and a social structure. They are also characterized by *social groups*. Each member in a society not only has his status roles and social class, he is also a member of a large number of groups. He always is, at least for a part of his life, a member of a family group, and he usually is a member of a community group, a city, or a town. Besides that he may be in a church group, an industrial group, a political group, a lodge, and many other kinds of groups. His behavior affects the group, and the group affects and controls his behavior.

CONFORMITY TO GROUP NORMS. Groups of which we are members influence our behavior in various ways, but probably the strongest and most pervasive of them are *group norms*. A norm, as the term implies, is a standard of behavior, but it is more than that. To understand exactly what it is we must refer again to the concepts of role and status.

A role, we have seen, is the behavior expected of us in a particular status. The accent should now be placed on the word "expected." A group can *expect* certain behavior from us because it confers its *disapproval* on us if we do not do what is expected. Since most of us acquire a need for social approval (see page 95), and hence do not wish to incur disapproval, we do what is expected of us. In a word, we conform to our group's expectations.

Some role expectations are limited to a few people. In my role as a father, for example, I conform largely to the expectations of my family, though there are certain ways of behaving "as father" that most members of my culture expect of me. In addition, there are certain ways I am expected to behave merely as a "gentleman,"

a citizen, or member of my social class. *Widely shared expectations among most members of a group, class, or culture are group norms.* These norms concern my general status as a member of a group. Being a member of many groups—family, university, community, church, and so on—I have many sets of group norms, or expected roles, I must meet. I must somehow *conform* to these norms or suffer the disapproval of the group members who set the norms.

Group norms seem to emerge, like statuses and social structure, wherever a group is formed. A group exists whenever there is any interaction between individuals. By interaction we mean any conversation, exchange of goods and services, or any joint efforts which could tend to cast group members into any kind of status. The longer people interact, and the more they interact, the more they tend to adopt common ways of interpreting the world and common standards for the behavior of each group member. In other words, group norms to which individuals feel a pressure to conform develop whenever there is any kind of continued interaction among people.

A now classic experiment [Sherif, 1958] in social psychology illustrates how shared ways of perceiving situations, i.e., group norms, may develop with continued social interaction:

The subjects were placed in a totally dark room and were asked to judge how far a point source of light seemed to move. Since the walls of the room were not visible, there was no physical frame of reference available to aid in making these judgments. In part of the experiment, individuals were shown the light for the first time in a group situation, and each person expressed his opinion aloud for the others to hear. The group members soon began to influence one another. Their judgments at first did not agree very well, but as they listened to one another's opinions, they seemed to agree that the light moved within a certain range. Each group developed its own range of judgments, i.e., its own way of perceiving this situation. Later, when each of the group members was asked to make his judgments alone, they still judged the movement to be within the range that had been agreed upon in the group. Thus, in the group, the subjects learned to interpret the ambiguous situation in a given way, and the learning carried over into their judgments when they were alone.

This experiment can serve as a model that helps explain many different kinds of social influences, including the adoption of certain cultural patterns. In their interaction, members of a society develop a common way of perceiving their world and the things in it. Perhaps even the Tchambuli conception of women as naturally businesslike and men as artistic arose in this way.

From shared perceptions, it is only a short step to shared rules or norms governing the behavior of group members in each status position. The difference is that norms have a *demand* quality. Not only does an individual tend to see and act the way other group members do, but he *must*. To enforce the demand, the group members devise different degrees of punishment ranging all the way from capital punishment for major crimes to something so innocuous as a social snub. In between are many tangible and effective forms of demanding conformity to group norms. Some years ago, for example, a white physician in Florida was fired from his post as county physician for having lunch with a Negro nurse. The doctor's behavior deviated from the norms then held regarding proper white-Negro relations, so social and economic punishment befell the violator. Women who smoked in public during the nineteenth and early twentieth centuries suffered a less severe punishment. They were simply excluded from "polite society."

FACTORS AFFECTING CONFORMITY. There are at least two good reasons why people tend to conform to group norms. One has already been stressed: people who go against

the norms suffer social disapproval or punishment in varying degrees. This fact is widely known, and motivates a good deal of conformity. Pressure to conform, however, is not limited to those we know or to those known to have the power to enforce the norms. The desire for social approval is so ingrained and so generalized to members of the group or community that we may even desire approval from complete strangers. This fact was demonstrated in one of the earliest experiments in social psychology [Allport, 1924]. Subjects in the experiment tended to give less extreme judgments when they were in the presence of other people than when they were alone. We can only surmise that this was because they feared that extreme judgments would bring disapproval from others about them, and they sought to avoid disapproval even though the others were strangers.

A second reason for social conformity is equally obvious. An individual may "go along" with the opinions of his group because he believes these opinions are correct, or at least probably correct.

It is important to distinguish between these two bases for conforming behavior even though it is at times difficult to tell *why* a given person may be conforming. Since conformity is regarded as "cowardly," people may be reluctant to say why they agree with the opinions of others, even if they know. This reluctance may be illustrated by the following experiment [Asch, 1958]:

Subjects were asked to make judgments concerning the length of lines. Each experimental session typically employed only one actual subject in a group of people who had been coached to express certain opinions. Hence, the real subject often faced a situation in which his eyes told him one thing while the others in the group agreed that something else was correct. Only a minority of the subjects consistently yielded to the erroneous group opinion. Later interviews with those who conformed to the majority opinion suggested that most of these "comformists" thought something was wrong with their eyesight and that the majority was probably correct.

Several years later two experimenters [Deutsch and Gerard, 1955] repeated this study in its essential details but added some other experimental conditions:

In one of these conditions, the subjects were led to believe that they could express their opinions anonymously after learning the judgments of the others. Under this condition, subjects yielded much less to the erroneous majority than did subjects in the "nonanonymous" condition. Even so, a few of the "anonymous" subjects conformed to the group. Thus most of the subjects who expressed the majority opinion apparently did so in order not to appear different (hence in order not to incur disapproval?), rather than because they believed the majority to be correct.

It is not always easy, as these experiments show, to disentangle the two chief reasons for conforming—fear of disapproval and belief that the group is correct. Indeed, both factors are probably at work in most situations in which people conform to group norms.

In addition to these factors, there are others that affect conforming behavior. We shall discuss three: (1) attraction to the group, (2) perceived consensus within the group, and (3) acceptance by the group. Each of these factors, as we shall see, involves some combination of fear of disapproval and belief in the group's opinion.

Attraction to the group. If a person is strongly attracted to the group, either because he likes it or because he somehow sees it as meeting his needs, he is more inclined to conform to it than if he is not attracted to it. And the greater his attraction, i.e., the more he wants to belong to the group, the more likely he is to agree with the opinions of the other members of the group. This conclusion is based on experiments, but it also grows out of daily experience. We usually have a higher regard for the opinions of people we like than for those of people we do not like. This is particularly the case if we have no objective way of determining whether the opinions are correct, as we often do not.

Fear of disapproval is certainly one of the reasons we do this. The punishment we may suffer by being rejected or disapproved by a group is obviously more serious if it is meted out by a group we would really like to belong to. Hence, even when there is no question of the correctness of a standard, we tend to conform to the norms of groups that are attractive to us. This point is illustrated in the following experiment [Berkowitz, 1954]

Things were so arranged that some subjects developed a high liking for two other people in their group, while other subjects developed less liking for these two people. The subjects were then put to work on a task. However, in some instances, the other group members made it known that they wanted a high level of productivity on the task, thus establishing a group norm for high productivity. In other instances, the group members indicated that they wanted low productivity, thus setting a group norm for low productivity. In other words, the experimental variables were liking versus disliking other group members and high productivity versus low productivity as group norms. How well the subjects did on the tasks yielded a measure of conforming behavior. The results were that the subjects who liked other members of their group conformed more to the group norms, whether these were for high or low productivity, than the subjects who had considerably less liking for their group members.

Perceived consensus within the group. Another important factor affecting conformity is the amount of agreement existing among the group members. If an individual sees that the others about him are unanimously agreed on a certain opinion or course of behavior, he is more likely to conform to their views than if he believes the group members are not in complete accord. This conclusion is borne out by several experiments. In one, mentioned above, each subject was asked to express his estimate of the length of lines, with most of the other people in his group having been coached to give other opinions. The subject was much less likely to conform to the group judgments when there was one other person who also differed from the group than when all the other group members were in agreement that one answer was correct [Asch, 1958; see Fig. 16.5].

One reason for this result, it seems, is that deviation from a unanimously agreed upon point of view may bring greater disapproval than nonconformity to a less agreed upon opinion. Of course, it also is true that the person can more readily believe an opinion is correct if it is held by most of the other members of the group [Festinger et al., 1952].

Orientation to the group. Another factor in conformity is the orientation of the individual to the group he is in. This orientation can vary in a number of ways, but we shall mention two: (1) One is the degree to which he feels accepted or rejected by the group. (2) The other is orientation to people in the group versus orientation to the tasks to be performed by group members.

The first of these, feelings of acceptance or rejection by the group, is of interest because it determines whether a person's conformity is real or only something professed in public. If a person feels rejected by his group, he is probably going to be motivated more by fear of disapproval than by a belief that the group may be correct. And if a person goes along with the views of others because he is afraid of being rejected by them, it stands to reason that he is not likely to adopt their views as his own. He is like a boy who expects to be punished for misbehavior. When threatened with punishment, the boy may accede to his parents' wishes only because he believes he may be

MOST PEOPLE CONFORM TO THE OPINIONS OF OTHERS:

FIGURE 16.5. An experiment on conformity to group opinion. At top, the rules are explained to the subject. He is told to judge the length of lines presented to him. He does not know the other subjects are "stooges." In the second picture, he makes a judgment with which the rest unanimously disagree. Next time, he attends more carefully, but they disagree again. By the fourth picture, he is showing the strain of regularly disagreeing with the other "subjects." By this time, most subjects in his situation are conforming to the opinion of the majority. This subject, however, holds out (last picture); he says "he has to call them as he sees them" [Asch, 1955; William Vandivert, *Scientific American*].

caught, not because he believes they are correct. Similarly, the person primarily motivated by the desire to avoid disapproval may conform only publicly just to keep from being caught. Privately he may continue to hold the disapproved views. On the other hand, an individual who is attracted to his group, or who believes its opinions are correct, will tend to adopt its views as his own.

What we are saying, in brief, is that conformity motivated by fear of disapproval is only superficial. It is not true conformity. This notion can be tested, and has been, by varying the motivation to avoid disapproval. That can be done by making the individual feel either accepted or rejected by his group. If he feels rejected, he should, according to this idea, have a greater fear of disapproval. The following experiment [Dittes and Kelley, 1956] demonstrates this point:

Some subjects in the experiment were treated in such a way that they felt rejected by the group. Others were made to feel accepted. The degree to which they conformed to group opinion was then measured. The result was that subjects with low acceptance "toed the line" in the group. Feeling on the verge of being outcasts, they went to great lengths to conform to the group. This conformity, however, was only a public, superficial conformity. Privately, they conformed less than those who felt accepted. Apparently, their low acceptance by the group caused them to dislike the others in the group, and this dislike was not conducive to true conformity.

We see then that where fear of disapproval is strong, conformity is not likely to

be real. Outward conformity, but not inward conformity, is usually the result.

A second way in which orientation to the group affects conformity has to do with whether a person is group-oriented or task-oriented. Some people working in a group are much more concerned with the task the group has to accomplish—with getting things done—than with their personal relations with group members. This may come about because the individual is typically task-oriented rather than group-oriented, because he is seriously interested in the purposes of the group, or because people in the group somehow make him feel this way. In any case, we might expect the task-oriented person to be much less affected by group pressures for conformity than the person who is group-oriented, that is, concerned about his personal relations with the group. This expectation has been borne out by research [Thibaut and Strickland, 1956]:

The investigators manipulated things so that some of their subjects were group-oriented and others were task-oriented. The task-oriented subjects were told that their purpose in being there was to find the best answer to an assigned problem. The group-oriented subjects were made conscious of their personal relations with the other group members so that they became more concerned with their acceptability to the other members. All the subjects were then asked to express their opinions about the best solution to the problem. After that, they were placed under varying degrees of pressure to adopt the views of certain other members of the group. The degree to which the two kinds of subjects yielded to this pressure was then

measured. The group-oriented subjects, who were concerned about their personal relations with other people in the group, tended to be influenced by this pressure. Indeed, for them, the greater the pressure, the more they conformed. This was not the case, however, for task-oriented subjects.

We have discussed group norms and conformity behavior at some length because these are basic concepts in understanding group influences on the individual. In fact, the pervasive control that society exercises over our lives—the theme with which we opened this chapter—is exerted very largely through such group norms and our motivation to comply with them. But there are also other aspects of social influences that we should consider. One of these is communication.

COMMUNICATION WITHIN THE GROUP. People in groups usually talk. Some of the talk has the purpose merely of killing time, being friendly, or communicating simple messages. Much of the communication within a group, however, is designed, intentionally or otherwise, to influence members of the group. Indeed, almost all communication among members of a group has some influence on its members' behavior. It is of interest therefore to consider communication as an influence on members of a group. Some of the same factors that govern tendencies to conform also influence communications in a group [Festinger, 1950].

Attraction to the group, we saw above, is a factor in conforming behavior. It is also a factor in the effectiveness of communications within a group. If the members of a group are highly attracted to the group and hold somewhat different opinions, they will communicate with one another more and attempt to influence one another more than if they are not so attracted [Back, 1958].

Perhaps this conclusion seems obvious. After all, there is nothing strange about our talking more, or communicating more, with the people and groups we like. Not so obvious, however, is the reason for this behavior. One factor, apparently, is that any disagreement with people we like is more disturbing than disagreement with people or groups that do not attract us. And the greatest volume of communication in a group is between those whose views differ the most. This has been true at least of the communications sent during the relatively brief time of experiments conducted on group communications.

At first thought, results like these may be puzzling. In everyday life we generally prefer to discuss issues with people holding opinions similar to our own. Republicans, for example, discuss politics almost exclusively with other Republicans, while Democrats talk about politics mainly with those of their own leanings [Lazarsfeld et al., 1944].

There are a number of reasons, however, why everyday communication may be different from communication in laboratory groups. These reasons shed some light on the factors at work in social communication. One factor, already mentioned, is that experimental group members usually communicate with one another for only a relatively brief time. Since the period is short, many of them do not have time to find out whether or not those who disagree with them will change their minds. Once subjects do decide that a deviate is going to persist in his opinion, they indicate less desire to talk to him [Schachter, 1951]. A similar process influences our political conversations. Most of us have learned that we cannot change other people's political beliefs, no matter how correct or brilliant our points may be, so we do not try. In a sense, we may have learned to "write off" people who hold differing opinions.

Another factor to consider is the degree of confidence a person has in his opinion. A person is less likely to communicate with people whose beliefs are very different from his own when he is not too certain he is right than if he is confident that he is. Several experiments support this conclusion.

One will be presented as an example [Brodbeck, 1956]:

Subjects in the experiment listened to a tape-recorded speech by a legal expert on the issue of wire tapping by law-enforcement agencies. For some in the group, the speech agreed with opinions they already held, and they generally indicated confidence in the correctness of their views. For other subjects, however, the expert's views differed from their own, and many said they now had less confidence in their initial beliefs. Then, in the next phase of the study, the subjects were assembled in small groups to discuss the issue further, with each person's views clearly identified for the other group members to see. The experimenter asked the subjects to indicate which group members they would prefer to discuss the issue with. Those people who were relatively uncertain that their opinions were correct were much more likely to want to talk to others holding similar beliefs than the people who were confident their own views were right.

Perhaps the explanation of these results is obvious. The person who is not sure of his own opinion may want to communicate with others of his opinion simply in order to find support. The individual with more confidence in his position may feel no such need for support. This suggests, then, that we tend to avoid discussing controversial issues with people who disagree with us because we are afraid they will shake our already shaky confidence in our beliefs.

COMMUNICATION STRUCTURES. Communications within a group are affected not only by whom the individuals in the group *wish* to talk to, but also by whom they are *permitted* to talk to. Most groups do not allow free-for-all discussions. They have chairmen to govern who may talk and when. They may also have rules about who may talk to whom. The workingman seldom gets a chance to talk to the company president. A junior executive may talk to his boss, but ordinarily he cannot go over his boss's head to the boss's boss. Thus the channels of communication are normally limited in certain ways. The pattern of closed and open communication channels in a group is known as the *communication structure*.

Let us take as an example two different groups of men, each organized to solve a particular business problem. In one group,

THE COMMUNICATION STRUCTURE OF A GROUP IS ITS PATTERN OF
OPEN AND CLOSED COMMUNICATION CHANNELS:

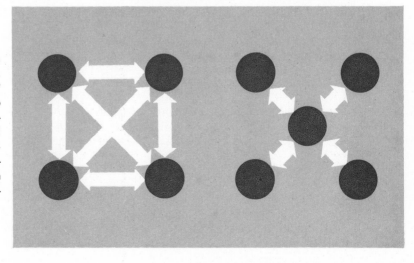

FIGURE 16.6. Two types of communication structure. On the right, the "star" pattern in which group members may communicate only with a central person; on the left, a completely connected ("com-con") structure in which each person may communicate with everyone else.

each member is free to talk to anyone else in the group. Since each person is "completely connected" with everyone else, social psychologists sometimes refer to this type of communication structure as a "com-con." Quite different is a structure in which each group member can communicate with a central person but not with anybody else. If they want to send messages to each other, they must do it through the central person, who can relay it on or not as he sees fit. This pattern is usually known as a "star" communication structure. Obviously, there may be many other kinds of structures, but for simplicity we shall discuss only these two (see Figure 16.6).

Is one structure better than another for getting a job done? Unfortunately, there is no simple, clear-cut answer. We have done many experiments comparing the two structures, and the results seem to depend upon a number of things. Two of the most significant factors are the difficulty or complexity of the job to be done and the work load given to each of the group members. One thing we can say with assurance, however, is that people feel better in the com-con structure than in the star pattern.

People in the com-con structure generally find their jobs more satisfying and have higher morale than the noncentral members of the star pattern [Shaw, 1955].

The reason usually given for this difference is that the com-con pattern gives group members more *independence* [Shaw, 1955]. In the com-con, all group members are equally dependent upon one another in doing their job. To put it another way, each is relatively independent of the others in his group. A person can talk to whomever he wishes; he can get the information or opinion he wants from any member at any time. This is not the case for the noncentral members of the star structure. They must depend entirely upon the central person for the information needed to get their work done. Most people in our society, however, desire some degree of independence in their jobs. They want to believe they have some say over the way they do their work. Communication structures that frustrate this desire tend to make them dissatisfied. This hypothesis is supported by the following experiment [Trow, 1957]:

Before the experiment began, a personality test was administered to measure each subject's need for independence. In addition, each subject was led to believe that he occupied either a central or a peripheral (noncentral) position in a communication network. Within each of these positions, some people were made to believe that they did not depend upon another group member, while the others were made dependent upon him. The results: job satisfaction was affected by making the subjects either independent of or dependent upon others. It was not affected merely by giving them either the central or peripheral position. Furthermore, it was affected most in those subjects with a relatively strong need for independence. These subjects were happiest when they were independent of other group members in doing their job and unhappiest when they had to rely on others for information.

Superficially, the star communication structure looks somewhat like an authoritarian group in which the group is dominated by a "dictator" or boss, and the com-con resembles a democratic group in which individuals have "freedom of speech." Indeed, communication is more restricted in an authoritarian group than in a democratic one. Again, however, the underlying difference is more related to feelings of independence, and the different climate these feelings create, than to the communication structure per se. Individuals in a democratic group can better satisfy their needs for independence. Consequently, they are generally happier. Students of Kurt Lewin [Lewin et al., 1939] have experimentally produced these different climates in children's play groups:

The experimenters created three kinds of groups: autocratic groups, democratic groups,

FIGURE 16.7. Authoritarian, democratic, and laissez-faire groups. In the authoritarian group (top), the leader tells the children exactly what to do. In the democratic group (middle), he acts as a consultant. In the laissez-faire group (bottom), the leader helps only when asked; children are often bored or break into horseplay [Ronald Lippitt].

and laissez-faire groups (see Figure 16.7). In the democratic groups, the leader acted as a consultant; he suggested, persuaded, and helped, but refrained from domineering. In the autocratic groups, he ordered and commanded, permitting no suggestions from group members. In the laissez-faire groups, he paid little or no attention to the group members, letting them do whatever they wanted to.

The laissez-faire groups, as one might expect, accomplished relatively little that was constructive; they were frequently bored, or they broke into horseplay. In the democratic groups, as compared with both the others and particularly with the autocratic groups, there was less hostility, more enjoyment, and more constructive work, and the group did not fall apart when the leader left it. The experimenters point out, however, that there were some exceptions to the superiority of the democratic climate.

Leadership

One of the most important characteristics of groups is that they have *leaders*. One person may get himself out of a burning building, but 500 school children cannot be evacuated without some coordination. Children can play individually as long as they are climbing ropes or "skinning the cat," but in most games they need a leader. You can play football without a captain, but it is much more fun if someone calls signals. Anarchists may be efficient individualists when assassinating kings and derailing trains, but anarchism applied to a military organization would result in many dead heroes and few victories. Moral: groups need leaders if they are to pull together effectively in a team.

LEADERS AND SOCIAL CHANGE.   Although students of human affairs have long tried to evaluate the role of leaders in group behavior, they have not been able to reach agreement on the matter. Writers from Carlyle to Marx have leaned toward one or another of two extreme opinions about leaders: (1) Leaders are necessary; history hinges on their actions. (2) Leaders are merely the expression of popular needs; they ride the tide of history, but they do not influence it.

The first view may be called the "leader principle" or the "great-man theory" of history. It holds that masses of people drift along in aimless confusion until a gifted leader assumes command and tells them what to do. The "man on horseback" is always a dramatic figure. He may accomplish social change (good or bad), but the truth of the matter is that he *appears* to accomplish much more than he actually does. It is said, for example, that Hitler conquered Poland and that Hitler slaughtered millions of people. Literally speaking, Hitler did not do any of these things. Mostly he just talked. But would these things have happened without Hitler? We do not know, for history is an uncontrolled experiment. Yet under the great-man theory of history, Hitler gets credit for *causing* the events.

The second opinion might be called the *sociological view*. It says that history makes or selects the man, not vice versa. Social and cultural developments are considered to follow their own laws, and the presence of a particular person as leader is purely coincidental. A society is regarded as a sprawling organism, adapting slowly to environmental change. Its habits and customs are its culture. If a social organism finds itself at war, a peace leader will not be tolerated; a nation in defeat demands a quisling type of leader. No leader can be at variance with the needs of the group and remain its leader. According to this view, then, it was not Hitler, but the German people who overran Poland and slaughtered the Jews. Extreme adherents of this view will not even admit the temporary influence of the leader. To them, he may be the people's voice, but never their brain.

There are arguments for and against each of these views of leadership. Neither can be proved or disproved. We have reason to believe that the truth lies somewhere between the two. Social change is probably a function of *leaders, groups,* and *situations,* all of which interact to determine the outcome. Leaders usually make some difference, sometimes great and sometimes small. On the other hand, the needs and attitudes of groups determine whom they will select or follow as their leaders. Of course, the behavior of both leaders and groups depends upon the situations they face.

Psychologists have no business playing the role of historian and explaining history. They can, however, conduct experiments on leadership in different kinds of groups and situations. One of these experiments [Haythorn, 1958] shows how leaders and followers interact to affect each other:

Four-man groups were assembled, with one member as the appointed leader. The groups were formed so that the personalities of the leader and his followers differed. First the subjects were given a personality test designed to measure their "authoritarian" tendencies, that is, the extent to which they desired a clear-cut authority structure in society. By using the results of this test, the experimenter established four types of groups: (1) highly authoritarian leaders with highly authoritarian followers, (2) highly authoritarian leaders with less authoritarian followers, (3) less authoritarian leaders with highly authoritarian followers, and (4) less authoritarian leaders with less authoritarian followers. Then the discussions that took place in these groups were studied. The discussions, it turned out, were affected both by the personality of the leader and the personalities of the followers. Groups with authoritarian leaders were more formal in structure and had a more unequal division of the work than the groups whose leaders were less authoritarian in personality, regardless of the followers' personalities. The followers, however, had some influence on the leaders' behavior. Regardless of their own personalities, leaders who had authoritarian followers behaved in a more autocratic manner than leaders with less authoritarian followers. The leader and group affected each other.

PERSONALITIES OF LEADERS. This brings us to the question of what personality traits, if any, characterize leaders. Our libraries are filled with well-meaning books, containing nothing but highly opinionated advice on the subject; they are usually intended for the young males of our society about to be initiated into the glories of adulthood. Opinions unrelated to facts are next to worthless for a science, and that is what most popular writing on leadership is. In recent years, however, scientists have been studying the question, and we are now beginning to get some facts.

In many of their studies, scientists have sought to isolate those personality characteristics that are possessed by leaders but not by nonleaders. By and large, the results of the research have been inconsistent [Jenkins, 1947], partly because too many different kinds of "leaders" have been grouped together, as if there were only one kind of leadership. Clearly, the person who is the leader of an intellectual group concerned with abstract ideas must be different from the individual who leads, say, an athletic club. To get a picture of leaders and leadership, we must consider the situation confronting the group, for the situation in which a leader leads determines to a considerable extent the personal qualities he must have.

This is not to say that leaders of any two groups will necessarily not have any traits in common or that the person who emerges as the leader of one group is not likely to become the leader of any other group. Indeed, it is possible to list some general qualities that often distinguish people who emerge as leaders. By and large, *leaders are more likely to be active participators in their groups, are dependable, persistent, verbally facile, self-confident, and socially popular* [Stogdill, 1958]. Each of these characteristics will be discussed below. Having these qualities, however, does not ensure leadership in every group. But if the situation is right, the person who possesses this combination of traits will probably win a position of leadership.

FORMAL AND INFORMAL LEADERS. Before we can understand *why* these traits may be important and in what situations they are most effective, we must understand more clearly *who* a leader is. Basically, of course, *a leader is a person who influences a group to follow the course of action he advocates,* but we generally restrict the term to those who *frequently* are successful influencers. They must get group members to adopt their proposals more than once or even a few times. Even when another person comes up with an idea that influences the group throughout its meeting, the leader's approval is necessary to sanction the idea. Hence in this situation, the leader is really the major influencer; he has influenced the acceptance of the idea.

Next we must distinguish two basic types of leaders—types in the sense that there are different reasons for their being successful influencers.

Formal leaders. One type of leader is the *formal leader*. A formal leader influences his group primarily because he occupies a formally recognized status. He is the president, chairman, or king. It is his usual role to attempt to influence, and it is the followers' role to follow. Frequently, of course, the followers accept the formal leader's ideas because the leader has authority over them; he dispenses rewards and punishments.

As we have seen, influence based upon the threat of punishment is not likely to be long lasting. The followers will obey orders only as long as they fear getting caught. This is not very effective leadership, though in some situations, such as a battle, it may be essential. Generally, a leader is most effective when his followers accept his ideas because they truly believe in them. In any case, the formal leader ultimately derives his authority and influence from the position he occupies.

The following experiment [Raven and French, 1958] demonstrates how an individual's formal status can affect other group members' acceptance of his proposals:

In this study, one person (the investigator's confederate) attempted to influence the real subjects under two different conditions. There were different groups of subjects for each of the conditions. In one condition, he apparently usurped the leadership role when it was not "legally" granted him by the group. In the other, he supposedly was elected to this role. His attempts to influence the group were much more successful when he was elected by the group. From this result, the investigators concluded that, "the election procedure is a formal means for designating the legitimate occupant of an office and for investing him with the legitimate power of that office."

Informal leaders. The second type of leader is the *informal leader.* An informal leader may frequently be quite a successful influencer of his group, yet his influence is not derived from a formal position. More than anything else, the others in the group follow his lead because his personal qualities convince them that they can satisfy their own needs by accepting his ideas. For this to happen, the group members must be unsure of how to attain their goals on their own. Since they cannot cope with the problems facing the group, they turn to the informal leader for ways of achieving their group goals.

But why does a group in this situation turn to one particular person? What are the important personal qualities he must possess? One quality certainly is his proficiency, as the group perceives it, in handling the tasks confronting the group. Of course, it often happens that a group has no sure way of knowing this. Then, in the absence of any objective means for evaluating an individual's task competence, the group frequently relies on the person's past performance. It is as if the group members say, "He has been right before; the chances are he is right now." This is probably one good reason why a person who has done well in the past is more likely to be a successful influencer on subsequent occasions than a person who had not done a good job earlier [Mausner, 1954].

Past performance, however, is not the only basis for accepting an informal leader's ideas. Liking him is another, just as it is in conforming behavior. A person who is well liked has a much better chance of having his ideas accepted, and thus of influencing people, than one who is less popular. Partly for this reason, social skills and personal popularity often characterize the person chosen for a position of leadership. In addition, the leader's job frequently involves promoting and maintaining harmonious relations among the members of his group. Hence, a socially skillful, popular person is better able to achieve these friendly relations within the group than a less socially skillful person.

As one might expect, the person who is highly popular with the members of one group is more likely to be popular with other groups. A person who has social skills and is likable can recruit friends from a wide range of people—but, of course, he may not appeal to or attract everybody. This means, then, that the individual who emerges as leader in one group may well become a leader in other groups, assuming that the tasks and the people involved in these groups are relatively similar [Bell and French, 1950].

There is evidence, finally, that the assertive individual is more likely to be chosen leader than the less assertive person, at least in the first stages of the group's existence. The assertive person is the individual who talks a great deal and advances a relatively large number of ideas. If he is not arrogant and aggressive in asserting himself, his active participation makes him stand out in the group. This, of course, increases his chances of being chosen as the leader. Talking and participating in the group also helps it by giving it ideas for coping with its problems. Further, since the assertive person usually presents his ideas with a great deal of confidence in their correctness, the members of the group come to feel that his ideas are indeed correct.

There are dangers, of course, in one's being too assertive. The individual who continues to dominate a group's activities over a number of sessions may well begin to frustrate some of its members' needs for independence. As a group proceeds with its work, many of its original problems are solved and the situation becomes less ambiguous. When this happens, other members want to have more control over their own activities. They no longer need so many ideas as they did at first. At this point, the very assertive person may lose his initial popularity if he continues to assert himself. For this reason, the adroit leader will perceive that it is time to let the other members of the group have more say in what they do.

Summary

1. Cultures of different societies tend to have characteristic patterns. These are widely shared ways of behaving, together with the beliefs that accompany them.

2. Cultures tend to resist change, but changes do come about. Whether the changes are slow or rapid depends upon such factors as the society's attitudes toward social change, its technological developments, and the intermingling of peoples.

3. Members of a culture are generally unaware of the extent to which culture shapes their habits and values. Each person has his own subculture and is greatly influenced by the smaller groupings to which he belongs as well as by the major segments of the larger culture.

4. Individuals in a society tend to be unequal in their ability to satisfy the needs of the group. This fact is largely the reason for the development of social structure.

5. Social structures are made up of different statuses. Individuals occupying a particular status are expected to play an appropriate role. A person may have several statuses and roles. Occasionally these conflict, but more often they supplement each other or are compartmentalized.

6. Characteristic statuses tend to be arranged on a prestige scale which becomes the basis for a division into social classes. There are several correlates of social class: socioeconomic differences, occupational differences, and social privileges such as greater freedom to talk and to deviate from the standards of the group and the ability to influence others.

7. Members of social classes also differ in their child-rearing practices, in occupational goals, in their dominant motivations, and in their attractiveness to others.

8. Group norms are expected ways of behaving that are widely shared by most members of a group, class, or culture. They have a demand quality; hence most people conform to them. Group norms seem to emerge wherever there is continued interaction among people.

9. People tend to conform to group norms because (a) they fear disapproval by members of the group, and (b) they are inclined to believe that the group is right.

10. Some of the principal factors affecting degrees of conformity to group norms are (*a*) attraction to the group, (*b*) the perceived consensus within the group, and (*c*) orientation to the group. The last-named factor refers to feelings of acceptance or rejection by the group and to whether the individual is task-oriented or group-oriented.

11. How much a person attempts to communicate in a group and to influence other members of the group largely depends upon such things as (*a*) the attractiveness of the group and (*b*) the confidence he has in his own opinion.

12. The channels of communication in a group are usually limited in certain ways. How they are limited determines the communication structure. In a star structure, group members may communicate only with one central person; in a com-con structure, they may communicate with anyone. People in the latter structure usually are more satisfied and have higher morale.

13. Most groups function well in complex situations only when they have leaders. A leader is a person who frequently influences other members of the group because he is regarded by them as better able than others to satisfy, or help satisfy, the needs of the group.

14. Since leadership depends on the group and the situation, relatively few qualities distinguish leaders from nonleaders. In general, however, leaders tend to be active participators in group activities and to be more dependable, persistent, verbally facile, self-confident, and socially popular than nonleaders.

Suggestions for further reading

Benedict, R. *Patterns of culture*. Boston: Houghton Mifflin, 1934.
A classical description and analysis, written by a social anthropologist, of patterns of culture in primitive societies.

Cartwright, D., and Zander, A. *Group dynamics* (2d ed.). Evanston, Ill.: Row, Peterson, 1960.
A collection of recent research reports dealing with the behavior of people in groups, together with some theoretical interpretations of such behavior.

Festinger, L., Schachter, S., and Back, K. *Social pressures in informal groups*. New York: Harper, 1950.
A theoretical analysis of social influence processes plus a report of research with "natural" groups.

Hartley, E., and Hartley, R. *Fundamentals of social psychology*. New York: Knopf, 1955. Chaps. 8–11.
A discussion of cultural and other social influences on human development and behavior, making use of psychological, sociological, and anthropological material.

Kluckhohn, C. *Mirror for man*. New York: McGraw-Hill, 1949. (Also published as a paperback, Premier Books, by Fawcett Publications, 1957.)
A popular survey of cultural differences in behavior and attitudes by an eminent social anthropologist.

Krech, D., and Crutchfield, R. S. *Theory and problems of social psychology*. New York: McGraw-Hill, 1948. Chaps. 10 and 11.
A text on social psychology containing chapters on social groups and leadership.

Maccoby, E., Newcomb, T. M., and Hartley, E. *Readings in social psychology* (3d ed.). New York: Holt, Rinehart and Winston, 1958.
A representative sampling of research and viewpoints in all areas of present-day social psychology.

Newcomb, T. M. *Social psychology*. New York: Dryden, 1950.
A general introduction to social psychology which attempts to integrate different psychological approaches.

Sherif, M., and Sherif, C. *An outline of social psychology* (rev. ed.). New York: Harper, 1956. Chaps. 5–8.
A discussion of the development of group norms and social structures based upon both experimental research and observation of "real-life" groups.

Warner, W. L., and Lunt, P. S. *The social life of a modern community*. New Haven, Conn.: Yale Univer. Press, 1941.
An intensive study of class structure and social attitudes in a New England city.

Attitudes, beliefs, & social prejudice

Aｌｔｈｏｕｇｈ ｔｈｅ ａｔｔｉｔｕｄｅｓ of other people are never seen or felt—they are only inferred—they make a great difference in almost everyone's life. To the person in business or politics they may mean the difference between success or failure. The businessman depends upon the favorable attitudes of his customers toward his products and services to keep his business going. The politician must have favorable attitudes toward his personality, abilities, and political behavior in order to count on his reelection. Each of us similarly strives to create favorable attitudes and to eliminate unfavorable attitudes toward us among our friends, associates, employers, and others. There are, indeed, very few acts or decisions in everyday affairs that do not somehow take account of the way in which attitudes may be affected.

Nature of attitudes

An attitude is usually defined by psychologists as a *tendency to respond positively* (favorably) *or negatively* (unfavorably) to certain objects, persons, or situations. Although this is an adequate definition, we must have two other things in mind in order to comprehend the nature of an attitude: *categories* and *goals*. An attitude, like the behavioral response it stands for, tends to place its stimulus object in one category or another. It is a kind of discrimination in that the stimulus is reacted to as though it were a member of one class of stimuli, but not a member of other classes of stimuli. This discrimination or categorization of the stimulus object is related to the individual's goals. Hence, to understand attitudes, we must consider the process of categorizing things and the relation of the categories formed to a person's motives and goals.

CATEGORIES AND GOALS.

To clarify this conception of attitudes, let us consider the hypothetical case of a Mr. Smith who has a negative attitude toward Democrats.

One day Mr. Smith finds he has a new neighbor, Mr. Jones. Very soon after their meeting, Mr. Smith hears Mr. Jones say some kind words about the former president, Harry Truman. Chances are that one of Smith's first responses will be to classify his neighbor as a Democrat—put him in the category of Democrat. Unless (or until) he gets to know his neighbor better, he will regard Jones as being fairly similar to other people in the same category. Stimuli placed together in one category are considered essentially equivalent. But more than this, since Smith does not care for Democrats, we may surmise that Democrats represent some sort of threat to his goals. He may believe, for example, that Democrats are trying to bring on socialism (which is threatening to him) and that their taxation program will thwart his ambition to become a wealthy man. Out of this motivation grows mild dislike for Jones. Of course, Smith is not responding to Mr. Jones as a person in his own right. He does not know Jones well enough to know what his unique characteristics are. He is reacting to him as a Democrat, as a member of a threatening or potentially punishing category of people.

Now we can see better what it means to say that an attitude is a tendency to respond positively or negatively to something. The hypothetical Mr. Smith has a negative attitude toward his neighbor. But the reason for this attitude is that he has placed his neighbor in a category with other things to which he reacts unfavorably because they threaten his goals. Conversely, if Mr. Jones had done or said something to classify him with Mr. Smith's positive goals and rewards, the attitude toward him would have been positive.

NEGATIVE ATTITUDES AND SOCIAL PREJUDICE.

Another way to look at Mr. Smith's behavior is to say that he is "prejudiced." This term today generally means a negative attitude toward a minority group such as Jews or Negroes. But this is a sociological definition, not a psychological one. If we consider only the *operation* of the social prejudice, it does not differ from other negative attitudes. Mr. Smith might have classified Mr. Jones as, say, a Jew if he had seen some sign of "Jewishness"; and if he had been anti-Semitic, he would have disliked his neighbor for being in *this* category. Psychologically, in terms of the way the attitude operates, social prejudice is but a special instance of negative attitudes.

Etymologically, the word "prejudice" means "pre-judgment." In this sense, prejudice means applying a previously formed judgment to some person, object, or situation. In Mr. Smith's case, he had a pre-formed judgment about Democrats that he applied to Mr. Jones. This judgment might just as well have been positive as negative, and so might the prejudice. In either case, Mr. Smith's prejudice toward his neighbor stems from the category into which he placed the neighbor. (If the prejudgment were favorable, "good things" would be related to the category, instead of "bad things.")

CATEGORIES AND STEREOTYPES.

There is another important consequence of classifying people into categories; it involves erroneous thinking and beliefs. Since Mr. Smith does not regard Mr. Jones as a unique person, but classifies him as a Democrat, he may be wrong about Mr. Jones. The Democratic party actually has all sorts of people in it. Mr. Jones may be a Democrat, but nevertheless opposed to socialism. If Mr. Smith's category, Democrat, includes only people who favor socialism, he will be wrong if he thinks his neighbor advocates socialism. Consequently he will be attributing to Mr. Jones characteristics he does not have.

In this particular instance, the error is in having an oversimplified view of the category of Democrat. The category should be composed of subcategories, that is, of different kinds of Democrats. Remember, stimuli included within the same category are considered essentially equivalent. People in one general category are assumed to be all alike. In this case, they are regarded as sharing the same political beliefs, when actually Democrats vary widely in their opinions.

This kind of thinking often leads to what has been called a *stereotype*. A stereotype is any widespread, oversimplified, and hence erroneous belief [Krech and Crutchfield, 1948]. Generally, too, it concerns a category of people. One illustration of such a stereotype is the notion that redheads have fiery tempers. This is a stereotype because it is widespread, at least in some cultural groups, and it is oversimplified. Actually, some redheads are quick-tempered, and some are not. Other stereotypes are prevalent about blonds, scientists, Italians, Jews, Irish, and many other groups.

In 1932, investigators at Princeton University systematically studied the attitudes of their students toward various national groups. They asked the subjects to indicate the traits characterizing each particular group. In Table 17.1 are some of the results. In looking over this table, you might judge from your own experience whether the stereotypes revealed there still exist today.

Some years later, another investigator studied stereotypes in a somewhat different way. This study is described below:

The investigator showed photographs of college girls, selected to be "ethnically non-specific," to 100 male and female college students and to 50 older male subjects. He asked his subjects to rate the girls on a number of qualities such as beauty, intelligence, character, and ambition. Two months later the same photographs were shown to the subjects, but together with other photographs in order to confuse their memories. The subjects were again asked to judge the girls. This

TABLE 17.1. Some of the most common traits supposedly possessed by various racial and national groups.

Group trait	Per cent of college students in sample attributing trait to group
Germans:	
Scientifically minded	78
Industrious	65
Stolid	44
Intelligent	32
Italians:	
Artistic	53
Impulsive	44
Passionate	37
Musical	32
Jews:	
Shrewd	79
Mercenary	49
Industrious	48
Intelligent	29
Ambitious	21
Negroes:	
Superstitious	84
Lazy	75
Happy-go-lucky	38
Irish:	
Pugnacious	45
Quick-tempered	39
Witty	38
Honest	32

time, though, they were given names at random, i.e., without regard to the girls' actual ethnic background. Five had Jewish names, five Irish, five Italian, and the remainder Anglo-Saxon names.

The new ratings were influenced by these names. Judgments of the supposedly Jewish girls, for example, clearly conformed to the stereotype of Jews shown in Table 17.1. In contrast to the way the girls had been rated before they were given names, they were now judged to be less beautiful and to have less character, but as being more intelligent and more ambitious. This pattern of changes did not occur for the supposedly Irish and Italian girls.

Jews, of course, are frequently believed to be intelligent and ambitious. Table 17.1 shows that these traits are often part of the stereotype of Jews. In the above experiment, then, the name given to the girl served to place her in a particular category (Jew). As a result, other qualities were attributed to her that are associated with this category. (Jews are ambitious. She is a Jew. She must be ambitious.)

The phenomenon just described is not limited to ethnic or racial groups. Whenever we encounter a situation, we tend to place the stimuli in it, whether they be people, objects, or symbols, into what seem to us to be appropriate categories. Once we classify them this way, we react to them as we would to other stimuli similarly classified (cf. stimulus generalization and concept formation). A stereotype, then, is just a particular type of category—one that concerns certain groups. The characteristics of the categories are widely agreed upon and are oversimplifications of reality.

BELIEFS, ATTITUDES, AND OPINIONS. In everyday usage, the terms *belief, attitude,* and *opinion* are very close together in meaning—so close that they are frequently used almost interchangeably. It is possible, however, to make distinctions among them. A belief is *the acceptance of a statement or proposition.* It does not necessarily imply an attitude of being "for" or "against." I believe that the sun will rise tomorrow morning. Some people believe in men wearing hats in church. Such beliefs can be held without the emotional tinge of an attitude. In between belief and attitude is something vague called an opinion. It usually involves some sort of belief and also some attitude of "pro" or "con," though the attitude may not be strong and the belief may be poorly formulated.

In actual practice, the distinction among these terms is not of very much value. Most beliefs and opinions are closely linked with attitudes. Indeed, they are often rationalizations for attitudes. In any case, it is hard to disentangle them. For that reason, beliefs and opinions also typically involve the classification of things into categories that are related to one's goals.

Development of attitudes and beliefs

Now that we understand what attitudes and beliefs are, we are in a position to discuss how they are formed and changed. In this section, we shall consider the development of attitudes and beliefs in children and adolescents. In the next section, we shall treat other factors influencing attitudes that are particularly important in adulthood. In the section following that one, we shall consider attitude change through education and propaganda. The last two sections of the chapter will cover attitude measurement and the special problem of racial attitudes and conflicts.

CULTURE. We learned in Chapter 16 that culture consists of the customs and traditions of a people and the attitudes and beliefs they have about important aspects of life. We also learned that these customs, traditions, attitudes, and beliefs influence each individual in many diverse ways through his social class, his social groups, his schools, his family, and so on. Since the individual experiences all these influences simultaneously, or at least in the course of a day or a week, it is difficult to separate them one from another. *In toto,* however, they shape his attitudes and beliefs.

Cross-cultural comparisons. One of the ways to assess the influence of culture on attitudes is to determine whether societies differ in their patterns of beliefs and attitudes. There obviously are pitfalls in talking about these differences, for it is easy to indulge in stereotypes and oversimplifications that lose sight of complex realities. If, for example, we were to say that Germany is an "authoritarian society," we would be expressing such a stereotype. There are, of course, Germans who prefer authoritarian forms of government and who believe that a few strong leaders generally have the right to tell others what to do. But this does not mean that every German possesses these attitudes or that other national groups do not have them.

It is possible, nevertheless, to ask whether Germans (or members of any other society) are relatively similar in their beliefs and different *on the average* from people in other societies. In this statistical sense, we can discuss group differences scientifically. And we can say that one society differs from another on a given characteristic when differences *between* societies are appreciably greater than differences *within* the societies.

Unfortunately, few investigations of differences between nations and societies rest on this statistical footing. Most of them are haphazard observations of relatively few members of a national group without evidence that they are representative of their society. Moreover, the writers ordinarily do not confine their conclusions to the few people studied, but instead they generalize uncritically to the entire society. The dangers of such an uncontrolled and unsystematic approach can be illustrated by the following fictitious, but somewhat typical, case.

Suppose an observer, who had a pet notion that Americans were an extremely hostile people, were to visit two or three classrooms in your school. He might happen to see several incidents in which students were critical of the view advocated by their instructor. Feeling that his theory had been confirmed, he might then go back home and write a paper. In it he might conclude that Americans generally are extremely hostile toward their parents because of their having been subjected to harsh toilet-training practices when they were between one and two years of age. This aggressiveness, he might maintain, is generalized to all authority figures, so that Americans have a compulsion to attack, question, and devalue anyone in a position of power over them.

Let us see what this fictitious observer has done: (1) He has interpreted (as aggression) a few incidents entirely from the point of view of his theoretical bias without realizing that other interpretations are possible. (2) He has regarded the behavior he saw as typical of members of our society in general without determining whether this behavior is indeed widespread or common in this country. (3) He has assumed, without the benefit of any scientific evidence, that the behavior pattern has its roots in certain childhood experiences (toilet training). (4) He has assumed that these childhood experiences are common to most Americans, again without any evidence.

This compendium of errors, of course, does not mean that scientific research on national and societal differences is impossible. It is presented to highlight the difficulties of such research and to indicate some of the things to be wary of in making such comparisons. Scientific investigations can be conducted, but they are expensive and require a good deal of careful work. One study [McGranahan, 1946] carried out shortly after the Second World War illustrates more adequately controlled procedures, although its results must be interpreted with caution:

One hundred and ninety-one German youths between 14 and 18 years old from the town of Bad Hamburg were interviewed, and their answers were compared with the responses given by a matched sample of American youngsters from the supposedly comparable town of Oak Park, Illinois. There were differences in the frequency of authoritarian-like beliefs in the two groups. A greater proportion of the Bad Hamburg adolescents felt that people "who unjustly criticized the government of a country" should be thrown in jail (36 per cent of the German youths to 21 per cent of the Oak Park adolescents). A greater proportion also felt that newspapers should report not what they wished, but only what they thought to be "for the good of the people" (43 per cent to 17 per cent).

These and other differences found between the two national groups appear to support a theory that Germans have a greater tendency toward authoritarian social organization than Americans have. By themselves, however, the results of this study do not prove such a theory. We do not know the extent to which the samples were representative of Germans and Americans in general, or even of German and American youngsters. It also is possible that similar differences would not be obtained today. The study does point to average differences between the two samples at the time, but also indicates that there were differences of opinion within each sample. All German interviewees are not authoritarian, even though many had the tendency to be, nor was the tendency entirely absent in the American sample.

Even when we assume that national or cultural differences in attitudes and beliefs do exist, we face the important problem of tracing the origin of these differences to their roots. The cross-cultural comparisons of primitive societies described in the last chapter are a beginning in this direction.

Cultural influences on attitudes. Another way to assess the influence of culture on attitudes is to correlate attitudes with cultural differences within a society. If a certain attitude is held more generally among individuals in one cultural category than among those in another category, it may be presumed that the culture influences the attitude. An illustration of such a correlation is to be found in a study sponsored some years ago by the Social Science Research Council [1947]. It concerned attitudes toward armed imperialism. About one thousand individuals were asked the question, "Some people say we should use our Army and Navy to make other countries do what we think they should. How do you feel about that?" As can be seen in Table 17.2, people generally disapproved of this point of view, but it is interesting that those with a college educa-

TABLE 17.2. The relationship of education, income, and religion to attitudes toward armed imperialism. Individuals were asked the question: "Some people say we should use our Army and Navy to make other countries do what we think they should. How do you feel about that?" [Social Science Research Council, 1947].

Respondents	General approval, per cent	General disapproval, per cent	No response, per cent	Number of respondents
Education:				
Grade school	19	57	24	500
High school	13	77	10	455
College	8	83	9	213
Income:				
Under $2,000	19	58	23	440
$2,000 to $3,999	16	73	11	478
$4,000 and more	8	86	6	216
Religion:				
Protestant	14	70	16	855
Catholic	18	68	14	245

tion and those in the higher economic brackets disapproved more than those of lesser education and income. There was no substantial difference, however, between those of Protestant and those of Catholic religious affiliation. From such a study, it may be concluded that educational and socioeconomic influences probably are important in determining attitudes toward the use of our Armed Forces.

In recent years a very large number of studies correlating attitudes and culture have been conducted [Murphy et al., 1937]. Almost any public-opinion poll, when analyzed according to the educational status, income level, religious background, etc., of the group questioned, yields information about such a relation. And there have been many experimental studies conducted in colleges. On some questions, such as birth control, war, and political issues, religious influences prove to be important: Catholics are usually more conservative than Jews, and those with religious training are usually more conservative than those without religious training.

In almost all beliefs and attitudes, socioeconomic status tends to be important. The upper socioeconomic classes tend to be more "liberal" regarding war and the use of force, as in the study we cited, but they tend to be more conservative in political and economic views. Perhaps this means, as other writers have noted [Allinsmith and Allinsmith, 1948], that there are at least two varieties of "liberalism," one in economic affairs, the other in noneconomic matters. The middle and upper social strata are more conservative than the lower classes in political-economic attitudes, but may be less conservative in other beliefs, such as those dealing with international relations. Other instances of social-class influences on attitudes and beliefs were cited in the last chapter (page 510).

We should not jump to the conclusion, however, that individuals simply take over the attitudes characteristic of their class or group, for this is not true. We must remember that the correlations are seldom very high; rather they usually indicate only moderate statistical tendencies. Such an imperfect correlation is to be expected, because the individual is exposed to numerous cultural influences and to many different attitudes and beliefs. Though a person may be of one religious training, he ordinarily associates with people of other religious backgrounds. Although he may be of one socioeconomic status, he usually has some contact with members of other socioeconomic groups. In these and other ways, his culture is by no means homogeneous. Even if it were, there are enough differences among members of any particular cultural group to expose him to a variety of attitudes and beliefs.

FAMILY INFLUENCES.   In the melee of cultural forces continuously playing on an individual, there are some that are especially important because they mediate between the individual and his culture. These are influences from his parents and his associates. A child's parents are products of the culture; their attitudes and beliefs have been influenced, and continue to be influenced, by the culture. Because their social contacts, their reading, their entertainment, and their other relations with the culture are considerably wider and more diverse than those of the child, they are more directly influenced by the culture than he is. Yet, considered together, they spend a good many hours of the day in contact with the child, all the while controlling his behavior and attempting to instill in him particular attitudes and beliefs. It is not surprising, then, that the *attitudes and beliefs of the child tend to correlate with those of his parents.*

In one study [Hirschberg and Gilliland, 1942] conducted with 200 college students at Northwestern University, for example, the attitudes of the students toward the New Deal administration, toward economic depression, and toward God correlated with the attitudes of the parents to the extent of .29 to .58.

One eminent student of American political behavior has reviewed a number of investigations of parental influence on political attitudes [Hyman, 1959]. He notes that the studies almost invariably find some degree of similarity between the parents' political beliefs and those of their children, providing "considerable evidence against the theory that political attitudes are formed generally in terms of rebellion and opposition to parents." Furthermore, this research shows that the similarity between parents and children generally is greater for political-party preference than for political beliefs. As a practical matter, the writer maintains, a man is born into his political party almost to the same extent that he may be regarded as being born into the membership of his church. He adopts his family's political party almost to the degree that he adopts its religion.

One major reason for this similarity in attitudes is that children tend to be in the same socioeconomic stratum as their parents. If a person were to enter a different social class from the one occupied by his parents, he might change his party preference.

Bearing on this point is a survey [Hyman, 1959] of college graduates in which changes in political orientation were related to social mobility. Among those graduates who came from Democratic (i.e., relatively low-income) families, the proportion who were Democrats themselves decreased sharply the higher their own income rose. This pattern was not revealed by the graduates who came from Republican families and who were earning less than their parents. For these people, a decline in social class did not alter their preference for the Republican party.

There also is reason, however, to believe that parents, as well as social class, influence political attitudes. For example, a national survey conducted during the 1952 presidential campaign found that the individual was likely to be indifferent to the two major political parties if his parents also were indifferent to them.

Familial influences, of course, affect more than our political attitudes. They may also determine, among other things, our attitudes toward other racial and religious groups.

In a set of interviews with white grammar school children about their attitudes toward Negroes, one investigator got such responses as these [quoted from Horowitz, 1936]:

First-grade girl: Mama tells me not to play with black children, keep away from them. Mamma tells me, she told me not to play with them. . . .

Second-grade girl: Colored children. Mother doesn't want me to play with colored children. . . . I play with colored children sometimes and Mamma whips me.

Second-grade boy: Colored children, mother and daddy tell me. They tell me not to play with colored people or colored persons' things.

Third-grade girl: Mother told me not to play with them because sometimes they have diseases and germs and you get it from them.

PEER INFLUENCES. As the individual grows older he meets more and more people outside his family group and becomes increasingly independent of his parents for the satisfaction of his needs. This does not mean that he now is independent of people generally; rather, he looks to his own efforts and also to people outside the family for gratifications that formerly were provided by members of his family. He relies on peers, friends, and acquaintances for the satisfaction of his desires for companionship and entertainment. He also may seek them out in order to obtain emotional and social support, wanting their consolation when plans go wrong, their reassurance that his behavior is proper, and their agreement that his opinions are correct. These friends and acquaintances thus become important influences on his attitudes and beliefs.

Two major reasons for this influence were cited in the last chapter. The individual may express the opinions and do the things advocated by his associates because (1) he believes their opinions and actions probably are correct and/or (2) he fears that his deviation may lead to disapproval and rejection. Whatever the reasons operating in any given case, the outcome is that an individual's peers may shape his views, as well as his behavior, more than his parents do, particularly when he has a great deal of contact with his peers.

One of the most famous investigations in social psychology [Newcomb, 1943] shows how a young person's peers may influence his political and economic beliefs to such an extent that family influences become secondary:

This study was conducted with the girls at Bennington College in Vermont in the mid-thirties. Most of the students entering the college as freshmen came from the upper and middle socioeconomic class and held the conservative political and economic views of their families. The highly self-contained college community to which they came, however, was at that time strongly "New Dealish" (liberal) in its political sentiments. What happened to the freshman "conservatives" in this environment? Attitude surveys revealed that the longer the girls remained in college the more liberal they generally became. Thus, as juniors and seniors they were more liberal than they had been when they were freshmen and sophomores.

Of course, there were individual differences in the degree to which the girls took over the attitudes of their peers. The girls who were regarded by their peers as most closely identified with the community were the ones who developed the most pro–New Deal beliefs. The girls who remained conservative despite the widespread liberalism among their fellow students generally were unable or unwilling to participate fully in college life. Often they were socially withdrawn, either because they were insecure and lacked social skills or because they had met frustrations at Bennington. Some girls did not enter into college life fully because they had strong attachments to other groups, such as their families. Whatever the reason, the girls who did not adopt the prevalent beliefs at Bennington usually participated least in the activities of their peers.

Adult attitudes and beliefs

So far we have described three sets of influences on the development of attitudes in the child and adolescent. These were culture, family, and peer groups, which continue to be important throughout the person's life. In adulthood, however, still other factors assume increasing importance in shaping and maintaining the attitudes of the individual: (1) his personality, (2) the information he receives, (3) the statements and attitudes of authorities to which he is exposed, and (4) the small informal groups, called primary groups, of which he is a member. These factors will be discussed in this section.

PERSONALITY. To recognize that the culture molds attitudes and beliefs is not to say that the culture simply gives or transmits them to the inert, passive individual. Whether attitudes are formed or not often depends upon the personality of the individual. Some individuals at any particular time are relatively immune to many attitudes and beliefs but are particularly susceptible to others. Thus much depends upon the personality of the individual who is exposed to cultural influences. This fact is demonstrated in several studies of the relationship between personality, on the one hand, and attitudes and beliefs, on the other.

Personality traits. You will remember from the chapter on personality that traits can be rated by persons who know an individual fairly well or by special tests that have been constructed for the purpose. One test measures a person's relative introversion or extroversion, another his relative dominance or submission in social situations, and still others are available to measure other traits. If we give such tests to a group of people and at the same time determine their attitudes on a number of issues, it is possible to correlate attitudes with personality traits.

In one study [Dexter, 1939], attitudes on

a number of political and social issues were used to divide students into "radical," "conservative," and more moderate groups. Correlating these attitudes with personality traits, the investigator found the women students who were radical in attitudes and beliefs to be more introverted, more self-sufficient, and more dominant than other women students in their groups. Such personality traits, it appears, enable a person more easily to adopt beliefs and attitudes that are less conventional.

Unfortunately, however, there are few general rules that can be applied to personality and attitudes. What may be "radical" attitudes for one cultural group may be the conventional attitudes for another. Thus the personality characteristics which in one group accompany certain attitudes may in another group be correlated with other attitudes. The important point is that the particular attitudes and beliefs a person adopts frequently are related to his personality characteristics.

This last sentence, the reader will note, does *not* claim that an individual's personality characteristics *always* determine the nature of his beliefs and attitudes. In many cases, a person adopts the attitudes and beliefs of others about him regardless of his traits. As indicated in the last chapter, this is particularly likely if he knows relatively little about the object or issue, if the others about him are in agreement, and if they are not disliked.

Personality traits seem to be most strongly related to attitudes when the groups around a person permit people to hold a variety of alternative opinions on a given issue. If a person's associates do not insist that only one course of action is socially proper in a given situation, then his personality traits are more likely to determine his attitudes. When, on the other hand, social pressures are great, the attitudes he expresses may hinge on his desire to conform. This in turn may arise from his attraction to the group.

The ethnocentric personality. There are many parts of the United States where cultural norms do not define particular minority groups, such as Negroes and Jews, as inferior or threatening. These regions, nevertheless, still contain a fair share of socially prejudiced people. It is not likely that these people developed their dislike for the minority groups simply through unpleasant experiences with them, because they tend to be strongly prejudiced against every minority group, not just one, and the pattern of prejudice is so frequent and so distributed throughout the country that we cannot attribute it to direct encounters with minority groups. The prejudiced people are not likely to have met all the groups they dislike. A better explanation for their negative attitudes is that, because of their personality characteristics, they distrust and dislike others who are different.

Light has been shed on the nature of these personality traits by a famous, large-scale study [Adorno et al., 1950] conducted by a team of social scientists at the University of California:

By studying and testing a large sample of people, the investigators found that some people could be described as generally prejudiced because they were biased against a wide variety of groups. These prejudiced people tended to glorify in a very extreme fashion the particular groups to which they belonged (including the United States). At the same time, they were hostile toward the groups in which they had no membership. They were given the name *ethnocentric*. Highly ethnocentric individuals then were singled out for further investigation. By administering many psychological tests both to them and to less prejudiced people, it was possible to determine how their personalities differed from those of the less ethnocentric group.

This research and later studies have presented a composite portrait of the highly ethnocentric person:

1. *He is an authoritarian.* Supposedly because he sees the world and most of the

people in it as dangerous and unfriendly, he seeks security by submitting uncritically to a powerful authority as if to gather strength from the authority. For this reason, an ethnocentric individual frequently is referred to as having an "authoritarian personality." Such a person is likely to hold beliefs such as the following [Adorno et al., 1950; Allport and Kramer, 1946]: "The world is a hazardous place in which men are basically evil and dangerous," and "We do not have enough discipline in our American way of life." The authoritarian person wants people to do whatever the proper authorities tell them to do. He also frequently wants a definite social hierarchy in which everybody has his place and knows who is leader and who is follower.

2. *He is rigidly moralistic.* This ethnocentric individual usually also seeks security in strict adherence to standards of morality and propriety. He feels he is safe as long as he is conventional and shuns the behavior that middle-class people generally regard as socially unacceptable. He also condemns harshly people who violate his moral code.

In one of the California studies highly prejudiced (ethnocentric) and less prejudiced women were asked, "What is the most embarrassing experience you've had?" The ethnocentric women usually said that it was some public violation of social rules and regulations. In contrast, the less prejudiced group said that their most embarrassing experiences involved failures in interpersonal relations, such as not living up to a friend's expectations.

3. *He strongly represses socially disapproved tendencies within himself and projects them to others.* Anxiously concerned with being conventional and proper, this person not only tries to avoid doing anything socially disapproved, but he is uncomfortable at the idea that he might *want* to do these things. Although less ethnocentric people can readily admit that they have sexual wishes or aggressive inclinations, the highly prejudiced individual frequently denies both to himself and to others that he has such

impulses. But more than this, these disapproved tendencies often are attributed to (i.e., projected to) other people, particularly to minority groups. It is as if the highly prejudiced person told himself, "*I* don't have these sexual or aggressive desires, the Negro (or other minority group) does."

One tendency that ethnocentric individuals have and at the same time disapprove is hostility toward parents. According to the California investigators, highly prejudiced people often have had harsh and unrealistically demanding parents. Stern treatment by their parents leaves them with aggressive feelings, yet they dare not express such feelings.

In the study of prejudiced women mentioned above, the psychologists found that these women openly expressed great admiration for their parents, but nevertheless revealed through personality tests hidden aggressive inclinations toward them. The less prejudiced women, on the other hand, more freely admitted occasionally disliking their parents.

4. *He often places people in oversimplified, black-and-white categories.* The highly ethnocentric person generally does not make fine distinctions among people. He is likely to agree with such statements as, "There are only two kinds of people, the weak and the strong." For him, people fall into only a small number of classes. Thus, members of a minority group are "all alike." Furthermore, these categories are simple and clear-cut: people are all bad or all good. He is not so likely as his less prejudiced peers to believe that both good and bad traits can exist simultaneously in the same person [Steiner, 1954].

5. *He frequently possesses conservative political and economic attitudes.* This conservatism does not seem to be "true" conservatism, such as might be expressed by some eighteenth-century philosophers or by many present-day advocates of a laissez-faire economy. Rather, it masks a readiness to employ force in order to attain political and economic goals. In extreme cases, the highly

ethnocentric person may make patriotic speeches, but act as an antidemocratic agitator in attempting to realize his political aims.

We may summarize the picture of the ethnocentric, authoritarian person by quoting from the conclusions of one group of investigators [Allport and Kramer, 1946] doing work in this field:

Prejudiced responses are not dissociated from the total pattern of personal life. The person who views the world as a jungle, where the traveler must choose to become "the diner or else the dinner" . . . who is authoritarian in his outlook, who has no disposition to sympathize with the underdog, who rejects legislative attempts to protect minority groups, who feels no shame at his own prejudices—such a person includes prejudices in his style of life.

INFORMATION.   A person's beliefs, we have indicated, are based on what he regards as facts. To understand, then, how he acquires his beliefs and related attitudes, we should consider how he acquires his facts.

It goes almost without saying that the typical individual does not have available to him in his own experience all the facts he needs to form an attitude, opinion, or belief about the many problems he confronts. In trying to decide whether to vote for Republicans or Democrats, he seldom has seen the candidates in person or knows at firsthand how the candidates have behaved or performed in particular situations. In forming an opinion about Negroes, he seldom has had very much contact with Negroes. In all kinds of matters he lacks many of the facts that he really ought to have to be able to make his decision intelligently.

Not only is there a relative scarcity of facts, but those that are available are frequently misleading. A person who forms an opinion about Negroes may have picked up the "fact" that Negroes when given intelligence tests tend to score lower than whites. What he may not know is that such Negroes have had inferior schooling and poor socio-economic circumstances or that they were much less motivated in taking the tests—all very relevant facts in evaluating the statement that their scores were lower. In a good many circumstances, a little knowledge is a dangerous thing because it leads to beliefs that are not justified when all the facts are known. Yet people regularly are called upon to form opinions with only a few of all the relevant facts available. Consequently they acquire erroneous beliefs and opinions and, indirectly, prejudiced attitudes.

AUTHORITIES.   Since we have relatively few firsthand facts upon which to base our beliefs, we find ourselves trusting authorities instead of facts. Indeed, many so-called "facts" are not facts at all in terms of firsthand experience; they are merely statements of authorities about facts. There is nothing inherently wrong with our relying on authority, for we could hardly manage otherwise. We are forced to rely on the statements of experts, authorities, or "eye-witness" reports. Such specialization of knowledge has been essential in the development of our complex civilization.

Reliance on authority, however, has its disadvantages. For one thing, *it is difficult for even the most conscientious person to report facts objectively* all the time. The attitudes and beliefs of the authority often affect his perception of a fact and the way he reports it to us. Moreover, the authority may be ignorant of other facts and thus not present them to us, but without them we cannot form a correct opinion. Often authorities disagree among themselves on the facts, and we must choose between two conflicting authorities.

Adding to our difficulties in forming correct opinions is the tendency of authorities *to acquire prestige and status outside their special fields of competence.* People often regard the successful businessman as the person best qualified to manage in government; actually business and government require rather different knowledge and skills for their successful operation. The man who has acquired a great reputation as a physicist will be listened to when he pronounces on religion and politics. Yet he is usually no more qualified in these matters than many persons in other fields of endeavor. All kinds of authorities make this mistake—and it is an easy one to make—with the result that people unwittingly base their beliefs on statements made by persons who are not real authorities on the matter at hand.

Another obstacle to forming correct beliefs and opinions is the tendency of some authorities *deliberately to distort the facts* in order to have us believe what they want us to believe. The manufacturer may know very well all the facts about his product, but he has his advertiser present us with only certain facts that lead us to form attitudes favorable to his product. The political leader may be intimately aware of corruption among some of his party's members, but he tells only the "good" facts about his administration in order to instill in us a favorable opinion that will reelect him next time. In this society, the deliberate selection and distortion of facts is practiced in almost every aspect of life as a means of encouraging erroneous beliefs that are advantageous to the purveyor of the facts.

PRIMARY GROUPS. Sociologists often use the term *primary groups* to identify those small-sized groups with whom we have many frequent and informal contacts, such as family, friends, and associates. They are primary in the sense that they often have an important effect on our attitudes and beliefs. It usually is through these primary groups that cultural factors and authorities shape our view of the world about us.

Studies of American voting behavior have documented the influence of an individual's family, friends, and associates upon his political attitudes and actions. The influence seems to stem partly from the fact that a sizable proportion of the American electorate is relatively unconcerned with politics and election campaigns, even during presidential elections. They often do not bother to read newspaper and magazine articles dealing with the issues and the candidates, nor do they want to listen to political speeches on radio or television. Nevertheless, these people do acquire some information about the campaign in informal conversations with friends and associates.

An intensive survey [Lazarsfeld et al., 1944] of political opinions in Erie County, Ohio, during the 1940 presidential election showed that there are politically active and interested people in every social stratum. These people follow the campaign rather avidly, absorb political information from the mass media, and then transmit the information to their friends, neighbors, and coworkers in the course of informal discussions with them. Since these people are so important in shaping the political beliefs of others, particularly if the others are relatively indifferent, neutral, or undecided (these three political characteristics usually go together), the investigators say they function as "opinion leaders."

These informal primary groups do more than serve as a medium for transmitting information. As we saw in the last chapter, they can influence the opinions of the group members. Naturally, this is also true for political attitudes and opinions. A study [Kitt and Gleicher, 1950] of the voting process, which was conducted in Elmira, New York, during the 1948 national election, is described below:

In August before the election, citizens of Elmira were asked, among other things, how each of their three closest friends would vote. Most of the people who could identify their friends' opinions reported that their friends were in agreement in preferring one or the other of the candidates. When asked their own opinion, they tended to support the candidate their friends preferred. Thus, "more than 90 per cent of the respondents with three Republican friends show some degree of Republican vote inclination themselves." This figure declined to only 68 per cent Republican for those people who said one of their three closest friends was a Democrat. Similar tendencies in favor of the Democrats were obtained among those people whose friends preferred the Democratic candidate.

Later on in the campaign, some of the people were interviewed to see whether their opinions had changed. In some cases, of course, they had. In the majority of these cases, the shifts were in the direction of increasing agreement among members of the friendship group. The findings are summarized in Table 17.3.

TABLE 17.3. August to October shifters in Elmira, New York, during the 1948 election.

Political inclination of three closest friends in August	Shifted toward Republicans by October, per cent	Shifted toward Democrats by October, per cent
RRR	56	44
RRD } DDR }	49	51
DDD	39	61

Attitude change and propaganda

Now let us consider the question of attitude changes and how they are brought about through education and propaganda. We shall first discuss some of the factors which make attitudes resistant to change—factors in the self-preservation of attitudes. After that we can survey the psychological aspects of deliberate attempts to change attitudes through education, propaganda, and advertising.

PRESERVATION OF ATTITUDES. We might expect that as a person's culture changes, as his personality matures, and as he becomes better informed, his attitudes and beliefs would change. They do. On the other hand, they do not change so rapidly as one might expect, because they have a way of resisting change and preserving themselves once they have been well formed. There are three principal reasons for the self-preservation of attitudes: (1) selective interpretation, (2) avoidance of information that might change attitudes and beliefs, and (3) social pressures for the preservation of attitudes.

Selective interpretation. Attitudes and beliefs tend to be preserved because they alter the perception of new experiences; they emphasize those facts that fit in with existing attitudes and beliefs and deemphasize those that do not. If I think that Negroes are dirty people and I see a Negro coming home from work in his work clothes, I may notice immediately the fact that his clothes are soiled. A white man in exactly the same state may not be noticed at all, or if so, he may be perceived as a person coming home from a hard day's work. If an individual is strongly opposed to government spending and sees the newspaper heading, "Congress appropriates 20 billion dollars for Armed Forces," he may perceive the 20 billion dollars as an instance of big government spending, but ignore or forget that it is for the defense of the country. If, on the other hand, a person is strongly concerned about adequate defense of the United States, he may perceive this headline as an instance of Congress providing for our defense, but take no note of the amount of money involved. Thus, of the facts presented, a person tends to perceive selectively those which fit in with or are relevant to his attitudes and beliefs and to pay little attention to other facts. In this way, has attitudes and beliefs are reinforced and strengthened, rather than changed, by his perceptions.

This concept can be understood readily in terms of the categorization process described in the first part of this chapter. A person with anti-Negro attitudes not only associates Negroes with threats and unpleasant events, but also attributes unfavorable qualities to the class of people termed "Negroes." This category has "bad" qualities for him. Seeing a person who belongs to this category, he infers that the person has the unfavorable characteristics which he thinks are generally possessed by other members of that class. So the soiled work clothes are interpreted as meaning "Negroes are dirty." There is a different interpretation of the white worker's soiled clothes. "Dirty" and other similar negative traits for many people may not be part of the category "white." Thus, when the worker is assigned to this latter class of people the state of his clothes is interpreted in a different way.

Similarly, the newspaper headline concerning government spending is interpreted in a manner consistent with the individual's category of "government." If this category includes the quality "too big," the headline is seen as meaning, Here is another example of big government.

Most social situations are relatively ambiguous; frequently it is possible to interpret them in a wide variety of ways. This ambiguity increases the likelihood that an attitude or belief will persist, since it enables the individual to interpret the situation (or whatever the stimulus appropriate to the attitude happens to be) in a manner consistent with his attitude. Interpreting it in this way, he perceives the situation as supporting his views.

Avoidance of information. For one reason or another, people often are so reluctant to change their attitudes and beliefs that they try to avoid information that is inconsistent with these attitudes and beliefs. Such information appears to make them too uncomfortable. In any case, there are plenty of illustrations in everyday life of this widespread tendency to withdraw from everything that conflicts with what one already believes: The person who is a confirmed liberal refuses to read conservative magazines or newspapers. The person who is prejudiced against Jews has nothing to do with them, and thus never gives himself a chance to acquire facts about them that might alter his prejudice. The person who dislikes the views of the Hearst press, or Westbrook Pegler, or the *Reader's Digest*,

or Walter Winchell refuses to read them or listen to them. Thus he avoids coming into contact with attitudes and beliefs that conflict with his own. On the other hand, he exposes himself only to viewpoints that agree with his own, and thus further strengthens the attitudes and beliefs that he already holds.

In the cases we have just mentioned the person has the opportunity to avoid physically the information that might disturb him. The same resistance, however, is also encountered even when the individual is a member of a "captive audience" and has to listen to or read material opposed to his opinions.

This point was dramatically illustrated in the following experiment [Levine and Murphy, 1943]:

The experiment was conducted with college students. Some of the students were favorable to communist ideas, some were not. All listened to the reading of some passages, part of which were favorable to communism and part of which were not. Later the students were tested to determine how much they had learned from the passages. The students who were favorable to communism had learned much more of the material that was favorable to their point of view than of the material which was not. On the other hand, the students who were opposed to communism had learned better the passages that supported their opinion.

This experiment demonstrates how people can resist disturbing information even though they are forced to come into contact with it. Paraphrasing an old saying, we might conclude, You can lead a person to information, but you can't make him learn it. If this information is opposed to his attitudes or beliefs he will learn it much more slowly than he will material that is congenial to his attitudes.

Social support. Still another powerful influence for preserving attitudes and beliefs is the *social approval of associates*. As we have already pointed out, an individual tends to share his attitudes and beliefs with the members of his particular group or culture. The need for social approval is ordinarily a fairly strong motivation (page 512). So long as a person's attitudes agree with those of his associates he will tend to secure their approval. On the other hand, if he expresses attitudes and beliefs contrary to theirs, he incurs their displeasure and disapproval. Thus, he punishes himself and thwarts his desire to be approved. Consequently, he consciously or unconsciously wants to believe the same things his friends do in order to have their approval. Since he already tends to have their attitudes and beliefs by virtue of having common cultural influences, the need for social approval lends additional support to his attitudes and makes it much more difficult for him to change them.

PROPAGANDA. This resistance to change, nevertheless, does not wholly prevent attitudes and beliefs from being changed by the impact of daily events and by a constant bombardment of propaganda. Indeed, propaganda—now a familiar household word—is the deliberate attempt to influence attitudes and beliefs. Since propaganda is so often used by dictators and others who have ulterior and socially questionable purposes, the term has come to have a rather odious connotation. In principle, however, propaganda is not necessarily either good or bad (see Figure 17.1). It can be used to correct attitudes and beliefs so that they are nearer to the "facts" just as well as it can be used to distort them so that they are further from the facts. Moreover, it is not possible to make any really clear-cut distinction between education and propaganda. In education, we try to emphasize the facts, but these facts nevertheless must always be interpreted. In interpreting them, the teacher has a chance to intrude his own biased attitudes and beliefs, with the result that education changes people's attitudes and beliefs. In practice, though, we regard education as a

FIGURE 17.1. Education or propaganda? A cartoon appearing in a daily newspaper designed to build a favorable attitude toward increasing teachers' salaries [Walt Partymiller; *Gazette and Daily*, York, Pa.]

legitimate attempt to change attitudes and beliefs, as well as to inculcate knowledge, in the direction of the facts, whereas propaganda typically is designed to change them in the direction favorable to the purposes of the propagandist whether these are or are not in accord with the facts (see Figure 17.2).

Many different devices are used by propagandists to influence attitudes and beliefs. We shall discuss only a few of these techniques under the following headings: (1) loaded words, (2) suggestion, and (3) needs.

Loaded words. In Chapter 9 we saw that words serve as symbols to represent objects and experiences. Since we experience directly few of the facts necessary to form attitudes and beliefs, most of our information about the world is conveyed through words chosen by someone else to symbolize events. The chooser of words—the advertiser, newspaper reporter, magazine writer, radio commentator, politician—has a very rich language to employ, one which gives him a great deal of latitude in how he may describe a fact or idea to us. There are a

FIGURE 17.2. An example of propaganda. Stalingrad workmen stand before a display of posters urging more production and projecting advances in such fields as coal, steel, and oil during the current seven-year plan [David Bird].

multitude of relatively neutral words that accurately describe facts without evoking attitudes one way or another. There are also many words that, through previous attitude formation, can be expected to evoke about the same attitude in most of the people who hear them.

These loaded words are the stock in trade of the propagandist. If he wishes to evoke an unfavorable attitude, he may use such words as "czarism," "dictatorship," "regimentation," "agitator," and "brain trust," to which the overwhelming majority of Americans react with strongly negative attitudes. If the propagandist wishes to create a favorable attitude, describing exactly the same set of events, he may use such words as "democracy," "freedom," "regulation," "taxpayer," and "advisers," all of which are regarded favorably by the great majority of the people.

You are probably familiar with such loaded words in the newspapers, magazines, and broadcasts to which you regularly attend. If you happen to agree with the point of view being expressed, you probably do not notice the loaded words and you may, indeed, think of them as factually accurate, but if you disagree with the point of view, you are more likely to notice the loaded words as propaganda or distortion of the truth. The person who has no strong attitudes or beliefs on the subject can have his attitudes influenced very easily by the loaded words he reads or listens to. Let us give one example from a rather old, but careful psychological study [Sargent, 1939]:

The investigator selected 40 terms from the news column of the *Chicago Tribune*, 20 of which were used by the newspaper in reporting policies it did not support and 20 of which were used in connection with events or policies it did support. To these 40 terms, the

CHAPTER SEVENTEEN

investigator added 10 neutral terms. He presented these terms in a mixed order to several groups of people, including parent-teachers, college students, high school alumni, laborers, and white-collar workers. He asked each person to indicate whether he liked, disliked, or had no feeling about the word. From the results each word could be assigned a score representing the "feeling tone" for the word; -100 was extremely unfavorable, and $+100$ extremely favorable. Here are some of the feeling-tone values he obtained in this study:

Czarism	-84	Cooperation	$+95$
Dictatorship	-84	Freedom	$+92$
Domination	-79	Reemployment	$+88$

There was no question but that the *Chicago Tribune* was successfully choosing words that evoked the strongly unfavorable or favorable attitudes it wished to evoke in support of its own views.

In a follow-up study, the investigator chose 12 loaded terms from the *Chicago Tribune* and 12 terms from the *New York Times* used in reporting exactly the same events in the two newspapers. As before, he determined feeling-tone values for these words. In Table 17.4 are the feeling-tone values for pairs of words used in describing the same events. Again it was clear that the same news was being slanted one way by one newspaper and another way by the other newspaper. Thus loaded words were being used to create the desired attitudes toward the events being reported.

Suggestion. Psychologists define *suggestion* as the *uncritical acceptance of a statement.* This is to say that a person may accept a belief, form an attitude, or be incited to action merely by accepting what someone else says and without requiring facts or other proof. The skilled advertiser, propagandist, and political leader know this and employ it to their advantage in changing beliefs and attitudes. They know rather well, moreover, under what circumstances suggestion is likely to work.

One of these is to make use of *prestige.*

If an advertiser wishes to sell a certain brand of cigarettes, he tries to use the fact that some famous person smokes these cigarettes. Similarly, politicians make liberal use of the names of George Washington, Abraham Lincoln, and other respected leaders to attempt to gain acceptance of their own ideas. If you watch television for just a few hours or motor down nearly any highway in the United States looking at billboards, you will see that prestige is used in many instances to influence people to buy some product, to vote a political ticket, or to alter their attitudes and behavior in other ways.

To a certain extent, prestige suggestion is merely an instance of our reliance on authorities for the facts behind our beliefs. Since the line between facts and beliefs is often a hazy one, it is natural that we sometimes accept a belief uncritically simply because we are forced to rely on authorities. To a certain extent, prestige suggestion also involves identification with some leader or idol. The girl who would like to be beautiful may have Marlene Grable as her model of beauty, and if Marlene uses Beautiface Cold Cream, the girl is likely to use it too as her way of aspiring to the beauty of the model. Prestige suggestion also plays on already existing attitudes and uses them to form new attitudes. If people have a generally un-

TABLE 17.4. Feeling-tone values for terms used by the *Chicago Tribune* and the *New York Times* in describing the same events [Sargent, 1939].

Chicago Tribune		New York Times	
Term	**Value**	**Term**	**Value**
Radical	-53	Progressive	$+92$
Regimentation	-53	Regulation	$+32$
Government witch-hunting	-38	Senate investigation	$+57$
The dole	-35	Home relief	$+27$
Alien	-35	Foreign	0

favorable attitude toward Communists, the suggestion may be made that such and such a political belief is "communistic" or endorsed by the Communist press. This is a way of taking an existing attitude and turning it toward another—often innocent—victim. Much of the name calling or "smearing" that we see in the political arena deliberately or unconsciously makes use of such suggestion.

Another important aspect of prestige suggestion, however, is that it *alters a person's perception of an object or situation.* When a prestige suggestion is attached to a thing, he views it in a new light. The following study [Asch et al., 1940] illustrates this point:

Students were asked to rank such professions as business, dentistry, journalism, medicine, and politics according to (1) the amount of intelligence they thought the profession required and (2) the social usefulness of the profession. Some students did this without being given any suggestion. Other groups of students were given suggestions by being told that another group of students had, say, ranked politics highest (or lowest). These suggestions were rather effective. The group that was told that politics had been ranked low by others also ranked it low, and those who were told that others had ranked it high also ranked it high. When these groups were later asked specifically what politicians they had in mind when making their rankings, the group ranking politics low said they had in mind politicians such as "Tammany Hall politicians" and the "usual neighborhood politicians." Those ranking politics high had in mind national politics and gave such examples as Roosevelt, Hull, Stimson, Lehman, La Guardia. Thus the effect of the suggestion was to get the students to think of the better or poorer examples of politicians and to express their attitudes accordingly.

"Everybody's doing it," or "More people smoke Nocoff cigarettes than any other cigarette" are examples of *social* suggestion, another kind of suggestion that is often rather effective. It appeals to the general tendency to conform and also to a person's lack of confidence in his own judgment. In many circumstances, we find ourselves uncertain about what we think or should think, and thus we are inclined to go along with the crowd or accept almost any other suggestion made by our peers. Our uncertainty may be due to inexperience or merely to our having no prior attitudes and beliefs. On the other hand, it may be due to the *ambiguity* of the objects or situations to which we are to react. As we have seen before, when there are a great many possible interpretations of a situation, the individual frequently adopts the same way of looking at it that others around him have adopted, particularly when they are well agreed or when they are attractive to him.

NEEDS. Perhaps it goes without saying that suggestion, as well as other methods of altering attitudes and beliefs, must fit in with a person's needs. The reader will remember that attitudes involve relationships between the category into which the object of an attitude is placed and the individual's goals or values. Thus things we regard favorably are related to pleasant events or to attaining some positive goal, and things we regard unfavorably are associated with threats and unpleasant events. It follows from this that to develop or change an attitude a category of objects or issues must be associated with an individual's goals or values. If necessary, such goals and values may even be created so that they can be related to the attitude category.

Much of today's advertising attempts to establish such relationships. By associating a particular brand of cold cream with the Hollywood beauty, Marlene Grable, the advertiser in essence tells his audience that the use of this cold cream may lead (i.e., be related) to the goal of becoming like this actress. A girl who develops a positive attitude toward the cold cream because of the advertisement sees some connection between this beauty aid and her goals (either of improving her looks or of being like Marlene Grable). Obviously, there would be little use in advertising beauty aids in a society of women who did not value their looks. Madison Avenue would first have to create a need in these women for beauty enhancement before it could sell them the product as a means of satisfying the need.

Need arousal. For this reason propagandists often go to some trouble to *create* needs. Advertisers also try to do this in order to enlarge the market for their products. To sell washing machines, they may emphasize how much washday drudgery is saved by the washing machine, then go on to emphasize the advantages of their particular washing machine. Even in labor-management relations, where there seems to be no need or problem, management may find it necessary to foment labor troubles, to fabricate stories of the dangers of labor uprising, etc., in order to get people to favor legislation designed to restrict labor.

Several recent psychological experiments illustrate the widespread implications of this approach to attitude change. Two such investigations demonstrate that it is possible to alter attitudes toward an issue by changing the perceived relationships between the issue and the audience's goals and values.

In one of these studies [Carlson, 1956], the experimenter changed college students' attitudes toward racially desegregated housing. He did this by convincing them that such housing would facilitate the attainment of certain goals (such as improving American prestige in the eyes of other nations) and would not interfere with the attainment of other goals (for example, would not necessarily lower property values).

In a later experiment [Di Vesta and Merwin, 1960] students who were high in achievement motivation were given talks on "teaching as a career." A speech that highlighted the connection between teaching and the satisfaction of achievement needs influenced their attitudes more than other speeches that did not play up this connection, even

though all talks contained favorable assertions about teaching. In other words, the speech that changed attitudes toward teaching most was one that made the audience aware of the relationship between this category and their own needs.

Another experiment [Weiss and Fine, 1958] shows that the same principle can be applied to negative goals as well as to positive ones:

One group of subjects was exposed to a humiliating and insulting experience designed to arouse their hostility, while another group was given a nonfrustrating and satisfying experience. Half of each of these groups then read a message urging harshly punitive treatment of juvenile delinquents; the other halves of the two groups read a communication stating that America should be very lenient in dealing with her allies. The study showed that the angered people were more likely than the nonangered subjects to accept the idea of treating delinquents harshly. On the other hand, they were somewhat less likely to be convinced that the United States should be lenient toward her allies. The audience apparently most readily adopted the opinions congenial to its emotional state, and at the same time tended to resist communications urging behavior inconsistent with its needs.

Defensive avoidance. From the point illustrated here it is only a short step to the "common-sense" notion frequently used in safety campaigns. This is the idea that you can get people to obey safety instructions by frightening them about the dangers of not doing so. It is behind such slogans as "Speed kills" or the din of statistics we hear daily on radio and TV about the number of traffic fatalities. It assumes that frightened people are more likely to heed appeals to drive safely. Unfortunately, the experimental evidence on this point is not encouraging. Indeed, the "scare 'em" approach may actually block, rather than aid, the acceptance of the appeal, as the following study [Janis and Feshbach, 1953] demonstrates:

High school students listened to lectures on dental hygiene under one of three conditions: strong fear arousal, moderate fear arousal, or minimal fear arousal. Under the strong-fear condition, subjects were made very anxious about the state of their mouths, while under the minimal-fear conditions no attempt was made to create this anxiety. In all conditions, the students were urged to adopt certain dental practices. The results, however, demonstrated that the higher the level of fear arousal the *less* likely the students were to accept the communicator's point of view.

The explanation for the results of this experiment and others that show about the same thing seems to be that fear arousal produces a "defensive-avoidance" reaction. To defend itself against the threat created by the message, the audience avoids accepting the communicator's conclusions. It is as if the members of the audience believed other people would get hurt or die, but not they.

Examples of defensive avoidance can be found in everyday life. There is the story of the cigarette smoker who said he was so disturbed by the newspaper articles on how smoking produced lung cancer that he was going to stop reading newspapers. This chap was not only avoiding the disturbing information, he was also maintaining that other people might come down with lung cancer, but not he.

This is not to say, of course, that people will always avoid accepting fear-arousing messages. Under some conditions they may not resist the communicator's conclusions even though he creates anxiety in them. Whether they do or not undoubtedly depends on their perceived probability of being hurt. Relatively few people, for example, actually come down with lung cancer, and comparatively few are hurt or killed in automobile accidents. So it is possible for the person to tell himself that the warnings he hears do not really apply to him. If, on the other hand, he knows or feels that he is in real danger, he is not so likely to shrug off

or resist the warnings. Tell a seasoned Arctic explorer that he must have the proper boots or he will be certain to develop frostbite, and he very likely will accept, rather than avoid, the message.

The measurement of attitudes and opinions

Since attitudes, opinions, and beliefs determine so greatly how individuals will react to social situations, it is not strange that there should be considerable interest in the precise measurement of attitudes. Leaders in government and public life would like to know people's attitudes and beliefs. Those who conduct business affairs must similarly know customers' attitudes and beliefs. Then, too, leaders and research workers in the field of education, knowing that much of education is a matter of affecting attitudes as well as knowledge, want to know the effects of various educational practices and environments on attitudes and beliefs.

ATTITUDE SCALES. The educator and research worker have relatively favorable conditions for investigating attitudes, because they usually have access to groups of students who can be studied rather intensively. Their methods, therefore, have been more accurate and detailed than those which, for practical reasons, have been developed for use in the political and commercial fields. Among the methods employed by educators and research workers are some that provide relatively accurate scales for the measurement of attitudes. We shall describe two.

Thurstone. One method of measuring attitudes was devised by L. L. Thurstone [Thurstone and Chave, 1929]. It involves the following steps: First some issue toward which attitudes might be measured must be defined. War is an example of such an issue. Once the issue has been defined, the next step is to collect as many statements as possible that might be relevant to the issue. In order to be useful in measurement, such statements must be simple and unambiguous, and they must distinguish between people holding different attitudes. Such statements as, "When war is declared, we must enlist," or "Wars are justifiable only when waged in defense of weaker nations," are specific enough and clear enough to evoke approval or disapproval and thus to determine attitudes toward different aspects of war.

After statements have been collected that are thought to bear on the issue, the next step is to present them to a large number of judges, preferably a hundred or more. Each judge is asked to sort these statements into 11 piles, representing a scale from an extremely favorable attitude toward the issue to an extremely unfavorable attitude toward it. Thus *scale values* for the different statements are established. That is to say, each statement is assigned a number that indicates to what degree approval or disapproval of the statement represents an attitude that is favorable or unfavorable to the object or issue. After all the judging is done, a limited number of statements, say, 20 are selected that (1) show reasonably good agreement among judges, and (2) have scale values that spread out along the continuum from 1 to 11 (see Table 17.5).

Once constructed, the attitude scale may be administered to any group we desire. The person taking it is instructed to check the statements with which he agrees. One way of scoring the results is to average the scale values of the items checked by an individual. In this way, we get a numerical measure of the person's attitudes and beliefs concerning the issue in question.

Likert scale. There are several other methods of constructing attitude scales. All involve starting with a relatively large number of statements and then selecting from them the statements that prove to be the most reliable indicators of a given attitude. We shall describe one such method developed by Likert [1932].

A series of statements are presented to subjects with the instruction to indicate their reaction to each in one of the following

TABLE 17.5. Some illustrative items from a scale for measuring attitudes toward war. Using a scale from 1 to 11, several judges rate each item for the degree to which it indicates an attitude toward or against a course of action. The median rating (see page 412) of the judges is the scale value assigned to the item [Droba, 1930].

Scale value	Item
1.3	1. A country cannot amount to much without a national honor, and war is the only means of preserving it.
2.5	2. When war is declared, we must enlist.
5.2	3. Wars are justifiable only when waged in defense of weaker nations.
5.4	4. Peace and war are both essential to progress.
5.6	5. The most that we can hope to accomplish is the partial elimination of war.
8.4	6. The disrespect for human life and rights involved in a war is a cause of crime waves.
10.6	7. All nations should disarm immediately.

ways: strongly approve, approve, undecided, disapprove, or strongly disapprove. Their responses are then analyzed to see how they correlate with each other (see Chapter 13). Items that correlate highly with each other— for example, when an individual strongly approves one statement and also strongly approves another, or vice versa—are considered to be relevant to the attitude being considered. When items do not correlate with other items, they are rejected as not being relevant to the attitude scale. In this way, two things are accomplished: (1) poor statements are discarded, and (2) the statements left in the test involve certain clusters of items.

We can illustrate these steps by describing Likert's construction of an attitude scale on foreign wars. Starting with a large number of items and giving them to a sample population, he discarded many that did not correlate with the total score. When his analysis was finished, he found that he had two clusters of items; one cluster seemed to concern problems of imperialism in foreign affairs and the other internationalism in such affairs. Thus he obtained a scale that could be broken down into two sets of attitudes toward foreign affairs, those toward *imperialism* and those toward *internationalism*.

To consider the construction of attitude scales in more detail is beyond the scope of this book. We have presented two of the more typical, widely used methods, but there are many variations on these methods and other scaling techniques. The end result of any method is to obtain a "test" which is a reasonably reliable and valid measure (see Chapter 13) of some attitude or attitudes. Once such a scale has been developed, it can then be used for a variety of purposes. Most of the facts that were presented in the first two sections of this chapter concerning the effect on attitudes of culture, socioeconomic status, family, and education were obtained by using attitude scales. Many of the conclusions drawn about prejudice also were based on the use of such scales.

PUBLIC OPINION AND MARKET RESEARCH. Although relatively few people, other than students of psychology, have heard of attitude scales, most citizens of the United States are now familiar with another kind of attitude measurement, the public-opinion poll. For them such a poll is an attempt to forecast the outcome of political elections. These forecasts, they have learned, may be fairly accurate when the election is not too close. In a close election, however, the polls may be wrong. Since polls are sometimes wrong or do not give good predictions, many people are inclined not to trust them.

Unfortunately, the public's concept of the public-opinion poll is greatly oversimplified. The most notable polling "failure," the 1948 forecast that the Republican presidential candidate, Thomas E. Dewey, would be elected, was not entirely due to inherent shortcomings of the polling method. Some of the blame can be attributed to inadequacies in the particular procedures employed by the commercial polling agencies [Mosteller et al., 1949]. Over the years, as several critics have pointed out, these procedures have rather consistently overestimated the Republican vote. The errors in procedure could have been corrected, but only at an increased financial expense to the agencies.

In defense of the pollsters, however, the 1948 election was also an extraordinary one. In the first place, an unusually large number of people did not make up their minds about how they would vote until just before the election. In contrast to previous or subsequent elections, most of these people finally voted for the Democratic candidate. Secondly, to add to the pollsters' problems, a surprisingly large proportion of voters changed their voting intentions just before the election, particularly in the farm states. In the elections both prior to and since 1948, neither of these things has happened on such a scale. In the meantime, commercial polling agencies have also improved their procedures somewhat. They are now rarely more than a few percentage points off in forecasting the winning candidates' margin of victory in a national election. Consequently, politicians are making increasing use of public-opinion surveys, not only to determine their chances of being elected, but also to guide their campaign strategy.

Predicting elections is only one—and probably the most difficult—of the uses of a public-opinion poll. It is being used regularly to assess attitudes on many problems, such as acreage allotments for farmers, cost of living, programs of road building, the United Nations, buying of United States government bonds, profits of businessmen, inflation and deflation, unemployment, and a host of other problems of concern to people [Likert, 1947]. Polls are being conducted both by agencies of the government and by groups of psychologists such as the National Opinion Research Center, American Institute of Public Opinion, and the University of Michigan Survey Research Center. These serve various business groups, as well as advertising and manufacturing groups, and in addition conduct research of their own.

Questions. Unlike attitude scales, polls must be made with people who represent a fair sample of some particular group, such as those who vote in a particular district, those who farm, those who buy Mouthwash A, or those who smoke. Such people cannot easily be induced to sit down and fill out any complicated attitude scale. They must be interviewed in a face-to-face situation, their interest and cooperation must be secured without imposing too much on their time or their privacy, and they must be asked questions which are rather simple and quickly covered.

To meet these limitations of the poll, it is customary to keep the interview brief and to have each question cover some particular attitude. Thus, in a public-opinion poll, a single question must serve as a measure of an attitude, whereas many statements can be used in the attitude scale. Although more than one question may be used in a poll, the number of questions or items must be greatly restricted. For this reason, the phrasing of a question is a matter of major importance and makes a great difference in the outcome of the poll (see Figure 17.3).

In general, questions developed for use in polls are of two types: the *fixed-alternative question* and the *open-end question*. The first type of question gives the respondent a fixed number of alternatives. For example, "Would you like to see more control over labor unions, less control, or about as much as there is now?" The open-end question allows the respondent to phrase his own answer in his own words. As you can readily imagine, it is sometimes difficult to decide what the answers to open-end questions mean. In practice, the interviewer has a number of possible alternatives to the question already coded, and after listening to the respondent, he simply checks one of the possibilities. These alternatives have usually been worked out by having a trial run on a small group of subjects, and then classifying their answers into some limited number of categories.

It might seem that the fixed-alternative question is preferable to the open-end question. Certainly it is simpler to use in an interview situation, and interviewers need very little training to be able to present it and to record the answers. One difficulty with this type of question, however, is that it greatly restricts the respondent's answer, often forcing him to answer in a way that does not reflect his true opinion. In the example above about control of labor, the respondent might think that in some respects labor ought to be more controlled and in others less so. Such an attitude is not the same as saying that control ought to remain pretty much as it is, yet he has no way of expressing his real attitude. Another difficulty with the fixed-alternative question is that minor differences in wording can greatly affect the result, often leading to complete misinterpretations of respondents' attitudes.

After the Second World War two leading polling agencies asked the following questions at about the same time:

"After the war would you like to see the United States join some kind of world organization, or would you like to see us stay out?" (National Opinion Research Center, January, 1945.)

"Do you think that the United States should join a world organization with police power to maintain world peace?" (American Institute of Public Opinion, April, 1945.)

There is no reason to believe that sentiment changed drastically between January and April, 1945, or that the populations sampled had very different views. However, 64 per cent said "yes" to the first question

FIGURE 17.3. Steps in public-opinion polling [U.S. Bureau of the Census; American Institute of Public Opinion].

and 81 per cent to the second question, while 26 per cent said "no" to the first and 11 per cent said "no" to the second. It is quite likely that the phrase "to maintain world peace" greatly increased the affirmative answers, because the pollsters know that inserting any phrase which by itself is generally approved increases the number of approvals of the question as a whole.

Because of the importance of wording, the pollsters do a great deal of research to arrive at their questions. Often they run a preliminary poll on small groups in which they use several different phrasings of a question; they then study the results to see what difference the phrasing makes. From such preliminary studies, they attempt to frame the alternatives that are most likely to give people a chance to express their attitudes. They try to avoid phrasings that are likely to give a spuriously high or spuriously low percentage of any particular answer. They must also try, in so far as time permits, to use different questions either in the same poll or in succeeding polls to be able to interpret the results that they obtain.

Sampling. Once a public-opinion poll has been prepared, the next question concerns the people to whom it should be given. In most polling, we should like to characterize the attitudes of some particular population. Sometimes this population is all adults in the United States. More often, however, we are interested in some restricted population. Even in political elections we need to know results district by district, because the outcome of elections is determined not by the national result, but rather by congressional districts, electoral districts, and states. In other instances, the population may be farmers, retail-store owners, taxpayers, schoolteachers, etc.

Whatever the population, it is almost always impractical to poll the whole group, simply because the group is too large. We are therefore faced with the problem of sampling some individuals from the total population. Of course, in the end, we wish to draw conclusions about the whole population from the relatively small sample. Statisticians, fortunately, have worked out rather dependable rules for inferring from a sample to a population. Just how accurate such inference is depends upon a number of factors. In general, though, it is possible to use a sample of several hundred cases and predict with relative accuracy what the response of the whole population might be. To do this the sample must be so drawn that it is truly representative of the population. Practical people, ignorant of statistical methods, often wonder how one can draw conclusions about a whole population from a small sample. Actually, there is no difficulty at all as long as the sample is truly representative. It is this matter of representative sampling, on which so much stands or falls, that is the major problem of the pollsters.

There are, in general, two ways of constructing samples so that they are reasonably representative of the population: (1) probability sampling and (2) quota sampling.

In *probability sampling,* each individual in the population has a known probability of being included in the sample. As a result, the probable degree of error in generalizing the findings from the sample to the population can be computed statistically.

To illustrate this approach, let us suppose that some organization wanted to survey opinions among all the property owners in a large community. This is the population to which they want to generalize the sample's findings and the sample must be representative of this population. The pollster, then, might go to the tax office, secure complete lists of those who own property, arrange the names randomly, and pick every *n*th name (every tenth, one-hundredth, one-thousandth, etc.) from the list. In this way, each property owner, has a one-in-*n* chance of being included in the sample.

The method of *sampling from lists* is widely used when the target population has been recorded on a list. The great danger in this method is that the list may not represent the population. This was the case in the famed *Literary Digest* poll that so badly predicted the election results in 1936 [Newcomb, 1950]. That poll made use of telephone lists, and its results probably represented fairly well how telephone subscribers

were going to vote. The trouble was that slightly over half the voters in the United States at that time were telephone subscribers. These were the economically favored members of the population, who had different political attitudes from the rest of the voters. It usually happens that lists of property owners, telephone subscribers, utility users, etc., represent the higher socioeconomic strata of society and cannot be taken as representative of the population as a whole.

Another major difficulty in sampling from lists, obviously, is that the population we are interested in may not be on a list. There is no list, for example, of every eligible voter in the United States, and it would be much too expensive to compile one. If the pollster wanted to forecast how the nation would vote in a presidential election he would have to adopt another procedure. Generally, he must do something else whenever there is no good list of the population of interest.

A frequent alternative is to sample from areas instead of population lists. The investigation of the 1948 presidential campaign in Elmira, New York, mentioned earlier, utilized the *area-sampling* procedure. The city was divided into a large number of smaller areas, such as city blocks. Each of these sampling units was then given a number at random. One number (area) in three was then selected for further study and a list of dwelling units in each area was prepared. Using this list, the research workers randomly selected a certain number of dwelling units (apartments or houses) to be visited within each of the areas.

In other studies, polling agencies may select addresses so that they are randomly divided among different geographical areas which represent various socioeconomic strata and other demographic factors in the same proportion that they exist in the population. The interviewers are then sent to specified addresses.

This area-sampling method assures about the most representative sample one can expect to get and therefore yields very accurate results. However, it is expensive because it means considerable travel for interviewers, who often must make many repeated calls before they find their respondents at home. The logic of the procedure demands that a person who has been randomly chosen to be included in the sample must be interviewed even if he is not at home when the first visit is made. People who are at home during the day or who are easily accessible are not necessarily similar in all respects to people who are away from home or who are less accessible to the interviewer. Omission of these not-at-home people introduces a bias into the sample so that it is no longer completely representative of the population [Hilgard and Payner, 1944].

The second of two general methods of sampling, *quota sampling,* is based on the assumption that a sample will be an accurate miniature of a larger population if important sociological groups are represented in the sample in the same proportion that they occur in the population. To achieve this type of representation the polling agency sets quotas for certain categories such as age, sex, socioeconomic status, and geographical region. Interviewers are then told how many interviews they must conduct with respondents in each category. The interviewers are left some discretion as to how they manage to fill their quota. By establishing quotas in this way, the agency hopes to obtain a fair cross section of the population. Interviewers, however, when given a choice, usually select the person who seems somewhat more cooperative or the house that seems somewhat better kept. Thus biases can creep into the sample. Wherever such biases have anything to do with attitudes, the quota-sampling method gives inaccurate results. This is one of the reasons why attempts to predict national elections encounter a certain amount of unknown error.

From this brief account of public-opinion polling, one can see that constructing and administering a poll is no simple matter. Considerable knowledge and experience with the measurement of attitudes, together with statistical skills, is required to design and carry out a poll. It is thus not advisable for the inexpert persons to try his hand at carrying out a poll. Under the supervision of well-trained persons, public-opinion polls can provide considerable information with relatively little error. In the hands of a novice, they are likely to give only misinformation.

Market research. Closely related to public-opinion polling is a specialized field that has grown greatly in the last 25 years—market research. The principal difference between the two is the kind of attitudes one is attempting to measure. In market research, *attitudes concerning specific products or the advertising of products* are measured rather than attitudes toward public issues. In addition, market research often *elicits specific information,* such as what brand of mouthwash a housewife last purchased, what advertising she has noticed recently, what magazines she reads regularly, or what radio programs she listens to. Such factual information, together with information about people's likes and dislikes of particular products, enables advertisers to devise more acceptable advertising. It also enables manufacturers to design products that will be more favorably received. Aside from these differences, however, the methods and the problems of market research are very much like those of public-opinion polling.

AUDIENCE MEASUREMENT. Advertisers, of course, are interested not only in what they advertise and how they advertise, but also in the medium through which they advertise—the newspaper, magazine, radio, and television. In fact, these media are wholly or partly financed by the proceeds from advertising. All parties concerned would like to know the extent of the audiences for their advertising. Hence, in recent years, attempts to measure the size, nature, and attitudes of audiences have increased considerably.

Many of the leading magazines, for example, continually conduct surveys to determine how many people are reading their magazines and what kind of people they are—their buying habits, their educational level, their hobbies, and their reading habits. In addition, they may find out just what parts of a magazine are read most often, what kinds of stories are most popular, and what advertising is most noticed, so that they may know better the effectiveness of advertising of different types placed in different positions in the magazine.

Radio and television stations have a somewhat different problem. They must first of all find out how many people and what kind of people are tuned in on them at different times of the day and for which types of programs. The most common method of doing this is to call houses by telephone (using the method of lists) and ask such questions as the following [Hooper, 1946]:

1. Were you listening to the radio (or watching television) just now?

2. To what program were you listening, please?

3. What station, please?

4. What is advertised?

5. How many men, women, and children in your home were actually listening?

From polls of this sort, one can derive a "Hooper rating," stating what percentage of homes have their sets tuned in to a particular station. Such ratings are quite important in the advertiser's decision whether he is reaching the size and kind of audience he wishes to reach with the program he is offering and the money he is paying for it.

Racial attitudes and conflicts

The word *race,* in ordinary usage, means *a group of human beings having common and distinctive innate physical characteristics.* It is a much-debated issue, with which we shall not deal here, whether there are any races at all and, if so, which ones and how many there are [Klineberg, 1954]. However, when we talk of racial conflict we shall refer to social conflict resulting from prejudice against any social group having some distinctive common characteristic, whether that common characteristic be race, religion, national origin, or something else. Most of the illustrations in this section will be drawn from anti-Negro prejudice in the United States, both because this is the kind of prejudice that is most intense in this country and because it has been best studied by psychologists and others. But the same principles which apply to conflict between Negroes and whites also apply to other "racial" conflicts.

ACQUIRING PREJUDICES. What is a prejudice? Earlier we defined it as an unfavorable attitude toward some person, living thing, or inanimate object. As we use it here, however, it refers to *a hostile attitude toward some social group.* Thus any attitude of hostility toward Negroes, Germans, politicians, Communists, or any other group is a prejudice. In other words, it does not matter whether the prejudice has some objective basis or not. If it is hostility toward a group, it is a prejudice.

Prejudices are attitudes, and just like any

other attitudes, they obey the principles of attitude formation and maintenance which were discussed earlier. In particular, *they are learned*. It is very important to ask how prejudices are learned, since one of the best ways of eradicating them is to prevent their being learned in the first place.

Logically, there are two possible ways in which a prejudice could be learned: (1) *from contact with the object of the prejudice* or (2) *from contact with others who have the prejudice*. Prejudices are, in fact, learned in both ways, but various studies indicate that *they are more commonly acquired by contact with people who have them*.

One study [Horowitz and Horowitz, 1938] of rural Tennessee children showed that their parents warned them to avoid Negro children and even objects which had been handled by Negro children, and that the parents sometimes punished their children severely for violating these warnings. A good many studies have shown that there is a high correlation between the attitudes of parents and those of their children, regardless of which attitudes are studied (although some attitudes show higher correlations than others) [Newcomb and Svehla, 1938].

Parents are not the only teachers of prejudice. Schoolmates, teachers, and general communication media like newspapers and television are also effective. In addition, most of the people we meet try to influence our attitudes. Hence we are continuously exposed to teachers of prejudice. If all these different sources repeat the same message, then it is no wonder that so many young children accept it.

A particularly dramatic demonstration of the fact that prejudice is usually learned from contact with the prejudiced rather than with the people against whom it is directed is the very strong anti-Communist prejudice now held by almost all Americans. Very few Americans have ever met a Communist. What they know about Communists they have learned from newspapers, TV, and other public information media. If it became desirable—as it was in the Second World War, when the Russians were our allies—to create a more favorable attitude toward Communists, the public information media would probably be used effectively for this end.

The first thing that a child learns about a prejudice is that the object group is "bad." Later he learns more specific things about the group.

One study showed, for example, that young Southern white children believed Negroes to be lower than whites in many traits, including the "trait" of religiousness [Blake and Dennis, 1943]. Older children showed a much more discriminating pattern of beliefs about Negroes; for example, they rated Negroes as more religious than whites.

Prejudice may grow out of personal experience with the group against which it is directed, but this source of prejudice is probably rare. In fact, direct contact with the group is sometimes a cure for prejudice.

The Army, for example, tried the experiment of creating mixed Negro and white units during the Second World War. Both before and after the whites saw service in such units, their attitudes toward Negroes were measured. In almost all cases the whites were less prejudiced after their experience in mixed units than they had been before. And the Negroes in mixed units, incidentally, proved to be quite effective in combat, unlike many Negroes in segregated units [Rose, 1946].

SUPPORTS FOR PREJUDICE. Once learned, prejudices are not allowed to die out through forgetting or disuse. Rather they continue to serve the *purpose of gratifying an individual's needs*. In addition, they so alter his perception and memory, as we indicated earlier, that his everyday experiences tend to support his prejudices. Consequently, between his needs and his perceptions, an individual usually maintains his prejudices at full strength.

Needs. Probably the need best served by prejudice is the need for *status*. A prejudice creates a social hierarchy in which the prejudiced person has a superior status. If one is prejudiced against Negroes, for example, he believes that Negroes are inferior to him and therefore that he is superior to them. Some people need to think well of themselves—to think themselves better than others (see Chapter 3). The poorest, least-educated, most unimportant white in a backwoods Southern town has the consolation of "knowing" that he is mentally, morally, and socially superior to most of the residents of his area.

Prejudice also serves the need to express *aggression*. Psychologists have good reason to believe, as we have pointed out in Chapters 4 and 5, that hostility (or aggression) usually originates in the frustration of needs. This notion is certainly consistent with ordinary experience, for we frequently see people irritated or angry because they have failed to get what they want or because something or somebody has obstructed their efforts.

Aggression resulting from frustration can often be simply vented at whatever is doing the frustrating. When a person of superior status or a situation beyond one's control does the frustrating, however, the aggression must be expressed in some other way. The consequence is *displaced aggression* (see Chapter 5).

In an experiment [Sears et al., 1940] in which psychologists deprived students for a prolonged period of sleep, food, cigarettes, and even permission to talk, one subject vented his aggression in hostile drawings. In other instances, the aggression may be expressed in prejudice against some "inferior" group that cannot retaliate. Such displaced aggression is illustrated by the lieutenant bawling out the sergeant, the sergeant working it out on the private, and the private kicking the dog. It is illustrated more scientifically in an experiment with boys at a summer camp who were frustrated by not being allowed to go to the movies. Before and after the frustration, their attitudes toward Mexicans and Japanese were measured, and these measurements showed that subjects were considerably more prejudiced after frustration than before [Miller and Bugelski, 1948].

Scapegoating. Such displaced aggression is particularly significant in racial conflict. In this case it is called *scapegoating*. The prejudiced person who suffers economic, social, or political frustrations may displace his aggression against some convenient object, and the most convenient object is likely to be the group against whom he already has a prejudice. This is particularly likely if he can so distort the facts that the group seems responsible for his frustrations. A most notable example of this sort of displacement is the German persecution of the Jews in the 1930s. Hitler was able to convince his followers (who were presumably anti-Semitic to begin with) that the Jews were responsible for most of Germany's economic and social woes. Thus he made Jews the scapegoats of displaced aggression.

Scapegoating, then, may be the displacement of hostility onto some minority group, but aggression that cannot be directed against the frustrator is not necessarily displaced onto a minority group. Many people do not exhibit the displaced aggression (prejudice) described above in boys in a summer camp. When that experiment was repeated in other populations, prejudice against minority groups did not always increase.

Some of the factors affecting the likelihood of scapegoating can be discussed here, although a full treatment of them is beyond our scope. One way of better understanding scapegoating is through the concept of *stimulus generalization* (see Chapter 7). A frustrator who arouses hostility in a person can be regarded as an original stimulus giving rise to the response of aggression. As we have seen in our discussion of stimulus generalization in conditioning experiments, once the organism has learned to make this response, then other stimuli can elicit it. The greater the similarity between these other stimuli and the original stimulus, the greater the likelihood they will produce the response. Thus, people similar to the original frustrator may also arouse hostility within the frustrated person.

This similarity need not be a physical one. Hostility may be generalized when there is little or no physical resemblance between the frustrator and the people it is turned toward. To the angered person, the similarity may be qualitative. For example, the only thing they may have in common is that he dislikes them both. Thus hostility can be generalized from the frustrator to another object because a dislike for both is the quality that makes them similar [Berkowitz and Holmes, 1959]. This analysis suggests that the summer-camp boys may have had some prior dislike for Mexicans and Japanese, and that the same result would not be obtained if subjects had no prior dislike for a particular group.

The main point in this analysis so far is that *hostility will be displaced from the frustrator to the person most similar to him when the frustrator is not available for direct attack* (for example, because of his absence). There is a somewhat different prediction to be made when the angered person is afraid to strike at the frustrator because the frustrator might retaliate. In this case the person may inhibit his aggression both toward the frustrator or toward other people very similar to him. Instead he will be most likely to attack others who appear to possess some intermediate degree of similarity to the frustrator.

The angered individual's personality traits may also affect the likelihood of his displacing his hostility onto minority groups. Our earlier discussion of the highly ethnocentric individual implied that this type of person has a readiness to displace aggression. It may be that the highly ethnocentric individual has learned to attack others who are relatively powerless, particularly minority groups, as a way of reducing aggressive

tensions within himself. Thus, the prejudice may be an outlet for pent-up aggression.

In one experiment among children prejudiced against Negroes, for example, those who were relatively free of repressed aggression learned much more easily not to be prejudiced. The only effect of educational procedures on those with aggressive personality patterns was to make them still more prejudiced, both against their teachers and against society in general [Mussen, 1950]. The value of education as a corrective for prejudiced attitudes is thus limited by the kind of person who is "educated."

Perception and judgment. Prejudice is supported not only by needs but also by *changes in perception and judgment.* We discussed this point above, but it should be reviewed again because it is germane to the preservation of prejudice. Prejudice alters perception so that we tend to see what we want to see or what we believe we are going to see. If we believe that Negroes are dirty and stupid, we take special note of instances of dirtiness or stupidity among Negroes while paying little attention to similar instances among whites or to outstanding examples of cleanliness or brilliance among Negroes. Indeed, with practice, we become quite skilled at perceiving only that which is consistent with our prejudices.

One experiment illustrates the way in which prejudice can distort the judgment and interpretation of situations [Cooper and Jahoda, 1947]. In this study, subjects were shown a series of cartoons involving a character dubbed Mr. Biggott. Subjects were asked to give their reactions to the cartoons. One subject, known to be prejudiced, interpreted the cartoon in Figure 17.4 as follows: If Mr. Biggott is only a sixth-generation American, he is a newcomer and is not entitled to put on airs.

Social handicaps. In the list of conditions that maintain prejudice, last but not least are the social effects of prejudice itself. To the extent that prejudice is permitted to operate in social affairs, to that extent it produces a world that is exactly what the preju-

MR. BIGGOTT

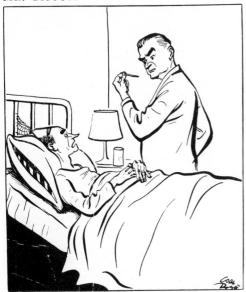

"In case I should need a transfusion, doctor, I want to make certain I don't get anything but blue, sixth-generation American blood!"

FIGURE 17.4. Examples of Mr. Biggott cartoons used in the study of prejudice [American Jewish Committee and Carl Rose].

MR. BIGGOTT

Mr. Biggott: "Was it necessary, Reverend, to emphasize the Lord's—er—Jewish background in your sermon?"

diced person expects it to be. People with anti-Negro prejudices, for example, believe that Negroes are less intelligent than whites. Believing that, they prevent Negroes from getting adequate schooling, library facilities, housing, and other cultural opportunities. The result, of course, is a social handicap for Negroes that prevents them from being as educated and as "intelligent" as whites. Thus the prejudice becomes "true." It creates the social conditions that justify the prejudice. This is obviously a vicious circle in which the effects of prejudice help to maintain the prejudice by providing an observable basis for it.

SOCIAL EFFECTS OF PREJUDICE. We have just noted one of the effects of prejudice—the creation of social conditions that confirm the prejudice. But let us look at the social consequences of prejudice in greater detail.

Perhaps the most significant effect of prejudice is that prejudiced people avoid those against whom they bear a prejudice. This fact applied on a scale affecting thousands or millions of people has a very simple result—*segregation*. In the Middle Ages, and also in Eastern Europe in recent times, Jews were required to live in ghettos. Nowadays we do not have so many ghettos, but we in America do have large areas in which only Negroes live and much larger ones where Negroes are not permitted to live. But segregation is not only a matter of where Negroes live. It also prohibits them from shopping in certain white stores, attending white places of entertainment, using white public facilities, including railroad cars and the front seats in buses, and, most important of all, from taking many jobs. Sometimes segregation is carried to ridiculous extremes. Upper-caste Hindus feel defiled if they eat

FIGURE 17.5. Teachers can combat prejudice by not teaching it and by ignoring racial differences [Hunter College Elementary School].

with low-caste Hindus. Probably the most concerted program of segregation of Negroes in the modern world is South Africa's program of almost complete segregation—*apartheid*.

Segregation with equal facilities is theoretically possible. The United States Supreme Court in 1896 therefore decided that separate, but equal, facilities were permissible. In practice, however, it does not work. Inevitably the segregated minority is forced to use inferior facilities under inconvenient, uncomfortable, or unsanitary conditions, because segregation permits majority groups to "take out" their prejudices on the minority. Becoming convinced of this fact, the Supreme Court finally ruled in 1954 against segregation in education. This ruling simply gave legal recognition to the social fact that segregated facilities are seldom equal.

PREVENTING RACIAL CONFLICT. We have seen that racial conflict has its roots in racial prejudice. To prevent or alleviate racial conflict requires, then, that we try to combat racial prejudice. From our analysis of prejudice, it is fairly easy to formulate several rules for coping with it. These rules, however, are easier to state than they are to apply:

1. *Prevent parents and teachers from teaching prejudices to children.* This is difficult to do but has been accomplished more and more in recent years (see Figure 17.5).

2. *Remove the supports for the prejudice and provide prejudiced persons with evidence contrary to the prejudice.* This is not likely to be very effective because of the distorting effects of prejudice on perception and judgment.

3. *Make prejudice conflict with other strong needs.* The campaigns, extensively used during the Second World War, which attempted to convince people that it is unpatriotic, irreligious, or undemocratic to be prejudiced were quite effective. This technique can backfire, though. If a person is propagandized to believe that prejudice is undemocratic, he may react not by rejecting prejudice, but by rejecting the underlying concept of democracy.

4. *Teach people not to be prejudiced.* This works fairly well, but it is difficult to get adults into an educational situation which is aimed at changing their prejudices. Consequently, disguised education is likely

FIGURE 17.6. Interaction among members of mixed groups, especially groups of children or of people working together, usually tends to reduce prejudice [Glenn Mitchell].

to be most effective. Television's casual acceptance of Negroes is an excellent example of one way to do this.

5. *Bring potentially conflicting groups together.* The success of the Army's mixed units indicates that contact helps to reduce prejudice (see Figure 17.6). However, it is important to make sure that the contact is not with the worst examples of the group against which the prejudice is directed.

Summary

1. An attitude is a tendency to respond positively or negatively to certain objects, persons, or situations. It represents a stimulus discrimination in which things are put into categories related to the person's goals.

2. A prejudice is a special case of a negative attitude in which the object is usually a minority group. In prejudice, a person usually holds an oversimplified, and hence erroneous, view of the category into which he has placed the minority group. Widely shared erroneous beliefs are called stereotypes.

3. Although in principal one can distinguish between beliefs and attitudes—a belief is the acceptance of a statement or proposition without necessarily being for or against it—in practice most beliefs are emotionally tinged and are hard to disentangle from attitudes.

4. Culture shapes the development of attitudes and beliefs. Making cross-cultural comparisons of attitudes, however, is hazardous, for differences within a culture may be greater than differences between cultures. Attitudes frequently correlate with socioeconomic and other differences.

5. Cultural influences on attitudes are transmitted largely through the family and peer groups. The attitudes of children tend to correlate with those of their parents and the persons with whom they associate.

6. Attitudes tend to be related to personality traits. One personality pattern, called the ethnocentric personality, is prejudiced against all minority groups, is authoritarian in viewpoint, and tends to place people in oversimplified "black-and-white" categories.

7. Since the information a person gets is frequently distorted or inadequate, his attitudes and beliefs are often similarly distorted. They are also influenced by the particular authorities on whom he relies for information.

8. Primary groups, which consist of friends and close associates, help shape a person's attitudes.

9. Once formed, attitudes are relatively resistant to change. They tend to be preserved by (a) selective interpretation and perception of information, (b) avoidance of information conflicting with existing attitudes, and (c) social approval or disapproval of one's associates.

10. Both education and propaganda influence and change attitudes, but propaganda is a deliberate attempt to alter attitudes in a direction favorable to the purposes of the propagandist. Three important devices of the propagandist are (a) loaded words, (b) suggestion, and (c) appeal to or creation of needs.

11. Loaded words, that is, emotionally toned words chosen to create the desired attitude, are the stock in trade of the propagandist.

12. Suggestion is the uncritical acceptance of a statement or idea. In prestige suggestion, statements are made about prestigeful people; in social suggestion, the statement that "everybody's doing it" appeals to one's desire to conform in situations where one's own feelings may be ambiguous.

13. Much propaganda and advertising attempt to influence attitudes by appealing to needs. In general, a favorable attitude can be created by arousing a need and relating it to the object of the attitude. Attempts, however, to change attitudes by frightening people, as in safety campaigns, frequently are ineffective.

14. Several methods of measuring attitudes have been developed. An attitude scale provides a precise measure of the degree of an attitude toward an issue, but it can be used only with people who have the time and interest to take it.

15. For many practical purposes, we are limited to the public-opinion poll, which consists of a series of questions answered in a brief personal interview. The phrasing of questions, the context in which they are asked, and representative sampling are all extremely important to the results obtained.

16. Prejudices may be learned either from the object of the prejudice or, more commonly, from contact with others who have the prejudice.

17. Once learned, prejudices are preserved and supported by (a) the needs they help satisfy, (b) the fact that they provide a means of scapegoating, that is, of displacing aggression for which there might otherwise be no outlet, (c) distortion in perception and judgment that make the prejudice seem "true," and (d) creating social handicaps for minority groups which appear to justify the prejudice.

18. The principal social consequences of prejudice are segregation and inferior facilities for the minority group.

Suggestions for further reading

Allport, G. W. *The nature of prejudice.* Cambridge, Mass.: Addison-Wesley, 1954. A readable summary and analysis of the literature on group prejudice.

Campbell, A., Converse, P. E., Miller, W. E., and Stokes, D. E. *The American voter.* New York: Wiley, 1960. A discussion of factors affecting voting behavior as discovered by attitude-survey techniques.

Harding, J., Kutner, B., Proshansky, H., and Chein, I. Prejudice and ethnic relations. In G. Lindzey (ed.), *Handbook of social psychology*. Cambridge, Mass.: Addison-Wesley, 1954.
A summary of research up to 1954 on factors affecting the development and lessening of ethnic prejudices.

Hovland, C. I. Effects of the mass media of communication. In G. Lindzey (ed.), *Handbook of social psychology*. Cambridge, Mass.: Addison-Wesley, 1954.
A useful summary of research on the effectiveness of mass media in changing attitudes, and a review of experiments dealing with procedures for altering beliefs.

Hyman, H. *Political socialization*. Glencoe, Ill.: Free Press, 1959.
A review of work dealing with the formation and change of political beliefs and attitudes.

Katz, D., Cartwright, D., Eldersveld, S., and Lee, A. M. (eds.). *Public opinion and propaganda*. New York: Dryden, 1954.
A collection of readings in the areas of communication, propaganda, and public opinion.

Krech, D., and Crutchfield, R. S. *Theory and problems of social psychology*. New York: McGraw-Hill, 1948, Chaps. 5–9.
How attitudes and beliefs operate, how they are measured and studied, and some procedures for changing them.

Mosteller, F., Hyman, H., McCarthy, P. J., Marks, E. S., and Truman, D. B. *The pre-election polls of 1948*. New York: Social Science Research Council, 1949.
An analysis of the reasons for the failure of polls to predict the election of Harry Truman in 1948.

Parten, M. *Surveys, polls, and samples*. New York: Harper, 1950.
An introduction to polling and survey techniques.

Schettler, C. *Public opinion in American society*. New York: Harper, 1960.
A consideration of the nature, formation, and operation of public opinion from the point of view of a political scientist.

Vocational adjustment

T HE PROBLEMS OF business, industry, government, and the world of work are touched upon by many subjects the student has an opportunity to study. Psychology is one of them. Almost every facet of vocational life has its psychological aspects. In this chapter we have chosen five vocational areas to which psychological knowledge can be, and has been, effectively applied. These are (1) the selection of employees, (2) the supervision and management of employees, (3) factors involved in job satisfaction, (4) factors involved in working efficiently, and (5) engineering for human use. These are some of the important topics in the field known as *industrial psychology*. In addition, the student should realize that our discussion of

aptitudes and interests in Chapter 14 also has a bearing on vocational adjustment, both in helping the person make the best vocational choice and in helping an employer choose the best person for a particular job.

Employee selection

An individual has the task of choosing the vocation or job that suits his aptitudes and interests, and the employer has the problem of choosing the right employee for his particular job. The employee, on the one hand, runs the risk of unhappiness and failure if he makes a mistake. The employer, on the other hand, may waste money in lowered efficiency and may disrupt the organization of his work if he picks the wrong people to fill his jobs. Thus both employee and employer are interested in avoiding mistakes or at least in keeping them to a minimum.

JOB ANALYSIS. In order to know who can do his work best, an employer must first know exactly what work it is he wants done. No one can tell who the best man for a job is without knowing what the job itself is. The process of finding out what a job is has been called *job analysis.* Many people are inclined to think that this is a simple matter, that all one has to do is let a workman or supervisor tell you what the job entails. Experience shows that this is not enough.

In one classical study, for example, secretaries were asked to write down during the course of each day's work exactly everything they did [Charters and Whitley, 1924]. When their notes were collected and tabulated, it turned out that their jobs included over eight hundred distinguishable duties. Neither the secretaries nor their supervisors could remember beforehand more than a fraction of these duties.

There are several different methods of doing job analyses. Some are better suited than others to a particular job; some are more expensive than others and are undertaken only when the expense is justified by the expected benefits. The following are the principal methods:

1. Employees write down everything they do in the course of a typical day or week. This is the method that was used in the example cited above.

2. An expert job analyst takes over the job for a few days and does it himself to see what it entails.

3. Motion pictures are taken of the work and are later analyzed in detail. This method is especially suitable for repetitive jobs such as those on an assembly line.

4. Some measure of the production or output of the job is used. This may be appropriate for machinists and carpenters, whose efforts are reflected in finished products.

Most job analyses are made in such a way that a complete list of duties can be compiled. These lists, as in the case of secretarial duties cited above, are often rather long. Then the question arises, What duties are the most important? Many duties do not distinguish one job from another, or if they do, they are not important because almost anyone can do them, and hence they do not spell success or failure in the job. For this reason, psychologists have recently devised a method called *critical incidents* [Flanagan, 1951]. In applying this method, the analyst attempts to determine those aspects of the job that are critical for its best performance.

The method is especially applicable to jobs where safety is a consideration, such as driving a truck or piloting an airplane. In these jobs, it is not what the person does most of the time that is important but what he does some of the time—in emergencies or especially dangerous situations—that determines whether he is successful, or in fact whether he and his equipment survive. The critical-incidents technique is also proving useful, however, in many other jobs, including industrial, secretarial, and managerial jobs.

Once a job analysis is completed, it can be used to write a *job description,* which is a detailed account of all the facts pertinent to a job. Job descriptions may then be compared to see which ones are different and which are essentially the same. All jobs having the same description are considered the same even if they have different names—and they often do, depending upon the region of the country or the particular business or industry. Jobs that are distinguishably different yet have certain similarities are grouped into *occupations.* Occupations, in turn, can be compared and classified into major occupational families.

The U.S. Employment Service has made studies of over 30,000 occupations in industry, business, and government and has classified them in the *Dictionary of Occupational Titles* [1949]. This invaluable dictionary shows how nearly all the jobs in the United States are classified into different occupations and gives the names and job specifications for each. It has served during and since the Second World War as a guide for fitting men to particular jobs and also as a way of finding out what and where our major manpower shortages are.

WORKER CHARACTERISTICS. The job description includes information about the job and about the worker who is needed to fill the job. On the one hand, it gives the kind of work performed, the amount of supervision given and received, the level of difficulty of the work, the standard of work required, the working conditions, and the machines, tools, equipment, and materials that the worker must use. On the other hand, it states the physical and psychological demands of the job, the amount of previous experience considered necessary, the requisite kind and amount of training—in a word, the *worker characteristics* required for a job.

Worker characteristics include a statement of how important each trait and ability is to the job. Each job requires its own particular combination of traits, interests, and abilities. A relatively complete list of the kinds of characteristics that may be included in such a statement are strength of hands, fingers, legs, and arms; dexterity of various kinds; keenness of the senses, such as depth of vision, color perception; memory for such things as faces, details, and oral and written instructions; arithmetic computation; intelligence; ability to express oneself orally; and ability to handle people. Figure 18.1 shows a standard War Manpower Commission form used during the Second World War and since for rating these various characteristics.

SELECTION METHODS. When an employer knows what worker characteristics are required for the jobs he wishes to fill, his next task is to select applicants for the job who meet these requirements or who best meet them. This is the process known as *personnel selection*. Since employers have been selecting employees for centuries and scientific methods have been available for only a few decades, it is natural that present-day methods of selection are a mixture of opinions and facts. Some of the facts are based on long employment experience and some on modern scientific research.

Application blanks. The most generally used source of information about the characteristics of a job applicant is the application blank. This may be made out by the applicant or by someone in an employment office who asks the applicant questions and records the answers on the blank. When used wisely, it is by far the simplest method of obtaining *some* of the desired information about the worker, such as age, sex, education, and most recent employment. Application blanks, however, are frequently loaded with items that have no relevancy to the job concerned, such as birthplace, height, weight, and number of brothers and sisters. Application blanks, moreover, do not allow one to appraise accurately the *quality* of such things as education and previous employment. Some applicants may have had considerable education and employment experience but may not have profited from them as much as they should have. So the application blank has its limitations.

Because the application blank is used so widely in selecting employees, it behooves the student and prospective employee to be prepared to supply the information that it may require. Even the best of memories may not be able to cope with all the questions on such a blank, so it is an excellent idea to make a list in advance of all the items that it may include and to keep available your records of such matters as beginning and ending dates of employment, name of supervisor, name of position held, and salaries received.

For the benefit of the student, Table 18.1 includes many of the items frequently called for on application blanks. It is a composite of many typical blanks.

Interviews. A second timeworn device used in selection is the employment inter-

JOB TITLE *ENGINE LATHE OPERATOR, FIRST CLASS*

Amount				CHARACTERISTICS REQUIRED	Amount				CHARACTERISTICS REQUIRED
O	C	B	A		O	C	B	A	
	✓			1. Work rapidly for long periods		✓			26. Arithmetic computation
	✓			2. Strength of hands		✓			27. Intelligence
	✓			3. Strength of arms		✓			28. Adaptability
	✓			4. Strength of back		✓			29. Ability to make decisions
	✓			5. Strength of legs			✓		30. Ability to plan
	✓			6. Dexterity of fingers			✓		31. Initiative
		✓		7. Dexterity of hands and arms			✓		32. Understanding mechanical devices
✓				8. Dexterity of foot and leg		✓			33. Attention to many items
		✓		9. Eye-hand coordination		✓			34. Oral expression
✓				10. Foot-hand-eye coordination	✓				35. Skill in written expression
	✓			11. Coordination of both hands		✓			36. Tact in dealing with people
	✓			12. Estimate size of objects		✓			37. Memory of names and persons
	✓			13. Estimate quantity of objects		✓			38. Personal appearance
		✓		14. Perceive form of objects		✓			39. Concentration amidst distractions
	✓			15. Estimate speed of moving objects		✓			40. Emotional stability
	✓			16. Keenness of vision		✓			41. Work under hazardous conditions
	✓			17. Keenness of hearing		✓			42. Estimate quality of objects
✓				18. Sense of smell		✓			43. Unpleasant physical conditions
✓				19. Sense of taste		✓			44. Color discrimination
	✓			20. Touch discrimination		✓			45. Ability to meet and deal with public
		✓		21. Muscular discrimination	✓				46. Height
		✓		22. Memory for details (things)	✓				47. Weight
	✓			23. Memory for ideas (abstract)					48. ______
	✓			24. Memory for oral directions					49. ______
	✓			25. Memory for written directions					50. ______

FIGURE 18.1. A worker-characteristics form. The letters have the following meanings for satisfactory performance on the job: O, not required; C, a medium or low degree required; B, an above-average degree required; and A, a very high degree required [U.S. Department of Labor].

TABLE 18.1. Some information often requested on the application blank.

Name	Salary	Business and evening schools:
Address	Title of your job	Major course
Birthplace	Brief description of work	College:
Age	Supervisor	Major course
Height	(Same as other previous employment)	Degree received
Weight	Personal references:	Special abilities
Sex	Name	Honors received or offices held
Health	Address	Membership in organizations, societies, etc.
Physical defects	How long known and in what capacity	
Father's occupation	Occupation	Hobbies
Number of brothers and sisters	Education:	Places traveled
	Grade school:	Articles or books written
Most recent employment:	Name	Reason for wanting a job with company
Employer	Years	
Address	High school:	Date available for work
Dates of employment	Major course	

view. In 1947 a survey was conducted of personnel-selection practices used in 325 prominent industrial concerns, with the finding that 96 per cent of these concerns used an interview as part of their employment procedure [Spriegel and Wallace, 1948].

Despite its widespread use, the interview is very often not so good a selection device as its users might think (see related discussion in Chapter 15). One classic psychological study [Hollingworth, 1929], for example, illustrates what can happen under some circumstances.

Twelve sales managers interviewed 57 applicants for an actual job under realistic yet controlled conditions. The sales managers were experienced interviewers, because their regular positions required frequent interviewing, but they were not necessarily *trained*. They were allowed to conduct the interview as they saw fit. They were required to rank the applicants in order of desirability for the job, and when the interviewing was completed, their rankings were collected and compared. The results are shown in Table

18.2. There is very little agreement. Applicant A, for example, was ranked sixth by one interviewer and fifty-sixth by another. Applicant B was ranked as the best man by one interviewer and as the worst one by another.

These results are fairly typical of many studies of interviewing. Where interviews are conducted under "normal" conditions, there is very often little agreement among interviewers. This fact makes it clear that if the interview is to serve effectively as a selection method, certain precautions must be taken.

There are three principal factors that can make the difference between good interviewing and practically worthless interviewing:

1. The interviewer should know well the job about which he is interviewing.

2. He should acquire good technique. This is usually somewhat nondirective (see Chapter 6); the interviewer must draw out the applicant, rather than ask direct questions. On the other hand, he must be able to keep the interview on the track, and by the time he completes it he must know the answers to a predetermined list of questions.

3. He should be carefully selected for the task. Some people cannot put applicants at ease or establish rapport with them; others are simply poor judges of people under any circumstances.

Many interviews do not meet these important conditions and are therefore untrustworthy. If the conditions are met, however, the interview can be a valuable aid in selection [Ghiselli and Brown, 1955].

Letters of recommendation. The letter of recommendation, like the application blank and interview, is widely used in the selection of employees. This is particularly true in selecting students for colleges and professional schools and in selecting clerical, white-collar, and professional personnel.

Though widely used, the letter of recommendation is subject to the same limitations as those of the application and interview and to a few additional ones. Those who write such letters are usually busy people who toss them off as one of many chores in a day's work. The writer may not know very much about the job for which the applicant is applying or about the standards of performance required in the job. He is inclined also to be lenient in his evaluation of the applicant, since the applicant will be working for *someone else.* Furthermore, since the writer is often chosen as a recommender because of his high rank in supervision, he may not know very much about the applicant. Finally, the words that are used to describe such traits as honesty, reliability, and initiative are rather vague, meaning dif-

ferent things to different people. It is extremely difficult to use them in a way that discriminates between well-qualified and unqualified applicants.

The users of recommendations have long been aware of their shortcomings and in recent years have taken steps to remedy them. The "letter" now often includes a check list of traits on which the recommender is asked to rate the applicant. This has the advantage of brevity and of giving ratings that may be compared for different applicants. It has the disadvantages, however, of being rather stereotyped, of permitting the recommender to omit important information, and of encouraging leniency in the rating of the applicant. To offset these limitations, recommendation blanks that call for ratings on traits also often ask the recommender to make comments freely as he would in a letter. Even so, the recommendation is seldom a highly reliable source of information for selecting employees.

Trade tests. Applications, interviews, and recommendations are the three most common sources of information used in selecting employees, especially for the more remunerative occupations. The benefits of scientific tests are not as widely exploited as they might be, but they are being used more and more each year for all sorts of occupations from the semiskilled to the executive classes. A variety of tests are being used, but the two kinds that have proved most valid are the trade tests and the aptitude tests.

The trade test is an achievement test; it

TABLE 18.2. Sample results of a study of the effectiveness of the interview. Twelve sales managers interviewed fifty-seven applicants, then ranked them for suitability for the job. These are the ranks assigned to three applicants. Agreement among interviewers is clearly not satisfactory [Hollingworth, 1929].

Applicant	Interviewer											
	1	2	3	4	5	6	7	8	9	10	11	12
A	33	46	6	56	26	32	12	38	23	22	22	9
B	53	10	6	21	16	9	20	2	57	28	1	26
C	43	11	13	11	37	40	36	46	25	15	29	1

measures (or attempts to measure) just how good a person is at his trade. It is usually given orally by an employment interviewer, but it may be administered as a paper-and-pencil test. It usually consists of a few items that correlate well with degree of knowledge and experience in a particular job. Of the large number of trade tests available today, many were constructed by expert job analysts in the U.S. Employment Service as part of a program to provide a relatively complete list of tests [Stead et al., 1940].

Some of the questions on a trade test require definitions. A carpenter, for example, may be asked, "What do you mean by a shore?" (Answer: "An upright brace.") Some deal with methods used in the trade. A plumber, for example, may be asked, "What are the most commonly used methods of testing plumbing systems?" (Answer: "Air, water, smoke, peppermint.") Other questions deal with use, procedures, location, names, purpose, and number. An example of number as a basic element in a question is, "How many jaws has a universal chuck?" (Answer: "Three.")

Questions and tests of this type have been prepared, standardized, and validated for most of the common trades. They usually have a high validity in that they distinguish well the different levels of accomplishment within the trade. These, for convenience, are divided into three grades: the expert, who has had long experience in the trade;

the apprentice, who is in the process of learning it; and the related worker, who by working with or around experts and apprentices has picked up a limited knowledge of the trade.

In Table 18.3 is evidence of how well a trade test can distinguish among these three grades of training. In this case the trade is painting. In the highest-scoring category we find that 78 per cent are experts, while no related workers make high scores. On the other hand, few experts make low scores, although nearly all related workers do.

Aptitude tests. We have already described aptitude tests in Chapter 14. They can be used both to advise a person about his vocational abilities and to help the employer determine who is best suited for his jobs (see Figure 18.2).

The employer is faced, however, with the problem of deciding which of hundreds of possible aptitude tests is most valid for a particular job. To do that he must first consider, as we have previously explained, the worker characteristics essential for that job. This problem has been met by the construction of *psychographs*.

There are two kinds of psychographs, job psychographs and individual psychographs. *Job psychographs,* illustrated in Figure 18.3, show the traits and abilities required in a job or a family of jobs. It is drawn up, as can be seen in the illustration, in terms of percentages of the population. The amount of a trait or ability required in a job is defined by the percentage of people in a population who have as much as, or more than, is necessary. To make this kind of representation as simple as possible, the U.S. Employment Service has distinguished three grades of abilities. The A grade is the amount possessed by only the upper 2 per cent of the population; the B grade, the amount possessed by the next 28 per cent; and the C grade, the amount possessed by the remaining 70 per cent. These three grades are close enough for most purposes of weighing the traits or abilities required.

Quite a few occupations have been inves-

TABLE 18.3. Distribution of scores made on "Trade Questions for Painters" by expert painters, apprentices, and related workers [Stead et al., 1940]:

Score group	Distribution, per cent		
	Experts	Apprentices	Related workers
9–15	78	17	0
6–8	14	40	0
0–5	8	43	96

tigated to determine whether there is a particular pattern of abilities by which each might be distinguished. In Figure 18.3 are the profiles of three occupations: office clerk, garage mechanic, and retail salesman. The scores along the top and the bottom of the psychograph are based upon a standard sample of men drawn from all occupational levels. Clerks seem to score higher than the average person on tests of intelligence, clerical ability, and manual dexterity but are about average in mechanical ability. Contrast this score with that of the garage mechanic.

To select an employee, one must know whether an applicant's abilities correspond with those stated in the profile, or job psychograph, of required abilities. This means that some way must be found of constructing an *individual psychograph* for the applicant and matching this with the job psychograph. In some circumstances, this may be done by rating the applicant with information obtained from the application blank, interview, and recommendation. Better yet, it may be done by tests selected to measure the required abilities.

VALIDITY IN SELECTION. Whatever method or combination of methods is used to select employees, the validity of the selection procedure is always a problem (see Chapter 13). In the practical world, one cannot always do things as they should be done, and often it may prove too expensive or may require too much research to determine whether one's selection procedures are valid. Nevertheless, it must be recognized that one can be sure of validity only when he has properly followed the necessary procedures (pages 425, 436, and 460) for establishing the validity of a method for predicting a criterion with a particular population. Anything less is risky. Sometimes one can make a good guess from knowing that the procedures have proved valid in what appears to be a similar set of circumstances. Research experience, however, indicates that procedures are not necessarily valid simply

FIGURE 18.2. Examples of vocational-aptitude tests. On the peg board, the testee's job is to put the pegs and washers in the appropriate places on the board as speedily as possible. On the form board, his task is to place the forms correctly in the various spaces, again as rapidly as possible (Grundy, Three Lions). [New York Univer. Testing and Advisement Center].

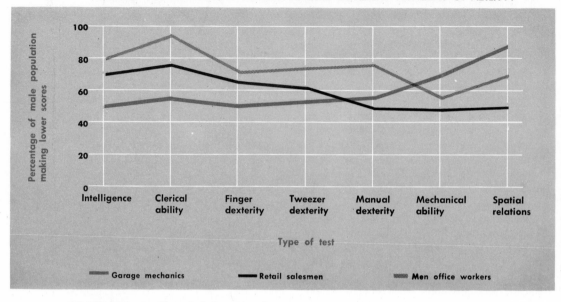

FIGURE 18.3. Profiles of abilities for three occupations. The scale is a percentile scale based upon a standard sample of men drawn from all occupational levels. The scores for each occupational group are average scores translated into the general percentile scale. Thus, the average male office worker is at the 80th percentile of the general population in intelligence, and the average garage mechanic stands at about the 80th percentile of the general population in spatial-relations ability [after Ghiselli and Brown, 1955].

because they look valid to the employer or to a psychologist. It is best, therefore, to be cautious and to make strenuous efforts to measure the actual validity of the procedures one uses in selecting employees.

Supervision

The selection of an employee and his acceptance of a job are just the beginning of the problems of vocational adjustment. After that it remains to be seen whether the employee will succeed in his work and whether the employer will be effective in supervising him. Millions of words—most of them no more than embellished common sense— have been written about "how to succeed." We shall not repeat many of them here. There are, however, certain principles of

effective supervision, as well as some scientific information about the satisfactions a person can have in his job.

If you are a college student, the chances are rather good that you will find that your vocation entails the supervision of people. Most college graduates in business and industry are primarily employed in supervisory work. But even doctors, lawyers, teachers, and others in independent work have secretaries, assistants, and students whom they will be called upon to supervise. Despite this fact, relatively few receive any systematic instruction in the art and science of supervision, and many supervisors are consequently poorly prepared for their jobs. The few principles that we sketch here are no substitute for a thorough training in supervision, but if heeded, they may help.

TRAINING. The supervisor is, first of all, a teacher. He starts teaching by instructing a new employee in his duties, and he continues to teach as new methods are introduced, as the organization undergoes change, and as day-by-day problems are solved. The most important part of the training, of course, is during the first few weeks that an employee is on the job, but it goes on after that, month in and month out. Whether the employee learns his job slowly or rapidly, correctly or incorrectly, and whether he keeps up as the work changes depends very much on the skill of the supervisor as a teacher.

Knowledge of results. Perhaps the most important principle a supervisor should keep in mind—and often does not—is that learning proceeds best when a person has knowledge of results. To know what he should be doing and to correct his mistakes, a person should know what he has just done and whether it is right or wrong. This point has been stressed in the chapter on human learning (Chapter 8). Knowledge of results is primarily a matter of knowing the outcome of one's work, whether it is good or bad, acceptable or unacceptable, accurate or inaccurate. Many illustrations of this principle could be drawn from practical experi-

ence in supervision, but one should suffice here [Lindahl, 1945]:

In this case the job involved operating a lathe in a highly skilled manner. The operator, in fact, had to learn an intricate pattern of hand and foot movements executed at a certain speed and with a certain form, rhythm, and pattern of pressures. Operators had trouble acquiring this skill until supervision stepped in and analyzed the problem. First an apparatus was built to provide a graphic record of the movements of a *skilled* operator. The record was then analyzed and labeled so that the trainee could see what movements were represented in the record. Then the trainees were asked to operate the machine so that they produced a record as much like that of the expert as possible. The results are shown in Figure 18.4. The trainees, once they had knowledge of their own results, learned considerably faster than they had learned before.

Relatively few problems in supervision require the construction of a recording machine to provide knowledge of results. More often the supervisor can supply the necessary knowledge by giving careful directions, pointing out mistakes as a teacher would,

KNOWLEDGE OF RESULTS AIDS TRAINING:

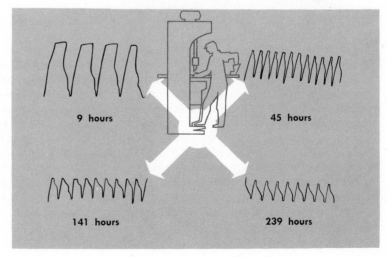

FIGURE 18.4. The records are of foot-action patterns in the operation of a disk-cutting machine. The person being trained has the record of an experienced operator as a guide and attempts to duplicate the record. Notice the great improvement in the course of 239 hours of supervised training [after Lindahl, 1945].

9 hours

45 hours

141 hours

239 hours

and telling the employee as often as possible just what the quality of his work is.

There are several other pointers, drawn from the psychology of learning, that the supervisor, in playing the role of a good teacher, should follow:

1. In general, guidance is much more effective early in learning than later; consequently it is better to show somebody how to do things right in the first place than it is to wait until after he has learned bad habits.

2. People usually master one thing at a time better than they master many things at a time. Therefore, training should be limited to a reasonable number of tasks and to a reasonable degree of complexity at any one time.

3. Transfer of training is a powerful ally to be enlisted. When a person has learned one task, then is the time to show him other tasks that are similar to it or other tasks that involve the same principle. In this way one can capitalize on positive transfer and avoid negative transfer (see Chapter 8).

We have run over these points hurriedly because they are all applications of principles presented in detail earlier. The alert supervisor will know well the principles of learning and will continually seek ways to use them in helping his employees work effectively.

COMMUNICATION.   Closely allied to the supervisor's role as a teacher is his responsibility for communication [Bellows, 1949]. Almost all instructions and information are transmitted to an employee through language, written or spoken. He learns what he is supposed to do and to know from the supervisor's words. Therefore, if the supervisor is to be effective, he must concern himself with language and with ways to use it effectively in communication. Unfortunately, supervisors are all too often unaware of the problem of communication. Here are three general principles to follow.

1. The supervisor makes sure to tell his employees what they need to know. He does not leave it to them to "read his mind" or to "pick up" what they should know. He sees to it that they are promptly and accurately informed of anything relevant to their work.

2. The supervisor dispenses his communications in small doses, for most people have a limited capacity to absorb very much information at a time. Hence long, involved communications are seldom read or listened to, and if they are, they are rarely digested. Only a few important points should be communicated at a time.

3. The supervisor learns to phrase his communications in simple, direct style. His employees are usually not so bright, well educated, or experienced as he. Even if they are, they are more likely to perceive the intended message correctly if it is phrased in the most straightforward manner.

Using simple language. This last point is worth amplifying. There are wide individual differences in the ability of people to express themselves comprehensibly. Some succeed in making language relatively easy to understand, and others make the task unbearably difficult. Research workers in language and psychology have studied this problem in some detail. The results of one study are described in a book by Rudolf Flesch [1946], called *The Art of Plain Talk*. Flesch has described the elements of language expression that, in general, make for ease of reading and comprehension. (We have used some of his principles in this book to help make it easier to understand.) These elements are as follows:

Number of words in a sentence. The shorter the sentence, the more easily it is comprehended.

Number of syllables in a word. The shorter the words—as measured by syllables but not necessarily by letters—the easier they are to understand.

Number of personal words and sentences. The greater the percentage of personal words and/or personal sentences, as distinguished from impersonal, abstract constructions, the easier the reading.

Flesch has combined these elements into

an index which anyone can compute by following his rules. The index is a fairly good measure, though not a perfect one, of the relative difficulty or ease with which a sample of writing or speech can be comprehended. Flesch has many examples of good versus poor communication as judged by his index, but one almost unintelligible sample of legal prose will serve as an illustration:

Ultimate consumer means a person or group of persons, generally constituting a domestic household, who purchase eggs generally at the individual stores of retailers or purchase and receive deliveries of eggs at a place of abode of the individual or domestic household from producers or retail route sellers and who use such eggs for their consumption as food.

Flesch comments:

That's a lot of words; let's try to cut down on them. Let's say just "people" instead of "a person or group of persons:" then let's leave out all those clauses with the word "generally" in them (they don't belong in a definition anyway); then let's say "eat" instead of "use for consumption as food." Now let's see what we have:

Ultimate consumers are people who buy eggs to eat them.

Note how well Flesch followed his own precepts in explaining how the communication could be made more comprehensible.

EVALUATION. Besides being a teacher and a communicator, the supervisor must be an evaluator. He must evaluate the worth of the jobs under his supervision and the worth of the employees holding those jobs.

The first of these evaluations is known as *job evaluation* and is an assessment of the remuneration to be offered and paid for a particular job. The traditional way of deciding what to pay is to accept the general market evaluation of a job. The supervisor finds out, for example, what secretaries or machinists currently are being paid and offers this when he wishes to employ a person for such a job. This is a relatively unscientific way of evaluating a job, and an employer who uses it as a basis for hiring often fails to get employees who have the necessary abilities. It also neglects the question of what is a fair compensation for the skills and abilities involved in a job. It is gradually being displaced by more systematic methods of evaluation; the evaluations are sometimes done by specialists in these methods.

The general aim of the specialists, called job evaluators, is to assess the worker characteristics required in a job and then set the pay scale according to the relative availability of these characteristics in the general population. If, for example, the job requires a degree of intelligence that is relatively rare, they set the pay for the job rather high on the scale, but if, on the other hand, it requires skills or abilities that almost everyone has, the pay will be relatively low. There are many different systems for arriving at such an evaluation, but in any case the aim is to assign a fair value to a job that is well done, not to a worker.

The second aspect of evaluation concerns the worker. Is he doing his job satisfactorily or not? Is he doing it unusually well? Could he do another job better than he is doing his present one? Is he worthy of promotion to another job? These are difficult questions that need to be answered fairly in order to reward the worker for his efforts and to make the most of his abilities in an organization. Again there are many methods for making a worker evaluation.

Production. In industries or businesses where employees produce something that is measurable, the evaluation can be made almost solely in terms of amount and quality of production. In addition, there are a good many fringe criteria that may be employed, such as seniority on the job, number of times a person is tardy for work, number of accidents, and amount of time required in training for a job. When such criteria are used, a way must be found of weighting each of them into some composite judgment, and there are systems for doing this.

Ratings. In many kinds of work, especially in office operations or work requiring initiative and responsibility, none of the production or fringe criteria may be adequate. Then supervisors must turn to some kind of *rating* made by the immediate supervisors or associates of the person (see Figure 18.5).

One of the common methods used, for example, in the civil service system and military establishment is the efficiency report. This is usually a rating of "excellent," "satisfactory," or "unsatisfactory" of several aspects of a person's work and is made out by the immediate supervisor. Because supervisors tend to be lenient, such ratings usually are inflated and therefore yield far too few "unsatisfactories" and far too many "excel-

---

EMPLOYEE PERFORMANCE AND WORK APPRAISAL FORM

Date.. 19

Judge the employee on the basis of the work now being done. Be sure that each characteristic is considered separately, regardless of where the appraisal falls on any of the other characteristics. Place a check (√) in the box below the group of words which best describes the individual, but only one check for each line. However, it is essential that every line be checked.

NAME.. JOB TITLE.................................. DEPT........................

How long under your supervision?.. Date of Employment?........................

1. Knowledge of Job: Consider knowledge essential to person's job.	Has an Exceptionally thorough knowledge of work ☐	Has good knowledge of work ☐	Requires Considerable coaching ☐	Has inadequate knowledge of work ☐
2. Quality of Work: Consider the ability to turn out work which meets quality standards.	Highest Quality ☐	Well Done ☐	Passable ☐	Poor ☐
3. Quantity of Work: Consider the volume of work produced under normal conditions.	Large Volume ☐	Good Volume ☐	Slightly Below Average Volume ☐	Unsatisfactory Volume ☐
4. Attendance & Punctuality: Consider frequency of absences as well as latenesses.	Record is Excellent ☐	Occasionally Absent or Late ☐	Frequently Absent or Late ☐	Undependable; Absent or Late Without Notice ☐
5. Attitude: Consider his attitude toward his work, company and associates, and his willingness to work with and for others.	Unusually Fine Attitude ☐	Good Attitude ☐	Passable ☐	Poor Attitude ☐
6. Judgment: Consider his ability to make decisions and to utilize working time to best advantage.	Justifies Utmost Confidence ☐	Applies Himself Well; Needs Little Supervision ☐	Needs Frequent Checking ☐	Cannot be relied upon; Needs constant Supervision ☐
7. Reliability: Consider the ability of the person to get the work out under pressure, and to follow job through to completion.	Can always be counted upon ☐	Generally can be counted on ☐	Unpredictable under Pressure ☐	"Cracks up" under pressure ☐
8. Flexibility — Adaptability: Consider the speed with which he learns and the amount of instruction required to teach him new duties.	Learns Fast ☐	Learns Reasonably Fast ☐	Slow to Learn ☐	Unable to Learn ☐
9. Personal Characteristics: Consider Appearance, Personality, Integrity, "Housekeeping".	Decidedly Favorable ☐	Good ☐	Passable ☐	Generally Unsatisfactory ☐

Appraised by.. Date.................... Reviewed by.. Date....................

(See other side)

FIGURE 18.5. An example of the kind of form commonly used to appraise the performance of employees.

lents" to be very useful in discriminating the worth of different employees.

To overcome the deficiencies of the simple efficiency report, psychologists have devised more precise methods. One is the *man-to-man* rating, in which the supervisor must compare each person with several other persons known to him or under his supervision. This method, although it forces a comparative rating of individuals, is handicapped by the fact that the supervisor is usually not equally familiar with the work of all who are compared. A second method is the *forced-choice* rating blank [Sisson, 1948]. This presents the supervisor with pairs of adjectives and asks him to check the member of each pair most descriptive of the individual. The members of the pair have been carefully chosen through research so that they appear equally attractive or unattractive to the supervisor but so that one is important and the other unimportant in determining the worth of an individual employee (see Figure 18.6). A supervisor often objects to the forced-choice technique, because he does not know whether his ratings will be favorable or unfavorable to the person being rated until they are scored in the front office. Research indicates, however, that the method is a good one *if* supervisors carefully and honestly make out the forced-choice forms.

These are just a sample of the scientific methods available for evaluating an employee's worth. The good supervisor accepts the responsibility, uses the best methods suitable to his problem, and is always on the alert for any better methods that he might use. In this way he can reward fairly people who are deserving and he can also maintain the effectiveness and morale of his group.

COUNSELING. We should mention briefly a fourth, and often unrecognized, psychological responsibility of the supervisor. This is counseling. Employees are not mere machines that may be broken in and then operated at high speed to produce all they can. Employees are people, and people have

INSTRUCTIONS: Read carefully each group of four phrases, then check the one that is most descriptive of the person being rated and also the one that is least descriptive of him.

	Most	Least
A. A go-getter who always does a good job	☐	☐
B. Cool under all circumstances	☐	☐
C. Doesn't listen to suggestions	☐	☐
D. Drives instead of leads	☐	☐
A. Always criticizes, never praises	☐	☐
B. Carries out order by "passing the buck"	☐	☐
C. Knows his job and performs it well	☐	☐
D. Plays no favorites	☐	☐
A. Constantly striving for new knowledge and ideas	☐	☐
B. Businesslike	☐	☐

FIGURE 18.6. These are some of forced-choice items formerly used by the United States Army on the job-proficiency section of an officer-efficiency report.

problems, as we have emphasized elsewhere in the book. These problems affect their work. A man's nagging wife, his personal relations with fellow workmen, his worries about his children's health, and countless other personal problems seriously affect his work and indirectly the work of his associates.

This fact was well demonstrated years ago in the famous Hawthorne study of the Western Electric Company [Roethlisberger and Dickson, 1939]. In this study it was revealed that personal problems had as much to do with factory production as any other single factor. The management discovered, too, after some experimentation, that a counseling system in which they listened to employees' problems and tried to render psychological help made the employees happier and more productive. Many other companies have also instituted and maintained regular counseling services.

We have seen elsewhere (Chapter 12) that counseling is an occupation that requires special skills and trained personnel if it is to be done most effectively. Where feasible, therefore, it is desirable to have members of the staff whose principal function is counseling. On the other hand, every supervisor should be aware of the personal problems of his employees. He should realize, for example, that when a workman starts coming in drunk, when a secretary becomes sulky and disgruntled, or when two men simply do not get along, the problem is one of emotional adjustment. He should try to understand what the problem is and offer some kind of help that will alleviate it.

Job satisfaction

In the chapter "Motivation," we emphasized that people have social as well as physiological needs. We may expect, consequently, that their efforts both at work and at play will be directed toward the satisfaction of all their needs, not just those for material things such as food, clothing, and housing. This expectation has been confirmed in many psychological studies of the satisfactions people derive (or fail to derive) from their work. In such studies employees have been asked what they considered most important to them in their jobs. Although the results vary somewhat from one locality to another and from one kind of work to another, we are justified in drawing some conclusions that generally apply to most people who work.

PAY.   For those of us who work for a living, pay or income is what lets us buy the material things we want. Without it, moreover, we could not live. You might think, therefore, that pay would head the list of things people consider important to them in their respective jobs. But this is not the case [Smith, 1957]. When asked to rank pay along with several other features of their jobs, most people rank it relatively low and very few rank it first (see Table 18.4).

Even when they rank pay high, they usually indicate that it is not just high pay that they want. Rather they want to be paid as well as other people doing the same work, or as well as other people in the same industry. Thus most people are more concerned about being paid fairly than about being paid a large amount. Fair treatment is more important than the amount of money received.

The fact that pay is seldom listed as the most important factor in working should not lead us to think that it is unimportant. Probably most people assume that they will be paid enough to take care of their basic necessities. Above that point, then, pay becomes relatively unimportant. If the pay scale were dropped far below its present level for a particular person, then pay would become important again. It is interesting to see, though, how often people decide which job to take or which to keep on grounds other than the pay they receive.

SECURITY.   Probably the factor most often stated as important in work is job security. People want to know that they will have steady work and that the work will continue for many years. They also want security in the personal sense; they want to work on safe jobs. They do not want to run the risk of losing their earning power because of accidents on the job.

The importance of security in job satisfaction partly explains why high pay is not an extremely important problem. Most people prefer a low salary which is guaranteed over a long period of time to a high salary which may not last long. Such concerns are typical of the human species. People are able to look well beyond immediate satisfactions and to anticipate satisfying their needs at some time in the future. They are more concerned about making a guaranteed minimum salary over a long period of time than they are about making the most money right now.

TABLE 18.4. What industrial workers say they want in a job. The table below is a summary of several different surveys. Different language and varying numbers of alternatives were used in the surveys. The factors named at the left have been paraphrased but represent approximately the areas covered. The numbers are rankings of the factors considered in each study.

	Women factory workers	Union workers	Nonunion workers	Men	Women	Employees of five factories
Steady work	1	1	1	1	3	1
Type of work				3	1	3
Opportunity for advancement	5	4	4	2	2	4
Good working companions	4			4	5	
High pay	6	2½	2	5½	8	2
Good boss	3	5½	5	5½	4	6
Comfortable working conditions	2	2½	3	8½	6	7
Benefits		5½	6	8½	9	5
Opportunity to learn a job	8					
Good hours	9	7½	7	7	7	
Opportunity to use one's ideas	7	7½	8			
Easy work	10					

GOOD WORKING CONDITIONS. Good working conditions are frequently listed as important considerations in working. People like to work in a clean and neat working area. If they work in an industrial plant, they want it to be one which makes them feel they are working in a pleasant environment of which they can be proud. Comfortable jobs are often important, and short hours are frequently preferred over higher pay.

The large class of people called white-collar workers is the best example of people to whom working conditions are more important than high pay. Office workers, clerks, and stenographers often earn much less money than they could if they were doing skilled manual labor, and yet they do not often change their job category. In addition, of course, white-collar workers usually have steady work and can look forward to a future of continued employment.

OPPORTUNITY FOR ADVANCEMENT. Another illustration of the fact that people are frequently more concerned about the future than about the present is that they usually give opportunity for advancement a high rating. A man often turns down a higher-paying job, for example, to take one which starts at a lower salary but which ensures early advancement. Sometimes the concern about advancement takes the form of wanting a guaranteed rate of promotion after a fixed period of time. In other instances people simply want to be assured that they will be told about opportunities for advancement and can compete for them. In still other cases, a person is most interested in the company's providing training opportunities for employees so that he can learn the skills necessary for advancement.

Regardless of the particular form the concern about advancement takes, it is clear that people are as interested in the future as they are in the present. It is also clear that concepts of fair play are important when people ask for equal opportunity for advancement or opportunity to learn. In such cases, people are not asking for a guarantee of advancement, but only for a fair chance. Nobody wants to work where the boss's son-in-law gets promoted regardless of his qualifications.

PERSONNEL RELATIONS.   Also important to most people are the personnel relations they have in their jobs [McGregor, 1960]. People want to work with companions and coworkers whom they like. They will work for a good boss, and quit when they don't like the boss. They want help from management in their work, and knowledge about how their work is progressing. They want to be sure that they have somebody to whom they can take their grievances and that they will get a fair deal when they have a grievance. For that reason, the organization which provides special means of handling grievances will always have an advantage in attracting workers. Last, but not least, they want recognition of the importance of their work. They want to be told when they are doing a good job and helped when they are doing a poor one, and they want to feel that their work and their effort to do better work are appreciated.

This factor of wanting appreciation for work has raised a good many problems for psychologists who have tried to do experiments in industry. In the Hawthorne experiments mentioned above, several girls were studied over the course of 2 years.

The girls were put in a separate room where many different working conditions could be controlled. First, the illumination was changed, and production immediately went up. Then other factors were changed: The girls were given rest periods, sometimes for 5 minutes and sometimes for 10 minutes. They were given free lunches, and at one time were allowed to go home early. Every time a change was made, production improved.

Then all the rest periods, free lunches, etc., were taken away, *and production went up still higher.*

What had happened here? The answer, it was learned later, was in the *attention* the girls were getting. Every time a change was made, the girls were reminded that other people were concerned with what they were doing, and this appreciation was what really made production go up.

All this points up the fact that people work for many things besides money. They want security, future opportunity, pleasant working conditions, and good relations with their coworkers and their bosses. Physiological factors are basic, but we should never forget that people also have complex motives that require satisfaction.

Efficiency in work

Having considered job satisfaction and the factors affecting it, we turn now to problems of efficiency in work. Employed adults usually spend half or more of their waking hours in some form of work. Aside from work in their employment, they are busy in such activities as studying, reading, writing, mowing the lawn, repairing the house, or fixing the car. In most such activities, there is the question of efficiency: What is the fastest way of getting work done with a minimum of effort? This question is in part a psychological question, for it concerns the conditions under which we are best able to think and to use our learned skills. We shall therefore consider these conditions.

THE WORK CURVE.   People seldom work at the same pace over a long period of time. Work has its ups and downs. For example, you probably do not study as effectively at the end of a long period of study as you do at the beginning. Indeed, you may not study as well at the beginning as you do after you have been at it for a little while. So you know that the efficiency of work changes during any considerable period of time.

When we have some measure of the efficiency of work and plot our measurements against the minutes or hours of the work period, the graph that results is called a *work curve*. Work curves are somewhat different for different types of work, but those in Figure 18.7 have been found in many industries and for many tasks.

The typical work curve in Figure 18.7 was obtained several years ago for a job involving heavy handwork. Notice that production was slightly better than average for the first hour of the day but it improved during the second hour. During the third hour it was still better than average, but it had dropped considerably from the second hour. And it dropped even more during the fourth hour. After the lunch period, production increased again, but then it dropped steadily for the rest of the afternoon.

Work curves of this general description are frequently found in industry and other working situations. The precise shape of the curve, however, depends on a number of factors which we shall discuss below. By studying the effect of these factors on the work curve, we have been able to analyze the curve into four components, each of which represents a factor in work. These four components are warming up, beginning spurt, end spurt, and fatigue. We shall consider the first three factors in this section, then devote the next section to a discussion of fatigue.

Warming up. A *warm-up effect* is one of the features that may appear in a work curve. It is illustrated in the top line of Figure 18.8. Most of us are familiar with the idea of warming up and deliberately make use of it. A boxer warms up before a fight by dancing around and shadow boxing. A runner runs back and forth lightly. Football players run a ball before going into a game. In these cases, the warming up is done before the athlete actually enters the game, because he knows that he will not be at his top performance if he does not warm up first.

This same type of warming up takes place in other types of activity, even in intellec-

THE TYPICAL WORK CURVE HAS ITS PEAK ABOUT MIDMORNING:

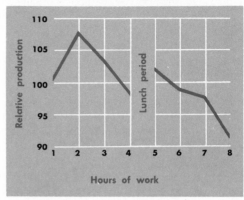

FIGURE 18.7. A typical work curve for heavy handwork. The curve is rather characteristic of work curves obtained for heavy work. The figures have been adjusted to let 100 stand for the average rate of production for the 8-hour day.

A WORK CURVE CAN BE ANALYZED INTO FOUR COMPONENTS:

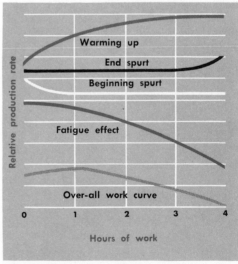

FIGURE 18.8. The components of the work curve. The shape of any particular work curve will depend on the relative importance of the various components.

tual activities such as studying for an examination or writing a term paper. When you first start to work, you are poorly organized; you are not really set for the job, and perhaps you fidget or even get up and walk around. The warming-up period may take longer for some people than for others, and it may take longer for some activities than for others. But warming up is of value in almost every type of activity.

Referring now to Figure 18.7, one can see that warming up accounts for the fact that production is greater during the second hour than during the first hour. If the warming up is very slow, the work curve may rise throughout the whole morning period. On the other hand, if it is very fast, it may be over in the first few minutes and not have any appreciable effect on the total productivity for the first hour.

Beginning spurt. The middle curve in Figure 18.8 illustrates another factor in work curves, the *beginning spurt*. This is exactly the opposite of the warming-up effect and can completely cancel it. We may start off a particular job with a great deal of enthusiasm and put our full effort into it. Then the realization that this job is going on for a long time hits us, and we slow down to a steadier pace—a pace more suitable for the long haul. After people have worked on the same job a good many times, they are less likely to show a beginning spurt. It is characteristic of a new job or activity and does not occur in some jobs.

End spurt. When activity is increased at the end of a job, we call it an *end spurt*. The end of the day brings with it an increased enthusiasm, and a final burst of energy sends production up. The end spurt commonly occurs in athletic events and probably represents the athlete's willingness to use up all the energy he has left, because he knows he need not save it for any later effort. A long-distance runner, for example, usually manages an extra burst of speed at the end of the run, and a boxer frequently fights more vigorously in the last round than he has in any preceding one.

Occasionally the end spurt at the end of a day is so large that it hits a peak of production for the day. When this happens, it is clear that the worker has not really been working at top effort all along. As we shall see in the discussion on fatigue, it is important to recognize the difference between what a man can do and what he is willing to do.

Effects of fatigue

The most important trend in a work curve usually represents fatigue. This is a general downward trend throughout the whole period of work. It is on this trend that effects of other factors such as warming up, beginning spurt, and end spurt are superimposed. Fatigue makes the efficiency of work fall far short of what one might expect by looking at the peaks of the work curve.

Fatigue is a common word, and we are therefore inclined to think that we know what it means. Certainly we feel fatigue, and we have many words to describe this feeling—tired, weary, exhausted, spent, worn out, beat, dead. Such subjective reports of fatigue probably make up the best definition of fatigue that can be offered at the present time. *Fatigue is a feeling of being tired.* As we shall see below, there is no completely consistent way of measuring fatigue.

OUTPUT. Sometimes fatigue is reflected in a decrement in performance. The decrement may be measured either by a decreased *output* of work or by increased *errors*. Usually decreased output is the decrement when the work is primarily physical. If a person is shoveling coal, he shovels less coal when he is fatigued than when he is not. If he is typing, he usually types fewer words per minute when he is fatigued than when he is rested. Here, we are talking about the amount of work accomplished, and it is easy to measure the amount. We can measure the weight of the coal shoveled or the number of words typed. When the activity or work is of a kind for which an amount can be measured, our first attempt to measure fatigue is always in terms of the amount of work done.

Typically, the amount at first drops slowly or imperceptibly. Then it drops faster and faster, as shown in Figure 18.8. If the work is kept up long enough, fatigue eventually becomes so great that no work at all can be done. We say that a person is completely exhausted when he is so fatigued that he can no longer work at all.

ERRORS AND TIME. In psychomotor work—work which involves skill, speed, or accuracy, as distinguished from physical work—there frequently is no decrement in amount of work done as fatigue increases. Sometimes this is because the work cannot be measured in amounts. Studying for an examination is an activity that can hardly be measured as an amount. At other times, the physical effort involved in the work is so slight that no change in amount occurs. In such cases, however, a measurement of errors frequently reveals fatigue when a measurement of amount does not. For example, when a person is receiving telegraphic code, his fatigue is reflected in an increase in the number of errors.

In one study [Mackworth, 1950], receivers made between three and four times as many errors in the third hour of receiving code as they did in the first hour. In a study of typing errors [Robinson and Bills, 1926], the time required to type successive lines was measured, and although the time required per line (a measure of amount of work) went up at first, it later went back down again. An analysis of the errors made, however, showed that the number of errors per line continued to increase long after the time per line leveled off.

Whether fatigue shows up as increased *time* taken to do a certain amount of work or as increased *errors* depends on the attitude or set of the worker. If he has been instructed to work for perfect accuracy, he can do so over a long period of time. Then as he becomes more and more fatigued, he must slow down in order to keep from making errors. If, on the other hand, the worker has been instructed to work primarily for speed, he may continue to work at the same rate for long periods of time but will make more and more errors.

Thus we see that fatigue can show itself in more ways than one, and we must be careful, in looking for the effects of fatigue, to examine all possible changes in performance. If we measure one thing and neglect another, we may find that there is no change in what we are measuring. The change may take place instead in some aspect of performance that we fail to measure. This is especially true when the worker knows what is going to be measured, for then he strives to keep his performance up in that particular respect. But if he is really fatigued, his work will deteriorate in some other way.

PHYSIOLOGICAL EFFECTS. We should note in passing, without going into details, that fatigue may be reflected in physiological performance. Muscle tension may increase, as may heart rate, blood pressure, and other measures of exertion. The amount of oxygen required to do a given amount of work may also increase. Hence physiological measures of these changes may indicate fatigue when there is little or no evidence in the behavior of the person.

FATIGUE AS A CHANGE IN MOTIVATION. There is still another way in which fatigue can show up. Suppose that you observe men at work over long periods of time and that their production continues to decline. You then have clear evidence of fatigue. Suppose that you now stop the men at work and give them some tests of ability. The chances are that you will find their ability to perform on these tests is as good after many hours of work as it was when they were fresh. You might also find that their work was being done with no loss in physiological efficiency. So the men are still able to work as well after many hours as in the first hour, but they actually do not work as well.

What then accounts for the decline in their production? You might be justified in supposing that it is due to a change in *motivation* rather than fatigue—that the men simply are not trying so hard as they might. Alternatively, you might say that to compensate for fatigue more motivation is required [Mackworth, 1948]. Both statements are correct.

This situation is shown schematically in Figure 18.9. The curve of work output continues to drop, but the curve of ability as measured by laboratory tests does not go down. What has changed is the person's feeling of what is necessary, or his willingness to work.

This effect of fatigue is very common in our everyday life. If you have been driving an automobile for several hours and are stopped and given a driving test, you probably will do as well as if you had not been driving for a long time. However, while you are actually driving, you probably change your idea of what is necessary. You are less alert, you do not slow down quite so soon when you approach an intersection, and you take more chances when you pass another car—not because you are unable to do the correct thing, but rather because it no longer seems quite so necessary to do so.

The term *vigilance* has been used to describe what diminishes in this effect, and it is very apt. You can do as well, but you are less vigilant.

It is the very nature of this effect of fatigue that makes it so important. If you have been digging a ditch for several hours, you are fatigued, and you know it. If you are driving a car, however, you do not realize that you are fatigued because the only effect of the fatigue has been to make you relax your standards of what you consider good performance. You do not drive as well because you think you do not have to, and when you have an accident because of carelessness you will be sure that you have done everything just as you should. But

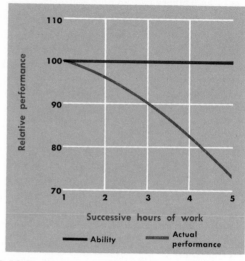

FIGURE 18.9. Tests may tell us that a worker's ability has not changed, but the fact that actual performance has declined during the course of the working period indicates that motivation has changed.

when you are tired, what you *think* you should do and what you *really* should do are often two different things.

SLEEP. One of the obvious ways to make a person tired or fatigued is to deprive him of sleep. By itself, loss of sleep is not the same thing physiologically as fatigue. Nevertheless, the sleep-deprived person, merely by remaining awake and active without the rest afforded by sleep, becomes a very fatigued person. It is therefore of interest to ask, What are the effects of sleep deprivation?

There are dozens of research studies on this question. They have run into the same problems that we have already encountered in other attempts to measure fatigue. If a man goes one night without sleep, it is hard to tell much difference the next day. He may confess that he is somewhat lightheaded, his attention may wander a little, and he may have an unusual desire to sit down or lie down. His performance, however, is likely to be about the same, for he can do a fair day's work, take examinations, answer letters, and otherwise function normally.

Suppose we keep the man up for still another night, and then another. In several studies, people have been kept from sleeping for three successive nights. On the fourth day, they have been given all sorts of tests—psychomotor, intelligence, arithmetic, etc. The interesting fact is that they can do just about as well on all these objective tests of efficiency as they could when they were rested. Rather prolonged loss of sleep, therefore, does not impair efficiency if we use systematic tests to measure it.

There are, nevertheless, profound effects that can be discovered in other ways. People tend to become silly, irritable, and restless. Some may even develop symptoms that resemble mental illness—symptoms such as delusions of grandeur or persecution, or false memories of people and of the passage of time. Their judgment becomes impaired, and if they drive cars they are more likely to take chances. In general, people who have been deprived of sleep for a long time show all the subtle symptoms of persons who have worked hard for too many hours or who suffer a little oxygen lack. Perhaps the most obvious symptom is that they do not want to work; indeed, all they want to do is lie down and go to sleep. So loss of sleep, like other effects of fatigue, does not change a person's capacity to perform, but it does change his willingness or motivation to perform.

WORK AND REST. We have seen that there are many factors that affect how we work. Fatigue is the most important of these factors. We can show its effects in many different ways. Since fatigue is so important, we are greatly concerned with ways of preventing it and means of overcoming it after it has occurred.

Recovery from fatigue. Perhaps the best way of learning how to prevent or overcome fatigue is to find out just how fast we recover from it. Figure 18.10 shows the results

RECOVERY FROM FATIGUE IS MOST RAPID DURING THE FIRST FEW MINUTES OF REST:

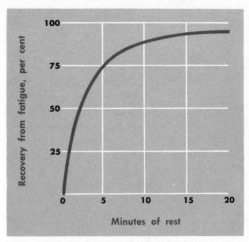

FIGURE 18.10. These are the results of a test for recovery from fatigue. Subjects lifted a weight with their fingers until they could no longer lift it. Then, after various periods of rest, they were required to lift the weight again. The curve shows how high, relative to first lifting, they could lift the weight after rest [after Manzer, 1927].

of an old experiment [Manzer, 1927] performed with university students.

The students were required to lift a weight with their fingers, and the height to which they lifted the weight was measured on each trial. They were required to continue lifting the weight until they could no longer lift it at all. Then they were given rest periods for various lengths of time, after which they were required to lift the weight again. The height to which they could lift the weight on the first trial after rest was a measure of the relative recovery from fatigue. If they still could not lift it at all, they had not recovered at all. If they could lift it as high as they had on the first trial previously, then the recovery was 100 per cent.

Figure 18.10 shows that recovery from fatigue is fairly rapid at first but then slows down considerably. Even after 20 minutes of rest, the students had not completely recovered from the fatigue. In fact, at the rate they were recovering, a total of 40 minutes would be required for them to get back to normal.

If the students were stopped before they had reached complete fatigue, and then given rest periods, recovery was much faster. For example, they might have been stopped when they were lifting the weight only 50 per cent as high as they had on the first trial. In this case recovery would be complete in a much shorter period of time. In fact, recovery from fatigue is so much faster after short periods of work than after long periods that much greater over-all efficiency can be obtained with short work periods than with long work periods.

For example, suppose you have a certain amount of snow that has to be shoveled. If you start right in and keep going until you can barely lift the shovel, you will have to stop and take a rest. It will require a long rest, however, for you to recover from your fatigue and get back to work. On the other hand, if you shovel for a little while, then rest for a little while, then shovel, etc., you never need very long rest periods, because recovery from fatigue is rapid when only a little work has been done. In this way you can shovel steadily for a much longer period of time, and you actually can get the whole job done much sooner than if you keep shoveling until you are completely fatigued.

Rest periods. There is a definite moral to this story: to stave off fatigue and still get work done, one should schedule rest periods often enough to keep from getting very tired. How often they should be and how long they should be depends on the kind of work. Heavy manual labor requires frequent and reasonably long rest periods. For sedentary work, rest periods do not need to be either so frequent or so long (see related discussion in Chapter 8 of periods of practice in learning).

In recent years industry has been applying these principles more and more by providing for regular rest periods throughout the workday. Industrial concerns have learned by experience as well as experiment that such rest periods allay fatigue and increase productivity, that necessary rest is not time lost but rather work gained. They often face the practical decision, however, of how long to make the periods and when to schedule them. Usually they have provided for periods of 10 to 15 minutes. By studying production records carefully it is possible to schedule the periods just before production tends to fall off. In the case of clerical and sedentary workers, one break about midmorning and another about midafternoon are usually about right.

One of the things we learn from studies of industrial fatigue is that it is better, usually, to schedule rest periods than to allow people to take them irregularly. In one study, for example, production was greater with scheduled periods than with irregular ones even though the total time taken in rest in the latter instance was slightly greater [McGehee and Owen, 1940]. The reason for this apparently lies in the set of a person for work. Most of us manage to adjust our level of effort to the total amount of work to be accomplished or to the total time we have to work. If, for example, you are starting to run a mile, you do not run as fast as if you are starting to run 100 yards. Likewise, if a person has 10 minutes to work, he is likely to work harder than if he has 2 hours to work. So when a person has a definite time to rest he is likely to pace himself at a little faster rate than if he works until he gets tired and voluntarily stops.

Length of the workday and workweek. Another factor in work efficiency is the length of the working day. The facts of this matter are very interesting. Many people assume, rather naturally, that if we want to get more from a particular worker, the thing to do is increase the number of hours per day or per week that he works. In recent years, however, it has become increasingly clear that there is a real limit to the number of hours most people can work in a day or week and still work with reasonable efficiency. Perhaps it is obvious that a man becomes less efficient *per hour* if he works 10 hours a day than if he works 8 hours a day. What was not realized for a long time, however, is that he can become so much less efficient that the total work done in a 10-hour day is less than the total work done in an 8-hour day.

A number of studies demonstrate both points [Ghiselli and Brown, 1955]. If maximum production per hour is what we want, then a workweek between 36 and 44 hours is best. If, however, we want the maximum production per workweek, a workweek between 48 and 54 hours is best. The reason for this difference is that the hourly efficiency drops when the workweek is increased from 40 to 50 hours, but the drop in efficiency is not great enough to offset the greater number of hours. If, however, the workweek is increased beyond this point, then the drop in hourly efficiency is so great that it completely offsets the increased number of hours.

Engineering for human use

In the technological age we live in, there is still another aspect of the adjustment of people to their work. This is their relationship to machines. Machines are taking over countless tasks formerly done by people, as well as doing things that never before were possible. It takes people, however, to run these machines, and the machines in turn control people's behavior. The net result is that people are doing more and more of their work with or through machines. They must somehow "get along" with machines, and do it well, in order to work safely and efficiently and to make machines do what they are intended for.

MAN-MACHINE PROBLEMS. This relationship of man to machines is generating new problems—problems of matching men and machines. One set of problems, which we have already mentioned, concerns selecting and training people for operating machines. Another set of problems concerns the design of machines for human use—designing them so that the man together with the machine gets his job done. The field of knowledge concerned with the solution of these problems has various names. One is *human engineering,* but this is often expanded to *human-factors engineering* in order to make clearer what is meant. Such engineering involves a number of disciplines, but the one of interest here is *engineering psychology.* This is a rapidly growing field of application of psychology—mostly experimental psychology—to problems of engineering design.

Engineering psychology got its start in the Second World War, when wartime demands brought psychologists in contact with engineering problems [Chapanis et al., 1949]. This contact demonstrated that psychology had information of use in engineering design, and could produce more when needed through appropriate experiments and tests. Thus engineering psychology began to flourish and has grown rapidly since. Today most of the larger industries concerned with designing complex systems, such as airplanes, missiles, communication systems, computers, and the like, employ engineering psychologists as members of their teams of engineers charged with designing such systems. It is now a field that boasts several textbooks and handbooks. We shall attempt here to give only a bird's-eye view of it.

The operation of machines may involve various kinds of work—physical, psychomotor, or mental—but it typically falls in the class of psychomotor tasks. Generally speaking, there are two ways to measure performance in such tasks: errors and amount of work. Conversely, when a man-machine combination fails to perform effectively, the failure may be due to errors made by the operator or to his being overloaded with more work than he can do. These two factors, of course, interact. By slowing down, a man usually can be more accurate;

by speeding up, he usually can handle a larger load of work but at the sacrifice of accuracy. Hence, the two factors and their interaction are the general problems of concern to the engineering psychologist. He attempts to design, or redesign, machines in such a way as to minimize errors and to maximize output. The relative importance of each depends on the machine and its purpose.

The work of engineering psychology can also be divided in another way into two general parts: displays and controls. Man may be regarded as a component in a man-machine system. As such a component, he receives "inputs" from the machine component as well as from his physical environment. In other words, he receives information through his senses. Such information is presented to him through some kind of *display*. On the other hand, his "output" consists of things he does to and with the machine to control its behavior. The "things" he uses for this purpose are *controls*. Thus most of the problems the engineering psychologist works with involve either displays or controls or both.

MAN COMPARED WITH MACHINES. We shall consider examples of the design of displays and controls. Before doing that, however, a more general question deserves some discussion. This is the question of how man compares with machines in ability to do different tasks. Despite the near-miraculous performance of some machines, there are still many things man can do better than machines. To design the best man-machine system, one must assign to each the things it can do best.

Sensing. There are some general statements that can be made about this comparison [Williams et al., 1956]. Man as a sensor is restricted in the range of the spectrum of light or sound to which he responds, whereas machines can be built to sense signals, for example, infrared, of which man is completely unaware. On the other hand, human sensitivity to many forms of physical energy is exceedingly acute and often is better than

that of a sensing device. Moreover, man's senses operate through a much wider range of intensities, giving good performance for very weak as well as very strong stimuli, as compared with sensing devices. It is important, however, to realize that one sense may be much better for assimilating a particular kind of information—for example, the eye is much superior to the ear in handling spatial information—and this must be considered in selecting and designing displays.

Data processing. In processing data—remembering and interpreting information—man also has advantages and disadvantages which compare with machines. Man is superior in the following respects: He does not need extensive programming, for example, as a computer does. He is more flexible, and can deal with unforeseen situations. He can exercise judgment, and quickly recall facts and methods of solving problems. However, machines are superior to men in the amount of detailed information they can store (remember), in the speed and accuracy with which they can arrive at answers, in sorting and classifying data, in giving reliable results in routine operations, and in working longer at high speed without being subject to fatigue, prejudice, or other factors that distort judgment and decisions.

Controlling. When it comes to controlling things, man is generally inferior to machines, and the controls he uses must be designed to take his limitations into account. He is relatively weak and slow. He is limited in the kind of movements he can make and in the number of controls he can operate either simultaneously or in quick succession. The time he can work without fatigue or wavering of attention is relatively short. For these reasons, the tasks assigned to human control must be carefully chosen and designed.

These statements are only general guides. Specific data of handbook proportions are available for determining how well human beings can perform on various sensing, judging, and control tasks [Woodson, 1954]. When available data do not answer specific questions, the engineering psychologist runs tests and experiments to obtain the needed answers. Then, together with other members of the design team, he draws up an over-all design of the man-machine system. This design prescribes, at least roughly, what is expected of the man and of the machine. It serves as a guide to the development of specific components in the system.

Knowing at least roughly what the man will be expected to do in a man-machine system, the engineering psychologist can next turn his attention to the design of the displays and controls involved in the man's tasks. In order to proceed with this assignment, he must somehow obtain a complete job description of the man's duties specified in terms of the information needed (for display) and the actions he must take (for control). There are several methods for obtaining a job description; some are like the procedures for preparing job analyses described earlier. Having accomplished that, the engineering psychologist is ready to proceed with the design of the displays and controls of the system.

DESIGN OF DISPLAYS. To design the displays that a man must use in any complicated system, the designer must first consider the chance of overloading one or more of the senses. The sense that is most often overloaded is vision; after that, hearing. Consider, for example, the picture of an airplane cockpit in Figure 18.11. You can readily see that the visual sense is overloaded; there are far too many dials here for a person to attend to. Indeed, studies show that many accidents or near accidents have occurred for this reason. Since this picture was taken, designers have improved cockpit design, especially in jet aircraft, by utilizing a number of human-engineering principles, some of which will be covered below.

Where one sense is overloaded, the engineering psychologist can devise ways of presenting some of the information through another sense. Simple warning signals, for example, are often better presented as auditory signals, e.g., a buzzer, than as lights. In

FIGURE 18.11. A problem in human engineering. Psychologists specializing in the field of human engineering rearrange and simplify levers, knobs, and dials so that the man who uses them can do his job more easily, more efficiently, and more safely [American Airlines].

some specialized cases, information may be presented as a vibration, say, of a control held continuously by the operator. Tradition and habit often hamper the acceptance of such alternatives, but they are being employed.

When a decision has been made about the mode of presenting information, the next step is to decide on the type of display to be used. Since most displays are visual, let us restrict ourselves to visual displays. In any complicated situation such as a cockpit, there may be dozens of displays. In designing a group of visual displays, the engineering psychologist must make several decisions.

Pictorial versus symbolic displays. One is whether a given display will be *pictorial* or *symbolic.* A pictorial display is one that reproduces with some realism the situation it represents. Maps, for example, are pictorial displays. In an aircraft, an artificial horizon indicator may be a pictorial display, for it pictures the position of a plane and its orientation with respect to a horizon. Symbolic displays are instruments that present information indirectly, usually by dials, pointers, or lights. The speedometer on a car is a symbolic display; so is a license plate. One displays speed, the other the identity of an automobile and its owner in numbers that symbolize, but do not picture, the thing represented.

Symbolic displays have the advantages of being simple, versatile, compact, and above all, accurate. Pictorial displays, on the other hand, can usually be interpreted more quickly than symbolic displays, with little or no training required on the part of the operator. If, for example, you are shown a map with a miniature car marked on it (pictorial display), you can tell quickly where the car is. Given the same information on dials showing longitude and latitude (symbolic display), you would need some training in the use of such a scheme in order to interpret the numbers quickly and correctly. To decide which type of display to use, the engineering psychologist must know what kind of people will be using the display and what will be required of them.

Kinds of indicators. There are many interesting problems in the design of pictorial displays, but symbolic displays are most frequently used, primarily because they are compact. Most practical problems therefore arise in connection with symbolic displays, particularly dials. In designing symbolic displays, the designer must first ask, What is the purpose of the display? In general, each display serves one of three purposes:

1. *Check-reading indicators.* A check-reading dial tells the operator whether something is on or off, working or not working. The blinker on the dash board of an automobile with turn indicators serves this purpose; it merely tells the driver whether the

indicator is working. Some automobiles use a red light to indicate whether oil pressure or battery charging is adequate or not. This is a check-reading indicator.

2. *Qualitative indicators.* Some indicators serve the purpose of telling the operator whether things are all right, and if not, in which direction they are off. The temperature indicator on most automobiles is such an indicator. It does not say exactly what the temperature is, for that doesn't matter, but it does tell whether the car is cold, is warmed up and in the normal range, or is getting too hot.

3. *Quantitative indicators.* Some information needs to be relatively precise. If, for example, we are to obey posted speed limits when driving, we need to know how fast we are going. The customary speedometer gives this information quantitatively.

The automobile has been used as an example because it should be familiar to the reader, but this classification of dials and indicators serves well for all sorts of visual symbolic displays. In order to avoid overloading an operator, it is important to know just what kind of indicator is necessary. If all that is required is check reading, an indicator showing more information than that should not be used. Similarly, a quantitative indicator should not be used when a qualitative one will do. Those who have observed the evolution of the modern automobile panel will realize that these principles are now being utilized more effectively than they were some years ago.

Dial design. Once the type of indicator has been chosen, the problem narrows down to the details of designing each dial for its intended purpose. This is not too much of a problem for check-reading or qualitative indicators, but it may be for quantitative indicators. For one thing, a choice must be made between a *counter* and a *dial.* (The odometer showing accumulated mileage is a counter; the speedometer usually is a dial.) We have experiments to show that counters usually can be read more quickly and accurately than dials. On the other hand, they may be impossible to use if the operator must set them to a prescribed number or read them while their readings are changing. Hence the choice again depends on the nature of the operator's task.

If the choice is a dial, then there are many types of dials to select from. In Figure 18.12, for example, are five different types of dials: round, semicircular, an open-window dial with the scale moving and the pointer fixed, a vertical dial with moving pointer, and a horizontal dial with moving pointer. This particular set of dials was subjected to extensive experimenter comparisons in which subjects made over a thousand readings. Their errors were subsequently analyzed [Sleight, 1948]. The result showed that the open-window dial was read with the greatest accuracy, and the vertical moving-pointer dial with the greatest number of errors. This result was obtained under a particular set of experimental conditions, and one cannot therefore generalize it to every situation. It nevertheless shows how one may go about selecting the proper type of dial for a particular task.

Another problem in dial design is how to make the scale divisions on the dial. A dial with relatively few marks on it is obviously difficult to read with any accuracy. On the other hand, a scale that is too finely divided can be confusing, hard to read, and likely to produce errors. Moreover, a human being is rather good at interpolation; he can estimate fairly accurately the position of a pointer between two marks. Psychologists have studied this matter in some detail and have figures available for the design of various dials. In general, for the typical dial used on a cockpit or automobile panel, the scale markings should be about half an inch apart. This design gives better accuracy than dials that are more or less cluttered with markings.

There are many other problems in the design of dial displays, especially when the information to be presented is complex and involves a large range of numbers. As a final example, however, of the design of displays for human use, let us consider a common

SOME DIALS ARE BETTER THAN OTHERS FOR A PARTICULAR PURPOSE:

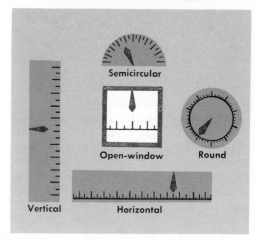

FIGURE 18.12. Five different shapes used in an experiment to compare dial shapes [after Sleight, 1948].

problem presented by a large number of dials.

In the upper part of Figure 18.13 is a display of dials as they might appear when arranged on a cockpit panel without regard to their use by people. Indeed such displays can be found in many situations today. Since each dial displays a different sort of information, the normal place of the point differs from dial to dial. One can see that it would be difficult and time-consuming for an operator to read each of these dials and determine whether things were all right or, if not, how they differed from what they ought to be.

The task can be greatly simplified by *patterning the dial display* [Woodson, 1954]. This can be done by orienting each dial so that the normal or usual position of a pointer is the same on every dial. Only when the dial indicates something different or unusual does the pointer move away from the usual position. Thus the task of reading the dials is simplified. At a glance, the operator can see which dials are "out of line" and then read them to find out what the discrepancy means. This principle is being incorporated in airplanes and other systems that involve displays of many dials.

DESIGN OF CONTROLS. We have discussed displays, and particularly dials, at some length in order to give a coherent, though still sketchy, picture of one aspect of engineering psychology. Although the design of controls is also a large subject, we shall treat it more briefly and give only a few points.

Classes of controls. The same distinction among classes of controls can be made as among classes of indicators. *On-off controls* are like check-reading indicators. A toggle switch used in controlling the lights at home is such a control. *Position controls* are like qualitative indicators. They are set in one of three or four positions. The station selector on a television set is an example. *Continuous controls* are like quantitative indicators. Changes in the thing controlled are proportional to the movement of the control. The foot brake and steering wheel of a car are examples.

Here, as with displays, the tasks of operators must be analyzed and a control selected that is sufficient for the job. In general, the engineering psychologist should not supply a continuous control if an on-off switch or a position control will do.

Placement of controls. The placement of controls often presents a problem, especially where a good many controls are necessary and space is at a premium. There are two reasons for this. One is that human beings are limited in the contortions they can make and still operate a control properly. Controls placed too close to the arms are easily knocked accidentally. Those that are too far away cause awkwardness of motion or force the operator to let up or lose contact with other controls being operated by the other hand or the feet. Those that are under seats or panels often cannot be turned or pushed properly.

Another factor in placing controls properly concerns habits the operator has previously acquired. If he is accustomed to finding a certain control in one place and he now finds it in another, he will need time to learn the new position and may

PATTERNING MAKES DIAL CHECKING MUCH EASIER:

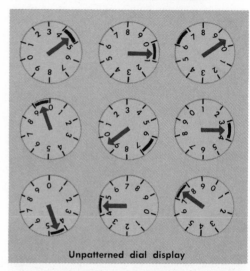

Unpatterned dial display

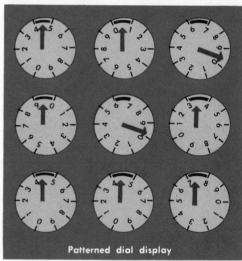

Patterned dial display

FIGURE 18.13. The patterning of dials. Patterning helps the operator to see at a glance which dials are not indicating their normal readings.

make some serious mistakes in the process. He is also likely to revert to old habits in times of emergency. This is illustrated by the following account:

CHAPTER EIGHTEEN

Some years ago in tracking down the causes of aircraft accidents, Air Force psychologists noted that a large number of accidents (or near accidents) occurred when pilots switched from one to another of the following planes: B-25, C-47, and C-82. In particular, errors made by the pilots often involved operating the wrong control. The trouble was that different but related controls were arranged in a different sequence on these various planes (see Figure 18.14). The throttle was on the left in the B-25 and in the center on the C-47 and C-82. The propeller control was in the center on the B-25, on the left in the C-47, and on the right in the C-82. The gas-mixture control was on the right in the B-25 and C-47, but on the left in the C-82.

The student may remember the discussion of negative transfer or habit interference in an earlier chapter (page 235). This is an example of it. Because of negative transfer, the pilots frequently operated controls as they had been accustomed to operate them in other planes they had flown. Serious efforts are made nowadays in airplane design to standardize the placement of controls.

Coding of controls. When it is not possible to do this or when the operator cannot readily see a control and might mistakenly operate the wrong one, it helps to *code* the controls by shape and/or size. (The coding of displays by color or size is also a useful device.) By making each of the controls discriminably different, the operator can tell by "feel" when he places his hand on the control whether he has the right one.

For the purpose of coding controls used in airplane cockpits, Air Force psychologists investigated a series of 22 possible shapes. This was about as many different ways as anyone could devise of making knobs or controls different from each other. These shapes were then used in a discrimination experiment in which blindfolded subjects attempted to identify each knob by feeling it. The confusions between various shapes were noted, and shapes that were confused more than 1

T   Throttle

P   Propellor

M   Gas mixture

FIGURE 18.14. Placement of controls on three different airplanes. The controls are for throttle, propeller, and fuel mixture. Because of lack of standard arrangement, pilots may make the mistake of operating the wrong control.

per cent of the time were eliminated. As a result, the 11 different shapes shown in Figure 18.15 were selected as suitable for use whenever it seemed desirable to use shape coding in the design of controls.

These are just a few of many ways in which psychology is being applied in the design of machines for human use. Sometimes the engineering psychologist does little more than employ common sense. His role is then one of a watchdog to see that human factors are not overlooked in meeting engineering objectives. More important, he also

FIGURE 18.15. Eleven shapes found to be best for shape coding of controls [after Jenkins, 1947].

draws on a stockpile of knowledge about human capacities and limitations and goes ahead to obtain more information through further experiments.

Comparatively, the number of engineering psychologists is not yet large. On a liberal count, there are only a few hundred. Several years ago, however, there were only a handful, so growth has been very rapid. At the present rate, it will be only a matter of time until engineering psychology is a large field that will be encountered and utilized in nearly every phase of our modern technology.

Summary

1. The first step in the scientific selection of employees is to make a job analysis to determine accurately the requirements of the job. Next, the characteristics a worker must have to do the job adequately are assessed.

2. Traditional methods of selecting employees through application blanks, interviews, and letters of recommendation are relatively unreliable unless precautions are taken to obtain the best results from them.

3. Trade tests may be helpful in selecting skilled workers. Aptitude tests also can be valid in selecting many types of employees if the tests are properly chosen and proved through careful research.

4. The duties of the supervisor of employees have several psychological aspects. One is to be a teacher and trainer, not only in breaking in a new employee, but also in day-by-day supervision.

5. The supervisor must also be able to communicate his instructions promptly and intelligibly and to keep employees informed on most matters that they feel concern them in their work.

6. He must also evaluate both the job and the worker on the job so that he can make the fullest use of the workers' abilities and reward them fairly for their accomplishments.

7. The supervisor, finally, must consider the personal and emotional problems of an employee, because these seriously affect performance; he must offer counseling or other aid that may alleviate problems.

8. Employees do not work for pay alone, but for the satisfaction of all their needs. In fact, once pay is reasonable and fair, other factors, such as job security, good working conditions, opportunity for advancement, and good personnel relations become considerably more important.

9. Work curves that are typical of the amount of work done during the course of a day have their ups and downs. They can be analyzed, however, into four principal components: (*a*) a warm-up effect, (*b*) a beginning spurt, (*c*) an end spurt, and (*d*) a fatigue effect.

10. Fatigue can be measured in a number of ways: (*a*) by amount of work produced, (*b*) by errors or quality of work, (*c*) by physiological effects, and (*d*) by changes in motivation.

11. Often, when there is not a measurable effect of fatigue on production, fatigue shows up as a lowered motivation for work or as a lowered standard of performance.

12. Recovery from fatigue is generally faster when the fatigue is mild than when it has become severe. Thus it is better to take short rests frequently than long rests infrequently.

13. If one attempts to lengthen the workday or the workweek, one finds that there is a point beyond which total production declines. Consequently, there is an optimum workday and workweek.

14. Engineering psychology is a rapidly growing field in which psychological methods and research are used to improve the design of machines so that they better fit the capabilities of the human operator.

15. Machines are being designed to take the place of human operators, yet there are several respects in which man is more efficient than any machine. To design the best man-machine system, one must assign to each the things it can do best.

16. Displays for conveying information to the human operator should make use of man's various senses in such a way that no one sense is overloaded. The displays should be designed to enable the operator to comprehend information rapidly but with a minimum of error.

17. Similarly, controls should be designed with the operator in mind. The man-machine system can be made to function best by (*a*) choosing the best type of control, (*b*) placing and arranging controls properly, and (*c*) coding the controls so that they can be identified without having to be seen.

Suggestions for further reading

Bingham, W. V. D., Moore, B. V., and Gustad, J. W. *How to interview* (rev. ed.). New York: Harper, 1959.
The revision of a standard text on interviewing.

Burtt, H. E. *Applied psychology* (2d ed.). Englewood Cliffs, N.J.: Prentice-Hall, 1957.
A textbook on various uses of applied psychology, including vocational adjustment and industrial applications.

Chapanis, A. *The design and conduct of human engineering studies*. Baltimore: Johns Hopkins Press, 1959.
A readable account of the methods used in human engineering.

Chapanis, A., Garner, W. R., and Morgan, C. T. *Applied experimental psychology*. New York: Wiley, 1949.
A text on human engineering, work, and efficiency.

Ghiselli, E. E., and Brown, C. W. *Personnel and industrial psychology* (2d ed.). New York: McGraw-Hill, 1955.
A widely used text covering the general field of industrial psychology.

Haire, M. *Psychology in management*. New York: McGraw-Hill, 1956.
A brief and interesting psychological analysis of the role of the manager and supervisor.

Karn, H. W., and Gilmer, B. von H. *Readings in industrial and business psychology*. New York: McGraw-Hill, 1952.
The selected writings of different authors, with emphasis on modern developments in the field.

Maier, N. R. F. *Principles of human relations*. New York: Wiley, 1952.
The importance of human relations in industry, and methods for improving them.

McCormick, E. J. *Human engineering*. New York: McGraw-Hill, 1957.
An introductory textbook on human engineering.

Shartle, C. L. *Occupational information* (rev. ed.). Englewood Cliffs, N.J.: Prentice-Hall, 1952.
A sourcebook of information about the nature and classification of different occupations.

Smith, H. C. *Psychology of industrial behavior*. New York: McGraw-Hill, 1957.
A textbook emphasizing the role of motivational and social factors in industry.

CHAPTER EIGHTEEN

Introduction to psychology

NERVOUS SYSTEM
& INTERNAL
ENVIRONMENT

PHYSIOLOGICAL
BASIS OF
BEHAVIOR

PART SEVEN
BIOLOGICAL BACKGROUND

CHAPTER NINETEEN

Nervous system & internal environment

AT THE BEGINNING OF THIS book we defined psychology as the "science of human and animal behavior." We have now completed a broad survey of much of that science. It should have become evident in the course of the survey that behavior has a physiological basis. Behavior itself is actually the contraction of muscles. The stimuli to which behavior is a reaction, directly or indirectly, have their effects through the various sense organs. In between the muscles and the sense organs, many events take place in the nervous system, the blood stream, and the various glands.

Without these intervening physiological events, there would be no behavior, for, as we shall see in this chapter and the next, we need only disturb these events in some way to alter or to abolish behavioral responses. We cannot, therefore, fully understand behavior, and hence psychology, until we know something about these events. Put another way, behavior has a physiological basis, and to round out our "introduction to psychology" we should study it. We might almost say that we should look for the physiological explanation of behavior, for we can explain or at least better understand some of the phenomena we have studied by knowing the physiological mechanisms that underlie them. At any rate, we shall learn what some of the physiological correlates of behavior are.

To do that we shall proceed in two stages. In this chapter we must learn a little physiology and anatomy. We must learn the names, the structures, and some of the functions of the organs that are important in behavior. Not much will be said about the sense organs because they have been considered at length in Chapters 10, 11, and 12. We shall, however, study the sensory pathways leading from the sense organs into and through the nervous system. In the last chapter of the book we shall consider how the functions of certain organs are related to behavior.

The internal environment

Almost every organ of the body has some connection with behavior to the extent that its normal function is required for the well-being of the individual. Some organs, however, are more involved in behavior than others, for they are directly involved in responding to a stimulus. These organs are the *sense organs,* the *nervous system,* and the *effectors.* Sometimes these three parts of the stimulus-response mechanism are referred to respectively as the *receptors, adjustors,* and *effectors.* Effectors are of two general types: the *muscles* and the *glands.* As indicated elsewhere (page 45), the effector glands are of two kinds: the *exocrine* or duct glands, such as the salivary glands, which empty their secretions into cavities of the body, and the *endocrine* or ductless glands, such as the thyroid gland, which empty their secretions into the blood stream. The endocrine glands are the glands of greatest interest to us because they have widespread effects on behavior.

Not all, though nearly all, of the endocrine glands have nervous connections. Hence not all are effectors. Apart, however, from whether or not they are effectors, their secretions circulating in the blood stream can affect, by stimulation or inhibition, the functioning of other glands. Their secretions can also affect, as we shall see shortly, the activities of many other tissues, including particularly the nervous system and the muscles. They consequently provide a kind of *internal environment* for the various organs of the body. Internal environment refers to *all those chemical, temperature, and stimulus conditons within the body that form an environment for its organs,* just as the atmosphere and the external world of stimuli constitute the external environment of the organism.

As implied by this definition, the internal environment encompasses more than the endocrine secretions. It also includes body temperature and various chemical conditions related to eating, drinking, excretion, and breathing, as well as conditions generated by the body's own chemical and physiological processes. It happens that various aspects of the internal environment profoundly affect behavior. We therefore should consider it more closely.

METABOLIC MACHINERY. The internal environment is important, first of all, because it supples energy to various organs of the body. Muscles, obviously, must obtain energy if they are to do their work. So also must the cells of the nervous system and of the sense organs. These organs, in fact, are somewhat like fuel-burning engines. They receive and store the food that is brought to them in the blood. Then they use the oxygen, transported in the blood by a substance in the red corpuscles known as *hemoglobin,* to burn their fuel, much as an engine burns its fuel. In this way the muscles are able to contract and the nervous system is able to generate and transmit nerve impulses.

The body is always burning fuel, even when it is quiet as in sleep. At times, however, a relatively greater supply of cellular fuel must be on hand for immediate use. The cells of the several tissues of the body therefore store fuel as well as burn it up. The two processes, of building up and of breaking down stores of energy, taken together are known as *metabolism.*

Metabolism is no simple matter. Since the food we eat is not in a form the body can use, it must be broken down—digested— into simple chemical packets that can pass through the walls of the intestines into the blood. Once there, it must be converted into

FIGURE 19.1. The names and positions in the body of the endocrine (ductless) glands that secrete hormones.

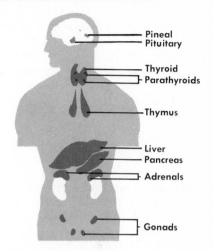

other forms and transported to convenient places for storage. Some is stored in the liver, some in the muscles, and some in other tissues of the body. This storing involves several chemical steps. Then, when it is needed, the fuel must be gotten out of storage—more chemical steps—and transported to its place of use. At that point, still other chemical steps are necessary to put it into a usable form.

So metabolism involves numerous chemical reactions and many different chemical materials. Food materials and the oxygen that is ultimately used to burn them are, of course, essentials in metabolism. A number of other substances enter into the process. These are the hormones, vitamins, and enzymes. Without these substances, metabolism could never run its course and our organs could not function. They are therefore of special interest to us.

HORMONES.   A *hormone is a chemical substance secreted by an endocrine gland* (page 74). This type of gland pours its secretion directly into the blood. There are a great many hormones. Although physiologists have not yet identified all of them, they do know many of them well, even to the point of being able to synthesize them. They also know what many of the hormones do in metabolism. In the accompanying illustration (Figure 19.1) are the names and positions in the body of the principal glands that produce hormones. We shall describe only those that have an important bearing on behavior.

Thyroid gland. The thyroid gland, located in the tissue of the neck around the windpipe, produces a hormone known as *thy-*

roxin. This hormone controls the general rate at which energy is produced in the body. If the amount of thyroxin is low, energy is burned slowly, even though the body may have ample food resources. The individual is sluggish and shows many medical signs of low metabolism. If there is too much thyroxin, the individual is usually extremely active and shows signs of high metabolism. Thyroxin, then, regulates metabolic rate.

Parathyroid glands. In the vicinity of the thyroid glands are two pairs of small glands, collectively called the *parathyroid glands*. Their hormone, called *parathormone*, regulates the level of calcium and phosphorus— two chemical elements important in nerve activity. Parathormone keeps the supply of calcium in the blood high and that of phosphorus relatively low. If there is a deficiency in parathormone, calcium levels are lowered and those of phosphorus rise.

Pancreatic gland. The pancreas is located along the lower wall of the stomach. It secretes the hormone *insulin,* a substance primarily responsible for the control of blood-sugar level. If insulin is deficient, blood sugar rises above normal amounts; if it is in excess, blood sugar falls below normal. The blood-sugar level, in turn, indicates how much sugar the tissues are able to get for fuel. When blood sugar is high, it means that not enough is getting out of the blood to the brain; as a result, the brain is "starving" for food. The converse is true when blood sugar falls because there is an excess of the hormone insulin. Thus insulin can affect how much sugar the brain gets for fuel and, in turn, for carrying out its functions.

Adrenal glands. We have already mentioned the adrenal glands in describing bodily changes in emotion (Chapter 4). These glands are located in the back of the body above the kidney. One part of them secretes a hormone called *adrenalin*. It is this hormone that is released in strong emotion. Another part, the cortical part, secretes a number of hormones, collectively known as *cortin*, which govern the level of sodium and the amount of water in the internal environment.

Gonads. The technical name for the sex glands of the male and female is *gonads.* In the male the gonads are called the *testes;* in the female, the *ovaries.* In each case they occur in pairs. They secrete several related hormones, but those of the male are somewhat different from those of the female. The sex hormones are not very active in young children. They come into play at puberty (when the child is about twelve years of age) and are responsible for the marked physical changes that take place in girls and boys at that time: growth of the breasts, the beginning of menstruation, growth of the beard, and changes of the voice—all the so-called "secondary sex characteristics" that distinguish girls from boys.

Pituitary gland. At first the sex hormones lie dormant under the control of the *pituitary gland.* It is not until the child is about eleven or twelve years old that the pituitary gland stimulates the gonads to secrete actively. The pituitary gland, in fact, secretes a number of hormones that stimulate or inhibit secretion in other glands of the body. It is for this reason that it is sometimes called the "master gland." In addition, the pituitary secretes other hormones that play a direct role in metabolism. One of these, the *growth hormone,* controls the general rate of growth in a child. If there is too little of it, he becomes a dwarf; if too much, a giant.

It may be seen from this brief survey that the hormones take part in many aspects of the body's metabolism. Biochemists have been conducting intensive research in recent years to find out precisely how hormones participate in the chemical steps of metabolism. They have discovered that rather small amounts of them are required to maintain normal metabolism and that little of them is burned up in the course of metabolism. They conclude, therefore, that hormones are agents that help or hinder certain chemical steps without directly supplying the energy for them [Dempsey, 1946].

ENZYMES. The hormones, however, are not alone in the job of regulating metabolic reactions. In fact, they probably work by increasing or decreasing the supply of other agents known as *enzymes.* Enzymes result from chemical reactions taking place in various cells of the body. These enzymes are the intermediate agents, or *catalysts,* that *regulate particular chemical steps in metabolism.* There are many known enzymes, and each takes part in a particular reaction. For example, in the chemical reactions required to get sugar to the brain or to make use of the by-products of the burning of sugar, there are several specific enzymes, each involved in some one step. If one of these enzymes should be deficient, the chemical reactions with which it is concerned are blocked. We shall see a little later (page 636) how such blocking may produce feeble-mindedness.

VITAMINS. Vitamins are a class of substances closely related to the enzymes. The public is now fully indoctrinated about the importance of vitamins and is consuming vast quantities of them annually—usually without knowing exactly why. Unlike the hormones and enzymes, vitamins are *not* produced in the body. Instead they must be imported in the foods that are normally eaten or in the capsules available at drugstores. Although the body needs only small traces of them, the vitamins *control certain vital chemical reactions in the body.* Indeed, modern biochemical research seems to show that vitamins probably join with other products in the body to make enzymes. In any event enzymes and vitamins are closely related.

GENES.   Three kinds of chemicals—the hormones, vitamins, and enzymes—are the agents that control the complex chemical machinery of the body. This hierarchy of controlling agents, in turn, is the product of genetic factors [Beadle, 1945]. We have already seen (Chapter 2) that the genes are the agents of heredity—the means by which physical characteristics are handed down from one generation to another. This transmission of hereditary characteristics has to be done by chemical reactions. The individual starts out as one cell, which multiplies and divides in various ways through many chemical reactions until eventually the tissues and organs of the body are formed. Hence genes determine the ultimate form of the body by working through the hormones, enzymes, and vitamins.

The chain of relationships between genes and behavior is sketched in Figure 19.2. Genes, besides reproducing themselves, either produce or catalyze the production of enzymes. These in turn catalyze various reactions involved in cellular metabolism, thus determining the form and function of cells. Various cells, interacting with each other, participate in the processes of morphogenesis—meaning the formation of structures—through which the organs of the body are fashioned. Some of these organs, as we have noted, participate in behavior. In the next chapter, we shall see how glandular secretions, enzymes, and vitamins may be

A CHAIN OF PROCESSES LINKS GENES AND BEHAVIOR:

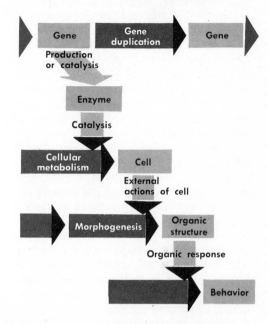

FIGURE 19.2. The chain of processes through which genes and enzymes are related to behavior [after Zubek and Solberg, 1954].

directly concerned in behavior. Let us turn now to the organ that is most important in behavior, namely, the nervous system, and the neurons that compose it.

Neurons and synapses

We have already explained how each individual begins life as a single cell (Chapter 2). This original cell divides and multiplies over and over again until the various organs of the body take form. In the multiplication, cells differentiate in structure and function, each coming to play a particular role in the body's activities. Although each organ of the body eventually consists of many kinds of cells, there is usually one kind that serves the principal function of the organ. In the case of the nervous system, this cell is the *neuron,* and its function is to conduct messages called nerve impulses.

NEURONS.   In Figure 19.3 is a schematic drawing of a neuron. Neurons actually vary a great deal in size and shape, and the one sketched is more typical of a motor neuron that extends out from the spinal column to a muscle than it is of other varieties of neurons. The diagram, however, brings out the essential features of different neurons. They all have two general parts: a *cell body* and *fibers*. The cell body contains structures that keep the neuron alive and functioning normally. Neuron fibers are of two types: *dendrites,* which are stimulated by neighboring neurons or by physical stimuli, and *axons,* which deliver nerve impulses to adjacent neurons or to an effector, such as a muscle. Dendrites and axons may be relatively long or very short, depending on the cells they connect with. Many of the neurons within the brain that serve as connectors between closely packed neurons have very short fibers. Other neurons, such as those serving the skin of the toes, have very long dendrites and shorter axons, while motor neurons, such as those connected with the muscles of the big toe, have very long axons and short dendrites.

Notice in the diagram of Figure 19.3 that the axon is surrounded by a sheath. This is known as the *myelin sheath*. It clothes most of the larger fibers in the nervous system if they extend out very far from the cell body, which is not sheathed. The very small fibers of the nervous system, especially many in the autonomic system (page 114), have no myelin sheath.

Despite intensive research on the question, the exact function of the myelin sheath is not yet known. It does seem to be necessary for the normal functioning of the fibers it covers. In the case of many fibers of the brain, the myelin sheath is not present at birth and the process of myelinating the fibers goes on for 1 or 2 years. Some scientists believe that this delayed myelinization of fibers may be responsible for the relatively slow maturation of many of the sensory and motor functions of the human infant (see page 54).

NERVE IMPULSES.   The neuron's principal function is *to conduct nerve impulses*. These are very brief pulses traveling along the fiber at a relatively fast speed—from about 1 to 100 meters a second. Such a pulse undoubtedly represents some chemical reaction within the fiber, but it also consists of an electrical change. This change can be recorded on a voltmeter if electrodes are placed on the neuron and led into a suitable amplifier. In Figure 19.4 is an electrical record of such an impulse. As it passes one of the two electrodes, a voltage deflection is registered in one direction; then as it passes the second electrode, the voltmeter deflects in the opposite direction. It takes about a thousandth of a second, more or less, to pass any particular point on the fiber.

In attempting to account for the voltage deflection that represents the nerve impulse, physiologists have carefully examined the nerve fiber in a variety of ways. From chemical studies they have learned that the membrane of the fiber is normally polarized; it has an excess of positive ions on the out-

THE NEURON IS THE BASIC UNIT OF THE NERVOUS SYSTEM:

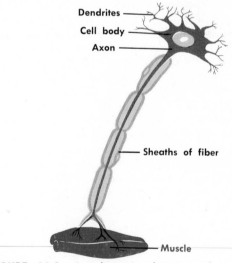

Dendrites —

Cell body —

Axon —

— Sheaths of fiber

— Muscle

FIGURE 19.3. A schematic drawing of a neuron.

CHAPTER NINETEEN

side and an excess of negative ions on the inside (see Figure 19.5). From electrical studies they have found that this polarization of the membrane is represented by a *resting potential* (voltage) across the membrane. This may be registered by placing one electrode on the outside of the membrane and a second electrode inside the fiber or at the end of a cut fiber (see Figure 19.5). What apparently happens, then, in a nerve impulse, is that the polarization of the membrane breaks down, which causes the resting potential to drop to zero (or even to swing in the opposite direction).

All-or-none law. Although many of the events in the membrane of the fiber are still obscure, some are known. When a stimulus is applied to the membrane, it disturbs the balance of ions across the membrane, causing the resting potential to drop. If the stimulus is weak, the drop is small, and it is short-lived, for the membrane is restored rather quickly to its normal resting level. If the stimulus is relatively strong, the drop in potential is complete and travels along the membrane to the very end of the fiber. It is this *potential change moving along a fiber* that we call the *nerve impulse.* Because such a propagated impulse represents a complete drop in resting potential or even a reversal, we say that it obeys an *all-or-none law;* it either occurs or does not, and there are no shades in between.[1]

Impulse size and speed. One should not take this last statement to mean that all impulses for all fibers are of the same size, for they are not. The resting potential, generated by ions adjacent to the membrane, varies with the size of the fiber in which it is found. It is large in large fibers, small in small fibers. Consequently the nerve impulse

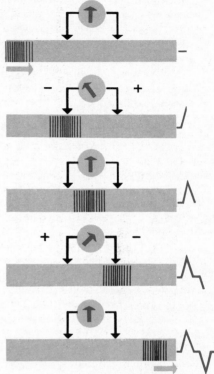

FIGURE 19.4. The electrical record of a nerve impulse. The arrow in the circle represents the needle of a voltmeter making a circuit with the nerve fiber through the two electrodes (arrows in contact with membrane). On the right and reading downward is the record of the swing of the needle as the impulse passes first one electrode, then the other [after Gardner, 1958].

varies with the size of fiber. In fact, it follows a rough rule of being proportional to the square of the fiber's diameter. The size of the nerve impulse also depends upon the condition of the fiber. If it is drugged, deprived of oxygen, fatigued, or otherwise in an abnormal state, its impulses will be altered accordingly. But whatever its condition, a fiber responds according to the all-or-none law. It gives its all or nothing at all. It

[1] In some experiments, the voltage change in the nerve impulse is greater than the resting potential. The reason for this is not yet clear. The resting potential, however, accounts for nearly all the nerve impulse.

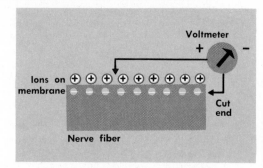

FIGURE 19.5. The resting potential of a nerve fiber. Positive ions are in excess on the outside of the nerve membrane and negative ions are in excess on the inside. As a consequence, there is a resting potential that may be measured by placing one electrode on the outside of the fiber and the other at the cut end of the fiber.

might also be pointed out that the speed at which an impulse travels depends on the condition of the fiber in much the same way as does impulse size. Large impulses travel faster than small ones.

Impulse rates. In some way that we do not yet fully understand, a fiber quickly recovers its balance once it has been discharged. Within a few thousandths of a second, it has restored its resting potential and is ready for any new stimulus that may come along. Even as it is recovering, it can be discharged if the stimulus is sufficiently strong. During this time, however, a stimulus must be considerably stronger than when the fiber is rested if it is to be effective. This period of recovery, requiring unusually strong stimuli, is known as the *refractory period.*

It is probably obvious that the length of the refractory period limits the rate of firing of a neuron. Just as the rifleman who can reload his gun faster can fire more often, so the neuron that recovers more quickly than another can deliver nerve impulses at a more rapid rate. The recovery rate of neurons varies with the same conditions that affect impulse size. The larger ones recover in about a millisecond and can fire as often as 1,000 times a second. Some of the smaller fibers can deliver impulses at the rate of only a few each second.

SYNAPTIC CONNECTIONS. Knowing that nerve impulses travel along fibers, it is

natural to ask where they come from and where they go to. This question has several answers. One is that impulses originate in the receptors of the various senses. Some receptors, like the rods and cones of the retina, the hair cells of the olfactory sense, and the free nerve endings of the skin and deep senses, are themselves specialized neurons. In them an external stimulus directly evokes an impulse. The receptors of some other senses are not neurons, but they are connected to neurons. When a stimulus disturbs them, they somehow trip off impulses in these neurons. In either case, whether the action is direct or indirect, the neuron conducting the impulse is called a *sensory neuron.*

At the end of each sensory neuron, the impulse comes to a gap which it cannot cross. *This gap, marking the end of one neuron and the beginning of another, is called a synapse.* Though an impulse cannot cross this synapse, its electrical field traverses the gap well enough to stimulate the adjacent neuron and to start a new impulse in its fiber. Thus a new impulse is tripped off at the synapse where the ends of two neurons are adjacent to each other.

Most sensory neurons extend all the way from a sense organ—no matter how far away this may be—to the central nervous system, which is contained within the bony case of the skull or spinal column. They therefore make their synapses within the central nervous system. In some instances, for example, in the eye, there are several synapses within the sense organ itself, and the neuron that enters the central nervous system is the third or fourth in a chain.

Within the central nervous system several arrangements of synapses are possible. Possibly in a few atypical cases, the sensory neuron synapses directly with a *motor* neuron which sends a fiber out to muscles or glands. More often, however, there are one or more intervening neurons called *association* neurons. We therefore think of the *simplest complete arrangement for a behavioral response to a stimulus as consisting of a sensory neuron, an association neuron, and a motor neuron*. This arrangement is called the *reflex arc* (see Figure 19.6) and is responsible for some of the more elementary reflexes.

The reflex arc, however, is not typical or common. Synaptic connections are almost always more complicated than that (see Figure 19.7). Often a number of sensory neurons make synapses with one association neuron; we saw examples of this in the ending of many rods and cones on bipolar cells of the retina (Chapter 11). This means that association neurons in the central nervous system often have relatively large *receptive fields;* they receive impulses from many receptors in a sense organ. Association neurons, moreover, may loop back on each other to form *recurrent nerve circuits*. In such an arrangement, impulses keep themselves going with little or no aid from incoming sensory impulses. In this way activity that is once started in the nervous system can continue indefinitely. This arrangement accounts for a considerable amount of nerve activity.

REFLEXES. Although the reflex arc represents the skeleton of the circuit involved in reflex reactions, most reflexes involve more than one intervening association neuron, often arranged in recurrent nerve circuits that prolong the action of the stimulus initiating the reflex. Reflex pathways of varying complexity are found in many parts of the nervous system. They are responsible for such reactions as the blink of the eyelid when the cornea of the eye is touched, the contraction of the pupil in bright light, salivation from food placed in the mouth, the pricking of the dog's ears when it hears an unfamiliar sound, and a host of other automatic reactions.

The reflexes just mentioned all involve pathways in the brain. Other reflexes involve only the spinal cord, and these can be classified into two general categories: the *flexion*

THREE SETS OF NEURONS ARE INVOLVED IN VERY SIMPLE REFLEXES:

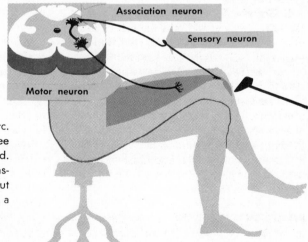

FIGURE 19.6. The sensory-motor reflex arc. Sensory neurons (in this case, in the knee tendon) conduct impulses into the spinal cord. These usually relay through intervening association neurons. Then impulses travel out over motor neurons to muscles to cause a reflex response.

reflexes and the *extension reflexes*. We have all observed our own flexion reflexes when we have inadvertently touched a hot stove or stepped on a sharp object. The reaction in each case is quickly to flex (bend) the limb concerned in order to withdraw it from the painful stimulus. Extension reflexes are even more common than flexion reflexes, but we are less aware of them because they are so "automatic." For example, when one's leg touches the ground, pressure on the foot reflexly extends and stiffens the leg to support one's weight. And when one lifts his foot off the ground, the opposite leg reflexly stiffens to support the body. The reflex in this latter case has its stimulus in the kinesthetic receptors of the flexed leg (see Chapter 12). Both are examples of extension reflexes. They aid us in standing, walking, and running, and they occur so regularly that we seldom notice them.

These are just a few examples of reflexes. More complex reflexes may involve several association neurons whose fibers extend some distance in the nervous system. One example is the scratch reflex which we observe in our household pets or even in ourselves. The scratch reflex happens to be a nicely timed alternation of flexion and extension reflexes.

RECIPROCAL INHIBITION. The timing and smoothness of reflex action depends on the way muscles are arranged and innervated (connected with nerve fibers). The muscles of the body and particularly those of the limbs are typically arranged in *antagonistic* pairs. One set of muscles extends the limb; another set, the antagonistic set, flexes it. The two sets of antagonistic muscles, however, seldom contract at the same time. When the extensor muscles contract, the flexor muscles relax, and vice versa. In this way, antagonistic muscles are kept from working against each other, and only one reflex is dominant at a time. This simultaneous contraction and relaxation of antagonistic muscles is called *reciprocal inhibition*.

Reciprocal inhibition is only a special case

NEURONS ARE ALMOST ALWAYS CONNECTED IN COMPLEX WAYS:

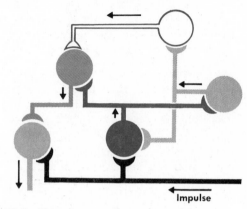

FIGURE 19.7. This diagram shows how neurons may form recurrent circuits that can maintain activity for some time after being activated by an impulse.

of inhibition. Inhibition is a general phenomenon of synaptic function in which impulses from one source can cause a neuron to be less excitable and thus not to respond to impulses from another source. Inhibitory impulses may come from the muscles (kinesthetic receptors) involved in a reflex and also from various other pathways and centers of the nervous system.

THE MOTOR UNIT. It is interesting to note that the size of a reflex action depends upon the way in which muscles are innervated. Muscular tissue, like nerve tissue, is made up of many cellular units, in this case called muscle fibers, which are connected with the axons of motor neurons. One axon, however, serves more than one muscle fiber by branching into a number of endings, each of which serves a muscle fiber. As a consequence, one impulse in one motor axon causes several muscle fibers to contract. All those connected with one axon contract as a group. Hence a motor axon and all the muscle fibers it serves is called a *motor unit*.

How large the motor unit is depends upon the *innervation ratio*. This is the ratio of muscle fibers to axons. In some parts of the body, the ratio is as high as 150:1; in others, it may be as low as 3:1. A high ratio, which is typical of the larger muscles of the body such as those used in walking, means a relatively large contraction. A low ratio, typical of smaller muscles such as those of the finger and eyelid, means relatively small contraction. The fineness and precision of movement of any particular muscle group therefore depends upon the innervation ratio. This limitation established by the innervation ratio applies, as we shall see, not only to reflex reactions, but also to learned skilled movements controlled at higher levels of the nervous system.

REACTION TIME. Every reaction to a stimulus requires a finite amount of time, and the time between stimulus and response is called *reaction time.* For simple reflexes, this time is of the order of $\frac{1}{10}$ second, though it varies with the reflex. For simple voluntary reactions, such as pushing a key when a light is flashed or a bell is sounded, the reaction time is roughly $\frac{2}{10}$ second. For more complex reactions, such as pushing the brake pedal on an automobile, reaction time is closer to 1 second.

From studies of nerve activity we know that reaction time depends mostly on the number of synapses involved in the reaction. Although it takes time for nerve impulses to travel along nerve fibers, the speed of travel is so fast that reaction times, if they were the limiting factor, would be much less than they are. Rather it is probably delay at the synapse that is the limiting factor, and the more synapses, the more delay. This is what accounts for relatively long reaction time and the greater reaction time for responses that involve many neurons and synapses of the nervous system.

The nervous system

The nervous system may be divided up in several ways, each of which provides a useful distinction. One is to distinguish between a central nervous system and a peripheral nervous system. The *central nervous system* is that part of the nervous system which *lies within the bony case formed by the skull and spine.* The neurons, or parts of neurons, together with other supporting tissues, enclosed within this bony case constitute the central nervous system; those that lie outside the case make up the *peripheral nervous system.* Other ways of distinguishing parts of the nervous system will be described later in this chapter.

PERIPHERAL NERVOUS SYSTEM. The peripheral nervous system consists in part of fibers of sensory and motor neurons. These fibers are always collected together in bundles called *nerves.* For most of the journey to and from the central nervous system, these nerves are both sensory and motor. Some of the nerves entering and leaving the skull, however, are only sensory or only motor. All nerves, moreover, usually divide just outside the central nervous system into two roots, a sensory root and a motor root (see Figure 19.8). They do this because they have different points of origin and departure within the central nervous system.

All that we have just said applies to *fibers* of the peripheral nervous system. This system, however, has two main divisions: the autonomic and the somatic systems. The *autonomic system* was discussed briefly in connection with emotion (Chapter 4). It is a motor system serving the blood vessels, heart, glands, and other internal organs of the body. It is stirred up in emotion. The *somatic system,* on the other hand, is both sensory and motor; it serves the various senses we have described and the skeletal muscles of the body involved in standing, walking, writing, and instrumental behavior in general.

Both the autonomic and somatic systems contain cell bodies as well as fibers. The cell bodies are collected together in groups called *ganglia.* Arranged along the spinal column are two series of ganglia; one consists of the

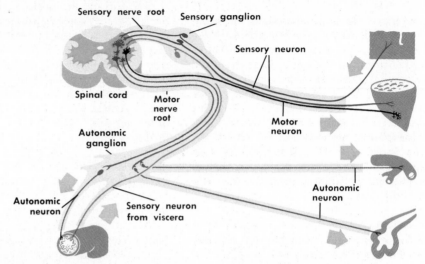

FIGURE 19.8. Pathways of the peripheral nervous system. Sensory neurons from the various receptors have their cell bodies in the dorsal spinal ganglia. The motor-nerve roots send fibers out to skeletal muscles and to autonomic ganglia. From the autonomic ganglia, fibers go to smooth muscles (e.g., intestine and blood vessels) and to various glands (both duct and ductless).

autonomic ganglia, containing cell bodies of the autonomic motor fibers, and the other consists of the *sensory ganglia* of the somatic system (see Figure 19.8). There are no motor ganglia of the somatic system, because the cell bodies of motor-nerve fibers are found inside the central nervous system.

CENTRAL NERVOUS SYSTEM. The neurons within the central nervous system are more or less segregated into centers and pathways. The pathways consist of bundles of fibers, and the centers are made up of cell bodies. Very frequently, however, the cell bodies in centers have very short fibers that synapse with neighboring neurons within the center. Fibers in the pathways also usually synapse with other neurons in these centers. The center, therefore, is something of a mixture of cell bodies and fibers. Centers have specific names depending on where they are and how they are arranged. Sometimes they

are called *nuclei,* in other cases *ganglia,* and in still others simply *areas.* We shall have occasion to use all three terms, but it should be remembered that they refer to *centers, or collections of cell bodies, where synapses are usually made.*

White and gray matter. A coincidence of nature makes it relatively easy to distinguish centers and pathways as one looks at the nervous system either with the naked eye or under a microscope. The normal color of a neuron is gray. As was mentioned above, however, most of the fibers in the nervous system have a myelin sheath around them and this is white. The cell bodies, on the other hand, do not have this sheath. Consequently, to the observer, pathways appear white and centers of cell bodies appear gray. For this reason we often refer to pathways as *white matter* and to centers as *gray matter.*

The spinal cord. The central nervous system is organized regionally into two principal parts: the *spinal cord* within the spinal column and the *brain* within the skull. In Figure 19.9 is a cross section of a spinal cord. Notice that its center is gray and its outside is white. The central gray thus consists of cell bodies of neurons, while conducting pathways are in the outside white. Notice that motor pathways bringing impulses down from the brain are toward the front of the body. The sensory, or ascending pathways, on the other hand, are in several bundles in the white matter; pathways for the deep senses are toward the back of the body; those for the skin senses are in two bundles on the side.

The spinal cord, generally speaking, has two functions: as a conduction path to and from the brain, and as an organ for effecting reflex action. Hardly any reflex is unaffected by impulses descending from the brain, yet many can be seen as purely spinal affairs when the brain is disconnected from the cord. In fact the extension, flexion, and scratch reflexes that we mentioned above, as well as the basic pattern of alternating steps in walking, are organized at the spinal level.

THE BRAIN.   Of the two principal parts of the nervous system, the spinal cord and the brain, the brain is the more interesting because it plays the central role in all complex activities: learning, thinking, perception, etc. Its part in these processes will be a subject of study in the next chapter. In order to understand it, however, we must first take time to outline the general structure of the brain. The principal divisions of the brain are diagrammed and labeled in Figure 19.10. They may be considered in three main groups: the hindbrain, midbrain, and forebrain.

1. Within the *hindbrain* are the *cerebellum* and the *medulla*. The medulla contains vital centers for breathing and heart rate, but it also includes centers that relay sensory impulses upward to the midbrain and

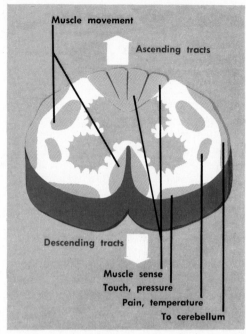

FIGURE 19.9.   A cross section of the spinal cord.

forebrain. The cerebellum is a center, but not the only center, for motor coordination; it helps make our movements smooth and accurate. By making use of vestibular and kinesthetic impulses, it also is an essential organ for maintaining posture and balance.

2. The *midbrain* is a sort of bridge connecting the forebrain and the hindbrain and therefore contains a number of tracts conveying impulses upward and downward, but it also has important centers in it for vision and hearing, and these will be mentioned again below.

3. The *forebrain* is the "highest" part of the brain. Though slow to develop in the animal kingdom, it eventually became the most highly developed part of the brain in man and the higher animals. As can be seen in the diagram of the brain (Figure 19.10), its mass is considerably greater than that of

the midbrain or hindbrain. Many parts of the forebrain are known to take part in complex behavior, but the parts of greatest interest to us fall into three main groups: the *cerebral cortex,* the *thalamus,* and three closely related structures forming one group known as the *hypothalamus, septum,* and *amygdala.* Outside the forebrain, running through the hindbrain and midbrain is another structure, the *reticular activating system,* whose importance has only recently been discovered. These four regions will be described in turn.

Cerebral cortex. A photograph of the human brain, such as you see in Figure 19.11, is more a picture of the cerebral cortex than of anything else, because the cortex encloses almost all the forebrain and midbrain. The cortex, as the picture shows, is like a rumpled piece of cloth that has many ridges and valleys. Anatomists call one of these ridges a *gyrus* (plural, gyri); a valley or crevice is sometimes called a *sulcus* (plural, sulci) and sometimes a fissure.

The large sulci or fissures can be used to mark off the cerebral cortex. Along the midline dividing the brain into two symmetrical halves, called cerebral *hemispheres,* is the *longitudinal fissure.* Running from this fissure across the top and down the sides of the two hemispheres is the *central sulcus.* All the cortex in front of this fissure is called the *frontal lobe,* and this lobe may be considered the expressive part of the brain because it contains motor centers for controlling movements and actions. The cortex behind the central sulcus has been called the *receptive* part of the cortex, because it contains the centers at which incoming sensory impulses arrive. (There are certain exceptions to these statements, but they serve as a reasonably good way of dividing the functions of the cerebral cortex.) Finally, along the side of each hemisphere is a crevice known as the *lateral sulcus.* The cortex below it and to the side of it makes up the *tem-*

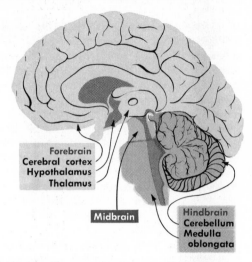

Forebrain
Cerebral cortex
Hypothalamus
Thalamus

Midbrain

Hindbrain
Cerebellum
Medulla
oblongata

FIGURE 19.10. The principal parts of the human brain.

poral lobe. There are still two other lobes of the cerebral cortex, making four lobes in all, that are not set off by any major fissures. These are the *parietal lobe* and *occipital lobe.* The parietal lobe lies immediately behind the central sulcus, and the occipital lobe is the cortex lying under the back of the skull. The functions of these various lobes will be described in the next chapter.

Thalamus. The thalamus (see Figure 19.10) lies just above the midbrain, well enveloped by the cortex and other structures of the forebrain. It is best thought of as a relay station, although some of its parts have other functions. Sensory impulses coming into the spinal cord, hindbrain, and midbrain make their way, after intervening synapses, to centers in the thalamus. In one case, vision, the sensory nerve goes directly to the thalamus, but usually thalamic centers relay impulses from below to various parts of the cortex—the receptive cortex.

Reticular activating system. The reticular activating system (RAS) will be mentioned out of order because its function parallels that of the thalamus (see Figure 19.12). It

FIGURE 19.11. The lobes of the cerebral cortex. Below, an actual photograph of a cerebral cortex [Gardner, 1958].

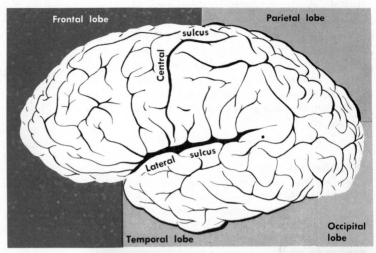

Frontal lobe

Parietal lobe

Central

sulcus

Lateral sulcus

Temporal lobe

Occipital lobe

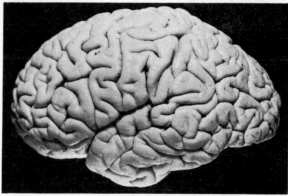

is a sensory relay station on the way to the cerebral cortex [Lindsley, 1958]. The thalamus, however, is a direct relay to the cerebral cortex, and its projection is quite specific. Visual impulses, for example, arrive at a visual center in the thalamus and are relayed to a visual area of the cortex. Hearing and the lower senses similarly have their own thalamic centers and their respective areas of projection on the cerebral cortex. This is not the case, however, with the RAS. This system is a relatively diffuse one. It receives impulses from sensory systems "on the side" as sensory fibers ascend to the thalamus. It also relays impulses to the cerebral cortex, but to a relatively large part of the cortex. Although more visual impulses may be relayed to the visual area of the cerebral cortex than to other areas, the RAS does not keep different impulses entirely separate from each other. Rather it is a general activating system for the cerebral cortex; hence its name.

The part of the RAS that relays sensory impulses to the cerebral cortex is called the *ascending* reticular activating system. (Another part, a descending system, sends impulses downward to the spinal cord.) In addition, the cerebral cortex also sends back impulses to the RAS. Thus the RAS and the cerebral cortex form a closed loop in which impulses in the RAS arouse the cerebral cortex, but those in the cortex in turn arouse the RAS. We shall see later the part played by the RAS in sleep and alertness.

Hypothalamus, septum, and amygdala. Of particular interest is a fourth region of the brain—in this case, the forebrain—containing a complex system of pathways and centers, all of which have technical names. In order, however, not to complicate our account unduly, we need note only that the three structures in this system that are most important in behavior, particularly emotion

FIGURE 19.12. Schematic diagram of the reticular activating system. The system (dark area) comprises an indirect sensory pathway (dark green arrows) to several areas of the cortex, receiving collaterals from the direct sensory pathway (light green arrows). Pathways also lead back (broken arrows) from the cortex to the reticular system, thus forming a loop.

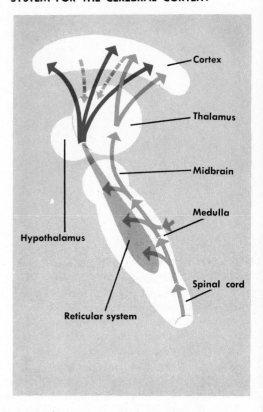

and motivated behavior, are the *hypothalamus, septum,* and *amygdala* [Brady and Bunnell, 1960]. The general size and position of the hypothalamus can be seen in Figure 19.10. As its name implies, it lies underneath the thalamus in a nook in the floor of the skull in a position that a surgeon can most easily reach by going through the roof of the mouth. Its comparatively small size, hardly larger than a peanut, should be noted, for this contrasts markedly with the large number of very important functions it has.

The relation of the hypothalamus to the septum and amygdala is diagrammed in Figure 19.13. The septum, which is also a relatively small structure, lies in front of and above the hypothalamus in the median plane. The amygdala (or amygdaloid nucleus) lies behind and somewhat to the side of the hypothalamus. Actually all three structures, like others in the brain, are symmetrically paired. The septum and hypothalamus, however, lie along the midline so that their two sides are adjacent. The amygdala is not a midline structure, and hence there are two amygdaloid nuclei, one on either side. The fact that all structures have two halves, however, should not be forgotten, for even within the midline structures, various nuclei are always found in pairs.

The precise connections between these structures are not yet known. They are connected with each other in both direct and roundabout ways, but both the septum and amygdala appear to send fibers into the hypothalamus. Those from the septum appear to be inhibitory, while those from the amygdala seem to be excitatory. In other words, activity in the septum inhibits the hypothalamus, whereas that in the amygdala apparently excites it.

Methods of study

The sections above provide a bird's-eye view of the organs and functions of greatest importance in behavior. Additional details will be supplied in the next chapter as they are needed.

The general problem of the psychophysiologist is to correlate structures and functions of the body with the events of behavior. To do this, he must ordinarily use a

THE LIMBIC SYSTEM IS IMPORTANT IN EMOTION:

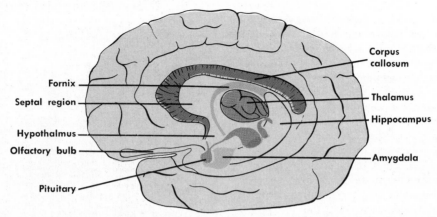

FIGURE 19.13. Some of the parts of the limbic system. Note particularly the septal region, amygdala, and hypothalamus [after Brady and Bunnell, 1960].

combination of methods of study, employing both those of the anatomist and physiologist and those of the psychologist. The methods of the psychologist are described extensively throughout this book, but the more biological methods are not. Hence, to understand what is coming in the next chapter, it is necessary to sketch those that are especially relevant.

NEUROANATOMICAL METHODS. To study the structure of the nervous system, the neuroanatomist must first find ways of distinguishing the fibrous pathways of the nervous system from the centers (nuclei and ganglia) containing cell bodies, and then of tracing the various connections among centers and pathways. In effect he attempts to learn what the wiring diagram of the nervous system is.

The very general features of such a diagram can be seen with the naked eye, once the nervous system has been exposed to view. Because, as we have already mentioned, a large proportion of the fibers of the nervous system are clothed in a white myelin sheath, while unmyelinated cell bodies are gray, one can tell roughly what is a pathway and what is a center merely by observing its color. By this method, however, one can tell

little or nothing about the connections between neurons, nor can one distinguish the "fine-grained" organization of centers and pathways into subdivisions. For this, other methods are required.

One is to *stain* the nervous system and then to study it closely under the microscope. A variety of stains are available for this purpose. Some stains are picked up only by the granules in the cell bodies and hence make the cell bodies stand out clearly from the fibers. Other stains are effective with fibers, usually by lodging in the myelin sheath of fibers, and enable one not only to distinguish cell bodies from fibers but to trace the pathways of fibers from beginning to end. A great deal has been learned about the nervous system with the aid of such stains.

Often staining methods are combined with a method of *degeneration*. When a fiber is cut, it always degenerates back to its cell body. This makes it possible to obliterate, at least temporarily, a fiber pathway. If one cuts it somewhere along its length, one can trace its course by noting degeneration of either the fibers or their cell bodies. In the case of most neurons in the central nervous system, degeneration from a cut fiber proceeds to affect the whole neuron and to result in its death. Thus by cutting a pathway, or part of a pathway, and determining which cell bodies degenerate and die, one can establish the relation of centers and pathways (see Figure 19.14). Peripheral neurons do not die in this way; given the proper conditions, they can regenerate. This difference between peripheral and central neurons is not fully understood, but it is helpful in the study of the nervous system.

The psychophysiologist frequently uses a similar method, the method of *extirpation,* in the study of the functions of various parts of the nervous system. He may remove, for example, a particular area of the cerebral cortex, a center in the thalamus, or simply cut a nerve or pathway, then measure the ability of an animal both before and after the operation to perform on some task, say, a visual discrimination. The results he obtains will often depend on how well he has succeeded in extirpating quite exactly the area concerned. He frequently cannot determine this when he is operating. So it is necessary at the end of an experiment to sacrifice the animal, prepare microscopic sections of the nervous system, stain them, and then map exactly the areas that have been destroyed.

Several methods of extirpating or destroying areas of the nervous system have been developed. The oldest one, and the one that is appropriate for relatively large, easily accessible areas, is simple excision (cutting out) with surgical instruments. This will not do, though, when the area is deep in the nervous system and relatively small. For this purpose, *electrolytic lesions* (injuries) are frequently employed. To make such a lesion, the psychophysiologist pushes a fine wire or needle, insulated along its sides but not at its tip, to the desired place, and runs a current through the needle and the tissue surrounding its tip. If the current is of sufficient intensity and duration, the tissue around the tip of the needle is destroyed. The size of a lesion made in this way depends upon the size of the needle tip, the amount of current,

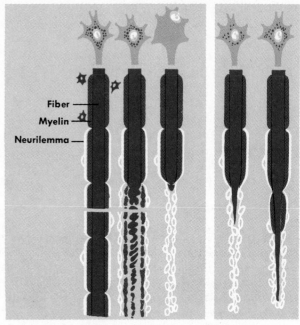

FIGURE 19.14. Schematic representation of the degeneration and subsequent regeneration of a nerve fiber and its cell body after the nerve fiber has been cut [after Gardner, 1958].

and the time it is on. The needle, being quite fine, usually does not destroy any significant amount of tissue along the path of its insertion.

ELECTRICAL RECORDING. As we have already noted, it is possible to record nerve impulses in neuron fibers by means of electrodes and a suitable amplifying and recording system. It is also possible to record disturbances of larger magnitude. These disturbances, called *potential changes,* or merely potentials, may consist of a great many nerve impulses (spike potentials) firing at about the same time and place summated in one or more waves. They may also consist of relatively slow rhythmic changes in the resting potentials of a large group of neurons. In any case, the recording of potentials has been used to obtain some useful information about the functions of the nervous system. In general, three levels or degrees of fineness of recording may be distinguished.

Electroencephalogram. The grossest method of recording, and one which can easily be done with the intact animal or human being, yields what is known as the *electroencephalogram* (EEG). To obtain an EEG, the investigator attaches two electrodes firmly to the scalp; the output of the electrodes is suitably amplified and recorded on a tape. The position of the electrodes makes some difference, for some of the potentials recorded in the EEG are much stronger in some areas of the brain than in others. But with a suitable placement, gross changes, called *brain waves,* may be recorded. The frequency and size of these waves change, as we shall see in the next chapter, with a number of conditions and can be correlated to some extent with what the subject is doing (see Figure 20.5 in Chapter 20).

Action potentials. A more refined method of recording is to place electrodes directly on or in the part of the nervous system being studied. In this case, one electrode is usually placed on the part of interest, while the second electrode is put at some neutral position in the body. The first or active electrode then picks up any potential changes in the region near its placement. The wave that is recorded is usually complex, consisting both of slow potentials and of masses of nerve impulses. It can be used to signal the presence of activity under the active electrode.

Electrical recording of this sort is valuable in "mapping" the nervous system. One can, for example, place an electrode on the cerebral cortex and then sound different tones. By determining which electrode placements show electrical activity in response to the sound of the tone, one can establish the limits of the auditory area of the cortex. Indeed, the method has been refined to the point of mapping the points on the cortex that respond most to each of many different tones.

The use of electrical recording to map areas of response in the nervous system often confirms or corrects conclusions reached from strictly neuroanatomical methods. In addition, however, it has frequently revealed areas and pathways that had escaped detection by neuroanatomical methods. Today, a considerable part of our knowledge of sensory and motor areas of the brain rests on this method of electrical recording.

Microelectrodes. The most refined of all electrical recording methods is the *microelectrode technique.* This employs an electrode that has been drawn out so finely that its tip is not much larger than the size of a single cell body. Hence, when it is inserted into the nervous system, it enables the experimenter to "see" and record spike potentials from individual neurons. Often more than one neuron contributes spike potentials to the record, but the one nearest the electrode gives the largest potential. By means of the all-or-none law, the experimenter can distinguish spikes of different size, knowing that they must come from different neurons. By recording impulses in this way, while presenting known stimuli either to the sense organs of the animal or to other specified regions of the nervous system, one can study the extremely "fine grain" of the nervous system and determine which neurons respond to a particular kind of stimulus. The method has been most useful in the study of sensory mechanisms. Examples of its use were cited in Chapter 11.

STIMULATION METHODS. Electrodes can be used to stimulate, as well as to record from, neural tissue. In fact, the same electrodes may sometimes be used at different times both for stimulation and for recording. More often, one pair is employed in one place for stimulation, and another pair at a different site is used for recording. In this way it is possible to trace activity in the nervous system from one point to another.

The stimulus used is usually an electrical pulse or series of pulses generated by a specially designed stimulator.

Probably the oldest use of the method of electrical stimulation is excitation of the so-called "motor areas" of the cortex (see Figure 20.2 in the next chapter). In fact it was with this method that these areas were first mapped. A neutral or inactive electrode is attached to the skull or body and the active electrode is touched to a point on the exposed surface of the cerebral cortex. Stimulation of the motor area of the cortex causes the subject to make various kinds of movements, because there is a pathway leading from the motor cortex downward to the muscles of the body. Stimulation at one point in the cortex causes one movement in a particular part of the body; stimulation at another point causes another movement somewhere else. By keeping track of the movements evoked by stimulation at various points, one can construct a map of the parts of the body controlled by different parts of the motor cortex (Figure 20.2).

In recent years, this method has been used in conscious human subjects to explore areas of the cortex concerned in sensation and memory [Penfield and Rasmussen, 1950]. This is done, of course, only when a patient is being operated on for some other reason, usually for the removal of a brain tumor.

The skull is opened under local anesthesia, so that the patient feels no pain and at the same time is fully conscious. Electrodes are then used to stimulate various points on the cortex while the patient reports what he experiences. The method yields considerable information about the functions of the cerebral cortex. It also enables the surgeon to remove a tumor while keeping to a minimum the damage to those areas most concerned in sensory experience and memory.

A method of permanently implanting electrodes for purposes of stimulation has been developed. A fine wire or needle, similar to one used for recording, is inserted in the brain. It is suitably attached to the skull with a socket or connection outside the skin. Then, when an experimenter wishes to stimulate the spot at the tip of the electrode, all he needs to do is hook up the connector to a stimulator (see Figure 19.15). This method is now commonly used in the study of the functions of the deeper parts of the brain. The stimulus applied through the electrode may be controlled either by the experimenter or by the subject. In certain sites, we shall see, electrical stimulation is definitely "pleas-

WITH PERMANENTLY IMPLANTED ELECTRODES, THE BRAIN CAN BE STIMULATED AT WILL:

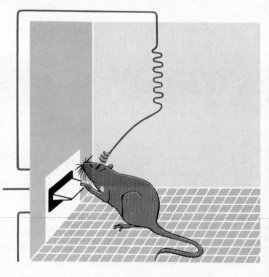

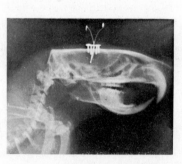

FIGURE 19.15. Diagram of method of implanting an electrode in the brain and using it as a self-stimulation circuit, and an X-ray photograph showing electrode assembly in position [Olds, 1956; University of Michigan].

ant" for a subject (either human or animal), and he will voluntarily close a switch delivering stimulation to himself [Olds, 1956].

Although the method of local stimulation usually employs an electrical stimulus, it can also be used with chemical stimuli. In that case, a small pipette is inserted instead of an electrode. Through the pipette, the experimenter can deliver small amounts of chemical substances in solution and study the response of the particular area to different substances. The method has not yet been used on a large scale, but it has been employed to advantage in experiments on the mechanism of thirst motivation.

HORMONAL AND BIOCHEMICAL METHODS. There are many different methods of studying the effects of various hormones and chemical substances on behavior and related functions, and they are not easily classified. Some of the methods worth mentioning, however, are outlined in the following paragraphs.

Gland removal. The oldest method of determining the function of an endocrine gland is the surgical removal of the gland. By choosing certain measurements to be made on the organism before and after the removal of the gland, the effects of removal can be determined. Some of these measurements may, of course, be behavioral. In the case of sex behavior, for example, the role of the male and female sex glands (gonads) has been studied by employing some measure of sexual activity such as number of copulations or number of items of sexual activity displayed in a period of time.

Replacement therapy. The method that complements gland removal and enables an experimenter to check on some of the conclusions drawn from gland removal is the method of replacement therapy. After a gland has been removed, the hormone of the gland is "replaced," usually by injecting it directly into the blood stream. This method is particularly useful where a gland secretes several different hormones, as many of the glands do, for it permits us to separate the effects of the different hormones. It is also convenient because it is reversible; simply by injecting the hormone or not injecting it, one can repeatedly compare the same animal with and without a particular hormone.

Summary

1. The internal environment consists of the chemical conditions in the blood and tissues that affect nervous functions. It is regulated by hormones, enzymes, and vitamins.

2. Hormones are produced by such endocrine glands as the pituitary, adrenal, thyroid, parathyroid, pancreatic, and gonadal. Hormones of these glands control the level of such materials as water, sugar, salt, calcium, phosphorus, and other minerals in the blood.

3. Hormones probably do their work by regulating the supply of enzymes, which are catalysts manufactured in the body that aid or hinder particular chemical reactions.

4. Helping the enzymes in this function are the vitamins; the organism obtains vitamins by eating foods in which they occur. Relatively small quantities of the hormones, enzymes, and vitamins are sufficient to carry on the regulation of the internal environment.

5. The basic unit of the nervous system is the neuron. It consists of a cell body, an axon, and one or more dendrites; the last two taken together are known as nerve fibers.

6. Stimulation of a nerve fiber generates a nerve impulse which obeys an all-or-none law; it either reaches full size or it does not propagate at all.

7. At the end of one fiber and at the beginning of another is a gap called the synapse. At this gap a new impulse is evoked as the old one dies out.

8. Neurons form many different kinds of synaptic connections. One arrangement is the reflex arc, consisting of a sensory neuron, an association neuron, and a motor neuron. Reflex arcs are involved in such reflexes as flexion and extension.

9. In most reflexes, muscles are arranged in antagonistic pairs, so that when one antagonist contracts, the other relaxes. This relaxation is brought about by reciprocal inhibition from impulses arriving over sensory fibers which originate in the contracting muscle.

10. A motor unit consists of one axon and several muscle fibers which it innervates. The innervation ratio, i.e., the number of muscle fibers innervated by an axon, determines the fineness or grossness of muscle movements.

11. The nervous system has two main divisions: (a) a peripheral system, which consists in turn of an autonomic system and a somatic system, and (b) the central nervous system contained within the bony cavities of the skull and spine.

12. The peripheral nervous system conveys impulses to and from the central nervous system. The latter system consists of centers and pathways in the brain and spinal cord. The spinal cord, in turn, conveys impulses to and from the brain, but it also is responsible for spinal reflexes.

13. The brain has three principal divisions: forebrain, midbrain, and hindbrain. Within these divisions, the parts of greatest psychological importance are the cerebral cortex, the thalamus, the reticular activating system, and a group of centers named the hypothalamus, the septum, and amygdala.

14. The methods of studying neural and glandular functions most often used to establish correlations with behavior are (a) the neuroanatomical methods of making experimental injuries in the nervous system and tracing the degeneration that results, (b) electrical recording of both gross and minute electrical activities of the nervous system, (c) electrical, and sometimes chemical, stimulation of selected regions of the brain, and (d) the surgical removal of endocrine glands coupled with the injection of hormones into the blood stream.

Suggestions for further reading

Brazier, M. A. B. *The electrical activity of the nervous system.* London: Pitman, 1951.
An elementary treatment of the electrical phenomena of the nervous system.

Field, J., Magoun, H. W., and Hall, V. E. (eds.). *Handbook of physiology: neurophysiology.* Vol. I. Washington, D.C., American Physiological Society, 1959.
Compendious, authoritative treatment of all aspects of nervous-system function.

Gardner, E. *Fundamentals of neurology* (3d ed.). Philadelphia: Saunders, 1958.
An introductory text on the structure and function of the nervous system.

Langley, L. L., and Cheraskin, E. *The physiology of man.* New York: McGraw-Hill, 1954.
A college textbook of physiology containing several chapters on the nervous and endocrine systems.

Morgan, C. T., and Stellar, E. *Physiological psychology* (2d ed.). New York: McGraw-Hill, 1950.
A standard text on the physiological mechanisms of behavior, with chapters on the nervous system and internal environment.

Stevens, S. S. (ed.). *Handbook of experimental psychology.* New York: Wiley, 1951. Chaps. 2–6.
Compact authoritative chapters on the physiology of the nervous system and the internal environment.

Physiological basis of behavior

$\mathbf{T}$HE PRECEDING CHAPTER provides the background that is necessary for understanding this one. Although the picture it gives of the nervous system and internal environment is extremely sketchy, it should suffice for our purpose here. In this chapter we shall study the physiological basis of the behavior we have been describing elsewhere in the book.

Sensory motor mechanisms

The sensory and motor pathways of the nervous system are relatively easy to trace by neuroanatomical methods. They have therefore been the object of more study than other regions, and their functions are rela-

tively well understood. Hence we begin with them.

The sensory and motor areas of the cortex are shown in Figure 20.1. Notice that the sensory areas lie in the cortex behind the central sulcus. The meaning of each of the terms used in the illustration will be explained as we go along. Man's cerebral cortex is shown in comparison with that of the chimpanzee and the dog to bring out the fact that the sensory and motor areas in the lower animals occupy a relatively larger part of the total cortex than they do in man. Put another way, more of the human cortex is concerned with functions that are not sensory or motor than is the cortex of the dog or chimpanzee. This may reflect the greater abilities of man in complex activities such as learning and thinking.

SKILLED MOVEMENTS.   Two areas of the cerebral cortex are of special importance in movement and motor functions. These are the *motor area* and the *premotor area,* lying in front of the central sulcus.

Various experiments show that the motor area is the "executive" area of the cortex. Through it an individual is able to execute different patterns of movement. In this area are motor neurons that send fibers downward to the motor neurons of the hindbrain and spinal cord, which activate skeletal muscles. Thus there is a direct, two-neuron link from the motor area to the peripheral musculature. The fact that this link is essential for the performance of coordinated movements has been demonstrated in two kinds of experiments.

One is direct electrical stimulation of the motor area. An electrical stimulus applied to this area in a conscious human being or in an animal under light anesthesia evokes observable movements somewhere in the body. The kind of movement and the place that it occurs depend on the point stimulated on the motor area. At the top of the area and around the bend into the longitudinal fissure between the two halves of the cortex, a stimulus produces movements of the leg. A little to the side of this, a stimulus evokes movements of the trunk. Still more to the side is a region in which stimulation causes movements of the hand and arm. At the side and bottom of the area, in the direction of the lateral sulcus (see Figure 19.11), movements of the face and mouth are evoked. By carefully plotting each point on the cortex that evokes a movement, an investigator can construct a map of the cortex; this map is illustrated schematically in Figure 20.2. It shows that the areas concerned with trunk and leg movements are relatively small; those for the hand are somewhat larger; and

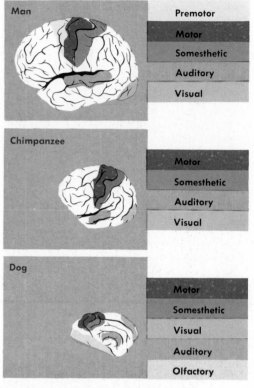

FIGURE 20.1. The cerebral cortex of the dog, the chimpanzee, and man. Note the size and positions of the visual, auditory, and somesthetic areas. The diagram also shows the motor areas of all three species and the large olfactory areas of the dog. Note, too, how large the brain of man is compared with that of the chimpanzee and the dog.

those for face and mouth movements are by comparison monstrous.

Another experiment demonstrating the functions of the motor area is one in which the areas are extirpated or otherwise destroyed. If, through surgery, cerebral hemorrhage, or other injury, some of this area is destroyed, a paralysis results. If the whole area on one side is damaged, then there is a relatively complete paralysis of one side of the body—the opposite side, because fibers from the motor area cross over from one side to the other in their descending paths. If only a part of the motor area is destroyed, a partial paralysis of the corresponding portion of the body results.

The other area in Figure 20.1 that has motor function is the one marked *premotor area*. This area is part of a complex system in the brain involving the cerebellum (see Figure 19.10) and subcortical centers of the forebrain. Its functions are therefore difficult to describe. Generally speaking, it regulates tension and posture in different parts of the body and facilitates specific movements under the control of the motor area. If the premotor area is removed or damaged, the individual's movements become awkward. He seems to know what he wants to do but has difficulty in doing it very well. Continuous tension in his extensor muscles prevents his making smooth, accurate movements.

There are other areas of the cerebral cortex that are involved in motor functions, and there are many centers outside the cerebral cortex that are concerned in movement. Their function, however, is not of special concern to the psychologist. We have described briefly the role of the motor and premotor area in order to give some idea of the mechanism of movement. Now let us turn to the sensory mechanisms.

SENSORY CENTERS AND PATHWAYS. In considering sensory mechanisms, one should keep in mind the ways in which the senses can be classified (Chapter 10). For our purposes, the most convenient classification is into four main groups: vision, hearing, somesthesis, and chemical senses. Somesthesis includes the skin senses of pressure, pain, warmth, and cold and the kinesthetic pressure sense. The chemical senses include taste and smell. Much that we have to say here is generally true of all senses within a group and sometimes of more than one group. (As was pointed out in Chapter 12, we probably

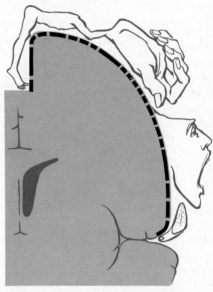

FIGURE 20.2. A homunculus showing the topographical organization of the motor area. Both the motor area in front of the central sulcus and the somesthetic area behind it are so arranged that the legs are represented near the top of the area, the arms in the middle, and the face and mouth near the bottom [after Penfield and Rasmussen, 1950].

have no direct experience of events in the vestibular sense organs. For that reason, the vestibular sense is not considered here.)

Three of these groups, namely, vision, hearing, and the chemical senses, are located in the head. It is to be expected, therefore, that their nerves, centers, and pathways would be found in the head and brain and would have nothing to do with the spinal cord. To give some idea of the nerves over which sensory information flows into the brain, Figure 20.3 has been presented. For accuracy, it gives the correct name of each of the 12 cranial nerves supplying the brain, but the important thing is to note the paths of each group of senses.

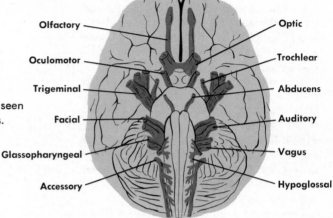

Olfactory — Optic

Oculomotor — Trochlear

Trigeminal — Abducens

Facial — Auditory

Glossopharyngeal — Vagus

Accessory — Hypoglossal

FIGURE 20.3. A diagram of the brain as seen from below, showing the cranial nerves.

The olfactory nerve leads off the olfactory organ behind the bridge of the nose and runs directly into the base of the cerebral cortex. The optic nerve emerges from the blind spot of the retina, proceeds through an opening in the eye socket, and ends in the thalamus. The auditory nerve and the taste nerves enter the hindbrain; from there impulses course upward to the midbrain and thalamus of the forebrain, whence they are projected to the cerebral cortex.

What is true of these groups of senses, however, does not apply entirely to the somesthetic senses located all over the body. Since these senses serve the head and face as well as the trunk and limbs, they have nerves which, like those of hearing and taste, enter the hindbrain, but they also have nerves entering the spinal cord throughout its whole length from the base of the spine to the base of the skull. These latter serve the sense organs of the body exclusive of the head. As we nave already seen, the spinal sensory nerves are part of reflex arcs and are involved in many spinal reflexes. In addition, however, they send branches coursing upward to the hindbrain where they join fibers from the somesthetic sense organs of the head. As a consequence, pathways for all the senses are found in the brain, whether they

enter directly or come up from the spinal cord.

Although smell and taste are chemical senses and are so closely related in human experience that we sometimes cannot tell whether we are tasting something or smelling it (see page 387), they do not have the same or even similar pathways in the brain. Smell pathways enter the base of the brain and end in the cortex there. Taste, on the other hand, has the same centers and pathways as the somesthetic senses of the head, even though it is a chemical rather than a somesthetic sense. There are separate centers for taste and somesthesis in the hindbrain, but fibers from the two sensory groups thereafter intermix so thoroughly that one cannot distinguish their centers and pathways in the thalamus and cerebral cortex, for they appear to be exactly the same.

All the senses except smell have relay centers in the thalamus. One center is for vision, another for hearing, and another for the combined senses of somesthesis and taste. These centers are called relay centers because they do not seem to have any special functions other than to relay impulses to the cerebral cortex. At the cortical level, there are again three main areas for the respective groups (see Figure 20.1). Just behind the

CHAPTER TWENTY

central sulcus is an area for somesthesis and taste. In the very back of the cortex in the occipital lobe is an area for vision. And in the wall of the lateral fissure in the temporal lobe is the area for hearing. We call these areas just named the *primary sensory areas* because they receive fibers in direct pathways from the respective sense organs. As we shall see in the next section, there are also some indirect pathways to other areas of the cortex.

Vision and hearing are different from the other senses in that they have additional centers in the midbrain. (Somesthetic fibers send some branches to the midbrain, but have no centers there.) On the roof of the midbrain are two pairs of bodies. The front pair is concerned in vision and the back pair in hearing. In lower animals such as the fish, which have no cerebral cortex to speak of, these midbrain centers are the principal centers for vision and hearing. In the mammalian animals, such as the rat, monkey, and man, these are alternative centers to those found in the cerebral cortex.

TOPOGRAPHICAL ARRANGEMENT. From this point on, we shall have nothing to say about the sense of smell because we as yet know so little about it and the statements we make about the other senses are generally not applicable to smell. It is characteristic of the other senses, however, that their centers have an orderly *topographical arrangement*—much like maps. In vision, for example, both the thalamic center and the primary cortical area are arranged so that different points on them represent different points on the retina. By recording with electrodes or using other anatomical techniques, one can show that for every point on the retina there is a corresponding point in the thalamus and cortical area. We often speak of this arrangement as *point-to-point projection*.

There is a similar, though perhaps not so accurate, projection in hearing and somesthesis. We have already seen that different frequencies of sound waves stimulate different places in the cochlea. This *tonotopic* organization is preserved in the auditory system, so that it holds for the auditory cortex as well as for the cochlea. If electrodes are placed on this cortex while different tones are sounded, the electrical recordings show an orderly arrangement of places on the cortex corresponding to those in the cochlea. A similar order prevails in the somesthetic cortex, but in this case it is parts of the body that are represented. The upper part of the somesthetic cortex outlined in Figure 20.1 represents the legs and lower parts of the body, the middle part the arms and trunk, and the lower part the head, face, mouth, tongue, etc. This arrangement parallels quite exactly the arrangement for movements in the motor area just across the central sulcus, illustrated in Figure 20.2. In summary, then, all the senses projected to the cortex via the thalamus are represented in a topographical way.

SENSORY EXPERIENCE. Knowing the centers and pathways of the various senses, we may go on to ask how they participate in sensory experience. To study this question we have two general methods: stimulation and destruction. One is used to excite different centers and pathways and the other to remove them.

The method of *stimulation* has been used with human subjects whose brains have been exposed under local anesthesia. While an electrical stimulus is applied, the subject is asked to report whatever he experiences [Penfield and Rasmussen, 1950]. The subject reports sensations of warmth or pressure when his somesthetic cortex is stimulated, visual experiences when his visual cortex is stimulated, and various sounds when his auditory cortex is the site of the stimulation. It is interesting, however, that he never reports *pain* when his somesthetic areas are stimulated. Pain is obtained only when the thalamus is somehow involved. It therefore appears that the pain fibers of the somesthetic system go only as far as the thalamus and do not reach the cortex.

Another method of studying the sensory functions of the brain is destruction of a particular center, testing the subject's sensory capacity both before and after the removal. This method, of course, is used ordinarily only with animals. It occasionally is used with human beings when injury or disease requires brain surgery. In general, experiments of this kind show that the cerebral cortex is concerned with the *spatial aspects* of perception, whereas subcortical centers are more important in the *intensity* of experience [Lashley, 1937]. This, however, is only a general statement, and therefore is not true in every detail.

Vision is probably the best example of this general rule. In all the animals that have been studied, the primary visual cortex is necessary to perceive patterns and visual detail [Kluever, 1942]. Remove this cortical area, and an animal cannot distinguish a triangle from a circle or vertical stripes from horizontal ones (see Figure 20.4). The same animal, however, can react to a light going on or off and can distinguish which of two panels is lighted. The ability to experience intensity, as distinguished from spatial details, is therefore a property of subcortical centers—presumably in the midbrain—rather than of the visual cortex. We should hasten to add, however, that in human beings the cortex seems to have taken over some of these subcortical functions, for when people lose their visual cortex they are reported to be completely blind, although we are not entirely certain of this.

In both hearing and the somesthetic senses, matters are not so clear. These senses do not play so great a part in space perception as vision does, and it has proved more difficult to tell just how much their cortical areas are involved. We do know, though, that removal of the appropriate cortical areas reduces sensitivity to stimuli. But the loss is not great. In fact, removal of all the forebrain and midbrain centers for these senses still leaves the animal with the capacity to

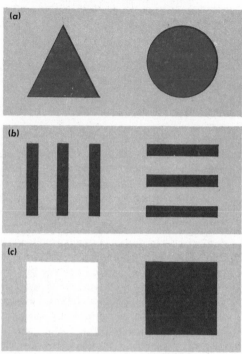

FIGURE 20.4. Visual perception in animals lacking the primary visual cortex. In the absence of the visual cortex, rats cannot distinguish pairs (a) and (b). They can, however, distinguish pair (c), for they are able to perceive the difference between black and white.

react to fairly strong stimuli. It therefore appears that all parts of these sensory systems, including those in the hindbrain, contribute something to sensory experience.

Motivation and emotion

What we have just said about sensory and motor mechanisms has been known for some time, and few startling advances have been recorded in recent years. This contrasts sharply with recent discoveries of mechanisms for motivation and emotion. For years, we knew little more than that certain motivational and emotional centers existed in the hypothalamus. Recently, a whole series of findings, coming on each other's heels, have quickly revealed details of the hypothalamic mechanisms as well as the participation of other, hitherto unsuspected centers and pathways. Consequently, much of what we have to report in this section was not known 20 years ago.

SLEEP AND AROUSAL. Sleep has already been described as one of the physiological needs (Chapter 3). Most animals must sleep in order to stay alive as well as to retain their normal capacities for doing other things. Many animals, including man, the birds, and some domestic animals, take one long period of sleep each day. Other animals, such as the rat, cat, and human babies, sleep more often, alternating a few hours of sleep with a few hours of waking. In any case, whether the periods of sleep be long or short, they always fall into some kind of rhythm or cycle of sleep and waking.

The question that has long puzzled scientists is, What accounts for these cycles of sleep and waking? One possibility, namely, that there are chemical substances in the blood and brain that bring on sleep, has already been discussed (Chapter 3), but we still know practically nothing about them. Two other possibilities, however, are more firmly established. One is that there may be centers in the brain for sleep and waking, and the other is that sensory stimulation from the environment and sense organs in the body may control or influence sleep.

Sleep and waking centers. That there may be centers for sleep in the brain was first suggested many years ago when patients were encountered who had abnormal tendencies to sleep (somnolence). In some of these patients, tumors or disease were found in the hypothalamus. Following this lead, experimental scientists paid particular attention to the hypothalamus, making controlled lesions (injuries) in various parts of the hypothalamus of animals. Their efforts were rewarded, for they found one relatively small center whose destruction caused pro-

nounced somnolence. Monkeys, for example, sleep almost continuously for 4 to 8 days after destruction of this center and are extremely drowsy for many months afterward [Ranson, 1939]. The monkeys can be aroused briefly by noises or other strong sensory stimulation, but when left alone they quickly fall asleep again. Similar results have been obtained with other animals, so there can be no doubt but that there is such a center in most animals [Nanta, 1946]. Since the destruction of this center causes somnolence, we presume that it keeps the animal awake when it is functioning normally. Therefore it is called a *waking center*.

Once the waking center had been established, one investigator asked whether there might not also be a *sleep center* [Nanta, 1946]. By exploring the hypothalamus with lesions placed in different spots, he located such a center some distance away from the waking center.

Destruction of the sleep center, the investigator found, keeps an animal (rat) from sleeping. Animals without this center eat, drink, and are otherwise normal but they have never been observed to sleep. Instead they stay awake and active until they are exhausted, and then fall into a coma and eventually die. In other experiments, this investigator destroyed both the waking center and the sleep center; he found that the result was somnolence, just as when he destroyed the waking center alone.

From this we may conclude that the waking center tends to be the dominant center and that sleep is probably produced by the sleep center's temporarily inhibiting the waking center.

Reticular activating system. This is by no means the whole story about sleep and waking. The rest of it has to do with the reticular activating system (RAS). But to tell it, we must first refer to the electroencephalogram (EEG), recorded from the skull of the intact subject. It has been known for some years now that the EEG pattern correlates with the state of arousal of a person.

As shown in Figure 20.5, the characteristic EEG of a normal, relaxed, but waking person is a rhythmic wave, called the *alpha wave,* of about 10 cycles per second. This pattern is obliterated or "blocked" by the onset of a light or sound. It is also wiped out when a person is apprehensive or anxious. In its place we see either no waves at all or an irregular pattern of small fast waves. The alpha rhythm also disappears as a person goes to sleep. At first, when he is drowsy the waves become slower and larger. As he sleeps more and more deeply, the waves further increase in size but become very slow and quite irregular.

These changes associated with sleep and waking can usually be relied upon, and have frequently been used, in determining objectively whether a person is drowsy or in deep sleep. They are also related to activities within the RAS, as the following experiment shows [Moruzzi and Magoun, 1949]:

The investigators were exploring the effects of direct electrical stimulation of the brain by placing electrodes in various positions and noting the effects of stimulation. They were surprised to find that stimulation of the RAS

did two things: First of all, it woke up a cat that was sleeping or drowsy, and it alerted one that was already awake. Secondly, it altered the EEG, producing the same changes in the EEG that accompany waking or arousal. It appeared then that the RAS was directly involved in the mechanism of waking and sleeping.

Further research brought out a number of additional facts. One, already mentioned (page 609), was that sensory impulses traveling toward the cerebral cortex could also be recorded in the RAS. This, together with the fact that stimulation of the RAS caused activity in the cerebral cortex, established the RAS as a separate relay station for sensory impulses. The investigators found that stimulation of the cerebral cortex evoked activity in the RAS, and thus demonstrated that there is a closed loop between cortex and RAS. They then went on to do other experiments using the method of extirpation [Lindsley et al., 1950].

The investigators cut the sensory pathways to the cortex, leaving those from the RAS to

BRAIN WAVES ARE DIFFERENT IN WAKING, DROWSINESS, AND SLEEP:

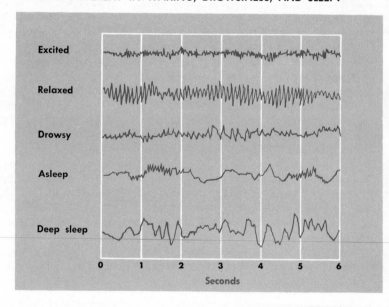

FIGURE 20.5. Brain waves typical of various states of alertness [after Jasper, 1941].

the cortex intact, and found that this operation had no effect on the sleep and waking pattern of a cat. The EEG pattern, as well as observation of the cat, indicated the typical waking state. On the other hand, when the RAS was severed, the cat fell into a sleeping state and tended to stay in it for long periods of time. How deep and prolonged the somnolence became depended on the level at which the RAS was cut. If the cut was made relatively high (near the junction of the midbrain and hypothalamus), thus blocking off practically all impulses from the RAS to the cerebral cortex, the somnolence was severe. If the cut was made lower down, thus leaving some RAS linked with the cortex, the somnolence were relatively slight.

How the RAS is related to the sleep and waking centers in the hypothalamus is not yet clear. Obviously there must be a close tie. It is plain, however, that the RAS is a basic arousal mechanism for the brain. Without its activation of the cortex, an individual remains somnolent, and even though sensory impulses reach the cortex by the thalamic route, they are not decoded by the cortex. This is the situation in sleep. The RAS, then, determines the general state of sleep or arousal of the organism.

EMOTION. The *hypothalamus* is a relatively small area, but it is much more influential than its size would indicate. When we study emotion, or indeed any other aspect of motivated behavior, we find again and again that it plays an important part.

Hypothalamus. The role of the hypothalamus in emotion was first well established by the now classic experiments of Cannon [1927] and Bard [1928]:

Using cats as their experimental animals, they made a series of sections through the forebrain, each time slicing off a little more until they had severed the entire forebrain from its connections with the midbrain and hindbrain. Usually only one level of section was used in any one subject and experiment.

Each animal was tested before and after operation for angry behavior by such procedures as pinching its tail, presenting a dog, blowing a bugle, etc. The characteristic behavior of angry cats includes growling, hissing, spitting, biting, lashing the tail, thrashing the forelegs, protruding the claws, urinating, and breathing rapidly. The investigators found that the essential pattern of angry behavior was always present as long as the hypothalamus was intact. When the hypothalamus was excluded by the operation, leaving only the midbrain and hindbrain, the pattern of rage response was broken up. The subjects sometimes displayed fragments of emotion, such as growling, hissing, or fur-ruffing, but without the hypothalamus they lost their characteristic pattern of anger.

The investigators concluded, then, that the hypothalamus is the area in which the various elements of hostile emotional behavior are organized into a pattern. This conclusion, however, has been modified by more recent research in which lesions have been made in the hypothalamus alone, leaving the rest of the forebrain intact [Bard and Mountcastle, 1947]. From what we have just said, one would expect such lesions to abolish patterns of angry behavior, but this is only partly true. The animals are more stolid, more somnolent, and generally more difficult to arouse than normal animals. The important fact, however, is that rage responses can sometimes be elicited from animals lacking the crucial hypothalamic centers. Apparently, then, the hypothalamus is not the only organizing center for emotion. There are others that participate in the same task.

Septum and amygdala. Two other centers for organizing emotion are now known to be the septum and the amygdala. Their role in emotion has been studied by making lesions in them and observing the effects on behavior. A number of experiments of this kind have been performed, usually on a rat or cat; they can be summarized as follows [King, 1958]:

A scale for rating the emotionality of a rat was developed. This merely translated into a point system the judgment of skilled raters of the degree of emotionality of the rat when subjected to several standard situations, such as having a pencil thrust at it. Ratings of emotionality were done before and after operation, and on a control group not subjected to any operation. One operative group was subjected to lesions in the septal region; another to lesions in the amygdaloid nuclei. All lesions had to be made bilaterally because of the symmetrical pairing of the structures.

Lesions in the septal region were followed by a great increase in ferocity. Formerly tame animals had to be handled with heavy gloves; they quickly attacked and bit a pencil thrust into their cage, and they were generally jumpy and ferocious. Lesions made in the amygdaloid area had just the opposite effect. Animals who were not very wild to begin with nevertheless became very placid; they would accept all kinds of irritation and rough handling without showing any rage. Later, in another experiment, some animals were subjected first to a septal operation, which made them ferocious, and then to an amygdaloid operation, which again made them calm and placid. This showed that the two regions oppose each other but that lack of both has about the same effect as lack of the amygdaloid area only.

The destruction of an area, of course, should produce results just the opposite of those produced by the normal function of the area. We may therefore conclude from the above experiments that the septal area normally inhibits ferocious behavior, while the amygdala normally excites it or makes it excitable. It is possible that the two areas exercise their function by acting on the hypothalamic centers for emotion. Thus we can think of the septum as inhibiting the hypothalamus and the amygdala as exciting it. This conclusion, however, has not at this writing been definitely proved. Nevertheless, we are making progress in understanding the centers and pathways involved in emotion.

PLEASURE AND PAIN. Another recent advance in our knowledge of the mechanisms of motivation comes from experiments with implanted electrodes. The technique was described on page 614. It involves inserting the tips of fine electrodes to a desired point deep in the brain and arranging an external connection that can be used by the experimenter to deliver at will brief electric shocks to the point selected. Such shocks may be used as reinforcement for some predetermined response on the part of the animal, such as pushing a lever, turning a wheel, or making a particular turn in a maze. The interesting thing about the experiments is that the central stimulation can serve either as a positive reinforcement or a negative reinforcement (page 201), depending among other things on the place in the brain which is stimulated. Experiments with both types of reinforcement have been done with rats, cats, and monkeys. We shall consider positive and negative reinforcement separately.

Pain. When a stimulus serves as a negative reinforcement, we may presume that it is painful or unpleasant in some way. Thus, in speaking of the negatively reinforcing effects of central stimulation, we shall use "pain" in the broad sense to include not only the kind of pain produced by peripheral stimulation of pain receptors, but anything that the individual attempts to escape or avoid—the opposite of pleasure. The negatively reinforcing effects of central stimulation are illustrated in the following experiments [Miller, 1958]:

The investigator used cats as subjects. Each cat was placed in an apparatus having a grill for a floor and a wheel in the side wall. Shock could be administered through the grill, and the cat could switch it off by turning the wheel. Cats in which brain electrodes had previously been implanted were trained to do this. Thus they learned to escape shock by turning a wheel. After they had learned this, central stimulation was substituted for shock given through the grill, and the central stimulation was continued until the cat turned the wheel. On the first few trials of this procedure, the cat seemed somewhat "surprised" and disorganized, but it quickly transferred the habit of wheel turning from peripheral to central stimulation. Evidently, the central stimulation was painful or unpleasant.

In another experiment, rats prepared with implanted electrodes were placed in a maze. As the rat wandered through the maze, the experimenter turned on a central shock whenever the rat entered an incorrect alley and kept it on until the rat left the alley and got into a correct one, at which time it was turned off. The rats learned the maze in much the same way that they would if electric shock had been administered peripherally at the wrong turn. Again central stimulation appeared to be negatively reinforcing.

Many different positions of the electrode have been used in various experiments in order to explore the brain for pathways and centers where stimulation has an unpleasant or painful effect. There are many such places, and we do not yet understand why all of them are effective. We expect, however, that the method will prove to be a valuable tool in mapping out the mechanisms of pain and unpleasantness in the brain.

Taken by themselves, the studies of unpleasant effects of central stimulation are not particularly surprising. After all, electric shock takes the place of normal methods of stimulation, and we might expect that we could produce about the same effects by central stimulation of pain pathways as we could by peripheral stimulation of pain receptors. In some cases, this is probably what is happening. In other cases, when electrodes are in positions not known to be near any pain pathways, a general unpleasantness appears to be the effect of central stimulation.

Pleasure. The unpleasant effects of central electrical stimulation are not particularly surprising to either the psychologist or the nonpsychologist, for we all know peripheral shock to be painful or annoying. What is

totally unexpected and surprising, however, is the fact that central stimulation can also be pleasant and can serve as positive reinforcement. This phenomenon can be described in the words of one of its discoverers [Olds, 1955, p. 83ff.]:

In the Fall of 1953, we were looking for more information about the reticular activating system. We used electrodes permanently implanted in the brain of a healthy, behaving rat. . . . Quite by accident, an electrode was implanted in the region of the anterior commissure [a structure near the septum].

The result was quite amazing. When the animal was stimulated at a specific place in an open field, he sometimes moved away but he returned and sniffed around that area. More stimulations at that place caused him to spend more of his time there.

Later we found that this same animal could be "pulled" to any spot in the maze by giving a small electrical stimulus *after* each response in the right direction. This was akin to playing the "hot and cold" game with a child. Each correct response brought electrical pulses which seemed to indicate to the animal that it was on the right track.

Still later, the same animal was placed on an elevated T maze. As there was an initial right turn preference, he was forced to the left and stimulated at the end of the left arm. After three such trials, he proceeded to make 10 consecutive runs to the left for electrical stimulation alone, with decreasing running times. Then the stimulus was stopped on the left, and 6 runs were forced to the right with electrical stimulation in the right arm. After this, the animal made 10 runs to electrical stimulation in the right arm. Up to this point, no food had been in the maze at all.

Following this experiment and other exploratory tests, the experimenters decided to study the phenomenon more systematically. They continued their studies by placing rats in a Skinner box (page 200), which provides for automatic recording of responses and for a very high rate of responding. The lever of the Skinner box actuated a switch that turned on central stimulation for the rat (see Figure 19.15). Rats were then prepared with several electrode placements, and Skinner-box records were made on each animal. After it was determined whether a particular placement was rewarding or not, the animal was sacrificed and the exact position of the electrode established by anatomical methods. As we might expect, the animals turned out to be aversive to some of the electrode positions; they avoided pushing the lever after they experienced some central stimulation. In this case the electrodes evidently were in pathways for pain or unpleasantness. Continuing the quotation from Olds [1955, pp. 90–91]:

The first large structure of the rat brain found to give consistently "rewarding" results was the septal area. . . . [septal] rats produce regular response rates for long periods of time [see Figure 20.6]. These rates vary from about one response for every two seconds to about one response for every ten seconds.

For a given rat, however, the rate is quite constant. Septal rats spend about three-quarters of their time responding at these steady rates even if left on acquisition up to four hours a day. When, on the other hand, the voltage is turned off so that responding no longer produces brain stimulation, bar-pressing stops quite abruptly. The animal scratches, grooms, or sleeps. If the experimenter turns the voltage back on and gives the animal one or two stimulations to show that it is on, the animal stops anything else he is doing, walks to the lever and starts responding again.

Of all the electrode positions that give this effect, most of them are in structures of the *limbic system*. This is the system that includes the septum and ties in closely with the hypothalamus. (See the diagram of the limbic system in Figure 19.13.) A few positions that are rewarding are outside this system.

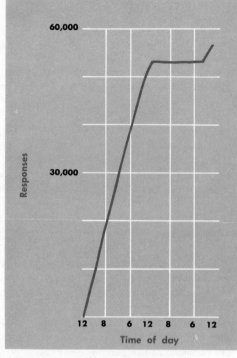

FIGURE 20.6. A record of bar-pressing in the Skinner box, with the reinforcement being mild electric shock within the brain. Beginning at noon one day, the rat stimulated itself at a rate of more than 2,000 responses an hour for 26 hours, then slept for 19 hours, and then resumed self-stimulation at the same rate [after Olds, 1958].

These initial experiments on the rewarding or pleasant effects of central stimulation have been described at some length because they are both interesting and important. They open up great possibilities for understanding better the motivational mechanisms of the brain as well as opportunities for practical applications of this knowledge. It is possible that the method of central stimulation will prove useful in the treatment of otherwise hopeless mental illness, though it is still too early to tell. The use of implanted electrodes for both positive and negative

CHAPTER TWENTY

reinforcement is also being coupled with the search for new therapeutic drugs. The purpose of this work is to find drugs that selectively act on certain emotional centers of the brain, and particularly to find those that enhance the rewarding effects, or reduce the punishing effects, of central stimulation. Thus the method serves as a screen for spotting new drugs that might prove beneficial in human use. Though the research is promising, it has not yet gone far enough to draw any general conclusions about it at this time.

NEEDS. When we discussed physiological needs in the chapter on motivation, we explained that they arose from chemical conditions in the body, but we did not say how these conditions expressed themselves in motivated behavior. That question, which we shall now take up briefly, leads us once again to the hypothalamus, for this center proves to be important in the physiological needs as well as in sleep and emotion. The three needs for which we know this to be true are sex, hunger, and thirst. We shall consider them in order.

Sexual behavior. Investigators interested in finding how the nervous system functions in sexual behavior have carried out experiments much like those we described above for emotional behavior. The following experiment [Dempsey and Rioch, 1939] is an example:

Sections were made at different levels through the forebrain and midbrain of female animals, and attempts were then made to induce typical mating behavior in the animals. Mating behavior was normal so long as the back part of the hypothalamus and a region behind the hypothalamus (called *mammillary bodies*) were left intact. If, however, the section passed through the midbrain behind these structures, the animals no longer engaged in full-fledged mating behavior.

Following this kind of experiment, the next logical step is to make restricted lesions in the hypothalamus. This has been done in several different animals, both male and female. In one fairly clear-cut experiment [Brookhart and Dey, 1941; Dey et al., 1940], lesions in the hypothalamus abolished sexual behavior in both male and female animals, and no amount of the hormones which normally induce sexual behavior (see Chapter 3) could reinstate it. From experiments such as these, physiologists have been led to believe that hormones excite the hypothalamus and associated structures and that it is from this point that sexual responses are organized.

Hunger. We have excellent evidence that hunger is also mediated by the hypothalamus. The principal technique used to provide this evidence has been to make relatively small lesions in the hypothalamus and to measure the effect of these lesions on eating. One center, located near the midline of the hypothalamus, restrains hunger and eating; when it is destroyed, animals develop voracious appetites [Brobeck, 1946].

Such animals, even before they recover from the operation, usually attack food ravenously and eat large quantities of it. Their immense appetites continue day after day; they gain weight rapidly and become so obese that they are about three times their normal weight. Then they slacken off somewhat and maintain their weight in this state. In Figure 20.7, you see the picture of a rat in which obesity was produced by a small lesion in the hypothalamus.

Experimenters have studied such animals to see just what has gone wrong with them. Their metabolism is normal, and so is just about everything else in the machinery of the body. Apparently the main thing wrong is that their appetites have gotten out of hand. It is probably this hypothalamic center that is deficient in some obese human beings. On the other hand, it is very likely that obesity in human beings is more often a matter of bad eating habits and personality difficulties than of a deranged hypothalamus.

It is interesting that there is a second center in the hypothalamus that has quite the opposite function. When experimenters make their lesions just a fraction of an inch to the side of the lesion that produces ravenous appetite, the result is that the animal has no appetite at all [Teitelbaum and Stellar, 1954]. Such animals, unless given special care, never touch food again and if left alone eventually die of "voluntary" starvation. By maintaining the animals through artificial means (stomach tubes) and offering them especially desirable food, such as chocolate bars, experimenters have been able to teach some of them to start eating again. The important point, though, is that in the case of hunger, as in that of sleep, there are two pairs of centers; one exercises a restraining influence, the other an exciting influence.

Thirst. We know considerably less about the central mechanisms of thirst, but they appear to be somewhat similar to those of sex and hunger. There is a region in the hypothalamus whose destruction makes animals extremely thirsty. This region sends down fibers to the pituitary gland, which plays an important role in water metabolism. In fact, destruction of one part of the pituitary causes a drastic increase in water consumption, known as *polydipsia*. This has been traced to a hormone of the pituitary that controls the excretion of water. When this hormone is lacking, water is excreted much more rapidly, and a deficit of water in the body results. The water deficit appears to be the cause of the increased thirst, for it precedes the appearance of thirst. This set of facts, however, does not lead us any nearer to the mechanism of thirst; we still do not know how a water deficit in the body causes thirst.

A good guess, though, is that the increased concentration of salts in the blood directly stimulates a thirst center in the hypothalamus. When the body loses water, by sweating or excretion, it tends to retain the salts normally found in the blood, so that their concentration increases. We do not know whether this condition directly stimulates the hypothalamus, but we do know that salt solutions applied to the proper point in the hypothalamus cause

FIGURE 20.7. An obese rat. This rat has a ravenous hunger and has almost doubled its weight as a result of a small surgical lesion made in the part of the hypothalamus concerned in hunger.

increased drinking. This point will be brought out in the next section.

Central stimulation. The method of central stimulation has been used to study the central mechanisms of sex, hunger, and thirst. We have not mentioned it before because it is more easily explained separately. It has been used in two forms: electrical stimulation, usually of points in or near the hypothalamus; and biochemical stimulation with solutions or hormones. Electrical stimulation has been used to study hunger; biochemical stimulation to study sex and thirst.

In one series of experiments [Miller, 1958], which we shall now describe, electrodes were implanted in the hypothalamus of rats:

When the electrodes were implanted at certain points, which seem to correspond fairly well with the regions whose destruction causes hunger, electrical stimulation produced what appeared to be an increase in hunger. This was demonstrated in a number of ways. After a rat had been thoroughly satiated on food, electrical stimulation was turned on. Shortly after that the rat resumed eating; if no edible objects were available, it would gnaw away on anything that happened to be around. When the stimulation was turned off, the rat stopped gnawing and eating. If milk was available during stimulation, the rat drank it. Stimulation, however, was producing hunger, rather than thirst, for the rat would not drink plain water.

The electrical stimulation could be used to motivate otherwise satiated rats to learn a response or to perform one already learned. The rat would run a simple T maze, rewarded at the end with food, during stimulation, but not before or afterward. It would similarly push a bar to obtain food in the familiar Skinner box during stimulation, then stop pushing and eating after the stimulation ceased. It appeared then that the electrical stimulation was producing a genuine hunger drive.

In an experiment [Andersson, 1953] using chemical stimulation, a goat was outfitted with a pipette whose tip was in the general region of the hypothalamus. The goat was given its fill of water, and then a tiny amount of salt solution was forced through the pipette. Thereupon the goat resumed drinking water vigorously.

A comparable, but opposite effect has been demonstrated with cats. Cats made thirsty by water deprivation stopped drinking when a small amount of plain water was injected [Miller, 1958]. Similar experiments have also been done with hormones [Fisher, 1956]. The injection of a minute quantity of male hormone at a place in the brain concerned with sexual behavior induced sexual behavior, and in some cases, maternal behavior. It is interesting, however, that electrical stimulation of the same site had no such effects. It would seem then that the neural cells involved are more sensitive to the right sort of chemical stimulation than to electrical stimuli.

Experiments of this kind have been introduced only in recent years, and it will be some time before they are fully exploited. Along with the experiments that employ the method of destruction, they point to rela-

tively specific centers, usually pairs of centers that balance each other and control the different physiological drives. So far, the emphasis has been on the hypothalamus, and we can be certain that this tiny region of the nervous system contains the centers that are, perhaps, the primary points of control. It is also certain, however, that other regions of the brain exert some influence over these centers, but it remains for future research to tell us what they are and how they fit into the mechanisms of motivation.

Learning and thinking

Perhaps the most interesting property of the nervous system is that it enables us to learn and to think. For that reason a great deal of research has been devoted to the neural mechanisms of learning and thinking. Such research has been pointed at two general questions, one pertaining to the microscopic level and the other to the macroscopic level. The first question is, What changes take place in neurons or their synaptic connections to make learning possible? Although it has been studied diligently, the question is still without a firm answer. The general opinion, although it is without direct proof, is that learning involves some sort of change in synapses that makes the passage of impulses easier than it was before. It may be that the fibers grow together at their juncture. But this is only a surmise. The other question concerns the centers and pathways of the nervous system: What parts of the nervous system are involved in any particular kind of learning? For the second question we have some answers, and shall deal with them in this section.

CONDITIONING. Conditioning is usually regarded as the simplest form of learning (see Chapter 7). For this reason, we might assume that an organism, if it can learn at all, can learn a conditioned response. Investigators have, therefore, used the conditioning method in attempting to discover what parts of the nervous system are capable of learning. Their method, typically, has been to remove some part of the nervous system—or at least to cut it off from the rest of the nervous system—and then to test the animal's capability of learning a conditioned reaction.

For many years it was thought that the highest part of the nervous system, the cerebral cortex, was necessary for even the most elementary conditioning to take place. Now we know that this is not so. Human beings born without a cerebral cortex and animals from whom it has been experimentally removed have both been conditioned. But there are limits to this conditioning. The normal animal learns to lift its paw promptly and smoothly when a signal warns him of impending shock. The decorticate animal, on the other hand, typically learns to squeal and squirm but does not acquire the smooth "adaptive" response [Culler, 1938]. The decorticate animal has therefore lost some of the skill one normally sees in conditioning, even though it can learn to respond to the conditioning stimulus.

There are many other experiments designed to determine whether certain sensory centers are necessary for a particular kind of conditioning. Is the visual cortex, for example, necessary for a visual conditioned reaction? In vision as well as the other senses, the answer seems to be "no." In the absence of the visual cortex, a dog may be conditioned to wink its eye when a light is flashed. (In this case, the unconditioned stimulus is a puff of air to the eyeball.) Nor is memory for the conditioned reaction disturbed when the visual cortex is removed. From these facts it seems evident that some conditioning normally takes place in subcortical centers.

DISCRIMINATIVE LEARNING. This statement is not true, however, of more complex learning. Suppose, for example, that the task for the animal is one of discrimination rather than conditioning. It may be required to choose between two windows, one lighted and the other unlighted, being rewarded for correct responses and punished for incorrect ones. An animal that is taught such a discrimination and then has its visual cortex removed "forgets" what it has learned. Yet, if given the opportunity to relearn the discrimination, it will do so in just about the same number of trials and errors as it required before operation [Lashley, 1935]. It would seem, consequently, that the sensory cortex is *not* necessary for *learning* a discrimination but is necessary for *remembering* it if it has been learned before injury to the brain. Apparently subcortical centers can take over learning functions normally carried on cortically.

We have used vision to illustrate the point, but there are numerous experiments with other senses giving about the same results. We do not yet understand just why one part of the nervous system can take over when another fails. The phenomenon nonetheless is important in understanding nervous function. It means that, within certain limits, there is an *equivalence of function*— a sort of built-in insurance—that offsets the handicap of injury to a particular center or area [Lashley, 1929].

This capacity of the nervous system, however, does not extend to every sort of learning. If we teach a rat to discriminate different patterns, such as a triangle versus a circle, and then destroy its cortex, it will never be able to relearn this discrimination. In this case the visual cortex is absolutely necessary for the ability to discriminate patterns, and no other part of the visual system can take over this capacity.

Besides the primary sensory areas there are other areas of the cerebral cortex that are involved in the learning of discriminations (see Figure 20.8). Just in front of and more or less surrounding the visual cortex is an area sometimes called the *visual association area* or (by anatomists) the *prestriate area.* Just behind the somesthetic area and occupying the principal part of the parietal lobe is the *parietal association area,* which is concerned in somesthetic learning. And an area near the primary auditory area of

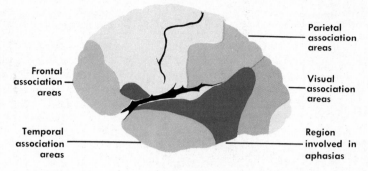

FIGURE 20.8. The association areas of the cerebral cortex. Aphasias, which are disorders of the linguistic functions, are discussed on page 634.

Parietal association areas

Frontal association areas

Visual association areas

Temporal association areas

Region involved in aphasias

the temporal lobe serves as an *auditory association area*. Each sense, therefore, has an area near its primary cortical area that may function as an association area.

We still have much to learn about these association areas, and it is not yet possible to ascribe to them really definite functions. There are, however, two general statements we can make about them. The first is that they sometimes have an equivalence of function with primary areas. This is demonstrated in the following study [Ades, 1946]:

The experimenter taught monkeys to make discriminations of size, color, and form. Then he removed their prestriate areas on both sides. After allowing sufficient time for surgical recovery, he tested them on the discrimination habits. He found that they had complete amnesia—loss of memory—for the habits. Upon extensive retraining, however, they could relearn the habits almost as quickly as they had learned them preoperatively. Thus the experimenter showed that the prestriate association areas were important in the original learning of the habit, but that the remainder of the visual system could take over this capacity in their absence. Similar results have been obtained for other association areas and the respective discriminations that depend upon them.

The second general statement we can make about sensory association areas of the cortex is that they are involved in the more complex sensory discriminations. The following experiment [Ruch et al., 1938] illustrates this statement:

The investigator taught a chimpanzee to discriminate a cone from a pyramid by touch alone. The animal could not see the objects and had to discriminate them by handling them. He also taught the chimpanzee the more difficult discrimination of a wedge from a pyramid. Then he removed the posterior parietal association area. After the operation, the animal lost both habits, but upon retraining was able to learn again the discrimination of the pyramid and cone. With no amount of retraining, however, could the animal again discriminate the wedge and pyramid—the more complex discrimination. Thus it appears that the association areas are necessary for learning difficult discriminations.

MEMORY DISORDERS. Although more definitive experiments on brain functions can be performed with animals than with man, human subjects naturally acquire a great many complex habits that can be taught to animals only with great labor or not at all. They can also be tested fairly extensively and easily once it is known that they have an injury. For that reason, much of our information about memory and brain functions has come from people who have suffered brain injury.

The disorders of memory that have been observed in the brain-injured have been divided into three general classes: aphasia, agnosia, and apraxia. An *aphasia* concerns language functions, including arithmetic and mathematics as well as words and names. Any loss of linguistic abilities and memories is called an aphasia. An *agnosia,* on the other hand, is nonlinguistic; it is a loss of memory for the meaning of objects, for example, loss of recognition of a fork or an automobile or a pencil—not their names but what they are used for. Finally, *apraxia* concerns movement; it is loss of memory for how to do things, such as how to throw a ball, open a door, dress oneself, or drive a car. Each of these memory disorders can be subdivided into a number of varieties. Aphasia, for example, can be divided into sensory aphasia, which is the inability to understand language, and motor aphasia, which is the inability to produce language through speech or writing. Most of these distinctions, however, will not concern us here.

The memory disorders can alternatively be classified into the *expressive* disorders and *receptive* disorders. In general, the expressive disorders (apraxias and motor aphasia) depend upon the frontal lobes, and the receptive disorders (agnosias and sensory aphasia) depend upon other lobes. When, for example, we encounter a person who can no longer speak or write words, though he understands them and is quite capable in other ways, we can be rather certain that he has sustained an injury or lesion in the frontal lobes. If, on the other hand, he does not recognize speech when he hears it or reads it, or does not recognize the names of familiar objects and people, the chances are high that his injury is farther back in the brain.

There is considerable disagreement among neurologists about how specifically we can assign memory disorders to particular areas of the cortex. It seems fairly certain, however, that there is an *area for speech* in the lateral frontal part of the cortex. When this area is obliterated, a person has speech aphasia; he no longer can remember how to make the sounds that are necessary to talk.

It is probably also true that farther up in the frontal lobe is an *area for writing*. This must be intact for a person to remember how to make the highly coordinated movements involved in writing language and in drawing. The localization of sensory aphasia and of the agnosias is more debatable, but some neurologists believe from their observations of a great many cases that the areas can be defined reasonably well.

The localization of memory functions in man, however, cannot be extremely specific because it is usually possible for a person to relearn what he has "forgotten." Just as in the case of sensory learning, there is some equivalence of the parts lost and those remaining. A person simply must start again the long laborious process of learning what took him months or years to learn in childhood. If he can no longer read, he must learn his alphabet again, then simple words, then phrases and more complex sentences. Unless the damage has been very great or unless he suffers another injury, as often happens to older people with cerebral hemorrhage, he has a good chance of at least partial recovery of the functions he has lost.

FRONTAL ASSOCIATION AREAS. In Figure 20.8, there are relatively large areas of the frontal lobe that are not concerned with specific memories but are nevertheless involved in intellectual processes. These have been called the *prefrontal areas* or the *frontal association areas.* Their removal in man or animals is followed by a number of important changes in ability and in personality. An inability to attend well to a task is one of the symptoms that follows destruction of the prefrontal areas.

This fact has often been demonstrated in experiments [Jacobsen, 1935; Harlow and Johnson, 1943] with monkeys that have been taught a delayed reaction.

The monkey is shown that food is under a particular object (see Figure 20.9). Then a screen is lowered in front of him so that he cannot stare at it. After an interval of time, the screen is raised; the monkey's task is then to select the correct object from among others. Normal monkeys can do this after delays of several minutes (see Chapter 7). Prefrontal monkeys—those lacking the prefrontal areas—usually fail if the delay is more than a few seconds. By turning lights out during the delay or doing other things to keep the animals from being distracted, the experimenter may be able to get some prefrontal animals to solve the problem.

We cannot say, then, that this problem can never be solved without the frontal lobes. However, it is much more difficult without them. From this experiment and other things we know about prefrontal animals, it appears that they have difficulty in attending to a task.

Human beings with injury to their prefrontal areas are able to solve the delayed-reaction problem, apparently because the task is much less difficult for them than it is for monkeys. In many other little ways, however, they exhibit difficulties in attending, planning, and keeping their minds on what they should be doing. They are more likely to shirk responsibility, not to worry about the future, to be inconsiderate of people, and to react impulsively to their present inclinations than are normal people. Some observers summarize all these changes by saying that the prefrontal areas have to do with a person's planning and regard for the future and that the person suffering damage to them loses much of his concern for the future.

In the late 1930s, when this conception of the function of the prefrontal areas was emerging, it suggested the possibility that some forms of mental illness might be treated by removing parts of the prefrontal areas or by cutting them off from lower centers of the brain. The operation as employed with human patients was called *prefrontal lobotomy* or, more generally, *psychosurgery* [Freeman and Watts, 1950]. It was sometimes performed on individuals who had become so worried, depressed, and

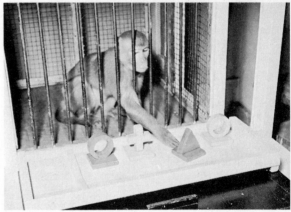

FIGURE 20.9. A monkey solving a delayed-reaction problem. Above, the monkey is shown the correct stimulus (gray triangle) and allowed to find food under it. After a delay, the monkey (below) is presented with several stimuli (gray circle, white cross, gray triangle, and white circle). He shows that he remembers which is correct by pushing back the gray triangle and obtaining food from the well beneath it [H. F. Harlow].

anxious about the future that they had become mentally ill and had not been helped by milder forms of treatment. Neurosurgeons sometimes reported that patients were considerably improved by the operation—enough in some cases to be discharged from treatments. But systematic studies of control, as well as operative cases, has not borne this out. In general, it appears that just about as many unoperated patients as operated patients improve over a period of months or years [Mettler, 1949]. The operation is therefore not regarded so favorably as it once was as a method of treating severe and otherwise incurable illnesses.

Intelligence

No sharp line can be drawn between learning and thinking, on the one hand, and intelligence, on the other. In fact, intelligence generally refers to the ability of an individual to learn and to solve problems. In human beings, however, we usually measure intelligence by means of tests that do not directly test ability to learn but rather measure the abilities that have been developed through previous learning. In animals, an attempt to obtain a crudely comparable measure has been made. We rate "intelligence" by measuring ability at some learning task or by determining the complexity of tasks the animals can learn to solve. In any case, we are concerned with the ability to learn, rather than with the learning process itself.

We can then go on to ask what physiological factors are important in intelligence. We do not yet know a great deal about this, but we have discovered some of the factors that account for *lack* of intelligence, namely, feeble-mindedness. In addition, there have been some so far unsuccessful attempts to find physiological means of improving intelligence. We shall discuss both.

FEEBLE-MINDEDNESS.   There are approximately four million people in the United States whose intelligence is so low that they can be considered feeble-minded (see Chapter 14). Some cases of feeble-mindedness are caused by injury to the brain at birth. The great majority of cases, however, are not so readily explained. Since low intelligence tends to run in families, many of the feeble-minded probably inherit a defective nervous system. In such instances, we may

suppose that the genes make something go wrong in the developing structure of the nervous system and in the internal environment on which it depends. So far, however, we are unable to say specifically in most cases just what has gone wrong.

There is one kind of feeble-mindedness, however, which is inherited and is known to be due to a defect in the internal environment. This is *phenylpyruvic oligophrenia* [Jervis, 1939]. It is relatively rare, but its genetic mechanism is reasonably clear. It seems to be caused by a *single defective gene* which is responsible for an *enzyme* necessary to utilize phenylpyruvic acid. This acid is a product in the brain's burning of fuel. Ordinarily it is disposed of by a chemical reaction controlled by a specific enzyme. If this reaction is blocked and the acid accumulates in the brain, the result is that the individual is feeble-minded. The diagnostic sign of such feeble-mindedness is excretion of phenylpyruvic acid, for some accumulated acid finds its way to the kidney, and individuals who excrete it are without exception feeble-minded.

The internal environment is also clearly involved in another type of feeble-mindedness, *cretinism* (see Figure 20.10). In this case, the deficiency is in the thyroid hor-

FIGURE 20.10. A 17-year-old boy with cretinism who resembles a 3-year-old child. The boy was born with a deficient thyroid gland. A deficiency of thyroid has caused stunted growth and mental retardation [E. Cheraskin].

mone. As we have already pointed out, the thyroid hormone regulates the rate of metabolism—the utilization of energy—and when it is deficient the brain and other tissues of the body cannot grow or function normally. The child suffering this deficiency becomes a cretin—a feeble-minded dwarf with a potbelly and thick, rough skin. Fortunately, we are able to recognize this disease reasonably early and to administer thyroid hormones to alleviate it. Some of the effects of thyroid deficiency on brain function are probably irreversible, especially if the deficiency is severe, but hormone therapy helps the cretin to develop more normally and to have more nearly normal intelligence than he would otherwise. Thyroid deficiency can develop in adults as well as in children. Then it is called *myxedema*.

Lack of oxygen (known as *anoxia*) is another important cause of feeble-mindedness. This is understandable, because the brain must have oxygen to get its energy and to maintain its normal function. If a person is deprived of adequate oxygen for long periods of time (or of all oxygen for a few minutes) and is still able to live, the chances are that he will suffer a serious loss in intelligence. Such cases occasionally occur in clinical practice, as when a person has nearly died of asphyxiation or has had the blood supply to his brain shut off too long while undergoing surgery.

Oxygen lack is most serious in the infant before it is born or at birth, because the brain is still being formed. It is during this time, too, that the chances of oxygen lack are high. Sometimes the blood supply to the fetus is inadequate, and thus causes oxygen lack. The *mongoloids,* one large class of the feeble-minded, are probably produced in this way [Ingalls, 1952]. In some instances, the mother may be given drugs that have the side effect of reducing the amount of oxygen that reaches the fetus. In other cases, the baby may be temporarily suffocated during delivery because the umbilical cord carrying oxygen from the mother is closed off before he starts breathing. In any event,

lack of oxygen before or during birth can play havoc with the nervous system, and the result can be feeble-mindedness.

We might say in passing that we have considerable evidence on this point from experiments with animals [Windle, 1958]. Rats and guinea pigs that are partially asphyxiated at birth fail to grow normally. They are unable to learn mazes or other problems at a normal rate. They show other neurological defects, such as partial paralysis, blindness, and deafness, as well as generally poor intelligence.

IMPROVING INTELLIGENCE. Perhaps the reader has wondered whether some drug or chemical substance might be used to improve intelligence. After all, we now have wonder drugs for almost "anything that ails you"; why not one for intelligence? Scientists have asked this question and have tried to find such a wonder drug. In the case of the cretin, we know that the trouble is a lack of thyroxin and that giving the cretin thyroxin early enough really does wonders. This is a special case, however, and the matter is not so simple when we come to other forms of feeble-mindedness or to the problem of improving the intelligence of normal people.

Many substances, along with the enzymes needed for their metabolism, are critical in brain processes; without them, brain function would be impaired and so would intelligence. If a deficiency in the amount and utilization of one of these substances impairs function, we may reasonably ask whether a surplus of it might be beneficial and hence might be used to improve intelligence. In time this question will be answered by research that systematically tests the effects of various substances known to take part in brain chemistry. To date, little research of this kind has been done. Research on the effects of two substances—glutamic acid and the vitamin thiamin—has, however, been carried out.

Glutamic acid. Glutamic acid is a decomposition product of protein. It and its related compounds are known to play an important role in the metabolism of most tissues, and in particular to take part in the removal of ammonia, a decomposition product, in brain tissue. For this reason, glutamic acid was chosen as a substance that might prove useful in improving intelligence, particularly the intelligence of retarded individuals. Research employing this acid at first seemed to show that it could improve the intelligence of children and the learning ability of rats. In two experiments, one with feeble-minded children and the other with rats, glutamic acid seemed to have beneficial effects. These studies were not altogether convincing, however, for they were not completely controlled. Several subsequent studies have failed to confirm them [Arbitman, 1952]. We must therefore look elsewhere for a substance or drug that might improve intelligence.

Thiamin. Biochemists know that thiamin (otherwise known as vitamin B$_1$) is necessary in one of the essential chemical reactions of the brain. It is therefore another candidate for improving intelligence. Research on it indicates that under some circumstances it may be effective.

In a study of orphanage children receiving thiamin daily for over a year, the children improved on many measures of skill, achievement, and intelligence in comparison with a control group receiving placebos [Harrell, 1947]. In another study of 90 mental defectives, about 15 per cent showed some improvement in intelligence following the regimen of thiamin [Rudolf, 1949]. It would appear from these studies that in some cases thiamin affords a slight improvement in intelligence, particularly if it is administered to very young children. After children reach the age of five or six, extra thiamin probably does no good. The results of experiments with rats suggest that the vitamin is helpful if given early enough in life [O'Neill, 1949]. Extra thiamin fed to the mother during pregnancy, and then to the pups after birth up until weaning, appears to improve greatly the ability of rats to learn

mazes. We do not yet know, however, whether these results can be applied to man.

As matters now stand, there is no wonder drug for feeble-mindedness or for improving intelligence. Such a drug, however, is not out of the question. It may be discovered in the near future.

Drugs and personality

In the last 30 years, we have witnessed remarkable advances in the treatment of infectious diseases. First the sulfa drugs, then penicillin, and now a long list of wonder drugs have either eliminated or provided rapid cures for diseases that used to kill or incapacitate millions of people. One of the distinguishing features of these drugs is that they fight relatively specific diseases. One drug combats a particular disease or a group of related diseases, but is relatively impotent against other diseases for which other drugs are more effective.

In the next 30 years, we may expect to see a parallel development of drugs with psychological effects. The hunt for such drugs has been in progress now for about ten years, and it is being prosecuted with great vigor and with some promising results. In fact, a new branch of pharmacology, called *psychopharmacology*, has already been born; it refers to the study of drugs that primarily affect behavior and personality. Research in this field is seeking to invent and to discover drugs that may, like the antibiotics, be used for particular purposes, such as to reduce anxiety, make the mentally ill more lucid, reduce fatigue, or activate the depressed.

At the moment, the field is in a more or less confused state. There has not been time to evaluate the usefulness of drugs already on hand; yet new drugs are making their appearance almost daily. The claims made for some of the drugs are grossly exaggerated, and even spurious. When all the evidence is in, many of these drugs will prove to be passing fads. On the other hand, exciting progress is being made, and we can be relatively certain that the future promises some dramatic breakthroughs in the treatment and control of behavior through drugs. For that reason, we shall summarize briefly the present status of psychopharmacology [Wikler, 1957].

Drugs with psychological effects fall roughly into two classes: *psychotomimetic drugs* and *psychotherapeutic drugs*. As the names imply, the first produces symptoms or effects that are similar in some respects to the symptoms of mental illness. They are mainly useful as research tools. The second class of drugs consists of those used in the treatment of behavior disorders or, more generally, for the purpose of gaining some improvement in behavior.

PSYCHOTOMIMETIC DRUGS. Consider first how some drugs affect us. Alcohol, if taken in sufficient quantity, frequently produces the incoherence and hallucinations that are also observed in psychoses. Nitrous oxide, or "laughing gas," can cause fits of uncontrollable emotions of the sort that occur only in the most severe mental disorders. Many of the narcotics put the drug addict into a trancelike state in which he "lives" his dreams and is completely out of touch with reality. In this respect he is not unlike some patients one sees in a schizophrenic ward. Even the simple lack of oxygen, such as that experienced at high altitude, causes a person to become confused, display poor judgment, and lose emotional control in much the same way that he does in personality disorders. There is, in fact, a long list of drugs, narcotics, and chemical conditions that can produce striking mental symptoms. This fact suggests the possibility that mental illness may be caused, in part, by some maladjustment in the internal environment.

The psychotomimetic drug that has recently received the most attention is *lysergic acid diethylamide*, more commonly known as LSD-25, or more briefly as just LSD [Ruben, 1957]. Its effects on human beings are described by some as a drug-produced psychosis, but this is probably an overstatement. In any case, it does seem to produce many of the symptoms of schizophrenia.

Descriptions of those who have taken LSD, or have observed the behavior of others who have taken it, include the following reactions: heightened anxiety, feelings of euphoria, changes in mood, silliness and giggling, flights of ideas and fantasy, visual illusions and hallucinations, inability to concentrate, feelings of depersonalization and detachment, and distortion of the sense of time. The particular effects observed vary of course with the dosage, but they also vary with the individual, with whether the person is in a dark room or a light room—more hallucinations are observed in the dark— and even with the personality of the experimenter or the people around the person under the influence of the drug. When he is alone the effects are different from when he is with other people. Some of these effects are shown in Figure 20.11.

Given to patients already suffering a psychosis, LSD is said to increase their psychotic symptoms and often to produce additional bizarre symptoms. Some psychiatrists have been trying it out as an aid in psychotherapy. They report that by making the patient somewhat more anxious and prone to fantasy, LSD helps the individual to talk more freely and to verbalize what otherwise would be repressed. It remains to be seen, though, whether the drug will be of value in therapy.

An objective evaluation of the evidence to date makes it clear that LSD is far from the perfect psychotomimetic drug. There are many differences between its effects and those of a real psychosis. There are other drugs, particularly the narcotics, that do almost as good a job, though a somewhat different one, in producing bizarre, psychosis-like behavior. Nevertheless LSD offers a promising lead in the study of the physiological mechanisms of the behavior disorders. Quite probably, more and better psychotomimetic drugs will be discovered in the pharmaceutical laboratories in the near future.

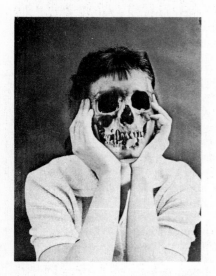

FIGURE 20.11. Some hallucinations and fantasies reported by individuals taking the drug LSD-25 [David Linton].

PSYCHOTHERAPEUTIC DRUGS. There are certain drugs that seem to help in mental illness. Injections of metrazol, for example, produce violent convulsions, which sometimes help to cure psychoses. Similarly, insulin (the hormone of the pancreas) given in heavy doses produces convulsions and a deep coma, which psychiatrists have found effective in dealing with some cases of psychosis.

Another drug that has been used in therapy for some years is sodium amytal. It affects metabolism in the brain. It is sometimes given to patients who have completely withdrawn from the world of reality. Patients may be so severely disordered that they do not move or speak, do not eat, and have to be tube-fed. Yet when given sodium amytal, they often show remarkable improvement. They get up briskly, talk eagerly and often coherently, and eat ravenously. Unfortunately, the effect of sodium amytal wears off after a short while, and the patient lapses back into a stupor. The drug, however, at least gives the doctor a chance to contact the patient, to talk to him, and to get a better idea of what may be wrong (see page 169).

One of the most recent and widely publicized additions to our inventory of psychotherapeutic drugs are the so-called "tranquilizers" or, more technically, the ataractic drugs. The number and names of these drugs are multiplying so rapidly that it is hard to keep up with them. Three that have been widely used are reserpine, chlorpromazine, and meprobamate, or Miltown. Different drugs have somewhat different effects, but in general they act as depressants of the sympathetic system, thereby tending to reduce anxiety and emotionality. Thus, they keep the anxious person from feeling so tense and miserable, and tend to quiet him down. It should be emphasized, however, that by themselves they do not reduce worry or the basic causes of anxiety. They consequently treat the symptom, not the illness.

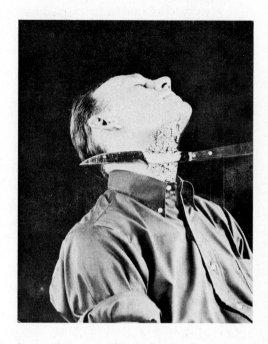

The fact that tranquilizers reduce anxiety and emotional behavior has been demonstrated in animal experiments. One experiment employed a technique now being used widely to assay the effects of drugs on emotional behavior.

The technique is to develop a conditioned emotional response (CER) in which the response is a suppression of bar pressing in a Skinner box. A rat is placed in a Skinner box on a schedule of partial reinforcement and taught to depress the bar to obtain food (or fluid). Then the animal is given a few conditioning trials in which a clicker is sounded for a period, followed at the end by an electric shock. In this way, anxiety (CER) is conditioned to the sound of the clicker. Thereafter, whenever the clicker goes on, the normal animal stops pushing the bar and does not resume pushing it again until the clicker stops. Hence, the CER can be measured as a cessation of bar pressing.

Figure 20.12 presents a graph showing the effects of two drugs on the CER [Brady, 1956.] Amphetamine (Benzedrine) is a stimulant that, like caffeine, tends to pep up an organism; reserpine is a tranquilizer; and saline serves as a control. The downward step in the curves marks the onset of the clicker, and the upward step marks its cessation. When this step is flat, it means that the rat stops pressing the bar during the sounding of the clicker. If it is not flat, but is still of less slope than the rest of the line, it indicates that the rat merely slowed its bar pressing.

The latter is the case for the normal saline control; the clicker-induced emotional response merely slows bar pressing. With the stimulant amphetamine, however, the record during periods of clicking is substantially flat, indicating that the rat's emotionality is heightened. Note, too, that bar pressing between periods of clicking is more rapid than normally; the recording line is much steeper. Quite the reverse happens with the tranquilizer reserpine. The general rate of respond-

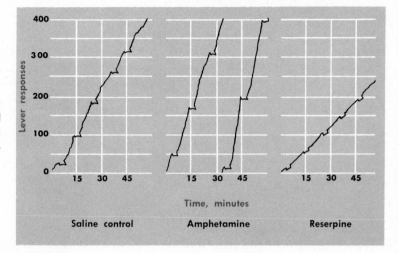

FIGURE 20.12. Effects of a stimulant (amphetamine) and a tranquilizer (reserpine) on a conditioned emotional response [after Brady, 1956].

ing is slower than normal—tranquilizers may have general sedation effects, especially in heavy doses—but it is just the same during both periods of time. In other words, the tranquilizer completely abolishes the conditioned emotional response to the clicker.

As one might suspect from the result of this experiment, tranquilizers tend to quiet down an organism. This is a most valuable effect when used with human patients. In some patients, the quieting effect of the tranquilizer is sufficient to release them from the hospital, for it was their agitated behavior that brought them there. In some cases, the quieting effect makes it possible for others to deal with them, and hence to conduct psychotherapy with them.

There have been a good many studies of the value of tranquilizers in the treatment and management of patients in hospitals. Many report that tranquilizers permit the hospital staff to do away with various forms of physical restraint otherwise needed with agitated patients. Many are extremely enthusiastic about the value of tranquilizers. Very few studies, however, have been conducted with any control groups or with "double-blind" techniques, in which neither the physician nor the patient is told which

patients are receiving the drug and which ones are not. The following study [quoted from Hollister et al., 1956, pp. 72–74] is a noteworthy exception:

The double blind technique was used in short-term studies of the effects of reserpine and chlorpromazine in groups of 24 to 42 patients. Studies were made of the action of reserpine in normal individuals, in patients hospitalized with anxiety, and in patients with chronic schizophrenic reactions. . . .

These drugs were found to have distinct value in the treatment of psychiatric patients. Patients hospitalized with anxiety reactions and mild schizophrenic reactions responded well to reserpine and a combination of reserpine and chlorpromazine. There was no advantage noted from the combined use of these drugs. It was felt that use of these drugs in adequate doses possibly shortened the period of hospitalization of this group of patients. A . . . schedule of reserpine produced improvement in two-thirds of treated patients with chronic schizophrenic reactions. A comparable dosage schedule of chlorpromazine to that of reserpine produced benefit in one-half of the treated patients with chronic schizophrenic reactions. Both drugs produced marked im-

CHAPTER TWENTY

provement in one-fourth of these patients. This improvement far surpassed that accomplished by previous forms of treatment in these patients.

Experience with these drugs thus far would indicate that they represent a significant advance in psychiatric medicine. Even the most hardened skeptic must admit that sometimes they achieve favorable results in patients who have not responded previously to other treatment. However, on the basis of double-blind studies, the enthusiast must revise downward his judgment concerning the frequency and the degree of beneficial results obtained. There remain many unanswered clinical questions concerning the proper selection of patients, the best dose for individual patients, and the optimal duration of treatment.

Use of these drugs promises to make more patients than ever before amenable to effective psychiatric rehabilitation. The trend toward making mental hospitals therapeutic, rather than custodial, institutions is bound to be accelerated by these agents.

Summary

1. Sensory areas of the cerebral cortex lie in the receptive cortex behind the central sulcus, and the motor areas lie in the expressive cortex in front of the central sulcus.

2. The motor area and premotor area are the two principal cortical areas concerned in movement and motor functions. Electrical stimulation of the motor area causes movements and the destruction of it causes paralysis. The area has a topographical representation of the body. The premotor area regulates tension and posture in different parts of the body.

3. Pathways for all the senses, except smell and the vestibular sense, proceed to the thalamus and are relayed to the cerebral cortex. Vision and hearing, in addition, have centers in the midbrain. Each of these senses has an orderly topographical arrangement in the cortex, representing a point-to-point projection of the sense organs.

4. If a sensory area of a person's cortex is electrically stimulated, he reports the corresponding sensory experience. If, on the other hand, it is removed, his ability to use the sense in space perception is usually lost. Intensity of experience, however, depends in part on subcortical centers.

5. Mechanisms for sleep, waking, and alertness include the hypothalamus, the reticular activating system, and the cerebral cortex. In the hypothalamus are centers for sleep and waking. The reticular system receives impulses from sensory systems and activates the cortex. The cortex also has return pathways to the reticular activating system.

6. The principal centers concerned in emotion are the hypothalamus, the septum, and amygdala. The septum appears to inhibit, and the amygdala to excite, the hypothalamus.

7. Direct electrical stimulation of the brain is sometimes painful or unpleasant, sometimes pleasant. Electrodes in certain positions serve as negative reinforcement in avoidance learning; in other positions, they are positively reinforcing, for animals will learn and repeatedly perform habits with electric shock to the brain as the only reinforcement. The septum is one of the best positions for this effect.

8. Centers for the major physiological needs of hunger, thirst, and sex exist in the hypothalamus. Usually they are in pairs; one member is excitatory, and the other inhibitory. Destruction of one member increases the need; destruction of the other greatly reduces it. Direct electrical or chemical stimulation of the appropriate centers can induce the need.

9. Conditioning can take place without the cerebral cortex. Many kinds of discrimination can also be learned without the

relevant cortical area. Memory for discrimination, however, is frequently lost when the relevant area is destroyed. After such destruction, memories may often be reestablished by further training. Thus subcortical centers in some cases are able to take over cortical functions in memory.

10. Fairly complex discriminative learning probably involves other areas of the cortex called sensory association areas. There are one or more such association areas for each sense. Memory disorders in man are related to damage in these areas. In general, expressive disorders depend upon the frontal lobes and receptive disorders on other lobes of the cerebral cortex.

11. The internal environment is important in learning and in intelligent behavior. Deficiencies of hormones and enzymes, as well as of oxygen, can produce feeble-mindedness. We have not yet found substances that can improve intelligence, although some day we may be successful.

12. Rapid progress is being made in the development of drugs for the study and treatment of personality disorders. Those which produce effects that mimic such disorders are psychotomimetic drugs; they include alcohol, anesthetics, and narcotics, but the best example is lysergic acid diethylamide (LSD-25 or LSD). Psychotherapeutic drugs used to aid in the treatment of personality disorders include sodium amytal and, more recently, the tranquilizers.

Suggestions for further reading

Beach, F. A. *Hormones and behavior.* New York: Hoeber-Harper, 1948.
A summary of experiments on the effects of hormones on behavior.

Morgan, C. T., and Stellar, E. *Physiological psychology* (2d ed.). New York: McGraw-Hill, 1950.
A standard text on the physiological mechanisms of behavior.

Stevens, S. S. (ed.). *Handbook of experimental psychology.* New York: Wiley, 1951. Chaps. 7, 12, 14, 20, 24, and 28.
Authoritative chapters on the physiological basis of development, motivation, learning, and perception.

Stone, C. P. (ed.). *Comparative psychology* (3d ed.). Englewood Cliffs, N.J.: Prentice-Hall, 1951. Chaps. 5 and 9.
Chapters on internal secretions and the neurology of learning.

Wenger, M. A., Jones, F. N., and Jones, M. H. *Physiological psychology.* New York: Holt, Rinehart and Winston, 1956.
An elementary textbook covering the nervous system, internal secretions, and the physiological correlates of behavior.

Wikler, A. *The relation of psychiatry to pharmacology.* Baltimore: Williams & Wilkins, 1957.
A comprehensive summary of recent literature on the effects of drugs on behavior.

Bibliography

Ades, H. W. (1946). Effect of extirpation of parastriate cortex on learned visual discrimination in monkeys. *J. Neuropath. exp. Neurol.,* **5,** 60–65.

Ades, H. W. (1959). Central auditory mechanisms. In J. Field et al. (eds.), *Handbook of physiology,* vol. I. Washington, D.C.: American Physiological Society.

Adolph, E. F. (1941). The internal environment and behavior. III. Water content. *Amer. J. Psychiat.,* **97,** 1365–1373.

Adorno, T. W., Frenkel-Brunswik, E., Levinson, D. J., and Sanford, R. N. (1950). *The authoritarian personality.* New York: Harper.

Alexander, F., and French, T. M. (eds.) (1946). *Psychoanalytic therapy.* New York: Ronald.

Allinsmith, W., and Allinsmith, B. (1948). Religious affiliation and politico-economic attitude. *Publ. Opin. Quart.,* **12,** 377–389.

Allport, F. H. (1924). *Social psychology.* Boston: Houghton Mifflin.

Allport, G. W. (1937). *Personality.* New York: Holt, Rinehart and Winston.

Allport, G. W. (1954). *The nature of prejudice.* Cambridge, Mass.: Addison-Wesley.

Allport, G. W., and Kramer, B. (1946). Some roots of prejudice. *J. Psychol.,* **22,** 9–39.

Allport, G. W., and Odbert, H. S. (1936). Trait names, a psycholexical study. *Psychol. Monogr.,* **47,** 1–171.

Allport, G. W., Vernon, P., and Lindzey, G. (1951). *A study of values.* Boston: Houghton Mifflin.

Anastasi, A., and Foley, J. P., Jr. (1958). *Differential psychology* (3d ed.). New York: Macmillan.

Andersson, B. (1953). The effect of injections of hypertonic NaCl solutions into different parts of the hypothalamus of goats. *Acta Physiol., Scand.,* **28,** 188–201.

Arbitman, H. D. (1952). The present status of glutamic acid therapy for mental deficiency. *Train. Sch. Bull.,* **48,** 187–199.

Asch, S. E. (1958). Effects of group pressure upon the modification and distortion of judgments. In E. E. Maccoby, T. M. Newcomb, and E. L. Hartley (eds.), *Readings in social psychology* (3d ed.). New York: Holt, Rinehart and Winston.

Asch, S. E. (1955). Opinions and social pressure. *Scient. Amer.,* **193,** 31–35.

Asch, S. E., Block, H., and Hertzman, M. (1940). Studies in the principles of judgments and attitudes. II. Determination of judgments by group and by ego standards. *J. soc. Psychol.*, **12,** 433–465.

Back, K. (1958) Influence through social communication. In E. E. Maccoby, T. M. Newcomb, and E. L. Hartley (eds.), *Readings in social psychology* (3d ed.). New York: Holt, Rinehart and Winston.

Baker, C. H., and Young, Phyllis (1960). Feedback during training and retention of motor skills. *Canad. J. Psychol.*, **14,** 257–264.

Bales, R. F. (1958). Task roles and social roles in problem-solving groups. In E. E. Maccoby, T. M. Newcomb, and E. L. Hartley (eds.), *Readings in social psychology* (3d ed.). New York: Holt, Rinehart and Winston.

Bard, P. (1928). A diencephalic mechanism for the expression of rage with special reference to the sympathetic nervous system. *Amer. J. Physiol.*, **84,** 490–515.

Bard, P., and Mountcastle, V. B. (1947). Some forebrain mechanisms involved in the expression of rage with special reference to suppression of angry behavior. *Res. Publ. Ass. nerv. ment. Dis.*, **27,** 362–404.

Bare, J. K. (1949). The specific hunger for sodium chloride in normal and adrenalectomized white rats. *J. comp. physiol. Psychol.*, **42,** 242–253.

Barker, R., Dembo, T., and Lewin, K. (1941). Frustration and regression, an experiment with young children. *Univer. Iowa Stud. Child Welf.*, **18,** no. 386.

Barker, R. G., and Wright, H. F. (1951). *One boy's day.* New York: Harper.

Bartlett, F. C. (1958). *Thinking: an experimental and social study.* London: G. Allen.

Bartlett, F. C. (1932). *Remembering: an experimental and social study.* London: Cambridge Univer. Press.

Beach, F. A. (1942). Sexual behavior of prepuberal male and female rats treated with gonadal hormones. *J. comp. Psychol.*, **34,** 285–292.

Beach, F. A. (1947a). Evolutionary changes in the physiological control of mating behavior in mammals. *Psychol. Rev.*, **54,** 297–315.

Beach, F. A. (1947b). A review of physiological and psychological studies of sexual behavior in mammals. *Physiol. Rev.*, **27,** 240–307.

Beach, F. A. (1949). *Hormones and behavior.* New York: Hoeber-Harper.

Beadle, G. E. (1945). Genetics and metabolism in neurospora. *Physiol. Rev.*, **25,** 643–663.

Bechterev. (1949). Cited in J. F. Dashiell, *Fundamentals of general psychology* (3d ed.). Boston: Houghton Mifflin. P. 509.

Bekesy, G. von. (1960). *Experiments in hearing.* New York: McGraw-Hill.

Bell, G., and French, R. (1950). Consistency of individual leadership position in small groups of varying membership. *J. abnorm. soc. Psychol.*, **45,** 764–767.

Bellows, R. M. (1949). *Psychology of personnel in business and industry.* Englewood Cliffs, N.J.: Prentice-Hall.

Benedict, R. (1934). *Patterns of culture.* Boston: Houghton Mifflin.

Berch, P. J. (1951). The influence of two variables upon the establishment of a secondary reinforcer for operant responses. *J. exp. Psychol.*, **41,** 62–73.

Berg, C. (1946). *Deep analysis.* London: G. Allen.

Berkowitz, L. (1954). Group standards, cohesiveness and productivity. *Hum. Relat.*, **7,** 509–519.

Berkowitz, L. (1957). Liking for the group and the perceived merit of the group's behavior. *J. abnorm. soc. Psychol.*, **54,** 353–357.

Berkowitz, L. (1959). Anti-Semitism and the displacement of aggression. *J. abnorm. soc. Psychol.*, **59,** 182–188.

Berkowitz, L., and Holmes, D. S. (1959). The generalization of hostility to disliked objects. *J. Pers.*, **27,** 565–577.

Berkowitz, L., and Howard, R. (1959). Reactions to opinion deviates as affected by affiliation need and group member interdependence. *Sociometry*, **22,** 81–91.

Bettelheim, B. (1943). Individual and mass behavior in extreme situations. *J. abnorm. soc. Psychol.*, **38,** 417–452.

Bexton, W. H., Heron, W., and Scott, T. H. (1954). Effects of decreased variation in the sensory environment. *Canad. J. Psychol.*, **8,** 70–76.

Blake, R., and Dennis, W. (1943). The development of stereotypes concerning the Negro. *J. abnorm. soc. Psychol.*, **38,** 525–531.

Bonney, M. E. (1944). Relationships between social success, family size, socioeconomic home background, and intelligence among school children in grades III and IV. *Sociometry*, **7**, 26–39.

Bordin, E. S. (1955). *Psychological counseling*. New York: Appleton-Century-Crofts.

Boring, E. G. (1942). *Sensation and perception in the history of experimental psychology*. New York: Appleton-Century-Crofts. Pp. 184, 196.

Boring, E. G. (1943). The moon illusion. *Amer. J. Phys.*, **11**, 55–60.

Boring, E. G. (ed.) (1945). *Psychology for the armed services*. Washington, D.C.: Combat Forces Press. P. 242.

Boring, E. G. (1953). A history of introspectionism. *Psychol. Bull.*, **50**, 169–189.

Boyd, D. A., Jr., and Nie, L. W. (1949). Congenital universal indifference to pain. *Arch. Neurol. Psychiat., Chicago*. **61**, 402–412.

Brady, J. V. (1956a). Assessment of drug effects on emotional behavior. *Science*, **123**, 1033–1034.

Brady, J. V. (1956b). Emotional behavior and the nervous system. *Trans. N. U. Acad. Sci.*, **18**, 601–612.

Brady, J. V. (1957). A comparative approach to the experimental analysis of emotional behavior. In P. H. Hoch and J. Zubin (eds.), *Experimental psychopathology*. New York: Grune & Stratton.

Brady, J. V. (1958). Ulcers in "executive" monkeys. *Scient. Amer.*, **199**, 95–100.

Brady, J. V., and Bunnell, B. N. (1960). Behavior and the nervous system. In R. H. Waters, D. A. Rethlinshafer, and W. E. Caldwell (eds.), *Principles of comparative psychology*. New York: McGraw-Hill. Chap. 12.

Bridges, K. M. B. (1932). Emotional development in early infancy. *Child Develpm.*, **3**, 324–341.

Brobeck, J. R. (1946). Mechanism of the development of obesity in animals with hypothalamic lesions. *Physiol. Rev.*, **26**, 541–559.

Brodbeck, May (1956). The role of small groups in mediating the effects of propaganda. *J. abnorm. soc. Psychol.*, **52**, 166–170.

Bronfenbrenner, U. (1958). Socialization and social class through time and space. In E. E. Maccoby, T. M. Newcomb, and E. L. Hartley (eds.), *Readings in social psychology* (3d ed.). New York: Holt, Rinehart and Winston.

Brookhart, J. M., and Dey, F. L. (1941). Reduction of sexual behavior in male guinea pigs by hypothalamic lesions. *Amer. J. Physiol.*, **133**, 551–554.

Brown, J. S. (1948). Gradients of approach and avoidance responses and their relation to motivation. *J. comp. physiol. Psychol.*, **41**, 450–465.

Browne, C. G. (1950). The concentric organization chart. *J. appl. Psychol.*, **34**, 375–377.

Bryan, W. L., and Harter, N. (1899). Studies on the telegraphic language: the acquisition of a hierarchy of habits. *Psychol. Rev.*, **6**, 345–375.

Burt, C., and Howard, M. (1956). The multiple factorial theory of inheritance and its application to intelligence. *Brit. J. statist. Psychol.*, **9**, 95–131.

Burtt, H. E. (1941). An experimental study of early childhood memory. *J. genet. Psychol.*, **58**, 435–439.

Bustanoby, J. H. (1947). *Principles of color and color mixing*. New York: McGraw-Hill.

Buxton, C. E. (1940). Latent learning and the goal gradient hypothesis. *Contr. psychol. Theor.*, **2**, No. 6.

Cameron, N. A., and Magaret, A. (1951). *Behavior pathology*. Boston: Houghton Mifflin.

Cannon, W. B. (1927). The James-Lange theory of emotions: a critical examination and an alternative theory. *Amer. J. Psychol.*, **39**, 106–124.

Cannon, W. B. (1929). *Bodily changes in pain, hunger, fear, and rage* (2d ed.). New York: Appleton-Century-Crofts.

Cannon, W. B. (1932). *The wisdom of the body*. New York: Norton.

Cannon, W. B. (1934). Hunger and thirst. In C. Murchison (ed.), *A handbook of general experimental psychology*. Worcester, Mass.: Clark Univer. Press. Pp. 247–263.

Carlson, E. R. (1956). Attitude change and attitude structure. *J. abnorm. soc. Psychol.*, **52**, 256–261.

Carmichael, L. (1927). A further study of

the development of behavior in vertebrates experimentally removed from the influence of environmental stimulation. *Psychol. Rev., 34,* 34–47.

Carr, H. A., and Watson, J. B. (1908). Orientation in the white rat. *J. comp. Neurol., 18,* 27–44.

Cason, H. (1930). Common annoyances: a psychological study of everyday aversions and irritations. *Psychol. Monogr.,* no. 182.

Cattell, R. B. (1942). The concept of social status. *J. soc. Psychol., 15,* 293–308.

Cattell, R. B. (1946). *Description and measurement of personality.* Yonkers, N.Y.: World.

Cattell, R. B. (1950). *Personality.* New York: McGraw-Hill.

Chapanis, A., Garner, W. R. and Morgan, C. T. (1949). *Applied experimental psychology.* New York: Wiley. Chap. 11.

Charters, W. W., Jr., and Newcomb, T. M. (1958). Some attitudinal effects of experimentally increased salience of a membership group. In E. E. Maccoby, T. M. Newcomb, and E. L. Hartley (eds.), *Readings in social psychology* (3d ed.). New York: Holt, Rinehart and Winston.

Charters, W. W., and Whitley, I. B. (1924). *Analysis of secretarial duties and traits.* Baltimore: Williams & Wilkins.

Clark, K. E. (1957). *America's psychologists.* Washington, D.C.: American Psychological Association.

Cofer, C. N. (1951). Verbal behavior in relation to reasoning and values. In H. Guetzkow (ed.), *Groups, leadership and men.* Pittsburgh: Carnegie Press.

Coleman, J. C. (1950). *Abnormal psychology and modern life.* Chicago: Scott, Foresman (2d ed., 1956).

Cook, B. S., and Hilgard, E. R. (1949). Distributed practice in motor learning: progressively increasing and decreasing rests. *J. exp. Psychol., 39,* 169–172.

Cook, T. W. (1934). Massed and distributed practice in puzzle solving. *Psychol. Rev., 41,* 330–355.

Cooper, E., and Jahoda, M. (1947). The evasion of propaganda: how prejudiced people respond to anti-prejudice propaganda. *J. Psychol., 23,* 15–25.

Cotzin, M., and Dallenbach, K. M. (1950).

"Facial vision": the role of pitch and loudness in the perception of obstacles by the blind. *Amer. J. Psychol., 63,* 485–515.

Cox, C. M. (1926). *Genetic studies of genius,* vol. II. Stanford, Calif.: Stanford Univer. Press.

Crocker, E. C. (1945). *Flavor.* New York: McGraw-Hill.

Cruze, W. W. (1935). Maturation and learning in chicks. *J. comp. Psychol., 19,* 371–409.

Culler, E. A. (1938). Recent advances in some concepts of conditioning. *Psychol. Rev., 45,* 134–153.

Davis, C. M. (1928). Self-selection of diet by newly weaned infants. *Amer. J. dis. Child., 36,* 651–679.

Davis, E. A. (1932). *The development of linguistic skill in twins, singletons with siblings, and only children from age five to ten years.* Minneapolis: Univer. of Minnesota Press.

Davis, F. C. (1932). The functional significance of imagery differences. *J. exp. Psychol., 15,* 630–661.

Davis, F. C. (1933). Effect of maze rotation upon subjects reporting different methods of learning and retention. *Univer. Calif. Los Angeles Publ. Educ., Phil., Psychol., 1,* 47–63.

Davis, K. (1947). Final note on a case of extreme isolation. *Amer. J. Sociol.,* 52, 432–437.

Day, E. J. (1932). The development of language in twins. I. A comparison of twins and single children. *Child Develpm., 3,* 179–199.

Dempsey, E. W. (1946). Metabolic function of the endocrine glands. *Annu. Rev. Physiol., 8,* 451–466.

Dempsey, E. W., and Rioch, D. McK. (1939). The localization in the brain stem of the oestrous responses of the female guinea pig. *J. Neurophysiol., 2,* 9–18.

Dennis, W. (1940). The effect of cradling practices upon the onset of walking in Hopi children. *J. genet. Psychol., 56,* 77–86.

Dennis, W. (1941). Spalding's experiment on the flight of birds repeated with another species. *J. comp. Psychol., 31,* 337–348.

Deutsch, A. (1946). *The mentally ill in*

America. New York: Columbia Univer. Press.

Deutsch, M., and Gerard, H. (1955). A study of normative and informational social influences upon individual judgment. *J. abnorm. soc. Psychol.,* **51,** 629–636.

Dexter, E. S. (1939). Personality traits related to conservatism and radicalism. *Charact. and Pers.,* **7,** 230–237.

Dey, F. L., Fisher, C., Berry, C. M., and Ranson, S. W. (1940). Disturbances in reproductive functions caused by hypothalamic lesions in female guinea pigs. *Amer. J. Physiol.,* **129,** 39–46.

Dictionary of Occupational Titles (2d ed.) (1949). Washington: U.S. Government Printing Office.

Dimmick, F. L., and Hubbard, M. R. (1939a). The spectral location of psychologically unique yellow, green, and blue. *Amer. J. Psychol.,* **52,** 242–254.

Dimmick, F. L., and Hubbard, M. R. (1939b). The spectral components of psychologically unique red. *Amer. J. Psychol.,* **52,** 348–353.

Dittes, J., and Kelley, H. (1956). Effects of different conditions of acceptance upon conformity to group norms. *J. abnorm. soc. Psychol.,* **53,** 100–107.

DiVesta, F. J., and Merwin, J. C. (1960). The effects of need-oriented communications on attitude change. *J. abnorm. soc. Psychol.,* **60,** 80–85.

Doll, E. A. (1936). *The Vineland Social Maturity Scale, revised condensed manual of instructions.* Vineland, N.J.: Smith Printing House.

Dollard, J., and Miller, N. E. (1950). *Personality and psychotherapy.* New York: McGraw-Hill.

Dorcus, R. M. (ed.) (1956). *Hypnosis and its therapeutic applications.* New York: McGraw-Hill.

Droba, D. D. (1930). *A scale for measuring attitude toward war.* Chicago: Univer. of Chicago Press.

Dunbar, H. F. (1954). *Emotions and bodily changes* (4th ed.). New York: Columbia Univer. Press.

Edwards, A. L. (1942). Retention of affective experiences: a criticism and restatement of the problem. *Psychol. Rev.,* **49,** 43–53.

Engen, T., Levy, N., and Schlosberg, H. (1957). A new series of facial expressions. *Amer. Psychol.,* **12,** 264–266.

Engen, T., Levy, N., and Schlosberg, H. (1958). The dimensional analysis of a new series of facial expressions. *J. exp. Psychol.,* **55,** 454–458.

English, H. B., and English, A. C. (1958). *A comprehensive dictionary of psychological and psychoanalytical terms.* New York: Longmans.

Ericksen, S. C. (1942). Variability of attack in massed and distributed practice. *J. exp. Psychol.,* **31,** 339–358.

Estes, W. K. (1944). Experimental study of punishment. *Psychol. Monogr.,* **57,** no. 263.

Eysenck, H. J. (1947). *Dimensions of personality.* London: Routledge.

Farris, E. J., and Griffiths, J. Q., Jr. (eds.) (1949). *The rat in laboratory investigation* (rev. ed.). Philadelphia: Lippincott.

Felix, R. H., and Kramer, M. (1953). Extent of the problem of mental disorders. *Ann. Amer. Acad. pol. soc. Sci.,* **286,** 5–14.

Festinger, L. (1950). Informal social communication. *Psychol. Rev.,* **57,** 271–282.

Festinger, L., Gerard, H., Hymovitch, B., Kelley, H., and Raven, B. (1952). The influence process in the presence of extreme deviates. *Hum. Relat.,* **5,** 327–346.

Fisher, A. (1956). Maternal and sexual behavior induced by intracranial chemical stimulation. *Science,* **124,** 228–229.

Fiske, D. W. (1949). Consistency of factorial structures of personality ratings from different sources. *J. abnorm. soc. Psychol.,* **44,** 329–344.

Fjeld, H. A. (1934). The limits of learning ability in Rhesus monkeys. *Genet. Psychol. Monogr.,* **15,** 403.

Flanagan, J. C. (1951). Defining the requirements of the executive's job. *Personnel,* **28,** 28–35.

Flesch, R. (1946). *The art of plain talk.* New York: Harper.

Ford, C. S., and Beach, F. A. (1951). *Patterns of sexual behavior.* New York: Hoeber-Harper.

Freeman, W., and Watts, J. W. (1950). *Psychosurgery* (2d ed.). Springfield, Ill.: Charles C Thomas.

French, N. R., and Steinberg, J. C. (1947). Factors governing the intelligibility of speech sounds. *J. acoust. Soc. Amer.*, **19**, 90–119.

Freud, S. (1938). *The basic writings of Sigmund Freud* (ed. by A. A. Brill). New York: Modern Library.

Frings, H., and Frings, Mable (1959). The language of crows. *Scient. Amer.*, **201** (5), 119–131.

Galton, F. (1907). *Inquiries into human faculty and its development* (2d ed.). New York: Dutton.

Gardner, E. (1958). *Fundamentals of neurology* (3d ed.). Philadelphia: Saunders.

Garfield, S. L. (1957). *Introductory clinical psychology*. New York: Macmillan.

Gates, A. I. (1917). Recitation as a factor in memorizing. *Arch. Psychol., N.Y.*, **6**, no. 40.

Geldard, F. A. (1953). *The human senses*. New York: Wiley.

Gerard, R. W. (1941). *The body functions*. New York: Wiley.

Gesell, A., and Thompson, H. (1929). Learning and growth in identical infant twins: an experimental study by the method of co-twin control. *Genet. Psychol. Monogr.*, **6**, 1–124.

Ghiselli, E. E., and Brown, C. W. (1955). *Personnel and industrial psychology* (2d ed.). New York: McGraw-Hill.

Gibson, Eleanor J., and Walk, R. D. (1960). The "visual cliff." *Scient. Amer.*, **202**, 64–71.

Gibson, J. J. (1929). The reproduction of visually perceived forms. *J. exp. Psychol.*, **12**, 1–39.

Gibson, J. J. (1950). *The perception of the visual world*. Boston: Houghton Mifflin.

Gibson, K. S., and Tyndall, E. P. T. (1923). Visibility of radiant energy. *Sci. Papers Bur. Standards*, **19**, no. 475.

Gifford, W. S. (1928). Does business want scholars? *Harper's Magazine*, **156**, 669–674.

Goldfarb, W. (1947). Variations in adolescent adjustment of institutionally reared children. *Amer. J. Orthopsychiat.*, **17**, 449–457.

Goldhammer, H., and Marshall, A. W. (1953). *Psychosis and civilization*. Glencoe, Ill.: Free Press.

Goodenough, F. (1949). *Mental testing: its history, principles, and applications*. New York: Holt, Rinehart and Winston.

Granit, R. (1959). Neural activity in the retina. In *Handbook of physiology*, vol. I. Washington, D.C.: American Physiological Society.

Griffin, D. R., and Galambos, R. (1941). The sensory basis of obstacle avoidance by flying bats. *J. exp. Zool.*, **86**, 481–506.

Guilford, J. P. (1954). *Psychometric methods* (rev. ed.). New York: McGraw-Hill.

Guilford, J. P. (1956). *Fundamental statistics in psychology and education* (3d ed.). New York: McGraw-Hill.

Guilford, J. P. (1959). *Personality*. New York: McGraw-Hill.

Hall, C. S. (1938). The inheritance of emotionality. *Sigma Xi Quart.*, **26**, 17–27.

Hall, C. S. (1951). What people dream about. *Scient. Amer.*, **184**, 60–63.

Hall, J. F. (1956). The relationship between external stimulation, food deprivation, and activity. *J. comp. physiol. Psychol.*, **49**, 339–341.

Halverson, H. M. (1931). An experimental study of prehension in infants by means of systematic cinema records. *Genet. Psychol. Monogr.*, **10**, 107–286.

Hanes, R. M. (1949). The construction of subjective brightness scales from fractionation data: a validation. *J. exp. Psychol.*, **39**, 719–728.

Hardy, J. D., Goodell, H., and Wolff, H. G. (1951). The influence of skin temperature upon the pain threshold as evoked by thermal radiation. *Science*, **114**, 149–150.

Harlow, H. F. (1951). Thinking. In H. Helson, *Theoretical foundations of psychology*. New York: Van Nostrand. P. 469.

Harlow, H. F. (1958). The nature of love. *Amer. Psychol.*, **13**, 673–685.

Harlow, H. F., and Johnson, T. (1943). Problem solution by monkeys following bilateral removal of the prefrontal areas. III. Test of initiation of behavior. *J. exp. Psychol.*, **32**, 495–500.

Harlow, H. F., and McClearn, G. E. (1954). Object discrimination learned by monkeys on the basis of manipulation motives. *J. comp. Physiol.*, **47**, 73–76.

Harrell, R. F. (1947). Further effects of added thiamine on learning and other processes. *Teach. Coll. Contr. Educ.,* no. 928.

Harrell, T. W., and Harrell, M. S. (1945). Army General Classification Test scores for civilian occupations. *Educ. psychol. Measmt,* **5,** 229–239.

Hartshorne, H., and May, M. A. (1928). *Studies in deceit.* New York: Macmillan.

Hassmann, M. (1952). Vom Erlernen unbenannter Anzahlen bei Eichhörnchen. *Z. Tierpsychol.,* **9,** 294–321.

Hathaway, S. R., and McKinley, J. C. (1943). *The Minnesota Multiphasic Personality Inventory* (rev. ed.). Minneapolis: Univer. of Minnesota Press.

Hayes, K. J., and Hayes, C. (1951). The intellectual development of a home-raised chimpanzee. *Proc. Amer. phil. Soc.,* **95,** 105–109.

Haythorn, W. (1958). The effects of varying combinations of authoritarian and equalitarian leaders and followers. In E. E. Maccoby, T. M. Newcomb, and E. L. Hartley (eds.), *Readings in social psychol* (3d ed.). New York: Holt, Rinehart and Winston.

Hebb, D. O. (1946). On the nature of fear. *Psychol. Rev.,* **53,** 259–276.

Hecht, S., and Williams, R. E. (1922). The visibility of monochromatic radiation and the absorption spectrum of visual purple. *J. gen. Physiol.,* **5,** 1–33.

Heidbreder, E. (1947). The attainment of concepts. III. The process. *J. Psychol.,* **24,** 93–138.

Heidbreder, E. (1948). The attainment of concepts. VI. Exploratory experiments on conceptualization at perceptual levels. *J. Psychol.,* **26,** 193–216.

Helmholtz, H. L. F. von. (1924). *Physiological optics* (trans. J. P. C. Southall), vol. II. Rochester, N.Y.: Optical Society of America.

Hess, E. H. (1959). Imprinting. *Science,* **130,** 133–141.

Hilgard, E. R. (1957). *Introduction to psychology* (rev. ed.). New York: Harcourt, Brace.

Hilgard, E. R., and Payner, S. L. (1944). Those not at home; riddle for pollsters. *Publ. Opin. Quart.,* **8,** 254–261.

Hilgard, Josephine R. (1953). Anniversary reactions in parents precipitated by children. *Psychiatry,* **16,** 73–80.

Hill, W. F. (1956). Activity as an autonomous drive. *J. comp. physiol. Psychol.,* **49,** 15–19.

Hirschberg, G., and Gilliland, A. R. (1942). Parent-child relationships in attitudes. *J. abnorm. soc. Psychol.,* **37,** 125–130.

Hollingshead, A. B. (1949). *Elmtown's youth.* New York: Wiley.

Hollingshead, A. B., and Redlich, F. C. (1958). *Social class and mental illness.* New York: Wiley.

Hollingworth, H. L. (1929). *Vocational psychology and character analysis.* New York: Appleton-Century-Crofts.

Hollister, L. E., Traub, L., and Beckman, W. G. (1956). Psychiatric use of reserpine and chlorpromazine: results of double-blind studies. In N. S. Kline (ed.), *Psychopharmacology.* Washington, D.C.: American Association for the Advancement of Science.

Honzik, C. H. (1936). The sensory basis of maze learning in rats. *Comp. Psychol. Monogr.,* **13,** No. 64.

Hooper, C. E. (1946). The coincidental method of measuring radio audience size. In A. B. Blankenship (ed.), *How to conduct consumer and opinion research.* New York: Harper.

Horney, K. (1937). *The neurotic personality of our time.* New York: Norton.

Horowitz, E. L. (1936). The development of attitudes toward the Negro. *Arch. Psychol., N.Y.,* **28,** No. 194.

Horowitz, E. L., and Horowitz, R. E. (1938). Development of social attitudes in children. *Sociometry,* **1,** 301–338.

Hovland, C. I. (1937). The generalization of conditioned responses. I. The sensory generalization of conditioned responses with varying frequencies of tone. *J. gen. Psychol.,* **17,** 125–248.

Howes, D. H., and Solomon, R. L. (1951). Visual duration threshold as a function of word-probability. *J. exp. Psychol.,* **41,** 401–410.

Hull, C. L. (1920). Quantitative aspects of the evolution of concepts. *Psychol. Monogr.,* no. 123.

Hull, C. L. (1943). *The principles of behavior.* New York: Appleton-Century-Crofts.

Humphrey, G. (1951). *Thinking: an introduction to its experimental psychology.*

New York: Wiley. Chaps. 2, 3, and 4.

Hunter, W. S. (1913). The delayed reaction in animals and children. *Behav. Monogr.*, vol. 2.

Hunter, W. S., and Nagge, J. W. (1931). The white rat and the double alternation temporal maze. *J. genet. Psychol.*, **39**, 303–319.

Hurvich, L. M., and Jameson, D. (1957). An opponent-process theory of color vision. *Psychol. Rev.*, **64**, 384–404.

Hurwitz, J., Zander, A., and Hymovitch, G. (1953). Some effects of power on the relations among group members. In D. Cartwright and A. Zander (eds.), *Group dynamics*. Evanston, Ill.: Row, Peterson.

Hyman, H. (1959). *Political socialization: a study in the psychology of political behavior*. Glencoe, Ill.: Free Press.

Inbau, F. E. (1942). *Lie detection and criminal investigation*. Baltimore: Williams & Wilkins.

Ingalls, T. H. (1952a). Biologic implications of mongolism. In Milbank Memorial Fund, *The biology of mental health and disease*. New York: Hoeber-Harper.

Ingalls, T. H. (1952b). Mongolism. *Scient. Amer.*, **186**, 60–66.

Jackson, T. A. (1942). Use of the stick as a tool by young chimpanzees. *J. comp. Psychol.*, **34**, 223–235.

Jacobsen, C. F. (1935). Functions of the frontal association areas in primates. *Arch. Neurol. Psychiat., Chicago*, **33**, 558–569.

Jacobson, L. E. (1932). The electrophysiology of mental activities. *Amer. J. Psychol.*, **44**, 677–694.

James, W. (1890). *Principles of psychology* (2 vols.). New York: Holt, Rinehart and Winston.

Janis, I., and Feshbach, S. (1953). Effects of fear-arousing communications. *J. abnorm. soc. Psychol.*, **48**, 78–92.

Jasper, H. H. (1941). Electroencephalography. In W. Penfield and T. Erickson (eds.), *Epilepsy and cerebral localization*. Springfield, Ill.: Charles C Thomas.

Jenkins, J. G., and Dallenbach, K. M. (1924). Oblivescence during sleep and waking. *Amer. J. Psychol.*, **35**, 605–612.

Jenkins, W. O. (1947a). The tactual discrimination of shapes for coding aircraft-type controls. In P. M. Fitts (ed.), *Psy-*

chological research on equipment design. Washington: U.S. Government Printing Office. Pp. 199–205.

Jenkins, W. O. (1947b). Review of leadership studies with particular reference to military problems. *Psychol. Bull.*, **44**, 54–79.

Jenkins, W. O., and Stanley, J. C. (1950). Partial reinforcement: a review and critique. *Psychol. Bull.*, **47**, 193–234.

Jersild, A. T., Markey, F. V., and Jersild, C. L. (1933). Children's fears, dreams, wishes, daydreams, dislikes, pleasant and unpleasant memories. *Child Develpm. Monogr.*, no. 12.

Jersild, A. T., and Ritzman, R. (1938). Aspects of language development: the growth of loquacity and vocabulary. *Child Develpm.*, **9**, 243–259.

Jervis, G. A. (1939). A contribution to the study of the influence of heredity on mental deficiency. The genetics of phenylpyruvic oligophrenia. *Proc. Amer. Ass. Stud. ment. Def.*, **44**, 13–24.

Jessner, L., and Ryan, V. (1941). *Shock treatment on psychiatry*. New York: Grune & Stratton.

Johnson, D. M. (1948). *Essentials of psychology*. New York: McGraw-Hill.

Johnson, D. M. (1955). *The psychology of thought and judgment*. New York: Harper.

Johnson, W. (1944). Studies in language behavior. I. A program of research. *Psychol. Monogr.*, **56**, 1–15.

Johnson, W. B., and Terman, L. M. (1940). Some highlights in the literature of psychological sex differences. *J. Psychol.*, **9**, 327–336.

Jones, H. E., and Conrad, H. S. (1933). The growth and decline of intelligence. *Genet. Psychol. Monogr.*, **13**, 223–298.

Jones, H. E., and Jones, M. C. (1928). A study of fear. *Childh. Educ.*, **5**, 136–143.

Jost, H., and Sontag, L. W. (1944). The genetic factor in autonomic nervous system function. *Psychosom. Med.*, **6**, 308–310.

Kagan, J., and Berkun, M. (1954). The reward value of running activity. *J. comp. Physiol.*, **47**, 108.

Kallman, F. J. (1951). Twin studies in relation to adjustive problems of man. *Trans. N.Y. Acad. Sci.*, **13**, 270–275.

Katz, D., Maccoby, N., and Morse, N. C. (1950). *Productivity, supervision, and morale in an office situation*. Ann Arbor, Mich.: Survey Research Center. Part I.

Katz, S. E., and Landis, C. (1935). Psychologic and physiologic phenomena during a prolonged vigil. *Arch. Neurol. Psychiat., Chicago,* **34,** 307–316.

Keller, F. S. (1937). *The definition of psychology.* New York: Appleton-Century-Crofts.

Kellogg, W. N., and Kellogg, L. A. (1933). *The ape and the child.* New York: McGraw-Hill.

Kennedy, J. L. (1939) A methodological review of extrasensory perception. *Psychol. Bull.,* **36,** 59–103.

Keys, A. B., Brozek, J., Heuschel, A., Mickelson, O., and Taylor, H. L. (1950). *The biology of human starvation.* Minneapolis: Univer. of Minnesota Press.

Kimble, G. A. (1956). *Principles of general psychology.* New York: Ronald.

Kimble, G. A., and Bilodeau, E. A. (1949). Work and rest as variables in cyclical motor learning. *J. exp. Psychol.,* **39,** 150–157.

King, F. A. (1958). Effects of septal and amygdaloid lesions on emotional behavior and conditioned avoidance responses in the rat. *J. nerv. ment. Dis.,* **126,** 57–63.

Kingsley, H. R., and Garry, R. (1957). *The nature and conditions of learning* (2d ed.). Englewood Cliffs, N.J.: Prentice-Hall.

Kinsey, A. C., Pomeroy, W. B., and Martin, C. E. (1948). *Sexual behavior in the human male.* Philadelphia: Saunders.

Kish, G. B. (1954). Learning when the onset of illumination is used as a reinforcing stimulus. *J. comp. physiol. Psychol.,* **48,** 261–264.

Kitt, A., and Gleicher, D. B. (1950). Determinants of voting behavior: a progress report on the Elmira election study. *Publ. Opin. Quart.,* **14,** 393–412.

Klapman, J. W. (1946). *Group psychotherapy.* New York: Grune & Stratton.

Kleitman, N. (1939). *Sleep and wakefulness.* Chicago: Univer. of Chicago Press.

Kline, L. W., and Johannsen, D. E. (1935). Comparative role of the face and of the face-body-hands as aids in identifying emotions. *J. abnorm. soc. Psychol.,* **29,** 415–426.

Klineberg, O. (1935). *Negro intelligence and selective migration.* New York: Columbia Univer. Press.

Klineberg, O. (1954). *Social psychology* (rev. ed.). New York: Holt, Rinehart and Winston.

Kluever, H. (1942). Visual mechanisms. In *Biological Symposia,* vol. VII. New York: Ronald.

Koehler, O. (1943). Zahl-versuche an einem Kolkraben und Vergleichsversuche an Menschen. *Z. Tierpsychol.,* **5,** 575–712.

Köhler, W. (1925). *The mentality of apes.* New York: Harcourt, Brace.

Köhler, W. (1947). *Gestalt psychology* (rev. ed.). New York: Liveright.

Krech, D., and Crutchfield, R. S. (1948). *Theory and problems of social psychology.* New York: McGraw-Hill.

Krech, D., and Crutchfield, R. S. (1958). *Elements of psychology.* New York: Knopf.

Krechevsky, I. (1932). "Hypotheses" versus "chance" in the pre-solution period in sensory discrimination-learning. *Univer. Calif. Publ. Psychol.,* **6,** no. 3.

Krechevsky, I. (1933). Hereditary nature of "hypotheses." *J. comp. Psychol.,* **16,** 99–116.

Lambert, W. W., Solomon, R. L., and Watson, P. D. (1949). Reinforcement and extinction as factors in size estimation. *J. exper. Psychol.,* **39,** 637–641.

Lancaster, Evelyn, with Poling, J. (1958). *The final face of Eve.* New York: McGraw-Hill.

Landis, C., and Hunt, W. A. (1939). *The startle pattern.* New York: Holt, Rinehart and Winston.

Lashley, K. S. (1929). *Brain mechanisms and intelligence.* Chicago: Univer. of Chicago Press.

Lashley, K. S. (1935). The mechanism of vision. XII. Nervous structures concerned in the acquisition and retention of habits based on reactions to light. *Comp. Psychol. Monogr.,* **11,** 43–79.

Lashley, K. S. (1937). Functional determinants of cerebral localization. *Arch. Neurol. Psychiat.,* **38,** 371–387.

Lashley, K. S. (1950). In search of the engram. *Symp. Soc. exp. Biol.,* vol. IV.

London: Cambridge Univer. Press. Pp. 454–482.

Lawrence, D. H. (1949). Acquired distinctiveness of cues. I. Transfer between discriminations on the basis of familiarity with the stimulus. *J. exp. Psychol.,* **39,** 770–784.

Lazarsfeld, P. F., Berelson, B. R., and Gaudet, H. (1944). *The people's choice.* New York: Duell, Sloan & Pearce.

Lazarus, R. S., and McCleary, R. A. (1951). Autonomic discrimination without awareness: a study of subception. *Psychol. Rev.,* **58,** 113–122.

Lecron, L. M., and Bordeaux, J. (1947). *Hypnotism today.* New York: Grune & Stratton.

Leonard, W. E. (1927). *The locomotive god.* New York: Appleton-Century-Crofts.

Levine, J. M., and Murphy, G. (1943). The learning and forgetting of controversial material. *J. abnorm. soc. Psychol.,* **38,** 507–517.

Lewin, K. (1935). *A dynamic theory of personality.* New York: McGraw-Hill.

Lewin, K., Lippitt, R., and White, R. K. (1939). Patterns of aggressive behavior in experimentally created social climates. *J. soc. Psychol.,* **10,** 271–299.

Lewis, M. M. (1936). *Infant speech: a study of the beginnings of language.* New York: Harcourt, Brace.

Licklider, J. C. R. (1944). The effects of amplitude distortion upon the intelligibility of speech. Harvard Univer., Psychoacoustic Laboratory, *OSRD Report No. 4217.* Washington, D.C.: Department of Commerce, Office of Technical Services.

Licklider, J. C. R. (1946). Effects of amplitude distortion upon the intelligibility of speech. *J. acoust. Soc. Amer.,* **18,** 429–434.

Licklider, J. C. R., and Miller, G. A. (1951). The perception of speech. In S. S. Stevens (ed.), *Handbook of experimental psychology.* New York: Wiley.

Likert, R. (1932). A technique for the measurement of attitudes. *Arch. Psychol., N.Y.,* no. 140.

Likert, R. (1947). The sample interview survey. In W. Dennis (ed.), *Current trends in psychology.* Pittsburgh: Univer. of Pittsburgh Press.

Lilly, J. C. (1956). Mental effects of reduction of ordinary levels of physical stimuli on intact healthy persons. *Psychiat. Res. Rep.,* **5,** 1–9.

Lindahl, L. G. (1945). Movement analysis as an industrial training method. *J. appl. Psychol.,* **29,** 420–436.

Lindsley, D. B. (1958). The reticular system and perceptual discrimination. In H. Jasper et al. (eds.), *Reticular formation and the brain.* Boston: Little, Brown.

Lindsley, D. B., Bowden, J. W., and Magoun, H. W. (1950). Behaviorial and EEG changes following chronic brain lesions in the cat. *EEG Clin. Neurophysiol.,* **2,** 483–498.

Linton, R. (1945). *The cultural background of personality.* New York: Appleton-Century-Crofts.

Lorge, I. (1930). Influence of regularly interpolated time intervals upon subsequent learning. *Teach. Coll. Contr. Educ.,* no. 438.

Luchins, A. (1954). Mechanization in problem solving: the effect of Einstellung. *Psychol. Monogr.,* **54,** No. 6.

Luckiesh, M. (1944). *Light, vision and seeing.* New York: Van Nostrand.

Lumsdaine, A. A., and Glaser, R. (eds.) (1960). *Teaching machines and programmed learning.* Washington, D.C.: National Education Association.

Lund, F. H. (1939). *Emotions.* New York: Ronald.

Lynd, R. S., and Lynd, H. M. (1929). *Middletown.* New York: Harcourt, Brace.

MacFarlane, D. A. (1930). The role of kinesthesis in maze learning. *Calif. Univer. Publ. Psychol.,* **4,** 277–305.

Mackworth, N. H. (1948). The breakdown of vigilance during prolonged visual search. *Quart. J. exp. Psychol.,* **1,** 6–21.

Mackworth, N. H. (1950). *Researches on the measurement of human performance.* London: Medical Research Council Report no. 268.

Maier, N. R. F. (1930). Reasoning in humans. *J. comp. Psychol.,* **10,** 115–143.

Maier, N. R. F. (1949). *Frustration.* New York: McGraw-Hill.

Manzer, C. W. (1927). Experimental investigation of rest pauses. *Arch. Psychol. N.Y.,* no. 90.

Masling, J., Greer, L., and Gilmore, R. (1955). Status, authoritarianism and sociometric choice. *J. soc. Psychol.,* **41,** 297–310.

Maslow, A. H. (1954). *Motivation and personality.* New York: Harper.

Masserman, J. H. (1943). *Behavior and neurosis.* Chicago: Univer. of Chicago Press.

Masserman, J. H. (1946). *Principles of dynamic psychiatry.* Philadelphia: Saunders.

Mausner, B. (1954). The effect of one partner's success in a relevant task on the interaction of observer pairs. *J. abnorm. soc. Psychol.,* **49,** 557–560.

Max, L. W. (1937). Experimental study of the motor theory of consciousness. IV. Action-current responses in the deaf during awakening, kinaesthetic imagery and abstract thinking. *J. comp. Psychol.,* **24,** 301–344.

McCarthy, Dorothea, A. (1930). *The language development of the preschool child.* Minneapolis: Univer. of Minnesota Press.

McCarthy, Dorothea A. (1946). Language development in children. In L. Carmichael (ed.), *Manual of child psychology.* New York: Wiley.

McClelland, D. C., Atkinson, J. W., Clark, R. A., and Lowell, E. L. (1953). *The achievement motive.* New York: Appleton-Century-Crofts.

McCrary, J. W., and Hunter, W. S. (1953). Serial position curves in verbal learning. *Science,* **117,** 131–134.

McGehee, W., and Owen, E. B. (1940). Authorized and unauthorized rest pauses in clerical work. *J. appl. Psychol.,* 24, 605–614.

McGeoch, J. A. (1936). The direction and extent of intra-serial association at recall. *Amer. J. Psychol.,* **48,** 221–245.

McGeoch, J. A., and Irion, A. L. (1952). *The psychology of human learning.* New York: Longmans.

McGranahan, D. V. (1946). A comparison of social. attitudes among American and German youth. *J. abnorm. soc. Psychol.,* **41,** 245–257.

McGraw, Myrtle B. (1935). *Growth: a study of Johnny and Jimmy.* New York: Appleton-Century-Crofts.

McGraw, Myrtle B. (1946). Maturation of behavior. In L. Carmichael (ed.), *Manual of child psychology.* New York: Wiley.

McGregor, D. (1960). *The human side of enterprise.* New York: McGraw-Hill.

McNemar, Q. (1942). *The revision of the Stanford-Binet scale.* Boston: Houghton Mifflin.

Mead, M. (1935). *Sex and temperament.* New York: Morrow.

Mettler, F. A. (ed.) (1949). *Selective partial ablation of the frontal cortex.* New York: Hoeber-Harper.

Miller, G. A. (1951). *Language and communication.* New York: McGraw-Hill.

Miller, G. A., Bruner, J., and Postman, L. (1951). In G. A. Miller, *Language and communication.* New York: McGraw-Hill.

Miller, G. A., and Selfridge, J. A. (1950). Verbal context and the recall of meaningful material. *Amer. J. Psychol.,* **63,** 176–185.

Miller, J. G. (1939). Discrimination without awareness. *Amer. J. Psychol.,* **52,** 562–578.

Miller, N. E. (1948a) Studies of fear as an acquirable drive. I. Fear as motivation and fear-reduction as reinforcement in the learning of new responses. *J. exp. Psychol.,* **38,** 89–101.

Miller, N. E. (1948b). Theory and experiment relating psychoanalytic displacement to stimulus-response generalization. *J. abnorm. soc. Psychol.,* **43,** 155–178.

Miller, N. E. (1958). Central stimulation and other new approaches to motivation and reward. *Amer. Psychol.,* **13,** 100–108.

Miller, N. E., and Bugelski, R. (1948). Minor studies of aggression. II. The influence of frustration imposed by the in-group on attitudes expressed toward out-groups. *J. Psychol.,* **25,** 437–452.

Millikan, G. A. (1948). Anoxia and oxygen equipment. In E. C. Andrus (ed.), *Advances in military medicine,* vol. I. Boston: Little, Brown. Chap. 24.

Moon, P., and Spencer, D. E. (1944). Visual data applied to lighting design. *J. opt. Soc. Amer.,* **34,** 605–617.

Moreno, J. L. (1946). *Psychodrama.* New York: Beacon House.

Morgan, C. D., and Murray, H. A. (1935). A method for investigating fantasies: the thematic apperception test. *Arch. Neurol. Psychiat.,* **34,** 289–306.

Morgan, C. T. (1939). Studies in vision. I. A technique for the study of visual discrimination in the rat. *J. comp. Psychol.,* **28,** 73–79.

Morgan, J. J. B., and Morton, J. T. (1944). The distortion of syllogistic reasoning produced by personal convictions. *J. soc. Psychol.,* **20,** 39–59.

Morphett, M. V., and Washburn, C. (1931). When should children begin to read? *Elem. Sch. J.,* **31,** 496–503.

Moruzzi, G., and Magoun, H. W. (1949). Brain stem reticular formation and activation of the EEG. *EEG Clin. Neurophysiol.,* **1,** 455–473.

Mosteller, F., et al. (1949). The pre-election polls of 1948. *Soc. Sci. res. Council Bull.,* no. 60.

Mowrer, O. H., and Jones, H. M. (1945). Habit strength as a function of the pattern of reinforcement. *J. exp. Psychol.,* **35,** 293–311.

Munn, N. L. (1950). *Handbook of psychological research on the rat.* Boston: Houghton Mifflin.

Munn, N. L. (1955). *The evolution and growth of human behavior.* Boston: Houghton Mifflin.

Murphy, G., Murphy, L. B., and Newcomb, T. M. (1937). *Experimental social psychology.* New York: Harper.

Murray, H. A. (1938). *Explorations in personality.* New York: Oxford Univer. Press.

Murray, H. A. (1943). *Thematic apperception test.* Cambridge, Mass.: Harvard Univer. Press.

Mussen, P. (1950). Some personality and social factors related to changes in children's attitudes toward Negroes. *J. abnorm. soc. Psychol.,* **45,** 423–441.

Nauta, W. J. H. (1946). Hypothalamic regulation of sleep in rats: an experimental study. *J. Neurophysiol.,* **9,** 285–316.

Newcomb, T. M. (1943). *Personality and social change.* New York: Dryden.

Newcomb, T. M. (1950). *Social psychology.* New York: Dryden.

Newcomb, T. M., and Svehla, G. (1938). Intra-family relationships in attitudes. *Sociometry,* **1,** 180–205.

Newman, E. B. (1939). Forgetting of meaningful material during sleep and waking. *Amer. J. Psychol.,* **52,** 65–71.

Newman, H. H., Freeman, F. N., and Holzinger, K. J. (1937). *Twins: a study of heredity and environment.* Chicago: Univer. Chicago Press.

Noble, C. E. (1952). The role of stimulus meaning (m) in serial verbal learning. *J. exp. Psychol.,* **43,** 437–446.

Noyes, A. P. (1948). *Modern clinical psychiatry* (3d ed.). Philadelphia: Saunders.

Oesterberg, G. (1935). Topography of the layer of rods and cones in the human retina. *Acta ophthal., Suppl.,* **61,** 1–102.

Office of Strategic Services, Assessment Staff. (1948). *Assessment of men: selection of personnel for the Office of Strategic Services.* New York: Holt, Rinehart and Winston.

Ogg, E. (1955). Psychologists in action. *Publ. Affairs Pamph.,* no. 229.

Olds, J. (1955). Physiological mechanisms of reward. In M. Jones (ed.), *Nebraska symposium on motivation,* vol. III. Lincoln, Neb.: Univer. of Nebraska Press. Pp. 73-139.

Olds, J. (1958). Self-stimulation of the brain. *Science,* **127,** 315–323.

O'Neill, P. H. (1949). The effect of subsequent maze-learning ability of graded amounts of vitamin B$_1$ in the diet of very young rats. *J. genet. Psychol.,* **74,** 85–95.

Orr, D. W. (1949). Psychiatric uses of sodium pentothal. *U.S. Nav. med. Bull.,* **49,** 508–516.

Osgood, C. E. (1952). The nature and measurement of meaning. *Psychol. Bull.,* **49,** 197–237.

Osgood, C. E. (1953). *Method and theory in experimental psychology.* New York: Oxford Univer. Press.

Osgood, C. E., Suci, G. J., and Tannenbaum, P. H. (1957). *The measurement of meaning.* Urbana, Ill.: Univer. of Illinois Press.

Pavlov, I. P. (1927). *Conditioned reflexes* (trans. by G. V. Anrep). London: Oxford Univer. Press.

Pavlov, I. P. (1928). *Lectures on conditioned reflexes.* New York: International Publishers.

Penfield, W., and Rasmussen, T. (1950). *The cerebral cortex of man.* New York: Macmillan.

Piéron, H. (1920). Researches comparatives sur la mémoire des formes et celle de chiffres. *Ann. Psychol.,* **21,** 119–148.

Pilgrim, F. J., and Patton, R. A. (1947). Patterns of self-selection of purified dietary components by the rat. *J. comp. physiol. Psychol.,* **40,** 343–348.

Poincaré, H. (1913). Mathematical creation. In *The foundations of science* (trans. by G. H. Halsted). New York: Science Press. Pp. 383–394.

Polyak, S. L. (1941). *The retina.* Chicago: Univer. of Chicago Press.

Postman, L., Bruner, J. S., and McGinnies, E. (1948). Personal values as selective factors in perception. *J. abnorm. soc. Psychol.,* **43,** 142–154.

Ramsay, A. O., and Hess, E. H. (1954). A laboratory approach to the study of imprinting. *Wilson Bull.,* **66,** 196–206.

Ranson, S. W. (1939). Somnolence caused by hypothalamic lesions in the monkey, *Arch. Neurol. Psychiat., Chicago,* **41,** 1–23.

Raven, B., and French, J. R. P. (1958). Group support, legitimate power, and social influence. *J. Pers.,* **26,** 400–409.

Reed, J. D. (1947). Spontaneous activity of animals. *Psychol. Bull.,* **44,** 393–412.

Reich, E. (1951). The game of "Gossip" analyzed by the theory of information. *Bull. mathemat. Biophys.,* **13,** 313–318.

Richardson, H. M. (1934). The adaptive behavior of infants in the utilization of the lever as a tool. *J. genet. Psychol.,* **44,** 352–377.

Richter, C. P. (1927). Animal behavior and internal drives. *Quart. Rev. Biol.,* **2,** 307–343.

Richter, C. P. (1936). Increased salt appetite in adrenalectomized rats. *Amer. J. Physiol.,* **115,** 155–161.

Richter, C. P. (1942–1943). Total self-regulatory functions in animals and human beings. *Harvey Lect.,* **38,** 63–103.

Riddle, O., Bates, R. W., and Lahr, E. L. (1935). Maternal behavior in rats induced by prolactin. *Proc. Soc. exp. Biol., N.Y.,* **32,** 730–734.

Riecken, H. (1958). The effect of talkativeness on ability to influence group solutions of problems. *Sociometry,* **21,** 309–321.

Riesen, A. H. (1950). Arrested vision. *Scient. Amer.,* **183,** 16–19.

Riggs, A. F. (1929). *Intelligent living.* New York: Doubleday.

Robinson, E. S., and Bills, A. G. (1926). Two factors in the work decrement. *J. exp. Psychol.,* **9,** 415–443.

Robinson, F. P. (1946). *Effective study* (rev. ed.). New York: Harper.

Roethlisberger, F. J., and Dickson, W. J. (1939). *Management and the worker.* Cambridge, Mass.: Harvard Univer. Press.

Rogers, C. R. (1951). *Client-centered therapy.* Boston: Houghton Mifflin.

Rogerson, C. H. (1931). *Play therapy in childhood.* New York: Oxford Univer. Press.

Rorschach, H. (1942). *Psycho-diagnostics.* Berne: Huber.

Rose, A. M. (1946). Army policies toward Negro soldiers. *Ann. Amer. Acad. pol. soc. Sci.,* **244,** 90–94.

Rosen, B. (1956). The achievement syndrome: a psychocultural dimension of social stratification. *Amer. soc. Rev.,* **21,** 203–211.

Ross, S., and Harriman, A. E. (1949). A preliminary study of the Crocker-Henderson odor-classification system. *Amer. J. Psychol.,* **62,** 399–404.

Ruben, L. S. (1957). The psychopharmacology of lysergic acid diethylamide (LSD 25). *Psychol. Bull.,* **54,** 479–489.

Ruch, T. C., Fulton, J. F., and German, W. J. (1938). Sensory discrimination in the monkey, chimpanzee, and man after lesions of the parietal lobe. *Arch. Neurol. Psychiat., Chicago,* **39,** 919–937.

Rudolf, G. de M. (1949). The treatment of mental defectives with thiamine. *J. ment. Sci.,* **95,** 910–915.

Sanford, F. H. (1951). Annual report of the executive secretary (Amer. Psychol. Assn.). *Amer. Psychol.,* **7,** 686–696.

Sargent, S. S. (1939). Emotional stereotypes in the *Chicago Tribune. Sociometry,* **2,** 69–75.

Schachter, S. (1951). Deviation, rejection and communication. *J. abnorm. soc. Psychol.,* **46,** 190–207.

Schjelderup-Ebbe, T. (1935). Social behavior of birds. In C. Murchison (ed.), *Handbook of social psychology.* Worcester, Mass.: Clark Univer. Press.

Schlosberg, H. (1954). Three dimensions of emotion. *Psychol. Rev.,* **61,** 81–88.

Scott, E. M., and Verney, Ethel L. (1949).

Self-selection of diet. IX. The appetite for thiamine. *J. Nutrition,* **37,** 81–92.

Scott, J. P. (1958). *Animal behavior.* Chicago: Univer. of Chicago Press.

Sears, R. R. (1936). Experimental studies of projection. I. Attribution of traits. *J. soc. Psychol.,* **7,** 151–163.

Sears, R. R., Hovland, C. I., and Miller, N. E. (1940). Minor studies in aggression. I. Measurement of aggressive behavior. *J. Psychol.,* **9,** 277–281.

Sells, S. B. (1936). The atmosphere effect: an experimental study of reasoning. *Arch. Psychol., N.Y.,* no. 200.

Selye, H. (1950). *The physiology and pathology of exposure to stress.* Montreal: Acta, Inc.

Seward, J. P. (1949). An experimental analysis of latent learning. *J. exp. Psychol.,* **39,** 177–186.

Shaffer, L. F. (1947). Fear and courage in aerial combat. *J. consult. Psychol.,* **11,** 137–143.

Shaffer, L. F., and Shoben, E. J., Jr. (1956). *The psychology of adjustment* (rev. ed.). Boston: Houghton Mifflin.

Sharp, Agnes A. (1938). An experimental test of Freud's doctrine of the relation of hedonic tone to memory revival. *J. exp. Psychol.,* **22,** 395–418.

Shaw., M. E., and Gilchrist, J. (1956). Intragroup communication and leader choice. *J. soc. Psychol.,* **43,** 133–138.

Shaw, M. E. (1955). A comparison of two types of leadership in various communication nets. *J. abnorm. soc. Psychol.,* **50,** 127–134.

Sheffield, F. D., and Roby, T. B. (1950). Reward value of a non-nutritive sweet taste. *J. comp. physiol. Psychol.,* **43,** 471–481.

Sheldon, W. H., and Stevens, S. S. (1942). *The varieties of temperament.* New York: Harper.

Sherif, M. (1958). Group influences upon the formation of norms and attitudes. In E. E. Maccoby, T. M. Newcomb, and E. L. Hartley (eds.), *Readings in social psychology* (3d ed.). New York: Holt, Rinehart and Winston.

Sherman, M. C., Sherman, I. C., and Flory, C. D. (1936). Infant behavior. *Comp. Psychol. Monogr.,* **12,** no. 4.

Shirley, M. M. (1933a). *The first two years, a study of twenty-five babies,* vol. I. *Postural and locomotor development.* Minneapolis: Univer. of Minnesota Press.

Shirley, M. M. (1933b). *The first two years, a study of twenty-five babies,* vol. II. *Intellectual development.* Minneapolis: Univer. of Minnesota Press.

Siegal, S. (1956). *Nonparametric statistics for the behavioral sciences.* New York: McGraw-Hill.

Sisson, E. D. (1948). Forced choice—the new Army rating. *Personnel Psychol.,* **1,** 365–381.

Skinner, B. F. (1938). *The behavior of organisms.* New York: Appleton-Century-Crofts.

Skinner, B. F. (1958). Teaching machines. *Science,* **128,** 969–977.

Skinner, B. F. (1959). *Cumulative record.* New York: Appleton-Century-Crofts.

Skinner, B. F. (1960). Pigeons in a pelican. *Amer. Psychol.,* **15,** 28–37.

Skodak, M., and Skeels, H. M. (1949). A final follow-up of one hundred adopted children. *J. genet. Psychol.,* **75,** 3–19.

Sleight, R. B. (1948). The effect of instrument dial shape on legibility. *J. appl. Psychol.,* **32,** 170–188.

Smith, H. C. (1957). *Psychology of industrial behavior.* New York: McGraw-Hill.

Smith, J. R. (1941). The frequency growth of the human alpha rhythms during normal infancy and childhood. *J. Psychol.,* **11,** 177–198.

Smith, M. E. (1935). A study of the speech of eight bilingual children of the same family. *Child Develpm.,* **6,** 19–25.

Snyder, F. W., and Pronko, N. H. (1952). *Vision with spatial vision.* Wichita, Kan.: Univer. of Wichita Press.

Social Science Research Council (1947). *Public reaction to the atomic bomb and world affairs.* Ithaca, N.Y.: Cornell Univer. Press.

Solomon, R. L., and Wynne, L. C. (1953). Traumatic avoidance learning: acquisition in normal dogs. *Psychol. Monogr.,* **67,** no. 4 (whole no. 354).

Solomon, R. L., and Wynne, L. C. (1954). Traumatic avoidance learning: anxiety conservation and partial irreversibility. *Psychol. Rev.,* **61,** 353–385.

Spence, K. W. (1951). Theoretical interpretations of learning. In C. P. Stone (ed.), *Comparative Psychology* (3d ed.). Englewood Cliffs, N.J.: Prentice-Hall.

Spriegel, W. R., and Wallace, R. F. (1948). Recent trends in personnel selection and induction. *Personnel,* 77–88.

Stagner, R. (1948). *Psychology of personality* (2d ed.). New York: McGraw-Hill.

Stead, W. H., et al. (1940). *Occupational counseling techniques.* New York: American Book.

Steggerda, F. R. (1941). Observations on the water intake in an adult man with dysfunctioning salivary glands. *Amer. J. Physiol.,* **132,** 517–521.

Steiner, I. (1954). Ethnocentrism and tolerance of trait inconsistency. *J. abnorm. soc. Psychol.,* **49,** 349–354.

Stevens, S. S. (1939). Psychology and the science of science. *Psychol. Bull.,* **36,** 221–263.

Stevens, S. S. (1951). *Handbook of experimental psychology.* New York: Wiley.

Stevens, S. S. (1957). On the psychophysical law. *Psychol. Rev.,* **64,** 153–181.

Stevens, S. S., and Volkmann, J. (1940). The relation of pitch to frequency: a revised scale. *Amer. J. Psychol.,* **53,** 329–353.

Stogdill, R. M. (1948). Personal factors associated with leadership: a survey of the literature. *J. Psychol.,* **25,** 35–71.

Stone, C. P. (1932). Wildness and savageness in rats of different strains. In K. S. Lashley (ed.), *Studies in the dynamics of behavior.* Chicago: Univer. of Chicago Press.

Stouffer, S. A. (1949). An analysis of conflicting social norms. *Amer. sociol. Rev.,* **14,** 707–717.

Strodtbeck, F., James, R., and Hawkins, C. (1958). Social status in jury deliberations. In E. E. Maccoby, T. M. Newcomb, and E. L. Hartley (eds.), *Readings in social psychology* (3d ed.). New York: Holt, Rinehart and Winston.

Strong, E. K., Jr. (1938). *Vocational interest blank for men (revised), Form M.* Stanford, Calif.: Stanford Univer. Press.

Stroud, J. B. (1940). Experiments on learning in school situations. *Psychol. Bull.,* **37,** 777–807.

Swift, E. J. (1918). *Psychology and the day's work.* New York: Scribner.

Teitelbaum, P., and Stellar, E. (1954). Recovery from the failure to eat produced by hypothalamic lesions. *Science,* **120,** 894–895.

Terman, L. M. (1943). In R. G. Barker, J. S. Kounin, and H. F. Wright (eds.), *Child behavior and development.* New York: McGraw-Hill. Chap. 17.

Terman, L. M. (1950). *Psychological factors in marital happiness.* New York: McGraw-Hill.

Terman, L. M., et al. (1925). *Genetic studies of genius,* vol. I. *Mental and physical traits of a thousand gifted children.* Stanford, Calif.: Stanford Univer. Press.

Terman, L. M., and Merrill, M. A. (1937). *Measuring intelligence.* Boston: Houghton Mifflin.

Terman, L. M., and Oden, M. H. (1959). *The gifted group at mid-life: thirty-five years' follow-up of the superior child.* Stanford, Calif.: Stanford Univer. Press.

Thibaut, J., and Strickland, L. (1956). Psychological set and social conformity. *J. Pers.,* **25,** 115–129.

Thigpen, C. H., and Cleckley, H. M. (1957). *The three faces of Eve.* New York: McGraw-Hill.

Thompson, W. R., and Melzack, R. (1956). Early environment. *Scient. Amer.,* **194,** 38–42.

Thompson, W. R., and Solomon, L. M. (1954). Spontaneous pattern discrimination in the rat. *J. comp. physiol. Psychol.,* **47,** 104–107.

Thorndike, E. L. (1932). *The fundamentals of learning.* New York: Teach. Coll.

Thurstone, L. L. (1938). Primary mental abilities. *Psychometr. Monogr.,* no. 1.

Thurstone, L. L., and Chave, E. J. (1929). *The measurement of attitudes.* Chicago: Univer. of Chicago Press.

Thurstone, L. L., and Thurstone, T. G. (1941). Factorial studies of intelligence. *Psychometr. Monogr.,* no. 2.

Tiegs, E. W., and Katz, B. (1941). *Mental hygiene in education.* New York: Ronald.

Tinbergen, N. (1951). *The study of instinct.* London: Oxford Univer. Press.

Tolman, E. C. (1939). Prediction of vicarious trial and error by means of the schematic sowbug. *Psychol. Rev.,* **46,** 318–336.

Tolman, E. C., and Honzik, C. H. (1930).

Introduction and removal of reward and maze performance in rats. *Univer. Calif. Publ. Psychol.,* **4,** 257–275.

Tomkins, W. (1931). *Universal Indian sign language.* San Diego, Calif.: William Tomkins.

Trow, D. (1957). Autonomy and job-satisfaction in task-oriented groups. *J. abnorm. soc. Psychol.,* **54,** 204–209.

Tsang, Y. C. (1938). Hunger motivation in gastrectomized rats. *J. comp. Psychol.,* **26,** 1–17.

Tyler, L. E. (1956). *The psychology of human differences* (2d ed.). New York: Appleton-Century-Crofts.

Underwood, B. J. (1957). Interference and forgetting. *Psychol. Rev.,* **64,** 49–60.

U.S. Employment Service. (1944). *Training and reference manual for job analysis.* Washington: Government Printing Office.

Verney, E. B. (1947). The antidiuretic hormone and the factors which determine its release. *Proc. roy. Soc.,* **135,** 24–106.

Von Frisch, K. (1950). *Bees: their vision, chemical senses, and language.* Ithaca, N.Y.: Cornell Univer. Press.

Wake, F. R. (1950). Changes of fear with age. Unpublished doctor's dissertation, McGill Univer., 1950. Cited in J. P. Zubek and P. A. Solberg (1954), *Human development.* New York: McGraw-Hill.

Wald, G. (1959). The photoreceptor process in vision. In *Handbook of physiology,* vol. I. Washington, D.C., American Physiological Society.

Wallas, G. (1926). *The art of thought.* New York: Harcourt, Brace.

Wangensteen, O. H., and Carlson, A. J. (1931). Hunger sensations in a patient after total gastrectomy. *Proc. Soc. exp. Biol., N.Y.,* **28,** 545–547.

Wapner, S., Werner, H., and Chandler, K. A. (1951). Experiments on sensory-tonic field theory of perception. I. Effect of extraneous stimulation on the visual perception of verticality. *J. exp. Psychol.,* **42,** 341–346.

Warden, C. J. (1931). *Animal motivation studies. The albino rat.* New York: Columbia Univer. Press.

Warden, C. J., Jenkins, T. N., and Warner, L. H. (1936). *Comparative psychology,* vol. III. New York: Ronald.

Warner, W. L., et al. (1949). *Democracy in Jonesville, a study in quality and inequality.* New York: Harper. P. 22.

Warner, W. L., and Lunt, P. S. (1941). The social life of a modern community. New Haven, Conn.: Yale Univer. Press.

Washburn, R. W. (1929). A study of smiling and laughing of infants in the first year of life. *Genet. Psychol. Monogr.,* **6,** 397–539.

Watson, J. B. (1925). *Behaviorism.* New York: Norton.

Watson, J. B., and Rayner, R. (1920). Conditioned emotional reactions. *J. exp. Psychol.,* **3,** 1–14.

Wechsler, D. (1949). *Wechsler intelligence scale for children.* New York: Psychological Corp.

Wechsler, D. (1955). *The Wechsler adult intelligence scale manual.* New York: Psychological Corp.

Wechsler, D. (1958). *The measurement and appraisal of adult intelligence* (4th ed.). Baltimore: Williams & Wilkins.

Weiss, W., and Fine, B. J. (1958). The effect of induced aggressiveness on opinion change. In E. E. Maccoby, T. M. Newcomb, and E. L. Hartley (eds.), *Readings in social psychology* (3d ed.). New York: Holt, Rinehart and Winston.

Welker, W. I. (1956). Some determinants of play and exploration in chimpanzees. *J. comp. Physiol.,* **49,** 84–89.

Wendt, G. R. (1951). Vestibular function. In S. S. Stevens (ed.), *Handbook of experimental psychology.* New York: Wiley. Chap. 31.

Werner, H., and Kaplan, E. (1950). Development of word meaning through verbal context: An experimental study. *J. Psychol.,* **29,** 251–257.

Wertheim, T. (1894). Ueber die indirekte Schschaerfe. *Z. Psychol.,* **7,** 172–187.

Wertheimer, M. (1959). *Productive thinking* (rev. ed.). New York: Harper.

Wever, E. G. (1949). *Theory of hearing.* New York: Wiley.

Whiting, J. W. M., Kluckhohn, R., and Anthony, A. (1958). The function of male initiation ceremonies at puberty. In E. E. Maccoby, T. M. Newcomb, and E. L. Hartley (eds.), *Readings in social psychology* (3d ed.). New York: Holt, Rinehart and Winston.

Wikler, A. (1957). *The relation of psychiatry to pharmacology*. Baltimore: Williams & Wilkins.

Wilkins, L., and Richter, C. P. (1940). A great craving for salt by a child with cortico-adrenal insufficiency. *J. Amer. med. Ass.*, **114**, 866–868.

Williams, A. C., Jr., Adelson, M., and Ritchie, M. (1956). A program of human engineering research on the design of aircraft instrument displays and controls. Wright Air Development Center, *WADC Tech. Rep.* 56–526.

Windle, W. F. (ed.) (1958). *Neurological and psychological deficits of asphyxia neonatorum*. Springfield, Ill.: Charles C Thomas.

Witkin, H. A. (1959). The perception of the upright. *Scient. Amer.*, **200**, 50–56.

Wolfe, J. B. (1936). Effectiveness of token rewards for chimpanzees. *Comp. Psychol. Monogr.*, **12**, no. 60.

Wolff, H. G., and Wolf, S. (1948). *Pain*. Springfield, Ill.: Charles C Thomas.

Wolfle, D. (1948). Annual report of the executive secretary (Amer. Psychol. Assn.). *Amer. Psychol.*, **3**, 503–510.

Woodson, W. E. (1954). *Human engineering guide for equipment designers*. Berkeley, Calif.: Univer. of California Press.

Woodworth, R. S., and Schlosberg, H. (1954). *Experimental psychology* (rev. ed.). New York: Holt, Rinehart and Winston.

Yerkes, R. M. (1943). *Chimpanzees*. New Haven, Conn.: Yale Univer. Press.

Young, F. M. (1941). An analysis of certain variables in a developmental study of language. *Genet. Psychol. Monogr.*, **23**, 3–141.

Young, P. T. (1944). Studies of food preference, appetite, and dietary habit. I. Running activity and dietary habit of the rat in relation to food preference. *J. comp. Psychol.*, **37**, 327–370.

Zeller, A. F. (1950). An experimental analogue of repression. II. The effect of individual failure and success on memory measured by relearning. *J. exp. Psychol.*, **40**, 411–422.

Zubek, J. P., and Solberg, P. A. (1954). *Human development*. New York: McGraw-Hill.

Glossary

THIS GLOSSARY defines all important terms and phrases used in the book. It includes both technical terms and common words used in a special or restricted sense in psychology. In each case, the meaning given is that used in the book. For other meanings, more complete definitions, and terms not used in the book, see H. B. English and A. C. English. *A comprehensive dictionary of psychological and psychoanalytical terms.* New York: Longmans, Green, 1958.

A

Ability. A general term referring to any knowledge, skill, or capacity that can be demonstrated by measurements.

Ability test. A test used to predict future achievement or achievement in another situation.

Absolute judgment. A method of making sensory measurements in which the observer estimates the magnitude, or some other characteristic, of a single stimulus.

Absolute threshold. The smallest amount of a stimulus that can be perceived. *See also* Differential threshold.

Abstraction. A learning process in which an individual learns to disregard some properties of objects and to respond only to certain properties that the objects have in common. It is the process through which concepts (*q.v.*) are formed.

Accommodation. A change in the shape of the lens of the eye that focuses the image of an object on the retina. It compensates for the distance of the object from the observer.

Achievement. Accomplishment on a test of knowledge or skill; also a personal motive.

Achievement test. Any test used to measure present knowledge or skills.

Achromatism. Total color blindness (*q.v.*); extremely rare.

Acquired fear. A learned fear.

Acquired need. A learned motive or drive. *Cf.* Physiological needs.

Activator. A drug used to increase the activity level of a person otherwise depressed or withdrawn.

Activity. A general term covering restlessness, exploration, and miscellaneous responses to environmental stimuli; considered to be a general drive (*q.v.*).

Adaptation. A change in the sensitivity of a

sense organ due to stimulation or lack of stimulation. In general, all senses become less sensitive as they are stimulated and more sensitive in the absence of stimulation. *See also* Dark adaptation.

Adjustment. The relationship that exists between an individual and his environment, especially his social environment, in the satisfaction of his motives. *See also* Method of adjustment.

Adrenal glands. A pair of endocrine glands located on the top of the kidneys. They secrete the hormones of adrenalin and cortin.

Adrenalin. A hormone secreted by the adrenal glands. It mimics the action of the sympathetic system, and it is secreted in strong emotion.

Affectional drive. A general drive (*q.v.*) to have contact with and be close to another organism.

Affective reactions. Psychotic reactions marked by extremes of mood, e.g., depression or manic elation. *See also* Manic-depressive psychosis.

Affiliative needs. Needs to associate with or belong with other people.

Aggression. A general term applying to feelings of anger or hostility. Aggression functions as a motive which is often frustration.

Agnosia. Inability to recognize objects and their meaning, usually owing to damage to the brain. *See also* Aphasia, Apraxia.

Alarm reaction. The first stage of the general-adaptation syndrome (*q.v.*), in which a person reacts vigorously to a stressful situation.

Albedo. The percentage of light falling on a surface that is reflected by the surface. In brightness constancy, the relative albedos of object and background, rather than albedo of the object, is perceived.

Alcoholic psychosis. A psychosis developing as a result of prolonged alcoholism. It is characterized by defects of memory, disorientation, delusions, and other symptoms similar to those seen in senile psychosis (*q.v.*).

All-or-none law. The principle that a nerve impulse is either evoked at full strength or not evoked at all.

Alternation. An experimental method in which the subject is required to alternate responses in a pattern such as left-right-left-right or left-left-right-right. The method has been used in the study of thinking in animals and children. *See also* Delayed alternation, Delayed reaction.

Amnesia. Generally any loss of memory; specifically, a neurotic reaction in which a person forgets his own identity and is unable to recognize familiar people and situations. *See also* Dissociative reaction.

Amoeba. One kind of single-celled animal.

Amphibia. A class of vertebrates that includes, frogs, toads, and salamanders.

Amplitude. The intensity at any given instant of an acoustic or electric wave.

Amplitude distortion. Any distortion of the pattern of intensities making up a series of sounds. *See also* Center clipping, Peak clipping.

Amygdala. A structure of the forebrain connected with the hypothalamus and concerned in emotion.

Anal stage. The stage, according to psychoanalytic theory, during which the child's interest centers on anal activities.

Animistic reasoning. Reasoning based on coincidences of nature. For example, if there is a thunderstorm on the day a boy plays hooky from school, then according to animistic reasoning, the boy's truancy caused the thunderstorm.

Anomalous color defect. Color weakness in which a person is able to discriminate colors when they are vivid but is color-blind when they are poorly saturated. There are the same varieties of anomalous color defect as there are of color blindness (*q.v.*).

Anoxia. Lack of sufficient oxygen to maintain normal metabolism.

Anxiety. A vague fear, acquired through learning and through stimulus generalization, often a consequence of frustration.

Anxiety reactions. One of the major classes of neurosis, characterized by anxiety.

Aperiodic sound. A complex sound consisting of waves of various heights and widths appearing in a random order. *See also* Random noise; *cf.* Periodic sound.

Apes. A group of animals resembling man and including monkeys, gorillas, chimpanzees, and baboons.

Aphasia. A language defect ordinarily due to damage or disease of the brain. It may be a sensory disorder consisting of some impairment in reading or understanding of speech, or it may be a motor disorder consisting of an impairment in the writing or speaking of language. *See also* Agnosia, Apraxia.

Apparent movement. Movement that is perceived because the observer sees an object in successively different positions rather than because the object is seen to move. For example, motion pictures are really rapidly presented stationary pictures but are perceived as moving.

Approach-approach conflict. Conflict in which a person is motivated to approach two different goals that are incompatible.

Approach-avoidance conflict. Conflict in which a person is both attracted and repelled by the same goal.

Apraxia. A memory disorder, due to brain injury, characterized by inability to remember the performance of skilled movements such as driving a car, dressing oneself, or playing baseball. *See also* Agnosia, Aphasia.

Aptitude. Ability to profit by training. *See also* Scholastic aptitude, Vocational aptitude.

Area and block sampling. A sampling procedure, used in surveys and public-opinion polls, in which the interviewer is sent to specific addresses previously selected from a detailed map. *See also* Sampling, Survey methods.

Arithmetic mean. One measure of central tendency, commonly called the average, computed by summing all the scores in a frequency distribution, then dividing by the number of scores. *Cf.* Median.

Association. A general term referring to any connection formed through learning.

Association area. A general term for an area of the cerebral cortex concerned in learning and memory.

Association neuron. A neuron, usually within the central nervous system, which occupies a position between sensory and motor neurons.

Associative process. A process within the organism that is some part or fraction of an original, either unlearned or previously learned, process.

Astigmatism. Irregularities in the shape of the cornea or other structures of the eye

transmitting light to the retina, which cause parts of an image projected on the retina to be out of focus.

Attention. Focusing on certain aspects of current experience and neglecting others. Attention has a focus in which events are clearly perceived and a margin in which they are less clearly perceived.

Attitude. A tendency to respond either positively or negatively to certain persons, objects, or situations. *See also* Set.

Attitude scale. A method of measuring attitudes which typically consists of a set of items, each having a preestablished scale value, to be checked with favor or disfavor by the testee.

Attribute. The perceived quality or aspect of a stimulus; a psychological dimension of sensory experience.

Audience measurement. Measurement of the characteristics of the people who read a periodical or listen to radio and television programs, designed to assist advertisers in determining what and how to advertise in a particular medium.

Audiogram. A graph representing the absolute threshold of hearing at different frequencies.

Audiometer. A device for measuring the audiogram, used to detect deafness.

Auditory canal. The canal leading from the outside of the head to the eardrum; also called the external auditory meatus.

Auditory nerve. The nerve leading from the cochlea and conducting auditory impulses to the brain. The term is often used loosely to refer to the eighth cranial nerve, which contains nerve fibers for the vestibular sense as well as for hearing.

Authoritarian personality. The traits that characterize an individual who seeks security in authority and wants a social hierarchy in which everybody has and knows his place. *See also* Ethnocentric personality.

Autonomic changes. Changes in heart rate, blood pressure, breathing, etc., controlled by impulses in the autonomic system.

Autonomic system. A division of the nervous system serving the endocrine glands and the smooth muscles. It controls internal changes in the body during emotion as well as other functions that are essential to homeostasis.

Avoidance-avoidance conflict. Conflict in which a person is caught between two negative goals. As he tries to avoid one goal, he is brought closer to the other, and vice versa.

Avoidance learning. Learning to avoid a noxious stimulus, e.g., shock, by responding appropriately to a warning signal.

Axon. A nerve fiber transmitting impulses from the cell body to an adjacent neuron or to an effector.

B

b **wave.** A wave obtained in the electroretinogram and used as a measure of retinal sensitivity to light.

Basic anxiety. A concept in Karen Horney's theory of personality; anxiety learned as a reaction to a variety of tension-laden situations giving rise to neurotic needs.

Basic motives. A set of motives that can be used generally to describe and compare the motives of different people.

Basilar membrane. The membrane in the cochlea on which the organ of Corti is located. Its motion is important in hearing.

Basket nerve ending. A specialized structure at the root of hairs on the body. It is regarded as a sense organ for pressure or touch.

Beginning spurt. The tendency for the work curve to be elevated briefly at the beginning of a period of work. *Cf.* Warming up.

Behavior disorder. *See* Mental disorder.

Behavioral sciences. The sciences most concerned with human and animal behavior. The principal behavioral sciences are psychology, sociology, and social anthropology, but they also include certain aspects of history, economics, political science, physiology, zoology, and physics.

Behaviorism. A viewpoint held early in the twentieth century by some experimental psychologists who were opposed to the method of introspection and proposed that psychology be limited to the study of observable behavior.

Belief. The acceptance of a statement or proposition. It does not necessarily involve an attitude (*q.v.*), although it may.

Binaural. Pertaining to the simultaneous use of the two ears.

Binocular. Pertaining to the simultaneous use of the two eyes.

Bipolar cell. A neuron (*q.v.*) with a single axon and a single dendrite; in the eye, a cell connecting the rods and cones (*q.v.*) of the first retinal layer with the ganglion cells (*q.v.*) of the third layer.

Bisection. A method of constructing a sensory scale (*q.v.*) in which the observer sets a stimulus so that it is perceived to be half-way between two other stimuli.

Blind spot. The point on the retina where fibers leave the eyeball to form the optic nerve. There are no photosensitive receptors at this point. However, the blind spots of the two retinas are not on corresponding points; hence a person can see with one eye what he cannot see with the other.

Brain. The part of the nervous system encased in the skull. It is the site of centers for sensory experience, motivation, learning, and thinking.

Brain waves. Electrical fluctuations of the brain normally recorded from the skull. *See also* Electroencephalogram.

Brightness. A dimension of color that refers to the relative degree of whiteness, grayness, or blackness of the color, as distinguished from hue and saturation (*q.v.*). The term is also used to refer to the perceived intensity of a light.

Brightness constancy. A phenomenon of perception in which a person perceives an object as having the same brightness whether it be in bright or in dim illumination. For example, snow looks white in moonlight, and coal appears black in sunlight, even though, under these circumstances, coal reflects more light than snow.

Bril. A subjective unit of visual brightness.

C

CA. *See* Chronological age.

Cafeteria feeding. A method used to study specific hungers. Different kinds of food are offered to a subject, and he chooses the ones he wants.

Castration. Operative removal of the male gonads, used experimentally to study the effects of reducing sex hormones. *Cf.* Ovariectomy.

Catatonia. A state of muscular rigidity, seen in certain cases of schizophrenia. In the catatonic state, a person may remain fixed in a position for minutes or hours.

Cathode-ray oscilloscope. An electrical device which translates a sound wave into a picture that may be viewed on a screen.

Center clipping. Amplitude distortion in which sounds below a certain intensity are eliminated. It greatly reduces speech intelligibility. *Cf.* Peak clipping.

Centile score. The percentage of the scores in a distribution that are equal to or less than the obtained score; sometimes called percentile score. The centile score is a convenient method of expressing a score so that its relative meaning can be understood without knowing the original units of measurement.

Central nervous system. The part of the nervous system enclosed in the bony case of the skull and backbone. *Cf.* Peripheral nervous system.

Central stimulation. Electrical or chemical stimulation of some region of the brain, usually in the waking animal, by means of a permanently implanted electrode or pipette.

Central sulcus. A fissure in the cerebral cortex dividing the frontal lobe from the parietal lobe.

Cerebral cortex. A large mass of gray matter, which is part of the forebrain, lying in folds near the interior surface of the skull.

Cerebral hemispheres. Two symmetrical halves of the cerebral cortex and their associated structures.

Chaining. Learning of a series of responses in which the stimulus arising from one response is associated with the next response in the series.

Chemical senses. The senses of taste and smell.

Chemotherapy. The treatment of a neurosis or psychosis with a drug or chemical substance, e.g., with a tranquilizer (*q.v.*).

Chimpanzee. One of the higher apes; a primate.

Choroid coat. The middle layer of the wall of the eyeball, dark in color and opaque. It reduces stray light which might other-wise enter the eyeball from the side and blur vision.

Chromosomes. Colored bodies seen under the microscope in the nucleus of the cells of the body. They contain genes.

Chronological age (CA). Age in years. *Cf.* Mental age.

Ciliary muscle. A muscle attached to the lens of the eye which thickens the lens when it contracts and flattens the lens when it relaxes. It controls accommodation.

Classical conditioning. Learning that takes place when a conditioning stimulus is paired with an unconditioned stimulus.

Client-centered therapy. A nondirective therapy (*q.v.*) developed by Carl Rogers, which typically is not so intensive or prolonged as psychoanalysis.

Clinical methods. Methods of collecting data in which information is obtained about people who come to physicians and psychologists for assistance.

Clinical psychology. A branch of psychology concerned with psychological methods of recognizing and treating mental disorders and problems of adjustment.

Closure. The tendency for gaps to be perceived as filled in. For example, the dotted outline of an object may be recognized almost as easily as a continued outline of it.

Cochlea. A bony cavity, coiled like a snail shell, containing receptor organs for hearing. It contains three canals: vestibular, tympanic, and cochlear.

Cochlear canal. One of the canals in the cochlea.

Coefficient of contingency. A measure of correlation that may be computed from nominal measurements, i.e., when individuals have been classified in categories. Symbol: C. *See also* Coefficient of correlation, Rank-difference correlation.

Coefficient of correlation. A number between $+1.00$ and -1.00 expressing the degree of relationship between two sets of measurements arranged in pairs. A coefficient of $+1.00$ (or -1.00) represents perfect correlation, and a coefficient of .00 represents no correlation at all. Symbol: r.

Color blindness. A defect that makes a person unable to tell the difference between two or more colors that most other people can easily distinguish. Total color blindness is very rare, but two-color vision occurs in 1 out of 15 men. There are three kinds of color blindness: protanopia, deuteranopia, and tritanopia (*q.v.*).

Color circle. An arrangement of colors in which hues are spokes of a wheel and saturation is represented by radial distance on the spokes.

Color solid. A three-dimensional diagram representing the relationships of hue, saturation, and brightness in the perception of color.

Color unit. A neural element of the retina, probably a neuron, from which microelectrode (*q.v.*) records of activity are recorded; presumed to be involved in color vision.

Communication structure. The pattern of closed and open channels of communication within a group of individuals.

Compensation. A defense mechanism in which an individual substitutes one activity for another in an attempt to satisfy frustrated motives. It usually implies failure or loss of self-esteem in one activity and the compensation of this loss by efforts in some other realm of endeavor.

Complementary colors. Pairs of hues that, when mixed in proper portions, are seen as gray.

Compulsion. An irrational, useless act that constantly intrudes into a person's behavior; seen in psychasthenia.

Concept. An internal process representing a common property of objects or events, usually represented by a word or name.

Conditioning. A general term referring to the learning of some particular response. *See also* Classical conditioning.

Conditioning stimulus. The stimulus that is originally ineffective but that, after pairing with an unconditioned stimulus, evokes the conditioned response. *See also* Classical conditioning.

Conduction deafness. Deafness due to an impairment of the conduction of sounds to the cochlea.

Cone. A photosensitive receptor in the retina, shaped like a cone and most sensitive under daytime conditions of seeing. Cones are closely packed in the fovea and are the important receptors in color vision.

Conflict of motives. *See* Motivational conflict.

Constancy. *See* Perceptual constancy.

Constant stimuli. A method of obtaining sensory thresholds in which preselected intensities, or values of a stimulus, are presented to an observer for comparison with a standard stimulus.

Constitutional theory. The theory of Sheldon that temperament and physical constitution are correlated.

Contiguity. *See* Law of contiguity.

Contingency. See Coefficient of contingency.

Continuation. The tendency to perceive objects as forming a line, curve, or other continuous pattern. *See also* Grouping.

Contour. The line of demarcation perceived by an observer whenever there is a marked difference between the brightness or color in one place and that in an adjoining region.

Contrast. A marked difference in stimulation, as between light and dark, silence and noise, and hot and cold; also, more specifically, the difference in brightness between an object and its immediate surround.

Contrast threshold. *See* Differential threshold.

Control. Used in two senses: (1) The group or condition in an experiment that is similar in all respects to the experimental group or condition except that it does not include the experimental variable. (2) Any stick, switch, wheel, or other device used by an individual to operate a device or machine.

Controlled sampling. Sampling (*q.v.*) according to some plan that provides for certain numbers of people in each category according to their incidence in the population sampled.

Convergence. Turning the eyes inward toward the nose as objects are brought closer to the eyes.

Conversion reaction. A neurotic reaction in which motivational conflict has been converted into physical symptoms, so that the person appears to have various ailments that have no physical basis.

Cornea. The outermost, transparent layer of the front of the eye.

Correlation coefficient. Any coefficient of correlation, but usually the coefficient *r* computed from scores on two distributions. *See also* Coefficient of correlation.

Rank-difference correlation, Coefficient of contingency.

Cortex. A rind or covering. *See also* Cerebral cortex.

Cortical. Pertaining to a cortex; usually refers to the cerebral cortex, but can also refer to the cortex of other structures, e.g., the adrenal gland.

Cortin. A general term for the hormones secreted by the cortical part of the adrenal glands. It governs, among other things, levels of sodium and water in the internal environment.

Counseling. The giving of advice and assistance to individuals with vocational or personal problems. It often involves some psychotherapy.

Cranial nerves. The nerves serving the brain. There are 12 cranial nerves, some sensory, some motor, and some of mixed function.

Cretinism. A physical disorder caused by insufficient thyroxin in infancy and childhood. It results in dwarfism and feeble-mindedness, but it can be alleviated or cured by feeding thyroxin.

Criterion. In the evaluation of tests, the job or performance that a test is supposed to predict; in learning, the level of performance considered to represent relatively complete learning.

Critical incidents. A technique of making a job analysis by compiling instances that are critical for doing the job satisfactorily, as distinguished from those representing work that can be done by almost anybody and are not important in determining whether a job is done satisfactorily.

Cue-producing response. A response which serves as a kinesthetic stimulus for another response. It may be either an observable response or an implicit response.

Culture. The customs, habits, and traditions that characterize a people or a social group. It includes the attitudes and beliefs that the group has about important aspects of its life.

Culture pattern. Widely shared ways of behaving in a society together with the beliefs that accompany them.

Curiosity. A tendency to prefer or to respond to novel stimulation; considered to be a general drive. *See also* Exploratory drive, Manipulative drive.

D

Daltonism. Color blindness (*q.v.*).

Dark adaptation. The increase in sensitivity of the eye that takes place when the eye is allowed to remain in the dark.

Deaf-mute. A person who is completely deaf and consequently unable to talk. Such a person, however, ordinarily can be taught how to talk.

Decibel. The unit of measurement used to express the intensity of a sound. It is a relative measure which has meaning only when some reference level is given. It is $\frac{1}{10}$ of a bel, which is the logarithm of the ratio of two sounds having intensities of 10 to 1. The reference level ordinarily employed in hearing is 0.0002 dyne per square centimeter.

Decorticate. Lacking the cerebral cortex.

Deep senses. The kinesthetic sense, vestibular sense, and organic sense.

Defense mechanism. A reaction to frustration that defends the person against anxiety and serves to disguise his motives, so that he deceives himself about his real motives and goals. For examples, *see* Displacement, Reaction formation, Repression.

Degeneration. A method of studying injury or damage in the nervous system. When a nerve fiber is cut, it degenerates back to the cell body, and degenerative changes take place in the cell body; from these changes the cell bodies and pathways affected can be determined.

Delayed alternation. A variation on the alternation method in which a subject is required to wait for an interval between each response in a series of alternations. *See also* Alternation, Delayed reaction.

Delayed reaction. A type of experiment in which a subject is shown the correct stimulus along with incorrect stimuli but must wait for an interval before having an opportunity to make the correct choice. This kind of experiment has been used to study thinking in animals and children.

Delusion. A groundless, irrational belief or thought, usually of grandeur or of persecution. It is characteristic of paranoia.

Dendrite. A nerve fiber that normally is

stimulated by an external physical stimulus or by the impulse brought to it by an axon (*q.v.*).

Dependency need. The need to depend on other people for advice, counsel, and moral support.

Dependent variable. The variable that changes as a result of changes in the independent variable (*q.v.*). For example, if the number of errors made in typing increases as the environmental temperature becomes hotter, errors in typing are the dependent variable.

Depressive disorder. A mental disorder characterized by anxiety, guilt feelings, self-deprecation, or suicidal tendencies.

Depth perception. Perception of the relative distance of objects from the observer.

Descriptive statistics. Statistical measures that summarize the characteristics of a frequency distribution or the relationship between two or more distributions. *Cf.* Interpretative statistics.

Desensitization. Generally, a weakening of a response, usually an emotional response, with repeated exposure to a situation; more specifically, a method used in psychotherapy to enable a person to be comfortable in situations in which he was previously highly anxious.

Deuteranope. A partially color-blind person who is unable to distinguish red and green. *See also* Protanope, Tritanope.

Deviation score. The difference between the score obtained and the mean of the distribution that includes the obtained score. Symbol: x.

Dichromatism. Partial color blindness (*q.v.*) consisting of two-color vision. All colors are seen as shades of two hues.

Differential reinforcement. Reinforcement of one stimulus but not of another. Such reinforcement is used experimentally to establish a discrimination. *See also* Discriminative learning.

Differential threshold. The smallest difference in a stimulus that can be perceived. *See also* Absolute threshold.

Directive therapy. Therapy in which the therapist prescribes remedies and courses of action much as a physician prescribes medicine. It was used extensively in the early history of psychotherapy. *Cf.* Nondirective therapy.

Discriminative learning. Learning to respond positively to one stimulus and negatively to another.

Displacement. The disguising of the goal of a motive by substituting another in place of it.

Display. Any means of presenting information to a person.

Dissociative reaction. A neurotic reaction involving repression in which certain aspects of personality and memory are compartmentalized and function more or less independently, e.g., amnesia and multiple personality (*q.v.*).

Distribution. *See* Frequency distribution.

Dol. A subjective unit of pain.

Dominant gene. A gene whose hereditary characteristics are always expressed. *Cf.* Recessive gene.

Dominator. A neural unit in the retina having a spectral sensitivity curve like that of day vision or night vision.

Dream analysis. The analysis of the content of dreams to obtain information about the source of a person's emotional problems; sometimes used in psychoanalysis.

Drive. A term implying an impetus to behavior or active striving; often used synonomously with motive or need (*q.v.*). *See also* General drive.

Drive-reduction theory. The theory that the satisfaction or alleviation of a drive is necessary for a response to be learned.

Dynamic range. In sound and hearing, the total range of intensities of sound emitted by a loudspeaker or a human voice.

E

Educational psychology. A field of specialization concerned with psychological aspects of teaching and of formal learning processes in school.

EEG. *See* Electroencephalogram.

Effectors. Organs of response; muscles and glands.

Ego. In psychoanalysis, a term referring to the self and to ways of behaving and thinking realistically. The ego delays the satisfaction of motives when necessary, and directs motives into socially acceptable channels. *See also* Id, Superego.

Eidetic imagery. Extremely detailed imagery; a sort of projection of an image on a mental screen. Such imagery is more common in children than in adults and is greater in some individuals than in others.

Electroencephalogram (EEG). A record of electrical fluctuations in the brain (brain waves), usually obtained by placing electrodes on the skull.

Electrolytic lesion. A lesion, usually in the nervous system, made by passing weak current into an area through an electrode.

Electromagnetic radiation. A general term referring to a variety of physical changes in the environment, including light, radio waves, X rays, and cosmic rays. It travels at approximately 186,000 miles per second and can be specified in terms of either wavelength or frequency of vibrations.

Electroretinogram (ERG). The record of electrical activity obtained from the eye when it is exposed to light.

Embryo. A young organism in the early stages of development. In man, it refers to the period from shortly after conception until 2 months later. *Cf.* Fetus.

Empirical. Founded on experiments, surveys, and proven facts, as distinguished from that which is asserted by argument, reasoning, or opinion.

End spurt. A tendency to give a final spurt of effort at the end of a period of work. It is a factor in the shape of the work curve.

Endocrine glands. Glands that secrete substances called hormones directly into the blood. The thyroid gland is an example. *Cf.* Exocrine glands.

Engineering psychology. An applied field of psychology concerned with psychological factors in the design and use of equipment.

Enzyme. An organic catalyst regulating particular chemical steps in metabolism.

ERG. *See* Electroretinogram.

Escape learning. Learning to escape from a noxious or unpleasant situation by making an appropriate response.

ESP. *See* Extrasensory perception.

Ethnocentric personality. The traits that characterize an individual who is generally hostile or prejudiced toward most groups to which he does not belong. *See also* Authoritarian personality.

Exhaustion. The third stage of the general-adaptation syndrome (*q.v.*), in which a person is no longer able to endure stress.

Exocrine glands. Glands that secrete through ducts into cavities of the body, e.g., salivary glands. *Cf.* Endocrine glands.

Exorcism. The attempt to cast out demons or evil spirits by such acts as prayer, religious rites, medicines, or whipping.

Experimental method. A scientific method in which conditions that are likely to affect a result are controlled by the experimenter. It involves dependent and independent variables.

Exploratory drive. A tendency to explore a novel environment; is considered a general drive not clearly distinguishable from curiosity or manipulative drive.

Expressive disorder. A general term for any disorder, usually caused by brain damage, in which a person does not know how to do things, including talking, that were once familiar to him. *Cf.* Receptive disorder.

Extension reflex. A reflex in which a limb is straightened. *Cf.* Flexion reflex.

Extensional meaning. Meaning that can be established by pointing to objects or events; sometimes called ostensive meaning; distinguished from intentional meaning.

External auditory meatus. *See* Auditory canal.

Extinction. The procedure of presenting the conditioning stimulus without reinforcement to an organism previously conditioned; also the diminution of a conditioned response resulting from this procedure. *See also* Primary reinforcement.

Extinction curve. A graph of the diminution of previously learned responses during the course of extinction (*q.v.*).

Extirpation. The removal of a part, usually of the nervous system.

Extrasensory perception (ESP). Perception that purportedly takes place outside of sensory channels.

F

Face validity. The appearance of validity (*q.v.*) in a test because of the similarity of the test to the job to be performed.

Face validity is not, however, necessarily true validity. Tests should always be examined with validating procedures to determine whether they are, in fact, valid.

Factor analysis. A general statistical method, involving coefficients of correlation, that isolates a few common factors in a large number of tests, ratings, or other measurements.

Familial feeble-mindedness. *See* Primary feeble-mindedness.

Fantasy. Daydreaming and imagining a world of one's own, often used as a defense mechanism. Carried to the extreme, fantasy is characteristic of schizophrenia.

Father figure. An instance of transference in which a person is regarded as though he were a father.

Fatigue. A general term referring to the effects of prolonged work or lack of sleep, probably best defined as a feeling of being tired. Fatigue, however, is often reflected in a decrement in performance.

Feeble-mindedness. A general term applying to the condition of individuals who are both mentally deficient and retarded in social and occupational skills. *See also* Mental deficiency.

Fetus. A young organism in the later stages of prenatal development. In man, it refers to the period from 2 months after conception until birth. *Cf.* Embryo.

Figure-ground perception. Perception of objects or events as standing out clearly from a background. For example, pictures hang *on* walls, words are *on* a page, and an automobile travels *on* a road.

Fissure. *See* Sulcus.

Fixation. A rigid habit developed by repeated reinforcement or as a consequence of frustration.

Fixed-interval schedule. A schedule of partial reinforcement (*q.v.*) in which a response made after a certain interval of time is reinforced.

Fixed-ratio schedule. A schedule of partial reinforcement (*q.v.*) in which every *n*th response is reinforced.

Flexion reflex. A reflex in which a limb is bent. *Cf.* Extension reflex.

Fluency. The amount of language or the number of words that a person can produce in any given time. It is one of the factors measured in intelligence tests.

Folkways. Conventions and habitual behavior that serve to perpetuate social values.

Forced choice. A method for evaluating the effectiveness of a worker by forcing an informed judge to choose one phrase as more or less descriptive of the worker than another phrase.

Forebrain. The most forward of three divisions of the brain. In man and higher animals, it is the most highly developed part of the brain. It includes the cerebral cortex, thalamus, and hypothalamus. *See also* Hindbrain, Midbrain.

Forgetting. A partial or total loss of retention of material previously learned.

Formal-discipline theory. *See* Mental-faculty theory.

Formal group. A social group that has a relatively permanent structure of positions, jobs, and roles.

Fourier analysis. The analysis of a complex tone into sine-wave components, each specified in terms of frequency and intensity.

Fovea. A central region of the retina where cones are closely packed together and visual acuity is at its best. The fovea is the part of the retina that is used when one looks directly at an object.

Fractionation. A method of constructing sensory scales (*q.v.*) in which an observer judges the value of a stimulus that is some fraction, e.g., half, of another stimulus.

Fraternal twins. Twins who develop from two different fertilized eggs (ova), and who consequently may be as different in hereditary characteristics as ordinary brothers and sisters. *Cf.* Identical twins.

Free association. The technique of requiring a patient in psychotherapy to say whatever comes to his mind, regardless of how irrelevant or objectionable it may seem.

Free nerve endings. Nerve endings that are not associated with any special structures. They are found in the skin, blood vessels, and many parts of the body. They are regarded as sense organs for pain and probably also for pressure.

Free-response method. A method of measuring the meaning of concepts in which a person is asked to describe or define a concept.

Frequency. One of the dimensions of vibrational stimuli, such as light or sound. It is most often used with sound and is stated in number of cycles per second, which is the number of alternations in air pressure per second. It is a physical measure of a sound wave, as distinguished from the psychological attribute of pitch.

Frequency composition. The composition of complex tones as specified by Fourier analysis (*q.v.*).

Frequency distribution. A set of measurements arranged from lowest to highest (or highest to lowest) and accompanied by a count (frequency) of the number of times each measurement or class of measurements occurs.

Frequency polygon. A frequency distribution represented by plotting a point on a graph for each frequency of each score, or class of scores, and connecting the points with straight lines.

Frontal association area. Part of the frontal lobe lying in front of the motor and premotor areas; also called prefrontal area. It functions in attention, planning, and expressive aspects of memory.

Frontal lobe. The part of the cerebral cortex lying in front of the central sulcus. It contains areas involved in motor functions, attention, and planning behavior.

Frustration. The thwarting of motivated behavior directed at a goal.

Frustration tolerance. Ability to tolerate frustration and its accompanying anxiety. It is characteristic of well-adjusted people and is something to be learned in achieving mental health.

Functional autonomy. The ability of certain motives to continue functioning without further reinforcement of the conditions under which they were learned. *See also* Learned goal.

Functional psychosis. A psychosis that has no known organic basis in disturbance, damage, or disease of the brain. *Cf.* Organic psychosis.

Functionalism. A viewpoint taking the middle course among introspectionism, behaviorism, and gestalt psychology. Functionalists proposed that all activities serving some function, including both behavior and experience, be studied by psychologists.

Fundamental. In hearing, the lowest frequency in a complex tone.

G

Galvanic skin response (GSR). A change in the electrical resistance of the skin, occurring in emotion and in certain other conditions.

Ganglion. A collection of the cell bodies of neurons.

Ganglion cell. The cell body of a neuron located in a nucleus or ganglion of the nervous system; also, in the eye, the cell found in the third layer of the retina. Fibers of the retinal ganglion cells make up the optic nerve.

General-adaptation syndrome. A sequence of physiological reactions to prolonged physical or emotional stress; consists of three stages: the alarm reaction, resistance to stress, and exhaustion (*q.v.*).

General drive. A drive that is unlearned but is not aroused by a specific physiological need.

Generalization. The phenomenon of an organism's responding to all situations similar to one in which it has been conditioned, for example, giving a galvanic skin response to high-pitched tones when one has been conditioned with electric shocks to respond to low-pitched tones. *See also* Stimulus generalization.

Genes. The essential elements in the transmission of hereditary characteristics, carried in chromosomes. *See also* Dominant gene, Recessive gene.

Genital stage. A stage in development, according to psychoanalytic theory, during which the adolescent displays heterosexual interests.

Germ cell. An egg or sperm cell.

Gestalt psychology. A viewpoint, developed by German psychologists, that considered introspectionism and behaviorism too atomistic and emphasized the importance of configuration and insight in perception.

Gland. An organ that secretes. There are two general types, endocrine glands and exocrine glands (*q.v.*).

Glutamic acid. An acid believed to be concerned in metabolism of the nervous system. It has been used without success to improve intelligence.

Goal. The place, condition, or object that satisfies a motive.

Golgi tendon organs. Receptors located in tendons that are activated when the muscle to which the tendon is attached contracts, putting tension on the tendon.

Gonads. The sex glands, which are the testicles in the male and the ovaries in the female. They determine secondary sex characteristics such as growth of the breasts, beginning of menstruation, growth of the beard, and change of the voice and also influence sexual motivation.

Gradient. In the study of motivational conflict, the increasing strength of a goal, the nearer one is to the goal. Other things being equal, the avoidance gradient for negative goals is steeper than the approach gradient for positive goals.

Gradient of reinforcement. The concept that the closer a response is in time and space to a reinforcement, the more the response is strengthened.

Gray matter. Nervous tissue without any covering. It usually consists of cell bodies of neurons. *Cf.* White matter.

Group. *See* Social group.

Group norm. A widely shared expectation or standard of behavior among most members of a group, class, or culture.

Group test. A test that may be administered to a group of people at one time.

Group therapy. A specialized technique of psychotherapy, consisting of a group of patients discussing their personal problems under the guidance of a therapist.

Grouping. The tendency to perceive objects in groups rather than as isolated elements. Grouping is determined by such factors as nearness, similarity, symmetry, and continuation of objects.

Growth hormone. A hormone secreted by the pituitary gland and controlling the general rate of growth of the body.

GSR. *See* Galvanic skin response.

Gust. A subjective unit of taste.

Gyrus. A ridge in the cerebral cortex of the brain. *Cf.* Sulcus.

H

Habituation. The tendency of a response to weaken with repeated presentation of a stimulus; similar to desensitization (*q.v.*).

Hallucination. An image that is regarded by the person as real sensory experience. Hallucinations are diagnostic of certain mental disorders, such as schizophrenia.

Harmonics. Components of complex tones that are multiples of the fundamental frequency.

Hebephrenia. A state characterized by childishness and regressive behavior, seen in some cases of schizophrenia. The hebephrenic person may behave in almost every way as though he were a small child.

Helmholtz resonance theory. A theory of pitch that assumes different parts of the basilar membrane (*q.v.*) to resonate to different sound frequencies. *See also* Place theory.

Hering theory. *See* Opponent-colors theory.

Higher-order conditioning. Conditioning of a response to a stimulus by pairing the stimulus with another stimulus to which the response has previously been conditioned.

Hindbrain. The third of three divisions of the brain. It includes the medulla, which is a vital center for breathing, heartbeat, etc., and the cerebellum, which is a center for motor coordination. It also contains pathways passing between the spinal cord and other parts of the brain. *See also* Forebrain, Midbrain.

Histogram. A frequency distribution represented by erecting bars whose heights vary with the frequencies of the scores or classes of scores.

Homeostasis. The tendency of the body to maintain a balance among internal physiological conditions, such as temperature, sugar, air, and salt.

Hormones. Secretions of endocrine glands that help or inhibit certain chemical steps in the body.

Hostility. *See* Aggression.

Hue. The aspect of a color that is determined by the dominant wavelength and that enables us to discriminate blue from red, red from yellow, and so on, as distinguished from brightness and saturation (*q.v.*).

Human engineering. In psychological usage, the field of specialization concerned with the design of equipment and of tasks performed in the operation of equipment; sometimes called engineering psychology.

Hunger. A drive stemming from a physiological need for food.

Hyperphagia. Eating abnormally large quantities of food; associated with injuries in certain regions of the hypothalamus.

Hypnosis. A trancelike state resembling sleep in which a person is extremely susceptible to the suggestion of the hypnotist.

Hypochondriasis. A neurotic reaction in which a person is excessively concerned with his physical welfare or constantly complaining of minor ailments; seen in anxiety reactions.

Hypomania. A disturbance characterized by elation and excitement without any clear external cause. *See also* Manic-depressive psychosis.

Hypothalamus. A region in the floor of the brain just above the throat that is part of the forebrain. It contains centers for the regulation of sleep, temperature, thirst, hunger, and emotion.

Hypothesis. A process inferred to be operating when an organism repeatedly responds in the same way to a stimulus situation without being reinforced for the response or being told what is correct.

Hysteria. A kind of neurosis marked by conversion reactions (*q.v.*).

I

Id. In psychoanalytic theory, the aspect of personality concerned with instinctual reactions for satisfying motives. The id seeks immediate gratification of motives with little regard for the consequences or for the realities of life. *See also* Ego, Superego.

Identical twins. Twins who develop from the same fertilized egg (ovum). They have exactly the same kinds of chromosomes and genes and hence the same hereditary characteristics. *Cf.* Fraternal twins.

Idiot. A person with an intelligence quotient of 20 or less.

Illusion. A perception that does not agree with other, more trustworthy perceptions.

Image. A representation in the brain of sensory experience. Images are involved in thinking (*q.v.*).

Imageless thought. Thought occurring without the presence of images. The phrase refers particularly to a theory of the nature of thinking entertained by a group of German psychologists about 1900.

Imbecile. A person with an intelligence quotient between 20 and 50.

Imitation. Copying the behavior of another.

Implicit response. A minute muscle movement ordinarily detectable only by special electrical or mechanical recording methods. Implicit responses, miniatures of large, observable movements, are acquired in previous learning and involved in thinking.

Imprinting. Very rapid learning that takes place in some animals, notably birds, at a certain early stage of development.

Impulse. Sometimes used in psychoanalysis to refer to motive, but usually refers to the nerve impulse.

Incentive. A term approximately synonymous with goal, but implying the manipulation of a goal to motivate the individual. Money, for example, is used as an incentive to motivate people to work.

Incidental learning. Learning without an incentive and without reinforcement. *See also* Latent learning.

Incubation. A stage in creative thinking during which the problem is put aside and unconscious factors permitted to work.

Independent variable. The variable that may be selected or changed by the experimenter and is responsible for changes in the dependent variable (*q.v.*). For example, if errors made in typing depend on environmental temperature, temperature is the independent variable.

Individual psychograph. A profile of an individual's traits and abilities. It may be compared with a job psychograph (*q.v.*) to determine whether the individual is fitted for a particular job.

Individual test. A test that can be given to only one individual at a time, e.g., the Stanford-Binet intelligence test.

Industrial psychology. A field of specialization concerned with methods of selecting, training, counseling, and supervising personnel in business and industry. It sometimes includes problems of increasing efficiency in work and of redesigning machines to suit better the capacities of the worker. *See also* Human engineering.

Inferiority complex. A concept put forth by

Alfred Adler; an attitude developed out of frustration in striving for superiority.

Informal group. A social group having no formal or permanent structure and consisting of people who happen to be assembled together at a particular time. Sometimes, however, the members of a formal group (e.g., the employees of a company) may constitute an informal group that is different from the one prescribed by the formal structure of the organization.

Inhibition. A general concept of a hypothetical nervous state; a decreasing tendency to respond with repetition of a response.

Inner ear. *See* Cochlea, Vestibular sense.

Innervation ratio. The ratio of muscle fibers to axons serving the fibers. A high ratio is typical of larger muscles, a small ratio of smaller muscles, e.g., fingers and eyelid, involved in fine, precise movements.

Insight. In learning and problem solving, the relatively sudden solution of a problem; in psychotherapy, the understanding of one's own motives and their origins.

Insight therapy. Treatment of a personality disorder by attempting to uncover the deep causes of the patient's difficulty and to help him rid himself of his defense mechanisms. It represents an attempt to guide the patient in self-understanding of his motives and his resources for satisfying them. Sometimes it is called uncovering therapy. *Cf.* Supportive therapy.

Instinctive. Pertaining to complex, unlearned patterns of behavior motivated by a physiological drive.

Instinctive behavior. A complex pattern consisting of reflexes, taxes, and instinctive movements.

Institutional ways. The laws of a society used to enforce social values considered essential to the society's way of life.

Instrumental behavior. Behavior that typically accomplishes a purpose, usually the satisfaction of a need, e.g., working for a living.

Instrumental learning. Learning to make a response that is instrumental in satisfying a need. It is sometimes referred to as instrumental conditioning.

Insulin. A hormone secreted by the pancreas and concerned in controlling the amount of sugar in the blood; used in insulin-shock therapy.

Insulin shock. A method, infrequently used today, for treating severe psychosis; causes convulsions and coma.

Intelligence. A general term covering a person's abilities on a wide range of tasks involving vocabulary, numbers, problem solving, concepts, and so on. As measured by a standardized intelligence test, it generally involves several specific abilities, with special emphasis on verbal abilities.

Intelligence quotient (IQ). A number obtained by dividing chronological age into mental age and multiplying by 100. This rule applies only to children; more complex methods are used to compute the intelligence quotient for teen-agers and adults.

Intensity. A general term referring to the amount of physical energy stimulating a sense organ. It is expressed in physical units appropriate to the kind of energy involved.

Intentional meaning. Meaning of a word derived by using other words, e.g., its dictionary meaning.

Interference. A factor in learning and forgetting; the incompatibility of two learned associations.

Internal environment. The environment of the nervous system, including the temperature of the body, oxygen, food supplies, minerals, hormones, and related substances that are important in the functioning of the nervous system.

Interpretative statistics. Statistical measures that permit inferences about the population from which a particular sample of measurements is drawn. *Cf.* Descriptive statistics.

Interval scale. A scale in which differences between numbers may be regarded as equal, e.g., $3 - 1 = 4 - 2$.

Introspection. A method of psychological experimentation in which a subject is presented with some stimulus, such as a colored light, and asked to give a detailed report of his sensations; seldom used at the present time.

Introspectionism. A viewpoint held early in the twentieth century by one group of experimental psychologists who employed the method of introspection. It regarded sensation as the important psychological element in consciousness and attempted to analyze mental content.

Inventory. A detailed questionnaire that provides specific information about a person's likes, dislikes, habits, preferences, and so on. It usually refers to a personality or interest test.

Invertebrates. In general, animals that are not vertebrates, such as worms, shellfish, insects, and other animals without segmented backbones.

Involutional melancholia. An organic psychosis, often transitory, whose chief symptoms are depression, a frivolous regression to the clothes and manners of younger days, and somewhat paranoid accusations against one's friends and even oneself. It is seen most frequently in women undergoing menopause.

Iodopsin. A photosensitive substance found in the cones of the retina of chickens; presumed to be involved in human cone vision.

IQ. *See* Intelligence quotient.

Iris. The set of muscles, controlled by the autonomic system, that varies the amount of light admitted to the eye by narrowing or enlarging the pupil. It gives the eye its distinctive color, such as blue or brown.

J

Job. A set of activities performed by an individual worker. Several individuals, however, may do the same kind of work and be said to have the same job.

Job analysis. The process of finding out what constitutes a particular job. It is carried out with a variety of different methods, according to the type of job being analyzed.

Job description. A statement of the significant characteristics of a job and of the worker characteristics (*q.v.*) necessary to perform the job satisfactorily.

Job evaluation. The assessment of the remuneration to be offered or paid for a particular job.

Job psychograph. A profile of the traits and abilities required in a job or a family of jobs. *Cf.* Individual psychograph.

Just noticeable difference (jnd). *See* Differential threshold.

K

Kinesis. An undirected, unlearned reaction to a stimulus. *Cf.* Taxis.

Kinesthetic receptors. Sense organs located in the muscles, tendons, and joints that convey impulses to the brain when muscles are contracted or stretched.

Knowledge of results. A person's knowledge of how he is progressing in training or in the performance of his job. It is usually necessary for the most rapid learning and for the best performance of the job.

Kymograph. A device which makes a record of movement. It may be used to measure heartbeat, body sway, breathing, finger tremor, etc.

L

Landolt ring. A test object used in measurements of visual acuity, consisting of an incompleted circle.

Latent learning. Learning that becomes evident only when the occasion arises for using it. *See also* Incidental learning.

Lateral sulcus. A fissure in the cerebral cortex dividing the temporal lobe from the frontal and parietal lobes.

Law of contiguity. The principle that two events must occur close together in time and space to be associated in learning.

Learned goal. A goal that has been acquired through learning, as distinguished from a physiological goal.

Learning. A general term referring to a relatively permanent change in behavior that is the result of past experience. It includes conditioning, instrumental learning, and perceptual learning.

Learning curve. Any graphical representation of progress in learning.

Learning set. A kind of transfer of training (*q.v.*) in which a subject becomes increasingly adept at learning problems of the same general type.

Lesion. Any damage or change in a tissue due to injury or disease.

Level of aspiration. The level at which a person sets certain goals.

Level of performance. The achievement of a person, as distinguished from his level of aspiration.

Lie detector. A popular name for a device designed to detect guilt. It usually involves measures of breathing, heart rate, blood pressure, and galvanic skin response.

Light. The portion of the visible spectrum (*q.v.*) of electromagnetic radiation. It may be specified by wavelength and intensity.

Light-compass reaction. An unlearned reaction in which an animal uses some source of light, such as the sun, as a compass for maintaining transverse orientation. The reaction in bees enables them to navigate between a food source and the hive.

Linear perspective. The perception of faraway objects as close together and of nearby objects as far apart. It is an important factor in depth perception.

Loaded words. Words having an emotional tone, used by propagandists and advertisers for creating and maintaining attitudes.

Logical thinking. Reasoning carried out according to the formal rules of logic; not very common in human thinking.

Loudness. A psychological attribute of tones, related to intensity but not directly proportional to it.

Luminosity. The perceived brightness of a visual stimulus. *See also* Luminosity curve.

Luminosity curve. A curve depicting the threshold at different wavelengths. The luminosity curve for daylight vision has its greatest sensitivity at about 555 millimicrons; the comparable curve for night vision has its greatest sensitivity at about 505 millimicrons. *See also* Cone, Rod.

M

MA. *See* Mental age.

Maladjustment. A broad term covering not only the psychoneuroses and psychoses but also mild disturbances in which a person is anxious or behaves peculiarly.

Mammals. The class of vertebrates that nourish their young with milk.

Manic-depressive psychosis. A psychosis characterized by extremes of mood. In the manic state, the person may be extremely active, elated, and/or aggressive; in the depressed state, he may feel melancholy, worthless, guilty, and hopeless.

Manipulative drive. A tendency to explore and manipulate objects; considered to be a general drive not clearly distinguishable from curiosity or exploratory drive.

Man-to-man rating. A method of evaluating workers by having informed judges compare individuals two at a time and rate one as better than the other. It is a specific case of the method of paired comparisons (*q.v.*).

Market research. Research consisting of surveys conducted in much the same manner as public-opinion polls but with the purpose of measuring attitudes concerning specific products, the effectiveness of advertising, and the relative preferences of consumers for different brands.

Masking. The deleterious effect of one sound on a person's ability to hear other sounds simultaneously.

Maternal behavior. Behavior concerned with giving birth to young, nursing them, and caring for them. Maternal behavior in animals presents many examples of truly instinctive behavior.

Maturation. The completion of developmental processes in the body. Maturation is governed both by heredity and by environmental conditions.

Maze. A device used in animal and human learning experiments that has blind alleys and a correct path. It presents the subject with the task of taking a path through it without entering any blind alleys.

Mean. *See* Arithmetic mean.

Measurement. The assignment of numerals or numbers to objects or events according to rules.

Mechanical-ability test. A vocational-aptitude test for predicting success in jobs requiring mechanical ability.

Median. The middle score in a frequency distribution when all scores are ranked from highest to lowest (or lowest to highest). It is one measure of central tendency. *Cf.* Arithmetic mean.

Mediating process. An associative process connecting previously learned processes and responses.

Medical therapy. The treatment of an illness by using medicines, drugs, or surgery. *Cf.* Psychotherapy.

Meissner corpuscle. A specialized structure in the skin regarded as a sense organ for pressure or touch.

Mel. A subjective unit of pitch.

Mental age (MA). The age at which the average child passes tests equivalent in difficulty to those passed by a child to which a mental age is assigned. It is a relative measure of mental growth. For example, if a five-year-old child does as well on an intelligence test as the average child of seven, his mental age is 7. *See also* Intelligence quotient.

Mental deficiency. The condition of individuals who have an intelligence quotient of less than 70. There are three grades of mental deficiency: morons, imbeciles, and idiots (*q.v.*).

Mental disorder. A general term referring to the more severe personality disorders, usually implying a psychosis, rather than a neurosis, though its usage is not hard and fast. It means about the same thing as mental illness.

Mental-faculty theory. The theory that formal education generally develops mental faculties so that a person is better able to solve all sorts of problems. The theory is sometimes called formal-discipline, theory or the doctrine of formal discipline.

Mental health. A general term referring to personal adjustments relatively free of neurotic and psychotic symptoms.

Mental hygiene. A general term, similar in meaning to mental health, which refers to the maintenance of satisfying personal adjustments.

Mental illness. *See* Mental disorder.

Metabolism. A general term referring to chemical processes in the cells of the body. It includes the assimilation of food, the storing of energy, the utilization of energy, the repairing of tissues, and the disposition of cellular wastes.

Meter. A unit of length in the metric system; 39.37 inches.

Method of adjustment. A method of obtaining sensory thresholds in which the observer adjusts the intensity of a stimulus until he just barely senses it or distinguishes the difference between it and a standard stimulus.

Method of rating. A method that requires a person to assign comparative adjectives or numbers on a scale to indicate preferences, judgments, or opinions. *See also* Rating.

Metrazol. A drug which causes convulsions, infrequently used today in the treatment of psychoses.

Microelectrode. An electrode so small that it can provide a record of electrical activity in a single neuron or sensory cell.

Midbrain. The middle of three divisions of the brain. It contains reflex centers for hearing and vision, pathways to and from the forebrain, and several other centers. *See also* Forebrain, Hindbrain.

Middle ear. A bony cavity containing ossicles which link the eardrum to the cochlea.

Millimicron. A unit of measurement used with light and other electromagnetic radiations. It is usually abbreviated mμ. "Milli" means one-thousandth, and "micron" means one-millionth of a meter.

Mode. The most frequent score or category in a distribution of measurements.

Mode of adjustment. The characteristic way in which an individual attempts to satisfy his motives.

Modulator. A neural unit of the retina having a relatively narrow range of sensitivity to wavelengths of the spectrum; presumed to take part in color vision.

Mongoloid. A type of feeble-mindedness (*q.v.*) characterized by mongolian facial features; not hereditary. Mongolism is believed to be due to insufficient oxygen or to a similar condition affecting metabolism in the early stages of prenatal development.

Monocular. Pertaining to the use of only one eye. *Cf.* Binocular.

Mores. Customs that enforce social values having ethical or moral significance. Violation brings strong social disapproval.

Moron. A feeble-minded person with an intelligence quotient of 50 to 70.

Motivation. A general term referring to behavior instigated by needs and directed toward goals.

Motivational conflict. A conflict between two or more motives resulting in the frustration of a motive. Most motivational conflict involves acquired motives.

Motive. A term implying a need and the direction of behavior toward a goal; often used synonymously with need or drive (*q.v.*).

Motor area. An area of the cerebral cortex lying just in front of the central sulcus. It is concerned in the execution of skilled movements. Damage to the area, if sufficiently great, produces paralysis.

Motor neuron. A neuron conveying impulses away from the central nervous system toward a muscle or gland.

Motor unit. A motor axon together with the muscle fibers it serves. *See also* Innervation ratio.

Multiple personality. A dissociative reaction (*q.v.*) in which a person displays two or more relatively distinct personalities, each with its own set of memories. *See also* Amnesia, Dissociative reaction.

Munsell system. A system of denoting colors in steps of hue, saturation, and brightness that are equidistant in terms of ability to discriminate them.

Mutation. A change in a gene and hence in the characteristic it determines.

Myelin sheath. A white covering around some fibers of the nervous system.

N

Narcoanalysis. Analysis of a person's memories, usually involving a traumatic experience, and of his emotional problems under the influence of a sleep-inducing drug, e.g., sodium amytal.

Narcosis. Sleep or sleepiness caused by drugs, e.g., sodium amytal.

Nationalism. A set of attitudes, held by numbers of people, that are prejudicial to foreigners and other countries. It includes a feeling that one's own country is superior in manners, morals, and way of life.

Natural observation. The observation of events as they occur in nature or in the course of human affairs without exercising experimental controls and without using methods of systematic sampling.

Need. Any lack or deficit within the individual, either acquired or physiological (*q.v.*); often used synonymously with drive or motive (*q.v.*). See also Social needs.

Negative acceleration. The characteristic of a curve that is steep at its beginning but becomes increasingly flat as it approaches its end. Learning curves are typically of this shape.

Negative transfer. The negative effect on learning in one situation because of previous learning in another situation. It is due to incompatible responses being required in the two situations.

Nerve. A bundle of nerve fibers.

Nerve deafness. Deafness due to an impairment of the sense organs or of the nerves concerned in hearing. It is also called perception deafness or perceptual deafness.

Nerve fiber. An axon or a dendrite of a neuron. It conducts nerve impulses.

Nerve impulse. An electrical change in the membrane of a nerve fiber, propagated along the length of the fiber. It is the basic message unit of the nervous system and obeys an all-or-none law (*q.v.*).

Nervous system. The brain, spinal cord, and nerves serving the various sense organs, endocrine glands, and muscles of the body.

Neurasthenia. A neurotic reaction in which the person complains of general nervousness, fatigue, and insomnia; often accompanied by depression, feelings of inadequacy, and inability to work.

Neuron. The cell that is the basic unit of the nervous system. It conducts nerve impulses and consists of dendrite(s) (*q.v.*), cell body, and axon (*q.v.*).

Neurosis. A mental or personality disorder, less severe than a psychosis (*q.v.*), in which a person is unusually anxious, miserable, troubled, or incapacitated in his work and his relations with other people. Also called psychoneurosis.

Neurotic need. According to Horney, a learned need for something connected with the alleviation of basic anxiety.

Nominal scale. A scale in which numbers are assigned to objects or persons only to distinguish those that are alike from those that are different, e.g., postal zone numbers. The numbers of a nominal scale may not be used additively.

Nondirective therapy. Psychotherapy in which the patient is dominant and given the greatest possible opportunity to express himself. The method is based on the principle that the patient must learn how to solve his own problems and cannot have them solved for him by the therapist. *Cf.* Directive therapy.

Nonsense figure. A set of lines, marks, or contours having little or no meaning. *Cf.* Nonsense syllable.

Nonsense syllable. A syllable, usually of three letters, constructed so as to resemble meaningful English as little as possible. Nonsense syllables are used in learning experiments as new or unfamiliar material.

Normal curve. A bell-shaped frequency distribution, also called the normal-probability curve, which is an ideal approximated by many distributions obtained in psychology and biological sciences. It can be derived mathematically from the laws of chance.

Norms. An average or standard, or a distribution of measurements, obtained from a large number of people. It permits the comparison of an individual score with the scores of comparable individuals.

Nucleus. A collection of cell bodies of neurons within the central nervous system; also a structure within the neuron containing chromosomes. Plural: nuclei.

O

Obsession. A seemingly groundless idea that constantly intrudes into a person's thoughts; seen in obsessive-compulsive reactions.

Obsessive-compulsive reaction. A neurosis or neurotic reaction characterized by obsessions and/or compulsions (*q.v.*).

Occipital lobe. The part of the cerebral cortex lying at the back of the head. It contains the highest centers for vision.

Oddity method. A method used for various purposes in which three or more stimuli are presented and the subject is asked to indicate which stimulus is different.

Oldsightedness. Farsightedness characteristic of old age and typically increasing beyond the age of forty.

Olfactorium. A specially designed room free of all odors except those introduced in measured quantities by an experimenter. It is used in the study of smell.

Ommatidia. Elements of the complex eye of the insect and certain other invertebrates. Each element is a complete structure capable of responding to light, even when other elements are destroyed or covered.

Open-end question. The type of question that allows a respondent to answer in his own words.

Operant behavior. Behavior, usually occurring without a known stimulus, that has some consequence, i.e., operates on the environment; e.g., bar-pressing that supplies food or turns off a light.

Opinion. Acceptance of a statement accompanied by an attitude of pro or con; in practice, difficult to distinguish from an attitude or belief (*q.v.*).

Opponent-colors theory. The theory that human color vision depends on three pairs of opposing processes: white-black, yellow-blue, and red-green.

Opsin. A breakdown product of rhodopsin in rod vision.

Optic nerve. The nerve formed by axons of the ganglion cells of the retina. It leaves the eye at the blind spot and ends in relay centers of the thalamus.

Oral stage. The stage, postulated in psychoanalytic theory, during which an infant's satisfactions center around his mouth and sucking.

Order of skill. A type of motor ability, such as control of neck muscles, control of trunk and upper limb muscles, etc., observed in the development of infants.

Ordinal scale. A scale in which numbers are assigned to objects or persons so as to rank them in order according to some quality or magnitude, e.g., ranking students 1, 2, 3, etc., according to their grades.

Organ of Corti. The organ containing receptors for hearing, located on the basilar membrane which separates the vestibular and tympanic canals of the cochlea.

Organic psychosis. A psychosis known to be caused or aggravated by some damage or disease of the brain. *Cf.* Functional psychosis.

Organic senses. Sense organs located in the

internal organs of the body, such as receptors for cold and warmth in the stomach.

Ossicles. Three bones in the middle ear, through which sound is conducted from the eardrum to the oval window of the cochlea.

Otolith organs. Sense organs found in chambers near the cochlea. They are sensitive to gravity and to the position of the head; they are part of the vestibular sense.

Oval window. The entrance to the cochlea through which sound vibrations pass from the ossicles of the middle ear to the canals of the cochlea.

Ovariectomy. Operative removal of the female ovaries, used experimentally to study the effect on behavior of a reduction in sex hormones. *Cf.* Castration.

Overcompensation. According to Adler, an overreaction to feelings of inferiority so that a person becomes superior in things in which he otherwise would not be.

Ovum. The cell formed in the ovary of the female which, when fertilized by the sperm of the male, may develop into a new individual. Plural: ova.

P

Pacinian corpuscle. A specialized structure serving as a receptor for pressure, located below the skin, in joints, and other deep parts of the body.

Paired-associate learning. Learning in which the subject must respond with one word or syllable when presented with another word or syllable.

Paired comparisons. A method of measurement in which things or people are taken two at a time and a judgment is made as to which is greater than the other, better than the other, etc.

Pancreas. An endocrine gland, located along the lower wall of the stomach, which secretes the hormone insulin. This hormone controls blood-sugar level.

Parallel bars. A test object used in measurements of visual acuity in place of the letters of the familiar eye chart.

Paramecium. A single-celled animal shaped like a slipper.

Paranoia. A personality disorder marked by extreme suspiciousness of the motives of others, often taking the form of elaborate beliefs that they are plotting against the person. *See also* Projection.

Parasympathetic system. A subdivision of the autonomic system that generally functions to conserve the resources of the body. It acts antagonistically to the sympathetic system (*q.v.*).

Parathormone. The hormone secreted by the parathyroid glands.

Parathyroid glands. Two pairs of endocrine glands located on the thyroid glands of the neck. They secrete hormones concerned in the regulation of calcium and phosphorus levels in the body.

Parietal lobe. The part of the cerebral cortex lying immediately behind the central sulcus. It contains areas involved in somesthesis and somesthetic memory.

Part learning. Learning, usually in the sense of memorizing, in which learning is divided into smaller units and each unit is separately learned. *Cf.* Whole learning.

Partial reinforcement. Reinforcement of some proportion of unconditioned responses (in conditioning) or of instrumental responses (in instrumental learning).

Peak clipping. Amplitude distortion in which the peaks of sound above a certain intensity are "clipped off" or eliminated in some way from the sound. It has little effect on intelligibility of speech, and coupled with compensatory amplification, it can be used to increase intelligibility. *Cf.* Center clipping.

Peer. An equal in a given respect; an associate at roughly the same level.

Perception. A general term referring to the awareness of objects, qualities, or events stimulating the sense organs.

Perception deafness. *See* Nerve deafness.

Perceptual constancy. A general term referring to the tendency of objects to be perceived in the same way despite wide variations in the manner of viewing them. *See also* Brightness constancy, Shape constancy, Size constancy.

Performance. As generally used in psychology, nonlinguistic ability. Performance tests are so constructed that they do not handicap a person who speaks no English or who has verbal deficiencies.

Periodic sound. A complex sound consisting of repetitive patterns of waves. *Cf.* Aperiodic sound, Random noise.

Peripheral nervous system. The part of the nervous system lying outside the skull and the backbone. *Cf.* Central nervous system.

Personality. The traits, modes of adjustment, and ways of behaving that characterize the individual and his relation to others in his environment.

Personality disorder. A general term referring to a neurosis or psychosis. *See also* Mental disorder.

Personality structure. In general, the unique organization of traits, motives, and ways of behaving that characterizes a particular person; in psychoanalysis, the conception of the personality in terms of id, ego, and superego.

Phallic stage. The third stage in development, according to psychoanalytic theory, during which the child becomes interested in his sexual organs and forms a romantic attachment (Oedipus complex) to the parent of the opposite sex.

Phase difference. The difference in pressure (negative or positive) between two tones at any particular instant. A tone coming from a person's left, for example, and heard simultaneously by the two ears, is in a different part of its cycle of vibration when it strikes the left ear than when it strikes the right ear. Consequently, there is a phase difference between the two ears.

Phenomenology. The study of the phenomena of human experience and behavior without elaboration or analysis into elements.

Phenylpyruvic oligophrenia. A type of feeble-mindedness that is inherited and that is caused by a lack of an enzyme for utilizing phenylpyruvic acid, a product of brain metabolism. It is recognized by the presence of phenylpyruvic acid in the urine.

Philology. The study of the history and development of languages.

Phobia. An intense, irrational fear, usually acquired through conditioning to an unpleasant object or situation.

Phoneme. A speech sound that is distinguishable from other speech sounds used in a particular language.

Phonetics. The study of the sounds made in speech.

Photochromatic interval. The interval of intensities, representing the difference between rod and cone sensitivities, in which light but not color is perceived.

Photosensitive substances. Chemical substances in the rods and cones of the retina that are decomposed by light and initiate the visual process.

Physiological needs. Needs arising from some lack or deficit in the body, as distinguished from acquired needs (*q.v.*).

Pictorial display. A display that reproduces with some realism the situation it represents. *Cf.* Symbolic display.

Pinna. The part of the external ear that protrudes from the head; the structure which in common parlance is called simply the ear.

Pitch. A psychological attribute of tones, related to frequency but not directly proportional to it.

Pitch scale. A curve depicting the relationship between physical frequency and perceived pitch.

Pituitary gland. A gland located beneath the hypothalamus that secretes a number of hormones which stimulate or inhibit other glands of the body. It also secretes a growth hormone that controls general rate of growth of the body.

Place theory. A theory of pitch, widely accepted, that assumes different places on the basilar membrane (*q.v.*) to be activated by different frequencies of a sound stimulus.

Plateau. A flat portion in a learning curve (*q.v.*) representing a temporary slowing of progress in learning.

Play therapy. A technique for the study of personality and for the treatment of personality problems in children. It permits the child to express his conflicts in play. *See also* Release therapy.

Point-to-point projection. *See* Topographical arrangement.

Polarized membrane. The membrane of a nerve fiber that has an excess of positive ions on its outside and an excess of negative ions on its inside. In the passage of the nerve impulse, this polarized membrane is temporarily depolarized.

Poll question. The type of question, used in

public-opinion polls, that gives the respondent a fixed number of alternatives.

Polydipsia. Drinking abnormally large quantities of water.

Positive transfer. More rapid learning in one situation because of previous learning in another situation. It is due to a similarity of the stimuli and/or responses required in the two situations.

Posthypnotic suggestion. Suggestion made by the hypnotist while a person is in a hypnotic trance but carried out after his awakening from the trance.

Power. In psychological usage, the ability to control or influence the behavior of others; a social need.

Power test. A test not limited in time, or a test having a nominal time limit, designed to measure ability, irrespective of speed of taking the test. *Cf.* Speed test.

Predisposition. In the study of personal adjustment, a tendency that is inherited or has a biological basis to develop certain personality disorders. Some individuals, for example, seem to have a biological predisposition for schizophrenia.

Prefrontal areas. *See* Frontal association area.

Prefrontal lobotomy. The surgical interruption of pathways from the frontal association areas, often performed in extreme cases of mental disorder after other forms of therapy have failed. The operation, sometimes called psychosurgery, tends to allay anxiety and worry.

Prehension. The grasping of objects with the hands, the fingers, or (in the case of some monkeys) the tail.

Prejudice. Literally, a prejudgment; more generally, an emotionally toned attitude for or against an object, person, or group of persons. Typically, it is a hostile attitude that places a person or group at a disadvantage.

Premotor area. An area of the cerebral cortex lying just in front of the motor area. It is concerned with posture and the execution of skilled movements.

Prenatal. Before birth.

Presbyopia. Oldsightedness; farsightedness of advancing age.

Prestige. The feeling of being better than other persons with whom one compares oneself. The prestige need is a social need

to achieve prestige. The need is frequently exploited with propaganda and social techniques.

Prestriate area. An area of the cerebral cortex lying near the primary visual area, concerned in visual memory.

Primary feeble-mindedness. Feeble-mindedness having no known organic basis. Usually it is correlated with feeble-mindedness in other members of the family and is therefore considered to have a hereditary basis. Sometimes it is called familial feeble-mindedness. *Cf.* Secondary feeble-mindedness.

Primary goal. The unlearned goal of a physiological or general drive, e.g., food or water. *See also* Primary reinforcement.

Primary group. A small group with which a person has frequent informal contacts, such as family, friends, associates.

Primary reinforcement. In conditioning, the presentation of the unconditioned stimulus immediately following the conditioning stimulus; in instrumental learning, the presentation of an incentive satisfying a physiological motive immediately following the instrumental response.

Primary sensory area. An area of the cerebral cortex to which fibers transmit impulses from the receptors of a particular sense. There are primary sensory areas for each of the senses except pain, the vestibular sense, and smell.

Primates. Monkeys, man, and closely related species of animals.

Proactive inhibition. *See* negative transfer.

Programmed learning. Self-instruction by means of a carefully designed series of questions which, through immediate reinforcement, motivates and enhances the learning process. *See also* Teaching machine.

Projection. The disguising of a source of conflict by ascribing one's own motives to someone else; prominent in paranoia.

Projective methods. Methods used in the study of personality, in which a subject is presented with a relatively ambiguous stimulus and asked to describe it in a meaningful way or to tell a story about it.

Prolactin. A hormone secreted by the pituitary gland. It stimulates the development of the breasts and is concerned in maternal behavior.

Propaganda. The deliberate attempt to influence attitudes and beliefs.

Protanope. A partially color-blind person who is unable to distinguish red and green and who is also weak in sensitivity to the red end of the spectrum. *Cf.* Deuteranope, Tritanope.

Pseudo conditioning. The strengthening of a response by prior presentation of some alerting stimulus, e.g., a siren; not true conditioning. *See also* Sensitization.

Pseudo-isochromatic plates. Plates consisting of colored dots so arranged that the color-blind person sees either no pattern at all or a different pattern of dots from the normal person. They are used as a test for color blindness.

Pseudo words. Words constructed by choosing letters at random according to the frequency with which these letters are used in language and to the probability of one particular letter following another.

Pseudophone. A device used in experiments on perception to reverse the reception of sound by the two ears. It carries sound normally reaching the right ear to the left ear, and vice versa.

Psychasthenia. An emotional disturbance characterized by irrational thoughts and/or strong compulsions (*q.v.*) to repeat seemingly meaningless acts.

Psychiatry. A branch of medicine specializing in the diagnosis and treatment of mental illness.

Psychoanalysis. Primarily a method of psychotherapy developed by Sigmund Freud, but also a theory of the development and structure of personality. As a psychotherapy, it is rather nondirective in approach and emphasizes the techniques of free association (*q.v.*) and the phenomenon of transference (*q.v.*).

Psychodrama. A specialized technique of psychotherapy in which patients act out the roles, situations, and fantasies relevant to their personal problems. Psychodrama is usually conducted in front of a small audience of patients.

Psychograph. A profile of traits and abilities involved in the performance of a job. *See also* Individual psychograph, Job psychograph.

Psychology. The science that studies the behavior of animals and human beings.

Psychomotor test. A test involving movement and coordination; usually a vocational-aptitude test.

Psychoneurosis. *See* Neurosis.

Psychopathic deviate. An individual with a personality disorder characterized by antisocial, amoral conduct.

Psychopharmacology. The study of the effects of drugs on behavior and psychological functions.

Psychosis. A mental or personality disorder, more severe than a neurosis (*q.v.*) and often requiring custodial care.

Psychosomatic illness. A bodily disorder precipitated or aggravated by emotional disturbance.

Psychosurgery. *See* Prefrontal lobotomy.

Psychotherapeutic drug. A drug having beneficial effects in treating mental illness or emotional disturbances.

Psychotherapy. The treatment of mental illness and mild adjustment problems by means of psychological techniques. *Cf.* Medical therapy.

Psychotomimetic drug. A drug that induces some of the symptoms of psychosis.

Public-opinion poll. A method of surveying opinions on certain issues by selecting a sample of the population and interviewing each member of the sample.

Punctate sensitivity. In the study of the skin senses, greater sensitivity in certain spots of the skin than in others. It is a phenomenon that distinguishes four primary senses among the skin senses.

Punishment. The application of an unpleasant stimulus for the purpose of eliminating undesirable behavior.

Pupil. The aperture through which light is admitted to the eye; altered in size by the action of the iris muscles.

Pure tone. A simple sine-wave tone.

Purkinje effect. A change in the perception of color as the eye shifts from daylight to twilight levels of adaptation.

Q

Quota sampling. A method of sampling (*q.v.*) in which the polling agency sets quotas for certain categories, such as age, sex, and socioeconomic status, and then permits the interviewer to select the particular individuals who satisfy the quota requirements.

R

Race. A group of human beings having common and distinctive innate physical characteristics.

Random noise. A noise consisting of a random mixture of many different frequencies that are not multiples or harmonics of each other.

Random sampling. Selecting samples of individuals, objects, or measurements solely by chance. *See also* Sampling.

Range. The difference between the highest score and the lowest score in a frequency distribution. It is a crude measure of the variability of a distribution.

Rank-difference correlation. A method of computing correlation when individuals have been separately ranked on two different variables. Symbol: ρ

RAS. *See* Reticular activating system.

Rating. A general term for the method in which a judge or observer rates the amount of aptitude, interest, ability, or other characteristic that an individual is considered to have.

Ratio scale. A scale in which equal ratios may be regarded as equal, e.g., $4:2 = 10:5$.

Rationalization. The interpretation of one's own behavior so as to conceal the motive it expresses and to assign the behavior to some other motive.

Reaction formation. The disguising of a motive so completely that it is expressed in a form that is directly opposite to its original intent.

Reaction time. The time from the onset of a stimulus until the organism responds.

Reality principle. In personal adjustment, the principle of setting attainable goals and of finding practicable ways of eliminating motivational conflicts and hence of satisfying motives; in psychoanalysis, a function served by the ego.

Reasoning. Thinking in which one attempts to solve a problem by combining two or more elements from past experience.

Recall. A method of measuring retention in which the subject must reproduce with a minimum of cues something that he has previously learned.

Receptive disorder. A general term for a disorder, usually caused by brain damage, in which a person cannot recognize or remember the meaning of sensory stimuli, such as words or familiar objects. *Cf.* Expressive disorder.

Receptive field. The area from which a neuron receives impulses. Because many sensory neurons often make synapse with a single association neuron, the latter may have a relatively large field from which it receives impulses.

Recessive gene. A gene whose hereditary characteristics are not expressed when it is paired with a dominant gene (*q.v.*).

Reciprocal inhibition. The relaxation of a muscle simultaneously with the contraction of its antagonist.

Recognition. A method of measuring retention in which the subject is required only to recognize the correct answer when it is presented to him along with incorrect answers, e.g., in a true-false or multiple-choice examination.

Recollection. A general term meaning about the same thing as recall, i.e., remembering past events and their related circumstances.

Recurrent nerve circuit. An endless loop made by the synapses of neurons, permitting nerve impulses to circle back to the point from which they originate.

Reflex. A relatively rapid and consistent unlearned response to a stimulus. It is ordinarily not conscious or subject to voluntary control.

Reflex reserve. The total number of learned responses that can be expected to occur during a prolonged extinction (*q.v.*).

Refractory period. A brief period during and after the discharge of a nerve impulse when unusually strong stimuli are required to evoke another impulse.

Regression. A retreat to earlier or more primitive forms of behavior, frequently encountered in children and adults faced with frustration.

Regulatory behavior. Behavior that aids in maintaining a homeostatic balance by leading to the satisfaction of physiological needs.

Reinforcement. *See* Primary reinforcement, Secondary reinforcement.

Release therapy. Similar to play therapy (*q.v.*); useful with older children and adults. It may consist of finger painting, games, or other unstructured activities. It general purpose is to permit the expression of deep-seated motivational conflicts.

Releasers. Stimulus situations that trigger instinctive (*q.v.*) movements.

Reliability. The self-consistency of a method of measurement, or the degree to which separate, independent measurements of the same thing agree with each other. Reliability is usually expressed by a coefficient of correlation (*q.v.*) representing the relationship between two sets of measurements of the same thing. *See also* Validity.

Replacement therapy. Compensation for the effects of gland removal or deficiency by administration of the gland's hormone.

Representative sampling. Sampling (*q.v.*) so as to obtain a fair cross section of a population without introducing biases that make the sample unrepresentative.

Repression. A psychological process in which memories and motives are not permitted to enter consciousness but are operative at an unconscious level. Repression is one of several reactions to frustration and anxiety. It serves as a means of altering conscious motives and goals.

Resistance. A phenomenon observed in psychotherapy, exhibited as an inability to remember important events in one's past or to talk about certain anxiety-charged subjects. Resistance may be indicated by a blocking of free associations or by a person's steering away from certain subjects during free association (*q.v.*).

Resistance to stress. The second stage of the general-adaptation syndrome in which a person endures stress without showing any observable impairment.

Respondent conditioning. *See* Classical conditioning.

Resting potential. An electrical difference, found in the inactive nerve fiber, between the outside and the inside of the polarized membrane. It is temporarily abolished during the passage of a nerve impulse.

Retention. The amount correctly remembered. The principal methods of measuring retention are savings, recognition, and recall.

Reticular activating system (RAS). A network of cell bodies and fibers extending through the medulla, midbrain, hypothalamus and thalamus, forming an indirect sensory pathway to the cerebral cortex.

Retina. The photosensitive layer of the eye on which images of objects are projected. It contains receptors, known as rods and cones, and nerve cells that convey impulses to the brain.

Retinal disparity. A slight difference in the images of an object projected on the retinas of the two eyes. It arises from the fact that the two eyes view the object from slightly different angles.

Retinene. A breakdown product of the photosensitive substances involved in vision.

Retroactive inhibition. The harmful effect of learning or activity on the retention of previous learning; a special case of negative transfer (*q.v.*).

Rhodopsin. A photosensitive substance found in the rods of man and many animals.

Rod. A photosensitive receptor in the retina, long and cylindrical like a rod, and most sensitive in nighttime conditions of seeing. It is probably not involved in color vision.

Role. A pattern of behavior that a person in a particular social status (*q.v.*) is expected to exhibit.

Rotary pursuitmeter. A device used in human learning experiments that requires the subject to keep a stylus on a moving spot while the spot rotates on a circular platform.

Rotation nystagmus. Movement of the eyes, slowly in one direction and quickly in the other, caused by rotation of the head.

S

Safety needs. According to Maslow, needs for security, stability, and order that are less important than physiological needs but take precedence over needs for belonging, esteem, and self-actualization.

Sampling. The process of selecting a set of individuals or measurements from a large population of possible individuals or measurements. Almost all frequency distributions in psychology are samples. *See also* Controlled sampling, Quota sampling, Random sampling, Representative sampling.

Sampling error. The error due to chance differences in selecting a sample from a population.

Saturation. A dimension of color that refers to the amount or richness of a hue, as distinguished from brightness or hue (*q.v.*); e.g., a red that is barely distinguishable from a gray is low in saturation.

Savings. A method of measuring retention in which the subject learns again what he previously learned. Savings are measured by the difference between the number of trials or errors originally required to learn and the number required in relearning.

Scale of measurement. In general, a set of numbers assigned to some aspect of objects or events according to some rule. The term is also used in a more limited sense to refer to a well-standardized test, such as the Wechsler Intelligence Scale for Children.

Scale value. In the measurement of attitudes, a number assigned to a statement representing the degree to which approval or disapproval of the statement indicates a favorable or unfavorable attitude toward the subject of the statement.

Scapegoating. The displacement of aggression to a convenient group or class. It is a defense mechanism that operates as a prejudice against racial, religious, or other groups.

Scatter diagram. A plot of the scores made by the same individuals on two different variables providing a visual picture of the degree of correlation between the variables.

Schizophrenia. One of the psychoses, characterized by fantasy, regression, hallucinations, delusions, and general withdrawal from contact with the person's environment.

Scholastic aptitude. Ability to succeed in some specified type of formal schooling. For example, college aptitude refers to aptitude for doing college work.

Sclerotic coat. The white outermost coat of the eyeball. It gives way in the front of the eye to the transparent cornea.

Secondary feeble-mindedness. Feeble-mindedness due to birth injury, to disease, or to damage in the brain. *Cf.* Primary feeble-mindedness.

Secondary goal. A goal learned through association with a primary goal. *See also* Secondary reinforcement.

Secondary reinforcement. The reinforcing effect of a stimulus that has been paired with a primary reinforcement (*q.v.*).

Security. The feeling of being safe against loss of status, friends, loved ones, income, etc. The need to feel secure is an important social need.

Self-actualization. According to Maslow, the highest need in man's hierarchy of needs; the name for Maslow's motivational theory of personality.

Self-selection. Selection of specific foods when offered in cafeteria feeding (*q.v.*).

Self-stimulation. Central stimulation, usually electrical, of the brain, administered by the animal's pressing a bar or switch.

Semantic differential. A method of measuring the meaning of a concept in which the person rates the concept on one or more bipolar scales.

Semantics. The study of the meaning of words and sounds.

Semicircular canals. Three canals found near the cochlea in each ear. They are sensitive to rotation and to changes in the position of the head; they are part of the vestibular sense.

Senile psychosis. An organic psychosis that tends to appear in some individuals with advancing age; characterized by defects of memory, general disorientation, and delusions. *See also* Alcoholic psychosis.

Sensitization. A phenomenon similar to learning in which a response is facilitated by an intense or unpleasant stimulus. For example, an animal that has become habituated to a loud sound may again show fright if the sound is preceded by an electric shock.

Sensory area. An area of the brain concerned in sensory functions. It is usually an area of the cerebral cortex. *See also* Primary sensory area.

Sensory neuron. A neuron that conveys nerve impulses away from sense organs into the central nervous system. It usually has its cell body in a ganglion just outside the central nervous system.

Sensory scale. A curve or function showing the relationship of perceived magnitude to physical units of stimulation, usually intensity.

Septum. A midline structure of the brain near the corpus collosum, concerned in emotion.

Serial anticipation. A learning method in which items are arranged in a series and the subject must anticipate the next item in the series.

Serial learning. Learning to make a series of responses in exact order.

Serial-position effect. The effect of the position of an item in a series on the rate of learning the item. The middle items in a series are usually the most difficult.

Set. A readiness to react in a certain way when confronted with a problem or stimulus situation.

Sex differences. Differences between men and women in interests, abilities, etc.

Sex hormones. Hormones secreted by the gonads and responsible for secondary sex characteristics such as the male's beard and the female's breasts. They are involved in sexual motivation.

Sex-linked characteristic. A hereditary characteristic controlled by a gene carried on the chromosome that determines sex, for example, color blindness (*q.v.*).

Shape constancy. The tendency to perceive the "true" shape of an object even when the image on the retina is distorted. For example, a circle is seen as a circle even when viewed at an acute angle.

Shock therapy. The treatment of mental disorder by some agent causing convulsion and/or coma. Such agents include insulin, metrazol, and electric shock to the brain.

Sibling. A brother or sister.

Sign. Any stimulus that stands for something else. *See also* Symbol.

Signal. A stimulus used to indicate that the time and place for something to happen is at hand.

Significance. A probability statement of the likelihood of obtaining a given difference or correlation between two sets of measurements by chance.

Sine wave. The simplest kind of sound wave, generated by a vibrating object moving back and forth freely like a pendulum. *See also* Fourier analysis.

Situation test. A test in which a person is observed in some real-life situation, e.g., in managing a group of men in the building of a small bridge.

Situational therapy. The treatment of a personality problem by changing the person's situation—his work, his way of life, or his relationships with family and associates.

Size constancy. The tendency to perceive the size of familiar objects as constant even when viewed at a distance that makes the image of them on the retina very small. For example, a man 100 feet away is perceived as being as large as the same man nearby.

Skewness. The degree to which a frequency distribution departs from a symmetrical shape. The curve of a distribution that has its longer tail on the right is said to be skewed to the right.

Skin senses. The senses of pain, warmth, cold, and pressure located in the skin.

Sleep center. A center in the hypothalamus whose destruction results in chronic insomnia. Animals in which the sleep center has been destroyed stay awake until they die of exhaustion. *Cf.* Waking center.

Smell prism. A three-dimensional diagram representing six primary odors and their mixture.

Smooth muscle. Muscle that under the microscope exhibits no stripes. It is found in blood vessels, intestines, and certain other organs. *Cf.* Striped muscle.

Social anthropology. The social or behavioral science that studies cultural customs, habits, and beliefs, chiefly of primitive societies but also of modern societies and communities.

Social approval. A common, frequently strong motive in human beings.

Social attitude. An attitude held in common with a number of other persons, as distinguished from personal attitudes, which may be unique to a single individual.

Social class. A grouping of people on a scale of prestige in a society according to their social status. It is determined by many factors, such as nature of occupation, kind of income, moral standing, family genealogy, social relationships and organizations, and area of residence.

Social facilitation. Increased motivation and effort arising from the stimulus provided by other people.

Social group. Any group of people, formal or informal, assembled or dispersed, who are related to each other by some common interest or attachment. When a social group is defined in a more limited sense as people in a face-to-face relationship, other dispersed groups such as unions are defined as social organizations or institutions.

Social institution. A collection of objects, customary methods of behavior, and techniques of enforcing such behavior on individuals, e.g., a union, an army, or a political party.

Social maturity. The degree of development of social and vocational abilities. It may be measured by the Vineland Social Maturity Scale, from which a social-maturity quotient can be computed in much the same way as an intelligence quotient is obtained.

Social needs. Needs, usually learned, that require the presence or reaction of other people for their satisfaction. *See also* Affiliative needs, Status needs.

Social psychology. A field of specialization concerned with attitudes, beliefs, and psychological factors in group behavior.

Social structure. A general term referring to the fact that each society typically assigns ranks to its members, expects them to do certain kinds of work and to have certain attitudes and beliefs.

Social technique. Behavior that makes use of other people to achieve satisfaction of a need.

Social value. A learned goal involving one's relationship to society and other people.

Social worker. A person with advanced training in sociology, abnormal psychology, and social science, who investigates the family and social background of persons with personality problems and who assists the psychotherapist by maintaining contact with a patient and his family. The social worker is often a member of a psychiatric team consisting also of psychiatrists and clinical psychologists.

Socialization. Learning to behave in a manner prescribed by one's family and culture and to adjust in relationships with other people.

Society. A group of individuals, as large as several countries or as small as a portion of a community, that have a distinguishable culture.

Sociogram. A diagram showing preferences and aversions among members of a group; a way of depicting the structure of an informal group.

Sociometric test. A set of ratings made by members of a group, from which a sociogram may be constructed.

Sodium amytal. A drug that, given in light doses, tends to make a person talk more freely. It is sometimes used as a "truth drug" and as a means, in psychotherapy, of making withdrawn patients temporarily more communicative.

Somatic system. The part of the nervous system serving the sense organs and the skeletal muscles.

Somesthesis. The senses of the skin and of kinesthesis.

Somnolence. A tendency to sleep all the time.

Sone. A subjective unit of loudness.

Sound-pressure level (SPL). The intensity of a tone expressed in decibels (*q.v.*) above a reference level.

Sound wave. Alternating increases and decreases in pressure propagated through a medium, usually air. It may be regarded as a vibration having a certain frequency (or wavelength) and a certain intensity.

Spaying. *See* Ovariectomy.

Specific hunger. A hunger for a specific kind of food. *See also* Cafeteria feeding.

Spectral-absorption curve. A curve representing the absorption, and hence the sensitivity, of a photochemical substance at different wavelengths.

Spectral sensitivity. Sensitivity of the eye, often measured by the absolute threshold (*q.v.*), at different wavelengths of the spectrum.

Speed test. A test limited in time and favoring the person who can do tasks quickly. *Cf.* Power test.

Sphincter. Smooth muscle whose action controls elimination from such organs as the stomach, bladder, and bowels.

Spinal cord. The part of the nervous system encased in the backbone. It is a reflex center and a pathway for impulses to and from the brain.

SPL. *See* sound-pressure level.

Spontaneous discrimination. A discrimination learned without any specific learning procedure and without any identifiable reinforcement.

S-R association. Stimulus-response association; a learned connection between a stimulus and a response.

S-S association. Stimulus-stimulus or sensory-sensory association; a learned association between two stimuli.

Standard deviation. A precise measure of the variability of a frequency distribution (*q.v.*), computed by squaring the deviation of each score from the arithmetic mean (*q.v.*), summing the resulting squares, dividing by the number of scores, and finally taking the square root of the resulting quantity. In other words, it is the root-mean-square of the deviations from the mean. Symbol: σ.

Standard score. In the strict sense, a score equivalent to a z score, but often a score obtained by multiplying a z score by an arbitrary constant (e.g., 10 or 20) and adding the result to an arbitrary mean (e.g., 50 or 100). It permits a direct comparison with scores made by a standardization group.

Standardization. The establishment of uniform conditions for administering a test and interpreting test results. A large number of individuals are tested in the same way to provide norms (*q.v.*) with which to compare any particular test score.

Standardization group. The group of people on which a test is standardized. To interpret individual scores on a test, one should know the characteristics of the standardization group.

Startle pattern. An extremely rapid reaction to a sudden, unexpected stimulus (e.g., a gunshot), relatively consistent from person to person. It consists in part of a closing of the eyes, a widening of the mouth, and a thrusting forward of the head and neck.

Static senses. The part of the vestibular senses responding to gravity and to position of the head.

Status. In motivation, a social motive; in a social structure, a position representing differences that are important in the exchange of goods and services and in the satisfaction of needs in a society. *See also* Role.

Status needs. Needs to achieve a status with respect to other people in a group. They include more specific needs, such as needs for prestige, power, and security.

Stereotype. A fixed set of greatly oversimplified beliefs that are held generally by members of a group.

Stimulus. Any object, energy, or energy change in the physical environment that excites a sense organ.

Stimulus generalization. The tendency to react to stimuli that are different from, but somewhat similar to, the stimulus used as a conditioning stimulus.

Striped muscle. Muscle that, under the microscope, appears to be striped. It is found in the muscles of the skeleton, such as those that move the trunk and limbs. *Cf.* Smooth muscle.

Subcortical centers. Centers of the brain below the cerebral cortex.

Subitizing. Perceiving at a glance the number of objects present. Many animals and people can subitize objects up to approximately seven.

Sublimation. The use of a substitute activity to gratify a frustrated motive. Freud believed, for example, that a frustrated sex drive could be partially gratified by channeling it into some aesthetic activity.

Subliminal perception. Perception of a stimulus or some feature of a stimulus, as measured by a response, without conscious awareness of the perception.

Subvocal speech. Talking that is inaudible to others, but sufficiently stimulating (kinesthetically) to oneself to permit an internal conversation. It is one kind of implicit response involved in thinking.

Suggestion. The uncritical acceptance of an idea. Suggestion is used in psychotherapy to effect temporary relief of neurotic symptoms, particularly hysterical symptoms. It is also used generally by propagandists and advertisers to change or maintain attitudes and beliefs.

Sulcus. A crevice in the cerebral cortex; sometimes called a fissure. *See also* Central sulcus, Lateral sulcus.

Superego. In psychoanalytic theory, that

which restrains the activity of the ego and the id (*q.v.*). The superego corresponds closely to what is commonly called conscience; it keeps a person working toward ideals acquired in childhood.

Superiority. According to Adler, a major striving of the person. Failure to achieve superiority may generate an inferiority complex.

Superstition. A belief concerning natural phenomena that is widely held but is demonstrably false.

Supportive therapy. Treatment of a personality problem by listening to a person's problems, suggesting courses of action, and reassuring him about what he has done or proposes to do. Such therapy may be effective in mild or temporary disturbances. *Cf.* Insight therapy.

Survey methods. Methods of collecting data by sampling a cross section of people, e.g., questioning a large number of married couples about factors in marital happiness, or conducting a public-opinion poll; distinguished from experimental methods.

Survey Q3R. A method of study in which the sequence is survey, question, read, recite, and review.

Symbol. A stimulus that represents something else by reason of relationship, association, convention, etc. A symbol may be an external stimulus, e.g., a spoken word, or an internal process, e.g., an image involved in thinking. The latter may also be called a symbolic process (*q.v.*).

Symbolic display. Any means of presenting information indirectly, as by a dial, pointer, or light. *Cf.* Pictorial display.

Symbolic process. A representative process standing for previous experience; essential in thinking.

Sympathetic system. A subdivision of the autonomic system most concerned in emotional states. It mobilizes the body for action and acts antagonistically to the parasympathetic system (*q.v.*).

Synapse. The juncture of two neurons. It is not a direct connection, but rather a place where the fibers of the two neurons come into close proximity with one another.

Syndrome. A pattern of personality characteristics and their underlying causes in the life history of the person.

T

T score. *See* Standard score.

Tabes dorsalis. One type of syphilitic infection of the central nervous system, principally of the spinal cord, in which pathways of the kinesthetic senses degenerate.

Taboos. The do's and don't's of a particular society, strongly inculcated into most members of that society.

Taxis. An unlearned, directed reaction to a stimulus in which the animal moves toward or away from the stimulus. *Cf.* Kinesis.

Teaching machine. A mechanical or electronic device which presents programmed material. *See also* Programmed learning.

Telephone theory. A theory of pitch that assumes that frequencies of impulses in the auditory nerve represent frequencies of the sound stimulus.

Temperament. The aspects of personality pertaining to mood, activity, general level of energy, interest in food, exercise, and intellectual activities.

Temporal lobe. The part of the cerebral cortex lying on the side of the head beneath the lateral fissure. It contains centers for hearing, speech perception, and related memories.

Temporal maze. A maze so constructed that the subject keeps returning to the same choice point but must turn left or right each time according to some sequence established by the experimenter. Such a maze has been used in conjunction with the alternation method, in which a sequence of simple or double alternation (*q.v.*) is required.

Test. A sample of the performance of a person on a task or set of tasks.

Thalamus. An area in the forebrain concerned with relaying nerve impulses to the cerebral cortex.

Theory. In science, a principle or set of principles that explains a number of facts and predicts future events and outcomes of experiments.

Therapy. The treatment of an illness. *See also* Medical therapy, Psychotherapy.

Thiamin. Vitamin B_1. It is concerned in the utilization of sugars by the brain.

Thinking. Processes that are representative of previous experience; consisting of images, minute muscle movements, and other activities in the central nervous system. *See also* Image, Implicit response.

Thirst. A drive stemming from a physiological need for water.

Thought experiment. A type of experiment employed by early experimental psychologists in an attempt to discover the nature of thought. *See also* Imageless thought.

Threshold. *See* Absolute threshold, Differential threshold.

Thyroid gland. An endocrine gland in the neck, which produces the hormone thyroxin.

Thyroxin. The hormone secreted by the thyroid gland. It controls the general rate at which energy is produced in the body; it is a regulator of metabolism.

Timbre. The tonal quality that enables us to distinguish different musical instruments and voices having the same fundamental frequency. It is determined by the frequencies comprising a sound, especially the harmonics.

Tonotopic organization. A topographical arrangement of auditory areas of the brain corresponding to different parts of the cochlea and consequently to different frequencies of stimulation.

Topographical arrangement. A spatial arrangement of the nervous system that corresponds to a similar arrangement of the sense organs or of the muscles of the body. Cortical areas for the various senses and for motor functions are topographically arranged.

Trace process. A memory lasting for a brief period and serving as a stimulus-cue.

Trade test. An achievement test that measures a person's knowledge of important elements in his trade.

Trait. An aspect of personality that is reasonably characteristic of a person and distinguishes him in some way from many other people.

Transfer of training. More rapid learning in one situation because of previous learning in another situation (positive transfer, *q.v.*); or slower learning in one situation because of previous learning in another situation (negative transfer, *q.v.*). *See also* Stimulus generalization.

Transference. In psychotherapy and especially psychoanalysis, the reenactment of previous relationships with people and principally of the parent-child relationship. In psychoanalysis, the therapist becomes the object of transference; the transference aids in the analysis because it permits the patient to express toward the therapist attitudes and feelings he has held toward other people.

Tranquilizer. Any one of several drugs used to reduce anxiety.

Trial and error. A phrase describing attempts to learn, or to solve a problem, by trying alternative possibilities and eliminating those that prove to be incorrect. Such behavior is characteristic of instrumental learning and is involved in some thinking.

Tritanope. A partially color-blind person who appears to be unable to see blue.

Truth serum. A narcotic drug such as sodium amytal used to make a person's past experiences and emotional difficulties more accessible to a therapist.

Tympanic membrane. Another name for eardrum.

Type. A class of individuals alleged to have a particular trait; but a concept not accepted as valid by psychologists because individuals cannot be grouped together into a few discrete classes.

Type-token ratio. The ratio of the number of different words a person uses to the total number of words in a sample of his speech or writing. It is one index of verbal diversification.

U

Unconscious motivation. Motivation that can be discerned in a person's behavior but that he cannot report and does not perceive.

Unconscious processes. Psychological processes or events of which a person is unaware.

Unique color. A pure color judged not to be tinged with any other hue. There are four unique colors: blue, green, yellow, and red.

V

Valence. A term proposed by Lewin to refer to the attraction or repulsion of a goal. It is indicated by a plus or minus sign. Goals with negative valences are those a person fears or tries to avoid; those with positive valences are those he seeks to attain.

Validity. The extent to which a method of measurement measures what it is supposed to measure. Validity is expressed in terms of a coefficient of correlation (*q.v.*) representing the relationship of a set of measurements to some criterion.

Value. A learned goal.

Variable. One of the conditions measured in an experiment. *See also* Dependent variable, Independent variable.

Vector. A term proposed by Lewin to mean the resultant of motivational forces when a person is attracted and/or repelled by different goals; in psychology, analogous to "vector" as used in physics.

Veg. A subjective unit of weightiness.

Verb-adjective ratio. The ratio of the number of verbs used to the number of adjectives used in a sample of speech or writing. It varies with conditions of measurements and with personality characteristics. It is one index of verbal diversification.

Verbal diversification. The degree to which different words and different constructions of words are employed in a person's language.

Vertebrates. Animals with segmented backbones. The group includes fishes, amphibia, reptiles, birds, and mammals.

Vestibular sense. The sense of balance and movement, consisting of two groups of sense organs: the semicircular canals and the otolith organs.

Vicarious trial and error (VTE). Behavior in which the organism substitutes partial responses, correct or incorrect, for completed, reinforced responses.

Visible spectrum. Those electromagnetic radiations that are visible, extending from less than 400 to nearly 800 millimicrons.

Visual acuity. Ability to discriminate fine differences in visual detail. It may be measured with the physician's eye chart or by more precise tests, such as the Landolt ring (*q.v.*) or parallel bars.

Visual cycle. The cycle of decomposition and regeneration of photosensitive substances in rod and cone vision.

Visual purple. *See* Rhodopsin.

Vitamin. A substance essential to metabolism but not manufactured in the body, so that it must be obtained in food.

Vocabulary. A general and somewhat vague term referring to the words a person knows. However, the words he can recognize are more numerous than those he uses; and those he uses in writing are more numerous than those he uses in everyday speech. Hence, size of vocabulary varies greatly with the circumstances under which it is measured.

Vocational aptitude. Aptitude for learning a specified vocation. For example, clerical aptitude is the ability to learn a clerical vocation.

VTE. *See* Vicarious trial and error.

W

Waking center. A center in the hypothalamus whose destruction results in somnolence. *Cf.* Sleep center.

Warming up. The tendency for the work curve to rise at the beginning of a period of work; opposite in effect to the beginning spurt (*q.v.*). It is a factor in the shape of the work curve.

White matter. Nerve fibers covered with a white sheath. The peripheral part of the spinal cord is white matter; so are several different regions of the brain. Its presence indicates tracts of nerve fibers, as distinguished from cell bodies. *Cf.* Gray matter.

Whole learning. Learning, usually in the sense of memorizing, in which the entire learning material is studied before going through it again. *Cf.* Part learning.

Word association. A method of testing or measuring in which a person is given a stimulus word and asked to respond with a word he associates with it.

Work curve. A line representing some measure of work for some given period of time.

Worker characteristics. The physical and psychological characteristics required of a person in a particular job. They are best stated in terms of the proportion of the population having the required degree of the characteristic.

Work-sample performance test. A test consisting of a sample of the work for which a person is being evaluated.

Y

Young-Helmholtz theory. The theory that human color vision depends on three receptors, a "blue" receptor, a "green" receptor, and a "red" receptor.

Z

z score. A score obtained by dividing the standard deviation (*q.v.*) into the deviation of an obtained score from the arithmetic mean (*q.v.*) of the frequency distribution (*q.v.*). It is convenient for the comparison of scores without regard to the units of measurement employed.

Name index

Subject index

American Council on Education (ACE) Psychological Examination, 444, 459
American Institute of Public Opinion, polls of, 549
American Psychologist, 27
Amnesia, 149, 150, 664
  case, 150
Amoeba, 664
Amphetamine, effects, 641
Amphibia, 664
Amplitude, 664
  of speech sounds, 395
Amplitude distortion, 665
  of speech, 395
Amygdala, 609, 664
  role in emotion, 625
Anal stage, 664
  in personality development, 490
Anal syndrome, 490
Anger, development, 107
  expression, 108
  as social technique, 111
  stimuli for, 111
Animal behavior and behaviorism, 9
Animal psychology, 23
Animals, complex processes in, 288
  as detectors, 24
  (*See also* specific animals)
Animistic reasoning, 280, 664
Annoyance, common, 108
Anomalous color defect, 348, 664
Anoxia, 664
  and feeble-mindedness, 637
Anticipation in maze learning, 218
Anxiety, 664
  accepting, 182
  bodily changes in, 117–120
  and frustration, 136
  and hostility, 113 .
  reduction with alcohol, 138
  sources, 113
Anxiety reactions, 144–147, 664
  case, 144
Anxiety theory of personality, 491
Apartheid program, 558
Aperiodic sound, 372, 664
Apes, 664
  language in, 39
  reared in darkness, 52
  (*See also* Chimpanzee; Monkey; Primates)
Aphasia, 288, 633, 634, 664
Apparent movement, 313, 665
Appetite (*see* Hunger)
Application blanks in employee selection, 564–566
Approach-approach conflict, 129, 665
Approach-avoidance conflict, 130, 665
Approach gradient, 132
Apraxia, 634, 665

Aptitude, 458–464, 665
  for logical thinking, 461
  scholastic, 458, 459
  vocational, 459–462
Aptitude tests, definition, 437
  in employee selection, 568
  use, 461
  validation, 460
Arapesh personality, 484
Area and block sampling, 665
Arithmetic mean, 412, 665
Armed Forces Qualification Test (AFQT), 444
Armed imperialism, attitudes toward, 531
Army Alpha Test, age differences on, 453
  of intelligence, 443
Army Beta Test, 443
Army General Classification Test (AGCT), 429
  as aptitude test, 459
  description, 443, 444
Art, definition, 2
Assertiveness and leadership, 523
Association, 665
  of concepts, 272
  in language development, 60
  in learning, 188
  and meaning, 257
  remote, 232
Association areas, 665
Association neuron, 603, 665
Association theory of learning, 190
Associationism, 188
Associative process, 665
Astigmatism, 340, 665
Atmosphere effect in reasoning, 280
Atomism, opposition to, 10
Attention, 665
  and perception, 299–332
  role of, 307–309
  shifting, 307
Attention-rejection, rating, 122
Attitude, 526–561, 665
  toward armed imperialism, 531
  change, 539–546
  definition, 112
  development, 529–534
  as emotional habit, 112
  measurement, 546–553
  nature, 526–529
  parental, 485
  and personality, 471
  preservation, 539
  toward products, 552
  of social classes, 509
Attitude scale, 546–548, 665
Attribute, 665
  of pitch, 369
  sensory, 303
Audience measurement, 553, 665
Audiogram, 382, 665

Deuteranope, 348, 670
Development, of behavior, 29–64
  of emotion, 101
  of organs, 44
  of personality, 481–485
  sensory motor, 53–56
  steps in, 44
  timing, 44
Deviation score, 670
Diabetes, hunger in, 73
Dials, shapes, 589
    design, 588
    patterning, 589, 590
Dichromatism, 348, 670
Dictionary of Occupational Titles, 563, 649
Differential reinforcement, 211, 670
Differential threshold, 670
  definition, 302
Direction of sounds, 279
Directive therapy, 171, 670
Discrimination, of auditory intensity, 376
  without awareness, 304
  of concepts, 271
  conditioned, 210
  after cortical lesions, 622
  of frequency, 376
  in language, 257
  in maze learning, 217
  and prestriate areas, 633
  sensory, 300–307
  spontaneous, 213
Discriminative learning, 211, 670
  in concept formation, 266
  physiological basis, 632
Diseases, psychosomatic, 119
Displacement, 141, 670
Display, 670
  design, 587–589
  of information, 586
Dissociative reaction, 149–151, 670
  (*See also* Amnesia; Multiple personality)
Dissonance, 378, 379
Distance perception in hearing, 381
Distortion, amplitude, of speech, 395, 665
  visual, 325, 326
Distress in infant, 103
Distribution, 670
  of measurements, 405–411
  of practice, 224, 225
Doctor's degree in psychology, 25
Dog, cortex, 618
  reared in isolation, 53
Dol, 670
Dominant characteristic, 31
Dominant gene, 31, 670
Dominator, 670
  in retina, 363
Double alternation, 291
Dream analysis, 670
  in psychoanalytic therapy, 175

Drive, 670
  and activity, 77
  definition, 66
  comparative strength, 84
  physiological, 68–77
  substitution, 93
Drive-reduction theory of learning, 190, 670
Drugs, and personality, 638–643
  tranquilizing, 120
Ducklings, imprinting in, 51
Dynamic range, 670
  of speech, 397

Ear, structure, 373–376
Eardrum, 373
Economic status (*see* Social classes; Socio-economic status)
Ectoderm, 44
Ectomorphy, 493
Education, and attitudes, 531
  psychology in, 21
  transfer in, 235
Educational psychology, 21, 670
EEG (electroencephalogram) 613, 624, 671
Effectors, 670
  classification, 596
Egg cell, 29
Ego, 489, 670
Eidetic imagery, 229, 230, 671
  and thinking, 261
Election prediction, 548
Electrical activity of retina, 360
Electrical recording from nervous system, 612, 613
Electrical stimulation, of brain, 630, 667
  of hypothalamus, 631
Electroencephalogram (EEG), 613, 624, 671
Electrolytic lesion, 612, 671
Electromagnetic radiation, 671
  as stimulus, 334
Electromagnetic spectrum, 335
Electroretinogram (ERG), 360, 671
Electroshock therapy, 168
Embryo, 671
Emotion, 100–126
  bodily states in, 113–120
  definition, 101
  development, 101
  differentiation, 102
  and hypothalamus, 625, 626
Emotional expression, 121–124, 184
  changes in, 105
Emotional habits, 109–113
Emotional motives, 109–113
Emotional situations, 123
  change in, 105
Empirical, 671
Empiricism in science, 4
Employee evaluation, 574
Employee selection, 562–570

Involutional melancholia, 677
  predisposition to, 482
Iodopsin, 358, 677
IQ (*see* Intelligence quotient)
Iris of eye, 335, 677
Ishihara test of color blindness, 349
Isolation, and development, 49
  of puppies, 53
  and sensory deprivation, 52

Job, 677
Job analysis, 563, 677
Job description, 563, 677
Job evaluation, 573, 677
Job psychograph, 677
  in employee selection, 568
Job satisfaction, 576–578
Johns Hopkins University Psychological Laboratory, 7
Jonesville study, 507
Just noticeable difference (jnd), 302, 677

Kinesis, 677
Kinesthesis, 301
Kinesthetic receptors, 301, 677
Kinesthetic senses, 322, 391
Kittens, sequential behavior in, 292
Knowledge of results, 225, 677
  in college study, 247
  with teaching machines, 248
  in work, 571
Kuder Preference Record as vocational interest test, 463, 464
Kwakiutl Indians, culture, 501
Kymograph, 677
  use in studying suggestibility, 478

Laboratories, psychological, 8
Laissez-faire group, 519
Landolt ring, 353, 677
Language, of bees, 289
  and communication, 281–288
  defective, 288
  disorders, 633, 634
  meaning, 285
  and social values, 91
  study, 281
  and thinking, 254–297
  units, 282
  use in supervision, 572
  (*See also* Speech perception)
Language development, 59–62
  in isolation, 49
Latent learning, 211–213, 677
Lateral fissure, 608, 677
Laughter, 123
  development, 105
Law, of contiguity, 189, 677
  of effect in learning, 190

Leaders, intelligence, 449
Leadership, 519–523
Learned drive, fear as, 89
Learned goal, 677
Learning, in animals, 5
  avoidance, 205–209
  curves, 222, 677
  definition, 187, 677
  of discriminations, 211
  of emotional reactions, 104
  factors in, 188–194
  human, 221–253
  by insight, 215
  instrumental, 199–205
  latent, 211
  maturation, 50
  of motives, 88
  and perception, 327
  perceptual, 210–215
  physiological basis, 631–636
  principles, 187–220
  programmed, 246–252
  reactions to frustration, 134
  of secondary goals, 89
  set, 276, 677
  stages in, 205
  two-factor theory, 206
  (*See also* Forgetting; Memory; Retention)
Learning to learn, 276
Learning principles in industry, 572
Learning program, 249
Lecture notes, taking, 245
Leipzig, University of, 7
Lens, accommodation, 339
Lesion, 678
  of nervous system, 612
Level, of aspiration, 97, 678
  of performance, 97, 678
Liberalism, attitudes, 532
Libido, 489
Lie detector, 678
  nature, 116
Life history use in therapy, 170
Light, 334, 678
  and visual acuity, 355
Light-compass reaction, 289, 678
Likert attitude scale, 547
Linear perspective, 678
  in depth perception, 314
Literary Digest poll, 551
Loaded words, 541, 678
Locomotion, development, 56
Logic, of measurement, 401
  rules, 279
Logical Analysis Device (LAD), 461
Logical reasoning, 277–281
Logical thinking, 279, 678
  aptitude for, 461
Longitudinal fissure, 608

Loudness, 678
  as attribute, 371
Lower senses, 367, 383–393
Luminosity, 678
Lysergic acid diethylamide (LSD-25) as hallucinogenic drug, 639

Machines, compared with man, 586, 587
  design, 587–592
Maladjustment, 678
Mammals, 678
  maternal pattern in, 38
Man compared with machines, 586, 587
Man-machine problems, 585
Man-to-man rating, 678
  of employees, 575
Manic-depressive psychosis, 678
  predisposition to, 482
Manipulative drive, 678
  in chimpanzees, 80
Market research, 548, 678
  polling in, 552
Marriage, and affiliation, 94
  study, 15
Masking, 678
  of sounds, 378
Massed practice, 224
Master's degree in psychology, 25
Maternal behavior, 678
  of rat, 37
Maternal drive, 76
  strength of, 85
Maturation, 678
  of behavior, 29–64
  concept, 43
  of emotions, 104
  of perception, 324
Maze, 678
  types, 215, 216
Maze learning, 215–219
Mean, 412, 678
Meaning, of concepts, 270
  in context, 286
  extensional, 285
  index, 286
  intentional, 285
  of language, 285
  of meaning, 257
  in visual memories, 229
Meaningfulness, in learning, 227
  of material, retention, 237
  of words, 231
Measurement, 678
  definition, 402
  kinds, 402–405
  method, 403
  in psychology, 401–434
  in science, 6
Measurements, distribution, 405–411

Measurements, prediction from, 429, 430
  uses, 405
Measures, of ability, 435–438
  of frequency distributions, 411–415
Mechanical-ability test, 460, 678
Median, 678
  as measure, 412
Median age of attaining skills, 55
Mediating process, 258, 679
  in thinking, 260
Medical therapy, 166, 679
  for mental illness, 167
Medulla, 607
Meissner corpuscle, 679
  of skin, 389
Mel, 369, 679
Memory disorders and brain function, 633
Memory images, 228
Memory processes, 228–234, 445
  (See also Forgetting; Learning; Retention)
Men and women, differences between, 452
Mental age (MA), 679
  concept, 439
  of mentally deficient, 447
  and reading readiness, 49
Mental deficiency, 447–449, 679
  (See also Feeble-mindedness)
Mental disease (see Mental disorder; Mental illness)
Mental disorder, 144–157, 679
  definition, 160
  and inheritance, 482
  and sensory isolation, 87
  (See also Mental illness)
Mental-faculty theory, 679
  of transfer, 236
Mental health, 679
  problems, 160–169
  and readjustment, 160–186
Mental-health movement, 165
Mental-health programs, 181
Mental hygiene, 679
Mental illness, 679
  diagnosis, 180
  prevalence, 161
  and social class, 162
Mentally gifted, 449–452
Mesoderm, 44
Mesomorphy, 493
Metabolism, 596, 679
Meter, 679
Method, of adjustment, 679
  clinical, 15
  experimental, 12
  of introspection, 8
  of natural observation, 6, 11
  of rating, 679
  survey, 14

716   SUBJECT INDEX

Metrazol, 679
  as therapy, 168
Mice, light motivation in, 79
Microelectrode, 679
  in study of nervous system, 613
Midbrain, 607, 679
Middle ear, 373, 679
Millimicron, 334, 679
Minnesota Multiphasic Personality Inventory
    (MMPI), description, 475
Mr. Biggott cartoons on racial prejudice, 557
MMPI, 475
Mode, 412, 679
  of adjustment, 473, 679
Modulator, 363, 679
  in retina, 363
Mongoloid, 637, 679
Monkey, avoidance learning, 209
  delayed response, 635
  sex drive, 75
  somnolence, 623
  ulcers, 118
Monocular, 679
Monocular cues in depth perception, 314
Moon illusion, 323
Moralistic attitudes, 536
Mores, 679
Moron, 447, 679
Mother surrogates for monkeys, 82
Motion pictures, apparent movement in, 313
Motion sickness, 393
Motivation, 679
  as aid in learning, 191
  changes in, with fatigue, 581, 582
  definition, 66
  in learning, 190
  mechanisms, 622–631
  nature, 65–68
  and perception, 329
  in problem solving, 273
  to study, 242
Motivational conflict, 112, 127–144, 680
Motivational cycle, 66
Motives, 680
  and adjustment, 183
  in attention, 309
  classification, 67, 473
  complex, 94–97
  conflict of, 128–134
  definition, 66
  modification, 87–94
  as personality characteristics, 472
  understanding, 183
Motor, definition, 53
Motor area, 680
  of cerebral cortex, 618
Motor development sequence, 54–56
Motor movement from stimulation, 614
Motor neuron, 603, 680

Motor unit, 604, 680
Mouth, dryness, and thirst, 70
Movement, and attention, 308
  in depth perception, 316
Müller-Lyer illusion, 300
Multiple determination, genetic, 33
Multiple personality, 680
  case, 150
Munsell Book of Color, 346, 347
Munsell system, 680
  of color, 346
Muscle activity in thinking, 263
Muscle sense, 367
Mutation, 34, 680
Myelin sheath, 680
  of neurons, 600
Myxedema, 637

Narcoanalysis, 169, 680
Narcosis in psychotherapy, 168
National Opinion Research Center, polls of, 549
National Science Foundation, surveys by, 19
National Science Foundation Register, 26
Nationalism, 680
Natural observation, 6, 680
  in psychoanalysis, 11
Natural sciences, training in, 25
Navaho Indians, personality, 484
Navy General Qualification Test (NGQT), 445
Near point of vision, 341
Nearsightedness, 340
Need, 680
  arousal with propaganda, 545
  definition, 66
  and food preference, 72
  physiological basis, 629–631
  and prejudice, 555
  and propaganda, 544
  self-actualization, 492
Need theory of personality, 492
Negative acceleration, 680
Negative correlation, scatter diagram, 420
Negative goal, definition, 67
  fear of, 79
Negative transfer, 235, 680
Negroes, attitudes toward, 533, 539, 554
  intelligence in, 457, 458
  prejudice toward, 556
Nerve, 606, 620, 680
Nerve fiber, 600, 680
Nerve deafness, 383, 680
Nerve impulse, 600–602, 680
Nervous system, 680
  development, 45
  methods of study, 610–615
  structure, 599–616
Neurasthenia, 680
  case, 145
Neuroanatomical methods, 611, 612

Neuron, 599–602, 680
  structure, 600
Neurosis, 144–151, 680
  definition, 144
  evidence, 161
  kind, and social class, 163
Neurotic need, 680
  concept, 491
Neurotic reactions, 144–151
Nominal measurement, 402
  correlation, 417
Nominal scale, 402, 680
Nondirective therapy, 173, 680
Nonsense figure, 230, 681
Nonsense form, 230, 231, 681
Nonsense material, retention, 237
Nonsense syllable, 230, 681
Normal curve, 408–411, 681
Norms, 681
  for development, 55
  group conformity to, 511
Nose structure, 383
Nucleus, 606, 681
Number, meaning, 402
Number factor in intelligence, 445

Obesity, neural structures in, 629, 630
Objects, perception, 309–313
Observation methods, 12
Obsession, 681
  definition, 146
Obsessive-compulsive reaction, 146–148, 681
Obstacles, internalizing, 131
Occipital lobe, 608, 681
Occupations, and abilities, 570
  and intelligence, 455
  social status of, 507
Ochlophobia, 146
Oddity method, 681
  of measuring concepts, 271
Odors, classification, 384
Oedipus complex, 490
Office of Strategic Services, personality testing in, 477
Office of Strategic Services Assessment Staff, 477, 656
Oldsightedness, 340, 681
Olfactorium, 681
Olfactory nerve, 620
Ommatidia, 681
Open-end question, 549, 681
Open-field tests, in monkeys, 83
  of rats, 102
Operant behavior, 200, 681
Opinion, 681
  discussion, 516
  measurement, 546–553
  relation to attitude, 529
Opinion effect on reasoning, 280
Opponent-colors theory, 362, 681

Opsin, 358, 681
Optic nerve, 338, 620, 681
Oral fixation, 490
Oral stage, 681
  of personality development, 490
Oral syndrome, 490
Order of skill in development, 55, 681
Orderliness in animals, 292
Ordinal measurement, 403
  correlation, 418
Ordinal scale, 403, 681
Organ of Corti, 374, 681
Organic psychosis, 152, 156, 157, 681
Organic senses, 367, 390, 681
Organization, study of, 15
Organizations, scientific, 18
Ossicles, 373, 682
Otis Self-Administering Test of Mental Ability (Otis SA), 444–446
Otolith organs, 391–393, 682
Output in work, 580
Oval window, 374, 682
Ovariectomy, 682
Ovaries, 598
Overcompensation, 491, 682
Ovum, 682
  period, 29, 44

Pacinian corpuscle, 682
  in kinesthesis, 390
Pain, from central stimulation, 626
  as drive, 68
  mechanism, 621
  sensitivity to, 389
Paired-associate learning, 240, 682
Paired comparisons, 403, 682
Pancreas (pancreatic gland), 597, 682
Papillae of taste buds, 386
Parallel bars, 682
  and visual acuity, 353
Paramecium, 682
Paranoia, 682
  measurement, 475
Paranoid reactions, 153
Paranoid schizophrenia, case, 155
Parasympathetic system, 682
  in emotion, 114
Parathormone, 597, 682
Parathyroid glands, 597, 682
Parents, role, in personality development, 485
  in prejudice, 554
Parietal association area, function, 632
Parietal lobe, 608, 682
Parrots, language in, 40
Part learning, 227, 682
Partial reinforcement, 202–205, 682
  and avoidance learning, 207
  of conditioned responses, 198
  and extinction, 203
Pay in employment, 576

Public-opinion poll, 685
Punctate sensitivity, 388, 685
Punishment, 685
    of anger, 111
    and avoidance learning, 207
    effectiveness, 207–210
    during extinction, 207
Pupil of eye, 335, 685
Pure tone, 368, 685
Purkinje effect, 351, 685

Quota sampling in polling, 552, 685

Raccoon, delayed reaction in, 260
Race, 553, 686
Racial attitudes, 553–559
Racial stereotypes, 528
Random noise, 373, 686
Random sampling, 686
    in measurement, 422
Range, 686
    as measure, 413
Rank as status motive, 95
Rank-difference correlation, 686
    coefficient, 431
Rank-ordering, 404
Rat, emotionality, 101
    food selection, 72
    hypotheses in, 214
    rigidity in, 135
Rating, 686
    of employees, 574
Rating scale, personality, 479
    temperament, 494
Ratio scale, 404, 686
Rationalization, 142, 686
Reaching movements, development, 56
Reaction formation, 140, 686
Reaction-getting habit, learning, 91
Reaction time, 605, 686
    braking, 408
Readiness for learning, 48
Reading, eye movements in, 356
    versus recitation, 226
Reading readiness and mental age, 49
Reality principle, 686
    in adjustment, 182
Reasoning, 277–281, 686
    distortions in, 280
Reasoning factor in intelligence, 445
Recall, 686
    and essay examinations, 246
    method, 236
Receptive disorder, 686
    and brain function, 634
Receptive field, 686
    of neurons, 603
Receptor, definition, 301
    processes in vision, 357–366

Receptor, sensitivity, 301
    smell, 383
    taste, 385
    (*See also* Sense organs; Senses)
Recessive characteristic, 32
Recessive gene, 31, 686
Reciprocal inhibition, 604, 686
Recitation, and reading, 226
    in study, 244
Recognition, 686
    method, 236
Recognition tests, examinations as, 246
Recollection, 686
Recommendation letters, 567
Recurrent nerve circuit, 604, 686
Reeducation in psychotherapy, 171
Reflex, 603, 604, 686
    and pain, 69
Reflex reserve, 686
    and extinction, 208
Refractory period, 602, 686
Regression, 686
    definition, 137
Regulatory behavior, 686
    in homeostasis, 68
Reinforcement, 687
    of conditioned response, 196
    and extinction, 206
    and frustration, 134
    gradient, 217
    implications, 204
    in instrumental learning, 201
    partial, 202–205
    and performance, 213
    principle, 196
    secondary, 201
Rejection by group, 514
Release therapy, 178, 687
Releasers, 687
Reliability, 687
    of tests, 424, 436
Religion and attitudes, 531
Remote associations, 232
    in verbal learning, 233
Repetition, and attention, 308
    in experiments, 12
Replacement therapy, 615, 687
Representative process, symbol, 254–257, 692
    thinking, 254–297, 693
Representative sampling, 421, 687
Repression, 687
    in avoidance-avoidance conflict, 130
    case, 139
    description, 138–140
    and forgetting, 242
    in hysterical reactions, 149
    of motives, 97
Research, in science, 5

Sensitivity, of eye, 334, 349–352
  to pressure, 389
  of skin, 388
  smell, 385
  taste, 386
Sensitization, 192, 688
Sensory areas of cerebral cortex, 621, 622, 688
Sensory associations in learning, 188
Sensory attribute, 369
Sensory centers of cortex, 619–621
Sensory deprivation and isolation, 52
Sensory discrimination, 300–307
Sensory experience in cortical centers, 621
Sensory ganglia, 606
Sensory isolation, effects, 86
Sensory magnitude versus physical magnitude, 304
Sensory motor development, 53–56
Sensory motor mechanisms, 617–622
Sensory-motor reflex arc, 603
Sensory neuron, 602, 688
Sensory scale, 303, 689
Sensory stimulation and activity, 78
Sentences, meaning, 287
Septum, 609, 689
  role in emotion, 625
  and self-stimulation, 628
Serial anticipation method, 230, 689
Serial learning, 230, 689
Serial-position effect, 689
  in verbal learning, 232
Set, 689
  and attention, 309
  definition, 262
  in problem solving, 273
Sex, and fear, 133
  and intelligence, 61
  and language development, 61
Sex determination, 32
Sex differences, 689
  in intelligence, 452
Sex drive, 74
  and activity, 77
  in humans, 76
  and marriage, 15
Sex glands, maturation, 46
Sex hormones, 689
  and motivation, 75
Sex-linked characteristics, 32, 689
Sexual behavior and hypothalamus, 629
Shadows in depth perception, 315
Sham drinking and thirst, 70
Shape constancy, 320, 689
Shock therapy, 168, 689
Siamese twins, sleep in, 74
Siblings, 689
  intelligence in, 41
Sign, 689
  and symbol, 254–257
Signal, 255, 689

Significance, 689
  of differences, 423
Similarity, in object perception, 310
  in transfer of training, 234
Sine wave, 368, 689
Situation test, 689
  of personality, 476
Situational therapy, 170, 689
Size and attention, 308
Size constancy, 321, 689
Skewed distributions, 411
Skewness, 689
  of distribution, 411
Skilled movements and motor cortex, 618
Skills, acquiring, 221–228
  development, 55
Skin senses, 367, 387–390, 689
  development, 54
Skin structure, 389
Skinner box, 200, 209
  and central stimulation, 627, 628
  extinction in, 203
Sleep, and arousal, 623
  as drive, 74
  loss and work, 582
  and retention, 239
Sleep center, 623, 689
Sleep deprivation, effects, 74
Sleep-tension, 122
Smell prism, 384, 689
Smell receptors, 384
Smell sensitivity, 385
Smiling, development, 105
Smooth muscle, 689
Snellen chart, 352
Social anthropology, 3, 689
Social approval, 689
  and attitudes, 540
  and conformity, 512
  need for, 95
Social attitude, 112, 689
Social change and leaders, 520
Social class, 506–508, 689
  and behavior, 509–511
  and mental illness, 162
Social disapproval versus hostility, 134
Social facilitation, 690
Social frustration in children, 108
Social group, 511–519, 690
Social handicaps of prejudice, 556
Social influences, on behavior, 499–525
  on language development, 61
Social institution, 690
Social learning of values, 91
Social maturity, 690
  of mentally deficient, 447
Social needs, 94–96, 690
Social psychology, 23, 690
Social Science Research Council, 531, 658
Social sciences, training in, 25

Social status of occupations, 507
Social structure, 503–511, 690
Social suggestion, 544
Social support for attitudes, 540
Social technique, 91, 111, 690
    fear as, 110
Social value, 90, 690
Social worker, 20, 180, 690
Socialization, 690
Society, 690
Society for Mental Hygiene, 166
Socioeconomic status, 508
    and attitudes, 531
    and intelligence, 456
    and language development, 62
Sociogram, 690
Sociological view of leadership, 520
Sociometric test, 690
Sodium amytal, 690
    use in therapy, 169, 640
Solitary confinement, effects, 86
Somatic system, 605, 690
Somatotonia, 494, 495
Somesthesis, 690
    neural mechanism, 620
Somnolence, 623, 690
Sone, 690
Sound, stereophonic, 318
Sound-pressure level (SPL), 371, 690
Sound wave, 368, 690
Space factor in intelligence, 445
Space perception, auditory, 379–381
    visual, 313, 320
Spaying, 690
    and activity, 77
Species differences in behavior, 39
Specific food aversions, 73
Specific hunger, 72, 73, 690
Spectral absorption in retina, 359
Spectral-absorption curve, 359, 690
Spectral sensitivity, 690
    of eye, 350
Speech area of cortex, 634
Speech perception, 393–398
Speed test, 690
    of intelligence, 437
Spelling, teaching, 250
Sphincter, 690
Spinal cord, 606, 607, 690
Spontaneous discrimination, 213, 691
Spontaneous recovery of conditioned response, 197
Spurts in work, 580
S-R association, 189, 691
S-S association, 188, 691
Stammering, 288
Standard deviation, 691
    definition, 413
    of standardization group, 427

Standard score, 414, 691
    of standardization group, 427
Standardization, 691
    of tests, 436
Standardization group, 426, 436, 691
    characteristics, 427
Stanford-Binet test, compared with Vineland Scale, 448
    description, 438–441
    example, 438, 439
    limitations, 440
    reliability, 419
    verbal content, 446
Startle pattern, 121, 691
Static senses, 321, 691
Status, 691
    of authorities, 537
    need for, 95
    and role, 504
Status needs, 691
Status system, 96
Stereophonic sound, 318
Stereoscope, 318
Stereotype, 691
    social, 527–529
Stimulation, of cortex, 621
    of nervous system, 613
Stimuli, similarity, 234
Stimulus, 691
    for hearing, 368
    for vision, 334
Stimulus generalization, 691
    and maze learning, 218
    and prejudice, 555
Stimulus-response associations in learning, 189
Stomach contractions, in emotion, 115
    and hunger, 71
Striped muscle, 691
Strong Vocational Interest Blank, 462
Structuralism, 8
Study techniques, 242–246
Stupidity and frustration, 135
Stuttering, 288
Subcortical centers, 607–610, 618, 691
Subcutaneous sensibility, 390
Subitizing, 691
    in animals, 293
Sublimation, 691
    and compensation, 142
Subliminal perception, 304, 691
Subvocal speech, 691
    in thinking, 263
Success and need achievement, 97
Suggestibility measurement, 478
Suggestion, 691
    in propaganda, 543
    in therapy, 172
Sulcus, 608, 691
Superego, 489, 691

Superiority, 692
  and compensation, 491
Superstition, 692
Supervision of work, 570–576
Supportive therapy, 170, 692
Suppression of anger, 111
Surround and visual acuity, 355
Survey in study, 243
Survey methods, 14, 692
Survey Q3R method, 243, 692
Swallowing reactions in chick, 47
Symbol, 254–257, 692
Symbolic display, 587, 692
Symbolic process, 692
  (*See also* Thinking)
Symmetry in object perception, 310
Sympathetic system, 692
  in emotion, 114
Synapse, 602–604, 692
Synaptic connections, 602–604
Syndrome, 692
Syphilis and psychosis, 157

T scores, 414, 692
  profile, 416
  of Wechsler tests, 441
Tabes dorsalis, 692
Taboos, 692
Talking rate, 397
Tasks, sampling, 426
Taste bud, 386
Taste receptors, 385
Taste sensitivity, 386
Taste qualities, 385
Tastes, classification, 386
Taxis, 692
Tchambuli, cultural pattern, 500
Teachers, limitations, 246
Teaching machines, 247–249, 692
Telephone theory, 692
  of hearing, 375
Temperament, 493–495, 692
Temperature, body, 68
Temperature stimulation, 389
Temporal lobe, 608, 692
Temporal maze, 692
Tendon organ, 391
Test norms, 426
Testes, 598
Tests, 692
  characteristics, 424–430, 436
  in clinical psychology, 16
  intelligence, 438–444
  of interests, 462–464
  interpretation, 446
  kinds, 437
  pencil-and-paper, of personality, 474
Textbooks, programmed, 247
Thalamus, 608, 692

Thalamus, relay centers in, 620
Thematic Apperception Test (TAT), 480
  and motives, 472
Theory, 692
  in psychology, 17
Therapy, 692
  client-centered, 173
  directive, 171
  kinds, 167–171
  trends in, 166, 167
Thiamin, 693
  and intelligence, 638
Thinking, 254–297, 693
Thinking process, 259–264
Thirst, 693
  mechanism, 69, 630
  strength, 85
Thought experiment, 261, 693
Threshold, 693
  absolute, 301
  of hearing, 376, 377
  visual, 349–352
Thurstone attitude scale, 546
Thwarting, 128
Thyroid gland, 597, 693
Thyroxin, 597, 693
Timbre, 693
  tone complexity, 372
Time difference in auditory localization, 379
Tones, loudness, 370
  pitch, 369
  pure, 368
Tonotopic organization, 621, 693
Topographical arrangement, 693
  of cortex, 621
Touch sensitivity, 388
Trace process, 260, 693
Trade test, 693
  in employee selection, 567, 568
Training, of employees, 571
  parental, 485
  transfer of, 234–236
  of twins, 52
Trait theory of personality, 493
Traits, definition, 468, 693
  factor analysis, 469, 470
  personality, 468
Tranquilizers, 693
  and anxiety, 120
  use, 640–642
  in therapy, 169
Transfer, in concept formation, 268
  principles, 234
  in problem solving, 276
  of training, 234–236, 693
  in industry, 572
Transference, 693
  in psychoanalysis, 176

Treatment of feeble-minded, 448
  (*See also* Psychotherapy)
Trial and error, 693
  in problem solving, 275
Tritanope, 348, 693
Truth serum, 169, 693
Twins, emotionality, 102
  IQ, reared apart, 42
  language development, 61
  maturation, 48, 52
  mental disease, 483
Tympanic membrane, 374, 693
Type, 693
  personality, 470
Type-token ratio, 285, 693

Ulcers and anxiety, 118
Unconditioned response, definition, 196
  of fear, 88
Unconditioned stimulus, definition, 196
Unconscious factors in problem solving, 274
Unconscious motivation, 97, 693
Unconscious processes, 693
Unique colors, 342, 693
United States Air Force, human engineering
  in, 23
U.S. Department of Labor, work character-
  istics form, 565, 660
U.S. Employment Service, 568, 660
  occupational information, 563
  tests used, 22, 462
University of Michigan Survey Research Cen-
  ter polls, 549
Uterus, 44

Vacillation in avoidance-avoidance conflict, 130
Valence, 128, 694
Validation of vocational-aptitude tests, 460
Validity, 694
  of personality tests, 474, 475
  in selection, 569
  of tests, 425, 426, 436
Value, 694
  Allport-Vernon-Lindzey Study, 476
Variability, of behavior in learning, 191
  measures, 412
Variable, 694
  in experiments, 13
Vector, 128, 694
Veg, 303, 694
Verb-adjective ratio, 285, 694
Verbal associations in memory, 230
Verbal comprehension factor in intelligence,
  445
Verbal context, 282
Verbal diversification, 284, 694
Verbal reasoning, 278
Verbal tests of intelligence, 437, 441
Vertebrates, 694
Vertical-horizontal illusion, 300

Vestibular receptors, 301, 391
Vestibular sense, 367, 694
  organs, 391, 392
  reactions to, 392
Veterans Administration, psychology in, 20–22
  tests, 462
Vicarious trial and error (VTE), 258, 694
Vigilance in work, 582
Vineland Social Maturity Scale for mentally
  deficient, 448
Viscerotonia, 494, 495
Visibility and photochemical events, 359
  luminosity, 678
  (*See also* Sensitivity)
Visible spectrum, 334, 335, 694
Vision, 333–366
  centers, 621
  after cortical lesions, 622
  development, 54
  near point, 341
  restriction, 52
  stimulus, 334
  (*See also* Perception)
Visual acuity, 352–357, 694
Visual association area of cortex, 622, 632
Visual cycle, 358, 694
Visual discrimination and prestriate areas, 633
Visual memory, 229
Visual perception in chimpanzees, 53
  (*See also* Perception)
Visual purple, 358, 694
Vitamins, 598
  A, 358, 694
  B, specific hunger for, 73
  B_1, and intelligence, 638
Vocabulary, 284, 694
Vocal expression in emotion, 121
Vocalization in infant, 58
Vocational adjustment, 562–594
Vocational aptitudes, 459–462, 569, 694
Voice quality, 397
Volley theory of hearing, 375
Vowels in speech sounds, 394
VTE (vicarious trial and error), 694

WAIS (*see* Wechsler Adult Intelligence scale)
Waking and retention, 239
Waking center, 623, 694
Warming up, 694
  effect in work, 579
Warmth, as drive, 68
  sense of, 388
Wechsler Adult Intelligence Scale, 441, 442
  age differences on, 453
White matter, 694
  in nervous system, 606
Whole learning, 227, 694
WISC (Wechsler Intelligence Scale for Chil-
  dren), 442
Witchcraft and mental illness, 164